Writers' & Artists' YEARBOOK 2013

Writers' & Artists' YEARBOOK 2013

ONE HUNDRED AND SIXTH EDITION

A directory for writers, artists, playwrights, designers, illustrators and photographers

B L O O M S B U R Y

LONDON • NEW DELHI • NEW YORK • SYDNEY

50 Bedford Square, London WC1B 3DP

Bloomsbury Publishing, London, New Dehli,
New York and Sydney
www.bloomsbury.com

This book is produced using paper that is made from wood grown in managed, sustainable forests. It is natural, renewable and recyclable. The logging and manufacturing processes conform to the environmental regulations of the country of origin.

A CIP catalogue record for this book is available from the British Library.

ISBN 978-1-4081-5749-7

Writers' & Artists' editorial team
Editor Alysoun Owen
Editorial Assistant Celeste Ward-Best
Articles Editor Barbara Cheney
Listings Editors Lisa Carden, Rebecca Collins, Lauren Simpson
Database editing Virginia Klein
Database Manager Martin Dowling

Typeset by QPM from David Lewis XML Associates Ltd

Printed and bound by CPI Group (UK) Ltd, Croydon CR0 4YY

This edition of the *Writers' & Artists' Yearbook* is dedicated to the memory of Michael Legat (1923–2011), who was a valued contributor to the *Yearbook* for over 15 years. After a long and successful publishing career, Michael became a full-time writer and author of *An Author's Guide to Publishing* and *Understanding Publishers' Contracts.*

About the *Yearbook*

The Editor welcomes readers to this edition of the *Writers' & Artists' Yearbook*.

The *Writers' & Artists' Yearbook* was first published in 1906 and, as the unofficial 'bible' of the media and publishing industries, it has firmly established itself as the first port of call for all writers and artists as well as aspiring writers and artists. Inside these covers you will find the details of hundreds of societies, companies and other organisations across the media industries – publishers of books, newspapers and magazines, literary agents, prize-giving bodies and literary festivals. The listings are independently vetted, checked and updated every year.

The articles throughout the *Yearbook* are written by experts in their fields: prize-winning novelists, writers for stage, screen and radio, poets and non-fiction authors; established illustrators; literary agents and publishing professionals; lawyers and financial experts. Together, the articles provide a mix of practical advice and inspirational insight.

New for 2013

The *Yearbook* has been extensively reviewed and this year we have more new and expanded articles than ever before. They range from *Notes from a successful romantic novelist* (page 242) from Katie Fforde, to *Writing for the theatre* (page 395) from playwright David Eldridge and an indispensable how-to guide on *Writing for magazines* from Hero Brown (page 3).

Getting into print has never been more achievable with the expansion of self-publishing and electronic formats. And at the same time, securing a deal with a literary agent and a mainstream publisher may seem more elusive than ever. To set the context, Tom Tivnan's *A year in view of the publishing industry* (page 313) casts an eye over the publishing world as a whole and Philip Jones' *Electronic publishing* (page 581) gives a digest of trends and developments in this fast-moving arena. We have new articles on *Writing memoir* (page 266), *Understanding publishing agreements* (page 287), *Copyright questions* (page 639) and the legal minefield of *The laws of Privacy and Confidentiality* (page 664). Maggie Gee reminds us *Why libraries matter* (page 621) and there are two new articles on the editing process: *Perfect proofs* (page 611) and *Who will edit your book?* (page 299), which emphasise the value of reviewing and editing your own work.

For even more writing advice and up-to-the minute comment, visit the newly relaunched *Writers' & Artists'* website (www.writersandartists.co.uk), where you can sign up for our regular newsletter and competitions, share your work with other aspiring writers, find out about editorial services we offer and see additional listings.

I hope that, whatever your stage as a writer, you will feel inspired by the advice within these pages.

Alysoun Owen
Editor

Contents

Praise for the *Writers' & Artists' Yearbook*

'The one-and-only, indispensable guide to the world of writing'
William Boyd

'Essential reading ... the A–Z of how to survive in publishing'
Kate Mosse

'The wealth of information ... is staggering'
The Times

'A must for established and aspiring authors'
The Society of Authors

'Even established writers can feel as though they're climbing a mountain. Think of the *Writers' & Artists' Yearbook* as your Sherpa'
Ian Rankin

'Much, much better than luck'
Terry Pratchett

Foreword

Lawrence Norfolk is the author of *Lemprière's Dictionary* (1991), *The Pope's Rhinoceros* (1996), *In the Shape of a Boar* (2001) and *John Saturnall's Feast* (2012), which have sold over a million copies and been translated into 24 languages. He is the winner of the Somerset Maugham Award and the Budapest Festival Prize for Literature and his work has been short-listed for the International IMPAC Dublin Literary Award, the James Tait Black Memorial Prizes and the Jewish Quarterly–Wingate Prize for Literature. In 1993 he was on *Granta* magazine's list of 'Best of Young British Novelists'. In 1992, Lawrence reported on the war in Bosnia for *NEWS* magazine, Austria, and since then his journalism has appeared in newspapers and magazines throughout Europe and the USA.

It is easier for an unpublished writer to find a needle in a haystack than an agent. And easier for a camel to pass through the eye of that needle than for an unagented writer to find a publisher. That is the received wisdom. But it begs an obvious question. If it's so impossible to get published, where do all the books come from?

The first step to an answer is the *Yearbook* in your hands. Within its covers you will find everything you need to know about the business of being a writer. The actual writing, of course, you have to do yourself. You will also need some luck. But these pages will guide you to the place where your luck, when it comes, will count and where your writing, when it emerges, will be read.

My own path to that place began 25 years ago, when I was (I wince to recall) 'thinking about being a writer'. I had been given a ticket to the London Book Fair and my then-girlfriend (a forceful individual) had told me that this was my chance. I should go there and get a publisher. Or an agent. Or both. Then I could write that book I'd always been thinking of writing.

'That book' at the time was a one-page outline of a story about a dead dictionary-writer ensnared in a plot fabricated by the secret masters of the East India Company. But off I went with my ticket and my sheet of A4 to walk up and down the crowded aisles. All the publishers' stands were guarded by terrifying receptionists so I hovered instead around the agents. At last, after my hovering had started to seem like lurking, a woman stepped forward and asked me what I wanted. I remember the odd, slightly quizzical expression that stole over her face as I explained how I was 'thinking of becoming a writer'.

That expression, I now know, was disbelief, though whether at my nerve or naivety, I'm still not sure. Explaining that she was at the Fair to sell the work of writers she already represented, not to acquire more writers, she sent me gently but firmly on my way. It was then that I had one of two great strokes of good fortune. The woman noticed my single sheet of paper.

'What's that?'

'The story I want to write. It's about a dead dictionary-writer and the East India Company....'

The quizzical expression faded. She might even have looked interested. When I had finished, she reached forward and took my piece of paper. (The single sheet, I realised much later, was my one smart move that day. No agent lacks for things to read.) I ambled off down the aisle, pleased and surprised. An agent was going to read my work.… Then, just as I was about to disappear into the crowd, I had my second stroke of luck. I heard a shout of 'Come back!'

The woman was beckoning. Had she decided on the spot to represent me? Or suddenly remembered that publisher who just happened to be looking for a novel about a dead dictionary-writer? She was pointing to my synopsis.

'You haven't written your name on this.'

'No.'

'Or a telephone number.'

I conceded that there was none.

'Or an address. How are we meant to get in touch with you? How are you meant to get in touch with us? You haven't taken our card.'

Another step and I would have been gone. I probably would never have written my novel, or been published. As it was I took the card. It read, 'Carole Blake: Blake Friedmann Literary Agency'.

Carole and I have now been together for 25 years (you can find her on page 431) and our relationship is pretty much the same as the one that was forged that day on the floor of the London Book Fair. I write. Carole takes care of everything else. It is a simple arrangement and, for that reason, a very stable one.

It needs to be.

The life of a writer, I have discovered since that fateful meeting, while it appears to involve sitting at a desk and writing, is actually more like riding a spectacularly ramshackle rollercoaster. This *Yearbook* is your ticket. No one can do the writing for you or help you with the luck. But as you scale the peaks and plunge into the troughs these pages will provide support, comfort and sound advice. And if that fails, you can always scream.

Welcome aboard.

Lawrence Norfolk

Newspapers and magazines

Getting started

Of the titles included in the newspapers and magazines section of this *Yearbook*, almost all offer opportunities to the writer. Many publications do not appear in the lists because the market they offer for the freelance writer is either too small or too specialised, or both. To help writers get started, we offer some guidelines for consideration before submitting material.

Study the market

• The importance of studying the market cannot be overemphasised. It is an editor's job to know what readers want, and to see that they get it. Thus, freelance contributions must be tailored to fit a specific market; subject, theme, treatment, length, etc must meet the editor's requirements. This is discussed further in *Writing features for newspapers and magazines* on page 8 and *Writing for magazines* on page 3.

• Magazine editors frequently complain about the unsuitability of many submissions, so before sending an article or feature, always carefully study the editorial requirements of the magazine – not only for the subjects dealt with but for the approach, treatment, style and length. These comments will be obvious to the practised writer but the beginner can be spared much disappointment by buying copies of magazines and studying their target market in depth.

• For additional information on markets, see the UK volume of *Willings Press Guide*, which is usually available at local reference libraries.

Check with the editor first

• Before submitting material to any newspaper or magazine it is advisable to first contact the relevant editor. The listings beginning on page 11 give the names of editors for each section of the national newspapers. A quick telephone call or email to a magazine will establish the name of the relevant commissioning editor.

• Most newspapers and many magazines expect copy to be sent by email.

• Editors who accept postal submissions expect them to be well presented: neatly typed, double spaced, with good margins, on A4 paper is the standard to aim at. Always enclose an sae (stamped addressed envelope) for the return of unsuitable material.

• It is not advisable to send illustrations 'on spec'; check with the editor first. See *Picture agencies and libraries* on the *Writers' & Artists'* website (www.writersandartists.co.uk) for listings. For a list of publications that accept cartoons see page 739.

Explore the overseas market

• The lists of overseas newspapers and magazines in the *Yearbook* contain only a selection of those journals which offer a market for the freelance writer. For fuller listings, refer to *Willings Press Guide* Volume 2 (Europe) and Volume 3 (World). The overseas market for stories and articles is small and editors often prefer their fiction to have a local setting. Some editors require their contributors to be residents of that country.

• Some overseas magazine titles have little space for freelance contributions but many of them will consider outstanding work.

• It is worth considering using an agent to syndicate material written for the overseas market. Most agents operate on an international basis and are more aware of current market requirements. Listings for *Syndicates, news and press agencies* start on page 110.

Understand how newspapers and syndicates work

• The larger newspapers and magazines buy many of their stories, and the smaller papers buy general articles, through well-known syndicates. Another avenue for writers is to send printed copies of their stories published at home to an agent for syndication overseas.
• For the supply of news, most of the larger UK and overseas newspapers depend on their own staff and press agencies. The most important overseas newspapers have permanent representatives in the UK who keep them supplied, not only with news of special interest to the country concerned, but also with regular summaries of British news and with articles on events of particular importance. While many overseas newspapers and magazines have a London office, it is usual for manuscripts from freelance contributors to be submitted to the headquarters' editorial office overseas. Listings of *National newspapers UK and Ireland* start on page 11.

Payment

• The *Yearbook* has always aimed to obtain and publish the rates of payment offered for contributions by newspapers and magazines. Many publications, however, are reluctant to state a standard rate, since the value of a contribution may be dependent not upon length but upon the standing of the writer or of the information given. Many other periodicals prefer to state 'by negotiation' or 'by arrangement', rather than giving precise payment information.

See also...

- *Writing for magazines*, page 3
- *Writing features for newspapers and magazines*, page 8
- *Regional newspapers UK and Ireland*, page 19
- *Newspapers are listed together with magazines for Australia* (page 97), *Canada* (page 102), *New Zealand* (page 104), *South Africa* (page 106) and *USA* (page 109)

Writing for magazines

Hero Brown gives some tips on how to break into the competitive world of writing for magazines.

Ask magazine journalists what it was like working in the Eighties and early Nineties and they'll tell you a tale of fabulous fees and eager commissioning editors. These days, with economic hard times still bruising the UK and magazine advertising revenues badly affected, the climate has changed. Only the leanest, most street-smart of magazines survive. Editors commission more features in-house, they're more diligent at using up their back catalogue of purchased features, and they think more carefully about the features they commission.

What does this mean for journalists trying to write for magazines? Simply that it's tougher now to get your break into the industry. But don't despair. Bright journalists with great ideas are always in demand, so if you're up for the fight, read on.

The Three Commandments

Whether you're writing for magazines, newspapers or online, there are three cardinal rules that you must never forget (or beware the consequences with an irate editor). Not very creative rules, I grant you, and yes, they sound so simple... but you'd be surprised how often journalists fail at this basic hurdle. Make life easy for yourself and ingratiate yourself to the features desk by doing the following:

• **Write to length.** The editor and designer have worked out how many pages of the magazine your feature will take up and given you a word count accordingly – let's say 1,000 words. If you've enjoyed crafting your feature so much that you can't bear to cut back your 2,000-word masterpiece, what you are actually handing over is a feature two magazine pages longer than the one asked of you. Quite an assumption! You've also given the features editor a whole lot of extra work and hassle too, because halving your copy (yes, it will happen!) is not so much an edit but a rewrite as the feature will have to be chopped up and stuck together again, and your beautifully wrought Titian might end up looking like a chipped mosaic.

• **Spell-check your copy.** Spell-checking is just what it says on the tin. But if you don't do it (and scan your grammar while you're at it) it looks lazy and unprofessional.

• **File on time**. This is vital: print-runs don't wait for the muse to hit you. If you file late, the editorial team falls behind, and the sub-editor works late into the night... Not a good idea if you want to be recommissioned.

Work out your strengths

There are so many magazines published in the UK that deciding who to contact for work can feel overwhelming. Rather than panicking and flitting between dozens of potential magazines, take some time to think about what you really want. Which magazines do you like best, and why? What subjects are you most interested in, or knowledgeable about (not necessarily the same thing)? And what are your own writing strengths? If you're good at putting people at ease, perhaps you'll be talented at finding and interviewing case studies. If you're meticulous about detail and like to get under the skin of a story, perhaps investigative features are your strength. If you have great contacts in the fashion industry, then style journalism is a potential place to start.

Let's assume that you've worked out the type of features you'd like to write and the publication that best fits your interest and outlook. Now it's time to research. Buy the magazine regularly and look strategically at the types of articles that appear – generally, there's a format that will be repeated in each issue. For example, women's glossies broadly tend to include a celebrity interview, features on health, beauty, something news-led, an emotional case-study feature, and perhaps a first-person viewpoint. Work out why a certain feature exists, and then pitch for that slot. Read rival magazines too – it's no good pitching an idea that was in another publication the previous month.

Work out the lead times for magazines – often they work two months ahead, so any ideas you pitch will have to be at least that far in advance or they won't be relevant. Stay up to date with news, search the internet, view potential stories from unusual angles. If an idea has already been written, look at it from the reverse; see if there's a different spin you can put on it to make it more relevant or fresh.

Pitching your idea

As in other industries, experience is important in journalism, and brilliant as you undoubtedly are, you're unlikely to get the *Vogue* cover story at your first stab (or your second!). If you haven't been published before, or only a little, you need patience, perseverance and some tenacity. There are some simple ways to help yourself to reach your goal. Before you pitch your idea, do yourself a favour and find out who edits the magazine section you want to write for. Trust me when I say it's very irritating for busy editors to be asked by writers who they should send their ideas to. If you can't be bothered to research that, an editor will wonder what else can't you be bothered to research properly.

When you pitch the idea, you can telephone, email or, if you're being super gung-ho, text (good luck with that one!). Personally, I'd be wary of cold-calling your feature proposal. If you catch an editor on a bad day he or she might not give you a decent chance to explain your idea. Perhaps the safer route is to send a brief synopsis of your idea via email. A couple of paragraphs is ample, but make sure you include evidence of why the idea is new, different, worth publishing – it shows you've already taken time to research the feature, and instils confidence. Use a headline and strapline to 'sell' the synopsis – it's a great way of getting an editor to visualise the piece in the magazine.

Once you've emailed your idea, try to be patient. The desire to check your email hourly to see if you've had a response will leave you slumped and disconsolate within days (I know, I used to do it myself). The reality is that, unlike newspapers with their fast turnarounds, magazines often only have features meetings weekly or even fortnightly so it's unlikely you'll hear back immediately. Simply check the relevant editor has received your proposal once you've emailed it, ask when the next features meeting will be held and then if you can't stand the wait, call afterwards to hear the verdict.

Common sense

If you've been researching a great idea, the last thing you want to happen is for it to be stolen from you. However, it's counter-productive to be too coy about your ideas. From the editor's point of view, it's impossible to commission an idea that's padlocked in a lead box. For the writer, the danger is that refusing to divulge your idea properly leaves you sounding paranoid or pretentious, and therefore more trouble than you're worth. If you respect the publication, the odds are you'll also be able to respect its editors, but if you still feel uncomfortable about handing over the crown jewels, perhaps do some research on the journalists you best trust before getting in touch. Don't forget that you will have an email record and timeline of your correspondence as a protection against someone taking your idea.

Close, but no cigar

Be prepared that if you're pitching an idea to a magazine but have no published work to date, it's possible (though by no means inevitable) that you won't be commissioned straight away. Assuming you have piqued the editor's interest, one of two things may happen. Firstly, if the idea is of interest, you may be offered a fee for the idea. This means you'll get paid an agreed amount, but the editor will get someone more experienced to write it. If you have lots of ideas, this can be a good way to make money and work your way into an editor's little black book.

The other option is that you may be asked to write the feature 'on spec'. In other words, the editor likes your idea but wants you to write and submit the feature before deciding if it's well written enough to go in the magazine. You are perfectly within your rights to politely decline and take your feature to other publications – the editor will understand fully. If other editors offer the same response, you can either see it as a shameful affront on your journalistic integrity, or you can shake your brain into action and see it for what it is – an opportunity.

If you're starting out, you need to show confidence in your own ability and take every chance you can find to get published. Even if the feature doesn't quite hit the mark, you'll get free advice on how to improve and perhaps another shot with the same editor. If you agree to write on spec, it's worth asking at this early stage what the fee would be if your feature is accepted. This will allow you to work out whether you want to do the work involved, and also gives you peace of mind that you have a written agreement (an email confirmation is fine) that you will be paid, should your feature be published.

If you do happen to be commissioned in full from the beginning, make sure you have a contract. This is sent from the magazine, stating your name, address, feature you're writing, fee that you're being paid and deadline. Usually you just sign it, send it back to the magazine and keep a copy.

Make yourself indispensable

Work experience, though usually embarked upon for love not money, is an excellent way of giving yourself a head start in journalism, and magazines always seem to find room for an extra pair of hands to help at the coal face. Competition is fierce, so you need to work your contacts, beautify your CV, and make a compelling argument for why it should be you rather than the 300 other journalists who deserve an internship.

If you make it into the building, well done, you're halfway to your goal. Next, make sure you're super-nice at all times, never balk at making tea, grit your teeth through any casual condescension, and trust me, eventually you'll be given the chance to write something. Even if it's 150 words in the news section, suddenly you're a published journalist and your prospects immediately perk up. Editors can see you have staying power, persistence and potential. Hopefully you've also made some useful contacts, not just at your magazine but at the magazine next door, and the ones above and below your floor.

Get connected

If you've had a couple of commissions, fantastic. Now's the time to set yourself up on LinkedIn (www.linkedin.com) and make formal connections with the editors you've dealt with. A whole swathe of magazine editors will be able to see the publications you've written for, and what sort of person you're like to deal with. Gorkana (www.gorkana.com/uk) is another great resource for journalists. There's a whole section on magazine jobs, permanent and freelance, from glossies to weeklies, style to sports, plus a massive PR directory if you need help with specific stories. Just register for regular updates.

You'll need an online presence too. The days of lugging around a plastic file of yellowing clippings is long gone. If you're already published, set up a simple website to showcase your work. It will look slight at first, but it only takes a few good commissions to look more beefy.

Blogging

Blogging is another simple but effective way to showcase your writing. Last year I started a blog called Muddy Stilettos – 'the urban guide to the countryside' around Buckinghamshire/Oxfordshire where I live. It's become a whopping big advert for my writing and I've won a lot of commissions off the back of it. So again, be strategic. Think about the publications you want to write for and tune your blog accordingly to make it a must-read. Find out about writing with SEO (search engine optimisation), tagging and social media in mind. If you end up writing for online magazines, these are all skills that will help you get commissioned or taken on permanently.

Negotiating fees

Unless you're a big name journalist, too much foot-stomping about money will just result in a weary sigh from your editor who will probably remind you of your relative inexperience. Feature fees are often worked out on word count – generally it's around £300 per 1,000, but it entirely depends on the publication and the editor involved. Sometimes it's a flat fee for a certain feature slot and there's no getting around it. Of course, there's nothing to stop you asking nicely for an extra £50 or £100 if you think the fee is too low – your editor may well respect you for it. If there's some travel involved, that can be a legitimate way to bolster the money.

As you become more established, you may feel more comfortable negotiating a higher rate. It's entirely a personal decision and you'll sense when you've pushed it as far as you can. If you really feel you've been taken for a ride, you can get in touch with the National Union of Journalists to find out the minimum freelance rates you can expect. However, if you talk to other journalists, most will regale you with stories of early work written for little money, just for the experience. In a sense, the experience is the fee and it really is valuable in its own right.

Diversify or specialise?

Many journalists enjoy researching and writing about lots of different subjects, and find the idea of being a specialist – for example, a health or interiors journalist – limiting. But there are definite benefits of focusing on a single area in journalism. Namely, if you become the expert, you are in demand. And if you're in demand, your rates are substantially higher. Eventually, you may be able to move into different media if you so wish, such as television and radio, and at that point, ironically, you may well be able to diversify into other areas. It may seem premature to be thinking about this if you're only just getting to the point of being published, but it's worth considering now in terms of pitching ideas and gaining contacts in the right areas. If you're not sure, and want to go with the flow, that's OK too.

If you're still not having any luck...

Ask for help. A good editor will take a minute out of their day to explain to you exactly what they need and why you are not offering the right story. He or she may suggest other publications that better suit your style of writing – maybe they see a quality in you that you can't yet see yourself. Don't lose confidence but keep an open mind, and whatever you do, keep writing, keep pitching ideas, keep networking. With talent and a sprinkle of luck, that magical magazine commission will arrive in the end.

Hero Brown is a former magazine editor at the *Independent on Sunday* and deputy editor of *Red* magazine. She now freelances for *Marie Claire*, *Red*, the *Observer* and the *Sunday Telegraph* among others. Read her blog at www.muddystilettos.co.uk.

See also...

- *Writing features for newspapers and magazines*, page 8
- *Marketing yourself online*, page 587
- *Writing a blog*, page 594
- *Copyright questions*, page 639
- *UK copyright law*, page 643
- *The laws of Privacy and Confidentiality*, page 664
- *Defamation*, page 668

Writing features for newspapers and magazines

Merope Mills outlines a route to success for prospective feature writers to follow.

Newspapers and magazines are experiencing their most profound change in a century. Every title – be it broadsheet, tabloid or glossy magazine – is finding its way in these increasingly digital times. It's a revolution that is both frightening and exciting in equal measure. ABC figures are largely in decline but online 'unique users' are, mostly, on the up. Feature writers these days can reach enormous audiences from around the world, but finances at many titles have never been tighter. For several years now, budgets have been cut, staff numbers slashed and freelances' contracts have been terminated. But just when you think it's all doom and gloom for print, there are unexpected success stories – such as the launch of the *Independent's* sister title *i*; the launch of the free magazines *Stylist* and *ShortList*, and the huge popularity of the now free *Evening Standard*.

No one could accurately predict what shape the industry will take a few years from now, but one thing is for sure: every title needs great writers, ideas and well-written content. But be it for the print or online arm of its operation, making the right approach, especially if you are unknown to an editor, is more essential than ever.

Starting out

If you're new to writing, the best thing you can do is play to your strengths. Do your friends tell you your emails make them fall off their chairs laughing? Then maybe a humorous column beckons. Do you have specialist knowledge? A green-fingered writer might be able to spot a gap in the market in a gardening title, for example. When starting out in journalism, it is often best to stick to factual journalism that you can write about entertainingly. Most comment and analysis columnists these days are personalities who already carry authority – novelists, television celebrities or journalists who have built up a reputation across many years. If you're at the start of your career, your opinion (though extremely valid) will count for very little unless it's backed up by something solid. The majority of newspaper and magazine freelances are feature writers as news reporters tend to be on staff.

The internet

As a freelance writer, the internet is your friend. A newspaper or magazine has a finite number of pages and therefore a limited number of people that can write for it. Its online equivalent, on the other hand, can accommodate many more voices. If you have a niche subject and a valid angle on a story and the newspaper or magazine editor can't accommodate you in print, they may be able to include your piece online.

If you already have your own blog, so much the better. In the newspaper industry, it used to be traditional for writers to work their way up the ladder through local papers. Today, the talent seems increasingly to come from the internet. Its advantages are plain: a writer with a blog has a stash of readily available, easily accessible cuttings that clearly establish their identity. Better still for an editor, if it's a good blog it may even have built up its own raft of followers who would keenly follow the blogger if they were to shift to print.

The rise of Twitter presents endless opportunities for the freelance writer. The trick is learning how to exploit it. The master at this, in my opinion, is the freelance writer Sali Hughes – who appears regularly in womens' magazines such as *Red* and *Grazia*, as well as writing comment pieces for the *Guardian*. When I found her on Twitter she seemed smart and funny, so I became one of her many thousands of followers. Eventually, off the back of that digital relationship, I hired her for the beauty column in *Weekend*. She told me that Twitter is invaluable to her freelance career: one of her editors will see something she's tweeted and then ask her to write a longer feature on the subject. She is also comfortable having conversations with her readers – both on Twitter and 'below the line' (with people who comment on her column). Embracing new technology and fostering a community of fans in this way is a fantastic example of how to make social media work for you.

Ideas

Good ideas are the essence of a good journalist. But you must avoid the obvious. Don't write to a magazine or newspaper editor suggesting an interview with Madonna – it's likely they've already had that idea and probably aren't casting around for writers. If you're just starting out, think laterally. Look in the less obvious sections or supplements for columns that an editor might struggle to fill. In a travel magazine or newspaper travel section, for example, you probably won't be able to bag a 2,000-word commission on a Maldives beach holiday, but there may be a small regular section on B&Bs or budget holidays around the UK that grander, established writers probably won't be pitching for. Don't be shy of writing about yourself and your own experiences. Again, the rise of the internet means that newspapers and magazines increasingly see the value of readers' stories and contributions. Look for those 'first person' slots and think if you've got a good personal story that would suit. From tiny acorns like that, whole careers can grow. Once you've established contact and written something, however small, bigger things may well flourish.

Respond quickly to time-sensitive ideas that are the lifeblood of newspaper features and weekly magazines, and if there is something in the news or something trending on Twitter that you think you can spin a feature out of – act fast. When something is big news or goes viral and you have an idea, get in quick – before someone beats you to it.

Contacting the publication

Whether you are published or unpublished, the most important thing is to write a convincing email or letter. Keep your idea succinct – no more than two paragraphs. (Think of it like the newspaper or magazine's standfirst. On publication, they have to sell the idea to the readers in a few brief sentences – so you should be able to do the same.) If you've written before, include a few links to your most relevant work. Lots of people tell me they write for the *Guardian*, but all too often I find myself searching the archive for their byline, never to find it. It's so much easier to point to your work within your pitch.

It sounds obvious, but make sure your idea is right for the publication you're contacting. Don't blanket-email every title you can think of with the same idea, hoping that somewhere it will stick. It's good for an editor to know that you're familiar with their product and that you're suggesting an idea specifically for their section and readership. I get way too many ideas that are a completely wrong fit for the *Guardian*. It's a waste of everybody's time.

Above all, the most important thing you can do is *read* the publication you're pitching to, before getting in contact.

It's a writer's instinct to send things to the editor of the publication, but there's often someone else who will consider your idea quicker and give you an answer. Perhaps it's the deputy editor, the commissioning editor or the features editor. If it's a more specific idea – to do with fashion, health or food, for example – find out who is in charge of that area and contact them. Make a call first to see who the best person to receive your pitch is, if you're not sure. Always address them by name. If you can't be bothered to write a personal email, it doesn't suggest you're likely to be a thorough journalist.

Style

Again, read the publication, and writers you particularly admire. They might be owned by the same company – Murdoch's News International – but there's a world of difference between writing for the *Sun* and *The Times*. They might both deal in celebrity and fashion, but *Grazia* and *Vogue* have completely different styles and sections. You must adapt to the publication, and think about whether the way you've written a piece is suitable.

There is no formula to writing features you can follow for every publication, but it is common to start a piece with some 'colour'. This means beginning a piece by focusing on one anecdote or one particular person's story or quote before broadening it out to explain why their tale matters and what it represents. By the third or fourth paragraph there should really be an explanation of what trend/event/issue your piece is about. The body of any feature should have enough case studies (usually at least three people) to back up the facts and opinions that make the thrust of the piece.

Money

You've had an idea accepted – now what? The first thing to do is agree a fee. Most commonly you will be offered the publication's lineage fee (a standard rate, paid by the word). This can vary widely, so make sure you're happy with this before you start. The National Union of Journalists (www.nuj.org.uk) offers a guide tofreelance rates that is worth checking. Also make it clear if you will be submitting expenses receipts and give a rough estimate of what these might be, so your editor can budget for them. Establish who owns copyright beforehand, in case you want to sell second rights to another publication. Having said that, most titles have a syndication service and are more likely to be able to place it elsewhere for you, taking a cut if they do. This is worth investigation.

Deadlines and editing

Don't miss a deadline – even if you are sure that the piece won't be printed imminently. You probably aren't familiar with the title's production schedule and deadlines are usually there for a reason, so don't ignore them. It's also better to be open to your editor's thoughts and rewriting suggestions. Their job is to make the piece better, not worse, so it's in everyone's best interest not to be a prima donna about your copy. If you're not sure of the reason for the changes, just ask.

Breaking into the industry isn't easy, but writing for newspapers and magazines can have many rewards – from meeting interesting people, to seeing your name in print for the first time, to receiving a cheque for your first published piece of work. All you need is a nice style, some good ideas and a little bit of luck!

Merope Mills is editor of the *Guardian's Weekend* magazine.

National newspapers UK and Ireland

Daily Express

Northern & Shell Building, 10 Lower Thames Street, London EC3R 6EN
tel 020-8612 7000
website www.express.co.uk
Editor Hugh Whittow
Daily Mon–Fri 50p, Sat 80p
Supplements **Daily Express Saturday**

Exclusive news; striking photos. Leader page articles (600 words); facts preferred to opinions. Payment: according to value.

City Editor Peter Cunliffe
Deputy Editor Michael Booker
Diary Editor Lizzie Catt
Environment Editor John Ingham
Features Editor Fergus Kelly
Literary Editor Caroline Jowitt
News Editor Geoff Maynard
Political Editor Macer Hall
Sports Editor Bill Bradshaw
Women's Editor Tina Moran

Daily Express Saturday Magazine

Editor Graham Bailey
Free with paper
Magazine.

Daily Mail

Northcliffe House, 2 Derry Street, London W8 5TT
tel 020-7938 6000 *fax* 020-7937 3251
email managingeditor@dailymail.co.uk
website www.dailymail.co.uk
Editor Paul Dacre
Daily Mon–Fri 50p, Sat 80p
Supplements **Weekend**

Founded 1896.

City Editor Alex Brummer
Diary Editor Richard Kay
Education Correspondent Laura Clark
Features Editor Leaf Kalfayan
Foreign Editor David Harding
Health Editor Justine Hancock
Business & Property Correspondent Becky Barrow
Literary Editor Sandra Parsons
Moneymail Editor James Coney
News Editor Ben Taylor
Picture Editor Paul Silva
Political Editor James Chapman
Showbiz Editor Sara Nathan
Head of Sport Lee Clayton
Travel Editor Mark Palmer
Weekend Editor Nicole Mowbray

Daily Mirror

1 Canada Square, Canary Wharf, London E14 5AP
tel 020-7293 3000
email mirrornews@mirror.co.uk
website www.mirror.co.uk
Editor Richard Wallace
Daily Mon–Fri 45p, Sat 65p
Supplements **The Ticket, We Love Telly!, Your Life**

Top payment for exclusive news and news pictures. Freelance articles used, and ideas bought: send synopsis only. 'Unusual' pictures and those giving a new angle on the news are welcomed; also cartoons. Founded 1903.

Business Editor Graham Hiscott
Head of Content Chris Bucktin
Deputy Head of Content Barry Rabbetts, Shiraz Lalani
Health Editor Emily Cook
Letters Editor Fiona Parker
Picture Editor Ian Down
Political Editor Bob Roberts
Sports Editor Dominic Hart

Daily Record

1 Central Quay, Glasgow G3 8DA
tel 0141 309 3000 *fax* 0141 309 3340
email reporters@dailyrecord.co.uk
London office 1 Canada Square, Canary Wharf, London E14 5AP
tel 020-7293 3000
website www.dailyrecord.co.uk
Daily Mon–Fri 40p, Sat 65p
Supplements **Saturday, Living, TV Record, Road Record, Recruitment Record**

Topical articles, from 300–700 words; exclusive stories of Scottish interest and exclusive colour photos.

Executive Editor Bob Caldwell
Features Editor Melanie Harvey
Sports Editor Jim Traynor

Saturday

Editor Jayne Savva
Free with paper
Lifestyle magazine and entertainment guide. Reviews, travel features, shopping, personalities. Payment: by arrangement. Illustrations: colour.

Daily Star

Express Newspapers, Northern & Shell Building, 10 Lower Thames Street, London EC3R 6EN
tel 020-8612 7000 *fax* 020-8612 7401
email news@dailystar.co.uk
website www.dailystar.co.uk
Editor Dawn Neesom
Daily Mon–Fri 30p, Sat 60p
Supplements **Hot TV**

Hard news exclusives, commanding substantial payment. Major interviews with big-star personalities;

short features; series based on people rather than things; picture features. Payment: by negotiation. Illustrations: line, half-tone. Founded 1978.

Music Editor Kim Dawson
Sports Editor Howard Wheatcroft
Deputy Editor (news) John McJannet

Daily Star Sunday

Express Newspapers,
The Northern and Shell Building,
10 Lower Thames Street, London EC3R 6EN
tel 0208-612 7424 *fax* 0208-612 7401
website www.dailystarsunday.co.uk
Editor Gareth Morgan
Sun £1
Supplements **OK! Extra**

Opportunities for freelances.

The Daily Telegraph

111 Buckingham Palace Road, London SW1W 0DT
tel 020-7931 2000 *fax* 020-7931 2938
email dtnews@telegraph.co.uk
website www.telegraph.co.uk
Editor Tony Gallagher
Daily Mon–Fri £1.20, Sat £2
Supplements **Arts & Books, Business2 & Jobs, Gardening, Motoring, Property, Sport, Telegraph Magazine, Television & Radio, Travel, Weekend, Your Money**

Articles on a wide range of subjects of topical interest considered. Preliminary letter and synopsis required. Length: 700–1,000 words. Payment: by arrangement. Founded 1855.

Arts Editor Sarah Crompton
City Editor Richard Fletcher
Education Editor Graeme Paton
Environment Editor Geoffrey Lean
Fashion Editor Lisa Armstrong
Features Editor Genevieve Fox
Foreign Editor David Munk
Health Features Editor Rebecca Smith
News Editor Hugh Dougherty
Picture Editor Lucy Verey
Political Editor Robert Winnett
Public Policy Editor Andrew Porter

Electronic Telegraph

email et@telegraph.co.uk
website www.telegraph.co.uk
Editor Richard Fletcher
Daily Free to internet subscribers

Based on *The Daily Telegraph*. Founded 1994.

Telegraph Magazine

Editor Michele Lavery
Free with Sat paper

Short profiles (about 1,600 words); articles of topical interest. Preliminary study of the magazine essential. Illustrations: all types. Payment: by arrangement. Founded 1964.

Financial Times

1 Southwark Bridge, London SE1 9HL
tel 020-7873 3000 *fax* 020-7873 3076
email news.desk@ft.com
website www.ft.com
Editor Lionel Barber
Daily Mon–Fri £2.50, Sat £3
Supplements **Business Books, Companies & Markets, FT Digital Business, FTfm, FT Global Traveller, FT Reports, House and Home, How To Spend It, FT Weekend, Money**

Articles of financial, commercial, industrial and economic interest. Length: 800–1,000 words. Payment: by arrangement. Founded 1888.

Arts Editor Jan Dalley
Banking Editor Patrick Jenkins
Deputy Editor Martin Dickson
Travel Editor Tom Robbins
International Affairs Editor Quentin Peel
Arts Editor Neville Hawcock
Investment Correspondent Kate Burgess
Lex Editor John Authers
Political Editor George Parker
Special Reports Editor Michael Skapinker
US Managing Editor Gillian Tett
FT Weekend Editor Caroline Daniel
World News Editor Shawn Donnan

The Guardian

King's Place, 90 York Way, London N1 9GU
tel 020-3353 2000
email national@guardian.co.uk
1 Scott Place, Manchester M3 3GG
tel 0161 908 3898 *fax* 0161 832 7200
website www.guardian.co.uk/commentisfree
Editor Alan Rusbridger
Daily Mon–Fri £1.20, Sat £2.10
Supplements **Education, Film & Music, G2, The Guide, Review, Media, Society, Weekend, Family, Work, Money**

Few articles are taken from outside contributors except on its feature and specialist pages. Illustrations: news and features photos. Payment: from £295.72 per 1,000 words; £125–£350 (depending on size) for illustrations. Founded 1821.

Arts Editor Melissa Denes
Business Editor Fiona Walsh
Commentisfree.com Editor Natalie Hanman
Deputy Editor Ian Katz / Katherine Viner
Economics Editor Larry Elliott
Education Editor Jeevan Vasagar
Fashion Editor Jess Cartner-Morley
Features Editor Charlotte Northedge /Clare Margetson
Women's Editor Jane Martison
Music Editor Casper Llewellyn-Smith
The Guide Editor Paul McInnes
Head of International News Charles English
Head of National News Nick Hopkins

Literary Editor Claire Armitstead
Media Editor Janine Gibson
Head of Media and Technology Dan Sabbagh
Head of Politics Will Woodward
Head of Society, Health, Education Patrick Butler
Review Editor Lisa Allardice
Society Editor Alison Benjamin
Head of Sport Paul Johnson
Technology Editor Charles Arthur
Travel Editor Isabel Choat

Guardian Unlimited
website www.guardian.co.uk
Director of Digital Content Emily Bell

Weekend
Editor Merope Mills, *Commissioning Editor* Becky Barnicoat
Free with Sat paper

Features on world affairs, major profiles, food and drink, home life, the arts, travel and leisure. Also good reportage on social and political subjects. Illustrations: b&w photos and line, cartoons. Payment: apply for rates.

The Herald

Herald & Times Group, 200 Renfield Street, Glasgow G2 3QB
tel 0141 302 7000 *fax* 0141 302 7007
email news@theherald.co.uk
Englishoffice 58 Church Street, Weybridge, Surrey KT13 8DP
tel (01932) 821212
website www.heraldscotland.com
Editor Jonathan Russell
Daily Mon–Fri £1, Sat £1.30

Articles up to 1,000 words. Founded 1783.
Arts Editor Keith Bruce
Business Editor Ian McConnell
Diary Editor Ken Smith
Weekend Features Editor Garry Scott
Digital Editor Calum MacDonald
News Editor Ian Marland
Sports Editor Donald Cowey

The Independent

Northcliffe House, 2 Derry Street, London W8 5HF
tel 020-7005 2000 *fax* 020-7005 2999
email newseditor@independent.co.uk
website www.independent.co.uk
Editor-in-Chief Chris Blackhurst
Daily Mon–Fri £1.20, Sat £1.60
Supplements **Business Review, Education, The Information, Arts & Books Review, Property Supplement, Save & Spend, Traveller**

Occasional freelance contributions; preliminary letter advisable. Payment: by arrangement. Founded 1986.
Arts Editor David Lister
Business & City Editor Ian King
Comment Editor Katherine Butler
Education Editor Richard Garner
Environment Editor Mike McCarthy
Features Editor Susie Rushton
Foreign Editor Archie Bland
Health Editor Jeremy Laurance
Literary Editor Boyd Tonkin
Media Editor Ian Burrell
News Editor Oliver Duff
Picture Editor Lynn Cullen
Political Editor Andrew Grice
Sports Editor Matt Gatward

The Independent Magazine
email magazine@independent.co.uk
Editor Susie Rushton
Free with Sat paper

Profiles and illustrated articles of topical interest; all material commissioned. Preliminary study of the magazine essential. Length: 500–3,000 words. Illustrations: cartoons; commissioned colour and b&w photos. Payment: by arrangement. Founded 1988.

Independent on Sunday

Northcliffe House, 2 Derry Street, London W8 5TT
tel 020-7005 2000 *fax* 020-7005 2047
email sundaynews@independent.co.uk
website www.independent.co.uk
Executive Editor Lisa Markwell, *Editor-in-Chief* John Mullin, *Editor-at-Large* Raymond Whitaker
Sun £1.80
Supplements **Business, The New Review**

News, features and articles. Illustrated, including cartoons. Payment: by negotiation. Founded 1990.
Arts Editor Mike Higgins
Assistant Editor David Randall
Business Editor Maggie Pagano
Deputy Editor James Hanning
Foreign Editor David Randall
Executive Editor (News) Peter Victor
Picture Editor Sophie Batterbury
Political Editor Jane Merrick
Sports Editor Marc Padgett
Executive Editor Lisa Markwell

The New Review
tel 020-7005 2000 *fax* 020-7005 2027
Editor Bill Tuckey
Free with paper

Original features of general interest with potential for photographic illustration. Material mostly commissioned. Length: 1,000–5,000 words. Illustrations: transparencies. Payment: £150 per 1,000 words.

Irish Daily Star

Independent Star Ltd, Level 5, Building 4, Sandyford Road, Dundrum Town Centre, Dublin 16, Republic of Ireland
tel +353 (0)1 4993400

email news@thestar.ie
website www.thestar.ie
Editor Michael O'Kane
Daily Mon–Sat €1.40

General articles relating to news and sport, and features. Length: 1,000 words. Illustrations: colour photos. Payment: by negotiation. Founded 1988.

Senior Deputy Editor Danny Smyth
Deputy Editor Des Gibson
Picture Editor Brian Dowling
Political Editor Catherine Halloran
Group Sports Editor Eoin Brannigan

Irish Examiner

City Quarter, Lapps Quay, Cork, Republic of Ireland
tel +353 (0)21 4272722 (newsroom)
fax +353 (0)21 4275477
email editor@examiner.ie
website www.irishexaminer.ie
Editor Tim Vaughan
Daily Mon–Sat €1.80

Features. Material mostly commissioned. Length: 1,000 words. Payment: by arrangement. Founded 1841.

Executive Editor Dolan O'Hagan
Features Editor Vickie Maye
News Editor John O'Mahony
Picture Editor John O'Donovan
Sports Editor Tony Leen

Irish Independent

27–32 Talbot Street, Dublin 1, Republic of Ireland
tel +353 (0)1 7055333 *fax* +353 (0)1 8720304
email info@independent.ie
website www.independent.ie
Editor Gerard O'Regan
Daily Mon–Sat €1.90, Sat €2.25

Special articles on topical or general subjects. Length: 700–1,000 words. Payment: editor's estimate of value.

Business Editor Maeve Dineen
Education Editor John Walshe
Executive Editor Features Frank Coughlan
News Editor Shane Doram
Sports Editor Dave Courtney
Motoring Editor Eddie Cunningham
Health Correspondent Eilish O'Regan
News Editor Shane Doran
Political Editor Fionnan Sheehan
Security Editor Tom Brady

The Irish Times

The Irish Times Building, PO Box 74,
24–28 Tara Street, Dublin 2, Republic of Ireland
tel +353 (0)1 6758000 *fax* +353 (0)1 6758035
email editor@irishtimes.com
website www.irishtimes.com
Editor Geraldine Kennedy
Editor-in-Chief Kevin O'Sullivan
Daily Mon–Fri €1.90, Sat, €2.25
Supplements **The Irish Times Magazine (Sat), Healthplus (Tue), Business This Week (Fri), Go Travel (Sat), Sport (Mon, Wed, Sat)**

Mainly staff-written. Specialist contributions (800–2,000 words) by commission on basis of ideas submitted. Payment: at editor's valuation. Illustrations: photos and line drawings.

Deputy Editor Denis Staunton
Business Editor John McManus
Arts Editor Shane Hegarty
Features Editor Conor Goodman
Foreign Editor Patrick Smyth
News Editor Kevin O'Sullivan
Picture Editor David Sleator or Frank Miller
Sports Editor Roddy O'Sullivan

The Irish Times on the Web

website www.irishtimes.com
Online Editor Hugh Linehan

Mail on Sunday

Northcliffe House, 2 Derry Street, London W8 5TT
tel 020-7938 6000 *fax* 020-7937 3829
email editorial@mailonsunday.co.uk
website www.mailonsunday.co.uk
Editor-in-Chief Geordie Greig
Sun £1.50
Supplements **The Mail on Sunday 2, Live, You**

Articles. Payment: by arrangement. Illustrations: line, half-tone; cartoons. Founded 1982.

Financial Mail Editor Lisa Buckingham
Features Editor Sian James
Literary Editor Susanna Gross
News Editor David Dillon
Picture Editor Sam Reilly
Political Editor Simon Walters
Sports Editor Malcolm Vallerius

Financial Mail on Sunday

tel 020-7938 6984
Editor Lisa Buckingham, *Personal Finance Editor* Jeff Prestridge
Part of main paper
City, industry, business, and personal finance. News stories up to 1,500 words. Payment: by arrangement. Full colour illustrations and photography commissioned.

Live Magazine

tel 020-7938 6033 *fax* 020-7937 7488
Editor Gerard Greaves
Free with paper
Interviews, entertainment-related features and TV listings. Length: 1,000–3,000 words. Illustrations: colour photos. Founded 1993.

Review

Editor Nick Pyke
Investigative journalism; reportage; features; and film, TV, book and theatre reviews.

You

Editor Sue Peart, *Deputy Editor* Catherine Fenton
Free with paper

Women's interest features. Length: 500–2,500 words. Payment: by arrangement. Illustrations: full colour and b&w drawings commissioned; also colour photos.

Morning Star

(formerly Daily Worker)
People's Press Printing Society Ltd,
William Rust House, 52 Beachey Road,
London E3 2NS
tel 020-8510 0815 *fax* 020-8986 5694
email newsed@peoples-press.com
website www.morningstaronline.co.uk
Editor (Deputy) Richard Bagley
Daily Mon–Sat £1

Newspaper for the labour movement. Articles of general interest. Illustrations: photos, cartoons, drawings. Founded 1930.

Arts & Media Editor Cliff Cocker
News Editor Adrian Roberts
Political Editor John Haylett
Sports Editor Greg Leedham
Features Editor Ros Sitwell

The Observer

Kings Place, 90 York Way, London N1 9GU
tel 020-3353 2000 *fax* 020-3353 3189
website www.observer.co.uk
Editor John Mulholland
Sun £2.20
Supplements **Observer Magazine, Observer Food Monthly, The New Review, Sport**

Some articles and illustrations commissioned. Payment: by arrangement. Founded 1791.

Art Director Carolyn Roberts
Arts Editor Sarah Donaldson
Business Editor Heather Stewart
Cash Editor Lisa Bachelor
City Editor Richard Wachman
Comment Editor Robert Yates
Fashion Editor Jo Jones
Assistant Editor (National & International News) Julian Coman
Home News Editor Lucy Rock
Literary Editor William Skidelsky
OFM Editor Allan Jenkins
Picture Editor Greg Whitmore
Political Editor Toby Helm
Readers' Editor Stephen Pritchard
The New Review Editor Jane Ferguson
Sports Editor Matthew Hancock
Head of Travel Andy Pietrasik

Observer Magazine

tel 020-3353 4451
Editor Ruarioh Nicoll
Free with paper

Commissioned features. Length: 2,000–3,000 words. Illustrations: first-class colour and b&w photos. Payment: NUJ rates; see website for details.

The Observer Online

website www.observer.co.uk

The People

(formerly Sunday People)
1 Canada Square, Canary Wharf, London E14 5AP
tel 020-7293 3000 *fax* 020-7293 3517
email peoplenews@mgn.co.uk
website www.people.co.uk
Editor Lloyd Embley
Sun £1
Supplements **The SP, Take it Easy**

Features Editor Caroline Waterston
News Editor Lee Harpin
Political Editor Nigel Nelson
Sports Editor James Brown

Exclusive news and feature stories needed. Investigative and campaigning issues. Features and human interest stories as speciality. Strong sports following. Payment: rates high, even for tips that lead to published news stories.

Take it Easy

Editor Hanna Tavner
Free with paper

Scotland on Sunday

108 Holyrood Road, Edinburgh EH8 8AS
tel 0131 620 8620 *fax* 0131 620 8491
email newssos@scotlandonsunday.com
website www.scotlandonsunday.co.uk
Editor Ian Stewart
Sun £1.70

Features on all subjects, not necessarily Scottish. Payment: varies. Founded 1988.

News Editor Jeremy Watson
Political Editor Eddie Barnes

Spectrum Magazine

Editor Fiona Leith
Free with paper

The Scotsman

Barclay House, 108 Holyrood Road,
Edinburgh EH8 8AS
tel 0131 620 8620 *fax* 0131 620 8616
email newsdeskts@scotsman.com
website www.scotsman.com
Editor John McLellan
Daily Mon–Fri £1, Sat £1.30
Supplements **Saturday Magazine, Critique, Property, Motoring, Recruitment**

Considers articles on political, economic and general themes which add substantially to current information. Prepared to commission topical and controversial series from proved authorities. Length: 800–1,000 words. Illustrations: outstanding news pictures, cartoons. Payment: by arrangement. Founded 1817.

Arts Editor Andrew Eaton
Business Editor Terry Murden

Books Editor David Robinson
Education Correspondent Chris Marshall
Foreign Editor Rob Corbidge
Group News Editor Frank O'Donnell
Group Political Editor Eddie Barnes
Saturday Magazine Editor Alison Gray
Group Sports Editor Donald Walker

The Scottish Sun

News International Newspapers, Scotland, 6th Floor, Guildhall, 57 Queen Street, Glasgow G1 3EN
tel 0141 420 5200 *fax* 0141 420 5248
email scoop@thesun.co.uk
website www.thescottishsun.co.uk
Editor Andrew Harries
Daily Mon–Fri 30p, Sat–Sun 50p
Supplements **Fabulous**

Scottish edition of *The Sun*. Illustrations: transparencies, colour and b&w prints, colour cartoons. Payment: by arrangement. Founded 1985.

The Sun

3 Thomas More Square, London E98 1XY
tel 020-7782 4000
email news@the-sun.co.uk
website www.the-sun.co.uk
Editor Dominic Mohan
Daily Mon–Fri 30p, Sat–Sun 50p
Supplements **Cashflow, The TV Mag, Fabulous**

Takes freelance material, including cartoons. Payment: by negotiation. Founded 1969.
Deputy Editor Simon Cosyns
Business Editor Steve Hawkes
Features Editor Sean Hamilton
Health Editor Emma Little
Letters Editor Amanda Greenley
Political Editor Tom Newton Dunn
Showbiz Editor Gordon Smart
Sports Editor Mike Dunn
Travel Editor Lisa Minot
Women's Editor Sally Brook

The Sunday Business Post

80 Harcourt Street, Dublin 2, Republic of Ireland
tel +353 (0)1 6026000 *fax* +353 (0)1 6796496
email sbpost@iol.ie
website www.thepost.ie
Editor Cliff Taylor
Sun €2.70

Features on financial, economic and political topics; also lifestyle, media and science articles. Illustrations: colour and b&w photos, graphics, cartoons. Payment: by negotiation. Founded 1989.
Agenda Editor Fiona Kelly
Business Editor Richard Curran
Technology Editor Adrian Weckler
Marketing Editor Catherine O'Mahony
News Editor Martha Kearns
Political Correspondents Pat Leahy, Niamh Connolly
Property Editor Gillian Nelis

Sunday Express

Northern & Shell Building, 10 Lower Thames Street, London EC4R 6EN
tel 020-8612 7000 *fax* 0871 434 7300
email news.desk@express.co.uk
website www.express.co.uk/Sunday
Editor Martin Townsend
Sun £1.20
Supplements **'S' Sunday Express, Property, Review, Sport, Travel, Financial**

Exclusive news stories, photos, personality profiles and features of controversial or lively interest. Length: 800–1,000 words. Payment: top rates. Founded 1918.
Features Editor Amy Packer
Comment Editor Graham Ball
News Editor Stephen Rigley
Deputy Political Editor Kirsty Buchanan
Sports Editor Scott Wilson

'S' Sunday Express

tel 0871 520 7297 *fax* 0871 520 7599
Editor Louise Robinson
Free with paper

Sunday Herald

200 Renfield Street, Glasgow G2 3QB
tel 0141 302 7800 *fax* 0141 302 7863
website www.sundayherald.com
Editor Richard Walker
Sun £1.30
Supplements **Business, Sport, Sunday Herald Magazine, Scottish Review of Books, Fresh**

News and stories about Scotland, its characteristics and people. Opportunities for freelances with quality contacts. Founded 1999.
Business Editor Colin Donald
Digital Editor David Milne
Features Editor Allan Burnett
Magazine Editor Susan Flockhart
Assistant News Editor John Bynorth
Investigations Editor Paul Hutcheon
Sports Editor Jonathan Jobson

Sunday Independent

27–32 Talbot Street, Dublin 1, Republic of Ireland
tel +353 (0)1 7055333 *fax* +353 (0)1 7055779
website www.independent.ie
Editor Anne Harris
Sun €2.70

Special articles. Length: according to subject. Illustrations: topical or general interest, cartoons. Payment: at editor's valuation.
Business Editor Nick Webb
Associate Editor Willie Kealy
Deputy Editor Jody Corcoran
Life Magazine Editor Brendan O'Connor
Sports Editor John Greene

Sunday Mail

1 Central Quay, Glasgow G3 8DA
tel 0141 309 3000 *fax* 0141 309 3587

email mailbox@sundaymail.co.uk
London office 1 Canada Square, Canary Wharf, London E14 5AP
website www.sundaymail.com
Editor Allan Rennie
Sun £1.30
Supplements **Entertainment, Fun on Sunday, Jobsplus!, 7-Days, Right at Home**

Exclusive stories and pictures of national and Scottish interest; also cartoons. Payment: above average.
Deputy Editor Jim Wilson
Health Editor Dr Gareth Smith
News Editor Brendan McGinty
Picture Editor Andrew Hosie
Supplements Editor Liz Cowan
Showbiz Editor Billy Sloan
Sports Editor George Cheyne

Sunday Mirror

1 Canada Square, Canary Wharf, London E14 5AP
tel 020-7293 3000 *fax* 020-7293 3939
email news@sundaymirror.co.uk
website www.mirror.co.uk
Editor Tina Weaver
Sun £1
Supplements **Celebs On Sunday, Homes and Holidays**

Concentrates on human interest news features, social documentaries, dramatic news and feature photos. Ideas, as well as articles, bought. Payment: high, especially for exclusives. Founded 1963.
Head of Content (Features) Jill Main
Head of Content (News) Nick Buckley
Deputy Editor James Scott
Head of Content (Pictures) Ben Jones
Sport Editor David Walker

Sunday Post

D.C. Thomson & Co. Ltd, 144 Port Dundas Road, Glasgow G4 0HZ
tel 0141 332 9933 *fax* 0141 331 1595
email mail@sundaypost.com
Albert Square, Dundee DD1 9QJ
tel (01382) 223131 *fax* (01382) 201064
website www.sundaypost.com
Editor Donald Martin
Sun £1.20
Supplements **Post Plus**

Human interest, topical, domestic and humorous articles, and exclusive news. Payment: on acceptance.

The Sunday Post Magazine

tel (01382) 223131 *fax* (01382) 201064
Editor Jan Gooderham
Monthly Free with paper
General interest articles. Length: 1,000–2,000 words. Illustrations: colour transparencies. Payment: varies. Founded 1988.

Sunday Telegraph

111 Buckingham Palace Road, London SW1W 0DT
tel 020-7931 2000
email stnews@telegraph.co.uk
website www.telegraph.co.uk
Editor Ian MacGregor
Sun £2
Supplements **Business, City, Home & Living, Money & Jobs Sport, Travel**

Occasional freelance material accepted.
City Editor Tim Woodward
Comment Editor Chris Deerin
Deputy Editor Tim Jotischky
Diary Editor Tim Walker
Foreign Editor David Wastell
Literary Editor Michael Prodger
News Editor Hugh Dougherty
Picture Editor Mike Spillard
Political Editor Patrick Hennessy
Seven Editor Ross Jones
Sports Editor Peter Mitchell
Travel Editor Maggie O'Sullivan

Stella

tel 020-7931 3649 *fax* 020-7931 3427
email stella@telegraph.co.uk
Editor Anna Murphy
Free with paper
All material is commissioned. Founded 1995.

The Sunday Times

3 Thomas More Square, London E98 1XY
tel 020-7782 5000 *fax* 020-7782 5731
email newsdesk@sunday-times.co.uk
website www.thesundaytimes.co.uk
Editor John Witherow
Sun £2.20
Supplements **Appointments, Business, Culture, Ingear, Home, Money, News Review, Sport, Style, The Sunday Times Magazine, Travel**

Special articles by authoritative writers on politics, literature, art, drama, music, finance and science, and topical matters. Payment: top rate for exclusive features. Founded 1822.
Deputy Managing Editor Kathleen Herron
Culture Editor Helen Hawkins
Economics Editor David Smith
Literary Editor Andrew Holgate
News Editor Nick Hellen
Sports Editor Alex Butler
Travel Editor Christine Walker

The Sunday Times Magazine

tel 020-7782 7000
Editor Sarah Baxter
Free with paper
Articles and pictures. Illustrations: colour and b&w photos. Payment: by negotiation.

The Times

3 Thomas More Square, London E98 1XY
tel 020-7782 5000 *fax* 020-7782 5988
email home.news@thetimes.co.uk
website www.thetimes.co.uk

Editor James Harding
Daily Mon–Fri £1, Sat £1.50
Supplements **Books, Body & Soul, Bricks & Mortar, Crème, Football Handbook, The Game, The Knowledge, Money, Times 2, Times Law, The Times Magazine, Times Sport, Travel, Arts and Entertainment, Fashion**

Outside contributions considered from: experts in subjects of current interest and writers who can make first-hand experience or reflection come readably alive. Phone appropriate section editor. Length: up to 1,200 words. Founded 1785.

Executive Editor Alex O'Connell
Deputy Editor Keith Blackmore
Education Editor Greg Hurst
Foreign Editor Richard Beeston
Health Editor Martin Barrow
Home News Editor Robert Cole
Industrial Correspondent Angela Jameson
Literary Editor Erica Wagner
Media Editor Ben Webster
Political Editor Roland Watson
Saturday Times Editor Louise France
Science Editor Hannah Devlin
Sports Editor Tim Hallissey
Travel Editor Jane Knight
Times 2 Editor Emma Tucker

The Times Magazine
Editor Louise France
Free with Sat paper

Features. Illustrated.

Wales on Sunday

6 Park Street, Cardiff CF10 1XR
tel 029-2024 3600
email newsdesk@mediawales.co.uk
website www.icwales.co.uk
Editor Simon Farrington
Sun £1
Supplements **Life on Sunday, Sport on Sunday**

National Sunday newspaper of Wales offering comprehensive news, features and entertainments coverage at the weekend, with a particular focus on events in Wales. Accepts general interest articles, preferably with a Welsh connection. Founded 1989.

News Editor Nick Rippington
Sports Editor Paul Abbandonato

Regional newspapers UK and Ireland

Regional newspapers are listed in alphabetical order under region. Some will accept and pay for letters to the editor, brief fillers, and gossip paragraphs, as well as puzzles and quizzes. See also *Writing features for newspapers and magazines* on page 8.

BELFAST

Belfast Telegraph

124–144 Royal Avenue, Belfast BT1 1EB
tel 028-9026 4000
fax 028-9055 4506 (news only), 028-9055 4517 (features), 028-9055 4508 (sport)
email editor@belfasttelegraph.co.uk, newseditor@belfasttelegraph.co.uk
website www.belfasttelegraph.co.uk
Editor Mike Gilson
Group Managing Editor Paul Connolly
Daily Mon–Sat 70p

An Independent News & Media publication. Any material relating to Northern Ireland. Payment: by negotiation. Founded 1870.

Irish News

113–117 Donegall Street, Belfast BT1 2GE
tel 028-9032 2226 *fax* 028-9033 7505
website www.irishnews.com
Editor Noel Doran
Daily Mon–Sat 70p

Articles of historical and topical interest. Payment: by arrangement. Founded 1855.

News Letter

Ground Floor, Metro Building,
6-9 Donegall Square South, Belfast BT1 5JA
tel 028-9089 7700
email newsdesk@newsletter.co.uk
website www.newsletter.co.uk
Editor Darwin Templeton
Daily 68p

Pro-Union. Founded 1737.

Sunday Life

124–144 Royal Avenue, Belfast BT1 1EB
tel 028-9026 4000 *fax* 028-9055 4507
email sinews@sundaylife.co.uk
website www.sundaylife.co.uk
Editor Martin Breen
Sun £1.10

Items of interest to Northern Ireland Sunday tabloid readers. Payment: by arrangement. Illustrations: colour and b&w pictures and graphics. Founded 1988.

CHANNEL ISLANDS

Guernsey Press and Star

PO Box 57, Braye Road, Vale, Guernsey GY1 3BW
tel (01481) 240240 *fax* (01481) 240235
website www.thisisguernsey.com/guernsey-press
Editor Richard Digard
Daily Mon–Sat 45p

News and feature articles. Length: 500–700 words. Illustrations: colour and b&w photos. Payment: by negotiation. Founded 1897.

Jersey Evening Post

PO Box 582, Five Oaks, St Saviour, Jersey JE4 8XQ
tel (01534) 611611 *fax* (01534) 611622
email news@jerseyeveningpost.com
website www.thisisjersey.com
Editor Chris Bright
Daily Mon–Sat 50p

News and features with a Channel Islands angle. Length: 1,000 words (articles/features), 300 words (news). Illustrations: colour and b&w. Payment: £110 per 1,000 words. Founded 1890.

CORK

Evening Echo (Cork)

Evening Echo Publications Ltd, City Quarter, Lapps Quay, Cork, Republic of Ireland
tel +353 (0)21 4272722 *fax* +353 (0)21 4802135
email [firstname.lastname]@eecho.ie
website www.eveningecho.ie
Editor Maurice Gubbins
Daily Mon–Sat €1.50

Articles, features and news for the area. Illustrations: colour prints.

DUBLIN

Evening Herald

Independent House, 27–32 Talbot Street, Dublin 1, Republic of Ireland
tel +353 (0)1 7055722
email hnews@independent.ie
website www.herald.ie
Editor Stephen Rae
Daily Mon–Sat €1

Articles. Payment: by arrangement. Illustrations: line, half-tone, cartoons.

EAST ANGLIA

Cambridge News

Winship Road, Milton, Cambs. CB24 6PP
tel (01223) 434437 *fax* (01223) 434415

email newsdesk@cambridge-news.co.uk
website www.cambridge-news.co.uk
Group Editorial Director Colin Grant *Editor* Paul Brackley
Daily Mon–Sat 50p (Sat 55p)

The voice of the Cambridge region – news, views and sport. Illustrations: colour prints, b&w and colour graphics. Payment: by negotiation. Founded 1888.

East Anglian Daily Times

30 Lower Brook Street, Ipswich, Suffolk IP4 1AN
tel (01473) 230023 *fax* (01473) 324871
website www.eadt.co.uk
Editor Terry Hunt
Daily Mon–Fri 60p, Sat £1.20

Features of East Anglian interest, preferably with pictures. Length: 500 words. Illustrations: colour, b&w. Payment: negotiable. Illustrations: NUJ rates. Founded 1874.

Eastern Daily Press

Prospect House, Rouen Road, Norwich NR1 1RE
tel (01603) 628311 *fax* (01603) 623872
London office House of Commons Press Gallery, House of Commons, London SW1A 0AA
tel 020-7219 3384 *fax* 020-7222 3830
website www.edp24.co.uk
Editor Peter Waters
Daily Mon–Fri 60p, Sat £1.20

Limited market for articles of East Anglian interest not exceeding 900 words. Founded 1870.

Ipswich Star

Archant Regional, Press House,
30 Lower Brook Street, Ipswich, Suffolk IP4 1AN
tel (01473) 230023 *fax* (01473) 324850
website www.ipswichstar.co.uk
Editor Nigel Pickover
Mon–Thurs 60p, Fri 60p

Norwich Evening News

Prospect House, Rouen Road, Norwich NR1 1RE
tel (01603) 628311 *fax* (01603) 623872
website www.eveningnews24.co.uk
Editor Tim Williams
Daily Mon–Sat 50p

Interested in local news-based features. Length: up to 500 words. Payment: NUJ or agreed rates. Founded 1882.

EAST MIDLANDS

Burton Mail

Burton Daily Mail Ltd, 65–68 High Street,
Burton on Trent DE14 1LE
tel (01283) 512345 *fax* (01283) 515351
email editorial@burtonmail.co.uk
website www.burtonmail.co.uk
Editor Kevin Booth
Daily Mon–Sat 40p

Features, news and articles of interest to Burton and south Derbyshire readers. Length: 400–500 words. Illustrations: colour and b&w. Payment: by negotiation. Founded 1898.

Chronicle & Echo, Northampton

Northamptonshire Newspapers Ltd, Upper Mounts, Northampton NN1 3HR
tel (01604) 467000 *fax* (01604) 467200
Editor David Summers
Daily Mon–Sat 48p

Articles, features and news – mostly commissioned – of interest to the Northampton area. Length: varies. Payment: by negotiation. Founded 1931.

Derby Telegraph

Northcliffe House, Meadow Road, Derby DE1 2BH
tel (01332) 291111 *fax* (01322) 253027
website www.thisisderbyshire.co.uk
Editor Steve Hall
Daily Mon–Sat 40p

Articles and news of local interest. Payment: by negotiation.

The Leicester Mercury

St George Street, Leicester LE1 9FQ
tel 0116 251 2512 *fax* 0116 253 0645
website www.thisisleicestershire.co.uk
Acting Editor-in-Chief Richard Bettsworth
Daily Mon–Sat 40p

Occasional articles, features and news; submit ideas to editor first. Length/payment: by negotiation. Founded 1874.

Nottingham Post

Castle Wharf House, Nottingham NG1 4AB
tel 0115 948 2000
email newsdesk@nottinghameveningpostgroup.co.uk
website www.thisisnottingham.co.uk
Editor Malcolm Pheby
Daily Mon–Sat 38p

Material on local issues considered. Founded 1878.

Peterborough Evening Telegraph

Telegraph House, 57 Priesgate,
Peterborough PE1 1JW
tel (01733) 555111 *fax* (01733) 588737
email eteditor@peterboroughtoday.co.uk
website www.peterboroughtoday.co.uk
Editor Mark Edwards
Daily Mon–Sat 45p

LONDON

Evening Standard

Northcliffe House, 2 Derry Street, London W8 5EE
tel 020-3367 7000

website www.thisislondon.com
Editor Geordie Greig
Daily Mon–Fri Free

Founded 1827.

ES Magazine
Executive Editor Andrew Barker
Weekly Free with paper on Fri
Feature ideas, exclusively about London. Payment: by negotiation. Illustrations: all types.

Homes and Property
Editor Janice Morley
Weekly Free with paper on Wed
UK property. Payment: by negotiation.

NORTH

Carlisle News and Star
CN Group, Newspaper House, Dalston Road, Carlisle CA2 5UA
tel (01228) 612600 *fax* (01228) 612640
website www.newsandstar.co.uk
Editor David Helliwell
Mon–Sat 50p

Evening Chronicle
ncjMedia Ltd, Groat Market, Newcastle upon Tyne NE1 1ED
tel 0191 201 6446 *fax* 0191 232 2256
email ec.news@ncjmedia.co.uk
website www.chroniclelive.co.uk
Editor Darren Thwaites
Daily Mon–Sat 45p

News, photos and features covering almost every subject of interest to readers in Tyne & Wear, Northumberland and Durham. Payment: by prior arrangement.

Evening Gazette
Gazette Media Company Ltd, 105–111 Borough Road, Middlesbrough TS1 3AZ
tel (01642) 245401
email news@eveninggazette.co.uk
website www.gazettelive.co.uk
Editor Chris Styles
Daily Mon–Sat 44p

News, and topical and lifestyle features. Length: 600–800 words. Illustrations: line, half-tone, colour, graphics, cartoons. Payment: £75 per 1,000 words; scale rate or by agreement for illustrations. Founded 1869.

Hartlepool Mail
Northeast Press Ltd, New Clarence House, Wesley Square, Hartlepool TS24 8BX
tel (01429) 239333 *fax* (01429) 869024
email mail.news@northeast-press.co.uk
website www.hartlepoolmail.co.uk, www.peterleemail.co.uk
Editor Joy Yates
Daily Mon–Sat 43p

Features of local interest. Length: 500 words. Illustrations: colour, b&w photos, line. Payment: by negotiation. Founded 1877.

The Journal
Groat Market, Newcastle upon Tyne NE1 1ED
tel 0191 232 7500 *fax* 0191 201 6044
email jnl.newsdesk@ncjmedia.co.uk
website www.journallive.co.uk
Editor Brian Aitken
Daily 55p

News, sport items and features of topical interest considered. Payment: by arrangement.

North-West Evening Mail
Newspaper House, Abbey Road, Barrow-in-Furness, Cumbria LA14 5QS
tel (01229) 840150
fax (01229) 840164, (01229) 832141
website www.nwemail.co.uk
Editor Jonathan Lee
Daily Mon–Fri 48p, Sat 50p

Articles, features and news. Length: 500 words. Illustrations: colour photos and occasional artwork. Covering the whole of South Cumbria. Founded 1898.

The Northern Echo
Priestgate, Darlington, Co. Durham DL1 1NF
tel (01325) 381313 *fax* (01325) 380539
website www.thenorthernecho.co.uk
Editor Peter Barron
Daily Mon–Sat 48p

Articles of interest to North-East and North Yorkshire; all material commissioned. Preliminary study of newspaper advisable. Length: 800–1,000 words. Illustrations: line, half-tone, colour – mostly commissioned. Payment: by negotiation. Founded 1870.

The Shields Gazette
Chapter Row, South Shields, Tyne & Wear NE33 1BL
tel 0191 427 4800 *fax* 0191 456 8270
website www.shieldsgazette.com
Editor John Szymanski
Daily Mon–Sat 48p

The Sunday Sun
Groat Market, Newcastle upon Tyne NE1 1ED
tel 0191 201 6201 *fax* 0191 201 6180
email scoop.sundaysun@ncjmedia.co.uk
website www.sundaysun.co.uk
Editor Matt McKenzie
Sun £1

Key requirements: immediate topicality and human sidelights on current problems. Particularly welcomed are special features of family appeal and news stories of special interest to the North of England. Length: 200–700 words. Payment: normal lineage rates, or by arrangement. Illustrations: photos. Founded 1919.

Sunderland Echo

Echo House, Pennywell, Sunderland,
Tyne & Wear SR4 9ER
tel 0191 501 5800 *fax* 0191 534 7497
website www.sunderlandecho.com
Editor Rob Lawson
Daily Mon–Sat 48p

Local news, features and articles. Length: 500 words. Illustrations: colour and b&w photos, line, cartoons. Payment: by negotiation. Founded 1875.

NORTH WEST

The Blackpool Gazette

Blackpool Gazette and Herald Ltd, Avroe House,
Avroe Crescent, Blackpool Business Park,
Squires Gate, Blackpool FY4 2DP
tel (01253) 400888 *fax* (01253) 361870
email editorial@blackpoolgazette.co.uk
website www.blackpoolgazette.co.uk
Editor David Helliwell
Daily Mon–Sat 45p

Local news and articles of general interest, with photos if appropriate. Length: varies. Payment: on merit. Founded 1929.

The Bolton News

Newspaper House, Churchgate, Bolton,
Lancs. BL1 1DE
tel (01204) 537270 *fax* (01204) 537068
email newsdesk@theboltonnews.co.uk
website www.thisisbolton.co.uk
Editor-in-Chief Ian Savage
Daily Mon–Sat 43p

Founded 1867.

Lancashire Evening Post

Oliver's Place, Preston PR2 9ZA
tel (01772) 254841 *fax* (01772) 880173
email lep.newsdesk@lep.co.uk
website www.lep.co.uk
Editor Simon Reynolds
Daily Mon–Sat 50p

Topical articles on all subjects. Area of interest: Wigan to Lake District, Lancs., and coast. Length: 600–900 words. Illustrations: colour and b&w photos, cartoons. Payment: by arrangement.

Lancashire Telegraph

Newspaper House, High Street, Blackburn,
Lancs. BB1 1HT
tel (01254) 678678 *fax* (01254) 680429
website www.lancashiretelegraph.co.uk
Editor Kevin Young
Daily Mon–Sat 43p

Will consider general interest articles, such as property, motoring and finance. Payment: by arrangement. Founded 1886.

Liverpool Echo

PO Box 48, Old Hall Street, Liverpool L69 3EB
tel 0151 227 2000 *fax* 0151 472 2474
website www.liverpoolecho.co.uk
Editor Alastair Machray
Daily Mon–Fri 49p, Sat 62p

Articles of up to 600–800 words of local or topical interest; also cartoons. Payment: according to merit; special rates for exceptional material. Connected with, but independent of, the *Liverpool Daily Post*. Articles not interchangeable.

Manchester Evening News

MEN Media, Mitchell Henry House,
Hollinwood Avenue, Chadderton OL9 8EF
tel 0161 832 7200 *fax* 0161 211 2030 (editorial)
website www.manchestereveningnews.co.uk
Editor Maria McGeoghan
Daily Mon–Sat 47p

Feature articles of up to 1,000 words, topical or general interest and illustrated where appropriate, should be addressed to the Features Editor. Payment: on acceptance.

Oldham Evening Chronicle

PO Box 47, 172 Union Street, Oldham,
Lancs. OL1 1EQ
tel 0161 633 2121 *fax* 0161 652 2111
email news@oldham-chronicle.co.uk
website www.oldham-chronicle.co.uk
Editor David Whaley
Daily Mon–Fri 47p

News and features on current topics and local history. Length: 1,000 words. Illustrations: colour and b&w photos and line. Payment: £20–£25 per 1,000 words; £16.32–£21.90 for illustrations. Founded 1854.

SCOTLAND

The Courier and Advertiser

D.C. Thomson & Co. Ltd, 80 Kingsway East,
Dundee DD4 8SL
tel (01382) 223131 *fax* (01382) 454590
London office 185 Fleet Street, London EC4A 2HS
tel 020-7400 1030 *fax* 020-7400 1089
website www.thecourier.co.uk
Editor Richard Neville
Daily Mon–Sat 44p

Founded 1801 and 1816.

Dundee Evening Telegraph and Post

80 Kingsway East, Dundee DD4 8SL
tel (01382) 223131 *fax* (01382) 454590

email newsdesk@eveningtelegraph.co.uk
London office 185 Fleet Street, London EC4A 2HS
tel 020-7400 1030 *fax* 020-7400 1089
website www.eveningtelegraph.co.uk
Daily Mon–Fri 40p

Evening Express (Aberdeen)

Aberdeen Journals Ltd, PO Box 43, Lang Stracht, Mastrick, Aberdeen AB15 6DF
tel (01224) 690222 *fax* (01224) 341820
website www.eveningexpress.co.uk
Editor Alan McCabe
Daily Mon–Sat 45p

Lively evening paper. Illustrations: colour and b&w. Payment: by arrangement.

Evening News (Edinburgh)

108 Holyrood Road, Edinburgh EH8 8AS
tel 0131 620 8620 *fax* 0131 620 8696
website www.edinburghnews.com
Editor Frank O'Donnell
Daily Mon–Sat 48p

Features on current affairs, preferably in relation to the circulation area. Women's talking points; local historical articles; subjects of general interest; health, beauty and fashion.

Glasgow Evening Times

200 Renfield Street, Glasgow G2 3QB
tel 0141 302 7000 *fax* 0141 302 6699
website www.eveningtimes.co.uk
Editor Tony Carlin
Daily Mon–Sat 50p

Founded 1876.

Inverness Courier

New Century House, Stadium Road, Inverness IV1 1FG
tel (01463) 233059 *fax* (01463) 238223
email editorial@inverness-courier.co.uk
website www.inverness-courier.co.uk
Editor Robert Taylor
Tue 65p, Fri 85p

Articles of Highland interest only. Unsolicited material accepted. Illustrations: colour and b&w photos. Payment: by arrangement. Founded 1817.

Paisley Daily Express

Scottish and Universal Newspapers Ltd, 14 New Street, Paisley, Renfrewshire PA1 1YA
tel 0141 887 7911 *fax* 0141 887 6254
website www.paisleydailyexpress.co.uk
Editor John Hutcheson
Daily Mon–Sat 45p

Articles of Paisley interest only. Considers unsolicited material.

The Press and Journal

Lang Stracht, Aberdeen AB15 6DF
tel (01224) 690222
email pj.editor@ajl.co.uk
website www.pressandjournal.co.uk
Editor Damian Bates
Daily Mon–Fri 60p, Sat 70p

Contributions of Scottish interest. Payment: by arrangement. Illustrations: half-tone. Founded 1747.

SOUTH EAST

The Argus

Argus House, Crowhurst Road, Hollingbury, Brighton BN1 8AR
tel (01273) 544544 *fax* (01273) 566114
email news@theargus.co.uk
website www.theargus.co.uk
Group Editor Michael Beard
Daily Mon–Sat 45p

Established 1880.

Echo

Newspaper House, Chester Hall Lane, Basildon, Essex SS14 3BL
tel (01268) 522792 *fax* (01268) 469281
email echonews@nqe.com
website www.echo-news.co.uk
Editor Martin McNeill
Daily Mon–Fri 43p

Mostly staff-written. Only interested in local material. Payment: by arrangement. Founded 1969.

Medway Messenger

Medway House, Ginsbury Close, Sir Thomas Longley Road, Medway City Estate, Strood, Kent ME2 4DU
tel (01634) 227800 *fax* (01634) 715256
website www.kentonline.co.uk
Editor Bob Bounds
Mon 60p, Fri 90p

Emphasis on news and sport from the Medway Towns. Illustrations: line, half-tone.

The News, Portsmouth

The News Centre, London Road, Hilsea, Portsmouth PO2 9SX
tel 023-9266 4488 *fax* 023-9267 3363
email newsdesk@thenews.co.uk
website www.portsmouth.co.uk
Editor Mark Waldron
Daily Mon–Sat 50p

Articles of relevance to South-East Hampshire and West Sussex. Payment: by arrangement. Founded 1877.

Oxford Mail

Newspaper House, Osney Mead, Oxford OX2 0EJ
tel (01865) 425262 *fax* (01865) 425554
email news@nqo.com
website www.oxfordmail.co.uk

Editor Simon O'Neill
Daily 40p

Reading Post

8 Tessa Road, Reading, Berks. RG1 8NS
tel 0118 918 3000 *fax* 0118 959 9363
email editorial@reading-epost.co.uk
website www.getreading.co.uk
Editor Andy Murrill
Daily Mon–Fri 45p

Topical articles based on current local news. Length: 800–1,200 words. Payment: based on lineage rates. Illustrations: half-tone. Founded 1965.

The Southern Daily Echo

Newspaper House, Test Lane, Redbridge, Southampton SO16 9JX
tel 023-8042 4777 *fax* 023-8042 4545
email newsdesk@dailyecho.co.uk
website www.dailyecho.co.uk
Editor Ian Murray
Daily 40p

News, articles, features, sport. Length: varies. Illustrations: line, half-tone, colour, cartoons. Payment: NUJ rates. Founded 1888.

Swindon Advertiser

100 Victoria Road, Old Town, Swindon SN1 3BE
tel (01793) 528144 *fax* (01793) 542434
email newsdesk@swindonadvertiser.co.uk
website www.swindonadvertiser.co.uk
Editor Gary Lawrence
Daily Mon–Sat 42p

News and information relating to Swindon and Wiltshire only. Considers unsolicited material. Founded 1854.

SOUTH WEST

The Citizen

6-8 The Oxebode , Gloucester GL1 2RZ
tel (01452) 420621 *fax* (01452) 420664
website www.thisisgloucestershire.co.uk
Editor Ian Mean
Daily Mon–Fri 40p, Sat 45p

Local news and features for Gloucester and its districts. Length: 1,000 words (articles/features), 300 words (news). Illustrations: colour. Payment: by negotiation.

Daily Echo

Richmond Hill, Bournemouth BH2 6HH
tel (01202) 554601 *fax* (01202) 292115
email newsdesk@bournemouthecho.co.uk
website www.bournemouthecho.co.uk
Editor Tony Granville
Daily Mon–Fri 45p, Sat 65p

Established 1900.

Dorset Echo

Fleet House, Hampshire Road, Weymouth, Dorset DT4 9XD
tel (01305) 830930 *fax* (01305) 830956
email newsdesk@dorsetecho.co.uk
website www.dorsetecho.co.uk
Editor Toby Granville
Daily Mon–Fri 35p, Sat 45p

News and occasional features (1,000–2,000 words). Illustrations: b&w photos. Payment: by negotiation. Founded 1921.

Express & Echo

Express & Echo News & Media, Heron Road, Sowton, Exeter EX2 7NF
tel (01392) 442211 *fax* (01392) 442287
website www.thisisexeter.co.uk
Editor Andy Phelan
Weekly Thurs £1

Features and news of local interest. Length: 500–800 words (features), up to 400 words (news). Illustrations: colour. Payment: lineage rates; illustrations: by negotiation . Founded 1904.

Gloucestershire Echo

Third Floor, St James's House, St James's Square, Cheltenham, Glos. GL50 3PR
tel (01242) 278000
email echo.news@glosmedia.co.uk
website www.thisisgloucestershire.co.uk
Editor Kevan Blackadder
Daily Mon–Fri 42p, Sat 50p

Specialist articles with Gloucestershire connections; no fiction. Founded 1873.

The Herald

17 Brest Road, Derriford Business Park, Plymouth PL6 5AA
tel (01752) 765500 *fax* (01752) 765527
email news@theplymouthherald.co.uk
website www.thisisplymouth.co.uk
Editor Bill Martin
Daily Mon–Sat 45p

Local news, articles and features. Will consider unsolicited material. Welcomes ideas for articles and features. Illustrations: colour and b&w prints.

Herald Express

Harmsworth House, Barton Hill Road, Torquay, Devon TQ2 8JN
tel (01803) 676767 *fax* (01803) 676228
website www.thisissouthdevon.co.uk
Editor Jim Parker
Weekly Thurs £1

The Post

Temple Way, Bristol BS2 0BU
tel 0117 934 3000 *fax* 0117 934 3570
website www.thisisbristol.co.uk
Editor-in-chief Mike Norton

Daily Mon–Fri 45p

Takes freelance news and articles. Payment: by arrangement. Founded 1932.

Sunday Independent

The Sunday Independent Newspapers Ltd, Webbs House, Tindle Suite, Liskeard, Cornwall PL14 6AH
tel (01579) 342174 *fax* (01579) 341851
email newsdesk@sundayindependent.co.uk
website www.sundayindependent.co.uk
Editor John Noble
Sun 70p

News features on West Country topics; features/articles with a nostalgic theme; short, quirky news briefs (must be original). Length: 600 words (features/articles), 300 words (news). Illustrations: colour, b&w. Payment: by arrangement. Founded 1808.

Western Daily Press

Bristol Evening Post and Press Ltd, Temple Way, Bristol BS99 7HD
tel 0117 934 3000 *fax* 0117 934 3574
email wdeditor@bepp.co.uk
website www.westerndailypress.co.uk
Editor Tim Dixon
Daily Mon–Fri 45p, Sat 70p

National, international or West Country topics for features or news items, from established journalists, with or without illustrations. Payment: by negotiation. Founded 1858.

The Western Morning News

17 Brest Road, Derriford, Plymouth PL6 5AA
tel (01752) 765500 *fax* (01752) 765535
website www.thisisdevon.co.uk, www.thisiscornwall.co.uk
Editor Alan Qualtrough
Daily Mon–Fri 50p, Sat 75p

Articles plus illustrations considered on West Country subjects. Founded 1860.

WALES

The Leader

NWN Media Ltd, Mold Business Park, Wrexham Road, Mold, Flintshire CH7 1XY
tel (01352) 707707 *fax* (01352) 700048
website www.leaderlive.co.uk
Editor Barrie Jones
Mon–Fri 48p

South Wales Argus

South Wales Argus, Cardiff Road, Maesglas, Newport, Gwent NP20 3QN
tel (01633) 777023 *fax* (01633) 777202
email newsdesk@gwent-wales.co.uk
website www.southwalesargus.co.uk
Editor Kevin Ward
Daily Mon–Sat 40p

News and features of relevance to Gwent. Length: 500–600 words (features); 350 words (news). Illustrations: colour prints and transparencies. Payment: £30 (features), £20 (news) per item; £20–£25 (photos). Founded 1892.

South Wales Echo

6 Park Street, Cardiff CF10 1XR
tel (02920) 223333
email echo.newsdesk@walesonline.co.uk
website www.walesonline.co.uk
Editor Tim Gordon
Daily Mon–Fri 50p, Sat 58p

Evening paper: news, sport, features, showbiz, news features, personality interviews. Length: up to 700 words. Illustrations: photos, cartoons. Payment: by negotiation. Founded 1884.

South Wales Evening Post

PO Box 14, Adelaide Street, Swansea SA1 1QT
tel (01792) 510000 *fax* (01792) 514697
email postbox@swwp.co.uk
website www.thisissouthwales.co.uk
Editor-in-Chief Spencer Feeney
Daily 40p

Western Mail

6 Park Street, Cardiff CF10 1XR
tel 029-2022 3333 *fax* 029-2058 3652
website www.walesonline.co.uk
Editor Ceri Gould
Daily Mon–Fri 35p

Articles of political, industrial, literary or general and Welsh interest are considered. Illustrations: topical general news and feature pictures, cartoons. Payment: according to value; special fees for exclusive news. Founded 1869.

WEST MIDLANDS

Birmingham Mail

6th Floor, Fort Dunlop, Fort Parkway, Birmingham B24 9FF
tel 0121 234 5536 *fax* 0121 233 0271
London office 1 Canada Square, Canary Wharf, London E14 5AP
tel 020-7293 3000 *fax* 020-7293 3793
website www.birminghammail.net
Editor David Brookes
Daily Mon–Sat 42p

Features of topical Midland interest considered. Length: 400–800 words. Payment: by arrangement. Founded 1870.

The Birmingham Post

6th Floor, Fort Dunlop, Fort Parkway, Birmingham B24 9FF

tel 0121 234 5301 *fax* 0121 234 5667
London office 22nd Floor, 1 Canada Square, Canary Wharf, London E14 5AP
tel 020-7293 3455 *fax* 020-7293 3400
website www.birminghampost.net
Editor Alun Thorne
Weekly £1.25

Authoritative and well-written articles of industrial, political or general interest are considered, especially if they have relevance to the Midlands. Length: up to 1,000 words. Payment: by arrangement.

Coventry Telegraph

Corporation Street, Coventry CV1 1FP
tel 024-7663 3633 *fax* 024-7655 0869
website www.coventrytelegraph.net
Editor Darren Parkin
Daily Mon–Sat 45p

Topical, illustrated articles with a Coventry or Warwickshire interest. Length: up to 600 words. Payment: by arrangement.

Express & Star

51–53 Queen Street, Wolverhampton WV1 1ES
tel (01902) 313131 *fax* (01902) 319721
email newsdesk@expressandstar.co.uk
website www.expressandstar.com
Editor Adrian Faber
Daily Mon–Sat 42p

Founded 1874.

The Sentinel

Staffordshire Sentinel News & Media Ltd, Sentinel House, Etruria, Stoke-on-Trent ST1 5SS
tel (01782) 602525 *fax* (01782) 602616
email editor@thesentinel.co.uk
website www.thisisthesentinel.co.uk
Editor Michael Sassi
Daily Mon–Sat 40p

Articles and features of topical interest to the north Staffordshire/south Cheshire area. Illustrations: colour and b&w. Payment: by arrangement. Founded 1873.

Shropshire Star

Waterloo Road, Ketley, Telford TF1 5HU
tel (01952) 242424 *fax* (01952) 254605
website www.shropshirestar.com
Editor Keith Harrison
Daily Mon–Sat 42p

Evening paper: news and features. No unsolicited material; write to Features Editor with outline of ideas. Payment: by arrangement. Founded 1964.

Sunday Mercury

6th Floor, Fort Dunlop, Fort Parkway, Birmingham B24 9FF
tel 0121 234 5493 *fax* 0121 234 5877
website www.sundaymercury.net
Executive Editor Paul Cole
Sun £1.10

News specials or features of Midland interest. Illustrations: colour, b&w, cartoons. Payment: special rates for special matter.

Worcester News

Berrows House, Hylton Road, Worcester WR2 5JX
tel (01905) 748200 *fax* (01905) 429605
website www.worcesternews.co.uk
Editor Peter John
Daily Mon–Sat 42p

Local and national news, sport and features. Will consider unsolicited material. Welcomes ideas for articles and features. Length: 800 words (features), 300 words (news). Payment: by negotiation. Illustrations: colour jpg files.

YORKSHIRE/HUMBERSIDE

Evening Courier

PO Box 19, King Cross Street, Halifax HX1 2SF
tel (01422) 260200 *fax* (01422) 260341
email editor@halifaxcourier.co.uk
website www.halifaxcourier.co.uk
Editor Tim Robinson
Daily Mon–Sat 50p

Grimsby Telegraph

80 Cleethorpe Road, Grimsby, North East Lincs. DN31 3EH
tel (01472) 360360 *fax* (01472) 372257
email newsdesk@grimsbytelegraph.co.uk
website www.thisisgrimsby.co.uk
Editor Michelle Lalor
Daily Mon–Sat 40p

Considers general interest articles. Illustrations: line, half-tone, colour, cartoons. Payment: by arrangement. Founded 1897.

The Huddersfield Daily Examiner

56 John William Street, Huddersfield HD1 1ER
tel (01484) 430000 *fax* (01484) 437789
email editorial@examiner.co.uk
website www.examiner.co.uk
Editor Roy Wright
Daily Examiner 49p, Weekend Examiner 62p

No contributions required at present. Founded 1851.

Hull Daily Mail

Blundell's Corner, Beverley Road, Hull HU3 1XS
tel (01482) 327111 *fax* (01482) 315353
website www.thisishullandeastriding.co.uk
Editor Neil Hodgkinson
Daily Mon–Fri 45p, Sat 48p

Lincolnshire Echo

Ground Floor, Witham Wharf, Brayford Wharf East Lincoln LN5 7HY

tel (01522) 820000 *fax* (01522) 804493
website www.thisislincolnshire.co.uk
Editor Steven Fletcher
Weekly Thurs £1

The Press

Newsquest York, PO Box 29, 76–86 Walmgate, York YO1 9YN
tel (01904) 653051 *fax* (01904) 612853
email newsdesk@thepress.co.uk
website www.yorkpress.co.uk
Managing Editor Steve Hughes
Daily Mon–Sat 48p

Articles of North and East Yorkshire interest. Length: 500–1,000 words. Payment: by arrangement. Illustrations: line, half-tone. Founded 1882.

Scarborough Evening News

17–23 Aberdeen Walk, Scarborough, North Yorkshire YO11 1BB
tel (01723) 363636 *fax* (01723) 383825
website www.scarborougheveningnews.co.uk
Editor Ed Asquith
Weekly Thurs 37p

Sheffield Star

York Street, Sheffield S1 1PU
tel 0114 276 7676 *fax* 0114 272 5978
website www.thestar.co.uk
Editor Jeremy Clifford
Daily Mon–Sat 47p

Well-written articles of local character. Length: about 500 words. Payment: by negotiation. Illustrations: topical photos, line drawings, graphics, cartoons. Founded 1887.

Telegraph & Argus

Hall Ings, Bradford BD1 1JR
tel (01274) 729511 *fax* (01274) 723634
email newsdesk@telegraphandargus.co.uk
website www.telegraphandargus.co.uk
Editor Perry Austin-Clarke
Daily Mon–Sat 48p

Daily paper: news, articles and features relevant to or about the people of West Yorkshire. Length: up to 1,000 words. Illustrations: line, half-tone, colour. Payment: features from £15; line from £5, b&w and colour photos by negotiation. Founded 1868.

Yorkshire Evening Post

PO Box 168, Wellington Street, Leeds LS1 1RF
tel 0113 238 8917 *fax* 0113 238 8535
website www.yorkshireeveningpost.co.uk
Editor Paul Napier
Daily Mon–Sat 45p

News stories and feature articles. Illustrations: colour and b&w, cartoons. Payment: by negotiation. Founded 1890.

Yorkshire Post

Wellington Street, Leeds LS1 1RF
tel 0113 243 2701 *fax* 0113 238 8537
London office 292 Vauxhall Bridge Road, London SW1V 1AE
tel 020-7963 7646
website www.yorkshirepost.co.uk
Editor Peter Charlton
Daily Mon–Fri 60p, Sat £1
Supplements **Yorkshire Post Magazine**

Authoritative and well-written articles on topical subjects of general, literary or industrial interests. Length: max. 1,200 words. Payment: by arrangement. Founded 1754.

Magazines UK and Ireland

Listings for regional newspapers start on page 19 and listings for national newspapers start on page 11. For quick reference, magazines are listed by subject area starting on page 699.

Accountancy

145 London Road, Kingston-upon-Thames, Surrey KT2 6SR
tel 020-8247 1379 *fax* 020-8247 1481
email accountancynews@wolterskluwer.co.uk
website www.accountancylive.com
Editor Sara White
Monthly £99 p.a.; 2 years, £178.20; 3 years, £237.60. Overseas subs: 1 year, £112; 2 years, £201.60; 3 years, £268.80

Articles on accounting, taxation, audit, financial, legal and other subjects likely to be of professional interest to accountants in practice or industry, and to top management generally. All feature ideas to be submitted by email in the form of a brief, bullet-pointed synopsis. Founded 1889.

Accountancy Age

Incisive Media, 32–34 Broadwick Street, London W1A 2HG
tel 020-7316 9000 *fax* 020-7316 9250
email news@accountancyage.com
website www.accountancyage.com
Editor Kevin Reed
Weekly £95 p.a.

Articles of accounting, financial and business interest. Illustrations: colour photos; freelance assignments commissioned. Payment: by arrangement. Founded 1969.

Accounting & Business

Association of Chartered Certified Accountants, 29 Lincolns Inn Fields, London WC2A 3EE
tel 020-7059 5000 *fax* 020-7059 5050
email info@accaglobal.com
website www.accaglobal.com
Editor Chris Quick
10 p.a. £10, £85 p.a.

Journal of the Association of Chartered Certified Accountants. Features accountancy, finance and business topics of relevance to accountants and finance directors. Length: 1,100 words. Illustrated. Founded 1998.

Acumen Literary Journal

6 The Mount, Higher Furzeham, Brixham, South Devon TQ5 8QY
tel (01803) 851098
email patriciaoxley6@gmail.com
website www.acumen-poetry.co.uk
Editor Patricia Oxley
3 p.a. (Jan/May/Sept) £5.50, £15.50 p.a.

Poetry, literary and critical articles, reviews, literary memoirs, etc. Send sae with submissions. Payment: small. Founded 1985.

Aeroplane Monthly

IPC Media Ltd, The Blue Fin Building, 110 Southwark Street, London SE1 0SU
tel 020-3148 4100
website www.aeroplanemonthly.com
Editor Michael Oakey
Monthly £3.99

Articles and photos relating to historical aviation. Length: up to 3,000 words. Illustrations: line, half-tone, colour, cartoons. Payment: £60 per 1,000 words, payable on publication; photos £10–£40; colour £80 per page. Founded 1973.

Aesthetica Magazine

PO Box 371, York YO23 1WL
tel (01904) 629137
website www.aestheticamagazine.com
Editor Cherie Federico
Bi-monthly £3.95

International art and culture magazine featuring articles on visual arts, film, performance and music. For freelance opportunities, contact the editor. Founded 2002.

Africa-Asia Confidential

Asempa Ltd, 73 Farringdon Road, London EC1M 3JQ
tel 020-7831 3511 *fax* 020-7831 6778
website www.africa-asia-confidential.com
Editor Patrick Smith
Monthly £49 p.a. students, £271 p.a. institutions, £319 p.a. companies

News on the Africa–Asia axis. Unsolicited contributions welcome but must be exclusive and not published elsewhere. Length: 1,200 words (features), 600 words (briefings). Payment: from £200 per 1,000 words. No illustrations. Founded 2007.

Africa Confidential

Asempa Ltd, 73 Farringdon Road, London EC1M 3JQ
tel 020-7831 3511 *fax* 020-7831 6778
website www.africa-confidential.com
Editor Patrick Smith
Fortnightly £737 p.a.

News and analysis of political and economic developments in Africa. Unsolicited contributions welcomed, but must be exclusive and not published elsewhere. Length: 1,200-word features, 200-word pointers. Payment: from £300 per 1,000 words. No illustrations. Founded 1960.

Africa: St Patrick's Missions

St Patrick's, Kiltegan, Co. Wicklow,
Republic of Ireland
tel +353 (0)59 6473600 *fax* +353 (0)59 6473622
email africa@iol.ie
website www.spms.org
Editor Rev. Tim Redmond
9 p.a. £10 p.a. (€12)

Articles of missionary and topical religious interest. Length: up to 1,000 words. Illustrations: colour.

African Business

IC Publications Ltd, 7 Coldbath Square,
London EC1R 4LQ
tel 020-7841 3210 *fax* 020-7841 3211
email editorial@africasia.com
website www.africasia.com
Editor Anver Versi
Monthly £3.00, £40 p.a.

Articles on business, economic and financial topics of interest to businessmen, ministers, officials concerned with African affairs. Length: 1,000–1,400 words; shorter coverage 500 words. Illustrations: line, half-tone, cartoons. Payment: £90–£100 per 1,000 words; £1 per column cm for illustrations. Founded 1978.

Agenda

The Wheelwrights, Fletching Street, Mayfield,
East Sussex TN20 6TL
tel/fax (01435) 873703
email editor@agendapoetry.co.uk
website www.agendapoetry.co.uk
Editor Patricia McCarthy
Quarterly. £28 p.a. (£35 libraries, institutions and overseas); £22 OAPs/students

Poetry and criticism. Study the journal and visit the website for submission details before submitting work via email to submissions@agendapoetry.co.uk. Young poets and artists aged 16–38 are invited to submit work for online broadsheets.

AIR International

Key Publishing Ltd, PO Box 100, Stamford,
Lincs. PE9 1XQ
tel (01780) 755131 *fax* (01780) 751323
email airint@keypublishing.com
Editor Mark Ayton
Monthly £4.20, £41 p.a.

Technical articles on aircraft; features on topical aviation subjects – civil and military. Length: up to 3,000 words. Illustrations: colour transparencies/prints, b&w prints/line drawings. Payment: £50 per 1,000 words or by negotiation; £20 colour, £10 b&w. Founded 1971.

All Out Cricket

Unit 3–23 Kennington Court, 1–3 Brixton Road,
London SW9 6DE
tel 020-3176 0187
website www.alloutcricket.com
Editor Andy Afford
12 p.a. £3.95, £45 p.a.

Magazine of the Professional Cricketers' Association. Humour, insight, expert commentary interviews, photography and lifestyle. Email editor with ideas first. Payment by negotiation. Founded 2004.

Amateur Gardening

IPC Media Ltd, Westover House, West Quay Road,
Poole, Dorset BH15 1JG
tel (01202) 440840 *fax* (01202) 440860
website www.amateurgardening.com
Editor Tim Rumball
Weekly £2.00

No longer accepts any form of unsolicited material. Founded 1884.

Amateur Photographer

(incorporating Photo Technique)
IPC Media Ltd, The Blue Fin Building,
110 Southwark Street, London SE1 0SU
tel 020-3148 5000
email amateurphotographer@ipcmedia.com
website www.amateurphotographer.co.uk
Editor Damien Demolder
Weekly £2.60, £127.50 p.a.

Unsolicited editorial submissions are not encouraged. Founded 1884.

Ambit

17 Priory Gardens, London N6 5QY
tel 020-8340 3566
email info@ambitmagazine.co.uk
website www.ambitmagazine.co.uk
Editor Martin Bax, *Poetry Editors* Henry Graham, Carol-Ann Duffy, *Prose Editor* Geoff Nicholson, *Art Editor* Mike Foreman
Quarterly £9 (single copy), £12/€16 (Rest of Europe), £14/€22 (Rest of World); £28 p.a. (UK), £32/€40 (Rest of Europe), £38/$64 (Rest of World)

Poetry, short fiction, art, poetry reviews. New and established writers and artists. Welcomes unsolicited prose, poetry and artwork. Payment: by arrangement. Illustrations: line, half-tone, colour. Founded 1959.

Android Magazine

Imagine Publishing Ltd, Richmond House,
33 Richmond Hill, Bournemouth BH2 6EZ
website www.littlegreenrobot.co.uk
Editor Andy Betts
Monthly £4.99

Magazine focused solely on the Android operating system for phones and tablet PCs. Includes features, tips, tutorials and tweaking information, as well as app and hardware reviews. Unsolicited material not accepted but pitches are welcome via email.

Angler's Mail

IPC Media Ltd, The Blue Fin Building,
110 Southwark Street, London SE1 0SU

tel 020-3148 4159 *fax* 020-3148 8129
email anglersmail@ipcmedia.com
website www.anglersmail.com
Editor Tim Knight, *Features Editor* Richard Howard
Weekly £1.80

News items about coarse fishing. Payment: by agreement.

Angling Times

Bauer Consumer Media, Bushfield House, Orton Centre, Peterborough PE2 5UW
tel (01733) 395106 *fax* (01733) 465844
email rich.lee@bauermedia.co.uk
website www.gofishing.co.uk/Angling-Times
Editor Richard Lee
Weekly £1.60, £60 p.a.

Articles, pictures, news stories, on all forms of angling. Illustrations: line, half-tone, colour. Payment: by arrangement. Founded 1953.

Apollo

22 Old Queen Street, London SW1H 9HP
tel 020-7961 0150
email editorial@apollomag.com
website www.apollo-magazine.com
Editor Oscar Humphries
Monthly £5.95

Scholarly and topical articles of about 2,000–3,000 words on art, architecture, ceramics, photography, furniture, armour, glass, sculpture, and any subject connected with art and collecting. Interviews with collectors. Exhibition and book reviews, articles on current developments in museums and art galleries, regular columns on the art market and contemporary art. Payment: by arrangement. Illustrations: colour. Founded 1925.

Aquila

New Leaf Publishing Ltd, PO Box 2518, Eastbourne, East Sussex BN21 2BB
tel (01323) 431313 *fax* (01323) 731136
email info@aquila.co.uk
website www.aquila.co.uk
Editor Jackie Berry
Monthly £40 p.a.

Dedicated to encouraging children aged 8–13 to reason and create, and to develop a caring nature. Short stories and serials of up to three parts. Occasional features commissioned from writers with specialist knowledge. Approach in writing with ideas and sample of writing style, with sae. Length: 700–800 words (features), 1,000–1,100 words (stories or per episode of a serial). Payment: £75 (features); £90 (stories), £80 (per episode). Founded 1993.

The Architects' Journal

EMAP Construct, Greater London House, Hampstead Road, London NW1 7EJ
tel 020-7728 5000
website www.architectsjournal.co.uk
Editor Kieran Long
Weekly £4, £150 p.a.

Articles (mainly technical) on architecture, planning and building accepted only with prior agreement of synopsis. Illustrations: photos and drawings. Payment: by arrangement. Founded 1895.

Architectural Design

John Wiley & Sons, 25 John Street, London WC1N 2BS
tel 020-8326 3800
Editor Helen Castle
6 double issues p.a. £24.99 (print, single issue), £120 p.a.; *AD* app for iPad single issue £9.99, £44.99 for subscription (£7.50 each)

International architectural publication comprising an extensively illustrated thematic profile and magazine back section, *AD Plus*. Uncommissioned articles not accepted. Illustrations: drawings and photos, line (colour preferred). Payment: by arrangement. Founded 1930.

The Architectural Review

EMAP Construct, Greater London House, Hampstead Road, London NW1 7EJ
tel 020-7728 4592
website www.architectural-review.com
Editor Catherine Slessor
Monthly £9.99, £110 p.a.

Articles on architecture and the allied arts (urbanism, design, theory, history, technology). Writers must be thoroughly qualified. Length: up to 3,000 words. Payment: by arrangement. Illustrations: photos, drawings, etc. Founded 1896.

Architecture Today

161 Rosebery Avenue, London EC1R 4QX
tel 020-7837 0143 *fax* 020-7837 0155
website www.architecturetoday.co.uk
Editor Chris Foges
10 p.a. £4.50, £45 p.a.

Mostly commissioned articles and features on today's European architecture. Length: 200–800 words. Illustrations: colour. Payment: by negotiation. Founded 1989.

Art Business Today

The Fine Art Trade Guild, 16–18 Empress Place, London SW6 1TT
tel 020-7381 6616 *fax* 020-7381 2596
email abt@fineart.co.uk
website www.artbusinesstoday.co.uk
5 p.a. £28 p.a.

Distributed to the fine art and framing industry. Covers essential information on new products and technology, market trends and business analysis. Length: 800–1,600 words. Illustrations: colour photos, cartoons. Payment: by arrangement. Founded 1905.

Art Monthly

4th Floor, 28 Charing Cross Road,
London WC2H 0DB
tel 020-7240 0389 *fax* 020-7497 0726
email info@artmonthly.co.uk
website www.artmonthly.co.uk
Editor Patricia Bickers
10 p.a. £4.40, £44 p.a.

Features on modern and contemporary visual artists and art history, art theory and art-related issues; exhibition and book reviews. All material commissioned. Length: 750–1,500 words. Illustrations: b&w photos. Payment: features £100–£200; none for photos. Founded 1976.

The Art Newspaper

70 South Lambeth Road, London SW8 1RL
tel 020-3416 9000
website www.theartnewspaper.com
Editor Jane Morris
11 p.a. £85 p.a. (monthly; print and print + digital), £45 (monthly; digital only)

International coverage of visual art, news, politics, law, exhibitions with some feature pages. Length: 200–1,000 words. Illustrations: b&w photos. Payment: £350+ per 1,000 words. Founded 1990.

Art Quarterly

The Art Fund, Millais House, 7 Cromwell Place,
London SW7 2JN
tel 020-7225 4800 *fax* 020-7225 4848
email info@artfund.org
website www.artfund.org
Editor Charlotte Mullins
Quarterly Free to members

Magazine of the Art Fund. Features on current events in the art world and extensive coverage of the Art Fund's campaigns and grant-giving activities.

Art Review

Art Review Ltd, 1 Sekforde Street, London EC1R 0BE
tel 020-7107 2760 *fax* 020-7107 2761
email editorial@artreview.com
website www.artreview.com
Editor Mark Rappolt
Monthly £5.50, £29 p.a.

Modern and contemporary art and style features and reviews. Proposals welcome. Payment: from £350 per 1,000 words. Illustrations: colour. Founded 1949.

The Artist

The Artists' Publishing Co. Ltd, Caxton House,
63–65 High Street, Tenterden, Kent TN30 6BD
tel (01580) 763673
Editor Sally Bulgin
Monthly £3.70

Practical, instructional articles on painting for all amateur and professional artists. Payment: by arrangement. Illustrations: line, half-tone, colour. Founded 1931.

Artists & Illustrators

Unit 19, 15 Lots Road, London SW10 0QJ
tel 020-7349 3150 *fax* 020-7349 3160
email info@artistsandillustrators.co.uk
website www.artistsandillustrators.co.uk
Editor Steve Pill
Monthly £3.75

Practical and inspirational articles for amateur and professional artists. Length: 500–1,500 words. Illustrations: hi res digital images, hand-drawn illustrations. Payment: variable. Founded 1986.

AS Magazine

Suite 404, Albany House, 324 Regent Street,
London W1B 3HH
tel 020-7622 6670 *fax* 020-7636 2323
email editor@asmagazine.co.uk
website www.amateurstagemagazine.co.uk
Editor Douglas Mayo
Monthly £2.40

Articles on all aspects of the amateur theatre, preferably practical and factual. Length: 600–2,000 words. Illustrations: photos, line drawings. Payment: none. Founded 1946.

Assent

Room E701, Kedleston Road, University of Derby,
Derby DE22 1GB
Poetry Editor Julia Gaze
3 p.a. £4, £12 p.a. (£20 overseas); cheques payable to 'Derby University'

Poems, reviews, articles. Payment: complimentary copy. Founded 1946.

Astronomy Now

Pole Star Publications, PO Box 175, Tonbridge,
Kent TN10 4ZY
tel (01732) 446110 *fax* (01732) 300148
email editorial2011@astronomynow.com
website www.astronomynow.com
Editor Keith Cooper
Monthly £5.25

Specialises in translating exciting astronomy research into articles for the lay reader. Also covers amateur astronomy with equipment reviews and observing notes. Send sae for writers' guidelines. Length: 1,000–2,000 words. Payment: 15p per word; from £10 per photo. Founded 1987.

Athletics Weekly

PO Box 614, Farnham, Surrey GU9 1GR
tel (01733) 808550 *fax* (01733) 808530
email jason.henderson@athleticsweekly.com
website www.athleticsweekly.com
Editor Jason Henderson
Weekly £2.95

News and features on track and field athletics, road running, cross country, fell and race walking. Material mostly commissioned. Length: 300–1,500 words. Illustrations: colour and b&w action and head/shoulder photos, line. Payment: varies. Founded 1945.

Attitude

Ground Floor, 211 Old Street, London EC1V 9NR
tel 020-7608 6446 *fax* 020-7608 6320
email attitude@attitude.co.uk
website www.attitude.co.uk
Editor Matthew Todd
13 p.a. £4.25, £29.25 p.a. (print edition), £24.99 p.a. (iPad edition)

Men's style magazine aimed primarily, but not exclusively, at gay men. Covers style/fashion, interviews, reviews, celebrities, humour. Illustrations: colour transparencies, b&w prints. Payment: £150 per 1,000 words; £100 per full page illustration. Founded 1994.

The Author

84 Drayton Gardens, London SW10 9SB
tel 020-7373 6642
website www.societyofauthors.org/author
Editor Andrew Rosenheim
Quarterly £12

Organ of the Society of Authors. Commissioned articles from 1,000–2,000 words on any subject connected with the legal, commercial or technical side of authorship. Little scope for the freelance writer: preliminary letter advisable. Illustrations: line, occasional cartoons. Payment: by arrangement. Founded 1890.

Auto Express

Dennis Publishing Ltd, 30 Cleveland Street, London W1T 4JD
tel 020-7907 6000 *fax* 020-7907 6234
email editorial@autoexpress.co.uk
website www.autoexpress.co.uk
Editor David Johns
Weekly £2.25

News stories, and general interest features about drivers as well as cars. Illustrations: colour photos. Payment: features £350 per 1,000 words; photos, varies. Founded 1988.

Autocar

Haymarket Publishing Ltd, Teddington Studios, Broom Road, Teddington, Middlesex TW11 9BE
tel 020-8267 5630 *fax* 020-8267 5759
email autocar@haymarket.com
website www.autocar.co.uk
Editor Chas Hallett
Weekly £3.10

Articles on all aspects of cars, motoring and the motor industry: general, practical, competition and technical. Illustrations: line (litho), colour and electronic (Illustrator). Press day news: Thursday. Payment: varies; mid-month following publication. Founded 1895.

Aviation News

Key Publishing, PO Box 100, Stamford PE9 1XQ
tel (01780) 751323
email editor@aviation-news.co.uk
website www.aviation-news.co.uk
Editor David Baker
Monthly £4.10

Covers all aspects of aviation. Many articles commissioned; will consider competent articles exploring fresh ground or presenting an individual point of view on technical matters. Illustrated, mainly with photos. Payment: by arrangement.

BackTrack

Pendragon Publishing, PO Box 3, Easingwold, York YO61 3YS
tel/fax (01347) 824397
email pendragonpublishing@btinternet.com
website www.pendragonpublishing.co.uk
Editor Michael Blakemore
Monthly £3.95

British railway history from 1820s to 1980s. Welcomes ideas from writers and photographers. Articles must be well researched, authoritative and accompanied by illustrations. Length: 3,000–5,000 words (main features), 500–3,000 words (articles). Illustrations: colour and b&w. Payment: £30 per 1,000 words, £18.50 colour, £10 b&w. Founded 1986.

Balance

Diabetes UK, 10 Parkway, London NW1 7AA
tel 020-7424 1000 *fax* 020-7424 1001
email balance@diabetes.org.uk
website www.diabetes.org.uk
Editor Angela Coffey
Bi-monthly £3.95

Articles on diabetes and related health and lifestyle issues. Length: 1,000–1,500 words. Payment: by arrangement. Illustrations: colour. Founded 1935.

The Banker

FT Business, 1 Southwark Bridge, London SE1 9HL
tel 020-7873 3000
email brian.caplen@ft.com
website www.thebanker.com
Editor-in-Chief Brian Caplen
Monthly £595 p.a. (includes online access), £525 (print only)

Global coverage of retail banking, corporate banking, banking technology, transactions services, investment banking and capital markets, regulation, and top 1,000 bank listings.

Baptist Times

PO Box 54, 129 Broadway, Didcot, Oxon OX11 8XB
tel (01235) 517677

website www.baptisttimes.co.uk
Editor Paul Hobson
Website only.

Religious or social affairs, news, features and reviews. Founded 1855.

BBC magazines – see Inside the BBC, page 382

BBC Countryfile Magazine
website www.bbccountryfile.com

BBC Easy Cook
website www.bbcmagazines.com/ads/easycook

BBC Gardeners' World
website www.gardenersworld.com

BBC Good Food
website www.bbcgoodfood.com

BBC Good Homes
website www.bbcgoodhomes.com

BBC History Magazine
website www.bbchistorymagazine.com

BBC Music Magazine
website www.bbcmusicmagazine.com

BBC Top Gear
website www.topgear.com

BBC Wildlife
website www.wildlifemagazine.com

Focus
website www.focusmag.co.uk

Gardens Illustrated
website www.gardensillustrated.com

Homes & Antiques
website www.homesandantiques.com

Sky at Night Magazine
website www.skyatnightmagazine.com

What to Wear
website www.bbcmagazines.com/whattowear

The Beano

D.C. Thomson & Co. Ltd, 2 Albert Square, Dundee DD1 9QJ
email mstirling@dcthompson.co.uk
185 Fleet Street, London EC4A 2HS
tel 020-7400 1030 *fax* 020-7400 1089
Editor Michael Stirling
50 p.a. £1.50

Comic strips for children aged 6–12. Series, 11–22 pictures. Artwork only. Payment: on acceptance.

Bella

H. Bauer Publishing, Academic House, 24–28 Oval Road, London NW1 7DT
tel 020-7241 8000 *fax* 020-7241 8056
Editor Julia Davis
Weekly 89p

Women's magazine with celebrity interviews, exclusive photos, real life stories, high street fashion, diet advice, health, food and travel. Payment: by arrangement. Founded 1987.

Best

Hearst Magazines UK, 33 Broadwick Street, London W1F 0DQ
tel 020-7339 4500 *fax* 020-7339 4580
email best@natmags.co.uk
Editor Jackie Hatton, *Features Editor* Charlotte Seligman
Weekly 89p

Short stories. No other uncommissioned work accepted, but always willing to look at ideas/outlines. Length: 1,000 words for short stories, variable for other work. Payment: by agreement. Founded 1987.

Best of British

Church Lane Publishing Ltd, The Clock Tower, 6 Market Gate, Market Deeping, Lincs. PE6 8DL
tel (01778) 342814, 380906 *fax* (01778) 342814
email info@bestofbritishmag.co.uk
website www.bestofbritishmag.co.uk
Editor Caroline Chadderton
Editor-in-Chief Ian Beacham
Monthly £3.75

Nostalgic features about life in the 1940s, 1950s and 1960s together with stories celebrating interesting aspects of Britain today. Length: max. 1,200 words. Illustrations: colour and b&w. Payment: at editor's discretion. Founded 1994.

The Big Issue

1–5 Wandsworth Road, London SW8 2LN
tel 020-7526 3200 *fax* 020-7526 3201
email info@thebigissue.com
website www.bigissue.com
Editor-in-Chief John Bird
Weekly £2.50

Features, current affairs, reviews, interviews – of general interest and on social issues. Length: 1,000 words (features). No short stories or poetry. Illustrations: colour and b&w photos and line. Payment: £160 per 1,000 words. Founded 1991.

The Big Issue Cymru

55 Charles Street, Cardiff CF10 2GD
tel 029-2025 5670 *fax* 029-2025 5673
email editorial@bigissuecymru.co.uk
website www.bigissuecymru.co.uk
Editor Rachel Howells
Weekly £1.50

The Welsh edition of *The Big Issue*. Content is relevant to Wales: some articles are taken from the main London edition but news, features, arts and music coverage are locally sourced. Considers unsolicited material. Welcomes ideas for articles and features. No poetry or short stories. Length: 1,000–1,500 words (articles/features), 200–400 words (news). Illustrations: colour and b&w prints and artwork. Payment: by arrangement. Founded 1994.

The Big Issue in the North

The Big Issue in the North Ltd, The Big Life Group, 123 Moss Lane East, Manchester M15 5DD
tel 0161 831 5550
website www.bigissueinthenorth.com
Editor Kevin Gopal
Weekly £2

Articles of general interest and on social issues; arts features and news covering the north of England. No fiction or poetry, except by the homeless. Contact the editorial department to discuss ideas. Length: 1,000 words (features/articles), 300–500 (news), 700 (arts features). Payment: £120 per 1,000 words/12p per word. Colour transparencies, puzzles and quizzes. Founded 1992.

The Big Issue in Scotland

31 Queensferry Street, Edinburgh EH2 4QS
tel 0141 352 7260 *fax* 0141 333 9049
email editorial@bigissuescotland.com
website www.bigissuescotland.com
Editor Paul McNamee
Weekly £2.50

Features on social issues, human rights, the environment, injustice, Scotland, medical, health and crime plus news and arts coverage. Also international features/news. Length: 1,000–2,000 words (articles); 300–400 words (news). Illustrations: colour and b&w. Payment: £120 per 1,000 words; £60 per photo/illustration. Founded 1993.

Bike

Bauer Consumer Media, Media House, Lynchwood, Peterborough PE2 6EA
tel (01733) 468181 *fax* (01733) 468196
email bike@bauermedia.com
website www.bikemagazine.co.uk
Editor Tim Thompson
Monthly £4.10

Motorcycle magazine. Interested in articles, features, news. Length: articles/features 1,000–3,000 words. Illustrations: colour and b&w photos. Payment: £140 per 1,000 words; photos per size/position. Founded 1971.

Bird Watching

Bauer Consumer Media, Media House, Lynchwood, Peterborough PE2 6EA
tel (01733) 468201
website www.birdwatching.co.uk
Editor Sheena Harvey
Monthly £4.10

Broad range of bird-related features and photography, particularly looking at bird behaviour, bird news, reviews and UK birdwatching sites. Limited amount of overseas features. Emphasis on providing accurate information in entertaining ways. Send synopsis first. Length: up to 1,200 words. Illustrations: emailed jpgs and photo images on CD, bird identification artwork. Payment: by negotiation. Founded 1986.

Birding World

Sea Lawn, Coast Road, Cley next the Sea, Holt, Norfolk NR25 7RZ
tel (01263) 740913 *fax* (01263) 741014
email steve@birdingworld.co.uk
website www.birdingworld.co.uk
Editor Steve Gantlett
Monthly £49 p.a. (£56 p.a. Europe; £59 p.a. rest of the world, airmail)

Magazine for keen birdwatchers. Articles and news stories about mainly European ornithology, with the emphasis on ground-breaking new material and identification. Length: up to 3,000 words (articles); up to 1,500 words (news). Illustrations: good quality colour photos of birds. Founded 1987.

Birdwatch

Solo Publishing Ltd, The Chocolate Factory, 5 Clarendon Road, London N22 6XJ
tel 020-8881 0550
website www.birdwatch.co.uk
Editor Dominic Mitchell
Monthly £4.10

Topical articles on all aspects of birds and birding, including conservation, identification, sites and habitats, equipment, overseas destinations. Length: 700–1,500 words. Illustrations: high-res jpgs (300 dpi at 1,500 pixels min. width) of wild British and European birds considered; submit on CD/DVD. Artwork by negotiation. Payment: from £50 per 1,000 words; colour: photos £15–£40, cover £75, line by negotiation; b&w: photos £10, line £10–£40. Founded 1991.

Bizarre

Dennis Publishing, 30 Cleveland Street, London W1T 4JD
tel 020-7907 6000 *fax* 020-7907 6439
email bizarre@dennis.co.uk
website www.bizarremag.com
Editor David McComb
Monthly £3.50

Features on strange events, adventure, cults, weird people, celebrities, etc. Study the magazine for style before submitting ideas by post or fax. No fiction. Payment: 20p per word. Colour transparencies and prints: £200 per dps, £125 per page. Founded 1997.

Black Beauty & Hair

Hawker Publications, 2nd Floor, Culvert House, Culvert Road, London SW11 5DH

tel 020-7720 2108 *fax* 020-7498 3023
email info@blackbeautyandhair.com
website www.blackbeautyandhair.com
Editor Irene Shelley
Bi-monthly £3, £15 p.a.

Beauty and style articles relating specifically to the black woman; celebrity features. True-life stories and salon features. Length: approx. 1,000 words. Illustrations: colour and b&w photos. Payment: £100 per 1,000 words; photos £25–£75. Founded 1982.

Black Static

TTA Press, 5 Martins Lane, Witcham, Ely, Cambs. CB6 2LB
website www.ttapress.com
Editor Andy Cox
Bi-monthly £3.95 (£21 for 6 issues)

New horror and dark fantasy stories. Also features interviews with, and profiles of, authors and film-makers. Send sae with all submissions. Considers unsolicited material and welcomes ideas for articles and features. Length: 3,000–4,000 words (articles and features), short stories unrestricted. Illustrations: send samples and portfolios. Payment: by arrangement. Founded 1994.

Bliss

Panini UK Ltd, Brockbourne House, 77 Mount Ephraim, Tunbridge Wells, Kent TN4 8BS
tel (01892) 500100 *fax* (01892) 545666
email bliss@panini.co.uk
website www.mybliss.co.uk
Editor Leslie Sinoway
Monthly £2.75

Glamorous young women's glossy magazine. Bright, intimate, A5 format, with real life reports, celebrities, beauty, fashion, shopping, advice, quizzes. Payment: by arrangement. Founded 1995.

Blueprint

Progressive Media Markets, 6–14 Underwood Street, London N1 7JQ
tel 020-7549 2542
website www.blueprintmagazine.co.uk
Acting Editor Peter Kelly, *Associate Editor* Tim Abrahams
12 p.a. £4.75, £49 p.a.

Magazine for architects and designers. Interested in articles, features and reviews. Length: up to 2,500 words. Illustrations: colour and b&w photos and line. Payment: negotiable. Founded 1983.

BMA News

British Medical Association, BMA House, Tavistock Square, London WC1H 9JP
tel 020-7383 6122 *fax* 020-7383 6566
Editors Caroline Winter-Jones, Carol Harris
49 p.a. £92 p.a.

News and features. Length: 700–2,000 words (features), 100–300 words (news). Illustrations: any colour and b&w artwork. Payment: by negotiation. Founded 1966.

Bodyfit

Aceville Publications Ltd, 25 Phoenix Court, Hawkins Road, Colchester CO2 8JY
tel (01206) 505972
email info@bodyfitmagazine.co.uk
Editor Naomi Abeykoon
10 p.a. £2.60

Features on health and emotional weight-loss issues. Length: 800 or 1,400 words. No unsolicited MSS at this time. Send feature summary by email in first instance. Freelance entries occasionally accepted. Payment: by arrangement. Founded 1972.

The Book Collector

(incorporating Bibliographical Notes and Queries)
PO Box 6431, London W1A 2BJ
tel 020-7297 4889 *fax* 020-7297 4866
email editor@thebookcollector.co.uk
website www.thebookcollector.co.uk
Editorial Board Nicolas Barker (Editor), A. Edwards, J. Fergusson, T. Hofmann, D. McKitterick, Joan Winterkorn
Quarterly £50 p.a., £60 Europe (€76.50 by credit card only), £65/US$105 Rest of World (airmail)

Articles, biographical and bibliographical, on the collection and study of printed books and MSS. Payment: for reviews only. Founded 1952.

Book World Magazine

Christchurch Publishers Ltd, 2 Caversham Street, London SW3 4AH
tel/fax 020-7351 4995
email leonard.holdsworth@btinternet.com
Editor Leonard Holdsworth
Monthly £5

Special features and reviews of interest to serious book collectors, booksellers and librarians. Articles and ideas for articles welcome. Illustrations: b&w and colour. Payment: by negotiation. Established 1980.

Books Ireland

11 Newgrove Avenue, Dublin 4, Republic of Ireland
tel +353 (0)1 2692185
email booksi@eircom.net
Editor Jeremy Addis, *Features Editor* Shirley Kelly
Monthly (exc. Jan, July, Aug) €3.50, €35 p.a.

Reviews of Irish-interest and Irish-author books, articles of interest to librarians, booksellers and readers. Length: 800–1,400 words. Payment: €100 per 1,000 words. Founded 1976.

The Bookseller

VNU Entertainment Media Ltd, 5th Floor, Endeavour House, 189 Shaftesbury Avenue, London WC2H 8TJ

tel 020-7420 6006 *fax* 020-7420 6103
email felicity.wood@thebookseller.co.uk
website www.thebookseller.com
Editor-in-Chief Neill Denny, *Features Editor* Tom Tivnan
Weekly £4.40, £170 p.a.

Journal of the UK publishing, bookselling trade and libraries. While outside contributions are welcomed, most of the journal's contents are commissioned. Length: about 1,000–1,500 words. Payment: by arrangement. Founded 1858.

Bowls International

Key Publishing Ltd, PO Box 100, Stamford, Lincs. PE9 1XQ
tel (01780) 755131 *fax* (01780) 751323
Editor Patrick Hulbert
Monthly £3.40

Sport and news items and features; occasional, bowls-oriented short stories. Illustrations: colour transparencies, b&w photos, occasional line, cartoons. Payment: sport/news approx. 25p per line, features approx. £50 per page; colour £25, b&w £10. Founded 1981.

Brass Band World Magazine

Impromptu Publishing Ltd, 2nd Floor, Century House, 11 St Peter's Square, Manchester M2 3DN
tel 0161 236 9526 *fax* 0161 247 7978
email capital@btconnect.com
website www.brassbandworld.com
Editor Carol Jarvis
Monthly £3.85

Artlcles, features and news of brass bands internationally. Reviews of concerts and contests, personality profiles, tips, and news from colleges for students, players and audiences. Payment: negotiable. Founded 1981.

British Birds

4 Harlequin Gardens, St Leonards on Sea TN37 7PF
tel (01424) 755155
email editor@britishbirds.co.uk
website www.britishbirds.co.uk
Editor Dr Roger Riddington
Monthly £51 p.a. (£58 p.a. overseas)

Publishes major papers on identification, behaviour, conservation, distribution, ecology, movements, status and taxonomy with official reports on: rare breeding birds, scarce migrants and rare birds in Britain. Payment: token. Founded 1907.

British Chess Magazine

44 Baker Street, London W1U 7RT
tel 020-7486 8222 *fax* 020-7486 3355
website www.bcmchess.co.uk
Editor John Saunders
Monthly £3.70, £38 p.a.

Authoritative reports and commentary on the UK and overseas chess world. Payment: by arrangement. Founded 1881.

British Deaf News

British Deaf Association, Bushell Street Mill, Bushell Street, Preston, Lancs. PR1 2SP
tel (01772) 259725 *fax* (01772) 561610
email bdn@bda.org.uk; membership@bda.org.uk (membership enquiries)
website www.bda.org.uk
Editor Alison Gudgeon
Monthly £2, £20 p.a. UK individuals, £30 p.a. UK organisations

Membership magazine for the British Deaf Association. Interviews, features, reviews, articles, news items, regular columns. Payment: by arrangement. Illustrations: line, half-tone. Founded 1872.

The British Journal of Photography

32–34 Broadwick Street, London W1A 2HG
tel 020-7316 9000 *fax* 020-7316 9003
email bjp.editor@bjphoto.co.uk
website www.bjp-online.com
Editor Simon Bainbridge
Monthly £6.99

Focus on all aspects of professional photography: articles on fine art, commercial, fashion, social and press, alongside technical reviews of the latest software and equipment. Founded 1854.

British Journalism Review

Sage Publications, 1 Oliver's Yard, 55 City Road, London EC1Y 1SP
tel 020-7324 8500 *fax* 020-7324 8600
email editor@bjr.org.uk
website www.bjr.org.uk
Editor Bill Hagerty
Quarterly £36 p.a. (overseas rates on application)

Comment/criticism/review of matters published by, or of interest to, the media. Length: 1,500–3,000 words. Illustrations: b&w photos. Payment: by arrangement. Founded 1989.

British Medical Journal

BMJ Publishing Group, BMA House, Tavistock Square, London WC1H 9JR
tel 020-7387 4499 *fax* 020-7383 6418
email fgodlee@bmj.com
website www.bmj.com
Editor Dr Fiona Godlee
Weekly Free to members of BMA; for subscription details see website

Medical and related articles. Payment: by arrangement. Founded 1840.

British Philatelic Bulletin

Royal Mail, 35–50 Rathbone Place, London W1T 1HQ

fax 020-7441 4744
email john.r.holman@royalmail.co.uk
website www.royalmail.com/stamps
Editor J.R. Holman
Monthly £1.20

Articles on any aspect of British philately – stamps, postmarks, postal history; also stamp collecting in general. Length: up to 1,500 words (articles); 250 words (news). Payment: £75 per 1,000 words. Illustrations: colour. Founded 1963.

British Woodworking

Freshwood Publishing, Ampney St Peter, Cirencester, Glos. GL7 5SH
tel (01285) 850481
email nick.gibbs@britishwoodworking.com
website www.britishwoodworking.com
Editor Nick Gibbs
Bi-monthly £3.50, £18.50 p.a.

Articles and features for woodworking hobbyists. Includes projects, news and wood-related articles. Length: 2,500 words. Payment: by arrangement.

Broadcast

Greater London House, Hampstead Road, London NW1 7EJ
tel 020-7728 5512 *fax* 020-7728 5555
email lisa.campbell@emap.com
website www.broadcastnow.co.uk
Editor Lisa Campbell
Weekly £4.95

For people working or interested in the UK and international broadcast industry. News, features, analysis and opinions. Covers the latest developments in programming, commissioning, digital, technology and post-production. Illustrations: colour, b&w, line, cartoons.

Building

Building Magazine, UBM Information Ltd, 3rd Floor, 245 Blackfriars Road, London SE1 9UY
tel 020-7560 4000 *fax* 020-7560 4004
email building@ubm.com
website www.building.co.uk
Editor Tom Broughton
Weekly £2.90

Covers all aspects of the construction industry from architecture to development to social housing, industrial and manufacturing aspects of the building industry. Will consider articles on architecture at home and abroad; also news and photos. Payment: by arrangement. Founded 1842.

Building Design

UBM Information Ltd, Ludgate House, 245 Blackfriars Road, London SE1 9UY
tel 020-7921 5000 *fax* 020-7921 8244
email buildingdesign@ubm.com
website www.bdonline.co.uk
Editor Amanda Baillieu
Subscription only

News and features on all aspects of building design. All material commissioned. Length: up to 1,500 words. Illustrations: colour and b&w photos, line, cartoons. Payment: £150 per 1,000 words; illustrations by negotiation. Founded 1970.

The Burlington Magazine

14–16 Duke's Road, London WC1H 9SZ
tel 020-7388 8157 *fax* 020-7388 1230
email editorial@burlington.org.uk
website www.burlington.org.uk
Editor Richard Shone
Monthly £16.50

Deals with the history and criticism of art; book and exhibition reviews; illustrated monthly Calendar section. Potential contributors must have special knowledge of the subjects treated; MSS compiled from works of reference are unacceptable. Length: 500–5,000 words. Payment: up to £140. Illustrations: colour images. Founded 1903.

Buses

Key Publishing Ltd, Foundry Road, Stamford, Lincs. PE9 2PP
tel (01780) 484630 *fax* (01780) 763388
Editor Alan Millar, PO Box 14644, Leven KY9 1WX
tel (01333) 340637
email buseseditor@btconnect.com
website www.busesmag.com
Monthly £4.10

Articles of interest to both road passenger transport operators and bus enthusiasts. Preliminary enquiry essential. Illustrations: digital, colour transparencies, half-tone, line maps. Payment: on application. Founded 1949.

Business Life

85 Strand, London WC2R 0DW
tel 020-7550 8000
email businesslife@cedarcom.co.uk
website www.cedarcom.co.uk
Editor Tim Hulse
Monthly

Free inflight magazine for British Airways passengers. Articles and features of interest to the European business traveller. All material commissioned; approach in writing with ideas. Founded 1986.

Business Traveller

Panacea Publishing, Cardinal House, 39–40 Albemarle Street, London W1S 4TE
tel 020-7647 6330
email editorial@businesstraveller.com
website www.businesstraveller.com
Editor Tom Otley
10 p.a. £3.95, £42.95 p.a.

Articles, features and news on consumer travel aimed

at individual frequent international business travellers. Submit ideas with recent clippings and a CV. Length: varies. Illustrations: colour for destinations features; send lists to Deborah Miller, Picture Editor. Payment: on application. Founded 1976.

Cambridgeshire Journal

Cambridge Newspapers Ltd, Winship Road, Milton, Cambridge CB24 6PP
tel (01223) 434419 *fax* (01223) 434415
email alice.ryan@cambridge-news.co.uk
Content Editor Alice Ryan
Monthly £2.45

Articles, features and news of interest to Cambridgeshire: history, people, events, natural history and other issues. Also regional lifestyle, i.e. gardens, homes and fashion. Founded 1994.

Campaign

Haymarket Business Publications Ltd, 174 Hammersmith Road, London W6 7JP
tel 020-8943 5000
website www.campaignlive.co.uk
Editor Claire Beale
Weekly £3.70

News and articles covering the whole of the mass communications field, particularly advertising in all its forms, marketing and the media. Features should not exceed 2,000 words. News items also welcome. Press day, Wednesday. Payment: by arrangement.

Canals, Rivers + Boats

PO Box 618, Norwich NR7 0QT
tel (01603) 708930
email chris@themag.fsnet.co.uk
Editor Chris Cattrall
Monthly £3.50

Articles on UK inland waterways and cruising features, DIY articles and historical features. Length: 1,500 words max (articles/features), 300 words (news). Payment: £100-150 (inc. illustrations). Text: Word Document format files. Illustrations: hi-res jpg files required. Founded 1978.

Candis

Newhall Publications Ltd, Newhall Lane, Hoylake, Wirral CH47 4BQ
tel 0151 632 3232
email fiction@candis.co.uk
website www.candis.co.uk
Editor Debbie Attewell
Monthly £3.50 Subscription only

Commissions one 2,500 word short story each month by a well known published author. Unsolicited material is no longer received and will be returned unread. Writers willing to share a personal life story or experience for real lives feature may send a synopsis to editor@candis.co.uk. Also covers health, news, celebrity interviews, family issues, fashion and beauty.

Car

Bauer Consumer Media, 3rd Floor, Media House, Lynchwood, Peterborough PE2 6EA
tel (01733) 468379 *fax* (01733) 468660
Editor Phil McNamara
Monthly £4.20

Top-grade journalistic features on car driving, car people and cars. Length: 1,000–2,500 words. Payment: minimum £350 per 1,000 words. Illustrations: b&w and colour photos to professional standards. Founded 1962.

Car Mechanics

Broadway Court, Broadway, Peterborough PE1 1RP
tel (01733) 347559 *fax* (01733) 891342
email cm.ed@kelsey.co.uk
website www.carmechanicsmag.co.uk
Editor Martyn Knowles
Monthly £3.85

Practical articles on maintaining, repairing and uprating modern cars for DIY plus the motor trade. Always interested in finding new talent for our rather specialised market but study a recent copy before submitting ideas or features. Email outlining feature recommended. Payment: by arrangement. Illustrations: line drawings, colour prints, transparencies or digital images. Supply package of text and pictures.

Caravan Magazine

Warners Group Publications, The Maltings, Bourne, Lincs. PE10 9PH
tel (01778) 391000
email johns@warnersgroup.co.uk
website www.caravanmagazine.co.uk
Managing Editor John Sootheran
Monthly £3.80

Lively articles based on real experience of touring caravanning, especially if well illustrated by photos. Payment: by arrangement. Founded 1933.

Caring Business

CMP Information, Ludgate House, 245 Blackfriars Road, London SE1 9UY
tel 020-7921 5000
website www.careshow.co.uk
Editor Olufunmi Majekodunmi
Monthly £64 p.a.

Specialist contributions relating to the commercial aspects of nursing and residential care, including hospitals. Payment: £50 per 1,000 words. Illustrations: line, half-tone. Founded 1985.

Carousel – The Guide to Children's Books

Ephraim Phillips House, 54–76 Bissell Street, Birmingham B5 7HP

tel 0121 622 7458
email carousel.guide@virgin.net
website www.carouselguide.co.uk
Editor David Blanch
3 p.a. £11.85 p.a. (£17 p.a. Europe; £20 p.a. rest of world)

Reviews of fiction, non-fiction and poetry books for children, plus in-depth articles; profiles of authors and illustrators. Length: 1,200 words (articles); 150 words (reviews). Illustrations: colour and b&w. Payment: by arrangement. Founded 1995.

Cat World

Ancient Lights, 19 River Road, Arundel BN18 9EY
tel (01903) 884988 *fax* (01903) 885514
website www.catworld.co.uk
Editor Laura Quiggan
Monthly £2.95

Bright, lively articles on any aspect of cat ownership. Articles on breeds of cats and veterinary articles by acknowledged experts only. No unsolicited fiction. All submissions by email or on disk. Illustrations: colour prints, transparencies, tiffs. Payment: by arrangement. Founded 1981.

Caterer & Hotelkeeper

Reed Business Information Ltd, Quadrant House, The Quadrant, Sutton, Surrey SM2 5AS
tel 020-8652 3500 *fax* 020-8652 8973
email catererneews@rbi.co.uk
Editor Mark Lewis
Weekly £3.10

Articles on all aspects of the hotel and catering industries. Length: up to 1,500 words. Illustrations: line, half-tone, colour. Payment: by arrangement. Founded 1874.

The Catholic Herald

Herald House, Lambs Passage, Bunhill Row, London EC1Y 8TQ
tel 020-77448 3602 *fax* 020-7256 9728
email editorial@catholicherald.co.uk
website www.catholicherald.co.uk
Editor Luke Coppen
Weekly £75 p.a. (print only), £85 p.a. (digital and print versions)

Independent newspaper covering national and international affairs from a Catholic/Christian viewpoint as well as church news. Length: articles 800–1,200 words. Illustrations: photos of Catholic and Christian interest. Payment: by arrangement.

Catholic Pictorial

36 Henry Street, Liverpool L1 5BS
tel 0151 522 1007 *fax* 0151 522 1008
email p.heneghan@rcaol.co.uk
Editor Peter Heneghan
Monthly £1

News and photo features (maximum 800 words plus illustration) of Merseyside, regional and national Catholic interest only; also cartoons. Has a strongly social editorial and is a trenchant tabloid. Payment: by arrangement. Founded 1961.

Catholic Times

Gabriel Communication, Landmark House, 4th Floor, Station Road, Cheadle, Hulme SK8 7JH
tel 0161 488 1700 *fax* 0161 488 1701
email kevin.flaherty@totalcatholic.com
website www.totalcatholic.com
Editor Kevin Flaherty
Weekly £1

News (400 words) and news features (800 words) of Catholic interest. Illustrations: colour and b&w photos. Payment: £30–£80; photos £50. Relaunched 1993.

Ceramic Review

63 Great Russell Street, London WC1B 3BF
tel 020-7183 5583 *fax* 020-3137 0924
email editorial@ceramicreview.com
website www.ceramicreview.com
Editor Bonnie Kemske
6 p.a. £6.30, £36 p.a.

High-quality magazine containing critical features, reviews and practical information on ceramics around the world. Welcomes article proposals: critical, profile, technical, historical or experiential; also looking at the role of ceramics within contemporary culture.

CGA Magazine

CGA, Chalke House, Station Road, Codford, Warminster BA12 0JX
tel (01985) 850706 *fax* (01985) 850378
email enquiries@thecga.co.uk
website www.thecga.co.uk
Editor Melanie Tibbs
8 p.a. Controlled circulation: members only

Magazine of the Country Gentlemen's Association. News and features coveringa mix of events, interviews, leisure, food, homes and gardens and travel. Some outside contributors used. Payment: by arrangement. Founded 1893.

Chapman

4 Broughton Place, Edinburgh EH1 3RX
tel 0131 557 2207
email chapman-pub@blueyonder.co.uk
website www.chapman-pub.co.uk
Editor Dr Joy Hendry
3 p.a. £24 p.a.

New poetry, short stories, reviews, criticism, articles on Scottish culture or general cultural matters. Featured artist in each issue. Illustrations: line, half-tone, cartoons. Payment: £8 per page; illustrations by negotiation. Founded 1970.

Chartered Secretary

ICSA Information & Training Ltd, 16 Park Crescent, London W1B 1AH

tel 020-7612 7045 *fax* 020-7612 7034
email chartsec@icsa.co.uk
website www.charteredsecretary.net
Editor Rachael Johnson, *Assistant Editor* Gareth Pearce
Monthly £90 p.a. (free to members)

Official magazine of The Institute of Chartered Secretaries and Administrators. Practical and topical articles (2,000+ words) on law, governance, finance and management affecting company secretaries and other senior administrators in business, not-for-profit sector, local and central government and other institutions in Britain and overseas.

Chat

IPC Connect Ltd, The Blue Fin Building, 110 Southwark Street, London SE1 0SU
tel 020-3148 5000
website www.ipcmedia.com
Editor Gilly Sinclair
Weekly 84p

Tabloid weekly for women. Includes reader's letters, tips and true life features. Payment: by arrangement. Founded 1985.

Child Education PLUS

Book End, Range Road, Witney OX29 0YD
tel (01926) 887799 *fax* (01926) 883331
email childed@scholastic.co.uk
website www.scholastic.co.uk/childedplus
Publishing Director Paula Hubbard
Bi-monthly £19.98 p.a.

For teachers concerned with the education of children aged 4–11. Articles by specialists on practical teaching ideas and methods. Length: 600–1,200 words. Payment: by arrangement. Profusely illustrated with photos and artwork; also two A2 colour posters. Founded 1924.

Church of England Newspaper

Religious Intelligence Ltd, 14 Great College Street, London SW1P 3RX
tel 020-7878 1001 *fax* 020-7878 1031
email cen@churchnewspaper.com
website www.churchnewspaper.com
Editor Colin Blakely
Weekly £1.25

Anglican news and articles relating the Christian faith to everyday life. Evangelical basis; almost exclusively commissioned articles. Study of paper desirable. Length: up to 1,000 words. Illustrations: photos, line drawings, cartoons. Payment: c. £40 per 1,000 words; photos £22, line by arrangement. Founded 1828.

Church Times

13–17 Long Lane, London EC1A 9DJ
tel 020-7776 1060 *fax* 020-7776 1086
email news@churchtimes.co.uk
website www.churchtimes.co.uk
Editor Paul Handley
Weekly £1.40

Articles on religious topics are considered. No verse or fiction. Length: up to 1,000 words. Illustrations: news photos, sent promptly. Payment: £100 per 1,000 words; Periodical Publishers' Association negotiated rates for illustrations. Founded 1863.

CIRCA

The Priory, John Street West, Dublin 8, Republic of Ireland
tel/fax +353 (0)1 6401585
email editor@recirca.com
website www.recirca.com
Editor Peter FitzGerald
Quarterly €25 p.a. (Rep. of Ireland, Northern Ireland), €34.50 outside RoI and NI

Covers contemporary visual arts in Ireland with news, reviews, previews, interviews and feature articles. The magazine is dedicated to reflecting visual culture as it unfolds throughout Ireland while also reporting on important developments further afield. Welcomes proposals for feature articles: email ideas or texts to the editor.

Classic Boat Magazine

The Chelsea Magazine Co., Liscartan House, 127-131 Sloane Street, London SW1X 9AS
tel 020-8726 8000 *fax* 020-8726 8195
email cb@ipcmedia.com
website www.classicboat.co.uk
Editor Dan Houston
Monthly £4.40

Cruising and technical features, restorations, events, new boat reviews, practical, maritime history; news. Study of magazine essential: read 3–4 back issues and send for contributors' guidelines. Length: 500–2,000 words. Illustrations: colour and b&w photos; line drawings of hulls. Payment: £75–£100 per published page. Founded 1987.

Classic Cars

Bauer Consumer Media, Media House, Lynchwood, Peterborough Business Park, Peterborough PE2 6EA
tel (01733) 468000 *fax* (01733) 468888
website www.classiccarsmagazine.co.uk
Editor Phil Bell
Monthly £4.20

Specialist articles on older cars. Length: from 500–4,000 words (subject to prior contract). Illustrations: half-tone, colour. Payment: by negotiation.

Classic Rock

Future Publishing Ltd, 30 Monmouth Street, Bath BA1 2BW
tel (01225) 442244 *fax* (01225) 446019
website www.classicrockmagazine.com
Editor in Chief Scott Rowley, *Editor* Siân Llewellyn

13 p.a. £4.99

'The definitive voice in rock journalism', focusing on hard rock, heavy metal and the older generation of 'Rockers'. Features the real stories behind rock legends with in-depth profiles, interviews, news overviews, tour dates, retrospective articles and reviews.

Classical Music

Rhinegold Publishing Ltd, 241 Shaftesbury Avenue, London WC2H 8TF
tel 020-7333 1742 *fax* 020-7333 1769
email classical.music@rhinegold.co.uk
website www.rhinegold.co.uk
Editor Keith Clarke
Fortnightly £3.95

News, opinion, features on the classical music business. All material commissioned. Illustrations: colour photos and line; colour covers. Payment: minimum £100 per 1,000 words; from £50 for illustrations. Founded 1976.

Classics Monthly

Future Excite, 30 Monmouth Street, Bath BA1 2BW
tel/fax (01225) 442244
Editor Gary Stretton
Monthly £3.99

News photos and stories of classic car interest and illustrated features on classic car history, repairs, maintenance and restoration. Study magazine before submitting material. Features must have high level of subject knowledge and technical accuracy. Length: up to 2,000 words (features); 200 words (news). Illustrations: colour and b&w. Payment: £120 per 1,000 words plus £100 per set of supporting photos (features); £120 per 1,000 words plus photos based on £100 per page (news). Founded 1997.

Climb Magazine

David Pickford, Climb Magazine, Greenshires Publishing, 160-164 Barkby Road, Leicester LE16 8FZ
tel (0116) 2022600
email climbmagazine@gmail.com
website www.climbmagazine.com
Editor David Pickford
12 p.a. £3.50

Climbing magazine covering mainly British rock climbing. Features all aspects of climbing worldwide from bouldering to mountaineering. Contact Editor to discuss requirements. Founded 1987.

Climber

The Maltings, West Street, Bourne, Lincs. PE10 9PH
tel (01778) 391000 *fax* (01778) 394748
email climbercomments@warnersgroup.co.uk
website www.climber.co.uk
Editor Andy McCue
Monthly £3.50

Articles on all aspects of rock climbing/ mountaineering in Great Britain and abroad, and on related subjects. Study of magazine essential. Length: 1,500–2,000 words. Illustrations: colour transparencies. Payment: according to merit. Founded 1962.

Closer

Bauer Consumer Media, Endeavour House, 189 Shaftsbury Avenue, London WC2H 8JG
tel 020-7437 9011
email closer@closermag.co.uk
website www.closeronline.co.uk
Editor Lisa Burrow
Weekly £1.40

Women's entertainment magazine with true-life stories and celebrity articles, letters, listings and reviews. Payment by negotiation.

Coin News

Token Publishing Ltd, Orchard House, Duchy Road, Heathpark, Honiton, Devon EX14 1YD
tel (01404) 46972 *fax* (01404) 44788
email johnm@tokenpublishing.com
Editor John W. Mussell
Monthly £3.65

Articles of high standard on coins, tokens, paper money. Send text in digital form. Length: up to 2,000 words. Payment: by arrangement. Founded 1964.

Commando

D.C. Thomson & Co. Ltd, 80 Kingway East, Dundee DD4 8SL
tel (01382) 223131 *fax* (01382) 322214
4 per fortnight £1.50

Fictional stories set in time of war told in pictures. Scripts: about 135 pictures. Synopsis required as an opener. New writers encouraged; send for details. Payment: on acceptance.

Commercial Motor

Reed Business Information Ltd, Quadrant House, The Quadrant, Sutton, Surrey SM2 5AS
tel 020-8652 3500 *fax* 020-8652 8988
website www.roadtransport.com
Editor Justin Stanton
Weekly £1.80, £110 p.a.

Technical and road transport articles only. Length: up to 1,500 words. Payment: varies. Illustrations: drawings and photos. Founded 1905.

Community Care

Reed Business Information Ltd, Quadrant House, The Quadrant, Sutton, Surrey SM2 5AS
tel 020-8652 3500 *fax* 020-8652 4739
email comcare.children@rbi.co.uk, comcare.adults@rbi.co.uk
website www.communitycare.co.uk
Editor Bronagh Miskelly

Weekly £2.45

Articles, features and news covering the Social Services sector.

Company

Hearst Magazines UK, National Magazine House, 72 Broadwick Street, London W1V 2BP
tel 020-7439 5000 *fax* 020-7312 3797
website www.company.co.uk
Editor Victoria White
Monthly £2

Articles on a wide variety of subjects, relevant to young, independent women. Most articles are commissioned. Payment: usual magazine rate. Illustrated. Founded 1978.

Computer Arts

Future Publishing Ltd, Computer Arts, 30 Monmouth Street, Bath BA1 2BW
tel (01225) 442244
email ca.mail@futurenet.co.uk
website www.computerarts.co.uk
Editor Rob Carney
Monthly £6

Magazine for digital artists and designers with in-depth tutorials together with tips for web design, typography, 3D, animation, motion graphics and multimedia. Also reviews the latest hardware and software releases and includes interviews with the leading figures in the global design world.

Computer Weekly

Reed Business Information Ltd, Quadrant House, The Quadrant, Sutton, Surrey SM2 5AS
tel 020-8652 3500 *fax* 020-8652 8979
email computer.weekly@rbi.co.uk
website www.computerweekly.com
Editor Brian McKenna
Weekly £3.35

Feature articles on IT-related topics for business/ industry users. Length: 1,200 words. Illustrations: b&w and colour photos, line, cartoons. Payment: £253 per 1,000 words; negotiable for illustrations. Founded 1966.

Computeractive

Incisive Media, 32–34 Broadwick Street, London W1A 2HG
tel 020-7316 9000
website www.computeractive.co.uk
Editor Paul Allen
Fortnightly £1.79

Magazine offering 'simple clear advice' on computers with workshops, product reviews, internet news and group tests.

Condé Nast Traveller

Condé Nast Publications Ltd, Vogue House, Hanover Square, London W1S 1JU
tel 020-7499 9080 *fax* 020-7493 3758
email cntraveller@condenast.co.uk
website www.cntraveller.com
Editor Sarah Miller
Monthly £3.99

Lavishly photographed articles on all aspects of travel, featuring exotic destinations and those close to home. Specialist pieces include food and wine, motoring, health, foreign correspondents, travel news, hotels. Illustrations: colour. Payment: by arrangement. Founded 1997.

Contemporary

Studio 56, 4 Montpelier Street, London SW7 1EE
tel 020-7019 6205
website www.contemporary-magazine.com
Editor Brian Muller
Monthly £5.95

International magazine with extensive coverage of visual arts, architecture, fashion, film, photography, books, music, dance and sport. Also includes interviews, profiles and art news from around the world. Length: varies. Illustrations: colour transparencies, hi-res scans. Payment: £100 per 1,000 words; none for photos. Founded 1997; relaunched 2002.

Contemporary Review

(incorporating the Fortnightly)
Contemporary Review Co. Ltd, PO Box 1242, Oxford OX1 4FJ
tel (01865) 201529 *fax* (01865) 201529
email editorial@contemporaryreview.co.uk
website www.contemporaryreview.co.uk
Editor Dr Richard Mullen
Institutional £55 p.a.; individual £44 p.a.

Independent review dealing with questions of the day, chiefly politics, international affairs, religion, literature and the arts. Mostly commissioned, but with some scope for freelance authors with authoritative knowledge. TS returned only if sae enclosed. Intending contributors should study journal first. Length: 2,000–3,000 words. No illustrations. Payment: £5 per page (500 words), 2 complimentary copies. Founded 1866.

Cosmopolitan

National Magazine House, 72 Broadwick Street, London W1F 9EP
tel 020-7439 5000
Editor-in-Chief Louise Court
Monthly £3.50

Articles. Commissioned material only. Payment: by arrangement. Illustrated. Founded 1972.

Cotswold Life

Archant Life South, Cumberland House, Oriel Road, Cheltenham, Glos. GL50 1BB
tel (01242) 216050 *fax* (01242) 255116

email editorial@cotswoldlife.co.uk
website www.cotswoldlife.co.uk
Editor Mike Lowe
Monthly £3.25

Articles on the Cotswolds, including places of interest, high-profile personalities, local events, arts, history and food. Unsolicited ideas welcome.

Country Homes and Interiors

IPC Media Ltd, The Blue Fin Building,
110 Southwark Street, London SE1 0SU
tel 020-3148 5000
Editor Rhoda Parry
Monthly £3.90

Articles on country homes and gardens, interiors, food, lifestyle. Payment: from £250 per 1,000 words. Founded 1986.

Country Life

IPC Media Ltd, The Blue Fin Building,
110 Southwark Street, London SE1 0SU
tel 020-3148 4444
website www.countrylife.co.uk
Editor Mark Hedges, *Deputy Editor* Rupert Uloth
Weekly £3.20

Illustrated journal chiefly concerned with British country life, social history, architecture and the fine arts, natural history, agriculture, gardening and sport. Length: about 1,000 or 1,300 words (articles). Illustrations: mainly colour photos. Payment: according to merit. Founded 1897.

Country Living

Hearst Magazines UK, National Magazine House,
72 Broadwick Street, London W1F 9EP
tel 020-7439 5000
email (features team) features@countryliving.com; (interiors/home) emporium@countryliving.co.uk
website www.allaboutyou.com
Editor Susy Smith
Monthly £3.90

Up-market home-interest magazine with a country lifestyle theme, covering interiors, gardens, crafts, food, wildlife, rural and green issues. Do not send unsolicited material or valuable transparencies. Illustrations: line, half-tone, colour. Payment: by arrangement. Founded 1985.

Country Smallholding

Archant Regional Ltd, Fair Oak Close,
Exeter Airport Business Park, Clyst Honiton,
Exeter EX5 2UL
tel (01392) 888481 *fax* (01392) 888449
email editorial.csh@archant.co.uk
website www.countrysmallholding.com
Editor Simon McEwan
Monthly £3.60

The magazine for smallholders. Practical, how-to articles, and seasonal features, on organic gardening, small-scale poultry and livestock keeping, country crafts, cookery and general subjects of interest to smallholders and others. Approach the Editor in writing or by phone or email with ideas. Length: up to 1,200 words. Payment: on application. Founded 1975 as *Practical Self-Sufficiency*.

Country Walking

Bauer Consumer Media, Media House, Lynchwood, Peterborough Business Park, Peterborough PE2 6EA
tel (01733) 468205
website www.LFTO.com
Editor Vincent Crump
Monthly £3.99

Features. Length: 1,000 words on average. Illustrations: digital images. Payment: by arrangement. Founded 1987.

The Countryman

Country Publications Ltd, The Water Mill,
Broughton Hall, Skipton,
North Yorkshire BD23 3AG
tel (01756) 701381 *fax* (01756) 701326
email editorial@thecountryman.co.uk
Editor Paul Jackson
Monthly £3.25

Every area of rural life. Copy must be trustworthy, well-written, brisk, cogent and light in hand. Articles up to 1,200 words. Skilful sketches of life and character from personal knowledge and experience. Dependable natural history based on writer's own observation. Really good matter from old unpublished letters and MSS. Study magazine before submitting material. Illustrations: b&w and colour photos and drawings, but all must be exclusive and out of the ordinary. Payment: approx. £75 per 1,000 words. Founded 1927.

craft&design Magazine

PO Box 5, Driffield, East Yorksshire YO25 8JD
tel (01377) 255213
email info@craftanddesign.net
website www.craftanddesign.net
Editor Angie Boyer
Bi-monthly £5.95, £35 p.a.

Articles, features and news on craft makers and other areas of the craft industry. Aims to promote quality craftsmanship. Welcomes ideas for articles and features. Length: 1,000 words (articles and features). Payment £100 per 1,000 words. Illustrations: colour prints, transparencies or digital images on CD. See website for all editorial copy dates. Founded 1983.

Crafts Magazine

44A Pentonville Road, London N1 9BY
tel 020-7806 2538 *fax* 020-7837 0858
email editorial@craftscouncil.org.uk
website www.craftsmagazine.org.uk
Editor Grant Gibson

Bi-monthly £6.20

Magazine for contemporary craft, published by the Crafts Council. Specialist features, craft news and reviews, archive articles from the magazine's 35-year history, and contributors from iconic institutions such as the V&A, Royal College of Art and Central St Martins. Submissions for review should include pictures and applicants should be mindful of the lead times associated with a bi-monthly schedule.

The Cricketer

70 Great Portland Street, London WA1 7UW
tel 020-7460 5200
email magazine@thecricketer.com
website www.thecricketer.com
Editor Andrew Miller
Monthly £3.95

Cricket articles of exceptional interest (unsolicited pieces seldom used). Length: up to 3,000 words. Payment: by arrangement. Illustrations: half-tone, colour.

Criminal Law & Justice Weekly (incorporating Justice of the Peace)

LexisNexis, 35 Chancery Lane, London WC2A 1EL
tel 020-7400 2828
email diana.rose@lexisnexis.co.uk
website www.criminallawandjustice.co.uk
Consulting Editor John Cooper QC, *Magazine Editor* Diana Rose
Weekly £339 p.a.

Delivers information and acts as a resource for the criminal law professional and those working within the courts. Articles on criminal and local government law and associated subjects including family law, criminology, medico-legal matters, penology, police, probation. Founded 1837.

Critical Quarterly

Newbury, Crediton, Devon EX17 5HA
tel (01359) 242375 *fax* (01359) 242880
website www.criticalquarterly.com
Editor Colin MacCabe
Quarterly £30 p.a.

Fiction, poems, literary criticism. Length: 2,000–5,000 words. Study magazine before submitting MSS. Payment: by arrangement. Founded 1959.

Crystal Magazine

3 Bowness Avenue, Prenton, Birkenhead CH43 0SD
tel 0151 608 9736
email christinecrystal@hotmail.com
website www.christinecrystal.blogspot.com
Editor Christine Carr
Bi-monthly £18 p.a. (UK), £20 p.a. (overseas)

Poems, stories (true and fiction), articles. £10 to writer of most popular piece. Also includes Wordsmithing, a humorous and informative look into the world of writers and writing; readers' letters; subscribers' news; Crystal Companions, an opportunity for Crystallites (subscribers) to get in touch; competitions. Founded 2001.

Cumbria Magazine

Country Publications Ltd, The Water Mill, Broughton Hall, Skipton, North Yorkshire BD23 3AG
tel (01756) 701381 *fax* (01756) 701326
email editorial@cumbriamagazine.co.uk
Features editor Kevin Hopkinson
Monthly £2.35

Articles of genuine rural interest concerning the Lake District and surrounding areas, and its people. Short length preferred. Illustrations: first-class photos. Payment: £70 per 1,000 words. Pictures extra. Founded 1951.

Custom Car

Kelsey Publishing Ltd, Cudham Tithe Barn, Berry's Hill, Cudham, Kent TN16 3AG
tel (01959) 541444 *fax* (01959) 541400
email cc.ed@kelsey.co.uk
website www.kelsey.co.uk
Editor David Biggadyke
Monthly £3.85

Hot rods, customs and drag racing. Length: by arrangement. Payment: by arrangement. Founded 1970.

Custom PC

Dennis Publishing Ltd, 30 Cleveland Street, London W1T 4JD
tel 020-7907 6000 *fax* 020-7907 6835
website www.custompc.co.uk
Editor Alex Watson
Monthly £3.75

Magazine covering performance PC hardware, technology and games with full-page and DPS single product reviews, group tests, and practical and technical features.

Cycle Sport

IPC Media Ltd, Leon House, 233 High Street, Croydon CR9 1HZ
tel 020-8726 8462 *fax* 020-8726 8499
email cyclesport@ipcmedia.com
website www.cyclesport.co.uk
Managing Editor Robert Garbutt, *Deputy Editor* Edward Pickering
Monthly £4

Articles and features on European professional racing. Specially commissions most material but will consider unsolicited material. Welcomes ideas for articles and features. Length: 1,500–2,500 words. Illustrations: transparencies, colour and b&w artwork and cartoons, digital images. Payment: £120 per 1,000 words; £50–£150 illustrations. Founded 1991.

Cycling Weekly

IPC Media Ltd, Leon House, 233 High Street, Croydon CR9 1HZ
tel 020-8726 8453 *fax* 020-8726 8499
email cycling@ipcmedia.com
website www.cyclingweekly.co.uk
Editor Robert Garbutt
Weekly £2.85

Racing and technical articles. Illustrations: topical photos with a cycling interest considered; cartoons. Length: not exceeding 2,000 words. Payment: by arrangement. Founded 1891.

Cyphers

3 Selskar Terrace, Ranelagh, Dublin 6, Republic of Ireland
tel +353 (0)1 4978866 *fax* +353 (0)1 4978866
website www.cyphers.ie
€21/$36 for 3 issues

Poems, fiction, translations. Payment: €15 per page. Submissions cannot be returned unless accompanied by postage (Irish stamps or International Reply Coupons.) Founded 1975.

Dairy Farmer

Riverbank House, Angel Lane, Tonbridge TN9 1SE
tel (01732) 377273
email peter.hollinshead@ubm.com
website www.farmersguardian.com
Editor Peter Hollinshead
14 p.a. £3.75

In-depth, technical articles on all aspects of dairy farm management and milk marketing. Length: normally 800–1,400 words with colour photos. Payment: by arrangement.

Dalesman

Country Publications Limited, The Water Mill, Broughton Hall, Skipton, North Yorkshire BD23 3AG
tel (01756) 701381 *fax* (01756) 701326
email editorial@dalesman.co.uk
Editor Paul Jackson
Monthly £2.50

Articles and stories of genuine interest concerning Yorkshire (1,000 words). Payment: £70 per 1,000 words plus extra for useable photos/illustrations. Founded 1939.

Dance Today

The Dancing Times Ltd, 45–47 Clerkenwell Green, London EC1R 0EB
tel 020-7250 3006 *fax* 020-7253 6679
email dancetoday@dance-today.co.uk
website www.dance-today.co.uk
Editor Nicola Rayner
Monthly £1.95

Ballroom, popular and social dancing from every aspect, ranging from competition reports to dance holiday features, health and fitness articles, and musical reviews. Well-informed freelance articles are used, but only after preliminary arrangements. Payment: by arrangement. Illustrations: action photos preferred, colour only. Founded 1956.

Dancing Times

The Dancing Times Ltd, 45–47 Clerkenwell Green, London EC1R 0EB
tel 020-7250 3006 *fax* 020-7253 6679
email dt@dancing-times.co.uk
website www.dancing-times.co.uk
Editor Jonathan Gray
Monthly £2.95

Ballet, contemporary dance and all forms of stage dancing from general, historical, critical and technical angles. Well-informed freelance articles used occasionally, but only after preliminary arrangements. Payment: by arrangement. Illustrations: occasional line, action photos preferred; colour welcome. Founded 1910.

The Dandy

D.C. Thomson & Co. Ltd, Albert Square, Dundee DD1 9QJ
tel (01382) 223131 *fax* (01382) 322214
PO Box 305, London NW1 1TX
tel 020-7400 1030 *fax* 020-7400 1089
Editor Craig Graham
Fortnightly £1.99

Comic strips and features for boys aged 7–10 years. Picture stories with 7–10 pictures per page, 1–4pp per story. Promising artists are encouraged. Payment: on acceptance.

Dare

The River Group, 1 Neal Street, London WC2H 9QL
tel 020-7306 0304 *fax* 020-7306 0303
Editor Charley Williams
Free

Superdrug magazine. Predominently features aspirational yet affordable beauty and fashion.

Darts World

MB Graphics, 25 Orlestone View, Ham Street, Ashford, Kent TN26 2LB
tel (01233) 733558
website www.dartsworld.com
Editor Michael Beeken
Monthly £2.95

Articles and stories with darts theme. Illustrations: half-tone, cartoons. Payment: £40–£50 per 1,000 words; illustrations by arrangement. Founded 1972.

The Dawntreader

132 Hinckley Road, Stoney Stanton, Leics. LE9 7NE
email dawnidp@btinternet.com
website www.indigodreams.co.uk

Editors Ronnie Goodyer and Dawn Bauling
Quarterly £4, £15 p.a.

Poetry, short stories and articles encompassing themes of the mystic, myth, legend, landscape, nature and love. New writers welcome. No payment. Sae essential. Founded 2007.

Decanter

IPC Inspire, The Blue Fin Building,
110 Southwark Street, London SE1 0SU
tel 020-3148 5000
email editor@decanter.com
website www.decanter.com
Editor Guy Woodward
Monthly £4

Articles and features on wines, wine travel and food-related topics. Welcomes ideas for articles and features. Length: 1,000–1,800 words. Illustrations: colour. Payment: £250 per 1,000 words. Founded 1975.

delicious.

Axe & Bottle Court, 3rd Floor, 70 Newcomen Street, London SE1 1YT
tel 020-7803 4115 *fax* 020-7803 4101
email info@deliciousmagazine.co.uk
website www.deliciousmagazine.co.uk
Editor Karen Barnes
Monthly £3.60

Articles on food, recipes, preparation, trends, chefs, wine and ingredients. Ideas welcome. Founded 2003.

Derbyshire Life and Countryside

Archant Life, 61 Friargate, Derby DE1 1DJ
tel (01332) 227850 *fax* (01332) 227860
email joy.hales@derbyshirelife.co.uk
website www.derbyshire.greatbritishlife.co.uk
Editor Joy Hales
Monthly £3.15

Articles, preferably illustrated, about Derbyshire life, people, places and history. Length: up to 800 words. Some short stories set in Derbyshire accepted; no verse. Payment: according to nature and quality of contribution. Illustrations: photos of Derbyshire subjects. Founded 1931.

Descent

Wild Places Publishing, PO Box 100,
Abergavenny NP7 9WY
tel (01873) 737707
email descent@wildplaces.co.uk
website www.wildplaces.co.uk
Editor Chris Howes
Bi-monthly £4.50

Articles, features and news on all aspects of cave and mine sport exploration (coalmines, active mining or showcaves are not included). Submissions must match magazine style. Length: up to 2,000 words (articles/features), up to 1,000 words (news). Illustrations: colour. Payment: on consideration of material based on area filled. Founded 1969.

Devon Life

Archant Life South, Archant House, Babbage Road, Totnes, Devon TQ9 5JA
tel (01803) 860910 *fax* (01803) 860926
email devonlife@archant.co.uk
website www.devon.greatbritishlife.co.uk
Editor Jane Fitzgerald
Monthly £3.45

Articles on all aspects of Devon, including inspiring people, fascinating places, beautiful walks, local events, arts, history and food. Some articles online, plus a lively community of Devon bloggers. Unsolicited ideas welcome. Founded 1963.

The Dickensian

The Dickens Fellowship,
The Charles Dickens Museum, 48 Doughty Street, London WC1N 2LX
fax (01227) 827001
email M.Y.Andrews@kent.ac.uk
Editor Prof. Malcolm Andrews, School of English, Rutherford College, University of Kent, Canterbury, Kent CT2 7NX
3 p.a. £19 p.a. £25 p.a. institutions (reduced rate for Dickens Fellowship members)

Welcomes articles on all aspects of Dickens's life, works and character. Payment: none. Send hard-copy contributions only (enclose sae if return required) and editorial correspondence to the Editor. For house-style conventions, see www.dickensfellowship.org/dickensian.

Digital Camera

Future Publishing Ltd, 30 Monmouth Street, Bath BA1 2BW
tel (01225) 442244 *fax* (01225) 446019
website www.digitalcameraworld.com
Editor Geoff Harris
Monthly £4.99

Practical guide to creating better photographs. Each issue contains inspirational images, expert techniques and essential tips for capturing great images and on how to perfect them on a computer. Also includes reviews of the latest cameras, accessories and software.

Digital Camera Essentials

Imagine Publishing Ltd, Richmond House,
33 Richmond Hill, Bournemouth BH2 6EZ
tel (01202) 586200
email DCBsite@imagine-publishing.co.uk
website www.digicambuyer.co.uk
Editor Debbi Allen
Monthly £3.99

Comprehensive buyer's guide for all levels of camera with reviews, buying advice and shooting tips.

Director

116 Pall Mall, London SW1Y 5ED
tel 020-7766 8950 *fax* 020-7766 8840
email director-ed@iod.com
website www.director.co.uk
Editor Lysanne Currie, *Depty Editor* Amy Duff
Monthly £3.50, £42 p.a.

Authoritative business-related articles. Send synopsis of proposed article and examples of printed work. Length: 500–2,000 words. Payment: by arrangement. Illustrations: colour. Founded 1947.

Disability Now

(published by Scope)
6 Market Road, London N7 9PW
tel 020-7619 7323 *minicom* 020-7619 7332
fax 020-7619 7331
email editor@disabilitynow.org.uk
website www.disabilitynow.org.uk
Editor Ian Macrae
Monthly £1.80 (free to qualifying individuals); tape version free to people with visual impairment or severe disability

Newspaper for people with different types of disability, carers and professionals, and anyone interested in disability. News and comment on anything of interest in the disability field: benefits, services, equipment, jobs, politics, motoring, holidays, sport, relationships, the arts. All regular contributors have a disability (unless they are a parent of someone with a disability). Preliminary letter or email desirable. Founded 1984.

Diva

Millivres Prowler Ltd, Spectrum House, Unit M, 32-34 Gordon House Road, London NW5 1LP
tel 020-7424 7400 *fax* 020-7424 7401
email edit@divamag.co.uk
website www.divamag.co.uk
Editor Jane Czyzselska
Monthly £3.65

Lesbian life and culture: articles and features. Length: 200–2,000 words. Illustrations: colour. Payment: £15 per 100 words; variable per photo; variable per illustration. Founded 1994.

Diver

55 High Street, Teddington, Middlesex TW11 8HA
tel 020-8943 4288 *fax* 020-8943 4312
email enquiries@divermag.co.uk
website www.divernet.com
Editor-in-Chief Nigel Eaton, *Editor* Steve Weinman
Monthly £3.99

Articles on sub aqua diving and related developments. Length: 1,500–2,000 words. Illustrations: colour. Payment: by arrangement. Founded 1953.

DIY Week

Faversham House Group Ltd, 232A Addington Road, South Croydon CR2 8LE
tel 020-8651 7100 *fax* 020-8651 7117
website www.diyweek.net
Editor Will Parsons
Fortnightly £102 p.a.

Product and city news, promotions and special features of recent developments in DIY houseware and garden retailing. Payment: by arrangement. Founded 1874.

Dogs Today

The Doghouse, 4 Bonseys Lane, Chobham, Surrey GU24 8JJ
tel (01276) 858880 *fax* (01276) 858860
website www.dogstodaymagazine.co.uk
Editor Beverley Cuddy
Monthly £3.75

Study of magazine essential before submitting ideas. Interested in human interest dog stories, celebrity interviews, holiday features and anything unusual – all must be entertaining and informative and accompanied by illustrations. Length: 800–1,200 words. Illustrations: colour, preferably digital. Payment: negotiable. Founded 1990.

The Dolls' House Magazine

Guild of Master Craftsman Publications Ltd, 86 High Street, Lewes, East Sussex BN7 1XN
tel (01273) 488005
website www.thegmcgroup.com
Monthly £47.88 p.a.

Dorset Life – The Dorset Magazine

7 The Leanne, Sandford Lane, Wareham, Dorset BH20 4DY
tel (01929) 551264 *fax* (01929) 552099
email office@dorsetlife.co.uk
Editor Joël Lacey
Monthly £2.45

Articles (about 1,200 words), photos (colour) and line drawings with a specifically Dorset theme. Payment: by arrangement. Founded 1967.

Drapers

Emap Inform, Greater London House, Hampstead Road, London NW1 7EJ
tel 020-7728 5000 *fax* 020-7812 3760
website www.drapersonline.com
Editor Jessica Brown
Weekly £3.20

Business editorial aimed at fashion retailers, large and small. Payment: by negotiation. Illustrations: colour and b&w photos. Founded 1887.

The Dublin Review

PO Box 7948, Dublin 1, Republic of Ireland
tel/fax +353 (0)1 6788627
website www.thedublinreview.com
Editor Brendan Barrington
Quarterly €34 p.a. (€45 overseas; £36 UK; $60 US)

Essays, memoir, reportage and fiction for the intelligent general reader. Payment: by arrangement. Founded 2000.

Early Music

c/o Faculty of Music, University of Cambridge,
11 West Road, Cambridge CB3 9DP
tel (01223) 335178
email earlymusic@oxfordjournals.org
website http://em.oxfordjournals.org
Editor Francis Knights
Quarterly £63 p.a.

Lively, informative and scholarly articles on aspects of medieval, renaissance, baroque and classical music. Payment: £20 per 1,000 words. Illustrations: line, half-tone, colour. Founded 1973.

East Lothian Life

1 Beveridge Row, Belhaven, Dunbar,
East Lothian EH42 1TP
tel (01368) 863593 *fax* (01368) 863593
website www.eastlothianlife.co.uk
Editor Pauline Jaffray
Quarterly £3

Articles and features with an East Lothian slant. Length: up to 1,000 words. Illustrations: b&w photos, line. Payment: negotiable. Founded 1989.

Eastern Art Report

EAPGROUP International Media,
Eastern Art Publishing Group, PO Box 13666,
London SW14 8WF
tel 020-8392 1122 *fax* 020-8392 1422
email ear@eapgroup.com
website www.eapgroup.com
Publisher/Editor-in-Chief Sajid Rizvi
Bi-monthly £6, £30 p.a. (individual), £60 p.a. (institutions)

Original, well-researched articles on all aspects of the visual and performing arts, cinema and digital media – Asian and diasporic, Buddhist, Islamic, Judaic, Indian, Chinese and Japanese; reviews. Length of articles: min. 1,500 words. Illustrations: colour or b&w, high-resolution digital format. No responsibility accepted for unsolicited material. Payment: by arrangement. Founded 1989.

Easy Living

Condé Nast Publications UK Ltd,
68 Old Bond Street, London W1S 4PH
tel 020-7499 9080
email easylivingeditorial@condenast.co.uk
website www.easyliving.co.uk
Editor Susie Forbes
Monthly £3.60

Women's magazine that 'optimises time without compromising on style', covering fashion, the home, beauty and health, recipes, and relationships. Founded 2005.

The Ecologist

Unit 102, Lana House Studios,
116–118 Commercial Street, London E1 6NF
tel 020-7422 8100 *fax* 020-7422 8101
email editorial@theecologist.org
website www.theecologist.org
Editor Andrew Wasley
10 p.a. £3.50

News, news investigations, features and green living advice pieces bought in. Proposal first in most cases. Payment: various. Particularly interested in exclusive investigations on populist consumer issues. See website for examples.

Economica

STICERD, London School of Economics,
Houghton Street, London WC2A 2AE
tel 020-7955 7855 *fax* 020-7955 6951
Editors Prof. F. Caselli, Prof. F. Cowell,
Dr A. Michaelides, Prof. P.N. Sorensen
Quarterly £209 per volume (subscription rates on application)

Learned journal covering the fields of economics, economic history and statistics. Payment: none. Founded 1921; New series 1934.

The Economist

25 St James's Street, London SW1A 1HG
tel 020-7830 7000 *fax* 020-7839 2968
website www.economist.com
Editor John Micklethwait
Weekly £4.00

Articles staff-written. Founded 1843.

The Edge

Unit 138, 22 Notting Hill Gate, London W11 3JE
tel 0845 456 9337
website www.theedgemagazine.co.uk
Editor David Clark
Quarterly £5

Reviews and features: film (indie, arts), books, popular culture. Fiction: see magazine or website for examples/tone. For guidelines send sae or see website. Payment: negotiable. For sample issue, send cheque payable to 'The Edge'.

Edinburgh Review

22a Buccleugh Place, Edinburgh EH8 9LN
tel 0131 651 1415 *fax* 0131 651 1415
email edinburgh.review@ed.ac.uk
website www.edinburghreview.org.uk
Editor Alan Gillis
3 p.a. UK price: £20 p.a. (£35 institutions); Non-UK price: £28 p.a. (£43 institutions)

Submissions by post only: fiction, poetry and clearly written articles on literary and cultural themes. Payment: by arrangement. Founded 1969.

Education Journal

Devonia House, 4 Union Terrace, Crediton,
Exeter EX17 3DY

tel (01363) 774455 *fax* (01363) 776592
email info@educationpublishing.com
website www.educationpublishing.com
Editor Demitri Coryton
11 p.a. £3.65

Features on policy, management and professional development issues. Major documents and reports gutted down to a brief digest; documents and research listings. Research section combining original reports and updates on research projects. Coverage of parliamentary debates and answers to parliamentary questions, giving statistical data by LEA. Reference section that includes coverage of all circulars, conference reports and opinion column. Length: 1,000 words. Illustrations: photos, cartoons. Payment: by arrangement. Founded 1903; relaunched 1996.

Electrical Review

6 Laurence Pountney Hill, London EC4R 0BL
tel 020-7933 8999 *fax* 020-7933 8998
email elinorem@electricalreview.co.uk
website www.electricalreview.co.uk
Editor Elinore MacKay
Monthly £3.50, £160 p.a.

Technical and business articles on electrical and control engineering; outside contributions considered. Electrical news welcomed. Illustrations: photos and drawings, cartoons. Payment: according to merit. Founded 1872.

ELLE (UK)

Hachette Filipacchi UK, 64 North Row, London W1K 7LL
tel 020-7150 7000 *fax* 020-7150 7670
website www.elleuk.com
Editor Lorraine Candy
Monthly £3.80

Commissioned material only. Payment: by arrangement. Illustrations: colour. Founded 1985.

Embroidery

The Embroiderers' Guild, 1 King's Road, Walton-on-Thames, Surrey KT12 2RA
tel (01260) 273891
email jo.editor@btinternet.com
website www.embroiderersguild.com/embroidery
Editor Joanne Hall
6 p.a. £4.90, £29.40 p.a.

News and illustrated features on all aspects of embroidery in contemporary design, fashion, illustration, interiors, art, general textiles and world embroidery. Features on internationally renowned makers, artists and designers working with textiles, stitch and embroidery. News covering exhibitions, books, interiors and products, plus event listings, book and exhibition reviews, and opportunities.

Empire

Bauer Consumer Media, Endeavour House, 189 Shaftesbury Avenue, London WC2H 8JG
tel 020-7295 5000
website www.empireonline.com
Editor Mark Dinning
Monthly £3.99

Guide to film on all its platforms: articles, features, news. Length: various. Illustrations: colour and b&w photos. Payment: approx. £300 per 1,000 words; varies for illustrations. Founded 1989.

Energy Engineering

Gillard Welch Ltd, 6A New Street, Warwick, Warks. CV34 4RX
tel (01926) 408242 *fax* (01926) 408206
email steve@energyengineering.co.uk
website www.energyengineering.net.co.uk
Editor Steve Welch
12 p.a. £9

'For innovators in technology, manufacturing and management': features and news. Contributions considered on all aspects of engineering. Illustrations: colour. Founded 1866.

The Engineer

Centaur Communications Ltd, St Giles House, 50 Poland Street, London W1F 7AX
tel 020-7970 4437 *fax* 020-7970 4189
email jon.excell@centaur.co.uk
website www.theengineer.com
Editor Jon Excell
Fortnightly £3.70, £75 p.a.

Features and news on innovation and technology, including profiles, analysis. Length: up to 800 words (news), 1,000 words (features). Illustrations: colour transparencies or prints, artwork, line diagrams, graphs. Payment: by negotiation. Founded 1856.

Engineering in Miniature

TEE Publishing Ltd, The Fosse, Fosse Way, Radford Semele, Leamington Spa, Warks. CV31 1XN
tel (01926) 614101 *fax* (01926) 614293
email info@engineeringinminiature.co.uk
website www.engineeringinminiature.co.uk
Managing Editor C.L. Deith
Monthly £3.10

Articles containing descriptions and information on all aspects of model engineering. Articles welcome but technical articles preferred. Payment dependent on pages published. Founded 1979.

The English Garden

Archant House, Oriel Road, Cheltenham, Glos. GL50 1BB
email theenglishgarden@archant.co.uk
Editor Tamsin Westhorpe
Monthly £3.99

Features and photography on gardens in the English style, plant genera and garden design. Length: 800 words. Illustrations: colour photos and artwork. Payment: variable. Founded 1997.

Envoi

Meirion House, Glan yr afon, Tanygrisiau, Blaenau Ffestiniog, Gwynedd LL41 3SU
tel (01766) 832112
website www.cinnamonpress.com
Editor Jan Fortune
3 p.a. £15 p.a.

New poetry, including sequences, collaborative works and translations; reviews; articles on modern poets and poetic style. Sample copy: £5. Payment: complimentary copy. Founded 1957.

Erotic Review (eZine)

ER Magazine, 31 Sinclair Road, London W14 0NS
email editor@ermagazine.org
website www.eroticreviewmagazine.com
Editor Jamie Maclean
12 p.a. subscription only

Sophisticated erotic lifestyle and fiction eZine for sensualists and libertines. Commissions features: 500-2,500 words; short fiction: 1,000–5,000 words. Illustrations and cartoons. Payment details can be obtained on request. Founded 1995.

Esquire

National Magazine House, 72 Broadwick Street, London W1F 9EP
tel 020-7439 5000 *fax* 020-7439 5675
website www.esquire.co.uk
Editor Alex Bilmes
Monthly £4.25

Quality men's general interest magazine – articles, features. No unsolicited material or short stories. Length: various. Illustrations: colour and b&w photos, line. Payment: by arrangement. Founded 1991.

Essentials

IPC Media Ltd, The Blue Fin Building, 110 Southwark Street, London SE1 0SU
tel 020-3148 7211
Editor Jules Barton-Breck
Monthly £2.70

Features, fashion, health, beauty, cookery, travel, consumer. Illustrations: colour. Payment: by negotiation. Founded 1988.

Essex Life

Fairfax House, North Station Road, Colchester, Essex CO1 1RJ
tel/fax (07834) 101686
email julian.read@archant.co.uk
Editor Julian Read
Monthly £3.45

No unsolicited material. Founded 1952.

Eventing

IPC Inspire, The Blue Fin Building, 110 Southwark Street, London SE1 0SU
tel 020-3148 5000 *fax* 020-3148 8127
email julie_harding@ipcmedia.com
Editor Julie Harding
Monthly £3.95

News, special reports, gossip, profiles, topical features, event reports (from grassroots leve to four-star in the UK and abroad), opinion pieces and 'Through the Keyhole' features – all connected to the sport of horse trials. Mostly commissioned, but all ideas welcome. Length: up to 1,500 words. Illustrations: colour and b&w, mostly commissioned. Payment: by arrangement. Founded 1984.

Evergreen

PO Box 52, Cheltenham, Glos. GL50 1YQ
tel (01242) 537900 *fax* (01242) 537901
Editor Stephen Garnett
Quarterly £3.95

Articles about Great Britain's heritage, culture, countryside, people and places. Length 250–2,000 words. Illustrations: digital; colour transparencies only accepted when accompanying articles. Payment: £15 per 1,000 words, £4 poems (12–24 lines). Founded 1985.

Everyday Practical Electronics

Wimborne Publishing Ltd, 113 Lynwood Drive, Merley, Wimborne, Dorset BH21 1UU
tel (01202) 880299 *fax* (01202) 843233
email editorial@wimborne.co.uk
website www.epemag.com
Editor Matt Pulzer
Monthly £4.40

Constructional and theoretical articles aimed at the student and hobbyist. Length: 1,000–5,500 words. Payment: £55–£90 per 1,000 words. Illustrations: line, half-tone. Founded 1971.

Executive PA

15-17 Blackfrairs Lane, London EC4V 6ER
tel 020-7236 1118 *fax* 020-7489 5809
website www.executivepa.net
Editor Cora Lydon
Quarterly £21 p.a.

Business to business for working senior secretaries. Length: 700–1,400 words. Illustrations: colour. Payment: £140 per 1,000 words. Founded 1991.

Families First

(formerly Home & Family)
The Mothers' Union, Mary Sumner House, 24 Tufton Street, London SW1P 3RB
tel 020-7222 5533
email familiesfirst@themothersunion.org
Editor Catherine Butcher
Bi-monthly £2.50

Short articles on parenting, marriage, family life, Christian faith, fair trade and community life. Payment: from £80 per 1,000 words. Illustrations:

colour photos and occasionally illustrations. Few unsolicited articles are accepted. Enclose sae. Founded 1954.

Family History Monthly

Unit 101, 140 Wales Farm Road, London W3 6UG
tel (0208) 752 8181 *fax* (0208) 752 8185
email jen.newby@metropolis.co.uk
Editor Jen Newby
Monthly £3.75

Articles on all aspects of genealogy and British social history plus listings, news and reviews. Ideas welcome. Particularly interested in articles on social, military and economic history since 1750, practical genealogy research features and family history case studies in first person. Does not publish anything above 3,000 words. Submit 100-200 word feature ideas via email. Contact editor for guidelines. Payment: details available on request. Founded 1995.

Family Law Journal

Jordan Publishing Ltd, 21 St Thomas Street, Bristol BS1 6JS
tel (0117) 923 0600 *fax* (0117) 925 0486
website www.jordanpublishing.co.uk
Monthly £45

Articles concerning developments and practical issues in family law, written for and by lawyers working in the field. Length from 1,500 words, no payment, no illustrations. Founded 1971.

Family Tree

61 Great Whyte, Ramsey, Huntingdon, Cambs. PE26 1HJ
tel (01487) 814050 *fax* 0871 288 2286
email editorial@family-tree.co.uk
website www.family-tree.co.uk
Editor Helen Tovey
Every 4 weeks £4.75, £45 p.a.

Articles on any genealogically related topics. Payment: by arrangement. Founded 1984.

Farmers Weekly

Reed Business Information, Quadrant House, The Quadrant, Sutton, Surrey SM2 5AS
tel 020-8652 4911 *fax* 020-8652 4005
email farmers.weekly@rbi.co.uk
website www.fwi.co.uk
Editor Jane King
Weekly £2.55

Articles on agriculture from freelance contributors will be accepted subject to negotiation. Founded 1934.

Feminist Review

Palgrave Macmillan, Brunel Road, Houndmills, Basingstoke, Hants RG21 6XS
tel (01256) 329242 *fax* (01256) 810526
website www.feminist-review.com
Edited by a Collective, supported by a group of corresponding editors
3 p.a. £46

Aims to unite research and theory with political practice and contribute to the development of both as well as the exploration and articulation of the socio-economic realities of women's lives. Welcomes contributions from the spectrum of contemporary feminist debate. Empirical work – both qualitative and quantitative – is particularly welcome. In addition, each issue contains some papers which are themed around a specific debate. Founded 1979.

FHM (For Him Magazine)

Bauer Consumer Media, Endeavour House, 189 Shaftesbury Avenue, London WC2H 8JG
tel 020-7182 8000 *fax* 020-7182 8021
email general@fhm.com
website www.fhm.com
Editor Joe Barnes
Monthly £3.90

Features, fashion, grooming, travel (adventure) and men's interests. Length: 1,200–2,000 words. Illustrations: colour and b&w photos, line and colour artwork. Payment: by negotiation. Founded 1987.

The Field

IPC Inspire, The Blue Fin Building, 110 Southwark Street, London SE1 0SU
tel 020-3148 4772
website www.thefield.co.uk
Editor Jonathan Young
Monthly £4.20

Specific, topical and informed features on the British countryside and country pursuits, including natural history, field sports, gardening and rural conservation. Overseas subjects considered but opportunities for such articles are limited. No fiction or children's material. Articles, length 800–2,000 words, by outside contributors considered; also topical 'shorts' of 200–300 words on all countryside matters. Illustrations: colour photos of a high standard. Payment: on merit. Founded 1853.

Film Ireland

Filmbase, Curved Street, Temple Bar, Dublin 2, Republic of Ireland
tel +353 (0)1 6796716 *fax* +353 (0)1 6796717
email editor@filmbase.ie
website www.filmireland.net
Editor Niamh Creely
Bi-monthly €6

Aims to be an open and pluralist forum for the exchange of ideas and news on film-making and cinema, both Irish and international. Special reports, interviews and reviews; acts as a unique archival mirror of film activity in Ireland. Founded 1987.

Film Review

Visual Imagination Ltd, 9–10 Blades Court, Deodar Road, London SW15 2NU

tel 020-8875 7417 *fax* 020-8875 1588
email filmreview@visimag.com
website www.visimag.com/filmreview, www.filmreviewonline.com
Editor Nikki Baughan
Every 4 weeks £3.99

Features and interviews on mainstream cinema; film and DVD reviews. No fiction. Length: 1,000–3,000 words (features), 350 words (reviews). Illustrations: colour and b&w. Payment: £80 per 1,000 words; £20 for first image, £10 per additional image. Founded 1950.

Financial Adviser

Financial Times Business, 1 Southwark Bridge, London SE1 9HL
tel 020-7775 3000
email hal.austin@ft.com
website www.ftadviser.com
Editor Hal Austin
Weekly £99 p.a. Free to financial intermediaries working in financial services

Topical personal finance news and features. Length: variable. Payment: by arrangement. Founded 1987.

FIRE

PO Box 100, Chichester PO18 8HD
tel (01243) 576444 *fax* (01243) 576456
website www.fire-magazine.com
Editor Andrew Lynch
Monthly £10.30, £76 p.a.

Articles on firefighting and fire prevention from acknowledged experts only. Length: 600 words. No unsolicited contributions. Illustrations: dramatic firefighting or fire brigade rescue colour photos. Also *Fire International*. Payment: by arrangement. Founded 1908.

Fishing News

INTRAFISH, Nexus Place, 25 Farringdon Street, London EC4A 4AB
tel 020-7029 5712 *fax* 020-7029 5749
email editor@fishingnews.co.uk
website www.fishingnews.co.uk
Editor Cormac Burke
Weekly £2.10

News and features on all aspects of the commercial fishing industry. Length: up to 1,000 words (features), up to 500 words (news). Illustrations: colour and b&w photos. Payment: negotiable. Founded 1913.

Flight International

Reed Business Information Ltd, Quadrant House, The Quadrant, Sutton, Surrey SM2 5AS
tel 020-8652 3842 *fax* 020-8652 3840
website www.flightinternational.com
Editor Michael Targett
Weekly £2.85

Deals with all branches of aerospace: operational and technical articles, illustrated by photos, engineering cutaway drawings; also news, paragraphs, reports of lectures, etc. News press days: Thurs, Fri. Illustrations: tone, line, colour. Payment: by agreement. Founded 1909.

Flora International

The Fishing Lodge Studio, 77 Bulbridge Road, Wilton, Salisbury, Wilts. SP2 0LE
tel (01722) 743207 *fax* (01722) 743207
email floramag@aol.com
Editor Maureen Foster
Bi-monthly £3.95

Magazine for flower arranging and floristry; also features flower-related crafts and flower arrangers' gardens. Unsolicited enquiries and suggestions welcome on any of these subjects. Send brief synopsis together with sample illustrations attached. Illustrations: transparencies, colour prints or high-res files on CD or email. Payment: £60 per 1,000 words, £10–£20 illustrations. Founded 1974.

Fly Fishing & Fly Tying

Rolling River Publications, The Locus Centre, The Square, Aberfeldy, Perthshire PH15 2DD
tel (01887) 829868 *fax* (01887) 829856
email MarkB.ffft@btinternet.com
website www.flyfishing-and-flytying.co.uk
Editor Mark Bowler
12 p.a. £3.25

Fly-fishing and fly-tying articles, fishery features, limited short stories, fishing travel. Length: 800–2,000 words. Illustrations: colour photos. Payment: by arrangement. Founded 1990.

Folio

2nd Floor, Bristol News and Media, Temple Way, Bristol BS99 7HD
tel 0117 942 8491 *fax* 0117 934 3566
email editor@foliomagazine.co.uk
website www.foliomagazine.co.uk
Editor Mike Gartside
Monthly Free

Articles, features, interviews and news on people, places and events with a local connection (Bristol and Bath area). No short stories or poems. Unsolicited material considered. Length: 600–2,000 words (features), variable (news). Illustrations: colour and b&w. Payment: by negotiation. Founded 1994.

Fortean Times

Box 2409, London NW5 4NP
tel 020-7907 6235 *fax* 020-7907 6139
email david_sutton@dennis.co.uk
website www.forteantimes.com
Editor David Sutton
13 p.a. £4.25

Journal of strange phenomena, experiences, related

'... editing for authors who care about their readers ...'
aesop
www.copyedit.co.uk
1970–2013
Based in Oxford, established for just over forty years, All Editorial Services Online for Publishers & Writers, is the home of professional editorial services in the UK
Among many other editorial services, AESOP offers: copyediting, proofreading, indexing, research, rewrites, ghostwrites, novelisation, thesis and dissertation editing for any kind of text destined for paper/electronic publication
contact: martin noble mart@copyedit.co.uk
aesop 28 Abberbury Road, Oxford OX4 4ES 01865 429563

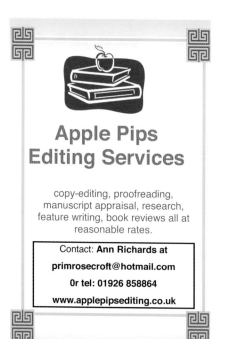

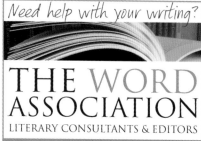

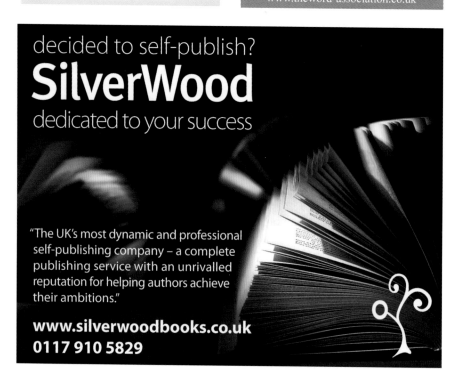

CAMBRIDGE
PUBLISHING MANAGEMENT

Neil Miller's Books
Why pay £7000 to have your novel published ?

www.yps-publishing.co.uk
The one-stop-shop for self publishers
Copy editing
Proof-reading
Full book design service
Printing & binding
Promotion & marketing
Book distribution
Online bookshop
eBooks and Apps
Book trailers
York Publishing Services Ltd
tel. 01904 431213
enquiries@yps-publishing.co.uk
Recommended by the Writers' & Artists' Yearbook

University of Chichester

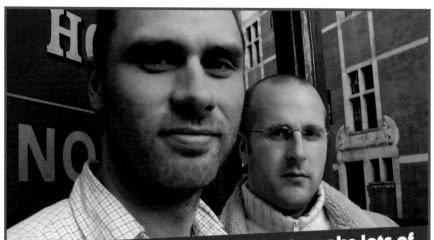

subjects and philosophies. Includes articles, features, news, reviews. Length: 500–5,000 words; longer by arrangement. Illustrations: colour photos, line and tone art, cartoons. Payment: by negotiation. Founded 1973.

Fortnight – An Independent Review of Politics and the Arts

11 University Road, Belfast BT7 1NA
tel 028-9023 2353 *fax* 028-9023 2650
website www.fortnight.org
Editor Rudie Goldsmith
Monthly £2.50

Current affairs analysis, reportage, opinion pieces, cultural criticism, book reviews, poems. Illustrations: line, half-tone, cartoons. Payment: by arrangement. Founded 1970.

FourFourTwo

Haymarket, Teddington Studios, Broom Road, Teddington, Middlesex TW11 9BE
tel 020-8267 5848 *fax* 020-8267 5061
website www.fourfourtwo.magazine.co.uk
Editor David Hall
Monthly £4.50

Football magazine with 'adult' approach: interviews, in-depth features, issues pieces, odd and witty material. Length: 2,000–3,000 (features), 100–1,500 words (Up Front pieces). Illustrations: colour transparencies and artwork, b&w prints. Payment: £200 per 1,000 words. Founded 1994.

France

Archant House, Oriel Road, Cheltenham, Glos. GL50 1BB
tel (01242) 216050 *fax* (01242) 216094
email editorial@francemag.com
website www.francemag.com
Editor Carolyn Boyd
Monthly £3.99

Informed quality features and articles on the real France, ranging from cuisine to culture to holidays exploring hidden France. Length: 800–2,000 words. Payment: £100 per 1,000 words; £50 per page/pro rata for illustrations. Founded 1989.

Freelance Market News

8-10 Dutton Street, Manchester M3 ILE
tel 0161 819 9919 *fax* 0161 819 2842
email fmn@writersbureau.com
website www.freelancemarketnews.com
Editor Angela Cox
11 p.a. £29 p.a.

Information on UK and overseas publications with editorial content, submission requirements and contact details. News of editorial requirements for writers. Features on the craft of writing, competitions, letters page. Founded 1968.

The Friend

173 Euston Road, London NW1 2BJ
tel 020-7663 1010 *fax* 020-7663 1182
email news@thefriend.org
website www.thefriend.org
Editor Ian Kirk-Smith
Weekly £76 p.a. (paper + online), £48 p.a. (online only)

Material of interest to Quakers and like-minded people; political, social, economic, environmental or devotional, considered from outside contributors. Length: up to 1,200 words. Illustrations: b&w or colour prints, b&w line drawings and cartoons by email preferred. Payment: not usually but will negotiate a small fee with professional writers. Founded 1843.

Frieze

1 Montclare Street, London E2 7EU
tel 020-3372 6111 *fax* 020-3372 6115
email editors@frieze.com
website www.frieze.com
8 p.a. £5.95, £33.50 p.a.

Magazine of European contemporary art and culture including essays, reviews, columns and listings. Frieze Art Fair is held every October in Regent's Park, London, featuring over 150 of the most exciting contemporary art galleries in the world. Founded 1991.

Full House

Hubert Burda Media UK, The Tower, Phoenix Square, Colchester, Essex CO4 9HU
tel (01206) 851117 *fax* (01206) 849079
website www.fullhousemagazine.co.uk
Editor Dave Claridge
Weekly 55p

Women's magazine with real-life features and puzzles. Founded 2005.

The Furrow

St Patrick's College, Maynooth, Co. Kildare, Republic of Ireland
tel +353 (0)1 7083741 *fax* +353 (0)1 7083908
email furrow.office@may.ie
website www.thefurrow.ie
Editor Rev. Ronan Drury
Monthly €3.50

Religious, pastoral, theological, social articles. Length: up to 3,500 words. Payment: average €20 per page (450 words). Illustrations: line, half-tone. Founded 1950.

Galleries

Barrington Publications, Riverside Studios, Crisp Road, London W6 9RL
tel 020-8237 1180
email features@galleries.co.uk
website www.galleries.co.uk
Editor Andrew Aitken
Monthly £28 p.a.

Art listings and editorial magazine describing current

exhibitions and stock of commercial and public art galleries, galleries for hire and art services.

GamesMaster

Future Publishing Ltd, 30 Monmouth Street, Bath BA1 2BW
tel (01225) 442244 *fax* (01225) 446019
email gamesmaster@futurenet.co.uk
Editor-in-Chief Robin Alway
Every 4 weeks £3.99

The UK's longest running video games magazine, covering the biggest and best games across all formats.

The Garden

4th Floor, Churchgate, New Road, Peterborough PE1 1TT
tel 0845 260 0909 *fax* (01733) 341633
email thegarden@rhs.org.uk
Editor Chris Young
Monthly £4.25

Journal of The Royal Horticultural Society. Features of horticultural or botanical interest on a wide range of subjects. Commissioned material only. Length: 1,200–2,500 words. Illustrations: 35mm or medium format colour transparencies, occasional b&w prints, botanical line drawings; digital images. Payment: varies. Founded 1866.

Garden Answers

Bauer Consumer Media Ltd, Media House, Lynchwood, Peterborough Business Park, Peterborough PE2 6EA
tel (01733) 468000 *fax* (01733) 468888
email gardenanswers@bauermedia.co.uk
Editor Geoff Stebbings
Monthly £3.60

Some commissioned features and articles on all aspects of gardening. Study of magazine essential. Approach by letter with examples of published work. Length: approx. 750 words. Illustrations: colour transparencies, digital images and artwork. Payment: by negotiation. Founded 1982.

Garden News

Bauer Consumer Media Ltd, Media House, Lynchwood, Peterborough Business Park, Peterborough PE2 6EA
tel (01733) 468000
email gn@bauermedia.co.uk
website www.gardennewsmagazine.co.uk
Editor Clare Foggett
Weekly £1.99

Up-to-date information on everything to do with plants, growing and gardening. Illustrations: line, colour, cartoons. Payment: by negotiation. Founded 1958.

Gay Times – GT

Spectrum House, 32–34 Gordon House Road, London NW5 1LP
tel 020-7424 7400 *fax* 020-7424 7401
email edit@gaytimes.co.uk
website www.gaytimes.co.uk
Editor Darren Scott
Monthly £4.20

Celebrity, gay lifestyle, health, parenting, music, film, technology, current affairs, opinion, culture, art, style, grooming, features and interviews. Length: up to 2,000 words. Payment: by arrangement. Founded 1984.

Geographical

1.17 QWest, Great West Road, Brentford, Middlesex, TW8 0GP
tel 020-8332 8434 *fax* 020-8332 8438
email magazine@geographical.co.uk
website www.geographical.co.uk
Editor Geordie Torr
Monthly £4.50

Magazine of the Royal Geographical Society (with IBG). Covers culture, wildlife, environment, science and travel. Illustrations: top-quality hi-res digital files, vintage material. Payment: by negotiation. Founded 1935.

Geographical Journal

Royal Geographical Society (with the Institute of British Geographers), 1 Kensington Gore, London SW7 2AR
tel 020-7591 3026 *fax* 020-7591 3001
email journals@rgs.org
Editor Prof. Klaus Dodds
4 p.a. £192 p.a. print and online, £174 print only

Papers range across the entire subject of geography, with particular reference to public debates, policy-oriented agendas and notions of 'relevance'. Illustrations: photos, maps, diagrams. Founded 1893.

Gibbons Stamp Monthly

Stanley Gibbons Ltd, 7 Parkside, Ringwood, Hants BH24 3SH
tel (01425) 472363 *fax* (01425) 470247
email hjefferies@stanleygibbons.co.uk
website www.stanleygibbons.co.uk
Editor Hugh Jefferies
Monthly £3.60

Articles on philatelic topics. Contact the Editor first. Length: 500–2,500 words. Payment: by arrangement, £60 or more per 1,000 words. Illustrations: photos, line, stamps or covers.

Glamour

6–8 Old Bond Street, London W1S 4PH
tel 020-7499 9080 *fax* 020-7491 2551
email editor@glamourmagazine.co.uk
website www.glamourmagazine.com
Editor Jo Elvin
Monthly £2

Lifestyle magazine containing fashion, beauty, real-life features and celebrity news aimed at women aged 18–34. Feature ideas welcome; approach with brief outline. Length: 500–800 words. Payment: by arrangement. Founded 2001.

Go Girl Magazine

Egmont Magazines, 239 Kensington High Street, London W8 6SA
tel 020-7761 3500
website www.gogirlmag.co.uk
Editor Emma Prosser
Every 3 weeks £2.50

Magazine for 7–11-year-old girls including fashion, beauty, celebrity news and gossip. Payment: by arrangement. Founded 2003.

Golf Monthly

IPC Inspire, The Blue Fin Building, 110 Southwark Street, London SE1 0SU
tel 020-3148 5000
email golfmonthly@ipcmedia.com
website www.golf-monthly.co.uk
Editor Michael Harris
Monthly £3.70

Original articles on golf considered (not reports), golf clinics, handy hints. Illustrations: half-tone, colour, cartoons. Payment: by arrangement. Founded 1911.

Golf World

Bauer Media, Media House, Lynchwood, Peterborough Business Park, Peterborough PE2 6EA
tel (01733) 468000 *fax* (01733) 468843
email chris.jones@bauermedia.co.uk
website www.golf-world.co.uk
Editor Chris Jones, *Acting Managing Director* Steve Prentice
Monthly £4.10

Expert golf instructional articles, 500–3,000 words; general interest articles, personality features 500–3,000 words. No fiction. No unsolicited material. Payment: by negotiation. Illustrations: line, half-tone, colour, cartoons. Founded 1962.

The Good Book Guide

Editorial Office 33 Whitebeam Close, Colden Common, Winchester SO21 1AJ
tel (01962) 712507
email fiona@thegoodbookguide.com
Customer Services 1A All Hallows Road, Bispham, Blackpool, Lancs. FY2 0AS
tel 0121 314 3539 *fax* 020-3070 0343
email enquiries@thegoodbookguide.com
Managing Director Graham Holmes *Editorial Director* Fiona Lafferty
10 p.a. Subscription only. Annual subscription rates: UK £29; Europe £35.75; Rest of the World £40.25

Review magazine recommending and selling the best books published in the UK.

Good Housekeeping

National Magazine House, 72 Broadwick Street, London W1F 9EP
tel 020-7439 5000 *fax* 020-7439 5616
email goodh.mail@hearst.co.uk
website www.goodhousekeeping.co.uk
Editorial Director Lindsay Nicholson
Monthly £3.80

Articles on topics of interest to intelligent women. No unsolicited features or stories accepted. Homes, fashion, beauty and food covered by staff writers. Payment: magazine standards. Illustrations: commissioned. Founded 1922.

GQ

Condé Nast Publications, Vogue House, Hanover Square, London W1S 1JU
tel 020-7499 9080 *fax* 020-7495 1679
website www.gq-magazine.co.uk
Editor Dylan Jones
Monthly £3.95

Style, fashion and general interest magazine for men. Illustrations: b&w and colour photos, line drawings, cartoons. Payment: by arrangement. Founded 1988.

Granta

12 Addison Avenue, London W11 4QR
tel 020-7605 1360 *fax* 020-7605 1361
website www.granta.com
Editor John Freeman
Quarterly £12.99, £29.95 p.a.

Original literary fiction, non-fiction, memoir, reportage and photography. Study magazine before submitting work. No academic essays or reviews. Length: determined by content. Illustrations: photos. Payment: by arrangement. Founded 1889; reconceived 1979.

Grazia

Bauer Consumer Media, Endeavour House, 189 Shaftesbury Avenue, London WC2H 8JG
tel 020-7437 9011 *fax* 020-7520 6599
email graziadaily@graziamagazine.co.uk
website www.graziadaily.co.uk
Editor-in-Chief Jane Bruton
Weekly £1.95

Women's magazine with the latest trends, gossip, fashion and news in bite-size pieces.

Green Futures

Overseas House, 19–23 Ironmonger Row, London EC1V 3QN
email post@greenfutures.org.uk
website www.greenfutures.org.uk
Editor-in-Chief Martin Wright
Quarterly £24 p.a. personal, £34 non-profit organisations, £57 p.a. businesses (subscription only)

Articles and features on environmental solutions and sustainable futures for people in government, business and higher education. Specially commissions most material. Welcomes ideas for news stories and features. Illustrations: high-res digital photos. Send material to Katie Shaw, Editorial and Marketing Coordinator. Founded 1996.

Greetings Today

(formerly Greetings Magazine)
Lema Publishing, 1 Churchgates, The Wilderness, Berkhamsted, Herts. HP4 2AZ
tel (01442) 289930 *fax* (01442) 289950
website www.greetingstoday.co.uk
Editor Ella Hoyos
Monthly £45 p.a. (other rates on application)

Trade magazine with articles, features and news related to the greetings card industry; includes Artists Directory for aspiring artists wishing to attract the eye of publishers. Mainly written in-house; some material taken from outside. Length: varies. Illustrations: line, colour and b&w photos. Payment: by arrangement. Founded 1999; first published 1972.

The Grocer

William Reed Publishing Ltd, Broadfield Park, Crawley, West Sussex RH11 9RT
tel (01293) 613400 *fax* (01293) 610333
website www.thegrocer.co.uk
Editor Adam Leyland
Weekly £1.95

Trade journal: articles or news or illustrations of general interest to the grocery and provision trades. Payment: by arrangement. Founded 1861.

Grow Your Own

25 Phoenix Court, Hawkins Road, Colchester CO2 8JY
tel (01206) 505979 *fax* (01206) 505905
email lucy.halsall@aceville.co.uk
website www.growfruitandveg.co.uk
Editor Lucy Halsall
Monthly £3.99

Magazine for kitchen gardeners of all levels of expertise. Will consider unsolicited material. Welcomes ideas for articles and features. Length: 1,000 words (articles), 1,500 words (features) 200 words (news). Illustrations: transparencies, colour prints and digital images. Payment: varies.

Guiding Magazine

17–19 Buckingham Palace Road, London SW1W 0PT
tel 020-7834 6242 *fax* 020-7828 8317
email guiding@girlguiding.org.uk
website www.girlguiding.org.uk
Editor Jane Yettram
Quarterly

Official magazine of Girlguiding UK. Articles of interest to women of all ages, with special emphasis on youth work and the Guide Movement. Illustrations: line, half-tone, colour. Payment: £300 per 1,000 words. Please contact editor with proposal first.

Guitarist

Future Publishing UK, 30 Monmouth Street, Bath BA1 2BW
tel (01225) 442244 *fax* (01225) 446019
website www.guitarist.co.uk
Editor Mick Taylor
13 p.a. £5.25

Aims to improve readers' knowledge of the instrument, help them make the right buying choices and assist them in becoming a better player. Ideas for articles welcome. Founded 1984.

H&E naturist

New Freedom Publications Ltd, Burlington Court, Carlisle Street, Goole, East Yorkshire DN14 5EG
tel (01405) 760298 *fax* (01405) 763815
email editor@henaturist.net
website www.henaturist.net
Editor Sam Hawcroft
Monthly £3.95

Articles on naturist travel, clubs, beaches and naturist lifestyle experiences from the UK, Europe and the world. Length: 800–1,200 words. Illustrations: prints and digital images featuring naturists in natural settings; also cartoons, humorous fillers and features with naturist themes. Payment: by negotiation but guidelines for contributors and basic payment rates available on request.

Hairflair & Beauty

Freebournes House, Freebournes Road, Witham, Essex CM8 3US
tel (01376) 534534 *fax* (01376) 534546
Editor Jane MacArthur
Bi-monthly £2.99

Hair, beauty and health for the 18–40 age group. Not currently accepting freelance submissions or illustrations. Founded 1985.

HAMPSHIRE – The County Magazine

A&D Media Ltd, Jesses Farm, Snow Hill, Dinton, Wilts. SP3 5HN
tel (01722) 717028
Editor Mark Allen, *Deputy Editor* Geoffrey Williams
Monthly £2.99

Factual articles concerning all aspects of Hampshire, past and present. Length: 600–1,500 words. Payment: by arrangement. Illustrations: mainly colour photos. Founded 1960.

Harper's Bazaar

National Magazine House, 72 Broadwick Street, London W1F 9EP
tel 020-7439 5000 *fax* 020-7439 5506
website www.harpersbazaar.co.uk
Editor Lucy Yeomans
Monthly £3.99

Features, fashion, beauty, art, theatre, films, travel, interior decoration – some commissioned. Founded 1929.

Health Club Management

Leisure Media Company Ltd, Portmill House, Portmill Lane, Hitchin, Herts. SG5 1DJ

tel (01462) 431385 *fax* (01462) 433909
email healthclub@leisuremedia.com
website www.health-club.co.uk
Editor Kate Cracknell
Monthly £36 p.a.

Official publication of the Fitness Industry Association. Articles on the operation of health clubs, day spas, fitness and sports centres. Items on consumer issues and lifestyle trends as they affect club management are welcomed. Length: up to 1,500 words. Illustrations: colour and b&w photos. Payment: by arrangement. Founded 1995.

Healthy

The River Group, 1 Neal Street, London WC2H 9QL
tel 020-7420 6502
website www.healthy-magazine.co.uk
Editor Jane Druker
9 p.a. £1.75

Holland & Barrett magazine. Health and nutrition information, features, tips, news and recipes, all from a holistic health angle. Ideas from freelances welcome, with a view to commissioning. It does not do product reviews, won't mention products not available in Holland & Barrett and cannot mention cite any brand names in the copy. Email ideas in first instance. Payment by negotiation. Founded 1996.

Heat

Bauer Consumer Media, Endeavour House, 189 Shaftesbury Avenue, London WC2H 8JG
tel 020-7437 9011
email heatEd@heatmag.com
website www.heatworld.com
Editor Lucie Cave
Weekly £1.65

Features and news on celebrities. Founded 1999.

Hello!

Wellington House, 69–71 Upper Ground, London SE1 9PQ
tel 020-7667 8700 *fax* 020-7667 8716
Editor Rosie Nixon
Weekly £2

News-based features – showbusiness, celebrity, royalty; exclusive interviews. Payment: by arrangement. Illustrated. Founded 1988.

Hertfordshire Countryside

Beaumonde Publications Ltd, PO Box 5, Hitchin, Herts. SG5 1GJ
tel (01462) 422014 *fax* (01462) 422015
email martin@hertscountryside.co.uk
Editor Sandra Small
Monthly £2.25

Articles of county interest. No poetry, puzzles or crosswords. Length: approx. 1,000 words. Payment: negotiable. Founded 1946.

Hi-Fi News

IPC Inspire, Leon House, 233 High Street, Croydon CR9 1HZ
tel 020-8726 8311 *fax* 020-8726 8397
email hifinews@ipcmedia.co.uk
website www.hifinews.com
Editor Paul Miller
Monthly £4

Articles on all aspects of high-quality sound recording and reproduction; also extensive record review section and supporting musical feature articles. Audio matter is essentially technical, but should be presented in a manner suitable for music lovers interested in the nature of sound. Length: 2,000–3,000 words. Illustrations: line, half-tone. Payment: by arrangement. Founded 1956.

High Life

Cedar Communications Ltd, 85 Strand, London WC2R 0DW
tel 020-7550 8000
email high.life@cedarcom.co.uk
website www.cedarcom.co.uk
Editor Kerry Smith
Monthly Free £37 p.a.

Inflight consumer magazine for British Airways passengers. Articles on entertainment, travel, fashion, business, sport and lifestyle. Founded 1973.

History Today

25 Bedford Avenue, London WC1B 3AT
tel 020-3219 7810
email admin@historytoday.com
website www.historytoday.com
Editor Paul Lay
Monthly £5.20

History in the widest sense – political, economic, social, biography, relating past to present; world history as well as British. Length: 3,500 words (articles); 600–1,200 words (news/views). Illustrations: prints and original photos. Do not send original material until publication is agreed. Accepts freelance contributions dealing with genuinely new historical and archaelogical research. Payment: by arrangement. Send sae for return of MS. Founded 1951.

Home Words

77 Verulam Road, St Albans AL3 4DJ
tel (01727) 833400 *fax* 020-7776 1086
email terence@harrowweald.org
website www.churchtimes.co.uk
Editor Terence Handley-MacMath
Monthly 5p

Leading national insert for C of E parish magazines. Articles of interest to parishes; poems. Items should bear the author's name and address; include return postage or send by email. Length: up to 450 words, accompanied by photos/illustrations. Payment: by arrangement. Founded 1905.

Homes and Gardens

IPC Magazines Ltd, The Blue Fin Building, 110 Southwark Street, London SE1 0SU

tel 020-3148 5000
email hgcontactus@ipcmedia.com
website www.housetohome.co.uk/homesandgardens
Editor Deborah Barker
Monthly £3.90

Articles on home interest or design, particularly well-designed British interiors (snapshots should be submitted). Length: articles, 900–1,000 words. Illustrations: all types. Payment: generous, but exceptional work required; varies. Founded 1919.

Horse & Hound

IPC Inspire, 9th Floor, The Blue Fin Building, 110 Southwark Street, London SE1 0SU
tel 020-3148 4562 *fax* 020-3148 8127
email jenny_sims@ipcmedia.com
website www.horseandhound.co.uk
Editor Lucy Higginson
Weekly £2.60

Special articles, news items, photos, on all matters appertaining to equestrian sports. Payment: by negotiation.

Horse and Rider

Headley House, Headley Road, Grayshott, Surrey GU26 6TU
tel (01428) 601020 *fax* (01428) 601030
email djm@djmurphy.co.uk
website www.horseandrideruk.com
Editor Nicky Moffatt
Monthly £3.70

Sophisticated magazine covering all forms of equestrian activity at home and abroad. Good writing and technical accuracy essential. Length: 1,500–2,000 words. Illustrations: photos and drawings, the latter usually commissioned. Payment: by arrangement. Founded 1959.

Hortus

Bryan's Ground, Stapleton, Nr Presteigne, Herefordshire LD8 2LP
tel (01544) 260001 *fax* (01544) 260015
email all@hortus.co.uk
website www.hortus.co.uk
Editor David Wheeler
Quarterly £38 p.a. (£44 Europe, £48 rest of world)

Articles on decorative horticulture: plants, gardens, history, design, literature, people; book reviews. Length: 1,500–5,000 words, longer by arrangement. Illustrations: line, half-tone and wood-engravings. Payment: by arrangement. Founded 1987.

Hot Press

13 Trinity Street, Dublin 2, Republic of Ireland
tel +353 (0)1 2411500 *fax* +353 (0)1 2411539
email info@hotpress.ie
website www.hotpress.com
Editor Niall Stokes
Fortnightly €3.50

High-quality, investigative stories, or punchily written offbeat pieces, of interest to 16–39 year-olds, including politics, music, sport, sex, religion – whatever's happening on the street. Length: varies. Illustrations: colour with some b&w. Payment: by negotiation. Founded 1977.

House & Garden

Vogue House, 1 Hanover Square, London W1S 1JU
tel 020-7499 9080 *fax* 020-7629 2907
Editor Susan Crewe
Monthly £3.70

Articles (always commissioned), on subjects relating to domestic architecture, interior decorating, furnishing, gardens and gardening, exhibitions, travel, food and wine.

House Beautiful

Hearst Magazines UK, National Magazines House, 72 Broadwick Street, London W1F 9EP
tel 020-7439 5000 *fax* 020-7439 5141
email julia.goodwin@natmags.co.uk
website www.allaboutyou.com/housebeautiful
Editor Julia Goodwin
Monthly £3.20

Specialist features for the homes of today. Unsolicited manuscripts are not accepted. Illustrated. Founded 1989.

Housebuilder

Byron House, 7–9 St James's Street, London SW1A 1EE
tel 020-7960 1630 *fax* 020-7960 1631
website www.house-builder.co.uk
Editor Ben Roskrow
10 p.a. £7, £85 p.a.

Official Journal of the Home Builders Federation published in association with the National House-Building Council. Technical articles on design, construction and equipment of dwellings, estate planning and development, and technical aspects of house-building, aimed at those engaged in house and flat construction and the development of housing estates. Preliminary letter advisable. Length: articles from 500 words, preferably with illustrations. Payment: by arrangement. Illustrations: photos, plans, construction details, cartoons.

HQ Poetry Magazine

(The Haiku Quarterly)
39 Exmouth Street, Swindon SN1 3PU
tel (01793) 523927
Editor Kevin Bailey
3-4 p.a. £2.80 (4 issues £10 p.a., £13 non-UK)

International in scope, publishes both experimental and traditional work. About one third of the content is devoted to haikuesque and imagistic poetry. Also includes review section and articles. Payment: small. Founded 1990.

ICIS Chemical Business

Reed Business Information, Quadrant House, The Quadrant, Sutton, Surrey SM2 5AS
tel 020-8652 3500 *fax* 020-8652 3375
email icbeditorial@icis.com
website www.icischemicalbusiness.com
Editor Joseph Chang
Weekly £293.30 p.a. (online subscription saving 30%)

Articles and features concerning business, markets and investments in the chemical industry. Length: 1,000–2,000 words; news items up to 400 words. Payment: £150–£200 per 1,000 words.

Icon Magazine

Media 10, Crown House, 151 High Road, Loughton, Essex IG10 4LF
tel (01992) 570030 *fax* (01992) 570031
website www.iconeye.com
Editor Christopher Turner
Monthly £5.00

Articles on new buildings, interiors, innovative design and designers. Payment by negotiation. Founded 2003.

Ideal Home

IPC Media Ltd, The Blue Fin Building, 110 Southwark Street, London SE1 0SU
tel 020-3148 5000 *fax* 020-3148 8121
Editorial Director Isobel McKenzie-Price
Monthly £3.40

Lifestyle magazine, articles usually commissioned. Contributors advised to study editorial content before submitting material. Payment: according to material. Illustrations: usually commissioned. Founded 1920.

Improve Your Coarse Fishing

Bauer Media, Media House, Lynchwood, Peterborough PE2 6EA
tel (01733) 468000 *fax* (01733) 468300
email kevin.green@bauermedia.co.uk
website www.gofishing.co.uk
Editor Kevin Green
Monthly £3.35

Articles on technique and equipment, the best venues, news and features. Ideas welcome by email. Founded 1991.

InStyle

IPC Southbank, The Blue Fin Building, 110 Southwark Street, London SE1 0SU
tel 020-3148 5000 *fax* 020-3148 8166
Editor Eilidh MacAskill
Monthly £3.70

Fashion, beauty and celebrity lifestyle magazine for style-conscious women aged 25–44. Rarely accepts unsolicited material. Founded 2001.

Index on Censorship

60 Farringdon Road, London EC1R 3GA
tel 020-7324 2522
email jo@indexoncensorship.org
website www.indexonline.org
Editor Jo Glanville
Quarterly £9.50, £32 p.a.

Articles up to 3,000 words dealing with all aspects of free speech and political censorship. Illustrations: b&w, cartoons. Payment: £75 per 1,000 words. Founded 1972.

Inside Soap

Hachette Filipacchi (UK) Ltd, 64 North Row, London W1K 7LL
tel 020-7150 7000 *fax* 020-7150 7683
website www.insidesoap.co.uk
Editor Steven Murphy
Weekly £1.55

Gossip and celebrity interviews with soap and popular TV characters on terrestrial and satellite channels. Submit ideas by email in first instance. Payment by negotiation.

Inspire Magazine

CPO, Garcia Estate, Canterbury Road, Worthing, West Sussex BN13 1BW
tel (01903) 264556 *fax* (01903) 537321
email russbravo@cpo.org.uk
website www.inspiremagazine.org.uk
Editor Russ Bravo
Monthly free/donation; available in churches

Magazine with 'good news' stories of Christian faith in action and personal testimonies. Length: 400–700 words (features). Freelance articles used rarely. Payment: up to £85.

Insurance Age

Incisive Media, 32–34 Broadwick Street, London W1A 2HG
tel 020-7316 9115 *fax* 020-7316 9313
email martin.friel@incisivemedia.com
website www.insuranceage.com
Editor Martin Friel
Monthly £5

News and features on general insurance and the broker market, personal, commercial, health and Lloyd's of London. Payment: by negotiation. Founded 1979.

Insurance Brokers' Monthly

Insurance Publishing & Printing Co., 7 Stourbridge Road, Lye, Stourbridge, West Midlands DY9 7DG
tel (01384) 895228
website www.brokersmonthly.co.uk
Editor John Sadler
Monthly £88 p.a.

Articles of technical and non-technical interest to insurance brokers, intermediaries and others engaged in the general insurance industry. Length: 700–1,500 words. Payment by arrangement. Founded 1950.

InterMedia

International Institute of Communications, 24–25 Nutford Place, London W1H 5YN
tel 020-7723 7210 *fax* 020-7723 6982
email s.mcclelland@iicom.org
Editor Stephen McClelland
Bi-monthly £95 p.a.

International journal concerned with policies, events, trends and research in the field of communications, broadcasting, telecommunications and associated issues, particularly cultural and social. Preliminary letter essential. Illustrations: b&w line. Payment: by arrangement. Founded 1970.

International Affairs

The Royal Institute of International Affairs, Chatham House, 10 St James's Square, London SW1Y 4LE
tel 020-7957 5728
email swolf@chathamhouse.org.uk
Editor Caroline Soper
6 p.a. £73 p.a. individuals, £434 p.a. institutions

Serious long-term articles on international affairs; approx. 50 books reviewed each issue. Preliminary letter advisable. Article length: average 7,000 words. Illustrations: none. Payment: by arrangement. Founded 1922.

Interzone

TTA Press, 5 Martins Lane, Ely, Cambs. CB6 2LB
website www.ttapress.com
Editor Andy Cox
Bi-monthly £3.95 (£21 for 6 issues)

Science fiction and fantasy short stories, articles, interviews and reviews. Read magazine before submitting. Length: 2,000–6,000 words. Illustrations: colour. Payment: by arrangement. Founded 1982.

Investors Chronicle

Number One, Southwark Bridge, London SE1 9HL
tel 020-7873 3000
website www.investorschronicle.co.uk
Editor Jonathan Eley
Weekly £4.10, £145 p.a.

Journal covering investment and personal finance. Occasional outside contributions for features are accepted. Payment: by negotiation.

Ireland's Own

Channing House, Upper Rowe Street, Wexford, Republic of Ireland
tel +353 (0)53 9140140 *fax* +353 (0)53 9140192
email irelands.own@peoplenews.ie
Editors Phil Murphy, Sean Nolan
€1.50

Short stories: non-experimental, traditional with an Irish orientation (1,800–2,000 words); articles of interest to Irish readers at home and abroad (750–900 words); general and literary articles (750–900 words). Monthly special bumper editions, each devoted to a particular seasonal topic. Suggestions for new features considered. Payment: varies according to quality and length. Founded 1902.

Irish Arts Review

State Apartments, Dublin Castle, Dublin 2, Republic of Ireland
tel +353 (0)1 6793525 *fax* +353 (0)1 6334417
website www.irishartsreview.com
Editor John Mulcahy
Quarterly €56, €75 (UK)

Magazine committed to promoting Irish art and heritage around the world with reviews of Irish painting, design, heritage, sculpture, architecture, photography and decorative arts.

Irish Farmers Journal

Irish Farm Centre, Bluebell, Dublin 12, Republic of Ireland
tel +353 (0)1 4199530 *fax* +353 (0)1 4520876
email edit@farmersjournal.ie
website www.farmersjournal.ie
Editor Matthew Dempsey
Weekly €2.50

Readable, technical articles on any aspect of farming. Length: 700–1,000 words. Payment: £100–£150 per article. Illustrated. Founded 1948.

Irish Journal of Medical Science

Royal Academy of Medicine, Frederick House, 19 South Frederick Street, Dublin 2, Republic of Ireland
tel +353 (0)1 6334820 *fax* +353 (0)1 6334918
email journal@rami.ie
website www.ijms.ie
Send material to Prof. David Bouchier-Hayes
Quarterly €42, €156 p.a. Ireland and EU, €192 non-EU

Official Organ of the Royal Academy of Medicine in Ireland. Original contributions in medicine, surgery, midwifery, public health, etc; reviews of professional books, reports of medical societies, etc. Illustrations: line, half-tone, colour.

Irish Medical Times

24–26 Upper Ormond Quay, Dublin 7, Republic of Ireland
tel +353 (0)1 8176300 *fax* +353 (0)1 8176335
email editor@imt.ie
website www.imt.ie
Editor Dara Gantly
Weekly €5.10, €236 p.a.

Medical articles. Length: 850–1,000 words. Payment: £100 per 1,000 words.

Irish Pages: A Journal of Contemporary Writing

The Linen Hall Library, 17 Donegall Square North, Belfast BT1 5GB

tel 028-9043 4800
email editor@irishpages.org
website www.irishpages.org
Editor Chris Agee
Bi-annual £10/€14

Poetry, short fiction, essays, creative non-fiction, memoir, essay reviews, nature writing, translated work, literary journalism, and other autobiographical, historical and scientific writing of literary distinction. Publishes in equal measure writing from Ireland and abroad. Accepts unsolicited submissions by post only. Payment: pays only for certain commissions and occasional serial rights. Founded 2002.

The Irish Post

c/o Loot Limited, Suite A, 1 Lindsey Street, London EC1A 9HP
tel 020-87900 4193 *fax* 020-8741 3382
website wst.co.uk
Weekly (Wed) £1.30

Coverage of all political, social and sporting events relevant to the Irish community in Britain. Also contains a guide to Irish entertainment in Britain.

Irish Printer

care of Maev Martin, Broom House, Mulgrave Street, Dun Laoghaire, Co. Dublin, Republic of Ireland
tel +353 (0)1 7642700 *fax* +353 (0)1 7642750
website www.irishprinter.ie
Editor Maev Martin
Monthly €99.79 p.a.

Technical articles and news of interest to the printing industry. Length: 800–1,000 words. Illustrations: colour and b&w photos. Payment: €140 per 1,000 words; photos £30. Founded 1974.

Irish Tatler

Harmonia Ltd, Rosemount House, Dundrum Road, Dublin 14
tel +353 (0)1 2405300 *fax* +353 (0)1 6619757
email jcollins@harmonia.ie
website www.harmonia.ie
Editor Jessie Collins
Monthly €2.10, €24 p.a.

General interest women's magazine: fashion, beauty, interiors, cookery, current affairs, reportage and celebrity interviews. Length: 2,000–4,000 words. In association with ivenus.com. Payment: by arrangement.

Jane's Defence Weekly

Sentinel House, 163 Brighton Road, Coulsdon, Surrey CR5 2YH
tel 020-8700 3700 *fax* 020-8763 1007
website jdw.janes.com
Editor Peter Felstead
Weekly £305 p.a. print, £1,1195 p.a. online, £505 p.a. digital

International defence news; military equipment; budget analysis, industry, military technology, business, political, defence market intelligence. Payment: minimum £200 per 1,000 words used. Illustrations: colour. Founded 1984.

Jane's Police Review

Jane's Information Group, 133 Houndsditch, London EC3A 7AH
tel 020-3159 3579 *fax* 020-3159 3276
email ppr@janes.com
website www.policereview.com
Editor Chris Herbert
Weekly £1.95, £92 p.a.

News and features of interest to the police and legal professions. Length: 200–1,500 words. Illustrations: colour photos, line, cartoons. Payment: NUJ rates. Founded 1893.

Jewish Chronicle

25 Furnival Street, London EC4A 1JT
tel 020-7415 1500 *fax* 020-7405 9040
email editorial@thejc.com
website www.thejc.com
Editor Stephen Pollard
Weekly £1.50

Authentic and exclusive news stories and articles of Jewish interest from 500–1,500 words are considered. Includes a lively arts and leisure section and regular travel pages. Payment: by arrangement. Illustrations: of Jewish interest, either topical or feature. Founded 1841.

The Jewish Quarterly

ORT House, 126 Albert Street, London NW1 7NE
tel 020-74267 9442 *fax* 020-7443 5159
email editor@jewishquarterly.org
website www.jewishquarterly.org
Editor Rachel Lasserson
Quarterly £4.95, £25 p.a. (£35 Europe, £45 overseas)

Articles of Jewish interest, literature, history, music, politics, poetry, book reviews, fiction. Illustrations: colour. Founded 1953.

Jewish Telegraph

Telegraph House, 11 Park Hill, Bury Old Road, Prestwich, Manchester M25 0HH
tel 0161 740 9321 *fax* 0161 740 9325
email manchester@jewishtelegraph.com
1 Shaftesbury Avenue, Leeds LS8 1DR
tel 0113 295 6000 *fax* 0113 295 6006
email leeds@jewishtelegraph.com
tel 0151 475 6666
email liverpool@jewishtelegraph.com
May Terrace, Giffnock, Glasgow G46 6LD
tel 0141 621 4422 *fax* 0141 621 4333
email glasgow@jewishtelegraph.com
website www.jewishtelegraph.com
Editor Paul Harris

Weekly Manchester 60p, Leeds 55p, Liverpool 35p, Glasgow 60p

Non-fiction articles of Jewish interest, especially humour. Exclusive Jewish news stories and pictures, international, national and local. Length: 1,000–1,500 words. Payment: by arrangement. Illustrations: line, half-tone, cartoons. Founded 1950.

Journal of Alternative and Complementary Medicine

Fern Lodge, 5 Cotterill Street, Hereford HR4 0HH
tel (01432) 353656 *fax* (01432) 354010
Editor Dr K.A. Jobst
Monthly £200 p.a.

Feature articles on complementary and alternative medicine, paradigm, practise and policy (up to 3,000 words) and news stories (up to 500 words). Unsolicited material welcome but not eligible for payment unless commissioned. Illustrations: line, half-tone, colour. Payment: by negotiation. Founded 1983.

Junior

Magicalia Publishing Ltd, 15–18 White Lion Street, London N1 9PG
tel 020-7843 8800
email editorial@juniormagazine.co.uk
website www.juniormagazine.co.uk
Editor Catherine O'Dolan
Monthly £3.50

Glossy up-market parenting magazine aimed at mothers of children aged 0–8 and reflects the shift in today's society towards older mothers and fathers who have established their careers and homes. Intelligent and insightful features and the best in fashion. Specially commissions most material. Welcomes ideas for articles and features. Payment: £150 per 1,000 words (articles/features/short fiction), £300 per feature (colour and b&w photos/artwork). Founded 1998.

Kent Life

28 Teville Road, Worthing, West Sussex BN11 1UG
tel (01622) 762818 *fax* (01622) 663294)
email sarah.sturt@kent-life.co.uk, michael.palmer@kent-life.co.uk
website www.kent-life.co.uk
Editor Sarah Sturt, *Assistant Editor* Michael Palmer
Monthly £2.95

Local lifestyle magazine 'celebrating the best of county life'. Features local people, social events and entertainment and promotes local towns and villages, walks and heritage. Welcomes ideas for articles and features, length: 1,000 words (articles/features). Illustrations: hi-res jpgs preferred, colour and b&w prints, colour artwork. Payment: negotiable.

Kerrang!

Bauer Media Group, Endeavour House, Shaftesbury Avenue, London WC2H 8JG
tel 020-7182 8406 *fax* 020-7312 8910
website www.kerrang.com
Editor James McMahon
Weekly £2.20

News, reviews and interviews; music with attitude. All material commissioned. Illustrations: colour. Payment: by arrangement. Founded 1981.

Kids Alive! (The Young Soldier)

The Salvation Army, 101 Newington Causeway, London SE1 6BN
tel 020-7367 4911 *fax* 020-7367 4710
email kidsalive@salvationarmy.org.uk
website www.salvationarmy.org.uk/kidsalive
Editor Justin Reeves
Weekly 50p (£25 p.a. including free membership of the Kids Alive! Club)

Children's magazine: pictures, scripts and artwork for cartoon strips, puzzles, etc; Christian-based with emphasis on education re addictive substances. Payment: by arrangement. Illustrations: half-tone, line and 4-colour line, cartoons. Founded 1881.

Kitchen Garden

Mortons Media Group Ltd, Media Centre, Morton Way, Horncastle, Lincs. LN9 6JR
tel (01507) 529396 *fax* (01507) 529495
email sott@mortons.co.uk
website www.kitchengarden.co.uk
Editor Steve Ott
Monthly £3.90

Magazine for people with a passion for growing their own vegetables, fruit and herbs. Includes practical tips and inspirational ideas. Specially commissions most material. Welcomes ideas for articles and features. Length: 700–2,000 (articles/features). Illustrations: colour transparencies, prints and artwork; all commissioned. Payment: varies. Founded 1997.

Koi

Origin Publishing, Tower House, Fairfax Street, Bristol BS1 3BN
tel 0117 927 9009 *fax* 0117 934 9008
email beckierodgers@originpublishing.co.uk
website www.koimag.co.uk
Editor Beckie Rodgers
Every 4 weeks £3.95

A practical and informative guide to keeping Koi as a hobby, from pond construction to Koi health care. Also includes features on the hobby in Japan. Length 800–1,700 words (articles), 2,000–3,000 words (features), 150 words (news). Payment: £80–£170 (articles), £200–£300 (features). Illustrations: colour.

The Lady

39–40 Bedford Street, London WC2E 9ER
tel 020-7379 4717 *fax* 020-7836 4620
email editors@lady.co.uk
website www.lady.co.uk

Editor Matt Warren
Weekly £2.00

Features, interviews, comment, columns, arts and book reviews, fashion, beauty, interiors, cookery, health, travel and pets. Plus classified ads, holiday cottages and pages of puzzles. No unsolicited manuscripts, please; brief pitches by email. Founded 1885.

Lancashire Magazine

Oyston Mill, Strand Road, Preston PR1 8UR
tel (01772) 761277 *fax* (01772) 739202
email info@lancashiremagazine.co.uk
website www.lancashiremagazine.co.uk
www.lancashiremagazine.tv
Editor Anthony Skinner
Monthly £1.95, £10 p.a.

Articles about people, life and places in all parts of Lancashire. Length: 700–1,000 words. Payment: £70–£100. Illustrations: full colour. Founded 1977.

Lancet

32 Jamestown Road, London NW1 7BY
tel 020-7424 4910 *fax* 020-7424 4911
email editorial@lancet.com
website www.thelancet.com
Editor Dr Richard Horton
Weekly £160 p.a. (print and online), £140 p.a. (online only)

Research papers, review articles, editorials, correspondence and commentaries on international medicine, medical research and policy. Material may be submitted directly through a dedicated online system. Founded 1823.

The Lawyer

79 Wells Street, London W1T 3QN
tel 020-7970 4000 *fax* 020-7970 4640
email editorial@thelawyer.com
website www.thelawyer.com
Editor Catrin Griffiths
Weekly £2.95

News, articles, features and views relevant to the legal profession. Length: 600–900 words. Illustrations: as agreed. Payment: £125–£150 per 1,000 words. Founded 1987.

Legal Week

32–34 Broadwick Street, London W1A 2HG
tel 020-7316 9000 *fax* 020-7316 9278
email alex.novarese@incisivemedia.com
website www.legalweek.com
Editor Alex Novarese
Weekly £4.40

News and features aimed at business lawyers. Length: 750–1,000 words (features), 300 words (news). Payment: £200 upwards (features), £75–£100 (news). Considers unsolicited material and welcomes ideas for articles and features. Founded 1999.

Leisure Painter

Caxton House, 63–65 High Street, Tenterden, Kent TN30 6BD
tel (01580) 763315 *fax* (01580) 765411
email ingrid@tapc.co.uk
website www.painters-online.co.uk
Editor Ingrid Lyon
Monthly £3.50

Instructional articles on painting and fine art. Payment: £75 per 1,000 words. Illustrations: line, half-tone, colour, original artwork. Founded 1967.

LGC (Local Government Chronicle)

Emap Public Sector, Greater London House, Hampstead Road, London NW1 7EJ
tel 020-7728 5000 *fax* 020-7728 3700
email lgcnews@emap.com
website www.lgcplus.com
Editor Emma Maier
Weekly £4.40

Aimed at senior managers in local government. Covers politics, management issues, social services, education, regeneration, industrial relations and personnel, plus public sector finance and Scottish and Welsh local government. Length: 1,000 words (features). Illustrations: b&w and colour, cartoons. Payment: by arrangement. Founded 1855.

Life and Work: The Magazine of the Church of Scotland

121 George Street, Edinburgh EH2 4YN
tel 0131 225 5722 *fax* 0131 240 2207
email magazine@lifeandwork.org
Editor Lynne McNeil
Monthly £1.80

Articles not exceeding 1,200 words and news; occasional stories and poetry. Study the magazine and contact the Editor first. Payment: by arrangement. Illustrations: photos and colour illustrations.

Lincolnshire Life

County House, 9 Checkpoint Court, Sadler Road, Lincoln LN6 3PW
tel (01522) 527127 *fax* (01522) 842000
email editorial@lincolnshirelife.co.uk
website www.lincolnshirelife.co.uk
Editor Josie Thurston
Monthly £2.60

Articles and news of county interest. Approach in writing. Length: up to 1,500 words. Illustrations: colour photos and line drawings. Payment: varies. Founded 1961.

The Linguist

The Chartered Institute of Linguists, Saxon House, 48 Southwark Street, London SE1 1UN
tel 020-7940 3101 *fax* 020-7940 3125

email linguist.editor@googlemail.com
website www.iol.org.uk/linguistmagazine
Editor Miranda Moore
Bi-monthly £41 p.a. (free to Chartered Institute of Linguists members)

Articles of interest to professional linguists in translating, interpreting and teaching fields. Articles usually contributed, but payment by arrangement. All contributors have special knowledge of the subjects with which they deal. Length: 1,500–2,000 words.

The List

14 High Street, Edinburgh EH1 1TE
tel 0131 550 3050 *fax* 0131 557 8500
email editor@list.co.uk
website www.list.co.uk
Editor Jonathan Ensall
Monthly £2.50, £40 p.a. (with LIST card), £30 p.a. (without LIST card)

Events guide for Glasgow and Edinburgh covering film, theatre, music, clubs, books, city life, art, and TV and video. Publishes special issues to support major arts events and festivals. Considers unsolicited material and welcomes ideas. Length: 200 words (articles), 800 words and above (features). Illustrations: transparencies and colour prints. Payment: £20 (articles), from £60 (features); £25–£50. Founded 1985.

The Literary Review

44 Lexington Street, London W1F 0LW
tel 020-7437 9392 *fax* 020-7734 1844
email editorial@literaryreview.co.uk
website www.literaryreview.co.uk
Editor Nancy Sladek
Monthly £3.50, £35 p.a.

Reviews, articles of cultural interest, interviews, profiles, monthly poetry competition. Material mostly commissioned. Length: articles and reviews 800–1,500 words. Illustrations: line and b&w photos. Payment: £25 per article; none for illustrations. Founded 1979.

Living France Magazine

Archant Life, Archant House, Oriel Road, Cheltenham, Glos. GL50 1BB
tel (01242) 216050 *fax* (01242) 216094
email editorial@livingfrance.com
website www.livingfrance.com
Editor Eleanor O'Kane
13 p.a. £3.99

Articles on travel, property and aspects of living in France, from having a baby to setting up utilities. Interviews with expats also featured. Founded 1990.

Loaded

Vitality Publishing, 3rd floor, 207 Old Street, London EC1V 9NR
tel 020-7608 6300 *fax* 020-7608 6320
website www.loaded.co.uk
Editor Andy Sherwood
Monthly £3.60

Magazine for men aged 18–30. Music, sport, sex, humour, travel, fashion, hard news and popular culture. Address longer features (2,000 words) to Features Editor, and shorter items to Handbook Editor. Payment: by arrangement. Founded 1994.

LOGOS

5 Beechwood Drive, Marlow, Bucks. SL7 2DH
tel (01628) 483371 *fax* (01628) 477577
email editor@logosjournal.com
website www.logos-journal.org
Editor Emeritus Gordon Graham
Editor Charles Levine (*email* logos-editor@att.net, *tel* (01718) 577 1175)
Quarterly £48 p.a. (£120 p.a. institutions)

In-depth articles on publishing, librarianship and bookselling with international or interdisciplinary appeal. Length: 3,500–7,000 words. Payment: 10 offprints/copy of issue. Founded 1990.

The London Magazine: A Review of Literature and the Arts

Administration 11 Queen's Gate, London SW7 5EL
email admin@thelondonmagazine.org
website www.thelondonmagazine.org
Editor Steven O'Brien
Bi-monthly £6.95, £33 p.a.

Poems, stories (2,000–5,000 words), memoirs, critical articles, features on art, photography, theatre, music, architecture, etc. Sae essential (3 IRCs from abroad). Submissions by email accepted. No payment offered. First published in 1732.

London Review of Books

28 Little Russell Street, London WC1A 2HN
tel 020-7209 1101 *fax* 020-7209 1102
email edit@lrb.co.uk
Editor Mary-Kay Wilmers
Fortnightly £3.50

Features, essays, poems. Payment: by arrangement.

Lothian Life

Larick House, Whitehouse, Tarbert, Argyll PA29 6XR
tel (01880) 730360
website www.lothianlife.co.uk
Editor Susan Coon
Online publication only

Articles, profiles, etc with a Lothians angle. Length: 500–2,000 words. Founded 1995.

MacUser

Dennis Publishing Ltd, 30 Cleveland Street, London W1T 4JD
tel 020-7907 6000
email mailbox@macuser.co.uk
website www.macuser.co.uk

Editor in Chief Adam Banks
Fortnightly £3.99

News, reviews, tutorials and features on Apple computer products and topics of interest to their users. Commissioned reviews of products compatible with Mac computers required. Occasional requirement for features relating to Mac-based design and publishing and general computing and internet issues. Ideas welcome. Length: 2,000–5,000 words (features), approx. 500 words (news), 300–2,500 words (reviews). Illustrations: commissioned from Mac-based designers. Payment: £190 per 1,000 words; competitive (artwork). Founded 1985.

Macworld

IDG London, 101 Euston Road, London NW1 2RA
tel 020-7756 2877
email karen_haslam@macworld.co.uk
website www.macworld.co.uk
Editor Karen Haslam
14 p.a. £5.99

All aspects of Apple Macintosh computing, primarily for professional users: industry news, product testing, tips and how-to features. Specially commissions most material. Welcomes ideas for articles and features. Digital pictures only. Founded 1989.

Management Today

Teddington Studios, Broom Road, Teddington, Middx. TW11 9BE
tel 020-8267 5462
Editor Matthew Gwyther
Monthly £4.70

Company profiles and analysis – columns from 1,000 words, features up to 3,000 words. Payment: £350 per 1,000 words. Illustrations: colour transparencies, always commissioned. Founded 1966.

Marie Claire

IPC Media Ltd, The Blue Fin Building, 110 Southwark Street, London SE1 0SU
tel 020-3148 7513
email marieclaire@ipcmedia.com
website www.marieclaire.co.uk
Editor Helen Russell
Monthly £3.50

Feature articles of interest to today's woman; plus fashion, beauty, health, food, drink and travel. Commissioned material only. Payment: by negotiation. Illustrated in colour. Founded 1988.

Market Newsletter

Bureau of Freelance Photographers, Focus House, 497 Green Lanes, London N13 4BP
tel 020-8882 3315
email info@thebfp.com
website www.thebfp.com
Editor John Tracy
Monthly £54 p.a. UK (£70 overseas); free to members of BFP

Current information on markets and editorial requirements of interest to writers and photographers. Founded 1965.

Marketing Week

Centaur Communications, 50 Poland Street, London W1F 7AX
tel 020-7970 4000 *fax* 020-7970 6722
website www.marketingweek.co.uk
Editor Mark Choueke
Weekly £3.95

Aimed at marketing management. Accepts occasional features and analysis. Length: 1,000–2,000 words. Payment: £250 per 1,000 words. Founded 1978.

Maxim

Dennis Publishing Ltd, 30 Cleveland Street, London W1T 4JD
tel 020-7907 6000 *fax* 020-7907 6020
email Stuart_Messham@dennis.co.uk
website www.maxim.co.uk
Editorial Director Stuart Messham
Monthly £3.70

Glossy men's lifestyle magazine with news, features and articles. All material is commissioned. Length: 1,500–2,500 words (features), 150–500 words (news). Illustrations: transparencies. Payment: by negotiation. Founded 1995.

Mayfair

Paul Raymond Publications, 3rd Floor, 207 Old Street, London EC1V 9NR
tel 020-7608 6300 *fax* 020-7608 6380
email mayfair@paulraymond.com
website www.paulraymond.com
Editor Matt Berry
Monthly £4.30

Classic British adult magazine containing features ranging from those on motorbikes and celebrities to those of a more explicit nature, as well as several photo sets. Short stories. Welcomes ideas for articles and features. Length: 1,200–1,500 words. Illustrations: colour, cartoons. Payment: negotiable. Founded 1965.

MBUK (Mountain Biking UK)

Future Publishing Ltd, 30 Monmouth Street, Bath BA1 2BW
tel (01225) 442244 *fax* (01225) 446019
email mbuk@futurenet.com
website www.bikeradar.com
Editor Danny Walter
Every 4 weeks £4.20

Magazine for mountain bike enthusiasts with features, reviews, news and world and domestic racing coverage.

Medal News

Token Publishing Ltd, Orchard House, Duchy Road, Heathpark, Honiton, Devon EX14 1YD

tel (01404) 46972 *fax* (01404) 44788
email info@tokenpublishing.com
website www.tokenpublishing.com
Editor John Mussell
10 p.a. £3.50

Well-researched articles on military history with a bias towards medals. Send text in digital form. Length: up to 2,000 words. Illustrations: if possible. Payment: by arrangement; none for illustrations. Founded 1989.

Media Week

Haymarket Publishing Ltd, 174 Hammersmith Road, London W6 7JP
tel 020-8267 4055
website www.mediaweek.co.uk
Editor Jeremy King

No subscription charge.

Online B2B magazine covering news, analysis, features and interviews on the UK media industry. Readership: 100,000 unique users per month. Founded 1985.

Men Only

Paul Raymond Publications, 3rd Floor, 207 Old Street, London EC1V 9NR
tel 020-7608 6300 *fax* 020-7608 6380
email menonly@paulraymond.com
Editor Matt Berry
Monthly £4.30

High-quality glamour photography; explicit sex stories (no erotic fiction); male interest features – sport, humour, entertainment, hedonism. Proposals welcome. Payment: by arrangement. Founded 1971.

Men's Health

Natmag Rodale Ltd, 33 Broadwick Street, London W1F 0DQ
tel 020-7339 4400 *fax* 020-7339 4444
website www.menshealth.co.uk
Editor Morgan Rees
10 p.a. £3.80

Active pursuits, grooming, fitness, fashion, sex, career and general men's interest issues. Length 1,000–4,000 words. Ideas welcome. No unsolicited MSS. Payment: by arrangement. Founded 1994.

Methodist Recorder

122 Golden Lane, London EC1Y 0TL
tel 020-7251 8414
email editorial@methodistrecorder.co.uk
website www.methodistrecorder.co.uk
Managing Editor Moira Sleight
Weekly £1.95

Methodist newspaper; ecumenically involved. Limited opportunities for freelance contributors. Preliminary letter advised. Founded 1861.

Military Modelling

PO Box 6018, Leighton Buzzard LU7 2RS
tel/fax (01525) 850938
email kelvin.barber@myhobbystore.com
website www.militarymodelling.com
Editor Kelvin Barber
Monthly £4.40

Articles on military modelling. Length: up to 2,000 words. Payment: by arrangement. Illustrations: line, half-tone, colour.

Minor Monthly

Custom Creations, 43 Astbury Avenue, Poole, Dorset BH12 5DU
tel (01202) 469199
email russ@poundbury.co.uk
website www.minormonthly.com
Editor Russ Harvey
Monthly £2.40

Magazine for the Morris Minor owner and enthusiast: news, features, profiles and workshops. Specially commissions most material but will consider unsolicited material. Length: 1,000 words (articles/features). Illustrations: colour prints. Payment: negotiable. Founded 1995.

Mixmag

Development Hell Ltd, 90–92 Pentonville Road, London N1 9HS
tel 020-7078 8400 *fax* 020-7833 9900
email mixmag@mixmag.net
website www.mixmag.net
Editor Nick DeCosemo
Monthly £4.20

Dance music and clubbing magazine. No unsolicited material. Payment: £200 per 1,000 words. Illustrations: colour and b&w. Founded 1984.

Mizz

Panini UK, Brockbourne House, 77 Mount Ephraim, Tunbridge Wells TN4 8AR
tel (01892) 500100 *fax* (01892) 545666
email mizz@panini.co.uk
website www.mizz.com
Editor Karen O'Brien
Fortnightly £2.50

Articles on any subject of interest to girls aged 10–14. Approach in writing. Payment: by arrangement. Illustrated. Founded 1985.

Model Boats

MyHobbyStore Ltd, PO Box 718, Orpington, Kent BR6 1AP
tel 0844 412 2262 *fax* (01689) 899266
website www.modelboats.co.uk
Editor Paul Freshney
Monthly £4.15

Founded 1964.

Model Engineer

MyHobbyStore Ltd, PO Box 718, Orpington, Kent BR6 1AP

tel (01929) 463358
Editor David Clark
Fortnightly £2.95

Detailed description of the construction of models, small workshop equipment, machine tools and small electrical and mechanical devices; articles on small power engineering, mechanics, electricity, workshop methods, clocks and experiments. Payment: £50 per page. Illustrations: line, half-tone, colour. Founded 1898.

Modern Language Review

Modern Humanities Research Association,
c/o 1 Carlton House Terrace, London SW1Y 5AF
email mlr@mhra.org.uk
website www.mhra.org.uk
Quarterly £22 p.a. (individual), £126 (institutions)

Articles and reviews of a scholarly or specialist character on English, Romance, Germanic and Slavonic languages and literatures. Payment: none, but offprints are given. Founded 1905.

Mojo

Bauer Media Group, Endeavour House,
189 Shaftesbury Avenue, London WC2H 8JG
tel 020-7208 3443 *fax* 020-7182 8596
email mojo@bauermedia.co.uk
website www.mojo4music.com
Editor Phil Alexander
Monthly £4.50

Serious rock music magazine: interviews, news and reviews of books, live shows and albums. Length: up to 10,000 words. Illustrations: colour and b&w photos, colour caricatures. Payment: £250 per 1,000 words; £200–£400 illustrations. Founded 1993.

Moneywise

Standon House, 21 Mansell Street, London E1 8AA
tel 020-7680 3600
website www.moneywise.co.uk
Editor Johanna Gornitzki
Monthly £3.95

Financial and consumer interest features, articles and news stories. No unsolicited MSS. Length: 1,500–2,000 words. Illustrations: willing to see designers, illustrators and photographers for fresh new ideas. Payment: by arrangement. Founded 1990.

More!

Bauer Media Group, Endeavour House,
189 Shaftesbury Avenue, London WC2H 8JG
tel 020-7208 3165 *fax* 020-7208 3595
website www.moremagazine.co.uk
Editor Chantelle Horton
Weekly £1.50

Celebrities, fun, gossip and sexy features, how-to articles aimed at young women. Study of magazine essential. Length: 900–1,100 words. Illustrated. Founded 1988.

Mother & Baby

Bauer Media Group, Endeavour House,
189 Shaftsbury Avenue, London WC2H 8JG
tel 020-7347 1869
website www.askamum.co.uk
Editor Kathryn Blundell
Monthly £2.70

Features and practical information including pregnancy and birth and babycare advice. Expert attribution plus real-life stories. Length: 1,000–1,500 words (commissioned work only). Payment: by negotiation. Illustrated. Founded 1956.

Motor Boat and Yachting

IPC Media Ltd, The Blue Fin Building,
110 Southwark Street, London SE1 0SU
tel 020-3148 4651 *fax* 020-3148 8127
email mby@ipcmedia.com
website www.mby.com
Editor Hugo Andreae
Monthly £4.50

General interest as well as specialist motor boating material welcomed. Features up to 2,000 words considered on all sea-going aspects. Payment: varies. Illustrations: high-resolution photos. Founded 1904.

Motor Boats Monthly

IPC Media Ltd, 9th Floor, The Blue Fin Building,
110 Southwark Street, London SE1 0SU
tel 020-3148 4664
email mbm@ipcmedia.com
website www.motorboatsmonthly.co.uk
Editor Carl Richardson
Monthly £4.65

News on motorboating in the UK and Europe, cruising features practical guides and anecdotal stories. Mostly commissioned – send synopsis to the Editor. Length: news up to 200 words, features up to 4,000 words. Illustrations: digital colour. Payment: by arrangement. Founded 1987.

Motor Caravan Magazine

IPC Inspire, Leon House, 233 High Street,
Croydon CR9 1HZ
tel 020-8726 8248 *fax* 020-8726 8299
website www.motorcaravanmagazine.co.uk
Editor Victoria Bentley
Monthly £3.50

Touring, products, motorhome tests, practical features. Length: up to 2,000 words. Payment: £60 per page. Founded 1985.

Motor Cycle News

Bauer Media Group, Media House,
Peterborough Business Park, Lynchwood,
Peterborough PE2 6EA
tel (0845) 601 1356 *fax* (01733) 468028
email mcn@motorcyclenews.com
website www.motorcyclenews.com

Editor Marc Potter
Weekly £1.99

Features (up to 1,000 words), photos and news stories of interest to motorcyclists. Founded 1955.

Motorcaravan Motorhome Monthly (MMM)

Warners Group Publications, West Street, Bourne, Lincs. PE10 9PH
tel (01778) 39115492439
email danielattwood@warnersgroup.co.uk
website www.outandaboutlive.co.uk
Editor Daniel Attwood
Monthly £3.90

Articles including motorcaravan travel, owner reports and DIY. Length: up to 2,500 words. Payment: by arrangement. Illustrations: line, half-tone, colour prints and transparencies, high-quality digital. Founded 1966 as *Motor Caravan and Camping*.

Mslexia

PO Box 656, Newcastle upon Tyne NE99 1PZ
tel 0191 233 3860 *fax* 0191 233 3882
email postbag@mslexia.co.uk
website www.mslexia.co.uk
Editorial Director Debbie Taylor
Quarterly from £20.75 p.a.

Magazine for women writers which combines features and advice about writing with new fiction and poetry by women. Considers unsolicited material. Length: up to 2,200 words (short stories), or up to four poems of no more than 40 lines each, in any style, which must relate to current themes (or adhere to poetry or short story competition rules). Also accepts submissions for other areas of the magazine, including Pen Portrait, Monologue, etc., variously themed and unthemed. Articles/features by negotiation. Illustrations: mono art, photos, colour transparencies. Payment: by negotiation. Founded 1998.

Muscle & Fitness

Weider Publishing, 10 Windsor Court, Clarence Drive, Harrogate, North Yorkshire HG1 2PE
tel (01423) 504516 *fax* (01423) 561494
website www.muscle-fitness-europe.com
Editor Chris Lund
Monthly £4.00

A guide to muscle development and general health and fitness. Founded 1988.

Music Teacher

Rhinegold House, 20 Rugby Street, London WC1N 3QZ
tel (07785) 613 145 *fax* 020-7333 1736
email music.teacher@rhinegold.co.uk
website www.rhinegold.co.uk
Editor Christopher Walters
Monthly £7.45

Information and articles for both school and private instrumental teachers, including reviews of books, music, CD-Roms and other music-education resources. Articles and illustrations must both have a teaching, as well as a musical, interest. Length: articles 600–1,700 words. Payment: £120 per 1,000 words. Founded 1908.

Music Week

Intent Media London, 1st Floor, Suncourt House, 18-26 Essex Road, London N18 LR
email musicweeksupport@intentmedia.co.uk
website www.musicweek.com
Editor Tim Ingham
Weekly £5.15, £235 p.a.

News and features on all aspects of producing, manufacturing, marketing and retailing music. Payment: by negotiation. Founded 1959.

Musical Opinion

1 Exford Road, London SE12 9HD
tel 020-8857 1582
email musicalopinion@hotmail.co.uk
website www.musicalopinion.com
Editor Robert Matthew-Walker
Bi-monthly £4.50, £28 p.a.

Suggestions for contributions of musical interest, scholastic, educational, anniversaries and ethnic. DVD, CD, opera, festival, book, music reviews. Illustrations: colour photos. Founded 1877.

Musical Times

7 Brunswick Mews, Hove, East Sussex BN3 1HD
Editor Antony Bye
4 p.a. £18.75 (£75 p.a.)

Musical articles, reviews, 500–6,000 words. All material commissioned; no unsolicited material. Illustrations: music. Founded 1844.

My Weekly

D.C. Thomson & Co. Ltd, 80 Kingsway East, Dundee DD4 8SL
tel (01382) 223131 *fax* (01382) 452491
email myweekly@dcthomson.co.uk
PO Box 305, London NW1 1TX
tel 020-7400 1030 *fax* 020-7400 1089
Weekly 89p

Modern women's magazine aimed at 50+ age group. No unsolicited MSS considered. Send ideas or pitches to relevant department editor. Payment by negotiation. Illustrations: colour. Founded 1910.

My Weekly Pocket Novel

D.C. Thomson & Co. Ltd, 80 Kingsway East, Dundee DD4 8SL
tel 0800 318846
email myweekly@dcthomson.co.uk
Editor Maggie Seed

4 p.m. £1.99

50,000-word romantic stories for women. Payment: on acceptance; competitive for the market. No illustrations.

The National Trust Magazine

The National Trust, Heelis, Kemble Drive, Swindon SN2 2NA
tel (01793) 817716
email magazine@nationaltrust.org.uk
website www.nationaltrust.org.uk
Editor Sue Herdman
3 p.a. £3.95 Free to members

Lifestyle title with focus on the National Trust, encompassing interiors, gardens, food, UK travel, wildlife, environment, topical features and celebrity content. No unsolicited articles. Length: 1,000 words (features), 200 words (news). Illustrations: colour transparencies and artwork. Payment: by arrangement; picture library rates. Founded 1932.

Natural World

Think Publishing Ltd, The Pall Mall Deposit, 124–128 Barlby Road, London W10 6BL
tel 020-8962 3020 *fax* 020-8962 8689
Editor Rupert Paul, *Publisher* Ian McAuliffe
3 p.a. Free to members

National magazine of the Wildlife Trusts. Short articles on the work of the UK's 47 wildlife trusts. Unsolicited MSS not accepted. Length: up to 1,200 words. Payment: by arrangement. Illustrations: line, colour. Founded 1981.

Nature

Macmillan Magazines Ltd, The Macmillan Building, 4 Crinan Street, London N1 9XW
tel 020-7833 4000 *fax* 020-7843 4640
email nature@nature.com
website www.nature.com/nature
Editor Philip Campbell
Weekly £2.65, £135 p.a.

Devoted to scientific matters and to their bearing upon public affairs. All contributors of articles have specialised knowledge of the subjects with which they deal. Illustrations: line, half-tone. Founded 1869.

NB Magazine

RNIB, 105 Judd Street, London WC1H 9NE
tel 020-7391 2070
email nbmagazine@rnib.org.uk
Editor (Acting) Paul Cottam
Monthly £3.75

Articles on eye health and sight loss for professionals. Published in clear print, braille, audio CD and email editions. 48pp, contains advertising. Length: from 500 words. Payment: by arrangement. Illustrations: hi-res jpg files on disk only. Founded 1930; as *Beacon* 1917, then *New Beacon*.

.net

Future Publishing Ltd, Beaufort Court, 30 Monmouth Street, Bath BA1 2BW
tel (01225) 442244 *fax* (01225) 732295
website www.netmag.co.uk
Editor Dan Oliver
Monthly Digital issue, £4.16, Print, £5.99

Articles, features and news on the internet. Length: 1,000–3,000 words. Payment: negotiable. Illustrations: colour. Founded 1994.

New Humanist

The Rationalist Association, Merchants House, 5-7 Southwark Street, London SE1 1RQ
tel 020-3117 0630 *fax* 020-7407 7962
email info@newhumanist.org.uk
website www.newhumanist.org.uk
Editor Caspar Melville
Bi-monthly £5.50

Articles on current affairs, philosophy, science, literature, religion and humanism. Length: 500–1,500 words. Illustrations: colour photos. Payment: nominal. Founded 1885.

New Internationalist

55 Rectory Road, Oxford OX4 1BW
tel (01865) 811400 *fax* (01865) 793152
email ni@newint.org
website www.newint.org
Editors Vanessa Baird, Chris Brazier, Hazel Healy, Dinyar Godrej
Monthly £4.45, £39.85 p.a.

World issues, ranging from food to feminism to peace – examines one subject each month. Length: up to 2,000 words. Illustrations: line, half-tone, colour, cartoons. Payment: £230 per 1,000 words. Founded 1973.

New Law Journal

LexisNexis Butterworths, Halsbury House, 35 Chancery Lane, London WC2A 1EL
tel 020-7400 2580 *fax* 020-7400 2583
email newlaw.journal@lexisnexis.co.uk
website www.newlawjournal.co.uk
Editor Jan Miller
48 p.a. £7.65, £319 p.a.

Articles and news on all aspects of civil litigation and dispute resolution. Length: up to 1,800 words. Payment: by arrangement.

New Media Age

Centaur Media plc, St Giles House, 50 Poland Street, London W1F 7AX
020-7970 4000 *fax* 020-7970 4863
website www.nma.co.uk
Editor Justin Pearse
Weekly £99 p.a.

Magazine devoted to interactive media, marketing and advertising. Founded 1996.

New Musical Express (NME)

(incorporating Melody Maker)
IPC Ignite, The Blue Fin Building, 110 Southwark Street, London SE1 0SU

tel 020-3148 5000
website www.nme.com
Editor Krissi Murison
Weekly £2.40

Authoritative articles and news stories on the world's rock and movie personalities. Length: by arrangement. Preliminary letter or phone call desirable. Payment: by arrangement. Illustrations: action photos with strong news angle of recording personalities, cartoons. Founded 1952.

New Scientist

Lacon House, 84 Theobalds Road, London WC1X 8NS
tel 020-7611 1200 *fax* 020-7611 1250
email news@newscientist.com
website www.newscientist.com
Editor Jeremy Webb
Weekly £3.50

Authoritative articles of topical importance on all aspects of science and technology. Potential contributors should study recent copies of the magazine and initially send only a 200-word synopsis of their idea. NB: Does not publish non-peer reviewed theories, poems or crosswords. Payment: varies but average £300 per 1,000 words. Illustrations: all styles, cartoons; contact art dept.

New Statesman

(formerly New Statesman & Society)
7th Floor, John Carpenter House, 7 Carmelite Street, London EC4Y 0AN
tel 020-7936 6400 *fax* 020-7305 7304
email info@newstatesman.co.uk
website www.newstatesman.co.uk
Editor Jason Cowley
Weekly £4.95

Interested in news, reportage and analysis of current political and social issues at home and overseas, plus book reviews, general articles and coverage of the arts, environment and science seen from the perspective of the British Left but written in a stylish, witty and unpredictable way. Length: strictly according to the value of the piece. Illustrations: commissioned for specific articles, though artists' samples considered for future reference; occasional cartoons. Payment: by agreement. Founded 1913.

New Theatre Quarterly

Oldstairs, Kingsdown, Deal, Kent CT14 8ES
email simontrussler@btinternet.com
Editors Simon Trussler, Maria Shevtsova
Quarterly £30, £65 p.a.

Articles, interviews, documentation, reference material covering all aspects of live theatre. An informed, factual and serious approach essential. Preliminary discussion and synopsis desirable. Payment: by arrangement. Illustrations: line, half-tone. Founded 1985; as *Theatre Quarterly* 1971.

New Welsh Review

PO Box 170, Aberystwyth, Ceredigion SY23 1WZ
tel (01970) 628410
email submissions@newwelshreview.com
website www.newwelshreview.com
Editor Gwen Davis
Quarterly £5.99, £23.96 p.a.

Literary – critical articles, creative non-fiction, short stories, poems, book reviews and profiles. Especially, but not exclusively, concerned with Welsh writing in English. Length: up to 3,000 words (articles). Send by email or hard copy with a sae for return of material. Decisions within 3 months of submission. Illustrations: colour. Payment: £68 per 1,000 words (articles); £28 per poem, £100 per short story, £47 per review. Founded 1988.

The New Writer

PO Box 60, Cranbrook, Kent TN17 2ZR
tel (01580) 212626
email admin@thenewwriter.com
website www.thenewwriter.com
Editor Suzanne Ruthven *Publisher* Merric Davidson
4 p.a. £4.50 plus monthly e-news bulletin

Features, short stories from guest writers and from subscribers, poems, news and reviews. Seeks forward-looking articles on all aspects of the written word that demonstrate the writer's grasp of contemporary writing and current editorial/publishing policies. Length: approx. 1,000 words (articles), longer pieces considered; 1,000–2,000 words (features). Payment: £20 per 1,000 words (articles), £10 (stories), £3 (poems). Founded 1996.

newbooks magazine

4 Froxfield Close, Winchester SO22 6JW
tel (01962) 620320
email guy@newbooksmag.com
website www.newbooksmag.com
Publisher Guy Pringle
Bi-monthly £22.50 p.a.

The magazine for readers and reading groups. Includes extracts from new books, articles and features about and by authors, how the book trade works and how books reach publication and find a readership. Check out our website or email for a free introductory copy.

The Newspaper

Young Media Holdings Ltd, PO Box 400, Bridgwater TA6 9DT
tel 0845 094 0646
website www.thenewspaper.org.uk
Managing Editor Phil Wood
6 p.a. Subscription only

Newspaper aimed at 8–14-year-old schoolchildren for use as part of the National Curriculum. Contains similar columns as in any national daily newspaper. Not currently looking for new writers/articles. Founded 2000.

Now

IPC Connect, The Blue Fin Building,
110 Southwark Street, London SE1 0SU
tel 020-3148 5000 *fax* 020-3148 8110
website www.nowmagazine.co.uk
Editor Sally Eyden
Weekly £1.10

Celebrity gossip, news, fashion, beauty and lifestyle features. Most articles are commissioned or are written by in-house writers. Founded 1996.

Nursery Education Plus

FREEPOST (SCE 2665), Scholastic Education,
Windrush Park, Range Road, Witney,
Oxon IX29 0YD
tel (01993) 893456 *fax* (01993) 893222
email earlyyears@scholastic.co.uk
website www.scholastic.co.uk/nurseryedplus
Editor Tracey Brand
Monthly £4.25, £51 p.a.

News, features, professional development and practical theme-based activities for professionals working with 0–5 year-olds. Activity ideas based on the Early Learning Goals. Material mostly commissioned. Length: 500–1,000 words. Illustrations: colour and b&w; colour posters. Payment: by arrangement. Founded 1997.

Nursery World

Haymarket Media Group, 174 Hammersmith Road,
London W6 7JP
tel 020-8267 8401
email news.nw@haymarket.com
website www.nurseryworld.co.uk
Editor Liz Roberts
Weekly £2.95, £99 p.a. (credit card), £84 p.a. (Direct Debit)

For all grades of primary school, nursery and child care staff, nannies, foster parents and all concerned with the care of expectant mothers, babies and young children. Authoritative and informative articles, 800 or 1,300 words, and photos, on all aspects of child welfare and early education, from 0–8 years, in the UK. Practical ideas, policy news and career advice. No short stories. Payment: by arrangement. Illustrations: line, half-tone, colour.

Nursing Times

EMAP Public Sector, Greater London House,
Hampstead Road, London NW1 7EJ
tel 020-7728 5000
website www.nursingtimes.net
Editor Alastair McLellan
Weekly £1.60

Articles of clinical interest, nursing education and nursing policy. Illustrated articles not longer than 2,000 words. Press day: Friday. Illustrations: photos, line. Payment: NUJ rates; by arrangement for illustrations. Founded 1906.

Nuts

IPC Media Ltd, The Blue Fin Building,
110 Southwark Street, London SE1 0SU
tel 020-3148 5000
email nutsmagazine@ipcmedia.com
website www.nuts.co.uk
Editor Dominic Smith
Weekly £1.90

Lads' magazine featuring sport, news, TV, women and true stories.

Official UK Playstation 2 Magazine

Future Publishing UK, 30 Monmouth Street,
Bath BA1 2BW
tel (01225) 442244 *fax* (01225) 732285
website www.playstation.co.uk
Editor Nick Ellis
13 p.a. £5.99

Non-technical magazine for the Playstation owner. Payment: by arrangement. Founded 1995.

OK!

Northern & Shell Building, 10 Lower Thames Street,
London EC3R 6EN
tel 0871 434 1010 *fax* 0871 434 7305
website www.ok.co.uk/home
Editor Lisa Byrne
Weekly £2.60, £50.49 p.a.

Exclusive celebrity interviews and photographs. Submit ideas in writing. Length: 1,000 words. Illustrations: colour. Payment: £150–£250,000 per feature. Founded 1993.

Old Tractor

Kelsey Publishing Ltd, Cudham Tithe Barn,
Berry's Hill, Cudham, Kent TN16 3AG
tel (01959) 541444 *fax* (01959) 541400
email ot.mag@kelsey.co.uk
website www.oldtractor.co.uk
Editor Peter Love
Monthly £3.75, £45 p.a.

Articles and features on tractors and agricultural engineering for the enthusiast, the collector and the serious historian. Ideas welcome but an in-depth knowledge of the subject is essential. Payment by negotiation. Founded 2003.

The Oldie

65 Newman Street, London W1T 3EG
tel 020-7436 8801 *fax* 020-7436 8804
email editorial@theoldie.co.uk
website www.theoldie.co.uk
Editor Richard Ingrams
Monthly £3.75

General interest magazine reflecting attitudes of older people but aimed at a wider audience. Features (600–1,000 words) on all subjects, as well as articles for specific sections. Be familiar with the magazine prior to submitting work. See website for further guidelines. Enclose sae for reply/return of MSS. No poetry. Illustrations: welcomes b&w and colour cartoons. Payment: approx. £100–£150 per 1,000 words; £100 for cartoons. Founded 1992.

Opera

36 Black Lion Lane, London W6 9BE
tel 020-8563 8893 *fax* 020-8563 8635
email editor@opera.co.uk
website www.opera.co.uk
Editor John Allison
13 p.a. £4.99

Reviews of opera from the UK and around the world, including profiles of opera's greatest performers and a comprehensive calendar of productions and events. Length: up to 2,000 words. Payment: by arrangement. Illustrations: photos.

Opera Now

Rhinegold House, 20 Rugby Street,
London WC1N 3QZ
tel 020-7333 1729 *fax* 020-7333 1736
email opera.now@rhinegold.co.uk
website www.rhinegold.co.uk
Editor Ashutosh Khandekar
Monthly £4.95

Articles, news, reviews on opera. All material commissioned only. Length: 150–1,500 words. Illustrations: colour and b&w photos, line, cartoons. Payment: £120 per 1,000 words. Founded 1989.

Orbis International Literary Journal

17 Greenhow Avenue, West Kirby, Wirral CH48 5EL
tel 0151 625 1446
email baldock.carole@googlemail.com
website www.kudoswritingcompetitions.com
Editor Carole Baldock
Quarterly £5 (£5/€10/$11 overseas), £17 p.a. (£20/€30/$36 overseas)

Poetry, prose (1,000 words), news, reviews, views, letters. Up to 4 poems by post; via email, overseas only, up to 2 in body (no attachments). Enclose sae/2 IRCs with all correspondence. Payment: £50 for featured writer. £50 Readers' Award: for piece(s) receiving the most votes (4 winners submitted to Forward Poetry Prize, Single Poem Category); £50 split between 4 (or more) runners-up. Founded 1968.

OS Magazine

Peebles Media Group, Bergius House, Clifton Street, Glasgow G3 7LA
tel 0141 567 6000 *fax* 0141 331 1395
email km.mcallister@peeblesmedia.com
website www.osmagazine.co.uk
Editor Mike Travers
Bi-monthly £37 p.a.

Serious features on anything of interest to senior secretaries and executive PAs. No unsolicited MSS; ideas only. Illustrations: colour transparencies and prints. Payment: by negotiation. Founded 1986.

Other Poetry

10 Prospect Bank Road, Edinburgh EH6 7NR
email editors@otherpoetry.com
website www.otherpoetry.com
Editors Peter Armstrong, Peter Bennet, James Roderick Burns, Malcolm Carson, Jo Colley
3 p.a. £5.00, £14 for 3 issues

Poetry, reviews, articles. Submit 4-5 poems pasted into the body of an email (no attachments) to the email address above; query reviews and articles. Payment by subscription. Founded in 1979.

Our Dogs

1 Lund Street, Trafford Park, Manchester M16 9EJ
tel 0870 731 6500 *fax* 0870 731 6501
email editorial@ourdogs.co.uk
website www.ourdogs.co.uk
Editor Alison Smith
Weekly £2.20

Articles and news on the breeding and showing of pedigree dogs. Illustrations: b&w photos. Payment: by negotiation; £10 per photo. Founded 1895.

Park Home & Holiday Caravan

Park Home & Holiday Caravan, Kelsey Publishing, Cudham Tithe Barn, Berry's Hill, Cudham, Kent, TN16 3AG
tel (01959) 543 530 *fax*
email phhc@ipcmedia.com
Editor Alex Melvin
Monthly (12 p.a.) £2.95

Informative articles on residential mobile homes (park homes) and holiday static caravans – personal experience articles, site features, news items. No preliminary letter. Payment: by arrangement. Illustrations: line, half-tone, colour transparencies, digital images, cartoons. Founded 1960.

PC Advisor

IDG Communications Ltd, 101 Euston Road, London NW1 2RA
tel 020-7756 2800
email matt_egan@idg.co.uk
website www.pcadvisor.co.uk
Editor Matt Egan
Monthly Digital issue £3.99, DVD edition £4.99

Aimed at PC-proficient individuals who are looking for IT solutions that will enhance their productivity at work and at home. Includes information on the latest hardware and software and advice on how to use PCs to maximum effect. Features are commissioned; unsolicited material may be considered. Length: 1,500–3,000 words (features). Illustrations: colour artwork. Payment: dependent on feature type. Founded 1995.

PC Plus

Future Publishing Ltd, 30 Monmouth Street, Bath BA1 2BW

tel (01225) 442244
email martin.cooper@futurenet.co.uk
website www.pcplus.co.uk
Editor Martin Cooper
13 p.a. £5.99 (print), £2.99 (iPad edition)

For the discerning, dedicated computing enthusiast who loves technology, the magazine includes tutorials and features, and the DVD carries full software products, essential utilities and bonus video material. Each issue is made up of opinion, analysis, and hardware and software labs verdicts.

PC Pro

Dennis Publishing Ltd, 30 Cleveland Street, London W1T 4JD
tel 020-7907 6000
email news@pcpro.co.uk
website www.pcpro.co.uk
Editor Barry Collins
Monthly £5.99 (DVD edition), £4.99 (CD edition)

In-depth industry comment and news, reviews and tests, aimed at IT professionals and enthusiasts. Email feature pitches to editor@pcpro.co.uk.

Peace News

5 Caledonian Road, London N1 9DY
tel 020-7278 3344 *fax* 020-7278 0444
email editorial@peacenews.info
website www.peacenews.info
Editors Milan Rai, Emily Johns
10 p.a. £13 p.a.

Political articles based on nonviolence in every aspect of human life. Illustrations: line, half-tone. No payment. Founded 1936.

Pensions World

LexisNexis, Quadrant House, The Quadrant, Sutton, Surrey SM2 5AS
tel 0845 370 1234 *fax* 020-8212 1988
email stephanie.hawthorne@lexisnexis.co.uk
website www.pensionsworld.co.uk
Editor Stephanie Hawthorne
Monthly £129 p.a.

Specialist articles on pensions, investment and law. No unsolicited articles; all material is commissioned. Length: 1,400 words. Payment: by negotiation. Founded 1972.

People Management

Personnel Publications Ltd, 17 Britton Street, London EC1M 5TP
tel 020-7324 2729 *fax*
email editorial@peoplemanagement.co.uk
website www.peoplemanagement.co.uk
Editor Rob MacLachlan
Monthly £8.75, £105 p.a.

Magazine of the Chartered Institute of Personnel and Development. News items and feature articles on recruitment and selection, training and development; pay and performance management; industrial psychology; employee relations; employment law; working practices and new practical ideas in personnel management in industry and commerce. Length: up to 2,500 words. Payment: by arrangement. Illustrations: contact art editor.

People's Friend

D.C. Thomson & Co. Ltd, 80 Kingsway East, Dundee DD4 8SL
tel (01382) 223131 *fax* (01382) 452491
Send material to The Editor, Angela Gilchrist
Weekly 95p

Fiction magazine for women of all ages. Serials (60,000–70,000 words) and complete stories (1,500–3,000 words) of strong romantic and emotional appeal. Considers stories for children. Includes knitting and cookery. No preliminary letter required. Illustrations: colour. Payment: on acceptance. Founded 1869.

People's Friend Pocket Novel

D.C. Thomson & Co. Ltd, 80 Kingsway East, Dundee DD4 8SL
tel (01382) 223131 *fax* (01382) 452491
email tsteel@dcthomson.co.uk
Editor Tracey Steel
2 p.m. £1.99

45,000–50,000-word family and romantic stories aimed at 30+ age group. Payment: by arrangement. No illustrations.

Period Living

Centaur Special Interest Media, 2 Sugar Brook Court, Aston Road, Bromsgrove, Worcs. B60 3EX
tel (01527) 834 435
email period.living@centaur.co.uk
website www.periodliving.co.uk
Editor Sarah Whelan
Monthly £3.70

Articles and features on decoration, furnishings, renovation of period homes; gardens, crafts, decorating in a period style. Illustrated. Payment: varies, according to work required. Founded 1990.

The Photographer

PO Box 9337, Witham, Essex CM8 2UT
tel (01296) 642020
email editor@bipp.com
website www.bipp.com
Editor Jonathan Briggs
Bi-monthly £5.25, £30 p.a. (UK residents), £65 p.a. (overseas), free to all BIPP members

Journal of the BIPP covering conventional and digital imaging and images. Authoritative reviews, news, views and high-quality photographs.

Pick Me Up

IPC Connect Ltd, The Blue Fin Building, 110 Southwark Street, London SE1 0SU

tel 020-3148 5000 *fax* 020-3148 8112
email pickmeup@ipcmedia.com
website www.pickmeupmagazine.co.uk
Editor Gilly Sinclair
Weekly 68p

Upbeat women's magazine containing real-life stories and puzzles.

Picture Postcard Monthly

15 Debdale Lane, Keyworth, Nottingham NG12 5HT
tel 0115 937 4079 *fax* 0115 937 6197
email reflections@postcardcollecting.co.uk
website www.postcardcollecting.co.uk
Editor Brian Lund
Monthly £2.60, £34 p.a.

Articles, news and features for collectors of old or modern picture postcards. Length: 500–2,000 words. Illustrations: colour and b&w. Payment: £27 per 1,000 words; 50p per print. Founded 1978.

The Pink Paper

Millivres Prowler Group, Spectrum House, 32–34 Gordon House Road, London NW5 1LP
tel 020-7424 7400 *fax* 020-7424 7401
email editorial @pinkpaper.com
website www.pinkpaper.com
Editor Peter Lloyd
Fortnightly Online only

National newspaper for lesbians and gay men. Features (500–1,000 words) and news (100–500 words) plus lifestyle section (features 350–1,000 words) on any gay-related subject. Founded 1987.

Planet

PO Box 44, Aberystwyth, Ceredigion SY23 3ZZ
tel (01970) 611255 *fax* (01970) 611197
email planet.enquiries@planetmagazine.org.uk
website www.planetmagazine.org.uk
Editor (Acting) Emily Trahair
Quarterly £6.75

Articles on culture, society, Welsh current affairs and international politics, as well as short fiction, poetry, photo essays and review articles. Article length: 2,000–4,000 words. Payment: £50 per 1,000 words. Submissions by post or email. For articles, email enquiry in first instance. Founded 1970.

PN Review

(formerly Poetry Nation)
School of Critical University Studies, 6 University Gardens, Glasgow G12 8QH; Carcanet Press Ltd, 4th Floor, Alliance House, 30 Cross Street, Manchester M2 7AQ
tel 0161 834 8730 *fax* 0161 832 0084
email info@carcanet.co.uk
website www.pnreview.co.uk
Editor Michael Schmidt
6 p.a. £6.99, £36 p.a.

Poems, essays, reviews, translations. Submissions by post only. Payment: by arrangement. Founded 1973.

Poetry Ireland Review/Éigse Éireann

32 Kildare Street, Dublin 2, Republic of Ireland
tel +353 (0)1 6789815 *fax* +353 (0)1 6789782
email poetry@iol.ie
website www.poetryireland.ie
Editor John F. Deane
Quarterly €9.99; €45 p.a. (Britain & Ireland)

Poetry. Features and articles by arrangement. Payment: €40 per contribution; €75 reviews. Founded 1981.

Poetry London

81 Lambeth Walk, London SE11 6DX
tel/fax 020-7735 8880
email admin@poetrylondon.co.uk
website www.poetrylondon.co.uk
Editors Colette Bryce, Scott Verner, Martha Kapos, Tim Dooley
3 p.a. £8, £20 p.a.

Poems of the highest standard, articles/reviews on any aspect of modern poetry. Comprehensive listings of poetry events and resources. Contributors must be knowledgeable about contemporary poetry. Payment: £20 minimum. Founded 1988.

Poetry Review

22 Betterton Street, London WC2H 9BX
tel 020-7420 9883 *fax* 020-7240 4818
email poetryreview@poetrysociety.org.uk
website www.poetrysociety.org.uk
Editor Fiona Sampson
Quarterly £30 p.a., £50 institutions, schools and libraries

Poems, features and reviews. Send no more than 6 poems with sae. Preliminary study of magazine essential. Payment: £50+ per poem.

Poetry Wales

57 Nolton Street, Bridgend CF31 3AE
tel (01656) 663018
email info@poetrywales.co.uk
website www.poetrywales.co.uk
Quarterly £5, £20 p.a. (£30 institutions)

Poetry, criticism and commentary from Wales and around the world. Payment: by arrangement. Founded 1965.

Police Journal

Vathek Publishing, Bridge House, Dalby, Isle of Man IM5 3BP
tel (01624) 844056 *fax* (01624) 845043
website www.vathek.com
Quarterly £131 p.a. (print only) £158 (print and online) £117 (online only)

Articles of technical or professional interest to the Police Service throughout the world. Payment: none. Illustrations: line drawings. Founded 1928.

The Political Quarterly

Wiley-Blackwell, 9600 Garsington Road, Oxford OX4 2DQ

tel (01865) 776868 *fax* (01865) 714591
website www.wiley.com
Editors Andrew Gamble, Tony Wright MP
4 p.a. £288 p.a. premium print and online rate institutions, £27 p.a. individuals

Topical aspects of national and international politics and public administration; takes a progressive, but not a party, point of view. Send articles to Assistant Editor. Length: average 5,000 words. Payment: about £125 per article. Founded 1930.

PONY Magazine

Headley House, Headley Road, Grayshott, Surrey GU26 6TU
tel (01428) 601020 *fax* (01428) 601030
website www.ponymag.com
Editor Janet Rising
13 p.a. £3.25

Lively articles and short stories with a horsy theme aimed at readers aged 8–16. Technical accuracy and young, fresh writing essential. Length: up to 800 words. Payment: by arrangement. Illustrations: drawings (commissioned), photos, cartoons. Founded 1949.

Post

32–34 Broadwick Street, London W1A 2HG
tel 020-7316 9000
email postmag@incisivemedia.com
website www.postonline.co.uk
Editor Lynn Rouse
Weekly £6.70

Commissioned specialist articles on topics of interest to insurance professionals; news. Illustrations: colour photos and illustrations, colour and b&w cartoons and line drawings. Payment: £200 per 1,000 words; photos £30–£120, cartoons/line by negotiation. Founded 1840.

Poultry World

Reed Business Information, Quadrant House, The Quadrant, Sutton, Surrey SM2 5AS
tel 020-8652 4020 *fax* 020-8652 4006
email poultry.world@rbi.co.uk
website www.fwi.co.uk/poultry
Editor Philip Clarke
Monthly £3.30

Articles on poultry breeding, production, marketing and packaging. News of international poultry interest. Payment: by arrangement. Illustrations: photos, line.

PR Week

22 Bute Gardens, London W6 7HN
tel 020-8267 4370
email danny.rogers@haymarket.com
website www.prweek.com
Editor Danny Rogers
45 issues p.a. £3.80

News and features on public relations. Length: approx. 800–3,000 words. Payment: £250 per 1,000 words. Illustrations: colour and b&w. Founded 1984.

Practical Boat Owner

Westover House, West Quay Road, Poole, Dorset BH15 1JG
tel (01202) 440820
email pbo@ipcmedia.com
website www.pbo.co.uk
Editor Sarah Norbury
Monthly £4.20

Yachting magazine. Hints, tips and practical articles for cruising skippers. Send synopsis first. Payment: by negotiation. Illustrations: photos or drawings. Founded 1967.

Practical Caravan

Haymarket Magazines, Teddington Studios, Teddington Lock, Broom Road, Teddington TW11 9BE
tel 020-8267 5629 *fax* 020-8267 5725
email practical.caravan@haymarket.com
website www.practicalcaravan.com
Editor Rob Ganley
Monthly £4.10

Caravan-related travelogues, caravan site reviews; travel writing for existing regular series; technical and DIY matters. Illustrations: colour. Payment negotiable. Founded 1967.

Practical Fishkeeping

Media House, Lynchwood, Peterborough Business Park, Peterborough PE2 6EA
tel (01733) 468000
website www.practicalfishkeeping.co.uk
Editor Matt Clarke
13 p.a. £3.50

Practical fishkeeping in tropical and coldwater aquaria and ponds. Heavy emphasis on inspiration and involvement. Good colour photography always needed, and used. No verse or humour, no personal biographical accounts of fishkeeping unless practical. Payment: by worth. Founded 1966.

Practical Parenting & Pregnancy

Immediate Media Co. Ltd, 15–18 White Lion Street, London N1 9PD
tel 020-7843 8800
website www.madeformums.com
Editor Daniella Delaney
Monthly £2.99

Articles on parenting, baby and childcare, health, psychology, education, children's activities, personal birth/parenting experiences. Send feature ideas by email to lara.brunt@immediatemedia.co.uk. Illustrations: colour photos, line; commissioned only. Payment: by agreement. Founded 1987.

Practical Photography

Bauer Media Group, Media House, Lynchwood, Peterborough PE2 6EA

tel (01733) 468000 *fax* (01733) 468387
website www.photoanswers.co.uk
Editor-in-Chief Andrew James
Monthly £3.99

Aimed at anyone who seeks to take excellent quality pictures. Excellent potential for freelance pictures: must be first rate – technically and pictorially – and have some relevance to photographic technique. Freelance ideas for words welcome (the more unusual ideas stand the greatest chance of success). Send synopsis of feature ideas in first instance. Payment: negotiable but typically £80 per page pro rata for images and £120–£140 per 1,000 words. Founded 1959.

Practical Wireless

PW Publishing Ltd, Arrowsmith Court, Station Approach, Broadstone, Dorset BH18 8PW
tel 0845 803 1979 *fax* (01202) 659950
email rob@pwpublishing.ltd.uk
website www.pwpublishingltd.uk
Editor Rob Mannion
Monthly £3.50, £38 p.a.

Articles on the practical and theoretical aspects of amateur radio and communications. Constructional projects. Telephone or email for advice and essential PW author's guide. Illustrations: in b&w and colour; photos, line drawings and wash half-tone for offset litho. Payment: by arrangement. Founded 1932.

Practical Woodworking

MyHobbyStore Ltd, PO Box 718, Orpington, Kent BR6 1AP
tel (01689) 869876 *fax*
website www.getwoodworking.com
Editor Neil Mead
Bi-Monthly £4.99

Articles of a practical nature covering any aspect of woodworking, including woodworking projects, tools, joints or timber technology. Illustrated.

The Practising Midwife

66 Siward Road, Bromley BR2 9JZ
tel 020-8313 9617
website www.thepractisingmidwife.com
Editor Laura Yeates
Monthly £60 p.a. (£57 direct debit), £36 p.a. students (£34.20 DD), newly qualified midwives £50 (£47.50 DD)

Disseminates research-based material to a wide professional audience. Research and review papers, viewpoints and news items pertaining to midwifery, maternity care, women's health and neonatal health with both a national and an international perspective. All articles submitted are anonymously reviewed by external acknowledged experts. Length: 1,000–2,000 words (articles); 150–400 words (news); up to 1,000 words (viewpoints). Illustrations: colour transparencies and artwork. Payment: by arrangement. Founded 1991.

The Practitioner

Practitioner Medical Publishing Ltd, 10 Fernthorpe Road, London SW16 6DR
tel 020-8677 3508 *fax* 020-8664 7429
email editor@thepractitioner.co.uk
website www.thepractitioner.co.uk
Editor Corinne Short
Monthly £85 p.a., £138 p.a. overseas

Articles on advances in medicine of interest to GPs and vocational registrars, and others in the medical profession. Founded 1868.

Prediction

Vitality Publishing Ltd, 3rd floor, 207 Old Street, London EC1V 9NR
tel 020-8726 8000 *fax*
email prediction@predictionmagazine.com
website www.predictionmagazine.co.uk
Editor Alexandra Wenman
Monthly £3.25

Articles on astrology and all esoteric and mind, body, spirit subjects. Length: up to 3,000 words. Payment: by arrangement. Illustrations: large-format colour transparencies or photos. Founded 1936.

Press Gazette

John Carpenter House, John Carpenter Street, London EC4Y 0AN
tel 020-7936 6432
website www.pressgazette.co.uk
Editor Dominic Ponsford
Weekly £3, £115 p.a.

News and features of interest to journalists and others working in the media. Length: 1,200 words (features), 300 words (news). Payment: approx. £230 (features), news stories negotiable. Founded 1965.

Pride

Pride House, 55 Battersea Bridge Road, London SW11 3AX
tel 020-7228 3110 *fax* 020-7228 3121
email info@pridemagazine.com
website www.pridemagazine.com
Publisher C. Cushnie
Monthly £2.80

Lifestyle magazine incorporating fashion and beauty, travel, food and entertaining articles for the woman of colour. Length: 1,000–3,000 words. Illustrations: colour photos and drawings. Payment: £100 per 1,000 words. Founded 1991; relaunched 1997.

Prima

Hearst Magazines UK, National Magazine House, 72 Broadwick Street, London W1F 9EP
tel 020-7439 5000 *fax* 020-7312 4100
Editor Maire Fahey
Monthly £2.95

Articles on fashion, home, crafts, health and beauty, cookery; features. Founded 1986.

Prima Baby & Pregnancy

Immediate Media Co. Ltd, 15–18 White Lion Street, London N1 9PG
tel 020-7312 3852 *fax* 020-7312 3744
website www.babyexpert.com
Editor Elaine Griffiths
Monthly £2.80

Magazine for women covering all aspects of pregnancy and childbirth and life with children aged up to 3 years; plus health, fashion. Length: up to 1,500 words. Illustrations: colour transparencies. Payment: by arrangement. Founded 1994.

Private Eye

6 Carlisle Street, London W1D 3BN
tel 020-7437 4017 *fax* 020-7437 0705
email strobes@private-eye.co.uk
website www.private-eye.co.uk
Editor Ian Hislop
Fortnightly £1.50, £28 p.a.

Satire. News and current affairs. Payment: by arrangement. Illustrations and cartoons: colour or b&w. Founded 1961.

Professional Photographer

Archant House, Oriel Road, Cheltenham GL50 1BB
tel (01242) 216050 *fax* (01232) 216094
Editor Adrian Scorey
Monthly £4.20

Features and interviews covering all aspects of professional photography. Gear tests by professional photographers. Length: 1,000–2,000 words. Illustrations: colour and b&w digital files. Payment: typically £200. Founded 1961.

Prospect Magazine

Prospect Publishing Ltd, 2 Bloomsbury Place, London WC1A 2QA
tel 020-7255 1281 *fax* 020-7255 1279
email editorial@prospect-magazine.co.uk
website www.prospect-magazine.co.uk
Editor Bronwen Maddox
Monthly £4.50

Political and cultural monthly magazine. Essays, features, special reports, reviews, short stories, opinions/analysis. Length: 3,000–6,000 words (essays, special reports, short stories), 1,000 words (opinions). Illustrations: colour and b&w. Payment: by negotiation. Founded 1995.

Psychologies

Hearst Magazines UK, National Magazine House, 72 Broadwick Street, London W1F 9EP
tel (01858) 438856
email PsychologiesClub@psychologies.com
website www.psychologies.co.uk
Editor Louise Chunn *Deputy Editor* Clare Longrigg
Monthly £3.80

Women's magazine with a focus on 'what we're like, not just what we look like' with features covering relationships, family and parenting, personality, behaviour, health, wellbeing, beauty, society and social trends, travel, spirituality and sex. Welcomes new ideas by email which fit into one of these areas, and suggestions should offer a combination of psychological insight and practical advice.

Pulse

CMP Medica Ltd, Ludgate House, 245 Blackfriars Road, London SE1 9UY
tel 020-7921 8102 *fax* 020-7921 8132
email feedback@pulsetoday.co.uk
website www.pulsetoday.co.uk
Editor Jo Haynes
Weekly Free on request

Articles and photos of direct interest to GPs. Purely clinical material can only be accepted from medically qualified authors. Length: 600–1,200 words. Payment: £150 average. Illustrations: b&w and colour photos. Founded 1959.

Q Magazine

Bauer Media Group, Endeavour House, 189 Shaftesbury Avenue, London WC2H 8JG
tel 020-7437 9011
email qmail@qthemusic.com
website www.q4music.com
Editor Paul Rees
Monthly £3.99

Glossy music guide. All material commissioned. Length: 1,200–2,500 words. Illustrations: colour and b&w photos. Payment: £350 per 1,000 words; illustrations by arrangement. Founded 1986.

RA Magazine

Royal Academy of Arts, Burlington House, Piccadilly, London W1J 0BD
tel 020-7300 5820 *fax* 020-7300 8032
website www.ramagazine.org.uk
Editor Sarah Greenberg
Quarterly £4.95 (£20 p.a.)

Visual arts and culture articles relating to the Royal Academy of Arts and the wider British and international arts scene. Length:150–1,800 words. Illustrations: consult the Editor. Payment: average £250 per 1,000 words; illustrations by negotiation. Founded 1983.

Racing Post

Floor 23, 1 Canada Square, Canary Wharf, London E14 5AP
tel (01635) 246505 *fax*
email editor@racingpost.co.uk
website www.racingpost.com
Editor Bruce Millington
Mon–Fri £1.70, Sat £1.90, Sun £1.80, Digital edition £1.10

News on horseracing, greyhound racing and sports betting. Founded 1986.

Radio Times

Media Centre, 201 Wood Lane, London W12 7TQ
tel 020-8433 1200 *fax* 020-8433 3160
email feedback@radiotimes.com
website www.radiotimes.com
Editor Ben Preston
Weekly £1.40

Articles that preview the week's programmes on British TV and radio. All articles are specially commissioned – ideas and synopses are welcomed but not unsolicited MSS. Length: 600–2,500 words. Payment: by arrangement. Illustrations: mostly in colour; photos, graphic designs or drawings.

Rail

Bauer Media Ltd, Lynchwood,
Peterborough Business Park, Peterborough PE2 6EA
tel (01733) 468000
email rail@bauermedia.co.uk
website www.railmagazine.com
Managing Editor Nigel Harris
Fortnightly £3.30

News and in-depth features on current UK railway operations. Length: 2,000–3,000 words (features), 250–400 words (news). Illustrations: colour and b&w photos and artwork. Payment: £75 per 1,000 words; £10-£40 per photo except cover (£100). Founded 1981.

Railway Gazette International

DVV Media UK Ltd, NINE, Sutton Court Road,
Sutton, Surrey SM1 4SZ
tel 020-8652 5200 *fax* 020-8652 5210
email editor@railwaygazette.com
website www.railwaygazette.com
Editor Chris Jackson
Monthly £96 p.a.

Deals with management, engineering, operation and finance of railway, metro and light rail transport worldwide. Articles of business interest on these subjects are considered and paid for if accepted. No 'enthusiast'-oriented articles. Phone or email to discuss proposals. Illustrated articles, of 1,000–2,000 words, are preferred. A preliminary letter is required.

The Railway Magazine

Media Centre, Morton Way, Horncastle,
Lincs. LN9 6JR
tel (01507) 529589 *fax* (01507) 528980
email railway@mortons.co.uk
website www.railwaymagazine.co.uk
Editor Nick Pigott
Monthly £3.95

Illustrated magazine dealing with all railway subjects; no fiction or verse. Articles from 1,500–2,000 words accompanied by photos. Preliminary letter desirable. Payment: by arrangement. Illustrations: colour transparencies, half-tone and line. Founded 1897.

Reach Poetry

Indigo Dreams Publishing Ltd, 132 Hinckley Road,
Stoney Stanton, Leics. LE9 7NE
email ronnie@indigodreams.co.uk
website www.indigodreams.co.uk
Editor Ronnie Goodyer
Monthly £4.25, £48 p.a.

Unpublished and original poetry. Submit up to 3 poems for consideration by post (include sae for reply) or email. New poets encouraged. No payment; £50 prize money each issue. Founded 1998.

Reader's Digest

157 Edgware Road, London W2 2HR
tel 020-053 4500
email theeditor@readersdigest.co.uk
website www.readersdigest.co.uk
Editor-in-Chief Gill Hudson
Monthly £3.49, £42 p.a.

Original anecdotes – £100 for up to 150 words – are required for humorous anecdotes.

Real People

Hearst Magazines UK, National Magazine House,
72 Broadwick Street, London W1F 9EP
tel 020-7339 4570
email samm.taylor@hearst.co.uk
website www.realpeoplemagazine.co.uk
Editor Samm Taylor
Weekly 69p

Magazine for women with real-life tales of ordinary people coping with extraordinary events, plus puzzles section.

Reality

Redemptorist Communications, 75 Orwell Road,
Rathgar, Dublin 6, Republic of Ireland
tel +353 (0)1 4922488 *fax* +353 (0)1 49227999
email info@redcoms.org
website www.redcoms.org
Editor Rev. Gerry Moloney CSSR
Monthly €1.70

Illustrated magazine for Christian living. Illustrated articles on all aspects of modern life, including family, youth, religion, leisure. Length: 1,000–1,500 words. Payment: by arrangement; average £50 per 1,000 words. Founded 1936.

Record Collector

The Perfume Factory, Room 101,
Diamond Publishing, 140 Wales Farm Road,
London W3 6UG
tel 020-8752 8172 *fax* 020-8752 8186
website www.recordcollectormag.com
Editor-in-Chief Ian McCann
Monthly £4.90

Covers all areas of music, with the focus on collectable releases and the reissues market. Specially commissions most material but will consider unsolicited material. Welcomes ideas for articles and features. Length: 2,000 (articles/features), 200 (news). Illustrations: transparencies, colour and b&w prints, scans of rare records; all commissioned. Payment: negotiable. Founded 1980.

Red

Hearst Magazines, National Magazine House, 72 Broadwick Street, London, W1F 9EP
tel 020-7150 7600 *fax* 020-7150 7684
website www.redonline.co.uk
Editor-in-chief Sam Baker, *Send material to* Lindsay Frankel, Features Director
Monthly £3.80

High-quality articles on topics of interest to women aged 25–45: humour, memoirs, interviews and well-researched investigative features. Approach with ideas in writing in first instance. Length: 900 words upwards. Illustrations: transparencies. Payment: NUJ rates minimum. Founded 1998.

Red Pepper

Socialist Newspaper (Publications) Ltd, 1B Waterlow Road, London N19 5NJ
email office@redpepper.org.uk
website www.redpepper.org.uk
Co-editors Michael Calderbank, James O'Nions, Emma Hughes
Bi-monthly £3.95

Independent radical magazine: news and features on politics, culture and everyday life of interest to the left and greens. Material mostly commissioned. Length: news/news features 200–800 words, other features 800–2,000 words. Illustrations: photos, graphics. Payment: for investigations, otherwise only exceptionally. Founded 1994.

REFORM

(published by United Reformed Church)
45 Great Peter Street, London SW1P 3LT
tel 020-7799 6699
fax 020-7916 2021 (FAO 'REFORM')
email reform@urc.org.uk
Editor Kay Parris
10 issues p.a. £2, £20 p.a.

Articles of religious or social comment. Illustrations: graphic artists/illustrators. Payment: by arrangement. Founded 1972.

Report

ATL, 7 Northumberland Street, London WC2N 5RD
tel 020-7930 6441
email report@atl.org.uk
website www.atl.org.uk/report
Editors Alex Tomlin, Charlotte Tamvakis
9 p.a. £2.50, £15.50 p.a., £27 p.a. overseas, Free to members

The magazine from the Association of Teachers and Lecturers (ATL). Features, articles, comment, news about nursery, primary, secondary and further education. Payment: minimum £120 per 1,000 words.

Restaurant Magazine

Broadfield Park, Crawley RH11 9RT
tel (01293) 613400
email editorial@restaurantmagazine.co.uk
website www.bighospitality.co.uk
Editor William Drew
Monthly £5.00

Articles, features and news on the restaurant trade. Specially commissions most material. Welcomes ideas for articles and features. Illustrations: colour transparencies, prints and artwork. Payment: variable. Founded 2001.

Retail Week

EMAP Retail, Greater London House, Hampstead Road, London NW1 7EJ
tel 020-7728 5000
website www.retail-week.com
Editor Tim Danaher
Weekly £2.75, £137.50 p.a.

Features and news stories on all aspects of retail management. Length: up to 1,400 words. Illustrations: colour photos. Payment: by arrangement. Founded 1988.

The Rialto

PO Box 309, Aylsham, Norwich NR11 6LN
website www.therialto.co.uk
Editor Michael Mackmin
3 p.a. £5.50, £19 p.a. (£16 low income)

For poets and poetry. Submit up to 6 poems; sae essential. Payment: by arrangement. Founded 1984.

Right Start

PO Box 481, Fleet, Hants. GU51 9FA
tel (07867) 574590
email lynette@rightstartmagazine.co.uk
website www.rightstartmagazine.co.uk
Editor Lynette Lowthian
Bi-monthly £2.50, £10.90 p.a.

Features on all aspects of preschool and infant education, child health and behaviour. No unsolicited MSS. Length: 800–1,500 words. Illustrations: colour photos, line. Payment: varies. Founded 1989.

Royal National Institute of Blind People (RNIB)

105 Judd Street, London WC1H 9NE
tel 020-7388 1266 *fax* 020-7388 2034
textphone 0845 758 5691
email shop@rnib.org.uk
website www.rnib.org.uk

Published by the Royal National Institute of Blind People, the following titles are available via email and in braille, unless otherwise stated. *3FM*, *Access IT*, *Aphra*, *Big Print newspaper* (large print only), *Blast Off!* (children's magazine), *Braille at Bedtime* (7–11 years; braille), *Broadcast Times* (email only), *Channels of Blessing*, *Chess Magazine* (braille), *Compute IT*, *Contention*, *Conundrum*, *Cricket Fixtures*, *Daisy TV Listings* (Daisy format), *Daisy Radio Listing* (Daisy format), *Football Fixtures* (email, Daisy and braille), *Good Vibrations, Insight* (clear print, audio CD, braille, email), *The Max* (boys aged 16–19), *Missy* (girls aged 12–15), *Money Matters, Music Magazine* (disk and braille), *NB* (print, email, Daisy, audio , *New Product Guide* (braille, large print, email, Daisy), *Piano Tuners' Quarterly, Progress, Proms Guide, Pure* (girls aged 16–19), *Radio Guide, Ready, Steady, Read* (for new readers of braille in braille only), *Scientific Enquiry, Shaping Up, Shop Window, Shop Window Christmas Guide, Short Stories, SP, Television Guide, Upbeat, V* (boys aged 12–15), *Vision* (clear print, email, braille, Daisy format).

Rugby World

IPC Media Ltd, 9th Floor, The Blue Fin Building, 110 Southwark Street, London SE1 0SU
tel 020-3148 4708
Editor Owain Jones
Monthly £4.10

Features and exclusive news stories on rugby. Length: approx. 1,200 words. Illustrations: colour photos, cartoons. Payment: £120. Founded 1960.

Runner's World

Natmag Rodale Ltd, 33 Broadwick Street, London W1F 0DG
tel 020-7339 4400 *fax* 020-7339 4420
website www.runnersworld.co.uk
Editor Andy Dixon
Monthly £4.30

Articles on running, health and fitness, and nutrition. Payment: by arrangement. Illustrations: line, half-tone, colour. Founded 1979.

Running Fitness

Kelsey Publishing Group, PO Box 978, Peterborough PE1 9FL
tel (01959) 530530
email rf.ed@kelsey.co.uk
website www.runningfitnessmag.co.uk
Editor David Castle
Monthly £2.99, £31.80 p.a.

Practical articles on all aspects of running lifestyle, especially road running training and events, and advice on health, fitness and injury. Illustrations: colour photos, cartoons. Payment: by negotiation. Founded 1985.

RUSI Journal

Whitehall, London SW1A 2ET
tel 020-7747 2600
email publications@rusi.org
website www.rusi.org
Editor Emma De Angelis
Bi-monthly; available as part of RUSI membership (from £135 p.a.) or a subscription in conjunction with RUSI Whitehall Papers.

Journal of the Royal United Services Institute for Defence and Security Studies. Articles on international security, military science, defence technology and procurement, and military history; also book reviews and correspondence. Length: 3,000–3,500 words. Illustrations: colour photos, maps and diagrams.

Safety Education Journal

Royal Society for the Prevention of Accidents, 28 Calthorpe Road, Edgbaston, Birmingham B15 1RP
tel 0121 248 2000 *fax* 0121 248 2001
website www.rospa.com
Editor Janice Cave
3 p.a. £12.50 p.a. for members of Safety Education Department (£15 p.a. non-members)

Articles on every aspect of good practice in safety education including safety of teachers and pupils in school, and the teaching of road, home, water, leisure and personal safety by means of established subjects on the school curriculum. All ages. Published in electronic form only. Founded as *Child Safety* 1937; became *Safety Training* 1940; *Safety Education* 1966.

Saga Magazine

Saga Publishing Ltd, The Saga Building, Enbrook Park, Sandgate, Folkestone, Kent CT20 3SE
tel (01303) 771523 *fax* (01303) 776699
website www.saga.co.uk/magazine
Editor Katy Bravery
Monthly £24.95 p.a. Subscription only

General interest magazine aimed at the intelligent, literate 50+ reader. Wide range of articles from human interest, 'real life' stories, intriguing overseas interest (not travel), some natural history, celebrity interviews, photographic book extracts – all relevant to 50+ audience. Articles mostly commissioned or written in-house, but genuine exclusives welcome. Illustrations: colour, digital media; mainly commissioned but top-quality photo feature suggestions sometimes accepted. Payment: competitive rate, by negotiation. Founded 1984.

Sainsbury's Magazine

Seven, 3-7 Herbal Hill, London EC1R 5EJ
tel 020-7775 7775 *fax* 020-7775 7705
website www.sainsburysmagazine.co.uk
Editor Helena Lang
Monthly £1.60

Features: general, food and drink, health, beauty, homes; all material commissioned. Length: up to 1,500 words. Illustrations: colour and b&w photos and line illustrations. Payment: varies. Founded 1993.

Sarasvati

132 Hinckley Road, Stoney Stanton, Leics. LE9 7NE
email dawnidp@btinternet.com
website www.indigodreams.co.uk
Editors Dawn Bauling and Ronnie Goodyer
Bi-monthly £4.25, £24 for 6 issues

International poetry and short story magazine. New

writers/poets encouraged. Several pages given to each published subscriber. Founded 2008.

The School Librarian

1 Pine Court, Kembrey Park, Swindon SN2 8AD
tel (01793) 530166 *fax* (01793) 481182
email info@sla.org.uk
website www.sla.org.uk
Editor Steve Hird
Quarterly £85 p.a.

Official journal of the School Library Association. Articles on school library management, use and skills, and on authors and illustrators, literacy, publishing. Reviews of books, CD-Roms, websites and other library resources from preschool to adult. Length: 1,800–3,000 words (articles). Payment: by arrangement. Founded 1937.

Scientific Computing World

Europa Science Ltd, The Spectrum Building, The Michael Young Centre, Purbeck Road, Cambridge CB2 8PD
tel (01223) 211147 *fax* (01223) 211107
website www.scientific-computing.com
Editor Beth Sharp
6 p.a. £11, £95 p.a., Free to qualifying subscribers

Features on hardware and software developments for the scientific community, plus news articles and reviews. Length: 800–2,000 words. Illustrations: colour transparencies, photos, electronic graphics. Payment: by negotiation. Founded 1994.

The Scots Magazine

D.C. Thomson & Co. Ltd, 80 Kingsway East, Dundee DD4 8SL
tel (01382) 223131
email mail@scotsmagazine.com
website www.scotsmagazine.com
Monthly £1.99

Articles on all subjects of Scottish interest and poetry, but must also be Scottish. Illustrations: colour and b&w photos. Articles paid on acceptance: unsolicited material considered. Preliminary enquiries advised. Founded 1739.

The Scottish Farmer

Newsquest, 200 Renfield Street, Glasgow G2 3QB
tel 0141 302 7732 *fax* 0141 302 7799
email alasdair.fletcher@thescottishfarmer.co.uk
Editor Alasdair Fletcher
Weekly £99 p.a. (print), £49.99 (online only)

Articles on agricultural subjects. Length: 1,000–1,500 words. Payment: £80 per 1,000 words. Illustrations: line, half-tone, colour. Founded 1893.

Scottish Field

Special Publications, Craigcrook Castle, Craigcrook Road, Edinburgh EH4 3PE
tel 0131 312 4550 *fax* 0131 312 4551
email editor@scottishfield.co.uk
Editor Richard Bath
Monthly £3.60

Scottish lifestyle magazine: interiors, food, travel, wildlife, heritage, general lifestyle. Founded 1903.

Scottish Home and Country

42 Heriot Row, Edinburgh EH3 6ES
tel 0131 225 1724 *fax* 0131 225 8129
email magazine@swri.demon.co.uk
website www.swri.org.uk
Editor Liz Ferguson
Monthly £1.58, £19.70 p.a.

Articles on crafts, cookery, travel, personal experience, rural interest, women's interest, health, books. Length: up to 1,000 words, preferably illustrated. Illustrations: colour prints/transparencies, b&w, hi-res jpg files, cartoons. Payment: by arrangement. Founded 1924.

Scottish Memories

Celebrate Scotland, 5th floor, 31-32 Park Row, Leeds LS1 5JD
tel 0113 200 2939
email info@scottish-memories.co.uk
website www.scottish-memories.co.uk
Editor Matthew Hill
Monthly £3.20

Features on any aspect of Scottish nostalgia or history, from primeval times to the 1990s. Contact the Editor with an outline in first instance. Length: 1,000 words. Illustrations: colour and b&w. Payment: £70 per 1,000 words; £20 per photo. Founded 1993.

Screen International

EMAP Media, Greater London House, 1 Hampstead Road, London NW1 7EJ
tel 020-7728 5000
email conor.dignam@emap.com
website www.screendaily.com
Editor Conor Dignam
Weekly £3.60 (£160 p.a.)

International news and features on the international film business. No unsolicited material. Length: variable. Payment: by arrangement.

Sea Angler

Bauer Media, Media House, Lynchwood, Peterborough Business Park, Peterborough PE2 6EA
tel (01733) 395147 *fax* (01733) 468843
Editor Mel Russ
Monthly £3.45

Topical articles on all aspects of sea-fishing around the British Isles. Payment: by arrangement. Illustrations: colour. Founded 1973.

Sea Breezes

Media House, Cronkbourne, Tromode, Douglas, Isle of Man IM4 4SB

tel (01624) 696573 *fax* (01624) 661655
website www.seabreezes.co.im
Editor A.C. Douglas
Monthly £3.25

Factual articles on ships and the sea past and present, preferably illustrated. Length: up to 4,000 words. Illustrations: line, half-tone, colour. Payment: by arrangement. Founded 1919.

SelfBuild & Design

151 Station Street, Burton on Trent, Staffs. DE14 1BG
tel (01584) 841417
email ross.stokes@sbdonline.co.uk
website www.sbdonline.co.uk
Editor Ross Stokes
Monthly £3.99

Articles on house construction for individual builders. Welcomes ideas for articles. Payment: £100–£200 per 1,000 words. Illustrations: colour prints, transparencies and digital.

Sewing World

Traplet Publications Ltd, Traplet House, Pendragon Close, Malvern WR14 1GA
tel (01684) 588500 *fax* (01684) 594888
email sw@traplet.co.uk
Editor Wendy Gardiner
Monthly £4.95

Magazine for sewing machine enthusiasts. Articles and step-by-step projects. Length: 1,000–1,500 words (articles). Illustrations: colour. Payment: £100 per article including illustrations. Founded 1995.

SFX Magazine

Future Publishing Ltd, 30 Monmouth Street, Bath BA1 2BW
tel (01225) 442244
email sfx@futurenet.co.uk
website www.sfx.co.uk
Editor Dave Bradley, *Features Editor* Nick Setchfield
Every 4 weeks (13 p.a.) £4.50

Sci-fi and fantasy magazine covering TV, films, DVDs, books, comics, games and collectables. Founded 1995.

Ships Monthly

Kelsey Publishing Group, Cudham Tithe Barn, Berry's Hill, Cudham, Kent TN16 3AG
tel (01959) 541444
Editor Nicholas Leach
Monthly £3.95

Illustrated articles of shipping interest – both mercantile and naval, preferably of 20th and 21st century ships. Well-researched, factual material only. No short stories or poetry. 'Notes for Contributors' available. Mainly commissioned material; preliminary letter essential, with sae. Payment: by arrangement. Illustrations: half-tone and line, colour transparencies, prints and digital images on CD with thumbprint contact sheet. Founded 1966.

Shooting Times and Country Magazine

IPC Inspire, The Blue Fin Building, 110 Southwark Street, London SE1 0SU
tel 020-3148 4741 *fax* 020-3148 8179
email steditorial@ipcmedia.com
website www.shootingtimes.co.uk
Editor Alastair Balmain
Weekly £2.20

Articles on fieldsports, especially shooting, and on related natural history and countryside topics. Unsolicited MSS not encouraged. Length: up to 2,000 words. Payment: by arrangement. Illustrations: photos, drawings, colour transparencies. Founded 1882.

The Shop: A Magazine of Poetry

Skeagh, Schull, Co Cork, Republic of Ireland
email theshop@theshop-poetry-magazine.ie
website www.theshop-poetry-magazine.ie
Editors John Wakeman, Hilary Wakeman
3 p.a. €25/£16.50 p.a. Ireland, £20/€30/US$40 rest of world

Poems on any subject in any form and occasional essays on poetry, especially Irish poetry. No submissions by email. Illustrations welcome. Length: 2,000–3,000 words (essays); any (poems). Payment: by arrangement. Founded 1999.

Shout

185 Fleet Street, London EC4A 2HS
tel 020-7400 1030 *fax* 020-7400 1089
website www.shoutmag.co.uk
Editor Maria Welch
Fortnightly £2.50

Magazine for girls 11–14 years. Pop, film and 'soap' features and pin-ups; general features of teen interest; emotional features, fashion and beauty advice. Payment: on acceptance. Founded 1993.

The Shropshire Magazine

Shropshire Newspapers, Ketley, Telford TF1 5HU
tel (01952) 242424 *fax* (01952) 254605
website www.shropshiremagazine.com
Editor Neil Thomas
Monthly £2.50

Articles on topics related to Shropshire, including countryside, history, characters, legends, education, food; also home and garden features. Length: up to 1,500 words. Illustrations: colour. Founded 1950.

Sight and Sound

BFI, 21 Stephen Street, London W1T 1LN
tel 020-7255 1444 *fax* 020-7436 2327
website www.bfi.org.uk/sightandsound
Editor Nick James
Monthly £3.95

Topical and critical articles on world cinema; reviews of every film theatrically released in the UK; book reviews; DVD reviews; festival reports. Length: 1,000–5,000 words. Payment: by arrangement. Illustrations: relevant photos, cartoons. Founded 1932.

The Sign

c/o 77 Verulam Road, St Albans AL3 4DJ
tel (01727) 833400
website www.churchtimes.co.uk
Editor Terence Handley MacMath
Monthly 5p

Leading national insert for C of E parish magazines. Articles of interest to parishes; poems. Items should bear the author's name and address; return postage essential or send by email. Length: up to 450 words, accompanied by photos/illustrations. Payment: by arrangement. Founded 1905.

Ski + Board

The Ski Club of Great Britain, The White House, 57–63 Church Road, London SW19 5SB
tel 020-8410 2000 *fax* 0845 458 0781
email arnie.wilson@down-hill.co.uk
website www.skiclub.co.uk
Editor Arnie Wilson
Monthly in winter (Oct–Jan) £4.10

Articles, features, news, true life stories, ski tips, equipment reviews, resort reports – all in connection with skiing and snowboarding. Currently not seeking new commissions. Payment: up to £250 per 1,000 words; £50–£200 per photo/illustration. Founded as *Ski Survey* 1972.

The Skier and Snowboarder Magazine

Mountain Marketing Ltd, PO Box 386, Sevenoaks, Kent TN13 1AQ
tel (0776) 867 0158
email skierandsnowboarder@hotmail.com
Editor Frank Baldwin
5 p.a. (July-May) £2

Ski features, based around a good story. Length: 800–1,000 words. Illustrations: colour action ski photos. Payment: by negotiation. Founded 1984.

Slightly Foxed

Slightly Foxed Ltd, 67 Dickinson Court, 15 Brewhouse Yard, London EC1V 4JX
020-7549 2121, 020-7549 2111, 0870 199 1245
email all@foxedquarterly.com, gailpirkis@foxedquarterly.com
website www.foxedquarterly.com
Publisher/Co-editor Gail Pirkis
Quarterly £9, £11 overseas, Rest of World £12; Subscription: UK £36 p.a., Europe £44 p.a., Rest of World £48 p.a.

Informal and independent-minded magazine of book reviews. Each issue contains 96pp of recommendations for books of lasting interest, old and new, both fiction and non-fiction – books that have inspired, amused, and sometimes even changed the lives of the people who write about them. Unsolicited submissions are welcome; see website for guidelines.

Slimming World Magazine

Clover Nook Road, Alfreton, Derbyshire DE55 4RF
tel (01773) 546071
email editorial@slimmingworld.com
website www.slimmingworldmagazine.com
Editor Elise Wells
7 p.a. £2.75 (£1.95 group members)

Magazine about healthy eating, fitness and feeling good with real-life stories of how Slimming World members have changed their lives, recipes and menu plans, health advice, beauty and fitness tips, features, competitions and fashion.

Smallholder

Hook House, Wimblington March, Cambs. PE15 0QL
tel (01354) 741538 *fax* (01354) 741182
email liz.wright@smallholder.co.uk
website www.smallholder.co.uk
Editor Liz Wright
13 p.a. £3.75

Articles of relevance to small farmers about livestock and crops, organics, conservation, poultry, equipment. Items relating to the countryside considered. Email for guidelines. Send for specimen copy. Length: single-page article 700 words; DPS 1,200–1,400 words with pictures. Payment: by negotiation; more for commissions and technical livestock articles.

Snooker Scene

Hayley Green Court, 130 Hagley Road, Halesowen, West Midlands B63 1DY
tel 0121 585 9188 *fax* 0121 585 7117
email clive.everton@talk21.com
website www.snookerscene.com
Editor Clive Everton
Monthly £3, £30 p.a.

News and articles about the snooker and billiards scene for readers with more than a casual interest in the games. Payment: by arrangement. Illustrations: photos. Founded 1971.

Solicitors' Journal

Waterlow Professional Publishing, 6–14 Underwood Street, London N1 7JQ
tel 020-7490 0049 *fax* 020-7324 2366
email editorial@solicitorsjournal.co.uk
website www.solicitorsjournal.com
Editor Jean-Yves Gilg
Weekly (48 p.a) £239 p.a.

Articles, by practising lawyers or specialist journalists, on subjects of practical interest to solicitors. Articles on spec should be sent on disk or by email. Length:

up to 1800 words. Payment: by negotiation. Founded 1856.

The Songwriter

International Songwriters Association, PO Box 46, Limerick City, Republic of Ireland
tel +353 (0)61 228837
email jlliddane@songwriter,iol.ie
website www.songwriter.co.uk
Editor James D. Liddane
Quarterly

Articles on songwriting and interviews with songwriters, music publishers and recording company executives. Length: 1000–10,000 words. Payment: by arrangement. Illustrations: photos. Founded 1967.

Songwriting and Composing

Sovereign House, 12 Trewartha Road, Praa Sands, Penzance, Cornwall TR20 9ST
tel (01736) 762826 *fax* (01736) 763328
email songmag@aol.com
website www.songwriters-guild.co.uk
General Secretary Carole Jones
Quarterly Free to members

Magazine of the Guild of International Songwriters and Composers. Short stories, articles, letters relating to songwriting, publishing, recording and the music industry. Payment: negotiable upon content £25–£60. Illustrations: line, half-tone. Founded 1986.

The Spark Magazine

Blue Sax Publishing Ltd, 86 Colston Street, Bristol BS1 5BB
tel 0117 914 3434
email editor@thespark.co.uk
website www.thespark.co.uk
Commissioning Editor Vicki West
Quarterly Free

'A free thinking magazine about positive change for the West Country.' Features on health, the environment, social and community issues. Welcomes ideas for features and articles with a regional angle. See website for guidelines. Length: varies, from 52pp +. Illustrations: colour throughout. Payment: £10 per 100 words. Founded 1993.

Spear's Wealth Management Survey (WMS)

John Carpenter House, John Carpenter Street, London EC4Y 0AN
tel 020-7936 6445
email info@spearmedia.co.uk
website www.spearmedia.co.uk, www.spearwms.com
Editor William Cash
Bi-monthly £100 p.a.

Provides an informative, entertaining, objective guide to all aspects of wealth management and the high-net-worth (HNW) lifestyle. Readership mostly comprises individuals who hold over £5 million in financial assets. Length: 700–2,000 words (articles and features). Colour and b&w cartoons. Payment: 40p per word; £150 for cartoons. Founded 2003.

The Spectator

22 Old Queen Street, London SW1H 9HP
tel 020-7961 0200
email editor@spectator.co.uk
website www.spectator.co.uk
Editor Fraser Nelson
Weekly £3.50, £111 p.a.

Articles on current affairs, politics, the arts; book reviews. Illustrations: colour and b&w, cartoons. Payment: on merit. Founded 1828.

Spirit & Destiny

H. Bauer Publishing, Academic House, 24–28 Oval Road, London NW1 7DT
tel 020-7241 8000 *fax* 020-7241 8056
website www.spiritandestiny.co.uk
Editor Rhiannon Powell
Monthly £3.10

'For women who want the best possible future.' Entertaining and informative women's interest magazine with additional features on astrology and psychic matters, holistic therapies and alternative lifestyles. Founded 2002.

The Squash Player

460 Bath Road, Longford, Middlesex UB7 0EB
tel (01753) 775511 *fax* (01753) 775512
email editor@squashplayer.co.uk
website www.squashplayer.co.uk
Editor Ian McKenzie
Bi-monthly £24 p.a.

Covers all aspects of playing squash. All features are commissioned – discuss ideas with the Editor. Length: 1,000–1,500 words. Illustrations: unusual photos (e.g. celebrities), cartoons. Payment: £75 per 1,000 words; £25–£40 for illustrations. Founded 1971.

Staffordshire Life Magazine

Staffordshire Newspapers Ltd, The Publishing Centre, Derby Street, Stafford ST16 2DT
tel (01785) 257700 *fax* (01785) 253287
email editor@staffordshirelife.co.uk
website www.staffordshirelife.co.uk
Editor Louise Elliott
12 p.a. £2.25 (digital edition), £18 p.a.

County magazine for Staffordshire. Historical articles; features on county personalities. No short stories. Contact the Editor in first instance. Length: 500–800 words. Illustrations: colour transparencies and prints. Founded 1948; relaunched 1980.

The Stage

Stage House, 47 Bermondsey Street, London SE1 3XT
tel 020-7403 1818 *fax* 020-7939 8478

email editor@thestage.co.uk
website www.thestage.co.uk
Editor Brian Attwood
Weekly £1.60

Original and interesting articles on professional stage and broadcasting topics may be sent for the Editor's consideration. Length: 500–900 words. Payment: £100 per 1,000 words. Founded 1880.

Stamp Magazine

MyHobbyStore, Hadlow House, 9 High Street, Green Street Green BR6 6BG
tel (01689) 869905
Editor Guy Thomas
Monthly £3.55

Informative articles and exclusive news items on stamp collecting and postal history. Preliminary letter. Payment: by arrangement. Illustrations: line, half-tone, colour. Founded 1934.

Stand Magazine

School of English, University of Leeds, Leeds LS2 9JT
tel 0113 233 4794
email stand@leeds.ac.uk
website www.standmagazine.org
Managing Editor Jon Glover
Quarterly £6.50 plus p&p, £25 p.a.

Poetry, short stories, translations, literary criticism. Send sae/IRCs for return. Payment: £20 per 1,000 words (prose); £20 per poem. Founded 1952.

Staple

114–116 St Stephen's Road, Nottingham NG2 4JS
Editor Wayne Burrows
3 p.a. £25 p.a. (£35 overseas)

Poetry, fiction, articles and reviews. Payment: £10–25 fiction/articles. Founded 1982.

Star Trek Magazine

Titan Magazines, Titan House, 144 Southwark Street, London SE1 0UP
tel 020-7620 0200 *fax* 020-7803 1803
website www.titanmagazines.com/t/star-trek
Editor Paul Simpson
13 p.a. £27.99

Up-to-date news about every aspect of *Star Trek*, including all TV series and films, cast interviews, behind-the-scenes features and product reviews. Payment: by arrangement. Founded 1995.

The Strad

Newsquest Magazines, 2nd Floor, 30 Cannon Street, London EC4M 6YJ
tel 020-7618 3095 *fax* 020-7618 3483
email thestrad@thestrad.com
website www.thestrad.com
Editor Ariane Todes
12 p.a. £6.50, £54.95 p.a.

Features, news and reviews for string instrument players, teachers, makers and enthusiasts – both professional and amateur. Specially commissions most material but will consider unsolicited material. Welcomes ideas for articles and features. Length: 1,000–2,000 (articles/features), 100–150 (news). Payment: £150–£300 (articles/features), varies for news. Illustrations: transparencies, colour and b&w prints and artwork, colour cartoons; some commissioned. Founded 1890.

Studies, An Irish quarterly review

35 Lower Leeson Street, Dublin 2, Republic of Ireland
tel +353 (0)1 6766785 *fax* +353 (0)1 7758598
email studies@jesuit.ie
website www.studiesirishreview.com
Editor Rev. Bruce Radley SJ
Quarterly €10

General review of social comment, literature, history and the arts. Published by the Irish Jesuits. Articles written by specialists for the general reader. Critical book reviews. Preliminary letter. Length: 4,000 words. Founded 1912.

Stuff

Haymarket Ltd, Teddington Studios, Broom Road, Teddington, Middlesex TW11 9BE
tel 020-8267 5036 *fax* 020-8267 5019
email stuff@haymarket.com
website www.stuff.tv
Editor Tom Dunmore
Monthly £4.35, £39.99

Articles on gadgets, gear, technology, lifestyle, news and reviews. Payment by negotiation. Founded 1996.

Suffolk Norfolk Life

Today Magazines Ltd, The Publishing House, Station Road, Framlingham, Suffolk IP13 9EE
tel (01728) 622030 *fax* (01728) 622031
email todaymagazines@btopenworld.com
website www.suffolknorfolklife.com
Editor Richard Bryson
Monthly £3.30, £27 p.a.

Articles relevant to Suffolk and Norfolk – current topics plus historical items, art, leisure, etc. Considers unsolicited material and welcomes ideas for articles and features. Send via email. Length: 900–1,500 words. Illustrations: transparencies, digital colour and b&w prints, b&w artwork and cartoons. Payment: £40–£80 per article. Founded 1989.

Surrey Life

c/o 28 Teville Road, Worthing, West Sussex BN11 1UG
tel (01903) 703730
email editor@surreylife.co.uk
website http://surrey.greatbritishlife.co.uk
Editor Caroline Harrap
Monthly £3.15

Articles on Surrey, including places of interest, high-profile personalities, local events, arts, history and food. Founded 1970.

Swimming Times Magazine

Swimming Times Ltd, SportPark, Pavilion 3, 3 Oakwood Drive, Loughborough, Leics. LE11 3QF
tel (01509) 640230 *fax* (01509) 618701
email swimmingtimes@swimming.org
website www.swimming.org/swimmingtimes
Editor Peter Hassall
Monthly £2.80 plus p&p

Official journal of the Amateur Swimming Association and the Institute of Swimming. Reports of major events and championships; news and features on all aspects of swimming including synchronised swimming, diving and water polo, etc; accompanying photos where appropriate; short fiction with a swimming theme. Unsolicited material welcome. Length: 800–1,500 words. Payment: by arrangement. Founded 1923.

The Tablet

1 King Street Cloisters, Clifton Walk, London W6 0GY
tel 020-8748 8484 *fax* 020-8748 1550
email thetablet@thetablet.co.uk
website www.thetablet.co.uk
Editor Catherine Pepinster
Weekly £2.80

Catholic weekly: religion, philosophy, politics, society, books and arts. International coverage. Freelance work commissioned: do not send unsolicited material. Length: various. Illustrations: cartoons and photos. Payment: by arrangement. Founded 1840.

Take a Break

H. Bauer Publishing Ltd, Academic House, 24–28 Oval Road, London NW1 7DT
tel 020-7241 8000 *fax* 020-7241 8056
email tab.features@bauer.co.uk
website www.takeabreak.co.uk
Editor Rebecca Fleming
Weekly 84p

Lively, tabloid women's weekly. True life features, health and beauty, family; lots of puzzles. Payment: by arrangement. Illustrated. Founded 1990.

Take a Break's Take a Puzzle

H. Bauer Publishing, Academic House, 24–28 Oval Road, London NW1 7DT
tel 020-7241 8000 *fax* 020-0207 241 8030
email take.puzzle@bauer.co.uk
website www.puzzlemagazines.co.uk/takeapuzzle
Editor Guy Haslam
Monthly £2

Puzzles. Fresh ideas always welcome. Illustrations: colour transparencies and b&w prints and artwork. Work supplied on Mac-compatible disk preferred. Payment: from £25 per puzzle, £30–£90 for picture puzzles and for illustrations not an integral part of a puzzle. Founded 1991.

TATE ETC

Tate, Millbank, London SW1P 4RG
tel 020-7887 8724 *fax* 020-7887 3940
email tateetc@tate.org.uk
website www.tate.org.uk/tateetc
Editor Simon Grant
3 p.a. £5

Independent visual arts magazine: features, interviews, previews and opinion pieces. Length: up to 3,000 words but always commissioned. Illustrations: colour and b&w photos. Payment: negotiable.

Tatler

Vogue House, Hanover Square, London W1S 1JU
tel 020-7499 9080 *fax* 020-7409 0451
website www.tatler.co.uk
Editor Catherine Ostler
Monthly £3.70

Smart society magazine favouring sharp articles, profiles, fashion and the arts. Illustrations: colour, b&w, but all commissioned. Founded 1709.

Taxation

Quadrant House, The Quadrant, Sutton SM2 5AS
tel 020-8212 1949
email taxation@lexisnexis.co.uk
website www.taxation.co.uk
Editor Mike Truman
Weekly £7.70

Updating and advice concerning UK tax law and practice for accountants and tax experts. All articles written by professionals. Length: 2,000 words (articles). Payment £150 per 1,000 words. Founded 1927.

The Teacher

National Union of Teachers, Hamilton House, Mabledon Place, London WC1H 9BD
tel 020-7380 4708 *fax* 020-7387 8458
email teacher@nut.org.uk
website www.teachers.org.uk/teacher-online
Editor Elyssa Campbell-Barr
6 p.a. Free to NUT members

Articles, features and news of interest to all those involved in the teaching profession. Length: 650 words (single page), 1,200-1,300 (double page). Payment: NUJ rates to NUJ members. Founded 1872.

Technology Ireland

Enterprise Ireland, The Plaza, East Point Business Park, Dublin 3, Republic of Ireland
tel +353 (0)1 7272954 *fax* +353 (0)1 7272086
email technology.ireland@enterprise-ireland.com
website www.technologyireland.ie

Editor Kathy Burke
6 p.a. €54 plus VAT p.a.

Articles, features, reviews, news on current business, innovation and technology. Length: 1,500–2,000 words. Illustrations: line, half-tone, colour. Payment: varies. Founded 1969.

Television

Kildare House, 3 Dorsett Rise, London EC4Y 8EH
tel 020-7822 2810
email publications@rts.org.uk
website www.rts.org.uk
Editor Steve Clarke
Monthly £8, £82 p.a.

Articles on the technical aspects of domestic TV and video equipment, especially servicing, long-distance TV, constructional projects, satellite TV, video recording, teletext and viewdata, test equipment, monitors. Payment: by arrangement. Illustrations: photos and line drawings for litho. Founded 1950.

Tempo

Cambridge University Press,
The Edinburgh Building, Shaftesbury Road,
Cambridge CB2 8RU
Editorial address PO Box 171, Herne Bay,
Kent CT6 6WD
email macval@compuserve.com
Editor Calum MacDonald
Quarterly £87/$145 p.a. (online and print), £74/$126 p.a. (online only; institutions)

Authoritative articles on contemporary music. Length: 2,000–4,000 words. Payment: by arrangement. Illustrations: music type, occasional photographic or musical supplements.

The TES

26 Red Lion Square, Holborn WC1R 4HQ
tel 020-3194 3000
fax 020-3194 3202 (news), 020-3194 3200 (features)
email newsdesk@tes.co.uk, features@tes.co.uk
website www.tes.co.uk
Editor Gerard Kelly
Weekly £1.70, £45 p.a.

Education newspaper. Articles on education written with special knowledge or experience; news items; books, arts and equipment reviews. Check with the news or picture editor before submitting material. Outlines of feature ideas should be emailed. Illustrations: suitable photos and drawings of educational interest, cartoons. Payment: standard rates, or by arrangement.

TES Magazine

Weekly Free with TES

Magazine for teachers focusing on their lives, inside and outside the classroom, investigating the key issues of the day and highlighting good practice. Length: 800 words max.

The TES Cymru

Sophia House, 28 Cathedral Road, Cardiff CF11 9LJ
tel 029-2066 0201 *fax* 029-2066 0207
email cymru@tes.co.uk
website www.tes.co.uk/cymru
Editor Gerard Kelly
Weekly £1.70, £45 p.a.

Education newspaper. Articles on education, teachers, teaching and learning, and education policy in Wales. Length: up to 800 words (articles). Illustrations: line, half-tone. Payment: by arrangement. Founded 2004.

The TESS

Thistle House, 21–23 Thistle Street,
Edinburgh EH2 1DF
tel 0131 624 8333 *fax* 0131 467 8019
website www.tes.co.uk/scotland
Editor Neil Munro
Weekly £1.50

Education newspaper. Articles on education, preferably 800–1,000 words, written with special knowledge or experience. News items about Scottish educational affairs. Illustrations: line, half-tone. Payment: by arrangement. Founded 1965.

TGO (The Great Outdoors) Magazine

30 Cannon Street, London EC4M 6YJ
tel 0141 302 7736 *fax* 0141 302 7799
email emily.rodway@tgomagazine.co.uk
website www.tgomagazine.co.uk
Editor Emily Rodway
13 p.a. £44.95 p.a.

Articles on walking or lightweight camping in specific areas, mainly in the UK, preferably illustrated with photography. Length: 700–2,000 words. Payment: by arrangement. Illustrations: colour. Apply for guidelines. Founded 1978.

that's life!

H. Bauer Publishing Ltd, Academic House,
24–28 Oval Road, London NW1 7DT
tel 020-7241 8000 *fax* 020-7241 8008
email stories@thatslife.co.uk
website www.thatslife.co.uk
Editor Sophie Hearsey
Weekly 70p

Dramatic true life stories about women. Length: average 1,000 words. Illustrations: colour photos and cartoons. Payment: up to £1,000. Founded 1995.

Third Way

13–17 Long Lane, London EC1A 9PN
tel 020-7776 1071 *fax* 020-7776 1087
email editor@thirdway.org.uk
website www.thirdwaymagazine.co.uk
Editor Simon Jones
10 p.a. £4.95, £38 p.a.

Aims to present biblical perspectives on the political,

social and cultural issues of the day. Payment: by arrangement on publication. Email submissions preferred. Founded 1977.

This England

PO Box 52, Cheltenham, Glos. GL50 1YQ
tel (01242) 537900 *fax* (01242) 537901
email editor@thisengland.co.uk
website www.thisengland.co.uk
Editor Stephen Garnett
Quarterly £4.50

Articles about England's traditions, customs and places of interest. Regular features on towns, villages, the English countryside, notable men and women, and readers' recollections. Length 250–2,000 words. Illustrations: digital; colour transparencies only accepted when accompanying articles. Payment: £25 per 1,000 words, £10 poems (12–24 lines). Founded 1968.

Time Out London

Time Out Group Ltd, Universal House, 251 Tottenham Court Road, London W1T 7AB
tel 020-7813 3000 *fax* 020-7813 6001
email timeout@cisubs.co.uk
website www.timeout.com
Acting Editor Mark Frith
Weekly £3.25

Listings magazine for London covering all areas of the arts, plus articles of consumer and news interest. Illustrations: colour and b&w. Payment by negotiation. Founded 1968.

The Times Educational Supplement – see The TES

The Times Educational Supplement Scotland – see The TESS

Times Higher Education

26 Red Lion Square, London WC1R 4HQ
tel 020-3194 3000 *fax* 020-3194 3300
website www.timeshighereducation.co.uk
Editor Ann Mroz
Weekly £1.95

Articles on higher education written with special knowledge or experience, or articles dealing with academic topics. Also news items. Illustrations: suitable photos and drawings of educational interest. Payment: by arrangement. Founded 1971.

TLS (The Times Literary Supplement)

3 Thomas More Square, London E98 1BS
tel 020-7782 4985 *fax* 020-7782 4966
website www.the-tls.co.uk
Editor Peter Stothard
Weekly. £2.70

Will consider poems for publication, literary discoveries and articles on literary and cultural affairs. Payment: by arrangement.

Today's Golfer

Bauer Media, Media House, Lynchwood, Peterborough Business Park, Peterborough PE2 6EA
tel (01733) 468000 *fax* (01733) 468843
email andy.calton@bauermedia.co.uk
website www.todaysgolfer.co.uk
Editor-in-Chief Andy Calton
Monthly £4.20, £54.60 p.a.

Specialist features and articles on golf instruction, equipment and courses. Founded 1988.

Top Santé Health & Beauty

Bauer Consumer Media, Endeavour House, 189 Shaftesbury Avenue, London WC2H 8JG
tel 020-7520 6592
website www.topsante.co.uk
Editor Ellie Hughes
Monthly £2.90

Articles, features and news on all aspects of health and beauty. Ideas welcome. No unsolicited features. Payment: illustrations by arrangement. Founded 1993.

Total Film

Future Publishing Ltd, Beauford Court, Bath BA1 2BW
tel 020-7042 4839
email jane.crowther@futurenet.com
website www.totalfilm.com
Editor Jane Crowther
Monthly £3.99, £37.99 p.a.

Movie magazine covering all aspects of film. Email ideas before submitting material. Not seeking interviews or reviews. Length: 400 words (news items); 1,000 words (funny features). Payment: £150 per 1,000 words; up to £1,500 per picture. Founded 1996.

Total Off-Road

151 Station Street, Burton on Trent, Staffs. DE14 1BG
tel (01283) 742950 *fax* (01283) 742957
email editorial@toronline.co.uk
Editor Alan Kidd
Monthly £3.50, £39 p.a.

Features on off-roading: competitions, modified vehicles, overseas events. Length 1,200–3,000 words. Payment: £100 per 1,000 words. Illustrations: colour and b&w prints, transparencies and digital images. keen to hear from photographers attending UK/ overseas off-road events. Preliminary email strongly advised.

Total Politics

Westminster Tower, 3 Albert Embankment, London SE1 7SP
tel 020-7091 1260
email editorial@totalpolitics.com
website www.totalpolitics.com
Editor Ben Duckworth

Monthly £3.99, £27 p.a.

Magazine for politicians and people interested in politics. Looking for relevant articles and features. Length: up to 2,200 words. Illustrations: colour and b&w photos and bespoke artwork. Payment: negotiable. Founded 2008.

Trail

Bauer Consumer Meda Ltd, 1 Lincoln Court, Lincoln Road, Peterborough PE1 2RF
tel (01733) 468363
email trail@bauermedia.co.uk
website www.trailroutes.com
Editor Simon Ingram
Monthly £3.90

Outdoor activity magazine focusing mainly on high level walking with some scrambling and climbing. Some opportunities for freelances. Good ideas welcome.

Traveller

Traveller & Publishing, 4th Floor, 45-49 Brompton Road, London SW3 1DE
tel 020-7581 6156
email traveller@and-publishing.co.uk
website www.traveller.org.uk
Editor Amy Sohanpaul
3 p.a. Free to members of WEXAS, the traveller's club; back issues £6.95

Adventurous and authentic travel writing. Narrative features describe personal journeys to remarkable places. Unsolicited material considered if prose and pictures are excellent. See website for guidelines. Length: 1,000 words. Illustrations: transparencies, b&w prints plus hi res digital images. Payment: £200 per 1,000 words; colour £50 (£150 cover). Founded 1970.

Tribune

Woodberry, 218 Green Lanes, London N4 2HB
tel 020-8800 4281 *fax*
email mail@tribunemagazine.co.uk
website www.tribunemagazine.co.uk
Editor Chris McLaughlin, *Deputy Editor* Keith Richmond, *Arts Editor* George Osgerby
Weekly £2

Political, literary, with Socialist outlook. Informative articles (about 900 words), news stories (250–300 words). No unsolicited reviews or fiction. Payment: by arrangement. Illustrations: cartoons, photos.

Trout and Salmon

Bauer Media, Media House, Lynchwood, Peterborough PE2 6EA
tel (01733) 468000 *fax* (01733) 468843
email troutandsalmon@bauermedia.co.uk
Editor Andrew Flitcroft
13 p.a. £3.40, £44.20 p.a.

Articles of good quality with strong trout or salmon angling interest. Length: 400–2,000 words, accompanied if possible by good quality colour prints. Payment: by arrangement. Illustrations: line, colour transparencies and prints, cartoons. Founded 1955.

Truck & Driver

Road Transport Media Ltd, 9 Sutton Court Road, Sutton, Surrey SM1 4SZ
tel 020-8912 2141
Editor Colin Barnett
Monthly £2.85

News, articles on trucks, personalities and features of interest to truck drivers. Words (on disk or electronically) and picture packages preferred. Length: approx. 1,500 words. Illustrations: colour transparencies, digital and artwork, cartoons. Payment: negotiable. Founded 1984.

Trucking

Future Publishing Ltd, 30 Monmouth Street, Bath BA1 2BW
tel (01225) 442244
email steev.hayes@futurenet.co
website www.truckingmag.com
Editor Steev Hayes
Monthly £3.25

For truck drivers, owner–drivers and operators: news, articles, features and technical advice. Length: 750–2500 words. Illustrations: mostly 35mm digital. Payment: by negotiation. Founded 1983.

The Trumpet

44A Selby Road, London E11 3LT
tel 020-8522 6600 *fax* 020-8522 6699
email info@the-trumpet.com
website www.the-trumpet.com
Editor-in-Chief Femi Okutubo
Fortnightly Free (Subscription £60 p.a.)

Newspaper for Africans in the Diaspora. Founded 1995.

TVTimes Magazine

IPC Media Ltd, The Blue Fin Building, 110 Southwark Street, London SE1 0SU
tel 020-3148 5615 *fax* 020-3148 8115
website www.tvtimes.co.uk
Editor Ian Abbott
Weekly £1.20

Features with an affinity to ITV, BBC1, BBC2, Channels 4 and 5, satellite and radio personalities and TV generally. Length: by arrangement. Photographs: commissioned only. Payment: by arrangement.

U magazine

Rosemount House, Dundrum Road, Dublin 14, Republic of Ireland
tel +353 (0)1 2405300
website www.harmonia.ie
Editor Jennifer Stevens

Fortnightly €1.50

Fashion and beauty magazine for 18–25 year-old Irish women, with celebrity interviews, talent profiles, real-life stories, sex and relationship features, plus regular pages on the club scene, movies, music and film. Also travel, interiors, health, food, horoscopes. Material mostly commissioned. Payment: varies. Founded 1978.

Ulster Business

Greer Publications, 5B Edgewater Business Park, Edgewater Road, Belfast Harbour Estate, Belfast BT3 9JQ
tel 028-9078 3200 *fax* 028-9078 3210
email davidelliot@greerpublications.com
website www.ulsterbusiness.com
Editor David Elliott
Monthly £27.50 p.a.

Feature-based magazine with general business-related editorial for management level and above. Specially commissions most material but will consider unsolicited material. Welcomes ideas for articles and features. Length: 800 words (articles), 1,500 words (features). Payment: £60–£80 (articles), £120 (features). No illustrations required. Founded 1987.

Ulster Grocer

Greer Publications, 5B Edgewater Business Park, Belfast Harbour Estate, Belfast BT3 9JQ
tel 028-9078 3200 *fax* 028-9078 3210
Editor Louise Murphy
Monthly Controlled circulation

Topical features (1,000–1,500 words) on food/grocery retailing and exhibitions; news (200 words) with a Northern Ireland basis. All features commissioned; no speculative articles accepted. Illustrations: colour photos. Payment: features £275, product news £160. Founded 1972.

Under 5

Pre-school Learning Alliance, The Fitzpatrick Building, 188 York Way, London N7 9AD
tel 020-7697 2500 *fax* 020-7697 8607
website www.pre-school.org.uk
Editor Mandy Murphy
10 p.a. £30 p.a.

Articles on the role of adults, especially parents/preschool workers, in young children's learning and development, including children from all cultures and those with special needs. Length: 600–1,200 words. Founded 1962.

The Universe

4th Floor, Landmark House, Station Road, Cheadle, Hulme SK8 7JH
tel 0161 488 1700 *fax* 0161 488 1701
email joseph.kelly@thecatholicuniverse.com
website www.totalcatholic.com
Editor Joe Kelly
Weekly £1, £57 p.a.

Catholic Sunday newspaper. News stories, features and photos on all aspects of Catholic life required; also cartoons. Send sae with MSS. Payment: by arrangement. Founded 1860.

Vanity Fair

The Condé Nast Publications Ltd, Vogue House, Hanover Square, London W1S 1JU
tel 020-7499 9080 *fax* 020-7409 0783
website www.vanityfair.com
Editor-in-Chief Graydon Carter
Monthly £4.40

Media, glamour and politics for grown-up readers. No unsolicited material. Payment: by arrangement. Illustrated.

The Vegan

The Vegan Society, Donald Watson House, 21 Hylton Street, Birmingham B18 6HJ
tel 0121 523 1730 *fax* 0121 523 1749
email editor@vegansociety.com
website www.vegansociety.com
Editor Rosamund Raha
Quarterly £2.50, £10 p.a.

Articles on health, nutrition, cookery, vegan lifestyle, land use, animal rights. Length: approx. 1,000 words. Payment: by arrangement. Illustrations: photos, cartoons, line drawings – foods, animals, livestock systems, crops, people, events; colour for cover. Founded 1944.

Venue

Venue Publishing, Bristol News & Media, Temple Way, Bristol BS99 7HD
tel 0117 942 8491 *fax* 0117 942 0369
email editor@venue.co.uk
website www.venue.co.uk
Editor David Higgitt
Weekly £1.50

Listings magazine for Bristol and Bath combining comprehensive entertainment information with local features, profiles and interviews. Length: by agreement. Illustrations: colour. Payment: £9.90 per 100 words. Founded 1982.

Vintage Tractor & Countryside Heritage

Unit 101, The Perfume Factory, 140 Wales Farm Road, London W3 6UG
tel/fax (01778) 342814
email stuart@gibbardtractors.co.uk
website www.vtmag.co.uk
Editor Stuart Gibbard *tel* (01406) 380740
Monthly £3.80

Features on the golden age of tractors and nostalgic countryside matters from the days when life was simpler and farming was at the heart of every village. Unrivalled historical content, nostalgic photographs and fascinating interviews with people who were there at the time. Length: max. 2,000 words. Illustrations: colour and b&w. Payment: at editor's discretion. Founded 1981.

Viz

Dennis Publishing, 30 Cleveland Street,
London W1T 4JD
tel 020-7907 6000 *fax* 020-7907 6020
email viz@viz.co.uk
website www.viz.co.uk
Editor Hampton Doubleday
10 p.a. £3.20

Cartoons, spoof tabloid articles, spoof advertisements. Illustrations: half-tone, line, cartoons. Payment: £300 per page (cartoons). Founded 1979.

Vogue

Vogue House, 1 Hanover Square, London W1S 1JU
tel 020-7499 9080 *fax* 020-7408 0559
email vogue.com.editor@condenast.co.uk
website www.vogue.co.uk
Editor Alexandra Shulman
Monthly £4.10

Fashion, beauty, health, decorating, art, theatre, films, literature, music, travel, food and wine. Length: articles from 1,000 words. Illustrated.

The Voice

GV Media Group, Moorfoot House, 1st Floor East,
221 Marsh Wall, London E14 9FH
tel 020-7510 0340 *fax* 020-7510 0341
email newsdesk@the-voice.co.uk
website www.voice-online.co.uk
Editor Steve Pope
Weekly 85p

Weekly newspaper for black Britons. Includes news, features, arts, sport and a comprehensive jobs and business section. Illustrations: colour and b&w photos. Open to ideas for news and features on sports, business, community events and the arts. Founded 1982.

Young Voices

website www.young-voices.co.uk
Editor Dionne Grant
Monthly, 2nd Tues of each month £2.40

News, features, reviews, showbiz highlights and current affairs for 11–19 year-olds. Founded 2003.

walk

The Ramblers' Association, 2nd Floor,
Camelford House, 87–90 Albert Embankment,
London SE1 7TW
tel 020-7339 8540 *fax* 020-7339 8501
email dominic.bates@ramblers.org.uk
website www.walkmag.co.uk
Editor Dominic Bates
Quarterly £3.60 Free to members

Magazine of the Ramblers' Association. Articles on walking, access to countryside and related issues. Material mostly commissioned. Length: up to 1,500 words. Illustrations: colour photos, preferably high quality, digitally supplied. Payment: by agreement. Founded 1935.

Wallpaper

IPC Media Ltd, The Blue Fin Building,
110 Southwark Street, London SE1 0SU
tel 020-3148 5000 *fax* 020-3148 8119
email contact@wallpaper.com
website www.wallpaper.com
Editor-in-Chief Tony Chambers
12 p.a. £4

Interiors, architecture, fashion, entertainment and travel. Payment: by arrangement. Founded 1996.

Wanderlust

PO Box 1832, Windsor SL4 1YT
tel (01753) 620426
website www.wanderlust.co.uk
Editor Dan Linstead, *Publisher* Lyn Hughes
8 p.a. £3.60

Features on independent, adventure and special-interest travel. Visit www.wanderlust.co.uk/about for 'Guidelines for contributors'. Length: up to 2,500 words. Illustrations: high-quality colour slides or digital. Payment: by arrangement. Founded 1993.

The War Cry

The Salvation Army, 101 Newington Causeway,
London SE1 6BN
tel 020-7367 4900 *fax* 020-7367 4710
email warcry@salvationarmy.org.uk
website www.salvationarmy.org/warcry
Editor Major Nigel Bovey
Weekly 20p, £26 p.a.

Voluntary contributions: Human interest stories of personal Christian faith. Founded 1879.

Waterways World

Waterways World Ltd, 151 Station Street,
Burton-on-Trent DE14 1BG
tel (01283) 742950 *fax* (01283) 742957
website www.waterwaysworld.com
Editor Richard Fairhurst
Monthly £3.75

Feature articles on all aspects of inland waterways in Britain and abroad, including historical material; factual and technical articles preferred. No short stories or poetry. See website for 'Notes for WW Contributors'. Payment: £70 per page (including illustrations). Illustrations: digital, colour transparencies or prints, line. Founded 1972.

Wedding Magazine

Hubert Burda Media Ltd, Swan House,
37–39 High Holborn, London WC1V 6AA

tel 020-7421 5000 *fax* 020-3148 8117
email wedding@burdamagazines.co.uk
Editor Catherine Westwood
Bi-monthly £26 p.a.

Ideas and inspiration for modern brides. Fashion and beauty, information for grooms, real life weddings, planning advice, gift list ideas and honeymoon features. Unsolicited features not accepted. Founded 1985.

The Week

30 Cleveland Street, London W1T 4JD
tel 020-7907 6000 *fax*
email editorialadmin@theweek.co.uk
website www.theweek.co.uk
Editor Caroline Law, *Editor-in-chief* Jeremy O'Grady
Weekly £2.75, £89.99 p.a. (print only), £96 p.a. (print + iPad editions), £75.99 (iPad edition only)

Magazine that distils the best from the British and foreign press into 44pp, including news, art, science, business, property and leisure. Founded 1995.

The Weekly News

D.C. Thomson & Co. Ltd, 80 Kingsway East, Dundee DD4 8SL
tel (01382) 223131
email weeklynews@dcthomson.co.uk
137 Chapel Street, Manchester M3 6AA
tel 0161 834 5122
144 Port Dundas Road, Glasgow G4 0HZ
tel 0141 332 9933
Weekly 95p

Real-life dramas of around 500 words told in the first person. General interest fiction. Payment: on acceptance.

Weight Watchers Magazine

The River Group, 1 Neal Street, London WC2H 9QL
tel 020-7306 0304 *fax* 020-7836 6646
email wwmagazine@riverltd.co.uk
Editor Mary Frances
12 p.a. £2.75, £1.90 for members

Features: health, beauty, news; food-orientated articles; success stories: weight-loss, motivation, wellbeing. All material commissioned. Length: up to 3pp. Illustrations: colour photos and cartoons. Payment: by arrangement.

What Car?

Haymarket Motoring Magazines Ltd, Teddington Studios, Broom Road, Teddington, Middlesex TW11 9BE
tel 020-8267 5688 *fax* 020-8267 5750
email editorial@whatcar.com
website www.whatcar.com
Group Editor Steve Fowler
Monthly £4.99, £47.35 p.a.

Road tests, buying guide, consumer stories and used car features. No unsolicited material. Illustrations: colour and b&w photos, line drawings. Payment: by negotiation. Founded 1973.

What Laptop

2 Balcombe Street, London NW1 6NW
tel 020-7042 4000
website www.whatlaptop.co.uk
Editor Alex Bentley
Monthly £3.99

News, reviews and help for anyone who wants to buy or has bought a laptop or handheld computer. Discuss ideas for features with the Editor in first instance; ideas for features are welcomed. Length: up to 1600 words. Payment: by arrangement. Founded 1999.

What's on TV

IPC Media Ltd, 6th Floor, The Blue Fin Building, 110 Southwark Street, London SE1 0SU
tel 020-3148 5000 *fax* 020-3148 8116
website www.whatsontv.co.uk
Editor Colin Tough
Weekly 49p

Features on TV programmes and personalities. All material commissioned. Length: up to 250 words. Illustrations: colour and b&w photos. Payment: by agreement. Founded 1991.

WI Life

(formerly WI Home & Country)
104 New King's Road, London SW6 4LY
tel 020-7731 5777 *fax* 020-7736 4061
Editor Neal Maidment
8 p.a. as part of the WI subscription

Journal of the National Federation of Women's Institutes for England and Wales. Publishes material related to the Federation's and members' activities with articles of interest to members, mainly written in-house and by WI members. Illustrations: colour photos and artwork. Payment: by arrangement.

Windows: The Official Magazine

Future Publishing Ltd, 30 Monmouth Street, Bath BA1 2BW
tel (01225) 442244 *fax* (01225) 446019
website www.officialwindowsmagazine.com
Editor Andrew Ifans
Every 4 weeks £5.25, £45.99 p.a.

Magazine about Microsoft's operating system with guides for the beginner and articles on how to get the most from your PC. Also reviews and advice for buying the best and most appropriate hardware and software.

Woman

IPC Connect, The Blue Fin Building, 110 Southwark Street, London SE1 0SU
tel 020-3148 5000 *fax* 020-3148 8113
Editor Karen Livermore
Weekly 93p

News, celebrity and real life features, of no more than 1,000 words. Particular interest in celebrity and diet exclusives. Payment: by negotiation. Digital images only. Read magazine prior to submission. Fiction not published. Founded 1937.

Woman Alive

(formerly Christian Woman)
Christian Publishing and Outreach, Garcia Estate, Canterbury Road, Worthing, West Sussex BN13 1BW
tel (01903) 604352
email womanalive@cpo.org.uk
website www.womanalive.co.uk
Editor Jackie Harris
Monthly £2.50

Aimed at women aged 25 upwards. Celebrity interviews, topical features, Christian issues, profiles of women in interesting occupations, Christian testimonies and real life stories, fashion, beauty, travel, health, crafts. All feature articles should be illustrated. Length: 750–1,600 words. Payment £70–£125. Founded 1982.

Woman & Home

IPC Southbank Ltd, The Blue Fin Building, 110 Southwark Street, London SE1 0SU
tel 020-3148 5000
Editor Sue James
Monthly £3.50

Centres on the personal and home interests of the lively minded mature, modern woman. Articles dealing with fashion, beauty, leisure pursuits, gardening, home style; features on topical issues, people and places. Fiction: complete stories from 3,000–4,500 words in length. Illustrations: commissioned colour photos and sketches. Non-commissioned work is not accepted and cannot be returned. Founded 1926.

Woman's Own

IPC Media Ltd, The Blue Fin Building, 110 Southwark Street, London SE1 0SU
tel 020-3148 5000 *fax* 020-3148 8127
Editor (Acting) Jayne Marsden
Weekly 92p

Modern women's magazine aimed at the 35–50 age group. No unsolicited features or fiction. Illustrations: colour and b&w: interior decorating and furnishing, fashion. Address work to relevant department editor. Payment: by arrangement.

Woman's Way

Harmonia Ltd, Rosemount House, Dundrum Road, Dublin 14, Republic of Ireland
tel +353 (0)1 2405300 *fax* +353 (0)1 6619757
email atoner@harmonia.ie
website www.harmonia.ie
Editor Áine Toner
Weekly €1.35/£1.35

Human interest, personality interviews, features on fashion, beauty, celebrities and investigations. Founded 1963.

Woman's Weekly

IPC Connect, The Blue Fin Building, 110 Southwark Street, London SE1 0SU
tel 020-3148 5000 *fax* 020-3148 8113
Editor Diane Kenwood
Weekly 87p

Lively, family-interest magazine. Includes one three- or four-part fiction serial, averaging 3,500 words each instalment, of general emotional interest, and several short stories of 1,000–2,000 words of general emotional interest. Stories up to 7,000 considered for Fiction Special. Celebrity and strong human interest features, health, finance and consumer features, plus beauty, diet and travel; also inspirational and entertaining personal stories. Payment: by arrangement. Illustrations: full colour fiction illustrations, small sketches and photos. Founded 1911.

Woman's Weekly Fiction Special

IPC Connect, The Blue Fin Building, 110 Southwark Street, London SE1 0SU
tel 020-3148 5000
Editor Gaynor Davies
12 issues p.a. £1.95

Minimum 20 stories each issue of 1,000–7,000 words of varied emotional interest, including romance, humour and mystery. Payment: by arrangement. Illustrations: full colour. Founded 1998.

The Woodworker

MyHobbyStore Ltd, Hadlow House, 9 High Street, Green Street Green, Orpington, Kent BR6 6BG
tel (01689) 869876
website www.getwoodworking.com
Editor Mike Lawrence
Monthly £3.75

For the craft and professional woodworker. Practical illustrated articles on cabinet work, carpentry, wood polishing, wood turning, wood carving, rural crafts, craft history, antique and period furniture; also wooden toys and models, musical instruments; timber procurement, conditioning, seasoning; tool, machinery and equipment reviews. Payment: by arrangement. Illustrations: line drawings and digital photos. Founded 1901.

The Word

Development Hell Ltd, 90–92 Pentonville Road, London N1 9HS
tel 020-7520 8625 *fax* 020-7833 9900
email mail@wordmagazine.co.uk
website www.wordmagazine.co.uk
Editor Mark Ellen
Monthly £4.90, £50 p.a.

Music magazine focusing on music legends and their lives. Founded 2003.

World Fishing Magazine

The Old Mill, Lower Quay, Fareham PO16 0RA
tel (01329) 825335 *fax* (01329) 825330
email thills@worldfishing.net
website www.worldfishing.net
Editor Carly Wills
Monthly £117.50 p.a.

International journal of commercial fishing. Technical and management emphasis on catching, processing and marketing of fish and related products; fishery operations and vessels covered worldwide. Length: 500–1,500 words. Payment: by arrangement. Illustrations: photos and diagrams for litho reproduction. Founded 1952.

The World of Interiors

The Condé Nast Publications Ltd, Vogue House, 1 Hanover Square, London W1S 1JU
tel 020-7499 9080 *fax* 020-7493 4013
website www.worldofinteriors.co.uk
Editor Rupert Thomas
Monthly £4.70

All material commissioned: send synopsis/visual reference for article ideas. Length: 1,000–1,500 words. Illustrations: colour photos. Payment: £500 per 1,000 words; photos £125 per page. Founded 1981.

World Soccer

IPC Inspire, The Blue Fin Building, 110 Southwark Street, London SE1 0SU
tel 020-3148 5000 *fax* 020-3148 8128
website www.worldsoccer.com
Editor Gavin Hamilton
Monthly £3.60

Articles, features, news concerning football, its personalities and worldwide development. Length: 600–2,000 words. Payment: by arrangement. Founded 1960.

The World Today

Chatham House, 10 St James's Square, London SW1Y 4LE
tel 020-7957 5712 *fax* 020-7957 5710
email wt@chathamhouse.org.uk
website www.theworldtoday.org
Editor Alan Philips, *Assistant Editor* Agnes Frimston
Monthly £35 p.a. (£118 p.a. institutions, £28 p.a. students)

Analysis of international issues and current events by journalists, diplomats, politicians and academics. Length: 1,000–1,800 words. Payment: nominal. Founded 1945.

Writers' News

5th Floor, 31–32 Park Row, Leeds LS1 5JD
tel 0113 200 2929 *fax* 0113 200 2928
website www.writersnews.co.uk
Editor Jonathan Telfer
Monthly £44.90 p.a. (£39.90 p.a. CC/DD), inc. subscription to *Writing Magazine*

News, competitions, markets. Length: up to 350 words. Illustrations: colour, line, half-tone. Payment: by arrangement. Founded 1989.

Writing Magazine

Warners Group Publications, 5th Floor, 31–32 Park Row, Leeds LS1 5JD
tel 0113 200 2929 *fax* 0113 200 2928
website www.writers-online.co.uk
Editor Jonathan Telfer
Monthly £3.90, £39.90 p.a. (by Direct Debit; £45 p.a. otherwise. Includes *Writers' News*.)

Writing Magazine includes articles on all aspects of writing. Length: 400–1500 words. Illustrations: full colour, line, half-tone. Payment: by arrangement. Founded 1992. *Writers' News* (now part of *Writing Magazine*) features news competitions and market information. Length: up to 350 words. Illustrations: full colour, line, half-tone. Payment: by arrangement. Founded 1989.

Yachting Monthly

IPC Media Ltd, The Blue Fin Building, 110 Southwark Street, London SE1 0SU
tel 020-3148 5000 *fax* 020-3148 8128
email yachting_monthly@ipcmedia.com
website www.yachtingmonthly.com
Editor Kieran Flatt
Monthly £4.40

Articles on all aspects of seamanship, navigation, the handling of sailing craft, and their design, construction and equipment. Well-written narrative accounts of cruises in yachts. Length: up to 1,500 words. Illustrations: colour transparencies and prints, cartoons. Payment: quoted on acceptance. Founded 1906.

Yachting World

IPC Media Ltd, The Blue Fin Building, 110 Southwark Street, London SE1 0SU
tel 020-3148 5000 *fax* 020-3148 8127
email yachting_world@ipc.media.com
website www.yachtingworld.com
Editor David Glenn
Monthly £4.50

Practical articles of an original nature, dealing with sailing and boats. Length: 1,500–2,000 words. Payment: varies. Illustrations: digital files, drawings, cartoons. Founded 1894.

Yachts and Yachting

196 Eastern Esplanade, Southend-on-Sea, Essex SS1 3AB
tel (01702) 582245 *fax* (01702) 588434
email editorial@yachtsandyachting.com
website www.yachtsandyachting.com

Editor Gael Pawson
Monthly £4.30, £42 p.a.

Technical sailing and related lifestyle articles. Payment: by arrangement. Illustrations: line, half-tone, colour. Founded 1947.

Yoga & Health

PO Box 16969, London E1W 1FY
tel 020-7480 5456 *fax* 020-7480 5456
email janesill@aol.com
website www.yogaandhealthmag.co.uk
Editor Jane Sill
Monthly £3

Payment: by arrangement. Founded 1983.

Yorkshire Life

1200 Century Way, Thorpe Park, Leeds LS15 8ZA
tel 0113 251 5027 *fax* 0113 251 5100
website www.yorkshirelife.co.uk
Editor Esther Leach
Monthly £2.75

Articles on Yorkshire, including places of interest, high-profile personalities, local events, arts, history and food. Unsolicited ideas welcome. Founded 1946.

Yorkshire Ridings Magazine

Oyston Mill, Strand Road, Preston PR1 8UR
tel (01772) 761277 *fax* (01772) 761277
Editor Anthony Skinner
Bi-monthly £1.40

Articles exclusively about people, life and character of the 3 Ridings of Yorkshire. Length: up to 1,000 words. Payment: £70-£100. Illustrations: colour, b&w photos; prints preferred. Founded 1964.

You & Your Wedding

Immediate Media Co. Ltd, 15–18 White Lion Street, London N1 9PD
tel 020-7843 8800
email yywinfo@natmags.co.uk
website www.youandyourwedding.co.uk
Editor Miranda Eason
Bi-monthly £4.99

Articles, features and news covering all aspects of planning a wedding. Submit ideas by email. Illustrations: colour. Payment: negotiable.

Your Cat Magazine

BPG (Stamford) Ltd, Buckminster Yard, Buckminster, Grantham, Lincs. NG33 5SD
tel (01780) 766199
email editorial@yourcat.co.uk
website www.yourcat.co.uk
Editor Sue Parslow
Monthly £3.25

Practical advice on the care of cats and kittens, general interest items and features, plus true-life tales, celebrity interviews and fiction (commission only). Length: 800–1,500 words (articles), 200–300 (news). Founded 1994.

Your Dog Magazine

BPG (Stamford) Ltd, Buckminster Yard, Buckminster, Grantham, Lincs. NG33 5SD
tel (01780) 766199
email editorial@yourdog.co.uk
website www.yourdog.co.uk
Editor Sarah Wright
Monthly £3.60

Articles and information of interest to dog lovers; features on all aspects of pet dogs. Length: approx. 1,500 words. Payment: £140 per 1,000 words. Founded 1994.

Your Horse

Bauer Media, Media House, Lynchwood, Peterborough PE2 6EA
tel (01733) 395056
email julie.brown@bauermedia.com
Editor Julie Brown
Every 4 weeks £3.80

Practical horse care, riding advice and inspiration for riders and owners. Send feature ideas with examples of previous published writing. Specially commissions most material. Welcomes ideas for articles and features. Length: 1,500 words. Payment: £140 per 1,000 words. Founded 1983.

Yours

Bauer Consumer Media, Media House, Peterborough Business Park, Peterborough PE2 6EA
tel (01733) 468000
email yours@bauermedia.co.uk
website www.yours.co.uk/Yours-Magazine-News
Editor Valery McConnell
Fortnightly £1.40

Features and news about and/or of interest to the over-50s age group, including nostalgia and short stories. Study of magazine essential; approach in writing in the first instance. Length: articles up to 1,000 words, short stories up to 1,000 words. Payment: at the Editor's discretion or by agreement. Founded 1973.

Zest

Hearst Magazines UK, National Magazine House, 72 Broadwick Street, London W1F 9EP
tel 020-7439 5000 *fax* 020-7312 3750
email zest.mail@natmags.co.uk
website www.zest.co.uk
Editor Mandie Gower, *Send material to* zest.mail@natmags.co.uk
Monthly £3.40

Health and beauty magazine. Commissioned material only: health, fitness and beauty, features, news and shorts. Length: 50–2,000 words. Illustrations: colour and b&w photos and line. Payment: by arrangement. Founded 1994.

Zoo

Bauer Consumer Media, Endeavour House,
189 Shaftesbury Avenue, London, WC2H 8JG
tel 020-7295 5000 *fax* 020-7208 3574
email info@zooweekly.co.uk
website www.zootoday.co.uk
Editor Damian McSorley
Weekly £1.80

Entertainment magazine for young men with news, sport, photos, stories, jokes, listings and reviews. Founded 2004.

Newspapers and magazines overseas

Listings are given for newspapers and magazines in Australia (below), Canada (page 102), New Zealand (page 104) and South Africa (page 106). For information on submitting material to the USA see page 109. Newspapers are listed under the towns in which they are published.

AUSTRALIA

(Adelaide) Advertiser

31 Waymouth Street, Adelaide, SA 5000
tel +61 (0)8 1300 130 370 *fax* +61 (0)8 8206 3669
website www.news.com.au/adelaidenow
Editor Mel Mansell
Daily Mon–Fri $1.10, Sat $1.80

Descriptive and news background material, 400–800 words, preferably with pictures; also cartoons. Founded 1858.

(Adelaide) Sunday Mail

31 Waymouth Street, Adelaide, SA 5000
postal address GPO Box 339, Adelaide, SA 5001
tel +61 (0)8 1300 130370 *fax* +61 (0)8 8206 3646
website www.news.com.au/adelaidenow
Editor Megan Lloyd
Sun $2.00

Founded 1912.

AQ – Australian Quarterly

Australian Institute of Policy and Science, PO Box M145, Missenden Road NSW 2050
tel +61 (0)2 9810 5642 *fax* +61 (0)2 9810 2406
website www.aips.net.au
Editor James Morris
6 p.a. $72 p.a. individuals/schools, $120 p.a. organisations ($145 Asia/Oceania; $165 elsewhere)

Peer-reviewed articles for the informed non-specialist on politics, law, economics, social issues, etc. Length: 3,500 words preferred. Payment: none. Founded 1929.

Art & Australia

Art & Australia Pty Ltd, 11 Cecil Street, Paddington NSW 2021
email editorial@artandaustralia.com.au
website www.artandaustralia.com
Publisher/Editor Eleonora Triguboff
$80 p.a.

Articles with a contemporary perspective on Australia's traditional and current art, and on international art of Australian relevance, plus exhibition and book reviews. Length: 2,000–3,000 words (articles), 600–1,200 words (reviews). Payment: $500 per 1,000 words. Illustrations: colour tiff files. Founded 1916 as *Art in Australia*.

Art Monthly Australia

LPO Box 8321, ANU Acton, ACT 0200
tel +61 (0)2 6125 3988 *fax* +61 (0)2 6125 9794
email art.monthly@anu.edu.au
website www.artmonthly.org.au
Editor Maurice O'Riordan
10 p.a. March–Dec $9.95

Contemporary visual arts: reviews, commentary, news and book reviews. Specially commissions most material but will consider unsolicited material. Welcomes ideas for articles and features. Length: negotiable. Payment: $300 (AUD) per 1,000 words. Founded 1987.

Artlink

PO Box 8141, Station Arcade, Adelaide, South Australia 5000
tel +61 (0)8 8212 8711
email info@artlink.com.au
website www.artlink.com.au
Quarterly $14

Thematic art magazine linking art and society. Relevant articles and ideas welcome. Payment: $300 per 1,000 words. Email CV and examples of work.

The Australian Financial Review

Fairfax Business Media, GPO Box 55, Melbourne, Victoria 3001
tel +61 (0)2 9282 2512
website www.afr.com
Editor Kathy Bail
London office 1 Bath Street, London EC1V 9LB
tel 020-7688 2777 *fax* 020-7688 3499
Daily Mon–Sat $3

Investment business and economic news and reviews; government and politics, production, banking, commercial, and Stock Exchange statistics; company analysis. General features in Friday *Weekend Review* supplement.

Australian Flying

Yaffa Publishing Group, GPO Box, Sydney, NSW 2001
tel +61 (0)2 9281 2333 *fax* +61 (0)2 9281 2750
email info@yaffa.com.au
website www.australianflying.com.au
Editor Steve Hitchin
6 p.a. $7.75

Covers the Australian light aircraft industry. Payment: by arrangement.

Australian Geographic

54 Park Street, Sydney, NSW 2000
tel +61 (0)2 9263 9813 *fax* +61 (0)2 9263 9810

website www.australiangeographic.com.au
Editor Ian Connellan
Quarterly $59.95 p.a.

Articles and features about Australia, particularly life, technology and wildlife in remote parts of the country. Material mostly commissioned. Length: articles, 300–800 words, features, 2,000–3,000 words. Illustrations: all commissioned. Payment: from $500 per 1,000 words; illustrations by negotiation. Founded 1986.

Australian Home Beautiful

Pacific Magazines, 35–51 Mitchell Street, McMahons Point, NSW 2060
tel +61 (0)2 9464 3218 *fax* +61 (0)2 9464 3263
website www.housebeautiful.com.au
Editor Wendy Moore
Monthly $59 p.a.

Interior decoration, furnishing, gardening, cookery, etc. Unsolicited MSS not accepted. Founded 1925.

Australian House and Garden

Level 10, 54 Park Street, Sydney, NSW 2000
tel +61 (0)2 9282 8456 *fax* +61 (0)2 9267 4912
email jsanford@acpmagazines.com.au
website www.acp.com.au
Editor Lisa Green
Monthly $6.95

Factual articles dealing with interior decorating, home design, gardening, wine, food. Preliminary letter essential. Payment: by arrangement. Illustrations: line, half-tone, colour. Founded 1948.

Australian Journal of Politics and History

School of Political Science and International Studies, University of Queensland, St Lucia, Queensland 4072
tel +61 (0)7 3365 3163 *fax* +61 (0)7 3365 1388
website www.blackwellpublishing.com, www.polsis.uq.edu.au
Editor Ian Ward and Andrew Bonnell
4 p.a. $101/£59 p.a. individuals; $231/£225 institutions

Australian, European, Asian, Pacific and international articles. Special feature: regular surveys of Australian Foreign Policy and State and Commonwealth politics. Length: 8,000 words max. Illustrations: line, only when necessary. Payment: none.

Australian Photography

Yaffa Publishing Group, 17–21 Bellevue Street, Surry Hills, NSW 2010
tel +61 (0)2 9281 2333 *fax* +61 (0)3 9690 8636
email robertkeeley@yaffa.com.au
Editor Robert Keeley
Monthly $6.75

Illustrated articles: picture-taking techniques, technical. Length: 1,200–2,500 words with colour and/or b&w prints or slides. Payment: $80 per page. Founded 1950.

Australian Powerboat

Yaffa Publishing Group, 17–21 Bellevue Street, Surry Hills, NSW 2010
tel +61 (0)2 9281 2833 *fax* +61 (0)2 9281 2750
Editor Mick Fletoridis
6 p.a. $75 p.a.

Articles and news on boats and boating, racing, water skiing and products. Length: 1,500 words (articles), 200 words (news). Illustrations: colour (transparencies preferred). Payment: $100 per 1,000 words; from $30. Founded 1976.

The Australian Women's Weekly

ACP Magazines Ltd, 54 Park Street, Sydney, NSW 2000
tel +61 (0)2 9282 8000 *fax* +61 (0)2 9267 4459
postal address GPO Box 4178, Sydney, NSW 2000
Editor-in-Chief Helen McCabe
Monthly $6.90

Fiction and features. Length: fiction 1,000–5,000 words; features 1,000–4,000 words plus colour or b&w photos. Payment: according to length and merit. Fiction illustrations: sketches by own artists and freelances.

Aviation Business

17–21 Bellevue Street, Surry Hills, NSW 2010
tel +61 (0)2 9281 2333 *fax* +61 (0)2 9281 2750
email dougnancarrow@aviationbusiness.com.au
website www.aviationbusiness.com.au
Editor Doug Nancarrow
6 p.a. $80 p.a.

Aviation business magazine for industry professionals focusing on Asia Pacific. Welcomes ideas for features. Length: 800–2,000 words (features). Payment: on application. Illustrations: digital images only. Founded 1918.

The Big Issue Australia

GPO Box 4911, Melbourne, Victoria 3001
tel +61 (0)3 9663 4522 *fax* +61 (0)3 9663 4252
email editorial@bigissue.org.au
website www.bigissue.org.au
Editor Alan Attwood
Fortnightly $5, $155 p.a.

Profiles and features of general interest and on social issues and entertainment, arts reviews. One annual fiction edition. Length: 1,000–2,500 words (features), up to 900 words (news), 200 words (reviews). Payment: 15c per word (features), $30 (reviews). Founded 1996.

Bookseller + Publisher

Level One, 607 St Kilda Road, Melbourne, Victoria 3004
tel +61 (0)3 8517 8333 *fax* +61 (0)3 8517 8399

email bookseller.publisher@thorpe.com.au
website www.booksellerandpublisher.com.au
Editor-in-Chief Matthia Dempsey
6 p.a.

Founded 1921.

(Brisbane) The Courier-Mail

Queensland Newspapers Pty Ltd,
Cr. Mayne Road and Campbell Street, Bowen Hills, Brisbane, Queensland 4006
tel +61 1300 304 020 *fax* +61 (0)7 3666 6696
website www.couriermail.com.au
Editor Michael Crutcher
Mon-Sat $1

(Brisbane) The Sunday Mail

News Queensland, PO Box 130, 28 Mayne Road, Bowen Hills, Brisbane, Queensland 4001
tel +61 1300 304 020 *fax* +61 (0)7 3666 6787
email thompsons@qnp.newsltd.com.au
Editor Scott Thompson
Sun $2 GST inc.

Anything of general interest. Length: up to 1,500 words. Illustrations: line, photos, b&w and colour, cartoons. Rejected MSS returned if postage enclosed.

Camera

Nextmedia, 55 Chandos Street, St Leonards, NSW 2065
tel +61 (0)2 9901 6100 *fax* +61 (0)2 9901 6166
website www.next.com.au, www.avhub.com.au
Editor Paul Burrows
Bi-monthly $6.95

Magazine for amateur photographers and digital imaging enthusiasts covering techniques, test reports, new products. Considers unsolicited material. Welcomes ideas for articles and features. Length: 750–1,500 words (features/articles). Illustrations: colour prints and transparencies. Payment: $300–$500. Founded 1979.

Cordite Poetry Review

PO Box 393, Carlton South, Victoria 3053
email cordite@cordite.org.au
website www.cordite.org.au
Editor Kent MacCarter
3 p.a. Free

Publishes on the internet poetry by new and emerging Australian authors, alongside feature articles, reviews, news, interviews, blog posts, gossip items, audio poetry and special competitions. Welcomes material from overseas writers (no payment). Length: 100–3,000 words (articles and features). Payment: $50–$100; $50 per poem. Illustrations: colour and b&w. Submissions by email only. Founded 1997.

Dance Australia

Yaffa Publishing Group, 17–21 Bellevue Street, Surry Hills, NSW 2010
tel +61 (0)2 9281 2333 *fax* +61 (0)2 9281 2750
email dance@yaffa.com.au
website www.yaffa.com.au
Editor Karen van Ulzen
Bi-monthly $7.25

Articles and features on all aspects of dance in Australia. Material mostly commissioned, but will consider unsolicited contributions. Illustrations: b&w and colour photos, line drawings, cartoons. Payment: $200 per 1,000 words; illustrations by negotiation. Founded 1980.

Dolly

54–58 Park Street, Sydney, NSW 2000
tel +61 (0)2 9282 8000 *fax* +61 (0)2 9267 4361
website www.ninemsn.com.au/dolly
Editor Tiffany Dunk
Monthly $5.95

Features on teen fashion, health and beauty, personalities, music, social issues and how to cope with growing up, etc. Length: not less than 1,000 words. Illustrations: colour, b&w, line, cartoons. Payment: by arrangement. Founded 1970.

Harper's Bazaar

ACP Publishing Pty Ltd, 54 Park Street, Sydney, NSW 2000
tel +61 (0)2 9282 8000 *fax* +61 (0)2 9267 4361
email bazaar@acpmagazines.com.au
website www.harpersbazaar.com.au
10 p.a. $7.95

Fashion, health and beauty, celebrity news, plus features. Length: 3,000 words. Illustrations: colour and b&w photos. Founded 1998.

Island

PO Box 210, Sandy Bay, Tasmania 7006
tel +61 (0)3 6226 2325
email island.magazine@utas.edu.au
website www.islandmag.com
Editor Dale Campisi

Short stories, poetry and essays of social, environmental and cultural significance. Submission guidelines available on website. Online submissions only. Payment: $100 per poem, $150 for short stories, $150 per 1,000 words for articles.

(Launceston) The Examiner

Box 99, PO Launceston, Tasmania 7250
tel +61 (0)3 633 67111 *fax* +61 (0)3 633 47328
website www.examiner.com.au
Editor M. Gilmour
Daily $1.30

Accepts freelance material. Payment: by arrangement.

Meanjin

Melbourne University Publishing,
187 Gratton Street, Carlton, Victoria 3053
tel +61 (0)3 9342 0300 *fax* +61 (0)3 9342 0399

email meanjin@unimelb.edu.au
website www.meanjin.com.au
Editor Sally Heath
Quarterly $105 (overseas)

Cultural commentary, fiction, poetry, essays and discussion of contemporary issues, e.g. biography, drugs, travel. See website for submission guidelines. Payment: $50 per poetry item, min. $100 prose. Founded 1941.

(Melbourne) The Age

The Age Company Ltd, 655 Collins Street, Docklands, Melbourne, Victoria 3008
tel +61 (0)3 8667 2000 *fax* +61 (0)3 8667 2332
Editor-in-Chief Paul Ramadge
Daily Mon–Fri $1.70, Sat $2.70, Sun $2.20

Independent liberal morning daily; room occasionally for outside matter. *Good Weekend* and *Sunday Life* (illustrated weekend magazines); *Insight*; *Life & Style* (includes literary reviews). Accepts occasional freelance material.

(Melbourne) Herald Sun

HWT Tower, 40 City Road, Southbank, Melbourne 3006
tel +61 (0)3 9292 2000 *fax* +61 (0)3 9292 2112
website www.news.com.au/heraldsun
Editor Bruce Guthrie
Send material to Peter Helme, Syndications Manager
Daily Mon–Fri $1.10, Sat $1.50, Sun $1.70

Accepts freelance articles, preferably with illustrations. Length: up to 750 words. Illustrations: half-tone, line, cartoons. Payment: on merit.

(Melbourne) Sunday Herald Sun

HWT Tower, 40 City Road, Southbank, Melbourne 3006
tel +61 (0)3 9292 2963 *fax* +61 (0)3 9292 2080
website www.heraldsun.com
Editor Damon Johnston
Weekly $2.00

Accepts freelance articles, preferably with illustrations. Length: up to 2,000 words. Illustrations: colour. Payment: on merit.

Natural Health and Vegetarian Life

Skiptons Arcade, Suite 28, 541 High Street, Penrith, NSW 2750
email info@health.org.au
website www.health.org.au, www.veg-soc.org
Editors Roger French, Mark Berriman

Magazine of the Natural Health Society of Australia and the Australian Vegetarian Society. Welcomes contributions. Length: 700–2,500 words.

NW Magazine

54 Park Street, Sydney, NSW 2000
tel +61 (0)2 9282 8285 *fax* +61 (0)2 9264 6005
Editor Lisa Sinclair
Weekly $4.95

News and features on celebrities, food, new products, fashion and astrology. Illustrated. Payment: by negotiation. Founded 1993.

OK! Magazine

Northern and Shell, PO Box 4088, Sydney, NSW 2001
tel +61 (0)2 8622 9222
website www.okmagazine.com.au
Weekly

Exclusive celebrity interviews and photographs. Founded 2004.

Overland

PO Box 14428, Melbourne, Victoria 8001, Australia
tel +61 (0)3 9919 4163 *fax* +61 (0)3 9687 7614
email overland@vu.edu.au
website www.overland.org.au
Editor Jeff Sparrow
Quarterly $54 p.a. ($96 overseas)

Literary and cultural. Australian material preferred. Payment: by arrangement. Illustrations: line, half-tone, cartoons.

People Magazine

Civic Tower, Level 18, 66–68 Goulburn Street, Sydney, NSW 2000
tel +61 (0)2 9288 9648 *fax* +61 (0)2 9283 7923
Editor Shane Cubis
Weekly $4.40

National weekly news-pictorial. Mainly celebrity stories. Photos depicting glamour, show business, unusual occupations, rites, customs. Payment: $300 per page, text and photos.

(Perth) The Sunday Times

34 Stirling Street, Perth, Western Australia 6000
tel +61 (0)8 9326 8212 *fax* +61 (0)8 9221 1121
website www.sundaytimes.news.com.au
Editor Sam Weir
Sun $2.20

Topical articles to 800 words. Payment: on acceptance. Founded 1897.

(Perth) The West Australian

50 Hasler Road, Osborne Park, Western Australia 6017
tel +61 (0)8 9482 3111 *fax* +61 (0)8 9482 3177
website www.thewest.com.au
Editor Brett McCarthy
Daily Mon–Fri $1.30, Sat $2.30

Articles and sketches about people and events in Australia and abroad. Length: 300–700 words. Payment: Award rates or better. Illustrations: line, half-tone. Founded 1833.

Positive Words

PO Box 798, Heathcote 3523, Victoria, Australia
email positivewordsmagazine@live.com.au
Editor Sandra James

Monthly $5.50, $55.00 p.a.

Creative writing. Email for submission details or send 3 x IRC for sample copy. Length: short stories up to 1,000 words; poetry (one page). Payment: complementary copy.

Quadrant

Suite 2/5 Rosebery Place, Balmain, NSW 2041
postal address PO Box 82, Balmain, NSW 2041
tel +61 (0)2 9818 1155 *fax* +61 (0)2 8580 4664
website www.quadrant.org.au
Editor Keith Windschuttle
Literary Editor Les Murray
Monthly $8.90

Articles, short stories, verse, etc. Prose length: 2,000–5,000 words. Payment: min. $100 articles/stories/reviews, $40 poems.

Reader's Digest (Australia)

GPO Box 5030, Sydney, NSW 2001
tel +61 (0)2 9018 6227 *fax* +61 (0)2 9018 7250
Editor-in-Chief Thomas Moore
Monthly $5.99 (inc. GST)

Articles on Australian subjects by commission only. No unsolicited MSS accepted. Length: 2,000–3,000 words. Payment: up to $4,000 per article; $500 for 'My Story'; brief filler paragraphs, $50–$250. Illustrations: half-tone, colour.

Rock

Prime Creative Media, 11–15 Buckhurst Street, South Melbourne, Victoria 3205
tel +61 (0)3 9690 8766 *fax* +61 (0)3 9682 0044
email enquiries@primecreative.com.au
website www.rock.com.au
Editor Aaron Flanagan
Quarterly $8.99

Australian rockclimbing and mountaineering articles, features and news. See website for guidelines to contibutions. Length: 2,000 words (articles/features), 200 words (news). Payment: $100 per page (words and pictures). Founded 1978.

The Sun-Herald

Level 4, 1 Darling Island Road, Pyrmont, NSW 2009
tel +61 (0)2 9282 2833 *fax* +61 (0)2 9282 2151
website www.sunherald.com.au
Editor Simon Dulhunty
Weekly $2

Topical articles to 1,000 words; news plus sections on current affairs, entertainment, finance, sport and travel. Payment: by arrangement.

(Sydney) The Daily Telegraph

News Ltd, 2 Holt Street, Surry Hills, NSW 2010
tel +61 (0)2 9288 3000 *fax* +61 (0)2 9288 2608
website www.thetelegraph.com.au
Editor Paul Whittaker
Daily Mon–Fri $1, Sat $1.60

Modern feature articles and series of Australian or world interest. Length: 1,000–2,000 words. Payment: according to merit/length.

The Sydney Morning Herald

1 Darling Island Road, Pyrmont, NSW 2009
tel +61 (0)2 9282 2822
website www.smh.com.au
Editor Amanda Wilson
Literary Editor Susan Wyndham
Daily $1.20

Saturday edition has pages of literary criticism and also magazine articles, plus glossy colour magazine. Topical articles 600–4,000 words. Payment: varies, but minimum $100 per 1,000 words. Illustrations: all types. Founded 1831.

(Sydney) The Sunday Telegraph

News Ltd, 2 Holt Street, Surry Hills, Sydney, NSW 2010
tel +61 (0)2 9288 3000 *fax* +61 (0)2 9288 3311
website www.sundaytelegraph.com.au
Editor Neil Breen
Weekly $1.80

News and features. Illustrations: transparencies. Payment: varies. Founded 1935.

Traveltalk

PO Box 329, North Beach, Western Australia 6920
tel +61 (0)8 9240 3888 *fax* +61 (0)8 9240 2796
email editorial@traveltalk.biz
website www.traveltalknow.com
Editor Craig Sinclair
Quarterly $4.95

Travel news and features focusing on popular travel destinations, in Australia and international. Prefers to receive a list of ideas and sample of material initially. Length: 600 words (articles), 1,200–1,800 words (features), 150–450 words (news). Payment: 40 cents per published word. Founded 2002.

Vogue Australia

180 Bourke Road, Alexandria, NSW 2015
postal address Locked Bag 5030, Alexandria, NSW 2015
tel +61 (0)2 9353 6666 *fax* +61 (0)2 9353 6600
website www.vogue.com.au
Editor-in-Chief Kirstie Clements
Monthly $8.50

Articles and features on fashion, beauty, health, business, people and the arts of interest to the modern woman of style and high spending power. Ideas welcome. Length: from 1,000 words. Illustrations: colour and b&w. Founded 1959.

Wild

Prime Creative Media, 11–15 Buckhurst Street, South Melbourne, Victoria 3205
tel +61 (0)3 9690 8766 *fax* +61 (0)3 9682 0044

website www.wild.com.au
Editor Belinda Smith
6 p.a. $8.99

Australia's wilderness adventure magazine. Illustrated articles of first-hand experiences of the Australian wilderness, plus book and track reviews, and product tests. Email editor for guidelines and payment rates. Length: 2,500 words (articles), 200 words (news). Founded 1981.

Woman's Day

54–58 Park Street, Sydney, NSW 2000
tel +61 (0)2 9282 8508 *fax* +61 (0)2 9267 4360
Editor Fiona Connolly
Weekly $4

National women's magazine; news, show business, fiction, fashion, general articles, cookery, home economy, health, beauty.

CANADA

The Beaver: Canada's History Magazine

Bryce Hall, Main Floor, University of Winnipeg, 515 Portage Avenue, Winnipeg, Manitoba R3B 2E9
tel +1 204-988-9300 *fax* +1 204-988-9309
email editors@historysociety.ca
website www.thebeaver.ca
Editor Mark Reid
Bi-monthly $41.70 p.a. (taxes incl.)

Articles on Canadian history. Length: 1,500–3,000 words, with illustrations. Payment: on acceptance. Illustrations: b&w and colour archival photos or drawings. Founded 1920.

Canadian Bookseller

1255 Bay Street, Suite 902, Toronto, Ontario M5R 2A9
tel +1 416-467-7883 *fax* +1 416-467 7886
email editor@cbabook.org
website www.cbabook.org
Editor Emily Sinkins
Quarterly $37.80 (Canadian non-members)

Publishing industry news and contacts.

Canadian Literature

University of British Columbia, Buchanan E158, 1866 Main Mall, Vancouver, BC V6T 1Z1
tel +1 604-822-2780 *fax* +1 604-822-5504
email can.lit@ubc.ca
website www.canlit.ca
Editor Margery Fee
4 p.a. $52.50 p.a., $105 p.a. institutions, $130 p.a. outside Canada

Articles on Canadian writers and writing in English and French. No fiction. Length: up to 6,500 words. Payment: none. Founded 1959.

Canadian Screenwriter

366 Adelaide Street West, 401 Toronto, ON MSV 1R9
tel +1 416-979-7907 *fax* +1 416-979-9273
website www.wgc.ca/magazine
Editor David Kinahan
3 p.a. $40 CAD

Profiling screenwriters and their craft. Includes industry news, topical issues and insight into the profession of screenwriting in Canada.

Canadian Writer's Journal

PO Box 1178, New Liskeard, Ontario P0J 1P0
tel +1 705-647-5424 *fax* +1 705-647-8366
email cwj@cwj.ca
website www.cwj.ca
Editor Deborah Ranchuk
Bi-monthly $35 p.a.

News on markets and articles on writers' aspirations for dedicated apprentice and professional Canadian writers. Considers unsolicited material. Founded 1984.

Chatelaine

One Mount Pleasant Road, Toronto, Ontario M4Y 2Y5
tel +1 416-764-2424 *fax* +1 416-764-2431
website www.chatelaine.com
Editor Jane Francisco
Monthly $20 p.a.

Women's interest articles; Canadian angle preferred. Payment: on acceptance.

The Dalhousie Review

Dalhousie University, Halifax, Nova Scotia B3H 4R2
tel +1 902-494-2541 *fax* +1 902-494-3561
email Dalhousie.Review@dal.ca
website www.dalhousiereview.dal.ca
Editor Anthony Stewart
3 p.a. $22.50 p.a., $28 p.a. outside Canada

Articles on history, literature, political science, philosophy, sociology, popular culture, fine arts; short fiction; verse; book reviews. Usually not more than 3 stories and 10–12 poems in any one issue. Length: prose, up to 5,000 words; verse, less than 40 words. Contributors receive 2 copies of issue and 10 offprints of their work.

Descant

50 Baldwin Street, Toronto, Ontario M5T 1L4
tel +1 416-593-2557 *fax* +1 416-593-9362
email info@descant.ca
website www.descant.ca
Editor Karen Mulhallen
Quarterly $28 p.a.

Literary magazine: short fiction, poetry and essays, previously unpublished. Payment: $100 (articles and fiction) on publication. Illustrations: b&w. Founded 1970.

The Fiddlehead

Campus House, 11 Garland Court, UNB PO Box 4400, Fredericton, NB E3B 5A3

tel +1 506-453-3501
email fiddlehd@unb.ca
website www.thefiddlehead.ca
Editor Ross Leckie
Quarterly Can.$10, $30 p.a. Canada, $36 p.a. USA/ international

Reviews, poetry, short stories. Payment: approx. $40 per printed page. Founded 1945.

(Hamilton) The Spectator

44 Frid Street, Hamilton, Ontario L8N 3G3
tel +1 905-526-3333
website www.hamiltonspectator.com
Publisher Dana Robbins
Daily Mon–Fri $1, Sat $1.85

Articles of general interest, political analysis and background; interviews, stories of Canadians abroad. Length: 800 words maximum. Payment: rate varies. Founded 1846.

International Journal of Canadian Studies

250 City Centre, Suite 303, Ottawa, Ontario K1R 6K7
tel +1 613-789-7834 *fax* +1 613-789-7830
email Cristina.Frias@iccs-ciec.ca
website www.iccs-ciec.ca
Executive Director Cristina Frias
6 p.a. US$40 p.a., US$65 p.a. institutions

Major academic review of Canadian studies. Articles of general as well as scholarly interest on history, politics, literature, society, arts. Length: 7,000–10,000 words.

Inuit Art Quarterly

2081 Merivale Road, Ottawa, Ontario K2G 1G9
tel +1 613-224-8189 *fax* +1 613-224-2907
email iaq@inuitart.org
website www.inuitart.org
Editor Marybelle Mitchell
Quarterly $7.95

Features, original research, artists' profiles, news. Contributors are expected to have a thorough knowledge of the arts. Length: varies. Illustrations: colour and b&w photos and line. Payment: by arrangement. Founded 1985.

The Malahat Review

University of Victoria, PO Box 1700 STN CSC, Victoria, BC V8W 2Y2
tel +1 250-721-8524 *fax* +1 250-472-5051
email malahat@uvic.ca (queries only)
website www.malahatreview.ca
Editor John Barton
Quarterly $35 p.a. ($40 p.a. USA, $45 p.a. elsewhere)

Short stories, poetry, creative non-fiction, reviews. Payment: $30CAD per magazine page. Founded 1967.

Neo-opsis Science Fiction Magazine

4129 Carey Road, Victoria, BC V8Z 4G5
tel +1 250-881-8893
email neoopsis@shaw.ca
website www.neo-opsis.ca
Editor Karl Johanson
3 p.a. $7.95 ($8.95 USA, $11.50 UK)

Science fiction short stories, articles, opinion columns and reviews. Considers unsolicited short stories. Preferred length: up to 6,000 words. Unsolicited articles are no longer accepted; please follow guidelines online at www.neo-opsis.ca/guidelines. Illustrations: b&w cartoons. Payment: 2.5c per word with max. of $125 for short stories; $30 per illustration. Founded 2003.

Outdoor Canada

54 Patrick Street, Toronto, Ontario M5T 1V1
tel +1 416-599-2000
email editorial@outdoorcanada.ca
website www.outdoorcanada.ca
Editor Patrick Walsh
6 p.a. $23.70

Articles on Canada's best fishing and hunting adventures and destinations, conservation issues related to angling and hunting, plus news on gear and techniques. Send idea first. Length: 2,000–4,000 words for articles, 100–600 words for shorter features. Average payment .50 cent per word.

Photo Life

185 Rue St Paul, Quebec, QC G1K 3W2
tel +1-800-905-7468, +1-800-664-2739
email info@photolife.com
website www.photolife.com
Publisher Guy Poirier
6 p.a. $27 p.a.

Covers all aspects of photography of interest to amateur and professional photographers. Length: 800–1,500 words. Illustrations: colour and b&w photos. Payment: by arrangement. Founded 1976.

Queen's Quarterly

Queen's University, Kingston, Ontario K7L 3N6
tel +1 613-533-2667 *fax* +1 613-533-6822
email queens.quarterly@queensu.ca
website www.queensu.ca/quarterly
Editor Dr Boris Castel
Quarterly $6.50, $20 p.a., $40 p.a. institutions

A multidisciplinary scholarly journal aimed at the general educated reader – articles, short stories and poems. Length: 2,500–3,500 words (articles), 2,000 (stories). Payment: by negotiation. Founded 1893.

Quill & Quire

11 Queen Street East, Suite 302, Toronto, ON M5C 1S2
tel +1 416-364-3333 *fax* +1 416-595-5415
email info@quillandquire.com
website www.quillandquire.com
Editor Stuart Woods
12 p.a. $59.95 p.a. ($95 p.a. outside Canada)

Articles of interest about the Canadian book trade. Payment: from $100. Illustrations: line, half-tone. Subscription includes Canadian Publishers Directory (2 p.a.). Founded 1935.

Reader's Digest (Canada)

1125 Stanley Street, Montreal, QC H3B 5H5
tel +1 514-940-0751 *fax* +1 514-940-3637
email editor@readersdigest.ca
website www.readersdigest.ca
Monthly $24.97 p.a.

Original articles on all subjects of broad general appeal, thoroughly researched and professionally written. Outline or query only. Length: 3,000 words approx. Payment: from $2,700. Also previously published material. Illustrations: line, half-tone, colour.

(Toronto) The Globe and Mail

444 Front Street West, Toronto, Ontario M5V 2S9
website www.theglobeandmail.com
Editor John Stockhouse
Daily 70c

Unsolicited material considered. Payment: by arrangement. Founded 1844.

Toronto Life

111 Queen Street East, Suite 320, Toronto, Ontario M5C 1S2
tel +1 416-364-3333 *fax* +1 416-861-1169
email editorial@torontolife.com
website www.torontolife.com
Editor Sarah Fulford
Monthly $24 p.a.

Articles, profiles on Toronto and Torontonians. Illustrations: line, half-tone, colour. Founded 1966.

Toronto Star

1 Yonge Street, Toronto, Ontario M5E 1E6
tel +1 416-367-2000 *fax* +1 416-869-4328
London office Level 4A, PO Box 495, Virginia Street, London E1 9XY
tel 020-7833 0791
website www.thestar.com
Editor Michael Cooke
Daily Mon–Fri 30c, Sat $1, Sun 75c ($123 p.a.)

Features, life, world/national politics. Payment: by arrangement. Founded 1892.

(Vancouver) The Province

200 Granville Street, Suite 1, Vancouver, BC V6C 3N3
tel +1 604-605-2000 *fax* +1 604-605-2759
website www.theprovince.com
Editor-in-Chief Wayne Moriarty
Daily Mon–Fri $1, Sun $2

Founded 1898.

Vancouver Sun

200 Granville Street, Vancouver, BC V6C 3N3
tel +1 604-605-2000 *fax* +1 604-605-2308
website www.vancouversun.com
Editor-in-Chief Patricia Graham
Daily Mon–Thurs $1.12 + tax; Fri, Sat $2.25 + tax

Westcoast life arts magazine. Travel, Op-Ed pieces considered. Payment: by arrangement.

Winnipeg Free Press

1355 Mountain Avenue, Winnipeg, MB R2X 3B6
tel +1 204-697-7000 *fax* +1 204-697-7412
website www.winnipegfreepress.com
Publisher Bob Cox, *Editor* Margo Goodhand
Daily Sun–Thurs 80c, Fri $1, Sat $1.50

Some freelance articles. Founded 1872.

NEW ZEALAND

(Auckland) New Zealand Herald

PO Box 32, Auckland
tel +64 (0)9 379 5050 *fax* +64 (0)9 373 6421
website www.nzherald.co.nz
Editor Tim Murphy
Daily Mon–Fri $1.90, weekend $3

Topical and informative articles 800–1,100 words. Payment: by prior agreement. Illustrations: emailed images or prints. Founded 1863.

(Auckland) Sunday News

PO Box 1327, Auckland
tel +64 (0)9 925 9700
email editor@sunday-news.co.nz
website www.stuff.co.nz/sunday-times
Editor Mitchell Murphy
Sun $1.80

News, sport and showbiz, especially with NZ interest. Illustrations: colour and b&w photos. Founded 1963.

(Christchurch) The Press

Private Bag 4722, Christchurch
tel +64 (0)3 379 0940
email editorial@press.co.nz
website www.stuff.co.nz/the-press
Editor Andrew Holden
Daily Mon–Fri $1.40, Sat $2.60

Articles of general interest not more than 800 words. Illustrations: photos and line drawings, cartoons. Payment: by arrangement.

(Dunedin) Otago Daily Times

52 Stuart Street, PO Box 517 Dunedin, New Zealand
tel +64 (0)3 477 4760 *fax* +64 (0)3 474 7421
website www.odt.co.nz
Editor Murray Kirkness
Daily $1, Sat/Sun $1.50

Any articles of general interest up to 1,000 words, but preference is given to NZ writers. Topical illustrations and personalities. Payment: current NZ rates. Founded 1861.

Freelance

PO Box 1426, Palmerston North 4440
email nz.freelance.writers.assoc@gmail.com
website www.nzfreelancewriters.co.nz
Editor Alyson B. Cresswell
Quarterly $30; International members NZ$35

Magazine of the NZ Freelance Writers' Association. Welcomes ideas for articles on all genres of writing. Payment: $10 (490–900 words). Payment on acceptance.

Hawke's Bay Today

PO Box 180, Karamu Road North, Hastings 4156
tel +64 (0)6 873 0800 *fax* +64 (0)6 873 0812
email editor@hbtoday.co.nz
website www.hbtoday.co.nz
Editor Antony Phillips
Daily $1

Limited requirements. Payment: $30 upwards for articles, $30 upwards for photos.

(Invercargill) The Southland Times

PO Box 805, Invercargill
tel +64 (0)3 211 1130 *fax* +64 (0)3 211 1098
email news@stl.co.nz
website www.stuff.co.nz/southlandtimes
Editor F.L. Tulett
Daily Mon–Fri $1.20, Sat $1.60

Articles of up to 800 words on topics of Southland and Otago interest. Payment: by arrangement. Illustrations: colour, cartoons. Founded 1862.

Management Magazine

Mediaweb Ltd, PO Box 5544, Wellesley Street, Auckland 1141
tel +64 (0)9 845 5114 *fax* +64 (0)9 845 5116
email editor@management.co.nz
website www.management.co.nz
Monthly $6.95

Articles on the practice of management skills and techniques, individual and company profiles, coverage of organisational leadership and management trends and topics. A NZ/Australian angle or application preferred. Length: 2,000 words. Payment: by arrangement; minimum 30c per word. Illustrations: photos, line drawings.

The Nelson Mail

PO Box 244, 15 Bridge Street, Nelson 7040
tel +64 (0)3 546 2881 *fax* +64 (0)3 546 2802
website www.stuff.co.nz/nelson-mail
Editor Paul McIntyre

(New Zealand) Sunday Star-Times

PO Box 1327, Auckland 1140
tel +64 (0)9 302 1300 *fax* +64 (0)9 309 0258
email news@star-times.co.nz
website www.stuff.co.nz/sunday-star-times
Editor David Kerneys
Sun $2.50

New Zealand Woman's Day

100 Beaumont Street, Westhaven, Auckland 1010
tel +64 (0)9 308 2700 *fax* +64 0800 277412
email wdaynz@acmacpmagazines.co.nz
Editor Sido Kitchin
Weekly $4.20

Celebrity interviews, exclusive news stories, short stories, gossip. Length: 1,000 words. Illustrations: colour transparencies; payment according to use. Payment: by arrangement. Founded 1989.

NZ House & Garden

PO Box 6341, Wellesley Street, Auckland 1036
tel +64 (0)9 909 6913
website www.nzhouseandgarden.co.nz
Editor Kate Coughlan, *Associate Editor* Sally Duggan
Monthly $8.90

Glossy magazine that celebrates New Zealand's most interesting houses and beautiful gardens. Inspiration for food and entertaining, and a resource for decor and travel. Considers unsolicited material. Welcomes ideas for articles and features. Length: 500–1,000 words. Payment: $400–$600. Illustrations: colour transparencies. Founded 1994.

Takahe

Takahe Collective Trust, PO Box 13335, Christchurch 8141
email admin@takahe.org.nz
website www.takahe.org.nz
3 p.a. $30 p.a. ($40 p.a. international)

Quality short fiction 3,000 words maximum, poetry reviews and artwork. Founded 1989.

Taranaki Daily News

49–65 Currie Street, New Plymouth
tel +64 (0)6 759 0800 *fax* +64 (0)6 758 6849
email editor@tnl.co.nz
website www.taranakidailynews.co.nz
Editor Roy Pilott
Daily $1.20, Sat $1.60

Articles preferably with a Taranaki connection. Payment: by negotiation. Illustrations: half-tone, cartoons. Founded 1857.

The Timaru Herald

PO Box 46, Bank Street, Timaru 7940
tel +64 (0)3 684 4129
email editor@timaruherald.co.nz
website www.stuff.co.nz/timaru-herald
Editor David King
Daily 75c

Topical articles. Payment: by arrangement. Illustrations: colour or b&w prints.

(Wellington) The Dominion Post

PO Box 3740, 40 Boulcott Street, Wellington 6140
tel +64 (0)4 474 0000
fax +64 (0)4 474 0350, +64 (0)4 474 0185 (editor)

email editor@dompost.co.nz
website www.dompost.co.nz
Editor Bernadette Courtney
Daily Mon–Fri $1.50, Sat $2.50

General topical articles, 600 words. Payment: NZ current rates or by arrangement. News illustrations, cartoons. Founded 2002 with the merger of *The Dominion* and *The Evening Post.*

Your Home and Garden

Australian Consolidated Press (New Zealand) Ltd, PO Box 92512, Wellesley Street, Auckland 1036
tel +64 (0)9 308 2700 *fax* +64 (0)9 308 2878
Editor Leanne Moore
Monthly $7.40

Advice, ideas and projects for homeowners – interiors and gardens. Length: 1,000 words. Illustrations: digital images. Payment: 35c per word/$75 per transparency. Founded 1991.

SOUTH AFRICA

Africa Wild

Africa Wild Publishing (Pty) Ltd, PO Box 13333, Dowerglen, Ext. 7, 1612
tel +27 (0)11 454 0535 *fax* +27 (0)11 454 0538
email editor@africawildgroup.co.za
website www.africawildgroup.co.za
Editor-in-Chief Cheri-Ann Potgieter
11 p.a. R29,95

Travel magazine covering Southern Africa with articles on wildlife, conversation, nature and tourism.

Bona

Caxton Magazines, PO Box 1610, 2121 Parklands, KwaZulu-Natal
tel +27 (0)11 889 0600
website www.bona.co.za
Monthly R8,50

Articles on human drama, sport, music, health, social and consumer issues of interest to black people. Length: up to 1,000 words. Payment: on publication. Illustrations: colour jpgs or prints.

(Cape Town) Cape Times

Newspaper House, 4th Floor, 122 St George's Mall, Cape Town 8001
postal address PO Box 11, Cape Town 8000
tel +27 (0)21 488 4911 *fax* +27 (0)21 488 4744
website www.capetimes.co.za
Editor Alide Dasnois
Daily R6.80; Country edition R7.00

Contributions must be suitable for a daily newspaper and must not exceed 800 words. Illustrations: photos of outstanding South African interest. Founded 1876.

Car

PO Box 180, Howard Place 7450
tel +27 (0)21 530 3100 *fax* +27 (0)21 531 2212
email car@ramsaymedia.co.za
website www.cartoday.com
Editor Hannes Oosthuizen
Monthly R28,95

New car announcements with photos and full colour features of motoring interest. Payment: by arrangement. Illustrations: colour, cartoons. Founded 1957.

Daily Dispatch

Dispatch Media (Pty) Ltd, 35 Caxton Street, East London 5201
tel +27 (0)43 702 2000 *fax* +27 (0)43 743 5155
email letters@dispatch.co.za
postal address PO Box 131, East London 5200
website www.dispatch.co.za
Editor Phylicia Oppelt
Daily Mon–Sat R2,70

Newspaper for the Eastern Cape region. Features of general interest, especially successful development projects in developing countries. Contributions welcome. Illustrations: colour and b&w photographs, artwork, cartoons; provides research facility for a fee to authors and publications. Length: approx. 1,000 words (features). Payment: R500; R100 photographs. Founded 1872.

Destiny

Ndalo Media (Pty) Ltd, Bryanston Corner, 1st Floor, Building B, 18 Ealing Crescent (off Culross Road), CNR Main Road & Bryanston Drive, Bryanston 2191
PO Box 2077, Lonehill 2062
tel +27 (0)11 300 6700 *fax* +27 (0)11 300 6767
email destiny.editor@ndalomedia.com
website www.destinyconnect.com
Editor Khany Dhlomo
Monthly R26,95

Business and lifestyle for women. Aims to provide business and financial information that connects, supports and inspires women who are professionals, entrepreneurs, businesswomen and general business enthusiasts. Founded 2007.

Drum

Media 24, PO Box 653284, Benmore 2010
tel +27 (0)11 322 0877
website www.drum.co.za
Editor Makhosazana Zwane-Siguqa
Weekly R13,00

Family magazine with articles on celebrities, fashion and beauty, food and home, and advice, together with puzzles and TV listings. Include sae with submissions.

(Durban) The Mercury

Independent Newspapers KwaZulu-Natal Ltd, PO Box 47549, Durban 4023
tel +27 (0)31 308 2911
website www.themercury.co.za
Editor Angela Quintal

Daily Mon–Fri R4,80

Serious background news and inside details of world events. Length: 700–900 words. Illustrations: photos of general interest. Founded 1852.

Fairlady

Box 1802, Cape Town 8000
tel +27 (0)21 446 5131 *fax* +27 (0)21 446 5058
email flmag@fairlady.com
website www.fairlady.com
Editor Suzy Brokensha
Monthly R22,95

Magazine for women in their 30s covering beauty, fashion, food and interior design. Includes 8 features per issue for which it seeks topical stories written to style. Considers unsolicited material. Length: about 1,800 words. Illustrations: colour and b&w prints, colour artwork. Payment: R1.50 per word; R250 per photo, approx. R500 per illustration. Founded 1965.

Farmer's Weekly

368 Jan Smuts Avenue, Craighall 2196, PO Box 1797, Pinegowrie 2123
tel +27 (0)11 889 0836 *fax* +27 (0)11 889 0862
email farmersweekly@caxton.co.za
website www.farmersweekly.co.za
Editor Alita van der Walt
Weekly R13.95

Articles, generally illustrated, up to 1,000 words, on all aspects of practical farming and research with particular reference to conditions in Southern Africa. Includes women's section which accepts suitable, illustrated articles. Illustrations: line, half-tone, colour, cartoons. Payment: according to merit. Founded 1911.

Femina Magazine

Media24 Magazine Division, 7th Floor, Media City, 1 Heerengracht, Foreshore, Cape Town
tel +27 (0)21 446 5180
Editor Glynis O'Hara
Monthly R20,95

Magazine for women aged 40 and over with articles on culture, celebrities, parenting, relationships, real-life drama, popular science and human interest.

Garden and Home

Caxton House, 368 Jan Smuts Avenue, Craighall Park 2196
tel +27 (0)11 449 1010
email gardenhome@caxton.co.za
website www.gardenandhome.co.za
Editor Mary Jane Harris
Monthly R21,95

Well-illustrated articles on gardening suitable for southern hemisphere. Articles for home section on furnishings, decor ideas, food. Payment: by arrangement. Illustrations: half-tone, colour, cartoons.

Go!

8th Floor, Media City, 1 Heerengracht, Cape Town 8001
PO Box 1802, Cape Town 8000
tel +27 (0)21 446 1287
email editor@gomag.co.za
website www.gomag.co.za
Editor Barnie Louw
Monthly R20

Travel magazine covering Southern Africa with articles on places, food, photographing and equipment.

Ideas

PO Box 1802, Cape Town 8000
tel +27 (0)21 406 3185 *fax* +27 (0)21 406 2929
email ideased@media24.com
website www.ideasmag.co.za
Editor Terena Le Roux
Monthly R24,95

Features on beauty and fashion, food, knitting, needlecraft, crafts, home and garden, health and parenting. Length: up to 1,400 words (features/stories). Payment: R1,50 per word. Colour transparencies. Founded 1980.

Independent Newspapers Gauteng

PO Box 1014, Johannesburg 2000
tel +27 (0)11 633 9111 *fax* +27 (0)11 836 8398
website www.iol.co.za, www.star.co.za, www.pretorianews.co.za
Johannesburg **The Star** Daily R3,50
Saturday Star R4,20
Sunday Independent R9
Pretoria **Pretoria News** Daily R3,20

Accepts articles of general and South African interest; also cartoons. Payment: in accordance with an editor's assessment.

Independent Newspapers Kwa-Zulu Natal Ltd

18 Osborne Street, Greyville, Durban 4023
tel +27 (0)31 308 2400 *fax* +27 (0)31 308 2427
website www.iol.co.za, www.themercury.co.za, www.thepost.co.za
Durban **Daily News** Daily
The Mercury Daily
The Post Weekly R16,60 p.m.
Independent on Saturday

Accepts articles of general and South African interest; also cartoons. Payment: in accordance with an editor's assessment.

Independent Newspapers (South Africa) Ltd

PO Box 1014, Johannesburg 2000
tel +27 (0)11 633 2994 *fax* +27 (0)11 834 6059
website www.iol.co.za, www.capeargus.co.za
Cape Town **Argus** Daily R3,50

Saturday Argus R4
Sunday Argus R4,50
Cape Times Daily R3,80

Accepts articles of general and South African interest; also cartoons. Payment: in accordance with an editor's assessment.

(Johannesburg) Sunday Times

4 Biermann Avenue, Rosebank, Johannesburg 2196
tel +27 (0)11 280 3000
email tellus@sundaytimes.co.za
website www.timeslive.co.za
Editor Ray Hartley
Sun R16.00

Articles of political or human interest, from a South African angle if possible (max. 1,000 words and 2–3 photos). Shorter essays, stories and articles of a light nature from 500–750 words. Payment: average rate £100 a column. Illustrations: colour and b&w photos, line drawings.

Living and Loving

CTP Caxton Magazines, 4th Floor, Caxton House, 368 Jan Smuts Avenue, Craighall Park, Johannesburg
tel +27 (0)11 889 0621
postal address PO Box 218 Parklands 2121
website www.livingandloving.co.za
Editor Claire Huisamen
Monthly R24,95

Parenting magazine: from pregnancy to preschool. Articles about behaviour and development in the first 5 years of life. First-person parenting experiences – pregnancy and the growing child. Medical news/breakthroughs of interest to parents worldwide. Payment: by merit, on acceptance and publication. Founded 1970.

Men's Health

Touchline Media, PO Box 16368, Vlaeberg 8018
tel +27 (0)21 408 3800 *fax* +27 (0)21 408 1200
website www.mh.co.za
Editorial Director Jason Brown
Monthly R35

Magazine for men with articles on health, relationships, food, culture and finance.

Move!

Media24, PO Box 785266, Sandton 2146
tel +27 (0)11 263 4795
email mzwane@media24.com
website www.movemag.co.za
Editor Makhosazana Zwane-Siguqa
Weekly R7

Magazine for women with articles on celebrities, fashion and beauty, food and home, and advice, together with puzzles and TV listings. Include sae with all submissions.

O: The Oprah Magazine

21 St John's Street, Cape Town 8001
tel +27 (0)21 464 6200 *fax* +27 (0)21 465 8190
email info@assocmags.co.za
Editor in Chief Jane Raphaely
Monthly R26.95

Women's magazine with articles on Mind, Body & Spirit, health, food and style, all aimed to inspire.

People

CTP Ltd, Caxton House, 2nd Floor, 368 Jan Smuts Avenue, Craighall Park
Private Bag X005, Roosevelt Park 2129
tel +27 (0)11 889 0600 *fax* +27 (0)11 889 0794
website www.peoplemagazine.co.za
Editor Andrea Caknis
Weekly R12,95

Celebrity articles and gossip, real-life stories and TV listings.

Sailing

(incorporating SA Yachting)
PO Box 1849, Westville 3630
tel +27 (0)31 709 6087 *fax* +27 (0)31 709 6143
email sailing@iafrica.com
website www.sailing.co.za
Editor Richard Crockett
Monthly R210 p.a.

Articles and features for the safety of dinghy, cruising, keelboat and racing sailors. Welcomes ideas for articles and features. Will consider unsolicited material. Illustrations: colour.

Soul

PO Box 2930, Vanderbijlpark 1900
email venessa@finessemag.co.za
Editor-in-Chief Venessa Shueman
11 p.a. R13,95

Women's magazine with the focus on Mind, Body & Spirit themes.

Southern Cross

PO Box 2372, Cape Town 8000
tel +27 (0)21 465 5007 *fax* +27 (0)21 465 3850
email editor@scross.co.za
website www.scross.co.za
Editor Gunther Simmermacher
Weekly R5.50

National English-language Catholic weekly. Catholic news reports, world and South African. Length: 550 words (articles). Illustrations: photos of Catholic interest from freelance contributors. Payment: 40c per word; illustrations R55.

True Love

PO Box 784696, Sandton 2146
tel +27 (0)11 322 0880 *fax* +27 (0)11 322 0709
website www.truelove.co.za
monthly R18,95

Magazine for women with articles on health, Mind, Body & Spirit, careers and business, parenting, lifestyle, and fashion and beauty. Founded 1972.

The Witness

45 Willowton Road, Pietermaritzburg 3200
tel +27 (0)33 355 1111 *fax* +27 (0)33 355 1122
email fikile.moya@witness.co.za
Editor Fikile Moya
Daily R4.40

Accepts topical articles. All material should be submitted direct to the Editor in Pietermaritzburg. Length: 500–1,000 words. Payment: average of R600 per 1,000 words. Founded 1846.

World Airnews

PO Box 35082, Northway, Durban 4065
tel +27 (0)31 564 1319 *fax* +27 (0)31 563 7115
email tom@airnews.co.za
website www.airnews.co.za
Editor Tom Chalmers
Monthly £36 p.a.

Aviation news and features with an African angle. Payment: by negotiation.

Your Family

PO Box 473016, Parklands 2121, Gauteng
tel +27 (0)11 889 0600
website www.yourfamily.co.za
Editor Patti Garlick
Monthly R19,95

Cookery, knitting, crochet and homecrafts. Family drama, happy ending. Payment: by arrangement. Illustrations: continuous tone, colour and line, cartoons.

USA

American Markets Newsletter

1974 46th Avenue, San Francisco, CA 94116
email sheila.oconnor@juno.com
Editor Sheila O'Connor
6 p.a. £34 p.a. (£63 for 2 years)

Editorial guidelines for US, Canadian and other overseas markets, plus information on press trips, non-fiction/fiction markets and writers' tips. Free syndication for all subscribers. Sample issue £5.95 (payable to S. O'Connor).

Willings Press Guide

Cision UK Ltd, Chess House, 34 Germain Street, Chesham, Bucks. HP5 1SJ
tel 0870 736 0010 (UK), (01494) 797225 (international)
fax 0870 736 0011 (UK), (01494) 797224
email enquiries@willingspress.com
website www.willingspress.com
£420 3-volume set; £365 2 volumes; £255 1 volume

Three volumes contain details of over 50,000 newspapers, broadcasters, periodicals and special interest titles in the UK and internationally. Usually available at local reference libraries or direct from the publisher. Also available as an online product.

The Writer

Kalmbach Publishing Co., 21027 Crossroads Circle, PO Box 1612, Waukesha, WI 53187
tel +1 262-796-8776
email editor@writermag.com
website www.writermag.com
Monthly $32.95 p.a.

Contains articles of instruction on most writing genres, lists of markets for MSS, and special features of interest to fiction and non-fiction writers and freelance writers everywhere.

Writer's Digest

Writer's Digest, 4700 East Galbraith Road, Cincinnati, OH 45236
tel +1 513-531-2690 *fax* +1 513-891-7153
email writersdigest@fwmedia.com
website www.writersdigest.com
8 p.a. $24.96 p.a.

Magazine for writers who want to write better and sell more; aims to inform, instruct and inspire the freelance and fiction writer.

Writer's Digest Books

Writer's Digest, 4700 East Galbraith Road, Cincinannati, OH 45236
tel +1 513-531-2690 *fax* +1 513-531-2902
email writersdigest@fwmedia.com
website www.writersdigest.com

Publishes annually *Novel & Short Story Writer's Market, Children's Writer's & Illustrator's Market, Poet's Market, Photographer's Market, Artist's & Graphic Designer's Market, Guide to Literary Agents* and many other books on creating and selling writing and illustrations. Also *Writer's Digest* magazine (see above).

Syndicates, news and press agencies

Before submitting material, you are strongly advised to make preliminary enquiries and to ascertain terms of work. Strictly speaking, syndication is the selling and reselling of previously published work although some news and press agencies handle original material.

Academic File Information Services

EAPGROUP International Media,
Eastern Art Publishing Group, PO Box 13666,
London SW14 8WF
tel 020-8392 1122 *fax* 020-8392 1422
email afis@eapgroup.com
website www.eapgroup.com
Managing Editor Sajid Rizvi

Feature and photo syndication with special reference to the developing world and immigrant communities in the West. Founded 1985.

Advance Features

Stubbs Wood Cottage, Hammerwood,
East Grinstead, West Sussex RH19 3QE
tel (01342) 850480
email advancefeatures@aol.com
website www.advancefeatures.uk.com
Managing Editor Peter Norman

Crosswords: daily, weekly and theme; general puzzles. Daily and weekly cartoons for the regional, national and overseas press (not single cartoons).

AFP (Agence France-Presse)

Centre Point, 25th Floor,
101–103 New Oxford Street, London WC1A 1DD
tel 020-7010 8750 *fax* 020-7010 8751
email london.economics@afp.com
website www.afp.com

Major news agency with journalists in 165 countries and five regional headquarters.

Australian Associated Press

111 Buckingham Palace Road, London SW1W 0DT
tel 020-3262 0058 *fax* 020-7821 0851
email news.london@aap.com.au
website www.aap.com.au

News service to the Australian, New Zealand and Pacific Island press, radio and TV. Founded 1935.

Neil Bradley Puzzles

Linden House, 73 Upper Marehay, Ripley,
Derbyshire DE5 8JF
tel (01773) 741500 *fax* (01773) 741555
email bradcart@aol.com
Director Neil Bradley

Supplies visual puzzles to national and regional press; emphasis placed on variety and topicality with work based on current media listings. Daily single frame and strip cartoons. Founded 1981.

Brainwarp

PO Box 198, Birchwood, Warrington WA3 9AZ
mobile 07790 635208
email sarah@brainwarp.com
website www.brainwarp.com
Company Trixie Roberts, Tony Roberts, Sarah Simmons

Writes and supplies original crosswords, brainteasers, wordsearches, quizzes and word games to editors for the printed page. Does not accept work from external sources. Standard fees for syndicated puzzles. Customised work negotiable. Founded 1987.

Bulls Presstjänst AB

Fabrikörvägen 8, Box 1228, 13128 Nacka Strand,
Sweden
tel +46 8-55520600 *fax* +46 8-55520665
website www.bullspress.com

Bulls Pressedienst GmbH
Eysseneckstrasse 50, D-60322 Frankfurt am Main, Germany
tel +49 (0)69 959 270 *fax* +49 (0)69 959 27222
email sales@bullspress.de

Bulls Pressetjeneste A/S
Hammersborg torg 3, N-0179 Oslo, Norway
tel +47 2298 2660 *fax* +47 2220 4978
email henrik@bulls.no

Bulls Pressetjeneste
Ostbanegade 9, DK–2100 Copenhagen, Denmark
tel +45 3538 9099 *fax* +45 3538 2516
email kjartan@bulls.dk

Oy Fennopress Ab – a Bulls Company
Arabianranta 6, FIN–00560, Helsinki, Finland
tel +358 9-6129650 *fax* +358 9-656092
email sales@fennopress.fi

Bulls Press SP. z o.o.
17 Rejtana str. 24, 02–516 Warsaw, Poland
tel +48 22-845 9010 *fax* +48 22-845 9011
email office@bulls.com.pl

Bulls Press
Tornimäe 7–091, EE–10145 Tallinn, Estonia
tel +372 669 6737 *fax* +372 660 1313
email pilt@bulls.ee

Market newspapers, magazines, weeklies and advertising agencies in Sweden, Denmark, Norway, Finland, Iceland, Poland, The Baltic States, Germany, Austria and German-speaking Switzerland.

Syndicates human interest picture stories; topical and well-illustrated background articles and series; photographic features dealing with science, people, personalities, glamour; genre pictures for advertising;

condensations and serialisations of bestselling fiction and non-fiction; cartoons, comic strips, film and TV rights, merchandising and newspaper graphics online.

Cartoons & Wordgames

341 Stockport Road, Mossley,
Ashton-under-Lyne OL5 0RS
tel (01457) 834883 *fax* (01457) 838783
email email@wordgames.co.uk
website www.wordgames.co.uk
Managing Editor Tom Williams

Crosswords, puzzles, cartoons. Founded 1980.

Celebritext Ltd

PO Box 63628, London SW9 1BA
tel 020-8123 1730
email info@celebritext.com
website www.celebritext.com
Contact Lee Howard

Specialises in film, TV and music celebrity interviews. Commission: 50%. Founded 2000.

Copyline Scotland

Room 2, 28 Church Street, Inverness IV3 1EH
tel (01463) 710695 *fax* (01463) 713695
email copylinescotland@aol.com
Directors David Love, Maureen Love

Copywriting, writing press releases, covering news events for national and local media. Founded 1988.

Europa-Press

Fabrikörvägen 8, Box 1228, 13128 Nacka Strand, Sweden
tel +46 8-52210300 *fax* +46 8-52210300
email richard@europapress.se
website www.europapress.se
Director Richard Steinsvik

Market: newspapers, magazines, weeklies and websites in Sweden, Denmark, Norway, Finland, and the Baltic states. Syndicates high-quality features of international appeal such as topical articles, photo features – b&w and colour, women's features, short stories, serial novels, non-fiction stories and serials with strong human interest, comic strips.

Europress Features (UK)

18 St Chad's Road, Didsbury,
Nr Manchester M20 4WH
tel 0161 445 2945
email lauenbergandpartners@yahoo.com

Representation of newspapers and magazines in Europe, Australia, United States. Syndication of top-flight features with exclusive illustrations – human interest stories – showbusiness personalities. 30–35% commission on sales of material successfully accepted; 40% on exclusive illustrations.

FAMOUS*

13 Harwood Road, London SW6 4QP
tel 020-7731 9333 *fax* 020-7731 9330
email info@famous.uk.com
website www.famous.uk.com

Celebrity picture and feature agency. Supplies showbiz content to newspapers, magazines, websites, TV stations, mobile phone companies, books and advertisers worldwide. Represents celebrity journalists and photographers from LA, New York, Europe and Australia, syndicating their copy around the globe. Open to new material. Terms: 50%. Founded 1990.

ForesightNews

Centaur Media Plc, 79 Wells Street,
London W1T 3QN
tel 020-7190 7830 *fax* 020-7190 7858
email editorial@foresightnews.co.uk
website www.foresightnews.co.uk
Contact Nicole Hunt, *Editor* Rhys Morgan

Offers a vast fully searchable database of forthcoming news and events spanning 15 broad category areas and hundreds sub-categories including UK and EU politics, international news, business, crime, environment, defence and security, health, entertainment, royals and sport, delivering information to subscribers before it is reported.

Government News Network (GNN)

Room HR332, Hercules House, Hercules Road,
London SE1 7DU
tel 020-7261 8527 *fax* 020-7928 5696
website www.nds.coi.gov.uk

Government press office making national issues relevant to local audiences.

Graphic Syndication

4 Reyntiens View, Odiham, Hants RG29 1AF
tel (01256) 703004
email flantoons@btinternet.com
Manager M. Flanagan

Cartoon strips and single frames supplied to newspapers and magazines in Britain and overseas. Terms: 50%. Founded 1981.

Guardian/Observer Syndication

Kings Place, 90 York Way, London N1 9GU
tel 020-3353 2539 *fax* 020-3353 3167
email permissions.syndication@guardian.co.uk
website www.syndication.guardian.co.uk
Contact Helen Wilson

International syndication services of news and features from *The Guardian* and *The Observer*. Unable to syndicate content which hasn't been published in its own titles.

Hayters Teamwork

Image House, Station Road, London N17 9LR
tel 020-8808 3300 *fax* 020-8808 1122
email sport@hayters.com
website www.hayters.com
Managing Directors Nick Callow, Gerry Cox

Sports news, features and data supplied to all branches of the media. Commission: negotiable according to merit. Part of Info Strada. Founded 1955.

Headliners

Rich Mix, 35–47 Bethnal Green Road,
London E1 6LA
tel 020-7749 9360 *fax* 020-7729 5948
email enquiries@headliners.org
website www.headliners.org
Director Fiona Wyton

Offers young people aged 8–18 the opportunity to write on issues of importance to them, for newspapers, radio and TV. Founded 1995.

Independent Radio News (IRN)

Mappin House, 4 Winsley Street, London W1W 8HF
tel 020-7182 8591 *fax* 020-7182 8594
email news@irn.co.uk
website www.irn.co.uk
Managing Director Tim Molloy

National and international news.

International Fashion Press Agency

Penrose House, Birtles Road, Whirley,
Cheshire SK10 3JQ
tel (01625) 615323 *fax* (01625) 432284
Managing Director P. Bentham

Monitors and photographs international fashion collections and developments in textile and fashion industry. Specialist writers on health, fitness, beauty and personalities. Undertakes individual commissioned features. Supplies syndicated columns/ pages to press, radio and TV (NUJ staff writers and photographers).

International Press Agency (Pty) Ltd

Sunrise House, 56 Morningside, Ndabeni 7405,
South Africa
tel +27 (0)21 531 1926 *fax* +27 (0)21 531 8789
email inpra@iafrica.com
UK office 5 Cloister House, 53 Griffiths Road,
London SW19 1SS
tel 020-8767 4828
email uabarnett@inpra.co.uk
website www.inpa.co.za
Manager Mrs T. Temple
Managing Editor Mrs U.A. Barnett PhD

South African agents for many leading British, American and continental press firms for the syndication of press photos and features for the South African market. Founded 1934.

Joker Feature Service (JFS)

PO Box 253, 6040 AG, Roermond, The Netherlands
tel +31 475-337338 *fax* +31 475-315663
email info@jfs.nl
Managing Director Ruud Kerstens

Feature articles, serial rights, tests, cartoons, comic strips and illustrations, puzzles. Handles TV features, books, internet sites; also production for merchandising.

Knight Features

20 Crescent Grove, London SW4 7AH
tel 020-7622 1467 *fax* 020-7622 1522
website www.knightfeatures.com
Director Peter Knight, *Associates* Gaby Martin, Andrew Knight, Samantha Ferris

Worldwide selling of strip cartoons, puzzles, crosswords, horoscopes and serialisations. Agent in UK and Republic of Ireland for Universal Uclick and for Garfield. Founded 1985.

London at Large Ltd

Canal Studios, 3–5 Dunston Road, London E8 4EH
tel 020-7275 7667
email info@londonatlarge.com
website www.londonatlarge.com
Editor Chris Parkinson

Forward planner serving the media: lists press contacts for parties, celebrities, launches, premieres, music, film, video and book releases. Founded 1985.

London Press Service

23 Theydon Avenue, Woburn Sands,
Milton Keynes MK17 8PN
tel (01908) 587559
email londonpress@btconnect.com
Editor Dick Meredith

Newsfeatures about innovation, achievement, etc in the UK's business, scientific and technological sectors to help promote UK trade and attract inward investment. Part of BIS (Department for Business, Innovation and Skills). Commission: by arrangement. Founded 1950s.

Maharaja Features Pvt. Ltd (1969)

5/226 Sion Road East, Sion, Bombay 400 022, India
tel +91 22-24097951
email mahafeat@gmail.com
Editor Mrs R. Ravi, *Managing Editor* K.R.N. Swamy

Syndicates feature and pictorial material of interest to Asian readers to newspapers and magazines in India, UK and elsewhere. Specialises in well-researched articles on India by eminent authorities for publication in prestigious journals throughout the world. Also topical features. Length: 1,000–1,500 words. Illustrations: b&w prints, colour transparencies, digital photographs.

Market News International

1 Canada Square, 42nd Floor, Canary Wharf,
London E14 5DR
tel 020-7862 7404 *fax* 020-7862 7425
website www.marketnews.com

Provides news, data and analysis on financial markets from around the world.

National Association of Press Agencies (NAPA)

Suite 302, 3rd Floor, Queens Dock Business Centre, 67–83 Norfolk Street, Liverpool L1 0BG
tel 0870 240 0311 *fax* 0151 708 8079
email enquiries@napa.org.uk
website www.napa.org.uk
Directors Denis Cassidy, Chris Johnson, Matt Bell, Mark Solomons
Membership £250 p.a.

A network of independent, established and experienced press agencies serving newspapers, magazines, TV and radio networks. Founded 1983.

New Blitz Literary & TV Agency

Via di Panico 67, 00186 Rome, Italy
postal address CP 30047–00193, Rome 47, Italy
tel +39 06-4883268 *fax* +39 06-4883268
email blitzgacs@inwind.it
Manager Giovanni A.S. Congiu

Syndicates worldwide: cartoons, comic strips, humorous books with drawings, feature and pictorial material, topical, environment, travel. Average rates of commission 60/40%, monthly report of sales, payment 60 days after the date of sale.

PA Puzzles – see The Press Association

Photoshot

29–31 Saffron Hill, London EC1N 8SW
tel 020-7421 6000 *fax* 020-7421 6006
email info@photoshot.com
website www.photoshot.com
Managing Director Charles Taylor

Quality imagery. Collections include: UPPA – daily national and international business, political and establishment news; Starstock – live images of celebrity and entertainment personalities; Stay Still – celebrity portraiture; Talking Sport – live and archival sporting images; NHPA – nature; Photoshot Assignment – creative photographic commissions. Founded 1929.

Pixfeatures

5 Latimer Road, Barnet, Herts. EN5 5NU
tel 020-8449 9946 *fax* 020-8449 9946
Contact Peter Wickman

News agency and picture library. Specialises in selling pictures and features to British and European press.

The Press Association

292 Vauxhall Bridge Road, London SW1V 1AE
tel 0870 120 3200 *fax* 0870 120 3201
website www.pressassociation.co.uk
Chief Executive Clive Marshall, *Managing Director* Steven Brown

PA Entertainment Entertainment content including showbiz, lifestyle, food, fashion, health, property, travel, horoscopes, crosswords and cartoons

PA News Fast and accurate news, photography and information to print, broadcast and electronic media in the UK and Ireland.

PA Sport In-depth coverage of national and regional sports, transmitting a huge range of stories, results, pictures and updates every day.

PA Listings Page- and screen-ready information from daily guides to 7-day supplements on sports results, TV and radio listings, arts and entertainment, financial and weather listings tailored to suit requirements.

PA Digital Top quality content including news and sport for a wide range of multimedia customers.

PA WeatherCentre Continuously updated information on present and future weather conditions; consultancy services for media and industry. Founded 1868.

The Puzzle House

Ivy Cottage, Battlesea Green, Stradbroke, Suffolk IP21 5NE
tel (01379) 384656 *fax* (01379) 384656
email puzzlehouse@btinternet.com
website www.thepuzzlehouse.co.uk
Partners Roy Preston and Sue Preston

Supply original crosswords, quizzes and puzzles of all types. Commissions taken on any topic, with all age ranges catered for. Wide selection of puzzles available for one-off usage. Founded 1988.

Rann Communication

Level 1, 18–20 Grenfell Street, Adelaide, SA 5000, Australia
postal address GPO Box 958, Adelaide, SA 5000, Australia
tel +61 (0)8 8211 7771 *fax* +61 (0)8 8212 2272
website www.rann.com.au
Managing Director Chris Rann

Full range of professional PR, press releases, special newsletters, commercial and political intelligence, media monitoring. Welcomes approaches from organisations requiring PR representation or press release distribution. Founded 1982.

Reuters News

The Quadrangle, 180 Wardour Street, London W1A 4YG
tel 020-7437 9787
email general.info@thomsonreuters.com
website www.thomsonreuters.com

The largest international news agency – provides global information and news services to the world's newspapers, websites, TV networks, radio stations, as well as direct to business professionals in the financial, legal, tax and accounting, scientific, healthcare and media markets. Merged with Thomson Financial News in 2008.

Sirius Media Services

Suite 3, Stowmarket Business Centre, Needham Road, Stowmarket, Suffolk IP14 2AH

tel (01449) 678878 *fax* 0870 912 8041
website www.siriusmedia.co.uk

Crosswords, puzzles and quizzes.

Solo Syndication Ltd

17–18 Haywards Place, London EC1R 0EQ
tel 020-7566 0360 *fax* 020-7566 0388
Contact William Gardiner

Worldwide syndication of newspaper features, photos, cartoons, strips and book serialisations. Represents the international syndication of Associated Newspapers (*Daily Mail, Mail on Sunday, Evening Standard*) and Universal Press Syndicate, Creators Syndicate and the Christian Science Monitor Service in Africa and the Middle East.

Southern News Service

Exchange House, Hindhead, Surrey GU26 6AA
tel (01428) 607330 *fax* (01428) 606351
email denis@cassidyandleigh.com
Partners Denis Cassidy and Donald Leigh

News stories, features and court coverage. Full picture service, digital and ISDN. Public relations words and pictures. Founded 1960.

The Telegraph – Content Licensing & Syndication

Telegraph Media Group,
111 Buckingham Palace Road, London SW1W 0DT
tel 020-7931 1010 *fax* 020-7931 2867
email syndication@telegraph.co.uk
website www.telegraph.co.uk/syndication

News, features, photography & graphics, video, worldwide distribution and representation. Content licensing packages available for print or online use.

Thomson Financial News – see Reuters News

Visual Humour

5 Greymouth Close, Stockton-on-Tees TS18 5LF
tel (01642) 581847
email peterdodsworth@btclick.com
website www.businesscartoonshop.com
Contact Peter Dodsworth

Daily and weekly humorous cartoon strips; also single panel cartoon features (not gag cartoons) for possible syndication in the UK and abroad. Picture puzzles also considered. Submit photocopy samples only initially, with sae. Founded 1984.

WENN

35 Kings Exchange, Tileyard Road, London N7 9AH
tel 020-7607 2757 *fax* 020-7700 4649
email lloyd@wenn.com
website www.wenn.com

Provides the world's media with up-to-the-minute entertainment news and photos. Offices in Los Angeles, New York and Las Vegas. (Formerly World Entertainment News Network.)

Wessex News, Features and Photos Agency

Little Mead, Lower Green, Inkpen, Berks. RG17 9DW
tel (01488) 668308
email news@britishnews.co.uk
website www.britishnews.co.uk
Editor Jim Hardy

Freelance press agency with a network of writers and photographers across the UK. Providing real-life new stories and features for the national and international newspapers and magazines. Founded 1981.

Books

How to get published

The combined wisdom of the writers of the articles in this section of the *Yearbook* provide some of the most up-to-date and best practical advice you will need to negotiate your way through the two main routes to publication. Whether you opt for the traditional route via an agent or the self-publishing model, there are key things it would be useful to consider before you embark.

If you are unsure whether you have what it takes to write a book, see *Is there a book in you?* (page 279). Taking a writing course (see *Creative writing courses*, page 630) or joining a writing group, either online or in person, are both good ways to explore possibilities. Consider where it best suits you to write – see *The writer's ultimate workspace* (page 604), *Writers' retreats* (page 608) and *Why libraries matter* (page 621).

There is more competition to get published than ever before. Hundreds of manuscripts of would-be books land on the desks or appear in the in-boxes of publishers and literary agents every day. Both publishers and literary agents acknowledge that potential authors have to be really dedicated (or perhaps very lucky) in order to get their work published. So how can you give yourself the best chance of success?

1. Know your market

• Be confident that there is a readership for your book. Explore the intended market in advance of submitting your script so you are sure that your publishing idea is both commercially viable and desirable to the reading public, agent or publisher.

• Know your competition and review the latest publishing trends: look in bookshops, at ebook stores, at online book sites, take an interest in publishing stories in the media and above all *read*. See *A year in view of the publishing industry* on page 313.

2. Agent, publisher or do-it-yourself?

• First decide if you want to try and get signed by a literary agent and be published by a traditional publisher. Self-publishing in both print and electronically has never been easier, quicker or cheaper.

• If you opt for the agent/publisher route, then decide whether you prefer to approach an agent or to submit your material direct to a publisher. Many publishers, particularly of fiction, will only consider material submitted through a literary agent. See *'I think I need an agent'* on page 411, *How literary agencies work* on page 413, *How to get an agent* on page 416 and *Understanding publishing agreements* on page 287 for some of the pros and cons of each approach. Whether you choose to approach an agent or a publisher, your work will be subjected to rigorous commercial assessment.

• For information about self-publishing in print and electronically, consult *Doing it on your own* (page 290) and *Self-publishing in ebook* (page 294).

3. Choose the right publisher, agent or self-publishing route

• Study the entries in this *Yearbook*, examine publishers' lists and their websites, and look in the relevant sections in libraries and bookshops for the names of publishers which might be interested in seeing your material.

• A list of literary agents starts on page 429. See *Letter to an unsolicited author* on page 421 and *Making a successful submission to a literary agent* on page 418.
• Listings of publishers' names and addresses start on page 123. A list of *Publishers of fiction*, by genre, is on page 709 and a list of *Publishers of non-fiction* starts on page 714.
• The list of *Children's book publishers and packagers* on page 728 includes publishers of poetry for children and teenage fiction. A list of *Literary agents for children's books* is on page 737. See also the *Children's Writers' & Artists' Yearbook 2013* (Bloomsbury 2012) for more in-depth coverage of all aspects of writing and publishing for the children's and young adult markets.
• Publishers which consider poetry for adults are listed on page 736. See also *Getting poetry published* on page 335 and *Approaching a poetry publisher* on page 342.
• The electronic book market is growing dramatically. See *Electronic publishing* on page 581, *Self-publishing in ebook* on page 294, *A year in view of the publishing industry* on page 313 and *Print on demand* on page 317.
• Authors are strongly advised not to pay for the publication of their work. A reputable publishing house will undertake publication at its own expense, except possibly for works of an academic nature. See *Doing it on your own* on page 290 for an introduction to self-publishing, *Self-publishing in ebook* on page 294 and *Vanity publishing* on page 329.

4. Prepare your material well

• Presentation is important. No editor will read a handwritten manuscript. If your material is submitted in the most appropriate format a publisher will be more inclined to give attention to it. Many publishers' websites give guidance for new writers.
• Numerous manuscripts are rejected because of poor writing style or structure. A critique by an experienced editorial professional can help to iron out these weaknesses; see the *Writers' & Artists'* website (www.writersandartists.co.uk) for listings.
• It is understandable that writers, in their eagerness to get their work published as soon as possible, will send their manuscript in a raw state. Do not send your manuscript to a publisher until it is *ready* to be seen. Wait until you are confident that your work is as good as it can be. Have as your mantra: edit, review, revise and then edit again. See *Making a successful submission to a literary agent* on page 418.

5. Approach a publisher or literary agent in the way they prefer

• Submit your work to the right person within the publishing company or literary agency. Ring or email first to find out who is the best person to receive your work. If the listing in this *Yearbook* does not specify, also ask whether they want a synopsis (see *Writing a synopsis* on page 118) and sample chapters or the complete manuscript. Many publishers' and literary agents' websites give guidance on how to submit material, and should make clear if they accept unsolicited scripts, by email or only by post.
• Never send your only copy of the manuscript. Whilst every reasonable care will be taken of material in a publisher's possession, responsibility cannot be accepted if material is lost or damaged.
• Always include an sae with enough postage for the return of your material if sent by post, though most submissions tend to be electronic.

6. Write a convincing cover letter

• Compose your preliminary letter with care. It will be your first contact with an agent or publisher and needs to make them take notice of your book.

• When submitting a manuscript to a publisher, it is a good idea to let them know that you know (and admire!) what they already publish. You can then make your case about where your submission will fit in their list. Let them know that you mean business and have researched the marketplace. See *Understanding the publishing process* on page 215.

• What is the USP (unique selling point) of the material you are submitting? You may have an original authorial 'voice', or you may have come up with an amazingly brilliant idea for a series. If, after checking out the marketplace, you think you have something truly original to offer, then believe in yourself and be convincing when you offer it around.

7. Get out and network

• Writing can be a lonely business – don't work in a vacuum. Talk to others who write in the same genre or share a similar readership. You can meet them at literature festivals, conferences and book groups. Find out if there are any writer groups in your area and/or join an online book forum. Consider doing a course – see *Creative writing courses* on page 630.

• Go to a festival and be inspired! There are many literature festivals held throughout the year (see *Literature festivals* on page 571) at which both new and well-known authors appear.

8. Don't give up!

• Agents receive hundreds of manuscripts every week. For an agent and publisher, there are many factors that have to be taken into consideration when evaluating these submissions, the most important of which is 'Will it sell?' See *The state of commissioning* on page 283 and *Spotting a bestseller* on page 220.

• Be prepared to wait for a decision on your work. Editors and agents are very busy people so be patient when waiting for a response. Don't pester them too soon.

• Publishing is big business and it is ever more competitive. Even after an editor has read your work, there are many other people involved before a manuscript is acquired for publication. People from the sales, marketing, publicity, rights and other departments all have to be convinced that the book is right for their list and will sell.

• The harsh reality of submitting a manuscript to a publisher or literary agent is that you have to be prepared for rejection (see *Dealing with rejection* on page 601). But practically all successful authors have received such rejections from a publisher at some time so you are in good company.

• For advice from established writers on how they first got into print see the 'notes from successful authors' articles that start on page 226.

• Have patience and persevere. If the conventional route doesn't produce the results you were hoping for, consider the self-publishing route. Good luck!

Publishers' contracts

Following a publishing company's firm interest in a MS, a publisher's contract is drawn up between the author and the publisher (see *Understanding publishing agreements* on page 287). If the author is not entirely happy with the contract presented to them or wishes to take advice, he/she could ask their literary agent, the Society of Authors or the Writers' Guild of Great Britain to check the contract on their behalf – providing the author has an agent and/or is a member of those organisations. Or you can seek advice from a solicitor. Before consulting a solicitor, make sure that they are familiar with publishing agreements and can give informed advice. Many local firms have little or no experience of such work and their opinion can often be of limited value and the cost may outweigh any possible gains.

Writing a synopsis

When publishers and literary agents ask for a synopsis to be submitted, writers often misunderstand what is required. Rebecca Swift provides clarification.

The dictionary definition of 'synopsis' (derived from the Ancient Greek meaning) is 'a brief description of the contents of something'. The purpose of a synopsis is to inform a literary agent or publisher of the type of book you are writing/have written in a concise, appealing fashion, conveying that you are in command of your subject matter. If you want your manuscript to be given serious consideration, a good synopsis is a crucial part of your submission.

This *Writers' & Artists' Yearbook* will inform you that most publishing houses no longer accept direct submissions but those that do (usually the smaller houses) will most often ask for a cover letter, synopsis and sample chapters rather than a whole work in the first instance. The same applies to literary agents. To put it simply, the sample chapters are to show how you write, and the synopsis is to tell the reader what happens when they have finished reading them. This will help inform the publisher/literary agent whether they think it is worth their while to read more. Then, if they want to read more, they will ask you.

So, the bottom line is this – if you want to have your manuscript read in its entirety you must invest time in getting your cover letter and book synopsis right. I know from my experiences at The Literary Consultancy (TLC) that many writers can get disconcerted and nervous by having to produce a synopsis and there are usually two reasons why.

First, a writer might have an unwieldy story that they themselves are not 100% convinced by, or a non-fiction project that they do not really know enough about. If this is so, summarising can be difficult because the thinking through and planning of the project has not been thorough in the first place.

In this instance, I would urge the writer to question why this process is so difficult. If it is because the story is insufficiently clear, persuasive or gripping, then more work needs to be done to get the manuscript into the kind of shape that would persuade an agent or editor to consider it further.

Second, a writer might genuinely be able to write a good book but not be experienced in the art of summarising a work in an effective manner. A few might even consider the act of doing so demeaning. If this is the case, I would urge you to think not of yourself, but of the reader, and treat the project as a literary exercise which you should try to enjoy: a challenge and opportunity to show your work off in its essential form. It might help to refer to book blurbs, or plot summaries in reference books such as *The Oxford Companion to Literature*, or online, for example in Wikipedia.

In addition to letting a professional reader know what happens in your manuscript, the synopsis will also let them know at a glance if you have thought about how your work fits into the market. This is critical in non-fiction, less so with fiction, although with fiction awareness of what genre you have written in is vital. Also, if what you are writing coincides with any major anniversaries for example, or might have a marketing 'hook' of any other kind, this is important to mention if not within the synopsis itself, then within a cover letter (see below).

Fiction synopses

A fiction synopsis should comprise a brief summary followed by a more detailed synopsis. But before writing either of these, you must clarify which genre your work fits into.

The most important thing to realise about fiction in respect of how you present it to representatives of the publishing industry is that it breaks down into different types, or genres. For those who think that the obsession with genres is a modern phenomenon, the lines from Polonius' famous speech in *Hamlet* might serve to prove the opposite. He describes the actors who have come to court as 'The best actors in the world… for tragedy, comedy, history, pastoral, pastoral-comical, historical-pastoral, scene individable, or poem unlimited'. Some of these dramatic forms are familiar and others not. There are always more genres being invented or cross-fertilised. It can be difficult to keep up!

The most popular genres today are, broadly speaking: crime, thriller, psychological thriller, detective, sci-fi, horror, comic, chick lit, lad's lit, historical, saga, literary, experimental, graphic, erotic, fantasy, romantic, women's commercial fiction and literary–commercial crossover – or, as it's becoming more widely coined, 'lit lite'.

Classifying your novel within a genre can be a challenge. This is largely because when most people start to write a novel they do so without having studied the genre they are writing for. Although when you start to write you may feel free to explore, practise and experiment without thinking in terms of the defining limits of a genre, by the time you come to submitting your work to be published it is very important to know which genre your work fits into. In all art forms there are rule breakers, but almost inevitably – as in the cases of Picasso, Virginia Woolf and, more recently, the US writer Michael Cunningham – even the greatest 'artists' have studied the traditional forms/genres before taking any risks.

A good starting point is to read books you consider similar to the one you are writing that are already published, and note how they are classified on the back cover. By reading, and sometimes studying literature and writing through other routes, you will also learn the possibilities and limits offered by your chosen genre. The bad news is if you don't clarify what kind of book you have written, the chances are it will reflect in the text. If you don't clearly inform the agent or editor what your book is about and which category it falls into, it may all too quickly be labelled as a work which 'falls between stools', is impossible to market and so doesn't get considered any further.

Writing a brief summary

Having made it your top priority to identify what type of novel you have written, you can make a start on your all-important synopsis. All good synopses should begin with a brief summary of 30–75 words, the sort of thing which appears on a book's back cover. For example, had you written *Pride and Prejudice* today:

> *Pride and Prejudice* is a contemporary, literary romance about a woman who falls in love with a man she thinks she hates.

Or,

> *Pride and Prejudice*, a contemporary, literary novel, tells the story of Elizabeth Bennett, a proud, intelligent woman, one of five sisters, whose mother is committed to marrying her children off as a matter of urgency. Elizabeth meets Darcy, owner of a grand estate, but considers him overly proud, arrogant and undesirable. In time, she learns that he is not all that he appears to be, and revises her prejudice, before they fall deeply in love.

Both these examples, one short, one longer, serve to whet the appetite for more detail to follow.

An example of an ostensibly weak synopsis, which rambles and fails to emphasise the most important points quickly enough, might be:

> Set at some point in the 19th century, five sisters are looking for husbands. Or is Mary, really? Anyway, their mother is a real fuss pot and annoys everybody. Outside their house there are lots of fields and it is sometimes raining. The girls' father is gentle and kind, with grey hair but not good at standing up to his wife always. Mr Bingley is an important character who is very handsome, but is he as handsome as Mr Darcy? It is hard to tell!…

Hopefully you can see the clear differences between the two.

Writing a detailed synopsis

Following the brief summary should be a more detailed synopsis of 350–450 words. Literary agents do not want a detailed chapter-by-chapter breakdown (if they do, they'll ask for one) as reading them can be tiresome and difficult to follow. The main aim of the longer synopsis is to give a detailed overview which clearly and concisely conveys how the story flows and unfolds, and (very importantly) what is interesting about it. The longer synopsis should also reconfirm when the story is set (i.e. is it contemporary or historical?); the setting or background (e.g. is it Thatcher's government in its last throes or are we in a quiet Devonshire village where nothing ever happens, but there is a sense of impending doom?); inform the reader about the central character (i.e. what is interesting about them and what happens on their journey), as well as giving brief reference to other characters that are directly pivotal to the plot. The longer synopsis should also highlight the dramatic turning points and tell the reader of any other salient information which will help convey what kind of work it is, how well imagined are the characters involved and how well thought through and alluring is the plot.

Cover letter

Alongside the synopsis should also be an excellent, economically written and confident sounding cover letter. This should simply address a well-researched literary agent by name (never put a generic 'Dear Sir/Madam').

In this you should say that you are enclosing a novel called 'X', which is a thriller/ literary/coming-of-age/horror novel (identify genre). It does not matter if this is repeated on the synopsis page. You may also wish to refer to writers you feel you are similar too, although do be careful not to have misplaced arrogance in this. You might say, 'I write in the genre of John Grisham because he is a writer I read and hugely admire' or you might say, 'This is a novel in which *To Kill a Mocking Bird* meets *Crash*' or 'Harper Lee meets J.G. Ballard' – but do be sure that you have the talent to match claims like these. Otherwise, let the agent decide and they will help market you to the publisher, and the publisher will then help market you to the public. If you admire an agent for a particular reason, such as they publish a hero or heroine of yours, let them know.

Biographical note

If you have something interesting to say about yourself, such as that you have won a writing competition or have been published before in relevant publications, do include this briefly in the cover letter. It is for you to judge what is of particular interest about you, and how much to say, but you should also provide a fuller biographical note which sits well at the bottom of the synopsis page. As a guide, this should be 50–200 words. If you have been published, provide a summarised list of publications here. If you have not, or are trying to hide a career you think has gone off track and want to appear fresh, keep it brief and mention what you do, your age and anything that makes you sound interesting. If your career is related to your subject matter, then do say this. For example, 'I worked as a miner for 20 years' if your book is set in a mining community. Avoid listing technical publications as evidence of writing ability if you are submitting fiction. There is an enormous difference between writing technically and writing fiction, and if you don't seem to know this it is not impressive. This is different for non-fiction. As a rule, err on the side of brevity if necessary. If the reader loves your work they will be in touch to find out more about you. For help with learning how to self-market read *Marketing Your Book: An Author's Guide* by Alison Baverstock (A&C Black 2007, 2nd edn).

It should be noted that if the work is literary, there may be less emphasis on plot and more on the quality of the prose. Due to current climates and publishing trends, this is a difficult time to publish literary fiction without strong plots, although things undoubtedly will change.

Non-fiction synopses

A synopsis for a work of non-fiction performs a different function. The consideration of whether a non-fiction book has a potential market is generally more straightforward than for new fiction. In the case of non-fiction you should certainly have carefully researched your market before submission and ideally list the competitors in the field, outlining why your project is different and why you are the writer best positioned to write the book you have. Also, you should be able to list any marketing opportunities you believe your book may have, such as identifiable, or even guaranteed readers such as students if you teach a course, anniversary tie-ins and so on.

A literary agent is often prepared to sell a non-fiction work on synopsis and chapters only. This is an extreme rarity in the case of fiction. This is because it is easier for people to see if there is a gap in the market that can be filled by a non-fiction project, before the work is finished.

You may not need an agent for particular, more niche types of non-fiction book. In these cases publishers may well be prepared to take a direct submission from you. Again, this is because in the area of self-help or business books for example, the publisher of a list will know clearly what its gaps are. The list may have a standard format and you should certainly research this. Contact editors of specialised lists to find out if they have space for your idea, and so that they can let you know exactly how they like work to be presented before forming the project in your mind.

I think it best in general for the non-fiction writer to prepare two different types of proposal. The first would form an initial pitch and the second the follow-up proposal if the editor or literary agent asks to see more. Both documents need to be thoroughly persuasive as these may go directly towards securing a book deal.

Pitching for non-fiction

This should be no more than one or two pages. Include a brief summary (e.g. '*Flying High* is a book about the history of aeronautics' or '*My Name was Glory* is the biography of

Amanda Flemming, maid to Queen Gertrude and unknown holder of the Secret Chalice') and a description of the book content, with an argument for why it should be published now and why you are qualified to write it. Ideally, you should also include an overview of other work in the field, and argue why yours fills an important gap. In addition, you should include a chapter breakdown, giving a provisional title for each chapter with a brief summary (30–75 words, as a guide only) of the contents of each chapter to show how the book is structured throughout. Here also, spell out any ideas you have about how the book might be marketed. As non-fiction markets are more specific than fiction markets, it is useful for the author to let the agent or editor know what hooks there might be to help sell copies. As I have said, if you are lucky enough to have any guaranteed markets, such as students on a course you teach, do of course inform the industry of this.

If you can, estimate a word count for the work. For some pre-formatted non-fiction titles, there will be a word-length you will be expected to hit anyway. You will discover this as you research.

A more in-depth synopsis with sample chapter should include the initial pitch, but with any added material you can muster in terms of promoting your position as author or the book's market chances. Most importantly, in this second, longer pitch you need to show that you can write the book. Provide more in-depth chapter breakdowns (100–150 words each) and 5,000–10,000 words of polished, irresistibly clear and well-written text to show that you are capable of executing your intentions in a winning manner. Write the introduction and the opening chapter, if possible, to really show you mean business. Those two together would usually add up to 5,000–10,000 words.

Conclusion

Whilst it is worth spending time ensuring you have a good, short, confident cover letter and synopsis, it is important to stress that there is nothing as important to an editor than the quality of your writing and your ability to sustain the interest of a reader in the main body of the text. A synopsis is not a magic wand that will influence the real standard of a work. I have seen perfectly polished synopses followed by poor writing. The net result of this is that one feels excited, only to be let down, which is off-putting in itself. If you have the skill to write a gripping synopsis, use your energies wisely in advance of submitting to make sure that the book itself is as good as it can be. Focus, particularly, on fine-tuning the opening 50 pages. Your synopsis and summary should generally serve as a flag to indicate to the reader at what point the extract begins and a guide to the story beyond it. If the agent or publisher likes what they see well enough to ask for more... well done! Oh and good luck.

Rebecca Swift worked as an editor at Virago Press and writer, before co-founding The Literary Consultancy (www.literaryconsultancy.co.uk) with Hannah Griffiths in 1996. She has edited two books for Chatto & Windus, published poetry in *Staple*, *Vintage New Writing* and *Virago New Poets*, written an opera libretto, *Spirit Child*, and *Poetic Lives: Dickinson* (Hesperus Press 2011).

See also...

- *How to get published*, page 115
- *How to get an agent*, page 416
- *Making a successful submission to a literary agent*, page 418
- *Letter to an unsolicited author*, page 421

Book publishers UK and Ireland

*Member of the Publishers Association or Publishing Scotland
†Member of the Irish Book Publishers' Association

AA Publishing

AA Media Ltd, Fanum House, Basing View, Basingstoke, Hants RG21 4EA
tel (01256) 491524 *fax* 0161 488 7544
email aapublish@theaa.com
website www.theAA.com
Directors David Watchus (publisher), Richard Firth (production), Steve Wing (mapping & digital services), Terry Lee (sales & marketing)

Atlases, maps, leisure interests, travel including *Essential Guides*, *Spiral Guides*, *City Packs* and *Key Guides*. Founded 1979.

Abacus – see Little, Brown Book Group

Absolute Classics – see Oberon Books

Absolute Press – see Bloomsbury Publishing Plc

Academic Press – see Elsevier Ltd

Acorn Editions – see James Clarke & Co. Ltd

Addison-Wesley – see Pearson UK

Adlard Coles Nautical – see Bloomsbury Children's & Educational Division, Bloomsbury Publishing

Age UK

(formerly Age Concern Books)
Freepost (SWB 30375), Ashburton, Devon TQ13 7ZZ
tel 020-8765 7200 *fax* 020-8765 7211
website www.ageuk.org.uk
Commissioning Editor Peter Hooper

Age UK works with and for older people. Founded 1973.

Airlife Publishing – see The Crowood Press

Ian Allan Publishing Ltd

Riverdene Business Park, Molesey Road, Hersham, Surrey KT12 4RG
tel (01932) 266600 *fax* (01932) 266601
email info@ianallanpublishing.co.uk
website www.ianallanpublishing.com
Publishing Manager Nick Grant

Transport: railways, aircraft, shipping, road; naval, military and social history; reference books and magazines; sport and cycling guides; popular culture.

Classic Publications (imprint)
Military aviation.

Lewis Masonic (imprint)
Freemasonry.

Midland Publishing (imprint)
Transport: civil and military aviation.

Oxford Publishing Company (imprint)
Transport: railways, road.

Philip Allan – see Hodder Education Group

George Allen & Unwin Publishers – acquired by HarperCollins Publishers

J.A. Allen

Clerkenwell House, 45–47 Clerkenwell Green, London EC1R 0HT
tel 020-7251 2661 *fax* 020-7490 4958
email allen@halebooks.com
website www.allenbooks.co.uk
Publisher Lesley Gowers

Horse care and equestrianism including breeding, racing, polo, jumping, eventing, dressage, management, carriage driving, breeds, horse industry training, veterinary and farriery. Books usually commissioned but willing to consider any serious, specialist MSS on the horse and related subjects. Imprint of Robert Hale Ltd (page 144). Founded 1926.

Allen Lane – see Penguin Group (UK)

Allison & Busby Ltd

13 Charlotte Mews, London W1T 4EJ
tel 020-7580 1080 *fax* 020-7580 1180
email susie@allisonandbusby.com
website www.allisonandbusby.com
Publishing Director Susie Dunlop, *Sales & Digital Manager* Lesley Crooks

Fiction, general non-fiction, young adult. No unsolicited MSS accepted.

Allyn & Bacon – see Pearson UK

Alma Books

London House, 243–253 Lower Mortlake Road, Richmond, Surrey TW9 2LL
tel 020-8948 9550 *fax* 020-8948 5599
website www.almabooks.co.uk
Directors Alessandro Gallenzi, Elisabetta Minervini

Contemporary literary fiction, non-fiction, classics, poetry, drama. Around 60% English-language originals, 40% translations. No unsolicited MSS by email. Founded 2005.

Alma Classics

243–253 Lower Mortlake Road, Richmond, Surrey TW9 2LL
tel 020-8948 9547 *fax* 020-8948 5599
email agallenzi@almabooks.com
website www.almaclassics.com
Managing Director Alessandro Gallenzi

European, international and British fiction and plays, art, literary, music and social criticism, biography and autobiography, essays, humanities and social sciences, European classics. No unsolicited MSS. Inquiry letters must include a sae. Series include: *English National Opera Guides, New Writing and Writers.* Founded 2007.

The Alpha Press – see Sussex Academic Press

Amberley Publishing

The Hill, Stroud, Glos. GL5 4EP
tel (01453) 847800
website www.amberley-books.com
Chief Executive Alan Mabley, *Publishing Director* Jonathan Reeve, *Sales Manager* Stephen Lambe

General history and local interest; specialisations include biography, military history and transport history (railways, canals, maritime). Founded 2008.

Amgueddfa Cymru – National Museum Wales

Cathays Park, Cardiff CF10 3NP
tel 029-2057 3155 *fax* 029-2057 3321
email books@museumwales.ac.uk
website www.museumwales.ac.uk
Head of Publishing Mari Gordon

Books based on the collections and research of Amgueddfa Cymru for adults, schools and children, in both Welsh and English.

Andersen Press Ltd

20 Vauxhall Bridge Road, London SW1V 2SA
tel 020-7840 8703 (editorial), 020-7840 8701 (general) *fax* 020-7233 6263
email andersenpress@randomhouse.co.uk
website www.andersenpress.co.uk
Managing Director/Publisher Klaus Flugge, *Directors* Philip Durrance, Joëlle Flugge, Rona Selby (editorial picture books), Charlie Sheppard (editorial fiction), Clare Simms (publicity), Sarah Pakenham (rights), Mark Hendle (finance)

Children's books: picture books, junior and teenage fiction (send synopsis and first 3 chapters with sae); no short stories or poetry. International co-productions. Founded 1976.

The Angels' Share – see Neil Wilson Publishing Ltd

Anness Publishing

Head office, Blaby Road, Wigston, Leicester LE8 4SE
tel 0116 275 9086 *fax* 0116 275 9090
email info@anness.com
website www.annesspublishing.com, www.lorenzbooks.com, www.southwaterbooks.com
Managing Director Paul Anness, *Publisher* Joanna Lorenz

Practical illustrated books on lifestyle, cookery, crafts, reference, gardening, health and children's non-fiction. Founded 1988.

Anness Publishing

website www.annesspublishing.com

High-quality illustrated non-fiction: lifestyle, cookery, crafts, gardening.

Lorenz Books (hardback imprint)

website www.lorenzbooks.com

High-quality illustrated non-fiction: lifestyle, cookery, crafts, gardening.

Aquamarine (hardback imprint)

website www.aquamarinebooks.com

Lifestyle, cookery, crafts and gardening.

Southwater (paperback imprint)

website www.southwaterbooks.com

Illustrated promotional books on practical subjects.

Hermes House (promotional imprint)

website www.hermeshouse.com

Photolibrary of over 400,000 images generated in the process of developing 3,000 titles in the past 20 years.

Practical Pictures (image licensing)

website www.practicalpictures.com

Anova Books

The Old Magistrate's Court, 10 Southcombe Street, London W14 0RA
tel 020-7605 1400 *fax* 020-7605 1401
email customerservices@anovabooks.com
website www.anovabooks.com
Chairman Robin Wood, *Chief Executive* Polly Powell, *Operations & Production Director* David Proffit

Founded 2005; formerly Chrysalis Books Group.

Batsford (imprint)

Publisher Tina Persaud

Chess and bridge, art techniques, film, fashion and costume, practical craft, design, embroidery, heritage, woodwork.

Collins & Brown (imprint)

Publisher Katie Cowan

Lifestyle and interiors, cookery, gardening, photography, pet care, health and beauty, hobbies and crafts, including Good Housekeeping branded books.

Conway (inc. Brasseys Military, Putnam Aeronautical)

Publisher John Lee

History and highly illustrated reference books on

naval and maritime, aviation and military subjects, exploration, hobbies.

National Trust (imprint)
Acting Publisher Cathy Gosling
Heritage, gardens, cookery.

Pavilion (imprint)
Editorial Director Fiona Holman
Cookery, gardening, travel, wine, photography, art, popular culture, gift.

Portico (imprint)
Publisher Katie Cowan
Humour, popular culture, quirky reference, sport.

Robson Books (imprint)
General non-fiction, biography, music, humour, sport.

Salamander (imprint)
Packager of made-to-order books on cookery, crafts, military, natural history, music, gardening, hobbies, transport, sports, popular reference.

Anova Children's Books – see Pavilion Children's Books

Antique Collectors' Club Ltd

Sandy Lane, Old Martlesham, Woodbridge, Suffolk IP12 4SD
tel (01394) 389950 *fax* (01394) 389999
email info@antique-acc.com
website www.antiquecollectorsclub.com
Managing Director Diana Steel

Fine art, antiques, fashion, design, gardening and garden history, architecture. Founded 1966.

Anvil Press Poetry

Neptune House, 70 Royal Hill, London SE10 8RF
tel 020-8469 3033
email anvil@anvilpresspoetry.com
website www.anvilpresspoetry.com
Director Peter Jay

Poetry. Submissions only by post with sae. Enquire whether accepting submissions. Founded 1968.

Appletree Press Ltd†

The Old Potato Station, 14 Howard Street South, Belfast BT7 1AP
tel 028-9024 3074 *fax* 028-9024 6756
email reception@appletree.ie
website www.appletree.ie
Director John Murphy

Gift books, guidebooks, history, Irish interest, Scottish interest, photography, sport, travel. Founded 1974.

Aquamarine – see Anness Publishing

Aradia Books Ltd

15–16 Nassau Street, London W1W 7AB
tel 020-7436 9898
email info@arcadiabooks.co.uk
website www.arcadiabooks.co.uk
Publisher Gary Pulsifer, *Associate Publisher* Daniela de Groote, *Managing Editor* Angeline Rothermundt

Original fiction, fiction in translation, autobiography, biography, travel, gender studies, gay books. Publishers of José Eduardo Agualusa's *The Book of Chameleons*, winner of the Independent Foreign Fiction Prize 2007 and Dominique Manotti's *Lorraine Connection*, winner of the International Dagger 2008. Submissions via literary agents only. Founded 1996.

BlackAmber (imprint)
Black and Asian writing.

Bliss Books (imprint)
Popular fiction and non-fiction.

Euro Crime (imprint)
Quality crime from Europe.

The Maia Press (imprint)
Début fiction both in English and in translation.

Arc Publications

Nanholme Mill, Shaw Wood Road, Todmorden, Lancs. OL14 6DA
tel (01706) 812338 *fax* (01706) 818948
email arc.publications@btconnect.com
website www.arcpublications.co.uk
Directors Tony Ward, Angela Jarman, *Editors* John Kinsella (international), Jean Boase-Beier (translation), John W. Clarke (UK & Ireland), Angela Jarman (music)

Specialises in contemporary poetry and neglected work from the past: poetry from the UK and Ireland; world poetry in English; and bilingual translations (individual poets and anthologies). Refer to website for current publication list/catalogue and submissions policy. No unsolicited MSS.

Architectural Press – see Elsevier Ltd

Arcturus – see W. Foulsham & Co. Ltd

Arden Shakespeare – see Bloomsbury Academic & Professional Division, Bloomsbury Publishing

The Armchair Traveller *at the* bookHaus Ltd

70 Cadogan Place, London SW1X 9AH
tel 020-7838 9055
email info@hauspublishing.com
website www.thearmchairtraveller.com
Publisher Barbara Schwepcke

Publishes travel literature, travel guides and the *Traveller's History Series*.

Arrow Books Ltd – see The Random House Group Ltd

Ashgate Publishing Ltd

Wey Court East, Union Road, Farnham GU9 9PT
tel (01252) 736600 *fax* (01252) 736736

email info@ashgatepub.co.uk
website www.ashgate.com
Chairman Nigel Farrow, *Managing Director & Humanities Publishing Director* Rachel Lynch, *Social Sciences Publishing Director & President Ashgate US* Barbara Church
Humanities Ann Donahue (literary studies, 19th–20th centuries), Erika Gaffney (literary studies to 18th century; visual studies), Heidi Bishop (music), Sarah Lloyd (theology & religious studies), Thomas Gray (history), John Smedley (Publishing Director, Variorum imprint; history)
Social Sciences Alison Kirk (law), Guy Loft (aviation), Kirstin Howgate (international relations; politics), Val Rose (human geography; planning & design), Neil Jordan (sociology), Dymphna Evans (Publisher, reference and LIM)

Publishes a wide range of academic research in the social sciences and humanities, professional practice publications in the management of business and public services, and illustrated books on art, architecture and design. Founded 1967.

Gower (imprint)
website www.gowerpub.com
Publishing Director & Commissioning Editor Jonathan Norman
Business, management and training.

Lund Humphries (imprint)
website www.lundhumphries.com
Managing Director Lucy Myers
Art and architectural history.

Variorum (imprint)
Publishing Director John Smedley
History.

Ashmolean Museum Publications

Beaumont Street, Oxford OX1 2PH
tel (01865) 278010 *fax* (01865) 88070
website www.ashmolean.org
Contact Declan McCarthy

Fine and applied art of Europe and Asia, archaeology, history, numismatics. No unsolicited MSS. Photographic archive. Museum founded 1683.

Aslib (The Association for Information Management)

Howard House, Wagon Lane, Bingley BD16 1WA
tel (01274) 777700 *fax* (01274) 785201
email furtherinformation@aslib.com
website www.aslib.com

For books and journals contact Emerald *tel* (01206) 796351; for *Managing Information* magazine contact Graham Coult (editor), gcoult@aslib.com.

Atlantic Books

Ormond House, 26–27 Boswell Street, London WC1N 3JZ
tel 020-7269 1610 *fax* 020-7430 0916
email enquiries@atlanticbooks.co.uk
Ceo & Publisher Toby Mundy, *Editor-in-Chief* Ravi Mirchandani

Literary fiction, thrillers; history, current affairs, politics, reference, biography, memoir. Strictly no unsolicited submissions or proposals. Founded 2000.

Atlantic Europe Publishing Co. Ltd

Greys Court Farm, Greys Court, Henley-on-Thames, Oxon RG9 4PG
tel (01491) 628188 *fax* (01491) 628189
email info@atlanticeurope.com
website www.atlanticeurope.com, www.curriculumvisions.com
Director Dr B.J. Knapp

Children's primary school class books: science, geography, technology, mathematics, history, religious education. No MSS accepted by post; submit by email only with no attachments. Founded 1990.

Atom – see Little, Brown Book Group

Atrium – see Cork University Press

Attic Press – see Cork University Press

AudioGO Ltd

St James House, The Square, Lower Bristol Road, Bath BA2 3BH
tel (01225) 878000
website www.audiogo.co.uk
Directors Mike Bowen (managing), Jan Paterson (publishing)

Large print books and complete and unabridged audiobooks: general fiction, crime, romance, mystery/thrillers, westerns, non-fiction. Does not publish original books. Imprints include BBC Radio Collection, Cover to Cover Classics, BBC Cover to Cover, Chivers Audiobooks, Chivers Children's Audiobooks. Founded 2010 following the sale of BBC Audiobooks.

Aureus Publishing Ltd

Castle Court, Castle-upon-Alun, St Bride's Major, Vale of Glamorgan CF32 0TN
tel (01656) 880033 *fax* (01656) 880033
email info@aureus.co.uk
website www.aureus.co.uk
Director Meuryn Hughes

Rock and pop, autobiography, biography, sport; also music. Founded 1993.

Aurora Metro

67 Grove Avenue, Twickenham TW1 4HX
tel 020-3261 0000 *fax* 020-8898 0735
email info@aurorametro.com
website www.aurorametro.com
Director Rebecca Gillieron

Adult fiction, young adult fiction, biography, drama (including plays for young people), non-fiction, culture, cookery and translation. Submissions: send synopsis and 3 chapters as hard copy to: Neil Gregory, Submissions Editor at address above. Biennial Competition for women novelists, The Virginia Prize For Fiction. New imprint: Supernova Books.

Aurum Press Ltd

7 Greenland Street, London NW1 0ND
tel 020-7284 7160 *fax* 020-7485 4902
email [firstname.lastname]@aurumpress.co.uk
website www.aurumpress.co.uk
Directors David Graham (managing), Laurence Orbach, Mick Mousley

General adult non-fiction, illustrated and non-illustrated: history, sport, entertainment. Imprints: Argentum (photography), Jacqui Small (lifestyle), Union Books (literary non-fiction). Founded 1977.

Authentic Media Ltd

52 Presley Way, Milton Keynes MK8 0ES
tel (01908) 268500
email info@authenticmedia.co.uk
website www.authenticmedia.co.uk
Publisher Claire Ashurst

Biblical studies, Christian theology, ethics, history, mission, commentaries. Imprints: Paternoster, Authentic.

Avon – see HarperCollins Publishers

Award Publications Ltd

The Old Riding School, The Welbeck Estate, Worksop, Notts. S80 3LR
tel (01909) 478170 *fax* (01909) 484632
email info@awardpublications.co.uk

Children's books: full colour picture story books; early learning, information and activity books. No unsolicited material. Founded 1954.

Bernard Babani (publishing) Ltd

The Grampians, Shepherds Bush Road, London W6 7NF
tel 020-7603 2581/7296 *fax* 020-7603 8203
Director M.H. Babani

Practical handbooks on radio, electronics and computing.

Bailliere Tindall – see Elsevier Ltd (Health Sciences)

Duncan Baird Publishers

6th Floor, Castle House, 75–76 Wells Street, London W1T 3QH
tel 020-7323 2229 *fax* 020-7580 5692
website www.dbp.co.uk
Directors Duncan Baird (managing), Bob Saxton (editorial), Roger Walton (art), Severine Jeauneau (international sales), Vicky Pulley (financial), Anna Randall (UK sales)

Health and wellbeing, cookery, Mind, Body & Spirit, cultural reference. Founded 1992.

Bantam – see Transworld Publishers

Bantam Press – see Transworld Publishers

Bantam Press (children's) – see The Random House Group Ltd

Barefoot Books Ltd

294 Banbury Road, Oxford OX2 7ED
tel (01865) 3111000 *fax* (01865) 514965
email info@barefootbooks.co.uk
website www.barefootbooks.com/uk
Owner, Co-founder & Ceo Nancy Traversy, *Co-founder & Editor-in-Chief* Tessa Strickland, *Group Operations Director* Karen Janson

Children's picture books, apps and audiobooks: myth, legend, fairytale, cross-cultural stories. See website for submission guidelines. Founded 1993.

Barrington Stoke*

18 Walker Street, Edinburgh EH3 7LP
tel 0131 225 4113 *fax* 0131 225 4140
email info@barringtonstoke.co.uk
website www.barringtonstoke.co.uk
Chairman Ben Thomson, *Managing Director* Mairi Kidd, *Editor* Vicki Rutherford

Short fiction and non-fiction, specially adapted and presented for reluctant, struggling and dyslexic readers, aged 9–12 and 13+, with reading ages of 6–8. Short fiction (15,000 words) for adults with a reading age of 8. No picture books, no unsolicited submissions. Founded 1998.

Batsford – see Anova Books

BBC Audiobooks Ltd – see AudioGO Ltd

BBC Books – see The Random House Group Ltd

BBC Children's Books – see Penguin Group (UK)

BBC Worldwide Ltd – see page 382

Belair – see Folens Publishers

Bell & Hyman Ltd – acquired by HarperCollins Publishers

Berg Publishers – see Bloomsbury Publishing Plc

Berlin Academic – see Bloomsbury Academic & Professional Division, Bloomsbury Publishing

Berlin Verlag – see Bloomsbury Children's & Educational Division, Bloomsbury Publishing

Berlitz Publishing – see Insight Guides/Berlitz Publishing

BFI Publishing

Palgrave Macmillan, The Macmillan Building,
4 Crinan Street, London N1 9XW
tel 020-7833 4000
email bfipublishing@palgrave.com
website www.palgrave.com/bfi
Head of Publishing Rebecca Barden

Film, TV and media studies; general, academic and educational resources on moving image culture. Founded 1982.

BIOS Scientific Publishers – see Taylor and Francis Group

Birlinn Ltd

West Newington House, 10 Newington Road,
Edinburgh EH9 1QS
tel 0131 668 4371 *fax* 0131 668 4466
email info@birlinn.co.uk
website www.birlinn.co.uk
Directors Hugh Andrew, Neville Moir, William MacRobert, Jan Rutherford, Maria White

Scottish history, local interest/history, Scottish humour, guides, military, adventure, history, archaeology, sport, general non-fiction. Imprints: John Donald, Polygon. Founded 1992.

Polygon (imprint)

New international and Scottish fiction, poetry, short stories, popular Scottish and international general interest. No unsolicited poetry accepted.

John Donald (imprint)

Scottish academic titles.

Mercat Press (imprint)

Walking guides.

Birnbaum – see HarperCollins Publishers

A&C Black – see Bloomsbury Children's & Educational Division, Bloomsbury Publishing

Black Ace Books

PO Box 7547, Perth PH2 1AU
tel (01821) 642822 *fax* (01821) 642101
website www.blackacebooks.com
Publisher Hunter Steele, *Art, Publicity & Sales Director* Boo Wood

Fiction, Scottish and general; new editions of outstanding recent fiction. Some biography, history, psychology and philosophy. No submissions without first visiting website for latest list details and requirements. Imprints: Black Ace Books, Black Ace Paperbacks. Founded 1991.

Black & White Publishing Ltd*

29 Ocean Drive, Edinburgh EH6 6JL
tel 0131 625 4500 *fax* 0131 625 4501
email mail@blackandwhitepublishing.com
website www.blackandwhitepublishing.com
Directors Campbell Brown (managing), Alison McBride

Non-fiction: humour, biography, crime, sport, cookery, general. Fiction: classic Scottish, contemporary, crime, young adult (15+). Founded 1999.

Black Dagger Crime – see AudioGO Ltd

Black Dog Publishing London UK

10A Acton Street, London WC1X 9NG
tel 020-7713 5097 *fax* 020-7713 8682
email editorial@blackdogonline.com
website www.blackdogonline.com

Contemporary art, architecture, design, photography.

Black Lace – see Virgin Books (imprint, in partnership with Virgin Group), page 168

Black Swan – see Transworld Publishers

BlackAmber – see Aradia Books Ltd

Blackline Press

15 Lister Road, Ipswich IP1 5EQ
email info@blacklinepress.com
website www.blacklinepress.com
Proprietor Matt Smith

Specialises in football titles. Established 2009.

Blackstaff Press Ltd†

4C Heron Wharf, Sydenham Business Park,
Belfast BT3 9LE
tel 028-9045 5006 *fax* 028-9046 6237
email info@blackstaffpress.com
website www.blackstaffpress.com
Managing Editor Patsy Horton

Adult fiction, biography, history, memoir, sport, politics, cookery, natural history, humour and travel. See website for submission guidelines before sending material. Founded 1971.

Blackstone Press Ltd – acquired by Oxford University Press

Blackwater Press – see Folens Publishers

John Blake Publishing Ltd

(incorporating Metro Books and Smith Gryphon Ltd)
3 Bramber Court, 2 Bramber Road,
London W14 9PB
tel 020-7381 0666 *fax* 020-7381 6868

email words@blake.co.uk
website www.johnblakepublishing.co.uk

Popular non-fiction, including biographies, true crime, food and drink, health. No unsolicited fiction. Founded 1991.

Bliss Books – see Aradia Books Ltd

Bloodaxe Books Ltd

Highgreen, Tarset, Northumberland NE48 1RP
tel (01434) 240500 *fax* (01434) 240505
email editor@bloodaxebooks.com
website www.bloodaxebooks.com
Directors Neil Astley, Simon Thirsk

Poetry. Send sample of up to a dozen poems with sae. No email submissions or correspondence. No disks. Founded 1978.

Bloomsbury Publishing Plc*

50 Bedford Square, London WC1B 3DP
tel 020-7631 5600
website www.bloomsbury.com
Founder & Chief Executive Nigel Newton, *Executive Director* Richard Charkin, *Group Finance Director* Wendy Pallot, *Non-executive Chairman* Jeremy Wilson, *Non-executive Directors* Ian Cormack, Sarah Jane Thomson, *Company Secretary* Michael Daykin *Media enquiries* Katie Bond, Publicity Director, *tel* 020-7631 5670, *email* publicity@bloomsbury.com

Independent publicly quoted publishing house with 4 worldwide publishing divisions: Bloomsbury Adult, Bloomsbury Children's & Educational, Bloomsbury Academic & Professional and Bloomsbury Information. Offices in the UK, the USA (see page 194) and Australia (see page 183). No unsolicited MSS unless specified below. Founded 1986.

Absolute Press

Scarborough House, 29 James Street West, Bath BA1 2BT
tel (01225) 316013 *fax* (01225) 445836
email office@absolutepress.co.uk
website www.absolutepress.co.uk
Publisher Jon Croft, *Directors* Meg Avent (editorial), Matt Inwood (art)
Specialist food imprint: cookery, food-related topics, wine, lifestyle. No unsolicited MSS. Founded 1979.

Bloomsbury Adult Division

Managing Director Richard Charkin, *Group Editor-in-Chief* Alexandra Pringle
Worldwide publisher for fiction authors including Margaret Atwood, Nadine Gordimer, William Boyd, Richard Ford, Howard Jacobson, Donna Tartt. Non-fiction categories include biography/memoir, politics, science, history, philosophy and religion and also cookery, as well as reference books such as *Who's Who, Wisden Cricketers' Almanack* and *Reeds Nautical Almanac.* Market leaders in natural history, nautical and sports and fitness publishing, plus scholarly current affairs and religious titles.

Bloomsbury Children's & Educational Division

Managing Director Emma Hopkin, *Fiction Publishing Director and Editor-in-Chief* Rebecca McNally, *Nonfiction & Education Publishing Director* Jayne Parsons, *Editorial Director Illustrated Publishing* Emma Blackburn; Children's – *Deputy Editorial Director* Emma Mathewson, *Commissioning Editor* Ele Fountain Educational – *Commissioning Editors* Kate Paice (fiction), Helen Diamond (educational resources), Saskia Gwinn (non-fiction), Sheena Hodge (music) Imprints include A&C Black, Andrew Brodie, Featherstone Education, Continuum Education
Children's. Worldwide publisher for readers of all ages up to 18 years including *Harry Potter* series by J.K. Rowling. No unsolicited MSS; send a synopsis with 3 chapters.
Educational. Publishes around 80 titles per year for readers aged 4–14 including non-fiction, poetry and fiction. Publishes around 100 titles per year for teachers and practitioners in the areas of early years, music, teachers resources and professional development.

Bloomsbury Academic & Professional Division

website www.bloomsburyprofessional.com, www.bloomsburyacademic.com
Managing Director Jonathan Glasspool, *Publishing contacts* Martin Casimir (Bloomsbury Professional: law, tax & accountancy), Kathryn Earle (Berg Publishing, Fairchild Books & visual arts publishing), Jenny Ridout (drama, media & theatre studies), Anna Fleming (education, literary studies & linguistics), Jan-Peter Wissink (theology & biblical studies), Sarah Campbell (philosophy & religious studies), Frances Arnold (history), Charlotte Loveridge (Bristol Classical Press), Dr David Barker (politics, media studies & sound studies).
Publishes over 1,000 academic and professional titles, textbooks and print and digital reference works. Typical customers include students, scholars, schools, universities/other higher education establishments and professional firms. Imprints: Bloomsbury Academic, Bloomsbury Professional, Arden Shakespeare, Berg Publishers, Bristol Classical Press Continuum, Fairchild Books, Methuen Drama, T&T Clark.

Berg Publishers

50 Bedford Square, London WC1B 3DP
tel 020-7631 5600
website www.bergpublishers.com, www.bloomsbury.com
Non-fiction, reference (fashion studies, design studies, food studies, cultural studies, visual culture, social anthropology, film studies), poetry, music. Publishes approx. 180 titles each year. Imprint of Bloomsbury Academic & Professional division. Founded 1983.

Bloomsbury Information Division

website www.qfinance.com, www.bqfp.com.qa, www.qscience.com

Managing Director Kathy Rooney

Publishes approx. 60 titles annually in business, finance, language, crosswords, genealogy, reference and dictionaries. Also develops major information databases with external partners which are published in both digital and print.The division is responsible for Bloomsbury's business relationships with external partners such as the Qatar Foundation.

The Continuum International Publishing Group Ltd
50 Bedford Square, London WC1B 3DP
tel 020-7631 5600
website www.continuumbooks.com

Acquired by Bloomsbury Publishing Plc during 2011. Serious non-fiction, academic and professional, including scholarly monographs and educational texts and reference works in education, film, history, linguistics, literary studies, media studies, music, philosophy, politics; and in biblical studies, religious studies and theology. Imprints: Burns & Oates, Continuum, Network Continuum, T&T Clark International, Thoemmes Press, Mowbray.

Bloomsbury Verlag GmbH
Sold by Bloomsbury in April 2012.

Blue Guides Ltd

27 John Street, London WC1N 2BX
email editorial@blueguides.com
website www.blueguides.com

Blue Guides (cultural travel guidebooks), *Visible Cities* and *art/shop/eat* series.

BMJ Books – see Wiley-Blackwell

Boatswain Press Ltd – now Nautical Data Ltd

Bodleian Library Publishing

Osney One Building, Osney Mead, Oxford OX2 0EW
tel (01865) 283850 *fax* (01865) 277620
email publishing@bodleian.ox.ac.uk
website www.bodleianbookshop.co.uk
Head of Publishing Samuel Fanous

The Bodleian Library is the main library of the University of Oxford. The publishing programme creates trade and scholarly books on a wide range of subjects drawn from or related to the Library's rich collection of rare books, manuscripts, maps, postcards and other ephemera. Founded 1602.

The Bodley Head – see The Random House Group Ltd

Booth-Clibborn Editions

Studio 83, 235 Earls Court Road, London SW5 9FE
tel 020-7565 0688 *fax* 020-7244 1018
email info@booth-clibborn.com
website www.booth-clibborn.com

Illustrated books on art, popular culture, graphic design, photography. Founded 1974.

Bounty – see Octopus Publishing Group

Bowker

18–20 St Andrew's House, St Andrew Street, London EC4A 3AG
tel 020-7832 1770 *fax* 020-7832 1710
email sales@bowker.co.uk
website www.bowker.co.uk
Managing Director Doug McMillan

Publishes bibliographic information and management solutions designed to help publishers, booksellers and libraries better serve their customers. Creates products and services that make books easier for people to discover, evaluate, order and experience. Also generates research and resources for publishers, helping them understand and meet the interests of readers worldwide. Bowker, an affiliated business of ProQuest and the official ISBN agency for the US is headquartered in New Providence, New Jersey, with additional operations in the UK and Australia.

Boxtree – see Macmillan Publishers Ltd

Marion Boyars Publishers Ltd

26 Parke Road, London SW13 9NG
email catheryn@marionboyars.com
website www.marionboyars.co.uk
Director Catheryn Kilgarriff

Literary fiction, film, cultural studies, jazz, cookery. Not currently accepting submissions. Founded 1975.

Boydell & Brewer Ltd

Whitwell House, St Audrey's Park Road, Melton, Woodbridge, Suffolk IP12 1SY
tel (01394) 610600 *fax* (01394) 610316
email editorial@boydell.co.uk
website www.boydellandbrewer.com

Medieval studies, early modern and modern history, maritime history, literature, archaeology, art history, music, Hispanic studies. No unsolicited MSS. See website for submission guidelines. Founded 1969.

James Currey (imprint)
website www.jamescurrey.com

Academic studies of Africa and developing economies.

Bradt Travel Guides Ltd

23 High Street, Chalfont St Peter, Bucks. SL9 9QE
tel (01753) 893444 *fax* (01753) 892333
email info@bradtguides.com
website www.bradtguides.com
Publishing Director Adrian Phillips

Travel and wildlife guides with emphasis on unusual destinations and ethical/positive travel.

Brandon/Mount Eagle Publications†

(incorporating Brandon Book Publishers Ltd, 1982)
Cooleen, Dingle, Co. Kerry, Republic of Ireland
tel +353 (0)66 9151463 *fax* +353 (0)66 9151234
Publisher Steve MacDonogh

Fiction, biography, current affairs. No unsolicited MSS.

Books

Brasseys Military – see Anova Books

Nicholas Brealey Publishing

3–5 Spafield Street, London EC1R 4QB
tel 020-7239 0360 *fax* 020-7239 0370
email rights@nicholasbrealey.com
website www.nicholasbrealey.com
Managing Director Nicholas Brealey

Publishes subjects related to coaching, crossing cultures and the big ideas in business. Also popular psychology, science and philosophy, and includes an expanding travel writing/adventure list. Founded 1992 in London; also has offices in Boston.

Breedon Books Publishing Co. Ltd – see The Derby Books Publishing Company Ltd

Brilliant Publications

Unit 10, Sparrow Hall Farm, Edlesborough, Dunstable LU6 2ES
tel (01525) 222292 *fax* (01525) 222720
email info@brilliantpublications.co.uk
website www.brilliantpublications.co.uk
Managing Director Priscilla Hannaford

Practical resource books for teachers and others concerned with the education of children 0–13 years. All areas of the curriculum published, but specialises in modern foreign languages, art and design, developing thinking skills and PSHE. Some series of books for reluctant readers, aimed at children 7–11 years. No children's picture books, non-fiction books or one-off fiction books. See 'Manuscripts guidelines' on website before sending proposal. Founded 1993.

Bristol Classical Press – see Bloomsbury Academic & Professional Division, Bloomsbury Publishing

The British Library (Publications)*

Publishing Office, The British Library, 96 Euston Road, London NW1 2DB
tel 020-7412 7535 *fax* 020-7412 7768
email publishing_editorial@bl.uk
website www.bl.uk
Managers David Way (publishing), Lara Speicher (editorial)

Book arts, bibliography, music, maps, oriental, manuscript studies, history, literature, facsimiles, audio and multimedia. Founded 1979.

British Museum Company Ltd*

38 Russell Square, London WC1B 3QQ
tel 020-7323 1234 *fax* 020-7436 7315
email publicity@britishmuseum.co.uk
website www.britishmuseum.co.uk
Managing Director Brian Oldman, *Director of Publishing* Rosemary Bradley

General and specialist adult and children's books on art history, archaeology, history and world cultures. Division of The British Museum Company Ltd. Founded 1973.

Brockhampton Press – see Caxton Publishing Group

Andrew Brodie – see Bloomsbury Children's & Educational Division, Bloomsbury Publishing

Brown, Son & Ferguson, Ltd*

4–10 Darnley Street, Glasgow G41 2SD
tel 0141 429 1234 (24 hours) *fax* 0141 420 1694
email info@skipper.co.uk
website www.skipper.co.uk
Editorial Director Richard B.P. Brown

Nautical books, plays. Founded 1860.

Bryntirion Press

(formerly Evangelical Press of Wales)
Bryntirion, Bridgend CF31 4DX
tel (01656) 655886 *fax* (01656) 665919
email office@emw.org.uk
website www.emw.org.uk
Publications Officer Shâron Barnes

Theology and religion (in English and Welsh). Founded 1955.

Burns & Oates – see Bloomsbury Academic & Professional Division

Business Plus – see Headline Publishing Group

Buster Books – see Michael O'Mara Books Ltd

Butterworth-Heinemann – see Elsevier Ltd

Butterworths – see LexisNexis

Cadogan Guides – see New Holland Publishers (UK) Ltd

Calmann & King Ltd – see Laurence King Publishing Ltd

Cambridge University Press*

The Edinburgh Building, Shaftesbury Road, Cambridge CB2 8RU
tel (01223) 312393 *fax* (01223) 315052
email information@cambridge.org
website www.cambridge.org
Chief Operating Officer Peter Phillips, *Managing Director, Academic Publishing* Richard Fisher, *Managing Director, ELT* Michael Peluse, *Managing Director*, Hanri Pieterse

Anthropology and archaeology, art history, astronomy, biological sciences, classical studies, computer science, dictionaries, earth sciences, economics, educational (primary, secondary, tertiary), e-learning products, engineering, ELT, history, language and literature, law, mathematics, medical sciences, music, philosophy, physical sciences, politics, psychology, reference, technology, social sciences, theology, religion. Journals (humanities, social sciences, science, technical and medical). The Bible and Prayer Book. Founded 1534.

Campbell Books – see Macmillan Publishers Ltd

Canongate Books Ltd*

14 High Street, Edinburgh EH1 1TE
tel 0131 557 5111 *fax* 0131 557 5211
email info@canongate.co.uk
website www.canongate.net
Publisher Jamie Byng, *Directors* Douglas Doig (financial), Caroline Gorham (production), Jenny Todd (sales & marketing), Polly Collingridge (rights), Anya Serota (publishing), Nick Davies (non-fiction), Victoria Williams (audio publishing), *Senior Editor* Francis Bickmore (fiction).

Adult general non-fiction and fiction: literary fiction, translated fiction, memoir, politics, pop science, humour, travel, popular culture, history and biography. No unsolicited MSS. The independent audio publisher CSA WORD was acquired by Canongate in 2010, with audio now published under the Canongate label. Founded 1973.

Canopus Publishing Ltd

15 Nelson Parade, Bedminster, Bristol BS3 4HY
tel 0117 963 3366
email robin@canopusbooks.com
website www.canopusbooks.com
Directors Robin Rees, Tom Spicer, *Commissioning Editor* Jim Revill

Popular science and astronomy. Founded 1999.

Canterbury Press – see SCM Canterbury Press Ltd

Jonathan Cape – see The Random House Group Ltd

Jonathan Cape Children's Books – see The Random House Group Ltd

Capuchin Classics – see Stacey International

Carcanet Press Ltd

4th Floor, Alliance House, 30 Cross Street, Manchester M2 7AQ
tel 0161 834 8730 *fax* 0161 832 0084
email info@carcanet.co.uk
website www.carcanet.co.uk
Director Michael Schmidt

Poetry, *Fyfield* series, Oxford Poets, translations. Founded 1969.

Carlton Publishing Group

20 Mortimer Street, London W1T 3JW
tel 020-7612 0400 *fax* 020-7612 0401
email enquiries@carltonbooks.co.uk
website www.carltonbooks.co.uk
Chairman Jonathan Goodman, *Editorial Director* Piers Murray Hill

No unsolicited MSS; synopses and ideas welcome, but no fiction or poetry. Imprints: Carlton Books, André Deutsch, Goodman, Prion Books. Founded 1992.

Carlton Books (division)

Sport, music, history, military history, puzzles, lifestyle, fashion, popular culture, crime, children's interactive.

André Deutsch (division)

Autobiography, biography, history, current affairs.

Goodman (imprint)

Art and design.

Prion Books (division)

Humour, nostalgia.

Cassell Illustrated – see Octopus Publishing Group

Cassell Reference – see Weidenfeld & Nicolson

Caterpillar Books – see Magi Publications

Catholic Truth Society

40–46 Harleyford Road, London SE11 5AY
tel 020-7640 0042 *fax* 020-7640 0046
email info@cts-online.org.uk
website www.cts-online.org.uk
Chairman Rt Rev. Paul Hendricks, *General Secretary* Fergal Martin LLB, LLM

General books of Roman Catholic and Christian interest, liturgical books, missals, Bibles, prayer books, children's books and booklets of doctrinal, historical, devotional or social interest. MSS of 11,000–15,000 words with up to 6 illustrations considered for publication as booklets. Founded 1868.

Caxton Publishing Group

20 Bloomsbury Street, London WC1B 3JH
tel 020-7636 7171 *fax* 020-7636 1922
website www.caxtonpublishing.com
Director Finbarr McCabe

Reprints, promotional books, remainders. Imprints: Caxton Editions, Brockhampton Press, Knight Paperbacks.

CBD Research Ltd

15 Wickham Road, Beckenham, Kent BR3 5JS
tel 020-8650 7745 *fax* 020-8650 0768
email cbd@cbdresearch.com
website www.cbdresearch.com
Directors S.P.A. Henderson, A.J.W. Henderson

Directories, reference books, bibliographies, guides to business and statistical information. Founded 1961.

Chancery House Press (imprint)
Unusual non-fiction/reference works. Preliminary letter and synopsis with return postage essential.

Cengage Learning

Cheriton House, Andover SP10 5BE
tel (01264) 332424 *fax* (01264) 342745
email emea.editorial@cengage.com
website www.cengage.co.uk
Contact Publishing Director

Actively commissioning texts for further education and higher education courses in the following disciplines: IT, computer science and computer applications; accounting, finance and economics; marketing; international business; human resource management; operations management; strategic management; organisational behaviour; business information systems; quantitative methods; psychology; hairdressing and beauty therapy; childcare; catering and hospitality; motor vehicle maintenance. Submit proposal either by email or by post.

Century – see The Random House Group Ltd

The Chalford Press – see The History Press Ltd

Chambers Harrap Publishers Ltd – see Hodder Education Group

Chancery House Press – see CBD Research Ltd

Channel 4 Books – see Transworld Publishers

Chapman Publishing

4 Broughton Place, Edinburgh EH1 3RX
tel 0131 557 2207
email chapman-pub@blueyonder.co.uk
website www.chapman-pub.co.uk
Editor Joy Hendry

Poetry and drama: *Chapman New Writing Series*. Also the *Chapman Wild Women Series*. Founded 1970.

Paul Chapman Publishing – see SAGE Publications Ltd

Chartered Institute of Personnel and Development

CIPD Publishing, 151 The Broadway,
London SW19 1JQ
tel 020-8612 6200 *fax* 020-8612 6201
email publish@cipd.co.uk
website www.cipd.co.uk/bookstore
Head of Publishing Stephen Dunn

Personnel management, training and development.

Chatto & Windus – see The Random House Group Ltd

Cherrytree Books – see Zero to Ten Ltd

The Chicken House

2 Palmer Street, Frome, Somerset BA11 1DS
tel (01373) 454488 *fax* (01373) 454499
email chickenhouse@doublecluck.com
website www.doublecluck.com
Managing Director & Publisher Barry Cunningham, *Deputy Managing Director* Rachel Hickman

Fiction for ages 7+, picture books and teenage. No unsolicited MSS. See website for details of *The Times*/Chicken House Children's Fiction Competition. Part of Scholastic Inc.

Child's Play (International) Ltd

Ashworth Road, Bridgemead, Swindon,
Wilts. SN5 7YD
tel (01793) 616286 *fax* (01793) 512795
email office@childs-play.com
website www.childs-play.com
Chairman Adriana Twinn, *Publisher* Neil Burden

Children's educational books: board, picture, activity and play books; fiction and non-fiction. Founded 1972.

Chivers Press – see AudioGO Ltd

Christian Education*

(incorporating RE Today Services and International Bible Reading Association)
1020 Bristol Road, Selly Oak, Birmingham B29 6LB
tel 0121 472 4242 *fax* 0121 472 7575
email enquiries@christianeducation.org.uk
website www.christianeducation.org.uk

Publications and services for teachers of RE including *REtoday* magazine, curriculum booklets, training material for children and youth workers in the Church. Worship resources for use in primary schools. Activity Club material and Bible reading resources.

Chrysalis Books Group – now Anova Books

Churchill Archive – see Bloomsbury Academic & Professional Division, Bloomsbury Publishing

Churchill Livingstone – see Elsevier Ltd (Health Sciences)

Churchwarden Publications Ltd

PO Box 420, Warminster, Wilts. BA12 9XB
tel (01985) 840189 *fax* (01985) 840243
email enquiries@churchwardenbooks.co.uk
Directors J.N.G. Stidolph, S.A. Stidolph

Publisher of *The Churchwarden's Yearbook*. Care and administration of churches and parishes.

Cicerone Press

2 Police Square, Milnthorpe, Cumbria LA7 7PY
tel (01539) 562069 *fax* (01539) 563417
email info@cicerone.co.uk
website www.cicerone.co.uk
Managing Director Jonathan Williams

Guidebooks: walking, trekking, mountaineering, climbing, cycling in Britain, Europe and worldwide.

Cico Books – see Ryland Peters & Small

Cisco Press – see Pearson UK

T&T Clark International – see Bloomsbury Academic & Professional Division

James Clarke & Co. Ltd

PO Box 60, Cambridge CB1 2NT
tel (01223) 350865 *fax* (01223) 366951
email publishing@jamesclarke.co
website www.jamesclarke.co

Books and ebooks on: theology, philosophy, history and biography, biblical studies, literary criticism. Academic and reference books: dictionaries and encyclopaedias. Founded 1859.

The Lutterworth Press (subsidiary)

Books and ebooks on: history and biography, literature and criticism, science, philosophy, music, sport, art and art history, educational titles, biblical studies, theology, mission, religious studies, collecting, academic and reference books. Imprints: Acorn Editions, Patrick Hardy Books.

Classical Comics

PO Box 7280, Litchborough, Towcester NN12 9AR
tel 0845 812 3000
email info@classicalcomics.co.uk
website www.classicalcomics.com
Managing Director Clive Bryant

Graphic novel adaptations of classical literature.

Cló Iar-Chonnachta Teo.†

Indreabhán, Conamara, Co. Galway, Republic of Ireland
tel +353 (0)91 593307 *fax* +353 (0)91 593362
email cic@iol.ie
website www.cic.ie
Director Micheál Ó Conghaile, *General Manager* Deirdre O'Toole

Irish-language – novels, short stories, plays, poetry, songs, history; CDs (writers reading from their works in Irish and English). Promotes the translation of contemporary Irish fiction and poetry into other languages. Founded 1985.

Co & Bear Productions

63 Edith Grove, London SW10 0LB
tel 020-7351 5545 *fax* 020-7351 5547
email info@cobear.co.uk
website www.scriptumeditions.co.uk
Publisher Beatrice Vincenzini

High-quality illustrated books on lifestyle, photography, art. Imprints: Scriptum Editions, Cartago. Founded 1996.

Collins & Brown – see Anova Books

Collins Languages/COBUILD – see HarperCollins Publishers

Collins Gem – see HarperCollins Publishers

Collins Geo – see HarperCollins Publishers

Colourpoint Books

Colourpoint House, Jubilee Business Park, Jubilee Road, Newtownards, Co. Down, Northern Ireland BT23 4YH
tel 028-9182 6339 *fax* 028-9182 1900
email info@colourpoint.co.uk
website www.colourpoint.co.uk
Publisher Malcolm Johnston, *Head of Educational Publishing* Wesley Johnston, *Marketing* Jacky Hawkes

Irish, Ulster-Scots and general interest including local history; transport (covering the whole of the British Isles), buses, road and railways; educational textbooks and resources; fiction. Short queries by email. Full submission in writing including details of proposal, sample chapter/section, qualification/experience in the topic, full contact details and return postage. Imprints: Colourpoint Educational, Plover Fiction. Founded 1993.

The Columba Press†

55A Spruce Avenue, Stillorgan Industrial Park, Blackrock, Co. Dublin, Republic of Ireland
tel +353 (0)1 2942556 *fax* +353 (0)1 2942564
email info@columba.ie
website www.columba.ie
Publisher & Managing Director Fearghal O Boyle

Religion (Roman Catholic and Anglican) including pastoral handbooks, spirituality, theology, liturgy and prayer; counselling and self-help. Founded 1985.

Connections Book Publishing Ltd

St Chad's House, 148 King's Cross Road, London WC1X 9DH
tel 020-7837 1968 *fax* 020-7837 2025
email info@connections-publishing.com
website www.connections-publishing.com
Directors Nick Eddison, Ian Jackson, David Owen

Illustrated non-fiction books, kits and gift titles: broad, popular list including MBS, health, self-help, puzzles and relationships. Imprint: BOOKINABOX (gifts). Founded 1993.

Conran Octopus – see Octopus Publishing Group

Constable & Robinson Ltd*

3 The Lanchesters, 162 Fulham Palace Road, London W6 9ER

tel 020-8741 3663 *fax* 020-8748 7562
email enquiries@constablerobinson.com
website www.constablerobinson.com
Chairman Nick Robinson, *Managing Director* Pete Duncan, *Online Publishing Director* Nova Jayne Robinson, *Group Sales & Marketing Director* Martin Palmer, *Rights Director* Eryl Humphrey Jones, *Publicity Director* Samantha Evans, *Paperback Publisher* James Gurbutt

Unsolicited sample chapters, synopses and ideas welcome with return postage. No MSS; no email submissions. Founded 1795 (Constable).

Constable (imprint)

Current affairs, biography, history, humour, travel, photography.

Corsair (imprint)

Editorial Director James Gurbutt

Literary and commercial fiction.

Robinson (imprint)

Series-based publishing. Crime fiction (Krystyna Green), the *Mammoth* series (Duncan Proudfoot), the *Brief History* series (Leo Hollis), psychology and the *Overcoming* series (Fritha Saunders, Jamie Joseph).

Right Way (imprint)

Editor Judith Mitchell

Practical, how-to paperbacks and websites, including food and drink, gardening, self-help and pastimes.

Consumers' Association – see Which? Ltd

The Continuum International Publishing Group Plc – acquired by Bloomsbury Academic & Professional Division

Conway – see Anova Books

Thomas Cook Publishing

Unit 9, Coningsby Road, Peterborough PE3 8SB
tel (01733) 416477 *fax* (01733) 416688
email publishing-sales@thomascook.com
website www.thomascookpublishing.com
Head of Travel Books Lisa Bass

Travel guides, rail maps and timetables. Founded 1873.

Corgi – see Transworld Publishers

Corgi Children's Books – see The Random House Group Ltd

Cork University Press†

Youngline Industrial Estate, Pouladuff Road, Togher, Cork, Republic of Ireland
tel +353 (0)21 4902980 *fax* +353 (0)21 4315329
website www.corkuniversitypress.com
Publications Director Mike Collins

Irish literature, history, cultural studies, landscape studies, medieval studies, English literature, musicology, poetry, translations. Founded 1925.

Attic Press and Atrium (imprints)

email corkuniversitypress@ucc.ie

Books by and about women in the areas of social and political comment, women's studies. Cookery, biography and Irish cultural studies (trade).

Council for British Archaeology

St Mary's House, 66 Bootham, York YO30 7BZ
tel (01904) 671417 *fax* (01904) 671384
email info@britarch.ac.uk
website www.britarch.ac.uk
Director Mike Heyworth, *Publications Officer* Catrina Appleby

British archaeology – academic; practical handbooks; general interest archaeology. *British Archaeology* magazine. Founded 1946.

Country Books

(incorporating Ashridge Press)
Courtyard Cottage, Little Longstone, Bakewell, Derbyshire DE45 1NN
tel (01629) 640670
email dickrichardson@country-books.co.uk
website www.countrybooks.biz

Local history (new and facsimile reprints), ghost walk books, county quiz books, customs and folklore. Books for the National Trust, Chatsworth House, Peak District NPA, Derbyshire County Council. Established 1995.

Countryside Books

2 Highfield Avenue, Newbury, Berks. RG14 5DS
tel (01635) 43816 *fax* (01635) 551004
website www.countrysidebooks.co.uk
Partners Nicholas Battle, Suzanne Battle

Books of local or regional interest, usually on a county basis: walking, outdoor activities, local history; also heritage, genealogy, aviation and railways. Accepts proposals; submit outline and one chapter only to the Managing Director. Founded 1976.

Cover to Cover – see AudioGO Ltd

CRC Press – see Taylor and Francis Group

Creme de la Crime – see Severn House Publishers

Crescent Moon Publishing

PO Box 393, Maidstone, Kent ME14 5XU
tel (01622) 729593
email cresmopub@yahoo.co.uk
website www.crmoon.com
Director Jeremy Robinson *Editors* C. Hughes, B.D. Barnacle

Literature, poetry, arts, cultural studies, media, cinema, feminism. Submit sample chapters or 6 poems plus sae, not complete MSS. Founded 1988.

Cressrelles Publishing Co. Ltd

10 Station Road Industrial Estate, Colwall, Malvern, Herefordshire WR13 6RN
tel (01684) 540154
email simon@cressrelles.co.uk
website www.cressrelles.co.uk
Directors Leslie Smith, Simon Smith

General publishing. Founded 1973.

J. Garnet Miller (imprint)
Plays and theatre textbooks.

Kenyon-Deane (imprint)
Plays and drama textbooks for amateur dramatic societies. Plays for women.

New Playwrights' Network (imprint)
Plays for amateur dramatic societies.

Crown House Publishing Ltd

Crown Buildings, Bancyfelin, Carmarthen SA33 5ND
tel (01267) 211345 *fax* (01267) 211882
email books@crownhouse.co.uk
website www.crownhouse.co.uk
Chairman Martin Roberts, *Directors* David Bowman (managing), Glenys Roberts, David Bowman, Karen Bowman, Caroline Lenton

Publisher of Neuro-Linguistic Programming (NLP), hypnosis, counselling and psychotherapy, personal, business and life coaching, education, accelerated learning, thinking skills and personalising learning. Founded 1998.

Independent Thinking Press
Crown Buildings, Bancyfelin, Carmarthen SA33 5ND
tel (01267) 211345 *fax* (01267) 211882
email Caroline@independentthinkingpress.com
website www.independentthinkingpress.com
Publishing Director Caroline Lenton, *Commissioning Editor* Ian Gilbert
Publishes the thoughts and ideas of some of the UK's leading educational innovators including world-class speakers, award-winning teachers, outstanding school leaders and classroom revolutionaries.

The Crowood Press

The Stable Block, Ramsbury, Marlborough, Wilts. SN8 2HR
tel (01672) 520320 *fax* (01672) 520280
email enquiries@crowood.com
website www.crowood.com
Directors John Dennis (chairman), Ken Hathaway (managing)

Sport, motoring, aviation, military, martial arts, walking, fishing, country sports, farming, natural history, gardening, DIY, crafts, railways, model-making, dogs, equestrian and theatre. Founded 1982.

Airlife Publishing (imprint)
Aviation, technical and general, military, military history.

Benjamin Cummings – see Pearson UK

James Currey – see Boydell & Brewer Ltd

Curzon Press Ltd – now RoutledgeCurzon – see Taylor and Francis Group

Terence Dalton Ltd

Water Street, Lavenham, Sudbury, Suffolk CO10 9RN
tel (01787) 249290 *fax* (01787) 248267
Director T.A.J. Dalton

Non-fiction.

Darton, Longman & Todd Ltd

1 Spencer Court, 140–142 Wandsworth High St, London SW18 4JJ
tel 020-8875 0155 *fax* 020-8875 0133
email willp@darton-longman-todd.co.uk
website www.darton-longman-todd.co.uk
Editorial Director David Moloney

Spirituality, prayer and meditation; books for the heart, mind and soul; self-help and personal growth; biography; political, enviromental and social issues. Founded 1959.

Giles de la Mare Publishers Ltd

PO Box 25351, London NW5 1ZT
tel 020-7485 2533 *fax* 020-7485 2534
email gilesdelamare@dial.pipex.com
website www.gilesdelamare.co.uk
Chairman Giles de la Mare

Non-fiction: art, architecture, biography, history, music, travel. Telephone before submitting MSS. Founded 1995.

Dean – see Egmont UK Ltd

Dedalus Ltd

24 St Judith's Lane, Sawtry, Cambs. PE28 5XE
tel (01487) 832382
email info@dedalusbooks.com
website www.dedalusbooks.com
Chairman Juri Gabriel, *Directors* Eric Lane (managing), Robert Irwin (editorial), Mike Mitchell (translations)

Original fiction in English and in translation; Dedalus European Classics, Dedalus concept books. Founded 1983.

Richard Dennis Publications

The New Chapel, Shepton Beauchamp, Ilminster, Somerset TA19 0JT
tel (01460) 240044
email books@richarddennispublications.com
website www.richarddennispublications.com

Books for collectors specialising in ceramics, glass, illustration, sculpture and facsimile editions of early catalogues.

The Derby Books Publishing Company Ltd

(formerly Breedon Books Publishing Co. Ltd)
3 The Parker Centre, Mansfield Road, Derby DE21 4SZ
tel (01332) 384235 *fax* (01332) 292755
email submissions@dbpublishing.co.uk
website www.dbpublishing.co.uk
Directors Steve Caron (managing), Jane Caron (finance)

Football, sport, local history, heritage. No fiction. Unsolicited MSS welcome. Preliminary letter essential. Founded 2009.

André Deutsch – see Carlton Publishing Group

diehard

91–93 Main Street, Callander FK17 8BQ
tel (01877) 339449
website www.poetryscotland.co.uk
Director Sally Evans (editorial)

Scottish poetry. Founded 1993.

Digital Press – see Elsevier Ltd

Discovery Walking Guides Ltd

21 Upper Priory Street, Northampton NN1 2PT
tel (01604) 244869 *fax* (01604) 752576
email ask.discovery@ntlworld.com
website www.walking.demon.co.uk
Chairman Rosamund C. Brawn

'Walk!' walking guidebooks to UK and European destinations. 'Tour & Trail Super-Durable' large-scale maps for outdoor adventures. Bus & Touring Maps. 'Drive' touring maps. GPS The Easy Way. Digital 'Personal Navigator Files' for GPS users. Welcomes project proposals from technologically proficient walking writers. Founded 1994.

John Donald – see Birlinn Ltd

Dorling Kindersley – see Penguin Group (UK)

Doubleday Children's Books – see The Random House Group Ltd

Doubleday (UK) – see Transworld Publishers

The Dovecote Press Ltd

Stanbridge, Wimborne Minster, Dorset BH21 4JD
tel (01258) 840549 *fax* (01258) 840958
email online@dovecotepress.com
website www.dovecotepress.com
Editorial Director David Burnett

Books of local interest: *County in Colour* series, natural history, architecture, history. Founded 1974.

Little Toller Books (imprint)
Republishes classics of nature writing and rural life.

Dref Wen

28 Church Road, Whitchurch, Cardiff CF14 2EA
tel 029-2061 7860 *fax* 029-2061 0507
website www.drefwen.com
Directors Roger Boore, Anne Boore, Gwilym Boore, Alun Boore, Rhys Boore

Welsh language publisher. Original Welsh language novels for children and adult learners. Original, adaptations and translations of foreign and English language full-colour picture story books for children. Educational material for primary/secondary school children in Wales and England. Founded 1970.

University College Dublin Press†

Newman House, 86 St Stephen's Green, Dublin 2, Republic of Ireland
tel +353 (0)1 4779813, +353 (0)1 4779812
fax +353 (0)1 4779821
email ucdpress@ucd.ie
website www.ucdpress.ie
*Executive Editor*Noelle Moran

Irish studies, history and politics, literary studies, social sciences, sociology. Founded 1995.

Gerald Duckworth & Co. Ltd

First Floor, 90–93 Cowcross Street, London EC1M 6BF
tel 020-7490 7300 *fax* 020-7490 0080
email info@duckworth-publishers.co.uk
website www.ducknet.co.uk
Director Peter Mayer (publisher)

General trade publishers. Imprints: Duckworth, Duckworth Overlook, Nonesuch Press, Ardis. No unsolicited fiction submissions. Founded 1898.

Dunedin Academic Press

Hudson House, 8 Albany Street, Edinburgh EH1 3QB
tel 0131 473 2397 *fax* (01250) 870920
email mail@dunedinacademicpress.co.uk
website www.dunedinacademicpress.co.uk
Director Anthony Kinahan

Earth and environmental sciences, public health and social sciences (esp. chilren issues), history. See website for submission guidelines. Founded 2000.

Earthscan

Dunston House, 14A St Cross Street, London EC1N 8XA
tel 020-7841 1930 *fax* 020-7242 1474
email earthinfo@earthscan.co.uk
website www.earthscan.co.uk
Managing Director Jonathan Sinclair Wilson

Academic and professional: sustainable development, climate and energy, natural resource management, cities and built environment, business and economics, design and technology. Imprint of Earthscan Ltd.

Ebury Press – see The Random House Group Ltd

Eden – see Transworld Publishers

Edinburgh University Press*

22 George Square, Edinburgh EH8 9LF
tel 0131 650 4218 *fax* 0131 650 3286
email editorial@eup.ac.uk
website www.euppublishing.com
Chairman Ivon Asquith, *Chief Executive & Head of Sales* Timothy Wright, *Head of Book Publishing* Ms Jackie Jones, *Head of Book Marketing* Anna Glazier

Academic publishers of scholarly books and journals: African studies, film, media and cultural studies, Islamic and Middle Eastern studies, geography, history, law, linguistics, literary studies, philosophy, politics, Scottish studies, American studies, religious studies, sociology, classical and ancient history. Trade: Scottish language, literature and culture, Scottish history and politics.

Éditions Aubrey Walter/Gay Men's Press

99A Wallis Road, London E9 5LN
tel 020-8986 4854 *fax* 020-8533 5821
Publisher Aubrey Walter

Visual work by gay artists and photographers, usually in the form of a monograph showcasing one artist's work. Work may be submitted on disk, email, transparency, photocopy or photograph.

The Educational Company of Ireland†

Ballymount Road, Walkinstown, Dublin 12, Republic of Ireland
tel +353 (0)1 4500611 *fax* +353 (0)1 4500993
email info@edco.ie
website www.edco.ie
Executive Directors Martina Harford (Chief Executive), Robert McLoughlin, *Commissioning Editors* Robert Healy, Michele Staunton

Educational MSS on all subjects in English or Irish language. Trading unit of Smurfit Kappa Group – Ireland. Founded 1910.

Educational Explorers (Publishers)

Unit 5, Feidr Castell Business Park, Fishguard SA65 9BB
tel (01348) 874890 *fax* (01348) 874925
website www.cuisenaire.co.uk
Directors M.J. Hollyfield, D.M. Gattegno

Educational. Recent successes include: mathematics – *Numbers in Colour with Cuisenaire Rods*; languages – *The Silent Way*; literacy, reading – *Words in Colour*; educational films. No unsolicited material. Founded 1962.

Egmont UK Ltd*

The Yellow Building, 1 Notting Hill Village, 1 Nicholas Road, London W11 4AN
email info@egmont.co.uk
website www.egmont.co.uk

The UK's largest specialist children's publisher, publishing books from babies to teens, inspiring children to read. Publishes more than 30 million award-winning books, magazines, ebooks and apps each year. Authors include Michael Morpurgo, Andy Stanton, Enid Blyton, Julia Donaldson and Lemony Snicket. Characters include Winnie-the-Pooh, Tintin, Mr. Men, Thomas & Friends and Ben 10. Egmont has a growing portfolio of digital publishing which includes: the first Flips books for Nintendo DS, apps for iPhone and iPad, ebooks and enhanced ebooks and online virtual worlds. Egmont UK is part of the Egmont Group and owned by the Egmont Foundation, a charitable trust dedicated to supporting children and young people. It is Scandinavia's leading media group and Europe's largest children's publisher telling stories through books, magazines, film, TV, music, games and mobile in 30 countries throughout the world. Founded 1878.

Egmont Press

email childrensreader@euk.egmont.com

Picture book and gift (ages 0+), fiction (ages 5+). Authors include Michael Morpurgo, Enid Blyton, Andy Stanton, Michael Grant, Lemony Snicket, Kristina Stephenson, Giles Andreae, Jan Fearnley and Lydia Monks. Characters include Winnie the Pooh and Tintin.

Submission details: Please go to Egmont's website to see current submissions policy.

Egmont Publishing Group

email charcterpr@euk.egmont.com

Egmont Publishing Group is the UK's leading licensed character publisher of books and magazines for children from birth to teen. Books portfolio includes Thomas the Tank Engine, Mr Men, Fireman Sam, Ben 10, Bob the Builder, Baby Jake and Everything's Rosie and covers a wide range of formats from storybooks, annuals, novelty books to colouring, activity and sticker books. Magazines portfolio includes *Thomas & Friends, Disney Princess, Toy Story, Barbie, Ben 10, Tinker Bell, Fireman Sam, We Love Pop* and girls' pre-teen magazine *Go Girl* and boys' lifestyle title *Toxic.*

Eland Publishing Ltd

61 Exmouth Market, London EC1R 4QL
tel 020-7833 0762 *fax* 020-7833 4434
email info@travelbooks.co.uk
website www.travelbooks.co.uk
Directors Rose Baring, John Hatt, Barnaby Rogerson

Has a backlist of 125 titles in the areas of classic travel literature. No unsolicited MSS. Please email in first instance. Founded 1982.

Element – see Harper Thorsons, imprint of HarperCollins Publishers

11:9 – see Neil Wilson Publishing Ltd

Edward Elgar Publishing Ltd

The Lypiatts, 15 Lansdown Road, Cheltenham, Glos. GL50 2JA

tel (01242) 226934 *fax* (01242) 262111
email info@e-elgar.co.uk
website www.e-elgar.com
Managing Director Tim Williams

Economics, business, law, public and social policy. Founded 1986.

Elliot Right Way Books – see Constable & Robinson Ltd

Elliott & Thompson

27 John Street, London WC1N 2BX
tel 020-7831 5013
email nick@eandtbooks.com
website www.eandtbooks.com
Chairman Lorne Forsyth, *Publisher* Olivia Bays, *Publishing Executive* Nick Sidwell

History, biography, music, popular science, gift, sport, business, economics and adult fiction. Founded 2009.

ELM Publications and Training

Seaton House, Kings Ripton, Huntingdon, Cambs. PE28 2NJ
tel (01487) 773254 *fax* (01487) 773359
email elm@elm-training.co.uk
website www.elm-training.co.uk
Managing Director Sheila Ritchie

Business and management development books, packs and resources; training materials and training courses; some e-learning materials. Founded 1977.

Elsevier Ltd*

The Boulevard, Langford Lane, Kidlington, Oxford OX5 1GB
tel (01865) 843434 *fax* (01865) 843970
website www.elsevier.com
Ceo Health Sciences Division (Books & Journals) Michael Hansen, *Ceo Science & Technology (Books & Journals)* Herman van Campenhout

Academic and professional reference books; scientific, technical and medical books, journals, CD-Roms and magazines. No unsolicited MSS, but synopses and project proposals welcome. Imprints: Academic Press, Architectural Press, Bailliere Tindall, Butterworth-Heinemann, Churchill Livingstone, Digital Press, Elsevier, Elsevier Advanced Technology, Focal Press, Gulf Professional Press, JAI, Made Simple Books, Morgan Kauffman, Mosby, Newnes, North-Holland, Pergamon, Saunders. Division of Reed Elsevier, Amsterdam.

Elsevier Ltd (Butterworth Heinemann)*

The Boulevard, Langford Lane, Kidlington, Oxford OX5 1GB
tel (01865) 474010
website www.elsevierdirect.com
Managing Director Jim Donohue (Science & Technology Books)

Books and electronic products across business, technical, for students and professionals.

Elsevier Ltd (Health Sciences)*

The Boulevard, Langford Lane, Kidlington, Oxford OX5 1GB
tel (01865) 843434 *fax* (01865) 843970
website www.elsevier.com, www.elsevierhealth.com
Ceo Michael Hansen

Medical books and journals. No unsolicited MSS but synopses and project proposals welcome. Imprints: Bailliere Tindall, Churchill Livingstone, Elsevier, Mosby, Pergamon, Saunders.

Encyclopaedia Britannica (UK) Ltd

2nd Floor, Unity Wharf, 13 Mill Street, London SE1 2BH
tel 020-7500 7800 *fax* 020-7500 7878
email enquiries@britannica.co.uk
website www.britannica.co.uk
Managing Director Ian Grant, *VP of Operations* Jane Helps

Enitharmon Press/Enitharmon Editions

26B Caversham Road, London NW5 2DU
tel 020-7482 5967 *fax* 020-7284 1787
email info@enitharmon.co.uk
website www.enitharmon.co.uk
Director Stephen Stuart-Smith

Poetry, literary criticism, fiction, translations, artists' books. No unsolicited MSS. No freelance editors or proofreaders required. Founded 1967.

Lawrence Erlbaum Associates – see Taylor and Francis Group

Euro Crime – see Aradia Books Ltd

Euromonitor International plc

60–61 Britton Street, London EC1M 5UX
tel 020-7251 8024 *fax* 020-7608 3149
email info@euromonitor.com
website www.euromonitor.com
Directors T.J. Fenwick (managing), R.N. Senior (chairman)

Business and commercial reference, marketing information, European and International Surveys, directories. Founded 1972.

Europa Publications Ltd – see Taylor and Francis Group

Evangelical Press of Wales – see Bryntirion Press

Evans Publishing Group*

2A Portman Mansions, Chiltern Street, London W1U 6NR
tel 020-7487 0920 *fax* 020-7487 0921

email sales@evansbooks.co.uk
website www.evansbooks.co.uk
Directors Brian Jones (managing), A.O. Ojora (Nigeria), Danny Daly (finance), *UK Publisher* Su Swallow

Educational books, particularly preschool, school library and teachers' books for the UK, primary and secondary for Africa and the Caribbean. Submissions welcome but does not respond if unsuccessful. Part of the Evans Publishing Group. Founded 1908.

Everyman – see The Orion Publishing Group Ltd

Everyman's Library

Northburgh House, 10 Northburgh Street, London EC1V 0AT
tel 020-7566 6350 *fax* 020-7490 3708
website www.randomhouse.com/knopf/classics
Publisher David Campbell

Everyman's Library (clothbound reprints of the classics); *Everyman Pocket Classics; Everyman's Library Children's Classics*; *Everyman's Library Pocket Poets*; *Everyman Guides*; *P. G. Wodehouse*. No unsolicited submissions. Imprint of Alfred A. Knopf.

University of Exeter Press

Reed Hall, Streatham Drive, Exeter EX4 4QR
tel (01392) 263066 *fax* (01392) 263064
email uep@exeter.ac.uk
website www.exeterpress.co.uk
Publisher Simon Baker

Academic and scholarly books on history, local history (Exeter and the South West), archaeology, classical studies, English literature, film history, performance studies, medieval studies, maritime studies. Imprints include: University of Exeter Press, Bristol Phoenix Press, The Exeter Press. Founded 1958.

Helen Exley®

16 Chalk Hill, Watford, Herts. WD19 4BG
tel (01923) 474480 *fax* (01923) 818733/249795
website www.helenexleygiftbooks.com
Directors Dalton Exley, Helen Exley (editorial), Lincoln Exley, Richard Exley

Popular colour gift books for an international market. No unsolicited MSS. Founded 1976.

Expert Books – see Transworld Publishers

F&W Media International Ltd

Brunel House, Ford Close, Newton Abbot, Devon TQ12 4PU
tel (01626) 323200 *fax* (01626) 323319
email enquiries@fwmedia.co.uk
website www.fwmedia.co.uk
Managing Director James Woollam

A community-focused, creator of content (for books, e-books and digital downloads) and marketer of products and services for hobbyists and enthusiasts including crafts, hobbies, art techniques, writing books, gardening, natural history, equestrian, DIY, military history, photography. Founded 1960.

Faber and Faber Ltd*

Bloomsbury House, 74–77 Great Russell Street, London WC1B 3DA
tel 020-7927 3800 *fax* 020-7927 3801
website www.faber.co.uk
Chief Executive & Publisher Stephen Page, *Commercial Director* David Tebbutt, *Editorial Directors* Lee Brackstone, Walter Donohue, Julian Loose, Belinda Matthews, *Sales Director* Will Atkinson, *Publicity Director & Associate Publisher, Original Arts* Rachel Alexander, *Marketing Director* Jo Ellis, *Production Director* Nigel Marsh, *Rights Director* Jason Cooper, *Publishing Director Children's Books* Julia Heydon-Wells

High-quality general fiction and non-fiction, children's fiction and non-fiction, drama, film, music, poetry. Unsolicited submissions accepted for poetry only. For information on poetry submission procedures, ring 020-7465 0189, or consult the website. No unsolicited MSS.

Fabian Society

11 Dartmouth Street, London SW1H 9BN
tel 020-7227 4900 *fax* 020-7976 7153
email info@fabians.org.uk
website www.fabians.org.uk
General Secretary Andrw Harrup

Current affairs, political thought, economics, education, environment, foreign affairs, social policy. Also controls NCLC Publishing Society Ltd. Founded 1884.

CJ Fallon

Ground Floor, Block B, Liffey Valley Office Campus, Dublin 22, Republic of Ireland
tel +353 (0)1 6166400 *fax* +353 (0)1 6166499
email editorial@cjfallon.ie
website www.cjfallon.ie
Executive Directors Brian Gilsenan (managing), John Bodley (financial)

Educational textbooks. Founded 1927.

Falmer Press – now RoutledgeFalmer, see Taylor and Francis Group

Featherstone Education – see Bloomsbury Children's & Educational Division, Bloomsbury Publishing

David Fickling Books – see The Random House Group Ltd

Fig Tree – see Penguin Group (UK)

Findhorn Press Ltd

Delft Cottage, Dyke, Forres, Scotland IV36 2TF
tel (01309) 690582 *fax* (01317) 772711

email info@findhornpress.com
website www.findhornpress.com

Mind, Body & Spirit and healing. Founded 1971.

Fineleaf Editions

Moss Cottage, Pontshill, Ross-on-Wye HR9 5TB
tel 07951 939688
email books@fineleaf.co.uk
website www.fineleaf.co.uk
Editor Philip Gray

Landscape, nature, social history, fine art and poetry. Founded in 2005.

First and Best in Education

Earlstrees Court, Earlstrees Road, Corby, Northants NN17 4HH
tel (01536) 399011 *fax* (01536) 399012
email sales@firstandbest.co.uk
website www.shop.firstandbest.co.uk
Contact Anne Cockburn (editor)

Education-related books (no fiction). Currently actively recruiting new writers for schools; ideas welcome. Send sae with submissions. Founded 1992.

Fitzrovia Press Ltd

10 Grafton Mews, London W1T 5JG
tel 020-7380 0749
email info@fitzroviapress.co.uk, pratima@fitzroviapress.co.uk
website www.fitzroviapress.co.uk
Publisher Richard Prime, *Marketing Director* Pratima Patel

Fiction and non-fiction: Hinduism and creative writing grounded in Eastern philosophy that explores spirituality in the West. Submit outline plus sample chapter; no complete MSS. Founded 2008.

Five Star – see Profile Books Ltd (Serpent's Tail imprint)

Flame Tree Publishing

Crabtree Hall, Crabtree Lane, London SW6 6TY
tel 020-7386 4700 *fax* 020-7386 4701
email info@flametreepublishing.com
website www.flametreepublishing.com
CEO/Publisher Nick Wells, *Managing Director* Francis Bodiam

Culture, cookery and lifestyle. Part of Flame Tree Publishing Ltd. Facebook: Flame Tree Publishing. Twitter: flametreetweet. Currently not accepting unsolicited MSS. Founded 1992.

Floris Books*

15 Harrison Gardens, Edinburgh EH11 1SH
tel 0131 337 2372 *fax* 0131 347 9919
email floris@florisbooks.co.uk
website www.florisbooks.co.uk
Commissioning Editor Sally Polson

Religion, science, philosophy, holistic health, organics, Mind, Body & Spirit, Celtic studies, crafts; children's books: board, picture books, activity books. Founded 1978.

Kelpies (imprint)

Contemporary Scottish fiction from picture books (for 3–6 years) to novels (for 8–12 years). See website for submission details. Annual Kelpies Prize, see website.

Flyleaf Press†

4 Spencer Villas, Glenageary, Co. Dublin, Republic of Ireland
tel +353 (0)1 2854658
email books@flyleaf.ie
website www.flyleaf.ie
Managing Editor James Ryan

Irish family history. Founded 1988.

Focal Press – see Elsevier Ltd

Folens Publishers*

Waterslade House, Thame Road, Haddenham, Bucks. HP17 8NT
tel (01844) 576 8115 *fax* (01844) 296 666
email folens@folens.com
website www.folens.com
Managing Director Adrian Cockell, *Director of Publishing* Peter Burton, *Primary Publisher* Zoe Nichols, *Secondary Publisher* Abigail Woodman

Primary and secondary educational books. Imprints: Folens, Belair. Founded 1987.

Folens Publishers

Hibernian Industrial Estate, off Greenhills Road, Tallaght, Dublin 24, Republic of Ireland
tel +353 (0)1 4137200 *fax* +353 (0)1 4137282
email info@folens.ie
website www.folens.ie
Chairman Dirk Folens, *Managing Director* John O'Connor

Educational (primary, secondary, comprehensive, technical, in English and Irish). Founded 1956.

Blackwater Press (imprint)

General non-fiction, Irish interest. Founded 1993.

Footprint Handbooks

6 Riverside Court, Lower Bristol Road, Bath BA2 3DZ
tel (01225) 469141 *fax* (01225) 469461
email contactus@footprintbooks.com
website www.footprintbooks.com
Directors Andy Riddle (managing), Patrick Dawson (editorial), *Commissioning Editor* Alan Murphy

Travel guides.

W. Foulsham & Co. Ltd

The Oriel, Capital Point, 33 Bath Road, Slough, Berks. SL1 3UF

tel (01753) 526769 *fax* (01753) 535003
Managing Director B.A.R. Belasco, *Editorial Director* W. Hobson

Life issues. General know-how, cookery, health and alternative therapies, hobbies and games, gardening, sport, travel guides, DIY, collectibles, popular New Age. Imprints: Foulsham, Quantum. Founded *c.*1800.

Quantum (imprint)

Mind, Body & Spirit, popular philosophy and practical psychology.

Four Courts Press†

7 Malpas Street, Dublin 8, Republic of Ireland
tel +353 (0)1 4534668 *fax* +353 (0)1 4534672
email info@fourcourtspress.ie
website www.fourcourtspress.ie
Senior Editor Martin Fanning, *Marketing & Sales Manager* Anthony Tierney

Academic books in the humanities, especially history, Celtic and medieval studies, art, theology. Founded 1970.

Fourth Estate – see HarperCollins Publishers

Free Association Books

1 Angel Cottages, Milespit Hill, London NW7 1RD
email trevorebrown@hotmail.com
website www.fabooks.com
Publisher & Managing Director T.E. Brown

Social sciences, psychoanalysis, psychotherapy, counselling, cultural studies, social welfare, addiction studies, child and adolescent studies. No poetry, science fiction or fantasy. Founded 1984.

Free Press – see Simon & Schuster UK Ltd

W.H. Freeman – see Macmillan Publishers Ltd

Samuel French Ltd*

52 Fitzroy Street, London W1T 5JR
tel 020-7387 9373, 020-7255 4300 *fax* 020-7387 2161
email theatre@samuelfrench-london.co.uk
website www.samuelfrench-london.co.uk
Directors Nate Collins (chairman, USA), Vivien Goodwin (managing), Amanda Smith (editorial)

Publishers of plays and agents for the collection of royalties. Will consider full-length plays only if been performed professionally. One-act scripts, if received a production of some kind, should be submitted in full. Scripts not returned without a sae. Founded 1830.

The Friday Project – see HarperCollins Publishers

Frontline – see Pen & Sword Books Ltd

FT Prentice Hall – see Pearson UK

David Fulton – see Taylor and Francis Group

Gaia Books – see Octopus Publishing Group

Galaxy Children's Large Print – see AudioGO Ltd

The Gallery Press†

Loughcrew, Oldcastle, Co Meath, Republic of Ireland
tel +353 (0)49 8541779 *fax* +353 (0)49 8541779
email gallery@indigo.ie
website www.gallerypress.com
Editor/Publisher Peter Fallon

Poetry and drama – by Irish authors only at this time. Founded 1970.

Gallic Books

Worlds End Studios, 134 Lots Road, London SW10 0RJ
tel 020-7349 7112 *fax* 020-7351 5044
email info@gallicbooks.com
website www.gallicbooks.com
Managing Director Jane Aitken, *Editorial Director* Pilar Webb

French writing in translation. Only accepts submissions from French publishers or from agents representing French authors. Founded 2007.

Garland Science – see Taylor and Francis Group

J. Garnet Miller – see Cressrelles Publishing Co. Ltd

Garnet Publishing Ltd

8 Southern Court, South Street, Reading RG1 4QS
tel (01189) 597847 *fax* (01189) 597356
email arashhejazi@garnetpublishing.co.uk
website www.garnetpublishing.co.uk
Editorial Manager Arash Hejazi

Art, architecture, photography, fiction, religious studies, travel and general, mainly on the Middle East and Islam. Accepts unsolicited material only if relevant to Islam and the Middle East. Founded 1991.

Ithaca Press (imprint)

Postgraduate academic works, especially on the Middle East.

South Street Press (imprint)

Non-fiction, including *Behind the Headlines* series.

Gibson Square

47 Lonsdale Square, London N1 1EW
tel 020-7096 1100 *fax* 020-7993 2214
email info@gibsonsquare.com
website www.gibsonsquare.com
Publisher Martin Rynja

Non-fiction: female interest, general non-fiction, biography, current affairs, philosophy, politics, cultural criticism, psychology, history, travel, art history. Books must have the potential to engage in a debate; see website for guidelines or email to receive an automated response.

Gill & Macmillan Ltd†

Hume Avenue, Park West, Dublin 12, Republic of Ireland
tel +353 (0)1 5009500 *fax* +353 (0)1 5009596
website www.gillmacmillan.ie

Biography or memoirs, educational (primary, secondary, university), history, literature, cookery, current affairs, guidebooks, Irish-interest non-fiction. Founded 1968.

Ginn – see Pearson UK

GL Assessment

9th Floor East, 389 Chiswick High Road, London W4 4AL
tel 020-8996 3333 *fax* 020-8742 8767
email information@gl-assessment.co.uk
website www.gl-assessment.co.uk
Group Education Director Andrew Thraves

Testing and assessment services for education and health care, including literacy, numeracy, thinking skills, ability, learning support and online testing. Founded 1981.

Godsfield Press – see Octopus Publishing Group

The Goldsmith Press Ltd

Newbridge, Co. Kildare, Republic of Ireland
tel +353 (0)45 433613 *fax* +353 (0)45 434648
email viv1@iol.ie
website www.gerardmanleyhopkins.org
Directors V. Abbott, D. Egan, *Secretary* B. Ennis

Literature, art, Irish interest, poetry. Unsolicited MSS not returned. Founded 1972.

Gollancz – see The Orion Publishing Group Ltd

Gomer Press

Llandysul, Ceredigion SA44 4JL
tel (01559) 363090 *fax* (01559) 363758
email gwasg@gomer.co.uk
website www.gomer.co.uk, www.pontbooks.co.uk
Managing Director Jonathan Lewis, *Head of Publishing* Dylan Williams, *Editors* Elinor Wyn Reynolds (Adult, Welsh), Ceri Wyn Jones (Adult, English), Sioned Lleinau (Children's, Welsh), Viv Sayer (Children's, English)

History, travel, photography, biography, art, poetry and fiction of relevance to Welsh culture, in English and in Welsh. Picture books, novels, stories, poetry and teaching resources for children. No unsolicited MSS; prelimary enquiry essential. Imprint: Pont Books (English books for children). Founded 1892.

Goss & Crested China Club

62 Murray Road, Horndean, Waterlooville PO8 9JL
tel 023-9259 7440
email info@gosschinaclub.co.uk
website www.gosschinaclub.co.uk
Managing Director Lynda J. Pine

Crested heraldic china, antique porcelain. Milestone Publications – publishing and bookselling division of Goss & Crested China Club. Founded 1967.

Government Supplies Agency†

Publications Division, Office of Public Works, 51 St Stephen's Green, Dublin 2, Republic of Ireland
tel +353 (0)1 6476000 *fax* +353 (0)1 6610747

Irish government publications.

Gower – see Ashgate Publishing Ltd

Granta Books

12 Addison Avenue, London W11 4QR
tel 020-7605 1360 *fax* 020-7605 1361
website www.grantabooks.com
Executive Publisher Philip Gwyn Jones, *Sales & Marketing Director* Brigid MacLeod, *Finance Director* Craig Nicholson, *Publishing Director* Sara Holloway

Literary fiction, memoir, nature writing and travel. No submissions except via a reputable literary agent. An imprint of Granta Publications. Founded 1982.

Green Books

Dartington Space, Dartington Hall, Totnes, Devon TQ9 6EN
tel (01803) 863260 *fax* (01803) 863843
email edit@greenbooks.co.uk
website www.greenbooks.co.uk
Publisher John Elford

Environment (practical and philosophical). No fiction or children's books. No MSS; submit synopsis with covering letter, preferably by email. Founded 1987.

Green Print – see Merlin Press Ltd

Gresham Books Ltd

19/21 Sayers Lane, Tenterden, Kent TN30 6BW
tel (01580) 767596 *fax* (01580) 764142
email info@gresham-books.co.uk
website www.gresham-books.co.uk
Managing Director Nicholas Oulton

Hymn books, prayer books, service books, school histories and Companions.

Grub Street Publishing

4 Rainham Close, London SW11 6SS
tel 020-7924 3966, 020-7738 1008 *fax* 020-7738 1009
email post@grubstreet.co.uk
website www.grubstreet.co.uk
Principals John B. Davies, Anne Dolamore

Adult non-fiction: military, aviation history, cookery. Founded 1992.

Guild of Master Craftsman Publications Ltd

166 High Street, Lewes, East Sussex BN7 1XU
tel (01273) 477374 *fax* (01273) 478606
website www.thegmcgroup.com, www.ammonitepress.com
Joint Managing Directors Jennifer Phillips, Jonathan Phillips

Leisure and hobby subjects; practical, illustrated crafts, including photography, art, needlecrafts, dolls' houses and woodworking. Founded 1979.

Guinness World Records

3rd Floor, 184–192 Drummond Street, London NW1 3HP
tel 020-7891 4567 *fax* 020-7891 4501
website www.guinnessworldrecords.com

Guinness World Records, *GWR Gamer's Edition*, TV and brand licensing, records processing. No unsolicited MSS. A Jim Pattison Group company. Founded 1954.

Gulf Professional Press – see Elsevier Ltd

Gullane Children's Books

185 Fleet Street, London EC4A 2HS
tel 020-7400 1084 *fax* 020-7400 1037
email stories@gullanebooks.com
website www.gullanebooks.com
Publisher Simon Rosenheim

Picture and novelty books for children 0–8 years.

Hachette Children's Books*

338 Euston Road, London NW1 3BH
tel 020-7873 6000 *fax* 020-7873 6024
website www.hachettechildrens.co.uk
Managing Director Marlene Johnson

Children's non-fiction, reference, information, gift, fiction, picture, novelty and audiobooks. Unsolicited material is not considered other than by referral or recommendation. Formed by combining Watts Publishing with Hodder Children's Books in 2005. Part of Hachette UK (see page 144).

Hodder Children's Books (imprint)

Publishing Director Anne McNeil

Fiction, picture books, novelty, general non-fiction and audiobooks.

Orchard Books (imprint)

Publishing Director Megan Larkin

Fiction, picture and novelty books.

Franklin Watts (imprint)

Publishing Director Rachel Cooke

Non-fiction and information books.

Wayland (imprint)

Publishing Director Joyce Bentley

Non-fiction and information books.

Hachette UK*

338 Euston Road, London NW1 3BH
tel 020-7873 6000 *fax* 020-7873 6024
website www.hachette.co.uk
Chief Executive Tim Hely Hutchinson, *Directors* Jamie Hodder Williams (Ceo, Hodder & Stoughton, Headline, John Murray), Chris Emerson (Coo), Jane Morpeth (managing, Headline), Marlene Johnson (managing, Hachette Children's), Peter Roche (deputy Ceo/Ceo, Orion), Malcolm Edwards (managing, Orion), Alison Goff (Ceo, Octopus), Ursula Mackenzie (Ceo, Little, Brown Book Group), Pierre de Cacqueray (finance), Richard Kitson (commercial), Dominic Mahony (group HR), Malcolm Edwards (managing, Hachette Australia), David Young (Ceo, Hachette Book Group USA), Clare Harington (group communications)

Part of Hachette Livre SA since 2004. Hachette UK group companies: Hachette Children's Books (page 144), Headline Publishing Group (page 146), Hodder Education Group (page 147), Hodder & Stoughton (page 147), Hodder Faith (page 147), John Murray (page 157), Little, Brown Book Group (page 152), Octopus Publishing Group (page 159), Orion Publishing Group (page 160), Hachette Ireland, Hachette Australia (page 184), Hachette New Zealand (page 189), Hachette Book Publishing India Private Ltd.

Halban Publishers

22 Golden Square, London W1F 9JW
tel 020-7437 9300 *fax* 020-7437 9512
email books@halbanpublishers.com
website www.halbanpublishers.com
Directors Martine Halban, Peter Halban

General fiction and non-fiction; history and biography; Jewish subjects and Middle East. No unsolicited MSS considered; preliminary letter or email essential. Founded 1986.

Haldane Mason Ltd

PO Box 34196, London NW10 3YB
tel 020-8459 2131 *fax* 020-8728 1216
email info@haldanemason.com
website www.haldanemason.com
Directors Sydney Francis, Ron Samuel

Illustrated non-fiction books and box sets, mainly for children. No unsolicited material. Imprints: Haldane Mason (adult), Red Kite Books (children's). Founded 1995.

Robert Hale Ltd

Clerkenwell House, 45–47 Clerkenwell Green, London EC1R 0HT
tel 020-7251 2661 *fax* 020-7490 4958

email enquire@halebooks.com
website www.halebooks.com
Directors Gill Jackson (managing & editorial), John Hale (chairman), Robert Hale (production)

Adult general non-fiction and fiction. Founded 1936.

Halsgrove Publishing

Halsgrove House, Ryelands Business Park, Bagley Road, Wellington, Somerset TA21 9PZ
tel (01823) 653777 *fax* (01823) 216796
email sales@halsgrove.com
website www.halsgrove.com
Managing Director Julian Davidson, *Publisher* Simon Butler

Regional books for local-interest readers in the UK. Also illustrated books on individual artists. Founded 1986.

Hamish Hamilton – see Penguin Group (UK)

Hamlyn – see Octopus Publishing Group

Patrick Hardy Books – see James Clarke & Co. Ltd

Harlequin (UK) Ltd*

Eton House, 18–24 Paradise Road, Richmond, Surrey TW9 1SR
tel 020-8288 2800 *fax* 020-8388 2899
website www.millsandboon.co.uk
Directors Mandy Ferguson (managing), Stuart Barber (financial & IS), Angela Barnatt (production & operations), Kimberly Young (editorial), Tim Cooper (digital & marketing), Jackie McGee (human resources), Clare Somerville (retail sales & India).

Founded 1908.

Mills & Boon Historical™ (imprint)
Senior Editor L. Fildew
Historical romance fiction.

Mills & Boon Medical™ (imprint)
Senior Editor S. Hodgson
Contemporary romance fiction.

Mills & Boon Cherish™ (imprint)
Senior Editor Bryony Green
Commercial literary fiction.

Mira Books® (imprint)
Editorial Director Kimberley Young
Women's fiction.

Mills & Boon Riva™ (imprint)
Senior Editor Bryony Green
Contemporary romance fiction.

Mills & Boon Modern Romance™ (imprint)
Senior Editor Joanne Grant

HarperCollins Entertainment – see HarperCollins Publishers

HarperCollins Publishers*

77–85 Fulham Palace Road, London W6 8JB
tel 020-8741 7070 *fax* 020-8307 4440
also at Westerhill Road, Bishopbriggs, Glasgow G64 2QT
tel 0141 772 3200 *fax* 0141 306 3119
website www.harpercollins.co.uk
Ceo/Publisher Victoria Barnsley, *Publisher* Kate Elton

All fiction and trade non-fiction must be submitted through an agent, or unsolicited MSS may be submitted through the online writing community at www.authonomy.com. Owned by News Corporation. Founded 1819.

Avon
website www.avon-books.co.uk
Associate Publisher Caroline Ridding
Women's commercial fiction.

HarperFiction
Publisher Lynne Drew
General, historical fiction, crime and thrillers, women's fiction.

Voyager (imprint)
Publishing Director Jane Johnson
Fantasy/science fiction.

Harper NonFiction
Publisher Carole Tonkinson

HarperCollins (imprint)
Publishing Director David Brawn (Agatha Christie, J.R.R. Tolkien, C.S. Lewis)

HarperTrue (imprint)
Publisher Carole Tonkinson
True life stories. Established 2008.

HarperSport (imprint)
Publishing Director Nick Canham
Sporting biographies, guides and histories.

HarperCollins Audio (imprint)
Head of Audio Jo Forshaw
See page 208.

Harper Thorsons (imprint)
Publisher Carole Tonkinson

HarperCollins Children's Books
website www.harpercollinschildrensbooks.co.uk
Publisher Ann-Janine Murtagh
Quality picture books for under 7s; fiction for age 6+ to young adult; graphic novels; TV/film tie-ins; properties.

PRESS BOOKS
Executive Director David Roth-Ey

Fourth Estate (imprint)
Publishing Director/Publisher Nick Pearson
Fiction, literary fiction, current affairs, popular science, biography, humour, travel.

The Friday Project
email info@thefridayproject.co.uk
website www.thefridayproject.co.uk

Publisher Scott Pack
Books developed from popular websites with publishing initiatives that embrace new digital technology. Imprints: Friday Books, Friday Fiction, Friday Food, Friday Children's, Friday Instants.

HarperPress (imprint)
Publishing Directors Arabella Pike (non-fiction)

Collins (division and imprint)
Publisher Hannah MacDonald, *Publishing Director* Iain MacGregor, *Associate Publisher* Myles Archibald (natural history)
Guides and handbooks, Times World Atlases, phrase books and manuals on popular reference, art instruction, illustrated, cookery and wine, crafts, DIY, gardening, military, natural history, pet care, pastimes. Imprints: Collins, Collins Gem, Jane's, Times Books.

Collins Language (division and imprint)
Managing Director Robert Scriven, *Publishing Director* Elaine Higgleton (editorial)
Bilingual and English dictionaries, English dictionaries for foreign learners.

Collins Education (division)
Managing Director Nigel Ward
Books, CD-Roms and online material for UK primary and secondary schools and colleges.

Collins Geo (division and imprint)
Managing Director Sheena Barclay
Illustrated non-fiction: natural history, DIY, house and home, maps, atlases, street plans and leisure guides.

HarperTrue – see HarperCollins Publishers

Harvill Secker – see The Random House Group Ltd

Hawthorn Press
1 Lansdown Lane, Stroud, Glos. GL5 1BJ
tel (01453) 757040 *fax* (01453) 751138
email info@hawthornpress.com
website www.hawthornpress.com
'Books for a creative, peaceful and sustainable world'. Founded 1981.

Hay House Publishers
292B Kensal Road, London W10 5BE
tel 020-8962 1230 *fax* 020-8962 1239
email info@hayhouse.co.uk
website www.hayhouse.co.uk
Managing Director & Publisher Michelle Pilley, *Sales Director* Diane Hill
Mind, Body & Spirit, self-help, health. Head office in San Diego, California. Please send unsolicited MSS to submissions@hayhouse.co.uk or the address above marked 'submissions'. Founded 1984; in UK 2003.

Haynes Publishing
Sparkford, Yeovil, Somerset BA22 7JJ
tel (01963) 440635 *fax* (01963) 440001
website www.haynes.co.uk
Directors J.H. Haynes (founder director), J. Haynes (chairman), Jeremy Yates-Round (managing & sales), M. Minter, M.J. Hughes, G.R. Cook, J. Bunkum
Car and motorcycle service and repair manuals, car handbooks/servicing guides; DIY books for the home; car, motorcycle, motorsport and leisure activities.

Haynes Book Division (imprint)
email mhughes@haynes.co.uk
Editorial Director Mark Hughes
Cars, motorcycles and motorsport (including related biographies), plus other transport; practical books on home DIY and computing.

Haynes Motor Trade Division (imprint)
email mminter@haynes.co.uk
Editorial Director Matthew Minter
Car and motorcycle service and repair manuals and technical data books.

Headland Publications
Editorial office Tŷ Coch, Galltegfa, Llanfwrog, Ruthin, Denbighshire LL15 2AR
and 38 York Avenue, West Kirby, Wirral CH48 3JF
tel 0151 625 9128
email headlandpublications@hotmail.co.uk
website www.headlandpublications.co.uk
Editor Gladys Mary Coles
Poetry, anthologies of poetry and prose. No unsolicited MSS. Founded 1970.

Headline Publishing Group*
338 Euston Road, London NW1 3BH
tel 020-7873 6000 *fax* 020-7873 6024
email info@headline.co.uk
website www.headline.co.uk, www.hachettelivreuk.co.uk
Managing Director Jane Morpeth, *Director of Publishing* Marion Donaldson, *Publishing Director* Imogen Taylor
Commercial and literary fiction (hardback and paperback), and popular non-fiction including autobiography, biography, food and wine, gardening, history, popular science, sport, TV tie-ins. Publishes under Headline, Headline Review, Business Plus. Part of Hachette UK (see page 144).

William Heinemann – see The Random House Group Ltd

Heinemann – see Pearson UK

Christopher Helm – see Bloomsbury Children's & Educational Division, Bloomsbury Publishing

Books

The Herbert Press – see Bloomsbury Academic & Professional Division, Bloomsbury Publishing

Hermes House – see Anness Publishing

Nick Hern Books Ltd

The Glasshouse, 49A Goldhawk Road, London W12 8QP
tel 020-8749 4953 *fax* 020-8735 0250
email info@nickhernbooks.co.uk
website www.nickhernbooks.co.uk
Publisher Nick Hern, *Commissioning Editor* Matt Applewhite

Theatre and performing arts books, professionally produced plays, screenplays. Initial letter required. Founded 1988.

Hesperus Press Ltd

28 Mortimer Street, London W1W 7RD
tel 020-436 0869
email info@hesperuspress.com
website www.hesperuspress.com

Hesperus Press was established in 2002. In the 10 years since the press was founded, some 300 works by many of the greatest figures in worldwide literary history, including Dante, Dickens, Dostoevsky, Flaubert, Kafka, Tagore, Tolstoy and Woolf have been published. The list includes translations of contemporary foreign fiction, biographies, non-fiction and cultural histories. Founded 2002.

Hippo – see Scholastic Ltd

Hippopotamus Press

22 Whitewell Road, Frome, Somerset BA11 4EL
tel (01373) 466653 *fax* (01373) 466653
email rjhippopress@aol.com
Editors Roland John, Anna Martin

Poetry, essays, criticism. Submissions from new writers welcome. Founded 1974.

Historical™ – see Harlequin (UK) Ltd

The History Press Ltd

The Mill, Brimscombe Port, Stroud, Glos. GL5 2QG
tel (01453) 883300 *fax* (01453) 883233
website www.thehistorypress.co.uk
Directors Stuart Biles (Ceo), Gareth Swain (finance)

The History Press (imprint)

Head of Publishing & Digital Laura Perehinec, *Sales & Marketing* Tim Davies

Local, specialist and general history: military, aviation, maritime, transport, biography, archaeology, sport.

Phillimore (imprint)

British local history and genealogy.

Pitkin (imprint)

History, heritage, leisure, travel.

Spellmount (imprint)

Military history.

Hodder & Stoughton*

338 Euston Road, London NW1 3BH
tel 020-7873 6000 *fax* 020-7873 6024
website www.hodder.co.uk, www.hachettelivreukco.uk
Managing Director Jamie Hodder-Williams, *Deputy Managing Director* Lisa Highton, *Non-fiction* Rowena Webb, *Sceptre* Carole Welch, *Fiction* Carolyn Mays, *Audio* Rupert Lancaster

Commercial and literary fiction; biography, autobiography, history, humour, Mind, Body & Spirit, travel, lifestyle and cookery and other general interest non-fiction; audio. No unsolicited MSS or synopses. Publishes under Hodder & Stoughton, Sceptre, Mobius. Part of Hachette UK (see page 144).

Hodder Children's Books – see Hachette Children's Books

Hodder Education Group*

338 Euston Road, London NW1 3BH
tel 020-7873 6000 *fax* 020-7873 6325
website www.hoddereducation.co.uk, www.hachette.co.uk
Chief Executive Thomas Webster, *Finance Director* Alex Jones, *Managing Directors* David Swarbrick (consumer learning), C.P. Shaw (tertiary), Lis Tribe (schools), *Editorial Directors* Robert Sulley (science & international), Steve Connolly (digital publishing), Jim Belben (humanities & modern languages), *Business Operations Director* Alyssum Ross, *Sales & Marketing Directors* Janice Holdcroft (schools & FE), Tim Mahar (trade, HE & health sciences), *Directors* Paul Cherry (Philip Allan), John Mitchell (Hodder Gibson)

Medical (Hodder Arnold), consumer education and self-improvement (Hodder Education and Teach Yourself), school (Hodder Education, Hodder Gibson and Philip Allan), dictionaries, reference and language publishing (Chambers). Part of Hachette Ltd (see page 144).

Hodder Faith*

338 Euston Road, London NW1 3BH
tel 020-7873 6000 *fax* 020-7873 6024
email faitheditorialenquiries@hodder.co.uk
website www.hodderfaith.com
Managing Director Jamie Hodder-Williams

Bibles, Christian books, biography/memoir. Publishes New International Version (NIV) of the Bible, Today's New International Version (TNIV) of the Bible, New International Reader's Version (NIrV) of the Bible. Part of Hachette UK (see page 144).

Hodder Gibson*

2A Christie Street, Paisley PA1 1NB
tel 0141 848 1609 *fax* 0141 889 6315
email hoddergibson@hodder.co.uk
website www.hoddergibson.co.uk, www.hoddereducation.co.uk, www.hachettelivre.co.uk
Managing Director John Mitchell

Educational books specifically for Scotland. No unsolicited MSS. Part of Hachette UK (see page 144).

Hodder Headline Ltd – see Hachette UK

Hodder Wayland – see Hachette UK

Honno Ltd (Welsh Women's Press)

Honno, Unit 14, Creative Units, Aberystwyth Arts Centre, Penglais Campus, Aberystwyth, Ceredigion SY23 3GL
tel (01970) 623150 *fax* (01970) 623150
email post@honno.co.uk
website www.honno.co.uk
Editor Caroline Oakley

Literature written by women in Wales or women with a Welsh connection. All subjects considered – fiction, non-fiction, autobiographies. No poetry or works for children considered. Honno is a community co-operative. Founded 1986.

Hopscotch Educational Publishing Ltd

St Jude's Church, Dulwich Road, London SE24 0PB
tel 020-7501 6736 *fax* 020-7978 8316
email sales@hopscotchbooks.com
website www.hopscotchbooks.com
Publishing Manager Angela Morano-Shaw

National Curriculum teaching resources for primary school teachers. Founded 1997.

Step Forward Publishing Ltd

Early years teacher resources.

Quay Books

tel 020-7501 6705 *fax* 020-7978 8316
Editorial Manager Maria Anguita
Nursing, midwifery and medical.

House of Lochar

Isle of Colonsay, Argyll PA61 7YR
tel (01951) 200323
email lochar@colonsay.org.uk
website www.houseoflochar.com
Managing Director Georgina Hobhouse, *Editorial Director* Kevin Byrne

Scottish history, transport, Scottish literature. Founded 1995.

How To Books Ltd

Spring Hill House, Spring Hill Road, Begbroke, Oxford OX5 1RX
tel (01865) 375794
email info@howtobooks.co.uk
website www.howtobooks.co.uk
Publisher & Managing Director Giles Lewis, *Editorial Director* Nikki Read

Practical books that inspire in cookery, self-sufficiency and self-help reference. Subjects covered include cookery, vegetable and flower gardening, starting a small business, study skills and student guides, jobs and careers, lifestyle, personal transformation, creative writing, property, management skills and others. Book proposals welcome. Founded 1991.

Spring Hill (imprint)

Cookery and gardening.

Short-e Guides (imprint)

John Hunt Publishing Ltd

Laurel House, Station Approach, Alresford, Hants SO24 9JH
email office1@jhpbooks.net
website www.johnhuntpublishing.com
Director John Hunt

Global spirituality and Mind, Body & Spirit, history, religion and philosophy. See website for submission procedure. Imprints: O-Books, Zero Books, Moon Books, Circle Books. Founded 1989.

Hutchinson – see The Random House Group Ltd

Hutchinson Children's Books – see The Random House Group Ltd

Icon Books Ltd

The Omnibus Business Centre, 39–41 North Road, London N7 9DP
tel 020-7697 9695 *fax* (01763) 208080
email info@iconbooks.co.uk
website www.iconbooks.co.uk, www.introducingbooks.com
Directors Peter Pugh (chairman), Simon Flynn (managing), Duncan Heath (editorial), Andrew Furlow (sales & marketing), Najma Finlay (publicity)

Popular, intelligent non-fiction: *Introducing* series, literature, history, philosophy, politics, psychology, sociology, cultural studies, religion, science, current affairs, computers, women, anthropology, humour, music, cinema, linguistics, economics. Imprint: Wizard Books (children's, *Fighting Fantasy* gamebook series). Submission details: will consider unsolicited MSS (adult non-fiction only). Founded 1991.

Corinthian (imprint)

Sport.

ICSA Information & Training Ltd

16 Park Crescent, London W1B 1AH
tel 020-7612 7020 *fax* 020-7612 7034

email publishing@icsaglobal.com
website www.icsabookshop.co.uk
Joint Managing Directors Clare Grist Taylor, Susan Richards

Publishing company of the Institute of Chartered Secretaries and Administrators, specialising in information solutions for legal and regulatory compliance. Founded 1981.

Igloo Books Ltd

Cottage Farm, Mears Ashby Road, Sywell, Northants NN6 0BJ
tel (01604) 741116 *fax* (01604) 670495
email publishing@igloo-books.com
website www.igloo-books.com

Adult and children's: cookery, lifestyle, gift, trivia/crosswords, fiction, non-fiction (adult), novelty, board, picture, activity books, audio (children's), education. Not accepting submissions. Founded 2005.

The Ilex Press Ltd

210 High Street, Lewes, East Sussex BN7 2NS
tel (01273) 403124 *fax* (01273) 487441
website www.ilex-press.com

Highly illustrated technical books on digital photography, digital art and imaging, video and audio, web design, 3D art and design. See website before submitting MSS.

Imprint Academic

PO Box 200, Exeter EX5 5HY
tel (01392) 851550 *fax* (01392) 851178
email graham@imprint.co.uk
website www.imprint-academic.com
Publisher Keith Sutherland, *Managing Editor* Graham Horswell

Books and journals in politics, philosophy and psychology for both academic and general readers. Book series include *St Andrews Studies in Philosophy and Public Affairs*. Unsolicited MSS, synopses and ideas welcome with return postage only. Founded 1980.

In Pinn – see Neil Wilson Publishing Ltd

Independent Music Press

PO Box 69, Church Stretton, Shrops. SY6 6WZ
tel/fax (01694) 720049
email info@impbooks.com
website www.impbooks.com
Music Editor Martin Roach

Music: biography, youth culture/street style/subcultures. No unsoliticed MSS; submissions via literary agents only. Founded 1992.

Indepenpress Publishing Ltd*

25 Eastern Place, Brighton BN2 1GJ
tel (01273) 272758 *fax* (01273) 261434
email info@penpress.co.uk
website www.indepenpress.co.uk
Directors Lynn Ashman (managing), Grace Rafael (production)

Literary fiction, general fiction, children's fiction, selected non-fiction. Founded 1996.

Pulp Press (imprint)
Pulp fiction.

Pink Press (imprint)
Gay and lesbian fiction.

Indigo Dreams Publishing Ltd

132 Hinckley Road, Stoney Stanton, Leics. LE9 4LN
email publishing@indigodreams.co.uk
website www.indigodreams.co.uk
Editor Ronnie Goodyer, *Editor* Dawn Bauling

Publishes approx. 50–60 titles per year. Main subject areas include commercial, literary and historical fiction, biography and memoirs and poetry.

Infinite Ideas

36 St Giles, Oxford OX1 3LD
tel (01865) 514888 *fax* (01865) 514777
email info@infideas.com
website www.infideas.com/publishing.asp
Joint Managing Directors David Grant, Richard Burton

Lifestyle, *52 Brilliant Ideas* series (health, fitness, relationships; leisure and lifestyle; sports, hobbies and games; careers, finance and personal development), business books. *Infinite Success* series (re-interpreted personal development and business classics); *Feel Good Factory* series (lifestyle). Submit business book proposals directly to richard@infideas.com. Founded 2003.

Insight Guides/Berlitz Publishing

58 Borough High Street, London SE1 1XF
tel 020-7403 0284 *fax* 020-7403 0290
website www.insightguides.com, www.berlitzpublishing.com
Managing Director Katharine Leck

Travel, language and related multimedia. Founded 1970.

Institute of Public Administration†

Vergemount Hall, Clonskeagh, Dublin 6, Republic of Ireland
tel +353 (0)1 2403600 *fax* +353 (0)1 2698644
email rboyle@ipa.ie
website www.ipa.ie
Publisher Richard Boyle

Government, economics, politics, law, public management, health, education, social policy and administrative history. Founded 1957.

Inter-Varsity Press

Norton Street, Nottingham NG7 3HR
tel 0115 978 1054 *fax* 0115 942 2694

email sales@ivpbooks.com
website www.ivpbooks.com
Senior Commissioning Editor E. Trotter

Theology and religion.

Irish Academic Press Ltd†

2 Brookside, Dundrum Road, Dublin 14, Republic of Ireland
tel +353 (0)1 2989937 *fax* +353 (0)1 2982783
email info@iap.ie
website www.iap.ie

Scholarly books especially in 19th- and 20th-century history, literature, heritage and culture. Imprints: Irish University Press, Irish Academic Press. Merrion, founded 1974.

Ithaca Press – see Garnet Publishing Ltd

IWM (Imperial War Museums)

Lambeth Road, London SE1 6HZ
tel 020-7091 3064 *fax* 020-7416 5374
email mail@iwm.org.uk
website www.iwm.org.uk

IWM tells the stories of people who have lived, fought and died in conflicts involving Britain and the Commonwealth since 1914. Drawing on a unique collection, IWM publishes a large range of books linked to exhibitions and archives. Books are produced both in-house and in partnership with other publishers.

JAI – see Elsevier Ltd

Jane's – see HarperCollins Publishers

Jane's Information Group

163 Brighton Road, Coulsdon, Surrey CR5 2YH
tel 020-8700 3700 *fax* 020-8700 3751
website www.janes.com
Managing Director Scott Key

Professional business-to-business publishers in hardcopy and electronic multimedia of military, aviation, naval, defence, reference, police, geo-political. Consumer books in association with HarperCollins Publishers.

Jarrold Publishing – see The History Press Ltd

Jordan Publishing Ltd

21 St Thomas Street, Bristol BS1 6JS
tel 0117 923 0600 *fax* 0117 925 0486
website www.jordanpublishing.co.uk
Managing Director Caroline Vandridge-Ames

The company was founded in 1863 by Mr Richard Jordan, as a company registration and law stationery business operating from 123 Chancery Lane, London, in the heart of London's legal district. Today the company is the UK's leading privately owned law publisher and conference producer. Market leader in family law the company also has a strong presence in company, charities, employment, insolvency, private client, personal injury and civil litigation law. Portfolio includes loose leafs, major works, journals and textbooks available both online and in print format. Also provides high-quality conferences, seminars and online training. Founded in 1863.

Michael Joseph – see Penguin Group (UK)

Kenilworth Press – see Quiller Publishing Ltd

Kenyon-Deane – see Cressrelles Publishing Co. Ltd

Laurence King Publishing Ltd*

(formerly Calmann & King Ltd)
361–373 City Road, London EC1V 1LR
tel 020-7841 6900 *fax* 020-7841 6910
email enquiries@laurenceking.co.uk
website www.laurenceking.co.uk
Directors Laurence King (managing), Nicholas Perren (chairman), Simon Gwynn (marketing), Joanne Lightfoot (editorial), Philip Cooper (editorial), John Stoddart (financial)

Illustrated books on design, contemporary architecture, art, interiors and fashion for the professional, student and general market. Founded 1976.

Kingfisher – see Macmillan Publishers Ltd

Kingscourt – see McGraw-Hill Education

Jessica Kingsley Publishers*

116 Pentonville Road, London N1 9JB
tel 020-7833 2307 *fax* 020-7837 2917
email post@jkp.com
website www.jkp.com
Managing Director Jessica Kingsley

Psychology, psychiatry, arts therapies, social work, special needs (especially autism and Asperger Syndrome), education, law, practical theology and a small children's list focusing on books for children with special needs. Founded 1987.

Singing Dragon (imprint)

Focuses on oriental and complementary medicine, health, and Chinese martial arts.

Kluwer Law International

Zuidpoolsingel 2, 2408 ZE Alphen aan den Rijn, The Netherlands
tel +35 172-641-552
email sales@kluwerlaw.com
website www.kluwerlaw.com
Publisher Simon Bellamy

International law.

Books

Charles Knight – see LexisNexis

Knight Paperbacks – see Caxton Publishing Group

Kogan Page Ltd*

120 Pentonville Road, London N1 9JN
tel 020-7278 0433 *fax* 020-7837 6348
website www.koganpage.com
Chairman Phillip Kogan, *Directors* Helen Kogan (managing), Martin Klopstock (production), Mark Briars (financial), John Sadler (sales), Matthew Smith (editorial)

Training, business and management, human resource management, transport and distribution, marketing, sales, advertising and PR, finance and accounting, directories, small business, careers and vocational, personal finance, international business. Founded 1967.

Kube Publishing Ltd

(formerly the Islamic Foundation)
Markfield Conference Centre, Ratby Lane, Markfield, Leics. LE67 9SY
tel (01530) 249230 *fax* (01530) 249656
email info@kubepublishing.com
website www.kubepublishing.com
Managing Director Haris Ahmad

Books on Islam for adults and children.

Kudos Books – see Top That! Publishing plc

KyleBooks

23 Howland Street, London W1T 4AY
tel 020-7692 7215 *fax* 020-7692 7260
email general.enquiries@kylebooks.com
website www.kylecathie.com
Publisher & Managing Director Kyle Cathie

Health, beauty, food and drink, gardening, reference, style, design, Mind, Body & Spirit. Founded 1990.

Ladybird – see Penguin Group (UK)

Peter Lang Ltd

52 St Giles, Oxford OX1 3LU
tel (01865) 514160 *fax* (01865) 604028
email oxford@peterlang.com
website www.peterlang.com
Directors Antonio Albalá de Rivas (Ceo, Peter Lang Publishing Group), Fritz Schmutz (finance), Lucy Melville (managing/publishing), *Commissioning Editors* Hannah Godfrey, Christabel Scaife, Laurel Plapp

Academic: humanities and social sciences. Founded 2006.

Lawrence & Wishart Ltd

99A Wallis Road, London E9 5LN
tel 020-8533 2506 *fax* 020-8533 7369
email lw@lwbooks.co.uk
website www.lwbooks.co.uk
Directors Sally Davison (editorial), J. Rutherford, A. Greenaway, B. Kirsch

Cultural studies, current affairs, history, socialism and Marxism, political philosophy, politics, popular culture.

Legend Business Ltd

2 London Wall Buildings, London EC2M 5UU
tel 020-7448 5137
email info@legend-paperbacks.co.uk
website www.legendpress.co.uk
Directors Tom Chalmers (managing), Jonathan Reuvid

Business books.

Legend Press Ltd

2 London Wall Buildings, London EC2M 5UU
tel 020-7448 5137
email info@legend-paperbooks.co.uk
website www.legendpress.co.uk
Director Tom Chalmers (managing)

Contemporary fiction (not overly genre-specific).

Lewis Mason – see Ian Allan Publishing Ltd

LexisNexis

(formerly LexisNexis Butterworths)
Halsbury House, 35 Chancery Lane, London WC2A 1EL
tel 020-7400 2500 *fax* 020-7400 2842
email customer.services@lexisnexis.co.uk
website www.lexisnexis.co.uk

Division of Reed Elsevier (UK) Ltd. Founded 1974.

Butterworths (imprint)

Legal and tax and accountancy books, journals, looseleaf and electronic services.

Charles Knight (imprint)

Looseleaf legal works and periodicals on local government law, construction law and technical subjects.

Tolley (imprint)

Law, taxation, accountancy, business.

The Lilliput Press Ltd†

62–63 Sitric Road, Arbour Hill, Dublin 7, Republic of Ireland
tel +353 (0)1 6711647 *fax* +353 (0)1 6711233
email info@lilliputpress.ie
website www.lilliputpress.ie
Managing Director Antony T. Farrell

General and Irish literature: essays, memoir, biography/autobiography, fiction, criticism; Irish history; philosophy; Joycean contemporary culture; nature and environment. Founded 1984.

Frances Lincoln Ltd

4 Torriano Mews, Torriano Avenue, London NW5 2RZ
tel 020-7284 4009 *fax* 020-7485 0490
email reception@frances-lincoln.com
website www.frances-lincoln.com
Directors David Graham (managing), Maurice Lyon (editorial, children's books), Jon Rippon (finance), Gail Lynch (sales), Andrew Dunn (editorial, adult books)

Illustrated, international co-editions: gardening, architecture, environment, interiors, photography, art, walking and climbing, design and landscape, gift, children's books. Founded 1977.

Lion Hudson plc*

Wilkinson House, Jordan Hill Road, Oxford OX2 8DR
tel (01865) 302750 *fax* (01865) 302757
email info@lionhudson.com
website www.lionhudson.com
Managing Director Paul Clifford

Books for children and adults. Subject areas include Christian spirituality, reference, biography, history, contemporary issues and inspiration. Also specialises in children's bibles and prayer collections, as well as picture stories and illustrated non-fiction. Founded 1971 as Lion Publishing; merged with Angus Hudson Ltd in 2003.

Lion (imprint)

email info@lionhudson.com

Christian books for general readers: information and reference, history, spirituality and prayer, issues, self-help.

Monarch Books

email tonyc@lionhudson.com
Publisher Tony Collins

Christian books: biography, issues of faith and society, humour, church resources. Submit synopsis and 2 chapters with return postage.

Little, Brown Book Group*

100 Victoria Embankment, London EC4Y 0DY
tel 020-7911 8000 *fax* 020-7911 8100
email info@littlebrown.co.uk
website www.littlebrown.co.uk
Ceo Ursula Mackenzie, *Publisher* David Shelley, *Coo* Ben Groves-Raines, *Directors* Emily-Jane Taylor (finance), Richard Beswick (editorial), Antonia Hodgson (editorial), Robert Manser (group sales, publicity & marketing), Diane Spivey (rights)

Hardback and paperback fiction and general non-fiction. No unsolicited MSS. Part of Hachette UK (see page 144). Founded 1988.

Abacus (division)

Managing Director Richard Beswick

Trade paperbacks.

Atom (division)

website www.atombooks.co.uk
Publishing Director Tim Holman, *Editorial Director* Samantha Smith

Teen fiction with a fantastical edge.

Hachette Digital (division)

Editorial Director Sarah Shrubb; *Business Manager* Ben Goddard

CDs, downloads and ebooks. See page 208.

Little, Brown (division)

Managing Director Richard Beswick, *Publishing Director* Tim Whiting

General books: politics, biography, crime fiction, general fiction.

Orbit (division)

website www.orbitbooks.com
Publishing Director Tim Holman, *Editorial Director* Anne Clarke

Science fiction and fantasy.

Piatkus (division)

website www.piatkus.co.uk
Publishing Director, Non-fiction Tim Whiting, *Senior Commissioning Editor* Ann Lawrance, *Editorial Director, Fiction* Emma Beswetherick

Fiction and general non-fiction.

Sphere (division)

website www.twbookjuice.co.uk
Publisher Dan Mallory, *Associate Publisher (fiction)* Catherine Burke, *Publishing Director (non-fiction)* Adam Strange

Hardbacks and paperbacks: original fiction and non-fiction.

Virago (division)

website www.virago.co.uk
Publisher Lennie Goodings

Women's literary fiction and non-fiction.

Little Black Dress – see Headline Publishing Group

Little Books Ltd

73 Campden Hill Towers, 112 Notting Hill Gate, London W11 3QP
tel/fax 020-7792 7929
email info@maxpress.co.uk
website www.littebooks.net
Managing Director Max Hamilton Little

History, biography, fiction and gift books. No unsolicited MSS. Founded 2001.

Little Tiger Press – see Magi Publications

Liverpool University Press

4 Cambridge Street, Liverpool L69 7ZU
tel 0151 794 2233 *fax* 0151 794 2235

Books

email lup@liv.ac.uk
website www.liverpool-unipress.co.uk

French and Francophone studies, Hispanic and Lusophone studies, Liverpool interest titles, science fiction studies, art history, slavery studies and postcolonial studies. Founded 1899.

Logaston Press

Little Logaston, Logaston, Woonton, Almeley, Herefordshire HR3 6QH
tel (01544) 327344
email logastonpress@btinternet.com
website www.logastonpress.co.uk
Proprietors Andy Johnson, Karen Johnson

History, social history, archaeology and guides to rural West Midlands and Mid and South Wales. Welcomes submission of ideas: send synopsis first. Founded 1985.

Lonely Planet

BBC Media Centre (GHOS), 207 Wood Lane, London W12 7TQ
tel 020-7106 2100 *fax* 020-7106 2101
website www.lonelyplanet.com
Founders Tony Wheeler, Maureen Wheeler, *Managing Director* Douglas Schatz, *Regional Publisher* Imogen Hall

Country and regional guidebooks, city guides, pocket citybreak guides, *Discover* country guides, phrasebooks, walking guides, cycling guides, diving and snorkelling guides, pictorial books, healthy travel guides, wildlife guides, travel photography. Also a digital image library (Lonely Planet Images) and a TV company. London office established 1991.

Longman – see Pearson UK

Lorenz Books – see Anness Publishing

Luath Press Ltd

543/2 Castlehill, The Royal Mile, Edinburgh EH1 2ND
tel 0131 225 4326 *fax* 0131 225 4324
email gavin.macdougall@luath.co.uk
website www.luath.co.uk
Director Gavin MacDougall

Committed to publishing well-written books worth reading. Publishes modern fiction, history, travel guides, art, poetry, politics and more. Over 300 titles in print. Award-winning and shortlisted titles include Ann Kelley's *The Bower Bird* and Robert Alan Jamieson's *Da Happie Laand*. UK distributor HarperCollins. Founded 1981.

Lund Humphries – see Ashgate Publishing Ltd

The Lutterworth Press

PO Box 60, Cambridge CB1 2NT
tel (01223) 350865 *fax* (01223) 366951
email publishing@lutterworth.com
website www.lutterworth.com

Books and ebooks on: history and biography, literature and criticism, science, philosophy, music, sport, art and art history, educational titles, biblical studies, theology, mission, religious studies, collecting. Imprints: Acorn Editions, Patrick Hardy Books.

McGraw-Hill Education*

McGraw-Hill House, Shoppenhangers Road, Maidenhead, Berks. SL6 2QL
tel (01628) 502500
email emea_queries@mcgraw-hill.com
website www.mcgraw-hill.co.uk
Managing Director, Europe & South Africa John Donovan, *Managing Director MEA/EE* Thanos Blintzios, *Sales & Marketing Director MEA* Lefteris Souris, *Sales & Marketing Director MEA* Lefteris Souris, *General Manager Content & Digital Development EMEA* Shona Mullen, *Marketing Director Europe/South Africa* Alice Duijser, *Senior Marketing Manager UK Schools* Katie Donnison, *Sales & Marketing Director Professional/Medical/Open University Press* Jim Voute

Higher education: business, economics, computing, maths, humanities, social sciences, world languages. Professional: business, computing, science, technical, medical, general reference.

Kingscourt (imprint)

website www.kingscourt.co.uk

Primary and secondary education.

Open University Press (imprint)

email enquiries@openup.co.uk
website www.openup.co.uk

Social sciences.

Osborne (imprint)

Science, engineering, maths, computer science.

Macmillan Children's Books Ltd – see Macmillan Publishers Ltd

Macmillan Heinemann English Language Teaching – see Macmillan Publishers Ltd

Macmillan Publishers Ltd*

The Macmillan Building, 4 Crinan Street, London N1 9XW
tel 020-7833 4000 *fax* 020-7843 4640
website www.macmillan.com
Chief Executive Annette Thomas, *Directors* Julian Drinkall, S.C. Inchcoombe, D.J.G. Knight, Dr A. Thomas, J. Wheeldon, A. Forbes Watson, W.H. Farries, R. Gibb (Australia)

Pan Macmillan (division)

20 New Wharf Road, London N1 9RR
tel 020-7014 6000 *fax* 020-7014 6001

Books

website www.panmacmillan.com
Managing Director Anthony Forbes-Watson, *Publishers* Jon Butler (Macmillan non-fiction, Sidgwick & Jackson, Boxtree), Jeremy Trevathan (Macmillan fiction & Macmillan New Writing), Paul Baggaley (Picador)
Novels, literary, crime, thrillers, romance, science fiction, fantasy and horror. Autobiography, biography, business, gift books, health and beauty, history, humour, natural history, travel, philosophy, politics, world affairs, theatre, film, gardening, cookery, popular reference. Publishes under Macmillan, Tor, Pan, Picador, Sidgwick & Jackson, Boxtree, Macmillan Audio, Macmillan New Writing. No unsolicited MSS except through Macmillan New Writing. Founded 1843.

Macmillan (imprint)
Picador Publisher Paul Baggaley, *Non-Fiction Publisher* Jon Butler, *Fiction Publisher* Jeremy Trevathan, *Editorial Directors* Georgina Morley, Kate Harvey
Hardback commercial fiction including genre fiction, romantic, crime and thrillers. Hardback serious and general non-fiction including autobiography, biography, economics, history, military history, philosophy, politics and world affairs, popular reference titles.

Mantle (imprint)
Publisher Maria Rejt

Tor (imprint)
Science fiction, fantasy and thrillers published in hardback and paperback.

Pan (imprint)
Paperback imprint for Macmillan and Sidgwick & Jackson imprints. Founded 1947.

Picador (imprint)
Publisher Paul Baggaley, *Editorial Director* Kate Harvey
Literary international fiction, non-fiction and poetry published in hardback and paperback. Founded 1972.

Sidgwick & Jackson (imprint)
Publisher Jon Butler, *Editorial Director* Ingrid Connell
Hardback popular non-fiction including celebrity and show business to music and sport. Founded 1908.

Macmillan New Writing (imprint)
website www.macmillannewwriting.com
Editorial Director Will Atkins
Founded as a way of finding talented new writers who might otherwise go undiscovered. Publishes full-length novels by authors who have not previously published a novel. All genres considered and all submissions are assessed but MSS must be complete. No advance but the author pays nothing and receives a royalty of 20% on net sales. Send the complete novel by email via the website. Founded 2006.

Boxtree (imprint)
Publisher Jon Butler
Brand and media tie-in titles, including TV, film, music and internet, plus entertainment licences, pop culture, humour in hardback and paperback.

Macmillan Digital Audio (imprint)
Digital Director Sara Lloyd
Audio imprint for the entire Pan Macmillan list. See page 208.

Campbell Books (imprint)
Editorial Director Suzanne Carnell
Early learning, pop-up, novelty, board books for the preschool market.

Kingfisher (imprint)
tel 020-7014 6000 *fax* 020-7014 6001
Publishing Director Martina Challis
Children's books. Non-fiction: activity books, encyclopedias, general history, religion, art, music, philosophy, folklore, language, mathematics, nature, science and technology, novelty books, graded readers.

Young Picador (imprint)
Editorial Director Sarah Dudman
Literary fiction in paperback and hardback for the young adult market.

Palgrave Macmillan (division)*
Brunel Road, Houndmills, Basingstoke, Hants RG21 6XS
tel (01256) 329242 *fax* (01256) 479476
website www.palgrave.com
Managing Director Dominic Knight, *Publishing Directors* Margaret Hewinson (college), Sam Burridge (scholarly & reference), David Bull (journals)
Textbooks, monographs and journals in academic and professional subjects. Publishes in both hard copy and electronic formats.

W.H. Freeman (imprint)
tel (01256) 332807 *fax* (01256) 330688
Science, medicine, economics, psychology, sociology.

Macmillan Education Ltd (division)
Macmillan Oxford, 4 Between Towns Road, Oxford OX4 3PP
tel (01865) 405700 *fax* (01865) 405701
email info@macmillan.com
website www.macmillaneducation.com
Chief Executive Julian Drinkall, *Publishing Directors* Alison Hubert (Africa, Caribbean, Middle East, Asia), Kate Melliss (Spain), Sharon Jervis (Latin America), Sue Bale (dictionaries), Angela Lilley (international ELT)
ELT titles and school and college textbooks and materials in all subjects for the international education market in both book and electronic formats.

Made Simple Books – see Elsevier Ltd

Magi Publications

1 The Coda Centre, 189 Munster Road, London SW6 6AW
tel 020-7385 6333 *fax* 020-7385 7333
website www.littletigerpress.com, www.caterpillarbooks.com, www.stripespublishing.co.uk
Publishers Monty Bhatia, Jude Evans, Jane Harris, Jamie Asher

Children's picture books, novelty books, board books, pop-up books and activity books for preschool age to 7 years, and fiction for 6–12 years. See imprint websites for submissions guidelines. Imprints: Caterpillar Books (novelty), Little Tiger Press (picture books), Stripes (fiction). Founded 1987.

The Maia Press Ltd

15–16 Nassau Street, London W1W 7AB
tel 020-7436 9898
website www.maiapress.com

Original fiction by new and established authors. No unsolicited MSS. Part of Arcadia Books. Founded 2003.

Mainstream Publishing Co. (Edinburgh) Ltd*

7 Albany Street, Edinburgh EH1 3UG
tel 0131 557 2959 *fax* 0131 556 8720
email enquiries@mainstreampublishing.com
website www.mainstreampublishing.com
Directors Bill Campbell, Peter MacKenzie, Fiona Brownlee (marketing, publicity & rights), Ailsa Bathgate (editorial), Neil Graham (production), Douglas Nicoll (finance)

Biography, autobiography, art, sport, health, guidebooks, humour, current affairs, history, politics, true crime. Founded 1978.

Management Books 2000 Ltd

36 Western Road, Oxford OX1 4LG
tel (01865) 600738
email information@mb2000.com
website www.mb2000.com
Directors N. Dale-Harris, R. Hartman

Practical books for working managers and business professionals: management, business and lifeskills, and sponsored titles. Unsolicited MSS, synopses and ideas for books welcome.

Manchester University Press

Oxford Road, Manchester M13 9NR
tel 0161 275 2310 *fax* 0161 274 3346
email mup@manchester.ac.uk
website www.manchesteruniversitypress.co.uk
Chief Executive David Rodgers, *Editorial Director* Emma Brennan, *Director of Sales & Marketing* Simon Bell

Works of academic scholarship: literary criticism, cultural studies, media studies, art history, design, architecture, history, politics, economics, international law, modern-language texts. Textbooks and monographs. Founded 1904.

Mandrake of Oxford

PO Box 250, Oxford OX1 1AP
tel (01865) 243671
email mandrake@mandrake.uk.net
website www.mandrake.uk.net
Directors Mogg Morgan, Kim Morgan

Art, biography, classic crime studies, fiction, Indology, magic, witchcraft, philosophy, religion. Query letters only. Founded 1986.

Mango Publishing

PO Box 13378, London SE27 OZN
tel 020-8480 7771 *fax* 020-8480 7771
email info@mangoprint.com
website www.mangoprint.com

Poetry, fiction and non-fiction from the wider Caribbean region, the UK, the USA and Canada. Also translations of works not originally written in English. Founded 1995.

Manson Publishing Ltd*

73 Corringham Road, London NW11 7DL
tel 020-8905 5150 *fax* 020-8201 9233
email manson@mansonpublishing.com
website www.mansonpublishing.com
Managing Director Michael Manson

Medical, scientific, veterinary. Founded 1992.

Mantra Lingua TalkingPEN Ltd

Global House, 303 Ballards Lane, London N12 8NP
tel 020-8445 5123 *fax* 020-8446 7745
email info@mantralingua.com
website www.mantralingua.com, www.talkingpen.co.uk, www.birdmike.co.uk
Managing Directors R. Dutta, M. Chatterji

Innovative TalkingPEN technology to support language learning, literacy and other areas of the curriculum. Dual language books narrated in multiple languages by the TalkingPEN. Considers picture book MSS under 1,000 words, artwork submission, and non-fiction proposals. Founded 1984.

Marino Books – see The Mercier Press

Marshall Cavendish

5th Floor, 32–38 Saffron Hill, London EC1N 8FH
tel 020-7421 8120 *fax* 020-7421 8121
email info@marshallcavendish.co.uk
website www.marshallcavendish.co.uk
Managing Editor Susan McGing

English language teaching. Founded 1969.

Kenneth Mason Publications Ltd

The Book Barn, Westbourne, Hants PO10 8RS
tel (01243) 377977 *fax* (01243) 379136

email bookshop@kennethmason.co.uk
website www.kennethmason.co.uk
Directors Kenneth Mason (chairman), Piers Mason (managing), Michael Mason, Anthea Mason

Nautical, slimming, health, fitness; technical journals. Founded 1958.

Kevin Mayhew Ltd

Buxhall, Stowmarket, Suffolk IP14 3BW
tel (01449) 737978 *fax* (01449) 737834
email info@kevinmayhew.com
website www.kevinmayhew.com
Directors Kevin Mayhew (chairman), Barbara Mayhew

Christianity: prayer and spirituality, pastoral care, preaching, liturgy worship, children's, youth work, drama, instant art. Music: hymns, organ and choral, contemporary worship, piano and instrumental. Greetings cards: images, spiritual texts, birthdays, Christian events, musicians, general occasions. Contact Manuscript Submissions Dept before sending MSS/synopses. Founded 1976.

Meadowside Children's Books

185 Fleet Street, London EC4A 2HS
tel 020-7400 1084 *fax* 020-7400 1037
email info@meadowsidebooks.com
website www.meadowsidebooks.com
Publisher Paul Burgess
Publisher Simon Rosenheim

Picture books, junior fiction and young adult fiction. Founded 2002.

Medical™ – see Harlequin (UK) Ltd

Mentor Books†

43 Furze Road, Sandyford Industrial Estate, Dublin 18, Republic of Ireland
tel +353 (0)1 2952112 *fax* +353 (0)1 2952114
email admin@mentorbooks.ie
website www.mentorbooks.ie
Managing Director Daniel McCarthy, *Editor* Treasa O'Mahony

General: non-fiction, humour, biographies, politics, crime, history, guidebooks. Educational (secondary): languages, history, geography, business, maths, sciences. No unsolicited MSS. Founded 1980.

Mercat Press – see Birlinn Ltd

The Mercier Press†

Unit 3, Oak House, Riverview Business Park, Blackrock, Cork, Republic of Ireland
tel +353 (0)21 4614700 *fax* +353 (0)21 4614802
email info@mercierpress.ie
website www.mercierpress.ie
Directors J.F. Spillane (chairman), M.P. Feehan (managing), D. Crowley ACMA

Irish literature, folklore, history, politics, humour, academic, current affairs, health, mind and spirit, general non-fiction, children's. Founded 1944.

Merlin Press Ltd

99B Wallis Road, London E9 5LN
tel 020-8533 5800
email info@merlinpress.co.uk
website www.merlinpress.co.uk
Managing Director Anthony Zurbrugg

Radical history and social studies. Letters/synopses only.

Green Print (imprint)

Green politics and the environment.

Merrell Publishers Ltd

81 Southwark Street, London SE1 0HX
tel 020-7928 8880 *fax* 020-7928 1199
email mail@merrellpublishers.com
website www.merrellpublishers.com
Publisher Hugh Merrell, *Head of Editorial* Claire Chandler, *Head of Sales & Marketing* Mark Scott

High-quality illustrated books on all aspects of visual culture, including art, architecture, fashion photography and design. Unsolicited proposals welcomed but must be accompanied by return postage.

Methuen Drama – see Bloomsbury Academic & Professional Division, Bloomsbury Publishing

Methuen Publishing Ltd

8 Artillery Row, London SW1P 1RZ
tel 020-7802 0018 *fax* 020-7828 1244
website www.methuen.co.uk
Managing Director Peter Tummons, *Editor* Naomi Tummons

Literary fiction and non-fiction: biography, autobiography, travel, history, sport, humour, film, performing arts. No unsolicited MSS.

Politico's Publishing (imprint)

Politics, current affairs, political biography and autobiography.

Metro Books – see John Blake Publishing Ltd

Michelin Maps and Guides

Hannay House, 39 Clarendon Road, Watford, Herts. WD17 1JA
tel (01923) 205240 *fax* (01923) 205241
email travelpubsales@uk.michelin.com
website www.michelin.co.uk/travel
Commercial Director Ian Murray

Tourist guides, maps and atlases, hotel and restaurant guides.

Midland Publishing – see Ian Allan Publishing Ltd

Miller's – see Octopus Publishing Group

Mills & Boon Romance™ – see Harlequin (UK) Ltd

Milo Books Ltd

The Old Weighbridge, Station Road, Wrea Green, Preston PR4 2PH

tel (01772) 672900 *fax* (01772) 687727
email info@milobooks.com
website www.milobooks.com
Publisher Peter Walsh

True crime, sport, current affairs. Founded 1997.

Mira Books® – see Harlequin (UK) Ltd

Mitchell Beazley – see Octopus Publishing Group

Mobius – see Hodder & Stoughton

Modern Extra™ – see Harlequin (UK) Ltd

Modern Romance™ – see Harlequin (UK) Ltd

Monarch Books – see Lion Hudson plc

Morgan Kauffman – see Elsevier Ltd

Morrigan Book Company

Killala, Co. Mayo, Republic of Ireland
tel +353 (0)96 32555
email morriganbooks@gmail.com
Publishers Gerry Kennedy, Hilary Kennedy

Non-fiction: general Irish interest, biography, history, local history, folklore and mythology. Founded 1979.

Mosby – see Elsevier Ltd (Health Sciences)

Mount Eagle Publications Ltd – see Brandon/Mount Eagle Publications

Murdoch Books UK Ltd

Erico House, 6th Floor North,
93–99 Upper Richmond Road, London SW15 2TG
tel 020-8785 5995 *fax* 020-8785 5985
email info@murdochbooks.co.uk
website www.murdochbooks.co.uk

Non-fiction: homes and interiors, gardening, cookery, craft, DIY, narrative non-fiction, history, travel. Owned by Australian publisher Murdoch Books Pty Ltd.

John Murray (Publishers)*

338 Euston Road, London NW1 3BH
tel 020-7873 6000 *fax* 020-7873 6446
website www.johnmurray.co.uk, www.hachettelivre.co.uk
Directors Roland Philipps (managing), Eleanor Birne (non-fiction), Kate Parkin (fiction)

Quality commercial fiction and non-fiction: travel, history, entertainment, reference, biography and memoir, real-life stories. No unsolicited MSS without preliminary letter. Part of Hachette UK (see page 144).

Myriad Editions

59 Lansdowne Place, Brighton BN3 1FL
tel (01273) 720000
email info@myriadeditions.com
website www.myriadeditions.com
Directors Candida Lacey (managing), Bob Benewick, Judith Mackay

State of the World atlases, original fiction, innovative non-fiction and documentary comic books. Founded 1993.

National Trust – see Anova Books

Natural History Museum Publishing

Cromwell Road, London SW7 5BD
tel 020-7942 5336 *fax* 020-7942 5010
email publishing@nhm.ac.uk
website www.nhm.ac.uk/publishing
Head of Publishing Colin Ziegler

Natural sciences, entomology, botany, geology, mineralogy, palaeontology, zoology, history of natural history. Founded 1881.

Nautical Data Ltd

The Book Barn, White Chimney Row, Westbourne, Hants PO10 8RS
tel (01243) 389352 *fax* (01243) 379136
email enquiries@nauticaldata.com
website www.nauticaldata.com
Directors Piers Mason, Michael Benson-Colpi

Yachting titles.

NCVO Publications

(incorporating Bedford Square Press)
Regent's Wharf, 8 All Saints Street, London N1 9RL
tel 020-7713 6161 *fax* 020-7713 6300
email ncvo@ncvo-vol.org.uk
website www.ncvo-vol.org.uk
Head of Publications Emma Moore

Imprint of the National Council for Voluntary Organisations. Practical guides, reference books, directories and policy studies on voluntary sector concerns including management, employment, trustee development and finance. No unsolicited MSS accepted.

Nelson Thornes Ltd*

Delta Place, 27 Bath Road, Cheltenham, Glos. GL53 7TH
tel (01242) 267287 *fax* (01242) 253695
email cservices@nelsonthornes.com
website www.nelsonthornes.com
Managing Director Mary O'Connor

Print and electronic publishers for the educational market: primary, secondary, further education, professional. Part of the Infinitas Learning group.

New Beacon Books

76 Stroud Green Road, London N4 3EN
tel 020-7272 4889 *fax* 020-7281 4662
email newbeaconbooks@btconnect.com
website www.newbeaconbooks.co.uk

Directors Sarah White, Michael La Rose, Janice Durham

Small specialist publishers: general non-fiction, fiction, poetry, critical writings, concerning the Caribbean, Africa, African–America and Black Britain. No unsolicited MSS. Founded 1966.

New Cavendish Books

3 Denbigh Road, London W11 2SJ
tel 020-7229 6765 *fax* 020-7792 0027
email sales@newcavendishbooks.co.uk
website www.newcavendishbooks.co.uk

Specialist books for the collector; art reference, Thai guidebooks. Founded 1973.

River Books (associate imprint)

The art and architecture of Southeast Asia.

New Holland Publishers (UK) Ltd

Garfield House, 86–88 Edgware Road, London W2 2EA
tel 020-7724 7773 *fax* 020-7258 1293
email postmaster@nhpub.co.uk
website www.newhollandpublishers.com
Managing Director Steve Connolly

Illustrated non-fiction books on natural history, sports and hobbies, animals and pets, travel pictorial, travel maps and guides, reference, gardening, health and fitness, practical art, DIY, food and drink, outdoor pursuits, craft, humour, gift books. New proposals accepted (send CV and synopsis and sample chapters in first instance; sae essential).

Cadogan Guides (imprint)

email cadogan@nhpub.co.uk

Travel guides and travel literature.

New Island Books†

2 Brookside, Dundrum Road, Dundrum, Dublin 14, Republic of Ireland
tel +353 (0)1 2989937 *fax* +353 (0)1 2982783
email editor@newisland.ie
website www.newisland.ie
Publisher Edwin Higel

Fiction, poetry, drama, humour, biography, current affairs. Submissions by email to editor@newisland.ie. Send first 3 chapters as a word document together with a short synopsis. Please include details of any previous publications. Founded 1992.

New Playwrights' Network

10 Station Road Industrial Estate, Colwall, Nr Malvern, Herefordshire WR13 6RN
tel (01684) 540154
email simon@cressrelles.co.uk
website www.cressrelles.co.uk
Publishing Director Leslie Smith

General plays for the amateur, one-act and full length.

New Rider – see Pearson UK

New Theatre Publications/The Playwrights' Co-operative

2 Hereford Close, Woolston, Warrington, Cheshire WA1 4HR
tel 0845 331 3516, (01925) 485605 *fax* 0845 331 3518
email info@plays4theatre.com
website www.plays4theatre.com
Directors Ian Hornby, Alison Hornby

Plays for the professional and amateur stage. Submissions encouraged. Founded 1987.

Newnes – see Elsevier Ltd

Nexus – see Virgin Books (imprint, in partnership with Virgin Group), page 168

Nia – see The X Press

Nightingale Press

7 Green Park Station, Green Park Road, Bath BA1 1JB
tel (01225) 478444 *fax* (01225) 478440
email sales@manning-partnership.co.uk
website www.manning-partnership.co.uk
Directors Garry Manning (managing), Roger Hibbert (sales)

Humour, gift. Owned by the Manning Partnership Ltd. Founded 1997.

Nonsuch Publishing Ltd – see The History Press Ltd

North-Holland – see Elsevier Ltd

Northcote House Publishers Ltd

Horndon House, Horndon, Tavistock, Devon PL19 9NQ
tel (01822) 810066 *fax* (01822) 810034
email northcote.house@virgin.net
website www.northcotehouse.co.uk
Directors B.R.W. Hulme, A.V. Hulme (secretary)

Education and education management, educational dance and drama, literary criticism (*Writers and their Work*). Founded 1985.

W.W. Norton & Company

Castle House, 75–76 Wells Street, London W1T 3QT
tel 020-7323 1579 *fax* 020-7436 4553
email office@wwnorton.co.uk
website www.wwnorton.co.uk
Managing Director Edward Crutchley

English and American literature, economics, music, psychology, science. Founded 1980.

NWP – see Neil Wilson Publishing Ltd

Oak Tree Press†

19 Rutland Street, Cork, Republic of Ireland
tel +353 (0)21 4313855 *fax* +353 (0)21 4313496

email info@oaktreepress.com
website www.oaktreepress.com
Directors Brian O'Kane, Rita O'Kane

Business management, enterprise, accountancy and finance, law. Special emphasis on titles for small business owner/managers. Founded 1991.

Nubooks (imprint)
Ebooks.

Oberon Books

521 Caledonian Road, London N7 9RH
tel 020-7607 3637 *fax* 020-7607 3629
email info@oberonbooks.com
website www.oberonbooks.com
Managing Director Charles Glanville, *Publisher* James Hogan, *Editor* Andrew Walby

New and classic play texts, programme texts and general theatre and performing arts books. Founded 1986.

The O'Brien Press Ltd†

12 Terenure Road East, Rathgar, Dublin 6, Republic of Ireland
tel +353 (0)1 4923333 *fax* +353 (0)1 4922777
email books@obrien.ie
website www.obrien.ie
Directors Michael O'Brien, Ide ní Laoghaire, Ivan O'Brien

Ireland's leading independent book publisher. Adult: biography, politics, history, true crime, sport, humour, reference. Children's: fiction for all ages; illustrated fiction for ages 3+, 5+, 6+, 8+ novels (10+) – contemporary, historical, fantasy. No poetry, adult fiction or academic. Unsolicited MSS (sample chapters only), synopses and ideas for books welcome – submissions will not be returned. Founded 1974.

The Octagon Press Ltd

78 York Street, London W1H 1DP
tel 020-7193 6456 *fax* 020-7117 3955
email admin@octagonpress.com
website www.octagonpress.com
Director Anna Murphy

Travel, biography, literature, folklore, psychology, philosophy, with the focus on East–West studies. Welcomes single page book proposals via email. Unsolicited MSS not accepted. Founded 1960.

Octopus Publishing Group*

Endeavour House, 189 Shaftesbury Avenue, London WC2 8JY
tel 020-7632 5400 *fax* 020-7632 5405
email info@octopus-publishing.co.uk, publisher@octopus-publishing.co.uk (submissions)
website www.octopus-publishing.co.uk
Chief Executive Alison Goff, *Deputy Ceo & Group Sales & Marketing Director* Andrew Welham

Part of Hachette UK (see page 144).

Bounty (imprint)
email bountybooksinfo-bp@bountybooks.co.uk
Publishing & International Sales Director Polly Manguel
Promotional/bargain division of Octopus Publishing Group.

Cassell Illustrated (imprint)
Illustrated books for the international market specialising in popular culture.

Conran Octopus (imprint)
Quality illustrated books, particularly lifestyle, cookery, gardening.

Gaia Books (imprint)
The environment, natural living, health and the mind.

Godsfield Press (imprint)
email publisher@godsfieldpress.com
Mind, Body & Spirit with an emphasis on practical application.

Hamlyn (imprint)
Practical non-fiction, particularly cookery, health and diet, home and garden, sport, puzzles and reference.

Miller's (imprint)
Antiques and collectables.

Mitchell Beazley (imprint)
Quality illustrated books, particularly cookery, wine, gardening and the natural world.

Philip's (imprint)
email publisher@philips-maps.co.uk
Atlases, maps, astronomy, globes.

Spruce (imprint)
Illustrated books for the international market, specialising in cookery, gift and humour.

The Oleander Press

16 Orchard Street, Cambridge CB1 1JT
tel (01638) 500784
website www.oleanderpress.com
Managing Director Dr Jane Doyle

Travel, language, Libya, Arabia and Middle East, Cambridgeshire, history, reference, classics. MSS welcome with sae for reply. Founded 1960.

Michael O'Mara Books Ltd

16 Lion Yard, Tremadoc Road, London SW4 7NQ
tel 020-7720 8643 *fax* 020-7627 4900
email enquiries@mombooks.com
website www.mombooks.com
Chairman Michael O'Mara, *Managing Director* Lesley O'Mara, *Editorial Directors* Louise Dixon, Toby Buchan

General non-fiction: biography, humour, history. See website for submission guidelines. Imprint: Buster

Books (activity, novelty, fiction and non-fiction for children and novelty). Founded 1985.

Omnibus Press/Music Sales Ltd

14–15 Berners Street, London W1T 3LJ
tel 020-7612 7400 *fax* 020-7612 7545
email music@musicsales.co.uk
website www.omnibuspress.com
Chief Editor Chris Charlesworth

Rock music biographies, books about music. Founded 1976.

On Stream Publications Ltd†

Currabaha, Cloghroe, Blarney, Co. Cork, Republic of Ireland
tel +353 (0)21 4385798
email info@onstream.ie
website www.onstream.ie
Owner Rosalind Crowley

Cookery, wine, travel, human interest non-fiction, local history, academic and practical books. Founded 1986.

Oneworld Publications

185 Banbury Road, Oxford OX2 7AR
tel (01865) 310597 *fax* (01865) 310598
email info@oneworld-publications.com
website www.oneworld-publications.com
Director Juliet Mabey (publisher)

Fiction and general non-fiction: current affairs, politics, history, Middle East, business, popular science, philosophy, psychology, green issues, world religions and Islamic studies; literary fiction that sits at the intersection of the literary and commercial, showcasing strong voices and great stories. No unsolicited MSS; email or send proposal via website. Founded 1986.

Onlywomen Press Ltd

40d St Lawrence Terrace, London W10 5ST
tel 020-8354 0796
email onlywomenpress@btconnect.com
website www.onlywomenpress.com
Managing Director Lilian Mohin

Lesbian feminist fiction, non-fiction and books for children. Founded 1974.

Open Gate Press*

(incorporating Centaur Press, founded 1954)
51 Achilles Road, London NW6 1DZ
tel 020-7431 4391 *fax* 020-7431 5129
email books@opengatepress.co.uk
website www.opengatepress.co.uk
Directors Jeannie Cohen, Elisabeth Petersdorff, Sandra Lovell

Psychoanalysis, philosophy, social sciences, religion, animal welfare, the environment. Founded 1988.

Open University Press – see McGraw-Hill Education

Orbit – see Little, Brown Book Group

Orchard Books – see Hachette Children's Books

The Orion Publishing Group Ltd*

Orion House, 5 Upper St Martin's Lane, London WC2H 9EA
tel 020-7240 3444 *fax* 020-7240 4822
website www.orionbooks.co.uk
Directors Arnaud Nourry (chairman), Peter Roche (chief executive), Malcolm Edwards (deputy chief executive)

No unsolicited MSS; approach in writing in first instance. Part of Hachette UK (see page 144). Founded 1992.

Orion Paperbacks (division)

Managing Director Susan Lamb
Mass market fiction and non-fiction under Everyman, Orion and Phoenix imprints.

Orion Trade (division)

Directors Lisa Milton (managing), John Wood (fiction publishing)
Hardcover fiction (popular fiction in all categories), non-fiction and audio.

Gollancz (imprint)

Contact Simon Spanton
Science fiction and fantasy.

Orion Children's Books (division)

Publisher Fiona Kennedy
Fiction for younger and older readers, picture books.

Weidenfeld & Nicolson

See page 179.

Osborne – see McGraw-Hill Education

Oshun – see Random House Struik (Pty) Ltd

Osprey Publishing Ltd

Midland House, West Way, Botley, Oxford OX2 0PH
tel (01865) 727022 *fax* (01865) 727017
email info@ospreypublishing.com
website www.ospreypublishing.com
Directors Rebecca Smart (Ceo), Richard Sullivan (managing), John Bowman (finance), Kate Moore (editorial), Rufus Thurston (sales), Joanna Sharland (rights)

Illustrated history of war and warfare, and military aviation. Part of the Osprey Group. Founded 1968.

Oversteps Books Ltd

6 Halwell House, South Pool, Nr Kingsbridge, Devon TQ7 2RX

Books

tel (01548) 531969
email alwynmarriage@overstepsbooks.com
website www.overstepsbooks.com
Director/Managing Editor Dr Alwyn Marriage

Poetry. Email 3 poems that have been published, giving details of the magazines in which they appeared, the dates or issue numbers and the email addresses of the editors. Founded 1992.

Peter Owen Publishers

81 Ridge Road, , London N8 9NP
tel 020-7792 1873 *fax* 020-8341 7340
email aowen@peterowen.com
website www.peterowen.com
Directors Peter L. Owen (managing), Antonia Owen (editorial)

Arts, belles lettres, biography and memoir, literary fiction, general non-fiction, history, theatre and entertainment. No highly illustrated books. Do not send fiction without first emailing the Editorial Dept unless it is by an established novelist. No mass-market genre fiction, short stories or poetry; first novels almost never published.

Oxford Publishing Company – see Ian Allan Publishing Ltd

Oxford University Press*

Great Clarendon Street, Oxford OX2 6DP
tel (01865) 556767 *fax* (01865) 556646
email enquiry@oup.com
website www.oup.com
Ceo Nigel Portwood, *Group Finance Director* David Gillard, *Global Academic Business Managing Director* Tim Barton, *UK Children's & Educational Division Managing Director* Kate Harris, *ELT Division Managing Director* Peter Marshall, *UK Human Resources Director* Caroline James-Nock, *Academic Sales Director* Alastair Lewis

Archaeology, architecture, art, belles lettres, bibles, bibliography, children's books (fiction, non-fiction, picture), commerce, current affairs, dictionaries, drama, economics, educational (infants, primary, secondary, technical, university), encyclopedias, ELT, electronic publishing, essays, foreign language learning, general history, hymn and service books, journals, law, medical, music, oriental, philosophy, political economy, prayer books, reference, science, sociology, theology and religion; educational software; *Grove Dictionaries of Music & Art*. Trade paperbacks published under the imprint of Oxford Paperbacks. Founded 1478.

Palgrave Macmillan – see Macmillan Publishers Ltd

Pan – see Macmillan Publishers Ltd

Pan Macmillan – see Macmillan Publishers Ltd

Pandora Press – see Rivers Oram Press

Paper Tiger – see Anova Books

Paperbooks Publishing Ltd

2 London Wall Buildings, London EC2M 5UU
tel 020-7448 5137
email info@legend-paperbooks.co.uk
website www.legendpress.co.uk
Managing Director Tom Chalmers

Non-fiction.

Particular Books – see Penguin Group (UK)

Pavilion – see Anova Books

Pavilion Children's Books

10 Southcombe Street, London W14 0RA
tel 020-7605 1400 *fax* 020-7605 1401
website www.anovabooks.com
Publisher Ben Cameron

Children's books: from baby and picture books to illustrated classics and fiction. Part of the Anova Books Group. Submissions via an agent only.

Pavilion Publishing and Media Ltd

(Part of OLM Group)
Rayford House, School Road, Hove BN3 5HX
tel (01273) 623222 *fax* 0844 880 5062
email info@pavpub.com
website www.pavpub.com
Ceo, OLM Group Peter O'Hara, *Managing Editor* Kerry Boettcher

Health and social care training resources, books and assessment tools in a variety of fields including learning disability, mental health, vulnerable adults, housing, drugs and alcohol, staff development, children, young and older adults, and forensic services, aimed at front line workers, professionals and academics. Founded 1987.

Payne-Gallway – see Pearson UK

Peachpit Press – see Pearson UK

Pearson UK*

Edinburgh Gate, Harlow, Essex CM20 2JE
tel 0845 313 6666 *fax* 0845 313 7777
website www.pearsoned.co.uk
President Rod Bristow

Allyn & Bacon (imprint)
Higher education, humanities, social sciences.

BBC Active (imprint)
Learning resources for children and adults.

Cisco Press (imprint)
Cisco-systems authorised publisher. Material for networking students and professionals.

Benjamin Cummings (imprint)
Higher education, science.

FT Prentice Hall (imprint)
Business for higher education and professional.

Harcourt (imprint)
Educational resources for teachers and learners at primary, secondary and vocational level. Provides a range of published resources, teachers' support, and pupil and student material in all core subjects for all ages. Imprints: Ginn, Heinemann, Payne-Gallway, Raintree, Rigby.

Longman (imprint)
Education for higher education, schools, ELT.

New Riders (imprint)
Graphics and design.

Peachpit Press (imprint)
Internet and general computing.

Penguin Longman (imprint)
ELT.

Prentice Hall (imprint)
Academic and reference textbooks.

QUE Publishing (imprint)
Computing.

SAMS Publishing (imprint)
Professional computing.

Wharton (imprint)
Business.

York Notes (imprint)
Literature guides for students.

Pen & Sword Books Ltd

47 Church Street, Barnsley, South Yorkshire S70 2AS
tel (01226) 734555 *fax* (01226) 734438
email editorialoffice@pen-and-sword.co.uk
website www.pen-and-sword.co.uk
Managing Director Charles Hewitt, *Publishing Manager* Henry Wilson, *Commissioning Editors* Jamie Wilson, Phil Sidnell, Rupert Harding, *Publishing Director* Michael Leventhal

Military history, aviation history, naval and maritime, general history, local history. Imprints: Leo Cooper, Frontline Books, Pen & Sword Military Classics, Pen & Sword Aviation, Pen & Sword Naval & Maritime, Remember When, Seaforth, Pen & Sword Digital, Claymore, Wharncliffe Transport, and Pen & Sword Discovery.

Frontline (imprint)
Military history.

Wharncliffe (imprint)
Local history.

Penguin Group (UK)*

80 Strand, London WC2R 0RL
tel 020-7010 3000 *fax* 020-7010 6060
website www.penguin.co.uk
Chairman & Global Ceo John Makinson, *DK Ceo* Peter Field, *Penguin UK Ceo* Tom Weldon

Owned by Pearson plc.

Penguin General Books (literary division)
Managing Director Joanna Prior
No unsolicited MSS or synopses.

Viking (imprint)
Publishing Director Venetia Butterfield, *Editorial Directors* Tony Lacey, Eleo Gordon, Mary Mount, Joel Rickett, *Commissioning Editor* Will Hammond, *Editorial Assistant* Ben Brusey
Fiction and general non-fiction for adults. Founded 1925.

Portfolio (imprint)
Publishing Director Joel Rickett
Business. Launched 2010.

Hamish Hamilton (imprint)
Publishing Director Simon Prosser, *Assistant Editor* Anna Kelly
Fiction, belles lettres, biography and memoirs, current affairs, history, literature, politics, travel. No unsolicited MSS or synopses.

Fig Tree (imprint)
Publishing Director Juliet Annan, *Assistant Editor* Sophie Missing
Fiction and general non-fiction. No unsolicited MSS or synopses.

Penguin Ireland (imprint)
Irish Book Publishers' Association, 25 St Stephen's Green, Dublin 2, Republic of Ireland
tel +353 (0)1 6617695 *fax* +353 (0)1 6617696
email info@penguin.ie
website www.penguin.ie
Managing Director Michael McLoughlin, *Publishing Director* Patricia Deevy, *Editor* Brendan Barrington
Fiction and non-fiction, mainly of Irish origin, but published to travel beyond the Irish market. Unsolicited MSS accepted.

Michael Joseph (commercial division)
Managing Director Louise Moore, *Editors* Louise Moore (commercial women's fiction, celebrity non-fiction), Stefanie Bierwerth (crime fiction), Alex Clarke (commercial male fiction), Mari Evans (commercial historical fiction & women's fiction), Daniel Bunyard (commercial non-fiction, popular culture & military), Lindsey Evans (cookery), Katy Follain (commercial non-fiction & popular culture)

Penguin Press (division)
Managing Director Stefan McGrath, *Publishing Directors* Stuart Proffitt (Allen Lane), Simon Winder

(Allen Lane), *Classics Publisher* Adam Freudenheim, *Editorial Directors* Georgina Laycock (Allen Lane and Particular Books), Alexis Kirschbaum (Penguin Classics), Will Goodlad (Allen Lane), Helen Conford (Allen Lane and Particular Books)

Serious adult non-fiction, reference, specialist and classics. Imprint: Allen Lane. Series: *Penguin Classics, Penguin Modern Classics.* No unsolicited MSS or synopses.

Particular Books (imprint)
Publishing Director Helen Conford, *Editorial Director* Georgina Laycock

Non-fiction. Founded 2009.

Penguin Digital
Managing Director Anna Rafferty, *Head of Online Development* Jeanette Turmaine, *Head of Digital Marketing & Websites* Ashley Wilks, *Online Design Manager* Tom Johnson, *Digital Publisher* Nathan Hull

Children's Division
Managing Director, Penguin Children's Francesca Dow, *Puffin Publishing Director (fiction)* Sarah Hughes, *Puffin Editorial Director (picture books)* Louise Bolongaro, *Puffin Editorial Director (characters)* Kate Hayler, *Editorial Director, Classic Puffin* Elv Moody, *Publisher, Razorbill* Amanda Punter

Children's paperback and hardback books: wide range of picture books, board books and novelties; fiction; non-fiction and popular culture. No unsolicited MSS or synopses.

Razorbill (imprint)
Publisher Amanda Punter

Commercial teen fiction. Launched 2010.

BBC, Ladybird, Warne
Category Publisher, Warne Nicole Pearson, *Editorial Director, Ladybird* Heather Crossley, *Publisher, Media & Entertainment* Juliet Matthews, *Publishing Director, Media & Entertainment* Eric Huang, *Art Director, Media & Entertainment* Kirstie Billingham, *Creative Director* Ronnie Fairweather

Specialises in preschool illustrated developmental books for 0–6 years, non-fiction 0–8 years; licensed brands; children's classic publishing and merchandising properties. No unsolicited MSS.

Dorling Kindersley (division)
website www.dk.com
Deputy Ceo John Duhigg

Illustrated non-fiction for adults and children: gardening, health, medical, travel, food and drink, history, natural history, photography, reference, pregnancy and childcare, film and TV.

Brady (division)
Publisher Mike Degler, *Business Development Manager* Brian Saliba

Computer games strategy guides and collectors' editions.

Travel (division)
website www.traveldk.com, www.roughguides.com
Managing Director John Duhigg, *Publishing Director* Clare Currie, *Digital Publisher* Peter Buckley

Travel guides, illustrated travel books, phrasebooks and digital products; popular culture and lifestyle guides. Includes *Rough Guides* and *DK Eyewitness Travel.*

Penguin Longman – see Pearson UK

Pergamon – see Elsevier Ltd (Health Sciences)

Persephone Books

59 Lamb's Conduit Street, London WC1N 3NB
tel 020-7242 9292
email info@persephonebooks.co.uk
website www.persephonebooks.co.uk
Managing Director Nicola Beauman

Reprints of forgotten classics by 20th-century women writers with prefaces by contemporary writers. Founded 1999.

Phaidon Press Ltd

Regent's Wharf, All Saints Street, London N1 9PA
tel 020-7843 1000 *fax* 020-7843 1010
email enquiries@phaidon.com
website www.phaidon.com
Publisher Richard Schlagman, *Chairman* Andrew Price, *Directors* Amanda Renshaw (deputy publisher)

Visual arts, lifestyle and culture.

Philip's – see Octopus Publishing Group

Phillimore & Co. Ltd – see The History Press Ltd

Phoenix – see The Orion Publishing Group Ltd

Phoenix Yard Books

Phoenix Yard, 65 Kings Cross Road, London WC1X 9LW
tel 020-7239 4968
email info@phoenixyardbooks.com, submissions@phoenixyardbooks.com (submissions)
website www.phoenixyardbooks.com
Commissioning Editor Emma Langley

Picture books, poetry and fiction for 3–13 years. Specialism in character publishing. Particularly seeking character-based young fiction (6–9 years) and comics/graphic novel material. Detailed submissions guidelines can be found on the website. Please read fully before sending submissions. Founded 2009.

Piatkus – see Little, Brown Book Group

Pica Press – see Bloomsbury Children's & Educational Division, Bloomsbury Publishing

Picador – see Macmillan Publishers Ltd

Piccadilly Press

5 Castle Road, London NW1 8PR
tel 020-7267 4492 *fax* 020-7267 4493

email books@piccadillypress.co.uk
website www.piccadillypress.co.uk
Managing Director & Publisher Brenda Gardner

Early picture books, parental advice trade paperbacks, trade paperback children's fiction, young adult non-fiction and young adult fiction. Founded 1983.

Pimlico – see The Random House Group Ltd

Pink Press – see Indepenpress Publishing Ltd

Pipers' Ash Ltd

Pipers' Ash, Church Road, Christian Malford, Chippenham, Wilts. SN15 4BW
tel (01249) 720563 *fax* 0870 0568916
email pipersash@supamasu.com
website www.supamasu.com
Editorial Director Alfred Tyson

Poetry, short stories; historical novels, biographies, plays, translations, general non-fiction. New authors with talent and potential encouraged. Founded 1976.

Pitkin Publishing Ltd – see The History Press Ltd

The Playwrights Publishing Company

70 Nottingham Road, Burton Joyce, Notts. NG14 5AL
tel 0115 931 3356
email playwrightspublishingco@yahoo.com
website www.playwrightspublishing.com
Proprietors Liz & Tony Breeze

One-act and full-length drama published on the internet. Serious work and comedies, for mixed cast, all women or schools. Reading fee unless professionally produced or unwaged; sae required. Founded 1990.

Plexus Publishing Ltd

25 Mallinson Road, London SW11 1BW
tel 020-7924 4662 *fax* 020-7924 5096
email plexus@plexusuk.demon.co.uk
website www.plexusbooks.com
Directors Terence Porter (managing), Sandra Wake (editorial)

Film, music, biography, popular culture, fashion. Imprint: Eel Pie. Founded 1973.

Pluto Press

345 Archway Road, London N6 5AA
tel 020-8348 2724 *fax* 020-8348 9133
email pluto@plutobooks.com
website www.plutobooks.com
Chairman Roger van Zwanenberg, *Managing Director* Anne Beech, *Sales Director* Simon Liebesny, *Head of Marketing* Alec Gregory, *Publicity Manager* Jon Wheatley

Politics, anthropology, development, media, cultural, economics, history, Irish studies, Black studies, Islamic studies, Middle East, international relations.

Point – see Scholastic Ltd

The Policy Press

University of Bristol, 4th Floor, Beacon House, Queen's Road, Bristol BS8 1QU
tel 0117 331 4054 *fax* 0117 331 4093
email tpp-info@bristol.ac.uk
website www.policypress.co.uk
Director Alison Shaw, *Assistant Director* Julia Mortimer

Social science, specialising in social and public policy, criminology, social work and social welfare. Founded 1996.

Policy Studies Institute (PSI)

50 Hanson Street, London W1W 6UP
tel 020-7911 7500 *fax* 020-7911 7501
email psi-admin@psi.org.uk

Economic, cultural, social and environmental policy, political institutions, social sciences.

Politico's Publishing – see Methuen Publishing Ltd

Polity Press

65 Bridge Street, Cambridge CB2 1UR
tel (01223) 324315 *fax* (01223) 461385
website www.politybooks.com

Social and political theory, politics, sociology, history, media and cultural studies, philosophy, literary theory, feminism, human geography, anthropology. Founded 1983.

Polygon – see Birlinn Ltd

Pont Books – see Gomer Press

Poolbeg Press Ltd

123 Grange Hill, Baldoyle Industrial Estate, Dublin 13, Republic of Ireland
tel +353 (0)1 8321477 *fax* +353 (0)1 8321430
email info@poolbeg.com
website www.poolbeg.com
Directors Kieran Devlin (managing), Paula Campbell (publisher)

Popular fiction, non-fiction, current affairs. Imprint: Poolbeg. Founded 1976.

Portfolio – see Penguin Group (UK)

Portico – see Anova Books

Portland Press Ltd

Charles Darwin House, 12 Roger Street, London WC1N 2JL

tel 020-7685 2410 *fax* 020-7685 2469
email editorial@portlandpress.com
website www.portlandpress.com
Directors Caroline Black (managing), John Misselbrook (finance), John Day (IT), Adam Marshall (marketing)

Biochemistry and molecular life science books for graduate, postgraduate and research students. Illustrated science books for children: *Making Sense of Science* series. Founded 1990.

Portobello Books

12 Addison Avenue, London W11 4QR
tel 020-7605 1380
email mail@portobellobooks.com
website www.portobellobooks.com
Sales Director Brigid MacLeod, *Rights Director* Angela Rose, *Publisher* Philip Gwyn Jones, *Editorial Director* Laura Barber

Imprint of Granta Publications. Internationalist literature; activist non-fiction. Unsolicited submissions not accepted. Founded 2005.

T & AD Poyser – see Bloomsbury Children's & Educational Division, Bloomsbury Publishing

Preface Publishing – see The Random House Group Ltd

Prestel Publishing Ltd

4 Bloomsbury Place, London WC1A 2QA
tel 020-7323 5004 *fax* 020-7636-8004
email editorial@prestel-uk.co.uk
website www.prestel.com
Managing Director Andrew Hansen, *Commissioning Editor* Ali Gitlow

Art, architecture, photography, design, travel, cultural history and ethnography. Headquarters in Munich with offices in New York and London. Founded 1924.

Princeton University Press – Europe

6 Oxford Street, Woodstock, Oxon OX20 1TW
tel (01993) 814500 *fax* (01993) 814504
email admin@pupress.co.uk
website www.press.princeton.edu
Publishing Director – Europe Al Bertrand

Humanities, social sciences, and sciences. Part of Princeton University Press, USA. European office founded 1999.

Prion Books – see Carlton Publishing Group

The Professional and Higher Partnership

4 The Links, Cambridge Road, Newmarket CB8 0TG
tel (01638) 663456
email partners@professionalandhigher.com
website www.creativewritingstudies.wordpress.com, www.professionalandhigher.com
Directors Anthony Haynes, Karen Haynes

Publishes approx. 5 titles per year in academic and professional non-fiction (monographs, student guides) about creative writing or high education. Book proposal form available at www.creativewritingstudies.wordpress.com. No unsolicited MSS. Founded 2006.

Profile Books Ltd*

3A Exmouth House, Pine Street, London EC1R 0JH
tel 020-7841 6300 *fax* 020-7833 3969
email info@profilebooks.com
website www.profilebooks.com
Managing Director Andrew Franklin, *Publisher* Daniel Crewe

General non-fiction: history, biography, current affairs, popular science, politics, business, management, humour. Also publishers of *The Economist* books. No unsolicited MSS; phone or send preliminary letter. Founded 1996.

Serpent's Tail (imprint)

email info@serpentstail.com
website www.serpentstail.com
Publisher Peter Ayrton
Fiction and non-fiction; literary and non-mainstream work, and work in translation. No unsolicited MSS. Founded 1986.

Clerkenwell Press (imprint)

email info@clerkenwellpress.co.uk
Literary fiction in English and translation. No unsolicited MSS. Founded 2011.

Psychology Press*

27 Church Road, Hove, East Sussex BN3 2FA
tel 020-7017 6000 *fax* 020-7017 6717
website www.psypress.com

Psychology textbooks and monographs. Imprint of Taylor and Francis Group, an informa business.

Routledge (imprint)

website www.routledgementalhealth.com

Puffin – see Penguin Group (UK)

Pulp Press – see Indepenpress Publishing Ltd

Pushkin Press

12 Chester Terrace, London NW1 4ND
tel 020-854 0966
email books@pushkinpress.com
website www.pushkinpress.com
Publisher Melissa Ulfane

Literature in translation. Founded 1997.

Putnam Aeronautical – see Anova Books

Quadrille Publishing

5th Floor, Alhambra House,
27–31 Charing Cross Road, London WC2H 0LS

tel 020-7839 7117 *fax* 020-7839 7118
email enquiries@quadrille.co.uk
website www.quadrille.co.uk
Directors Alison Cathie (managing), Jane O'Shea (editorial), Helen Lewis (art), Vincent Smith (production)

Illustrated non-fiction: cookery, food and drink, gift and humour, craft, health and beauty, gardening, interiors, Mind, Body & Spirit. Founded 1994.

Quantum – see W. Foulsham & Co. Ltd

The Quarto Group, Inc.

230 City Road, London EC1V 2TT
tel 020-7700 9000 *fax* 020-7253 4437
email info@quarto.com
website www.quarto.com
Chairman & Ceo Laurence Orbach, *Chief Financial Officer* Mick Mousley, *Creative Director* Bob Morley, *Director of Publishing* David Breuer

Independent publishing group encompassing traditional and co-edition publishing. Co-edition books are licensed to third parties all over the world, with bestselling titles often available in 20+ languages. UK-based operations include the following autonomously run business units/imprints. See separate entries for Aurum Press Ltd and Jacqui Small on page 127 and RotoVision on page 170.

Marshall Editions

email james.ashton-tyler@quarto.com
Publisher James Ashton-Tyler

QED Publishing Ltd

email zetad@quarto.com
Associate Publisher Zeta Davies

Quantum Publishing Ltd

email sarah.bloxham@quarto.com
Publisher Sarah Bloxham

Quarto Children's Books Ltd

email quartokids@quarto.com, sueg@quarto.com
Publisher Sue Grabham, *Art Director* Jonathan Gilbert

Co-edition publisher of innovative Books-Plus for children. Highly illustrated paper-engineered, novelty and component-based titles for all ages, but primarily preschool (3+), 5–8 and 8+ years. Mainly non-fiction, early concepts and curriculum-based topics for the trade in all international markets. Opportunities for freelance paper engineers, artists, authors, editors and designers. Unsolicited MSS not accepted.

Quarto Publishing plc

email paulc@quarto.com
Publisher Paul Carslake

qu:id

email nigelb@quidpublishing.com
Publisher Nigel Browning

Quintessence

email mark.fletcherl@quarto.com
Publisher Mark Fletcher

Quintet Publishing Ltd

email mark.searle@quarto.com
Publisher Mark Searle

QUE Publishing – see Pearson UK

Quercus Publishing Plc

55 Baker Street, 7th Floor, South Block, London WIU 8EW
tel 020-7291 7200 *fax* 020-7291 7201
email enquiries@quercusbooks.co.uk
website www.quercusbooks.co.uk
Directors Mark Smith (Ceo), Mike McGrath (executive director group sales), Wayne Davies (executive director digital), David North (executive director & publisher), Paul Lenton (finance director), Jon Riley (editor-in-chief), Roisin Heycock (children's publishing), Caroline Proud (sales director), Ron Beard (key accounts), David Murphy (key accounts), Lucy Ramsey (publicity), Daniel Bouquet (rights & co-editions).

Fiction and non-fiction. Founded 2005.

Maclehose Press (imprint)

Publisher Christopher Maclehose

Jo Fletcher Books (imprint)

Publisher Jo Fletcher

Heron Books (imprint)

Publisher Susan Watt

Quest – see Top That! Publishing plc

Quiller Publishing Ltd

Wykey House, Wykey, Shrewsbury, Shrops. SY4 1JA
tel (01939) 261616 *fax* (01939) 261606
email info@quillerbooks.com
website www.countrybooksdirect.com
Managing Director Andrew Johnston

Kenilworth Press (imprint)

Equestrian (riding, training, dressage, eventing, show jumping, driving, polo). Publisher of BHS official publications.

Quiller Press (imprint)

Specialises in all country and country sports subjects, including fishing, shooting, cookery, humour, and all field sports.

The Sportsman's Press (imprint)

All country subjects and general sports including fishing, fencing, shooting, equestrian and gunmaking; wildlife art.

Swan Hill Press (imprint)

Country and field sports activities, including fishing, cookery, shooting, falconry, equestrian, gundog training, natural history, humour.

Radcliffe Publishing Ltd

70 Alston Drive, Bradwell Abbey, Milton Keynes MK13 9HG

tel (01235) 528820 *fax* (01235) 528830
email contact.us@radcliffemed.com
website www.radcliffe-oxford.com
Directors Gregory Moxon (managing), Gill Nineham (editorial), Margaret McKeown (financial)

Primary care, child health, palliative care, nursing, pharmacy, dentistry, counselling, healthcare organisation and management examination revision aids. Founded 1987.

Ragged Bears Publishing Ltd

Unit 14A, Bennett's Field Trading Estate, Southgate Road, Wincanton, Somerset BA9 9DT
tel (01963) 34300
email info@raggedbears.co.uk
website www.raggedbears.co.uk
Managing Director Henrietta Stickland

Preschool picture and novelty books, first chapter books to young teen fiction. Emailed submissions preferred but if posted send sae. Do not send original artwork. Imprint: Ragged Bears. Founded 1994.

Raintree – see Pearson UK

The Random House Group Ltd*

20 Vauxhall Bridge Road, London SW1V 2SA
tel 020-7840 8400
website www.randomhouse.co.uk
Chairman/Ceo Gail Rebuck, *Deputy Ceo* Ian Hudson, *Directors* Larry Finlay (RHCB & managing director, Transworld), Mark Gardiner (finance), Brian Davies (Ebury Publishing & managing director, overseas operations), Richard Cable (managing director, Vintage Publishing), Garry Prior (sales), Mark Williams (managing director distribution)

Subsidiary of Bertelsmann AG.

Group consists of 6 publishing companies comprising 40 imprints.

Random House Audio Books
tel 020-7840 8519 *fax* 020-7233 6127
Commissioning Editor Zoe Willis

See page 209.

Random House Digital
tel 020-7840 8400

Cornerstone (company)
Managing Director Susan Sandon, *Publicity Director* Charlotte Bush

No unsolicited MSS accepted.

Arrow Books Ltd (imprint)
tel 020-7840 8414 *fax* 020-7840 6127

Paperback fiction and non-fiction.

Century (imprint)
tel 020-7840 8569 *fax* 020-7233 6127
Publishing Director Ben Dunn, *Editorial Director* Jack Fogg, Kate Burke

Fiction, biography, autobiography, general non-fiction, true crime, humour.

Hutchinson (imprint)
tel 020-7840 8400 *fax* 020-7233 6127

Fiction: literary and women's fiction, adventure, crime, thrillers. Non-fiction: biography, memoirs, general history, politics, travel, current affairs.

Preface Publishing (imprint)
tel 020-7840 8424
email prefacesubmissions@randomhouse.co.uk
Publisher Trevor Dolby, *Publishing Director* Rosie de Courcy

Commercial fiction and non-fiction. Unsolicited MSS accepted by email.

Random House Books (imprint)
tel 020-7840 8451 *fax* 020-7840 6127
Publishing Director Nigel Wilcockson

Non-fiction: social and cultural history, current affairs, popular culture, reference, business and economics.

William Heinemann (imprint)
tel 020-7840 8400 *fax* 020-7233 6127
Publishing Director Jason Arthur

Fiction and general non-fiction: crime, thrillers, literary fiction, translations, history, biography, science.

Windmill Books (imprint)
tel 020-7840 8414 *fax* 020-7840 6127
website www.windmill-books.co.uk
Publishing Director Stephanie Sweeney

B-format paperback fiction and non-fiction.

Vintage Publishing (company)
Managing Director Richard Cable, *Deputy Managing Director* Faye Brewster, *Publisher* Dan Franklin, *Deputy Publishing Director* Rachel Cugnoni, *Publicity Director* Christian Lewis, *Marketing Director* Roger Bratchell

The Bodley Head (imprint)
tel 020-7840 8514 *fax* 020-7233 6117
Publishing Director Stuart Williams

Non-fiction: history, current affairs, politics, science, biography, economics.

Jonathan Cape (imprint)
tel 020-7840 8608 *fax* 020-7233 6117
Publishing Director Dan Franklin, *Deputy Publishing Director* Robin Robertson

Biography and memoirs, current affairs, drama, fiction, history, poetry, travel, politics, graphic novels, photography.

Chatto & Windus (imprint)
tel 020-7840 8745 *fax* 020-7233 6117
Publishing Director Clara Farmer, *Editorial Director* Becky Hardie

Belles lettres, biography and memoirs, current affairs, fiction, history, poetry, politics, philosophy, translations, travel. No unsolicited MSS.

Harvill Secker (imprint)
tel 020-7840 8893 *fax* 020-7233 6117
Publishing Director Liz Foley, *Editorial Director* Michal Shavit
English literature and world literature in translation. Non-fiction (history, current affairs, literary essays, music). No unsolicited MSS.

Pimlico (imprint)
tel 020-7840 8836 *fax* 020-7233 6117
Publishing Director Rachel Cugnoni
History, biography, literature. Exclusively in paperback. No unsolicited MSS.

Square Peg (imprint)
tel 020-7840 8894 *fax* 020-7233 6117
Publishing Director Rosemary Davidson
Eclectic, idiosyncratic and commercial non-fiction including humour, illustrated and gift books, food, nature, memoir, travel, parenting. Unsolicited MSS with sae.

Vintage (imprint)
tel 020-7840 8836 *fax* 020-7233 6117
Publishing Director Rachel Cugnoni, *Editorial Director Vintage Classics* Laura Hassan
Quality fiction and non-fiction. Predominantly in paperback. No unsolicited MSS.

Yellow Jersey Press (imprint)
tel 020-7840 8407 *fax* 020-7233 6117
Editorial Director Matthew Phillips
Sport and leisure activities. Unsolicited MSS (first 3 chapters only) accepted with sae.

Ebury Publishing (company)
website www.eburypublishing.co.uk
Managing Director Fiona MacIntyre, *Publisher* Jake Lingwood, *Publicity Director* Sarah Bennie, *Marketing Director* Diana Riley

BBC Books (imprint)
tel 020-7840 8400 *fax* 020-7840 8406
Senior Publishing Director Shirley Patton
TV and radio tie-ins and books linked to BBC brands and personalities.

Ebury Press (imprint)
tel 020-7840 8400 *fax* 020-7840 8406
Deputy Publisher Andrew Goodfellow, *Publishing Director Illustrated* Carey Smith, *Editorial Director Fiction* Gillian Green
General commercial non-fiction, autobiography, memoir, popular history, sport, travel writing, popular science, humour, film/TV tie-ins, music, popular reference, cookery, lifestyle, fiction.

Rider (imprint)
tel 020-7840 8400 *fax* 020-7840 8406
Publishing Director Judith Kendra
Inspirational titles across the spectrum of psychology, philosophy, international affairs, biography, current affairs, history, psychology, travel and spirituality.

Time Out (imprint, in partnership with Time Out Group)
tel 020-7840 8798 *fax* 020-7840 8406
Publishing Brand Manager Luthfa Begum
Travel, film, reference and lifestyle published in a unique partnership with *Time Out Guides*.

Vermilion (imprint)
tel 020-7840 8400 *fax* 020-7840 8406
Editorial Director Susanna Abbott
Personal development, health, diet, relationships, parenting.

Virgin Books (imprint, in partnership with Virgin Group)
tel 020-7840 8400
Publishing Director Ed Faulkner
Health and popular culture: entertainment, showbiz, arts, film and TV, music, humour, biography and autobiography, popular reference, true crime, sport, travel, memoir, environment. Imprints: Black Lace, Nexus.

Random House Children's Publishers UK (company)
61–63 Uxbridge Road, London W5 5SA
tel 020-8579 2652 *fax* 020-8231 6737
website www.kidsatrandomhouse.co.uk
Publisher, Fiction Annie Eaton, *Publisher, Colour & Licensing & RHCSE* Fiona MacMillan, *Editorial Director, Fiction* Becky Stradwick, *Editorial Director, Fiction* Kelly Hurst, *Deputy Publisher, Picture Books* Sue Buswell, *Licensing* Jacqui Butler, *Art Director* Margaret Hope
Picture books, novelty and gift books, preschool and pop-ups, fiction, non-fiction and audio CDs.

Imprints: Bantam Press, Bodley Head Children's Books, Jonathan Cape Children's Books, Corgi Children's Books, Doubleday Children's Books, David Fickling Books, Hutchinson Children's Books, Red Fox Children's Books, Tamarind. No unsolicited MSS or original artwork or text.

Tamarind Books (imprint)
61–63 Uxbridge Road, London W5 5SA
tel 020-8231 6800 *fax* 020-8231 6737
email info@tamarindbooks.co.uk
website www.tamarindbooks.co.uk
Deputy Publisher Sue Buswell
Multicultural children's picture books and posters. All books give a high positive profile to black children. Unsolicited material welcome with return postage. Founded 1987.

David Fickling Books (imprint)
31 Beaumont Street, Oxford OX1 2NP
tel (01865) 339000 *fax* (01865) 339009
email dfickling@randomhouse.co.uk
website www.davidficklingbooks.co.uk
Publisher David Fickling, *Editor* Bella Pearson
Picture books, fiction for 5–8 and 9–12 years, young

adult fiction and poetry. Will consider unsolicited MSS (first 3 chapters only); include covering letter and sae and allow 3 months for response. If possible, find an agent first. Founded 2000.

Transworld Publishers
See page 177.

Ransom Publishing Ltd

Radley House, 8 St Cross Road, Winchester SO23 9HX
tel (01962) 862307 *fax* (05601) 148881
email ransom@ransom.co.uk
website www.ransom.co.uk
Directors Jenny Ertle (managing), Steve Rickard (creative)

Books for reluctant and struggling readers covering high interest age/low reading age titles, quick reads, reading schemes. Range of accompanying workbooks and teacher's guides. Series include *Goal!*, *Boffin Boy*, *Dark Man*, *Trailblazers*, *Siti's Sisters*, *321 Go!* and *Cutting Edge*. Will consider unsolicited MSS. Email in first instance. Founded 1995.

RBI Search

(formerly Reed Business Information)
Windsor Court, East Grinstead House, Wood Street, East Grinstead, West Sussex RH19 1XA
tel (01342) 326972 *fax* (01342) 335860
email info@rbi.co.uk
website www.reedbusiness.com
Managing Director Jane Burgess

Online information specialists including leading search engines such as kellysearch.com and bankersalmanac.com covering industrial, financial, travel and media sectors, including gazetteers.com, hotelsearch and Kemps. Part of Reed Elsevier plc. Founded 1983.

The Reader's Digest Association Ltd

157 Edgware Road, London W2 2HR
tel 020-7053 4500
website www.readersdigest.co.uk
Managing Director C.J. Spratling, *Editor-in-Chief* Gill Hudson

Monthly magazine, condensed and series books; also DIY, computers, puzzles, gardening, medical, handicrafts, law, touring guides, encyclopedias, dictionaries, nature, folklore, atlases, cookery, music.

Reaktion Books

33 Great Sutton Street, London EC1V 0DX
tel 020-7253 1071 *fax* 020-7253 1208
email info@reaktionbooks.co.uk
website www.reaktionbooks.co.uk
Publisher Michael R. Leaman

Art history, design, architecture, critical biography, history, cultural studies, film studies, animal studies, modern music history, food history, natural history, Asian studies, popular science, sports history, travel writing, photography. Founded 1985.

Red Dress Ink™ – see Harlequin (UK) Ltd

Red Fox Children's Books – see The Random House Group Ltd

Thomas Reed – see Bloomsbury Children's & Educational Division, Bloomsbury Publishing

Reed Books – now Octopus Publishing Group

William Reed Directories

Broadfield Park, Crawley, West Sussex RH11 9RT
tel (01293) 613400 *fax* (01293) 610310
email directories@william-reed.co.uk
website www.william-reed.co.uk
Director John Lewis, *Content Manager* Leah Gale

Publishers of leading business-to-business directories and reports, including *The Retail and Shopping Centre Directory* and *The Grocer Directory of Manufacturers and Suppliers.*

Reed Educational and Professional Publishing Ltd – see Harcourt (imprint)

Reeds Nautical Almanac – see Bloomsbury Children's & Educational Division, Bloomsbury Publishing

Revenge Ink

Unit 13, Newby Road, Hazel Grove, Stockport, Cheshire SK7 5DA
email amita@revengeink.com
website www.revengeink.com
Editor Gopal Mukerjee (with Amita Mukerjee)
Director Amita Mukerjee

Founded by siblings Gopal and Amita Mukerjee, the company publishes adult fiction (all kinds) and prefers unsolicited, first-time novelists or established writers seeking a new outlet for edgier material. Considers poetry if presented in an original, creative manner. Currently publishes approx. 7 titles a year. Does not publish children's fiction or non-fiction titles such as cookbooks, gardens and how-to books. The company is aiming to create a non-fiction imprint for new research in philosophy, history, critical theory and political analysis. Submission guidelines can be found on the website. By email, preferably, send short sample and query first. Founded 2007.

Rider – see The Random House Group Ltd

Rigby – see Pearson UK

Rising Stars*

PO Box 105, Rochester, Kent ME2 4BE
tel 0800 091 1602 *fax* 0800 091 1603

email info@risingstars-uk.com
website www.risingstars-uk.com

Educational publisher of books and software for primary school age children. Titles are linked to the National Curriculum Key Stages, QCA Schemes of Work, National Numeracy Framework or National Literacy Strategy. Approach by email with ideas for publishing.

River Books – see New Cavendish Books

Rivers Oram Press

144 Hemingford Road, London N1 1DE
tel 020-7607 0823 *fax* 020-7609 2776
email ro@riversoram.com
website www.riversoram.com
Directors Elizabeth Rivers Fidlon (managing), Anthony Harris

Non-ficton: social and political science, current affairs, social history, gender studies, sexual politics, cultural studies. Founded 1991.

Pandora Press (imprint)

Feminist press. General non-fiction: biography, arts, media, health, current affairs, reference and sexual politics.

Roar Publishing – see Magi Publications

Robinson – see Constable & Robinson Ltd

Robson Books – see Anova Books

George Ronald

3 Rosecroft Lane, Oaklands, Welwyn, Herts. AL6 0UB
tel (01438) 716062 *fax* 0870 762 6242
email sales@grbooks.com
website www.grbooks.com
Managers E. Leith, M. Hofman

Religion, specialising in the Bahá'í Faith. Founded 1939.

RotoVision

Sheridan House, 112–116A Western Road, Hove, East Sussex BN3 1DD
tel (01273) 727268 *fax* (01273) 727269
email sales@rotovision.com
website www.rotovision.com

Illustrated books on design, photography and the performing arts. Part of the Quarto Group.

Rough Guides – see Penguin Group (UK)

Roundhouse Group

Unit B, 18 Marine Gardens, Brighton BN2 1AH
tel (01273) 603717 *fax* (01273) 697494
email sales@roundhousegroup.co.uk
website www.roundhousegroup.co.uk
Publisher Alan T. Goodworth

Art, photography and crafts; reference books. No unsolicited MSS. Founded 1991.

Route

PO Box 167, Pontefract, West Yorkshire WF8 4WW
tel (01977) 797695
email info@route-online.com
website www.route-online.com
Contact Ian Daley, Isabel Galan

Contemporary fiction (novels and short stories) and cultural non-fiction. Unsolicited MSS discouraged. See website for current guidelines.

Routledge-Cavendish – see Taylor and Francis Group

Routledge – see Psychology Press

Royal Collection Publications

Stable Yard House, St James's Palace, London SW1A 1JR
tel 020-7024 5584 *fax* 020-7024 5643
website www.royalcollection.org.uk
Publisher Jacky Colliss Harvey, *Commissioning Editor* Kate Owen, *Publishing Assistant* Nina Chang

Subjects from within the Royal Collection. Founded 1993.

Royal National Institute of Blind People (RNIB)

PO Box 173, Peterborough, Cambs. PE2 6WS
tel 0303 1239999 *fax* (01733) 375001
email shop@rnib.org.uk
website www.rnib.org.uk

Magazines, catalogues and books for blind and partially sighted people, to support daily living, leisure, learning and employment reading needs. Produced in braille, audio, large/legible print and email. For complete list of magazines see page 79. Founded 1868.

Ryland Peters & Small

20–21 Jockey's Fields, London WC1R 4BW
tel 020-7025 2200 *fax* 020-7025 2201
email info@rps.co.uk
website www.rylandpeters.com
Directors David Peters (managing), Cindy Richards (publishing), Julia Charles (editorial), Leslie Harrington (art), Denise Lie (rights), Danny Parnes (UK & export sales)

High-quality illustrated books on food and drink, home and garden, babies and children, gift books. Founded 1995.

Cico Books (imprint)

tel 020-7025 2280 *fax* 020-7025 2281
email mail@cicobooks.co.uk
website www.cicobooks.co.uk
Publisher Cindy Richards

Lifestyle and interiors, crafts and Mind, Body & Spirit. Founded 1999.

SAGE Publications Ltd*

1 Oliver's Yard, 55 City Road, London EC1Y 1SP
tel 020-7324 8500 *fax* 020-7324 8600
email info@sagepub.co.uk
website www.uk.sagepub.com

Social sciences, behavioural sciences, humanities, science, technology and medicine. Journals, books and electronic media for academic, educational and professional markets. Founded 1971.

St Pauls

St Pauls Publishing, 187 Battersea Bridge Road, London SW11 3AS
tel/fax 020-7978 4300
email editorial@stpaulspublishing.com
website www.stpaulspublishing.com

Theology, ethics, spirituality, biography, education, general books of Roman Catholic and Christian interest. Founded 1948.

Salamander – see Anova Books

Salariya Book Company Ltd

Book House, 25 Marlborough Place, Brighton BN1 1UB
tel (01273) 603306 *fax* (01273) 693857
email salariya@salariya.com
website www.salariya.com
Director David Salariya

Children's non-fiction. Imprints: Book House, Scribblers, Scribo. Founded 1989.

Salt Publishing

12 Norwich Road, Cromer, Norfolk NR27 0AX
email sarah-jayne@saltpublishing.com
website www.saltpublishing.com
Publishing Director Christopher Hamilton-Emery

Poetry, fiction and literary criticism and the Best British annual anthologies.

SAMS Publishing – see Pearson UK

Saunders – see Elsevier Ltd (Health Sciences)

Alastair Sawday Publishing Ltd

The Old Farmyard, Yanley Lane, Long Ashton, Bristol BS41 9LR
tel (01275) 395430 *fax* (01275) 393388
email info@sawdays.co.uk
website www.sawdays.co.uk, www.special-escapes.co.uk

Special Places to Stay series of guidebooks and *Fragile Earth Books* on global green issues. Founded 1994.

S.B. Publications

14 Bishopstone Road, Seaford, East Sussex BN25 2UB
tel (01323) 893498
email sbpublications@tiscali.co.uk
website www.sbpublications.co.uk
Proprietor Lindsay Woods

Local history, local themes (e.g. walking books, guides), specific themes. Founded 1987.

Scala Publishers

Northburgh House, 10 Northburgh Street, London EC1V 0AT
tel 020-7490 9900 *fax* 020-7336 6870
email sales@scalapublishers.com
website www.scalapublishers.com
Chairman David Campbell, *Directors* Henry Channon, Jan Baily, Antony White, *Director of Museum Publications US* Jennifer Wright, *Commissioning Editor UK* Jenny McKinley

Art, architecture, guides to museums and art galleries, antiques. Founded 1992.

Sceptre – see Hodder & Stoughton

Schofield & Sims Ltd

Dogley Mill, Fenay Bridge, Huddersfield HD8 0NQ
tel (01484) 607080 *fax* (01484) 606815
email post@schofieldandsims.co.uk
website www.schofieldandsims.co.uk
Chairman C.N. Platts

Educational: nursery, infants, primary; posters. Founded 1901.

Scholastic Ltd*

Euston House, 24 Eversholt Street, London NW1 1DB
tel 020-7756 7761 *fax* 020-7756 7795
website www.scholastic.co.uk
Chairman M.R. Robinson

Children's fiction and non-fiction and education resources for primary schools. Owned by Scholastic Inc. Founded 1964.

Scholastic Children's Books (division)

Euston House, 24 Eversholt Street, London NW1 1DB
tel 020-7756 7756 *fax* 020-7756 7795
email publicity@scholastic.co.uk
Directors Hilary Murray Hill (managing & publishing), Jill Sawyer (editorial, non-fiction), Clare Argar (editorial, fiction), Antonia Pelari (trade & rights), Lisa Edwards (publishing & commercial)

Activity books, novelty books, picture books, fiction for children 5–12 years, young adult fiction, series fiction and film/TV tie-ins. Imprints: Hippo, Point, Scholastic Fiction, Scholastic Non-fiction, Scholastic Press. Will consider unsolicited submissions: send synopsis and sample chapter only.

The Chicken House

See page 133.

Scholastic Educational Resources (division)

Book End, Range Road, Witney, Oxon OX29 0YD
tel (01993) 893456

Books

Managing Director, Publishing Hilary Murray Hill
Professional books, classroom materials and online resources for primary teachers.

Scholastic Book Clubs (division)
See page 332.

Scholastic Book Fairs (division)
See page 332.

Science Museum

Exhibition Road, London SW7 2DD
tel 0870 870 4771 *fax* 020-7942 4362
website www.nmsi.ac.uk, www.sciencemuseum.org.uk

History of science and technology, museum guides.

Science Navigation Group

34–42 Cleveland Street, London W1T 4LB
tel 020-7323 0323 *fax* 020-7580 1938
email info@sciencenavigation.com
website www.sciencenavigation.com
Chairman Vitek Tracz

Biological sciences, medicine, pharmaceutical science, internet communities, electronic publishing.

SCM Canterbury Press Ltd*

13–17 Long Lane, London EC1A 9PN
tel 020-7776 7540 *fax* 020-7776 7556
website www.scm-canterburypress.co.uk
Publishing Director Christine Smith

Theological books with special emphasis on text and reference books and contemporary theology for both students and clergy. Founded 1929.

Canterbury Press (imprint)
Norwich Books and Music, 13A Hellesdon Park Road, Norwich NR6 5DR
tel/fax (01603) 785925
Religious books for the general market, church resources and liturgy.

SCM Press (imprint)
Academic theology.

SCM Press – see SCM Canterbury Press Ltd

SCP Publishers Ltd

(trading as Scottish Cultural Press)
Unit 6, Newbattle Abbey Business Park, Newbattle Road, Dalkeith EH22 3LJ
tel 0131 660 6366 *fax* 0870 285 4846
email info@scottishbooks.com
website www.scottishbooks.com
Directors Brian Pugh, Avril Gray

Scottish non-fiction and Scots language, children's writing. Unsolicited MSS not accepted; send letter, telephone or email in first instance. Founded 1992.

Scottish Children's Press
Literature, history, archaeology, biography and environmental history.

Scripture Union

207–209 Queensway, Bletchley, Milton Keynes, Bucks. MK2 2EB
tel (01908) 856000 *fax* (01908) 856111
email info@scriptureunion.org.uk
website www.scriptureunion.org.uk
Director of Ministry Delivery Terry Clutterham

Christian books and Bible reading materials for people of all ages; educational and worship resources for churches; children's fiction and non-fiction; adult non-fiction. Founded 1867.

Seafarer Books Ltd

102 Redwald Road, Rendlesham, Woodbridge, Suffolk IP12 2TE
tel (01394) 420789
email info@seafarerbooks.com
website www.seafarerbooks.com
Commissioning Editor Patricia Eve

Books on traditional sailing and stories of the sea, mainly narrative.

Search Press Ltd

Wellwood, North Farm Road, Tunbridge Wells, Kent TN2 3DR
tel (01892) 510850 *fax* (01892) 515903
email searchpress@searchpress.com
website www.searchpress.com
Directors Martin de la Bédoyère (managing), Caroline de la Bédoyère (rights), Rosalind Dace (editorial)

Arts, crafts, leisure. Founded 1970.

Seren

57 Nolton Street, Bridgend CF31 3AE
tel (01656) 663018
email general@serenbooks.com
website www.serenbooks.com
Publisher Mick Felton

Poetry, fiction, drama, history, film, literary criticism, biography, art – mostly with relevance to Wales. Founded 1981.

Severn House Publishers

9–15 High Street, Sutton, Surrey SM1 1DF
tel 020-8770 3930 *fax* 020-8770 3850
email sales@severnhouse.com
website www.severnhouse.com
Chairman Edwin Buckhalter, *Publisher* Kate Lyall Grant

Hardcover, paperback, large print and ebook adult fiction for the library market: romances, mysteries, thrillers, detective, advance, war, science fiction. No unsolicited MSS; submissions via literary agents.

Shearsman Books

50 Westons Hill Drive, Emersons Green, Bristol BS16 7DF
tel 0117 957 2957

email editor@shearsman.com
website www.shearsman.com
Contact Tony Frazer

Contemporary poetry in English and in translation.

Sheldon Press – see Society for Promoting Christian Knowledge

Sheldrake Press

188 Cavendish Road, London SW12 0DA
tel 020-8675 1767 *fax* 020-8675 7736
email enquiries@sheldrakepress.co.uk
website www.sheldrakepress.co.uk
Publisher J.S. Rigge

History, travel, architecture, cookery, music; stationery. Founded 1979.

Shepheard-Walwyn (Publishers) Ltd

107 Parkway House, Sheen Lane, London SW14 8LS
tel 020-8241 5927
email books@shepheard-walwyn.co.uk
website www.shepheard-walwyn.co.uk, www.ethicaleconomics.org.uk
Director A.R.A. Werner

History, biography, political economy, perennial philosophy; illustrated gift books; Scottish interest. Founded 1971.

Shire Publications

Midland House, West Way, Botley, Oxford OX2 0PH
tel (01865) 811332 *fax* (01865) 242009
email shire@shirebooks.co.uk
website www.shirebooks.co.uk
Managing Director Rebecca Smart, *Publisher* Nick Wright

Discovering paperbacks, Shire Libraries, Shire Archaeology, Shire History and Shire Collections. Founded 1962.

Short Books Ltd

3A Exmouth House, Pine Street, London EC1R 0JH
tel 020-7833 9429 *fax* 020-7833 9500
email clemmie@shortbooks.co.uk
website www.shortbooks.co.uk
Editorial Directors Rebecca Nicolson, Aurea Carpenter

Non-fiction and fiction. No unsolicited MSS. Founded 2000.

Sidgwick & Jackson – see Macmillan Publishers Ltd

Sigma Press

Stobart House, Pontyclerc, Penybanc Road, Ammanford, Carmarthenshire SA18 3HP
tel (01269) 593100 *fax* (01269) 596116
email info@sigmapress.co.uk
website www.sigmapress.co.uk
Directors Nigel Evans, Jane Evans

Leisure: country walking, cycling, regional heritage, ecology, folklore; biographies. Founded 1979.

Silhouette® – see Harlequin (UK) Ltd

Simon & Schuster UK Ltd*

222 Gray's Inn Road, London WC1X 8HB
tel 020-7316 1900 *fax* 020-7316 0331/2
website www.simonandschuster.co.uk
Directors Ian Chapman (managing), Suzanne Baboneau (publishing), Ingrid Selberg (children's publishing)

Commercial and literary fiction; general and serious non-fiction; children's. No unsolicited MSS. Founded 1986.

Simon & Schuster (imprint)

Publishers Francine Lawrence, Mike Jones, *Fiction Publisher* Maxine Hitchcock

Adult non-fiction (history, biography, current affairs, science); illustrated non-fiction; mass market fiction; bespoke publishing.

Simon & Schuster Audioworks

Fiction, non-fiction and business.

Simon & Schuster Children's Publishing

Picture books, pop-up, novelty, fiction and non-fiction.

Smith Gryphon Ltd – see John Blake Publishing Ltd

Colin Smythe Ltd*

38 Mill Lane, Gerrards Cross, Bucks. SL9 8BA
tel (01753) 886000 *fax* (01753) 886469
website www.colinsmythe.co.uk
Directors Colin Smythe (managing & editorial), Leslie Hayward, Ann Saddlemyer

Irish biography, phaleristics, heraldry, Irish literature and literary criticism, Irish history. Founded 1966.

Snowbooks Ltd*

email info@snowbooks.com
website www.snowbooks.com
Directors Emma Barnes (managing), Rob Jones, *Publisher* Anna Torborg

Genre fiction: steampunk, fantasy, sci-fi and horror. General non-fiction. See website for submission guidelines. No postal submissions or calls please. Founded 2004.

Society for Promoting Christian Knowledge*

36 Causton Street, London SW1P 4ST
tel 020-7592 3900 *fax* 020-7592 3939
email publishing@spck.org.uk
website www.spckpublishing.co.uk
Director of Publishing Joanna Moriarty

Founded 1698.

Sheldon Press (imprint)
Popular medicine, health, self-help, psychology.

SPCK (imprint)
Theology and academic, liturgy, prayer, spirituality, biblical studies, educational resources, mission, gospel and culture.

Society of Genealogists Enterprises Ltd
14 Charterhouse Buildings, Goswell Road, London EC1M 7BA
tel 020-7251 8799 *fax* 020-7250 1800
email sales@sog.org.uk
website www.sog.org.uk
Chief Executive June Perrin

Local and family history books, software and magazines plus extensive library facilities.

Somerville Press Ltd
Dromore, Bantry, Co. Cork, Republic of Ireland
tel +353 (0)28 32873
email somervillepress@eircom.net
website www.somervillepress.com
Directors Andrew Russell, Jane Russell

Irish interest: fiction and non-fiction. Founded 2008.

South Street Press – see Garnet Publishing Ltd

Southwater – see Anness Publishing

Souvenir Press Ltd
43 Great Russell Street, London WC1B 3PD
tel 020-7580 9307/8
email sp.trade@ukonline.co.uk
Managing Director Ernest Hecht

Archaeology, biography and memoirs, educational (secondary, technical), general, humour, practical handbooks, psychiatry, psychology, sociology, sports, games and hobbies, travel, supernatural, parapsychology, illustrated books. No unsolicited fiction or children's books; initial enquiry by letter essential for non-fiction.

SPCK – see Society for Promoting Christian Knowledge

Spellmount Ltd – see The History Press Ltd

Sphere – see Little, Brown Book Group

Spon – see Taylor and Francis Group

Sportsbooks Ltd*
PO Box 422, Cheltenham, Glos. GL50 2YN
tel (01242) 256755 *fax* 0560 310 8126
email info@sportsbooks.ltd.uk
website www.sportsbooks.ltd.uk
Directors Randall Northam, Veronica Northam

Sport.

The Sportsman's Press – see Quiller Publishing Ltd

Spring Books – see How To Books Ltd

Springer-Verlag London Ltd*
236 Gray's Inn Road, Floor 6, London WC1X 8HB
tel 020-3192 2000
website www.springer.com
General Manager Beverley Ford

Medicine, computing, engineering, mathematics, chemistry, biosciences. Founded 1972.

Spruce – see Octopus Publishing Group

Stacey International
128 Kensington Church Street, London W8 4BH
tel 020-7221 7166 *fax* 020-7792 9288
email info@stacey-international.co.uk
website www.stacey-international.co.uk
Chairman Tom Stacey, *Managing Director* Struan Simpson, *Finance Director* Stephen Hill

Topical issues for *Independent Minds* series, encyclopaedic books on regions and countries, Islamic and Arab subjects, world affairs, children's books, art, travel, belles lettres, biography. Imprints: Capuchin Classics, Gorilla Guides. Founded 1974.

Capuchin Classics (imprint)
email info@capuchin-classics.co.uk
website www.capuchin-classics.co.uk
Contact Emma Howard
Enduring literary fiction, mostly 19th and 20th century. Founded 2008.

Stainer & Bell Ltd
PO Box 110, Victoria House, 23 Gruneisen Road, London N3 1DZ
tel 020-8343 3303 *fax* 020-8343 3024
email post@stainer.co.uk
website www.stainer.co.uk
Directors Keith Wakefield (joint managing), Carol Wakefield (joint managing & secretary), Amanda Aknai, Antony Kearns, Andrew Pratt, Nicholas Williams

Books on music, religious communication. Founded 1907.

Stenlake Publishing Ltd
54–58 Mill Square, Catrine Ayrshire KA5 6RD
tel (01290) 552233
email sales@stenlake.co.uk
website www.stenlake.co.uk
Managing Director Richard Stenlake

Local history, railways, transport, aviation, canals and mining covering Wales, Scotland, England, Northern Ireland, Isle of Man and Republic of Ireland. Founded 1997.

Stripes – see Magi Publications

Summersdale Publishers Ltd
46 West Street, Chichester, West Sussex PO19 1RP
tel (01243) 771107 *fax* (01243) 786300

email submissions@summersdale.com
website www.summersdale.com
Managing Director Alastair Williams, *Sales Director* Nicky Douglas, *Executive Commissioning Editor* Claire Plimmer

Popular non-fiction, particularly travel writing, humour and gift books. Also publishes ebooks and audiobooks. See website for guidelines. Founded 1990.

Sunflower Books

PO Box 36160, London SW7 3WS
tel/fax 020-7589 2377
email mail@sunflowerbooks.co.uk
website www.sunflowerbooks.co.uk
Directors P.A. Underwood (editorial), S.J. Seccombe

Travel guidebooks.

Sussex Academic Press

PO Box 139, Eastbourne, East Sussex BN24 9BP
tel (01323) 479220
email edit@sussex-academic.com
website www.sussex-academic.com
Editorial Director Anthony Grahame

Theology and religion, British history and Middle East studies. Founded 1994.

The Alpha Press (imprint)

International relations, Middle East studies, cultural studies, theatre, philosophy, literary criticism, biography, history with a special emphasis on Spanish history, first nations studies, Latin American studies, theology and religion, Jewish and Israel studies, Asian studies, art history.

Sutton Publishing – see The History Press Ltd

Swan Hill Press – see Quiller Publishing Ltd

Sweet & Maxwell*

100 Avenue Road, London NW3 3PF
tel 020-7393 7000 *fax* 020-7393 7010
website www.sweetandmaxwell.co.uk
Directors Peter Lake (managing), Ashley Doody (technology), Chris Elvin (customer operations), John Galvin (finance), Dick Greener (legal affairs), Hilary Lambert (commercial), Terri Hawksworth (sales & marketing), Giles Grant (strategy & business development), Mark Potter (human resources), Mark Seaman (editorial & production)

Law. Part of Thomson Reuters Ltd. Founded 1799; incorporated 1889.

Tamarind Books – see The Random House Group Ltd

Tango Books Ltd

PO Box 32595, London W4 5YD
tel 020-8996 9970 *fax* 020-8996 9977
email info@tangobooks.co.uk
website www.tangobooks.co.uk
Directors Sheri Safran, David Fielder

Children's fiction and non-fiction novelty books, including pop-up, touch-and-feel and cloth books. Maximum 500 words. No poetry. Submissions with sae or by email.

Tarquin Publications

Suite 74, 17 Holywell Hill, St Albans AL1 1DT
tel (01727) 833866 *fax* 0845 456 6385
email info@tarquinbooks.com
website www.tarquinbooks.com
Director Andrew Griffin

Mathematics and mathematical models, puzzles, codes and logic; paper cutting, paper engineering and pop-up books for intelligent children. No unsolicited MSS; send suggestion or synopsis in first instance. Founded 1970.

Taschen UK Ltd

5th Floor, 1 Heathcock Court, 415 Strand, London WC2R 0NS
tel 020-7845 8585 *fax* 020-7836 3696
email contact-uk@taschen.com
website www.taschen.com

Art, architecture, design, film, lifestyle, photography, popular culture, sex. Founded 1980.

Tate Publishing

The Lodge, Millbank, London SW1P 4RG
tel 020-7887 8869, 020-7887 8870 *fax* 020-7887 8878
email tgpl@tate.org.uk
website www.tate.org.uk
Merchandise Director Rosey Blackmore, *Sales & Rights Director*, Fiona MacDonald, *Head of Production*, Emma Woddiwiss

Publishers for Tate in London, Liverpool and St Ives. Exhibition catalogues, art books, children's books and diaries, posters, etc. Also product development, picture library and licensing. Division of Tate Enterprises Ltd. Founded 1995.

I.B.Tauris & Co. Ltd

6 Salem Road, London W2 4BU
tel 020-7243 1225 *fax* 020-7243 1226
website www.ibtauris.com
Chairman/Publisher Iradj Bagherzade, *Managing Director* Jonathan McDonnell

History, biography, politics, international relations, current affairs, Middle East, religion, cultural and media studies, film, art, archaeology, travel guides. Founded 1983.

Tauris Academic Studies (imprint)

Academic monographs on history, political science and social sciences.

Tauris Parke Books (imprint)

Illustrated books on architecture, design, photography, cultural history and travel.

Tauris Parke Paperbacks (imprint)

Non-fiction trade paperbacks: biography, history, travel, cinema, art, cultural history.

Taylor and Francis Group*

2 and 4 Park Square, Milton Park, Abingdon, Oxon OX14 4RN
tel 020-7017 6000 *fax* 020-7017 6699
email info@tandf.co.uk
website www.tandf.co.uk, www.informa.com
Managing Director, Taylor & Francis Books Jeremy North

Academic and reference books.

Routledge (imprint)

website www.routledge.com

Addiction, anthropology, archaeology, Asian studies, business, classical studies, counselling, criminology, development and environment, dictionaries, economics, education, geography, health, history, Japanese studies, library science, language, linguistics, literary criticism, media and culture, nursing, performance studies, philosophy, politics, psychiatry, psychology, reference, social administration, social studies/sociology, women's studies, law. Directories, international relations, reference, yearbooks.

Garland Science (imprint)

website www.garlandscience.com

Bioscience textbooks and scholarly works.

Psychology Press

See page 165.

Spon (imprint)

website www.sponpress.com

Architecture, civil engineering, construction, leisure and recreation management, sports science.

CRC Press (imprint)

website www.crcpress.com

Science: physics, mathematics, chemistry, electronics, natural history, pharmacology and drug metabolism, toxicology, technology, history of science, ergonomics, production engineering, remote sensing, geographic information systems, engineering.

Teach Yourself – see Hodder Education Group

The Templar Company Ltd

The Granary, North Street, Dorking, Surrey RH4 1DN
tel (01306) 876361 *fax* (01306) 889097
email info@templarco.co.uk, submissions@templarco.co.uk (submissions)
website www.templarco.co.uk
Managing & Creative Director Amanda Wood, *Sales & Marketing Director* Ruth Huddleston

Publisher and packager of high-quality illustrated children's books, including novelty books, picture books, pop-up books, board books, fiction, non-fiction and gift titles. Send submissions via email.

Tempus – see The History Press Ltd

Thames & Hudson Ltd*

181A High Holborn, London WC1V 7QX
tel 020-7845 5000 *fax* 020-7845 5050
email sales@thameshudson.co.uk
website www.thamesandhudson.com
Directors T. Neurath (chair), C. Kaine (deputy chair), J. Camplin (managing), L. Dietrich, T. Evans, C. Ferguson, C. Frederking, P. Hughes, B. Meek, J. Neurath, N. Palfreyman, C. Ridler

Illustrated non-fiction for an international audience, especially art, architecture, graphic design, garden and landscape design, archaeology, cultural history, historical reference, fashion, photography, ethnic arts, mythology, religion.

Think Books

Think Publishing Ltd, The Pall Mall Deposit, 124–128 Barlby Road, London W10 6BL
tel 020-8962 3020 *fax* 020-8962 8689
email watchdog@thinkpublishing.co.uk
website www.thinkpublishing.co.uk
Chairman Ian McAuliffe, *Chief Executive* Tilly Boulter

Specialises in books on the outdoors, gardening and wildlife. Publishes with the Wildlife Trusts, the Royal Horticultural Society and the Campaign to Protect Rural England, and others. Founded 2005.

Thoemmes Press – see Bloomsbury Academic & Professional Division

D.C. Thomson & Co. Ltd – Publications

2 Albert Square, Dundee DD1 9QJ
tel (01382) 223131
website www.dcthomson.co.uk
London office 185 Fleet Street, London EC4A 2HS

Publishers of newspapers and periodicals. Children's books (annuals), based on weekly magazine characters; fiction. For fiction guidelines, send a large sae to Central Fiction Dept.

Thomson Reuters – Round Hall

43 Fitzwilliam Place, Dublin 2, Republic of Ireland
tel +353 (0)1 6625301 *fax* +353 (0)1 6625302
email info@roundhall.ie
website www.roundhall.ie
Director & General Manager Catherine Dolan

Law. Part of Thomson Legal & Regulatory (Europe) Ltd.

Stanley Thornes (Publishers) Ltd – see Nelson Thornes Ltd

Tide Mill Press – see Top That! Publishing plc

Time Out – see The Random House Group Ltd

Time Warner – see Little, Brown Book Group

Times Books – see HarperCollins Publishers

Titan Books

144 Southwark Street, London SE1 0UP
tel 020-7620 0200 *fax* 020-7620 0032
email editorial@titanemail.com
website www.titanbooks.com
Publisher & Managing Director Nick Landau, *Editorial Director* Katy Wild

Graphic novels, including *Simpsons* and *Batman*, featuring comic-strip material; film/TV tie-ins and cinema reference books. No fiction or children's proposals, no email submissions and no unsolicited material without preliminary letter. Email or send large sae for current author guidelines. Division of Titan Publishing Group Ltd. Founded 1981.

Tolley – see LexisNexis

Top That! Publishing plc

Marine House, Tide Mill Way, Woodbridge, Suffolk IP12 1AP
tel (01394) 386651 *fax* (01394) 386011
email info@topthatpublishing.com
website www.topthatpublishing.com
Chairman Barrie Henderson, *Directors* David Henderson (managing), Simon Couchman (creative), Stuart Buck (production), Douglas Eadie (financial), Daniel Graham (editorial), Dave Greggor (sales)

Children's activity books, novelty books, picture books, fiction for 5–8 and 9–12 years, reference, gift books and early learning books. Adult non-fiction, humour, lifestyle and gift sets. Children's and adult book packaging for publisher's and retailers worldwide. Imprint: Top That!. Founded 1999.

Tor – see Macmillan Publishers Ltd

Torque – see The History Press Ltd

Transworld Publishers*

61–63 Uxbridge Road, London W5 5SA
tel 020-8579 2652 *fax* 020-8579 5479
email info@transworld-publishers.co.uk
website www.transworldbooks.co.uk
Managing Director Larry Finlay, *Publisher* Bill Scott-Kerr

Company of the Random House Group Ltd; subsidiary of Bertelsmann AG. No unsolicited MSS accepted.

Bantam Press (imprint)

Publishing Director Sally Gaminara

Fiction and general non-fiction: cookery, business, crime, health and diet, history, humour, military, music, paranormal, self-help, science, travel and adventure, biography, autobiography.

Black Swan (imprint)

Publisher Bill Scott-Kerr

Paperback quality fiction and non-fiction.

Transworld Sport, Cookery & Entertainment (imprint)

Publishing Director Doug Young

Channel 4 books and cookery. TV tie-ins.

Corgi (imprint)

Editorial Director Cat Cobain

Paperback general fiction and non-fiction.

Doubleday (UK) (imprint)

Publishing Director Marianne Velmans

Literary fiction and non-fiction.

Eden (imprint)

Publishing Director Susanna Wadeson

Environmental: the Eden Project.

Expert Books (imprint)

Expert Brand Manager Gareth Pottle

Gardening and DIY.

Transworld Ireland (imprint)

Publisher Eoin McHugh

Trentham Books Ltd

Westview House, 734 London Road, Oakhill, Stoke-on-Trent, Staffs. ST4 5NP
tel (01782) 745567 *fax* (01782) 745553
email tb@trentham-books.co.uk
Editorial office 28 Hillside Gardens, London N6 5ST
tel 020-8348 2174
website www.trentham-books.co.uk
Directors Dr Gillian Klein (editorial), Barbara Wiggins (executive)

Education (including specialist fields – multi-ethnic issues, equal opportunities, bullying, design and technology, early years), social policy, sociology of education, European education, women's studies. Does not publish books for use by parents or children, or fiction, biography, reminiscences and poetry. Founded 1978.

Troubador Publishing Ltd

9 Priory Business Park, Wistow Road, Kibworth, Leics. LE8 0RX
tel 0116 279 2299 *fax* 0116 279 2277
email enquiries@troubador.co.uk
website www.troubador.co.uk
Directors Jeremy Thompson (managing), Jane Rowland (editorial)

Fiction and non-fiction with specialist lists in Italian studies, Italian fiction in translation and communication ethics. Self-publishing imprint: Matador. Founded 1996.

TSO (The Stationery Office)

Head office St Crispins, Duke Street, Norwich NR3 1PD

tel (01603) 622211 *fax* 0870 6005533
website www.tso.co.uk
Chairman Miles Toulson-Clarke

Publishing and information management services: business, current affairs, directories, general, pharmaceutical, professional, reference, *Learning to Drive*.

Ulric Publishing

PO Box 55, Church Stretton, Shrops. SY6 6WR
tel (01694) 781354 *fax* (01694) 781372
email enquiries@ulricpublishing.com
website www.ulricpublishing.com
Directors Ulric Woodhams, Elizabeth Oakes

Non-fiction military and motoring history. Heritage Archive and Publishing Services. No unsolicited MSS. Founded 1992.

Ulverscroft Group Ltd*

The Green, Bradgate Road, Anstey, Leicester LE7 7FU
tel 0116 236 4325 *fax* 0116 234 0205
email m.merrill@ulverscroft.co.uk
website www.ulverscroft.co.uk

Large print books: fiction and non-fiction, Classics. Unabridged and abridged audio books: fiction and non-fiction.

Unicorn Press Ltd

66 Charlotte Street, London W1T 4QE
tel 07836 633377
email strathcarron@mac.com
website www.unicornpress.org
Publishers Hugh Tempest-Radford & Lord Strathcarron

Art reference: art history, architecture, artists' monographs, artists' biographies, gallery and museum catalogues. Founded 1994.

Merlin Unwin Books Ltd

Palmers House, 7 Corve Street, Ludlow, Shrops. SY8 1DB
tel (01584) 877456 *fax* (01584) 877457
email books@merlinunwin.co.uk
website www.merlinunwin.co.uk
Chairman Merlin Unwin, *Managing Director* Karen McCall

Countryside books. Founded 1990.

Usborne Publishing Ltd

Usborne House, 83–85 Saffron Hill, London EC1N 8RT
tel 020-7430 2800 *fax* 020-7430 1562
email mail@usborne.co.uk
website www.usborne.com
Directors Peter Usborne, Jenny Tyler (editorial), Robert Jones, Keith Ball

Children's books: reference, practical, craft, natural history, science, languages, history, geography, preschool, fiction. Founded 1973.

V&A Publishing

Victoria and Albert Museum, South Kensington, London SW7 2RL
tel 020-7942 2964 *fax* 020-7942 2967
email vapubs@vam.ac.uk
website www.vandashop.com
Head of Publishing Mark Eastment

Popular and scholarly books on fine and decorative arts, architecture, contemporary design, fashion and photography. Founded 1980.

Vallentine Mitchell

5th Floor, Middlesex House, 29/45 High Street, Edgware, Middlesex HA8 7UU
tel 020-8952 9526 *fax* 020-8952 9242
email info@vmbooks.com (general), editor@vmbooks.com (submissions)
website www.vmbooks.com
Directors Stewart Cass (managing), A.E. Cass, H.J. Osen, Hon. C.V. Callman

Jewish history, Judaism, Holocaust studies, Jewish culture, Jewish biography, Middle Eastern studies.

Variorum – see Ashgate Publishing Ltd

Veritas Publications†

Veritas House, 7–8 Lower Abbey Street, Dublin 1, Republic of Ireland
tel +353 (0)1 8788177 *fax* +353 (0)1 8786507
email publications@veritas.ie
website www.veritas.ie

Liturgical and Church resources, religious school books for primary and post-primary levels, biographies, academic studies, and general books on religious, moral and social issues.

Vermilion – see The Random House Group Ltd

Verso Ltd

6 Meard Street, London W1V 3HR
tel 020-7437 3546 *fax* 020-7734 0059
email enquiries@verso.co.uk
website www.verso.com
Directors Giles O'Bryen (managing), Rowan Wilson (sales & marketing), Robin Blackburn, Tariq Ali

Current affairs, politics, sociology, economics, history, philosophy, cultural studies. Founded 1970.

Viking – see Penguin Group (UK)

Vintage – see The Random House Group Ltd

Virago – see Little, Brown Book Group

Virgin Books – see The Random House Group Ltd

Virtue Books Ltd

Edward House, Tenter Street, Rotherham S60 1LB
tel (01709) 365005 *fax* (01709) 829982

email info@russums.co.uk
website www.virtue.co.uk
Directors Peter E. Russum, Margaret H. Russum

Books for the professional chef: catering and drink.

The Vital Spark – see Neil Wilson Publishing Ltd

Voyager – see HarperCollins Publishers

University of Wales Press

10 Columbus Walk, Brigantine Place,
Cardiff CF10 4UP
tel 029-2049 6899 *fax* 029-2049 6108
email press@wales.ac.uk
website www.uwp.co.uk

Academic and educational (Welsh and English). Specialises in Welsh and Celtic studies, selected fields within humanities and social sciences: European studies, political philosophy, literature. Founded 1922.

Walker Books for Young Readers, USA – see Bloomsbury Children's & Educational Division, Bloomsbury Publishing

Walker Books Ltd

87 Vauxhall Walk, London SE11 5HJ
tel 020-7793 0909 *fax* 020-7587 1123
website www.walker.co.uk
Directors David Heatherwick, Helen McAleer, Karen Lotz, Ian Mablin (non-executive), Roger Alexander (non-executive), Sarah Foster, Jane Harris, Jane Winterbotham, Alan Lee, John Mendelson, Hilary Berkman

Children's: picture books, non-fiction and novelty titles; junior and young adult fiction. Founded 1980.

Wallflower Press

4 Eastern Terrace Mews, Brighton BN2 1EP
email info@wallflowerpress.co.uk
website www.wallflowerpress.co.uk
Editorial Director Yoram Allon

Cinema and the moving image, including TV, animation, documentary and artists' film and video – both academic and popular. Contact by email in first instance. Founded 1999.

Warburg Institute

University of London, Woburn Square,
London WC1H 0AB
tel 020-7862 8949 *fax* 020-7862 8955
email warburg@sas.ac.uk
website www.warburg.sas.ac.uk

Cultural and intellectual history, with special reference to the history of the classical tradition.

Ward Lock Educational Co. Ltd

BIC Ling Kee House, 1 Christopher Road,
East Grinstead, West Sussex RH19 3BT
tel (01342) 318980 *fax* (01342) 410980
email wle@lingkee.com
website www.wardlockeducational.com
Directors Au Bak Ling (chairman, Hong Kong), Au King Kwok (Hong Kong), Au Wai Kwok (Hong Kong), Albert Kw Au (Hong Kong), *Company Secretary* Eileen Parsons

Primary and secondary pupil materials, Kent Mathematics Project: *KMP BASIC* and *KMP Main* series covering Reception to GCSE, *Reading Workshops*, *Take Part* series and *Take Part* starters, teachers' books, music books, *Target* series for the National Curriculum: *Target Science* and *Target Geography*, religious education. Founded 1952.

Warne – see Penguin Group (UK)

Warner/Chappell Plays Ltd – see Josef Weinberger Plays Ltd

Franklin Watts – see Hachette Children's Books

The Watts Publishing Group Ltd – see Hachette Children's Books

Waverley Books Ltd

144 Port Dundas Road, Glasgow G4 0HZ
tel 0141 567 2830 *fax* 0141 567 2831
email info@waverley-books.co.uk
website www.waverley-books.co.uk
Publishers Ron Grosset, Liz Small

Scottish-interest books. Part of the DC Thomson Group. Commission books for the trade market, as well as premiums.

Wayland – see Hachette Children's Books

Weidenfeld & Nicolson

(part of the Orion Publishing Group Ltd)
Orion House, 5 Upper St Martin's Lane,
London WC2H 9EA
tel 020-7240 3444 *fax* 020-7240 4822
Managing Director Lisa Milton, *Publisher* Alan Samson, *Publishing Director, Fiction* Kirsty Dunseath

Biography and autobiography, current affairs, history, travel, fiction, literary fiction, military history and militaria.

Weidenfeld & Nicolson Illustrated

Quality illustrated non-fiction: gardening, cookery, wine, art and design, health and lifestyle, history, popular culture, archaeology, British heritage, literature, fashion, architecture, natural history, sport and adventure.

Josef Weinberger Plays Ltd

12–14 Mortimer Street, London W1T 3JJ
tel 020-7580 2827 *fax* 020-7436 9016

email general.info@jwmail.co.uk
website www.josef-weinberger.com

Stage plays only, in both acting and trade editions. Preliminary letter essential.

Welsh Academic Press

PO Box 733, Cardiff CF14 7ZY
tel 029-2021 8187
email post@welsh-academic-press.com
website www.welsh-academic-press.com

Political studies, medieval Welsh and Celtic studies, Scandinavian and Baltic studies, education, history, employment and industrial relations. Founded 1994.

Wharncliffe – see Pen & Sword Books Ltd

Which? Ltd

2 Marylebone Road, London NW1 4DF
tel 020-7770 7000
email books@which.co.uk
Head of Which? Books Angela Newton

Part of Consumers' Association. Founded 1957.

Which? Books (imprint)

Restaurant guide (*The Good Food Guide*), computing, gardening, law, personal finance, property and key life events.

Whittet Books Ltd

1 St John's Lane, Stansted, Essex CM24 8JU
tel (01279) 815871 *fax* (01279) 647564
email mail@whittetbooks.com
website www.whittetbooks.com
Director George J. Papa, *Publisher* Shirley Greenall

Natural history, wildlfe, countryside, poultry, livestock, horses. Publishing proposals considered for the above lists. Please send outline, preferably by email. Founded 1976.

John Wiley & Sons Ltd*

The Atrium, Southern Gate, Chichester,
West Sussex PO19 8SQ
tel (01243) 779777 *fax* (01243) 775878
email customer@wiley.co.uk

Print and electronic products, specialising in scientific, technical and medical books and journals; professional and consumer books and subscription services; and textbooks and other educational materials for undergraduate and graduate students as well as lifelong learners. Global headquarters in Hoboken, New Jersey, with operations in the USA, Europe, Asia, Canada and Australia.

Wiley-Blackwell*

9600 Garsington Road, Oxford OX4 2DQ
tel (01865) 776868 *fax* (01865) 714591
website www.wiley.com
Senior Vice President Steve Miron

Books and journals in medicine, veterinary medicine, dentistry, nursing and physical and life sciences, social sciences, business and humanities. Journals are delivered online through the Wiley online library.

Neil Wilson Publishing Ltd*

G/2, 19 Netherton Avenue, Glasgow G13 1BQ
tel 0141 954 8007 *fax* 0560 150 4806
email info@nwp.co.uk
website www.nwp.co.uk
Managing Director Neil Wilson

Submissions by email only. Include covering letter, author CV, synopsis and sample chapter.

The Angels' Share (imprint)

website www.angelshare.co.uk
Whisky-related matters (leisure, reference, history, memoir); other food and drink categories.

11:9 (imprint)

website www.11-9.co.uk
Scottish Arts Council/National Lottery-funded project to bring new Scottish fiction writing to the marketplace. Not commissioning at present.

In Pinn (imprint)

website www.theinpinn.co.uk
The outdoors: travel, hillwalking, climbing.

NWP (imprint)

Scottish interest subjects including history, biography, true crime, culture and reference.

The Vital Spark (imprint)

website www.vitalspark.co.uk
Scottish humour.

Philip Wilson Publishers Ltd

109 Drysdale Street, London N1 6ND
tel 020-7033 9900 *fax* 020-7033 9922
email pwilson@philip-wilson.co.uk
website www.philip-wilson.co.uk
Chairman P. Wilson, *Director* S. Prohaska

Fine and applied art, collecting, museums. Founded 1975.

Windmill Books – see The Random House Group Ltd

Windsor Large Print – see AudioGO Ltd

John Wisden and Co. Ltd – see Bloomsbury Children's & Educational Division, Bloomsbury Publishing

Wizard – see Icon Books Ltd

WLR Media & Entertainment

6–14 Underwood Street, London N1 7JQ
website www.wilmington.com
Managing Director Polly Augherinos

Publications: *Hollis PR Annual*, *Hollis Sponsorship Newsletter*, *Hollis Europe* and *The Knowledge*.

Wolters Kluwer (UK) Ltd*

(formerly Croner.CCH Group Ltd)
145 London Road, Kingston-upon-Thames, Surrey KT2 6SR
tel 0844 561 8166 *fax* 020-8547 2638
email croner@wolterskluwer.co.uk, cch@wolterskluwer.co.uk
website www.croner.co.uk, www.cch.co.uk, www.wolterskluwer.co.uk

Human resources, health and safety, tax and accountancy, education and healthcare, manufacturing and construction. Looseleaf, consultancy and online information services. Founded 1948.

The Women's Press

27 Goodge Street, London W1T 2LD
tel 020-7636 3992 *fax* 020-7637 1866
email david@the-womens-press.com
website www.quartetbooks.co.uk/submissions.html

Books by women in the areas of literary and crime fiction, biography and autobiography, health, culture, politics, handbooks, literary criticism, psychology and self-help, the arts. No email submissions; see website for guidelines. Founded 1978.

Wooden Books

Signature, 20 Castlegate,
York YO1 9RP *or* Central Books, 99 Wallis Road, London E9 5LN
email info@woodenbooks.com
website www.woodenbooks.com
Directors John Martineau (managing), Anthony Brandt (secretary), Michael Glickman (overseas)

Magic, mathematics, ancient sciences, esoteric. Quality b&w illustrators may submit samples. Founded 1996.

Woodhead Publishing Ltd

80 High Street, Sawston, Cambridge CB22 3HJ
tel (01223) 499140 *fax* (01223) 832819
email wp@woodheadpublishing.com
website www.woodheadpublishing.com
Managing Director Martin Woodhead

Engineering, materials, welding, textiles, commodities, food science and technology, environmental science, mathematics, information and knowledge management (Chandos Publishing imprint). Founded 1989.

Wordsworth Editions Ltd

8B East Street, Ware, Herts. SG12 9HJ
tel (01920) 465167 *fax* (01920) 462267
email enquiries@wordsworth-editions.com
website www.wordsworth-editions.com
Managing Director Helen Trayler

Reprints of classic books: literary; children's classics; poetry; reference; Special Editions; mystery and supernatural. Because the company specialises in out-of-copyright titles, it is not able to consider new material for publication. Founded 1987.

The X Press

PO Box 25694, London N17 6FP
tel 020-8801 2100 *fax* 020-8885 1322
email vibes@xpress.co.uk
website www.xpress.co.uk
Editorial Director Dotun Adebayo, *Marketing Director* Steve Pope

Black interest popular novels, particularly reflecting contemporary ethnic experiences. *Black Classics* series: reprints of classic novels by black writers. Founded 1992.

Nia (imprint)

Literary black fiction.

Y Lolfa Cyf

Talybont, Ceredigion SY24 5HE
tel (01970) 832304 *fax* (01970) 832782
email ylolfa@ylolfa.com
website www.ylolfa.com
Director Garmon Gruffudd, *Editor* Lefi Gruffudd

Welsh-language popular fiction and non-fiction, music, children's books; Welsh-language tutors; Welsh and Celtic interest books in English. Founded 1967.

Yale University Press London*

47 Bedford Square, London WC1B 3DP
tel 020-7079 4900 *fax* 020-7079 4901
email [firstname.lastname]@yaleup.co.uk
website www.yalebooks.co.uk
Managing Director Robert Baldock, *Marketing Director* Kate Pocock, *Publishers* Gillian Malpass (art history), Sally Salvesen (architecture & decorative arts), Heather McCallum (trade books), *Head of Rights* Anne Bihan

Art, architecture, history, economics, political science, religion, history of science, biography, current affairs and music. Founded 1961.

Yellow Jersey Press – see The Random House Group Ltd

York Notes – see Pearson UK

Young Picador – see Macmillan Publishers Ltd

Zambezi Publishing Ltd

PO Box 221, Plymouth PL2 2YJ
tel (01752) 367300 *fax* (01752) 350453
email info@zampub.com
website www.zampub.com
Contact Sasha Fenton, Jan Budkowski

Mind, Body & Spirit. Founded 1999.

Zed Books Ltd

7 Cynthia Street, London N1 9JF
tel 020-7837 4014 (general) *fax* 020-7833 3960

email zed@zedbooks.net
website www.zedbooks.co.uk
Editors Ken Barlow, Tamsine O'Riordan

Social sciences on international issues; gender studies, politics, economics, development and environmental studies; area studies (Africa, Asia, Latin America, and the Middle East). Founded 1976.

Zero to Ten Ltd

327 High Street, Slough, Berks. SL1 1TX
tel (01753) 578499 *fax* (01753) 578488
email sales@evansbrothers.co.uk
Publishing Director Su Swallow

Non-fiction for children 0–10 years: board books, toddler books and first story books. Submissions welcome but does not respond to unsuccessful submissions. Part of the Evans Publishing Group. Founded 1997.

Cherrytree Books (imprint)
UK Publisher Su Swallow

Children's non-fiction illustrated books mainly for schools and libraries.

ZigZag Education

Unit 3, Greenway Business Centre, Doncaster Road, Bristol BS10 5PY
tel 0117 950 3199 *fax* 0117 959 1695
email submissions@publishmenow.co.uk
website www.zigzageducation.co.uk, www.publishmenow.co.uk
Development Director John-Lloyd Hagger, *Strategy Director* Mike Stephens

Teaching resources for UK secondary schools: English, maths, ICT, geography, history, science, business studies, politics. Founded 1998.

Book publishers overseas

Listings are given for book publishers in Australia (below), Canada (page 186), New Zealand (page 189), South Africa (page 190) and the USA (page 192).

AUSTRALIA

**Member of the Australian Publishers Association*

Access Press

PO Box 398, Carnarvon, West Australia 6701
tel +61 (0)8 9941 2265 *fax* +61 (0)8 9941 2298
Managing Editor Jenny Walsh

Australiana, biography, non-fiction. Commissioned works and privately financed books published and distributed. Founded 1974.

ACER Press

19 Prospect Hill Road, Private Bag 55, Camberwell, Victoria 3124
tel +61 (0)3 9277 5555 *fax* +61 (0)3 9277 5500
email info@acer.edu.au
website www.acer.edu.au
General Manager/Publisher Annemarie Rolls

Publisher of the Australian Council for Educational Research. Produces a range of books and assessments including professional resources for teachers, psychologists and special needs professionals.

Allen & Unwin Pty Ltd*

83 Alexander Street, Crows Nest, NSW 2065
postal address PO Box 8500, St Leonards, NSW 1590
tel +61 (0)2 8425 0100 *fax* +61 (0)2 9906 2218
email info@allenandunwin.com
website www.allenandunwin.com
Directors Patrick Gallagher (Chairman), Paul Donovan (Executive Director), Robert Gorman (Ceo), David Martin (finance), Sue Hines (trade publishing)

General trade, including fiction and children's books, academic, especially social science and history. Founded 1990.

Michelle Anderson Publishing Pty Ltd*

PO Box 6032, Chapel Street North, South Yarra 3141
tel +61 (0)3 9826 9028 *fax* +61 (0)3 9826 8552
email mapubl@bigpond.net.au
website www.michelleandersonpublishing.com
Director Michelle Anderson

General health and mind/body. Founded 2004.

Bloomsbury Publishing PTY Limited

(Sydney office of Bloomsbury Publishing)
Level 14, 309 Kent St, Sydney, NSW 2000
tel +61 (0)2 9994 8969
email csmanz@bloomsbury.com
website www.bloomsburyanz.com
Managing Director Kathleen Farrar

Supports the worldwide publishing activities of Bloomsbury Publishing: caters for the Australia and New Zealand territories. See Bloomsbury Adult, Bloomsbury Children's & Educational, Bloomsbury Professional & Academic and Bloomsbury Information on page 129.

Cambridge University Press Australian Branch*

477 Williamstown Road, Private Bag 31, Port Melbourne, Victoria 3207
tel +61 (0)3 8671 1400 *fax* +61 (0)3 9676 9966
email customerservices@cambridge.edu.au
website www.cambridge.edu.au
Chief Executive Stephen Bourne

Academic, educational, reference, English as a second language.

Cengage Learning Australia*

Level 7, 80 Dorcas Street, South Melbourne, Victoria 3205
tel +61 (0)3 9685 4111 *fax* +61 (0)3 9685 4199
website www.cengage.com.au

Educational books.

Dominie Pty Ltd

Drama (Plays & Musicals), 8 Cross Street, Brookvale, NSW 2100
tel +61 (0)2 9938 8686 *fax* +61 (0)2 9938 8690
email dominie@dominie.com.au
website www.dominie.com.au/drama

Australian representatives of publishers of plays and agents for the collection of royalties for Samuel French Ltd, Hanbury Plays, Samuel French Inc., The Society of Authors, Bakers Plays, Nick Hern Books, Pioneer Drama and Dominie Musicals.

EA Books

Engineers Media, PO Box 588, Crows Nest, NSW 2065
tel +61 (0)2 9438 5355 *fax* +61 (0)2 8823 6526
email eabooks@engineersmedia.com.au
website www.eabooks.com.au
Managing Editor Dietrich Georg

Publishing company of the Institution of Engineers Australia.

Elsevier Australia*

Tower 1, Level 12, 475 Victoria Avenue, Chatswood NSW 2067
tel +61 (0)2 9422 8500 *fax* +61 (0)2 9422 8501

email customerserviceau@elsevier.com
website www.elsevier.com.au
Managing Director Rob Kolkman

Science, medical and technical books. Imprints: Academic Press, Butterworth-Heinemann, Churchill Livingstone, Endeavour, Excerpta Medica, Focal Press, The Lancet, MacLennan and Petty, MD Consult, Morgan Kauffman, Mosby, Saunders, Science Direct, Syngress. Established 1972.

Hachette Australia Pty Ltd*

Level 17, 207 Kent Street, Sydney, NSW 2000
tel +61 (0)2 8248 0800 *fax* +61 (0)2 2848 0810
email auspub@hachette.com.au
website www.hachette.com.au
Directors Malcolm Edwards (managing), Chris Raine, David Cocking, Matt Richell, Fiona Hazard, Matt Hoy

General, children's. No unsolicited MSS.

HarperCollins Publishers (Australia) Pty Ltd Group*

postal address PO Box A565, Sydney South, NSW 1235
tel +61 (0)2 9952 5000 *fax* +61 (0)2 9952 5555
website www.harpercollins.com.au
Publishing Director Shona Martyn

Literary fiction and non-fiction, popular fiction, children's, reference, biography, autobiography, current affairs, sport, lifestyle, health/self-help, humour, true crime, travel, Australiana, history, business, gift, religion.

Kangaroo Press – see Simon & Schuster (Australia) Pty Ltd

Lantern – see Penguin Group (Australia)

Lawbook Co.

Level 5, 100 Harris Street, Pyrmont, NSW 2009
tel +61 (0)2 8587 7980 *fax* +61 (0)2 8587 7981
website www.thomsonreuters.com.au
Ceo Tony Kinnear

Law. Part of Thomson Legal.

LexisNexis Butterworths Australia*

Tower 2, 475–495 Victoria Avenue, Chatswood, NSW 2067
tel +61 (0)2 9422 2174 *fax* +61 (0)2 9422 2405
postal address Level 9, Locked Bag 2222, Chatswood Delivery Centre, Chatswood, NSW 2067
website www.lexisnexis.com.au
Publishing Director James Broadfoot

Accounting, business, legal, tax and commercial.

Lonely Planet*

90 Maribyrnong Street, Footscray, Victoria 3011
postal address Locked Bag 1, Footscray, Victoria 3011
tel +61 (0)3 8379 8000 *fax* +61 (0)3 8379 8111
website www.lonelyplanet.com
Ceo Matt Goldberg, *Publishing Director* Geoff Stringer

Country and regional guidebooks, city guides, pocket citybreak guides, *Discover* country guides, phrasebooks, walking guides, diving and snorkelling guides, pictorial books, healthy travel guides, wildlife guides, travel photography. Also a digital image library (Lonely Planet Images) and a TV company. Offices in London and Oakland, USA. Founded 1973.

McGraw-Hill Education*

Level 2, The Everglade Building, 82 Waterloo Road, North Ryde NSW 2113
postal address Private Bag 2233, Business Centre, North Ryde, NSW 1670
tel +61 (0)2 9900 1800 *fax* +61 (0)2 9900 1980
website www.macgraw-hill.com.au
Publishing Director Nicole Meehan, *Managing Director* Cindy Jones

Educational publisher: higher education, primary education and professional (including medical, general and reference). Division of the McGraw-Hill Companies. Founded 1964.

Macmillan Education Australia Pty Ltd*

Melbourne office Level 1, 15–19 Claremont Street, South Yarra, Victoria 3141
tel +61 (0)3 9825 1000 *fax* +61 (0)3 9825 1010
email mea@macmillan.com.au
Sydney office Level 25, BT Tower, 1 Market Street, Sydney, NSW 2000
tel +61 (0)2 9285 9200 *fax* +61 (0)2 9285 9290
website www.macmillan.com.au
Managing Director Stewart Gill, *Primary Literacy Publisher* Col Gillespie, *Primary Teacher Resource & Text Publisher* Sharon Dalgleish, *Primary Library Publisher* Carmel Heron, *General Manager Secondary* Peter Saffin

Educational books.

Melbourne University Publishing*

187 Grattan Street, Carlton, Victoria 3053
tel +61 (0)3 9342 0300 *fax* +61 (0)3 9342 0399
email mup-info@unimelb.edu.au
website www.mup.com.au
Ceo/Publisher Louise Adler

Academic, scholastic and cultural; educational textbooks and books of reference. Imprints: Miegunyah Press, Victory Books. Founded 1922.

National Archives of Australia*

PO Box 7425, Canberra Business Centre, ACT 2610
tel +61 (0)2 6212 3603 *fax* +61 (0)2 6213 3914
email angela.mcadam@naa.gov.au
website www.naa.gov.au
Publications Angela McAdam

Australia history (post Federation) and politics, genealogy, reference. Founded 1944; publishing books since 1989.

Pan Macmillan Australia Pty Ltd*

Level 25, 1 Market Street, Sydney, NSW 2000
tel +61 (0)2 9285 9100 *fax* +61 (0)2 9285 9190
email pansyd@macmillan.com.au
website www.macmillan.com.au
Directors James Fraser (publishing), Peter Phillips (sales), Andrew Farrell (publicity & marketing)

Commercial and literary fiction; children's fiction, non-fiction and character products; non-fiction; sport.

Penguin Group (Australia)*

250 Camberwell Road, Camberwell, Victoria 3124
tel +61 (0)3 9811 2400 *fax* +61 (0)3 9811 2620
postal address PO Box 701, Hawthorn, Victoria 3122
website www.penguin.com.au
Ceo Gabrielle Coyne, *Publishing Directors* Ben Ball, Julie Gibbs, Laura Harris

Fiction, general non-fiction, current affairs, sociology, economics, environmental, travel guides, anthropology, politics, children's, health, cookery, gardening, pictorial and general books relating to Australia. Imprints: Penguin Books, Lantern, Viking. Founded 1946.

University of Queensland Press*

PO Box 6042, St Lucia, Queensland 4067
tel +61 (0)7 3365 7244 *fax* +61 (0)7 3365 7579
email uqp@uqp.uq.edu.au
website www.uqp.com.au
General Manager Greg Bain

Non-fiction and academic in the fields of Australian history, Australian biography, Australian politics and current affairs, Australian social and cultural issues, and Australian indigenous issues. Australian fiction (adult, young adult and children's). Via agents only. Founded 1948.

Random House Australia Pty Ltd*

Level 3, 100 Pacific Highway, North Sydney, NSW 2060
tel +61 (0)2 9954 9966 *fax* +61 (0)2 9954 4562
email random@randomhouse.com.au
website www.randomhouse.com.au
Managing Director Margaret Seale, *Publishing Director* Niki Christer, *Children's Publisher* Zoe Walton, *Marketing Director* Brett Osmond, *Sales Director* Gavin Schwarcz, *Publicity Director* Karen Reid

General fiction and non-fiction; children's, illustrated. MSS submissions – for Random House and Transworld Publishing, unsolicited non-fiction accepted, unbound in hard copy addressed to Submissions Editor. Fiction submissions are only accepted from previously published authors, or authors represented by an agent or accompanied by a report from an accredited assessment service. Imprints: Arrow, Avon, Ballantine, Bantam, Black Swan, Broadway, Century, Chatto & Windus, Corgi, Crown, Dell, Doubleday, Ebury, Fodor, Heinemann, Hutchinson, Jonathan Cape, Knopf, Mammoth UK, Minerva, Pantheon, Pavilion, Pimlico, Random House, Red Fox, Rider, Vermilion, Vintage, Virgin. Subsidiary of Bertelsmann AG.

Scholastic Australia Pty Ltd*

76–80 Railway Crescent, Lisarow, Gostord, NSW 2250
tel +61 (0)2 4328 3555 *fax* +61 (0)2 4323 3827
website www.scholastic.com.au
Publisher Andrew Berkhut

Children's fiction and non-fiction. Founded 1968.

Simon & Schuster (Australia) Pty Ltd*

office Suite 19A, Level 1, Building C, 450 Miller Street, Cammeray, NSW 2062
postal PO Box 448, Cammeray, NSW 2062
tel +61 (0)2 9983 6600 *fax* +61 (0)2 9988 4293
website www.simonandschuster.com.au

Not accepting unsolicited material including MSS submitted via email or post.

Spinifex Press*

504 Queensberry Street, North Melbourne, Victoria 3051
postal address PO Box 212, North Melbourne, Victoria 3051
tel +61 (0)3 9329 6088 *fax* +61 (0)3 9329 9238
website www.spinifexpress.com.au
Managing Director Susan Hawthorne

Feminism and women's studies, art, astronomy, occult, education, gay and lesbian, health and nutrition, technology, travel, ebooks. No unsolicited MSS. Founded 1991.

UNSW Press*

University of New South Wales, UNSW Sydney, NSW 2052
tel +61 (0)2 9664 0900 *fax* +61 (0)2 9664 5420
email publishing@unswpress.com.au
website www.unswpress.com.au
Managing Director Kathy Bail, *Publisher* Phillipa McGuinness

Academic and general non-fiction. Politics, history, society and culture, popular science, environmental studies, Aboriginal studies. Includes imprints UNSW Press, New South and Choice. Founded 1962.

UWA Publishing*

UWA Publishing, University of Western Australia, M419, 35 Stirling Highway, Crawley 6009, Western Australia
tel +61 (0)8 6488 3670 *fax* +61 (0)8 6488 1027
email admin@uwap.uwa.edu.au
website www.uwap.uwa.edu.au
Director Terri-ann White

Fiction, general non-fiction, natural history, contemporary issues. Founded 1935.

Viking – see Penguin Group (Australia)

John Wiley & Sons Australia, Ltd*

42 McDougall Street, Milton, Queensland 4064
tel +61 (0)7 3859 9755 *fax* +61 (0)7 3859 9715

email aushighered@wiley.com
website www.wiley.com.au

Educational, technical, atlases, professional, reference, trade journals. Imprints: John Wiley & Sons, Jacaranda, Wrightbooks, Wiley-Blackwell, Frommer's, Jossey-Bass. Founded 1954.

Wiley-Blackwell Publishing*

Level 2, 155 Cremorne Street, Cremorne, Victoria 3121
tel +61 (0)3 9274 3100 *fax* +61 (0)3 9274 3101
email melbourne@wiley.com
website www.blackwellpublishing.com
Publishing Director Mark Robertson

Medical, healthcare, life, physical, earth sciences, professional.

CANADA

**Member of the Canadian Publishers' Council*
†Member of the Association of Canadian Publishers

Annick Press Ltd†

15 Patricia Avenue, Toronto, Ontario M2M 1H9
tel +1 416-221-4802 *fax* +1 416-221-8400
email annickpress@annickpress.com
website www.annickpress.com
Owner/Director Rick Wilks, *Associate Publisher* Colleen MacMillan, *Creative Director* Sheryl Shapiro

Preschool to young adult fiction and non-fiction. Founded 1975.

Boardwalk Books – see Dundurn Press

Butterworths Canada Ltd – see LexisNexis Canada Inc.

Castle Street Mysteries – see Dundurn Press

The Charlton Press

PO Box 820, Station Willowdale B, North York, Ontario M2K 2R1
tel +1 416-488-1418 *fax* +1 416-488-4656
email chpress@charltonpress.com
website www.charltonpress.com
President W.K. Cross

Collectibles, Numismatics, Sportscard price catalogues. Founded 1952.

D&M Publishers Inc†

2323 Quebec Street, Suite 201, Vancouver, BC V5T 4S7
tel +1 604-254-7191 *fax* +1 604-254-9099
email dm@dmpibooks.com
website www.dmpibooks.com
Executive Director Mark Scott

General list, including Greystone Books imprint: Canadian biography, art and architecture, natural history, history, native studies, Canadian fiction. Unsolicited MSS accepted. Founded 1971.

Dundurn Press†

3 Church Street, Suite 500, Toronto, Ontario M5E 1M2
tel +1 416-214-5544
email kmcmullin@dundurn.com
website www.dundurn.com
Publisher, Kirk Howard

Canadian history, fiction, non-fiction and young adult fiction. Founded 1972.

Boardwalk Books; Sandcastle Books (imprints)

Young adult fiction.

Castle Street Mysteries (imprint)

Mystery fiction.

Hounslow Press (imprint)

Popular non-fiction.

Simon & Pierre Publishing (imprint)

Theatre, drama, fiction, translations.

ECW Press Ltd†

2120 Queen Street E, Suite 200, Toronto, Ontario M4E 1E2
tel +1 416-694-3348 *fax* +1 416-698-9906
email info@ecwpress.com
website www.ecwpress.com
Publisher Jack David

Popular culture, TV and film, sports, humour, general trade books, biographies, guidebooks. Founded 1979.

Fitzhenry & Whiteside Ltd

195 Allstate Parkway, Markham, Ontario L3R 4T8
tel +1 800-387-9776 *fax* +1 800-260-9777
email godwit@fitzhenry.ca
website www.fitzhenry.ca
Publisher Sharon Fitzhenry

Trade, educational, children's books. Founded 1966.

Gold Eagle Books – see Harlequin Enterprises Ltd

Harlequin Enterprises Ltd*

PO Box 615, Fort Erie, Ontario L2A 5X3
tel +1 888-432-4879
email customer_ecare@harlequin.ca
website www.eharlequin.com
Publisher/Ceo Donna Hayes

Fiction for women, romance, inspirational fiction, African–American fiction, action adventure, mystery. Non-fiction for women, launching autumn 2008. Founded 1949.

Harlequin Books (imprint)

Contemporary and historical romance fiction in series.

Books

Silhouette Books (imprint)
Contemporary romance fiction in series.

Steeple Hill (imprint)
Director, Global Single Titles Editorial Margaret O'Neill Marbury
Contemporary inspirational romantic fiction in series.

Luna Books (imprint)
Romantic fantasy.

HQN Books (imprint)
Romantic single title fiction, contemporary and historical.

Mira Books (imprint)
Fiction for women, contemporary and historical dramas, family sagas, romantic suspense and relationship novels.

Gold Eagle Books (imprint)
Series action adventure fiction.

Worldwide Mystery (imprint)
General Manager, Kimani Press Glenda Howard
Contemporary mystery fiction. Reprints only.

Kimani Press (imprint)
Contemporary romance fiction in series.

Spice (imprint)
Executive Editor, Non-fiction Deborah Brody
Women's erotic fiction.

HarperCollins Publishers Ltd*

2 Bloor Street East, 20th Floor, Toronto, Ontario M4W 1A8
tel +1 416-975-9334
email hccanada@harpercollins.com
website www.harpercollins.ca
President David Kent

Literary fiction and non-fiction, history, politics, biography, spiritual and children's books. Founded 1989.

Hounslow Press – see Dundurn Press

HQN Books – see Harlequin Enterprises Ltd

Kids Can Press Ltd†

25 Dockside Drive, Toronto, Ontario M54 0B5
tel +1 416-479 7000 *fax* +1 416-479 5437
email customerservice@kidscan.com
website www.kidscanpress.com/canada
Editorial Director Yvette Ghione

Juvenile/young adult books. Founded 1973.

Kimani Press – see Harlequin Enterprises Ltd

Knopf Canada – see Random House of Canada Ltd

LexisNexis Canada Inc.*

123 Commerce Valley Drive East, Suite 700, Markham, Ontario L3T 7W8
tel +1 905-479-2665
email info@lexisnexis.ca
website www.lexisnexis.ca

Law and accountancy. Division of Reed Elsevier plc.

Lone Pine Publishing

231–96 Street, Edmonton, Alberta T6N 1G3
tel +1 780-433-9333 *fax* +1 780-433-9646
email info@lonepinepublishing.com
website www.lonepinepublishing.com
President Grant Kennedy, *General Manager* Shane Kennedy

Natural history, outdoor recreation and wildlife guidebooks, self-help, gardening, popular history. Founded 1980.

Luna Books – see Harlequin Enterprises Ltd

McClelland & Stewart Ltd†

1 Toronto Street, Suit 300, Toronto, Ontario M5C 2V6
tel +1 416-598-1114 *fax* +1 416-598-7764
email editorial@mcclelland.com
website www.mcclelland.com
President & Publisher Douglas Pepper

A division of of Random House of Canada Ltd. General. Founded 1906.

McGill-Queen's University Press†

1010 Sherbrooke Street West, Suite 1720, Montreal, Quebec H3A 2R7
tel +1 514-398-3750 *fax* +1 514-398-4333
email mqup@mcgill.ca
Queen's University, 144 Barrie Street, Kingston, Ontario K7L 3J9
tel +1 613-533-2155 *fax* +1 613-533-6822
email kingstonmqup@queensu.ca
website www.mqup.mcgill.ca

Academic, non-fiction, poetry. Founded 1969.

McGraw-Hill Ryerson Ltd*

300 Water Street, Whitby, Ontario L1N 9B6
tel +1 905-430-5000 *fax* +1 905-430-5020
website www.mcgrawhill.ca
President & Ceo David Swail

Educational and trade books.

Mira Books – see Harlequin Enterprises Ltd

Nelson Education*

1120 Birchmount Road, Scarborough, Ontario M1K 5G4
tel +1 416-752-9448 *fax* +1 416-752-8101
website www.nelson.com
President Greg Nordal, *Vice President, Market Development* Chris Besse, *Senior Vice President, Media Services* Susan Cline, *Vice President, Higher Education* James Reeve

Educational publishing: school (K–12), college and university, career education, measurement and guidance, professional and reference, ESL titles. Division of Thomson Canada Ltd. Founded 1914.

NeWest Press†

201 8540, 109 Street, Edmonton, AB T6G 1E6
tel +1 780-432-9427 *fax* +1 780-433-3179
email info@newestpress.com
website www.newestpress.com
Directors Doug Barbour (President), Don Kerr (Vice-President)

Fiction, drama, poetry and non-fiction. Founded 1977.

Oberon Press

205–145 Spruce Street, Ottawa, Ontario K1R 6P1
tel +1 613-238-3275 *fax* +1 613-238-3275
email oberon@sympatico.ca
website www.oberonpress.ca

General fiction, short stories, poetry, some biographies, art and children's. Only publishes Canadian writers.

Oxford University Press, Canada*

8 Sampson Mews, Suite 204, Don Mills, Ontario M3C 0H5
tel +1 416-441-2941 *fax* +1 416-444-0427
website www.oup.com
President David Stover

Educational and academic.

Pearson Canada*

(formerly Prentice Hall Canada and Addison-Wesley Canada)
26 Prince Andrew Place, Toronto, Ontario M3C 2T8
tel +1 416-447-5101 *fax* +1 416-443-0948
website www.pearsoned.ca
President Allan Reynolds

Academic, technical, educational, children's and adult, trade.

Penguin Group (Canada)*

90 Eglinton Avenue East, Suite 700, Toronto, Ontario M4P 2Y3
tel +1 416-925-2249 *fax* +1 416-925-0068
email online@ca.penguingroup.com
website www.penguin.ca

Literary fiction, memoir, non-fiction (history, business, current events). No unsolicited MSS; submissions via an agent only. Imprints: Penguin Canada, Viking Canada, Puffin Canada. Founded 1974.

Pippin Publishing Corporation

PO Box 242, Don Mills, Ontario M3C 2S2
tel +1 416-510-2918 *fax* +1 416-510-3359
email cynthia@pippinpub.com
website www.pippinpub.com
President/Editorial Director Jonathan Lovat Dickson

ESL/EFL, teacher reference, adult basic education, school texts (all subjects), general trade (non-fiction).

Random House of Canada Ltd*

1 Toronto Street, Suite 300, Toronto, Ontario M5C 2V6
tel +1 416-364-4449 *fax* +1 416-364-6863
website www.randomhouse.ca
Chairman John Neale

Adult and children's. Imprints: Canada, Doubleday Canada, Knopf Canada, Random House Canada, Seal Books, Vintage Canada. Subsidiary of Bertelsmann AG. Founded 1944.

Red Dress Ink – see Harlequin Enterprises Ltd

Ronsdale Press†

3350 West 21st Avenue, Vancouver, BC V6S 1G7
tel +1 604-738-4688 *fax* +1 604-731-4548
email ronsdale@shaw.ca
website www.ronsdalepress.com
Director Ronald B. Hatch

Canadian literature: fiction, poetry, biography, books of ideas, young adult novels. Founded 1988.

Sandcastle Books – see Dundurn Press

Silhouette Books – see Harlequin Enterprises Ltd

Simon & Pierre Publishing – see Dundurn Press

Spice – see Harlequin Enterprises Ltd

Steeple Hill – see Harlequin Enterprises Ltd

Thompson Educational Publishing†

20 Ripley Avenue, Toronto, Ontario M6S 3N9
tel +1 416-766-2763 *fax* +1 416-766-0398
email info@thompsonbooks.com
website www.thompsonbooks.com
President Keith Thompson, *Vice-President* Faye Thompson

Social sciences. Founded 1989.

University of Toronto Press†

10 St Mary Street, Suite 700, Toronto, Ontario M4Y 2W8
tel +1 416-978-2239 *fax* +1 416-978-4738
email publishing@utpress.utoronto.ca
website www.utpress.utoronto.ca
President John Yates, *Vice President Scholarly Publishing* Lynn Fisher

Founded 1901.

Tundra Books Inc.†

75 Sherbourne Street, 5th Floor, Toronto, Ontario M5A 2P9
tel +1 416-598-4786
email tundra@mccelland.com
website www.tundrabooks.com
Publisher Kathy Lowinger

High-quality children's picture books.

Women's Press

180 Bloor Street West, Suite 801, Toronto, Ontario M5S 2V6
tel +1 416-929-2774 *fax* +1 416-929-1926
email info@cspi.org
website www.womenspress.ca
Editor James MacNevin

The ideas and experiences of women: academic non-fiction. Owned by Canadian Scholars' Press. Founded 1987.

Worldwide Mystery – see Harlequin Enterprises Ltd

NEW ZEALAND

**Member of the Publishers Association of New Zealand (PANZ)*

Auckland University Press*

University of Auckland, Private Bag 92019, Auckland 1142
tel +64 (0)9 373 7528 *fax* +64 (0)9 373 7465
email press@auckland.ac.nz
website www.press.auckland.ac.nz
Director Dr Sam Elworthy

Archaeology, architecture, art, biography, business, health, New Zealand history, Maori and Pacific studies, poetry, politics and law, science and natural history, social sciences. Founded 1966.

David Bateman Ltd*

30 Tarndale Grove, Albany Business Park, Bush Road, Auckland
tel +64 (0)9 415 7664 *fax* +64 (0)9 415 8892
email bateman@batemanpublishing.co.nz
website www.batemanpublishing.co.nz
Directors Janet Bateman, Paul Bateman (joint managing), Paul Parkinson (joint managing)

Natural history, gardening, encyclopedias, sport, art, cookery, historical, travel, motoring, maritime history, business, art, lifestyle. Founded 1979.

Bush Press Communications Ltd

postal address PO Box 33029, Takapuna 0740, Auckland, New Zealand
office 41 Hauraki Road, Takapuna 0622
tel +64 (0)9 486 2667
email bush.press@clear.net.nz
website www.bushpress.com
Governing Director/Publisher Gordon Ell ONZM

NZ natural and historic heritage. Books on behalf of institutions, family and local histories. Founded 1979.

The Caxton Press*

PO Box 25088, 113 Victoria Street, Christchurch
tel +64 (0)3 366 8516 *fax* +64 (0)3 365 7840
email peter@caxton.co.nz
website www.caxton.co.nz
Director Peter Watson

Local history, tourist pictorial, Celtic spirituality, parent guide, book designers and printers. Founded 1935.

Cengage Learning New Zealand*

Unit 4B, Rosedale Office Park, 331 Rosedale Road, Albany, North Shore 0632
postal address PO Box 33376, Takapuna, North Shore 0740
tel +64 (0)9 415 6850 *fax* +64 (0)9 415 6853
Managing Director Tony Fisk, *Publisher* Alison Brook

Educational books.

Dunmore Press Ltd*

PO Box 25080, Wellington 6146
tel +64 (0)4 472 2705 *fax* +64 (0)4 471 0604
email books@dunmore.co.nz
website www.dunmore.co.nz
Director Sharmian Firth

Education, history, sociology, business studies, general non-fiction. Founded 1970.

Hachette New Zealand Ltd*

PO Box 100–749, North Shore Mail Centre, Auckland 0745
tel +64 (0)9 477 5550 *fax* +64 (0)9 477 5560
email admin@hachette.co.nz
Managing Director Kevin Chapman, *Editorial Director* Warren Adler, *Sales & Marketing Director* Melanee Winder

Sport, cooking, travel, general.

Halcyon Publishing Ltd

PO Box 360, Auckland 1140
tel +64 (0)9 489 5337 *fax* +64 (0)9 489 5218
email info@halcyonpublishing.co.nz
website www.halcyonpublishing.com
Managing Director/Publisher Graham Gurr

Hunting, shooting, fishing, outdoor interests. Founded 1982.

HarperCollins Publishers (New Zealand) Ltd*

31 View Road, Glenfield, Auckland 0627
tel +64 (0)9 443 9400 *fax* +64 (0)9 443 9403
email editors@harpercollins.co.nz
postal address PO Box 1, Shortland Street, Auckland
website www.harpercollins.co.nz
Managing Director Tony Fisk, *Publisher* Alison Brook

General literature, non-fiction, reference, children's.

Learning Media Ltd*

Level 4, Willeston House, 22–28 Willeston Street, Te Aro, Wellington PO Box 3293, Wellington 6140
tel +64 (0)4 472 5522 *fax* +64 (0)4 472 6444
email info@learningmedia.co.nz

An award-winning publisher, designer and developer of books, educational resources and interactive

Books

programmes for New Zealand and international markets. Texts published in English, Maori and 5 Pacific languages. Founded 1993.

LexisNexis NZ Ltd

181 Wakefield Street, Wellington 6011
tel +64 (0)4 385 1479 *fax* +64 (0)4 385 1598
email customer.service@lexisnexis.co.nz
postal address PO Box 472, Wellington 6140
website www.lexisnexis.co.nz
Publisher John Henton

Law, business, academic.

McGraw-Hill Book Company New Zealand Ltd*

Level 8, 56–60 Cawley Street, Ellerslie, Auckland
postal address Private Bag 11904, Ellerslie, Auckland 1005
tel +64 (0)9 526 6200
website www.mcgraw-hill.com

Educational publisher: higher education, primary and secondary education (grades K–12) and professional (including medical, general and reference). Division of the McGraw-Hill Companies. Founded 1974.

New Zealand Council for Educational Research

Box 3237, Education House, 178–182 Willis Street, Wellington 6011
tel +64 (0)4 384 7939 *fax* +64 (0)4 384 7933
email info@nzcer.org.nz
website www.nzcer.org.nz
Director Robyn Baker, *Publisher* David Ellis

Education, including educational policy and institutions, early childhood education, educational achievement tests, Maori education, curriculum and assessment. Founded 1934.

Otago University Press*

University of Otago, PO Box 56, Dunedin 9054
tel +64 (0)3 479 8807 *fax* +64 (0)3 479 8385
email university.press@otago.ac.nz
website www.otago.ac.nz/press
Publisher Wendy Harrex

New Zealand and Pacific history, social and cultural studies, as well as a wide range of scholarly to general books. Also publishes New Zealand's longest-running literary journal, *Landfall*. Founded 1958.

Pearson Education New Zealand Ltd*

Private Bag 102902, Rosedale, North Shore 0745, Auckland
tel +64 (0)9 442 7400 *fax* +64 (0)9 442 7401
email customer.service@pearsonnz.co.nz
website www.pearsoned.co.nz
General Manager Adrian Keane

New Zealand educational books.

Penguin Group (NZ)*

Private Bag 102902, Rosedale, North Shore 0745, Auckland
tel +64 (0)9 442 7400 *fax* +64 (0)9 442 7401
website www.penguin.co.nz
Managing Director Margaret Thompson, *Publishing Director* Geoff Walker

Adult and children's fiction and non-fiction. Imprints: Penguin, Viking, Puffin Books. Founded 1973.

Random House New Zealand Ltd*

Private Bag 102950, North Shore, Auckland 0745
tel +64 (0)9 444 7197 *fax* +64 (0)9 444 7524
email admin@randomhouse.co.nz
website www.randomhouse.co.nz
Managing Director Karen Ferns

Fiction, general non-fiction, gardening, cooking, art, business, health, children's. Subsidiary of Random House International, owned by the Bertelsmann group.

RSVP Publishing Company*

PO Box 47166, Ponsonby, Auckland 1144
tel/fax +64 (0)9 372 8480
email rsvppub@iconz.co.nz
website www.rsvp-publishing.co.nz
Managing Director/Publisher Stephen Ron Picard, *Sales & Marketing Director* Chris Palmer

Fiction, metaphysical, children's. Founded 1990.

Victoria University Press*

Victoria University of Wellington, PO Box 600, Wellington
tel +64 (0)4 463 6580 *fax* +64 (0)4 463 6581
email victoria-press@vuw.ac.nz
website www.victoria.ac.nz/vup
Publisher Fergus Barrowman, *Editor* Kyleigh Hodgson

Academic, scholarly books on NZ history, sociology, law; Maori language; fiction, plays, poetry. Founded 1974.

Viking Sevenseas NZ Ltd*

201A Rosetta Road, Raumati
tel +64 (0)4 902 8240 *fax* +64 (0)4 902 8240
email vikings@paradise.net.nz
Managing Director M.B. Riley

Natural history books on New Zealand only.

SOUTH AFRICA

**Member of the Publishers' Association of South Africa*

Ad Donker – see Jonathan Ball Publishers (Pty) Ltd

Jonathan Ball Publishers (Pty) Ltd*

PO Box 33977, Jeppestown 2043
tel +27 (0)11 601 8000 *fax* +27 (0)11 601 8183

email services@jonathanball.co.za
website www.jonathanball.co.za
Publishing Director Jeremy Boraine

Founded 1977.

Ad Donker (imprint)
Africana, literature, history, academic.

Jonathan Ball (imprint)
General publications, current affairs, politics, business history, business, reference.

Delta Books (imprint)
General South African trade non-fiction.

Sunbird Publishers (imprint)
Illustrated wildlife, tourism, maps, travel.

Cambridge University Press*

(African Branch)
Lower Ground Floor, Nautica Building, The Water Club, Beach Road, Granger Bay, Cape Town 8005
tel +27 (0)21) 412 7800 *fax* +27 (0)21 412 0594
email capetown@cambridge.org
website www.cambridge.org/africa
Publishing Director Hennette Calitz

Distance learning materials and textbooks for sub-Sahara African countries, as well as primary reading materials in 28 local African languages.

Clever Books Pty Ltd*

2nd Floor, Melrose Arch Piazza, 34 Whiteley Road, Melrose North 2116
tel +27 (0)11 731 3300 *fax* +27 (0)11 731 3500
postal Private Bag X19, Northlands 214
email info@cleverbooks.co.za
website www.cleverbooks.co.za
Managing Director Steven Cilliers

Educational titles for the RSA market. Owned by Macmillan South Africa. Founded 1981.

Delta Books – see Jonathan Ball Publishers (Pty) Ltd

Galago Publishing (Pty) Ltd

PO Box 1645, Alberton 1450
tel +27 (0)11 907 2029 *fax* +27 (0)11 869 0890
email lemur@mweb.co.za
website www.galago.co.za
Managing Director Fran Stiff, *Publisher* Peter Stiff

Southern African interest: military, political, hunting. Founded 1981.

Jacklin Enterprises (Pty) Ltd

Unit 19 Mifa Park, 399 George Road, Midrand 1684
tel +27 (0)11 265 4200 *fax* +27 (0)11 314 2984
email enquires@jacklinenterprises.com
Managing Director M.A.C. Jacklin

Children's fiction and non-fiction; Afrikaans large print books. Subjects include aviation, natural history, romance, general science, technology and transportation. Imprints: Mike Jacklin, Kennis Onbeperk, Daan Retief.

Juta & Company Ltd*

1st Floor, Sunclare Building, 21 Dreyer Street, Claremont 7708
tel +27 (0)21 659 2300 *fax* +27 (0)21 659 2360
email cserv@juta.co.za
website www.juta.co.za
Ceo Lynne du Toit

Academic, learning, health, law and electronic. Founded 1853.

University of KwaZulu-Natal Press*

Private Bag X01, Scottsville, 3209 KwaZulu-Natal
tel +27 (0)33 260 5226 *fax* +27 (0)33 260 5801
email books@ukzn.ac.za
website www.ukznpress.co.za
Publisher Debra Primo

Southern African social, political, economic and military history, gender, natural sciences, African poetry and literature, genealogy, education, biography. Founded 1948.

Maskew Miller Longman (Pty) Ltd*

PO Box 396, cnr Logan Way and Forest Drive, Pinelands 7405, Cape Town 8000
tel +27 (0)21 532 6000 *fax* +27 (0)21 531 8103
email customerservices@mml.co.za
website www.mml.co.za
Publishing Director Jacques Zakarian

Educational and general publishers.

NB Publishers (Pty) Ltd*

PO Box 879, Cape Town 8000
tel +27 (0)21 406 3033 *fax* +27 (0)21 406 3812
email nb@nb.co.za
website www.nb.co.za
Director Eloise Wessels, *Director* Musa Shezi

General: Afrikaans fiction, politics, children's and youth literature in all the country's languages, non-fiction. Imprints: Tafelberg, Human & Rousseau, Pharos and Kwela. Founded 1950.

New Africa Books (Pty) Ltd*

99 Garfield Road, Claremont, Cape Town 7700
tel +27 (0)21 674 4136 *fax* +27 (0)21 674 3358
email info@newafricabooks.co.za
postal address PO Box 46962, Glosderry 7702
website www.newafricabooks.co.za
Publisher Brian Wafawarowa

General books, textbooks, literary works, contemporary issues, children and young adult. Formed as a result of the merger of David Philip Publishers (founded 1971), Spearhead Press (founded 2000) and New Africa Educational Publishing.

David Philip (imprint)
Academic, history, social sciences, politics, biography, reference, education.

Spearhead (imprint)
Current affairs, also business, self-improvement, health, natural history, travel.

Oxford University Press Southern Africa*

Vasco Boulevard, N1 City, Goodwood, Cape Town 7460
tel +27 (0)21 596 2300 *fax* +27 (0)21 596 1234
email oxford.za@oup.com
postal address PO Box 12119, N1 City, Cape Town 7463
website www.oxford.co.za
Managing Director Lieze Kotze

Pan Macmillan South Africa*

Private Bag X19, Northlands, Johannesburg 2116
tel +27 (0)11 731 3440 *fax* +27 (0)11 731 3450
website www.panmacmillan.co.za
Managing Director Mrs Terry Morris

Imprints: Ravan Press, Picador Africa, Giraffe Books.

Random House Struik (Pty) Ltd

Wembley Square, First Floor, Solan Road, Gardens, Cape Town 8001
PO Box 1144, Cape Town 8000, South Africa
tel +27 (0)21 460 5400
email info@struik.co.za
website www.struik.co.za
Managing Director Steve Connollyn

General illustrated non-fiction: South African politics, sport, business and contemporary fiction. Founded 1962.

Oshun (imprint)
Life guides, memoirs and lighthearted entertainment for women.

Zebra Press (imprint)
Life guides, memoirs and lighthearted entertainment for women.

Shuter and Shooter Publishers (Pty) Ltd*

110 CB Downes Road, Pietermaritzburg 3201, KwaZulu-Natal
tel +27 (0)33 846 8700 *fax* +27 (0)33 846 8701
email sales@shuters.com
postal address PO Box 61, Mkondeni 3212, KwaZulu-Natal
website www.shuters.com
Managing Director Mrs P.B. Chetty

Core curriculum-based textbooks for use at foundation, intermediate, senior and further education phases. Supplementary readers in various languages; dictionaries; reading development kits, charts. Literature titles in English, isiXhosa, Sesotho, Sepedi, Setswana, Tshivenda, Xitsonga, Ndebele, isiZulu and Siswati. Founded 1925.

Sunbird Publishers – see Jonathan Ball Publishers (Pty) Ltd

Two Dogs

PO Box 53557, Kenilworth 7745
tel +27 (0)21 674 0211
email info@twodogs.co.za
website www.twodogs.co.za, www.burnetmedia.co.za
Publishing Manager Tim Richman

Innovative and irreverent non-fiction focusing on contemporary and lifestyle issues for South African men. Send proposals by email. Imprint of SchreiberFord Publications. Founded 2006.

Unisa Press*

University of South Africa, PO Box 392, Unisa, Mackleneuk, Pretoria 0003
tel +27 (0)12 429 3316 *fax* +27 (0)12 429 3449
email unisa-press@unisa.ac.za
website www.unisa.ac.za/press/
Director Elizabeth le Roux

Theology and all academic disciplines. Publishers of University of South Africa. Imprint: UNISA. Founded 1957.

Van Schaik Publishers*

PO Box 12681, Hatfield, Pretoria 0028
tel +27 (0)12 342 2765 *fax* +27 (0)12 430 3563
email vanschaik@vanschaiknet.com
website www.vanschaiknet.com
Ceo Leanne Martini

Texts for the tertiary and private FET markets in South Africa. Founded 1915.

Wits University Press*

PO Wits, 2050
tel +27 (0)11 484 5974 *fax* +27 (0)11 643 5769
email witspress@wup.wits.ac.za
postal address PO Wits, Johannesburg 2050
website www.witspress.wits.ac.za
Publisher Veronica Klipp

Zebra Press – see Random House Struik (Pty) Ltd

USA

**Member of the Association of American Publishers Inc.*

Abbeville Press, Inc.

137 Varick Street, New York, NY 10013
tel +1 212-366-5585 *fax* +1 212-366-6966
email abbeville@abeville.com
website www.abbeville.com
Publisher/President Robert Abrams

Fine art and illustrated books. Founded 1977.

ABC-Clio

130 Cremona Drive, Santa Barbara, CA 93117
tel +1 805-968-1911 *fax* +1 866-270-3856

Books

website www.abc-clio.com

Academic resources for secondary and middle schools, colleges and universities, libraries and professionals (librarians, media specialists, teachers). Founded 1971.

Abingdon Press

201 Eighth Avenue, PO Box 801, Nashville, TN 37202–0801
tel +1 800-251-3320 *fax* +1 800-836-7802
website www.abingdonpress.com
President Neil Alexander, *Vice President* Tammy Gaines

General interest, professional, academic and reference – primarily directed to the religious market; children's non-fiction. Imprint of United Methodist Publishing House.

Harry N. Abrams Inc.

115 West 18th Street, New York, NY 10011
tel +1 212-206-7715 *fax* +1 212-519 1210
email abrams@abramsbooks.com
website www.abramsbooks.com
Ceo/President Michael Jacobs

Art and architecture, photography, natural sciences, performing arts, children's books. No fiction. Founded 1949.

Ace – see Penguin Group (USA), Inc.

The University of Alabama Press

Box 870380, Tuscaloosa, AL 35487-0380
tel +1 205-348-5180 *fax* +1 205-348-9201
website www.uapress.ua.edu
Director Curtis L. Clark

American and Southern history, African–American studies, religion, rhetoric and communication, Judaic studies, literary criticism, anthropology and archaeology. Founded 1945.

Alpha – see Penguin Group (USA), Inc.

Amistad – see HarperCollins Publishers

Applause Theatre and Cinema Book Publishers

19 West 21st Street, Suite 201, New York, NY 10010
tel +1 212-575-9265 *fax* +1 212-575-9270
email info@applausepub.com
website www.applausepub.com
Publisher Michael Messina

Performing arts. Founded 1980.

Arcade Publishing

116 John Street, Suite 2810, New York, NY 10038
tel +1 212-475-2633 *fax* +1 212-353-8148
email arcadeinfo@arcadepub.com
website www.arcadepub.com
President/Editor-in-Chief Richard Seaver, *Publisher* Jeannette Seaver

General trade, including adult hardcover and paperbacks. No unsolicited MSS. Founded 1988.

ArcheBooks Publishing Inc.

6081 Silver King Boulevard, Suite 903, Cape Coral, FL 33914
tel +1 239-542-7595 (toll free) *fax* +1 239-542-0080
email info@archebooks.com
website www.archebooks.com
Publisher Robert E. Gelinas

Fiction and non-fiction (history and true crime). Send submissions via a literary agent. Founded 2003.

The University of Arkansas Press

McIlroy House, McIlroy Avenue, Fayetteville, AR 72701
tel +1 800-626-0090 *fax* +1 479-575-6044
email uapress@uark.edu
website www.uapress.com
Director Lawrence J. Malley

History, humanities, literary criticism, Middle East studies, African–American studies, poetry. Founded 1980.

Atlantic Monthly Press – see Grove/Atlantic Inc.

Avery – see Penguin Group (USA), Inc.

Avon – see HarperCollins Publishers

Back Bay Books – see Little, Brown & Company

Baker's Plays

7611 Sunset Boulevard, Hollywood, CA 90046
tel +1 323-876-0579 *fax* +1 323-876-5482
email info@bakersplays.com
website www.bakersplays.com
UK Agent Samuel French Ltd

Plays and books on the theatre. Also agents for plays. Division of Samuel French Inc. Founded 1845.

Ballantine Books – see Random House Inc.

Bantam Books – see Random House Inc.

Barron's Educational Series Inc.

250 Wireless Boulevard, Hauppauge, NY 11788
tel +1 800-645-3476 *fax* +1 631-434-3723
email fbrown@barronseduc.com
website www.barronseduc.com
Chairman/Ceo Manuel H. Barron, *President/Publisher* Ellen Sibley

Test preparation, juvenile, cookbooks, Mind, Body & Spirit, crafts, business, pets, gardening, family and health, art, study guides, school guides. Founded 1941.

Beacon Press

25 Beacon Street, Boston, MA 02108
tel +1 617-742-2110 *fax* +1 617-723-3097
website www.beacon.org
Director Helene Atwan

General non-fiction in fields of religion, ethics, philosophy, current affairs, gender studies, environmental concerns, African–American studies, anthropology and women's studies, nature. Founded 1854.

Bella Books

PO Box 10543, Tallahessee, FL 32302
tel +1 800-729-4992 *fax* +1 850-576-3498
website www.bellabooks.com

Lesbian fiction: mystery, romance, science fiction. Founded 1973.

Berkley Books – see Penguin Group (USA), Inc.

Bloomsbury Publishing USA

(New York office of Bloomsbury Publishing)
Suite 315, 175 Fifth Avenue, New York, NY 10010
tel +1 212-674-5151
email bloomsbury.kids@bloomsburyusa.com
website www.bloomsburyusa.com
Publishing Director George Gibson, *Other publishing contacts* Peter Ginna (non-fiction), Melanie Cecka (children's); *Chief Financial Officer* Peter DeGiglio

Supports the worldwide publishing activities of Bloomsbury Publishing Plc: caters for the US market. See Bloomsbury Adult, Bloomsbury Children's & Educational, Bloomsbury Professional & Academic, Bloomsbury Information on page 129.

R.R. Bowker*

630 Central Avenue, New Providence, NJ 07974
tel +1 908-286-1090
email info@bowker.com
website www.bowker.com
President & Ceo Annie M. Callanan

Bibliographies and reference tools for the book trade and literary and library worlds, available in hardcopy, on microfiche, online and CD-Rom. Reference books for music, art, business, computer industry, cable industry and information industry. Division of Cambridge Information Group.

Boyds Mills Press

815 Church Street, Honesdale, PA 18431
website www.boydsmillspress.com

Fiction, non-fiction, and poetry trade books for children and young adults. Founded 1991.

Burford Books

32 Morris Avenue, Springfield, NJ 07081
tel +1 888-672-5247 *fax* +1 973-258-0113
email info@burfordbooks.com
website www.burfordbooks.com
President Peter Burford

Outdoor activities: golf, sports, fitness, nature, travel. Founded 1997.

Cambridge University Press*

32 Avenue of the Americas, New York, NY 10013
tel +1 212-924-3900 *fax* +1 212-691-3239
email newyork@cambridge.org
website www.cambridge.org/us

Academic and professional; Cambridge Learning (ELT, primary and secondary education).

Candlewick Press

99 Dover Street, Somerville, MA 02144
tel +1 617-661-3330 *fax* +1 617-661-0565
email bigbear@candlewick.com
website www.candlewick.com
President/Publisher Karen Lotz, *Editorial Director/Associate Publisher* Liz Bicknell

Books for babies through teens: board books, picture books, novels, non-fiction, novelty books. Submit material through a literary agent. Subsidiary of Walker Books Ltd, UK. Founded 1991.

Cannongate US – see Grove/Atlantic Inc.

Center Street

Hachette Book Group USA, 237 Park Avenue, New York, NY 10017
email centerstreetpub@hbgusa.com
website www.hachettebookgroup.com

Books with traditional values for readers in the US heartland. Division of Hachette Book Group. Founded 2005.

University of Chicago Press*

1427 East 60th Street, Chicago, IL 60637
tel +1 773-702-7700 *fax* +1 773-702-2705
website www.press.uchicago.edu

Scholarly books and monographs (humanities, social sciences and sciences); general trade books; reference books; and 43 scholarly journals.

Chronicle Books

680 Second Street, San Francisco, CA 94107
tel +1 415-537-4200 *fax* +1 415-537-4460
email frontdesk@chroniclebooks.com
website www.chroniclebooks.com, www.chroniclekids.com
Chairman & Ceo Nion McEvoy, *Publisher* Christine Carswell

Cooking, art, fiction, general, children's, gift, new media, gardening, regional, nature. Founded 1967.

Coffee House Press

79 13th Avenue NE, Suite 110, Minneapolis, MN 55413
tel +1 612-338-0125 *fax* +1 612-338-4004
website www.coffeehousepress.org
Publisher Allan Kornblum

Literary fiction and poetry; collectors' editions. Founded 1984.

Collins – see HarperCollins Publishers

Columbia University Press

61 West 62nd Street, New York, NY 10023
tel +1 212-459-0600 *fax* +1 212-459-3677
email jc373@columbia.edu
website www.cup.columbia.edu
Associate Director Jennifer Crewe
For MSS submission information see www.cup.columbia.edu/static/ms_instructions

Scholarly, general interest, and professional books and upper-level textbooks in the humanities, social sciences, and earth and life sciences; reference works in print and electronic formats. Subjects include animal studies, Asian studies, conservation and environmental science, criminology, ecology, evolutionary studies, film, finance and economics, gender studies, history, international relations, journalism, literary and cultural studies, media studies, Middle East studies, neuroscience, paleontology, philosophy, political philosophy, political science, religion, social work. Publishes poetry, fiction and drama in translation only. Founded 1893.

Concordia Publishing House

3558 South Jefferson Avenue, St Louis, MO 63118
tel +1 314-268-1000
website www.cph.org
Publisher & Executive Director of Editorial Paul T. McCain

Religious books, Lutheran perspective. Few freelance MSS accepted; query first. Founded 1869.

Contemporary Books

130 East Randolph Street, Suite 400, Chicago, IL 60601
tel +1 800-621-1918
website www.mhcontemporary.com

Non-fiction. Imprints: Contemporary Books, Lowell House, Passport Books, VGM Career Books. Division of the McGraw-Hill Companies.

The Continuum International Publishing Group Inc. – acquired by Bloomsbury Academic & Professional Division

Cooper Square Publishing

4501 Forbes Boulevard, Suite 200, Lanham, Maryland 20706
tel +1 301-459-3366
website www.northlandpub.com

Part of the Rowman & Littlefield Publishing Group. Founded 1949.

Northland Publishing (imprint)

website www.northlandbooks.com

American Southwest themes including home design, cooking, and travel. Founded 1958.

Luna Rising (imprint)

website www.northlandbooks.com

Northland Publishing's bilingual (Spanish–English) imprint.

NorthWord Books for Young Readers (imprint)

11571 K–Tel Drive, Minnetonka, MN 55343
tel +1 952-933-7537 *fax* +1 952-933-3630
email mbohr@nbnbooks.com
website www.nbnbooks.com

Picture books and non-fiction nature and wildlife books in interactive and fun-to-read formats. Not accepting MSS at present. Founded 1989.

Rising Moon (imprint)

email editorial@northlandbooks.com
website www.northlandbooks.com

Illustrated, entertaining, and thought-provoking picture books for children, including Spanish–English bilingual titles. Founded 1998.

Two-Can Publishing (imprint)

website www.northlandbooks.com

Non-fiction books and multimedia products for children 2–12 years to entertain and educate. Not accepting MSS at present.

Cornell University Press*

(including ILR Press and Comstock Publishing Associates)
Sage House, 512 East State Street, Ithaca, NY 14850
tel +1 607-277-2338 *fax* +1 607-277-2374
email cupressinfo@cornell.edu
website www.cornellpress.cornell.edu
Director John G. Ackerman

Scholarly books. Founded 1869.

The Countryman Press

PO Box 748, Woodstock, VT 05091
tel ++1 802-457-4826
email countrymanpress@wwnorton.com
website www.countrymanpress.com
Editorial Director Kermit Hummel

Outdoor recreation guides for anglers, hikers, cyclists, canoeists and kayakers, US travel guides, New England non-fiction, how-to books, country living books, books on nature and the environment, classic reprints and general non-fiction. No unsolicited MSS. Division of W.W. Norton & Co. Inc. Founded 1973.

Crown Publishing Group – see Random House Inc.

DAW Books Inc.

375 Hudson Street, 3rd Floor, New York, NY 10014
tel +1 212-366-2096 *fax* +1 212-366-2090
email daw@us.penguingroup.com
website www.dawbooks.com
Publishers Elizabeth R. Wollheim, Sheila E. Gilbert

Science fiction, fantasy, horror, and paranormal: originals and reprints. Imprints: DAW/Fantasy,

DAW/Fiction, DAW/Science Fiction. Affiliate of Penguin Group (USA), Inc. Founded 1971.

Delacorte – see Random House Inc.

Dial Books for Young Readers – see Penguin Group (USA), Inc.

Tom Doherty Associates, LLC

175 5th Avenue, New York, NY 10010
tel +1 212-388-0100 *fax* +1 212-677-7456
email enquiries@tor.com
website www.us.macmillan.com/torforge.aspx

Fiction: general, historical, western, suspense, mystery, horror, science fiction, fantasy, humour, juvenile, classics (English language); non-fiction: adult and juvenile. Imprints: Tor, Forge, Orb, Starscope, Tor Teen. Founded 1980.

Dover Publications Inc.

31 East 2nd Street, Mineola, NY 11501
tel +1 516-294-7000 *fax* +1 516-742-6953
website www.doverpublications.com

Art, architecture, antiques, crafts, juvenile, food, history, folklore, literary classics, mystery, language, music, math and science, nature, design and ready-to-use art. Founded 1941.

Dutton – see Penguin Group (USA), Inc.

Dutton Children's Books – see Penguin Group (USA), Inc.

Faber and Faber, Inc. – see Farrar, Straus and Giroux, LLC

Facts On File Inc.

Infobase Publishing, 132 West 31st Street, New York, NY 10001
tel +1 800-322-8755 *fax* +1 800-678-3633
website www.factsonfile.com
Editorial Director Laurie E. Likoff

General reference books and services for colleges, libraries, schools and general public. Founded 1940.

Family Tree – see Writer's Digest Books

Farrar, Straus and Giroux, LLC

18th West 18th Street, New York, NY 10011
tel +1 212-741-6900 *fax* +1 212-633-9385
website www.fsgbooks.com, www.fsgoriginals.com
President/Publisher Jonathan Galassi

Hill and Wang (imprint)

Publisher Ileen Smith
General non-fiction, history, public affairs, graphic novels. Founded 1956.

North Point Press (imprint)

Literary non-fiction, with an emphasis on natural history, ecology, yoga, food writing and cultural criticism.

Faber and Faber, Inc.

18 West 18th Street, New York, NY 10011
tel +1 212-741-6900 *fax* +1 212-633-9385
website www.fsgbooks.com
Publisher Mitzi Angel
Fiction, general non-fiction, drama, poetry, film, music.

Firebird – see Penguin Group (USA), Inc.

Fodor's Travel Publications – see Random House Inc.

Samuel French Inc

45 West 25th Street, New York, NY 10010
tel +1 212 206 8990 *fax* +1 212 206 1429
email info@samuelfrench.com
website www.samuelfrench.com

Play publishers and authors' representatives (dramatic).

Getty Publications

1200 Getty Center Drive, Suite 500, Los Angeles, CA 90049
tel +1 310-440-6536 *fax* +1 310-440-7758
email booknews@getty.edu
website www.getty.edu

Art, art history, architecture, classical art and archaeology, conservation. Founded 1983.

David R. Godine, Publisher Inc.

15 Court Square, Suite 320, Boston, MA 02108
tel +1 617-451-9600 *fax* +1 617-350-0250
email info@godine.com
website www.godine.com
President David R. Godine

Fiction, photography, poetry, art, biography, children's, essays, history, typography, architecture, nature and gardening, music, cooking, words and writing, and mysteries. No unsolicited MSS. Founded 1970.

Gotham – see Penguin Group (USA), Inc.

Grand Central Publishing

(previously Warner Books Inc.)
237 Park Avenue, New York, NY 10017
tel +1 212-364-0600 *fax* +1 212-364-0928
email grandcentralpublishing@hbgusa.com
website www.hachettebookgroupusa.com

Fiction and non-fiction. Imprints: Aspect, Business Plus (business), Forever (romance), Vision (blockbuster fiction), Wellness Central (health and wellbeing), 5 Spot (women's fiction and non-fiction), Twelve, Springboard Press. Division of Hachette Book Group USA. Founded 1970.

Grosset & Dunlap – see Penguin Group (USA), Inc.

Grove/Atlantic Inc.*

841 Broadway, New York, NY 10003
tel +1 212-614-7850 *fax* +1 212-614-7886

website www.groveatlantic.com
Publisher Morgan Entrekin

Fiction, biography, autobiography, history, current affairs, social science, belles lettres, natural history. No unsolicited MSS. Imprints: Atlantic Monthly Press, Black Cat, Mysterious Press, Grove Press. Founded 1952.

Hachette Book Group USA

237 Park Avenue, 16th Floor, New York, NY 10017
website www.hachettebookgroup.com

Divisions: Center Street (see page 194), Grand Central Publishing (see page 196), Hachette Audio, Little, Brown and Company, Little, Brown and Company Books for Young Readers, Yen Press (see page 206). Imprints: Faith Words, Orbit, Windblown Media.

Orbit (imprint)

website www.orbitbooks.net

Science fiction and fantasy.

Harcourt Trade Publishers*

215 Park Avenue South, New York, NY 10003
tel +1 212-592-1034 *fax* +1 212-420-5850
website www.hmhbooks.com
President/Publisher Dan Farley, *Editorial Director* Liz Van Doren

Fiction and non-fiction (history and biography) for readers of all ages. Part of the Harcourt Houghton Mifflin Book Group.

HarperCollins Publishers*

10 East 53rd Street, New York, NY 10022
tel +1 212-207-7000
website www.harpercollins.com
President/Ceo Brian Murray

Fiction, history, biography, poetry, science, travel, cookbooks, juvenile, educational, business, technical and religious. No unsolicited material; all submissions must come through a literary agent. Founded 1817.

HarperCollins General Books Group (division)

President/Publisher Michael Morrison

Imprints: Amistad, Avon, Avon A, Avon Inspire, Avon Red, Caedmon, Collins, Collins Business, Collins Design, Collins Living, Ecco, Eos, Harper Mass Market, Harper Paperbacks, Harper Perennial, Harper Perennial Modern Classics, HarperAudio, HarperCollins, HarperCollins e-Books, HarperEntertainment, HarperLuxe, HarperOne, William Morrow, Morrow Cookbooks, Rayo.

HarperInformation (division)

Imprints: Access, HarperBusiness, HarperResource, William Morrow Cookbooks.

HarperSanFrancisco (division)

Imprint: HarperSanFrancisco.

HarperCollins Children's Books (division)

1350 Avenue of the Americas, New York, NY 10019
tel +1 212-261-6500
website www.harperchildrens.com
President/Publisher Susan Katz

Children's classic literature. Imprints: Amistad Press, Julie Andrews Collection, Joanna Cotler Books, Eos, Laura Geringer Books, Greenwillow Books, HarperChildren's Audio, HarperCollins Children's Books, HarperEntertainment, HarperTeen, HarperTrophy, Rayo, Katherine Tegen Books.

Harvard University Press*

79 Garden Street, Cambridge, MA 02138
tel +1 617-495-2600 *fax* +1 617-496-4677
email hup@harvard.edu
website www.hup.harvard.edu
Director William P. Sisler, *Editor-in-Chief* Susan Boehmer

History, philosophy, literary criticism, politics, economics, sociology, music, science, classics, social sciences, behavioural sciences, law.

Hastings House/Daytrips Publishers

PO Box 908, Winter Park, FL 32790-0908
tel +1 407-339-3600
email hastingsdaytrips@embarqmail.com
website www.hastingshousebooks.com
Publisher Peter Leers

Travel.

Hill and Wang – see Farrar, Straus and Giroux, LLC

Hippocrene Books Inc.

171 Madison Avenue, New York, NY 10016
tel +1 718-454-2366 *fax* +1 718-228-6355
email info@hippocrenebooks.com
website www.hippocrenebooks.com
President/Editorial Director George Blagowidow

International cookbooks, foreign language dictionaries, travel, military history, Polonia, general trade. Founded 1971.

Holiday House Inc.

425 Madison Avenue, New York, NY 10017
tel +1 212-688-0085 *fax* +1 212-421-6134
email info@holidayhouse.com
website www.holidayhouse.com
Vice President/Editor-in-Chief Mary Cash

General children's books. Send entire MS. Only responds to projects of interest. Founded 1935.

Henry Holt and Company LLC*

175 Fifth Avenue, New York, NY 10010
tel +1 646-307-5095 *fax* +1 212-633-0748
website www.henryholt.com, www.henryholtkids.com
President/Publisher Dan Farley

History, biography, nature, science, novels, mysteries; books for young readers; trade paperback line.

Imprints: Henry Holt, Metropolitan Books, Times Books, Holt Paperbacks. Founded 1866.

The Johns Hopkins University Press*

2715 North Charles Street, Baltimore, MD 21218–4319
tel +1 410-516-6900 *fax* +1 410-516-6968
email tcl@press.jhu.edu
website www.press.jhu.edu

History, literary criticism, classics, politics, environmental studies, biology, medical genetics, consumer health, religion, physics, astronomy, mathematics, education. Founded 1878.

Houghton Mifflin Harcourt*

222 Berkeley Street, Boston, MA 02116
tel +1 617-351-5000
website www.hmhco.com

Textbooks, instructional technology assessments, and other educational materials for teachers and students of all ages; also reference, and fiction and non-fiction for adults and young readers. Founded 1832.

HP Books – see Penguin Group (USA), Inc.

Hudson Street Press – see Penguin Group (USA), Inc.

Hyperion*

114 Fifth Avenue, New York, NY 10011
tel +1 800-242-7737
website www.hyperionbooks.com
President Robert Miller, *Vice-President/Publisher* Ellen Archer

General fiction and non-fiction, children's books. Division of Buena Vista Publishing, formerly Disney Book Publishing Inc. Founded 1990.

University of Illinois Press*

1325 South Oak Street, Champaign, IL 61820
tel +1 217-333-0950 *fax* +1 217-244-8082
email uipress@uillinois.edu
website www.press.illinois.edu
Director Willis G. Regier

American studies (history, music, literature, religion), working-class and ethnic studies, communications, regional studies, architecture, philosophy, women's studies, film, classics. Founded 1918.

Indiana University Press

601 North Morton Street, Bloomington, IN 47404–3797
tel +1 812-855-8817 *fax* +1 812-855-8507
email iupress@indiana.edu
website www.indiana.edu/~iupress
Director Janet Rabinowitch

Specialises in the humanities and social sciences: African, African–American, Asian, cultural, Jewish and Holocaust, Middle East, Russian and East European, and women's and gender studies; anthropology, film, history, bioethics, music, paleontology, philanthropy, philosophy, and religion. Imprint: Quarry Books (regional publishing). Founded 1950.

International Marine Publishing

PO Box 235, Thomaston, ME 04861
tel +1 207-354-4014
website www.internationalmarine.com
www.raggedmountainpress.com
Editorial Director Molly Mulhern

Imprints: International Marine (boats, boating and sailing); Ragged Mountain Press (sport, adventure/travel, natural history). A McGraw-Hill company.

Jove – see Penguin Group (USA), Inc.

University Press of Kansas

2502 Westbrooke Circle, Lawrence, KS 66045–4444
tel +1 785-864-4154 *fax* +1 785-864-4586
email upress@ku.edu
website www.kansaspress.ku.edu
Director Fred Woodward, *Editor-in-Chief* Michael Briggs, *Assistant Director/Marketing Manager* Susan K. Schott

American history (political, social, cultural, environmental), military history, American political thought, American presidency studies, law and constitutional history, political science. Founded 1946.

Knopf Doubleday Publishing Group – see Random House Inc.

Krause Publications

700 East State Street, Iola, WI 54990–0001
tel +1 800-258-0929
email info@krausebooks.com
website www.krausebooks.com
Publisher Dianne Wheeler

Antiques and collectibles: coins, stamps, automobiles, toys, trains, firearms, comics, records; sewing, ceramics, outdoors, hunting. Imprint of F&W Publications Inc.

Little, Brown & Company

1271 Avenue of the Americas, New York, NY 10020
tel +1 212-522-8700 *fax* +1 212-522-2067
email publicity@littlebrown.com
website www.hachettebookgroup.com

General literature, fiction, non-fiction, biography, history, trade paperbacks, children's. Founded 1837.

Back Bay Books (imprint)

Fiction and non-fiction. Founded 1993.

Little, Brown Books for Young Readers

website www.lb-kids.com, www.lb-teens.com
Publisher Megan Tingley, *Creative Director* Gail Doobinin

Picture books, board books, chapter books, novelty books and general non-fiction and novels for middle-grade and young adult readers.

Llewellyn Worldwide

2143 Wooddale Drive, Woodbury, MN 55125
tel +1 651-291-1970 *fax* +1 651-291-1908
email billk@llewellyn.com
website www.llewellyn.com
Publisher Bill Krause

New Age: alternative health and healing, astrology, earth-based religions, shamanism, Gnostic Christianity and Kabbalah; mystery novels and young adult novels. Founded 1901.

The Lyons Press

246 Goose Lane, Guilford, CT 06437
tel +1 203-458-4500
website www.lyonspress.com, www.globepequot.com
Associate Publisher Janice Goldklang

Fishing, hunting, sports, health and fitness, outdoor skills, animals/pets, horses, games, history/current affairs, military history, nature, games, reference and non-fiction. An imprint of Globe Pequot Press. Founded 1978.

McGraw-Hill Professional*

2 Penn Plaza, 12th Floor, New York, NY 10121
tel +1 212-904-2000
website www.mhprofessional.com, www.mgeducation.com

McGraw-Hill Business

Management, investing, leadership, personal finance.

McGraw-Hill Consumer

Non-fiction: from health, self-help and parenting, to sports, outdoor and boating books. Publishing partnerships include Harvard Medical School and Standard & Poor's.

McGraw-Hill Education

Test-prep, study guides, language instruction, dictionaries.

McGraw-Hill Medical

Harrison's and reference for practitioners and medical students.

McGraw-Hill Technical

Science, engineering, computing, construction references.

Macmillan

175 Fifth Avenue, New York, NY 10010
tel +1 646-307-5151
email press.inquiries@macmillanusa.com
website http://us.macmillan.com

Imprints: Bedford/St Martins; Farrar, Straus & Giroux; Farrar, Straus & Giroux BYR; Feiwel & Friends; :01 First Second; Henry Holt and Company; Henry Holt BYR; Macmillan Audio; Palgrave Macmillan; Picador; Scientific American Inc.; Square Fish; St Martin's Press (see page 204); Tor/Forge (see Tom Doherty Associates, LLC on page 196); W.H. Freeman; and Worth.

McPherson & Company*

PO Box 1126, Kingston, NY 12402
tel +1 845-331-5807 *fax* +1 845-331-5807
email bmcpher@verizon.net
website www.mcphersonco.com
Publisher Bruce R. McPherson

Literary fiction; non-fiction: art criticism, writings by artists, film-making; occasional general titles (e.g. anthropology). No poetry. No unsolicited MSS; query first. Distributed in UK by Central Books, London. Founded 1974.

The University of Massachusetts Press

PO Box 429, Amherst, MA 01004
tel +1 413-545-2217 *fax* +1 413-545-1226
email info@umpress.umass.edu
website www.umass.edu/umpress
Director Bruce Wilcox, *Senior Editor* Clark Dougan

Scholarly books and works of general interest: American studies and history, black and ethnic studies, women's studies, cultural criticism, architecture and environmental design, literary criticism, poetry, fiction, philosophy, political science, sociology, books of regional interest. Founded 1964.

The University of Michigan Press

839 Greene Street, Ann Arbor, MI 48104–3209
tel +1 734-764-4388 *fax* +1 734-615-1540
email um.press@umich.edu
website www.press.umich.edu/
Director Philip Pochoda

Scholarly and general interest works in literary and cultural theory, classics, history, theatre, women's studies, political science, law, American history, American studies, anthropology, economics, jazz; textbooks in English as a second language; regional trade titles. Founded 1930.

Microsoft Press*

One Microsoft Way, Redmond, WA 98052–6399
tel +1 425-882-8080 *fax* +1 425-936-7329
email 4bkideas@microsoft.com
website www.microsoft.com/learning/books/
Publisher Ben Ryan

Computer books. Division of Microsoft Corp. Founded 1983.

Milkweed Editions

1011 Washington Avenue South, Suite 300, Minneapolis, MN 55415
tel +1 612-332-3192 *fax* +1 612-215-2550
email editor@milkweed.org
website www.milkweed.org
Publisher Daniel Slager

Fiction, poetry, essays, the natural world, children's novels (8–14 years). Founded 1979.

University of Missouri Press

2910 LeMone Boulevard, Columbia, MO 65201
tel +1 573-882-7641 *fax* +1 573-884-4498
email upress@umsystem.edu
website www.umsystem.edu/upress
Director/Editor-in-Chief Beverly Jarrett

American and European history, African American studies, American, British and Latin American literary criticism, journalism, political philosophy, regional studies; short fiction. Founded 1958.

The MIT Press*

55 Hayward Street, Cambridge, MA 02142–1493
tel +1 617-253-5646 *fax* +1 617-258-6779
website www.mitpress.mit.edu
Director Ellen Faran

Architecture, art and design, cognitive sciences, neuroscience, linguistics, computer science and artificial intelligence, economics and finance, philosophy, environment and ecology, natural history. Founded 1961.

The Monacelli Press – see Random House Inc.

Morehouse Publishing Co.

PO Box 1321, Harrisburg, PA 17105
tel +1 717-541-8130 *fax* +1 717-541-8136
email morehouse@morehousegroup.com
website www.morehousepublishing.org
Executive Editor Nancy Fitzgerald

Religious books, spirituality. Imprint of Church Publishing Inc.

William Morrow – see HarperCollins Publishers

NAL – see Penguin Group (USA), Inc.

Thomas Nelson Publisher

PO Box 141000, Nashville, TN 37214
tel +1 800-251-4000
email publicity@thomasnelson.com
website www.thomasnelson.com
President & Ceo Michael Hyatt

Bibles, religious, non-fiction and fiction general trade books for adults and children. Founded 1798.

University of New Mexico Press

1312 Basehart Road SE, Albuquerque, NM 87106
tel +1 505-277-2346 *fax* +1 505-272-7141
email unmpress@unm.edu
website www.unmpress.com
Director Luther Wilson, *Managing Editor* Maya Allen-Gallegos

Western history, anthropology and archaeology, Latin American studies, photography, multicultural literature, poetry. Founded 1929.

The University of North Carolina Press*

116 South Boundary Street, Chapel Hill, NC 27514
tel +1 919-966-3561 *fax* +1 919-966-3829
email uncpress@unc.edu
website www.uncpress.unc.edu
Editor-in-Chief David Perry

American history, American studies, Southern studies, European history, women's studies, Latin American studies, political science, anthropology and folklore, classics, regional trade. Founded 1922.

North Light Books – see Writer's Digest Books

North Point Press – see Farrar, Straus and Giroux, LLC

Northland Publishing – see Cooper Square Publishing

NorthWord Books for Young Readers – see Cooper Square Publishing

W.W. Norton & Company Inc.*

500 Fifth Avenue, New York, NY 10110
tel +1 212-354-5500 *fax* +1 212-869-0856
website www.wwnorton.com
Editor-in-Chief Starling Lawrence

General fiction and non-fiction, music, boating, psychiatry, economics, family therapy, social work, reprints, college texts, science.

University of Oklahoma Press

2800 Venture Drive, Norman, OK 73069–8216
tel +1 405-325-2000 *fax* +1 405-325-4000
website www.oupress.com
Director B. Byron Price, *Editor-in-chief* Charles E. Rankin

American West, American Indians, classics, political science. Founded 1928.

Orbit – see Hachette Book Group USA

The Overlook Press*

141 Wooster Street, New York, New York 10012
tel +1 212-673-2210 *fax* +1 212-673-2296
website www.overlookpress.com
President & Publisher Peter Mayer

Non-fiction, fiction, children's books (*Freddy the Pig* series). Imprints: Ardis Publishing, Duckworth, Rookery Press. Founded 1971.

Oxford University Press*

198 Madison Avenue, New York, NY 10016
tel +1 212-726-6000
website www.oup.com/us
President Niko Pfund

Academic & Trade, Bibles, English Language Teaching, English as a Second Language, higher education, law, medicine, music, journals, online, reference.

Paragon House Publishers

1925 Oakcrest Avenue, Suite 7, St Paul, MN 55113–2619
tel +1 651-644-3087 *fax* +1 651-644-0997
email paragon@paragonhouse.com
website www.paragonhouse.com
Executive Director Gordon L. Anderson

Textbooks and general interest in philosophy, religion and non-fiction.

Peachtree Publishers

1700 Chattahoochee Avenue, Atlanta, GA 30318–2112
tel +1 404-876-8761 *fax* +1 404-875-2578
email hello@peachtree-online.com
website www.peachtree-online.com
President & Publisher Margaret Quinlin, *Submissions Editor* Helen Harriss

Children's picture books, novels and non-fiction. Adult non-fiction subjects include self-help, parenting, health, the South. No adult fiction.

Pelican Publishing Company*

1000 Burmaster Street, Gretna, LA 70053
tel +1 504-368-1175 *fax* +1 504-368-1195
email editorial@pelicanpub.com
website www.pelicanpub.com
Publisher/President Kathleen Calhoun Nettleton

Art and architecture, cookbooks, biography, history, business, children's, motivational, political science, social commentary, holiday. Founded 1926.

Penguin Group (USA), Inc.*

375 Hudson Street, New York, NY10014
tel +1 212-366-2000
email online@penguingroup.com
website www.us.penguingroup.com
President Susan Petersen Kennedy, *Ceo* David Shanks

Consumer books in both hardcover and paperback for adults and children; also maps, calendars, audiobooks and mass merchandise products. Adult imprints: Ace Books, Alpha Books, Avery, Berkley Books, Dutton, Amy Einhorn Books/Putnam, Gotham Books, HP Books, Hudson Street Press, Jove, New American Library, Penguin, Penguin Classics, The Penguin Press, Perigee Books, Plume, Portfolio, Prentice Hall Press, G.P. Putnam's Sons, Riverhead, Sentinel, Signet Classics, Jeremy P. Tarcher, Viking.

Ace

Editor-in-chief Ginjer Buchanan
Science fiction. Founded 1953.

Alpha

Vice-President & Publisher Marie Butler-Knight
Non-fiction and how-to guides, including the *Complete Idiot's Guides*. Founded 1991.

Avery

Publisher Megan Newman
Health, wellness, fitness, psychology, popular science.

Berkley Books

President, Publisher & Editor-in-chief Leslie Gelbman
Fiction and general non-fiction for adults. Imprints: Ace, Berkley, Jove. Founded 1955.

Dutton

President & Publisher Brian Tart
Fiction and non-fiction. Founded 1852.

Gotham

President & Publisher William Shinker
Business, current affairs, consumer reference, food writing, golf, health and fitness, memoirs, personal finance, popular culture, self-help, spirituality, sports, travel narrative, and narrative non-fiction. Founded 2003.

HP Books

Publisher, Vice-President & Senior Editor John Duff, *Associate Publisher & Editorial Director* Michael Lutfy
Self-help and how-to books: cooking, automotive, craft.

Hudson Street Press

Editor-in-chief Luke Dempsey
High-profile hardcover non-fiction. Founded 2003.

Jove

President, Publisher & Editor-in-chief Leslie Gelbman
Fiction.

NAL

Vice President/Publisher Kara Welsh
Fiction and general non-fiction. Imprints: DAW, NALAccent, NAL Caliber, NAL Jam, Onyx, Roc, Signet, Signet Eclipse.

Penguin

President & Publisher Kathryn Court
Fiction and non-fiction including literature, biography, memoir, history, science, business, psychology, popular reference and self-help. Founded 1935.

Penguin Press

President & Publisher Ann Godoff
Literary non-fiction and select fiction. Founded 2003.

Perigee

Publisher, Vice-President & Senior Editor John Duff
Fiction and non-fiction.

Plume

President Clare Ferraro
Non-fiction and fiction, including multicultural, gay and lesbian, literary. Founded 1970.

Portfolio

Editorial Director Jeffrey Krames
Business: management, leadership, marketing,

business narrative, investing, personal finance, economics, career advice. Founded 2001.

Prentice Hall Press
Publisher, Vice-President & Senior Editor John Duff
Business, health, and self-help/popular reference.

G.P. Putnam's Sons
Senior Vice-President, Publisher & Editor-in-chief Neil S. Nyren
Fiction and non-fiction.

Riverhead Books
Vice President & Executive Editor Sean McDonald and Sarah McGrath, *Executive Editor* Jake Morrissey
Literary fiction and quality non-fiction. Founded 1994.

Sentinel
Publisher Adrian Zackheim
Politics, history, public policy, culture, religion and international relations with a right-of-centre bias. Founded 2003.

Jeremy P. Tarcher
Vice-President & Publisher Joel Fotinos
Non-fiction, including health, psychology and philosophy.

Viking Press
President Clare Ferraro
Quality fiction and non-fiction. Founded 1925.

Penguin Books for Young Readers (division)
Children's picture books, board and novelty books, young adult novels, mass merchandise products. Imprints: Dial Books for Young Readers, Dutton Children's Books, Firebird, Grosset & Dunlap, Philomel, Price Stern Sloan, Puffin Books, G.P. Putnam's Sons Books for Young Readers, Razorbill, Speak, Viking Children's Books, Frederick Warne. Founded 1996.

University of Pennsylvania Press
3905 Spruce Street, Philadelphia, PA 19104–4112
tel +1 215-898-6261 *fax* +1 215-898-0404
email custserv@pobox.upenn.edu
website www.pennpress.org
Director Eric Halpern

American and European history, anthropology, art, architecture, business and economics, cultural studies, ancient studies, human rights, international relations, literature, Pennsylvania regional studies. Founded 1890.

Pennsylvania State University Press*
820 North University Drive, USB1, Suite C, University Park, PA 16802
tel +1 814-865-1329 *fax* +1 814-863-1408
email info@psupress.org
website www.psupress.org
Director Patrick Alexander

Art history, literary criticism, religious studies, philosophy, political science, sociology, history, Latin American studies and medieval studies. Founded 1956.

Perigee – see Penguin Group (USA), Inc.

The Permanent Press
4170 Noyac Road, Sag Harbor, NY 11963
tel +1 631-725-1101 *fax* +1 631-725-8215
website www.thepermanentpress.com
Directors Martin Shepard, Judith Shepard

Literary fiction. Imprint: Second Chance Press. Founded 1978.

Philomel – see Penguin Group (USA), Inc.

Plume – see Penguin Group (USA), Inc.

Popular Woodworking – see Writer's Digest Books

Portfolio – see Penguin Group (USA), Inc.

Potomac Books Inc.
22841 Quicksilver Drive, Dulles, VA 20166
tel +1 703-661-1548 *fax* +1 703-661-1547
email pbimail@presswarehouse.com
website www.potomacbooksinc.com
Publisher Samuel R. Dorrance

National and international affairs, history (military and diplomatic); reference, biography. Founded 1984.

Prentice Hall Press – see Penguin Group (USA), Inc.

Mathew Price Ltd
3213 Squireswood Drive, Carrollton, TX 75006
tel +1 972-484-0500
email info@mathewprice.com
email mathewp@mathewprice.com
website www.mathewprice.com
Chairman Mathew Price

Illustrated fiction and non-fiction children's books for all ages for the international market. Specialist in flap, pop-up, paper-engineered titles as well as conventional books. Unsolicited MSS accepted only by email. Founded 1983.

Price Stern Sloan – see Penguin Group (USA), Inc.

Princeton University Press*
Princeton, NJ 08540
tel +1 609-258-4900 *fax* +1 609-258-6305
postal address 41 William Street, Princeton, NJ 08540
website www.press.princeton.edu
Director Peter J. Dougherty, *Editor-in-Chief* Brigitta van Rheinberg

Books

Scholarly and scientific books on all subjects. Founded 1905.

Puffin Books – see Penguin Group (USA), Inc.

G.P. Putnam's Sons – see Penguin Group (USA), Inc.

Rand McNally

PO Box 7600, Chicago, IL 60680
tel +1 847-329-8100
website www.randmcnally.com
President/Ceo Rob Apatoff

Maps, guides, atlases, educational publications, globes and children's geographical titles and atlases in print and electronic formats.

Random House Inc.*

1745 Broadway, 10th Floor, New York, NY 10019
tel +1 212-782-9000 *fax* +1 212-302-7985
website www.randomhouse.com
Chairman/Ceo Markus Dohle

General fiction and non-fiction, children's books. Subsidiary of Bertelsmann AG.

Random House Publishing Group (division)

Imprints: Ballantine Books, Bantam Books, Delacorte, Dell, Del Rey, Del Rey/Lucas Books, The Dial Press, The Modern Library, One World, Presido Press, Random House Trade Group, Random House Trade Paperbacks, Spectra, Spiegel & Grau, Villard Books.

The Monacelli Press (division)

Architecture, fine art, interior design, landscape architecture, fashion, photography, graphic design. Founded 1994.

Crown Publishing Group (division)

General fiction, non-fiction, illustrated books. Imprints: Amphoto Books, Back Stage Books, Billboard Books, Broadway, Broadway Business, Crown, Crown Business, Crown Forum, Clarkson Potter, Broadway Business, Doubleday Religion, Harmony Books, Potter Craft, Potter Style, Ten Speed Press, Three Rivers Press, Tricycle Press, Shaye Areheart Books, Waterbrook Multnomah, Watson-Guptill.

Knopf Doubleday Publishing Group (division)

General fiction and non-fiction. Alfred A. Knopf, Anchor Books, Doubleday, Everyman's Library, Nan A. Talese, Pantheon Books, Schocken Books, Vintage.

Random House Audio Publishing Group (division)

For adults and children. Listening Library, Random House Audible, Random House Audio Assets, Random House Audio Dimensions, Random House Audio Roads, Random House Audio Voices, Random House Audio Price-less.

Random House Children's Books (division)

website www.randomhouse.com/kids, www.randomhouse.com/teens

Board books, activity books, picture books, novels for preschool children through to young adult. Divisions: Kids@Random (RH Children's Books), Golden Books.

Random House International (division)

The Random House Information Group (division)

Imprints: Fodor's Travel, Living Language, Prima Games, Princeton Review, Random House Puzzles and Games, Random House Reference, Sylvan Learning.

Random House Large Print (division)

Fiction and non-fiction in large print.

Rayo – see HarperCollins Publishers

Razorbill – see Penguin Group (USA), Inc.

Rising Moon – see Cooper Square Publishing

Riverhead Books – see Penguin Group (USA), Inc.

Rizzoli International Publications Inc.

300 Park Avenue South, New York, NY 10010
tel +1 212-387-3400 *fax* +1 212-387-3535
email publicity@rizzoliusa.com
website www.rizzoliusa.com
Publisher Charles Miers

Art, architecture, photography, fashion, gardening, design, gift books, cookbooks. Founded 1976.

Rodale Book Group*

733 Third Avenue, New York, NY 10017
tel +1 212-573-0300
website www.rodale.com

General health, women's health, men's health, senior health, alternative health, fitness, healthy cooking, gardening, pets, spirituality/inspiration, trade health, biography, memoir, current affairs, science, parenting, organics, lifestyle, self-help, how-to, home arts. Founded 1932.

Routledge

270 Madison Avenue, New York, NY 10016
tel +1 212-216-7800 *fax* +1 212-563-7854
website www.routledge.com
Vice President Sam Costanzo

Music, history, psychology and psychiatry, politics, business studies, philosophy, education, sociology, urban studies, religion, film, media, literary and cultural studies, reference, English language, linguistics, communication studies, journalism. Editorial office in the UK. Subsidiary of Taylor & Francis, LLC.

Running Press Book Publishers

2300 Chestnut Street, Suite 200, Philadelphia, PA 19103
tel +1 215-567-5080
email perseus.promos@perseusbooks.com
website www.perseusbooksgroup.com/runningpress
Publisher Chris Navratil, *Directors* Bill Jones (design), Frances Soo Ping Chow (RP Kids design), Greg Jones (editorial), Craig Herman (marketing)

General non-fiction, TV, film, humor, history, children's fiction and non-fiction, food and wine, pop culture, lifestyle, illustrated gift books, Miniature EditionsTM. Imprints: Running Press, Running Press Miniature Editions, Running Press Kids, Courage Books. Member of the Perseus Books Group. Founded 1972.

Rutgers University Press

PO Box 8895, Chapel Hill, NC 27515-8895
tel +1 800-848-6224 *fax* +1 800-272-6817
website www.rutgerspress.rutgers.edu
Directors Marlie Wasserman, *Editor-in-Chief* Leslie Mitchner

Women's studies, anthropology, film and media studies, sociology, public health, popular science, cultural studies, literature, religion, history of medicine, Asian–American studies, African–American studies, American history, American studies, art history, regional titles. Founded 1936.

St Martin's Press Inc.*

175 Fifth Avenue, New York, NY 10010
tel +1 212-677-7456 *fax* +1 212-674-6132
website www.stmartins.com

Trade, reference, college. No unsolicited MSS. Imprints: St. Martin's Press, Griffin, Minotaur, Thomas Dunne Books, and Truman Talley Books. Founded 1952.

Scholastic Inc.*

557 Broadway, New York, NY 10012
tel +1 212-343-6100
website www.scholastic.com
Editorial Director Elizabeth Szabla

Innovative textbooks, magazines, technology and teacher materials for use in both school and the home. Scholastic is a global children's publishing and media company. Founded 1920.

Sentinel – see Penguin Group (USA), Inc.

Sheridan House Inc.*

15200 NBN Way, Blue Ridge Summit, PA 17214
tel +1 800-462-6420 *fax* +1 301-306-0941
email custserv@rowman.com
website www.rowman.com
President James E. Lyons

Sailing, nautical, travel. Founded 1940.

Simon & Schuster Adult Publishing Group*

1230 Avenue of the Americas, New York, NY 10020
tel +1 212-698-7000 *fax* +1 212-698-7007
website www.simonandschuster.com
President & Ceo, Simon & Schuster Carolyn K. Reidy

General fiction and non-fiction. No unsolicited MSS. Imprints: Atria, Downtown Press, Fireside, Free Press, Howard Books, MTV®, Pocket Books, Scribner, Scribner Paperback Fiction, S&S Libros en Espanol, Simon & Schuster, Star Trek®, Strebor Books, Threshold Editions, Touchstone, Washington Square Press VHI®. Division of Simon & Schuster Inc. Founded 1924.

Simon & Schuster Children's Publishing Division*

1230 Avenue of the Americas, New York, NY 10020
tel +1 212-698-7200 *fax* +1 212-698-2793
website www.simonsayskids.com
Executive Publisher Jon Anderson, *Vice-President & Publisher* Valerie Garfield

Preschool to young adult, fiction and non-fiction, trade, library and mass market. Imprints: Aladdin Paperbacks, Atheneum Books for Young Readers, Libros para niños, Little Simon, Little Simon Inspirations, Margaret K. McElderry Books, Simon & Schuster Books for Young Readers, Simon Scribbles, Simon Pulse, Simon Spotlight. Division of Simon & Schuster, Inc. Founded 1924.

Soho Press Inc.

853 Broadway, New York, NY 10003
tel +1 212-260-1900 *fax* +1 212-260-1902
email soho@sohopress.com
website www.sohopress.com
Publisher Bronwen Hruska

Literary fiction, commercial fiction, mystery, memoir. Founded 1986.

Speak – see Penguin Group (USA), Inc.

Stackpole Books

5067 Ritter Road, Mechanicsburg, PA 17055
tel +1 717-796-0411 *fax* +1 717-796-0412
email sales@stackpolebooks.com
website www.stackpolebooks.com
Publisher Judith Schnell

Nature, outdoor sports, crafts and hobbies, history, military history, regional and travel. Founded 1935.

Stanford University Press*

1450 Page Mill Road, Palo Alto, CA 94304–1124
tel +1 650-723-9434 *fax* +1 650-725-3457
email info@www.sup.org
website www.sup.org

Scholarly (humanities and social sciences), professional (business, economics and management science), high-level textbooks. Founded 1925.

Ten Speed Press

1745 Broadway, 10th Floor, New York, NY 10019
tel +1 510-559-1600 *fax* +1 510-524-1052
email order@tenspeed.com
website www.randomhouse.com/crown/tenspeed
President Phil Wood, *Publisher* Lorena Jones

Career/business, cooking, practical non-fiction, health, women's interest, self-help, children's. Imprints: Celestial Arts, Crossing Press, Tricycle Press. Founded 1971.

University of Tennessee Press*

110 Conference Center Building, Knoxville, TN 37996
tel +1 865-974-3321 *fax* +1 865-974-3724
website www.utpress.org
Director Jennifer Siler

American studies: African–American studies, Appalachian studies, history, religion, literature, historical archaeology, folklore, vernacular architecture, material culture. Founded 1940.

University of Texas Press*

PO Box 7819, Austin, TX 78713–7819
tel +1 512-471-7233 *fax* +1 512-232-7178
email utpress@uts.cc.utexas.edu
website www.utexaspress.com
Director Joanna Hitchcock, *Assistant Director & Editor-in-Chief* Theresa May

Scholarly non-fiction: anthropology, classics and the Ancient World, conservation and the environment, film and media studies, geography, Latin American and Latino studies, Middle Eastern studies, natural history, ornithology, Texas and Western studies. Founded 1950.

Tor Books – see Tom Doherty Associates, LLC

Tuttle Publishing/Periplus Editions

Airport Business Park, 364 Innovation Drive, North Clarendon, VT 05759
tel +1 802-773-8930 *fax* +1 802-773-6993
email info@tuttlepublishing.com
website www.periplus publishinggroup.com
Ceo Eric Oey, *Publishing Director* Ed Walters

Asian art, culture, cooking, gardening, Eastern philosophy, martial arts, health. Founded 1948.

Two-Can – see Cooper Square Publishing

Viking Children's Books – see Penguin Group (USA), Inc.

Viking Press – see Penguin Group (USA), Inc.

Walker & Co.

175 Fifth Avenue, New York, NY 10010
tel +1 212-674-5151 *fax* +1 212-727-0984
website www.walkerbooks.com, www.bloomsburykids.com
Publisher Emily Easton (children's), George Gibson (adult)

General. Walker Books and Walker Books for Young Readers are imprints of Bloomsbury Publishing Plc (page 129).

University of Washington Press

4333 Brooklyn Avenue NE, Seattle, WA 98195–9570
postal address PO Box 50096, Seattle, WA 98145–5096
tel +1 206-543-4050 *fax* +1 206-543-3932
website www.washington.edu/uwpress
Director Patrick Soden

Anthropology, Asian–American studies, Asian studies, art and art history, aviation history, environmental studies, forest history, Jewish studies, literary criticism, marine sciences, Middle East studies, music, regional studies, including history and culture of the Pacific Northwest and Alaska, Native American studies, resource management and public policy, Russian and East European studies, Scandinavian studies. Founded 1909.

WaterBrook Multnomah Publishing Group

12265 Oracle Blvd, Suite 200, Colorado Springs, CO 80921
tel +1 719-590-4999 *fax* +1 719-590-8977
email info@waterbrookmultnomah.com
website www.waterbrookmultnomah.com
President Stephen Cobb

Fiction and non-fiction with a Christian perspective. No unsolicited MSS. Subsidiary of Random House Inc. Founded 1996.

Watson-Guptill Publications

c/o Random House, 1745 Broadway, New York, NY 10019
tel +1 212-782-9000, +1 212-572-6066
email info@watsonguptill.com
website www.watsonguptill.com, www.randomhouse.com/crown/watsonguptill

Art, crafts, how-to, comic/cartooning, photography, performing arts, architecture and interior design, graphic design, music, entertainment, writing, reference, children's. Imprints: Amphoto Books, Back Stage Books, Billboard Books, Watson-Guptill, Whitney Library of Design. Founded 1937.

Westminster John Knox Press

100 Witherspoon Street, Louisville, KY 40202–1396
tel +1 502-569-8400 *fax* +1 502-569-5113
website www.wjkbooks.com

Scholarly reference and general books with a religious/spiritual angle. Division of Presbyterian Publishing Corp.

John Wiley & Sons Inc.*

111 River Street, Hoboken, NJ 07030
tel +1 201-748-6000 *fax* +1 201-748-6088

email info@wiley.com
website www.wiley.com
President/Ceo William J. Pesce

Specialises in scientific, technical, medical and scholarly journals; encyclopedias, books and online products and services; professional/trade books, subscription products, training materials and online applications and websites; and educational materials for undergraduate and graduate students and lifelong learners. Founded 1807.

Workman Publishing Company*

225 Varick Street, New York, NY 10014
tel +1 212-254-5900 *fax* +1 212-254-8098
email info@workman.com
website www.workman.com
Editor-in-chief Susan Bolotin

Popular non-fiction: business, cooking, gardening, gift books, health, how-to, humour, parenting, sport, travel. Founded 1968.

Writer's Digest Books

10151 Carver Road, Suite 200, Cincinnati, OH 45242
tel +1 513-531-2690 *fax* +1 513-891-7185
email writersdigest@fwmedia.com
website www.writersdigest.com

Market directories, books and magazine for writers, photographers and songwriters. Imprint of F&W Media Inc. Founded 1920.

Family Tree (imprint)

Genealogy.

North Light Books (imprint)

Fine art, decorative art, crafts, graphic arts instruction books.

Popular Woodworking (imprint)

How-to in home building, remodelling, woodworking, home organisation.

Yale University Press*

PO Box 209040, New Haven, CT 06520-9040
tel +1 203-432-0960 *fax* +1 203-432-0948
website www.yale.edu/yup
Editorial Director Jonathan Brent

Scholarly books and art books.

Yen Press

Hachette Book Group, 237 Park Avenue, New York, NY 10017
email yenpress@hbgusa.com
website www.yenpress.com

Graphic novels and manga in all formats for all ages. Division of Hachette Book Group. Founded 2006.

Audio publishers

Many of the audio publishers listed below are also publishers of books.

Abbey Home Media Group Ltd

435–437 Edgware Road, London W2 1TH
tel 020-7563 3910 *fax* 020-7563 3911
email anne.miles@abbeyhomemedia.com
Managing Director Anne Miles

Specialises in the acquisition, production and distribution of quality audio/visual entertainment for children. Bestselling children's spoken word and music titles are available on CD in the Tempo range and include titles by Michael Rosen as well as *Postman Pat*, *Watership Down*, *Michael R*, *Baby Bright*, *Wide Eye*, *SuperTed* and *Golden Nursery Rhymes*.

AudioGO Ltd

St James House, The Square, Lower Bristol Road, Bath BA2 3BH
tel (01225) 878000 *fax* (01225) 310771
email info@audiogo.co.uk
website www.audiogo.co.uk
Managing Director Mike Bowen, *Publishing Director* Jan Paterson

Spoken word entertainment that can be enjoyed at listeners' convenience. Imprints include BBC Radio Collection, Cover to Cover Classics, BBC Cover to Cover, Chivers Audiobooks, Chivers Children's Audiobooks. Formed in 2010 following the sale of BBC Audiobooks.

Barefoot Books Ltd

294 Banbury Road, Oxford OX2 7ED
tel (01865) 311100 *fax* (01865) 514965
email info@barefootbooks.co.uk
website www.barefootbooks.co.uk
Editor-in-Chief Tessa Stickland

Narrative unabridged audiobooks, spoken and sung. Founded 1993.

Barrington Stoke*

18 Walker Street, Edinburgh EH3 7LP
tel 0131 225 4113 *fax* 0131 225 4140
email info@barringtonstoke.co.uk
website www.barringtonstoke.co.uk
Chairman Ben Thomson, *Managing Director* Mairi Kidd, *Editor* Vicki Rutherford

Short fiction and non-fiction, specially adapted and presented for reluctant, struggling and dyslexic readers, aged 9–12 and 13+, with reading ages of 6–8. Short fiction (15,000 words) for adults with a reading age of 8. No picture books, no unsolicited submissions. Founded 1998.

Beautiful Sounds

36–38 Glasshouse Street, London W1B 5DL
email info@beautifulsounds.co.uk
website www.beautifulsounds.co.uk

Produces audio digital downloads of books plus drama, interviews, live performance and debates. Division of The Beautiful Group. Founded 2008.

Bloomsbury Publishing Plc

50 Bedford Square, London WC1B 3DP
tel 020-7494 2111 *fax* 020-7734 8656
website www.bloomsbury.com
Contact Trâm-Anh Doan

A broad selection of literary fiction and non-fiction.

Canongate Audio Books

Eardley House, 4 Uxbridge Street, London W8 7SY
tel 020-8467 0852
website www.canongate.co.uk
Audio Director Victoria Williams

CDs of classic literature such as Jane Austen, Charles Dickens, D.H. Lawrence and P.G. Wodehouse; also current literary authors. Publishes approx. 25 titles per year and has 150 titles available, including many short stories. Founded 1991 as CSA Word; acquired by Canongate in 2010.

Chrome Dreams

PO Box 230, New Malden, Surrey KT3 6YY
tel 020-8715 9781 *fax* 020-8241 1426
email contactus@chromedreams.co.uk
website www.chromedreams.co.uk
Owner Rob Johnstone

Cló Iar-Chonnachta Teo.

Indreabhán, Conamara, Co. Galway, Republic of Ireland
tel +353 (0)91 593307 *fax* +353 (0)91 593362
email cic@iol.ie
website www.cic.ie
Ceo Micheál Ó Conghaile, *General Manager* Deirdre O'Toole

Irish-language novels, short stories, plays, poetry, songs; CDs (writers reading from their works), bilingual books. Promotes the translation of contemporary Irish poetry and fiction into other languages. Founded 1985.

Creative Content Ltd

Roxburghe House, 273–287 Regent Street, London W1B 2HA
tel 07771 766838
email ali@creativecontentdigital.com
website www.creativecontentdigital.com
Publisher Ali Muirden, *Editorial Director* Lorelei King

Publishes audio digital downloads, on-demand CDs and ebooks in the business, language improvement, self-improvement, lifestyle and crime fiction genres. Founded 2008.

57 Productions

57 Effingham Road, London SE12 8NT
tel/fax 020-8463 0866
email info@57productions.com
website www.57productions.com
Director Paul Beasley

Agency and production company specialising in contemporary poetry. Represents a wide range of writers and performers, including Jean 'Binta' Breeze, Adrian Mitchell and Patience Agbabi. Publishes CDs by John Hegley and Benjamin Zephaniah. Runs an online programme: www.iPoems.org, www.poetryjukebox.com and www.poetryvideojukebox.com. Founded 1992.

Hachette Digital

100 Victoria Embankment, London EC4Y 0DY
tel 020-7911 8056 *fax* 020-7911 8100 (publicity)
email becca.hargrove@littlebrown.co.uk
tel 020-7911 8044 *fax* 020-7911 8100 (editorial)
email sarah.shrubb@littlebrown.co.uk (editorial)
Editorial Director Sarah Shrubb

Audiobook list includes both unabridged and abridged titles from Little, Brown's bestselling authors such as Alexander McCall Smith, Patricia Cornwell and Mark Billingham, as well as classics such as Joseph Heller's *Catch-22*, John Steinbeck's *Of Mice and Men* and Hans Fallada's *Alone in Berlin*. Publishes approx. 60 audiobooks per year. Founded 2003.

Harper NonFiction

77–85 Fulham Palace Road, London W6 8JB
tel 020-8307 4706 *fax* 020-8307-4788 (editorial)
website www.harpercollins.co.uk
Publisher Carole Tonkinson

Commercial non-fiction imprint at HarperCollins with a list covering celebrity autobiography, cookery, tv tie-in, music, humour, sport, fashion, inspirational memoir, health and mind, body and spirit titles. The list includes Lorraine Pascale, Steve Coogan (as Alan Partridge), Frankie Boyle, Chris Evans, Russell Brand, Andre Agassi, Justin Bieber, Stephen Fry, Gordon Ramsay, Sophie Dahl, Cathy Glass and others.

HarperCollins Audio Books

77–85 Fulham Palace Road, London W6 8JB
tel 020-8741 7070
website www.harpercollins.co.uk
Director of Audio Jo Forshaw

Publishers of a wide range of genres including fiction, non-fiction, poetry, Classics, Shakespeare, comedy, personal development and children's, on both CD and download. Founded 1990.

Hodder & Stoughton Audiobooks

338 Euston Road, London NW1 3BH
tel 020-7873 6000 *fax* 020-7873 6024
website www.hodder.co.uk
Publisher Nick Coveney

Publishes authors from within the Hodder group as well as commissioning independent titles. List includes fiction and non-fiction. Authors include Stephen King, John Grisham, Elizabeth George, John le Carré, Alan Titchmarsh, Jean Auel, Al Murray, Jeffery Deaver, Jodi Picoult, Pam Ayres, Michael Parkinson, Peter Robinson, Chris Cleave, Miranda Hart and Michael Caine.

Isis/Soundings

Isis Publishing Ltd, 7 Centremead, Osney Mead, Oxford OX2 0ES
tel (01865) 250333 *fax* (01865) 790358
website www.isis-publishing.co.uk
Chief Executive Robert Thirlby

Complete and unabridged audiobooks: fiction, non-fiction, autobiography, biography, crime, thrillers, family sagas, mysteries, health, poetry, humour; large print books.

Library Magna Books Ltd

Magna House, Long Preston, Skipton, North Yorkshire BD23 4ND
tel (01729) 840225 *fax* (01729) 840683
website www.ulverscroft.co.uk
Managing Director Diane Allen

Audiobooks and large print books. Founded 1973.

Macmillan Digital Audio

20 New Wharf Road, London N1 9RR
tel 020-7014 6000 *fax* 020-7014 6001
email audiobooks@macmillan.co.uk
website www.panmacmillan.com
Digital Director Sara Lloyd

Adult fiction, non-fiction and autobiography, and children's. Established 1995.

Naxos AudioBooks

40A High Street, Welwyn, Herts. AL6 9EQ
tel (01438) 717808 *fax* (01438) 717809
email info@naxosaudiobooks.com
website www.naxosaudiobooks.com
Managing Director Nicolas Soames

Classic literature, modern fiction, non-fiction, drama and poetry on CD. Also junior classics and classical music. Founded 1994.

The Orion Publishing Group Ltd

5 Upper St Martin's Lane, London WC2H 9EA
tel 020-7240 3444 *fax* 020-7240 4822
email salesinformation@orionbooks.co.uk
Audio Publisher Pandora White

Adult and children's fiction and non-fiction. Founded 1998.

Penguin Audiobooks

80 Strand, London WC2R 0RL
tel 020-7010 3000

email audiobooks@penguin.co.uk
website www.penguin.co.uk/audio
Audio Publisher Jeremy Ettinghausen

Audiobooks list reflects the diversity of the Penguin book range, including classic and contemporary fiction and non-fiction, autobiography, poetry, drama and, in Puffin Audiobooks, the best of contemporary and classic literature for younger listeners. Authors include Nick Hornby, Claire Tomalin, Zadie Smith, Gervase Phinn, Dick Francis and Nicci French. Readings are by talented and recognisable actors. Over 300 titles are now available. Founded 1993.

Random House Audio Books

20 Vauxhall Bridge Road, London SW1V 2SA
tel 020-7840 8400
email audioeditorial@randomhouse.co.uk
website www.randomhouse.co.uk/audio
Editorial Director Zoe Willis

Authors include Jo Nesbø, Lee Child, Kathy Reichs, Andy McNab, Robert Harris, Jack Dee, James Patterson, Ruth Rendell, Karin Slaughter, Ian McEwan and Sebastian Faulks. Founded 1991.

Red Audio

7–14 Green Park, Sutton on the Forest,
York YO61 1ET
tel (01347) 810055 *fax* (01347) 812705
website www.red-audio.co.uk
Ceo & Editor Steve Parks

CDs and MP3 downloads of business topics such as marketing, start-ups, management and motivation. Publishes approx. eight titles per year; over 30 titles available. Part of Red Studios UK Ltd. Founded 2001.

Simon & Schuster Audio

Simon & Schuster UK, 1st Floor,
222 Gray's Inn Road, London WC1X 8HB
tel 020-7316 1900 *fax* 020-7316 0332
email enquiries@simonandschuster.co.uk
website www.simonandschuster.co.uk
Digital & Audio Publisher Kirsty McNeil

Fiction and non-fiction audiobooks. Fiction authors include Jackie Collins, Lynda La Plante and Tom Rob Smith. Non-fiction authors include Stephen Covey, Rhonda Byrne, Anthony Robbins and Spencer Johnson. Founded 1997.

SmartPass Ltd

15 Park Road, Rottingdean, Brighton BN2 7HL
tel (01273) 306203
email info@smartpass.co.uk
website www.smartpass.co.uk, www.spaudiobooks.com, www.shakespeareappreciated.com
Managing Director Phil Viner, *Creative Director* Jools Viner

SmartPass audio education resources present unabridged plays, poetry and dramatisations of novels as guided full-cast dramas for individual study and classroom use. Shakespeare Appreciated: full-cast unabridged plays with an explanatory commentary. SPAudiobooks: full-cast unabridged dramas of classic and cult texts.

Ulverscroft Group Ltd*

The Green, Bradgate Road, Anstey, Leicester LE7 7FU
tel 0116 236 4325 *fax* 0116 234 0205
email m.merrill@ulverscroft.co.uk
website www.ulverscroft.co.uk

Large print books: fiction and non-fiction, Classics. Unabridged and abridged audio books: fiction and non-fiction.

Walker Books Ltd

87 Vauxhall Walk, London SE11 5HJ
tel 020-7793 0909 *fax* 020-7587 1123
website www.walker.co.uk
Senior Editor Hannah Whitaker

Includes the bestselling fiction series *Alex Rider* and *The Power of Five* by Anthony Horowitz and titles by award-winning authors Michael Morpurgo, Mal Peet and Vivian French. Audio series for young children include *Listen and Join In!* – based on 12 classic picture books and featuring story readings, songs and activities – and the non-fiction picture book and CD series *Nature Storybooks*.

Book packagers

Many modern illustrated books are created by book packagers, whose particular skills are in the areas of book design and graphic content. In-house desk editors and art editors match up the expertise of specialist writers, artists and photographers who usually work on a freelance basis.

act-two ltd – now John Brown Group – Children's Division

Aladdin Books Ltd

2–3 Fitzroy Mews, London W1T 6DF
tel 020-7383 2084 *fax* 020-7388 6391
email sales@aladdinbooks.co.uk
website www.aladdinbooks.co.uk
Directors Charles Nicholas, Bibby Whittaker

Full design and book packaging facility specialising in children's non-fiction and reference. Founded 1980.

The Albion Press Ltd

113 High Street, Avebury, Marlborough, Wilts. SN8 1RF
tel (01993) 831094
email albion@indigogroup.co.uk
website www.hoap.co.uk
Director Bob Trubshaw

Specialises in Wiltshire and Leicestershire local interest titles; also folklore, mythology and social history. Publishes up to 10 titles a year. See website for submission details. Founded 1989.

Amber Books Ltd

Bradley's Close, 74–77 White Lion Street, London N1 9PF
tel 020-7520 7600 *fax* 020-7520 7606/7607
email enquiries@amberbooks.co.uk
website www.amberbooks.co.uk
Managing Director Stasz Gnych, *Deputy Managing Director* Sara Ballard, *Publishing Manager* Charles Catton, *Head of Production* Peter Thompson, *Design Manager* Mark Batley, *Picture Manager* Terry Forshaw

Book packager creating illustrated non-fiction books for adults and children. Works include multi-volume sets for schools and libraries, highly illustrated reference series on dinosaurs, animals and birds, and a military list. Children's titles created under Tiptoe Books imprint. Opportunities for freelances. Founded 1989.

Nicola Baxter Ltd

PO Box 215, Framingham Earl, Yelverton, Norwich NR14 7UR
tel (01508) 491111
email nb@nicolabaxter.co.uk
website www.nicolabaxter.co.uk
Director Nicola Baxter

Full packaging service for children's books in both traditional and digital formats. Happy to take projects from concept to finished work or supply bespoke authorial, editorial, design or commissioning services. Produces both fiction and non-fiction titles in a wide range of formats, for babies to young adults and experienced in novelty books and licensed publishing. Founded 1990.

Bender Richardson White

PO Box 266, Uxbridge, Middlesex UB9 5NX
tel (01895) 832444 *fax* (01895) 835213
email brw@brw.co.uk
website www.brw.co.uk
Directors Lionel Bender (editorial), Kim Richardson (sales & production), Ben White (design)

Specialises in children's and young people's natural history, science and family information. Opportunities for freelances. Founded 1990.

BLA Publishing Ltd

BIC Ling Kee House, 1 Christopher Road, East Grinstead, West Sussex RH19 3BT
tel (01342) 318980 *fax* (01342) 410980
Directors Au Bak Ling (chairman, Hong Kong), Albert Kw Au (Hong Kong)

High-quality illustrated reference books, particularly science dictionaries and encyclopedias, for the international market. Founded 1981.

The Book Guild Ltd

Pavilion View, 19 New Road, Brighton BN1 1UF
tel (01273) 720900 *fax* (01273) 723122
email info@bookguild.co.uk
website www.bookguild.co.uk
Directors Carol Biss (managing), Janet Wrench (production)

Offers a range of publishing options: a comprehensive package for authors incorporating editorial, design, production, marketing, publicity, distribution and sales; editorial and production only for authors requiring private editions; or a complete service for companies and organisations requiring books for internal or promotional purposes – from brief to finished book. Write for submission details. Founded 1982.

Bound Originals

Tithe Barn, Clouts Farm, Ide Hill Road, . Bough Beech, Kent TN8 7PH
tel (01732) 700839
email lucy@boundoriginals.co.uk
website www.boundoriginals.co.uk
Managing Director Lucy Hulme

Packages small gift books mainly for non-publishing companies, often corporate giveaways for branding purposes. Specialises in gift books, animals, lifestyle, art. Founded 2004.

Breslich & Foss Ltd

2A Union Court, 20–22 Union Road, London SW4 6JP
tel 020-7819 3990 *fax* 020-7819 3998
email sales@breslichfoss.co.uk
website www.breslichfoss.co.uk
Directors Paula G. Breslich, K.B. Dunning

Books produced from MSS to bound copy stage from in-house ideas. Specialising in crafts. Founded 1978.

John Brown Group – Children's Division

136–142 Bramley Road, London W10 6SR
tel 020-7565 3000 *fax* 020-7565 3060
email andrew.hirsch@johnbrownmedia.com
website www.johnbrownmedia.com
Ceo Andrew Hirsch (operations), Sara Lynn (creative)

Creative development and packaging of children's products including books, magazines, teachers' resource packs, partworks, CDs and websites.

Brown Wells & Jacobs Ltd

2 Vermont Road, London SE19 3SR
tel 020-8653 7670 *fax* 020-8653 7774
email graham@bwj-ltd.com
website www.bwj.org
Director Graham Brown

Design, editorial, illustration and production of high-quality non-fiction illustrated children's books. Specialities include pop-up and novelty books. Opportunities for freelances. Founded 1979.

Cambridge Publishing Management Ltd

Burr Elm Court, Main Street, Caldecote, Cambs. CB23 7NU
tel (01954) 214000
email initial.surname@cambridgepm.co.uk
website www.cambridgepm.co.uk
Managing Director Jackie Dobbyne, *Editorial Manager* Catherine Burch

Creative and highly skilled editorial and book production company specialising in complete project management of business, education, ELT, travel and illustrated non-fiction titles, from commissioning authors to delivery of final files to printer. Freelances should send their CVs to recruit@cambridgepm.co.uk. Founded 1999.

Carroll & Brown Ltd

20 Lonsdale Road, London NW6 6RD
tel 020-7372 0900 *fax* 020-7372 0460
email mail@carrollandbrown.co.uk
website www.carrollandbrown.co.uk
Managing Director Amy Carroll

Publishers and packagers of health, parenting, pregnancy and lifestyle titles. Opportunities for freelances. Founded 1989.

Cowley Robinson Publishing Ltd

(incorporating David Hawcock Books)
8 Belmont, Bath BA1 5DZ
tel (01225) 339999 *fax* (01225) 339995
email anna.sainaghi@cowleyrobinson.com
website www.cowleyrobinson.com
Directors Stewart Cowley, David Hawcock, Phil Fleming (finance)

Specialists in children's interactive novelty and paper-engineered formats for international co-editions. Information and early learning books for all age groups. Licence and character publishing formats. Founded 1998.

Creative Plus Publishing Ltd

2nd Floor, 151 High Street, Billericay, Essex CM12 9AB
tel (01277) 633005 *fax* (01277) 633003
email enquiries@creative-plus.co.uk
website www.creative-plus.co.uk
Managing Director Beth Johnson

Provides all editorial and design from concept to finished pages for books, partworks and magazines. Specialises in female interest, children's, gardening, illustrated non-fiction. Opportunities for freelances. Founded 1989.

Design Eye Ltd

226 City Road, London EC1V 2TT
tel 020-7812 8601 *fax* 020-7253 4370
email info@designeye.co.uk
website www.quarto.com/co_ed_designeye_uk.htm
Publisher Sue Grabham

Co-edition publisher of innovative Books-Plus for children. Highly illustrated, paper-engineered, novelty and component-based titles for all ages, but primarily children's preschool (3+), 5–8 and 8+ years. Mainly non-fiction, early concepts and curriculum-based topics for the trade in all international markets. Opportunities for freelance paper engineers, artists, authors, editors and designers. Unsolicited MSS not accepted. Founded 1988.

Diagram Visual Information Ltd

34 Elaine Grove, London NW5 4QH
tel 020-7485 5941 *fax* 020-7485 5941
email info@diagramgroup.com
website www.diagramgroup.com
Directors Bruce Robertson, Patricia Robertson

Research, writing, design and illustration of reference books, supplied as disks. Founded 1967.

Eddison Sadd Editions Ltd

St Chad's House, 148 King's Cross Road, London WC1X 9DH

tel 020-7837 1968 *fax* 020-7837 2025
email info@eddisonsadd.com
website www.eddisonsadd.com
Directors Nick Eddison, Ian Jackson, David Owen, Sarah Rooney

Illustrated non-fiction books, kits and gift titles for the international co-edition market. Broad, popular list including MBS, health, self-help and relationships. Incorporates BOOKINABOX Ltd. Founded 1982.

Edition

PO Box 1, Moffat, Dumfriesshire DG10 9SU
tel (01683) 220808
email jh@cameronbooks.co.uk
Director Jill Hollis

Illustrated non-fiction. Design, editing, typesetting and production from concept to finished book for galleries, museums, institutions and other publishers. Founded 1976.

Elwin Street Ltd

144 Liverpool Road, London N1 1LA
tel 020-7700 6785
email silvia@elwinstreet.com, pippa@elwinstreet.com
website www.elwinstreet.com
Director Silvia Langford, *Production Director* Angela Young, *Senior Editor* Pippa Crane

Illustrated non-fiction: reference, lifestyle, food, health and fitness, parenting, gift and humour.

Graham-Cameron Publishing & Illustration

The Studio, 23 Holt Road, Sheringham, Norfolk NR26 8NB
tel (01263) 821333 *fax* (01263) 821334
email enquiry@gciforillustration.com
and Duncan Graham-Cameron, 59 Hertford Road, Brighton BN1 7GG
tel (01273) 385890
website www.gciforillustration.com
Partners Helen Graham-Cameron, Duncan Graham-Cameron

Educational and children's books; information publications; sponsored publications. Illustration agency with 37 artists. Do not send unsolicited MSS. Founded 1985.

Hart McLeod Ltd

14 Greenside, Waterbeach, Cambridge CB25 9HP
tel (01223) 861495 *fax* (01223) 862902
email inhouse@hartmcleod.co.uk
website www.hartmcleod.co.uk
Directors Graham Hart, Joanne Barker

Primarily educational and general non-fiction with particular expertise in illustrated books, school texts, ELT and electronic and audio content. Opportunities for freelances and work experience. Founded 1985.

HL Studios Ltd

Riverside House, Two Rivers, Station Lane, Witney, Oxon OX28 4BH
tel (01993) 706273
email info@hlstudios.eu.com
website www.hlstudios.eu.com

Primary, secondary academic education (geography, science, modern languages) and co-editions (travel guides, gardening, cookery). Multimedia (CD-Rom programming and animations). Opportunities for freelances. Founded 1985.

Ivy Contract

210 High Street, Lewes, East Sussex BN7 2NS
tel (01273) 403120 *fax* (01273) 487441
email [surname]@ivy-group.co.uk
website www.ivy-group.co.uk
Creative Director Peter Bridgewater, *Managing Director* Stephen Paul

Provides full editorial, design (and where required, production) service to develop ideas owned by its publishing clients. Specialises in building entire lists of illustrated books in all subject areas; developing individual titles; designing jackets/covers; producing sales material; rebranding. Opportunities for freelances. Part of the Ivy Group.

The Ivy Press Ltd

210 High Street, Lewes, East Sussex BN7 2NS
tel (01273) 487440 *fax* (01273) 487441
email [surname]@ivy-group.co.uk
website www.ivy-group.co.uk
Creative Director Peter Bridgewater, *Managing Director* Stephen Paul

Packagers and publishers of illustrated trade books on art, lifestyle, popular culture, design, health and Mind, Body & Spirit. Opportunities for authors and freelances. Founded 1996.

Kipling Press Ltd

Gillie Cottage, Cucklington, Wincanton, Somerset BA9 9PT
email hugh@kipbooks.co.uk, susie@kipbooks
Directors Hugh Elwes, Susie Elwes

Packager of children's books. Founded 2010.

Lexus Ltd

60 Brook Street, Glasgow G40 2AB
tel 0141 556 0440 *fax* 0141 556 2202
email peterterrell@lexusforlanguages.co.uk
website www.lexusforlanguages.co.uk
Director P.M. Terrell

Language books, especially bilingual dictionaries, phrasebooks and schoolbooks, as publisher and packager. *Lexus Travelmate* and *Chinese Classroom* series. Founded 1980.

Little People Books

The Home of BookBod, Knighton, Radnorshire LD7 1UP

tel (01547) 520925
email littlepeoplebooks@thehobb.tv
website www.thehobb.tv/lpb
Directors Grant Jessé (production & managing), Helen Wallis (rights & finance)

Packager of audio, children's educational and textbooks, digital publications. Parent company: Grant Jessé UK.

Market House Books Ltd

Suite B, Elsinore House, 43 Buckingham Street, Aylesbury, Bucks. HP20 2NQ
tel (01296) 484911
email books@mhbref.com
website www.markethousebooks.com
Directors Jonathan Law (editorial), Anne Kerr (production)

Compilation of dictionaries, encyclopedias, and reference books. Founded 1970.

Marshall Editions Ltd

The Old Brewery, 6 Blundell Street, London N7 9BH
tel 020-7700 6764 *fax* 020-7700 4191
email JamesAshton-Tyler@marshalleditions.com
website www.marshalleditions.com
Publisher James Ashton-Tyler

Highly illustrated non-fiction for adults and children, including history, health, gardening, home design, pets, natural history, popular science.

Monkey Puzzle Media Ltd

11 Chanctonbury Road, Hove BN3 6EL
tel (01273) 279928 *fax* (01379) 588055
email info@monkeypuzzlemedia.com
Director Roger Goddard-Coote

Offers a full packaging service from concept or commission through to delivery of repro-ready pdf files. Specialises in high-quality illustrated children's and adult non-fiction and reference for trade, institutional and mass markets worldwide. Publishers' commissions undertaken. Produces approx. 60 titles each year. No unsolicited material accepted. Founded 1998.

Orpheus Books Ltd

6 Church Green, Witney, Oxon OX28 4AW
tel (01993) 774949 *fax* (01993) 700330
email info@orpheusbooks.com
website www.orpheusbooks.com
Executive Directors Nicholas Harris (editorial, design & marketing), Sarah Hartley (production & design)

Children's illustrated non-fiction/reference. Opportunities for freelance artists. Founded 1993.

Paragon Publishing

4 North Street, Rothersthorpe, Northants NN7 3JB
tel (01604) 832149
email mark.webb@tesco.net
website www.intoprint.net
Proprietor Mark Webb

Packagers of non-fiction books: architecture and design, educational and textbooks, electronic (academic and professional), languages and linguistics, sports and games. All editorial and design services to complete pdf files, iPad app, kindle, epub and print on demand — b&w and colour.

Playne Books Ltd

Park Court Barn, Trefin, Haverfordwest, Pembrokeshire SA62 5AU
tel (01348) 837073
email info@playnebooks.co.uk
Design & Production Director David Playne, *Editorial Director* Gill Playne

Specialises in highly illustrated adult non-fiction and books for very young children. All stages of production undertaken from initial concept (editorial, design and manufacture) to delivery of completed books. Currently not considering new unsolicited projects. Founded 1987.

Quantum Publishing

6 Blundell Street, London N7 8BH
tel 020-7700 6700 *fax* 020-7700 4191
email sarah.bloxham@quarto.com
website www.quarto.com
Publisher Sarah Bloxham

Packager of a wide range of non-fiction titles. Part of the Quarto Group. Founded 1995.

The Quarto Group, Inc.

230 City Road, London EC1V 2TT
tel 020-7700 9000 *fax* 020-7253 4437
email info@quarto.com
website www.quarto.com
Chairman & Ceo Laurence Orbach, *Chief Financial Officer* Mick Mousley, *Creative Director* Bob Morley, *Director of Publishing* David Breuer

Independent publishing group encompassing traditional and co-edition publishing. Co-edition books are licensed to third parties all over the world, with bestselling titles often available in 20+ languages. UK-based operations include the following autonomously run business units/imprints. See separate entries for Aurum Press Ltd and Jacqui Small on page 127 and RotoVision on page 170.

Marshall Editions

email james.ashton-tyler@quarto.com
Publisher James Ashton-Tyler

QED Publishing Ltd

email zetad@quarto.com
Associate Publisher Zeta Davies

Quantum Publishing Ltd

email sarah.bloxham@quarto.com
Publisher Sarah Bloxham

Quarto Children's Books Ltd

email quartokids@quarto.com, sueg@quarto.com
Publisher Sue Grabham, *Art Director* Jonathan Gilbert
Co-edition publisher of innovative Books-Plus for children. Highly illustrated paper-engineered, novelty

and component-based titles for all ages, but primarily preschool (3+), 5–8 and 8+ years. Mainly non-fiction, early concepts and curriculum-based topics for the trade in all international markets. Opportunities for freelance paper engineers, artists, authors, editors and designers. Unsolicited MSS not accepted.

Quarto Publishing plc
email paulc@quarto.com
Publisher Paul Carslake

qu:id
email nigelb@quidpublishing.com
Publisher Nigel Browning

Quintessence
email mark.fletcherl@quarto.com
Publisher Mark Fletcher

Quintet Publishing Ltd
email mark.searle@quarto.com
Publisher Mark Searle

Salamander – see Anova Books

Studio Cactus Ltd
Northgate Farm, Northgate Lane, Ellisfield, Basingstoke, Hants RG25 2QT
tel (01256) 409029
email mail@studiocactus.co.uk
website www.studiocactus.co.uk
Editorial Director Damien Moore, *Art Director* Amanda Lunn

High-quality illustrated non-fiction books for the international market. Undertakes book packaging/ production services, from initial concept to delivery of final disk or printed books. Founded 1998.

Tangerine Designs Ltd*
5th Floor, The Old Malthouse, Clarence Street, Bath BA1 5NS
website www.tangerinedesigns.co.uk

Packagers and international co-edition publishers of children's books. Brands include: *The Little Dreamers, Jolly Maties, Baby Eco, Little Eco.* Specialising in novelty books, book-plus and innovations. Submissions accepted from UK only; must enclose sae if return required. See website for submissions procedure. Founded 2000.

The Templar Company Ltd
The Granary, North Street, Dorking, Surrey RH4 1DN
tel (01306) 876361 *fax* (01306) 889097
email info@templarco.co.uk, submissions@templarco.co.uk (submissions)
website www.templarco.co.uk
Managing & Creative Director Amanda Wood, *Sales & Marketing Director* Ruth Huddleston

Publisher and packager of high-quality illustrated children's books, including novelty books, picture books, pop-up books, board books, fiction, non-fiction and gift titles. Send submissions via email.

Toucan Books Ltd
4th Floor, 111 Charterhouse Street, London EC1M 6AW
tel 020-7250 3388
website www.toucanbooks.co.uk
Directors Robert Sackville West, Ellen Dupont

International co-editions; editorial, design and production services. Founded 1985.

Tucker Slingsby Ltd
5th Floor, Regal House, 70 London Road, Twickenham TW1 3QS
tel 020-8744 1007 *fax* 020-8744 0041
email firstname@tuckerslingsby.co.uk
website www.tuckerslingsby.co.uk
Directors Janet Slingsby, Del Tucker

Highly illustrated children's books for the international market. Prints and delivers to co-edition publishers, distributors and whole-salers wordwide on a firm sale basis. Specialises in early learning, Bible stories, nursery rhymes, fairytales and picture books. Produces approx. 50 titles each year. No unsolicited MSS or artwork accepted. Founded 1992.

Windmill Books Ltd
1st Floor, 9–17 St Albans Place, London N1 0NX
tel 020-7424 5640 *fax* 020-7424 5641
Children's Publisher Anne O'Daly

Book, partwork and continuity set packaging services for trade, promotional and international publishers. Opportunities for freelances.

Working Partners Ltd
Stanley House, St Chad's Place, London WC1X 9HH
tel 020-7841 3939 *fax* 020-7841 3940
email enquiries@workingpartnersltd.co.uk
website www.workingpartnersltd.co.uk
Managing Director Chris Snowdon, *Operations Director* Charles Nettleton

Children's and young adult fiction series. Genres include: animal fiction, fantasy, horror, historical fiction, detective, magical, adventure. Unable to accept any MSS or illustration submissions. Pays advance and royalty; retains copyright on all work created. Selects writers from unpaid writing samples based on specific brief provided. Always looking to add writers to database: to register details visit www.workingpartnersltd.co.uk/wp/writers-literary-agents/. Founded 1995.

Working Partners Two (division)
Managing Director Charles Nettleton

Adult fiction. Aims to create novels across most adult genres for publication in the UK, USA and international houses. See above for submission guidelines. Founded 2006.

Understanding the publishing process

To someone who has never worked in publishing, the way a manuscript is transformed into a book may seem like magic but in reality, the process is fairly straightforward. Although no two publishing houses (big or small) do things in the same way, the real magic is the way that the different departments work together to give every book the best possible chance of success. Bill Swainson explains the process.

For the purposes of this article I have assumed a medium-sized publishing house, big enough to have a fairly clear division of roles – in smaller houses these roles frequently overlap – and I talk mainly about original (rather than paperback reprint) publishing.

To begin at the beginning. Communication is everything in publishing and while more and more business is done by email, publishers still receive a number of their submissions and send out packages and correspondence by post. So, the post-room staff, the computer wizards, the office management team, the receptionist who answers the telephone and welcomes visitors, all play a vital part in the process of making books. But it is the managing director or Ceo of a company who draws all the threads together and gives the company its direction and drive.

Editorial

Every editorial department has a similar staff structure: commissioning editors (sometimes called acquiring or acquisition editors) take on a book and become its champion in the company, copy-editors (sometimes called desk editors) do the close work on the manuscript, and editorial assistants support them.

Every publishing company acquires its books from similar sources: literary agents and scouts, other publishers throughout the world, a direct commission from editor to author and, very rarely, by unsolicited proposal. The in-house process goes something like this: the commissioning editor will make a case for taking on a book at an 'acquisitions meeting', which is attended by all the departments directly involved in publishing books, including sales, marketing, publicity and rights. Lively discussions take place and a final decision is determined from a mixture of commercial good sense (estimated sales figures, likely production costs and the author's track record) and taste – and every company's and every editor's taste is different. Negotiations with the author or the author's agent then take place and the advance and terms are agreed.

Shortly after acquisition, an 'advance information' sheet is drafted by the commissioning editor. This is the earliest attempt to harness the excitement that led to the book being signed, and it contains all the basic information needed by the rest of the company, including the title, ISBN, format, likely extent (number of pages), price, rights holder, sales points, short blurb and biographical note. It is the first of many pieces of 'copy' that will be written about the book, and will be used as the template for all others, such as a catalogue entry, jacket blurb and press release.

It is now that the book's journey really begins, with the finishing line some 10–12 months away. As soon as it arrives in the editorial department, the manuscript will receive a 'structural edit', which involves looking at the book as a whole. For fiction, this includes everything from its structure and narrative pacing to characterisation and general style, and in the case of non-fiction, looking at illustrations, appendices, bibliography, notes and index. The copy-editing is usually done when all the main structural editorial decisions have been made. While commissioning editors may see certain titles through from beginning to end, it is more likely the book will be passed to a member of their editorial team to manage once the 'structural edit' has been completed, while still keeping a watching brief on every aspect of publication. It is at this stage that the more detailed work begins.

The copy-edit is the next filtering process and is designed to catch all the errors and inconsistencies in the text, from spelling and punctuation to facts, figures and tics of style. In some publishing houses this work is done onscreen, but surprisingly many editors still prefer to work direct on the manuscript because it is easier to spot mistakes and see where decisions have been made along the way. Once the copy-edit has been completed, the author will be asked to answer any queries that may have arisen. When the commissioning editor, copy-editor and author are happy that the marked-up manuscript is in the best possible shape, it is passed to the production department to be designed and typeset.

From now on the book will shuttle between the editorial and production departments in the form of proofs, usually in three separate stages. First proofs are read by the author and a proofreader. This is the author's last chance to make any cuts or additions as amendments after this stage become tricky and expensive to implement. Both sets of amendments are then collated and sent to the production department to be made into second proofs. Second proofs, or 'revises', are checked against the collated first proofs and any last-minute queries are attended to. (If an index is to be included, it will be compiled at this stage.) The checked 'revised' proofs are then returned to the production department to be made into 'final' proofs. Final proofs are, in a perfect publishing world, what the name implies. They are checked against the second proofs, the index (if there is one) is proofread, the preliminary pages double-checked and when all is present and correct – the text is ready to be printed.

Design

The design department's work on a new book usually begins 10–12 months in advance of the publication date. Hardback jackets and paperback covers are publishing's main selling tools. People say you can't judge a book by its cover, but because most (if not all) buying decisions are made by the trade's buyers before the book is printed – up until that time the cover *is* the book. It's what makes the buyer believe in a book's potential enough to order it, and it's one of the most important things that makes a browsing customer pick up a book in the bookshop and pay for it at the till.

The design department also produces all other sales material that the marketing department decides it needs in order to make a good job of the 'sell-in', including catalogues, order forms, 'blads' (literally book layout and design, i.e. illustrated sales material), 'samplers' (booklets containing tantalising extracts), posters, book proofs (bound reading proofs) and advertisements. Much of this work is now done online on the company's website, or in the form of e-marketing campaigns.

Most companies try to develop a distinctive look for their books and it is the design department that creates it.

Production

The production department handles all aspects of book production including text design, although some of the very big companies have a separate department for this. This department styles (or formats) the copy-edited manuscript by drafting a brief known as a 'type specification', or 'spec' for short. The spec may be designed specifically for a unique book, or if the book is part of a series, the series spec unifies the look and feel of the books. The typescript is then usually despatched to an out-of-house typesetter, although some companies do their typesetting in-house. Meanwhile, the production manager (working with the commissioning editor and the designer) will choose the binding materials and any embellishments, such as headband, coloured or printed endpapers, or marker ribbon. The print run is also decided (based on advance sales and track record) and an order is placed with the printer.

Most publishing companies use only a few printers, negotiating the best possible rate per book depending on the volume of work they agree to place with the printer. A key role of the production department is to buy print at a rate that allows each tightly budgeted book to make money and, equally important (especially when a book takes off), to manage the supply of reprints so that the publisher's warehouse is never short of stock.

Sales

'Selling in' in the home market (Britain and Ireland) is done increasingly by key account or area managers working with the chain buyers, as well as by a team of sales representatives. The reps visit bookshops in their designated area and try to achieve the sales targets set for each book. The number of copies sold pre-publication is known as the subscription sale, or 'sub'.

Selling books effectively to bookshops, both chains and independents, and nowadays to supermarkets and internet and other retailers, takes time and careful planning. The British and Irish book trade has developed in such a way that the sales cycle has extended to cover the best part of a year. Even though the actual business of selling may not begin in earnest until eight or nine months prior to publication, the work of preparing sales material begins up to a year ahead. It can, however, be achieved in a shorter time frame and this allows a degree of flexibility for the publisher in case of a crisis or to take advantage of prime opportunities, such as issuing instant books on a burning topic of the day.

Many sales are also made in-house by phone, email, fax and the internet. Most publishers provide customers with the opportunity to buy their books either directly from their own websites or via a link to another bookselling website. Book clubs are another market for publishers that used to be much more important, but today they are faced with stiff competition from the internet and supermarkets.

Export sales are achieved using teams of international agents and reps organised by the in-house export sales department. While the bigger companies tend to have their own teams and the smaller companies use freelance agencies and reps, all face different challenges to the home sales team. Here format, discount, royalty rates, shipping and exchange rates are the key components. The margins are much tighter and it requires a lot of skill and *chutzpah* to generate significant sales and then to maintain a successful international presence.

Marketing

It could be said that the marketing department is the engine room of the sales department. It is responsible for originating all the sales material (catalogues, blads, samplers, etc) used by the sales team to persuade the buyers in the book trade to buy the company's books.

Marketing personnel also work alongside the sales department in dealing directly with the big bookshops on special promotions ('Book of the Month', 'Debut', 'Money off', etc) that are now such a common feature of the larger chains.

The marketing department also creates the advertising for the trade, such as the post-publication press advertisements that, along with reviews and other publicity, persuades customers to buy a particular book. It also organises the company sales conferences at which each new season's publishing is presented to the sales reps and overseas agents for the first time. The run-up to the sales conference and the event itself is an exciting time and stimulates many of the best ideas on how to sell new books.

Publicity

As the marketing department works to sell books with the emphasis on the 'sell-in', the publicity department works with the author and the media on 'free' publicity with the emphasis on the 'sell through'. This covers reviews, features, author interviews, bookshop readings and signings, festival appearances, book tours and radio and television interviews, and so on.

For each author and his or her book, the publicity department devises a campaign that will play to the book's or the author's strengths. For instance, best use will be made of written features or radio interviews for authors who are shy in public, just as full advantage will be made of public appearances for those authors who thrive on the thrill of showmanship. The publicist's careful work (which like much of publishing is a mixture of inspiration and enthusiasm on the one hand and efficient planning and flexibility on the other) is designed to get the best results for each individual author and book.

Rights

It is the aim of the rights department to make the best use of all the rights that were acquired when the contract was first negotiated between publisher and author or the author's agent.

While literary agents are understandably keen to handle foreign and serial rights, many publishing houses have well-developed rights departments with good contacts and are also well placed to sell the rights of a book. Selling rights is very varied and includes anything from dealing with requests for film or television rights, the sale of translation rights to other countries, or serial rights to a newspaper, to smaller requests for permission to reprint a poem or an extract. All are opportunities to promote the book and earn additional income for author and publisher, and at the time of first publication the rights, sales, marketing and publicity departments all work closely together.

Book fairs are key venues for the sale of foreign rights. At the Frankfurt Book Fair in October and at the London Book Fair in April, publishers and agents from all participating countries meet to form a rights bazaar. Here, commissioning editors have the opportunity to hear about and buy new books from publishing houses all over the world. Occasionally rights are sold on the spot, but it is more common for acquisition to be completed later.

Paperbacks

Paperbacks are published approximately a year after publication of the original edition and are a key part of publishing today. Publishing paperbacks requires a different skill to publishing in hardback, primarily in the marketing. Efforts are made to identify and broaden the likely market (readership) for a book, making sure that the cover and presentation will appeal to a wide audience, and being ingenious about positioning an author's books in the marketplace where they can be best seen, bought and read. The means used vary from in-store promotions and advertising campaigns to author-led publicity and renewed press coverage in the 'paperback round-ups'. But the energy that drives this inspired and careful work of reinvention comes from the paperback publisher's vision and passion for the book and the author and the list as a whole.

Ebooks

Almost all publishing houses have begun to respond to the challenge and opportunities of e-publishing. Smart phones, the Sony Reader, the Kindle, and iPad have started to transform the market for books and the reading experience. Two or three years ago e-readers were a rare sight, but now they seem to be everywhere. Whether they will increase the overall market or simply lead to a transfer of a proportion of sales from the printed word to the electronic word remains to be seen; reliable statistics are not yet available. What is clear though is that a significant and growing proportion of book sales are in electronic form (as much as 15% in the UK and over 20% and in the USA) and that publishers will have to devise lively marketing strategies to exploit these opportunities for their authors to the full.

Accounts

Every successful business needs a good finance department and most publishing houses split the work into two areas – purchase ledger and royalties. Purchase ledger deals with all incoming invoices associated with the company's business. The royalties department deals exclusively with author advances (payable on acquisition, and on delivery or publication of a book) and with keeping account of the different royalty percentages payable on book sales, serial deals, film rights, permissions, etc. This is done so that both author and agent can see that an accurate record has been kept against the day when the book earns back its advance (the point at which the royalties earned equal the advance paid) and the author starts earning additional income.

A special business

This article is a potted breakdown of the inner workings of a medium-sized company. Publishing is a business, and commercial considerations will be apparent in every department, but it is a very special kind of business, one which frequently breaks many of the accepted business rules and often seems to make no sense at all – just think of the hundreds of different lines, formats, price points and discounts. At times it shouldn't work – but somehow, miraculously, it does.

Bill Swainson has worked for small, medium and large publishers since 1976 and is currently a Senior Commissioning Editor at Bloomsbury Publishing Plc, where he edits non-fiction and fiction, including in translation.

See also...

- *A year in view of the publishing industry*, page 313
- *Who owns whom in publishing*, page 322
- *How literary agencies work*, page 413
- *Electronic publishing*, page 581
- *Perfect proofs*, page 611

Spotting a bestseller

Alexandra Pringle addresses the million dollar question of what makes a bestselling book.

Publishing, at least in the literary sector, is a strange combination of judgement, confidence, experience, instinct and sheer luck. It would be a wonderful and much simpler world if we could predict what people will want to read, or if we could separate our own taste from the publishing process. But publishing is infinitely complicated.

It is probably the case that statistically there are some editors who have a higher hit rate in choosing bestsellers than others; just as there are some people that go through life without bad things happening to them, who never slip over in the street or have a nasty divorce or have children who fail exams. But publishing, like life, is a messy business and one that is inevitably teeming with failure. For every book that sells over 100,000 copies there are dozens and dozens that sell fewer than 10,000.

Editors need to be optimists – they need to believe that every book they take on, which will entail hours and hours of work and thought and waking up in the middle of the night, has the chance to do something wonderful, to create the alchemy that will mean the book will do well, and could, just could, become that rare and wonderful thing, a bestseller.

Of course nowadays editors do not buy books in isolation. First they have to love the book, at best to distraction. Then they have to sell the book to colleagues in sales and marketing, publicity and rights. If there aren't enough people who respond to the book, its chances of making it out there are slim. And then the editor has to be a robust engine that will drag the book up hill and down dale, through every bit of its process, from the text to the cover blurb to the bound proof to the finished creature and then out into the world. Without that stubborn effort, that sheer will, a book, like a neglected plant, will weaken and wither.

There are roughly two sorts of bestsellers (other than those that are simply the next book by an already bestselling author): those that are 'created' and those that find their way slowly and surely.

The first sort happens when a book is acquired and every single person in the company feels they have a bestseller on their hands from the outset. This is often after a hard-fought, adrenalin-fuelled auction where different departments have had to pitch in with marketing and publicity plans, with jacket designs and editorial comments and blandishments to the author. This can give the book a terrific start because the machine is up and running: there is a vision of what the book is and how it can be published. On the other hand, it can create a high platform from which a book can crash: the press can dislike a book because they feel it has been hyped – an unrealistic expectation may have been created in the excitement of the auction.

The second kind of bestseller is often the sweetest. These books can be by unknown authors that find their way into the outside world through stealth, that can be ignored by bookshops and by the press when first published, but that are passed, like a secret, from person to person, and become bestsellers two, three or four years after first publication. We call these word-of-mouth bestsellers. We love them very much indeed.

Or they are by authors who you stay with and who stay with you like a strange old marriage, and who after many years of publishing (often small, exquisite books that receive wonderful reviews and no sales to speak of) and years of the editor believing and hoping, produce a book that sets the publishing company alight, that gives them something to go out and shout about, that in turn sets the world alight. These are pretty lovely, too, and a source of especial joy and satisfaction to the editor.

One thing is clear: you can throw a fortune at a book in marketing and advertising and touring the author and while it will ensure the book is noticed, it does not necessarily make it a bestseller. In the end people will only read what they want to read. It is vital never to underestimate the intelligence and the wilfulness of the reading public.

People talk of 'the market' but I have never understood what that means, nor how anyone can begin to judge what people will want by studying buying trends and graphs and types of books that sell. For there may be one book about a Victorian murder that sells hundreds of thousands of copies, or a book about mathematics that captures the imagination of the public, but those that slavishly follow that model, hoping to capture some of that particular stardust, are usually bitterly disappointed.

What I do understand is that people cannot publish well and publish cynically. Whether you publish romance novels or high literature, or thrillers or books on animals, or food books or novels from far-flung countries, or books on cars or fridges or knitting, you have to believe in them.

After all, in the end, and in the absence of clairvoyance, all an editor really has is their own taste, their own belief. It is from this that all else springs.

Rather like J.M. Barrie's *Peter Pan*, Peter, of course, being the editor and Tinkerbell the author:

'If you believe,' he shouted to them, 'clap your hands; don't let Tink die.'
Many clapped.
Some didn't.
A few beasts hissed.

Tink was saved. First her voice grew strong, then she popped out of bed, then she was flashing through the room more merry and impudent than ever. She never thought of thanking those who believed, but she would have liked to get at the ones who had hissed.

Alexandra Pringle is Editor-in-Chief at Bloomsbury Publishing Plc.

See also...

- *The state of commissioning,* page 283
- *Understanding the publishing process,* page 215
- *A year in view of the publishing industry,* page 313
- *Who owns whom in publishing,* page 322

One hundred years of fiction bestsellers

Alex Hamilton pulls out some plums from 20th century fiction bestsellers.

Among bestsellers published before the Great War half a dozen authors' names still echo faintly, though the bulk of their work is little read. Gene Stratton Porter's *Freckles*, based on her life in a cabin by a swamp, sold two million copies, but is valued today only as a collectors' first edition. Among them also was Winston Churchill – not the statesman, but the author of *Richard Carvel*, the story of a naval officer under Paul Jones, selling more than a million copies, and with *The Crisis* and *The Crossing* he proved himself to be what publishers always look for – a career novelist with a following.

Frank Norris likewise promised well, when his fifth book, *The Pit*, scaled the heights, but almost simultaneously he died of appendicitis at the age of 32. Meanwhile Conan Doyle, the stayer of this bunch, peaked with his most admired Sherlock Holmes tale, *The Hound of the Baskervilles*, and when tired of him launched a second serial character, Professor Challenger, in *The Lost World*. Even their huge popularity could not quite match the exotica of Elinor Glyn who, with five million sales of her novel of passion, *Three Weeks*, set a marker for all candidates for the Number One spot.

If unable to write a book selling five million, try writing five that sell one million. This was more or less a habit of prolific producers of Westerns, whose pioneers were Owen Wister with *The Virginians*, and the daddy of them all, Zane Grey, with *Riders of the Purple Range*. These were authors of a genre that celebrated adventure and individual heroics in a way of life that was virtually obsolete. Though not a Western writer, Jack London in this sense belongs with them: his *The Call of the Wild*, whose heroics were actually those of a dog, sold a million and a half, and *The Sea Wolf* and *White Fang* almost as many. He was reputed to be the best-paid writer in America. Zane Grey, the Englishman J.T. Edson and Louis L'Amour each wrote more than 100 titles and for the latter the publishers claim a world sale of 270 million copies. The Western went great guns, so to speak, until about 1970, when relentless film and television exploitation had virtually exhausted it.

Women and crime

The circumstances of long wars, when authors and readers are in the trenches and publishers' paper supplies are cut back, are a drag on bestselling books. All the same, there were women's names to conjure with in the Great War: Eleanor Porter, who passed the million mark with *Pollyanna*, the girl whose policy it was to be glad regardless; Ethel M. Dell of *The Way of an Eagle* and *Bars of Iron*, whose villains were hardly worse than her sadistic heroes; Mary Roberts Rinehart, first bestselling woman writer of detective fiction and, with *The Circular Staircase* and *K*, setting a rough-and-ready example for a later generation.

Their 'Golden Age' came in the Thirties and Forties. With a 350 million sales total Agatha Christie was top cat, marketed as 'A Christie for Christmas'. For some 50 years she always offered a puzzle, with her Belgian detective Hercule Poirot on hand to solve it until, like Conan Doyle, she took against her odd hero and switched to a second series character,

Miss Marple – with 66 detective stories published altogether. Most in demand were *The Murder of Roger Ackroyd* and *Murder on the Orient Express.* Belgium was not so much proud of Poirot as of the hundreds of brilliant atmospheric crime stories featuring Inspector Maigret by their author Georges Simenon, whose wife was rightly a martinet to scores of foreign translators (recording a thousand translations).

Other women crime writers climbing the ladder behind Christie included Margery Allingham and the New Zealander Ngaio Marsh; Dorothy L. Sayers, who fanned out the subdivisions of the genre editing her jumbo mystery anthologies, intrigued fans with *The Unpleasantness at the Bellona Club* and *Nine Tailors*, with their mandarin style and affected hero, Lord Peter Wimsey. All these and their equally popular male contemporarics, such as Erle Stanley Gardner (not far behind Christie), John Dickson Carr, S.S. Van Dine and Ellery Queen (who named his detective after himself), produced a relatively mild climate of crime compared with later developments, when the ethos (as with the Western in its declining years) turned nasty. Because of its capacity for change, the dexterity of its authors and the sheer bloody-mindedness of its personnel, the crime story has been the dominant genre of the century, even ahead of the romance in its many guises.

Between the wars

Between the wars the entertainers whom today we'd call 'brand names' were: P.G. Wodehouse, creator of *Jeeves* and frothy social comedies whose bubbles have not yet burst; E. Phillips Oppenheim, who lived luxury and deployed it in his high-life fiction, writing 100 books, mostly with a relay of mistresses on his yacht on the Riviera known as 'the floating double bed'; Rafael Sabatini, boisterous historical romantic, best known for *Captain Blood* and *The Sea Hawk*; Jeffrey Farnol, fey and sentimental, as in *The Chronicles of the Imp*; and Sapper, pseudonym for an ex-army officer who was the progenitor of a crude racist type of spy story, with *Bulldog Drummond* selling six million copies. The series was continued nine times after Sapper's death by another ex-army officer (much as Kingsley Amis and John Gardner kept James Bond going after the death of his creator, Ian Fleming). And who could resist the publisher's banner that declared, 'It is impossible not to be thrilled by Edgar Wallace'? He was a journalist able to turn his Dictaphone to any form in his 'factory of fiction', piling up 170 novels in three decades: African adventure with *Sanders of the River*, much melodrama – some, like *The Crimson Circle,* with a brilliant premise – and umpteen thrillers. On his death in 1931, when a packet of cigarettes cost 3d, a trade paperback 2s and a cottage £100, his royalties were running at £75,000 a year.

Beside the genre favourites, there were some *sui generis* storytellers with powerful appeal. Edna Ferber won a Pulitzer Prize in 1925 with *So Big*, followed it with *Show Boat,* and 25 years later when approaching 70, she came up with *Giant.* Pearl S. Buck also won a Pulitzer Prize (in 1932) with *The Good Earth*, which later won the Nobel Prize and led to five million sales. The Southern writer Erskine Caldwell won a $1,000 prize from the *Yale Review* for a short story, but his real money-spinners were *God's Little Acre* with eight million sales, and *Tobacco Road* with four million sales plus, as a play, the then longest stage run in American theatre history.

Two other big books, physically and commercially, were historical romances. At several hundred thousand words they seemed to be trying to reinstate the Victorian three-decker in one volume. Margaret Mitchell's *Gone with the Wind* sold eight million copies before the war, took her ten years to write and was her only book. Hervey Allen's *Anthony Adverse,* the baby-on-the-doorstep who grows up an adventurer, took him five years to write, but he was tougher than Mitchell and produced more hefty novels, even a trilogy, though never with the same *éclat*. By contrast James Hilton took only four days over *Goodbye Mr Chips*, a slight book to add to his other slight book, *Lost Horizon*, about a remote mountain paradise called Shangri-La, but both were commercial heavyweights.

The Second World War and after

The rising flow of big sellers was partly stalled by shortages in the Second World War. The force in fiction lay increasingly with Americans: John Steinbeck's *The Grapes of Wrath*, Ernest Hemingway's *For Whom the Bell Tolls* and the Lutheran minister Lloyd C. Douglas's novel deriving from the Crucifixion, *The Robe*, which accumulated four million sales. Near the end Kathleen Winsor added a saucy three million seller set in the time of Charles II, *Forever Amber*. The two British authors with similar results were Daphne du Maurier, whose *Rebecca* was brilliantly served by the Hitchcock movie (and *Frenchman's Creek* less well) and Somerset Maugham, a lifelong bestseller since 1915, with *The Razor's Edge*. Every one of the last dozen books mentioned was filmed, which of course prompted a second wave of sales.

In the immediate aftermath of the war there was no sudden eruption of blockbusters, despite the launch of new publishing houses and a growth in the number of titles that seems to have continued exponentially to the present day. However, two books carrying blatant messages had the rare distinction among bestsellers of being politically motivated: George Orwell's *Animal Farm*, followed by *1984*, which in 20 years each sold eight million copies. Between them appeared Norman Mailer's emotional response to the war, *The Naked and the Dead*, with a relatively modest three million sales.

The Fifties

In the Fifties the trade geared itself to a clutch of uncouth authors. The notable example is Mickey Spillane, who at one time had seven of his brutal thrillers in the Top 10, led by *I, the Jury*, all selling more than five million copies. Harold Robbins first showed at this time with *Never Love a Stranger* and *The Dream Merchants*, opening shots in a bombardment that for his total *oeuvre* eventually topped 150 million. Charts of two decades were overwhelmed by the glamour and snobbery of Ian Fleming's James Bond stories, starting with *Casino Royale*, and selling unbridled millions (40 plus) to this day. The archetypal blockbusters of the period were novels such as *Airport* and *Wheels* by Arthur Hailey, exploring the works of large organisations; *Peyton Place* by Grace Metalious, in tandem with its long-running television series, and slightly more serious, the vast doorstoppers by James Michener, *South Pacific* and *Hawaii*.

More lasting successes include *To Kill a Mockingbird* by Harper Lee, a classic of racist conflict in the American South, helped on beyond 10 million sales by its prescription for educational courses (William Golding's *Lord of the Flies* benefits in the same way); Joseph Heller's satire on military bureaucracy *Catch-22*, and the reclusive J.D. Salinger's *Catcher in the Rye*, a percentage of whose six million copies are said to have been urged by teenage girls on their boyfriends. Vladimir Nabokov's story of a middle-aged man's obsession with and seduction by a sub-teen girl, *Lolita*, seems to presage the imminent conflicts over censorship in the Sixties. The major test was the trial of Penguin Books in 1960, which ironically made a six million seller of perhaps the least of D.H. Lawrence's novels, *Lady Chatterley's Lover*, banned on its first publication 32 years earlier.

The Sixties

In the Sixties several books were boosted into orbit not so much by their actual sexual content as by the fuss that was made over it: *Candy* by Terry Southern, *Tropic of Cancer* by Henry Miller, *The Exhibitionist* by Henry Sutton, *Couples* by John Updike, *Portnoy's Complaint* by Philip Roth and *Myra Breckinridge* by Gore Vidal. Apart from Vidal, these writers' sales rarely returned to the highest level, despite their range and brilliance. The newcomers who appeared in the Top 10 and retained their position, as it were by right, were Irving Stone with his biographical novels, such as *The Agony and the Ecstasy* (about Michelangelo), Jacqueline Susann with the showbiz misery of *Valley of the Dolls* (10 million sales over 20 years), Mario Puzo with *The Godfather* (12 million), and two who changed the character of the thriller with their grasp of the intricacies of the Cold War: John le Carré opened with *The Spy Who Came in from the Cold*, while Len Deighton challenged Ian Fleming's picture of espionage with his first, *The Ipcress File*. For nearly 40 years there was always a new Deighton book high on the charts, until he called a halt on himself.

The Seventies and after

Other tireless British regulars over the last quarter of a century included the gothic romances of Victoria Holt, the adventures set in Africa by Wilbur Smith and the northern sagas of Catherine Cookson, whose paperback sales at her death had reached 55 million. Beginning with *The Day of the Jackal*, there was usually a million-selling thriller by Frederick Forsyth, and an automatic sale to half a million fans ready for the annual racecourse mystery from Dick Francis. Ahead of them all were the novels that Jeffrey Archer contrived from the extraordinary 'snakes and ladders' pattern of his own life, starting with *Not a Penny More, Not a Penny Less*. Across the Eighties some would rack up close on five million copies, though slightly shaded by the actual top seller of the decade, the humorous *Secret Diary of Adrian Mole Aged 13¾* by Sue Townsend.

Science fiction 'greats', cheered on by countless Sci-cons and Hugo and Nebula Awards, appreciate club support but also duck out, like Kurt Vonnegut with *Slaughterhouse Five* and J.G. Ballard with *Empire of the Sun*. Bestsellers include Isaac Asimov's *Foundation Trilogy*, John Wyndham's *The Day of the Triffids*, and Arthur C. Clarke's *2001*. Short stories are key to science fiction and the key anthologist is Brian Aldiss, prolific author of the *Helliconia Trilogy*. Fantasy's leaders are J.R.R. Tolkien's *Lord of the Rings* (12 million) and Terry Pratchett's *Discworld* novels, begun in 1983 with *The Colour of Magic*. (Pratchett's sales, all genres, surpass 25 million.)

Almost as many American as British authors figured every year in the 100 fastsellers from British publishers between 1980 and 2000. One phenomenon was Stephen King, the most read horror writer after William Blatty's 10 million for *The Exorcist*, always among the leaders with massive frighteners such as *IT* and *Pet Sematary*. The other who never missed was Danielle Steel, who would prefer that her novels were not called romances, and who, like King and Cookson, sometimes had two or three titles in the same list. In the Nineties John Grisham virtually took over the Number One spot with his thrillers about corporation lawyers and their illegal habits. As the millennium approached, however, he had to give way to J.K. Rowling. She with her *Harry Potter* series, and Dan Brown with his conspiracy thrillers, set an undreamt of pace for the 21st century.

Inevitably many unputdownable titles and storytellers are omitted from this fiction survey. Everyone will have a favourite that's been missed. Apologies from **Alex Hamilton**, who kept the *Guardian* Fastseller Chart for 25 years.

Notes on becoming a novelist

William Boyd reveals how his first novel came to be published.

In the early 1970s when I was at university I started to fantasise about becoming a novelist. The trouble was that I literally hadn't a clue about how to set about realising my vague but heartfelt dream. It's hard to imagine today – in this internet age, with hundreds of creative writing courses on offer, writers' blogs and literary festivals and all the rest – how arcane and remote the business of becoming a novelist appeared to be at that time. It seemed like trying to join some incredibly exclusive club. I didn't know anyone who was a writer or who was connected in any way to the publishing industry; I had no idea how to submit a book to a publishing company or even what job a 'literary agent' did.

However, I bought myself a typewriter and started to write. I wrote a novel and then another; I wrote student journalism, prose sketches and bad poems and even entered a play for a one-act play competition at my local theatre. In my random way I was actually doing the right thing, I now realise. I was writing as hard as I could, fulfilling my apprenticeship, making mistakes and learning from them.

Then in 1976 I moved to Oxford to do a PhD and for the first time met 'real' writers. Talking to them made the road to publication seem a little less obscure, a little less hit or miss. It struck me, then – and this also shows how times have changed – that my best chance of being published was through writing short stories and so I duly started to write short stories and send them off. I submitted stories to any magazine that published them – and there were quite a few in those days – literary magazines, women's magazines, the BBC's 'Morning Story' slot. I had my share of rejections but slowly but surely, over the next couple of years, I began to have stories published and broadcast. My stories appeared in *London Magazine*, *Company*, *Punch*, *Good Housekeeping*, *Mayfair* and the *Literary Review* amongst others. When I had had about nine stories published I thought – hang on, there's almost a short story collection here, and I decided to submit my stories to a publisher. In fact I sent my collected stories off to two publishers, simultaneously. I recommend this ploy – it saves a lot of time – and in the unlikely event they both reply positively it becomes what's known in Hollywood as a 'high-class problem' – the kind of problem no one complains about.

The publishers I chose were Jonathan Cape and Hamish Hamilton. Both of them were highly regarded and were also regular publishers of short story collections (again, how times have changed). As a last-minute afterthought I added a PS to my letters of submission relating the fact that I had written a novel featuring a character – an overweight, drunken, young diplomat called Morgan Leafy – that appeared in two of the short stories.

A few weeks later the magic letter arrived from Hamish Hamilton, from the managing director himself, Christopher Sinclair-Stevenson. He said he would like to publish my story collection. Even better, he said he'd also like to publish the novel I had written – but, crucially, he wanted to publish the novel first. Slight problem – slight high-class problem – I hadn't written the novel… So I told a white lie – I had to retype the manuscript in its entirety, I said – and in a torrid heat of creative dynamism wrote my novel *A Good Man in Africa* in about ten weeks and sent it off. And the rest, so to speak, is history. In 1981 my novel was published and, six months later, so was my short story collection. I didn't have an agent, I didn't know anyone influential, I had no introduction to an editor or publisher – I did it entirely on my own. And I'm still waiting for a reply from Jonathan Cape.

William Boyd is the author of 11 novels, several collections of short stories, screenplays and non-fiction writing; a memoir of his schooldays and the speculative memoir *Nat Tate: An American Artist*. His most recent novels are *Restless* (2006, winner of the Costa Book Award, Novel of the Year), *Ordinary Thunderstorms* (2009), and *Waiting for Sunrise* (Bloomsbury 2012). He is currently writing the new James Bond novel, due to be published in 2013.

Notes from a successful fiction author

Joanna Trollope shares her experiences of writing success.

I once said to a journalist – rather crossly – that it had only taken me 20 years to be an overnight success. This was in 1993, with my first number one (the paperback of *The Rector's Wife*) and the accompanying media assumption that I had come from nowhere to somewhere at meteoric speed.

People do, of course. Rare, rare people do, but most of us are trudging for years across the creative plateau, honing our skills and cajoling our sinking hearts and *hoping*. I wrote my first published book when my younger daughter was three. When *The Rector's Wife* appeared, she was almost 23, and there'd been ten books in the interim. Hardly *Bridget Jones*. Scarcely *White Teeth*.

But, on reflection, the long haul suited me. I learned about structure and dialogue and pace and characterisation at my own pace. I might have started with a readership so small it was almost invisible to the naked eye, but it grew, and it grew steadily in a manner that made it feel reliable, as is the case with long-term friendships. It also meant that when success came, it was absolutely lovely, no doubt about that, but there was no question of it turning my middle-aged head.

When I wrote my first published book in 1978 – a historical novel called *Eliza Stanhope* set around the battle of Waterloo – the publishing climate was very different to how it is now. Many of the great publishing individuals were still alive, agents were a scarcer breed and writing was not seen as a way to becoming instantly, absurdly rich (and, in my view, never should be). I sent my manuscript – poorly typed on thin paper – off to Hamish Hamilton in a brown paper parcel. It was politely returned. I sent it – heart definitely in sink – to Hutchinson. They wrote back – a letter I still have – and invited me, like a job interview, to 'come and discuss my future'.

Even if the rest is history, it is not easy or simple history. There weren't any great dramas, to be sure, no cupboards stuffed with rejection slips, no pulped copies (that came later), but what there was instead was a simply enormous amount of perseverance. I don't want to sound too austere, but I rather believe in perseverance when it comes to writing. As V.S. Pritchett once said, most people write better if they *practise*.

And I have to say that I am still practising. I think it very unlikely that I will ever feel I have got it right, and I would be uneasy if that feeling went away. After all, only a very few geniuses – Sophocles, Shakespeare – could claim to be prophets or inventors. Most writers are translators or interpreters of the human condition, but no more. A hefty dose of humility in writing seems to me both seemly and healthy.

Readers, after all, are no fools. Readers may not have a writer's gift of the arrangement of events and people and language, but they know about life and humanity all right. They may even know much more about both than the writer. So not only must they never be forgotten, but they must never be underestimated or patronised either.

Which is one of the reasons, in my case, why I research my novels. For the readers' sake, as well as my own, I have to be as accurate as possible about, say, being the child of a broken home, or the widow of a suicide, or a mistress or an adopted man in his thirties. So, once I've decided upon the theme of a novel (and those can have brewed in my brain for years or be triggered by a chance remark overheard on a bus) I go and talk to people who are in the situation that I am exploring. And I have to say that in all the years of working this way, no one has ever turned me down, and everyone has exceeded my expectations.

This habit has had an unlooked-for advantage. During all the years I've been writing, the business of promotion has grown and grown, and fiction is notoriously difficult to talk about in any medium. But the research gives me – and journalists – subject matter which is, to my relief, honourably relevant but, at the same time, miles away from the inexplicable private, frequently uncomfortable place where writing actually goes on. 'Tell me,' people say, not actually understanding what they are asking, 'Tell me how you write'. Pass.

Joanna Trollope is the author of 18 contemporary novels, including her latest number one bestseller, *The Soldier's Wife*, as well as a number of historical novels published under the name of Caroline Harvey, and a study of women in the British Empire called *Britannia's Daughters*. She lives in London.

Notes from a successful short story author

Chimamanda Ngozi Adichie shares her experiences of being a short story writer.

I have been writing since I was old enough to spell. It is difficult to say where it comes from, this urge to tell stories, and so I have convinced myself that it was simply meant to be. I like to think that I was born with a group of literary spirits hovering overhead and that they visit me from time to time to whisper in my ears. Writing has always been much more important to me than publishing and I think this is an important distinction to make, especially for beginning writers. When I start to write a story, I am not thinking of where it will be published, I am instead thinking of making it the best story it can be. Of course this sounds a bit simplistic, if not cliched, but I think writing stories is something that has to matter in a deep and metaphysical sense. You have to care about it, really care about it, and if that is the starting point of a good story, that story will definitely find a home.

I wrote a lot of poetry when I was younger – I even had a book of awful poems published in Nigeria when I was 15 – but I became drawn to the short story form after I moved to the United States to go to university. I am not entirely sure why but it was probably because I began to read more short stories. Most of my reading in Nigeria had been novels, although I first read and fell in love with Katherine Mansfield's stories when I was a teenager. So I began to write short stories. I joined an online writers' group where I read and critiqued the short stories of other writers – I found that very useful because it began to crystallise for me what I admired and did not admire in the form. I learned that I like realist fiction and that I am unwaveringly old-fashioned in my taste: I love fiction that has character and narrative at its heart. Postmodernism leaves me cold.

After I had written a few short stories, I then made the conscious decision that I wanted to be published. So I spent days at the library looking up information in books like the *Writers Market*, as well as magazines about writing. I needed to know how the whole thing worked. I didn't know, for example, that literary editors wanted stories to be double-spaced and it took me a while to figure out that the acronym 'sase' meant that one was required to include a self-addressed, stamped envelope. I bought a packet of envelopes. I double-spaced my stories. I copied out the names and addresses of a dozen literary journals and I sent off my stories. I remember the first sase that came back in the mail. I took it out of the mailbox, my hand slightly shaky because I thought that I was about to discover where my first published story would appear. It was, of course, a rejection. And the worst kind – a form rejection, which is a pre-typed letter that an assistant in a journal's paper-strewn office picks up from a ready pile on her desk, folds and slips into a sase. I was devastated. Other rejections came in slow succession, and with each form letter I read, I felt a little bit of my smug certainty melt away.

Why were those early stories rejected? Because some of them were just not good enough, and also because I had not targeted my stories properly. I had sent them to the best-known journals – always a good thing to do – but I had sent them only to the best-known journals. I had not considered the small, independent journals publishing wonderful fiction, edited by committed people but often unheard of. I decided to start over again. I revised some stories – and I find that reading the kind of fiction I love often helps me to see my own work in new ways. I read a lot of short stories while revising mine. The Ghanaian writer Ama Ata Aidoo is one of my favourite short story writers. Then I went back to the library, looked up the lesser-known journals in the writing reference books, and then read some of their back issues. I was often stunned by the quality of the work published. I knew I would be in good company if my story was published in any of them.

It took almost a year before my first acceptance letter came. Before that, though, the rejections became nicer; yes, it is in fact possible to get a nice rejection. A well-known editor wrote me a note – hand-written! – to say he liked my story, did not think it was right for his publication, but wanted me to send him something else. That was the kind of encouragement that made me perk up since writing is, sadly, in some ways an exercise in seeking validation. My first acceptance was for an online journal, called *Zoetrope Extra*, the online supplement of Francis Ford Coppola's print journal, *Zoetrope All-Story*. And then there was an acceptance from the *Iowa Review*. And then one from a journal in Canada.

I am still writing short stories and still find the process both frustrating and exhilarating. It has not become easier to write, if anything I find myself grumbling more and more about how the literary spirits are stingy about visiting. What is easier now is having access to publishing because I have an agent who sends my stories out. I still get rejections, of course, but I also now have editors contacting me to specifically ask for stories.

Because I write both novels and short stories, I am often asked about the differences between the two forms. I find short stories to be completely different from novels, obviously, but I don't think that short stories are the younger and less accomplished siblings of novels – which seems to be how some people look at them. They're equals, but different. To write a short story is to have very little space, to compress emotion, and because of that, I think that the form requires a kind of sustained focus that the novel doesn't necessarily require. And it also means that short stories have the potential to be powerful and affecting in ways that novels are not.

Chimamanda Ngozi Adichie was born in Nigeria in 1977. She is the author of a collection of short stories titled *The Thing Around Your Neck* (Fourth Estate 2009). Her novels include *Purple Hibiscus* (Harper Perennial 2003), for which she won the Orange Broadband Prize for Fiction in 2007; *Half of a Yellow Sun* (Harper Perennial 2006), which is being made into a film; and *Americanah* is due to be published by Fourth Estate in October 2012. Her work has been selected by the Commonwealth Broadcasting Association and the BBC Short Story Awards. Her website is www.l3.ulg.ac.be/adichie.

Notes from a successful comic author

Kathy Lette ponders the serious business of being a comic writer.

To be a comic author, there are many technical terms you first need to master. For example, did you know that 'brontosaurus' is an anthology of works by 19th century English sister authors? Then there's grammatical precision. A double negative is a complete no-no. Oh, and get an agent to deal with the financial side of things. Satirists are notoriously hopeless at handling money. We tend to spend half the time worrying about addition, half the time worrying about division and half the time worrying about subtraction. But for any budding comic author it would be easier if you could be strapped into a publishing simulator to experience the terrors and exhilaration, to see if you have what it takes. Because the list of requirements is gruelling. The honing of cheerfulness to chat show perfection. The haemorrhaging of charisma at book signings. The psychotic episodes which accompany concluding your comic masterpiece after you have stopped finding it funny. (Satires are like sausages – you really don't want to know what goes into making them. But creating one can sometimes prove as much fun as removing your own IUD with barbecue tongs.) Then there's the loneliness. I occasionally get so sick of my own company that even my imaginary friend gets bored and runs off to play with someone more interesting. Worst of all is the dreaded book tour which involves flying hundreds of miles from Dipstick, Ohio, to Buffalo Fart, Wyoming, for a one-minute slot on breakfast radio with a member of the 'Illiterati' whose reading material is limited to his bank balance and tarot cards.

Then there's the inane questions at book festivals. (1) Where do you get your ideas? And (2) Would you like to read my manuscript? And (3) What inspired you to write this comic novel? (Answer: The Inland Revenue. I thought I'd laugh my way to the bank.)

On the up side, writing a funny book is so much cheaper than therapy. Otherwise I'd be a permanent member of Couch Canyon. 'Poetic justice' is the only justice in the world – and I say that being married to a lawyer. A comic writer can always impale enemies on the end of a pen.

I first realised the wounding power of the pen as a teenager. The Aussie surfie males I grew up with disproved the theory of evolution – they were evolving into apes. These were the type of guys who thought 'sex drive' meant doing it in the car. I decided to exorcise my angst in a novel and shish-kebabed those boys on my Bic biro in a book called *Puberty Blues*. It was published when I was 19 and became a bestseller. It was furious, yes, but also bleakly funny. The success of the novel taught me how much more effective it is to comically kneecap the opposition.

In the ten novels I've written since, I've lampooned many subjects. *In Girls Night Out* I set my satirical sights on married men who think monogamy is something you make dining room tables out of. In *The Llama Parlour*, I took aim at Hollywood – a place where they say 'have a nice day' and then shoot you. In *Foetal Attraction*, I blew a literary raspberry at natural childbirth – a case of stiff upper labia. In *Mad Cows*, I wanted to barbecue the sacred cow that claims that motherhood is the ultimate fulfilment for a female. Yes, I love my children with a primal passion but, like all mums, am occasionally tempted to shove them back into the condom vending machine for a refund.

Altar Ego was the antidote to Bridget Jones, because I don't believe a woman should wait around to be rescued by a Knight in Shining Armani. It seems to me that a perfect marriage is like an orgasm – many of them are faked.

Nip'n'tuck was a fiesty attack on the facial prejudice older women endure and the cosmetic cowboys who want to disfigure us. (My mother told me never to pick my nose – especially from a catalogue!) I then penned *Dead Sexy* – a satire on the sex war. (Why do men like intelligent women? Because opposites attract.) *How To Kill Your Husband – and other handy household hints* was a cry for help for the generation of women who thought we were going to Have It All, but just ended up Doing It All. Even though women make up 50% of the workforce, we're still doing 99% of all the housework and childcare. The Dunkirk evacuation would have been easier to organise than a working mum getting her kids up and out of the house in the morning. Men may say they'd like to help more around the house, only they can't multi-task. This is just a biological cop out. Would any man have trouble multi-tasking at say, an orgy? (Men, take note, it is scientifically proven that no woman ever shot her husband while he was doing the vacuuming.)

To Love, Honour and Betray poses the theory that teenagers are God's punishment for having sex in the first place. Living with a teenage daughter is a lot like I imagine living with the Taliban would be. A mum is not allowed to laugh, dance, sing or wear short skirts. My top tip for mums of teens who say, 'I wish you'd just die,' is to take a big drag on a cigarette and a big gulp of wine and say, 'I'm doing my best darling'.

As you can see, I have a lot to get off my Wonderbra-ed chest. So, why use humour? Because if you can disarm with charm, you're more likely to get your message across. The author and critic Amanda Craig puts it more eloquently: 'Critics refuse to accept that literature can be profound, but also pleasurable; an experience which lifts the spirits while engaging the mind.' A thought backed up by no less than Dr Johnson, who observed, 'The true end of literature is to enable the reader better to enjoy life or better to endure it'.

Scientists tell us that laughter is innate; it originates in the oldest part of the brain, the hypothalamus. Biologists maintain that laughter increases our biological fitness. Anthropologists have revealed that the Eskimos hold laughing competitions and that women, in all cultures, laugh more often than men, *especially* in all-female groups. Why? Well, living with the male of the species, we have so much to laugh about. Firstly, there's the fact that hypochondria is Greek for man. (If any man says he's not a hypochondriac, well, that's the only disease he *doesn't* have.) Then there's the fact that many marriages break up for religious reasons – he thinks he's a God and well, she just doesn't. Not to forget the fact that women are still getting concussion from hitting our heads on the glass ceiling – and we're expected to clean it whilst we're up there. The female of the species is also the butt of God's biological joke, beginning with periods (when a girl gets taken hostage by her hormones) followed by pregnancy and childbirth (which requires you to stretch your birth canal the customary five kilometres) – then ending with the menopause. Then just when everything goes quiet, what happens? *You grow a beard.* Is that fair I ask you? Yes, for the female of the species it's probably a case of laugh or… your mascara runs.

Men always say that women can't tell jokes. Of course, this might be because we marry them. But perhaps one of the reasons men don't want to admit that women are funny is because they're terrified to think what we're being funny about. Boys, to put you at your ease, let me just say that on our all-girl gatherings, we don't just talk about the length of your appendages…. We also talk about the *width*, which, after childbirth is much, much more important.

So, as you can see, basically I just write down the way women talk when there are no men around. But the trouble with writing humorously is that it's so subjective. What one person finds funny, another finds fatuous, which can lead to some reviewer Rottweilering. And when it comes to criticism, if there were an Olympic Games for Hypocrisy, comic writers would win Gold. A glowing review, and we're sycophantic with praise – 'Critics! So perspicacious! Such literary taste and discernment!' Feelings explode in you like champagne. I once had a glowing review printed on a t-shirt and wore it for weeks. Hell, I had to be restrained from getting it tattooed onto my forehead. But when we get a *bad* review critics become no better than pond scum. 'Critics! Ugh! Cyborgs that eat human flesh are less alien than book reviewers!'

There's no need for a printed t-shirt now as you're running away to Goa to live naked in a hollowed-out tree with Lord Lucan. You begin to understand that there is a very fine line between book reviewing and homicide. Thoughts of murder cross your mind. The only thing which stops you is the hideously unflattering prison uniform. Although, you find yourself thinking, after a drink or two, at least the stripes are vertical, which would be vaguely slimming....

When you bump into a critic who has savaged your work, a few responses occur to you simultaneously: (1) Why can't you see her lobotomy scar? (2) How the hell does she fit her cloven hooves into those Prada shoes? But I suggest you simply shake his or her hand then say something like: 'It's really courageous of you to risk coming into contact with me *after the diagnosis*'.

That said, all writers need some constructive criticism – especially if you're writing comedy. How do you know if it's funny? My very scientific and high-tech test is to make an observation at the dinner table. If my female friends laugh, I write it down. But, it's pointless being precious about your material. I learnt this when writing for a sitcom for Columbia Pictures in Hollywood. Lines, jokes and whole scenes were rejected on a daily basis. All those hugely successful television sitcoms such as *Seinfeld*, *Frasier* and *Friends*, etc are all actually written by about ten people. They lock you in a windowless room, which I used to call the 'gag gulag', where you make jokes all day. It's like being a stand-up comedian, except you're sitting down. The hilarious writing staff I worked with were all Jewish. I became so Jewish when I worked there – big hair, high shoes, talking with my hands – that I feel guilty that I'm not. But that hothouse atmosphere taught me that there is always a better and funnier line.

The best thing about being a comic writer is that people expect you to be immature and disorganised. This means you get to work in your PJs all day, drink heavily on the job and have affairs and call it research. But I principally became a satirist as it involves no heavy lifting. Except for those writers who lift whole sections of other people's work and then call it their own. But hey, you can't have all work and no plagiarism, right?

But if you really want to be a comic writer, your most important assignment is to think of a witty epithet. Spike Milligan's was: 'I told you I was sick.' I think mine will be: 'Finally – a good plot.'

Kathy Lette has written 11 novels and two non-fiction books. Her latest non-fiction book is *Men – A User's Guide* (Bantam Press 2010). Her most recent novel is *The Boy Who Fell To Earth* (Transworld 2012).

Notes from a successful fantasy author

Terry Pratchett gives pointers on how to write successfully in the fantasy genre.

Since a lot of fiction is in some way fantasy, can we narrow it down to 'fiction that transcends the rules of the known world'? And it might help to add 'and includes elements commonly classed as magical'. There are said to be about five fantasy sub-genres, from contemporary to mythic, but they mix and merge and if the result is good, who cares?

If you want to write it, you've probably read a lot of it – in which case, stop (see below). If you haven't read any, go and read lots. Genres are harsh on those who don't know the history, don't know the *rules.* Once you know them, you'll know where they can be broken.

Genres are also – fantasy perhaps most of all – a big bulging pantry of plots, conceits, races, character types, myths, devices and directions, most of them hallowed by history. You're allowed to borrow, as many will have done before you; if this were not the case there would only ever have been one book about a time machine. To stay with the cookery metaphor, they're all just ingredients. What matters is how you bake the cake: every decent author should have their own recipe and the best find new things to add to the mix.

World building is an integral part of a lot of fantasy, and this applies even in a world that is superficially our own – apart, say, from the fact that Nelson's fleet at Trafalgar consisted of hydrogen-filled airships. It is said that, during the fantasy boom in the late Eighties, publishers would maybe get a box containing two or three three-runic alphabets, four maps of the major areas covered by the sweep of the narrative, a pronunciation guide to the names of the main characters and, at the bottom of the box, the manuscript. Please... there is no need to go that far.

There is a term that readers have been known to apply to fantasy that is sometimes an unquestioning echo of better work gone before, with a static society, conveniently ugly 'bad' races, magic that works like electricity and horses that work like cars. It's EFP, or Extruded Fantasy Product. It can be recognised by the fact that you can't tell it apart from all the other EFP.

Do not write it, and try not to read it. Read widely outside the genre. Read about the Old West (a fantasy in itself) or Georgian London or how Nelson's navy was victualled or the history of alchemy or clock-making or the mail coach system. Read with the mindset of a carpenter looking at trees.

Apply logic in places where it wasn't intended to exist. If assured that the Queen of the Fairies has a necklace made of broken promises, ask yourself what it looks like. If there is magic, where does it come from? Why isn't everyone using it? What rules will you have to give it to allow some tension in your story? How does society operate? Where does the food come from? You need to know how your world *works.*

I can't stress that last point enough. Fantasy works best when you take it seriously (it can also become a lot funnier, but that's another story). Taking it seriously means that there must be rules. If *anything* can happen, then there is no real suspense. You are allowed to make pigs fly, but you must take into account the depredations on the local bird life and the need for people in heavily over-flown areas to carry stout umbrellas at all times. Joking aside, that sort of thinking is the motor that has kept the *Discworld* series moving for nearly 30 years.

Somehow, we're trained in childhood not to ask questions of fantasy, like: how come only one foot *in an entire kingdom* fits the glass slipper? But look at the world with a questioning eye and inspiration will come. A vampire is repulsed by a crucifix? Then surely it can't dare open its eyes because everywhere it looks, in a world full of chairs, window frames, railings and fences, it will see something holy. If werewolves as Hollywood presents them were real, how would they make certain that when they turned back into human shape they had a pair of pants to wear? And in *Elidor*, Alan Garner, a master at running a fantasy world alongside and entwined with our own, memorably asked the right questions and reminded us that a unicorn, whatever else it may be, is also a big and very dangerous horse. From simple questions, innocently asked, new characters arise and new twists are put on an old tale.

G.K. Chesterton summed up fantasy as the art of taking that which is humdrum and everyday (and therefore unseen) and picking it up and showing it to us from an unfamiliar direction, so that we see it anew, with fresh eyes. The eyes could be the eyes of a tiny race of humans, to whom a flight of stairs is the Himalayas, or creatures so slow that they don't see fast-moving humanity at all. The eyes could even be the nose of our werewolf, building up an inner picture of a room by an acute sense of smell, seeing not just who is there now but who was there yesterday.

What else? Oh yes. Steer clear of 'thee' and 'thou' and 'waxing wroth' unless you are a genius, and use adjectives as if they cost you a toenail. For some reason adjectives cluster around some works of fantasy. Be ruthless.

And finally: the fact that it is a fantasy does not absolve you from all the basic responsibilities. It doesn't mean that characters needn't be rounded, the dialogue believable, the background properly established and the plots properly tuned. The genre offers all the palettes of the other genres, and new colours besides. They should be used with care. It only takes a tweak to make the whole world new.

Terry Pratchett OBE has written 39 novels in the *Discworld* series, the last 33 of which have all reached No 1 in the bestseller lists. His most recent book is a young adult novel, *Dodger*, set in a not quite historical 1840s London, due to be published in September 2012 by Doubleday. He has written 51 books and co-authored about 50 more, the most recent being a science fiction novel, *The Long Earth*, written with Stephen Baxter, to be published in June 2012. His novel, *Nation*, for young adult readers, was adapted for the Royal National Theatre and staged over the 2009 Christmas season. His young adult novel, *The Amazing Maurice and His Educated Rodents*, was the 2001 winner of the Carnegie Medal. A number of novels have appeared as mini-series on television and more are in preparation. He was knighted, for services to literature, in the 2009 New Year's Honours List.

Notes from a successful crime author

Mark Billingham shares his experiences of writing success.

I am a writer because I'm a reader. That I'm a *crime* writer, however, is probably down to a desire to get free books. I'd always written stuff of one sort or another: silly stories at school, terrible poetry at university, so-so plays for community theatre companies. I'd drifted into a career in stand-up and writing comedy for television but my passion as a reader was for crime fiction, primarily of the darker and more disturbing kind.

Devouring the work of my favourite writers from both sides of the Atlantic fired my imagination and fed my head and heart, but as I had also developed an obsession for collecting the first editions of these authors, it was doing very little for my bank balance. My wife made the choice quite a simple one: get the books for free or get a divorce.

I'm still amazed at how easy it was – how little time and effort was involved. A couple of phone calls to the publicity departments of several big publishers, a bit of blather about how I was reviewing for my local paper, and suddenly the books came tumbling through the letterbox: package after package carried manfully to the door by my less-than-delighted postman. I did indeed start to review for my local paper and soon I was writing longer pieces, then articles for national magazines, and it wasn't very long before I was asked if I'd like to interview a couple of crime writers – this was major!

I can vividly remember the enormous and terrifying thrill of interviewing such crime-writing giants as Michael Connelly and Ian Rankin, and I still get a secret buzz from the fact that I can now count them among my friends. (This, for me, remains one of the greatest pleasures in becoming a published writer; that if you're lucky, those whose work you've admired for many years can end up propping up bars with you in exotic countries at ungodly hours.) So, I was a reader who adored crime fiction, who was lucky enough to be writing *about* it and who, occasionally, talked to those who actually *wrote* it.

Writing it myself, however, at the time seemed completely out of the question. Talking now to unpublished writers, I discover that such terror at the thought of sitting down and writing a novel is hugely common. Some of them are like housebricks for heaven's sake! Now, I tell those as daunted as I was then, that if you write 1,000 words a day for a month, you're more or less a third of the way through a novel. It all sounds terribly straightforward of course, but it certainly didn't feel like that as I began trying to write my own crime novel.

One of the most common pieces of advice given to aspiring writers is to read, and it was at the point of starting what would become my first book, that I saw just how important this was. I was writing in an already overcrowded genre, and having read a great deal within it (or should that be *around* it?) I had a pretty good idea what not to write – that is, I knew those areas to which claims had already been successfully staked by others. Having decided therefore that my detective would not be a deerstalker-wearing cocaine fiend, or an Edinburgh-based Rolling Stones fan, I tried quite simply to write the sort of crime novel I enjoyed reading. I always imagine that such a stunningly basic notion would be obvious to all those who want to write. However, I'm constantly amazed to meet those claiming to have studied the industry carefully and to have spotted a sizeable gap on the bookshelves. Those who announce confidently that the world is finally ready for the crime-fighting antique-dealer/amateur veterinarian who, while not cooking and listening to opera, cracks tough cases with the help of a cat, in the mid-18th century Somerset countryside. If this is really what you're driven to write, then all power to you, but if you simply try and fill what you perceive to be a gap in the market, you're on a hiding to nothing.

I fully believed myself to be on a hiding to somewhat less than this, when I picked half a dozen agents from the *Writers' & Artists' Yearbook* and sent off the first 30,000 words of my novel. From this point on in the career path of almost any published writer, luck will play a part, and I must confess that I had more than my fair share of the very good sort.

Being taken on by an agent is wonderful, and if you're very fortunate, you will be taken on by a good one. Getting published is one thing but it helps if that publisher has enough faith in the book to spend a decent amount on marketing it – an amount so much more important than your advance. My still incomplete manuscript landed on all the right desks, and it was while in the incredible position of having to choose between agents, that I received the single best piece of advice I was given, or am able to pass on. Don't imagine that things are going well. Imagine that they are going badly. Imagine that *nobody* wants to publish your book, that the rejection letters come back in such numbers that the Royal Mail lays on special deliveries. When that happens, who will be the agent who will give you up as a bad lot, and who will be the one willing to fight? Which one will say 'well, if *they* don't want it I'm going to try X'? This is the agent to choose. In the course of any writer's life, a good agent, not to mention a good editor, will probably need to show more than once that they aren't afraid of a good scrap.

As far as further advice goes – beyond the encouragement to read and to write something every day – it is important to remember that lies (white or whoppers) and luck (of both kinds) may play a disproportionately large part in the way things turn out. Oh, and if you could avoid writing crime novels about a north London copper with a weakness for Tottenham Hotspur and Hank Williams, I'd be very grateful.

However, one small drawback to getting published and finding yourself trying to produce a book a year, is that you suddenly have far less time to read. This is hugely upsetting, and in my case doubly ironic considering that, with requests for reviews and endorsements, I now get more free books than ever. In fact, the only person unhappy about the way things turned out is my postman.

Mark Billingham is the author of an award-winning series of novels featuring London-based Detective Inspector Tom Thorne, the latest of which is *Rush of Blood*, due to be published by Little, Brown in August 2012. He has also worked for many years as a stand-up comedian but now prefers to concentrate on crime writing, as those that read the books are not usually drunk and can't throw things at him.

Notes from a successful contemporary women's novelist

Adele Parks shares her thoughts on writing and on submitting a manuscript for publication.

On an almost daily basis I'm asked whether I have any tips on how one goes about becoming a writer; it's a simple question yet so profound and tricky to answer. I understand that particular question and all the yearning, hope and passion behind it. It's difficult, sometimes overwhelming, being a secret and unpublished writer who is desperate to be discovered. I clearly remember, before I was published, standing in a Waterstones bookshop on Oxford Street, London, literally weeping in frustration as I stared at the plethora of published works; I wanted to know, what was the magic ingredient? Why were those books published and not mine?

In most careers, becoming a professional in a chosen field requires diligent study; earning the appropriate qualifications entitles one to be called a doctor, teacher or accountant, etc. But how does anyone know when they are entitled to call themselves a writer? There are no failsafe qualifications, even a degree in creative writing isn't that. Are you a writer the day you type your first words/pick up a pen? Or is it the day someone else reads and values your work? Or can you only be a fully fledged writer once you have an agent, a book deal, distribution and sales?

I believe writers are writers the day they describe themselves as such. I suppose that means I became a writer aged about seven; although it wasn't until much later that I realised that writing could be a career. From the moment I did realise it, all I wanted was to be a *published* author. Some people write for personal pleasure and have no desire to be publically recognised. That inner serenity is admirable but most writers crave the opportunity to share their work and gain some level of open appreciation. It's a little strange then, that while writers pine for acknowledgement, they often simultaneously nurture a dire shyness. I remember reluctantly confiding my secret desire to be a published writer to a select number of friends with a level of embarrassment and reticence that might have been more fitting if I was confessing to an addiction or unsocial disease (and maybe that's because, arguably, writing can be both addictive and unsocial!). I think my embarrassment stemmed from a lack of confidence. It seemed arrogant to say, 'I think I'm funny, interesting, creative or unique enough to entice people into giving up their time to actually read something I've written', which is exactly what writers are saying when they ask people to buy their books.

When I was in my late twenties I tragically lost a number of family members and friends in a short period of time. Grieving, I became acutely aware that time is finite and I realised that occasionally professing that one day I wanted to be a writer – whilst pursuing a day career in advertising – was never going to get me a book deal. I had to make the leap from viewing my writing as an interesting hobby and recognise it as a career I imperatively wanted to invest in.

Finding your own voice

I continued working in advertising but I wrote practically every evening after work, sometimes throughout the night, and I wrote at weekends and during my annual holidays too.

I strongly recommend that you write something every day, even if you're not in the mood, even if it's just for ten minutes (although more is advantageous!). If you're stuck for something to write about, set yourself simple tasks such as describing what you can see if you look out of the window, your earliest memory or your first kiss. It doesn't matter what you write, or even if you ever use these exercises in your novel, as it simply develops discipline.

My second tip is don't give up the day job. My heart sinks when people tell me that they've given up their salaried work so they can concentrate on their writing. Publishing is an incredibly precarious industry and rarely lucrative. It can take years to get noticed and not having a regular income can make it more stressful than it would be otherwise. Besides, I'm convinced that day-to-day interaction with my colleagues sharpened my writing. Because I write contemporary women's fiction it didn't make sense to cut myself off from my contemporaries, the very people who were inspiring me. Writing can become all-consuming but I really advise against becoming a hermit. Everything you see and do informs your writing. The more you experience, see, read and learn, the more ideas you'll have. No-one learns much by sitting at a desk waiting for 'the Muse' to knock on the door. Have fun: it shows in your work. If you don't enjoy what you're writing, it's unlikely anyone will enjoy reading it.

Don't waste time trying to imitate someone else's style because it's in vogue, no matter how successful that author has been. The chances are that by the time you finish writing your book, the wave will have passed. Remember, books hit the shelves about two years after they're written. The greatest challenge is to find your own style and voice, a challenge the best writers embrace.

Submitting your manuscript for publication

It can be difficult to know when your work is ready to be sent out into the big bad world. On the one hand, if you send your manuscript out too soon, you risk rejection because raw talent isn't enough if the work is riddled with structural or grammatical flaws. On the other hand, if you continually rewrite and revise – never finding a point when you are assertive enough to say, 'it's finished' – then you might miss out on a market opportunity or lose your confidence altogether. My only advice here is *be brave.* Trust yourself. As a writer you are, no doubt, a vociferous reader. You *do* know what makes a good book, you *can* judge. Don't kid yourself that you've written the next *War and Peace* because you probably haven't, but nor should you punish yourself for not having done so. Measure yourself against the published writers within your genre; be as encouraging and critical of your own work as you are of the writers you most admire.

I found it useful getting a second opinion on my work before I officially submitted it to anyone, although I've heard other authors strongly recommend against this. I entrusted my manuscript to a great friend to read. I knew she wouldn't allow me to waste my time if she didn't believe I had some molecule of talent; I also knew she would encourage and shore me up but not flatter unnecessarily or untruthfully. This friend is a rare beast. If, like me, you're lucky enough to have someone whose judgment you trust and value then do ask him or her to read through your work but don't take offence at any comments they make. Remember, they're doing you a favour by reading it and it's a difficult job. Be humble. Accept both praise and criticism with an equally open mind and act upon it where necessary.

It took me about a year to have a body of writing that I thought might be worthy of submission as a novel but then I hit a brick wall. Who should I submit work to? How should I present it? How could I convince anyone that this was *the* novel they *had* to read? I had no idea where to turn for advice. I didn't know any writers or anyone who worked in publishing. As a reader and writer I naturally turned to books for help. I scanned the shelves in my local bookshop and fell upon the big fat red book you're now holding, the *Writers' & Artists' Yearbook* (mine was the 1998 edition). Give yourself a huge tick as you've already recognised this invaluable tool, this portal.

It was news to me that I needed an agent and that it is practically impossible to get a fiction deal by directly approaching publishing houses – doing so would probably result in a collection of rejection letters (as well as the attached emotional baggage). Through the *Yearbook* I discovered that, generally, agents expect to see three chapters of your work, a CV and a synopsis. Personally, I think it's sensible to send your work to one agent at a time but this approach can be slow as it can take an agent a couple of months to respond to your submission; exclusivity requires patience. Actually, the entire business requires patience – that and persistence. It's of paramount importance to thoroughly research any agent you're thinking of approaching. Use the *Yearbook* as your first reference and then go online to investigate agents' websites. It's sometimes worth making a call to a potential agency and asking who you should approach (never send an open, 'To whom it may concern' type of note). Another tip for finding relevant agents is to look at the acknowledgements in the published novels you admire. Often, authors thank their agents and this may give you an idea about who to approach.

It's a strange business being a writer. You have to be a complex contradiction. Sensitive and open minded and yet thick skinned and, almost, cocksure. It's a certainty that you'll get some knock-backs along the way but don't ever give up hope. If you have a talent and you are persistent, I believe it will pay off eventually. Be realistic. Remember nothing is impossible, and not much is near impossible, so don't give up. Good luck!

Adele Parks has published ten *Sunday Times* top ten bestsellers in as many years and her work has been translated into over 20 different languages. Her latest novel is *About Last Night* (Headline Review 2011). Her website is www.adeleparks.com and you can follow her on Twitter @adeleparks.

Notes from a successful romantic novelist

Katie Fforde describes how she became published and why she likes writing romantic fiction.

If you want to get a group of writers into a panic, put them on a panel and then ask them, one at a time, what their working practice is. The first one answers confidently enough – after all they probably have several books on the shelves by this time. But the others listen in consternation, convinced that what they do is wrong and they are not proper writers even though the world is reading their books.

This is because there are as many writing methods as there are writers, and it's important to work out what kind of writer you are.

If you are reading this there is a chance that you are a writer; but in case you're not sure, do check. It's hard enough to write if you like doing it, but if you think you might prefer painting water colours or needlepoint, please try those first. At least you might get an acceptable still life or cushion relatively quickly. It takes a long time to write a novel.

I discovered I wanted to write – almost more than anything else in the world – as soon as I started. My mother had given me a writing kit for Christmas. This consisted of paper, pens, a dictionary, a thesaurus and yes, a copy of the *Writers' & Artists' Yearbook*, as well as Tipp-Ex and a nice box to keep it all in.

Having made a New Year's Resolution that I would start writing that year, I started in January. I cleaned the house, made sure my children were out of the way and put the first sheet of paper into my typewriter. When I'd got over my nerves – which I dealt with by starting to rewrite someone else's book – and began a story I'd had in my head for years, I realised what had been missing in my life for years. I had a lovely family, a lovely house and a lovely dog, and yet I wasn't content. What had been missing was a creative outlet.

One of the joys of starting to write is that no one needs to know you are doing it until you choose to tell them. Most other things people do require a bit of going out in public. While it would be a bit difficult to hide it from the people you live with, the rest of the world doesn't need to know. In fact, I suggest you don't tell anyone unless you're sure they will understand. There is nothing more irritating than being asked 'how the book is going' by people who assume you just need to write one to become a millionaire.

There are annoying examples of people who got their first novel published and became an instant bestseller – some of those authors are even my friends – but I prefer to think it's better to be a tortoise than a hare. If you get there the long slow way at least that way to know what you've done and can do it again. That said, I have a Pollyanna side to my nature and will always see the advantages to any of life's setbacks if I possibly can. It took me eight years before I found a publisher and ten years – from starting – before I had a book on the shelves.

Now that you're feeling a bit more positive about it, knowing how long it took me to achieve publication, I'll go on with my tips.

My top tip, which I'm assuming you do already, is to read a lot. I believe if you never ever went to any sort of writing course or never read a 'how to' book on writing, you would still be able to write to a publishable standard just by reading enough novels. It would take you longer, probably, because you could set yourself an impossibly high standard and consequently never become Henry James. But once you've decided what sort of book you want to write, which I hope would be the sort of book you want to read, read as many of the genre as you can fit into your busy life.

My second tip – which I sometimes describe as the gift I'd give to baby writers if I was a fairy godmother – is perseverance. This pig-headedness (a less polite but more accurate word) got me through receiving all those rejections. Every time I was rejected I became more determined that one day I would have a book published. But you do have to be very determined. I'd quite like to be a size ten, too, but I'm never going to be one because I don't want it quite enough.

My third tip, which I'll say more about later, is to emulate Nelson's favourite captains and be lucky.

So why did it take me so long? I think it does take quite a long time to learn to write – for most of us anyway – but also I was aiming at a market that wasn't quite suitable for me. I was trying to write for Mills & Boon. Like many people, I read these by the shelf-load and assumed, in my complete ignorance, that because they were easy to read they were easy to write. Not so! But I am eternally grateful to them because they sent me some very encouraging rejection letters and trying to fit my story into 50,000 words forced me to keep to the point. There is no room in those books for characters who have no function, for any little scene that doesn't further the plot or for a hero who isn't extremely attractive.

How did I finally get a book deal? This is where the luck comes in. I had been a member of the Romantic Novelists' Association for some years (I am now its President) and through its New Writers' scheme (which alas is now hugely oversubscribed) my writing came to the attention of an agent, who was new to the business and so had time to look for new writers and to work with them. This agent told me she couldn't do anything with the books I had been writing but that she liked my style and together we discussed what my next novel should be like. She asked for 100 pages before the end of the year. I felt I couldn't write what amounted to half a Mills & Boon novel and not check I was on the right track so I sent her the first chapter. She liked it and I got into the habit of sending her chunks which she would read and comment on, sometimes asking for changes, at other times saying, crack on with it. This wonderful woman had sold the novel before I'd finished it.

But then came the hard work. There is no tougher writing course than your first professional edit, and although it was hard – no actual blood but certainly sweat and tears – I pity writers who don't have this experience. My lovely story had too little plot and putting one in after it had been written was akin to putting in the foundations to a house after it is built. It is possible with the help of Acrow props and rigid steel joists, but it is not the way round to do it. Books need plots in the same way that bodies need skeletons and it's better to work out what yours is before starting.

My second huge stroke of luck after finding a wonderful agent was to be picked for the WHSmith Fresh Talent promotion. This meant cardboard cutouts of me and the other authors were in the window of every WHSmith shop in the country and our books were reviewed by almost every newspaper. This massive exposure was a terrific start to any writing career.

So what keeps me going nowadays, 20 or so books on? One thing is that I keep having ideas which I want to write and I think this is something that develops along with other neural pathways that you forge. My antennae are constantly twitching when I watch television, go to a party or sit on a train. I am fascinated by relationships and want to explore new ones, and I also like falling in love. If you write romantic fiction you have to fall in love with your hero or you can't expect your readers to. Falling in love with your hero is the affair you're allowed to have and it is a lot less complicated to arrange.

Why do people buy my books? It's hard to say but I'm very glad that they do. I think it's because readers can recognise themselves in my characters and this is the same whatever age you are – I have readers of all ages, from school age girls to elderly women. I and three other authors were asked this question at a literary festival recently and we none of us really knew. The general consensus was, life is tough for a lot of people and everyone needs a bit of escape. Some people like a nice gritty crime novel or an edge-of-the-seat thriller, but some like a story where you know the baby – and probably even the dog – is not going to die. You know you're guaranteed a few hours off from your own life in a safe place.

This is why I like writing romantic fiction. I enjoy spending time with people I like, to whom nice things happen. I like being able to choose the wallpaper and have the garden I could never have. I also like deciding it's time we had a good summer, and write about one.

And the very best thing about being a writer is meeting people who have enjoyed your books, read them to cheer themselves up when they were ill (although I do take it amiss when it's implied that you have to be ill to read my books) or going through some sort of hard time. That is the very best reward.

So, if you feel fit for the fight (as Bonnie Tyler might have said) gather your tools and do your research. First of all, decide what you like to read. Don't try and write anything just because it's the current favourite unless you love it. You probably won't succeed if your heart isn't in it; if you do you'll be stuck writing chaste romance novels when you yearn to write raunchy thrillers, and the market will have changed by the time it hits the shelves anyway.

And please do your research before you even think of submitting anything. It may seem blindingly obvious, but the number of people who send their work to any agent in this *Yearbook* without checking that they even handle fiction is enormous.

Be brave and get someone else to read at least part of your book before you submit it. It does have to be someone you can trust to be brutally frank, who will tell you if they don't know who any of the characters are, and if they couldn't care less. It's better to find out things like this before you let the professionals near it.

Make sure you present your script exactly as it's requested. Don't email books to agents who only want hard copy. Make sure the copy is clean and easy to read. Write a covering letter that will encourage the agent to look at the book and if a synopsis is asked for, write one. (Some people find it easier to write after the book is finished.)

If you are lucky enough to receive comments from an agent, take them to heart unless you know them to be wrong. If they say your characters come across as older than they are supposed to be, watch a bit of 'yoof' television and learn some modern slang. If they say no one wants to read about undertakers consider carefully if this is true. It's possible you've written the one that people would enjoy.

If you're brave enough to join a writers' group, make sure it's not a mutual appreciation society. It's more productive to be told your dialogue is poor than for people to wonder why on earth no one has yet snapped up your masterpiece.

Be in it for the long haul. If (or when) you're rejected, allow yourself a certain amount of time to gnash your teeth and eat chocolate and then get back to it. If you want it enough you will get there and there's no time to waste feeling sorry for yourself. Writing mustn't seem like a hobby, it must be your passion. Eventually it might also become your profession.

Katie Fforde's first book was *Living Dangerously* (1995) and she has written 17 novels since. Her hobbies, when she has time for them, are singing in a choir and flamenco dancing. Her website is www.katiefforde.com.

Notes from a successful historical novelist

Bernard Cornwell shares his experience of writing successful historical novels.

You are going to get things wrong. None of us mean to, but we do. There were no rabbits in King Arthur's Britain, which I knew, but a helpful reader (there's always a helpful reader) wrote to tell me there were no snowdrops either. Got that wrong.

So, how to write an historical novel? The real question is how to write a successful novel and I know only one answer. Story, story, story. You are *not* an historian, your job is to be a storyteller. If you set out to educate folk then you will probably bore them. Your job is to entertain them, and the way to do that is by telling a story. If your ambition is to inform readers of the intricacies of the Elizabethan religious settlement then be honest about that ambition and write a non-fiction history. But if you want a bestseller then devise a story with Jesuits in the shrubbery, secret chambers behind the linenfold panelling and the flames of Tyburn waiting for the tale's climax. Then, having written that book, write another with the same main characters. Write a series.

Why a series? Because the sales of the tenth book, or the twentieth, will encourage the sales of the first and the second and the rest. Series do not go out of print like standalone novels. I began to write because I had fallen in love with an American woman who could not come to live in Britain, which meant I had to emigrate to the United States. The fly in that romantic ointment was that the American government refused me a work permit, so I airily told my bride-to-be that I would make a living by writing novels. That was over 30 years ago and we're still married and I'm still writing, so it was not so desperate an idea as it seemed at the time. Yet it was desperate and, before emigrating, I sought advice. Peter Wolfe, a friend and the owner of his own publishing company, took me to lunch and told me never, never, to attempt fiction. He would not publish fiction. 'The market's too crowded,' he told me. So what do I do?, I asked him. You write a book, he said, called *My Friend the Cocker Spaniel*, a book full of good advice on how to raise, feed and exercise a Cocker Spaniel, and wherever puppies are sold and wherever dog food is sold and, indeed, wherever books are sold, *My Friend the Cocker Spaniel* will be on sale. He saw an objection coming and raised a hand to stop it. Once you've written *My Friend the Cocker Spaniel*, he continued, you go through the manuscript and you cross out the words Cocker and Spaniel and replace them with Dachshund. You have now written a second book called *My Friend the Dachshund*. Then you cross out Dachshund and put in Scottish Terrier. You get the idea. You write a series. I took that piece of Peter's advice even if I ignored his well meant injunction to avoid fiction.

I wrote historical fiction because I wanted to, because I liked it and because I was not capable of writing non-fiction. But I still needed help, so I did something which, in retrospect, seems obvious, but which very few aspiring writers actually do. I set out to learn how successful historical novelists wrote their books. I used three books: two of them were *Hornblower* novels by C.S. Forester and the third was *Imperial Governor* by George Shipway (an excellent and undervalued writer). I then disassembled those books. If you wanted the world to beat a path to your door by making a better mousetrap then the first thing you would do is discover how existing mousetraps work. You would take them apart, learn their secrets, and set out to do better. I am not saying I did better, but I did take those three books apart. I made huge charts which showed, paragraph by paragraph, where there was dialogue, where there was action, where there was flashback, where there was romance and so on. The charts revealed a structure. I did not slavishly copy the structure – indeed one reason to make the charts was a determination to use less of the things I disliked (flashback) and more of the things I liked, but when I found myself in difficulties with my first two or three books the charts were there to show me how successful writers had tackled the same problems. The answers to a lot of aspiring writers' problems are as close as the bookshelf. Use it.

Kurt Vonnegut once offered a splendid piece of advice. Every book starts with a question – a question the reader probably didn't know they wanted answered but the search for that answer is what will pull the reader through the book. That's the story. But too many historical novels begin by establishing a world. When I finished the third in my series of novels around Alfred the Great and his successors, I discovered I could tear 9,000 words out of a 10,000-word first chapter. Those words were delivering information I thought the reader needed but they slowed the story to a crawl, so they had to go. I don't know if pacing a story can be taught, or whether it is an intuitive thing, but I do know that pacing needs work and, even after 49 novels, I still have to do that work.

Can writing be taught? I have a thoroughly old-fashioned view of this, which is probably founded on prejudice rather than on informed opinion, but I do know writing is a solitary vice and believe that it is best practised in solitude. Writing can be encouraged, perhaps, but taught? To teach something implies there is something to be taught and that suggests that the activity can be reduced to, if not rules, maxims. But there are no rules except to tell a story. I have met dozens of folk who belong to writers' groups or pay for writing courses but the chief activity of both seems to be criticism and I am not sure criticism helps aspiring writers whose confidence is frail. Only three opinions matter. The first is your own. You write for yourself. You write the books you want to read. The second opinion which matters is that of the professional gatekeeper, whether agent or publisher, and their views on writing differ hugely from the folk who teach it. The third vital opinion is the reader, and on that your success depends. I accept that I probably do not understand creative writing courses. None were available when I was an aspiring author so I managed without. Writers I admire tell me such courses can be helpful, so I shall merely say that the majority of successful writers never submit to them. Draw your own conclusion.

The most frequent questions I am asked are about research: how do I do it? How much time do I spend on it? The questions are virtually unanswerable. I assume no one writes historical fiction unless they first love history, and so virtually all your reading is research. I still read more history for pleasure than any other kind of book. Of course research has to be focused, but the real danger is doing too much research. If you are writing a novel about Jesuits in the Elizabethan shrubbery then you need to know a lot about the religious settlement, about social life and probably clothes, but do you need to know about Tudor farming practices? Maybe you do, but you will discover that need as you write the book – and a great deal of research is done while the book is being written. To believe that you must equip yourself with an encyclopaedic knowledge of the Tudor world before you begin writing is to guarantee you won't begin. Get on with it! Tell the story! The gaps in your knowledge will show up soon enough and there will be time to fill them. On the other hand, doing too little research has obvious dangers and can also deprive you of good story ideas. When writing *Sharpe's Fury*, which is set in Cadiz in 1811, I discovered, in an extremely dry and academic history of the diplomatic relations between Britain and Spain, a reference to the fire-rafts with which the French had hoped to burn the British fleet in Cadiz Harbour. That single unexpected reference has already supplied 10,000 words of the new book. The whole plot for *Gallow's Thief* came from a single footnote in an academic history of crime and punishment. In the end you will have to decide how much research to do, but beware the danger of doing too much and so never starting the novel.

Then, having done the research, you must reject a great deal of it. There is a terrible impulse to put in everything, just to prove how much you know, but nothing kills an historical novel like long passages written straight from your notebooks. And sometimes you must reject the true history to make the story work. When I wrote *Sharpe's Company*, which is about the ghastly siege of Badajoz in 1812, I knew that no British soldiers had succeeded in penetrating any of the three breaches on the night of the assault. The feint attack worked instead and the major attacks were all failures. But the drama of the story was in those three breaches and, if Sharpe was involved, Sharpe would get through, so I changed the history. You have to confess such inventions in a note at the book's end because many readers rely on an historical novelist to teach them something about history. It is always a pleasure, of course, when history serves up a plot and a timeline that does not need changing, but history is rarely so generous.

Above all, have fun. You write because you want to, not because you're forced to. If you enjoy the story then your excitement and enjoyment will show in the novel. You are an entertainer, not an historian, so entertain. And remember the one immutable rule in a business without any rules – tell a story!

Bernard Cornwell is the author of more than 49 novels, most of them historical, of which the best known are the *Sharpe* series of books and the most recent is *Death of Kings*. His books have sold more than 20 million copies worldwide.

Notes from a successful biographer

Claire Tomalin shares her thoughts about what writing a successful biography entails.

A good biography is driven by the curiosity of the writer, a passion to get as close as possible to understanding what is going on in another life. Anyone can write a biography, provided they are prepared to put in a lot of work: research, reading, travel and, more than anything else, thought. As much as I dare to, I write for my own pleasure. I am fired by curiosity, by following a thread here, a filament there. I want to explore the past as one might explore a foreign country. In the process, I want to educate myself, and there is no better way to do this than to research, and then attempt to write a book.

Researching a biography can be even more fascinating than reading a story someone else has imagined, because of the detective element. You follow a trail that may lead to a series of closed doors or dead ends or, if you are lucky, to discoveries that change a part or the whole of the perspective on a person or a period. The central figure of a biography may become a prism through which you view a whole society, a whole period.

I am not sure about rules for biography, but I believe you must like your subject. Better still if you fall in love with her, or him, because there has to be an element of obsession. Devoting several years or decades of your own life to thinking and writing about someone else's life is like being married. There are ups and downs, days when you are irritated or disappointed, others when you are delighted and surprised. And you have to keep at it. This is alongside your real life, which tends to get sidelined while the notional, biographical marriage takes up increasing energy and space. Biographers do occasionally choose to write about someone they loathe and produce a hymn of hate, and that must be obsessive too. It is not something I would attempt. Serious dispassionate studies of monsters such as Stalin and Hitler are something different again, and make up a special category, requiring particular historical skills and iron nerves.

In both historical and literary biography it is important to create the world around your subject, both the physical and the intellectual. Context matters as much as character, and a biography that skimps on it is thin and unsatisfying. You need to let your reader see the houses, landscapes and cities, hear the noises in the streets, know what was being joked and argued about, how children were reared at the time, how people took their pleasures, how they wore their clothes and hair, what they disapproved of, what excited them, what they were ready to fight for, how the social classes interacted – and so on.

So you need a jackdaw mind, ready to search and pick about in many subjects – politics, painting and sculpture, topography, psychology, sociology, the theatre, fashion, military and naval history, medicine. For most of my books I have found myself in the Wellcome Library of Medical History, finding out about the illnesses of my subjects – from Katherine Mansfield's gonorrhoea to Pepys's kidney and bladder stones – and I have corresponded with physicians and surgeons, all wonderfully instructive and entertaining. You have to be a bit cautious too, because retired doctors enjoy making posthumous diagnoses and may get carried away (like the one who became convinced that Thomas Hardy and his wife had syphilis).

You must master the handwriting of your subject and other members of her/his circle. Carry a magnifying glass with you to help you with the tricky bits, and I find copying it helps me to learn a hand. It gets easier as you go on. You must also find your way about archives, county records, libraries and museums, parish records and the public record office – plus websites and Google. Sadly, many archives are now on microfiche, fiddly to use and cruelly hard on the eyes. When I was working on Pepys [*Samuel Pepys: The Unequalled Self*] I thought I was going blind myself – luckily I was wrong.

Do your own picture research. You should also suggest the order of the illustrations and caption them yourself, so interestingly that they will make a hesitant browser in a bookshop into a buyer. The advice came to me from my first editor, the late Tony Godwin, and I have followed it strictly. This is the journalistic side of your work, not to be despised.

You need academic skills too. You must write down all your sources carefully and legibly – book, volume, page, manuscript reference number, etc – as you go along, and keep them in a safe place. When I wrote my first book I was innocent of this, and it took me a long time to check my sources after I thought I had finished, returning to the British Library and other archives to do the work again. There was one reference I could not find, and naturally this was the one readers kept asking me about. Now I always put sources on my computer next to the quotation or fact as soon as I get back from a research trip – if you use a laptop you can do it at once. And never fail to back up your files! Another piece of advice from a scholarly friend: always read through and check quotations in your text at proof stage, to make sure you have copied them exactly, and indicated cuts. Sometimes there is no correct answer to a question. Hardy called his novel *Tess of the D'Urbervilles* in some editions and *Tess of the d'Urbervilles* in others, and reference books continue to give both: whichever you use, somebody will write pointing out your mistake.

If possible, visit the places where your subject lived, and walk where he or she walked. The historian Richard Cobb advised me to go on horseback, or at least on a bicycle, when researching subjects who lived before modern transport arrived, so as to see the landscape as they experienced it. He also told me I should make sure to search archives where there might just possibly be something of interest, however unlikely it seemed. Following his advice, I wrote to the town archives in Le Havre, which had been bombed flat in the Second World War, to ask if they had a record of the birth of Mary Wollstonecraft's daughter, Fanny, in 1794. Two weeks later an official envelope from the archivist arrived with a photocopy of Fanny's birth certificate (for '*le vingt cinquième jour Floréal l'an second de la république française*') which no one, it seemed, had looked at for nearly 200 years. It also certified that her parents were married, which they were not. I nearly cried with joy and tenderness for that little *Françoise*, who certainly never saw her own birth certificate.

Researching Mrs Jordan, I searched for material by writing to as many of her descendants as I could track down – she had 13 children – and found letters written by her sons in the first decade of the 19th century. The first batch were in a fairly remote country house, and their owner kindly brought them out in a dusty box in which they were crumbling away – I had arrived just in time. In a still more distant location there were other letters, and superb portraits of her I had never seen or heard of. More material surfaced after the hardback was published, with letters and portraits appearing as I went round giving talks about it, and successive editions of the paperback crammed in these extra discoveries. Biographies don't die, they become your life companions.

They also bring you friends. While researching Katherine Mansfield I was able to visit her friend Ida Baker, then in her nineties, living alone in a cottage in the New Forest, almost blind and very deaf, for a precious conversation about her memories. The discovery of an unknown short story by Mary Shelley in Italy took me to a 100-room house in San Marcello Pistoiese in the Apennines, still lived in by the great-granddaughter of the little girl for whom Mary Shelley had written her story. They were an enchanting family and greatly generous to me.

Not all research is so adventurous or such fun as this of course. There are long hours of tedious work, disappointments and moments of horror when you find that someone else is working on the same subject and is due to publish their book six months before yours. Since there is nothing you can do about this, you have to take it as calmly as you can. But do everything possible to avoid the double review, a dreadful thing which compares and contrasts your two efforts and is usually dull and likely to kill both books stone dead.

You will never write a definitive biography, because such a thing does not exist. New material appears, attitudes change. The best you can hope to do is approach your subject in good faith. There will always be things you don't know and can't find out. For me, the constraints of biography are part of the attraction, the tug between the known and the unknown, the fact that you have to accept that there are multitudinous gaps in what you know and which your narrative must deal with. One absolute rule must be that, when you speculate, declare that you are doing so, and give the grounds for your speculation – otherwise you are writing romantic fiction, not biography.

You may make money from a biography if you are lucky, but I doubt if that is the usual first reason for writing one. It occurs to me that we embark on the study of other people's lives for the same reason we read fiction, go to plays or watch films: to get the feeling of being inside another skin. As Katherine Mansfield wrote, 'one life is not enough'. And there is much more to it than that. It is a journey on which you explore another century, enlarge your understanding, perhaps do justice to a forgotten figure, and with any luck cast light on the variety of human activity and achievement. One Oxford academic complained that a biography was 'nosy', but I would say it is a condition of intelligent human beings to be curious about other lives – to be just that, nosy.

Claire Tomalin worked in publishing and then journalism for many years, becoming literary editor first of the *New Statesman* and then of the *Sunday Times*, which she left in 1986 in order to write full time. She is the author of *The Life and Death of Mary Wollstonecraft*, which won the Whitbread First Book Prize 1974; *Shelley and His World* (1992); *Katherine Mansfield: A Secret Life* (1988), *The Invisible Woman: The Story of Nelly Ternan and Charles Dickens* (1991), which won the NCR Book Award 1991, as well as the Hawthornden Prize and the James Tait Black Memorial Prize for Biography 1990; *Mrs Jordan's Profession* (1995); *Jane Austen: A Life* (1997); *Several Strangers* (1999), a collection of reviews and personal memoirs; *Samuel Pepys: The Unequalled Self* (2002), which won the Samuel Pepys Award and the Whitbread Book of the Year 2002; and *Thomas Hardy: The Time-Torn Man* (2006). She has edited selected *Poems of Thomas Hardy* (2006), *Poems of John Milton* (2008) and *Poems of John Keats* (2009) for Penguin Classics. Her most recent book is *Charles Dickens: A Life* (Viking 2011).

Ghostwriting

It is possible for an unknown writer to make a living as a full-time ghostwriter. Andrew Crofts shares some of his secrets on how to do it.

Why do it?

The greatest problem facing any professional writer is finding a steady supply of ideas and subjects so dazzlingly certain to appeal to the book-buying public that publishers are eager to buy. Not only are saleable ideas in short supply, it also takes an inordinate amount of time to research a new subject deeply enough to be able to sell it successfully. You might spend months researching a subject from a number of different sources and still be unable to find a buyer.

One answer is to collaborate with other people who lack writing skills and experience but have good stories to tell, either as fiction or non-fiction, or possess all the necessary information to create a book.

These people can be found in a number of places. They might be celebrities, who would impress publishers because of their notoriety, or ordinary people who have undergone extraordinary experiences. Alternatively, they might be experts in subjects that the public want to know more about, or they might be private individuals wanting to self-publish their own stories.

It's much easier for publishers to market books by celebrities or established experts than those by unknown writers. Apart from a handful of literary stars, few people buy books because of the authors' names, and the media have a limited amount of space in which to write about books. But if you write the autobiography of a soap star, controversial politician or sporting hero, the resulting book will be widely written and talked about in the media. While the author is spending several weeks being whistled around all day from breakfast television to late night television, the ghost can stay comfortably at home and get on with their next project.

The speed with which you can gather the information for a ghosted book means that you can produce far more publishable material in the course of a year than if you were researching each book in order to write them under your own name. Publishers are also willing to pay higher advances because they can see how they will market the book once it is written. Ghosting makes it quite possible for an unknown writer to make a good full-time living as an author. It also provides you with broad writing experience and helps you to build contacts in the publishing industry to whom you can then sell other projects of your own.

Of all the advantages that ghosting offers, however, the greatest must be the opportunities that ghosts get to meet people of interest. It's a licence to ask the sort of impertinent questions that you truly want to know the answers to, and to be allowed inside some of the most extraordinary stories.

Ghosting a book for someone is like being paid to be educated by the best teachers in the world. Imagine, for instance, being asked to ghost *The Origin of Species* for Darwin, or *The Decline and Fall of the Roman Empire* for Gibbon; being paid to learn everything that is in their heads and then turning their thoughts, words and notes into book form. Could there be a better form of education?

How to start

The first step could be to approach people you would like to ghost for and offer your services. That may mean your favourite celebrities, who you could write to care of their agents or television companies, or people you have read about in the press and who you think have stories that could be developed into books. It's usually possible to find some way of getting a letter or email to them. Alternatively, it may be someone wanting to write a book for private or limited circulation, a family history perhaps or the story of a regiment, a company or a club. These people can be approached directly with a suggested business plan for the writing and distribution of a book.

A more practical first step, however, might be to approach people who you come across in everyday life and who have an expertise that you think would be popular with a wider audience. If you've been on a course, for instance, find out if the trainer has thought of turning their message into book form. Would a garage mechanic who's good at explaining why your car isn't working be able to supply the material for a book on car maintenance? What about your doctor doing a book on healthcare for a specialist sector of the market? The options are endless.

Anyone who has access to a captive marketplace, like training companies or public speakers, has a ready-made market for books. There are companies who might want to produce books by their chief executives for distribution to employees as well as to the outside world and public relations departments who would relish the idea of getting their clients' messages to wider audiences. Private or 'bespoke' publishing is becoming an increasing force in the market. A ghost who can offer advice on aspects of self-publishing will have added another valuable string to their bow.

If you're already a writer in another field, approach your existing contacts. A show business journalist, for instance, has access to actors and singers. A sports writer can approach sportspeople they've interviewed in the past. People will nearly always prefer to work with a ghost they already know and trust and feel they have a rapport with, than with a stranger.

At the same time as approaching potential authors, you should also be letting the publishing world know that you're available to work as a ghost. Write to the literary agents and publishers listed in this *Yearbook* to let them know what your experience is and how they can contact you. They will often have clients who they know are not capable of doing their own writing.

How to sell projects

It's unusual for any publisher to buy a book idea without seeing a synopsis and some sample material. Once you're experienced you will sometimes be able to charge for writing synopses, but at the beginning it's probably wise to offer to do it for free in order to get projects off the ground.

A synopsis must be a hard-selling document that gives the publisher all the reasons why they should commission the book. It might be worth preparing a one- or two-page version first in order to catch their attention and then a longer document (5,000–10,000 words usually suffices) in order to get the message across. It must give the publishers confidence that the book will be written to a high standard and delivered on time. It must be something that their sales teams can immediately see how to sell. Give a brief biography of the author and demonstrate how promotable they will be.

Involve a literary agent, firstly because most publishers don't like dealing directly with authors and secondly because the agent can handle all the money side of the relationship, removing potential conflicts between the author and ghost.

Whenever possible, have one good agent representing both parties in the arrangement. The agent's prime interest will then be in getting the book well published, not in encouraging the ghost and the author to fight one another for larger shares of the resulting royalties. The agent can also act as a conciliatory go-between should the relationship between author and ghost break down.

Who pays the ghost?

How the ghost gets paid will depend largely on how speculative the project is and on the wishes of the author. It might be that the author is sufficiently confident of the book's success to suggest paying the ghost a fee. How much that fee will be depends on what the author can afford, what they are willing to pay and what the ghost is willing to do the job for. In other words, it's open for negotiation.

If the project already has a publisher and there is no speculative work involved, then it may be that the publisher will suggest a fee. Then there will be little or no room for negotiation. A writer starting out should accept any book that is offered, even if the money is low, simply in order to build up a track record.

Where there is no publisher involved at the outset, and the author has no money, then suggest splitting all the proceeds 50/50, which includes advances, royalties and foreign rights sales, serialisation fees and payments for film and television rights.

If the author is a celebrity and it's obvious the book will make a large amount of money the ghost might have to accept a lower percentage, or a percentage that will become lower once he or she has received a pre-agreed amount; for example the proceeds might be split 50/50 until the ghost has received £50,000, at which stage his or her share might then drop to 40%, and might then drop again at £100,000.

It would be unwise to write an entire book unless some money has been forthcoming, either from a publisher or from the author, but there are cases where even this risk is worth taking. With fiction it is nearly always necessary to write the whole book before any publisher will make an offer, making it a highly risky business. Go into it with your eyes open, knowing that it is closer to buying a lottery ticket than earning a living.

What skills does a ghost need?

Ghosts must suppress their own egos completely when working on an autobiography – a good discipline for any writer. You're fulfilling a similar function to a barrister in court, using your skills to plead the case of your client. Authors need ghosts who won't challenge them, but will simply listen to what they have to say and understand why they did what they did. If the ghost wishes to be critical of the subject then they must step back and create an objective biography, not an autobiography.

It is essential for the ghost to make the subject feel completely comfortable in his or her company. If they think the ghost is going to criticise them, judge them or argue with them they won't relax, open up or talk honestly. It's not the ghost's job to try to make them change their opinions about anything or anyone, but rather to encourage them to tell their story in the most interesting and coherent way possible. The ghost must be able to coax them off their hobbyhorses and persuade them to answer all the questions that the eventual readers are likely to ask. The author must not sound bitter. Part of the ghost's job is to ensure that the author remains attractive and interesting to the reader.

Once the voice is on tape the ghost then has to create what amounts to an 80,000-word monologue, just as a playwright might do, staying completely in the author's character at all times, using the sort of vocabulary the author would use and expressing the same views, ideas and prejudices.

It's important that a ghost is interested in the subject; otherwise the project will become unbearable. Imagine spending that much time talking to someone who bores you, and then having to go over it all again when you write it out.

A ghost must also be able to see the structure of a book from early on in the process. He or she then needs the ability to guide the subject into providing the right material, keeping them on track and clearing up any inconsistencies in the telling of the tale.

The ghosting process

Sometimes the author has already produced some written material that can provide the bulk of the background. More often the ghost will have a clean slate to work from.

How many hours of taping will be required depends on how succinct the author can be persuaded to be and how quickly the ghost can master the subject. I find that 10–20 hours of useful taping is generally enough to produce a strong first draft. For autobiographies it's important to get them to tell you the story chronologically, so that you know what they have and have not experienced at each stage of the tale. The sequence can always be changed for dramatic effect once the actual writing commences.

It is usually preferable to interview them on their own home ground, where they will be at their most relaxed and least guarded. You will also get a better idea of what their lives are like.

The first draft should be shown to no one until the author has okayed it; he or she has the final veto on what should and shouldn't be in the final draft. Only if the author is confident of this will they be completely open and honest with you. The ghost can advise and warn, but the author has the last word. (Once given the power to make changes they nearly always decide they can't actually think of a better way of putting things and leave the manuscript virtually untouched.) If there is arguing to be done, let it be done by the agent and the publisher.

A ghost must expect no glory. Enjoy the experience of researching and writing and of being paid to do pleasant work. Sometimes your name will get mentioned on the cover of a book and sometimes it will appear only on the flyleaf. Sometimes you will get a mention in the acknowledgements and sometimes your name will not appear at all. You may get billed as 'co-author', but it is more likely to say 'By Big Shot with Joe Bloggs' or 'as told to Joe Bloggs'. It's always useful to have your name there but it can never be allowed to become a problem if it disappears.

Why publishers use ghosts

Publishers like to use ghostwriters because they know they can rely on them as professionals. They want to know that the book will arrive on time in a publishable form, conforming as nearly as possible to the synopsis or the brief.

Frequently the authors of the books are busy people and hard to get hold of. Sometimes they are temperamental. The publishers consequently rely on the ghosts to act as go-betweens and to make the process of publication as smooth as possible.

The ghost is also the subject's best friend in the publishing business. During the long months when the agent is trying to sell the project and the phone doesn't ring, the ghost can assure them that this is perfectly normal and doesn't mean they will never find a publisher. When the publisher wants to change the title or favours a cover in the subject's least favourite colour, the ghost will again have to be there to assure them that it will all be okay on the night. Then, when the book comes out and the subject can't find it on the front table in any of their local bookshops, the ghost can explain the economics of the business to them and try to dissuade them from ringing the publisher and ranting and raving.

Ghosting is an endlessly varied, interesting and rewarding job – relish every opportunity you are given to practice it.

Andrew Crofts was described in the *Independent* as 'the king of modern ghosts'. He has published over 80 ghosted books, a dozen of which have been No 1 on the *Sunday Times* bestseller list. He is also the author of *The Freelance Writer's Handbook – How to make money and enjoy life* (Piatkus 2002) and *Ghostwriting* (A&C Black 2004). His website is www.andrewcrofts.com.

See also...

• *Writing a synopsis*, page 118

Notes from a successful travel author

Bestselling travel writer William Dalrymple explains the rise of the travel genre and gives guidance on how to write a travel book.

In the summer of 1973 a minor American novelist named Paul Theroux asked his publisher if they would be interested in a book about trains.

Trains mean travel – a travel book: it was a novel idea (at least in 1973) and the publishers liked it. In fact they liked it so much they gave Theroux an advance, his first, of £250. *The Great Railway Bazaar*, an account of a journey from London Victoria to Tokyo Central, was published in 1975. None of Theroux's novels had ever sold in any quantity. But the *Great Railway Bazaar* swiftly sold over 1.5 million copies in 20 different languages.

The book did more than revive Theroux's flagging literary career: it kick-started what was to be the most important publishing phenomenon of the 1980s. The success of *The Great Railway Bazaar* inspired Bruce Chatwin to give up his job on the *Sunday Times Magazine* and to head off to South America. The result – *In Patagonia* – was published in 1977, the same year Patrick Leigh Fermor produced his great masterpiece, *A Time of Gifts*. By the early 1980s Eland Books were busy reprinting the works of great 19th century travellers and Thomas Cook had announced its Travel Writing Award. Soon the travel sections in bookshops were expanding from a single shelf at the rear of the shop to a wall at the shop front, flanking fiction.

Two decades later, however, after several hundred sub-Therouxs have penned rambling accounts of every conceivable rail, road or river journey between Kamchatka and Patagonia, the climate has changed from enthusiasm to one of undisguised boredom. The reaction has yet to filter down from the book pages to the bookshops: the likes of Bill Bryson, Tony Hawks and Dave Gorman continue to dominate the bestseller lists. But what is certain is that travel writing has lost some of its chic.

This backlash is not the end of the line. But now that everyone travels, writing travel books is much more difficult than it used to be; while it's still fairly easy to write a travel book, to write a *good* travel book now takes real ingenuity. However fluent or witty your prose, it is simply no longer enough just to jump on a train: writers have had to dress up their journeys in some pretty fancy packaging if they want to be taken seriously. Certainly your proposal must be that much more spectacular than before.

The travel book is potentially a vessel into which a wonderfully varied cocktail of ingredients can be poured: politics, archaeology, history, philosophy, art, magic – whatever appeals to the author. You can cross-fertilise the genre with other literary forms: biography, or anthropological writing; or, perhaps more interesting still, following in Bruce Chatwin's footsteps and muddying the boundaries of fiction and non-fiction by crossing the travel book with some of the wilder forms of the novel. The result of this tendency has been a crop of some rather wonderful books by younger writers: Katie Hickman's travels with a Mexican circus (wonderful idea), William Fiennes's quest for the snow goose, Alice Albinia's *Search for the Source of the Indus*, and Jeremy Seal searching Turkey for the anthropology of the fez. Perhaps the best hybrid travel book is John Berendt's immensely successful *Midnight in the Garden of Good and Evil*, which is half travel writing and half murder mystery, but wholly enjoyable. Below are some hints on how you can get into print.

The concept

These days it's simply not enough to go off and write a book about travelling through France or Russia or Bolivia; it's certainly not the time to start putting in proposals about taking a dustbin cart to Borneo or a pogo stick to the Antarctic: the killing off of the Gimmicks School of Travel Writing is one of the more happy results of the recession (although Tony Hawks's hilarious parody of that sort of book, *Round Ireland with a Fridge*, is of course one of the bestselling travel books of the last few years).

To write about a country in a very general and unfocused way you have to be very good: Thubron can do it. But you have to be very good indeed to write a getting-into-the-soul-of-a-country travel book. An easier, less ambitious and more commercial option is the Relocation Book – about setting off from London or New York and building a new life for yourself in Tuscany, Spain or Provence. Peter Mayle's *A Year in Provence* kicked off a fashion for travel books of this sort and was followed by ex-Genesis drummer Chris Stewart's Andalucian memoir, *Driving Over Lemons* (and its sequel *A Parrot in the Pepper Tree*) and Frances Mayes's *Under the Tuscan Sun*, all of which got little critical attention but nevertheless turned into major bestsellers.

There is also a more serious strand of travel writing that aims to delve into the soul of a city. My own book on Delhi, *City of Djinns*, was written in the tradition of studies of remarkable cities such as Jan Morris's classic, *The World of Venice* and Geoffrey Moorhouse's wonderfully apocalyptic *Calcutta*.

If falling in love with a small fragment of the globe is as good a starting point for a travel book as any, then other passions can also provide a good take-off point. I think it's fair to say that to be a really interesting travel writer you've got to have some small obsession: Ryszard Kapuscinski loves revolutions and watching dictators fall; Redmond O'Hanlon likes birds, beasts and exotic diseases; Bruce Chatwin was on the lookout for ideas and for nomads. I don't think it really matters what your interest is – stamp collecting, train-spotting or whatever – as long as it's genuine and you can convey your enthusiasm for it, you've probably got the seed of a travel book in there.

The research

If your book is to have any sort of authority, a card index is a very useful tool for keeping track of your research. For my last two travel books, I kept two card indexes: one with anecdotes and references listed under places and one listed under themes. So for *From the Holy Mountain* one index contained a list of places I expected to pass through on and around my projected route (Istanbul, Aleppo, Damascus, etc) and the other a list of potential themes, which grew as I read (magic, monks, ghost stories, miracle stories, etc). So, when I came to write about a place or a theme, I had to hand a long list of the best stories I knew associated with each place.

Travel book shortlist

There is no better way to learn how to write travel books than simply to read other travel books. My own personal shortlist of the great travel books would include:

The Road to Oxiana by Robert Byron

Behind the Wall by Colin Thubron

Into the Heart of Borneo by Redmond O'Hanlon

Midnight in the Garden of Good and Evil by John Berendt

In Patagonia by Bruce Chatwin

The journey

Everyone goes about writing a travel book in a different way and I can only speak for myself when I talk of technique. For me the biggest mistake was to try to keep a logbook when I was exhausted at the end of the day. I think it is absolutely vital to have a notebook in your hands, always, and to scribble constantly: not so much full sentences, so much as lists of significant detail: the colour of a hillside, the shape of a tulip, the way a particular tree haunts a skyline. Creating fine prose comes later – back at home in front of the computer. On the road – even in a rickety bus or a bumpy jeep – the key is to get the raw material down before it is lost to memory.

Noting down dialogue is especially important – it's the key to any half-decent travel book and you simply can't remember the exact words even half an hour later, never mind at the end of an exhausting day. The travel writers I really admire have all kept exceptionally detailed notes: Theroux, Thubron, Chatwin. So the first golden rule is: get it down. If you can't write down dialogue immediately, or openly, find some stratagem to get around the problem. I know one travel writer who, when in customs posts and police stations, pretends to have a bad stomach in order to keep disappearing to the lavatory to note dialogue, as doing it openly would be inadvisable.

Dialogue is the heart and soul of modern travel writing, for if 19th century travel writing was principally about place – about filling in the blanks of the map and describing remote places that few people had seen – 21st century travel writing is all about people: exploring the extraordinary diversity that still exists in the world beneath the veneer of globalisation. As Jonathan Raban once remarked: 'Old travellers grumpily complain that travel is now dead and that the world is a suburb. They are quite wrong. Lulled by familiar resemblances between all the unimportant things, they meet the brute differences in everything of importance.'

The second golden rule is to be open to the unexpected. Often one can set oneself a task – perhaps to go and search out some aspect of a particular place – and not notice good material if it's not what one is looking for at that moment. For example, in 1990 I went to Simla to interview two 'Stayers On' who had lived in Delhi in the 1930s and would, I hoped, be able to recreate the lost world of the Raj for me. In the event, however, I arrived ten years too late: both the ladies had gone badly senile and now imagined that they were being persecuted by prostitutes who popped up from beneath the floorboards and put dope in their food. I failed to get anything at all usable about 1930's Delhi, and left the old ladies feeling disappointed that I had wasted an afternoon. It was only later when I told my wife, Olivia, about the meeting that she pointed out that the bizarre afternoon would in fact make an excellent sequence in itself. It duly became one of the very best – and much the strangest – sections in *City of Djinns.* If the art of travel writing is at least partly about spotting the significant moment and discarding the irrelevant, then you have to be constantly alert.

In the same way, you often come across the best stories when you least expect them: when you've ticked off your interviews and visits for the day and settle down to have a drink in a bar or eat dinner. So often its exactly when you close your notebook and settle down to relax that you stumble across the most intriguing characters and funniest anecdotes.

A final rule: when you are taking notes, try to encompass all the senses. When you write about a place, don't just give a physical description of somewhere: try to capture significant sounds and smells and the feel of a place. Also explore how your body responds to a particular location: in a hot climate, the roll of perspiration down the forehead, the grit of sand in your shoes, the grind of cicadas or the smell of frying chillies can recreate a much more immediate sense of place than a long description of what is physically there.

The same is true of building up a character: the way someone smells, or the timbre of their voice can help visualise a person much better than a lengthy description of their appearance. Most important of all is dialogue: a well-chosen snatch of conversation can bring a person to life in a single sentence.

The writing

Everyone has their own rhythm. When I'm actually writing a book – a process that takes me anything between six months and a year – I tend to be unusually disciplined. I get up early, finish my emails and chores by 8.30am and am at my desk writing by no later than 9.30am. I break for lunch, go for a walk and then come back and go through a printout of the morning's work at teatime, and continue correcting and planning the next day until about 7pm. Olivia is incredibly good at telling me when what I have written is boring. If your partner is no good at this, find a friend who is. Going over and over and over a piece of prose until it is as perfect as you can make it is as important as anything else in the formation of a book.

Evocative travel writing

Here are some of my favourite examples of exceptionally good evocations of place or people:

- For a short and perfect evocation of a city look at Bruce Chatwin's description of Buenos Aires at the beginning of *In Patagonia* (p7)
- For a totally different approach – as wonderfully purple as Chatwin is sparse – see Patrick Leigh Fermor's description of walking through a German winter in *A Time of Gifts* (pp117–8)
- For bringing a character to life in a single page, take a look at John Berendt's description of the Lady Chablis in *Midnight in the Garden of Good and Evil* (pp96–8), or two passages by Bruce Chatwin in *In Patagonia:* the hippy miner (p54) and the Scottish farmer (pp66–7)
- See also Eric Newby's famous description of the explorer Wilfred Thesiger on pp246–8 of *A Short Walk in the Hindu Kush.*

The selling

Find an agent for this: never try to do it for yourself. If you know any writers, however distantly, ask them for an introduction to their agent. Otherwise, look in the literary agents section (page 429) of this *Yearbook*. Send the agent a well-written covering letter asking whether they would like to look at the finished manuscript, plus a four- or five-page synopsis of the plot together with a short biographical paragraph about yourself. During the 1980s it was possible to get book contracts and advance payments before you had actually written your travel book but these days that is less and less likely to happen, and the writing of a book is by its nature a big financial gamble. Only go ahead with the project if you are really passionate about it. But if you have something to say, don't despair and don't let early rebuffs from agents or publishers put you off. If you can make it work, travel writing is one of the most enjoyable and stimulating ways of life imaginable – especially when you're young and single and able to leave home for great chunks of the year. Go for it!

William Dalrymple was born in Scotland and brought up on the shores of the Firth of Forth. He has written many award-winning and bestselling books including *In Xanadu, City of Djinns, From the Holy Mountain: A Journey in the Shadow of Byzantium*; *The Age of Kali* and *Nine Lives: In Search of the Sacred in Modern India.* He has also written and presented documentary series for television and radio. In 2002, William was awarded the Mungo Park Medal by the Royal Scottish Geographical Society for his 'outstanding contribution to travel literature'. *The Return of a King: Shah Shuja and the First Battle for Afghanistan* is due to be published by Bloomsbury in December 2012.

Notes from a successful non-fiction author

Simon Winchester shares his experiences of writing success.

The research is all done, the reading is complete. Files have been pored over, archives have been plundered. Those Who Know have been consulted. That Which Was Unknown has been explained and one fondly prays, made clear. I am, in consequence, or so I hope, now fully steeped in facts and awash with understanding. The book I have been planning for so very long is at last all in the forefront of my mind – structure, content, tone, pace and rhythm are all there. What now remains is simply – would that it were *simply* – to write it: 100,000 words, says the contract, due in just 100 days.

I live on a farm in the Berkshire Hills of western Massachusetts, and I have a small and ancient wooden barn, 100 yards or so from the main house. I have furnished it with books and a long desk on which are a variety of computers and two typewriters, one manual, the other electric. The farm is where I live. The barn is where I work. Each morning, well before the sun is up, I leave the comforts of the farm and enter this spartan, bookish little universe, and shut the allurements of domesticity behind me for the day. For a 100 days, in fact: for a 100 identical days of a solitary, writerly routine that, for me at least, is the only way I know to get a book properly and fully written.

Inside the barn I tend to follow an unvarying routine. First, as the dawn breaks, I spend two hours looking back over what I wrote the day before: I examine it with what I hope is a sharp and critical eye, checking it for infelicities of language, impropriety of grammar, expanding the inexact, refining the imprecise, making as certain as I can the minutiae of fact and detail. Only when I feel satisfied (never smug) that what I have on the screen represents as good a first draft as I can offer do I press the *print* button on the keyboard, and a few pages of A4 slither into the out-tray. Once that task is done I leave the barn and walk through the early sunlight back to the house for breakfast. I read the papers, drink enough coffee to kick-start both mind and body, and, at nine exactly, I head back again, this time to write for real.

I have a word counter at the top left of my computer screen. Purists may object, but my newspaper days have left me with deadline commitment, and this is the way that I like to work. Whenever I begin a book I set the counter with the start date, the number of words I have to write, the contract date and a very simple calculation – the number of words needed each day to meet the deadline. One hundred days, 100,000 words: 1,000 words each day is the initial goal. But things change: the writing life is imperfect, however noble the intentions. Some days are good and maybe I'll write 1,500 words, while others are much less satisfactory and, for a variety of reasons, I may write virtually nothing. So the following day's necessary word total will rise and fall depending on the achievement of the day before. It is that figure my system obliges me to set the night before that I'll see on my screen when I arrive in the cold dark before dawn: 1,245 words needed today, with 68 more days before the deadline? So be it.

I sit down, arrange my thoughts and hammer away without stopping for the next six hours – each day from nine in the morning until three in the afternoon. This is the solitary pleasure of writing – total concentration, pure lexical heaven. I write on, oblivious to everything around me. Except that I do know when I have done my six hours – because by the time the mid-afternoon is upon me, the sun will have shifted to the window in front of my desk, and in wintertime I have to suffer an uncomfortable hour or so of the sunset's glare. This gives me a perfect excuse to end this second stage of the day and do something quite different: a run along my country road, usually, followed by tea. By then it is six or so, the sun has fully set and the glare has been replaced by twilight glow. Then I return, for the day's third and final phase: planning for the next day.

I go back to my desk and arrange the papers, books and thoughts that I think I need for the next day's writing. Then I close down the computers – having been sure, of course, to have made the necessary calculations and set the counter to tell me how many words are due on the morrow – and walk back to the house. For a while I try to forget about the book (though I never can). I have dinner, go to a movie, have friends round – and am in bed, invariably, by midnight.

The next day it begins all over again. As before, I spend the first two hours of the morning looking back over what I have written in those six sunlit hours of the day before. As soon as I have tinkered and tweaked, I press *print*. I stack the A4 sheets neatly on the pile from the preceding day. Millimetre by millimetre, day by day, the pile grows taller and thicker, looking ever more substantial. In the first week it has the look and feel of a newspaper essay; after ten days or so, a magazine article; by a month, it's an outline, then chapter, a monograph, a dissertation – until finally, on one heaven-sent morning, I pick up the pile of paper and it has heft, weight and substance. And then it all changes.

The dream has been made solid. The former featherweight piece of ephemera has been transformed by time into a work-in-progress, a book-in-the-making. After a precisely calculated number of sunrises and sunsets, after yet more walks between barn and farmhouse, after setting and resetting the counter a score of times, and after hours spent reviewing and re-doing and printing and piling and collating and collecting – there, suddenly, is a finished product.

The pile of printed paper and digital confection of finished text will now be placed in the hands of the publisher, who by mysterious dint of designing, printing, binding and jacketing, will in due course turn it into a full-fledged book. *My* new book. After 100 days it is ready to be offered to the world. As for its fate – well, there lies ahead of it what will seem a lifetime of hoping – hoping that it will be lucky, do well and be loved by all. The wish and the prayer of any new parent, who has taken time and care to bring a newborn into the world. But that, of course, is another story. This is just the writing. What follows next is the reading, and that is much less exact of a science.

Simon Winchester OBE worked as a foreign correspondent for the *Guardian* and the *Sunday Times* for 30 years before turning to full-time writing. He is the author of more than 20 books, including *The Surgeon of Crowthorne, The Map that Changed the World, Krakatoa, A Crack in the Edge of the World, The Man Who Loved China* and *Atlantic: The Biography of an Ocean*. His most recent book is *The Alice Behind Wonderland* (Oxford University Press 2011). He divides his time between his small farm in the Berkshire Hills of western Massachusetts and New York.

Notes from a successful MBS author

William Bloom reveals the trials of writing for the mind, body & spirit market.

What's it all about? What's the meaning of life? What's my purpose? How am I meant to live? These Big Questions are at the heart of the Mind, Body & Spirit (MBS) movement and its books. Not surprisingly, the quality of answers ranges across a wide spectrum, from self-centred banality to wisdom. It was ever so with philosophy and religion.

Free of the pulpit and the university chair, yet attempting to wrestle with these core issues, the MBS movement – also known as New Age and holistic – is an easy target for critics who question its authority. As a popular movement it does not appear to have gravitas or roots or a secure intellectual method. It is also a very recent phenomenon. Just as each generation tends to decry the next generation's music, so philosophers and religionists do not like the look of this new creature in their territory. The glitterati, the media intellectuals, are also suspicious.

So, first things first, as an MBS author in the UK, expect no respect! Almost without exception, the book pages of the national media will not give you any space except perhaps to make some snobbish wisecracks. The media likes to make fun of New Age ideas. But far from being a small niche fashion, MBS is now a nationwide lifestyle approach, which the glitterati themselves may adopt when its design elements (e.g. feng shui) are attractive or its healthcare strategies (e.g. stress control using visualisation) are pragmatically useful. There are also books and authors who cross over between MBS and more mainstream niches, such as Elizabeth Gilbert's *Eat, Pray, Love* and the Dalai Lama's *The Art of Happiness.*

The cynicism of Grub Street is not helped by the number of authors in the MBS field whose work is indeed flaky, but, if you are a would-be MBS author or publisher, you cannot help but notice that books on angels, spooks and creating your own reality are nevertheless perennial sellers.

On the more positive side, however, MBS material often initiates and supports the very best in holistic and integrative healthcare. For example, the increasing awareness of the relationship between emotions, diet, social tensions and health has been pioneered by MBS bestsellers such as Deepak Chopra, Daniel Goleman and Louise Hay. The notion of self-managed healthcare is deeply embedded in the holistic approach. The philosophical connection between the concepts of sub-atomic physics and mysticism, the alliance of feminism and eco-spirituality, the inclusive recognition that all religious traditions share important core features – these valuable elements in today's culture have all been initiated and nurtured by MBS authors.

As a body of knowledge and cultural movement, MBS presents a general worldview that opposes, to one degree or another, mainstream traditional culture. From an MBS perspective, mainstream culture might be provocatively caricatured as patriarchal, uncomfortable with emotional literacy, devoted to a crude billiard ball model of the universe in which only the solid is real, and peculiarly narrow-minded when presented with any concepts that include altered states of consciousness, metaphysics or the notion of energy/vitality as an important force in human affairs. MBS presents a more fluid model of an interconnected, interdependent universe in which matter, energy and consciousness are aspects of the same spectrum and interchangeable.

To better understand the MBS field it is useful to place it in its historical context and see it as part of the democratisation of information. It is a cliché now to notice that a few hundred years ago enquirers into the meaning of life would have been severely restricted in their research. Predominantly illiterate and with travel so difficult, their enquiry would have been limited to local authorities. Priests and 'wise women' would have been sources of information and we can only guess at the quality of their answers. We can surmise that their responses would have been clothed mainly in their particular culture. There was no interfaith movement, nor much multiculturalism. To enquire fully into the big questions would have required literacy and travel, both scarce resources. Even if you possessed both, there was no centre of education that housed information on *all* the world's religious traditions and their techniques; nor for example was there a body of study which we now call psychology.

The mushrooming of literacy and communications since the 19th century has transformed that situation. Answers to the great questions can be found now in thousands of different sources. Over the last decades, for the first time in human history, the spiritualities, beliefs and philosophies of *all* cultures are now accessible. The sacred books of all traditions are available and there is at least one website that claims to provide the texts of all of them.

Teachings that were previously passed on one to one, teacher to student – such as tribal shamanic secrets or yoga techniques – are also now part of the public domain. The esoteric strategies of traditional faiths – for example meditation, visualisation, body posture and prayer – historically restricted to the mystics of those traditions, are also on public view.

This is no shallow revolution. Freedom of information has dismantled the dominating hierarchies of restricted information – in religion more than in any other domain of knowledge. Historically the power of religious organisations, of all faiths, was maintained by the claim that only an ordained few had access to the truth. At one level, in terms of literacy, this was indeed a horribly accurate statement. In terms of social status it was also violent and repressive.

MBS can, in my opinion, be seen as the cultural movement that is exploring and expressing this new-found freedom. All the old secrets are now on display. The dominance based on a monopoly of claimed truth or a monopoly of information is dismantled. The holistic movement is young and in its developmental stages. It is so young that it hardly even recognises itself, let alone takes itself seriously, which would be a good first step for a movement that wants others to take it seriously.

In this historical context of cultural upheaval, it is no wonder that traditional religionists survey this scene and decry the smorgasbord, the spiritual supermarket. The books and the general media offerings seem to offer no grounding in a stable community, a trustworthy tradition or a set of ethics.

Domains of MBS

- New Science
- Psychology
- Gaia – The Living Earth
- Holistic Health and Healing
- Feminism and the Goddess
- Shamanic and Magical Traditions
- Mystic and Esoteric Religion
- Modern Prophesy

To a degree these protests are justified. The inevitable forces of commercialisation and popularisation have indeed appropriated some precious spiritual jewels and bowdlerised them, sometimes beyond recognition. The dumbing down and smorgasbord aspects of MBS are easy targets. But that vulgarisation has always existed in the field of belief, from saints' bones and lascivious monks through to shrouds and cure-all snake oil.

The impression of being a spiritual supermarket is, when looked at more closely, a strength. One of the most positive features of MBS is its willing integration of many domains that participate in the enquiry for meaning. When I edited *The Penguin Book of New Age and Holistic Writing* in 2000, I organised these domains in a way that is still relevant (see box). In one form or another you will find similar sections, located close to each other, in most bookshops. What these books have in common is that they are all accessible to a popular audience and are not academic. Within each of the categories there are substantial bestsellers. Publishers, of course, are looking to repeat them. At the time of writing this article, authors such as Deepak Chopra, Neil Donald Walsh, Caroline Myss and Eckhart Tolle are performing strongly. In fact, one set of statistics suggests that Tolle has now sold more books than the Dalai Lama or the Pope. In the past, writers such as John Grey,M. Scott Peck and Louise Hay have topped the bestseller lists. As I mentioned above, there is currently a fashion for books on angels, spiritualist mediums, positive psychology, happiness and how to use the energy of thought for personal success. Previous flavours of the month have included subjects such as relationships, creativity, quantum physics, detoxing, past lives and energy medicine.

Is there a secret to success in this field? I once heard a cynical commissioning editor saying that the recipe for an MBS bestseller is to: (a) Tell people what they already know; (b) Wrap it up so that they think they are reading it for the first time; (c) Write it so that the reader feels intelligent for understanding the material and is therefore part of a cutting edge or spiritual elite. This means that pioneering authors, the originators of concepts, may be overshadowed by the more populist authors who transform original and unique material into a more accessible form. So another piece of advice for MBS authors seeking success is to not be original, but to develop the original material of others. (I am of course waiting philosophically for other authors to make a mint out of my work.) This, of course, is not always the case. Fritjof Capra's *Tao of Physics* and Daniel Goleman's *Emotional Intelligence* are good examples of bestselling and pioneering books.

So – as an MBS author, as in most literary fields, you have a wide range of options. You can offer your work as a flaky mishmash of half-baked truisms laid out on the supermarket smorgasbord of commercialised religion, psychology and philosophy. Or you can be part of an important cultural liberation movement in which adults, free of traditional prejudices and with an open heart and mind, are supported in exploring the most profound questions about life and its meaning.

William Bloom is one of the UK's most experienced teachers, healers and authors in the field of holistic development. His books include *The Endorphin Effect* (2001), *Feeling Safe* (2002) and *Psychic Protection* (1996), all published by Piatkus Little, Brown, and *Soulution: The Holistic Manifesto* (Hay House 2004). His latest book, *The Power of Modern Spirituality* was published by Piatkus Little, Brown in 2011. See more at www.williambloom.com.

Writing memoir

Irene Graham provides a guiding hand to those starting to write their life stories.

Memoir writing, a hybrid of autobiographical writing and personal essay, is growing up as a genre. Everyone has a story to tell. Writing memoir can be approached from a number of perspectives, depending on what the writer wants to achieve. It is therefore important to understand what is motivating you to write before embarking upon this worthwhile and rewarding form of writing. Memoir may be written as a therapeutic process; for family and friends; for publication; or to evoke life experiences for use in fiction. Knowing which is appropriate for you and the story you want to tell helps determine the development of your writing.

Getting started

Biographical, autobiographical and memoir writing differ from one another and demand qualities that the prospective writer should become familiar with before embarking on their writing journey. Biographical writing tells the life story of another person objectively. Memoirists can confuse writing the life story of their mother or father as they knew them with biographical writing. Autobiographical writing is generally written in chronological order. It is based on life experiences from birth to a given point in time that include perhaps hundreds of characters, places and events from the writer's entire life.

Memoir writing is not usually written in chronological order, although it can be. Memoir draws upon a particular subject matter, an incident, a specific period or event from the writer's life and focuses on the impact and challenges it subsequently had on their life. It could be about the life story of the memoirist's mother, father, friend or relative, from the writer's perspective. If a sibling told the story of your parents, it would be from the sibling's perspective and therefore the story would be totally different to the one you would tell. Because autobiographical writing encompasses an entire life and memoir forms part of a life story, an individual would generally have one autobiography but many memoirs.

Writing voice

Unlike fiction, where one can choose the point of view the story is written from, memoir is always written in the first person. The writer is the hero or heroine of the story, and the events and experiences all happened to the writer. Each person has an individual writing voice just like we have an individual singing voice. In writing, this is known as our unique or authentic writing voice.

Your writing voice can be nurtured by identifying with the reason for writing your memoir. It can then be strengthened as the writer develops the telling of his or her life experiences in their chosen subject matter. Someone's writing voice will alter dramatically when writing for publication as opposed to engaging with memoir writing for therapeutic purposes. A writing voice for publication requires wisdom in hindsight as the writer recounts the incidents of their life, however tragic or challenging, in a non-judgemental way which can include any amount of irony or other emotion. Jeannette Walls's memoir, *The Glass Castle*, is a powerful example of how to translate difficult and horrific family circumstances into a captivating story using a writing voice that serves to tell the reality of hardship. At one point, Walls recounts her battle with hunger without a hint of judgement towards her mother. 'If we asked Mom about food – in a casual way, because we didn't want to cause any trouble – she'd simply shrug and say she couldn't make something out of nothing. We kids usually kept our hunger to ourselves, but we were always thinking of food and how to get our hands on it.'

If, on the other hand, you chose to tell your life story using memoir writing to ultimately gain insight into painful and traumatic experiences – which writing as a therapeutic process allows – the description would have a completely different slant to it. The example given by Walls could be rewritten as: *Mum never provided food for us, we were always hungry. I could never understand how a mother could treat her kids this way; she never seemed to care, no matter how many times I broached this subject with her.*

Therefore, the writing voice in a therapeutic process allows the writer to whine, moan and be a victim of circumstance. I think this is the crucial distinction between a 'misery memoir' versus handling challenging life events with a mature and non-judgemental writing voice. Your tone, mood and attitude towards your subject matter play a significant part in how your writing voice is established. Other facets of writing voice include the choice of tense – past or present – and how best this element fits the particular story in question. Frank McCourt stated that when he started to write *Angela's Ashes* in the present tense he found his writing voice for that memoir. The memoirist needs to consider all these aspects of writing voice before starting to write so that their voice remains consistent throughout their story.

Published memoirs

Examples of published memoirs highlighted by subject matter include:

- *Burmese Lessons* by Karen Connelly – a story of life and love in war-torn Burma in the mid-1990s
- *The Year of Magical Thinking* by Joan Didion – reflections on the death of her husband and her daughter's illness
- *Marley & Me* by John Grogan – family life and how their dog made a difference to it
- *My Stroke of Insight* by Jill Bolte Taylor – a brain scientist's account of her personal experience of a brain haemorrhage and her path to recovery
- *Angela's Ashes* by Frank McCourt – childhood memories of life in Ireland before emigrating to the USA aged 19

Truth

The word 'memoir' attached to the work serves as an unspoken contract between the memoirist and the reader that they have written the truth. The writer must seek at all times to portray *their* truth about the event or incident. Another person recounting the same event will nearly always have a different slant on it, which will be their internal and emotional truth. There is never one real truth in any situation.

So is it possible in writing memoir for every exact detail to be the precise truth? The answer is most definitely no. Details become blurred. For example, when a man recalls his ex-wife stating to him, 'I want a divorce, you will never see your children again', he will write his emotional truth about this event. This same situation recalled by his ex-wife may vividly remember stating to her husband, 'I think I want a divorce which would mean you *may* never see your children again'.

It is impossible to remember every detail of our lives, of each event that took place right down to the actual dress or suit that someone wore, or perhaps the colour of the wallpaper in Aunt Sally's room when you were five years old. It is important therefore to be aware of the distinction between making up events – the significant moments that shaped your life which subsequently had an impact upon you and the lives of others – and the colour of Aunt Sally's wallpaper which has no real significance to the event in question. However, you should strive to be as accurate as possible with these details. If I remembered Aunt Sally's room to be musty with sparse furnishing and thread-worn carpet, it would resonate more with the story and the event if I included these details as I best remembered them, instead of setting a scene of grandeur.

It is also impossible to remember verbatim dialogue that took place between you and others. You may remember particular snippets of a conversation, or statements that subsequently had an affect on lives, but you may not remember the entire conversation. It is the line of dialogue that altered your life or the lives of others that is important. The other dialogue you may have to fill in, but not to the point where it turns the event into fiction. As you write, stay true to the experience as much as possible. In memoir events and people are not made up; if they are, it is a work of fiction.

Developing writing skills

Most writers would agree that thought, development and focus provide the backbone to their writing, before putting words on the page. Creativity also plays a huge role and it is equally important for our writing to nudge this into existence, to awaken it from its often dormant state. It is not realistic to think that writing is an automatic process which doesn't require tuition and guidance; it does – just like any art form. If you want to write memoir, learn how to do it and develop your writing skills. Set yourself a schedule and a time frame to complete your first story, so that it fits in with your lifestyle. Write a short memoir first and use the process to learn the craft. Writing exercises, establishing your tone and mood, playing with tenses and being aware of the subject matter enhances writing voice and will greatly serve to determine the quality of your writing. Don't be afraid to experiment.

Research the options for developing your writing and decide which approach would suit you – writing workshops, online courses, weekly classes at night school, weekend workshops or even a college programme. Read books on memoir. Write often. Join local writing groups. Read your work aloud. The only way to be a writer is to write.

When you complete your first story you can then look at your work and consider the next stage of development. Getting your work published is of course a worthy goal – whether it's a miniature memoir or a full-length book, if you have a story to tell and have told it well, publishing is always possible. Enjoy the process of being an apprentice writer.

Tips to establish your memoir writing journey

- Ascertain why you want to write your memoir
- Decide who you want to write your memoir for
- Research suitable options to learn the art of memoir writing
- Prepare your personal writing space and plan your personal writing schedule
- Gather your previous writings, if any, for future reference
- Don't get stuck in family research
- Enjoy the adventure!

Irene Graham is the founder of the Creative Writer's Workshop (www.thecreativewritersworkshop.com), which is based on right-brain/left-brain learning techniques, and is the founder and director of the Memoir Writing Club (www.thememoirwritingclub.com). She is also the author of *The Memoir Writing Workbook*.

Books published from blogs

Scott Pack explains the reality of how blogs become successful books.

'Washington sex blogger signs $300,000 book deal'. 'I blog, therefore I am £70,000 richer'. 'Blogger wins six-figure book contract'. 'Blogger's book turned into major TV series'.

Those are the headlines. Here is the reality. Brace yourself.

Most blogs are rubbish. They aren't read by anyone and are poorly written. They stand as much chance of being turned into books as the authors do of becoming the Pope. The internet is full of mindless drivel and finding something that would make a bestseller is like searching for a needle in a whole field of haystacks.

I didn't say it was impossible though.

The world of blogging has exploded in recent years and many in publishing see it as the potential next great breeding ground for writing talent. Because of this, unpublished writers are increasingly putting their work online in the form of blogs in the hope of a book deal. Like any other route to print, a chosen few will find success; most will remain ignored. So is it worth bothering in the first place and, if so, what are your chances of being spotted?

The traditional publishing model, at least as it currently stands, has authors sending work to agents. Agents sign up the manuscripts they think they can sell and then proceed to tout them round publishing houses in search of a tasty advance. Simple really. Of course, there is more to it than that and there are several variations on the theme but the bulk of new books published in the UK have taken that route.

And the truth is that most of the bloggers who have secured massive book deals have taken precisely that route as well. Blogging may be adding a new element to the world of contemporary literature, but it hasn't changed the face of publishing. At least, it hasn't yet.

You'd like to think in this day and age that editors spend loads of time scouring the web for the hottest new talent, one hand on the mouse, the other on the chequebook. In fact, most of them are far too busy publishing books to waste hours browsing the internet. They rely on others to do the browsing, filtering and touching up for them. And that is increasingly the role of the agent.

Agents are proving quite proactive when it comes to bloggers. Some of the more savvy ones are identifying blogs with a buzz behind them and approaching the authors with the lure of a possible book deal. But here's the thing. They aren't plucking these sites out of thin air, they are targeting blogs and bloggers that already have a big audience. Most of the successful bloggers with book deals put in a lot of time and hard work into their websites before they were signed up.

So don't expect to simply chuck up a couple of chapters of your first novel and then be inundated with offers from Penguin, Random House and HarperCollins. It ain't gonna happen. That doesn't mean you shouldn't do it. Getting your work online can be a great way to spread the word, find an audience and generate feedback. The simple discipline of writing every day, or a couple of times a week, can improve your skill as a writer. There is a lot to be said for blogging just for the sake of it. It is fun, it can be rewarding, and it might just be the start of something. But do make sure you go into it with realistic expectations.

And when it comes to expectations, it is probably best to ignore thoughts of a book deal altogether. Embrace the blogging form for what it is. Become the best blogger you can be. Offer your readers something different, entertaining and interesting. If you can please your audience then you have succeeded; anything else that happens is a bonus.

But what makes one blog stand out from another? How is it that some bloggers end up making a fortune and seeing their book top the bestseller charts while others languish on page 267 of a Google search? The answer is both simple and impossibly vague and is precisely the same when it comes to bestselling books – because people want to read them.

When you look at the more successful blooks (blogs turned into books) they aren't just versions of the blog cut and pasted into book form. In converting a blog to a book, authors and editors usually revert to a more traditional style of writing. Whereas blog posts tend to be episodic, and sometimes quite random in terms of content and running order, the best blooks have a narrative arc, they tell a story.

The experience of browsing a blog online is very different from reading a physical printed book and that is reflected in how they are put together. When an agent or a publisher identifies that a blog has book potential they are usually looking beyond the individual posts and focusing more on the quality of writing and the standard of story-telling, and they will have one eye on the size of the potential audience.

And the audience for the book is different to that of the online version. *The Intimate Adventures of a London Call Girl* by Belle de Jour is perhaps the most famous of recent blog-to-book success stories. The book has sold over 326,625 copies, the television series starring Billie Piper was watched by millions and it is a pretty good bet that the vast majority of those readers and viewers have never seen the blog upon which it is based. Publishers may be interested in your visitor stats and the fact that you have 1,000 page views a day but they cannot create a bestseller by simply selling copies of your book to your blog readers. They need to take your concept and sell it to the masses. The concept is the key.

Which is why a piece of fiction posted online, no matter how great a work of genius it may be, is probably not going to appeal to a publisher as much as *One Red Paperclip*, the story of an American guy who, starting with a red paperclip, kept swapping objects until he ended up with a house. Blogs about sex and the intimate goings on of their authors, have been some of the most popular and successful blooks of late. That bubble may well be about to burst but, when it does, it will be replaced with some other titillating subject, not a sudden surge of million-selling poetry books or works of philosophy.

If you are serious about starting a blog then you can probably have something online in a matter of minutes, but it would pay to do a bit of research first. Check out other bloggers who write on a similar subject. What can you do that is different? Are there any design features that you like and would like to emulate? What do you think others are doing right or wrong? Create the sort of site that you would want to visit.

It also makes sense to participate in other blogs. Read as much stuff as you can online and leave comments when you feel moved to do so. Most comments you leave will link back to your own site and a witty and incisive note on someone else's blog may have dozens of people visiting yours. The internet is a community and can be, by and large, a friendly one. People who like your writing will mention it on their sites and the more active you are the quicker word will spread.

For most people blogging is not the way to the Nobel Prize for Literature, neither is it a route to fame and fortune. It is simply what it is – a way of getting your words online. If you have something worthwhile to say then people will probably read it. If you are a wonderful writer then readers will spread the word and your audience will grow. If you have an unusual, original or intriguing and exciting concept that someone in a position of influence thinks they can make some money out of then, and probably only then, will you hear from an agent or publisher.

Having said that, if you venture into blogging with the intention of getting a book deal then you will probably fail. If you start a blog because you want to write and share your work with an online audience then you can only succeed.

Happy blogging.

Scott Pack is Publisher at The Friday Project, an imprint of HarperCollins. His own blog can be found at http://meandmybigmouth.typepad.com/scottpack.

See also...

- *Writing a blog*, page 594
- *Managing your online reputation*, page 591
- *Marketing yourself online*, page 587

Notes from a literary editor

Claire Armitstead gives an insight into the role of a literary editor.

The morning begins with a grey mail bag containing 20–30 books which jut out at angles, waiting to be shucked from their cardboard pods and stuck on to the shelves. This first daily arrival used to excite me but, though I still love the smell of new books, their relentlessness can be dispiriting. The sad truth is that, of the 400 or so books that are delivered to the office every week, fewer than 40 will make it into the review pages. As an Eeyorish colleague once mourned, 'Newspaper literary desks are where books go to die'.

The central part of any literary editor's job is working out which of these hundreds of hopefuls to despatch and which to spare for the next round. Some decisions are easy, but they are usually the outright rejections. We have two literary sections, the *Guardian Review* and the books pages of the *Observer News Review*. They have different personalities but neither review many celebrity biographies. Nor do we do self-help books or the misery memoirs that top the library charts year after year. Though we all have our quirks, there is quite a big crossover between the various newspaper review sections which means that thousands of the books published each year will never be reviewed in them. Perhaps surprisingly, none of us tend to review the books that sell the most – teen vampire fiction, for instance, or commercial thrillers. And even when we do – as the chief executive of a major publisher has remarked – we make no impact on their sales (though in certain arenas, for example history, I would argue that good reviews can make all the difference).

But to quibble about the impact of reviews on sales is to miss the whole point of book reviewing, which is a complicated negotiation between the culture of writing and reading. The role of the newspaper books pages is not to sell books: it is to entertain, inform and stimulate readers, some of whom have little time in their lives to actually read books at all. Review pages are part of the intellectual and imaginative life of the UK and – with the extra scope granted by www.guardian.co.uk and other websites – increasingly beyond it.

The most obvious function of the review is to tell people whether a book is good or bad. But there is a whole spectrum between those two extremes, and this is often where the character and colour of the books pages lie. A book may be well written but essentially dull or, conversely, badly written but packed with fascinating facts. Reviewers can offer a digest of the stuff people want to know about. They can mediate and simplify, bringing an academic thesis into the language of journalism and placing it within the available reading time of an ordinary person's working day. This is particularly true of non-fiction reviews, part of the purpose of which is to give a potted version of the book. After all, a reader can be very interested in advances in quantum physics and very unlikely to get through *A Brief History of Time* by Stephen Hawking.

Commissioning the reviews

Once the obvious books have been discarded, the literary editor needs to whittle down the dozens of more or less worthy contenders for the limited space available. At this stage, only hard discipline will do. The books are separated into original fiction and non-fiction, with a separate bookcase for paperback re-issues. There are three commissioning editors on my desk and we work on a 'buck-stops' basis: the buck for fiction commissioning stops with one editor, for non-fiction with another, and for paperbacks with a third. This is essential if the fantasy commissions of our brainstorming sessions are to translate into actual reviews. It does not mean that we are huddled away in our own little corners – on the contrary, the indefinable spark of a books desk depends on the hours that every editor is prepared to spend reading that marginal proof by an unknown writer on the bus home. The commissions I am proudest of are reviews of those completely unexpected gems that only emerge from the most conscientious scouting.

But there are logistical limits to this sort of eureka commission. There are only so many hours in a day to look for them; there is only so much money in the budget to pay people to do so. When I started this job 13 years ago, the *Guardian* books pages were over-commissioned by 50%, which meant that for every review that was used, another one was 'spiked'. This unfortunate state of affairs reflected a particular moment in publishing history when the rate at which books were produced had sped up beyond the capacity of any one set of books pages to give a comprehensive account of them. The margins are much tighter now, which means that we are less wasteful but the criteria for selection have to be very clear.

We are, of course, at a new turning-point in history today: the point at which bookshops are giving way to digital booksellers and the ebook is fast catching up with the printed versions. Newspapers have barely begun to acknowledge this transformation, though our own transformation has been almost as radical. Thirteen years ago, we were limited to reviews on paper; today we have a weekly books podcast, video interviews, a Twitter following of some 315,100 people all over the world, and a website devoted to children's books, chosen and reviewed by children themselves. Each medium has its own personality and potential. Consider the impact of a dedicated children's website on children's publishing – a literary sector that has traditionally struggled to get any coverage at all in newspapers. This shift towards reader-reviewing is also happening on our adult website. It means that for the first time in newspaper history, books are being reviewed by the people who buy and read them, rather than by hired hands.

But the newspaper is still central to what we do. We have space for eleven 200-word paperback reviews a week, so paperbacks are sent out to a regular roster of reviewers on a weekly basis. Big reviews of first editions are more tricky – I may know that we will carry an average of nine original fiction reviews and 10–11 non-fiction reviews, but until the review is actually in my hand, I can never be absolutely sure what it will be like – ecstatic, condemning, indifferent; even long or short.

This is where the job of a literary editor is closer to that of a news, rather than a features, editor. A features editor can set the agenda, simply by deciding how many words to commission on a subject and instructing a writer to write them. The job of review pages, in contrast, is to report on books – though the way in which this is done depends on a series of choices by the literary editors.

Placing the reviews

Once we have selected which books to send out, chosen a reviewer and taken delivery of their review, the next step is deciding where to place it and, just as importantly, what to place it with. For instance, nobody would want to read page after page of bad-tempered reviews (yet there are weeks when every piece that comes in seems to be disparaging). On the other hand, no one would trust pages in which every review was a rave. The challenge is to respect the opinion of the critic, while creating pages that have life and variety and which – in journalistic terms – 'talk to' each other. Occasionally, if the reviews coming up are in danger of being too dour, we will commission a 'turn' review, with the specific intent of bringing a bit of showbiz to the pages (though the good turn review can have its own crunchy wisdom, as when Professor Terry Eagleton wrote of Beckham's memoirs: 'One suspects that David Beckham wrote this book rather in the sense that the Pharaohs built the pyramids').

This sort of playful commissioning cannot be done lightly – it relies on an advance intelligence that enables the editor to see opportunities that a single critic might not spot. The same is true of spotting patterns and trends in publishing. In the last few years, for instance, there has been a fashion for calling everything a biography: in the past couple of years we've had biographies of food, of cities, of an ocean, the ordnance survey map and even of cancer.

Intelligence-gathering ranges from the diligent (the twice-yearly hack through all the publishing catalogues to compile a list of every upcoming book in the next season) to what might pass as mere partying (yes, publishers do still hold book launches, but no, they are not all about getting drunk and behaving badly). It is often at parties that the connections are made, and the hidden enthusiasms revealed so that, for instance, Paul Theroux ends up reviewing a book about bees. If I don't go out a couple of times a week, I don't feel I'm doing my job properly.

In the end, however, it all comes back to the solitary relationship between the critic and the book, and to the difficult negotiations between inside knowledge and independence, expertise and humility, seriousness and the willingness to entertain.

For a variety of social, historical and economic reasons, literary critics are regarded as more compromised than those in any other art form. There is some truth in this, if only because writers are always reviewed by other writers. There is none of the separation of crafts and industries that exists between, say, reviewer and actor or reviewer and concert pianist. Connected to this is the fact that there is no tradition in the UK of giving jobs to literary critics, as there is for other art forms, so most reviewers have 'day jobs' – usually their own writing, or some sort of teaching, both of which bring with them dependencies and compromises.

The most difficult part of the literary editor's job is steering a path between these conflicts of interest to that ideal reviewer, who will be knowledgeable but not compromised, and wise, reasonable and witty. But if it is the most difficult part, it is also the most important, because however much people love to hate critics – and however alienated the critic is from the culture of hype in which we now live – they are an essential part of the cultural ecology: the carrion birds, pecking away at mediocrity, dishonesty and rot and clearing a space for works of real quality.

Above every grey mailbag of books that arrives in the office sits a flock of invisible critics just waiting for the signal to plunge in their beaks. For that, we must all be profoundly grateful.

Claire Armitstead is head of books for the *Guardian*, the *Observer* and www.guardian.co.uk.

Notes from a successful crossover author

Neil Gaiman explains how he 'learned to stop worrying and became a crossover author'.

I didn't set out to be a crossover author, it just never occurred to me not to be. To put it another way, what I wanted to be was the kind of writer who told whatever stories he wanted in whatever medium he wanted, and I seem, more or less, to have got to that place. So, I can tell you how I did it. I'm just not sure I could tell you how you could do it too.

My first book was a children's book. I was about 22 when I wrote it, and I sent it to one publisher, and it came back with a nice note from the editor saying that it wasn't quite right for them, and I put it away for ever. I was a journalist for a while (it would be accurate to say that all I knew of being a journalist when I began was what I had gleaned from the 1983 edition of the *Writers' & Artists' Yearbook*). Then I wrote comics – mostly for grown-ups – and once I'd learned to write comics to my own satisfaction and thought it might be good fun to go and explore prose fiction, I was spoiled. The joy of writing comics is that it's a medium that people mistake for a genre: nobody seemed to mind whether I lurched from historical to fantasy to spy stories to autobiography to children's fiction, because it was all comics – a freedom that I treasured.

I started writing my first real children's book in 1991, a scary story for my daughter, Holly, called *Coraline*. I showed the first few chapters to my editor at Gollancz, Richard Evans. Now, Richard was a good editor and a smart man, and had just midwifed a book by Terry Pratchett and me, *Good Omens*, into existence. The next time I was in the Gollancz offices he took me to one side and said, 'Neil. I read the *Coraline* chapters, and I loved it. I think it's the best thing you've ever written. But I have to warn you, it's unpublishable'. I was puzzled: 'Why?' 'Well, it's a horror novel aimed at children and adults,' he told me, 'and I don't think we could publish a horror novel for children, and I really don't know how anyone could publish anything for adults and children at the same time.'

So I put the book away. I planned to keep writing it, in my own time, but there wasn't a lot of my own time about, and I managed about a thousand words on it during the next few years. I knew that unless someone was waiting for it, unless it had a chance of being read, I wasn't going to write it.

By now I had published a couple of books with Avon, and I sent it to my editor, Jennifer Hershey. 'It's great,' she said. 'What happens next?' I told her I wasn't really sure, but if she sent me a contract we would both find out! She did. The contract was for about 5% of what I'd got as an advance for my last novel, but it was a contract, and Jennifer said she would worry about how it was published when I handed it in.

Two years passed. I didn't have any more time, so I kept a notebook beside my bed and finished the book and handed it in. But I still had an adult novel, *American Gods*, to finish before *Coraline* would be published. Avon was taken over by HarperCollins, a publisher with a healthy children's publishing division, and somewhere in there it was decided that *Coraline* would be published by HarperCollins Children's. In the UK, the book was sold to Bloomsbury.

It was still a horror novel, still aimed at both adults and children, but the publishing landscape had changed in the previous handful of years. The success of the few books that had crossed over from children's fiction to the adult world – the Harry Potter books,Philip Pullman's *His Dark Materials*, the Lemony Snicket books – made it at least a feasible goal.

Coraline was published in the summer of 2002, which was, coincidentally, the first summer without a new Harry Potter book. Journalists had column inches to fill, and they wrote about *Coraline*, imagining a movement of adult novelists now writing children's books. In both the USA and the UK, it's fair to say, adults bought the book at first, not children. That came later, as teachers enjoyed reading it and began introducing it in schools, and news of it spread by word of mouth.

The Wolves in the Walls followed, written by me and illustrated by artist Dave McKean. A children's picture book, again, it was initially bought by adults who liked what I wrote and what Dave painted – essentially the graphic novel audience who had come with us from comics. But it was read to children, and became popular with them, and now most of the copies I sign at signings are for younger readers.

I don't think you can plan for something to be a crossover book. But you can do things to make it easier. In my case, it was useful that I already had a large readership, one that had followed me from comics into prose, and who didn't seem to mind that none of my prose books resembled each other very much, except in having been written by me. It was also wonderful that I had supportive publishers in the USA and the UK, who were willing to take different approaches to the material.

When I wrote *The Graveyard Book*, a book that began with me wondering what would happen if you took Kipling's *The Jungle Book* and relocated it to a graveyard, I wasn't really sure who I was writing it for. I just wanted it to be good. Dave McKean did a book cover for the US edition while I was still writing it, but once the book was done it was obvious that the cover was wrong. It looked like a book for ten year-olds, and only for ten-year-olds. While the book I'd written would work for children, it worked just as well for adults, and we didn't want to exclude them. With tremendous good humour, Dave went back to the drawing board and produced a dozen new sketches. One of them seemed perfect – it showed a gravestone, which became the outline of a boy's face in profile. It could as easily have been a children's book cover or the cover of a Stephen King book; no one picking it up would feel excluded. (Another of Dave's sketches, of a baby walking on a bloody knife-edge in which a graveyard could be seen, would have been perfect for a book aimed at adults, but was thought a bit too edgy for children.)

In the UK, Bloomsbury had come up with their own strategy: two editions of *The Graveyard Book*, one aimed at children, one at adults. The children's edition would be illustrated by Chris Riddell, the adult edition by Dave McKean – and Dave's baby-on-a-knife-edge cover was ideal for what they wanted, something that was unashamedly aimed at adults.

You can do your best to write a book for children that adults will like (or the other way around – in the USA the Young Adult Library Services awards celebrate the books for adults that young readers latch on to); you can try not to mess up the publishing end of things (that first cover for the US version of *The Graveyard Book*, which looked like a book that only 'middle grade readers' might have enjoyed would have been a mis-step); you can try to bring an existing audience with you, if you have one, and a way of letting them know what you've done. But I'm not sure that any of this will guarantee anything. Publishers are less intimidated by crossover books now that there have been many successes, but the mechanics of bookselling, the fact that books have to go somewhere in a bookshop, and that somewhere may be in a place that adults or children don't go, that the adult and children's divisions of publishers are staffed by different people in different groups who don't always talk to each other or have the same objectives (or even the same catalogues) – all of these things serve to make it harder to be a crossover author and encourage you to stay put, to write something people will know where to shelve, to write the same sort of thing you wrote before.

I suppose you become a crossover author by taking risks, but they had better be the kind of risks that you enjoy taking. Don't set out to be a crossover author. Write the books you have to write, and if you write one that crosses boundaries, that finds readers in a variety of ages and types, then do your best to get it published in a way that lets all of them know it's out there. Good luck.

Neil Gaiman is the *New York Times* bestselling author of the novels *Neverwhere, Stardust, American Gods, Anansi Boys* and *Good Omens* (with Terry Pratchett); the *Sandman* series of graphic novels; and the short story collections *Smoke and Mirrors* and *Fragile Things*. He is also the author of books for readers of all ages including the bestselling novel *The Graveyard Book*, the bestselling novels *Coraline* and *Odd and the Frost Giants*; the short story collection *M is for Magic* and the picture books *The Wolves in the Walls, The Day I Swapped My Dad for Two Goldfish*, and *Crazy Hair*, illustrated by Dave McKean; *The Dangerous Alphabet*, illustrated by Gris Grimly; and *Blueberry Girl*, illustrated by Charles Vess. He is the winner of numerous literary honours, including the Hugo, Bram Stoker, and World Fantasy Awards, and the Newbery Medal. Originally from England, he now lives in the USA. He is listed in the *Dictionary of Literary Biography* as one of the top ten living post-modern writers and he says he owes it all to reading the *Writers' & Artists' Yearbook* as a young man. Visit him at www.neilgaiman.com.

Notes from a successful children's author

J.K. Rowling shares her experiences of writing success.

I can remember writing *Harry Potter and the Philosopher's Stone* in a café in Oporto. I was employed as a teacher at the language institute three doors along the road at the time, and this café was a kind of unofficial staffroom. My friend and colleague joined me at my table. When I realised I was no longer alone I hastily shuffled worksheets over my notebook, but not before Paul had seen exactly what I was doing. 'Writing a novel, eh?' he asked wearily, as though he had seen this sort of behaviour in foolish young teachers only too often before. '*Writers' & Artists' Yearbook*, that's what you need,' he said. 'Lists all the publishers and... stuff' he advised before ordering a lager and starting to talk about the previous night's episode of *The Simpsons*.

I had almost no knowledge of the practical aspects of getting published; I knew nobody in the publishing world, I didn't even know anybody who knew anybody. It had never occurred to me that assistance might be available in book form.

Nearly three years later and a long way from Oporto, I had almost finished *Harry Potter and the Philosopher's Stone*. I felt oddly as though I was setting out on a blind date as I took a copy of the *Writers' & Artists' Yearbook* from the shelf in Edinburgh's Central Library. Paul had been right and the *Yearbook* answered my every question, and after I had read and reread the invaluable advice on preparing a manuscript, and noted the time-lapse between sending said manuscript and trying to get information back from the publisher, I made two lists: one of publishers, the other of agents.

The first agent on my list sent my sample three chapters and synopsis back by return of post. The first two publishers took slightly longer to return them, but the 'no' was just as firm. Oddly, these rejections didn't upset me much. I was braced to be turned down by the entire list, and in any case, these were real rejection letters – even real writers had got them. And then the second agent, who was high on the list purely because I like his name, wrote back with the most magical words I have ever read: 'We would be pleased to read the balance of your manuscript on an exclusive basis...'

J.K. Rowling is the bestselling author of the *Harry Potter* series (Bloomsbury), published between 1997 and 2007, which have sold over 450 million copies worldwide, are distributed in more than 200 territories, translated into 74 languages and have been turned into eight blockbuster films. The first in the series, *Harry Potter and the Philosopher's Stone*, was the winner of the 1997 Nestlé Smarties Gold Prize and *Harry Potter and the Goblet of Fire* (2000) broke all records for the number of books sold on the first day of publication. The seventh book in the series, *Harry Potter and the Deathly Hallows*, was published in 2007. *The Tales of Beedle the Bard* was published in 2008 in aid of the Children's High Level Group. J.K. Rowling has also written two small volumes that appear as the titles of Harry's schoolbooks within the novels: *Fantastic Beasts and Where to Find Them* and *Quidditch Through the Ages* (Bloomsbury) were published in March 2001 in aid of Comic Relief. September 2012 sees the publication of J.K. Rowling's first novel for adults, *The Casual Vacancy* (Little, Brown).

Is there a book in you?

Alison Baverstock examines what resources a writer needs to be a successfully published author.

One of the most disappointing things about finally getting a book professionally published is the reaction of other people. You might have imagined they would be impressed by your achievement. Think again. The reality is that most will use your success as a spur to their own aspirations, and rather than even *pausing* to admire what you have done, they will most likely come straight out with one of the following comments:

- 'That's something I have always planned to do';
- 'I've always felt there was a book in me too'; or even more frustratingly,
- 'Lucky you to have the time'.

The desire to have a book with one's name on the front cover is seemingly universal: so many people daydream that one day, somehow, this will appear. For some, the desire is for the object with their name on it; others anticipate that this will be the springboard to greater things: fame, riches and a celebrity lifestyle. And there really are lots of people wanting this. Competitions run in the media for new writers to achieve publication attract huge numbers of entrants.

Quite why it is such a common ambition is not hard to fathom. A book with your name on the cover is a solid achievement; it makes you feel both valid and validated (because others are investing in your talent). It offers significance and permanence amidst the 'changes and chances of this fleeting world'.

But given the vast disparity in numbers between those who want to try to get into print, and those who actually make it, how can you influence the process? Is it really true, as many suspect, that it is only the famous and well connected who get publishing deals, or will writing talent always win through?

Given that I have been a publisher, still work freelance within the industry (mainly running training courses on how to market books) and am also a writer (with 19 books and lots of articles to my name), I decided to try to theorise about *why* some people get into print and others do not; to define the resources would-be published writers need. Some necessary talents are obvious (can you write?) and some less so, but it's not necessarily true that having all the obvious qualifications for writing will guarantee you a publication deal. Those running creative writing courses often say that it's often not the best writers who get published; more likely it's those with the most self-belief or determination – or those who make pragmatic choices about the publishing house most likely to take them on. Here is my list of ten resources needed by would-be published writers:

1. Real determination

If you lack this core attribute, you are missing the one key requirement for getting published. Writing for publication demands an intense determination because so many things are stacked against you. There is huge competition – publishers and agents have vast numbers of would-be published writers to choose between; writing is hard and takes a long time; most writers earn little; there are bands of others helpfully telling you not to bother trying, as well as endless bothersome circumstances that present themselves, from manuscripts lost in the post to the editor who was about to commission your work changing job and moving to a publishing house that has no interest in the kind of book you want to write. Those who make it into print will be sustained by the knowledge that nothing matters to them more, and just keep going.

2. An ability to write what other people want to read

Canny observers might start by asking whether would-be published writers can write sufficiently well for publication. I am risking annoyance by dealing with this issue from the other side of the fence: placing emphasis on the consumer's judgement rather than sufficient a quota of literary merit.

In any case, there is *no* particular style of writing or mastery of literary structure that will guarantee an audience; writing that one person finds banal or staid may find a wider audience amongst those who relate to the story told or the characters described. So rather than displaying your ease with syntax to your potential publisher and feeling aggrieved that those who are less 'literary' than you get published, concentrate your energies on trying to prove that other people want to read what you are able to write.

Assemble proof. Find parallels. If your work compares in subject matter or style to a popular writer, name them. Many books these days are announced as having parents ('Jilly Cooper meets Joanna Trollope'). If your area of writing relates to a popular television programme or magazine, state how many people subscribe/watch and when. Tell the publisher how others respond to your work. For example, if you are writing for children, give readings in a local school and obtain feedback. If you are writing popular fiction, find out if your local newspaper would like to reproduce an extract and monitor the response. If you have just finished a novel, get friends to give you honest feedback on what they think, and if it is positive, pass it on with your manuscript to the publisher or agent you choose to approach.

3. Creativity

Few writers have an imagination to rival Shakespeare, but creativity is vital for the would-be writer, in whatever the field you choose to publish.

Whatever you are writing about, in whatever format, your decision on how to present your ideas is a creative one; there are many possibilities and as a writer you need to choose the style and format that you consider both most appropriate and interesting. Even if you are writing academic papers, the logic of presentation and the examples chosen to illustrate the points you want to make will come across best if they are selected with a creative sense of what will help to develop the reader's understanding, rather than just being the first ten that occur to you.

4. Support mechanisms for your writing

Some writers work best at times of personal turmoil; they find the spirit of 'this will show them!' helps them produce their best work. Others need tea, toast and sympathy at regular intervals. The most valuable support mechanism is money; writing is, most usually, badly paid and someone needs to be able to pay the rent/mortgage and provide enough money for food whilst you are busy crafting your masterpiece. The second most valuable support mechanism is usually appreciation: being shown that you are taken seriously is immensely helpful to a writer.

5. A writing habit

It is surprising how many people long to write but can never quite get down to it. Getting published demands self-discipline and self-knowledge; an understanding of when are your best times for writing and a determination to stick to the schedules you establish. Having a 'writing habit' means you prioritise your writing, where you do it, what time you get started, how long you stick at it, under what circumstances you can be disturbed – and, of course, how everyone else in your life is conditioned to respond to these things. If you are not willing to alter your priorities and put the writing first – not all the time, but when you have promised yourself you will – it will be very difficult to complete your book.

6. Something to write about

Few books arrive in the writer's imagination fully formed. The writers I talked to often mentioned the importance of the random in sparking ideas: an overheard conversation, a curious coincidence, an unexpected gift, and there was general agreement on the importance of novels developing best when characters you believed in started to shape events – rather than relying on plot alone for narrative development. Find someone who interests you and write about them, rather than dreaming up an exciting series of events and then deciding to whom they should happen. In your search for interesting ideas, try to lead an interesting life. Keep fit and healthy, eat well, listen to as wide a variety of people as possible, whether in print or socially. It's surprising how often the spark occurs when you least expect it.

7. An ability to present yourself as a writer

Years ago someone commented to me that 'other people take you at your own estimation'. It is true, but it's an area of real difficulty for many writers: we want our writing to be taken seriously, yet exposing our hopes of publication for general inspection feels as if we are tempting fate; will it compromise our ability to achieve anything? The ability to 'play the writer' on occasion demands self-confidence and the suspension of self-doubt – but will probably be well received by publishers and agents who are looking for not only someone who can write what others want to read, but who interviews well (for publicising the books) and is 'promoteable'. Don't forget that a publisher who decides to back your book is making an *investment* decision, on the grounds that you will, in the long or short term, make a profit for the publishing house that sponsored you.

8. The ability to deal positively with rejection

All writers get rejected – whether it is their initial ideas ('we can see no market for that'), their initial outline ('this does not fit our list at the present time') or their final draft ('editorial policy has changed and your book no longer fits our list as we are seeking to develop it. Please feel free to approach another house'). Even once accepted, having your precious manuscript edited can feel close to rejection – especially if it comes back covered with red ink and 'suggestions for change/development'.

What matters here is how you *deal* with rejection. A publisher's rejection is not a rejection of you or your ability to write, or indeed you as a person – although it may feel like all those things. Rather, it is a specific reader's response to what you sent at that particular time. Absorb all the advice you are given and try to do nothing in a hurry (certainly not a rude email back) but if you want to get published, don't let rejections grind you down. The publishing industry abounds with stories of the much-turned-down manuscript that went on to make a fortune (the *Harry Potter* series, *Day of the Jackal*, Mary Wesley, etc).

9. A wide knowledge of other people's books

Good writers are almost invariably well read: because why would you seek to contribute to the canon of published work if you do not respect the output of those who are already part of it? Some writers find that whilst writing a particular type of book, they read other things (maybe works in translation or non-fiction if they're writing fiction); others withdraw from reading while they're writing as it puts them off – then they are further motivated to get writing so they can get back to reading once they've finished their manuscript. Others have favourite writers who inspire them – one described reading Jane Austen as 'like having a blood transfusion'. And don't think that writing a particular type of book (children's titles or romantic fiction are commonly cited here) excludes you from being well read; such a view reveals a very patronising attitude towards just how hard it is to write any kind of book. Whatever you want to write, you do best if you understand how *other* writers develop ideas. Trying to write without the inspiration of reading yourself is like leaving the house without breakfast, the car without petrol, the hand-held console without batteries (you quickly run out of juice).

10. An understanding of how publishing works

A publishing house is not a charity. Publishers and agents are not in business to help you achieve personal satisfaction by writing a book; rather they exist to make products available to the reading public who will pay for access. Different houses commission different kinds of books in different formats according to their experience of the market, their customer base and their future plans. The more you know about this market the more specific you can make your pitch – and the more you are likely to be successful.

Conclusion

Most would-be published writers are pessimistic optimists. They are doubtful whether their writing will find its true appreciative audience – but they keep going just the same. Each of you can probably point to a published writer whose work got into print without the resources I have outlined: the celebrity whose book was written by someone else; the chick lit novel that for some reason caught popular imagination and having got loads of press coverage achieved huge sales – even though you personally thought it was rubbish.

It's true, chance is a great thing, but please don't assume that all celebrity books are instant hits or that press coverage is routinely unplanned. And so many of today's bestselling writers spent years of hard graft before they achieved the celebrity status that we now assume came overnight. For the vast majority of would-be published writers, it is the persistence of their slog, their self-belief and their determination that ultimately keeps them going and achieves the publishing deal. Faint heart never won fair lady. Good luck!

Alison Baverstock is a former publisher who has written 19 books. *Marketing Your Book: An Author's Guide* (A&C Black 2007, 2nd edn) gives writers guidance on how to present their work to agents, publishers and readers. *Is There a Book in You?* (A&C Black 2006) outlines the resources needed by writers and offers advice on how to achieve publication. Her most recent book is *The Naked Author: A Guide to Self-publishing* (A&C Black 2011). She teaches marketing – to authors, publishers and others – at Kingston University. Her website is www.alisonbaverstock.com.

See also...

- *Understanding the publishing process*, page 215
- *Writing a synopsis*, page 118
- *Spotting a bestseller*, page 220
- *Dealing with rejection*, page 601

The state of commissioning

Nicholas Clee spoke to six editors at different mainstream publishing houses to find out their thoughts on commissioning books for the current market.

It has never been so easy to get books published, and possibly never so difficult to pursue a career as an author. The two phenomena are related. The proliferation of small publishers and self-publishing operations, all potential outlets for authors who cannot find homes at the leading firms, is in part the result of the same trends that have brought about consolidation at the heart of the book industry. There is a polarisation, between niche markets and the mass market for which the publishing giants largely cater. Authors operating in the niches are seeing their incomes dwindle, while those lucky and talented enough to hit the bestseller lists are the industry's equivalents of Premier League footballers.

Those of us still entertaining ambitions to place books with mainstream houses have been watching these trends with alarm. We sense that publishers are commissioning more cautiously; that they are committing huge advances to prestige properties, but otherwise paying less generously; and that they are increasingly liable to drop authors rather than try patiently to nurture their careers.

To get a picture of the established publishers' commissioning policies, I asked six editors to talk about how they approached their jobs: Ingrid Connell of Macmillan, Daniel Crewe of Profile, Kate Mills of Orion, Alexandra Pringle of Bloomsbury, Simon Prosser of Hamish Hamilton, and my own editor, Selina Walker of Bantam Press at Transworld. Connell and Crewe are non-fiction editors, while Mills specialises in fiction; the others do both. Their thoughts, grouped under key questions, are below. First, a bit of preamble about how we got here.

The consolidation of book publishing gathered pace in the 1980s. It coincided with a similar trend in book retailing, with the growth of chains such as Waterstones and Ottakar's eventually producing mergers and acquisitions, leaving us with one national specialist bookseller (Waterstones), one national mixed-multiple bookseller (WHSmith), and one dominant online bookseller (Amazon). But this consolidated industry was until the mid-1990s operating with a pricing regime – the Net Book Agreement (NBA), under which prices on books could not be discounted – devised to support diversity. When the NBA went, supermarkets saw an opportunity to sell books as loss leaders, and Amazon was able to build its business by offering all books, and bestsellers particularly, at dramatically reduced prices. Bestselling titles – ranging from celebrity memoirs (Peter Kay, Dawn French), to J.K. Rowling's Harry Potter novels, to books selected for the Richard & Judy television book club (e.g. *The Kite Runner*, *The Interpretation of Murder*) – sold in quantities that the industry had never previously achieved. But the overall market did not grow by much. Below the top rank, the sales figures were lower than before.

This new market changed the economic model underlying book contracts. Retailers were more powerful, and demanded bigger discounts, along with contributions to marketing costs. Base discounts rose to 50% or higher, and publishers often conceded more than 60% in order to get books in prominent displays and in three-for-two promotions. These concessions ate into royalties: authors started receiving four-fifths, three-fifths or even less of the standard rates. Authors whose books broke sales records thought it a fair exchange, but the rest felt the pinch. Now it seems that aggressive marketing of ebooks may depress prices still further.

I asked the following questions to find out what, in these circumstances, authors can expect of publishers.

Are you commissioning less?

Some time ago, publishers decided that they could sell more copies of fewer titles. They seem to have taken that policy as far as it will go. 'Our numbers are staying exactly the same,' Alexandra Pringle says. 'Four new fiction titles a month is the maximum we can do, because otherwise they wouldn't get enough oxygen. There'll be a lead, a subsidiary lead, a "wild horse" [an unconventional title, which just might capture people's imaginations], and perhaps a genre title.'

Ingrid Connell says of Macmillan: 'We're not commissioning less – we've never had an overstuffed list', and Simon Prosser confirms: 'The Hamish Hamilton list has always been small and selective, and that hasn't changed.' Kate Mills says that Orion's numbers are also stable: 'We do 60 new [fiction] titles, in hardback or trade paperback, a year.'

Are you commissioning more conservatively?

'We're certainly commissioning more cautiously, and possibly more conservatively,' Selina Walker says. 'And we're pulling back from paying large advances when there's a substantial risk of not earning out [leaving a portion of the advance unearned by sales].' Simon Prosser says: 'It's harder to persuade yourself to take a risk on something you know is very left-field.'

As Daniel Crewe points out, publishers look at proposals in the knowledge that the number of large retailers that might back the subsequent books has diminished. Ingrid Connell gives an example:Borders was an enthusiastic supporter of books on music and popular culture; since the collapse of the chain, only a percentage of those sales has migrated elsewhere. Also, the decline in subscription figures, as booksellers cut their initial orders and reorder if necessary, has forced publishers to lower their print runs, to levels at which certain books become unviable. A paperback with a print run of only 2,000 copies is not, for a large publishing house, an attractive undertaking.

It can be easier to sign up new authors, who do not have compromising sales records and who may have stories that will attract publicity, than established ones. 'I had to turn down a book by a brilliant writer, because the BookScan numbers [the sales record of previous books] were too low,' Ingrid Connell says. 'You can't overcome that.' Some authors resort to pseudonyms. In the USA, novelist Patricia O'Brien received numerous rejections for her sixth novel before resubmitting it under the pseudonym Kate Alcott; an offer arrived within days.

What factors convince you to take on a book?

The potential support of booksellers has already been mentioned. While editors are aware of the risks of second-guessing booksellers' responses, they say that, more than ever before, they have to form a clear picture of how they can make a book appealing to readers. 'People who think they understand what the market will want are mad,' Alexandra Pringle says. 'You can't publish for the market. For us at Bloomsbury, it's whether a range of people are excited about a book – in editorial, in sales, in marketing, in publicity, and in rights. With novels, it helps if they're easy to talk about in a paragraph. How you're going to publish has to be a kind of three-dimensional picture in your head.'

'It's very interesting that Alexandra, from a more literary list, looks on it in the same way as I do,' says Selina Walker at Bantam Press. 'We all have to be, to use a horrible word, market-facing.'

What influence does this market-led approach exert on what gets published?

All the editors insist that there is still room on their lists for quirky books, and even for apparently uncommercial ones. Alexandra Pringle says: 'Georgina Harding [*The Solitude of Thomas Cave, The Spy Game*] is an exceptional writer, but she's also a quiet writer – you don't have an obvious hook to help get her into the trade. But we continue to publish her. We continued to publish Kamila Shamsie, selling about 5,000 copies of each title, and then we brought out *Burnt Shadows*, which has sold 100,000 copies to date.'

Selina Walker says: 'I'm a great believer that a really good book will break out and find a market, especially if you're passionate about it right from the start – as Stieg Larsson's novels did for Quercus, and as *American Wife* [Curtis Sittenfeld] and *The Book Thief* [Marcus Zusak] did for us.'

Daniel Crewe says: 'I believe that you can create markets for a book. It's increasingly common to start with a very low sub [initial order from booksellers] and find that a book goes on to sell very well. If the publicity and marketing are good, you can get booksellers to respond to a market you've created. It may sound very idealistic, but if a book is good enough you ought to be able to make it work.'

Simon Prosser took on for Hamish Hamilton *The Collected Stories of Lydia Davis*. A 700-page volume of short stories by a little-known American writer is not the most obviously commercial venture. But the stories have influential fans; and Prosser loves them too. 'You have to have complete passion for a book, take a deep breath, and hope that there is something you can do to help it find a way to readers.'

A book that attempts to exploit a formula will not necessarily charm editors. 'It's a mistake to see a bandwagon and jump on it,' Kate Mills says. 'A few years ago, when chick lit sales were declining, a few of those authors decided to try writing blockbusters instead. I don't think the books fared very well. The books that are most successful are the genre-busters and genre-creators, such as Kate Mosse's *Labyrinth* – her passion for that story seeped off the page. A few authors have tried to follow her, but they haven't succeeded.'

Readers seem to yearn for empathy, Ingrid Connell says. So they like books by people who have been on television, and who have become part of their everyday lives – a television star is more likely to sell books than a Hollywood star. Heartwarming or heartbreaking stories, involving people or pets, are also in vogue.

What are the qualities of a successful author?

Authors have to be 'market-facing' too, editors agree. Tweeting, blogging, Facebooking, giving talks, thinking of angles for media coverage: these are all activities that are likely to win publishers' thanks.

One of Kate Mills' authors, Veronica Henry, wrote a piece for the *Daily Mail* about the 'nasty surprises' she encountered on moving to Exmoor. The piece attracted more than 200 comments, many of them angry, on the *Mail* website. 'But Veronica is realistic that this is all part of what an author has to do.'

How precarious are authors' careers?

The editors concede that it is difficult to persist with authors whose books fail to sell strongly. 'We published three books by Alessandro Baricco and couldn't make them work,'

Simon Prosser says. 'Now Jamie [Byng, at Canongate] has taken him on – and that's good. I hope he's successful.' Alexandra Pringle says: 'We drop very few authors, but just occasionally you come to the conclusion that you'll have to let another publisher have a go.'

However, the editors say that they make efforts to manage their authors' careers. 'I find that I spend less of my time acquiring and more with authors who are already on the list,' Selina Walker says. 'For example, we published five books by Stephen Clarke [*A Year in the Merde*, etc], with diminishing sales, so we came up with the idea for a bigger book, *1000 Years of Annoying the French*. It was a *Sunday Times* top ten bestseller for weeks.'

'At Orion,' Kate Mills says, 'We have always prided ourselves on being a publisher of authors, not books – Ian Rankin is always held up as the great example. [Rankin published several novels with Orion before making his breakthrough.] If an author hasn't been selling well, we sit down and look at what we can do to improve things.'

The death of the midlist – occupied by authors whose books do not make the bestseller charts – has been a subject of debate for years. 'Midlist' has become almost a taboo word, a synonym for failure. But Kate Mills embraces it. 'To be midlist, solidly consistent, is no bad thing in this climate – although of course you hope that every author's career will have an upward trajectory. I can think of authors who might be classified as midlist but who are much loved, and we're delighted to have them.'

Are you optimistic?

Alexandra Pringle: 'I'm very optimistic. We're doing well. This is an exciting time for Bloomsbury.'

Simon Prosser: 'You couldn't stay in the business if you weren't an incorrigible optimist. I believe that people will carry on reading books and wanting stories, whether in print or on a Kindle or iPad – that's only a matter of format.'

There is every reason to be optimistic about books and reading. But, in spite of these editors' best hopes, the survival of the economic model of the industry that has sustained authors is less certain; and what will succeed it, no one knows.

Nicholas Clee is Joint Editor of the book industry information service BookBrunch (www.bookbrunch.co.uk).

See also...

- *A year in view of the publishing industry*, page 313
- *Who owns whom in publishing*, page 322
- *Spotting a bestseller*, page 220

Understanding publishing agreements

Publishers enter into a legal contract with authors or their agents when they sign them to publish their book. Gillian Davies demystifies some of the clauses in such agreements.

Publishing agreements are contracts and are governed by contract law, the defining feature of which is that it treats parties to the contract as being of equal standing. To put this in context, there are other areas of the law where it has been decided as a matter of policy that there is a 'weaker party' who needs to be protected. For example, in consumer law the consumer is regarded as being 'weaker' than an internet retailer; and in employment and discrimination law a person with disabilities or a pregnant employee is deemed 'weaker' than the employer. But this is not so with publishing agreements, albeit that we all know the reality of the situation is that the author/writer is the one (usually) who wants a publishing deal and the publisher, in certain circumstances, can take it or leave it so can dictate the terms.

If you have a literary agent, she or he should handle all these issues for you; and if you are a member of the Writers' Guild, the National Union of Journalists (NUJ) or the Society of Authors, they will help review the details of a contract. The main resource for lawyers in this field is *Clark's Publishing Agreements* (ed. Lynette Owen; Bloomsbury Professional 2010, 8th edn) which costs a hefty £160. It sets out standard form contracts for various kinds of publications. The contract for 'General book–author–publisher' has 35 clauses, some of which are 'legal nuts and bolts' and need not concern us too much – they are there to ensure the contract operates properly and can be enforced (e.g. 'Arbitration', 'Interpretation', 'Entire Agreement', '*Force majeure*', 'Notices').

What follows are some of the more significant clauses which will be key for writers. Whatever kind of contract you see, remember that in principle you can add, delete and amend any of the clauses in it. In practical terms, it will depend on how much clout you or your agent have as to whether your publisher will be happy to negotiate or not and, perhaps to a certain extent, on the time available.

Rights

Rights are multiple and sub-divisible. You can license them outright or in part (e.g. sound recording not images, script not film, illustrations not text, English translation not other languages), and do so for a set period of time or forever (i.e. the duration of the copyright). You can choose the territory (e.g. the film *Clockwork Orange* was not released in the UK but it was in France). You can grant exclusive or non-exclusive rights.

It is important that you license and do not *assign* your rights as assignation is almost impossible to reverse. If you must assign copyright, note that you would have a small chance of legal protection because the publisher may owe you 'fiduciary duties', i.e. be obliged to look after your best interests.

Most publishers will want 'all rights' and 'world rights', but you or your agent may want to negotiate to retain certain rights. Consider whether the publisher would consult you before transferring their rights to a third party: they should. Would the publisher act on your behalf if someone else is in breach of your copyright? Would the publisher protect your work to the best possible extent? For example, if the work is posted online, would it be tagged for permissions information to enable anyone who wants to reuse it to find you or the publisher in order to ask permission? Subsidiary rights include, for example, anthology rights.

Serial rights are generally offered as 'first' and 'second'. First serial rights are often retained by authors and refer to the right to publish elsewhere, for example in a magazine feature in advance of a book's publication. Second serial rights can belong to a different party and are often controlled by the publisher. They concern rights to reprint after the book's publication.

Delivery, acceptance and approval

The publisher will want to make sure it is not committing itself to publishing work which is not what it commissioned or not as expected and should of course be able to reject work which is poor, or which it considers to be factually incorrect or libellous. But what can you do if a publisher wants to reject your work because the economic climate has changed since you were commissioned, or it simply changes its mind because the market seems suddenly flooded with that kind of work? The Society of Authors used to advise writers to not sign 'acceptance' clauses for this type of reason, arguing that publishers should fully assess the work by asking for a synopsis and specimen chapters, rather than letting an author complete the work, submit it and have it rejected. You may be powerless to remove such a clause but it is something to be aware of.

Timing of publication may also be important. For example, if you are writing a law book and the publisher fails to get it to press within a reasonable time, the book may well be so out of date as to be useless, and consequently your reputation would suffer as well as sales. Another example may be that the publisher has budgetary reasons for the timing of publication or may want to link, for example, a sports book with an event such as the opening of the Olympic Games. These types of situations may be covered in a clause about 'Date of publication' or 'Publisher's responsibility to publish'.

Warranties and indemnities

With warranties and indemnities you 'warrant' to the publisher that you have done certain things like fact-checking, copyright clearance, checking there are no libellous statements, etc and promise to 'indemnify' them against any losses they may suffer as a result of anything like that happening after publication. I have seen some lawyer authors strike these out. In practice, you need to consider whether you would be in a financial position to indemnify a publisher against its loss – most individuals wouldn't be, especially against libel actions. (Remember, you cannot defame the dead but you can defame a business entity, so beware when writing blogs.) However, you may be confident that no issues will arise (famous last words); or you may be happy that you are 'decree proof' (no point suing you, you have no money); or you may have professional indemnity or another kind of insurance. Insurance is something authors and writers should consider if they focus on particular subjects (e.g. writing about medical dosages) or are of a certain profile.

Royalty advances and payment

An 'advance' is an advance on royalties which will be earned on book sales. This is different from a flat fee that is paid for a commission. Obviously, royalties are a very good thing if sales are to be significant, but they are perhaps less useful to authors whose markets are small, such as academic or specialised areas, or for children's authors who receive lower royalty rates (say 5% of the book's published price rather than the 10% a writer of fiction for adults might receive), albeit perhaps dealing with bigger volumes. Some novelists receive huge advances that are never recouped by the publisher; the writers will receive royalty statements reporting a deficit but most publishers do not expect that deficit to be repaid. Clarifying what would happen about an unrecouped advance is therefore crucial.

(Keep royalty statements for tax reasons: declare royalties as 'income' not 'other expenses'; losses/unrecouped advances are 'expenses' for income tax.)

If you are to receive royalties only, or an advance on royalties, it is important that someone is actually going to market the book. The clause 'Production and promotion responsibility' refers to this.

If the royalties payable to you are expressed as a percentage of estimated receipts (what the publisher actually earns from the sale of your book) rather than as a percentage of the book's published price, you will want to ask the publisher what they estimate receipts to be. However, the publisher may wish that information to be confidential.

Date of payment

As an author, when do you want to be paid? Probably on receipt by the publisher of your manuscript at the latest, if not on commission – depending on the job and your status. You do not want to be paid 'on publication' because for reasons beyond your control the book may never be published, for example due to the publisher going bust.

When does a publisher want to pay? Possibly not on receipt of the manuscript because there is still the copy-editing, typesetting and printing to carry out.

Payment in three stages is pretty standard – on signature; on delivery of the manuscript; and on the day of first UK publication. Four stages are also possible: as with three but with the third stage broken down into publication of hardback and of paperback editions.

The contract

As with most things in life, it is best to avoid contention, adversity and dispute where possible. Bear in mind that most publishers will be using a precedent form, i.e. a pro forma document. This may be historical or inherited from another part of the publishing group or a subsidiary/parent group and edited for your particular publication, so do not be surprised if it needs tweaking or renegotiating on issues which are important to you. Be firm and be understanding. The contract is possibly not the author's preferred focus, and it might also be a chore for the publisher.

Note too that you may have legal rights and remedies from areas of the law which are external to the contract, i.e. some things that are not explicitly written down in a contract may be enforceable by you under equity, breach of confidence, etc. The Contracts (Rights of Third Parties) Act 1999, for example, might be interpreted by lawyers to mean that if an author tells the publisher to 'pay my royalties to my friend', the friend gets the legal right to sue the publisher under the contract if this does not happen.

Publishing agreements are a minefield but if you can think about what is most important for you and your publication and its markets, and be aware of some of the issues noted above, you will at least be off to a good start.

Gillian Davies MA (Hons), LLB is the author of *Copyright Law for Artists, Designers and Photographers* (A&C Black 2010) and *Copyright Law for Writers, Editors and Publishers* (A&C Black 2011).

Doing it on your own

Reasons for self-publishing are varied. Many highly respected contemporary and past authors have published their own works. Peter Finch outlines the implications of such an undertaking.

Why bother?

You've tried all the usual channels and been turned down; your work is uncommercial, specialised, technical, out of fashion; you are concerned with art while everyone else is obsessed with cash; you need a book out quickly; you want to take up small publishing as a hobby; you've heard that publishers make a lot of money out of their authors and you'd like a slice – all reason enough. But be sure you understand what you are doing before you begin.

But isn't this cheating? It can't be real publishing – where is the critical judgement? Publishing is a respectable activity carried out by firms of specialists. Writers of any ability never get involved.

But they do. Start self-publishing and you'll be in good historical company: Horace Walpole, Balzac, Walt Whitman, Virginia Woolf, Gertrude Stein, John Galsworthy, Rudyard Kipling, Beatrix Potter, Lord Byron, Thomas Paine, Mark Twain, Upton Sinclair, W.H. Davies, Zane Grey, Ezra Pound, D.H. Lawrence, William Carlos Williams, Alexander Pope, Robert Burns, James Joyce, Anaïs Nin and Lawrence Stern. All these at some time in their careers dabbled in doing it themselves. William Blake did nothing else. He even made his own ink, handprinted his pages and got Mrs Blake to sew on the covers.

But today it's different?

Not necessarily. This is not vanity publishing we're talking about although if all you want to do is produce a pamphlet of poems to give away to friends then self-publishing will be the cheapest way. Doing it yourself today can be a valid form of business enterprise. Being twice shortlisted for major literary prizes sharpened Timothy Mo's acumen. Turning his back on mass-market paperbacks, he published *Brownout on Breadfruit Boulevard* on his own. Billy Hopkin's bestseller of Lancashire life, *High Hopes* (Headline), began as a self-published title, as did G.P. Taylor's children's book *Shadowmancer* (Faber), which topped the list of bestsellers for 15 weeks.

Can anyone do it?

Certainly. If you are a writer then a fair number of the required qualities will already be in hand. The more able and practical you are then the cheaper the process will be. The utterly inept will need to pay others to help them, but it will still be self-publishing.

Where do I start?

With research. Read up on the subject. Make sure you know what the parts of a book are. You will not need to become an expert but you will need a certain familiarity. Don't rush. Learn.

What about ISBN numbers?

International Standard Book Numbers – a standard bibliographic code, individual to each book published, are used by booksellers and librarians alike. They are issued by the Nielsen

ISBN Agency at a cost of £118.68 including VAT for ten, although prices are under review. Self-publishers may balk at this apparently inordinate expense but the ISBN is the device used by the trade to track titles and, if you are serious about your book, including one should be regarded as essential. There are full details of the Agency's services on its website (www.isbn.nielsenbook.co.uk); see also *FAQs about ISBNs* on page 297.

Next?

Put your book together – be it the printed-out pages of your novel, your selected poems or your story of how it was sailing round the world – and see how large a volume it will make. If you have no real idea of what your book should look like, go to your local bookshop and hunt out a few contemporary examples of volumes produced in a style you would like to emulate. Take your typescript and your examples round to a number of local printers and ask for a quote.

How much?

It depends. How long is a piece of string? Unit cost is important: the larger the number of copies you have printed the less each will cost. Print too many and the total bill will be enormous. Printing has gone through a revolution in recent years. The arrival of POD (print on demand) and other digital technologies have reduced costs and made short runs much more economic. But books are still not cheap.

Can I make it cost less?

Yes. Do some of the work yourself. If you want to publish poems and you are prepared to use a text set on your computer, you will make a considerable saving. Most word processing programs have publishing facilities which will enhance the look of your text. Could you accept home production, run the pages off on a copier, then staple the sheets? Editions made this way can be very presentable.

For longer texts savings, can be made by supplying the work as a digital file directly to a printer. But be prepared to shop around.

Who decides how it looks?

You do. No one should ever ask a printer simply to produce a book. You should plan the design of your publication with as much care as you would a house extension. Spend as much time and money as you can on the cover. It is the part of the book your buyer will see first. If you're stuck, employ a book designer.

How many copies should I produce?

Poetry books can sell about 200 copies, new novels sometimes manage 1,000, literary paperbacks 10,000, mass-market blockbusters half a million. But that is generally where there is a sales team and whole distribution organisation behind the book. When using traditional methods of production do not, on the one hand, end up with a prohibitively high unit cost by ordering too few copies. Fifty of anything is usually a waste of time. On the other hand, can you really sell 3,000? Will shops buy in dozens? They will probably only want twos and threes. Take care. Research your market first. If you worry then use POD as it allows for tiny print runs and avoids the risk of having to hold stock. The downside is that POD can significantly increase the unit cost.

How do I sell it?

With all your might. This is perhaps the hardest part of publishing. It is certainly as time consuming as both the writing of the work and the printing of it put together. To succeed here you need a certain flair and you should definitely not be of a retiring nature. If you intend selling through the trade your costing must be correct and worked out in advance. Shops will want at least 35% (with national chains asking for even more) of the selling price as discount. You'll need about the same again to cover your distribution, promotion and other overheads, leaving the final third to cover production costs and any profit you may wish to make. Multiply your unit production cost by at least four. Commerical publishers often multiply by as much as nine.

Do not expect the trade to pay your carriage costs. Your terms should be at least 35% post free on everything bar single copy orders. Penalise these by reducing your discount to 25%. Some shops will suggest that you sell copies to them on sale or return. This means that they only pay you for what they sell and then only after they've sold it. This is a common practice with certain categories of publications and often the only way to get independent books into certain shops; but from the self-publisher's point of view it should be avoided if at all possible. Cash in hand is best but expect to have your invoices paid by cheque at a later date. Phone the shops you have decided should take your book or turn up in person and ask to see the buyer. Letters and sample copies sent by post will get ignored. Get a freelance distributor to handle all of this for you if you can. But expect to be disappointed. Independent book representatives willing to take on a one-off title are as rare as hen's teeth. Expect to have to go it alone.

Successful selling through Amazon, the holy grail for many publishers, is easier than you might think. The company encourage individuals to include their titles on their website. Fulfilment of orders can be done either directly by the self-publisher or by them or, where there is sufficient demand, through Amazon's own warehouses. There is no financial risk but you will have to give Amazon a commission. Check their website for details. Worth doing? You'd be a fool not to.

What about promotion?

A vital aspect often overlooked by beginners. Send out as many review copies as you can, all accompanied by slips quoting selling price and name and address of the publisher. Never admit to being that person yourself. Invent a name: it will give your operation a professional feel. Ring up newspapers and local radio stations ostensibly to check that your copy has arrived but really to see if they are prepared to give your book space. Buying advertising space rarely pays for itself but good local promotion with 100% effort will generate dividends.

What about depositing copies at the British Library?

Under the Copyright Acts the British Library, the Bodleian Library, Oxford, the University Library, Cambridge, the National Library of Scotland, the Library of Trinity College Dublin and the National Library of Wales are all entitled to a free copy of your book which must be sent to them within one month of publication. One copy should go direct to the Legal Deposit Office at the British Library, Boston Spa, Wetherby, West Yorkshire LS23 7BY. The other libraries use the Agency for the Legal Deposit Libraries, 161 Causewayside, Edinburgh EH9 1PH (www.legaldeposit.org.uk). Contact them directly to find out how many copies they require.

And what if it goes wrong?

Put all the unsolds under the bed or give them away. It has happened to lots of us. Even the big companies who are experienced at these things have their regular flops. It was an adventure and you did get your book published. On the other hand you may be so successful that you'll be at the London Book Fair selling the film rights and wondering if you've reprinted enough.

Can the internet help?

The web is well on the way to taking the place of traditional print. No self-respecting author should be without their own personal website. From here you can advertise yourself and your works, and offer downloadable samples, or complete books. This method of self-promotion comes highly recommended. Self-publishers should get on board now.

The power of blogging and social networking should also not be ignored. Self-publishers will benefit enormously from setting up a Facebook page devoted to their titles, from sending out tweets pushing the works and from writing a blog about the whole process. None of this will cost anything more than time. Do it now.

The internet is also thick with operators offering to promote or publish work electronically. These range from companies which post sample chapters and then charge readers a fee for the complete work to professional ebook developers who offer books fully formatted for use on hand-held and other devices.

Peter Finch is a poet, author and psychogeographer. Until recently, he was Chief Executive of Literature Wales, the Literature Development Agency. He is a former bookseller and small publisher and author of the *How to Publish Yourself*. His website contains further advice for self-publishers (www.peterfinch.co.uk).

See also...

- *Self-publishing in ebook*, page 294
- *Helping to market your book*, page 306
- *Print on demand*, page 317
- *Vanity publishing*, page 329
- *Electronic publishing*, page 581
- *Marketing yourself online*, page 587
- *Managing your online reputation*, page 591

Further reading

Baverstock, Alison, *The Naked Author – The Complete Guide to Self-publishing*, A&C Black, 2011

Buchanan, Mike, *The Joy of Self-publishing: Self-publishing and Publishing with the Print-on-Demand and Digital Print Models of Lightning Source*, LPS Publishing, 2010

Finch, Peter, *How to Publish Yourself*, Allison & Busby, 4th edn, 2000

Hamilton, April, *The Indieauthor: Self-publishing Strategies Anyone Can Use*, Writers Digest Books, 2010

Kendall, Laura J., *How I Wrote, Self-published and Started My Books Online*, Kindle Edition, 2012

Lupton, Ellen, *Indie Publishing: How to Design and Produce Your Own Book*, Princeton University Press, 2008

Penn, Joanna, *From Idea to Book: Writing, Self-publishing and Print-on-demand... for Your Book*, Lulu, 2009

Ross, Marilyn and Collier, Sue, *The Complete Guide to Self-Publishing*, Writer's Digest Books, 5th edn, 2010

The Self-publishing Magazine, www.selfpublishingmagazine.co.uk

Self-publishing in ebook

In recent years the number of people self-publishing in ebook format has grown enormously. Nicholas Clee looks at why and how it is done.

Who would have imagined, in the days when the *Writers' & Artists' Yearbook* regularly offered dire warnings about vanity presses, that we would ever see a bestseller list on which five of the top ten titles were self-published? Yet that is the position at Amazon's Kindle store as I write. Some authors have sold tens of thousands of ebooks, even hundreds of thousands, through the Kindle platform and others. And they have not paid anything for the privilege. Vanity presses would charge thousands of pounds, print a few books if the author was lucky, and rarely sell any of them. The cost of uploading a file to Kindle and many other e-publishing platforms is zero.

The poster girl for ebook self-publishing is Amanda Hocking, a young (born in 1984) writer from Austin, Minnesota. Hocking writes prolifically in the fashionable genre – since the success of Stephenie Meyer's *Twilight* series – of paranormal romance. She began uploading her work in the *My Blood Approves* and *Trylle* series in April 2010, and a year later she had sold more than one million copies of nine novels, earning a reported $2 million. British authors, as sales of Amazon's Kindle e-reading device in particular boomed on this side of the Atlantic, began to take advantage of digital self-publishing services too, albeit not quite at the Hocking level. Stephen Leather, already a successful thriller writer with a long-term relationship with Hodder & Stoughton, brought out electronic editions of three previously unpublished titles, and following Christmas 2010 began selling about 2,000 ebooks a day, earning about £11,000 a month. During the 2011 Christmas season, the bestselling author at Amazon's UK Kindle store was Kerry Wilkinson, who had written and published three novels starring a Manchester Detective Sergeant called Jessica Daniels.

Why do it?

Why might you want to publish your own book with Kindle, and with other ebook platforms? The predominant reason for self-publishing has always been an inability to find a deal with a mainstream publisher, and it is certain to continue to be the story of self-publishing in the digital age. It was Amanda Hocking's original motivation, for example. But Stephen Leather turned to self-publishing because he saw a way to bring out his novellas, which can be difficult to sell in bookshops (especially if varying in genre from an author's main work) that his publisher had not wanted to sign up. Reasoning that he was entering the market just as new Kindle owners were keen to play with their new toy, he thought he had a chance to grab their attention, while making them aware of his other novels as well. Some authors go further than this: in the USA, novelists such as Barry Eisler and J.A. Konrath are arguing that they no longer need conventional publishers to reach wide readerships, and that they can earn more by going it alone. Self-publishing is, for some, a way of promoting themselves; for others, it is the new model under which they hope to pursue their writing careers.

The first attraction of e-publishing for 'indie' authors, as they have become known, is that it is straightforward. Platforms such as Kindle Digital Publishing, which is estimated to account for at least 90% of the market in the UK at present, and Smashwords, which distributes ebooks in a variety of formats, are free services, and simple to navigate. You could upload your text file and jacket in 30 minutes. The services do not ask for exclusivity, but Amazon insists that you should not price your ebook more cheaply elsewhere.

A second attraction, in theory, is the royalty rate. Amazon pays authors a royalty of 70% from the sale of ebooks priced at the equivalent of $2.99 and above. Unfortunately, the market to date has shown that indie authors cannot hope to sell ebooks carrying such price tags. *Locked In*, Kerry Wilkinson's first Jessica Daniel novel, is as I write (self-published authors tend to adjust their prices frequently in bids to attract new readers) 98p on the Kindle store. For each 98p sale, Wilkinson earns 34.3p (35%). (This is also the rate for sales overseas.) While this is a higher percentage than you would get from a mainstream publishing house (the leading publishers' top rates for ebook sales are mostly 25% of price received), it is not a great deal of money; and the mainstream house might be able to get away with higher retail prices.

What sells?

Stephen Leather found his audience by pricing low. But the strategy can have disadvantages, in addition to the low returns: 'I sold my book *Dreamer's Cat* for 99 cents,' he reports, 'but despite a warning about sexual and violent content, I have received a lot of bad reviews from readers saying they were shocked. Once I raised the price to £1.99 the bad reviews stopped coming. Readers began to take the time to read the sample, and those readers who didn't like the sexual content simply didn't buy the book.'

At the UK Kindle store, the bestselling indie titles are all fiction, and are thrillers or romances. In the USA, they are more varied. As the market matures, the profiles of readers who buy ebooks will converge with those of purchasers of print books. Nevertheless, the ebook bestseller lists may well continue to feature the kinds of books that conventional bookshops tend to ignore: Mills & Boon-style romances, for example. As Stephen Leather has demonstrated, e-reader owners are enthusiastic about novella-length works, which seems to repel print book buyers. Who knows, maybe even the long-neglected Western genre could make a comeback.

Marketing

The buzzword in the book world at present is 'discoverability'. How do you get your products noticed if you do not have a physical shop in which to display them? If this is a problem for mainstream publishers, which at least have marketing departments, it is a greater challenge for indie authors. Stephen Leather got active online, using Facebook and Twitter and raising his profile on various forums. But now he is somewhat sceptical about such activity: 'Every indie writer now has a blog, they have a Facebook presence which they use to constantly push their work (a quarter of my Facebook "friends" are writers who do nothing other than post about their books) and they spend hours on the various ebook forums. It's all about the marketing. They ask for other writers to tag their books, they get friends and family to post favourable reviews (it's amazing how many self-published ebooks start off with half a dozen five-star reviews on Amazon, mostly from readers who have only ever reviewed the one book) and they share tweets with other writers.... Does it work? In the early days of e-publishing it probably did, because it was a new phenomenon, but these days there are just too many writers out there promoting their work that you really can't see the wood for the trees.'

Stephen continues: 'I know what doesn't work. Visiting the various forums and posting about your book won't get it into the bestseller lists. Neither will paid advertising. Neither will a blog. The way to get your book onto the bestseller list is to write a book that people want to read. Word of mouth will do the rest. Too many indie writers seem to think that you can create a buzz by just pushing your book down people's throats.... Word of mouth happens because people read a book that they have enjoyed and they tell their friends. You can't create that, it's down to the quality of the book.'

The end of mainstream publishing?

So, should you self-publish your book online? It is free, and you will not be ripped off if you go with the likes of Amazon or Smashwords, so you have very little to lose. But you must be realistic about why you are doing it, and about what your expectations are. Stephen Leather, for one, would prefer you to keep your first novel, and maybe even your second and third, in your bottom drawer: 'Now any book can be published, no matter how awful. And I think that's bad for writers,' he says.

Leather's success, and Amanda Hocking's, does not show that mainstream publishers are now irrelevant for authors: far from it. Leather says that he may bring out more books as an indie author, but insists that his main career is with Hodder, and that the main point of self-publishing has been to find new readers for his thrillers: 'I would guess that 90% of the readers who have bought my self-published ebooks had never heard of my traditionally published thrillers. There has been a knock-on effect with a lot of those new readers going on to buy my thrillers from my publisher. Plus there has been a lot of media interest from newspapers, magazines and radio.'

In March 2010, Amanda Hocking signed a $2 million deal with St Martin's Press and also got a deal with St Martin's sister company, Pan Macmillan, in the UK. A conventional publishing arrangement, she wrote, would ensure that her books were more widely available, and were better edited; it would also provide 'career stability'. To date, more authors agree with her than with Barry Eisler and J.A. Konrath. Following the reports of his self-publishing successes, Kerry Wilkinson signed with Pan Macmillan too.

Aspiring authors will be combing the *Writers' & Artists' Yearbook* for agents to represent them to publishers for a good while yet.

Nicholas Clee is Joint Editor of the book industry information service BookBrunch (www.bookbrunch.co.uk).

See also...

- *Doing it on your own,* page 290
- *Electronic publishing,* page 581
- *Marketing yourself online,* page 587
- *Managing your online reputation,* page 591

FAQs about ISBNs

The Nielsen ISBN Agency for UK & Ireland receives a large number of enquiries about the ISBN system. The most frequently asked questions are answered here.

What is an ISBN?

An ISBN (International Standard Book Number) is a product identifier used by publishers, booksellers and libraries for ordering, listing and stock control purposes. It enables them to identify a specific edition of a specific title in a specific format from a particular publisher. The digits are always divided into five parts, separated by spaces or hyphens. The five parts can be of varying length and are as follows:

Contact details

Neilsen ISBN Agency for UK and Ireland
3rd Floor, Midas House, 62 Goldsworth Road, Woking GU21 6LQ
tel (01483) 712215 *fax* (01483) 712214
email isbn.agency@nielsen.com
website www.isbn.nielsenbook.co.uk

- Prefix element – distinguishes the ISBN from other types of product identifier which are used for non-book trade products; three-digit number that is made available by GS1 (Global Standards – required for barcodes). Prefixes that have already been made available by GS1 are 978 and 979, but there may be a further prefix allocation made in the future as required to ensure the continued capacity of the ISBN system.
- Group Identifier – identifies a national, geographic or language grouping of publishers. It tells you which of these groupings the publisher belongs to (not the language of the book).
- Publisher Identifier – identifies a specific publisher or imprint.
- Title Number – identifies a specific edition of a specific title in a specific format.
- Check Digit – this is always and only the final digit which mathematically validates the rest of the number.

Since January 2007 all ISBNs are 13 digits long. The older ten-digit format can be converted to the 13-digit format by adding the 978 EAN (European Article Number, i.e. a 'barcode') prefix and recalculating the check digit.

Do all books need to have an ISBN?

There is no legal requirement for an ISBN in the UK and Ireland and it conveys no form of legal or copyright protection. It is a product identifier.

What can be gained from using an ISBN?

If you wish to sell your publication through major bookselling chains, or internet booksellers, they will require it to have an ISBN to assist their internal processing and ordering systems. The ISBN also provides access to bibliographic databases such as Nielsen's database and information services, which are organised using ISBNs as references. These databases are used by the book trade – publishers, booksellers and libraries – for internal purposes, to provide information for customers and to source and order titles. ISBNs are also used by Nielsen's order routing (Nielsen BookNet TeleOrdering) and sales analysis services (Nielsen BookScan) to monitor book sales. The ISBN therefore provides access to additional marketing opportunities which assist the sales and measurement of books (including ebooks and other digital products).

Where can I get an ISBN?

ISBN prefixes are assigned to publishers in the country where they are based by the national agency for that country. The UK and Republic of Ireland Agency is run by Nielsen. The Agency introduces new publishers to the system, assigns prefixes to new and existing publishers and deals with any queries or problems in using the system. The Nielsen ISBN Agency for UK & Ireland was the first ISBN agency in the world and has been instrumental in the set up and maintenance of the ISBN. Publishers based elsewhere will not be able to get numbers from the UK Agency but may contact them for details of the relevant agency in their market.

Who is eligible for ISBNs?

Any organisation or individual who is publishing a qualifying product for general sale or distribution to the market is eligible (see below, 'Which products do not qualify for ISBNs?').

What is a publisher?

The publisher is generally the person or body which takes the financial risk in making a product available. For example, if a product went on sale and sold no copies at all, the publisher is usually the person or body which loses money. If you get paid anyway, you are likely to be a designer, printer, author or consultant of some kind.

How long does it take to get an ISBN?

In the UK and Ireland the 'Standard' service time is ten working days. There is also a 'Fast Track' service, which is a three-working day processing period.

How much does it cost to get an ISBN?

In the UK and Ireland there is a registration fee which is payable by all new publishers. The fees for ISBNs are subject to review so applicants should check with the Agency. A publisher prefix unique to you will be provided and allows for ten ISBNs. Larger allocations are available where appropriate.

ISBNs are only available in blocks. The smallest block is ten numbers. It is not possible to obtain a single ISBN.

Which products do not qualify for ISBNs?

Calendars and diaries (unless they contain additional text or images such that they are not purely for time-management purposes); greetings cards, videos for entertainment; documentaries on video/CD-Rom; computer games; computer application programs; items which are available to a restricted group of people, e.g. a history of a golf club which is only for sale to members or an educational course book only available to those registered as students on the course.

Can I turn my ISBN into a barcode?

Since ISBNs changed to 13 digits in 2007 it has been possible (with the appropriate software) to use the same number to generate a barcode. Information about barcoding for books is available on the Book Industry Communication website (www.bic.org.uk).

What is an ISSN?

An International Standard Serial Number is the numbering system for journals, magazines, periodicals, newspapers and newsletters. It is administered by the British Library, *tel* (01937) 546959.

Who will edit your book?

The person who works in a publishing company, reviewing and revising final manuscripts is not the only one to edit books. Editorial input can be given at any point in a book's creation, and anyone who offers it is potentially an editor. Following a traditional route to a book being published, several professional editors may contribute to the process. Cressida Downing explains who they are and highlights the value of editing.

The author

The author is the first 'editor' of their text, as they change, revise and rethink it. Authors are always very close to the work, so although they are best placed to make changes, they can find it hard to be dispassionate and understand what needs doing. It's useful for an author to put their writing away for a short period so that when they come to it fresh, it is almost as if they are divorced from the writing process and editing is easier.

Many authors are on Twitter, and use one of two hashtags as they work: either #amwriting or #amediting. A search for either will reveal a live congregation of writers all busy writing or editing, which can be a useful source for tips or just reassuring company.

The literary agent

Once a literary agent takes an author on, it is sometimes assumed that the author's work is done. It's very rare that the accepted manuscript is published just as it is. Agents take authors on because they like their work, but that is not the same as an uncritical acceptance of the text as it stands. Agent Carole Blake mentioned at a recent conference for writers that she helped one of her authors with 17 revisions of a book before she considered it ready to be submitted to publishers.

Publishers used to undertake more responsibility for turning the raw text of a manuscript into a marketable book, but as the competition has got tougher and publishers are under more pressure, agents are providing them with more polished work. So the second editor can be the literary agent. They can often see a book's potential but may feel it needs changing or tightening up, or even requires a different ending. It's a two-way process, with the author and agent sitting down together to discuss the work. For an agent to ask an author to change something, they have to be able to give reasons, and it has to be something the author wants to do. At this stage, an agent may bring in a freelance editor or consultant to help the author with the nitty-gritty of what needs doing, although not all agents offer this option.

Once the agent and author are both happy with the manuscript, it goes out for submission to editors at publishing houses. When a book is acquired, the author is taken on by an editor for their list. A good literary agent will know the different editors in all the publishing houses and the shape of the lists they are building, and can see how the author's work may fit into those lists. Many editors are feted in the industry for their editorial style and skill, and they can influence the nature of the publishing marketplace.

The publisher's editor and agent enter into a relationship, both intimately connected to the book and both are committed to getting the best possible finished work written by the author.

The publisher's editor

The editor in the publishing house has one of several titles: commissioning, acquistions or development editor, or 'publisher'. This is the person who is responsible for a 'list' of titles in a particular genre, for example cookery books, mind, body & spirit titles, or commercial fiction, or books aimed at a particular readership, such as young adults. The work of the commissioning editor is the next stage in the process. He or she will have their own suggestions for the author and the manuscript will get reworked again.

Different book manuscripts need varying degrees of editing. Sometimes it's down to a simple change of emphasis, or the rearrangement of a chapter or two. Other books may need a lot more work done on them. It's not uncommon for an editor to suggest a new ending, a different character, a different viewpoint or even a change of genre. It's all down to shaping; the author provides a rough diamond, and a good editor can decide how it can be cut and polished to make it sparkle, grab the attention of the reader and really complement its setting.

In addition to the commissioning editor, copy-editors are employed to work on the detailed editing of manuscripts: they dot 'is' and cross 'ts'. Copy-editors sometimes work in-house but are mainly freelance professionals. They will be asked to look at a full manuscript once the commissioning editor, agent and author are happy with the structure and content of the book: when it is ready for entering into the production stages and just needs a final and detailed review. The copy-editor looks out for inconsistencies, spelling errors, grammatical infelicities. They will be in touch with the author, who will have the final say as to what changes to his or her text are made, either direct or via the in-house editor.

Each editor has an invaluable role. They can look at a script with an independent, professional and fresh eye:

> 'My editor improved my book in places I didn't even realise needed improving. Almost every author I know is told at some point that their narrative drive is lacking or that the pace is off. This is one area that it's very difficult to judge [when it is] your own work. In neither case was it particularly difficult to remedy with some judicious suggestions from someone who was seeing it with fresher eyes.' – Christina Hopkinson, author of *The Pile at the Bottom of the Stairs*

An editor can act a bit like a book doctor who can pinpoint why it looks a bit pasty around the middle (needs flabby description removing) or why it's limping (plot a little unlikely here). The best editors identify a problem or weakness that the author was already aware of, but hadn't been able fully to diagnose.

The relationship between an author and their commissioning editor can be so vital that some authors have a 'key person' clause written into their contract. If an author signs to a publishing house, they are allocated an editor – *their* editor – and that relationship strengthens over time. If that editor moves on to another publishing house, the author can have a clause that allows them to move with the editor; so they are in effect tied to the editor rather than the publishing house.

Writers often worry that having their work edited would take away their essential 'voice'. When literary agents and editors talk about 'voice', it means more than just style; it is the author's flavour – it's the author – in written form. Editors don't do the rewriting – they send the author to explore in different directions or perhaps ask for a character to be written out or made stronger. But the work and the writing are done by the author. A good editor never sacrifices an author's voice.

Self-publishing

While the advent of ebooks and cheap technology has led to an explosion in self-published titles, the editing process has been rather sidelined. By definition, a self-published author won't have access to either an agent or editors in a publishing house, but it's vitally important to get work published in the best possible state. Books are being published which contain basic errors that could be picked up by a copy-editor, and which also lack structure and discipline.

> 'I think authors need editors, and if the market ever changes so much that we're all self-publishing to ebooks (as we are in my imagined dystopian future), I'd get a freelance editor whose judgement I trusted. I think authors need a second pair of eyes, a new perspective, to see what works and what doesn't. Even when I don't agree with my editor, thinking about the points she makes sharpens my perception. By the time I get to sending a "finished" book off, I have no idea whether it really works or not and I always hugely value someone else's opinion.' – Emily Barr, author of *Stranded* (and ten other novels)

An author can pay a professional, or ask a trusted friend, to give a fresh look at their work and give feedback on it. An editorial consultant can help an author avoid repetition of key phrases, sift chapters of unnecessary details, and point out inconsistency of tone or frequent changes of narrative viewpoint.

'Editors are needed for reassurance, confirmation, eliminating doubt, collaboration, streamlining, and the killing off of darlings.' – Penny Hancock, author of *Tideline*

Cressida Downing is a freelance editorial consultant (www.thebookanalyst.co.uk) who has worked in bookselling and publishing for over 20 years.

See also...

- *Understanding the publishing process*, page 215
- *Making a successful submission to a literary agent*, page 418
- *Perfect proofs*, page 611

Marketing, publicising and selling books

Publishers have their own staff to market, publicise and sell their books but authors can also contribute to this process. Katie Bond outlines how to be a publisher's 'dream author'.

Newspapers are full of discouraging stories about how publishers only want to take on novels by glamorous young things or misery memoirs or celebrity autobiographies. Let's quash that immediately: publishers want to publish the best books they can find in a wide variety of genres and sell the socks off them. In the selling process, a 'promotable author' can make a major difference and my aim here is to take you through the run-up to your publication and suggest how even the most 'normal' author can give their book a push.

Word-of-mouth sales

When a publisher signs up an author, it is said that every book must be sold three times: by the editor to the rest of the company, by the sales/marketing/publicity departments to the bookseller and by the bookseller to the consumer. The most powerful sales tool in publishing is word of mouth and this begins in-house. A commissioning editor can entice everyone in the company to read a book so that a hundred people are talking about it – every mention is a potential sale. A recent example is *The Kite Runner* by Khaled Hosseini. This was one of those slow-burn books that took two years to become an international bestseller and reading group favourite. Such was the passion of its editor, Arzu Tahsin, for this novel that everyone at Bloomsbury read it and was 100% behind the book. Everyone played a part in its success by recommending the book to friends – personal recommendation being the number one factor in influencing a purchase according to all book-buying surveys. If an author is aware of this, every person you meet – at your publishing house (whether they're in the accounts department, on reception or the Sales Director), in bookshops and libraries, or indeed anywhere in your professional capacity as 'an author' – becomes a VIP. I will never forgetWilliam Boyd – the first author I spoke to in my first job as a publicity assistant – asking and remembering my name and chatting to me when he called to speak to my boss. Having read and loved his books at university, I would have walked over hot coals to make sure that *The Blue Afternoon* was a success and any request of his was instantly top of my list. Geographical distance from your publisher may mean that you don't get the chance to visit them often but do try to meet as many people in different departments as possible, go to book launches and readings, keep an eye on your publisher's website so you're up to date with what they're doing, and find out if your local sales rep would like to meet up for coffee when they're next on your patch. The only caveat here is that publishers can become flustered by over-keen authors – one used to lurk outside our offices with 'surprise' cappucinos!

Marketing and publicity

Marketing is an umbrella term that includes all the work a publisher does to promote or sell a book. Traditionally 'marketing' is categorised as anything paid for (catalogues, advertising, posters and bookshop promotions) and 'publicity' (media coverage, bookshop events and festivals) is free. There will be a person in both marketing and publicity departments assigned to your book and creating good relationships with both of them – particularly the publicist (although obviously I'm biased here) is crucial. Ask your editor to let you know who they are and contact them as early as possible to meet up and decide on a marketing and publicity plan.

The sell-in

The sales process begins 6–9 months prior to publication when the sales team use the marketing and publicity plans to begin selling books to the head offices of the major book chains – from Waterstones to Tesco, Amazon and the wholesalers who supply independent bookshops. Closer to publication, local sales reps also sell books to individual bookshops in their areas although the front-of-store promotions (Read of the Week, Buy One Get One Free, Book of the Month) will be decided at head office level. The 'sell-in' is this process of persuading the bookshops to stock a particular book. The marketing department produces sell-in materials including six-monthly catalogues promoting the publisher's spring and autumn lists, and AIs (advance information sheets), bound proofs and glossy brochures on individual books. The initial print run for a book is based on the sell-in figures of advance orders placed for it. The speed at which a book can be reprinted (except highly illustrated and special format books) minimises the clash between publisher caution and author optimism and prevents lost sales if the initial print run sells out quickly.

The sell-out

This is the magic moment when a customer decides to buy a book. Marketing and publicity are geared towards boosting the sell-out in a myriad of ways from advertising and media coverage to book jacket design and bookseller recommendation. A recent survey reported in the *Bookseller* revealed, 'The consumer needs at least five positive mentions of a product as well as easy availability before he will buy'. With over 120,000 new titles being published in the UK every year, it's a crowded marketplace and clear signposting is essential to enable the book to reach its target readership.

The book jacket and author photograph

'Never judge a book by its cover' is an outdated maxim. This is the most important marketing tool of all and can make or break a publication. Even if your novel was inspired by an old family portrait, don't insist on having it on the cover if it isn't an eye-catching image. Conversely, do ransack old photograph albums, magazines and art galleries for images that you love and that you think are right for your book. Candida Crewe's memoir *Eating Myself* has an utterly arresting black-and-white close-up photograph of her doleful childhood face on the jacket – it was provided by her and taken by her mother. For the author photograph, definitely allow yourself a little vanity – a really good black-and-white portrait is a must for publicity purposes and you want to look your absolute best.

Publicity

Book publicity is incredibly varied and widespread from reviews to features, discussions to news stories, public appearances at bookshops, libraries and literary festivals to local stock signings and books for competition prizes. As a rough guide, a publicist starts work on book tours and magazine advertising as much as six months ahead of publication. Finished copies of a book are printed approximately 6–8 weeks prior to publication and this period is the key time for confirming the media coverage to run on publication. The publication date is the peg for the media, so coverage becomes increasingly unlikely months or even weeks after the publication date unless the book has taken off in a major way and its success becomes the story.

How authors can help

There is a limited amount that an author can do to help sales and marketing directly beyond being very nice to booksellers and librarians, providing details of any specialist sales outlets prior to publication and (gently, not forcefully) offering to sign copies of your book in bookshops after publication (having first checked anonymously that the bookshop does have copies in stock). If a bookshop doesn't have your book in stock, let your publisher know rather than complaining to the bookshop directly. Also avoid the temptation – however tantalising – of moving your book to a more prominent position on the shelves. One author was repeatedly caught doing this until WHSmith's head office threatened to send all copies of the book back to the publisher and refuse to stock it any more.

Authors can best focus their energies on publicity where their input is vital. A publicist will be working on anything from 2–10 books in any one month so their time is limited. You need to give your publicist as much information as possible on your book, yourself and any potential publicity angles (see below). Together you can then agree the timescale of the publicity campaign, achievable and optimistic goals, how publicity will best sell your book and discuss any potential pitfalls. Be honest with your publicist and tell them the full story even if you decide not to talk about it to the media. Your publicist can advise you on how much of your private life to mine for publicity and how to maximise your control over the coverage. First-time novelist Clare Allan chose to write newspaper articles about how her ten years as a patient in mental hospitals had informed her novel *Poppy Shakespeare,* rather than be interviewed. Trust your instincts and don't let journalists pressurise you. Jon McGregor was longlisted for the Man Booker Prize for his first novel *If Nobody Speaks of Remarkable Things.* A *Guardian* journalist and photographer went to interview him in Nottingham and on discovering that he'd washed up dishes in a local restaurant to support himself whilst writing the book, tried to persuade him to be photographed at the kitchen sink. Jon declined. It was a wise decision as otherwise this picture would have haunted him for years.

Pre-publication checklist for the 'dream author'

Your publicist is your primary contact for sales/marketing/publicity so the information below should be given to them to help plan the campaign.

- Make contact with the marketer, publicist and local sales rep at your publisher.
- Fill in the publisher's author questionnaire and write a 500–1,000-word piece about how you came to write your book and what's new and different about it (for examples look at the 'I am the author of' section on Amazon.co.uk).
- Make contact with your local bookshop, library, writers' groups, reading groups and literary festival and let them know that your book is being published.
- Research specialist sales outlets (e.g. wool shops for a book about knitting, football club fanzines for a book about football, or maritime museums for a novel about Nelson).
- Give the sales team any relevant information to drive sales regionally (e.g. if you're Welsh/Scottish/Irish or you lived in Cornwall for 20 years and have a huge network of family and friends there though you've recently moved to Derby).

• Make a list of any possible media angles relating either to yourself or the book.
• Make a list of any media contacts, both local and national.
• Research any anniversaries, exhibitions, television series or films that tie in with your book or the themes of your book and could create media hooks.
• If you're writing non-fiction, list what's new and newsworthy in your book (e.g. new source material or new angle). Differentiate your book from others on the same subject and list the other books in the same field.
• As you know your book best, suggest 1,000–3,000-word extracts that might work as standalone newspaper pieces.
• Write a description of your book in approximately 100–300 words (think book jacket copy style).
• If you think you could write newspaper articles, write paragraph pitches of ideas with potential word lengths. (Think of specific newspapers when you're doing this and be ruthless. Ask yourself if the feature is *really* relevant for the *Daily Mail's* Femail pages/*The Times'* Comment pages/the *Observer's* Food Monthly.)
• Write a list of the contemporary authors you admire and particularly any authors whose work is similar to yours as their readers might enjoy your book.
• Look at your publisher's website and see if there is additional material you can provide – on your book or a review of another book or article/feature.
• If the idea of standing up in front of people and talking about your book makes you feel queasy, ask your publisher for media and presentation training (budget permitting of course). Alternatively, go to other author events to see what works and what doesn't. (Shorter is *always* better and enlist the help of an honest friend for feedback.)
• Plan, prepare and practice your author event (from choosing the right passage for a reading from the book – one that is dramatic, self-contained, character-introducing, with the all-important want-to-read-on factor – to interacting with the audience). If you are nervous, write out your talk and repeat it aloud in front of the mirror at home.
• Listen or watch every television or radio programme before you go on it and always know the presenter's name.

Above all, charm, good manners and hard-working professionalism are the staple of the 'dream author' and will open promotional doors time and time again. Joanna Trollope, *doyenne* of the book tour, says: 'I think the advice I'd give to a first-time author is that *all* publicity (with some reservations, obviously, about the tabloids), however seemingly small, is worth doing because the whole process is really joining up the dots in a dot-to-dot picture (which *might* even turn out to be a little golden goose) and that whatever you do, do it with the best grace possible because no-one in your professional life will ever forget that you were a treat to deal with.' Finally, when your friends and family tell you how much they love your book, ask them for a favour: a rave review on Amazon never goes amiss.

Katie Bond has been Publicity Director at Bloomsbury since 1999 and has handled PR for many bestsellers including Sheila Hancock's *The Two of Us,* Margaret Atwood's *The Blind Assassin*, Donna Tartt's *The Little Friend* and J.K. Rowling's *Harry Potter* books, as well as winning the first British Book Award's Publicity Nibbie in 2005 for Susanna Clarke's *Jonathan Strange and Mr Norrell.*

See also...

- *Helping to market your book,* page 306
- *How to publicise your book,* page 310

Helping to market your book

Alison Baverstock offers guidance on how authors can help to enhance their publisher's efforts to sell their book. The information in this article is also relevant to self-publishers.

Having a book accepted for publication is immensely satisfying – all the more so if in the process you have amassed a thick pile of rejection letters spanning several years. At this stage, some authors decide that, having committed themselves to work with a professional publishing house, this is the end of their involvement in the process. They will move on thankfully to write their next book.

Once you have delivered your manuscript and it has been accepted for publication, a publisher should handle all aspects of your book's subsequent development, from copy-editing and production to promotion and distribution. But there is a sound pragmatism in remaining vigilant. When it comes to the marketing of your book, there is a huge amount that you can do to help it sell.

The challenging marketplace

Each year in the UK alone, over 150,000 books get published or come out in new editions. All compete for the attention of the same review editors, the same stock buyers in bookshops, and the largely static number of regular book-buying members of the general public. It follows that anything an author can do to help 'position' the book, to make it sound different, or just more interesting than those it competes with, will be a huge advantage.

The marketing of books is not usually an area of high spending and there are many reasons why. Books are relatively cheap (a paperback novel costs about the same as a cinema ticket, and much less than a round of drinks), the publishers' profit margins are low, booksellers claim a percentage of the purchase price as discount (35%) and supermarkets and online selling facilities claim more, and books sell in relatively small quantities (a mass market novel selling 15,000 copies may be considered a 'bestseller' – compare that with the sales figures for DVDs or computer games). Your publisher will probably try to make maximum use of (free) publicity to stimulate demand using low-cost marketing techniques. They are far more likely to arrange for the insertion of a simple leaflet as a loose insert in a relevant publication, or organise a specific mailing to members of a relevant society, than book television or billboard advertising. Your assistance in helping them reach the market could be valuable.

Examine your resources

Think in detail about what resources you have at your disposal that would help your book to sell, and then tell your publisher. Most publishers send you a publicity form about six months before publication, to obtain details of your book and to find out how you feel it can best be marketed. Whilst the publisher will probably not be able to fulfil all your ambitions (mass market advertising is not possible for every title), they will be particularly interested in your contacts. For example, were you at school with someone who is now a features writer on *The Times*? Even if you have not spoken since, they may still remember your name. Do your children attend the same school as a contact on your local paper? Do you belong to a society or professional organisation that produces a newsletter for members, organises a conference or regular dining club? How many friends do you have on

Facebook, followers on Twitter, or email contacts? All these communication channels provide opportunities for publishers to send information on your book to potential purchasers and sources of publicity.

Even greater things may be achieved if you set up the arrangements yourself. Can you arrange for an editorial mention of your book in a society journal (which will carry more weight than an advertisement) or organise for your publisher to take advertising space at a reduced rate? Remember that the less it costs your publishing house to reach each potential customer, the more of the market they will be able to cover out of their planned budgetary spend.

Offer a peg to your publisher

In trying to stimulate demand for a book, publishers try to achieve publicity (or coverage in the media) at the time of publication. The most usual way of getting this is for the in-house publicist to send a press release about you and your book to journalists in the hope that they will be sufficiently interested to write about you or, even better, decide to interview you.

Your publisher will need 'pegs' on which to hang stories about you and your book, and it is helpful if you volunteer these rather than waiting to be asked. So, think back over your career and life in general. What is interesting about you? Are there any stories that arise out of the research for the book; incidents that give a flavour of the book and you as a writer?

Try to look at your life as others might see it; events or capabilities you take for granted might greatly interest other people. For example, novelist Catherine Jones (Kate Lace) is married to a former soldier, and moved house 15 times in 20 years. In that time she has produced three children and has had appointments with over 40 different classroom teachers. She speaks about her life in a very matter of fact way, but when she wrote her first novel, *Army Wives* (Piatkus), the media were quite fascinated by a world about which they clearly knew nothing. They found military jargon particularly compelling, and this proved a wonderful (and headline-producing) peg on which to promote her book.

Make yourself available

For a mass market title, any publicity that can be achieved needs to be orchestrated at the time of publication. By this time the publisher will hopefully have persuaded booksellers to stock the book and copies will be in the shops. If the publicity is successful, but peaks before the books are available to buy, this prime opportunity has been missed. If there is no publicity on publication, and no consequent demand, the bookseller has the right to return the books to the publisher and receive a credit note. And in these circumstances it will be *extremely* difficult to persuade them to restock the title having been let down once.

Timing is therefore crucial, so make yourself available at the time of publication (this is not the time to take your well-earned break). Remember too that, unless you are a very big star, each newspaper or programme approached will consider its own requirements exclusively, and will not be interested in your own personal schedule. Not all journalists work every day, and even if they do they like to decide on their own priorities. If you ask for an interview to be rescheduled, it may be dropped completely.

Don't assume that only coverage in the national media is worth having as local radio and newspapers can reach a very wide audience and be particularly effective in prompting sales. You may be able to extend the amount of time and space you get by suggesting a competition or reader/listener offer. Local journalists usually have a much friendlier approach than those who work on the nationals, so if you are a novice to the publicity process this can be a much easier start – and an opportunity to build your confidence.

Contributing text for marketing

At several stages in the production process your publisher may request your input. You may be asked to provide text for the book jacket or for an author profile, to check information that will be included in the publisher's annual catalogue, or to provide biographical information for their website.

Think carefully about the words you have been asked for, who will read them and in what circumstances, and then craft what you write accordingly. For example, the text on a fiction book jacket (or 'blurb') should not retell the story or give away the plot; rather it should send signals that convey atmosphere, whet the appetite of the reader and show what kind of book they can expect. A non-fiction blurb should establish what the book will do for the reader and your qualifications for writing it. Potential buyers are likely to be reading the blurb in a hurry, perhaps whilst standing in a bookshop being jostled by other shoppers, so it is best to keep it brief.

A third party recommendation of your book will help enormously as this provides objective proof of what it is like and how useful it is. When books have come out as hardbacks, extracts from review coverage can be useful on the paperback edition. (Every author should keep a rigorous record of their review coverage, copies of which your publisher should send you. Things do sometimes go missing or get lost, and you are far more likely to remember the good ones, given that you are looking after a much smaller number of books than your publisher.) For previously unpublished authors, a relevant quotation is very helpful instead. Do you know anyone established in the appropriate field who could provide an endorsement for what you have written? It doesn't have to be from anyone famous, just someone relevant. For example, a children's book endorsed as a gripping read by a ten-year-old, or an educational text endorsed by a student who had just passed her exams could both be effective.

If you are asked to write website copy, be sure to look at the relevant site before you draft something. Think about the context in which your material will be seen and read (by whom, how often and for how long) and use this information as the basis for writing.

Marketing after publication

Although most of the effort in marketing your book will inevitably occur in the weeks leading up to publication (because next month's schedule will bring forward further titles that need the marketing department's attention), there is a great deal of opportunity to carry on selling your book afterwards.

So, if you are asked to speak at a conference or run a training course, ask if your book can be included in the package available to delegates, either as part of the overall price or at a reduced rate. Ask the publisher for simple flyers (leaflets) on your book which you can hand out on suitable occasions. Then ask the organisers to put a copy inside the delegate pack, on every seat, or in a pile at the back of the hall (or preferably all three!). Similarly, you could consider running a competition through a local newspaper or giving a talk in a bookshop or school.

Give your publisher the details of speaking engagements or conferences at which they could usefully mount a display of all their titles (your own included). Even though they published your book, you cannot reasonably expect them to be specialists in every specific field you know intimately, so give them *all* the details they need. For a conference this would include the full title (not just the initials you refer to it by), the organiser's address and contact numbers (not the chairperson's address to which you should send associated papers), the precise dates and times, and any associated deadlines (e.g. stand bookings placed before a certain date may be cheaper). Finally, try to plan ahead rather than passing on key details at the last minute (this is one of publishers' most common complaints about authors).

When authors get together they will moan about their publishers. But if that energy is channelled into helping promote the books, everyone benefits.

After ten years working in publishing **Alison Baverstock** set up her own marketing consultancy, specialising in running campaigns for the book trade and training publishers and authors to market more effectively. She is a well-established speaker on the book business and is Course Leader of the MA in Publishing at Kingston University. She is the author of *Marketing Your Book: An Author's Guide* (A&C Black 2007, 2nd edn) and *Is There a Book in You?* (A&C Black 2006), which offers would-be published writers a checklist of resources they must have if they want to get published. Her most recent book is *The Naked Author: A Guide to Self-publishing* (A&C Black 2011). Her website is www.alisonbaverstock.com.

See also...

- *Marketing, publicising and selling books*, page 302
- *How to publicise your book*, page 310
- *Marketing yourself online*, page 587
- *Managing your online reputation*, page 591

How to publicise your book

There are numerous ways that authors can, and have to, promote their books. Isabel Losada uses her website and a high Facebook presence to keep in touch daily with her readers. Here she talks about her ideas for author self-publicity.

There is a very annoying thing about publishing houses: they are publishing houses. Authors don't like this at all. We want them to be PR houses, promotional entrepreneurs and marketing experts. In an ideal world we would like entire publicity departments dedicated to promoting our books. Alas, this is not how it is.

Publicity departments

In one of my foreign publishing companies, my editor publishes 85 books a year. For every one published she looks at 10–15 books a week and reads at least five of them. The other two editors in this company each publish 75 and 60 books. This company has ONE publicity person who has responsibility for the promotion of 220 titles a year. So how many calls do you reckon he can make to try and sell an interview to the press? And imagine that your book is not about sport or sex… well it's a bleak picture ain't it? Or you may be lucky and your book is published by one of the major UK publishing houses, where perhaps two people work in the publicity department. Are you beginning to grasp the reality here?

The person most committed to getting your book out there is you. So don't moan about your publishing company, as many authors do – they have published your book after all. Get proactive and have fun with publicising your book. It's the only way to learn.

Be nice at all times to everyone as people who work in PR, publishing and marketing are under pressure and work very hard. What you need is cooperation. So, when you have a meeting with those who are working to promote your book, try to find out exactly what they are doing so that you can cover what they won't have time to do. Get as much information as you can, so you can help. For example, if you are going to visit a town as part of a promotional tour, it is relatively easy to fix up local radio interviews which can be done either in the town or 'down the line' from wherever you work or even from your home. Your publicity person won't have time to phone local newspapers but if you contact them with information about your event they will often be delighted. The best way to get people along to an event is to have someone you know who lives in the town rally their friends and for you to deal with local press and radio. It's hard work.

And that's the truth – you have to commit yourself to self-promotion both with time and with money. You have a tax allowance for advertising and promotion expenses, so surely it's worth producing postcards, for example, that show the front cover of your book, at your own expense. You can give them to those people at parties who insist on asking, 'What do you write?'. Sometimes they'll ask you to sign the card and then go out and buy the book. And you can find 100 other uses for the postcards too. So decide whether to spend your money on promotional tools or to give it to the tax man.

Never walk past a bookshop without going in to sign copies of your books. Be friendly to the booksellers. I once asked a bookseller where my books were and he said they had 75 copies in the basement. When I offered to sign them he looked at me wearily. It was a hot day and he evidently didn't want to go down to the basement and find them. 'Are you open to bribery?' I asked. 'If you will go and get them I will buy you an ice-cream.' 'Magnum please,' he replied and went off to get the books. While I signed books he ate his ice-cream. Having fun helps.

Websites, Facebook and Amazon

Then there is your website. Gotta have a website. And what is worse is that it's no good getting someone else to do it for you so that you aren't able to use it. You must be able to maintain it yourself and not have to ring someone (who's bound to be on holiday when you want them) every time you want to change or update something. Study other authors' websites. Some of them are truly dull – dead sites that just contain lots of downloadable pictures of the author and are evidently not designed for readers of the books. At the other end of the scale is www.neilgaiman.com, the genius of which few of us can ever aspire to. Neil Gaiman's website obviously takes up a lot of his time every day but for his fans the contact must be a continual source of pleasure and satisfaction. My own website (www.isabellosada.com) is basically an amateur site that I built with a couple of flashy touches which I was given help with. But it gives me huge pleasure and I reply to every email. Friendly emails from readers about how much they have enjoyed a book is a great way to start or end the day. So you gotta have a website.

The Amazon websites (www.amazon.com and www.amazon.co.uk) are important too. Thousands of people look at them and read the reader reviews. If a reader sends you a glowing email (to your website of course) about your book it's perfectly acceptable to ask them if they would mind repeating their accolade in the form of a reader review on Amazon. It's funny when authors write their own reviews because regular users at Amazon can tell the difference immediately. A review that says it's by 'a reader' and doesn't give the name is usually an author that hasn't done their homework and is writing their own reviews. And why do it? Genuine reviews from fans are much more interesting. But be warned: watching the rating on Amazon can drive authors crazy. One minute your book is at number 12 and the next it's at 5,756 and you think – how did that happen? It's obviously a deliberate plan to baffle us. If you are not on Facebook and using it effectively, you are a dinosaur. I prefer Facebook to a blog as a blog is all about you. Facebook is about others.

Publicity events

Keep all your press cuttings and put together your own list of reviews that are complimentary of your work. (Comments from any bad reviews can also be helpful – see 'Rejection letters' on my website.) This 'press pack' can then be sent to people when you want to introduce yourself and your work, for instance for interviews or literary festivals. Keep the details of all the people that you speak to and the conversations that you have with them. Who interviewed you and when? Don't assume that others will remember – they won't. I once did a radio interview with a regional station and I only realised at the last minute that the presenter had interviewed me twice before. I had no notes on this and could have inadvertently insulted him and humiliated myself. So keep notes.

When you do events, plan and prepare them like a professional entertainer would. Reading from your work is a skill that you may or may not have naturally. If you hate reading, don't do it. You'll be far more interesting and the audience will have a better time if you are happy. Have someone interview you about the book and your work instead. Check out the relevance to your audience. Ask them why they have come along. They may all secretly want to hear about your book before last. If you are promoting a book that is not your first, check that bookshops have copies of your backlist titles in stock too as there will always be people in the audience who will want those.

Go to other authors' events. By turning up for some of these you'll soon have a feel for what makes a good event and you may find other ways to support your fellow authors when you meet them.

Bookshops

If you have written a book about horses and there isn't a copy in a riding shop you visit – don't be surprised. Small shops don't necessarily have accounts with all the publishing companies. If your book on Buddhism isn't in the Buddhist monastery bookshop that you'd expect to find it in, you could offer the bookshop manager a copy, explain why you think the customers would enjoy the book and ask if he or she would consider it. Sometimes just asking gently works wonders.

Do not turn books that are spine side out face side out in shops. It will simply annoy the booksellers who will turn it back when you are gone. And do not move your books around the shop without first speaking to the manager of the shop. If you think your book is shelved in the wrong place this is a serious problem but needs to be dealt with from the top, i.e. by your publishing company. Getting cross with bookshops won't help as books are shelved according to the category printed on the back cover. So don't annoy booksellers, find out what supports them – they are your friends.

Self-promotion

Look out for opportunities to support the work of authors that you admire. You can use your website for this, for example by linking to other authors' pages if you are recommending their work. I have persuaded people to write articles about books I admire and even once persuaded a charity to promote a book to their 16,000 members. If you can benefit charities or causes that you support at the same time you are really making sense.

Always have a copy of your latest book about your person that you are happy to sell if someone asks. Sorry – but sometimes people (especially at parties) are thrilled that they can have a signed copy direct from the author. I know you are cringing, but it can be done gracefully and with a smile.

You may like to consider offering to visit book clubs that are reading your books. I am happy to go and talk at any club that will pay my travelling expenses (I once had an offer from Switzerland). I also sign books and will post them to anyone who asks me to (in return for a cheque, of course) and I often give away foreign edition copies from my website. (What else can I do with six copies in Greek?) So basically be reader friendly. And bookshop friendly. And publishing company friendly and editor and agent friendly.

Lastly, you have to believe passionately in your work and genuinely want everyone to read it. Don't write just because you have been asked to; wait until you have something to say. If you are passionate about what you write and your work makes a genuine and positive contribution, your readers will sell your books for you. And it's true – with a lot of help from you – that ultimately it's still word of mouth that will sell your books.

Isabel Losada is the author of *New Habits: Why Today's Women Become Nuns*, *The Battersea Park Road to Enlightenment* (translated into 16 languages), *For Tibet, With Love: A Beginner's Guide to Changing the World* (Bloomsbury), *One Hundred Reasons to be Glad* (Summersdale), *Men!* (Virgin) and *The Battersea Park Road to Paradise* (Watkins). She is also an actress and broadcaster and can be contacted through her website, www.isabellosada.com.

A year in view of the publishing industry

Tom Tivnan presents a round-up of book industry news and trends for 2011.

The three overriding themes that the book trade was focused on last year? Digital, digital and, oh yes, digital. Ebooks, apps and the myriad of sweeping, irrevocable changes the digital age is implementing on publishers and booksellers was the main topic of conversation in 2011 as the trade looked warily into its future. Interestingly, it is not so much as what to do with books themselves that troubles publishers any more – converting titles into ebooks, to a lesser extent apps, and 'repurposing' content into whatever digital format is required is now a matter of course. It has paid off, with most publishers at the end of last year seeing high triple digit percentage rises in digital revenue: Hachette UK (Britain's biggest publishing group), saw digital sales rise 500% to over £20 million, and Pan Macmillan reported an 800% year-on-year rise in ebook sales.

Those rises, we should underscore, were from some very low numbers. Even given the industry's preoccupation with digital, it is worth noting that the UK books market is still predominantly print. By the end of 2011, about 10%–12% of UK publisher revenue was coming from 'e', meaning, of course, that 88%–90% of the market is still the old-fashioned 'p'-books. In 2011, just under £1.59 billion was spent on print books through the industry sales monitor Nielsen BookScan, a fall of 6.3% (£106 million) from the previous year. It was a fairly miserable year across the board for print sales, with only four of the top 20 UK publishers improving on last year's performance (HarperCollins, Simon & Schuster, Scholastic and Usborne). Still, given that most publishers were reporting 10%–12% digital sales, that dip in print sales for many publishers was largely made up by ebooks.

No, what worries the trade is the frightening speed of change and the reversal of literally centuries of established business models. Particularly troubling for the industry is that at the moment most of the change is being led by just one 800-pound gorilla: Amazon. It is difficult to overestimate Amazon's power in the UK book trade. It accounts for about 30% of UK print books sales and, most crucially, it completely dominates the ebook market. Since its Kindle e-reader was launched in 2007 and its iPad-like tablet Kindle Fire in 2011, Amazon has swept the ebook competition aside and now controls about 85% of digital book sales in the UK. Its sales influence grew even more last year when it acquired The Book Depository, a UK-based online bookstore, which is extremely popular in Australia, a vital market for UK publisher exports.

If it was just in terms of pure selling, Amazon would be a force to reckon with. Yet, its power is increasing beyond retail. Amazon Publishing had a rather soft launch in 2009 with its self-publishing programme, AmazonEncore. Now that business has grown into seven imprints, and Amazon signalled its intent to fully enter direct competition with publishers last year when it hired 'traditional' books big hitter Larry Kirshbaum (he used to run the US-based Time Warner empire and his own literary agency) to run Amazon Publishing. The implications are obviously worrying to traditional publishers if the company which is becoming increasingly the main route to customers has a successful publishing programme – and one that often offers better royalty rates to authors.

Amazon's self-publishing programme – and to a far lesser extent other self-publishing websites like Smashwords and Lulu – has become increasingly profitable. Last year, two US self-published authors, John Locke and Amanda Hocking, joined a select group of traditionally published authors such as Stieg Larsson and James Patterson to sell more than a million Kindle books through Amazon.

Yet perhaps it is significant that last year both Hocking and Locke, despite making a large amount of money by self-publishing, both signed up to traditional publishers. Locke inked a deal with Simon & Schuster to have the publisher sell his physical books (but kept the rights to the ebooks himself), while Hocking's next four books (both 'e' and 'p') will be published by Pan Macmillan. This new era of publishing might be encapsulated by Stephen Leather, the British crime writer who has been very successfully published by Hodder. Last year, he took two older books that Hodder had previously rejected and self-published them through Amazon. He didn't do too shabbily; at one point the books were at number one and two on the Kindle chart and each was selling about 2,000 downloads a day.

Potter and more

One of the most dramatic, unexpected moves last year was J.K. Rowling splitting after 16 years with her agency Christopher Little. Rowling joined Neil Blair, who was her principle agent at Christopher Little, when he set up his new business, The Blair Partnership. The move was publishing's biggest gossip story of the year; most observers were taken by surprise, Little himself said he was 'angry and disappointed' and there were threats of lawsuits before the matter was settled out of court.

Outside of the gossip, the long-term effects of Rowling's move may bring about seismic changes. The main reason for Rowling's move was for her and Blair (and ex-HarperCollins digital boss Charlie Redmayne) to set up Pottermore.com, an all-singing, all-dancing virtual Harry Potter online world that sells a variety of digital products, including for the first time, her ebooks. Many eyes in the industry will be watching Pottermore to see if it – a project done primarily by author and agent without the help of a publisher – is viable financially. As by far the biggest selling author since records began, Rowling is in a class by herself. But there are other 'big brand' authors with loyal followings – Jamie Oliver, James Patterson, Julia Donaldson, *Wimpy Kid* creator Jeff Kinney and Stephen King to name but a few – who just might think of 'going it alone' if Pottermore proves to be a hit.

Pottermore is the vanguard for a number of new models that publishers, agents and authors are experimenting with. 'Crowd-funded' publisher Unbound, which launched in 2011, is another. Founded by *QI* writers John Mitchinson and John Pollard, and *Crap Towns* author Dan Kieran, Unbound requires authors to pitch their idea to readers on the publisher's website, and have 50 days to attract support through readers pledging money to fund the publication of the work. If enough money is pledged, the work will be published, primarily as an ebook or 'beautifully bound, limited edition hardback', or both, with each pledger's name inscribed in the back of the print edition.

It is not just new start-ups that are experimenting. Short stories have had a renaissance recently – the idea is that in the time-strapped modern world, people will turn to reading short fiction on mobile devices. To tap into this, both Penguin and Random House last year launched ebook-only short story lists with bespoke content written by the many writers across both company's lists. Other digital-only imprints are springing up throughout traditional publishers. Last October, Pan Macmillan set up Bello, which sells 'lost classics' ebooks from literary agency Curtis Brown's estates (the launch list had books from Vita Sackville-West and Gerald Durrell).

Daunting task

It is too early to tell whether these initiatives will make any money. But publishers are keen to experiment because they are nervous when they look to the high street. With closures of several chains in recent years, most notably Borders, a healthy and thriving Waterstones is ever more crucial to publishers. It was with almost universal cheer throughout publishing, therefore, when James Daunt took over as boss last year after the chain was bought from HMV by secretive Russian oligarch Alexander Mamut. Daunt, the founder of the high-quality, literary-minded mini-London chain Daunt Books – a business run remarkably like the early Waterstones – is seen in the trade as a 'bookseller's bookseller'. After a succession of people running Waterstones who came from supermarket and supply chain businesses, publishers rejoiced. Finally, a 'books guy' was in charge.

The honeymoon was short-lived. Particularly when that books guy started negotiating very toughly on terms, demanding greater discount from publishers. Yet it is a strategy Daunt must employ if Waterstones is to survive. Broadly, Daunt is trying to make each Waterstones into more of a 'local shop': getting away from centrally bought promotions, not trying to compete with Amazon and the supermarkets on price (one of his biggest decisions was to ditch the company's long-standing three-for-two promotion), allowing booksellers in the shops to purchase more of their own stock and curate their sections. The idea is to get Waterstones back to its roots, aping the on the shop floor bookseller-led ethos of the chain's early days in the 1980s; a move reflected by Daunt's decision to go back to the original name Waterstones, rather than Waterstone's.

What may help Waterstones' fortunes is if it decides to compete with the Kindle. In the USA, the world's biggest bookseller Barnes & Noble has taken a large chunk out of Amazon with launching its Nook e-reader and tablet. By actively promoting the device – B&N puts e-readers front of shop and has booksellers dedicated to selling it – Nook has claimed about 20%–25% of the US ebook market. Daunt has indicated that a Waterstones own brand e-reader would be out in summer or autumn 2012, but when this *Yearbook* went to press it had not been announced. In 2011, WHSmith announced a deal that it was selling the Kobo, a Canadian-based e-reader in the chain's shops. The Kobo's UK sales are not yet stratospheric, though bricks and mortar booksellers like WHSmith and Waterstones competing with Amazon on the digital side is essential for survival on the physical side.

It's still about the books

With the constant hand-wringing in the trade about the digital future, it is easy to forget about the books. And once again, it was a stonking year for Jamie Oliver. For the second year in a row and the third time in four years, the former Sainsbury's huckster, pride of Essex and scourge of fatties on both sides of the Atlantic, topped the year-end author chart by shifting £13.2 million in physical books through bookshop tills. In 2011, Oliver became only the second author since accurate records began in 1998 to top the author charts for consecutive years (Rowling, unsurprisingly, was the other: she was the bestselling author in seven out of the past 14 years, with a consecutive run of five years from 1999 to 2003). Since the beginning of 2010, a Jamie Oliver book has sold every 22 seconds in the UK.

There were breakout years for two genre authors: George R.R. Martin and Jo Nesbø. Epic fantasy maestro Martin had sales of £7.3 million in 2011 (a mere 2,145% rise from

2010), making him the second bestselling author within the fiction sector last year. He was helped by a new novel (his first since 2005), and the incredibly popular *A Game of Thrones* television adaptation which was screened on Sky Atlantic in April 2011. Nesbø is one of the many contenders to become TNSL (The Next Stieg Larsson). In fact, the Norwegian crime author surpassed Larsson in sales last year – in no small part thanks to Larsson's reinvigoration of the Scandinavia-set crime genre. Nesbø had a super year with support from Waterstones in particular and six of his novels sold more than 100,000 copies last year, whereas just one achieved the feat in 2010.

Children's print sales in general held up in 2011, down just 1% compared to the overall market's 6.3% slide. Two children's writers – *Gruffalo* author Julia Donaldson and *Wimpy Kid* creator Jeff Kinney – both have sales exceeding £10 million, a feat also achieved by only Jamie Oliver and James Patterson. Donaldson's sales grew for the fourth consecutive year in 2011, with the *Gruffalo* in its various incarnations accounting for a quarter of her £12.4 million total. An astonishing one in every ten preschool titles bought last year was written by Donaldson.

Like Martin, Kinney was helped by a film adaptation, and all seven of his *Diary of a Wimpy Kid* titles sold more than 200,000 copies last year for a total of £11 million. A rising children's author to watch is *Little Britain* star David Walliams. Worth £900,000 to booksellers in 2010, his sales more than tripled to just over £3 million last year. Three of his children's novels (*Gangsta Granny*, *Mr Stink* and *Billionaire Boy*, all published by HarperCollins) sold more than 100,000 copies last year.

Julian Barnes won the Man Booker Prize last year, but not before the prize itself had its annual bun fight. In 2011, the controversy was that the prize was accused of 'dumbing down' after a shortlist that had a couple of genre novels on it and ignored some bookies' favourites, including the rapturously reviewed *The Stranger's Child* by Allan Hollinghurst. Still, the furore helped Barnes – his *The Sense of a Ending* sold £1.5 million in 2011.

Back to Rowling. Since she ended the *Harry Potter* series in 2007, the question for most in the industry was: what is her next move? When it was revealed, like Pottermore, it was a bit of a surprise. She is writing a crime novel for adults which will be launched in September 2012. This is cheering for two reasons. One is that there has not truly been an 'event' book release – one that galvanises booksellers and gets reams of media attention – since Dan Brown's *The Lost Symbol* in 2009. It is a fillip the trade needs desperately. Secondly, that Rowling decided to move from *Harry Potter* publisher Bloomsbury to publish with Little, Brown is reason for optimism for publishers. Even the world's bestselling big brand author, at least for her new series, thinks there are still legs in the traditional publishing model yet.

Tom Tivnan is features and supplements editor of the *Bookseller*, and also the *Bookseller's* international editor. He wrote the text for *Tattooed by the Family Business* (Pavilion 2010). Previously a freelance writer, his work has appeared in the *Glasgow Herald*, the *Independent*, the *Daily Telegraph* and *Harper's Bazaar*. He has also worked as a bookseller for Blackwell in the UK and Barnes & Noble in the USA.

See also...

- *The state of commissioning*, page 283
- *Spotting a bestseller*, page 220
- *Print on demand*, page 317
- *Who owns whom in publishing*, page 322
- *Electronic publishing*, page 581

Books

Print on demand

David Taylor explains how print on demand is keeping books alive.

What is 'print on demand'?

Ever since mankind first started committing words to a physical form of delivery, whether on wood, stone, papyrus, illuminated text or moveable type, the method of supplying these for sale has largely followed a similar pattern: produce first and then sell. Of course, the risk in this is that the publisher can overproduce or underproduce. Overproduction means that the publisher has tied up cash in books that are waiting to be sold. Underproduction means that the publisher has run out and sales are being missed because the book is not available to buy.

If you walk around any publisher's distribution centre you will see huge quantities of books that have been printed and are awaiting sale, representing large amounts of cash tied up in physical inventory. This is often referred to as 'speculative inventory' because the publisher has printed the books in anticipation of selling them. One of the hardest decisions that a publisher has to make is how many copies of a title to print upon publication; equally hard is how many to reprint if the initial print run is sold. Get these wrong and it can cost the publisher dearly and, in some extreme cases, prove mortal to the business.

For others in the supply chain, this model is also deeply flawed. The author whose title sells well can fall into the limbo of 'out of stock' pending a reprint decision by the publisher. The bookseller, who has orders for a title but cannot supply them, also loses sales and disappoints customers. In some cases, those orders are of the moment and when that moment passes, so does the sale. Last but by no means least, the book buyer is frustrated as they are unable to buy the book that they wish to read.

The supply model is also famously inefficient characterised as it is by large amounts of speculative stock being printed, transported, stored in warehouses, transported again, returned from the bookseller if it does not sell and, in many cases, being pulped. Not only is this commercially inefficient, it is also environmentally costly involving large amounts of energy being used to print and transport books that may end their life as landfill.

In the mid 1990s, developments in the then emerging field of digital printing started to hold out the possibility that this traditional 'print first then sell' model might be changed to a more commercially attractive 'sell first and then print' model. Such a supply model was premised upon a number of things coming together.

- First, the technology of digital printing advanced to the stage where simple text-based books could be produced to a standard that was acceptable to publishers in terms of quality.
- Second, the speed of digital presses advanced so that a book could be produced upon the receipt of an order and supplied back to the customer within an acceptable timeframe.
- Third, models started to emerge which married these digital printing capabilities to wholesaling and book distribution networks such that books could be stored digitally, offered for sale to the market with orders being fulfilled on a 'print-on-demand' (POD) basis from a virtual warehouse rather than a physical warehouse full of speculative inventory. This hybrid model requires a highly sophisticated IT infrastructure to allow the swift

routing and batching of orders to digital print engines so that genuine single copy orders can be produced 'on demand'.

The first mover in developing this model was the US book wholesaler Ingram Book Group which, in 1997, installed a digital print line in their giant book wholesaling warehouse in Tennessee and started to offer a service to US publishers called Lightning Print. The service offered publishers the option of allowing Ingram to hold their titles in a digital format, offer them for sale via Ingram's vast network of bookselling customers and then print the title when it was ordered. In addition, the publisher signing up to the service could order copies for their own purposes.

Fifteen years on, Lightning Source, as the company is now called, has operations in the USA, the UK, Australia, a joint venture with Hachette in France, a research and training facility in Germany and agreements with POD vendors in Brazil and Germany. Lightning Source prints around two million books a month from a digital warehouse containing eight million titles from over 25,000 publishers. The average print run per order is around 1.8 copies.

POD publishers

Digital printing technology has developed at a staggering pace since the mid 1990s and the quality of digitally printed titles is now almost indistinguishable from titles printed using offset machines. The new generation of ink jet digital print engines are now starting to appear in the market and are taking the quality of digitally printed books to the next level, especially for full colour titles. Speed of production has also improved at amazing rates. For example, Lightning Source now produces books on demand for Ingram customers within four hours of receiving the order, thereby allowing orders to be shipped within 24 hours to the bookseller.

Whilst Ingram's Lightning Source is the clear global leader, other players have entered the market. In the UK, Antony Rowe established a POD operation in partnership with the UK's biggest book wholesaler, Gardners, in early 2000. Antony Rowe's POD facility supplies orders on demand for Gardner's bookselling customers using a very similar model to that of Ingram and Lightning Source in the USA. Other UK printers have been scrambling to enter the fast-growing POD space with significant investments being made in digital printing equipment. Rather ironically, the arrival of the ebook is fuelling the growth of POD as publishers move more titles into shorter print runs or opt to operate from a virtual stock position as they attempt to cope with the shift from 'p' to 'e'. The last thing a publisher wants is a warehouse full of titles that are increasingly selling in an 'e' format.

In Germany, the book wholesaler Libri has a POD operation, Books on Demand, which not only offers POD services to publishers, it also offers a self-publishing service to authors (see *Doing it on your own* on page 290). Lightning Source and Antony Rowe deal only with publishers. Books on Demand have recently extended their offer into both France and the Netherlands and have an arrangement with Ingram so that their self-published authors can use the Lightning Source network to get their titles into North America, the UK and Australia.

In the Australian market, the arrival of Lightning Source in mid 2011 has had a dramatic impact on Australian self-publishing companies. Now that they have a POD model in their market, they are actively growing their title base and are able to offer Australian authors easy access to a global selling network in addition to local services. One of the most significant moves in this area was the purchase in 2005 by Amazon of a small US POD business called Booksurge. Like Libri's Books on Demand model, Amazon also offers a self-publishing service to authors and is actively leveraging its dominance of the internet bookselling market to develop innovative packages for authors via this model and their Create Space brand. The consensus within the book trade appears to be that Amazon sees POD as a very important part of the way in which they manage their supply chain and as a key opportunity to improve service levels to their customers. Amazon is now also a publisher in the traditional sense of the word; it will be interesting to see how it blends its self-publishing offer with its traditional model.

As digital print technology has improved, many traditional book printers have tried to enter this market and offer POD. However, without significant investment in the IT infrastructure needed to deliver single copy production at scale and speed and without allying that capability to an established book distribution or wholesaling network, many of these offers are effectively ultra short-run printing offers and cannot replicate the genuine POD supply model of a single copy printed when an order is received. Increasingly, as well, that supply model needs to be built on a global scale to offer authors and publishers the maximum exposure for their titles.

What POD means for authors

POD is impacting aspiring and published authors in different ways. One of the by-products of the emergence of POD has been the birth of a whole set of new publishing models. Removing the need to carry speculative inventory has reduced the barriers to entry for organisations which want to enter the publishing space. For example, in the US market, Lightning Source's supply model has allowed a large number of self-publishing companies to flourish and to offer aspiring authors a wide range of services to allow them to get their work into print. These companies will typically use a POD service like Lightning Source to do the physical printing and distribution of a title; in addition, they may use Lightning to have these titles listed for sale via book wholesalers like Amazon and Gardners, internet booksellers like Amazon, and physical bookshop chains such as Barnes & Noble and Waterstones. Authors may also have the opportunity to order copies of their own titles. These companies will typically offer the aspiring author a set of support services covering editorial, marketing, design, etc.

The aspiring author

No longer does an author wanting to self-publish have to commit a large sum of money upfront to buy thousands of copies of his title and then have to sell them himself. The previously mentioned self-publishing organisations are large, sophisticated and have many tens of thousands of authors whose books are available for sale in mainstream book reselling outlets. In addition, there is a growing trend for what we might term traditional publishers to trawl self-published titles for potential; there have been several well-publicised cases of authors who started out by self-publishing before being picked up by one of the established publishing houses. There are also some signs that traditional publishers are starting to look at how they might build a self-publishing model into their traditional business.

The published author

The POD picture for the published author is a little more mixed. There is no doubt that traditional publishers are engaging more than ever before with the benefits that POD brings. The ability to reduce 'speculative inventory' (as defined at the beginning of this article) or get out of it completely, to ensure that sales are not missed, to reduce the risk of getting a reprint decision wrong, and even to bring titles back to life from the out-of-print graveyard, are all very attractive financial propositions. For the author who has a book already published, POD means sales are not missed and therefore royalties are forthcoming. Many books can languish in 'reprint under consideration' limbo for years: POD removes that category and ensures that books are available for sale. Probably the thorniest issue is around the decision to put a book out of print and here most author contracts have simply not caught up with the new technologies. Some contracts still require that the publisher has to keep physical inventory of a title to show that it is in print, yet many millions of books are in print and there is no physical inventory held anywhere. An author may therefore find their title being put out of print because of such a clause even though the publisher is willing to keep it in print but does not want to keep speculative inventory printed before an order is received.

The flip side of this, of course, is that a publisher might use POD to retain the rights to the title by printing a small amount of inventory when really the best thing for the author might be to allow the title to go out of print and get the rights back. There have been many cases where rights have reverted to the author who has then either set himself up as an independent publishing company or utilised the services of one of the self-publishing companies mentioned earlier. There have also been examples of literary agents using POD to offer a new publishing service to authors who may have the rights as the title has gone out of print at their original publisher.

In conclusion, the advice for both aspiring authors and published authors is to do your homework. For an aspiring author, look carefully at the various self-publishing organisations out there and do your sums. Are you better off using them or do you want to set up your own publishing company? For published authors, take a long hard look at how your contract defines 'out of print'. The old definition was typically based on 'no physical copies in existence': POD has made that irrelevant and your contract should reflect these new realities if you are to take full advantage of them.

And finally, here is one of the most delicious ironies of this whole model. The death of the physical book has been predicted many times now we live in a digital age. POD has digital technology at its core and yet it is giving life to one of the oldest products on the planet: the paper book. POD is set to be at the heart of the way in which paper books are published, printed and distributed for many years to come. Without this new model, there would be far fewer books available to buy and read and I, for one, think that the world would be a duller place for that.

David Taylor has spent most of his 27 years in the book trade in bookselling and is currently Senior Vice President, Content Acquisition International, Ingram Content Group and Group Managing Director, Lightning Source UK Ltd. He is also a Director of Lightning Source Australia and Lightning Source France.

ONLINE RESOURCES

This is a fast-moving area: sites and businesses appear and others cease year by year. Writers are reminded to check carefully what each service offers and to check all details of any contractual arrangements before entering into these. This *Yearbook* cannot be held responsible for any content on any of these sites.

Antony Rowe
website www.cpibooks.com/uk

An established printer offering short runs. There is a quote calculator on the site.

Author House
website www.authorhouse.com

US-based self-publishing site. The ebook publishing package is available from $349.

Authors Online
website www.authorsonline.co.uk

A Bedfordshire-based print and Kindle self-publishing venue. Their full standard service costs £725 and there are a lot of extras.

Blurb
website www.blurb.com/uk

Downloadable book-making software which is very easy to use. Starting price £2.95 for one book (pocket-sized).

CreateSpace
website www.createspace.com

The publishing engine of Amazon. Allows writers and users to self-publish and distribute books, DVDs, CDs, video downloads and MP3s on-demand.

Fast Print
website www.fast-print.net

About £146 for 25 copies of a 128pp book. Offers a calculator online.

Ingram
website www.ingrambook.com

The largest book wholesale distributor in the world, offering immediate access to more than 2 million titles. Offers wholesale distribution, print on demand, digital formats and full distribution services.

iUniverse
website www.iuniverse.com

A service for redeploying out-of-print books; the author contract should be checked carefully. Packages range from $899 to $4,499.

Lightning Source
website www.lightningsource.com

Established print-on-demand and ebook supplier. No prices given but there is an exhaustive list of FAQs.

Lulu
website www.lulu.com/uk

A showcase for services supplied by people in the book trade, with reliability ratings. A certain amount of free advice but it is necessary to register (free).

Pro Print
website www.proprintpublishers.co.uk

Cambridgeshire printer which offers a short-run print-on-demand service.

Smashwords
website www.smashwords.com

A book publishing and distribution platform for ebook authors, publishers, agents and readers. Offers multi-format, DRM-free ebooks. Free to register.

Unlimited Publishing
website www.unlimitedpublishing.com

A print-on-demand service for new and out-of-print titles. Short, non-fiction titles preferred. E-formats favoured.

Writers World
website www.writersworld.co.uk

A self-publishing resource for writers to publish their books by print on demand or ebook format. Quotation given on request. Free newsletter and chatroom.

Xlibris
website www.xlibris.com

Print-on-demand packages ranging from $499 to $15, 249 (for picture books) plus marketing packages. Has been in the market for 15 years.

See also...

- *Doing it on your own*, page 290
- *Self-publishing in ebook*, page 294
- *Vanity publishing*, page 329

Who owns whom in publishing

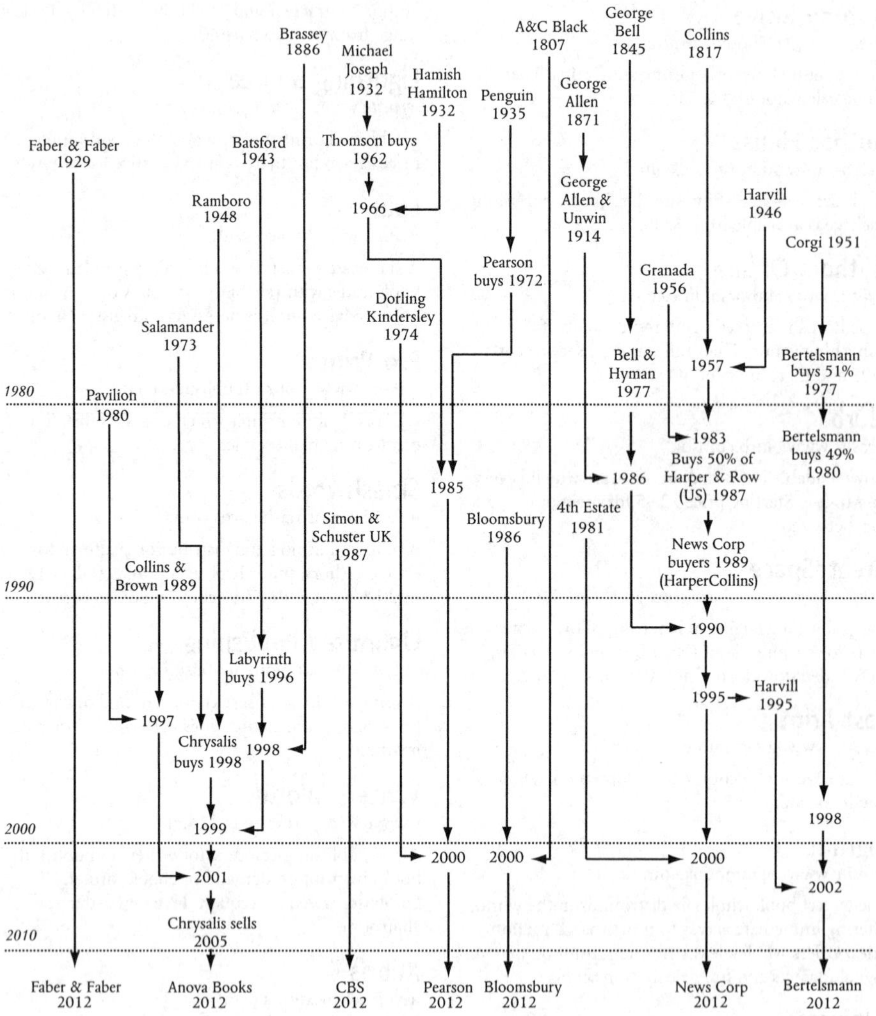

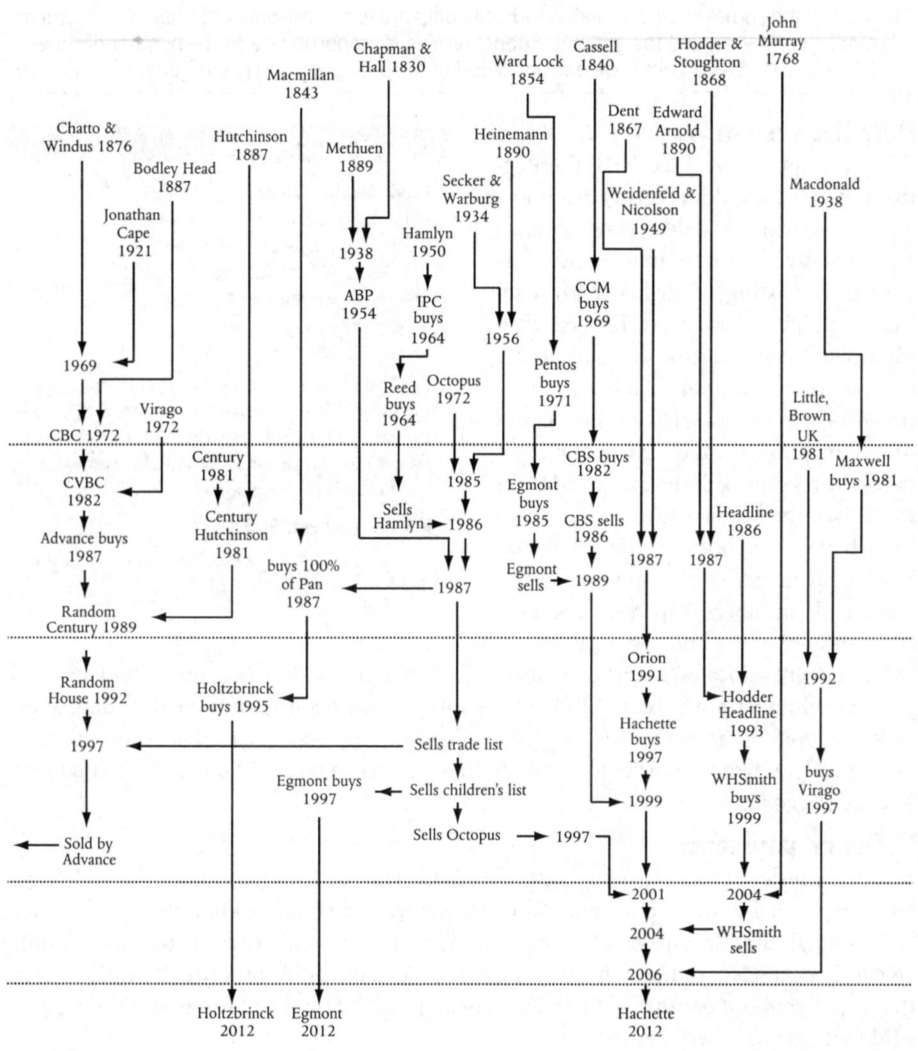
Chatto & Windus 1876
Bodley Head 1887
Jonathan Cape 1921
Hutchinson 1887
Macmillan 1843
Chapman & Hall 1830
Methuen 1889
Ward Lock 1854
Heinemann 1890
Secker & Warburg 1934
Cassell 1840
Dent 1867
Hodder & Stoughton 1868
Edward Arnold 1890
John Murray 1768
Weidenfeld & Nicolson 1949
Macdonald 1938
1938
Hamlyn 1950
ABP 1954
IPC buys 1964
1956
CCM buys 1969
1969
Pentos buys 1971
Reed buys 1964
Octopus 1972
Virago 1972
Little, Brown UK 1981
CBC 1972
Century 1981
CBS buys 1982
Maxwell buys 1981
CVBC 1982
1985
Egmont buys 1985
Century Hutchinson 1981
Sells Hamlyn
1986
CBS sells 1986
Headline 1986
Advance buys 1987
buys 100% of Pan 1987
1987
Egmont sells
1989
1987
1987
Random Century 1989
Orion 1991
1992
Random House 1992
Holtzbrinck buys 1995
Hodder Headline 1993
Hachette buys 1997
1997
Sells trade list
Egmont buys 1997
Sells children's list
1999
WHSmith buys 1999
buys Virago 1997
Sells Octopus
1997
Sold by Advance
2001
2004
2004
WHSmith sells
2006
Holtzbrinck 2012
Egmont 2012
Hachette 2012

Public Lending Right

Under the PLR system, payment is made from public funds to authors (writers, translators, illustrators and some editors/compilers) whose books are lent out from public libraries. Payment is made once a year, and the amount authors receive is proportionate to the number of times that their books were borrowed during the previous year (July to June).

How the system works

From the applications received, the Registrar of PLR compiles a register of authors and books, which is held on computer. A representative sample of book issues is recorded, consisting of all loans from selected public libraries. This is then multiplied in proportion to total library lending to produce, for each book, an estimate of its total annual loans throughout the country. Each year the computer compares the register with the estimated loans to discover how many loans are credited to each registered book for the calculation of PLR payments. The computer does this using code numbers – in most cases the ISBN printed in the book (see below).

Further information

Public Lending Right
PLR Office, Richard House, Sorbonne Close, Stockton-on-Tees TS17 6DA
tel (01642) 604699 *fax* (01642) 615641
website www.plr.uk.com, www.plrinternational.com
Contact The Registrar

Application forms, information, publications and a copy of its *Annual Report* are all obtainable from the PLR Office. See website for further information on eligibility for PLR, loans statistics and forthcoming developments.

PLR Management Board
Advises the Registrar on the operation and future development of the PLR scheme.

Parliament allocates a sum each year (£7.22 million for 2011/12) for PLR. This fund pays the administrative costs of PLR and reimburses local authorities for recording loans in the sample libraries (see below). The remaining money is then divided by the total registered loan figure in order to work out how much can be paid for each estimated loan of a registered book.

Limits on payments

If all the registered interests in an author's books score so few loans that they would earn less than £1 in a year, no payment is due. However, if the books of one registered author score so high that the author's PLR earnings for the year would exceed £6,600, then only £6,600 is paid. (No author can earn more than £6,600 in PLR in any one year.) Money that is not paid out because of these limits belongs to the fund and increases the amounts paid that year to other authors.

The sample

Because it would be expensive and impracticable to attempt to collect loans data from every library authority in the UK, a statistical sampling method is employed instead. The sample represents only public lending libraries – academic, school, private and commercial libraries are not included. Only books which are loaned from public libraries can earn PLR; consultations of books on library premises are excluded.

The sample consists of the entire loans records for a year from libraries in more than 30 public library authorities spread through England, Scotland, Wales and Northern

Ireland. Sample loans represent around 20% of the national total. All the computerised sampling points in an authority contribute loans data ('multi-site' sampling). The aim is to increase the sample without any significant increase in costs. In order to counteract sampling error, libraries in the sample change every three to four years. Loans are totalled every 12 months for the period 1 July–30 June.

An author's entitlement to PLR depends on the loans accrued by his or her books in the sample. This figure is averaged up to produce first regional and then finally national estimated loans.

ISBNs

The PLR system uses ISBNs (International Standard Book Numbers) to identify books lent and correlate loans with entries on the PLR Register so that payments can be made. ISBNs are required for all registrations. Different editions (e.g. 1st, 2nd, hardback, paperback, large print) of the same book have different ISBNs. See *FAQs about ISBNs* on page 297.

Authorship

In the PLR system the author of a book is the writer, illustrator, translator, compiler, editor or reviser. Authors must be named on the book's title page, or be able to prove authorship by some other means (e.g. receipt of royalties). The ownership of copyright has no bearing on PLR eligibility.

Co-authorship/illustrators. In the PLR system the authors of a book are those writers, translators, editors, compilers and illustrators as defined above. Authors must apply for registration before their books can earn PLR and this can be done via the PLR website. There is no restriction on the number of authors who can register shares in any one book as long as they satisfy the eligibility criteria.

Writers and/or illustrators. At least one must be eligible and they must jointly agree what share of PLR each will take based on contribution. This agreement is necessary even if one

Summary of the 29th year's results

Registration: authors. When registration closed for the 29th year (30 June 2011) there were 39,972 authors and assignees.

Eligible loans. Of the 300 million estimated loans from UK libraries, 129 million belong to books on the PLR register. The loans credited to registered books – 43% of all library borrowings – qualify for payment. The remaining 57% of loans relate to books that are ineligible for various reasons, to books written by dead or foreign authors, and to books that have simply not been applied for.

Money and payments. PLR's administrative costs are deducted from the fund allocated to the Registrar annually by Parliament. Operating the Scheme this year cost £703,000, representing some 10% of the PLR fund. The Rate per Loan for 2011/12 was 6.05 pence and was calculated to distribute all the £6.5 million available. The total of PLR distribution and costs is therefore the full £7.22 million which the Government provided in 2011/12.

The numbers of authors in various payment categories are as follows:

*313	payments at	£5,000–6,600
393	payments between	£2,500–4,999.99
826	payments between	£1,000–2,499.99
956	payments between	£500–999.99
3,640	payments between	£100–499.99
17,590	payments between	£1–99.99
23,718	TOTAL	

* Includes 211 authors whose book loans reached the maximum threshold

or two are ineligible or do not wish to register for PLR. The eligible authors will receive the share(s) specified in the application.

Translators. Translators may apply, without reference to other authors, for a 30% fixed share (to be divided equally between joint translators).

Editors and compilers. An editor or compiler may apply, either with others or without reference to them, to register a 20% share. An editor must have written at least 10% of the book's content or more than ten pages of text in addition to normal editorial work and be named on the title page. Alternatively, editors may register 20% if they have a royalty agreement with the publisher. The share of joint editors/compilers is 20% in total to be divided equally. An application from an editor or compiler to register a greater percentage share must be accompanied by supporting documentary evidence of actual contribution.

Dead or missing co-authors. Where it is impossible to agree shares with a co-author because that person is dead or untraceable, then the surviving co-author or co-authors may submit an application without the dead or missing co-author but must name the co-author and provide supporting evidence as to why that co-author has not agreed shares. The living co-author(s) will then be able to register a share in the book which reflects individual contribution. Providing permission is granted, the PLR Office can help to put co-authors (including illustrators) in touch with each other. Help is also available from publishers, writers' organisations and the Association of Illustrators.

Life and death. First applications may *not* be made by the estate of a deceased author. However, if an author registers during their lifetime the PLR in their books can be

Most borrowed authors

Children's authors

1	Daisy Meadows
2	Jacqueline Wilson
3	Francesca Simon
4	Julia Donaldson
5	Mick Inkpen
6	Adam Blade
7	Terry Deary
8	Fiona Watt
9	Roald Dahl
10	Lauren Child
11	Ian Whybrow
12	Enid Blyton
13	Lucy Cousins
14	Janet & Allan Ahlberg
15	Eric Hill
16	Tony Ross
17	Michael Morpurgo
18	Jeanne Willis
19	Vivian French
20	Jeremy Strong

Authors of adult fiction

1	James Patterson
2	Nora Roberts
3	Danielle Steel
4	M.C. Beaton
5	Clive Cussler
6	Josephine Cox
7	Tess Gerritsen
8	Anna Jacobs
9	Michael Connelly
10	Lee Child
11	Katie Flynn
12	Jodi Picoult
13	Alexander McCall Smith
14	Harlan Coben
15	Ian Rankin
16	Patricia Cornwell
17	David Baldacci
18	Jeffrey Deaver
19	Agatha Christie
20	John Grisham

These two lists are of the most borrowed authors in UK public libraries. They are based on PLR sample loans in the period July 2010–June 2011. They include all writers, both registered and unregistered, but not illustrators where the book has a separate writer. Writing names are used; pseudonyms have not been combined.

transferred to a new owner and continues for up to 70 years after the date of their death. The new owner can apply to register new titles if first published one year before, or up to ten years after the date of the author's death. New editions of existing registered titles can also be registered posthumously.

Residential qualifications. PLR is open to authors living in the European Economic Area (i.e. EU member states plus Norway, Liechtenstein and Iceland). A resident in these countries (for PLR purposes) must have their only or principal home there.

Eligible books

In the PLR system each edition of a book is registered and treated as a separate book. A book is eligible for PLR registration provided that:

• it has an eligible author (or co-author);

• it is printed and bound (paperbacks counting as bound);

• copies of it have been put on sale, i.e. it is not a free handout and it has already been published;

• it is not a newspaper, magazine, journal or periodical;

• the authorship is personal, i.e. not a company or association, and the book is not crown copyright;

• it is not wholly or mainly a musical score;

• it has an ISBN.

Statements and payment

Authors with an online account may view their statement online. Registered authors who do not have an online account receive a statement posted to their address if a payment is due.

Sampling arrangements

To help minimise the unfairness that arises inevitably from a sampling system, the scheme specifies the eight regions within which authorities and sampling points have to be designated and includes libraries of varying size. Part of the sample drops out by rotation each year to allow fresh libraries to be included. The following library authorities have been designated for the year beginning 1 July 2012 (all are multi-site authorities). This list is based on the nine government regions for England plus Northern Ireland, Scotland and Wales.

• East – Essex, Southend-on-Sea and Thurrock, Suffolk

• East Midlands – Northamptonshire

• London – Islington, London Libraries Consortium (Barking & Dagenham, Brent, Ealing, Enfield, Hackney, Havering, Kingston Upon Thames, Lewisham, Merton, Newham, Redbridge, Richmond Upon Thames, Tower Hamlets, Waltham Forest, Wandsworth), Sutton

• North East – Gateshead, Middlesbrough, South Tyneside

• North West & Merseyside – Blackburn with Darwen, Manchester, Salford

• South East – East Sussex, Portsmouth

• South West – Libraries West (Bath & North East Somerset, Bristol, North Somerset, Somerset, South Gloucestershire)

• West Midlands – Telford and Wrekin

• Yorkshire & The Humber – North Yorkshire, Rotherham

• Northern Ireland – The Northern Ireland Library Authority

- Scotland – East Ayrshire, North Lanarkshire, Scottish Borders
- Wales – Denbighshire and Flintshire, Vale of Glamorgan, Wrexham.

Participating local authorities are reimbursed on an actual cost basis for additional expenditure incurred in providing loans data to the PLR Office. The extra PLR work mostly consists of modifications to computer programs to accumulate loans data in the local authority computer and to transmit the data to the PLR Office at Stockton-on-Tees.

Reciprocal arrangements

Reciprocal PLR arrangements now exist with the German, Dutch, Austrian and other European PLR schemes. Authors can apply for overseas PLR for most of these countries through the Authors' Licensing and Collecting Society (see page 660). The exception to this rule is Ireland. Authors should now register for Irish PLR through the UK PLR Office. Further information on PLR schemes internationally and recent developments within the EC towards wider recognition of PLR is available from the PLR Office or on the international PLR website.

Vanity publishing

Mainstream publishers invest their own money in the publishing process. In contrast, vanity publishers require an up-front payment from the author to produce a book. Johnathon Clifford highlights the perils of vanity publishing.

My research into vanity publishing began in 1990 when a 12-year-old girl wrote to me stating she had found a publisher willing to publish her work. I telephoned the 'publisher' under the guise of an aspiring author, and this call was all it took for them to agree to publish my work. Their offer was 100 copies of a 38-page book for a fee of £1,900, with no need for them to see my poetry first.

Definition of vanity publishing

'Vanity publishing, also self-styled (often inaccurately) as "subsidy", "joint-venture", "shared-responsibility" or even "self" publishing, is a service whereby authors are charged to have their work published. Vanity publishers generally offer to publish a book for a specific fee, or offer to include short stories, poems or other literary or artistic material in an anthology, which the authors are then invited to buy.'

– Advertising Standards Authority definition of vanity publishing, 1997

Since then, I have written *Vanity Press & The Proper Poetry Publishers* (1991), a book based on feedback I received from vanity publishers, assisted the Advertising Standards Authority, and collaborated in making television and radio programmes. In 1999, I was invited to the House of Lords to talk about the problem of vanity publishing and the need for a change in the law to stop 'rogue traders' in the publishing world. However, it was not until 2008 that the law was suitably changed to enable the authorities to better curb the excesses of rogue vanity publishers, should they wish.

The perils of vanity publishing

'Vanity publisher' is a phrase I coined in the early 1960s when two American companies were advertising widely in the British press offering to publish poems for a payment of £9 and £12 per poem, respectively. Since then the term has extended its meaning to 'any company that charges a client to publish a book'.

Mainstream publishers invest in the marketing and promotion of a book and make their profit from its sales. In contrast, vanity publishers make their money from up-front charges. One of the main drawbacks of being published by a vanity publisher is its lack of credibility within the industry. The majority of booksellers and library suppliers are loath to handle vanity books and few reviewers are willing to consider a book published in this way. The Business Unit Director of one of the UK's biggest booksellers wrote in 1996: 'We do not buy from vanity publishers except in exceptional circumstances. Their books are, with one or two exceptions, badly produced, over-priced, have poor, uncompetitive jackets and usually have no marketing support.'

I have an extensive collection of documentation passed to me from authors who have approached one of the 100-plus vanity publishers operating in the UK. It consists of vanity publishers' initial promotional letters, subsequent written promises, the contracts and letters of complaint from the author, and the vanity publishers' response to those complaints. In recent years, court judgements have found that some vanity publishers are guilty of 'gross misrepresentation of the services they offer' and, as a result, some have been successfully sued and others forced into 'voluntary' liquidation – often only to swiftly reappear under different names.

How vanity publishers operate

Mainstream publishers never advertise for authors and almost never charge a client, whether known or unknown. Vanity publishers place advertisements wherever they possibly can inviting authors to submit manuscripts. Almost without exception, when authors submit work the vanity publisher will reply that they would like to publish the book but that, as an unknown, the author will have to pay towards the cost. Vanity publishers may tell the author they are very selective in the authors they accept and praise the work, but this is false flattery. I have not been able to find one person during the last 22 years who has been turned down by a vanity publisher – however poorly written their book is. The vanity publisher may state that this is the way many famous authors in the past set out, but this is untrue. Some famous well-respected authors *have* self-published but none of the 'famous authors' they quote started their writing career by paying a vanity publisher. The BBC programme *Southern Eye* reported that many authors had been sent exactly the same 'glowing report', whatever the subject or quality of their book.

Vanity publishers have charged aspiring authors anything from £1,800 up to (in one recorded instance) £20,000 for publishing their book. Many authors have borrowed thousands of pounds on the strength of promised 'returning royalties', as authors are often led to believe that sales through the vanity publisher's marketing department will recoup their outlay.

In December 1997, *Private Eye* ran an article about three authors, one of whom had paid £2,400 and the other two £1,800 each to a vanity publisher, on the basis that their books would command a 'high level of royalties'. These royalties amounted to £16.35, £21.28 and £47.30 respectively. When the authors complained they each received a threatening letter from the vanity publisher's solicitor. The same company's business practices were featured on the BBC programme *Watchdog* in November 2002.

Some vanity publishers ask their clients to pay a 'subvention', the *Collins English Dictionary* definition of which is 'a grant, aid, or subsidy, as from a government', and therefore it is a meaningless term when used in the context of vanity publishing. However the request for payment is worded, it is the author who will bear the full cost of publishing their book. Not a share of, or a subsidy towards, but the whole cost and a healthy profit margin on top.

Few vanity publishers quote for a specific number of copies, leaving the author with little idea what they are paying for. Vanity publishers may simply keep manuscripts 'on file' and only print on demand, making it difficult to deliver copies quickly enough to the outlets which *do* order them. Other companies propose that once book sales have reached a certain 'target' figure, the client's outlay will be refunded. The number of copies required to be sold is always well in excess of a realistic target.

Some companies claim that part of the service they offer is to send copies of books they 'publish' to Nielsen Books, the Copyright Receipt Office and the British Library. In fact, this is a legal requirement for all UK publishers. Other companies claim a 'special' relationship which enables them to supply information on your book to particular outlets on the internet. But Amazon.co.uk does not support this: 'Books are listed on Amazon.co.uk's website in a number of ways – we take feeds from BookData and Nielsens (who automatically update these details on our website) as well as from several wholesalers'.

Authors using a vanity publisher should be aware that once they have made the final payment, that vanity publisher doesn't need to sell a single copy of their book.

Self-publishing

Another way for an author to see their book in print is to self-publish. However, some vanity publishers may try to pass themselves off as self-publishers. For a book to be genuinely self-published, a name designated by the author as his or her publishing house must appear on the copyright page of the book as 'publisher' and the book's ISBN number must be registered by the ISBN Agency to that author as publisher.

All the copies of a self-published book are the property of the author. If an author does not wish to be involved with the sale and distribution of their book, this can be indicated in the 'Distributor (if different from Publisher)' section on the form sent to the ISBN Agency before publication.

On the title page of every book there is a paragraph which, in essence, states 'All rights are reserved. No part of this book can be stored on a retrieval system or transmitted in any form or by whatever means without the prior permission in writing from the *publisher*', i.e. not 'the author' who the vanity publisher may have persuaded their book is '*self*-published'.

Any company which publishes books under its own name or imprint cannot, by definition, claim to help authors to self-publish. The honest exception is where the publisher's address appears on the title page, the paragraph above states 'without prior permission of the copyright holder', and the author appears as copyright holder on the same page. True self-publishing gives authors much greater control over the production and dissemination of their books.

Aspiring authors should be careful not to be taken in by the promises of some vanity publishers which have so often proved false. The legal phrase 'Caveat Emptor' (Buyer Beware) here becomes 'Caveat Scriptor' – 'Author Beware!'

Johnathon Clifford may be contacted via his website, www.vanitypublishing.info, which was archived by the British Museum Library in 2009. There you will find a free Advice Pack designed to protect aspiring authors.

Recommended companies

Amolibros
Loundshay Manor Cottage, Preston Bowyer, Milverston, Taunton TA4 1QF
tel (01823) 401527
website www.amolibros.co.uk
Contact Jane Tatam

Authors On Line
19 The Cinques, Gamlingay, Sandy, Beds. SG19 3NU
tel (01767) 652005
website www.authorsonline.co.uk
Contact Richard Fitt

Matador Troubador Publishing Ltd
9 Priory Business Park, Wistow Road, Kibworth, Beauchamp, Leicester LE8 0RX
tel 0116-279 2299
website www.troubador.co.uk
Contact Jeremy Thompson

York Publishing Services Ltd
64 Hallfield Road, Layerthorpe, York YO31 7ZQ
tel (01904) 431213
website www.yps-publishing.co.uk
Contact Duncan Beal

Book clubs

Baker Books

Manfield Park, Cranleigh, Surrey GU6 8NU
tel (01483) 267888 *fax* (01483) 267409
email enquiries@bakerbooks.co.uk
website www.bakerbooks.co.uk

School book club for children aged 3–16. Operates in the UK and in English-medium schools overseas.

BCA

Hargreaves Road, Groundwell Ind. Estate, Swindon SN25 5BG
tel (01793) 723547 *fax* (01793) 747113
website www.member.booksdirect.co.uk

Books for Children, Fantasy & SF Book Club, The History Guild, Military and Aviation Book Society, The Railway Book Club, Books Direct, Omnibus.

Bibliophile

5 Datapoint, South Crescent, London E16 4TL
tel 020-7474 2474 *fax* 020-7474 8589
email orders@bibliophilebooks.com
website www.bibliophilebooks.com
Secretary Annie Quigley

To promote value-for-money reading. Upmarket literature and classical music on CD available from mail order catalogue (10 p.a.). Over 3,000 titles covering art and fiction to travel, history and children's books. Founded 1978.

The Book People Ltd

Park Menai, Bangor LL57 4FB
tel 0845 6024040 *fax* 0845 6064242
email sales@thebookpeople.co.uk
website www.thebookpeople.co.uk

Popular general fiction and non-fiction, including children's and travel. Monthly.

Cygnus Book Club

PO Box 15, Llandeilo, Carmarthenshire SA19 6YX
tel (01558) 825500, 0845 456 1577 *fax* (01558) 825517
email enquiries@cygnus-books.co.uk
website www.cygnus-books.co.uk

Includes psychology and self-help, diet, health and exercise, world religions, new economics and education, green issues, mythology, spirituality. Monthly. No unsolicited MSS.

The Folio Society

44 Eagle Street, London WC1R 4FS
tel 020-7400 4222 *fax* 020-7400 4242
website www.foliosociety.com

Fine editions of classic literature.

Letterbox Library

Unit 151 Stratford Workshops, Burford Road, London E15 2SP
tel 020-7503 4801 *fax* 020-7503 4800
email info@letterboxlibrary.com
website www.letterboxlibrary.com

Specialises in children's books that celebrate equality and diversity.

The Poetry Book Society

The Dutch House, 307–308 High Holborn, London WC1V 7LL
tel 020-7831 7468 *fax* 020-7831 6967
email info@poetrybooks.co.uk
website www.poetrybooks.co.uk, www.poetrybookshoponline.com, www.childrenspoetrybookshelf.co.uk

Runs a quarterly poetry book club, with poet selectors choosing the best new collection of the quarter, and the Children's Poetry Bookshelf, a three-times-yearly book club offering children's poetry to teachers, parents and grandparents. Also runs online poetry bookshop and distributes and sells CDs for the Poetry Archive. Awards the TS Eliot Prize for Poetry and, in partnership with the British Library, the Michael Marks Awards for Poetry Pamphlets. See also page 346.

Red House

PO Box 142, Bangor LL57 4ZP
tel 0845 606 4280 *fax* 0845 606 4242
email enquiries@redhouse.co.uk
website www.redhouse.co.uk

Helps parents to select the right books for their children at affordable prices. A free monthly magazine features the best of the latest titles on offer as well as young reader reviews and insights into the minds of popular children's writers. Sponsors the Red House Children's Book Award (page 563). Founded 1979.

Scholastic Book Clubs and Fairs

Euston House, 24 Eversholt Street, London NW1 1DB
tel 020-7756 7756 *fax* 020-7756 7799
email scbenquiries@scholastic.co.uk
website www.scholastic.co.uk, www.scholastic.co.uk

Leading schools book clubs and fairs. Offers primary and secondary clubs and fairs.

Scholastic Book Fairs

Westfield Road, Southam, Warks. CV47 0RA
tel 0845 603 9091 (freephone)
website www.scholastic.co.uk/bookfairs
Managing Director Steven Thompson

Sells directly to children, parents and teachers in schools through 25,000 week-long events held in schools throughout the UK.

Writers' Bookshelf

Writers' News, 5th Floor, 31–32 Park Row, Leeds LS1 5JD
tel 0113 200 2929 *fax* 0113 200 2928

Books and magazines for writers.

Poetry

Notes from a passionate poet

Benjamin Zephaniah describes his route to being published.

'How did you first get published?' and 'can you give me any advice on getting published?' must be the two questions I am most regularly asked as I go poeting around this planet. And what really gets me is that for most of my poetic life I have found them so hard to answer without doing a long talk on race and culture, and giving a lesson on the oral traditions of the Caribbean and Africa. I'm trying hard not to do that now but I have to acknowledge that I do come out of the oral tradition and to some extent I am still very much part of the Jamaican branch of that tradition, which has now established itself in Britain. In reality, getting published wasn't that hard for me: I came to the page from the stage. I didn't wake up one day and decide to join the oral tradition, I simply started performing in churches and community centres, on street corners and at political rallies, and I really didn't care about being published in books – I used to say I just want to be published in people's hearts. Now I don't want to sound like a royal seeking sympathy or a surgeon evaluating her or his work, I just feel there's something very special about hearing people recite a poem of yours back to you when you know that it has never been written down: it means that they must have heard me recite the poem and it had such an impact on them that it left an impression on their minds – but I say hearts because it sounds more sensitive.

Someone with a PhD once told me that the most important thing I could do was to get published, so for what seemed like an eternity (in fact it was just a couple of months) I became the most depressed kid on the block as the rejections flooded in, and I took each rejection very personally. I soon stopped punishing myself and went back to performing. Within the black and Asian communities there was a large network of venues to perform in and I was happy there, performing for 'my people'. But it wasn't long before I started to make a bit of a name for myself in what we now call the mainstream, and then the publishers came running back to me, many of them apologising and saying that the person who sent the rejection letter to me had now moved on and they weren't very good anyway. I didn't blame the publishers; I wasn't angry with them. It was a time when the British publishing industry simply didn't understand Reggae and Dub poetry, and the performance scene as we know it today had hardly taken root. It's not practical to advise all budding poets to go down the route that I chose. Some poets simply don't want to perform whilst others want something published before they take to the stage – they literally want something to cling to as they recite – but I have to say there is nothing like looking your audience in the face and delivering your work to them in person.

I used to be able to give a run down of the poetry publishing and performance scene in Britain in about 30 minutes, but not any longer, with the internet and all that, the universe has changed. Not only are there hundreds of ways to get your poetry published, you can now publish your performance and have a worldwide hit without ever actually having a book or leaving your bedroom. You don't even have to tread the boards to become a performance poet. The choice is now yours: you can be a Dub poet, a pub poet, a cyber poet, a graffiti poet, a rap poet, a naked poet, a space poet, a Myspace poet, or a street poet. You can be a geek poet, a YouTube poet, an underground poet, a Facebook poet, a sound poet, and if you like to keep it short you can be a Twitter poet. You can go any way you want, but you must never forget to be a poet. You must never forget why you started writing (or performing) and you must love your art. The love I had for words as a baby has never left me, and when I was getting all those rejection letters and feeling so unwanted, my love for poetry never waned.

And another thing: read poetry. Many people tell me that they love poetry but after a minute or so of investigation I find that they only love their own poetry, and in many cases they only understand their own poetry. You can get a lot of help from teachers or in workshops, but reading other people's poetry is the best way of understanding poetry, it is the best way of getting into the minds of other poets. This great book that you now have in your hands and learned people who understand the industry are able to give you much better advice on getting published than I can, and if you do get published your publisher or agent should be offering you all the practical help you need. But you have to have the passion, you have to have the inspiration, you have to be a poet. Stay true.

Benjamin Zephaniah has been performing poetry since he was 11 years old. He has also written 12 books of poetry, four novels, and recorded five music CD albums. He spends much of his time encouraging young people to write and perform poetry and has received 16 honorary doctorates in recognition of his work. His latest book is a martial arts travelogue called *Kung Fu Trip* (Bloomsbury 2011) and his last musical release is *Naked* (One Little Indian Records). He is currently Professor of Poetry and Creative Writing at Brunel University. His website is www.benjaminzephaniah.com.

Getting poetry published

Michael Schmidt examines the challenges for poets who wish to see their work published.

Start with this axiom: you have not come here to make money.

I write as a publisher who has spent over 40 years not making money out of poetry, and as a quondam poet whose rewards were never material, either. Money may be a consequence, but only in a few cases, usually obtained in the form of grants and bursaries, when a career is well beyond the point at which an article such as this is of interest.

In the old days, right up through the 1950s, there was a popular tradition of verse writing: people kept commonplace books for friends to write lines in when visiting. Or folk composed ballads, Christmas poems, dialect eclogues, limericks. Verse was part of social engagement. It took itself seriously in formal terms but made no pretence of being 'art'. There was a level of competence in making conventional verses, sometimes beyond English, in Latin or Greek, and most people could tell a good piece of verse from a bad one. Jane Austen's family was given to playful versing. In secondhand bookshops you find tomes with verse inscriptions. Like weekend painters, verse writers expressed themselves clearly and skilfully, bringing direct, strictly occasional pleasure to another person or a group. The ambition to Get Published At All Costs had not set in. Now it has; it has been endemic for three decades. The social space for verse has almost vanished, and with it the popular versifying skills. Such a loss has consequences. Dr Johnson in *The Life of Savage* reflects that 'negligence and irregularity, long continued, will make knowledge useless, wit ridiculous, and genius contemptible'. The creative writing culture of reception nowadays seems to be defined less as readership or audience, more as 'market'. Is this change regrettable? Yes. Has it brought any benefits? To the art of poetry, to poetry readership, very few.

Even today, weekend painters know their work will never hang in the Tate; amateur musicians (singers, instrumentalists, composers) content themselves with making music as an end in itself. But the occasional versifier is a dying breed, like the red squirrel, replaced by the interloping grey who, a year into writing, submits work to a dozen editors at once, declaring it to be original, relevant, topical. In the twinkling of an eye these strident creatures absorb, without troubling to learn names, the art of Chaucer, Spenser, Milton, Cowper, Dickinson, Walcott, Rich. Their opinion of modern poetry is low. But then they do not base their opinion on a very large sample. They will have heard of the market leaders and remember some of the poetry read at school.

As an editor at a small publishing house I receive over 2,000 full manuscripts a year (and many more submissions for *PN Review*). Telephone calls, letters and emails ask what kind of poetry we publish, whether we publish poetry at all, or how much it will cost to have poems printed. Few poets submitting are aware of the editorial contents of a poetry publisher's list, despite websites and other resources offering this information. Many have read, perhaps in this *Yearbook*, which publishers have a poetry list and try for publication, without doing a smidgen of research. Without reading. Few seem aware of how large a shoal of wannabe poets surrounds the little flotilla of publishers, editors and other validators. Poetry becomes a means to an end, not an end in itself: to be a poet, go for prizes, give readings and all the peripheral rewards which in the end poison and parch the individual spring, assuming it has more than illusory water in it.

Publishing in book form

An article of this kind usually proffers advice: how to present a manuscript, how to address an editor, what to expect from a contract, etc. I'd rather try to give writers who believe they have a body of publishable work a realistic sense of the chance of publication, and a realistic preparation for its aftermath, assuming the first goal is achieved. Better to counsel realism than foster illusion.

First, the chances of book publication. More than 2,000 new books of verse are published each year, but few are marketed or sold and fewer still reviewed. A list like the one I edit, with 36 poetry titles a year, accommodates at most four or five first collections, often fewer. Other substantial poetry publishers go for a year or five without adding new names to their lists. Few first collections sell over 1,000 copies. Indeed, some may sell fewer than 300. The book trade has become resistant to all but the market leaders in poetry; few independent presses get their poets even into some of the leading chains. One publisher who has set out to change the equation is Salt, with its short run and print-on-demand approach, and its website and Podcasts. Others have followed, notably Shearsman; and Arc is active in all sorts of ways.

The ecology of poetry publishing, as distinct from that of standard trade publishing, is based more and more narrowly on events. A poet can publish his or her own work, paying a printer to do the job and selling at readings. But then, who is going to invite a self-published poet to read? A poet can go to one of the vanity presses and pay a more substantial sum for the promise of exposure. Again, such publication capitalises on illusion and, as the title proclaims, vanity (see *Vanity publishing*, page 329).

There *are* new opportunities which can be valuable. Any poet is free to post work on the web, in both text and voice form, inviting response. It's quite cheap to do so and response is almost immediate. There are electronic magazines as well. In a sense, the withering away of the poetry book trade is a harbinger of the wider impact of the web. Unfortunately, the web is not discriminating and it is hard to know how a critical take on work self-published on the web will develop. At every stage, it seems to me, poets are tempted to succumb, in their eagerness for publication, to acts of desperation. Publish and

Poetry publishers

Anvil Press Poetry
See page 125.

Arc Publications
See page 125.

Bloodaxe Books Ltd
See page 129.

Carcanet
See page 132.

Dedalus Ltd
See page 136.

Enitharmon Press
See page 139.

Flambard Press
website www.flambardpress.co.uk

The Gallery Press
website www.gallerypress.com

The Poetry Business
See page 346.

Salt Publishing
See page 171.

Seren
See page 172.

Shearsman Books
See page 172.

be damned! Luck would be a fine thing. There is not even a sufficient audience to damn new work on the web. The question must be, how to publish and be sufficiently visible to *be* damned, or welcomed, as the case may be. But we are getting ahead of ourselves: the first question must be the quality of the work and the motive of the writer.

Before looking for a publisher, writers of verse (as of anything else) should interrogate themselves. *Why* do I want to be published in book form? Is it mere whim or is my work genuinely original? The only way you can answer these questions is by wide reading, not only of contemporaries but also of poets from the past. To be able to judge your art, you must understand it, as you would any other. What makes my work original? In a few instances subject matter in itself can be sufficiently interesting to justify a book, but this is rare: it has more to do with the accidents of birth and upbringing than with any choices a poet might make. Originality is expressed in diction, prosody and form. It need not be dazzling. Edward Thomas recognised Robert Frost's originality, reviewing *North of Boston* in 1914: 'This is one of the most revolutionary books of modern times, but one of the quietest and least aggressive. It speaks, and it is poetry.'

A poet who sets out to get published without understanding in depth the art practised, and the nature of the work intended for publication, is on a hiding to very little. Chances are that such a poet will make decisions that ensure the poetry remains unread.

Ask, before you solicit editorial judgment, to whom your poetry is likely to appeal: To friends and family? The local community (is it in dialect, locally relevant in some way)? To a religious group? Is your work sufficiently distinctive to appeal beyond those groups from which your identity is derived?

Seeking critical appraisal

If a spouse, relation, teacher or friend commends your verse, it will be gratifying, but how informed are they, and is their response to you as the writer or to the writing? Is it courtesy or real validation? Kind Sir John Betjeman used to write a note to anyone who sent him poems saying 'you show potential' or 'talent'. Thousands of poets thus commended would take his endorsement and include it for the next 20 years with each magazine and volume submission. The commendation of a kind writer is, alas, not worth the paper it is written on. If an established writer believes in your work, he or she will make it a mission to send your work to an editor.

It is important to get a critical purchase on your work, not to overestimate it. Some poets accept that their level is, say, among small magazines; they are content to exist there in a community of similarly committed writers. They do not try for the 'better' magazines, knowing they haven't a chance of getting in. They may blame those magazines as elitist and cliquish and no doubt some of them are, but elites and cliques that are permeable to quality. Finding one's level is an early stage in establishing peace of mind: always to aim too high and so to invite rebuff finally undermines self-respect.

Never ask an editor for comments and criticisms unless you are willing to take them. I am often asked for 'a serious appraisal'. When work seems genuinely interesting I offer detailed advice, and often receive back angry letters or defences of work I have risked commenting upon. A poem works or fails to work; no amount of argufying can convert an experienced reader. I may come to understand more clearly what the intention of a poem *was*, and therefore better to understand how far short it has fallen.

Magazines, the internet and broadcasting

Most editors advise new writers to seek publication in magazines first. This is mixed advice. It assumes the poet writes 'filler' poems, the fast food that can be served up in a weekly journal. If you are published in magazines the editor does not respect, it may diminish his or her respect for your work. It is crucial, especially if you are not prolific, to try for publication in places where (a) the work will be widely read, and (b) publication will increase your visibility. *The Times Literary Supplement* and *London Review of Books* have a curious and unpredictable taste; several specialised journals may be worth trying, *Agenda, Ambit, Iota, Kaffeeklatsch, Magma, Poetry, Poetry Review, The Reader, Rialto, Stand, Stride, Poetry London, The North, The Dark Horse* and *PN Review* among them. It is crucial to subscribe to journals you find congenial, read them regularly and get a sense of the wider world of contemporary publication. Do this not in a spirit of market research, more out of curiosity about the state of your art. Among overseas magazines worth close attention are *Chicago Review, Parnassus, Raritan* and *Threepenny Review*.

There are numerous opportunities to publish on the web in web-zines of varying quality. These include, among many dozens, the *Manchester Review, Jacket, Slate*, the *BowWow-Shop*, the *Literateur, The Wolf* and *THESHOp*. Publication in such e-magazines can be satisfying; it can also be dangerous for your copyright (the work can slip out of your control), though more and more editors are willing to credit the web as a place to look for poems. It is worth remembering that a poem first published on the web is unlikely to be published in a reputable magazine.

Broadcasting is as unpredictable a medium of dissemination as the web. There are slots for various kinds of poetry on radio: dramatic, lyric, etc. Look at the broadcasting schedules, familiarise yourself with the poetry programmes and producers, locally and nationally. On many networks a broadcast poem is heard by quite a large, if not a discriminating or informed, audience. Editors have been known to track down poems heard in broadcast, especially in the poet's own voice if that poet is a good performer.

The importance of market research

You can do your market research for a book publisher in your personal library of modern poetry books (you ought to have one, with books by favourite authors from a variety of imprints, and not just anthologies). Most have editorial priorities which are more or less coherent, expressed in anthologies or in the general choice offered. The chief imprints are Anvil, Bloodaxe, Cape, Carcanet, Chatto & Windus, Dedalus, Enitharmon, Faber, Gallery, Penguin, Picador, Salt, Seren and Shearsman among larger players, and Arc, Happenstance, Nine Arches, The Poetry Business, Reality Street, Salmon, Shoestring Press and Waywiser, among the smaller independents. Many other valuable outlets exist. The Poetry Book Society makes a convenient selection and has useful catalogues, but trusting a book club's choices is no safer for the poetry than for the fiction lover. Always read *beyond*.

In approaching journal editors or publishers it is important to indicate that you know who they are, and why you have chosen them over others. A brief letter is sufficient. If you practise multiple submissions, warn the editors to whom you write. Some editors follow a geological time-scale in replying. If you have not had a reply in six weeks, feel free to send your work elsewhere, but should the first editor accept it in the end, you must immediately withdraw it from other editors.

Success is slow: a hundred rejections may precede an acceptance. Or acceptance may never quite come. If it doesn't, how do you deal with failure? Many wannabe poets who cannot get visibly published develop a strategy of blame. It is not, they insist, the quality of the work that deprives them of readership, it is the cabals that control the avenues of transmission. Jonathan Swift knew this:

If on Parnassus' top you sit,
You rarely bite, are always bit:
Each poet of inferior size
On you shall rail and criticise…

Poetry magazines

Agenda
website www.agendapoetry.co.uk
A quarterly with a long, varied history, often surprising in its choices.

Ambit
website www.ambitmagazine.co.uk
Quarterly magazine that prints original poetry, short fiction, art and reviews.

The Dark Horse
website www.thedarkhorsemagazine.com
The best Scottish poetry magazine, international with a formal bias.

Iota
website www.iotapoetry.co.uk
Always interesting and uneven.

Kaffeeklatsch
website http://manualpoetry.co.uk
A new arrival with bright young editors.

Magma
website http://magmapoetry.com
An open and broad editorial remit.

Mslexia
website www.mslexia.co.uk
New writing by women.

The North
website www.poetrybusiness.co.uk
A poetry journal published by Smith-Doorstop and The Poetry Business in Huddersfield.

PN Review
website www.poetrysociety.org.uk/content/publications/review/
After 30-odd years, it is widely regarded as among the best publications for poetry, with a broad geographical and generic reach.

Poetry London
website www.poetrylondon.co.uk
An outstanding magazine for poetry, London listings and reviews.

Poetry Review
website www.poetryreview.org.uk
The journal of the Poetry Society.

Poets & Writers
website www.pw.org
A magazine on the craft and business of writing.

The Reader
website www.thereader.co.uk
A quarterly literary magazine.

The Riatlo
website www.therialto.co.uk
Long-established and with occasional surprises.

Stand
website www.people.vcu.edu/~dlatane/stand-maga/index.html
Resurrected and re-energised; a serious and entertaining magazine.

Stride Magazine
website www.stridemagazine.co.uk
Stride is a place to start.

USA

Chicago Review
website http://humanities.uchicago.edu/orgs/review

Parnassus
website http://parnassusreview.com

Raritan Literary Magazine
Rutgers – The State University of New Jersey, 31 Mine Street, New Brunswick, NJ 08903, USA
tel 732-932-7887 *fax* 732-932-7855

The Threepenny Review
PO Box 9131, Berkeley, CA 94709, USA
Submissions should be sent with an sae.

See also *Magazines UK and Ireland* starting on page 28 or *Poetry organisations* on page 346.

Other poets study 'the market' and try to follow the latest fashion. Runt-Raines, runt-Muldoons and Motions, have given way to runt-Duffys and Armitages. Aping success can seem to work: in my late 'teens, when the *New Statesman* had rejected me several times, I wrote a poem in what I took to be the style of Ted Walker, a poet popular with the magazine's poetry editor. Sure enough, my verse was accepted. I had the same experience with *Poetry Now* on radio. The editor loved what he called 'the macabre' and I delivered precisely that. Such poems, cynically composed, had a short half-life. Imitation is part of any serious apprenticeship, but publishing unacknowledged imitations, especially if they are written not to develop skills but to achieve publication, is a form of failure.

Dealing with success

Assuming the Muses of publication smile, how do you deal with success? Success can be failure postponed. A book is edited, designed, published, and then falls into a black hole of neglect. A book is published and receives negative reviews. A book is published, receives good reviews, but fails to sell. A book is published, receives good reviews, sells, but the next book does less well and there is a future of diminishing returns. The judge at the pearly gates will declare, 'It is the sort of verse which was modern in its time'.

Real success is rare and has little to do with the strategies outlined here. No poet living in the UK at this time makes a living solely from writing poems. Most write and teach, or write and perform, or have a day job, or write in other genres (novels, radio and television plays, journalism) as well as poetry. Assuming the poetry is good and/or well received, there will be invitations to perform. Fees vary from about £100 to £1,000, depending on the occasion and the venue. A poet who is a good performer will read once or twice a week for a period of time and sell more books than a poet who cannot perform convincingly, even if the latter's poems are better. Indeed some apparently substantial reputations are based on performance skills rather than on the quality of the poetry.

Real success is judged less by the marketplace, more by a culture of reception which gradually grows alert to new work and explores it. It may be, if the work you are writing is original and challenging, that you will have to develop your own means of transmission on paper (a magazine, a pamphlet or book publishing house) or on the web. As long as the vehicles you create exist to serve not only your own work, but poetry more widely, whether the writing of fellow radicals or neglected texts from the past that helped shape your perspectives and formal approaches. The creation of such vehicles means that you retain control of production and dissemination; eventually the endeavour, particular and general, is acknowledged, the work read. You are in dialogue with readers.

The endorsement of an Establishment consisting of the larger publishers, specialist lists, journals and the academy, is not a guarantee of quality. What is a guarantee is a readership which will go out of its way to get hold of your work – a poem in a magazine, a pamphlet,

Poetry online

A Public Space
website http://apublicspace.org

Contemporary Poetry Review
website www.cprw.com

Jacket
website www.jacketmagazine.com

Poetry Daily
website www.poems.com

an e-poem, a book – and will invest time and creative energy in reading you and taking bearings from what you propose.

It would be churlish of me not to mention that many poets spend their time and resources on entering competitions, and competitions are a way (the three or four major ones at least) of making yourself briefly visible. A competition-winning poem is not 'news that stays news', as Pound said poetry ought to be, but mere news. Mere news with money attached: not to be sneezed at. There is also the matter of fees and advances. For a 24-line poem published in a journal, payment will vary from £30 to £500, depending on the outlet. The advance for a book of poems, especially a first collection, will vary from £300 to £3,000, with the occasional mad exception.

In negotiating a publishing contract, it is worth remembering that the greatest value your poems will have in the long term for you, as for your publisher, is unlikely to be the book sales. What will matter in the end, assuming your work becomes established, is the subsidiary rights: anthology, quotation, broadcasting, electronic, translation. Several poetic estates live handsomely on subsidiary rights income. For three decades I have been publishing William Carlos Williams' poetry.

So much depends
upon
a red wheel
barrow…

Eight simple lines have earned Williams' estate, and his publisher, between £27 and £35 per week over that period.

Michael Schmidt OBE is editor of *PN Review* and director of Carcanet Press. He is Professor of Poetry at the University of Glasgow.

See also...

- *Notes from a passionate poet*, page 333
- *Approaching a poetry publisher*, page 342
- *Poetry organisations*, page 346

Approaching a poetry publisher

Roddy Lumsden outlines the route to getting a volume of poetry published and advises poets on when and how to approach a publisher.

If you follow the perils and pleasures of British poetry via the newspapers, you are excused for thinking things are in a bad way. The media rarely misses a chance to tell us how little we are selling or to report incidences of cronyism and infighting. Their interest is mainly in the peripheral areas of prizes and 'poetry celebrities'. In past editions of this *Yearbook*, this article noted optimistically that sales were better than reported and were thriving. However, there is no doubt that the economic situation has been having an effect on sales: books that might have sold 1,000 or more copies ten years ago are struggling to reach the break-even point, so publishers are tightening their belts.

Commercial publishers with poetry lists are currently more likely to drop poets than take them on – most have scaled down to a handful of books a year. Independent poetry presses are also being cautious. They still take on a small number of poets most years but, at a time when even well-known poets are not making them money, they are looking for poets who, via popular or specialist appeal, can market their work and sell hundreds of copies.

Large bookshops are stocking less poetry, alas, but other sales opportunities exist: smaller chains, specialist outlets, academic, library, overseas and online sales, and sales through poetry readings and courses. Although few poets can make a living from royalties and readings alone, there are certainly a few hundred British poets who make a comfortable, if far from lavish, living from poetry – universities, schoolwork, reviewing, residencies, editing, etc – or who combine this with other part-time employment. Given the unexpected rise in creative writing courses (there are now more than 600 full-time degree courses in creative writing in the UK, see page 630) which require experienced writers to pass on knowledge and techniques, there is now little need for poets to scrape by in an attic on a diet of lentils and divine inspiration.

Yet poetry publishing is a tricky business. Time was when a young chap had his mother type up his sheaf of poems – 20 or so would do – and sent them to the publisher, along with his note of recommendation from a mutual acquaintance at Cambridge and a list of a hundred friends and relatives who had vowed to purchase the slim volume. Things have changed. Until recent decades, few working-class or women writers would have considered attempting to publish. In recent years, at last, poetry books by women outnumber those by men, reflecting the fact that far more women write.

The postwar decades saw shifts in the ethos of British poets but changes affecting them in the century's latter decades were about 'infrastructure' – the rise of independent publishers, the creation of a circuit of poetry venues and literary festivals, government-backed subsidy and promotions, the stiffening of poetic factionalism, the confidence (and sheer numbers) of small magazines, the liberty/tyranny of the internet (with its bookselling and blogging, communities and catfights), the demise of 'broadsheet' interest, the desire for voices from outside the white middle class, the spread of residencies, commissions, fellowships and teaching opportunities.

In his 2004 T.S. Eliot lecture, Picador editor Don Paterson commented on the abundance of writers who, wanting a slice of these opportunities, push for publication before they are ready. Many writers, with hindsight, feel their first books lack cohesion. Another editor told me that many small press poets would have had a strong chance with bigger publishers had they been less impatient.

How much unpublished poetry is there? Let's look at some rough numbers. A late 1990s survey suggested 8% of the UK adult population had recently written a poem of some sort (of which two-thirds were women). Discounting the many who scribble in a diary or pen a quick verse in a card, we're still left with over a million writers who harbour some hope of publication. A few hundred poetry collections by individual writers are published most years. Most – admirable though they may be – are small-scale, from local presses, in pamphlet form, in small print runs. The better-known independent poetry presses (Anvil, Bloodaxe, Carcanet, Salt, Seren and others) publish over 150 books between them, while the few commercial presses (Cape, Chatto, Picador, Faber) venture only around 30 in total. However, these mainly comprise books by established poets from here or abroad (and new editions of work by deceased writers).

First books are few and far between, especially from bigger publishers. Having spoken to most poetry editors, and having done freelance editorial work too, I sympathise with publishers. Space for a debut sometimes comes at the expense of an older poet not selling well. It is difficult to promote a new poet – bookshops want anthologies, promoters want 'names'; despite all the opportunities listed above, poets have to work hard even after publication to make themselves known. Most first-timers are disappointed to find their collection is not met with a raft of reviews, shortlists and reading invitations. It is not unusual now for a poetry book to go unreviewed.

What publishers are looking for

So how do poets get published these days? Well, rarely from what is perceived to be the standard approach of simply submitting a manuscript to a publisher. My advice (and all editors and established poets will concur) is this: you *must* go through the hoops and tasks of learning your craft and proving yourself before considering an approach to a publisher. And no, you're not the exception, even if you are a brilliant young thing, or a late starter expecting short cuts. A first collection will contain 40–70 poems, and most poets will have written a few discarded efforts for each one that makes the cut.

Publishers will expect you to tell them where you have been published in magazine form. Broadly, your work should have appeared in several places. This should include well-established publications: vital though the little magazines are, you are frankly unlikely to be published in book form if the better-known periodicals are consistently turning down your poems. Publishers want you to have published substantially in good magazines and journals: a track record of magazine publications shows commitment to developing a manuscript and an effort to develop a readership for your work.

A few years ago, I went through several boxes of manuscripts for an independent press. These scripts had already been deemed worth a third look: most submissions are returned quickly since editors become adept at identifying substandard work. They don't often make mistakes, and would make fewer if the process wasn't clogged by those who send too soon. The manuscripts I read were generally impressive, carefully assembled by capable writers and much of it as good as work I'd recently seen in book form. But this publisher only has room for one or two debuts each year. My task was to look for exceptional, original manuscripts and after a while, I found myself growing impatient with poems which were well written but overfamiliar in style and subject matter.

If you do feel you are ready to approach a publisher, you must find out their current submissions policy (see the listings in this *Yearbook* and look at publishers' websites). Some of the bigger lists go through periods where they will not look at any unsolicited work. Some prefer sample submissions of a dozen poems only. Don't make common mistakes: email submissions are rarely allowed; full return postage must be supplied; never ask for an email response, or a detailed critique; keep your covering letter short and pertinent; never drop the name of someone who has praised your work unless you have the express permission to do so.

For younger poets, the Eric Gregory Awards (see page 553) have been an important step up for decades now, though far from a guarantee of publication. The annual awards, run by the Society of Authors, offer grants to the most promising poets (published or not) under 30. Competition success can be another way to attract notice to your work, especially the National Poetry competition (page 560). Every poet with serious ambitions should seek opportunities to recite their work and should make the effort to learn to read well, which does not require performance skills, just confidence and conviction.

How poets get published

Many people will whisper that it's 'who you know' that really counts. Well, certainly. This is not about nepotism and 'couch casting'; rather, if you are keen to progress, you will seek out peers and mentors where you can. Find a writing group run by a worthy tutor (preferably one with books out from a press you have heard of). You may not live in an area where good writing classes or writers-in-residence are available, but residential courses such as those run by the excellent Arvon Foundation (see page 630) have been a step towards many a successful publication (and grants are available for those with more promise than funds). Above all else, read lots of poetry which is contemporary and engaging, for that's what you will have to be – there is no market for the retro or pastiche. And read widely – many feel, with some validity, that larger British poetry presses can favour the anodyne and the commercial.

For myself, a few years of feverish reading, writing and showing work to university writers-in-residence and to other young poets lead to an Eric Gregory Award which was followed by interest from a major publisher (Faber, whose editor had been on the award panel). I spent five years carefully building up a manuscript. Faber then featured my work in an anthology of eight promising poets but turned down the manuscript. I worked hard to improve it and sent a pamphlet (which I cheaply self-published) to a few other publishers. I was quickly approached by Bloodaxe, who were familiar with my work via the Award and publication in magazines. Here are some examples of how other poets got published:

- Poet 'A' was a late starter and wrote in various ways. At a group, he found that poems in a certain style (which he had felt came too easy) were well received. He gladly went with this direction, and put effort into reading his poems aloud when he had the opportunity. A poetry editor saw him reading and asked to see his work.
- Poet 'B' had a reputation as a performance poet but had begun writing more formally. He read widely and joined a weekly group with a tutor whose poetry he admired and worked hard on developing a new style of writing. He then did an Arvon Foundation course with a tutor he had encountered before, who was so impressed with his new work, she recommended him to a publisher she was working with.

• Poet 'C' had placed poems in several magazines and had some commendations and prizes in a few competitions. She sent a dozen poems to a well-known publisher who asked to see more. She sent more for consideration, took some time off work to develop her manuscript and, in time, the book was accepted.

Most poets would prefer to be published by the bigger publishers with their distribution capabilities and the kudos which leads to their books being more widely read and reviewed. But regional presses can offer opportunities too: a poet I know is one of the 'best-known' poets in her region, does well from teaching and readings and sells up to 1,000 copies of her small press books, considerably more than some nationally known poets. And just as certain publishers have a geographical bent, some tend towards poetry in certain genres. A few small presses go for work with a 'performance' edge, while others make available the work of innovative and experimental poets.

One step at a time

To summarise, until you are ready to publish – in fact, until those whose judgement you trust recommend you try – you should concentrate on magazines and journals (and, if you wish, entering competitions). Joining the Poetry Society and the Poetry Book Society (see pages 346–347) are helpful steps. Find out which journals you appreciate and subscribe to them. Magazines constantly change (e.g. *Poetry London* was a low-level newsletter back in the 1990s and is now an impressive journal full of internationally known poets; see page 74); they appear and disappear overnight; they often have strong styles – you know not to send your quatrains on otters to a hard-boiled 'zine, yet this sort of thing happens frequently.

So take your time, find a mentor, or someone who'll be honest and astute about your poetry, build up a manuscript slowly, with lots of revision, read and read more, find opportunities for reading in public, go to a writing group if you can, do an Arvon Foundation course. And keep in mind that there is far more pleasure in writing than in seeing your name on the spine of a book.

Roddy Lumsden's volume of selected poems, *Mischief Night* (2004), his fifth poetry collection, *Third Wish Wasted* (2009), and *Identity Parade* (2010, an anthology of recent British and Irish poetry) are all published by Bloodaxe Books).

See also...

- *Publishers of poetry,* page 736
- *Getting poetry published,* page 335
- *Poetry organisations,* page 346
- *Notes from a passionate poet,* page 333

Poetry organisations

Poetry is one of the easiest writing art forms to begin with, though the hardest to excel at or earn any money from. Paul McGrane, Membership Manager at the Poetry Society, lists below the organisations which can help poets take their poetry further.

WHERE TO GET INVOLVED

The British Haiku Society

Longholm East Bank, Winglands, Sutton Bridge, Lincs. PE12 9YS
email enquiries@britishhaikusociety.org.uk
website www.britishhaikusociety.org.uk

The Society runs the prestigious annual James W. Hackett International Haiku Award and the annual British Haiku awards in two categories – haiku and haibun. It is active in promoting the teaching of haiku in schools and colleges, and is able to provide readers, course/workshop leaders and speakers for poetry groups, etc. Write for membership details. Founded 1990.

Commonword

6 Mount Street, Manchester M2 5NS
tel 0161 832 3777
email admin@cultureword.org.uk
website www.cultureword.org.uk

Commonword is a valuable resource for poets and writers in the North West. It provides support, training and publishing opportunities for new writers. It has helped to launch the careers of many of the region's leading poets and strives to seek out new talent in unexpected places.

Creative Arts East

Griffin Court, Market Street, Wymondham, Norfolk NR18 0GU
tel (01953) 713390
email enquiries@creativeartseast.co.uk
website www.creativeartseast.co.uk

Creative Arts East is a fast-growing arts development agency which provides practical support to the arts community in Norfolk; directly promotes tours, exhibitions, and one-off performances and readings by professional artists and companies; and develops community-based arts projects which address social issues around isolation and disadvantage.

The agency was formally launched in 2002, and was set up to combine the collective expertise and energy of four smaller arts organisations: Rural Arts East, Norfolk Arts Marketing, Wordwaves and Create! Members receive the Norfolk Literature Network newsletter containing information, news, events listings and competitions.

Literature Wales

(formerly Academi)
3rd Floor, Mount Stuart House, Mount Stuart Square, Cardiff Bay, Cardiff CF10 5FQ
tel 029-2047 2266
email post@literaturewales.org
website www.literaturewales.org

The Welsh National Literature Promotion Agency which has a huge resource available for poets and poetry. It organises events and tours, promotes poets and poetry, offers poetry advice, locates poetry publishers, offers financial help to poets and to organisers wishing to book poets, and much more. To take advantage of their services you have to live or be in Wales, which has the largest number of poets per 1,000 population anywhere in the Western World.

The Poetry Book Society

The Dutch House, 307–308 High Holborn, London WC1V 7LL
tel 020-7831 7468 *fax* 020-7831 6967
email info@poetrybooks.co.uk
website www.poetrybooks.co.uk, www.poetrybookshoponline.com, www.childrenspoetrybookshelf.co.uk

This unique book club for readers of poetry was founded in 1953 by T.S. Eliot, and is funded by Arts Council England. Every quarter, selectors choose one outstanding publication (the PBS Choice), and recommend 4 other titles, which are sent to members, who are also offered substantial discounts on other poetry books. The PBS also administers the T.S. Eliot Prize (see page 551), produces the quarterly membership magazine, the *Bulletin*, and provides teaching materials for primary and secondary schools. In addition, the PBS runs the Children's Poetry Bookshelf, offering children's poetry for 7–11 year-olds, with parent, school and library memberships and a child-friendly website. Write for details.

The Poetry Business

Bank Street Arts, 32–40 Bank Street, Sheffield S1 2DS
tel 0114 346 3037
email office@poetrybusiness.co.uk
website www.poetrybusiness.co.uk

Dedicated to helping writers reach their full potential by running supportive workshops.

The Poetry Can

12 Great George Street, Bristol BS1 5RH
tel 0117 933 0900
email admin@poetrycan.co.uk
website www.poetrycan.co.uk

The Poetry Can is one of the few literature organisations in the UK specialising in poetry. It organises events such as the Bristol Poetry Festival; runs a lifelong learning programme; offers information and advice in all aspects of poetry.

Poetry Ireland

32 Kildare Street, Dublin 2, Republic of Ireland
tel +353 (0)1 6789815 *fax* +353 (0)1 6789782
email poetry@iol.ie
website www.poetryireland.ie

Poetry Ireland is the national organisation dedicated to developing, supporting and promoting poetry throughout Ireland. It is the only professional and dedicated national organisation for literature in Ireland. For the past 32 years the organisation has supported poets and writers at all stages of their careers through both performance and publication opportunities, creating meaningful encounters between writers and the public. The organisation delivers through four core strands: Publication, Readings, the provision of an Information & Resource Service, and Education & Outreach. Through its Education & Outreach remit, Poetry Ireland offers a broad spectrum of services within the literary arts – from poetry to children's fiction, storytelling and drama.

Poetry on Loan

website www.lit-net.org/ponl

Poetry on Loan is a scheme to promote contemporary poetry through libraries in the West Midlands. There are 20 participating libraries and the scheme supports events, displays, stock collections and commissions. It also runs poetry projects for young people.

The Poetry Society

22 Betterton Street, London WC2H 9BX
tel 020-7420 9880 *fax* 020-7240 4818
email info@poetrysociety.org.uk
website www.poetrysociety.org.uk

The Poetry Society is Britain's leading voice for poets and poetry. Founded in 1909 to promote a more general recognition and appreciation of poetry, the Society has nearly 4,000 members. With innovative education, commissioning and publishing programmes, and a packed calendar of performances, readings and competitions, the Society champions poetry in its many forms.

The Society offers advice and information to all, with exclusive offers and discounts available to members. Every quarter, members receive copies of *Poetry Review* and the Society's newsletter, *Poetry News*. The Society also publishes education resources; organises high-profile events including an Annual Lecture and National Poetry Day celebrations; runs Poetry Prescription, a critical appraisal service available to members; and provides an education advisory and training service, school membership, youth membership and a website.

A diverse range of events and readings take place at the Poetry Cafe beneath the Society's headquarters in London's Covent Garden. The Society also programmes events and readings throughout the UK.

Competitions run by the Society include the annual National Poetry Competition, with a first prize of £5,000; the biennial Corneliu M. Popescu Prize for Poetry Translated from a European Language into English; the Ted hughes Award for New Work in Poetry; SLAMbassadors UK; and the Foyle Young Poets of the Year Award.

The Seamus Heaney Centre for Poetry

c/o School of English, Queen's University Belfast, Belfast BT7 1NN
tel 028-9097 1070
email g.hellawell@qub.ac.uk
website www.qub.ac.uk/schools/SeamusHeaney CentreforPoetry Facebook: Seamus Heaney Centre for Poetry

The Seamus Heaney Centre for Poetry (SHC) was established in 2003 and is designed to celebrate and promote poetry and artistic endeavour by poets from Northern Ireland. The Centre houses an extensive library of contemporary poetry volumes. It hosts regular creative writing workshops, a poetry reading group, and an ongoing series of readings and lectures by visiting poets and critics from all over the world. The SHC is chaired by the eminent poet, Ciaran Carson, and other resident poets include Medbh McGuckian.

Survivors Poetry

Studio 11, Bickerton House, 25–27 Bickerton Road, London N19 5JT
tel 020-7281 4654 *fax* 020-7281 7894
email info@survivorspoetry.org.uk
website www.survivorspoetry.org

A national charity which promotes the writing of survivors of mental distress. A Survivor may be a person with a current or past experience of psychiatric hospitals, ECT, tranquillisers or other medication, or a user of counselling services, a survivor of sexual abuse and any other person who has empathy with the experiences of survivors.

Tower Poetry Society

Christ Church, Oxford OX1 1DP
tel (01865) 286591
email info@towerpoetry.org.uk
website www.towerpoetry.org.uk

Tower Poetry exists to encourage and challenge everyone who reads or writes poetry. Funded by a generous bequest to Christ Church, Oxford, by the late Christopher Tower, the aims of Tower Poetry are to stimulate an enjoyment and critical appreciation of poetry, particularly among young people in education, and to challenge people to write their own poetry.

The Word Hoard

website www.wordhoard.co.uk

The Word Hoard is a not-for-profit cooperative of artists: writers, visual artists, makers, performers and musicians. Members have worked with text, music, performance, film and the visual arts in a variety of contexts with a huge range of people. They have also brought artists from abroad to the UK to play a part in projects and to work and teach around the country. Most of the projects have involved some kind of collaboration, between artists and between art forms.

WHERE TO GET INFORMATION

The first place to start is your local library. They usually have information about the local poetry scene. Many libraries are actively involved in promoting poetry as well as having modern poetry available for loan. Local librarians promote writing activities with, for example, projects like Poetry on Loan and Poetry Places information points in West Midlands Libraries.

Alliance of Literary Societies (ALS)

email l.j.curry@bham.ac.uk
website www.allianceofliterarysocieties.org.uk

The ALS is the umbrella organisation for literary societies and groups in the UK. Formed in 1973, it provides support and advice on a variety of literary subjects, as well as promoting cooperation between member societies. It produces an annual journal, *ALSo*….

Arts Council England

Head Office 14 Great Peter Street,
London SW1P 3NQ
tel 0845 300 6200
email chiefexecutive@artscouncil.org.uk
website www.artscouncil.org.uk

Arts Council England has 9 regional offices and local literature officers can provide information on local poetry groups, workshops and societies (see page 502). Some give grant aid to local publishers and magazines and help fund festivals, literature projects and readings, and some run critical services.

Arts Council of Wales

Bute Place, Cardiff CF10 5AL
tel 0845 8734 900 *fax* 029-2044 1400
email info@artswales.org.uk
website www.artswales.org.uk

The Arts Council of Wales is an independent charity, established by Royal Charter in 1994. It has 3 regional offices and its principal sponsor is the Welsh Assembly Government. It is the country's funding and development agency for the arts supporting and developing high-quality arts activities. Its funding schemes offer opportunities for arts organisations and individuals in Wales to apply, through a competitive process, for funding towards a clearly defined arts-related project.

National Association of Writers' Groups (NAWG)

PO Box 9891, Market Harborough LE16 0FU
email secretary@nawg.co.uk
website www.nawg.co.uk

NAWG aims to bring cohesion and fellowship to isolated writers' groups and individuals, promoting the study and art of writing in all its aspects. There are over 150 affiliated groups and more than 100 associate (individual) members across the UK.

The Northern Poetry Library

Morpeth Library, Gas House Lane, Morpeth, Northumberland NE61 1TA
tel 0845 600 6400 *fax* (01670) 500390
email ask@northumberland.gov.uk
website www.northumberland.gov.uk
Membership Free to anyone living in Northumberland, Tyne & Wear, Durham, Cleveland and Cumbria

The Northern Poetry Library has over 15,000 titles and magazines covering poetry published since 1945. For information about epic through to classic poetry, a full text database is available of all poetry from 600–1900. The library has free public internet access. Founded 1968.

The Poetry Library

Level 5, Royal Festival Hall, London SE1 8XX
tel 020-7921 0943/0664 *fax* 020-7921 0607
email info@poetrylibrary@org.uk
website www.poetrylibrary.org.uk, www.poetrymagazines.org.uk
Membership Free with proof of identity and current address

The principal roles of the Poetry Library are to collect and preserve all poetry published in the UK since about 1912 and to act as a public lending library. It also keeps a wide range of international poetry. Whenever possible it has 2 copies of each title available and a collection of about 40,000 titles in English and English translation. The Library also provides an education service (see under 'Help for young poets and teachers', below).

The Library runs an active information service, which includes a unique online noticeboard for lost quotations, and tracing authors and publishers from extracts of poems. Current awareness lists are available for magazines, publishers, competitions, groups, workshops and festivals on receipt of a large sae. The Library also stocks a full range of British poetry magazines as well as a selection from abroad and adds a wide range to these to its website at www.poetrymagazines.org.uk. The Library also has an exhibition space which hosts poetry and text-based art throughout the year. Open 11am–8pm Tuesday to Sunday. Founded in 1953 by the Arts Council.

The Poetry Trust

9 New Cut, Halesworth, Suffolk IP19 8BY
tel (01986) 835950
email info@thepoetrytrust.org
www.thepoetrytrust.org

The Poetry Trust is one of the UK's flagship poetry organisations, delivering a year-round live and digital programme, creative education opportunities, courses, prizes and publications. Over the last decade the Poetry Trust has been running creative workshops for teachers, and this extensive experience has been condensed into a free user-friendly handbook, *The Poetry Toolkit*. The Trust also produces *The Poetry Paper*, featuring exclusive interviews and poems.

The Scottish Poetry Library

5 Crichton's Close, Canongate, Edinburgh EH8 8DT
tel 0131 557 2876 *fax* 0131 557 8393
email reception@spl.org.uk
website www.spl.org.uk

The Scottish Poetry Library is the place for poetry in Scotland for the regular reader, the serious student or the casual browser. It has a remarkable collection of written works, as well as tapes and videos. The emphasis is on contemporary poetry written in Scotland, in Scots, Gaelic and English, but historic Scottish poetry – and contemporary works from almost every part of the world – feature too. They also have collections for the visually impaired. All resources, advice and information are readily accessible, free of charge. It holds regular poetry events, details of which are available on the library website. Founded 1984.

ONLINE RESOURCES

You can obtain a wealth of information at the click of a mouse these days. In addition to those listed above, good starting points are:

The Poetry Archive

website www.poetryarchive.org

The Poetry Kit

website www.poetrykit.org

The Poetry Society of America

website www.poetrysociety.org

WHERE TO GET POETRY BOOKS

See the Poetry Book Society, above. The Poetry Library provides a list of bookshops which stock poetry. In 2011 *The Independent* ran an article entitled 'The 50 Best bookshops' (*www.independent.co.uk/extras/indybest/arts-books/the-50-best-bookshops-6290989.html*). For second-hand mail order poetry books try:

Baggins Book Bazaar

19 High Street, Rochester, Kent ME1 1PY
tel (01634) 811651 *fax* (01634) 840591
email godfreygeorge@btconnect.com
website www.bagginsbooks.co.uk

Secondhand bookshop with over half a million books in stock.

The Poetry Bookshop

The Ice House, Brook Street, Hay-on-Wye HR3 5BQ
tel (01497) 821812
email sales@poetrybookshop.co.uk
website www.poetrybookshop.com

Peter Riley

27 Sturton Street, Cambridge CB1 2QG
tel (01223) 576422
email priley@waitrose.com
website www.aprileye.co.uk

Sweetens of Bolton

86 Deansgate, Bolton, Lancs. BL1 1BD
tel (01204) 528457 *fax* (01204) 522115

WHERE TO CELEBRATE POETRY

Festival information should be available from Arts Council England offices (see page 502). See also *Literature festivals* on page 571. As well as the list below, major poetry festivals each year include Ledbury, Beverley, Aldeburgh, and Cheltenham. Poetry also features strongly at the Glastonbury and Latitude Festivals.

The British Council

10 Spring Gardens, London SW1A 2BN
tel 020-7389 3194 *fax* 020-7389 3199
email arts@britishcouncil.org
website www.britishcouncil.org/arts-literature.htm

Send a large sae or visit the website for a list of forthcoming festivals.

Poems in the Waiting Room (PitWR)

Chair Wendy French, 4 Myton Road, London SE21 8EB
email pitwr@blueyonder.co.uk
website www.pitwr.pwp.blueyonder.co.uk

PitWR is a registered arts in health charity which supplies short collections of poems for patients to read while waiting to see their doctor. First established in 1995, the poems cover both the cannon of English verse and contemporary works – poetry from Quill to Qwerty.

Poetry-next-the-Sea

The New Cottage, Overy Road, Burnham Market, Norfolk PE31 8HH

tel (01328) 738243
email fmfraser@bmkt.freeserve.co.uk
website www.poetry-next-the-sea.com

The genesis of Poetry-next-the-Sea occurred in 1997, when John Coleridge reasoned that an annual poetry festival on the North Norfolk coast could be a viable addition to the already established festivals at Aldeburgh and King's Lynn, and which would also be within reach of the literary and arts audiences in Norwich and East Anglia. The newsletter of the Friends of Poetry-next-the-Sea is *Wavelength* (2 p.a.), which is intended to present Friends' opinions on Poetry-next-the-Sea and on poetry in general. The editors are actively seeking letters, comments, articles and reviews for this lively and informative publication, with the aim of establishing a lasting dialogue between the festival and its supporters.

StAnza: Scotland's International Poetry Festival

email info@stanzapoetry.org
website www.stanzapoetry.org

StAnza is international in outlook. Founded in 1988, it is held each March in St Andrews, Scotland's oldest university town. The festival is an opportunity to engage with a wide variety of poetry, to hear world class poets reading in exciting and atmospheric venues, to experience a range of performances where music, film, dance and poetry work in harmony, to view exhibitions linking poetry with visual art and to discover the part poetry has played in the lives of a diverse range of writers, musicians and media personalities. The simple intention of StAnza is to celebrate poetry in all its forms.

WHERE TO PERFORM

In London, Express Excess and Aromapoetry are 2 of the liveliest venues for poetry performances and they regularly feature the best performers. Poetry Unplugged at the Poetry Café is famous for its open mic nights (Tuesdays 7.30pm). Poetry evenings are held all over the UK and those listed below are worth checking out. Others can be found by visiting your local library or your Arts Council office, or by visiting the Landmarks of Britain section of the Poetry Society website (www.poetrysociety.org.uk/content/landmarks). The Poetry Library (www.poetrylibrary.org.uk) is also an excellent source for upcoming poetry events.

Apples and Snakes Performance Poetry and Spoken Word

The Albany, Douglas Way, London SE8 4AG
tel 0845 521 3460
email info@applesandsnakes.org
website www.applesandsnakes.org

Blind Poetics

32 West Nicolson Street, Edinburgh EH8 9DD
tel 07539 367467
email blindpoetics@gmail.com

Brewery Arts Centre

122a Highgate, Kendal, Cumbria LA9 4HE
(01539) 725133
email boxoffice@breweryarts.co.uk
website www.breweryarts.co.uk

Poetry events and open mic nights.

CB1 Poetry

32 Mill Road, Cambridge CB1 2AD
tel (01223) 363271 ext. 2725
email cb1poetry@fastmail.fm
website www.cb1poetry.org.uk

Clitheroe Books Open Floor Readings

29 Moor Lane, Clitheroe BB7 1BE
tel (01200) 444242
email joharbooks@aol.com
website www.roundstonebooks.co.uk

Coffee House Poetry

PO Box 16210, London W4 1ZP
tel 020-7370 1434
email coffpoetry@aol.com
website www.coffeehousepoetry.org

Dead Good Poets Society

email sarah@deadgoodpoetssociety.co.uk
website www.deadgoodpoetssociety.co.uk

Farrago Poetry

108 High Street, West Wickham, Kent BR4 0ND
tel 07905 078376
email farragopoetry@yahoo.co.uk
website http://london.e-poets.net

Farrago Poetry is a spoken word and performance poetry organisation based in London. It runs a range of events, from Spanish language poetry nights to events for elders, but is best known for pioneering slam poetry in the UK and for its links to the international performance poetry scene.

Hammer and Tongue

Hammer and Tongue HQ, The Old Music Hall, Oxford OX4 1JE
tel 07906 885069
email events@hammerandtongue.co.uk
website www.hammerandtongue.co.uk

Hit the Ode

website www.applesandsnakes.org

Spoken word poetry in Birmingham. Each Hit the Ode features an act from the West Midlands, one from elsewhere in the UK and one international guest.

Inky Fingers

website http://inkyfingersedinburgh.wordpress.com

A series of events in Edinburgh for people who love words.

Morden Tower

Back Stowell Street, West Walls,
Newcastle upon Tyne NE1 4XG
email mordentower@googlemail.com
website www.mordentower.org

Morden Tower is one of the UK's best known literary landmarks. Hundreds of poets have come from all over the world to give readings in this ancient turret room on Newcastle's city walls. Morden Tower readings started in 1964 and many poets have relished the experience of reading here with its fine acoustics, its warm, appreciative audiences and its gloriously battered architecture.

Poetry Café

22 Betterton Street, London WC2 9BX
tel 020-7420 9887
email poetrycafe@poetrysociety.org.uk

Swindon Open Mic

email hildasheehan@gmail.com
website http://swindonpoetryopenmic.blogspot.co.uk

Poets wishing to read or perform are invited to do so for up to 3 minutes. Takes place in the Reading Room at the Central Library, Regent Circus.

Tongues and Grooves

The Florence Arms, Florence Road, Southsea, Hants PO5 2NE
tel 07775 244573
email enquiries@tongues-and-grooves.org.uk
website www.tongues-and-grooves.org.uk

Weston Poets

The Carlton Centre, Carlton Road, Weston-Super-Mare
tel (01934) 426442
email marilynedbrooke@hotmail.com

COMPETITIONS

There are now hundreds of competitions to enter and as the prizes increase, so does the prestige associated with winning such competitions as the National Poetry Competition.

To decide which competitions are worth entering, make sure you know who the judges are and think twice before paying large sums for an anthology of 'winning' poems which will only be read by entrants wanting to see their own work in print. The Poetry Library publishes a list of competitions each month (available free on receipt of a large sae). See also *Getting poetry published* on page 335 and *Prizes and awards* on page 543.

Literary prizes are given annually to published poets and as such are non-competitive. An A–Z guide to literary prizes can be found on the Booktrust website (www.booktrust.org.uk). A current list of competitions can be found at www.poetrylibrary.org.uk/competitions

WHERE TO WRITE POETRY

Apples and Snakes

The Albany, Douglas Way, London SE8 4AG
tel 0845 521 3460
email info@applesandsnakes.org
website www.applesandsnakes.org

A vital performance poetry agency dedicated to giving 'voice to challenging, diverse and dynamic poets…' Presents fortnightly shows at the Albany and holds occasional workshops. Founded 1982.

The Arvon Foundation

Lumb Bank – The Ted Hughes Arvon Centre, Heptonstall, Hebden Bridge, West Yorkshire HX7 6DF
tel (01422) 843714 *fax* (01422) 843714
email lumbbank@arvonfoundation.org
The Arvon Foundation at Totleigh Barton, Sheepwash, Beaworthy, Devon EX21 5NS
tel (01409) 231338 *fax* (01409) 231144
email totleighbarton@arvonfoundation.org
The Arvon Foundation at Moniack Mhor, Teavarren, Kiltarlity, Beauly, Inverness-shire IV4 7HT
tel (01463) 741675 *fax* (01463) 741733
email moniackmhor@arvonfoundation.org
The Hurst – The John Osborne Arvon Centre, Clunton, Craven Arms, Shrops. SY7 0JA
tel (01588) 640658 *fax* (01588) 640509
email thehurst@arvonfoundation.org
website www.arvonfoundation.org

The Arvon Foundation's 4 centres run 5-day residential courses throughout the year to anyone over the age of 16, providing the opportunity to live and work with professional writers. Writing genres explored include poetry, narrative, drama, writing for children, song writing and the performing arts. Bursaries are available to those receiving benefits. Founded in 1968.

Camden Poetry Group

Contact Hannah Kelly, 64 Lilyville Road, London SW6

Meets in Hampstead one Saturday per month from 6.30pm. Examples of work should be sent with a covering letter before coming to the first meeting.

Cannon Poets

22 Margaret Grove, Harborne, Birmingham B17 9JH
email info@cannonpoets.co.uk
Meets at Moseley Community Development Trust, The Post Office Building, 149–153 Alcester Road, Moseley, Birmingham usually on the first Sunday of each month (except August) at 2pm
website www.cannonpoets.co.uk

Cannon Poets have met monthly since 1983. The group encourages poetry writing through:

• workshops run by members or visitors
• break-out groups where poems are subjected to scrutiny by supportive peer groups
• 10-minute slots where members read a selection of their poems to the whole group
• publication of its journal, *The Cannon's Mouth* (quarterly).

Members are encouraged to participate in poetry events and competitions.

Centerprise Literature Development Project

136–138 Kingsland High Street, London E8 2NS
tel 020-7254 9632 ext. 211, 214 *fax* 020-7923 1951
email info@centerprise.org.uk
website www.centerprisetrust.org.uk
Contact Eva Lewin, Catherine Johnson

Offers a range of creative writing courses, events, surgeries, advice and information resources plus links with other writers' organisations. Groups include the Women's Poetry Group and the Black Writers' Group. The project is committed to developing new writing from all community and ethnic groups.

City Lit

Keeley Street, London WC2B 4BA
tel 020-7492 2652, 020-7492 2600
email humanities@citylit.ac.uk
website www.citylit.ac.uk

Epsom Writers' Workshop

Epsom Centre, 1 Church Street, Epsom
Contact Stella Stocker *tel* 020-8668 3816

Kent & Sussex Poetry Society

Camden Centre, Market Square, Tunbridge Wells, Kent TN1 2SW
email info@kentandsussexpoetrysociety.org
website http://kentandsussexpoetrysociety.com

Lancaster University

Department of Continuing Education, Lancaster University, Ash House, Lancaster LA1 4YT
tel (01524) 592623
email conted@lancaster.ac.uk
website www.lancs.ac.uk

A range of part-time creative writing courses in various genres and at levels to suit both beginners and those with some experience.

The Poetry School

81 Lambeth Walk, London SE11 6DX
tel 020-7582 1679
email administration@poetryschool.com
website www.poetryschool.com

Teaches the art and craft of writing poetry. Offers courses, small groups and one-to-one tutorials, from one-day workshops to year-long courses, in London and a dozen more city locations. Activities for beginners to advanced writers, both unpublished and published. Learn how and what to write; how and where to publish; how to perform, teach and promote. Face-to-face, downloadable and online activities. Three new programmes a year.

Poets Anonymous

Contact Peter Evans, 70 Aveling Close, Purley, Surrey CR8 4DW
tel 020-8645 9956
email poets@poetsanon.org.uk
website www.poetsanon.org.uk

Meets at Woodside and South Norwood Social Club, Enmore Road, South Norwood SE25 5NQ on the first Friday of each month at 8pm, £2, and at the URC on the second Saturday of the month, 2.30–4pm, £1.50.

The Poet's House/Teach na hÉigse

Clonbarra, Falcarragh, County Donegal, Republic of Ireland
tel +353 (0)7 465470 *fax* +353 (0)7 465471
email phouse@iol.ie
website www.poetshouseireland.tripod.com

The Poet's House runs 3 ten-day poetry courses in July and August. An MA degree in creative writing is validated by Lancaster University, and the Irish Language Faculty includes Cathal O'Searcaigh. The poetry faculty comprises 30 writers, including Paul Durcan and John Montagu.

Shortlands Poetry Circle

Ripley Arts Centre, 24 Sundridge Avenue, Bromley
tel (01689) 811394
email shortlands@poetrypf.co.uk
website www.poetrypf.co.uk/shortlands.html

South Norwood Writers' Workshop

South Norwood Centre, Sandown Road, London SE24 4XC
Contact Stella Stocker *tel* 020-8668 3816

Surrey Poetry Centre (Wey Poets)

The Keep, 29 Castle Street, Guildford, GU1 3UW
email mjones.direct@gmail.com
Contact Martin Jones *tel* (01483) 504556

Meets on first and third Thursday of the month, 7.30–10pm.

Tŷ Newydd

Taliesin Trust, Tŷ Newydd, Llanystumdwy, Cricieth, Gwynedd LL52 0LW
tel (01766) 522811 *fax* (01766) 523095
email tynewydd@literaturewales.org
website www.tynewydd.org

Tŷ Newydd runs week-long writing courses encompassing a wide variety of genres, including poetry, and caters for all levels, from beginners to published poets. All the courses are tutored by published writers. Writing retreats are also available.

Wimbledon and Merton Poetry Group

Raynes Park Methodist Church, Worple Road, London SW20
Contact Russell Thompson *tel* (07969) 597967, 020-8942 3685
email zznsh@yahoo.co.uk

Meets on first Tuesday evening of each month.

GROUPS ON THE INTERNET

It is worth searching for discussion groups and chat rooms on the internet.

British–Irish Poets

website www.jiscmail.ac.uk/archives/british-irish-poets.html
Discussion list (innovative poetry).

Poetry Free-for-all

website www.everypoet.org/pffa

Post your poems and comment on others.

The Poetry Kit

website www.poetrykit.org/wkshops2.htm

List of online workshop/discussion sites.

Local groups

Local groups vary enormously so it is worth shopping around to find one that suits your poetry. Up-to-date information can be obtained from Arts Council England regional offices (see page 502).

The Poetry Library publishes a list of groups for the Greater London area which will be sent out on receipt of a large sae.

The Poetry Society organises local groups for its members – visit www.poetrysociety.org.uk/content/membership/stanzas/ for details.

HELP FOR YOUNG POETS AND TEACHERS

National Association of Writers in Education (NAWE)

PO Box 1, Sheriff Hutton, York YO60 7YU
tel/fax (01653) 618429
email paul@nawe.co.uk
website www.nawe.co.uk

NAWE is a national organisation, which aims to widen the scope of writing in education, and coordinate activities between writers, teachers and funding bodies. It publishes the magazine *Writing in Education* and is author of a writers' database which can identify writers who fit the given criteria (e.g. speaks several languages, works well with special needs, etc.) for schools, colleges and the community. Publishes *Reading the Applause: Reflections on Performance Poetry by Various Artists*. Write for membership details.

The Poetry Library

Children's Section, Royal Festival Hall, London SE1 8XX
tel 020-7921 0664
email info@poetrylibrary.org.uk
website www.poetrylibrary.org.uk

For young poets, the Poetry Library has about 4,000 books incorporating the SIGNAL Collection of Children's Poetry. It also has a multimedia children's section, from which cassettes and videos are available to engage children's interest in poetry.

The Poetry Library has an education service for teachers and writing groups. Its information file covers all aspects of poetry in education. There is a separate collection of books and materials for teachers and poets who work with children in schools, and teachers may join a special membership scheme to borrow books for the classroom.

Poetry Society Education

The Poetry Society, 22 Betterton Street, London WC2H 9BX
tel 020-7420 9894 *fax* 020-7240 4818
email education@poetrysociety.org.uk
website www.poetrysociety.org.uk

The Poetry Society has an outstanding reputation for its exciting and innovative education work. For over 30 years it has been introducing poets into classrooms, providing comprehensive teachers' resources and producing colourful, accessible publications for pupils. It develops projects and schemes to keep poetry flourishing in schools, libraries and workplaces. Schemes like Poets in Schools, Poet in the City and Poetry Places (a 2-year programme of residencies and placements, funded by the Arts Council's 'Arts for Everyone' lottery budget) have enabled the Poetry Society to give work to hundreds of poets and allowed thousands of children and adults to experience poetry for themselves.

Through projects such as the Respect Slam and The Foyle Young Poets of the Year Award the Poetry Society gives valuable encouragement and exposure to young writers and performers.

Schools membership offers publications, training opportunities for teachers and poets, a free subscription to *Poems on the Underground* and a consultancy service giving advice on working with poets in the classroom. *Poetryclass*, an INSET training project, employs poets to train teachers at primary and secondary level. Youth membership is available (for age 11–18) and provides advice on developing writing skills, access to publication on the Poetry Society website, quarterly issues of *Poetry News*, and poetry books and posters.

The Poetry Trust – see The Poetry Trust on page 349

Young Poets Network

website www.youngpoetsnetwork.org.uk

Aimed at young people up to 25.

YOUNG POETRY COMPETITIONS

Children's competitions are included in the competition list provided by the Poetry Library (free on receipt of a large sae).

Foyle Young Poets of the Year Award

The Poetry Society, 22 Betterton Street, London WC2H 9BX
tel 020-7420 9894 *fax* 020-7240 4818
email education@poetrysociety.org.uk
website www.poetrysociety.org.uk

Free entry for children 11–17 years with unique prizes. Annual competition. Poems must be written in English. Founded 2001.

SLAMbassadors

The Poetry Society, 22 Betterton Street, London WC2H 9BX
tel 020-7429 9894 020-7420 4818
email education@poetrysociety.org.uk
website http://slam.poetrysociety.org.uk

An annual poetry championship for 12–18 year olds. Young people across the UK are invited to enter by filming themselves performing a poem or rap and submitting it online for consideration by judges. Prizes include the opportunity to perfom at a showcase event, workshops with respected spoken word artists and further professional development opportunities. Established 2002.

Christopher Tower Poetry Prize

Christ Church, Oxford OX1 1DP
tel (01865) 286591
email info@towerpoetry.org.uk
website www.towerpoetry.org.uk/prize/

An annual poetry competition (open from November to March) from Christ Church, Oxford, open to 16–18 year-olds in UK schools and colleges. The poems should be no longer than 48 lines, on a different chosen theme each year. Prizes: £3,000 (1st), £1,000 (2nd), £500 (3rd). Every winner also receives a prize for their school.

FURTHER READING

Baldwin, Michael, *The Way to Write Poetry*, Hamish Hamilton, 1982, o.p.

Chisholm, Alison, *The Craft of Writing Poetry*, Allison & Busby, 1997, repr. 2001

Chisholm, Alison, *A Practical Poetry Course*, Allison & Busby, 1994

Corti, Doris, *Writing Poetry*, Writers News Library of Writing/Thomas & Lochar, 1994

Fairfax, John, and John Moat, *The Way to Write*, Penguin Books, 2nd edn revised, 1998

Finch, Peter, *How to Publish Your Poetry*, Allison & Busby, 4th edn, 1998

Forbes, Peter, *Scanning the Century: The Penguin Book of the Twentieth Century in Poetry*, Viking, 1999

Fulton, Len, *Directory of Poetry Publishers 2011–2012*, CD-ROM, Dustbooks, USA, 2011

Fulton, Len, *The International Directory of Little Magazines and Small Presses 2007–2008*, Dustbooks, USA, 2008

Hamilton, Ian, *The Oxford Companion to Twentieth-century Poetry*, Clarendon Press, 1994

Hyland, Paul, *Getting into Poetry: A Readers' & Writers' Guide to the Poetry Scene*, Bloodaxe, 2nd edn, 1992

Lee Brewer, Robert, *Poet's Market 2012*, Writer's Digest Books, USA, 2011

Livingstone, Dinah, *Poetry Handbook for Readers and Writers*, Macmillan, 1993, o.p.

O'Brien, Sean (ed), *The Firebox: Poetry from Britain and Ireland after 1945*, Picador, 1998, o.p.

Padel, Ruth, *52 Ways of Looking at a Poem: A Poem for Every Week of the Year*, Vintage, 2004

Padel, Ruth, *The Poem and the Journey: 60 Poems for the Journey of Life*, Vintage, 2008

Reading the Applause: Reflections on Performance Poetry by Various Artists, Talking Shop, 1999

Preminger, Alex, Terry V.F. Brogan, Frank J. Warnke (eds), *New Princeton Encyclopedia of Poetry and Poetics*, Princeton University Press, 3rd edn, 1993

Riggs, Thomas (ed.), *Contemporary Poets*, St James Press, 7th edn, 2003
Roberts, Philip Davies, *How Poetry Works*, Penguin Books, 2nd edn, 2000
Sampson, Fiona, *Writing Poetry: The Expert Guide*, Robert Hale, 2009
Sansom, Peter, *Writing Poems*, Bloodaxe, 1994, reprinted 1997
Sweeney, Matthew and John Williams, *Teach Yourself Writing Poetry*, Hodder and Stoughton, 3rd edn, 2009
Whitworth, John, *Writing Poetry*, A&C Black, 2006

See also...

- *Publishers of poetry*, page 731
- *Getting poetry published*, page 335
- *Approaching a poetry publisher*, page 342

Television, film and radio

Notes from a successful television screenwriter

Andrew Davies tells how he became a 'proper' writer.

I didn't begin as a screenwriter. I began as a poet. There was no television in the house I grew up in, and there was hardly any such thing as television drama. This was the early Fifties. There was a girl in our village called Jane Grant-Hughes, with a well-off dad, and they had a television. It was as big as a wardrobe with a tiny screen in the middle of it. I remember a bunch of us being invited round to Jane's house to watch a production of *The Merry Wives of Windsor*, and it was very grey and fuzzy and actually excruciatingly boring. The idea of anybody deliberately writing television drama seemed ludicrous to me.

I wanted to be a writer but my father, a teacher, sensibly pointed out that most writers didn't make anywhere near enough money to live on and I should have a job that paid the bills and write in my spare time. Like him, I became a teacher – I was attracted by the short hours and long holidays (time to write) but found that I enjoyed teaching and was quite good at it. I got home at 4.30pm and there were a couple of hours before my wife got home and I wrote in that time: short stories and radio plays mostly. There was a market for short stories in those days, not that I sold any, and there was a market for radio plays by new writers, and there still is (hint, hint). I was also writing poetry and articles for *Punch*, sketches and jokes for sketch shows, and a novel, everything, really. Hardly any of it sold, but I was enjoying myself. I always tried to make sure there was at least one thing *out there* with my hopes riding on it. (That's another thing I would recommend to the struggling writer.) When I did sell something, I spent the money immediately, on something specific. I remember I sold a couple of sketches to a radio programme called *Monday Night at Home* and bought a rather fine corduroy jacket with the proceeds.

The late Fifties and early Sixties were a good time for radio plays. There were a lot of poetic and experimental ones on the 'Third Programme' as Radio Three used to be called. Dylan Thomas and Louis MacNeice wrote radio plays; so did Pinter and Stoppard. And my first substantial sale was a radio play. It was based on an extraordinary time I'd spent on teaching practice in a benighted school deep in the Welsh valleys. Hilarious, touching, more than a little obscene, more than a little libellous as it turned out. (I guess another tip is: recognise when you've had a unique experience, and get all the juice you can out of it, but try to avoid getting sued.) The play was later successfully produced after I'd changed the names, physical characteristics and, in some cases, the sex of some of the teachers in the story; but it was a close-run thing, almost the end of my career before I'd even properly got started. That was in 1960.

I continued to write radio plays throughout the Sixties, acquiring an agent in the process. He came to me, not the other way round, and I graciously acceded to his plan to 'exploit me in all media' as he put it. It was the first time I had heard the word 'exploit' used in anything other than a pejorative sense. By 1965 we had a house and a puppy and a baby, and it seemed time to get a television as well. These were the days of the *Wednesday Play*, Dennis Potter, *Cathy Come Home*, and all that. I was entranced. I bought a book of television playscripts – I remember it included a wry little comedy by a guy I'd never heard of called Peter Nichols – and studied the layout and the length of scenes, the whole grammar of television drama. There weren't any creative writing courses or books on how to do it then. But study the best and steal from them has always been a good way to learn.

Early television success

I'm sure there must have been a couple of false starts, but the way I remember it is I sat down and wrote a play about a girl in a knicker factory and sent it off to the *Wednesday Play*, like doing the pools, really, and it was accepted – and produced. And it did very well. I really did think then that I was a made man… but it was FIVE YEARS before I sold another television play. I was still getting the radio plays done, and I could always kid myself I was a teacher really and just a hobby writer, but it was a tough time. And so the next bit of advice is that you have to like writing enough to keep going (that's the most important thing) and have faith in your own ability (also important) and dream the impossible dream (that's complete b******* , actually) and things may eventually get better.

For me they got better when a script editor called Louis Marks took a fancy to a half-hour script I'd written called 'Is That Your Body Boy?' and accepted it for a strand called *Thirty-Minute* (I keep nagging the BBC to revive the original half-hour play or film, so far with no success.) Anyway, that was done and got great reviews, and Louis Marks became a producer, and for some time his career and mine hung by the same slender thread as he continued to commission me to write single plays, often in 'anthology' series on a common theme. He also recommended me to other producers as fast, clever and cheap. (I am still reasonably fast and clever, I hope, but no longer cheap.) It's still a wonderful and important thing to find a producer who loves your work and will stick his (or nowadays more usually her) neck out for it, but these days producers have very little clout: all depends on the whim (or judgement as they prefer to think of it) of the commissioners.

By the mid-Seventies I was able to think of myself as an established writer, and this was consolidated when I was given the chance to adapt a sprawling Delderfield novel called *To Serve Them All My Days*, about a chap who gets invalided out of the First World War and spends what seems like the next hundred years teaching in a West Country boarding school. This established me as a writer who was capable of the long haul, and led to the commissioning of *A Very Peculiar Practice*, an original serial set in a campus university, which went out in the mid-Eighties, and is probably the television work of which I am most proud.

Becoming a 'proper' writer

It was at this time, 1986 to be precise, that I resigned from the day job at Warwick University and became a 'proper' writer. I celebrated this by suffering my first ever writer's block. Now I *had* to keep my family by writing, the thing seemed quite impossible. But fortunately I didn't have to suffer alone for too long: there were too many people who couldn't start their work until I had done mine, and I was coaxed out of my creative paralysis with the traditional application of bullying and whisky. Writer's block is all about performance anxiety, fear of failure, and there's a bit of it in every project – especially in the early stages. Experience and past successes don't help as much as you would think. And unless inspiration descends like a thunderbolt, I would advise you to take the traditional route: if you can't think of anything good, write something bad and rewrite it later.

Enough of such gloomy thoughts. What are the nice things about being a successful television writer? Money, obviously. Lunch at the Ivy is very nice. Fame can be a bit of a nuisance, though I guess most people would like to try it for a bit to see how it goes. Mostly, for me, the joy comes from working in a collaborative medium, which means that you are being stimulated by the bright ideas of producers and script editors; surprised by the creative flair of directors who do things you wouldn't have thought of with your work, but things that seem utterly right; actors who make your lines sound better than they really are. Just about my favourite part of the process is the 'readthrough'. It's the first time the actors come together, and it's the first time you get a feel for what the final thing will be like. And sometimes, if one of the actors can't make it, I get a chance to 'read in' – and when you're playing a scene with Gillian Anderson, say, life doesn't get much better, even if you're sitting in a draughty church hall, which is where these things always seem to take place.

But if you write for performance, that experience – seeing and hearing your words come alive off the page – is something all dramatists can experience, even if the production is by your local amateur group and never gets any further than that draughty church hall. In fact, that's the last bit of advice I'd give: if you write for performance, try to get it done somehow, even if it's just an informal reading with your friends. It's the best way to learn.

Andrew Davies has been writing for the screen since 1965. His television originals include *A Very Peculiar Practice, Getting Hurt, A Few Short Journeys of the Heart, Filipina Dreamgirls, Boudica (The Warrior Queen), The Chatterley Affair,* and the sitcom *Game On* (with Bernadette Davis). He has adapted *Middlemarch, Pride and Prejudice, Moll Flanders, Emma, Mother Love, House of Cards* (for which he won an Emmy award) *Vanity Fair, Wives and Daughters* and *Take a Girl Like You* for television. Also *Othello, The Way We Live Now* (for which he won a BAFTA) *Daniel Deronda, Dr Zhivago, Tipping the Velvet, He Knew He Was Right, Bleak House, The Line of Beauty, Northanger Abbey, A Room With a View, Fanny Hill, Affinity, Sense and Sensibility* and *Little Dorrit*. He has big-screen credits for *Circle of Friends, Bridget Jones's Diary, The Tailor of Panama* and *Bridget Jones: The Edge of Reason*. Most recently, he wrote the screenplay to *Mr Selfridge*, a ten-part series to be shown on ITV1 in 2013. Andrew was awarded a BAFTA Fellowship in 2002.

Adaptations from books

Although every writer wants to create their own work and find their own voice, adaptation is a good way both to generate income and to learn about how to write for other formats. It can also be a chance for a writer to raise their profile, with a successful adaptation sometimes leading to an original commission. Kate Sinclair explains.

Although every writer wants to create their own work and find their own voice, adaptation is a good way both to generate income and to learn about the disciplines of different media: how to write for other formats.

Writers may be approached to adapt their own work from one medium to another during their career. For example, John Mortimer originally wrote *A Voyage Round My Father* for the radio and later adapted it for stage, film and finally, for television. There are also opportunities for both writers and directors to adapt someone else's work from one performance medium to another or from a novel to any of the above.

Every year classic novels are made into adaptations for all media and it is a growing trend. These may be for the theatre, such as *War Horse* based on Michael Morpurgo's book or for radio such as *Life and Fate*, Vasily Grossman's novel adapted by Mike Walker and Jonathan Myerson (the Classic Serial, Radio 4). Television carries dramatisations like *Great Expectations* adapted by Sarah Phelps (BBC), and feature film screenplays such as Moira Buffini's adaptation of *Jane Eyre*, directed by Cary Fukunaga, or the award-winning *Tinker, Tailor, Soldier, Spy* by John Le Carre, adapted by Bridget O'Connor and Peter Straughan. Although these are usually costly to produce, involving large casts and – particularly in the visual media – the considerable expense of recreating the period in which they were written, they command loyal audiences and seem to be in steady demand. These classic projects also generate significant income both from DVD/video sales and from sales to overseas companies and networks. Some adapters are as well known as writers who concentrate on their own work. For example, Andrew Davies has become almost a household name for his television dramatisations of *Middlemarch*, *Bleak House* and, more recently, *Northanger Abbey* and *Little Dorritt*.

Producers in radio, television and film are also in regular contact with publishers and literary agents to keep abreast of contemporary novels which may work well in another format. I work as a producer and literary consultant and find books, both fiction and non-fiction, for screenwriters, directors or producers for feature films. Both television producers and film companies are also sent books with potential by the publicity departments of publishing houses and writers may also make direct approaches to producers and commissioners with material that they feel they can successfully transcribe for that particular medium. There is clearly a market for adaptations of all types. For example, I found *Slumdog Millionaire* for Film4 on reading 50 pages of an unpublished book, *Q&A* by Vikas Swamp. The added stimulus for the adapter is, as well as having a ready-made story, exploring technically how another writer writes – their use of language, the way they structure a narrative, their characterisation. It presents the opportunity to learn from the skill and subtlety of great writers together with the challenge of finding ways to transport a story from one form to another, with a multitude of creative possibilities to explore.

What to adapt, and why?

Just because a narrative works in one format doesn't guarantee that it will in another. Form and story are often inextricably bound together. Something works as a radio play precisely because it appeals to a listening audience and is able to exploit the possibilities of sound. A novel may be very literary and concentrate on a character's inner thoughts, and not on external action. While this may be fine for reading quietly alone, it could leave a theatre, television or film audience bored and longing for something to happen.

That said, the key ingredient is story and there are some stories which seem to work in almost any media and which have almost become universal (though different treatments bring out different aspects of the original). For example, Henry James's *The Turn of the Screw* was written as a novella. It subsequently became a much-performed opera, with a libretto by Myfanwy Piper and music by Benjamin Britten; an acclaimed film, retitled *The Innocents* with the screenplay by John Mortimer; and a television adaptation for ITV by Nick Dear. What makes a narrative like this transmute so successfully?

At the most basic level it must be dramatic. Radio, television and film, like the theatre, need drama to hold their audiences. Aristotle's premise that 'all drama is action', and should have protagonists whom we identify with, antagonists who oppose them, and the reversals, climaxes and resolutions which typify a dramatic structure. This is not necessarily the case for a novel; it is easy to be seduced by a tale that has personal resonance or beautiful language and forget the basic template which has, after all, worked for thousands of years. It may seem obvious, but reminding yourself of this when considering the suitability of any material for adaptation could spare you a rejection or a great deal of later reworking.

Knowing the media

The other important consideration is a detailed knowledge of the final medium. The adapter needs to understand why that particular story is specifically suited to it. Ideally they will have experience of writing for that form, as well as an awareness of the current market for the project. It is vital to know precisely what is currently being produced and by whom. Staff and policies change very quickly, so the more up-to-date your research is, the better your chance of creating a successful adaptation and being able to get it accepted.

If you are adapting for the theatre, how often do you go and when was the last time you saw a production that wasn't originally written for the stage? As well as observing how successful it was, both artistically and in box office terms, would you know whether that company or theatre regularly programmes adaptations, and if so, what sort? Do they, like Shared Experience, have a reputation primarily for classics, or do they, like the Young Vic, or The Royal Exchange, Manchester, produce versions of contemporary novels? Are you sufficiently aware of the tastes of the current artistic director and the identity of the theatre to know whether to send your project to the West Yorkshire Playhouse or the Arcola Theatre? This is not necessarily just a question of scale or level, but more a reflection of contemporary trends and the specific policy of each of these buildings. Whilst the overall remit of a theatre or company may remain the same – if they are funded to produce only new plays, it is unlikely that this will alter – individual personnel and fashions will change regularly and it is important to keep in touch.

Television and radio

The same holds true for all the other media and, if anything, is even more important in radio and television. All of the broadcast media are now subject to the rigorous demands of ratings, which in turn make for extremely precise scheduling. Channels have strong identities, and conversations with producers and commissioners will inevitably involve a discussion of which slot a project is suited to and what has recently been shown or broadcast. Up-to-the-minute knowledge of the work being produced by a company or broadcaster is therefore essential, and regularly seeing that work and being able to talk about it, even more so.

For example, BBC Radio 3's *Wire* is specifically for new work by contemporary writers and therefore isn't suitable for a classic adaptation of a novel. Radio 4 produces the Classic Serial on Sunday afternoons and *Women's Hour* has a regular serialisation slot that can be contemporary or classic and is often an adapted novel. Biographies, autobiographies and non-fiction works are also frequently abridged and read on Radio 4 at 9.45am on weekdays. For a detailed knowledge of this output there can be no substitute for studying the *Radio Times*, seeing what is programmed, and listening to what gets produced in which slots. Being able to envisage the eventual destination for a chosen adaptation helps you to choose the right project and place it successfully.

In television this process of research is more complex. As well as strong competition between the BBC and the larger independent broadcasters (ITV, Channel 4, Sky, etc) to secure an audience, there is also considerable rivalry between the hundreds of independent production companies to receive commissions. The ratings war means that scheduling is paramount and big dramatic adaptations are often programmed at exactly the same time on BBC TWO and ITV. Familiarity with the output of each channel is crucial when suggesting projects for adaptation, either to a commissioner or a production company. Again, watching dramatisations and noting what format they are in, who is producing them, and when they are being broadcast, is all part of the job.

It is helpful to know that, as a general rule, both adaptations and writing commissioned directly for television tend to be divided into several basic categories (not including soaps). Single dramas are usually high-profile, event pieces broadcast at prime times such as Bank Holidays and are about 90 minutes long. Series consist of a number of weekly parts shown over several weeks (3, 4, 6, and 8 are all common), each part lasting anywhere between 30 and 60 minutes. Finally, there are two-part dramas or high-profile pieces which take place on consecutive nights, sometimes five in a row, with each part between one and two hours long. The percentage of adaptations will generally be lower than newly commissioned drama, although this is entirely dependent upon the type of slot and the broadcaster. For example, the BBC has approximately double the budget per hour for drama that Channel 4 has, and produces many more dramatisations of classic novels, particularly recently. Likewise, ITV has currently been producing more contemporary drama in terms of adaptations with an emphasis on crime. Its period serials such as *Downton Abbey* have most recently been original drama rather than being book based. Channel 4, when it commissions adaptations, tends to focus on cutting-edge contemporary novels, such as *Any Human Heart* by William Boyd. And there are of course always exceptions to all these trends, which is why it is necessary to be an aware and regular viewer.

If you want to adapt for film, the nature of what will work and when, seems to be more open-ended, though it is of course important to go regularly to the cinema and know what has been produced recently. This may be to do with the nature of distribution – the fact that most films are on in a number of cinemas for several weeks – and the time it takes to make a film – often years between the initial idea and eventual screening. However, you still need to keep up to date with who is producing what and when. It is worth noting, though, that there is a very strong relationship between books and film, and that around 50% of all Oscar-winning films are based on books.

The rights

Once you have selected your material and medium, it is vital to establish who has the rights to the original and whether these are available for negotiation. Sometimes this involves a

Successful collaborations

Here is an entirely subjective list of my personal favourites among successful collaborations over the last 20 years, by way of example.

Film

Jane Eyre (Charlotte Bronte, screenplay Moira Buffini)
Tinker, Tailor, Soldier, Spy (John Le Carre, adaptation Bridget O'Connor and Peter Straughan
The Best Exotic Marigold Hotel (Deborah Moggach, screenplay Ol Parker)
The Social Network (Ben Mezrich, screenplay Aaron Sorkin)
127 Hours (Aron Ralston, screenplay Danny Boyle and Simon Beaufoy)
Up in the Air (Walter Kim, screenplay Jason Reitman and Sheldon Turner)
Slumdog Millionaire (Vikas Swamp, screenplay Simon Beaufoy)
The Diving Bell and the Butterfly (screenplay Ronald Harwood)
Motorcycle Diaries (Ché Guevara, screenplay Joe Rivera)
Enduring Love (Ian McEwan, screenplay Joe Penhall)
Trainspotting (Irvine Welsh, screenplay John Hodges)
Lord of the Rings (J.R.R. Tolkien, screenplay Fran Walsh)
The House of Mirth (Edith Wharton, screenplay Terence Davies)
Jude (George Eliot, screenplay Hossein Amini)
Persuasion (Jane Austen, screenplay Nick Dear)

Television

Great Expectations (Charles Dickens, adaptation Sarah Phelps)
Any Human Heart (William Boyd, adaptation William Boyd)
Lark Rise to Candleford (Flora Thompson, adaptation Bill Gallagher)
Bleak House (Charles Dickens, adaptation Andrew Davies)
Middlemarch (George Elliott, adaptation Andrew Davies)
The Forsyte Saga (John Galsworthy, adaptation Stephen Mallatratt)
Brideshead Revisited (Evelyn Waugh, adaptation John Mortimer)
The Buddha of Suburbia (Hanif Kureshi, adaptation Roger Michell and Hanif Kureshi)
Longitude (Dava Sobel, adaptation Charles Sturridge)

Theatre

War Horse (Michael Morpurgo, adaptation Nick Stafford)
Coram Boy (Jamilla Gavin, adaptation Helen Edmundson)
Nana (Emile Zola, adaptation Pam Gems)
The Magic Toyshop (Angela Carter, adaptation Bryony Lavery)

Radio

Life and Fate (Vasily Grossman, adaptation Mike Walker and Jonathan Myerson)
The Worst Journey in the World (Apsey Cherry-Garrod, adaptation by Stef Penny)
The Old Curiosity Shop (Charles Dickens, adaptation Mike Walker)

bit of detective work. If the writer is dead, it is necessary to find out whether there is an estate and if the work is still subject to copyright. Copyright law is extremely complex and varies around the world so it is essential to seek expert advice concerning the current rules for any potential project, depending on the country of origin (for further information see *UK copyright law*, page 643).

It is usually possible to begin the search for the copyright holder and source of rights from the imprint page of the novel, play, film script, etc. If this information is not given, try the publisher, the Society of Authors (see page 497) or the Authors' Licensing and Collecting Society (ALCS, page 660).

In the case of a living writer, you will need to establish who their literary agent is – if they have one – and contact them to see if adaptation is possible and how much it will cost. The scale of costs will depend upon the medium. Rights for a stage adaptation are often separate from film or television options. If a book or play has already been optioned, this means that it is probably not available for a period of at least 12–18 months. Should the purchaser of the option choose not to renew, or fail to produce the adaptation within the required timescale, rights may become available again. Many agreements include an extension clause for a further fixed time period, however, and this is particularly common in film as the end-product is rarely produced within 18 months.

Large film companies, particularly in Hollywood, will often buy the rights to a book or script outright, sometimes for a substantial sum. The proposed version may never get made but legally the original will not be available for adaptation by anyone else. If the writer or material is famous enough, or if they have a good agent, a time limit will be part of the original agreement. Complete buy-outs are less common in the UK.

The cost of acquiring rights varies significantly with the scale of the project, the profile of the writer and the intended medium. Usually an initial payment will be needed to secure the rights for a fixed period, followed by the same amount again, should an extension be necessary. In addition, there is nearly always some form of royalty for the original writer or estate in the form of a percentage of the overall profits of the final production, film, or broadcast. This will normally have a 'floor' (minimum amount or reserve) which must be paid whether or not the final work is financially successful and a 'ceiling' (purchase price). There may also be additional clauses for consultancy. With television, film or radio, there may be a further payment for repeat formats, and in the theatre the rate may well alter if the production transfers. Sometimes, with a low-budget production such as a fringe show or short film, a writer or estate will waive any initial rights fee and only expect a royalty. Whether you use a 'deal memo' to formalise your agreement or a more comprehensive 'long form agreement', it is always worth seeking expert help to make sure you have covered everything you need to.

Legalities aside, time spent forming a relationship with the writer of the original, or whoever manages their estate, has another much more important creative function, that of getting closer to the source material.

How to adapt

I don't believe it is possible to lay down a set of rules for adapting, any more than one could invent a meaningful template for creative writing. The only observation I can offer, therefore, is personal and a reflection of my own taste.

When I recommend or commission an adaptation, either for film, television or in the theatre, my first requirement is that something in the original story has hooked me and I want to see the original given another life and another audience. I have to be able to imagine that it has the potential to work dramatically in a different format and can often already see or hear fragments of it.

At this stage I ask myself a lot of questions about the material. How strong is the story and how engaging are the characters? Why should it be done in another medium? How is it possible to achieve the narrative, the characters, the tone, the sequences of action, in a way that is different but still truthful, a sort of creative equivalent, like a metaphor? For me, it is all about thinking laterally and being enthused about the new possibilities another form will generate from the original, or vice versa.

This process generally leads me back to the source, be it book, film or play, in order to dig over everything about it and its writer. As well as looking at other adaptations to see what parts of the original have been enhanced or cut, I like to meet and talk to the writer. If they are no longer alive I try to find out about them from books and/or people who knew them. I want to know what interested them; what were they thinking when they were writing; even what they looked at every day. If possible, I like to go and visit the places they have written about or the place in which they wrote. This process of total immersion helps me to get under the skin of the original.

While this is entirely personal, it raises an interesting question which I believe any adapter needs to answer for themselves. How closely do you wish to be faithful to the original material and how much do you intend to depart from it? Choosing not to stick closely to the source may be the most creative decision you make but you must understand why you are doing it and what the effect will be. After all, two different trains of thought, styles and imaginations need to be fused together for this transformation to be complete and it is important that the balance between them works. I once spoke to a writer who was commissioned to adapt a well-known myth for Hollywood. Several drafts later, when he had been asked to alter all the key elements of the story to the point where it was unrecognisable, he decided to quit. It was the right decision and the film was a flop.

While respect for the writer and the source material is fundamental, there are of course lots of examples where enormous lateral and creative changes have been made to make a story work to optimum effect in its new medium. What matters ultimately is the integrity of the final product. At its best, it is like a marriage of two minds, celebrating the talents of both writer and adapter in an equally creative partnership.

Kate Sinclair is the Film and TV Consultant for the Ampersand Agency. Previously she worked as Books Executive for Film4, where she found *Slumdog Millionaire* and *Brick Lane* for them. She was the Literary Consultant for the UK Film Council, a consultant for Aardman Animations, Free Range and See Saw Films and a Development Producer for Kudos Films, for whom she found *Salmon Fishing in the Yemen*. She has also worked as a theatre director and is currently producing, writing and directing her own feature film projects with her company, Feet Films Ltd.

See also...

• *Stories on radio*, page 377

Writing for television

Writing for television can be extremely rewarding. Anji Loman Field says that any writer with the right aptitude and attitude can succeed, and here she gives advice for screenwriters.

The market

There are various openings for new writers in television, but apart from competitions and special projects these are hardly ever advertised. The openings fall into five categories:

• **Single drama.** There are fewer slots nowadays for the single play – a 30- or even 60-minute one-off drama is highly unlikely to find a market. Occasionally broadcasters will gather single plays together under a collective banner but it's best to think of individual projects as either standalone television films, two-parters or even four-parters. It's always worth asking television companies for their guidelines on single drama and film. Check broadcasters' websites for current requirements.

• **Series and serials.** Although it has been known for a new writer to sell an original series or serial, it is a relatively rare occurrence – although with new channels popping up all the time it's worth keeping an eye on the market. Nevertheless, writers with a track record of writing for existing strands are far more likely to be taken seriously. Long-running soaps like *EastEnders*, *Doctors* and *Emmerdale* are sometimes in the market for new writers. If, after checking, the door is open, a good 'calling card script' is usually the way in. Submit an original piece of work in a similar genre that is at least an hour long and shows your ability to create believable characters, write sparkling dialogue and tell a compelling story. You may be invited to try out for one of these long-running shows.

• **Dramatisations/adaptations.** A new writer is extremely unlikely to be commissioned to adapt or dramatise someone else's work for television. However, if there's something you really want to adapt and you can afford to take out an 'option' on the rights (or already own them, if it is your own novel or play) then write the script on spec. If you have a good script and can show that you own the rights, you could succeed.

• **Situation comedy.** Sitcom is the one area where production companies and broadcasters are desperate for new talent to write for existing shows, and there are often competitions open to new writers. If you are a good comedy writer and market your work well, you will undoubtedly succeed (see 'Writing situation comedy' below).

• **Children's drama/comedy.** This is an important market for broadcasters and audiences, and long-running shows always need talented writers.

Completely new writers do occasionally sell ideas but are much more likely to sell the idea alone, i.e. the 'format rights', and will probably end up not writing the script. If you have a great calling card script or two, or have had a few episodes of something produced, your ideas will be taken much more seriously. At this stage you might well sell a project on the basis of a short outline or synopsis, and be paid to write the script(s).

Aptitude and attitude

The first prerequisite for writing for television is that you enjoy the medium, and actually watch the kinds of shows that you would be interested in writing for. A cynical approach will always show through. And before sitting down to write that first television script, arm yourself with the appropriate skills by examining the medium as a whole.

• **Record the kind of show you'd like to write for and analyse it**. How many scenes are there? What length are they? How much of the story happens 'off camera'? Knowing the answers to these questions will help you to understand the grammar of screen, and enable you to write a more professional script.
• **Study the structure of story telling**. There are plenty of books on the subject, and although it is never a good idea to follow structural paradigms to the letter, absorb as much information as possible so that the essential 'rules' on character, motivation and plot filter through into your writing.
• **Read scripts**. Some are published in book form, but a huge variety of scripts are also available from specialist bookshops such as Offstage (*tel* 020-7240 3883), the Screenwriter's Store (www.thescreenwritersstore.com) and the internet (e.g. www.bbc.co.uk/writersroom/scripts).
• **If you want to write sitcom, see as many live recordings of shows as possible**. This enables you to understand the techniques involved in television production, and particularly the physical constraints imposed by the studio. Free tickets for sitcom recordings are usually available – phone the broadcasters for information.
• **Be realistic**. Don't make your first project too ambitious in terms of screen time, locations or special effects. If you can 'contain the action' and make your first script affordable to shoot, it is far more likely to be taken seriously.

Learning the craft

Even the most successful and experienced screenwriters say they never stop learning. Some have been lucky enough to learn the skill of writing for the screen in a subliminal way. For example, Lynda La Plante (*Prime Suspect*) was an actress with plenty of opportunity for studying scripts and production techniques before she turned her hand to writing; John Sullivan (*Only Fools and Horses*) worked in the props department at the BBC on countless sitcoms, and used to take the scripts home to study. But there are other ways to learn.

Courses and workshops range from small self-help groups, where writers give each other feedback on their work, to full- and part-time screenwriting MA courses (see page 634). Script workshops are particularly useful. Evening classes are available at some local colleges, and there are even script workshops on the internet. Workshops can help in the following ways:
• **Discipline**. The hardest thing most writers ever have to do is sit down and face that blank screen or page. Joining a script workshop – where you *have* to deliver an outline or a treatment, or the next 20 pages of your script by a certain date – provides the push that so many writers need.
• **Feedback**. Reading and giving feedback on other people's work helps you to focus on getting your own script right. It is also good to get used to the idea of showing your own work to others and getting their feedback. Television writing is generally a collaborative process and writers need to be pleasant to work with, and receptive to ideas. Knowing when to argue a point and when to concede are crucial skills which can be developed in good writing workshops.
• **Rewriting**. Learn to Love the Rewrite. It is such a major achievement to finish a first draft that it tempting to rush to the post box and send it off to several production companies at once. *Four Weddings and a Funeral*, a Channel 4-funded project, went through 17 rewrites before finally reaching the screen. So before you post your masterpiece, leave it

to 'settle' for a few days and do something completely different to allow your head to clear. Then reread the script from beginning to end – from as objective a viewpoint as possible – and make necessary changes. Also get some reliable feedback. But be warned: knowing how to read and analyse a script properly is a particular skill. Unless they are equipped in this area, *never* ask your friends or relations to read your script. Their comments could either lull you into a false sense of security or destroy your confidence for ever. Feedback from other writers in your workshop group is best. There are some organisations (including Euroscript) which offer a professional script feedback service for a moderate fee.

All scripts must be typed and properly formatted if they are to be taken seriously. If you dread the practical aspects of getting your script onto the page it might be worth investing in a software program which can auto-format and number the pages and scenes, thus enabling you to move scenes around and restructure your script with ease. This allows you to concentrate wholly on the creative process and can therefore be quite liberating. Contact the Screenwriters' Store for details and advice.

Writing situation comedy

Situation comedy writing is the most lucrative area of television, and deservedly so. Have you ever tried making an audience laugh several times a minute for 25 minutes for at least six weeks running, and maybe (in the case of *Last of the Summer Wine*) for 20 long years?

Despite its name, sitcom is less about situation and much more about character. It is better to start with funny and engaging characters in mind and then (if it isn't part and parcel of the character) find the perfect situation in which to place them than it is to begin with the premise 'nobody's ever set a sitcom in a nuclear power station before'. It is not the setting that makes the audience laugh, it is the characters.

A good exercise in seeing if you can write funny material is to write an episode of an existing sitcom. If *Fawlty Towers* is your all-time favourite, study a few episodes and then try your own. It will never get made, but you'll learn a lot in the process – and a sample script like this can be useful as a calling card script.

Some of the broadcast companies issue guidelines on writing situation comedy – phone their comedy departments for information.

Competitions

Broadcasters occasionally run writing competitions or 'new writing initiatives'. Check BBC writersroom (see box) and other broadcasters' websites – and general screenwriters' websites – for up-to-date information. Also, watch out for annual awards run by organisations such as PAWS (Public Awareness of Science & Engineering, www.europaws.org) and BBC Talent (www.bbc.co.uk/newtalent). Details can be found in the trade press (*The Stage*, *Broadcast*, *Scriptwriter*) and via websites such as www.startintv.com as well as screenwriting organisations such as Euroscript. See also *Prizes and awards* on page 543.

Breaking in

Do you need an agent?

Many new writers are keen to get an agent before they attempt to sell anything, but this can be an arduous process and there are few agents prepared to take on a completely untried writer. The best way to get an agent is to first get an offer of a deal on a project. Most *bona fide* production companies and broadcasters will happily recommend a selection of agents to writers they want to do business with. If you can phone an agent and say 'so-and-so wants to option/commission my project and has recommended you as an agent' he or she is far more likely to be interested. And at that point you can pick and choose the agent who is right for you, rather than going with the first one to say 'yes'.

Selling yourself

Once you are sure you have a good script, where do you send it? If you've done your homework, you will already know which channel is the most likely to be interested. But sometimes it is better to send to an independent production company rather than directly to a broadcaster; check out the companies that are making the kind of show you've written and approach them first.

A preliminary letter or phone call can save you time and money because some smaller companies simply don't have the resources to read unsolicited material. If you feel that a certain production company is absolutely right for your project, write a letter giving a brief synopsis of the project and asking if they will read the script. If they agree, your script will join the 'solicited' pile. And if it fits the bill, they may even pick it up and develop it. But don't expect overnight results. It can sometimes take many months before scripts are read by small and/or busy companies.

Useful information

www.etbscreenwriting.com

A great, inspirational website run by international script consultant/tutor Laurie Hutzler.

www.twelvepoint.com

The online version of *Scriptwriter* magazine which is full of industry information and ideas for writers.

Arts Council England regional offices

Many regional offices offer grants that enable writers, producers and directors to make their projects (see page 502).

BFI (British Film Institute)

21 Stephen Street, London W1T 1LN
tel 020-7255 1444
email filmfundcoordinator@bfi.org.uk
website www.bfi.org.uk

Euroscript

Euroscript Ltd, 64 Hemingford Road,
London N1 1DB
tel (07958) 244656
email enquiries@euroscript.co.uk
website www.euroscript.co.uk

An independent, UK based, script development organisation for film and TV which offers analysis of screenplays from a team of screenwriters, producers and experienced teachers in the field. It also offers day-long training workshops focusing on different aspects of screenwriting and development.

Pact (Producers' Alliance for Cinema and Television)

3rd Floor, Fitzrovia House, 153–157 Cleveland Street, London W1T 6QW
tel 020-7380 8230
website www.pact.co.uk

Serves the feature film and independent TV production sector. Online fully searchable, password-protected *Directory*. (See page 528.)

The Spotlight

7 Leicester Place, London WC2H 7RJ
tel 020-7437 7631
email questions@spotlight.com
website www.spotlight.com

Publishes an annual handbook, *Contacts*, which contains useful information and contact addresses.

The Writers' Guild of Great Britain

40 Rosebery Avenue, London EC1R 4RX
tel 020-7833 0777 *fax* 020-7833 4777
email erik@writersguild.org.uk
website www.writersguild.org.uk

Trade union-affiliated organisation for professional writers. Negotiates rates for TV drama with the BBC and the ITV Network Centre. (See page 499.)

writersroom

website www.bbc.co.uk/writersroom

Information on opportunities for writers at the BBC.

Sending your script directly to a broadcaster can lead to a commission, but unless you target a particular producer whose work you admire you will probably have less control over who you work with. However, BBC writersroom remains a dedicated home for all unsolicited drama and comedy submissions. Their website offers a lot of writing tips and provides sample scripts to inform and inspire.

If you can get your work 'rehearse-read' by actors in front of an audience it will help your writing, and may even lead to discovery. Networking is as important for writers as it is for any other professionals. Many script readings are attended by development executives from television and production companies and there are frequent stories of individuals being picked up from such projects. Player–Playwrights (see page 529) organises rehearsed readings in London. Libraries may have details of local groups.

Development hell

This is the place between finding someone who wants to produce your script and waiting for the 'suits' at the television companies to give the final go-ahead for the project. In the meantime you will have been paid, perhaps just an option fee, or maybe a commission fee for a script or two. Either way, *never put all your eggs in one development basket.* Aim eventually to have several projects bubbling under for every one that comes to the boil.

A realistic optimism is required for this game. Don't believe anything wonderful will happen until you actually have that signed contract in front of you. In the meantime keep writing, keep marketing and, if you possibly can, keep making contacts in the industry. If you're good at schmoozing, go to as many industry events as possible and make new contacts. If you can send a script to a producer with a covering letter saying 'I heard your talk the other day…' you will immediately arouse interest.

The standard rejection letter is the worst part of this business. When it is accompanied by your returned script, looking decidedly unread, it is very easy to become disillusioned. The trick is to change your mental attitude so that if you don't receive at least one rejection letter in the post every day, you feel rejected! So long as you are absolutely sure that your work is good, keep sending it out. Sooner or later you'll get a nicer, more personalised rejection letter, and then eventually perhaps even a cup of tea with the producer….

Writing for television may look easy but huge amounts of work and commitment are required in order to succeed. If that doesn't put you off, and it is what you really want to do, then go for it. Good luck!

Anji Loman Field worked as researcher/producer of factual programming before switching to writing television, film and radio drama in the early 1990s. She became a regular writer for *EastEnders*, *Holby City* and *Doctors*, and has written several plays for Radio 4 as well as films for the German and Cambodian markets. She now runs an international production company (www.indevelopmentproductions.com). She has taught screenwriting at various establishments including the Royal College of Art, the London Institute and in Germany, Cambodia and Vietnam.

Further reading

Friedmann, Julian, *How to Make Money Scriptwriting*, Chicago University Press, 2000
Kelsey, Gerald, *Writing for Television*, A&C Black, 3rd edn, 1999
Seger, Linda, *Making a Good Script Great*, Samuel French Inc., 3rd edn, 2010
Vogler, Christopher, *The Writer's Journey*, Pan, 3rd edn, 2007

Notes from a successful soap scriptwriter

As the longest serving member of the *Archers'* scriptwriting team, Mary Cutler shares her thoughts about writing for soaps.

A few years ago I was introduced by a friend to someone struggling to establish herself as a playwright. 'I so envy you,' she said, 'writing for the *Archers*. I love soaps.' 'If you love soaps, maybe you should be writing them,' I suggested. I met her again some time later and she said, 'I want to thank you: I took your advice. I gave it a try, and now I'm writing for Emmerdale.' So there you are, dear readers. Ten magic words from me might transform your life. I will try to explore why you might love writing for soaps, or equally helpfully, I hope, why you might not.

I have been writing for the *Archers* for 33 years (the programme was first broadcast on Radio 4 in 1951) and such a long career is by no means unique in soaps. During these years I have had a guaranteed audience for my work, and what's more, an affectionate and engaged audience. I've worked collaboratively with some extremely talented people, while retaining control of my own words. I have had the opportunity to cover almost every dramatic situation – tragic, comic, social, political – I could ever have wanted to, in every possible dramatic form. Yes, you may ask – though I hope not as the question fills me with fury – but what about your own work? This is my own work. Who else wrote all those scripts?

The production process

The process of getting a script ready to be recorded starts with the monthly Monday script conference. This is attended by all the writers (there are 12 of us in the team at the moment) and the production team. We each have in front of us the large script pack which would have been emailed to us on the previous Friday. (It helps if you're a quick reader.) We meet to decide on the storyline for the next writing month, for which four of the writers present will each be writing a week's worth of episodes. But we all work on the storyline together – the writers, whether writing or not – and all the production team, at all levels. That is one of the things I like most. I have never felt plotting was a particular strength of mine, but if someone will give me a starting line I can run from it. The delight of a good script conference is when we start with a strong idea which everyone expands and improves on until it's a thing of beauty, and no one can remember whose idea it was first, and it doesn't matter.

To be part of this engrossing process you have to speak. Most soaps have a script conference element where you will be expected to voice, and if necessary, defend your ideas. That doesn't mean you have to shout, or talk all the time – indeed, these would be positive disadvantages. But you need to stand your ground, especially about what a character might or might not do, and also be ready to yield gracefully if you lose the argument. One of our characters was once torn between two lovers, and the team were, too. On the day of the final decision there was a bad hold-up on the motorway, and three writers rooting for one lover didn't arrive until midday, by which time the other had carried the day. Those writers each had to find their own way to make that decision work for them when they wrote their scripts.

After the script conference, the storyline is emailed two days later to all the writers and members of the production team to arrive on Wednesday evening. The writers for that month have until Tuesday to each write their synopsis, which is a scene-by-scene break down of what they intend to write in their six episodes. If it is a well-structured and imaginative synopsis, all that now needs to be written is the dialogue. A script editor speaks with each of the writers for that month on the following Thursday, and they then have ten days to write six scripts – an hour and a quarter's radio. Not everyone can work that fast. One of the best weeks of the *Archers* I ever heard was also that writer's last: he said he could never do it again in the time. It's not a case of locking yourself in your garret and seeing where the muse takes you. The storyline must be covered: while the writer for one week is working on their scripts, the writer for the following week's episodes is writing theirs starting from the point where the storyline is left on the previous week. As all the scripts are written simultaneously each writer needs to let the others know what they're doing. How each writer chooses to dramatise the story is entirely up to them, so there's a lot of scope for individual creative work. There are constraints on the structure of the programme, such as the financial restriction on the number of actors which can be used. Only two of our actors are on a regular contract, so writers may need to tell a story without a character being present because the actor is working elsewhere. Alternatively a writer may swap episodes within their week, or with other writers, to get the actors they need.

Until the script editor sees the writing for all four weeks, she can't tell if stories are going too fast or too slow, have become repetitive, or picked up the wrong tone. There may well be changes to be made following the synopsis discussion. It is only after the synopsis is agreed that the office starts ringing the actors to see if they are still available. Some of them may not be, in which case a writer may have to rethink their beautiful structure and clever stories. But those are just normal run-of-the-mill changes. When we lost the delightful and distinguished actress who played Julia Pargeter (who died suddenly and unexpectedly after a happy day in the recording studio) the team had to deal with not only their individual sorrow and distress, but the fact that this meant rewriting and re-recording scripts that had been completed in the studio, and rewriting those that were about to be recorded, as well as rethinking those that were about to be written. I had two days to turn round my part of this massive undertaking. When the foot-and-mouth crisis hit British farming in 2001 our fictional world was being rewritten practically day by day, so a good soap scriptwriter needs to be fast and flexible. When the Princess of Wales died our redoubtable editor had one day to get something appropriate on air.

My scriptwriting break

So how did scriptwriting for soaps become the job for me? I had always wanted to write, and had been writing since I was quite small. I thought I was going to be a novelist, and wrote several highly autobiographical, very literary quasi novels while at school and university. I should have noticed that the only person prepared to pay me was the editor of Jackie magazine to whom I sold three highly autobiographical, although not quite so literary, stories. Then at university I stopped having saleable teenage fantasies, and started having unsaleable literary ones. Real life took over – I decided my ambition to be a writer was a fantasy – I would concentrate on my burgeoning career as a teacher, and stop writing.

But I found I couldn't stop. When I realised how I think – rather than seeing images or words, I hear voices (a perpetual radio broadcast!) – I started to write radio plays. To my delight, I found that I could write dialogue till the cows came home(!) though whether it was about anything that would interest even the cows was another matter. I sent my radio plays to the BBC, and sometimes they came back with kind comments (once I was even invited to meet a producer) – and sometimes they just came back. But I persisted.

I am a life-long fan of the *Archers* (I remember Grace Archer dying when I was six and I used to play Phil Archer and his pigs with my little brothers – naturally I was Phil). When an old school friend started writing for the *Archers* I was fascinated to hear her first week on air: it simultaneously sounded like the *Archers* I had known and loved but also very like my friend – her sense of humour, her preoccupations. I idly wondered what I might find out about my own writing if I tried using these well-loved characters to express myself. So after I heard her Friday episode, I sat down to write the following Monday's, purely as a writing exercise and just for fun, and sent it off.

Some time later I received a letter from the recently appointed editor of the *Archers* saying that although he wasn't looking for new writers my script interested him. He also invited me to meet him. When I went to Pebble Mill the editor offered me a trial week, which I did in the Easter holidays. Following that he offered me a six-month contract. So my big break was a combination of persistence (I had been sending radio plays to the BBC for at least three years, and writing stories since I could hold a pencil) and sheer luck – the new editor *was* looking for new writers, despite what he'd said in his letter. (The *Archers* now has a rather more sophisticated method of finding new writers – see box.) My script also had the necessary ingredients of craft and, dare I say it, talent. I had, without knowing it, written a script of the right length, with the right number of scenes and the right number of characters – all those years of listening had given me a subliminal feel for the form. According to the editor, my first good line was two-thirds of the way down the first page. I can still remember it: 'She can get up a fair lick of speed when she's pushed'. (Maybe you had to be there but I still think it has a certain ring to it!) But it was also a script I wrote for fun for a programme I loved and admired.

Further information

The Archers Office
BBC, The Mailbox, Birmingham B1 1RF
Write to receive a Writer's Pack. NB: If you are asked to write a trial script this will be unpaid. Slots on the writing team do not come up often and at the time of writing there are no spaces.

Mary Cutler has been a scriptwriter for the *Archers* since 1979. She has dramatised five of Lindsey Davis's *Falco* novels for Radio 4, the last one being *Poseidon's Gold*, and three dramatic series – *Live Alone and Like It, Three Women and a Boat* and *Three Women and a Baby* for *Women's Hour*. She has also written for the stage and television, including some scripts for *Crossroads* before she was told that her particular talents did not quite fit its special demands. She'd still like to write a novel.

Writing drama for radio

Writing drama for radio allows a freedom which none of the other performing arts can give. Lee Hall guides the radio drama writer to submit a script which will be well received.

With upwards of 300 hours of radio drama commissioned each year, radio is constantly seeking new blood. It is no surprise to find that many of our most eminent dramatists, such as Pinter and Stoppard, did important radio work early in their careers.

Although the centrality of radio has been eclipsed somewhat by television and fringe theatre, it continues to launch new writers, and its products often find popular recognition in other media (e.g. the film version of Anthony Mingella's *Truly Madly Deeply*). Because radio is often cited as the discoverer and springboard of so many talents, this should not obscure the fact that many writers make a living primarily out of their radio writing and the work itself is massively popular, with plays regularly getting audiences of over 500,000 people.

For the dramatist, the medium offers a variety of work which is difficult to find anywhere else: serials, dramatisations, new commissions of various lengths (from a couple of minutes to several hours), musicals, soap operas, adaptations of the classics, as well as a real enthusiasm to examine new forms.

Because it is no more expensive to be in the Hindu Kush than to be in a launderette in Deptford, the scope of the world is only limited by the imagination of the writer. However, though radio drama in the Fifties and Sixties was an important conduit for absurdism, there is a perceived notion that radio drama on the BBC is domestic, Home Counties and endlessly trotting out psychological trauma in a rather naturalistic fashion. This is not a fair assessment of the true range of work presented. The BBC itself is anxious to challenge this idea and as the face of broadcasting changes, there is a conscious move to attract new audiences with new kinds of work.

Get to know the form

Listen to as many plays as possible, read plays that are in print, and try to analyse what works, what doesn't and why. This may seem obvious, but it is easy to fall back on your preconceived notions of what radio plays are. The more you hear other people's successes and failures, the more tools you will have to discriminate with when it comes to your own work.

Plays on radio tend to fit into specific time slots: 30, 60, 75, 90 minutes, and each slot will have a different feel – an afternoon play will be targeted at a different audience from one at 10.30pm.

A radio play will be chosen on artistic grounds but nevertheless a writer should be familiar with the market. This should not be seen as an invitation merely to copy forms or to try to make your play 'fit', but an opportunity to gain some sense of what the producers are dealing with. Producers are looking for new and fresh voices, ones which are unique, open new areas or challenge certain preconceptions. This is not to suggest you should be wilfully idiosyncratic but to be aware that it is the individuality of your 'voice' that people will notice.

Write what you feel strongly about, in the way that most attracts you. It should be bold, personal, entertaining, challenging and stimulating. Radio has the scope to explore drama that wouldn't get produced in theatres or on television, so treat it as the most radical forum for new writing. How many times have you listened to the radio with the sense that you've heard it all before? Never feel limited by what exists; instead be aware how your voice can enrich the possibilities of the future.

Who to approach

Opportunities for writing for radio in the UK are dominated by the BBC. Whilst there are increasing opportunities with independent stations, BBC Radio Drama overwhelms the field. Its output is huge. The variety of the work – from soaps to the classics – makes it the true national repertory for drama in its broadest sense. However, the BBC is increasingly commissioning productions from independent producers, so you can:

• Send your unsolicited script to the BBC writersroom (see page 382) where it will be assessed by a reader. If it is of interest they will put you in contact with a suitable producer.

• Approach a producer directly. This may be a producer at the BBC or at an independent company. Both will give a personal response based on their own taste, rather than an institutional one. Producers have a broad role: they find new writers, develop projects, edit the script, cast the actors, record and edit the play, and even write up the blurb for the *Radio Times*. Because of this intense involvement, the producer needs to have a strong personal interest in the writer or writing when they take on a project.

The system of commissioning programmes at the BBC is such that staff producers or independent production companies offer projects to commissioning editors to decide upon. Thus, a writer must be linked to a producer in the first instance to either get their play produced or get a commission for a new piece of work. Therefore, going direct to a producer can be a convenient short cut, but it requires more preparation.

Approaching a producer

Discovering and developing the work of new writers is only a small part of a producer's responsibilities, so be selective. Do your homework – there is little point in sending your sci-fi series to a producer who exclusively produces one-off period comedies.

To help decide which producer will be the most receptive to your work, become familiar with the work of each producer you are interested in and the type of writers they work with. Use the *Radio Times* to help with your research and listen to as many of their plays as possible. It is well worth the effort in order to be sure you send your play to the right person. If you can quote the reasons why you've chosen them in particular, it can only help to get a congenial reception. It will also give you confidence in their response, as the comments – good or bad – will be from someone you respect.

Submitting your work

Don't stuff your manuscript into an envelope as soon as you've written 'The End'. You owe it to yourself to get the script into the best possible state before anyone sees it. First impressions matter and time spent refining will pay dividends in attracting attention.

Ask a person you trust to give you some feedback. Try to edit the work yourself, cutting things that don't work and spending time revising and reinventing anything which you think could be better. Make sure that what you send is the best you can possibly do.

Producers have mountains of scripts to read. The more bulky your tome the less enthusiastically it will be received. (It's better to send a sparkling ten-page sample than your whole 300-page masterpiece.) Try to make the first scene excellent. The more you can surprise, engage or delight in the first few pages, the more chance the rest will be carefully read. The adage that a reader can tell whether a play is any good after the first three pages might be wholly inaccurate but it reflects a cynicism versed by the practice of script reading. The reader will probably approach your script with the expectation that it is unsuitable, and part of getting noticed is jolting them out of their complacency.

Have your script presentably typed. Make sure your letter of introduction is well informed and shows that you haven't just picked a name at random. Do not send it to more than one producer at a time, as this is considered bad etiquette. And don't expect an instantaneous response – it may take a couple of months before you receive a reply. Don't be afraid of calling up if they keep you waiting for an unreasonable length of time, but don't badger people as this will inevitably be counterproductive.

Finally

Don't be discouraged by rejection and *don't* assume that because one person has rejected your script that it is no good. It is all a question of taste. Use the criticism positively to help your work, not as a personal attack.

Lee Hall has written several plays for BBC Radio, including the award-winning *Spoonface Steinberg*, which he has since adapted for television and theatre. His most recent theatre productions include *The Pitmen Painters*, Live Theatre/Royal National Theatre 2007/8/9, Broadway 2010, West End 2011/12 (winner of the Evening Standard Best Play Award, TMA Best New Play Award) and *Billy Elliot – the Musical* (Olivier Award – Best Musical, nine Tony Awards inlcuding Best Book). His screenplays include *Warhorse* for Dreamworks, *Toast* for the BBC and *Billy Elliot* for Working Title Films, which was Oscar nominated.

Stories on radio

Getting a story read on BBC Radio 4 is very competitive. Di Speirs outlines how work is selected.

Before they were ever written down, we told stories to each other. And there remains a natural empathy between the written tale and the spoken word. The two make perfect partners in a medium where the imagination has free rein – in other words – radio. And that partnership is particularly effective on the BBC's spoken word station, BBC Radio 4, which plays host to more stories than any other UK network. Stories, of course, can and do appear in many guises there, from original plays to dramatised adaptations, but above all they work on air as themselves, read by some of the finest actors of our day and listened to by upwards of one million listeners on most slots.

There are two main reading slots for books on Radio 4: the morning non-fiction reading at 9.45am, which is repeated in the late evening, and every weekday evening a *Book at Bedtime* episode can lull you towards (although hopefully not to) sleep, just after *The World Tonight* at 10.45pm. There are also two slots a week, on Friday at 3.30pm and at 7.45pm on a Sunday where both commissioned and extant short stories are broadcast, and in 2012 there is the new Short Story Zone on Radio 4 Extra for five pieces from short story collections.

A number of different producers, both in-house and independent, produce readings for these slots – finding the books, getting them commissioned by Radio 4 and then producing the final programmes. The process of successfully translating the written work to the airwaves is as intimate as that of any editor within a publishing house. There is nothing like structuring the abridgement of a novel or a short story – which reduces an author's meticulously crafted work down to 2,000 words an episode – to focus the mind on the essential threads and hidden subtleties of a story, be it originally 3,500 perfectly chosen words or an intricately plotted 300-page novel. The author Derek Longman once described the abridging of his *Diana's Story* (one of the most popular readings ever on *Woman's Hour*) as akin to the book 'having gone on a diet'. You aim to retain the essence, but in a trimmer, slimmer version.

Once cut to the bone, finding the right voice to convey and enhance the story is crucial, as performance, in part, compensates for what has been lost. Casting is vital; so is direction in the studio where different stories demand very different approaches: listen to the output and you'll hear everything from a highly characterised monologue to a narrator-driven piece which demands the actor to also create a cast of dozens of distinct voices. From the cues that introduce a story, to the music that sets the right mood, a producer works to move a story from the author's original vision into a different but sympathetic medium. As authors mourn what is discarded, it is important to remember what is added by good quality production and top class performance. And of course to remember how effective readings are at taking a book to a whole new audience.

So how do you get your story on air and to all those eager listeners? What is Radio 4 looking for and what works best?

It would be disingenuous to say that it is any easier to get your work read on radio than to get it published. In truth, given the finite number of slots and the volume of submissions it's a tough call. But here are a few hints and guidelines that may help.

Book of the Week

The *Book of the Week* slot is the one that reflects current publishing more than any other. With 52 books a year broadcast on or very close to their original publication date, in five 13-minute episodes, the non-fiction remit is broad and the slot covers everything from biography to humour, politics to travel. Memoir is always an important part of the mix, but so too are good, accessible science books with a narrative thread that can engage the listener, and few subjects are out of bounds if the prose lifts off the page and can catch the attention of what is, by necessity, a largely active and busy audience at that time in the morning.

Submissions come through publishers and agents. The books need to sustain their story over five episodes but also work as individual episodes, for this is an audience that won't necessarily hear all of the book (though the BBC's 'Listen Again' facility is increasingly changing this pattern). Overly academic prose doesn't work, nor do too many names and facts. The key is a story and, as below, a voice.

Book at Bedtime

Book at Bedtime is a mix of classic and new fiction. The slot is mostly serialised fiction although occasional harder hitting short story collections – for instance by writers like Faber, MichelMichel Faber, Julie Orringer and Anne Enright – do find their way in, as do the odd weeks of poetry (*Paradise Lost* and *The Prelude* have been read in the past). The novels divide into, roughly, a third classic fiction; a third established names (e.g. new novels, usually transmitted on publication by popular writers, from William Trevor to Pat Barker, Tim Winton to Rose Tremain); and a third newer voices, including a high proportion of debut novels (Ross Raisin's *Waterline*, Kyung-sook Shin's *Please Look After My Mother*, Anna Funder's *All that I Am*, Amy Sackville's *The Still Point*) and some short stories (e.g. Polly Samson, Clare Keegan). What they all share is a quality of writing that works when you pare it to the core. Abridging a work will show up its literary qualities and its flaws – and there is nowhere to hide. Listen to the slot and you will be aware of both the variety (from classics to crime, domestic dramas to lyrical translations) and the quality of the writing.

There are few other hard-and-fast rules – a linear plot, with sub-plots that can be reduced or lost, is preferable – *The Vanishing Act of Esme Lennox* was a demanding listen in terms of jumps in time and place but the characters were so vivid and the story so powerful it worked; myriad characters are best avoided, but are manageable with a classic (where familiarity helps). Length is also an important issue. The usual run for a book is ten episodes over two weeks; for almost any novel over 350 pages this becomes a cut too far. Exceptions can be made but they are exceptions; *Atonement* by Ian McEwan, *Merival, A Man of His Time* by Rose Tremain and *The Interpretation of Murder* by Jed Rubenfeld all ran at 15 episodes, but for new work this is a rarity. (Short novels can run over five episodes.)

New book submissions

New novels are found almost entirely through submissions from agents and publishers to individual producers – the best ones both understand Radio 4 and know the predilections of the main players and play to their tastes. It is extremely rare that an author submits directly, even rarer for them to be successful in what is the most competitive readings slot of all. However, the passion of an individual agent or editor can make a real difference in getting a book read by the producer, which is the first step in the process. Bear in mind that in my office alone we receive upwards of 50 manuscripts and proof sets a week – a lot of work for a team of six. Having a reputable champion who can expand on why your novel really is potentially right for the slot is a genuine plus in getting to the top of the scripts pile.

We usually see work at the manuscript or proof stage; this is increasingly submitted online though this is not essential as many producers still prefer to read from paper. New titles are ideally broadcast at or near to the hardback publication date, and so producers need to see them in time to get them commissioned and made – ideally six to nine months in advance. And however passionate a producer is about an individual title, the choice is finally in the hands of the commissioning team at Radio 4 who know what else lies in the complex schedule across the network, and must always weigh individual merits against the broader picture.

What makes a good book to read on Radio 4?

Radio 4 is looking for the quality of the writing, coherence of plot (bear in mind though that complex sub-plots can sometimes be stripped out by skilful abridgers), a comprehensible, identifiable cast and perhaps above all, a sense of engagement with the listener. Although crime is always popular, broadcasting copious amounts of blood and gore at bedtime is unlikely to endear the BBC to the public. Psychological work – like *Engleby* by Sebastian Faulks – works better. Think too, when descriptions are cut, do the clues in the plot stand out like a sore thumb? Consider whether the subject matter is likely to fit with the Radio 4 audience – who are almost certainly much broader-minded and certainly more eclectic than you might imagine – and also highly literate. There is a very real desire to reflect as wide a range of fiction as possible – from a bestseller by Kate Long to a Bangladeshi debut from Tahmima Anan, from a suddenly discovered classic from Irene Nemirovsky to the cutting edge of David Mitchell. It's a broad spectrum but there are of course some issues surrounding language, violence and sexual content; these can be surmountable in many cases – judicious pauses are effective and radio is, after all, a medium that allows the imagination to fill in the blanks as far as you may want to. However, there is no point in submitting a novel filled with expletives or subject matter that will simply shock for the sake of it.

Think too about the voice of a novel – this applies, as much does here, to the short story too. It's an aural medium. Does your book have a 'voice' – can you hear it leaping off the page? Would you want to hear it read to you? And will that be easy to do? There are problems with any story or novel that veers from the third to the first person continually. It can be done – Anna Funder's *All That I Am* was a gift for three narrators, but remember that although every year Radio 4 runs several novels with multiple narrators, they are more expensive to produce and as budgets get ever leaner, slots are even more limited. Be realistic. The competition for this slot is the fiercest of all – and with approximately 26 titles a year, a good number of which are from the ever-popular classic canon, there are really only around 15 opportunities for the year's new titles.

Afternoon Story

Fifty-two weeks of the year, twice a week, Radio 4 broadcasts a short story – approximately 100 stories annually, are commissioned by producers around the country. The rest comprise of the retelling of old masters and selections from newly published collections, by writers such as Alice Munro, Jennifer Egan, Helen Simpson, Sana Kraskiov and Etgar Kerat. Like novels, these collections are submitted by publishers and agents.

The BBC is arguably the largest single commissioner of short stories in the UK, possibly even the world. It is hugely committed to the short story, that most difficult and often underrated of literary forms, and does provide an unparralleled opportunity for writers who want to explore the genre. However, as with *Book at Bedtime*, the competition here is severe.

Stories are usually grouped around a theme and often in runs of threes or fours. Each year there are stories broadcast from different literary festivals, such as Edinburgh, Latitude and Hay-on-Wye. Writers for these are often selected from the festival's own programme, either to write original material or to perform something they are already reading.

The majority of other weeks are commissioned by producers around a theme that they've discussed with the commissioning editor. The scope is very wide. There have been stories drawn from the three Benelux countries and others inspired by Tom Waits under the umbrella title 'The Heart of a Saturday Night'. A week of 'Heartbreak' was followed by a week of 'Passion' and later by 'Wedding Feasts', while thornier subjects such as 'Addiction' have allowed writers to explore a surprising variety of subjects from caffeine to love. 'Madame Bovary Speaks' allowed writers to play with various angles from Flaubert's novel while a returning series like 'Curly Tales' plays with the storytelling form and enjoys turning it upside down. These themed runs offer producers a wonderful opportunity to approach both well-known writers (who usually have a record in short story writing) and to give new writers – perhaps spotted in an anthology or a magazine, or because of a strong debut novel, or through the advocacy of an agent – a chance to get their work on air. Many acclaimed short story writers, like Jackie Kay, Helen Dunmore and Peter Ho Davies, have a long history with Radio 4, and are commissioned regularly because they understand the demands and the possibilities of the slot.

Unsolicited stories

I would love to say that the writers who send in unsolicited material have a good chance of getting their stories read. Some do – for instance the London unit runs a returning series called 'Opening Lines' and accepts submissions at a specific period during the year, and BBC Scotland produces a week of unsolicited 'Scottish Shorts' each year. Others get commissioned to write a story on a theme, rather than having their original idea read. But the short story is a demanding form and skill and practise is perhaps more vital here than anywhere else. Producers have a certain but sadly limited amount of time to work with an author in an editorial capacity. With only 2,000 words there's no room for waste and yet you must, as Alice Munro (the Canadian doyenne of the short story) says, 'create a world in a glance'. The subjects may be wide but the bar is high – the best writers in the country and beyond are writing for this slot and you have to match that standard. You may have a better chance of being considered by aiming your story locally (some local BBC radio stations run short fiction from time to time). Be aware of who works in your geographic area, as the Radio 4 slots reflect the regions and nations of the UK.

But above all, as with *Book at Bedtime*, listen to the slot to hear both the range and also what works well. Listen to how writers use the unique qualities of radio – the chance to write a powerful monologue or to use sound or location within a tale – to enhance their story, create a sense of place or person, to flesh out what is in reality a brief moment in time. There are real ways to be experimental in both storytelling and production and producers are always on the lookout for those alongside perfectly pitched and flawless prose.

Finally, for the past six years the BBC has been one of the partners, along with Booktrust, in the BBC National Short Story Award (see page 545), which was established to celebrate and foster the art of the short story. With an award of £15,000 to the winner is one of the largest in the world for a single story. We have received over 4,500 entries from published writers either from, or resident in, the UK since the award began, and from writers in English from around the globe in the Olympic year of 2012. It is certainly clear that the short story is alive and well across the UK and choosing the winners has been a tremendously hard task each time. If you are a published writer, do consider entering next time around. The BBC NSSA is part of the wider 'Story' campaign, run by Booktrust, which exists to support all short story writers (www.theshortstory.org.uk).

In all the readings slots, Radio 4 is looking for terrific writing, a good story and an ear-catching 'voice'. Despite the fierce competition, producers love to 'discover' new writers for the network and every year sees new talent getting their work on air. Keep listening, get to know the slots, and if you have a story – long or short – that demands to be read aloud, try to find a champion for it. Good luck.

Di Speirs worked in theatre and for the Australian Broadcasting Corporation before joining the BBC in 1991 as a producer for *Woman's Hour*. She edited the *Woman's Hour* serial for three years and produced the first ever *Book of the Week*. She is now Editor of the BBC London Readings Unit, responsible for around a third of the output in *Book of the Week*, a quarter of *Book at Bedtime*, as well as short stories on Radio 4, Radio 3 readings and *Woman's Hour* dramas, and *Afternoon Plays* adapted from novels and short stories. She has been instrumental in the BBC National Short Story Award since its inception in 2005 and is a regular judge on the panel. She was also a judge of the 2008 Asham Award and was the Chair of the Orange Award for New Writers in 2010.

Inside the BBC

The following information has been compiled as a guide for writers, artists, agents, publishers and all other media on how to make contact with the BBC. For more detailed information see the BBC website (www.bbc.co.uk).

The BBC is the largest broadcasting corporation in the world. Its purpose is to enrich people's lives with programmes that inform, educate and entertain. It is a public service broadcaster, established by a Royal Charter and funded by the licence fee that is paid by UK households.

The BBC uses the income from the licence fee to provide services including 8 national TV channels plus regional programming, 10 national radio stations, 39 local radio stations, an extensive website (www.bbc.co.uk), BBC Red Button interactive TV, BBC HD, BBC iPlayer, BBC Mobile and the BBC channel on YouTube. BBC World Service broadcasts internationally on radio, on TV and online, providing news and information in a range of languages. It is funded by a government grant, not from the licence fee.

The BBC has a commercial arm, BBC Worldwide, which operates a range of businesses including selling programmes around the world and publishing books, DVDs and merchandise. Its profits are returned to the BBC for investment in new programming and services.

The BBC is governed by the BBC Trust, which represents the interests of licence fee payers and sets the overall strategy. The Trust's Chairman is Lord Patten of Barnes. The BBC's Executive Board manages the day-to-day operation of the corporation and is made up of executive directors from within the BBC and 5 non-executive directors from outside:

Director-General Mark Thompson
Director, News Helen Boaden
Director, Audio & Music Tim Davie
Director, Vision George Entwistle
Director, Future Media Ralph Rivera
Chief Financial Officer Zarin Patel
Chief Operating Officer Caroline Thomson

The BBC structure

The BBC has 5 content divisions, 2 support departments and 3 commercial subsidiaries.

Content divisions:
- Vision, including Drama, Knowledge and Entertainment
- Audio & Music
- News Group including News, Nations, Global News
- Future Media
- BBC North including Sport, Children's and 5 Live.

Support departments:
- Operations (strategy, policy, distribution, property, legal affairs, fair trading, business continuity, marketing, communication & audiences and human resources)
- Finance & Business Affairs (financial planning & strategy).

Commercial subsidiaries:
- BBC Worldwide
- BBC Studios and Post Production
- BBC World News.

How to make contact

Submitting scripts

BBC writersroom

1st Floor, Grafton House, 379 Euston Road, London NW1 3AU
tel 020-7765 2703
website www.bbc.co.uk/writersroom

BBC writersroom is the first point of call at the BBC for unsolicited scripts and new writers. It champions new writing talent in films and TV single drama; TV series, serials and factual drama; TV sitcoms; radio drama; radio sitcoms; and children's drama.

BBC writersroom is on the lookout for writers of any age and experience who show real potential for the BBC. All eligible scripts are logged and assessed primarily for the talent of the writer and suitability of scripts for further development. If the opening 10pp hooks the attention of the reader, the script will be read fully and the writer will receive feedback. All other scripts are returned without feedback.

BBC writersroom runs schemes to target talent from a range of sources and promote writers across all BBC departments, channels and programmes. It works in partnerships with theatres, writer's organisations, screen agencies and the wider cultural industries. New writers are helped to develop their craft through the website and in open sessions around the country with the UK's best writing talent.

See website for more detailed information about BBC writersroom. Writers are strongly advised to read the guidelines and checklist on the website before submitting material.

Jobs and work placements/ experience

Recruitment BBC HR Direct, PO Box 1133, Belfast BT1 9GP
email careers@bbchrdirect.co.uk
website www.bbc.co.uk/careers/home

The BBC website provides information and advice

about how to get into the BBC and how to apply for BBC jobs, training schemes and work placements. Placements are available in most areas of the BBC across the UK. They are unpaid and can last anything from a few days to 4 weeks. In excess of 20,000 applications are received each year, so applicants must be able to demonstrate a keen interest in the placement.

Submitting programme ideas or formats

If you wish to submit an unsolicited idea to the BBC you need to team up with either a BBC in-house production department or contact an independent production company.

The development and production of a programme is a complex process, needing an in-depth understanding of the production system and involving many people as well as the creator of the original concept. Working with an independent production company or (in some areas) a production department provides this support.

Contacting a BBC production department

Unsolicited proposals (those which are unattached to any industry establishment) can only be accepted in the areas noted below, and should be sent to the relevant address.

Drama and narrative comedy scripts

Development Manager, BBC writersroom, Brock House, 3rd floor, 19 Langham Street, London W1A 3AA
website writersroom@bbc.co.uk

Note that comedy and drama ideas *must* be in the form of a fully written script; send an sae requesting guidelines.

Entertainment formats (quiz/game shows)

Format Entertainment Development Team, Room 4010, BBC Television Centre, Wood Lane, London W12 7RJ

Factual entertainment treatments

Factual Entertainment Development, Room 4010, BBC Television Centre, Wood Lane, London W12 7RJ

Interested in factual entertainment ideas only; does not accept proposals of a documentary or general factual nature.

Independent production companies

The best way of getting in touch with an independent production company is to do some research about the companies which produce the type of programmes you have an idea for. Many of these companies are members of Pact (Producers' Alliance for Cinema and Television, see page 528), which represents the independent sector. The *Pact Directory*, which can be accessed online for free, contains a whole host of useful information about UK independent producers and digital members, including the programmes they've produced, projects they have in development, distribution catalogues and rights available, key personnel and contact details, and brief company profiles (www.pact.co.uk).

Commissioning

TV including multi-platform

website www.bbc.co.uk/commissioning (select BBC Vision)

Programmes are commissioned by the genre teams. The genres are drama, comedy, entertainment, daytime and early peak, knowledge, CBBC, CBeebies, sport and programme acquisition. Each genre handles the entire process – editorial, business, finance and delivery. Contact details can be found on the website under the Who's Who section (www.bbc.co.uk/commissioning/whos-who). Programme requirements for the genres are updated regularly with development priorities on the website located within each of the genre pages in the What We Want section (www.bbc.co.uk/commissioning/tv/what-we-want).

Proposals for BBC network content on TV and all other video platforms (e.g. websites, mobile, interactive TV) must be submitted online through the e-Commissioning system and writers must first have teamed up with either an in-house production studio or an independent production company.

e-Commissioning enables the BBC to handle the huge volume of proposals it receives faster and more effectively. When registering for the system, suppliers should supply a short company profile including relevant industry experience of producing TV programmes or multi-platform content for a broadcaster, detailing relevant examples of productions and broadcasters. Approval of the registration is at the BBC's discretion.

Radio

website www.bbc.co.uk/commissioning/radio, www.bbc.co.uk/commissioinig/radio/how-we-work, www.bbc.co.uk/commissioinig/radio/pitching-ideas/proteus

Full information on the detailed commissioning process for each of the networks can be viewed by selecting the relevant network on the website. Before pitching a programme idea first review the website, particularly the How We Work section and the network to which you wish to pitch. New writers or writers without an agent or production company should explore the BBC writersroom (see above).

When a network invites programme proposals it requires them to be submitted via the Proteus system unless otherwise specified. An independent production company must therefore have access to Proteus before it can submit a programme proposal. New suppliers must first talk to the network that they wish to supply. If the network is interested in receiving programme proposals from that supplier, the company can then find out more about registering for the Proteus system via the website.

All contact details can be found under the Audio & Music section on the website.

BBC Vision

BBC Television Centre, Wood Lane,
London W12 7RJ
tel 020-8743 8000
Director, Vision George Entwistle

BBC Vision is responsible for commissioning, producing, scheduling and broadcasting the content of all the BBC's TV channels. It incorporates the service controllers, genre commissioners, in-house production and operations teams for BBC ONE, TWO, THREE, FOUR, CBBC, Cbeebies, the UKTV channels and BBC America. The service controllers are:

BBC ONE Danny Cohen
BBC TWO Janice Hadlow
BBC THREE Zai Bennett
BBC FOUR Richard Klein
Children's Joe Godwin
Daytime and Early Peak Liam Keelan

Genre commissioning

website www.bbc.co.uk/commissioning/whos-who, www.bbc.co.uk/commissiong/briefs/tv/browse-by-genre

Genre teams now commission all video content on all platforms including online, mobiles and interactive Red Button services, as well as for TV.

For more detailed information on each genre's commissioning team contacts and priorities for commissioning, see website.

Fiction

Comprises drama (including films), comedy and programme acquisition.

Head of Drama Commissioning Ben Stephenson
Controller, Comedy Commissioning Cheryl Taylor
Head of Series, Programme Acquisition Sue Deeks
Head of Films, Programme Acquisition Steve Jenkins

Entertainment

Controller, Entertainment Commissioning Mark Linsey

Knowledge

Controller, Knowledge Emma Swain
Controller, Learning Abigail Appleton

Vision Productions

Vision Productions is responsible for in-house programme making across factual, comedy, drama and entertainment from London, Manchester, Bristol and Birmingham.

Chief Creative Officer, Vision Productions Patrick Younge
Head of Comedy Productions Mark Freeland
Controller, Entertainment Productions Katie Taylor
Controller, Drama Production Nick Brown
Controller, Drama Productions & New Talent John Yorke
Controller, Drama Series & Serials Kate Harwood
Controller of Factual Productions Tom Archer
Controller, Production Operations Sally Debonnaire
Head of London Factual Karen O'Connor
Head of Natural History Unit, Bristol Andrew Jackson
Head of Factual, Birmingham and Manchester Nick Patten
Head of Bristol Factual Ben Gale
Head of Development Tessa Finch
Head of Production Talent Ian Critchley

Audio & Music

BBC Broadcasting House, Portland Place,
London W1A 1AA
tel 020-7765 4561
Director, Audio & Music Tim Davie

The Audio & Music division is responsible for the 5 national analogue networks (Radio 1, Radio 2, Radio 3, Radio 4 and BBC Radio Five Live) and the 5 digital stations (1Xtra, 6Music, Radio 4 Extra, Five Live Sports Extra and the Asian Network). It provides most of the music production for the BBC on national and World Service radio.

The TV Classical Music Television Unit is responsible for dance, performance and classical music on TV and TV Music Entertainment is responsible for popular music production across the BBC TV channels. Audio & Music Factual producers also provide speech programming covering a wide range of arts, science, features, drama and readings for domestic radio and the World Service. Other programmes are provided by Factual & Learning (Religion and the Natural History Unit), News, Sport and Light Entertainment. All BBC national radio stations are available on DAB radio, digital TV and via the internet.

Controller, Radio 1/1Xtra & Asian Network Ben Cooper
Controller, Radio 2 & 6Music Bob Shennan
Controller Radio 3, BBC Proms & Performing Groups Roger Wright
Controller, Radio 4 & Radio 4 Extra Gwyneth Williams
Controller, BBC Radio Five Live, 5 Live Sports Extra Adrian Van-Klaveren
Head of Programmes, 6Music Paul Rodgers
Head of Programmes, Radio 4 Extra Mary Kalemkerian
Head of BBC Asian Network Vijay Sharma

Radio Drama

Head of Radio Drama Alison Hindell
Editor, The Archers/Executive Producer, Radio Drama Vanessa Whitburn

Radio Entertainment

Head, Radio Light Entertainment Jane Berthoud

Audio & Music Factual

Controller of Production for Audio & Music Graham Ellis
Editor, Audio & Music Factual, Bristol Clare McGinn
Executive Editor (Regions), Audio & Music Factual Andrew Thorman
Editor, Audio & Music Factual, Manchester Ian Bent

Radio News

Head of Radio News Stephen Mitchell
Head of Radio Current Affairs Nicola Meyrick
Director, Global News Peter Horrocks

Radio Sport

Head of Radio Sport Gordon Turnbull
Executive Editor, Radio Sport Graeme Reid-Davies

News Group

Director Helen Boaden

The News Group comprises BBC News and the English Regions, BBC Global News and BBC Northern Ireland, BBC Scotland and BBC Wales (although the Directors of the Nations report directly to the Director General). It is responsible for the BBC's news and current affairs output on TV, radio and online, at local, national and international levels.

BBC News

BBC Television Centre, Wood Lane,
London W12 7RJ
tel 020-8743 8000
website www.bbc.co.uk/news

BBC News is the biggest news organisation in the world with over 2,000 journalists, 45 bureaus worldwide and 15 networks and services across TV, radio and new media, and incorporates the BBC English Regions. It also produces the news for the BBC World Service and BBC World News. These services are funded by commercial income and Foreign Office grants respectively, not by the licence fee.

Director, News Helen Boaden
Director, Global News Peter Horrocks
Head of Programmes, News Stephen Mitchell
Head of Newsroom Mary Hockaday
Head of Newsgathering Fran Unsworth
Deputy Head of Newsroom, Controller of BBC News Channel (inc. One O'clock News) Kevin Bakhurst
Head of Political Programmes, Analysis & Research Sue Inglish
Controller of Production, News Jenny Baxter
Controller, English Regions David Holdsworth
Executive Editor & Commissioning Editor for TV Current Affairs Clive Edwards
Executive Editor, Radio Current Affairs Nicola Meyrick

TV programmes

Editor, Six and Ten O'clock News James Stephenson
Editor, Newsnight Peter Rippon
Editor, Breakfast Alison Ford
Editor, Panorama Tom Giles

Radio programmes

Editor, Today Ceri Thomas
Editor, PM/Broadcasting House/The World This Weekend/The World at One Joanna Carr
Head of News Five Live Matt Morris
Editor, The World Tonight Alistair Burnett

Digital

BBC News Website, Editor Steve Herrmann
Social Media Editor, BBC News Chris Hamilton

BBC English Regions (includes Regional Television, Local Radio and BBC Local Online)

BBC Birmingham, The Mailbox, Royal Mail Street,
Birmingham B1 1RF
tel 0121 567 6767
Controller, English Regions David Holdsworth

The BBC's English Regions are responsible for 12 TV regional news operations across England along with related weekly current affairs output, 39 BBC local radio stations and 42 local websites providing news and information for their communities.

BBC Local Radio in England provides a primarily speech-based service of news, information and debate to local communities. Speech output is complemented by music. There is a strong emphasis on interactivity and audience involvement.

Chief Operating Officer Ian Hughes
Business Manager Laura Ellis
Head of Programming TV Craig Henderson
Head of New Media and New Services Laura Ellis
Head of Radio Development Chris Van, Kate Squire
Head of Sport Charles Runcie

For details of all the English Regional offices go to www.bbc.co.uk/local and select the region you are interested in. Then scroll down to the section Get In Touch which lists all relevant contact details.

BBC Global News

Director, BBC Global News Peter Horrocks

The BBC's international news services includes BBC World Service, BBC World News television and bbc.com/news, the BBC's international-facing online news site. The division also includes BBC Monitoring and the BBC World Service Trust.

BBC World Service

Bush House, PO Box 76, The Strand, London
WC2B 4PH

tel 020-7240 3456
website www.bbcworldservice.com

BBC World Service is an international multimedia broadcaster delivering a wide range of language and regional services on radio, TV, online and via wireless handheld devices. It uses multiple platforms to reach its weekly audience of 180 million globally (2010), including shortwave, AM, FM, digital satellite and cable channels. Its news sites include audio and video content and offer opportunities to join the global debate. BBC World Service offers its multilingual radio content to partner FM stations around the world and has numerous partnerships supplying content to news websites, mobile phones and other wireless handheld devices as well as TV channels. See website for more information.

BBC World News

Media Centre, 201 Wood Lane, London W12 7TQ
tel 020-8433 2419
website www.bbcworldnews.com, *International version* bbc.com/news

BBC World News, the BBC's commercially funded international 24-hour news and information channel, is owned and operated by BBC World News Ltd, a member of the BBC's commercial group of companies. It is available in more than 200 countries and territories worldwide, and around 300 million households and 1.8 million hotel rooms. The channel's content is also available on 118 cruise ships, 40 airlines, 39 mobile phone networks and a number of major online platforms including bbc.com/news. For further information on how to receive World News, download schedules or find out more about the channel, visit the BBC World News website.

Acting Controller of English, Global News Richard Porter
Head of Programmes Paul Gibbs
Commercial Director Colin Lawrence

BBC Northern Ireland

BBC Broadcasting House, Ormeau Avenue, Belfast BT2 8HQ
tel 028-9033 8000
website www.bbc.co.uk/ni
Director, BBC Northern Ireland Peter Johnston

BBCNI provides programmes and services for both local and network audiences. Its output is broad based with news and current affairs remaining a defining part, and extends across radio, TV and online. A sizeable proportion of non-news programming on local TV is sourced from the independent sector – reflecting BBCNI's role in supporting the creative industries. BBCNI's region-wide remit is supported by a network of news correspondents and studio facilities and BBC Radio Foyle, a dedicated service for audiences in the north-west. Locally produced programmes for network TV and radio are a developing feature of BBCNI's work – with all their creative and economic benefits – and includes current affairs, drama, factual entertainment and comedy.

Head of Programmes Ailsa Orr
Head of News Kathleen Carragher
Chief Operating Officer Mark Taylor
Head of Public Policy, Corporate and Community Affairs Mark Adair
Head of Drama Stephen Wright
Head of Marketing, Communications & Audiences Kathy Martin
Head of HR & Development Lawrence Jackson
Head of TV Current Affairs Jeremy Adams
Head of Entertainment & Events Mike Edgar
Head of Factual Doug Carnegie
Head of Radio Ulster Fergus Keeling
Editor, Sport Shane Glynn
Head of Multi-platform Commissioning Susan Lovell
Managing Editor, Learning, Language & Social Action Jane Cassidy
Editor, Radio Foyle Michael Tumelty

BBC Radio Ulster

BBC Broadcasting House, Ormeau Avenue, Belfast BT2 8HQ
tel 028-9033 8000

BBC Radio Foyle

8 Northland Road, Londonderry BT48 7JD
tel 028-7126 2244

BBC Scotland

40 Pacific Quay, Glasgow G51 1DA
tel 0141-422 6000
website www.bbc.co.uk/scotland
Director, Scotland Ken MacQuarrie

BBC Scotland is one of the most varied production centres outside London, providing BBC TV and radio networks with drama, comedy, entertainment, children's, leisure, documentaries, religion, education, arts, music, news, sport, current affairs and political coverage, as well as a wide range of online content, at its new state-of-the-art high definition digital headquarters.

BBC Scotland's TV Drama department produces work for the BBC's TV network and Scotland's only soap opera, *River City*. It collaborates with other organisations in the creative sector to support a range of schemes nurturing Scottish writing and directing talent for film and TV. BBC Radio Scotland's Drama department also produces distinctive work for the radio networks.

In addition to network contributions, BBC Scotland transmits around 900 hours of TV programming a year for Scottish audiences on BBC ONE and TWO Scotland, covering all of the major genres from a Scottish perspective and including Gaelic programming. BBC ALBA, launched in September 2008, offers a dedicated digital service for the Gaelic audience. It is operated, in partnership, by BBC Scotland and MG ALBA.

BBC Scotland provides the nation's two speech radio networks, Radio Scotland and Radio nan Gaidheal. There are local services for Orkney and Shetland and daily bulletins for listeners in the Highlands, Grampian, Borders, and the South West. Production work takes place at centres across the nation, from Dumfries to Lerwick.

Head of Programmes & Services Donalda MacKinnon
Chief Operating Officer Bruce Malcolm
Head of Marketing & Communications Mairead Ferguson
Head of Talent Division Donald-Iain Brown
Head of Public Policy & Corporate Affairs Ian Small
Head of HR & Development Wendy Aslett
Head of Strategy Catherine Smith
Head of Drama Chris Aird
Commissioning Editor, TV & Head of Sport & Comedy Ewan Angus
Head of Radio Jeff Zycinski
Head of News & Current Affairs John Boothman
Head of Children's Simon Parsons
Head of Factual Andrea Miller
Head of Learning and Executive Editor New Media Matthew Lee
Head of Radio Drama Bruce Young
Managing Editor, Gaelic Ishbel Maclennan
Head of Entertainment & Events Eileen Herlihy
Director, BBC Scottish Symphony Orchestra Gavin Reid
Head of Service, BBC ALBA Margaret Mary Murray

BBC Radio nan Gaidheal
Rosebank, 52 Church Street, Stornoway, Isle of Lewis HS1 2LS
tel (01851) 705000

BBC Inverness
7 Culduthel Road, Inverness IV2 4AD
tel (01463) 720720

BBC Radio Orkney
Castle Street, Kirkwall, Orkney KW15 1DF
tel (01856) 873939

BBC Radio Shetland
Pitt Lane, Lerwick, Shetland ZE1 0DW
tel (01595) 694747

BBC Radio Selkirk
Unit 1, Ettrick Riverside, Dunsdale Road, Selkirk TD7 5EB
tel (01750) 724567

BBC Radio Dumfries
lmbank, Lovers Walk, Dumfries DG1 1NZ
tel (01387) 268008

BBC Cymru/Wales
BBC Broadcasting House, Llandaff, Cardiff CF5 2YQ
tel 029-2032 2000
website www.bbc.co.uk/wales, www.bbc.co.uk/cymru
Director, BBC Wales Rhodri Talfan Davies

BBC Wales provides a wide range of services in Welsh and in English, on radio, TV and online. This includes more than 20 hours a week of programmes on BBC ONE Wales and BBC TWO Wales. Regular output includes the flagship news programme *Wales Today*, the current affairs strand *Week in Week Out*, homegrown and network drama such as *Doctor Who*, *Torchwood* and *Baker Boys*, a range of local and network factual programming including *Crimewatch*, as well as sport, including live rugby on *Scrum V*. Ten hours a week of Welsh-language programmes are shown on S4C, including the news programme *Newyddion* and the nightly soap opera *Pobol y Cwm*, and educational programmes. BBC Radio Wales, in English, and BBC Radio Cymru, in Welsh, each provide 20 hours a day of news, entertainment, music and sports output. Political coverage on all services continues to reflect the increasing importance of the National Assembly for Wales. BBC Wales produces a wide range of programmes for the BBC's network TV channels, and Radios 1, 2, 3 and 4. These include popular documentaries, drama, education and music programmes for audiences throughout the UK, including the biennial BBC Cardiff Singer of the World competition, accompanied by the BBC National Orchestra of Wales.

Acting Head of Programmes (English) Adrian Davies
Acting Head of Programmes (Welsh) Sian Gwynedd
Head of Strategy & Communications Rhodri Talfan Davies
Head of News & Current Affairs Mark O'Callaghan
Head of Broadcast Development Cathryn Allen
Head of TV Commissioning Elis Owen
Head of Drama Faith Penhale
Head of Sport Geoff Williams
Acting Head of Factual & Music Judith Winnan
Director, BBC National Orchestra of Wales David Murray
Editor, New Media Iain Tweedale
Editor, Radio Cymru Sian Gwynedd
Editor, Radio Wales Steve Austins

BBC North
Director Peter Salmon

The BBC North Group includes BBC Sport, Children's and 5 Live. In 2011 it relocated to Salford Quays and joined departments based in Manchester, as well as parts of Learning and Future Media, and became the BBC's second largest production hub.

BBC Sport
BBC Television Centre, Wood Lane, London W12 7RJ
tel 020-8743 8000
Director, Sport Barbara Slater

BBC Sport produces and, in conjunction with the

network TV channels and radio stations, broadcasts a range of live sport and related content to audiences across the country.

BBC Sport produces self-commissioning content across all platforms and invites tenders from independent producers as appropriate. Sports-related content is also created for and broadcast by BBC TV, BBC Radio, bbc.co.uk and local, national and regional services but is commissioned within those specific areas.

Head of TV Sport Philip Bernie
Head of Major Events Dave Gordon
Head of Radio Sport Gordon Turnbull
Head of Sports News Richard Burgess
Head of Interactive and Formula 1 Ben Gallop
Head of Sport Production Jackie Myburgh

Children's

Controller, Children's Joe Godwin

Children's is a self-commissioning, self-scheduling department that manages its own production unit and as such has a different structure to the rest of the BBC.

For more detailed information on CBBC and Cbeebies go to www.bbc.co.uk/commissioning and select BBC Vision, then select either Children's (CBBC) or (CBeebies).

CBBC

Controller Damian Kavanagh

CBBC is for primary school children aged 6–12 years. It offers a distinctive schedule of original drama, animation, comedy, news, factual programming and events on a variety of platforms as well as interactive applications (online, WAP, SMS, enhanced TV) that allow children to get involved, to connect with CBBC and to explore topics further. The CBBC channel runs 7am–7pm and CBBC output runs on BBC ONE and TWO.

Independent suppliers should send in proposals to Damian Kavanagh, and drama, acquisitions and animations enquiries should be made to Steven Andrew, but all submissions must be made via the e-Commissioning system.

CBeebies

Controller Kay Benbow

CBeebies is the BBC's first truly tri-media brand, offering TV, radio and web services on all digital platforms. CBeebies offers a rich portfolio of content on its website, through its TV outlets and most recently via radio on Radio 4 Extra. Therefore they are a multi-platform commissioner not just a TV commissioner.

CBeebies is a self-commissioning, self-scheduling department and now operates a rolling commissioning system. Independent suppliers should send all proposals to Kay Benbow (via e-Commissioning).

Enquiries concerning acquisitions and animations should be made to Kay Benbow (but proposals must be submitted via e-Commissioning).

The CBeebies digital TV channel (on satellite, cable and Freeview) is on-air 6am–7pm daily. CBeebies TV may also be found on BBC TWO which runs complementary schedules – sometimes simulcasting CBeebies on weekday mornings.

CBeebies radio is available on Radio 4 Extra (via a DAB radio or digital TV set-top box) 2–5pm daily, and programmes are available on the website for up to 7 days after initial broadcast.

BBC Future Media

Media Centre, 201 Wood Lane, London W12 7TQ
tel 020-8743 8000
website www.bbc.co.uk/commissioning (select Future Media)
Director, Future Media Ralph Rivera

The BBC is mandated by the BBC Trust to deliver 2 interactive services to licence fee payers – BBC Online and BBC Red Button. The terms are outlined in service licences, and the BBC's Future Media division is accountable for meeting those terms. More broadly, BBC Future Media is responsible for transforming the BBC for the digital age: conceiving, building and delivering non-linear digital products that deliver the BBC's interactive services, embracing new technologies for the benefit of the public (the BBC's sixth public purpose) and creating the digital public space that will guarantee access and give prominence to the BBC's digital services in the future.

In January 2011, BBC Online's operations were restructured around products that comprise teams from Future Media and the BBC's editorial divisions (such as BBC Vision). BBC Future Media has 4 General Managers, who work in partnership with the editorial divisions to develop and deliver the products.

General Manager, BBC Online Andy Conroy: Responsible for the day-to-day operational management of the service as a whole.
General Manager, News and Knowledge Phil Fearnley: Responsible for the delivery of 8 products: News, Weather, Sport, Homepage, Search, Knowledge & Learning, Children's (CBBC and CBeebies).
General Manager, Programmes On-Demand Daniel Danker: Responsible for the delivery of 2 products: TV & iPlayer and Radio & Music.

The BBC works with a wide range of third parties to deliver its digital services – both in technology and editorial – with just under £20m spent with external suppliers in 2009/10. Companies interested in finding out more should visit www.bbc.co.uk/commissioning.

BBC Worldwide

Woodlands, 80 Wood Lane, London W12 0TT
tel 020-8433 2000
website www.bbcworldwide.com
Chief Executive Officer John Smith

BBC Worldwide is the main commercial arm and a wholly owned subsidiary of the BBC. Its mission is to create, acquire, develop and exploit media content and brands around the world in order to maximise the value of the BBC's assets for the benefit of the UK licence payer.

BBC Worldwide provides a global showcase for the best of British creative talent including actors, journalists, presenters, writers, directors, musicians, designers and technicians. It sells programmes and formats produced by more than 500 different UK independent producers.

The company has 7 core businesses: Channels, Content & Production, Brands, Consumers & New Ventures, Digital, Sales & Distribution, BBC Magazines.

- **Global Brands** *Managing Director* Marcus Arthur
- **Worldwide Networks and Global iPlayer (inc. Channels)** *President* Jana Bennett
- **Content & Production** *Managing Director* Helen Jackson
- **Magazines** *Managing Director* Peter S. Phippen
- **Sales & Distribution** *Managing Director* Steve Macallister
- **Home Entertainment** *Managing Director* Paul Dempsey
- **Digital** *Director* Danie Heaf

TV Channels

The business comprises a portfolio of thematic and composite channels in the UK and around the world, some of which are joint-ventured with partner broadcasters such as Shaw Communications and Virgin Media. The UKTV joint venture with Virgin Media constitutes one of the biggest revenue streams for the Channels business while BBC America is the single largest channel, reaching 68 million homes.

UKTV

245 Hammersmith Road, London W6 8PW
tel 020-7299 6200
Director of Commissioning Jane Rogerson

Formed in 1997, UKTV is an independent commercial joint venture between BBC Worldwide, the commercial arm of the BBC, and Virgin Media. The network offers a broad range of distinctive programming on its 10 distinctive TV channels – Watch, G.O.L.D., Dave, Alibi, Eden, Blighty, Yesterday, Home, UKTV Food, and UKTV Gardens. UKTV currently operates 24 broadcast streams when multiplexes (+1s) and HD channels are taken into account, and complementary websites for every channel brand.

BBC America

tel +1 212-705-9644

BBC America showcases the best of the BBC's drama and entertainment programmes in North America. This digital cable and satellite channel does not directly commission programmes but occasionally invests in UK programmes in production to increase their suitability for the US market.

Other joint ventures: BBC Canada and BBC Kids (with Shaw Communications).

Other wholly owned channels: BBC Entertainment, BBC HD, BBC Knowledge, BBC Lifestyle, BBC World News, CBeebies, UKTV (Australia).

For more detailed information visit www.bbcworldwide.com/channels.

AudioGO Audiobooks

St James House, The Square, Lower Bristol Road, Bath BA2 3BH
tel (01225) 878000
website www.audiogo.co.uk

AudioGO is the new name for BBC Audiobooks Ltd, formed in July 2010 with BBC Worldwide retaining a 15% share in the business. It is the UK market leader with a heritage stretching back 20 years based on BBC Radio Collection, Cover to Cover and Chivers Audio Books. AudioGO plans to expand its catalogue, its distribution channels and to better exploit web and other emerging online retail opportunities.

Immediate Media (formerly BBC Magazines)

website www.immediatemedia.co.uk

Freelance contributions are regularly used by BBC Worldwide magazines but the use of unsolicited material is rare for some magazines as the editorial links closely with the BBC programme content.

For a full list of BBC Magazines and for contact information, visit the website.

Immediate Media Co. Ltd, London

BBC Worldwide, Media Centre, 201 Wood Lane, London W12 7TQ
tel 020-8433 1200

Magazines include *Radio Times, Top Gear, Gardeners' World, BBC Good Food, olive* and *Lonely Planet.*

Immediate Media Co. Ltd, Bristol

14th Floor, Tower House, Fairfax Street, Bristol BS1 3BN
tel 0117-927 9009

Magazines include *BBC Countryfile, BBC Focus, Gardens Illustrated, BBC History Magazine, Homes & Antiques, BBC Knowledge Magazine, BBC Music Magazine, BBC Sky at Night Magazine, Who Do You Think You Are? Magazine* and *BBC Wildlife.*

BBC broadcasting rights and terms

Contributors are advised to seek further details from the BBC, or online via the websites of the Writers' Guild of Great Britain (www.writersguild.org.uk) or the Society of Authors (www.societyofauthors.org).

Rights and terms – television

Specially written material

Fees for submitted material are paid on acceptance. For commissioned material, half the fee is paid on commissioning and half on acceptance as being suitable for television. All fees are subject to negotiation above the minima.

- Rates for one performance of a 60-minute original television play are a minimum of £8,544 for a play written by a beginner and a 'going rate' of £10,680 for an established writer, or *pro rata* for shorter or longer timings.
- Fees for a 50-minute episode in a series are a minimum of £6,480 for a beginner and a 'going rate' of £8,100 for an established writer.
- Fees for a 50-minute dramatisation are a minimum of £4,640 for a beginner and a 'going rate' of £5,800 for an established writer.
- Fees for a 50-minute adaptation of an existing stage play or other dramatic work are a minimum of £2,840 for a beginner and a 'going rate' of £3,550 for an established writer.
- Rates for specially written light entertainment sketch material range from £100 per minute for beginners with a 'going rate' of £150 for established writers.

Published material

- Prose works: £30.41 per minute.
- Poems: £36.48 per half minute.

Stage plays and source material for television

- Fees for stage plays and source novels are negotiable.

Rights and terms – radio

Specially written material

Fees are assessed on the basis of the type of material, its length, the author's status and experience in writing for radio. Fees for submitted material are paid on acceptance. For commissioned material, half the fee is paid on commissioning and half on acceptance as being suitable for broadcasting.

- Rates for specially written radio dramas in English (other than educational programmes) are £58.47 a minute for beginners and a 'going rate' of £89.05 a minute for established writers. This rate covers two broadcasts.
- Fees for specially written short stories range from £177 for 15 minutes.

Published material

Domestic radio

- Dramatic works: £17.66 per minute.
- Prose works: £17.66 per minute.
- Prose works required for dramatisation: £13.77 per minute.
- Poems: £17.66 per half minute.

World Service Radio (English)

• Dramatic works: £8.83 per minute for broadcasts within an eight-day period.
• Prose works: £8.83 per minute for broadcasts within an eight-day period.
• Prose works required for dramatisation: £6.87 per minute for broadcasts within an eight-day period.
• Poems: £8.83 per half minute for broadcasts within an eight-day period.
• Foreign Language Services are approximately one-fifth of the rate for English Language Services.

Television and radio

Repeats in BBC programmes

Further proportionate fees are payable for repeats.

Use abroad of recordings of BBC programmes

If the BBC licenses recordings of its programmes to overseas broadcasting organisations on their own networks or stations, further payments may accrue to the author, usually in the form of additional percentages of the basic fee paid for the initial performance or a royalty based on the percentage of the distributors' receipts. This can apply to both sound and television programmes.

Value Added Tax

There is a self-billing system for VAT which covers radio, World Service and television for programmes made in London.

Talks for television

Contributors to talks will usually be offered the standard television talks contract which grants to the BBC all rights in the contribution for all purposes without limitation.

Fees if applicable are arranged by the BBC contract teams (or programme makers) in London and the Regions.

Talks for radio

Talks contributors for domestic radio and World Service broadcasting may be offered either:
• the standard All Rights contract which grants all rights to the BBC as above; or
• an alternative form of All Rights agreement that takes all rights except print publication rights; or
• an NFC (No Fee Contract) where no payment is made which provides an acknowledgement that a contribution may be used by the BBC.
Fees if applicable are arranged by the contract teams (or programme makers) in London and the Regions.

See also...

- *The Society of Authors*, page 497
- *The Writers' Guild of Great Britain*, page 499

Other broadcasters

In addition to the BBC, other televisionbroadcasters produce their own programming and/or commission programming from independent producers. Here are the key contact details.

Independent national television

ITV plc

The London Television Centre, Upper Ground, London SE1 9LT
tel 020-7157 3000
website www.itv.com
Chief Executive Adam Crozier, *Director of TV, Channels and Online* Peter Fincham, *Managing Director, ITV Studios* Kevin Lygo

The ITV network is responsible for the commissioning, scheduling and marketing of network programmes on ITV1 and its digital channel portfolio, ITV2, ITV3, ITV4, CiTV. Programmes from ITV are provided by ITV's in-house production unit and by the independent sector. Network programming covers a full range of genres, including drama, entertainment, news, current affairs, factual, sport and children's programming.

Channel 4

124 Horseferry Road, London SW1P 2TX
tel 020-7396 4444
website www.channel4.com
Ceo David Abraham, *Chief Creative Officer* Jay Hunt

Channel 4 is a publicly owned, commercially funded public service broadcaster and transmits across the whole of the UK, except for some parts of Wales, which are covered by the Welsh language S4C. Channel 4 also operates a number of other services, including the free-to-air digital TV channels E4, More4, Film4 and 4Music, and an ever-growing range of online activities at channel4.com, Channel 4's bespoke video-on-demand service 4oD and standalone digital projects. As a publisher–broadcaster, Channel 4 does not produce its own programmes but commissions them from more than 300 independent production companies across the UK.

Channel 5

10 Lower Thames Street, London EC3R 6EN
tel 020-8612 7000
website www.channel5.com
Director of Programmes Jeff Ford

Channel 5 is a publisher–broadcaster and works with independent production companies to provide its programmes. They usually only accept programme proposals from independent production companies. Channel 5 brands include the original channel, 5; digital channels 5* and 5 USA, and video-on-demand service Demand 5.

ITN (Independent Television News Ltd)

200 Gray's Inn Road, London WC1X 8XZ
tel 020-7833 3000
website www.itn.co.uk
Chairman Maggie Carver, *Ceo* John Hardie

ITN is one of the world's leading news and multimedia content companies creating, packaging and distributing news, entertainment, factual and corporate content on multiple platforms to customers around the globe. As well as providing TV news, ITN operates 3 other divisions, ITN Source, ITN Productions and ITN Consulting.

Radió Telefís Éireann (RTÉ)

Donnybrook, Dublin 4, Republic of Ireland
tel +353 (0)1 2083111
website www.rte.ie
Director General Noel Curran, *Managing Director, TV* Glen Killane, *Managing Director, Radio* Clare Duignan

RTÉ is a Public Service Broadcaster, a non-profit-making organisation owned by the Irish people. RTÉ is Ireland's cross-media leader, providing comprehensive and cost-effective free-to-air TV, radio and online services. RTÉ operates 2 complementary TV channels, RTÉ One and RTÉ Two, and 4 radio stations, RTÉ Radio 1, RTÉ 2fm, RTÉ lyric fm and RTÉ Raidió na Gaeltachta. RTÉ also publishes Ireland's bestselling magazine, the *RTÉ Guide*, operates Ireland's leading teletext service, RTÉ Aertel, and provides up-to-date news, current affairs and entertainment information via Ireland's most popular media website, www.RTÉ.ie

S4C

Parc Ty Glas, Llanishen, Cardiff CF14 5DU
tel 029-2074 7444
website www.s4c.co.uk
Chief Executive Ian Jones, *Director of Content* Dafydd Rhys

Welsh language digital channel S4C is one of the UK's 5 public service broadcasters. A mixed-genre channel, programming includes drama, sport, children's factual, news, entertainment and culture. Programmes are commissioned from independent production companies with content also produced by BBC Wales and ITV Wales. The channel is only available on the digital TV platforms, plus broadband and has a video-on-demand service. There are subtitles for non-Welsh speakers and learners with signing for the deaf and the hard of hearing.

Independent regional television

The ITV network is made up of 15 regional licences, providing TV to viewers across the UK; 11 of the licences in England and Wales are owned by ITV Plc, providing local regional news and weather. STV Group Plc owns the 2 Scottish licences, STV Central and STV North; UTV and Channel Television own the licences for Northern Ireland and the Channel Islands respectively.

- **STV (North and Central)** *website* www.stv.tv
- **UTV** *website* www.u.tv
- **Channel Television Ltd** www.channelonline.tv
- **ITV Anglia** *website* www.itv.com/anglia
- **ITV Border** *website* www.itv.com/border
- **ITV Central** *website* www.itv.com/central
- **ITV Granada** *website* www.itv.com/granada
- **ITV London** *website* www.itv.com/london
- **ITV Meridian** *website* www.itv.com/meridian
- **ITV TyneTees** *website* www.itv/tynetees
- **ITV Wales** *website* www.itv.com/wales
- **ITV Westcountry and ITV West** *websites* www.itv.com/westcountry-west, www.itv.com/westcountry-east
- **ITV Yorkshire** *website* www.itv.com/yorkshire

Digital television providers

Digital TV offers a far wider choice of TV viewing with lots of extra channels, and uses digital technology to reduce the interference that may be experienced on analogue TV (the 5 channels received via standard TV aerial). By 2012, the UK's TV service will have switched to digital – for more information on the Digital Switchover visit www.digitaluk.co.uk. The main digital TV providers are listed below and for information on the channels available visit their websites.

British Sky Broadcasting (BSkyB)

Grant Way, Isleworth, Middlesex TW7 5QD
tel 0844 241 1542
website www.sky.com
Managing Director, Entertainment and News Sophie Turner-Laing, *Director of Programmes* Stuart Murphy

BSkyB (commonly marketed as Sky) is a British satellite broadcasting company that operates Sky Digital, a subscription TV service in the UK and Ireland. It offers the widest number of digital TV channels in the UK and 98% coverage of its satellite signal. It also owns channels Sky1 and 2, Sky Atlantic, Sky Arts 1 and 2, Sky Living, Sky Livingit and Sky Livingloves, Sky 3D, Sky News, Sky Sport News and various Sky movie, sport and HD channels. Sky commissions original programming from independent production companies.

Freesat

PO Box 6296, London W1A 3FF
tel 0844 225 0900
website www.freesat.co.uk

A not-for-profit joint venture with the BBC and ITV delivering 150+ free-to-air digital TV and radio channels, BBC iPlayer, and HD channels via a satellite dish.

On-demand pay television providers

BT Vision

website www.btvision.bt.com

On-demand digital TV for BT Total Broadband customers, with thousands of shows to watch on demand, including sports and children's, plus music videos and films. It is free of advertisements.

TalkTalk TV

Carphone Warehouse, 1 Portal Way, London W3 6RS
website www.talktalk.co.uk/tv

Users of this digital TV service watch live TV and on-demand content via a broadband-enabled phone line. TalkTalk TV is not available in all parts of the UK.

Top Up TV Anytime

tel 0844 415 2030
website www.topuptv.com

A digital terrestrial TV service that allows viewers to watch and record live TV, and watch extra content 'on demand'.

Smallworld Cable Ltd

3 Middlegate, White Lund Industrial Estate, Morecambe, Lancs. LA3 3BN

Suppliers of super-fast fibre optic broadband, digital TV and phone services via set-top boxes in Western Scotland and North West England.

Theatre

Writing for the theatre

From the perspective of a playwright, David Eldridge describes the process of writing a play, its production, through to a run at a theatre.

Writing the play

Ideas for plays can come from anywhere. Political anger, a riff of dialogue, an image, some experience in your life, a newspaper article, a dream or fantasy, or from a particular actor you admire. As Caryl Churchill says, 'What's the difference between an idea for a play [*sic*]? I think the only difference is that you want to make [it] into a play, the point at which [it] become[s] an idea for a play is when you get some sort of technical or physical way of turning it into a play'. Wherever your ideas for plays come from, the key thing is that you are fired up by your idea.

So you have your idea – a biting political satire or a fantastical farce fuelled by a lost dog – and you've decided whether it's going to be a stichomythic two hander or a surreally big cast piece. It could be that your story will be told in a form with which an audience is familiar and that inspires you – Chekhovian four act movement or a fragmented narrative inspired by the plays of Martin Crimp. But what next? Some writers are planners by nature and have everything mapped out on A4 or in notebooks, and spend weeks structuring the drama before any physical action or dialogue is written. Stephen Jeffreys and Simon Stephens are good examples of playwrights who work in this way. But for others, like Robert Holman or David Storey, often even thinking of the possible shape of a play is an anathema, and structuring is a block to them. They like to start with an image or a line, or even a blank page, and find out what 'it' is as they go along. I'm somewhere in the middle; I need to do a little bit of planning to get me going and to avoid false starts, but if there's too much plotting in advance it becomes drained of life. It's true, too, that each play I've written has been made in a different way. So it seems there's not only as many ways to write a play as there are playwrights, but each playwright may write differently from one play to the next.

In the absence of a right way to do it, the best thing is just to get on and do your own thing, what feels right for you – anything really, as long as you write. 'Don't get it right, get it written', is how it goes. I always remind myself that I'm under no obligation to show anyone what I've written, so I try not to fear anything. If what I write is rubbish, I can just chuck it away. If what I write is promising but not perfect, I can come back to it later and improve it. The main thing is to write and get to the end. And when you've got to the end, you go back to the beginning again and work on it until you can do no more.

Final draft to producer

When you feel your play is complete and that you've done all you can on it for now, what next? Resist reaching for the stamps or hitting the 'Send' button on your email, and have some time away from it – at least a week or two. Often after the intensive work on a first draft one comes back to it feeling refreshed both in perspective and in terms of renewed energy. And when you can do no more to improve your script, get one or two (certainly no more than three) people to read it. You need people who will read the script properly and give an honest and generous opinion. They may be a partner, a friend, a colleague or, if you are lucky enough to have such a connection, someone who works in the theatre. Choose your readers carefully because you don't want anyone who will focus solely on criticising your script and consequently demoralise you at this stage, and neither do you want unqualified praise as they think this is what you want to hear.

I tend to send out what is in reality a third draft. I usually do a second draft after leaving it for between two and four weeks and then a third draft, which is provoked a bit by the responses or questions of one or two trusted readers. That's my practice now as an established writer, just as it was when I started writing. Today, almost all my work is commissioned but when I first began writing and would send out a play unsolicited, I had some wise advice from playwright Mark Ravenhill. He said I should concentrate on submitting my play to two or three theatres where I believed the play might be of interest and welcome, and where I would like to work. I still think that's good advice. One must be realistic about how few plays that are sent unsolicited actually attract the attention of producing theatres. And plays that are sent unsolicited to too many theatres can often have a feeling of being dog-eared and rejected by everyone, making it harder for those plays to get on.

Since the mid-1990s, many theatres have grown substantive play development programmes and it is a normal requirement now for new plays to undergo substantial rewrites with the producer's notes in mind. Readings and workshops often take place to see how the scripts work with actors. There's a wide-ranging philosophical debate within the theatre about how much theatres ought to be actively involved in the rewriting of plays and what good it does. My feeling is that writers ought to take on the ideas of theatre professionals when they are good, to be unafraid of saying when you are unsure, and to say 'no' when you don't like the proposed changes to your script. While a network of collaboration brings a play to life, writers must take responsibility for their authorship. Active collaboration is good; passive concession is bad.

Around this time, it may be appropriate to get an agent. Most theatres will recommend agents and help you meet those who might be sympathetic to your work.

Rehearsals, production and previews

The play is going ahead. Often the first person you hear from is the theatre's director of marketing as they need to prepare the copy and images for your play for the season's brochure and other publicity. In new writing theatres it is normal for most elements of the pre-production and production of a play to involve the writer. This includes input on the choice of director and creative team, casting the actors, progress of the set design, the development of a marketing and sales strategy, press and media interviews, and even invitations to attend fundraising events for the theatre.

But of course the most significant contribution that the writer makes is to the rehearsal process, particularly in the first week of rehearsal. The acting company and creative team are hungry to mine the writer for every scrap of useful information which may help the play's production. The writer is very much at the centre of the process and what he or she says about their play or how it may be acted and staged has great power. I know from experience how invaluable a playwright's contribution can be to the production of his or her play, both from discussion of the text in rehearsals and from informal discussions during tea breaks, at lunch, or in the pub after rehearsals. Generally, most of what a writer says is useful but care needs to be taken not to squeeze the air out of the contributions of others.

Sometimes rewrites in rehearsals can be challenging. Changing the odd word or line isn't often contentious but when whole scenes are being cut or rewritten, the excitement of making the play better on the rehearsal room floor should be approached with caution. Actors tend to think of the script from their character's perspective rather than seeing the writer's whole vision. And, as the point of rehearsal is to practise something until it is right, I'd be wary of actors or directors who want to make changes too quickly.

After the first week or so it is usual and advisable for the writer to not attend rehearsals. The middle part of rehearsals become sticky and the actors may grapple with learning their lines. When the writer makes a return towards the end of rehearsals to see bits of the play worked without scripts or a run through, the writer's fresh perspective is very useful to the director.

As public performances approach, the playwright can make everyone feel good about the work by encouraging the company after rehearsals, buying the first drink in the pub, and making the tea during breaks. However, sometimes the writer has to be brave if things aren't right and late changes need to be made to adjust a performance or the staging, etc.

Some writers don't attend all the previews but I do as most directors continue working and rehearsing the play right up until opening night. You can learn a huge amount by watching the play with an audience, but I have two points of caution. Firstly, you have to be realistic about what is achievable before the opening night. Secondly, while it is important to learn from audience responses, particularly if the storytelling isn't clear or a joke doesn't work properly, I'd stay away from the discussion forums of theatre websites which are routinely populated by strange people who get off on abusing early performances of plays.

Opening nights are nerve-racking evenings for the writer and seeing the critics and guests forming a crush at the theatre bar can prompt the urge to run away, and for this reason some directors and playwrights don't watch their press night performances. I couldn't be absent as I feel I have to be there for my actors, but it is gruelling and all you can do is will the actors and stage crew on and keep your nerve.

The working writer

Hopefully, the play is a hit and it's a great experience. I tend to see the play once a week because you can learn so much from seeing it again and again and experiencing how it changes and grows over its run.

Often, however successful (or not) a first play is, just the fact that it has been produced will attract the interest of other theatre producers, often radio interviews and sometimes television. If your agent is doing their job, he or she will have brought some of these people to see your play with the hope of opening up future opportunities for you. Offers of commissions for rival theatres, finding yourself pitching radio, television and film ideas, and sometimes being approached to adapt an old play, book or film are all commonplace, particularly if your play is a success.

But the most important thing for the working playwright is to work on the next play. The longer you leave it after your first play closes the harder it gets to begin something new, and the bigger deal it will seem. So my advice is just to start where you began all those months and years ago and think about something which in some way intrigues you. And off you go.

David Eldridge is the author of *Under the Blue Sky*, *The Knot of the Heart*, *In Basildon* and many other plays and adaptations. His work has been performed at major new writing institutions, including the Royal Court Theatre, the Bush Theatre, and the National Theatre. In Spring 2012 his new version of *Miss Julie* by August Strindberg ran to critical acclaim at the Royal Exchange Theatre.

Theatre producers

This list is divided into London theatres (below), provincial theatres (page 402) and touring companies (page 406). See also *Writing for the theatre* on page 395 and *Literary agents for television, film, radio and theatre* on page 738.

There are various types of theatre companies and it is helpful to know what they include. Metropolitan new writing theatre companies are largely London-based theatres which specialise in new writing (Hampstead Theatre, Royal Court, Bush Theatre, Soho Theatre, etc). Regional repertory theatre companies are theatres based in towns and cities across the country which may do new plays as part of their repertoire. Commercial producing managements are unsubsidised profit-making theatre producers who may occasionally be interested in new plays to take on tour or to present in the West End. Small and/or middle-scale touring companies are companies (mostly touring) which may exist to explore or promote specific themes or are geared towards specific kinds of audiences.

Individuals also have a role. Independent theatre practitioners include, for example, actors who may be looking for interesting plays in which to appear, and independent theatre producers such as young directors or producers who are looking for plays to produce at the onset of their career. There are also drama schools and amateur dramatics companies.

LONDON

Bush Theatre

The Bush Theatre, Shepherds Bush Green, London W12 8QD
tel (admin) 020-8743 3584
email info@bushtheatre.co.uk, naiajohns@bushtheatre.co.uk
website www.bushtheatre.co.uk, www.bushgreen.org
Literary Administrator Naia Johns

Welcomes unsolicited full-length scripts. Scripts can also be sent online via www.bushgreen.org website. Commissions writers, including those at an early stage in their career. Produces over 8 premieres a year.

Michael Codron Plays Ltd

Aldwych Theatre Offices, Aldwych, London WC2B 4DF
tel 020-7240 8291 *fax* 020-7240 8467

Finborough Theatre

118 Finborough Road, London SW10 9ED
tel 020-7244 7439
email admin@finboroughtheatre.co.uk
website www.finboroughtheatre.co.uk
Artistic Director Neil McPherson

Presents new writing, revivals of neglected plays from 1800 onwards, music theatre and UK premieres of foreign work, particularly from Ireland, Scotland, the USA and Canada. Unsolicited scripts are accepted, but see literary policy on website before sending. Founded 1980.

Robert Fox Ltd

6 Beauchamp Place, London SW3 1NG
tel 020-7584 6855 *fax* 020-7225 1638
email info@robertfoxltd.com

Independent theatre and film production company. Stages productions mainly in the West End and on Broadway. Currently accepting submissions. Founded 1980.

Hampstead Theatre

Eton Avenue, London NW3 3EU
tel 020-7449 4200 *fax* 020-7449 4201
email literary@hampsteadtheatre.com
website www.hampsteadtheatre.com
Contact Literary Manager

The company's theatre, built in 2003, was designed with writers in mind, allowing for bold and flexible staging within an intimate auditorium. All plays are read but feedback is given only on plays that the theatre is interested in pursuing. It usually takes four months to respond. Unsolicited plays from writers based outside of the UK can not be considered. No plays accepted by email. See website for details of submission process and new writing initiatives.

Bill Kenwright Ltd

BKL House, 1 Venice Walk, London W2 1RR
tel 020-7446 6200 *fax* 020-7446 6222
email info@kenwright.com
website www.kenwright.com
Managing Director Bill Kenwright

Commercial producing management presenting revivals and new works for the West End and for touring theatres. Recent (or current) productions include: in the West End – *Blood Brothers*, *Hay Fever*, *Joseph & The Amazing Technicolor Dreamcoat*, *Whistle Down the Wind*, *The Crucible*, and *A Man for All Seasons*; on tour – *Blood Brothers*, *Festen*, *The Hollow*, and *This Is Elvis*.

King's Head Theatre

115 Upper Street, London N1 1QN
tel 020-7226 8561 *fax* 020-7226 8507
website www.kingsheadtheatre.com
Contact Adam Spreadbury-Maher, Artistic Director

Off-West End theatre producing premieres of plays and musicals.

Lyric Hammersmith

Lyric Square, King Street, London W6 0QL
tel 020-8741 6807 *fax* 020-8741 5965
email enquiries@lyric.co.uk
website www.lyric.co.uk
Artistic Director Sean Holmes, *Executive Director* Jessica Hepburn

West London's largest producing and receiving theatre. Unsolicited scripts for in-house productions not accepted.

Neal Street Productions Ltd

1st Floor, 26–28 Neal Street, London WC2H 9QQ
tel 020-7240 8890 *fax* 020-7240 7099
email post@nealstreetproductions.com
website www.nealstreetproductions.com
Contact Milly Leigh

Independent theatre and film producer of new work and revivals. No unsolicited scripts. Founded 2003.

New End Theatre Beyond

Studio One, 16 Castle Grove Drive, Moor Road, Leeds LS6 4BR
tel (0113) 275 2830
email briandaniels@newendtheatre.co.uk
Chief Executive/Artistic Director Brian Daniels

An independent theatre production company, previously known as the New End Theatre, London. Now producing and general managing selected plays for the stage. New writing preferred but with a producer or production finance attached. Scripts can be assessed for a negotiable fee and a production viability report prepared. In 2011/12, the company had three plays on UK national tours and two on extended small-scale runs with touring following. Founded 2011.

The Old Red Lion Theatre

418 St John Street, London EC1V 4NJ
tel 020-7833 3053 / 020-7837 7816
website www.oldredliontheatre.co.uk
Artistic Directors Henry Filloux-Bennett and Nicholas Thompson

Interested in contemporary pieces, especially from unproduced writers. No funding: incoming production company pays to rent the theatre. Sae essential with enquiries. Founded 1977.

Orange Tree Theatre

1 Clarence Street, Richmond, Surrey TW9 2SA
tel 020-8940 0141 *fax* 020-8332 0369
website www.orangetreetheatre.co.uk

Producing venue. New works presented generally come from agents or through writers' groups. The theatre asks that writers contact the theatre first by letter and do not send unsolicited scripts.

Polka Theatre

240 The Broadway, London SW19 1SB
tel 020-8543 8320 *fax* 020-8545 8365
email stephen@polkatheatre.com
website www.polkatheatre.com
Artistic Director Jonathan Lloyd

Exclusively for children aged 0–13, the Main Theatre seats 300 and the Adventure Theatre seats 70. It is programmed 18 months–2 years in advance. Theatre of new work, with targeted commissions. Founded 1967.

The Questors Theatre

Mattock Lane, London W5 5BQ
tel 020-8567 0011 *fax* 020-8567 2275
email enquiries@questors.org.uk
website www.questors.org
Executive Director Andrea Bath

Largest independent community theatre in Europe producing around 20 shows a year, specialising in modern and classical world drama. No unsolicited scripts.

The Really Useful Group

22 Tower Street, London WC2H 9TW
tel 020-7240 0880 *fax* 020-7240 1204
email online_team@reallyuseful.co.uk
website www.reallyuseful.com
Chairman Andrew Lloyd Webber

Owns seven West End theatres: Adelphi, Cambridge, Her Majesty's, London Palladium, New London, Palace, Theatre Royal Drury Lane. Founded 1978.

Royal Court Theatre

(English Stage Company Ltd)
Sloane Square, London SW1W 8AS
tel 020-7565 5050 *fax* 020-7565 5001
email info@royalcourttheatre.com
website www.royalcourttheatre.com
Literary Manager Chris Campbell

New plays.

Royal National Theatre

South Bank, London SE1 9PX
tel 020-7452 3100 *fax* 020-7452 3350

website www.nationaltheatre.org.uk
Associate Director (Literary) Sebastian Born

Limited opportunity for the production of unsolicited material, but submissions considered from the UK and Ireland. No synopses, treatments or email submissions. Send to Literary Department, together with a sae with return postage for the script.

Soho Theatre

21 Dean Street, London W1D 3NE
tel 020-7478 0117 *fax* 020-7287 5061
email jules@sohotheatre.com
website www.sohotheatre.com

Aims to discover and develop new playwrights, produce a year-round programme of new plays and attract new audiences. Producing venue (144-seat theatre) of new plays, cabaret and comedy. The Writers' Centre offers an extensive unsolicited script-reading service and provides a range of development schemes including the Writers' Attachment Programme, Open Access Workshops, the Verity Bargate Award (page 545), the Westminster Prize, a thriving Young Writers' Programme, commissions and seed bursaries and more. There is also a large self-contained studio space (Soho Upstairs) with 95-seat capacity, a new comedy and cabaret venue (Soho Downstairs) with a 150-seat capacity, plus theatre bar, restaurant, offices, rehearsal, writing and meeting rooms. Founded 1972.

Tabard Theatre

2 Bath Road, London W4 1LW
tel 020-8995 6035 *fax* 020-8994 5985
website www.tabardtheatre.co.uk

Theatre Royal, Stratford East

Gerry Raffles Square, London E15 1BN
tel 020-8534 7374 *fax* 020-8534 8381
website www.stratfordeast.com
Artistic Director Kerry Michael, *Executive Director* Mary Caws

Middle-scale producing theatre. Specialises in new writing: including developing contemporary British musicals. Welcomes new plays that are unproduced, full in length, and which relate to its diverse multicultural, Black and Asian audience.

The Tricycle Theatre Company

Tricycle Theatre, 269 Kilburn High Road, London NW6 7JR
tel 020-7372 6611 *fax* 020-7328 0795
website www.tricycle.co.uk
Artistic Director Nicolas Kent

Metropolitan new writing theatre company with particular focus on Black, Asian, Jewish and Irish writing. Script-reading service but fee charged for unsolicited scripts.

Triumph Proscenium Productions Ltd

First Floor, 18 Exeter Street, London WC2E 7DU
tel 020-7836 0186 *fax* 020-7379 4860

Unicorn Theatre

147 Tooley Street, London SE1 2HZ
tel 020-7645 0560 *fax* 020-7645 0550
website www.unicorntheatre.com
Artistic Director Purni Morell, *Executive Director* Anneliese Davidsen

Produces a year-round programme of theatre for children and young people (2–21 years). In-house productions of full-length plays with professional casts are staged across two auditoria, alongside visiting companies and education work. Unicorn rarely commissions plays from writers who are new to it, but it is keen to hear from writers who are interested to work with it in the future. Do not send unsolicited MSS. Send a short statement describing why you would like to write for the Unicorn and a CV or a summary of your relevant experience.

Warehouse Theatre

Dingwall Road, Croydon CR0 2NF
tel 020-8680 4060 (Box Office), 020-8681 1257 (Admin) *fax* 020-8688 6699
email info@warehousetheatre.co.uk
website www.warehousetheatre.co.uk
Artistic Director Ted Craig

South London's new writing theatre. Seats 100. Produces two to three in-house plays a year and co-produces with companies who share the commitment to new work. The theatre continues to build upon its tradition of discovering and nurturing new writers: activities include monthly writers' workshops and the annual International Playwriting Festival (see page 575). Unsolicited scripts are accepted but it is more advisable to submit plays via the Festival. Also hosts a youth theatre workshop, Saturday morning children's theatre and a community outreach programme.

Michael White

13 Duke Street St James's, London SW1Y 6DB

White Bear Theatre Club

138 Kennington Park Road, London SE11 4DJ
tel 020-7793 9193
email info@whitebeartheatre.co.uk
website www.whitebeartheatre.co.uk
Artistic Director Michael Kingsbury

Metropolitan new writing theatre company. Welcomes scripts from new writers. Founded 1988.

Young Vic Theatre Company

66 The Cut, London SE1 8LZ
tel 020-7922 2922
email info@youngvic.org
website www.youngvic.org
Artistic Director David Lan

Metropolitan producing theatre producing great plays of the world repertoire. Founded 1969.

PROVINCIAL

Abbey Theatre Amharclann na Mainistreach

26 Lower Abbey Street, Dublin 1, Republic of Ireland
tel +353 (0)1 8872200 *fax* +353 (0)1 8729177
email info@abbeytheatre.ie
website www.abbeytheatre.ie
Director Fiach MacConghail

Ireland's national theatre. Produces new plays and contemporary and classic drama from Irish and international writers.

Yvonne Arnaud Theatre Management Ltd

Millbrook, Guildford, Surrey GU1 3UX
tel (01483) 440077 *fax* (01483) 564071
email yat@yvonne-arnaud.co.uk
website www.yvonne-arnaud.co.uk
Contact James Barber

Producing theatre which also receives productions.

The Belgrade Theatre

Belgrade Square, Coventry CV1 1GS
tel 024-7625 6431 *fax* 024-7655 0680
email admin@belgrade.co.uk
website www.belgrade.co.uk
Contact Denise Duncombe

Repertory theatre producing drama, comedy and musicals.

Birmingham Repertory Theatre Ltd

Broad Street, Birmingham B1 2EP
tel 0121 245 2000 *fax* 0121 245 2100
website www.birmingham-rep.co.uk
Artistic Director Roxana Silbert, *Executive Director* Stuart Rogers, *Associate Directors* Ola Animashawun, Steve Ball, Tessa Walker

Pioneer of new plays: REP productions transfer regularly to London and tour nationally and internationally. Undergoing redevelopment as part of the new Library of Birmingham, and a new purpose-built auditorium is due to open in 2013. Learning and Participation department engages with over 10,000 young people each year through a variety of schemes.

The Bootleg Theatre Company

23 Burgess Green, Bishopdown, Salisbury, Wilts. SP1 3EL
tel (01722) 421476
website www.bootlegtheatre.co.uk
Contact Colin Burden

Metropolitan new writing theatre company and independent theatre practitioner. Stages two full-length plays a year. Also premieres short new plays at a small music venue, per year. Committed to new writing and welcomes unsolicited scripts. Recent and future productions include: *Girls Allowed* by Trevor Suthers, *Calling Time* by Derek Webb, *A Rainy Night in Soho* by Stephen Giles, and plays by Roger Goldsmith, Alec Taylor and John Foster. Founded 1985.

Bristol Old Vic

King Street, Bristol BS1 4ED
tel 0117 949 3993 *fax* 0117 949 3996
email admin@bristololdvic.org.uk
website www.bristololdvic.org.uk

Oldest theatre auditorium in UK (opened in 1766). See website for more details. Founded 1946.

The Byre Theatre of St Andrews

Abbey Street, St Andrews KY16 9LA
tel (01334) 475000 *fax* (01334) 475370
website www.byretheatre.com

Offers an exciting year-round programme of contemporary and classic drama, dance, concerts, comedy and innovative education and community events. Operates a blend of in-house and touring productions. Education programme caters for all ages with Youth workshops and Haydays (for 50+). Offers support for new writing through the Byre Writers, a well-established and successful playwrights group.

Chichester Festival Theatre

Oaklands Park, Chichester, West Sussex PO19 6AP
tel (01243) 784437 *fax* (01243) 787288
website www.cft.org.uk
Artistic Director Jonathan Church

Summer Festival Season April–Oct in Festival and Minerva Theatres together with a year-round education programme, autumn touring programme and youth theatre Christmas show. Unsolicited scripts are not accepted.

Clwyd Theatr Cymru

Mold, Flintshire CH7 1YA
tel (01352) 756331 *fax* (01352) 701558
email william.james@clwyd-theatr-cymru.co.uk
website www.clwyd-theatr-cymru.co.uk
Director Terry Hands, *Literary Manager* William James

Produces a season of plays each year performed by a core ensemble, along with tours throughout Wales (in English and Welsh). Plays are a mix of classics, revivals, contemporary drama and new writing. Considers plays by Welsh writers or with Welsh themes. Also the home of Clwyd Theatr Cymru Theatre for Young People (www.ctctyp.co.uk).

Colchester Mercury Theatre Ltd

Balkerne Gate, Colchester, Essex CO1 1PT
tel (01206) 577006 *fax* (01206) 769607
email info@mercurytheatre.co.uk
website www.mercurytheatre.co.uk
Contact (Playwrights' Group) Tony Casement

Regional repertory theatre presenting works to a wide audience. Produces some new work, mainly commissioned. Runs local Playwrights' Group for adults with a serious commitment to writing plays.

The Coliseum Theatre

Fairbottom Street, Oldham OL1 3SW
tel 0161 624 1731
Chief Executive Kevin Shaw

Interested in new work, particularly plays set in the North. The Coliseum employs a reader to read all submitted scripts, which should be clearly typed and include a page of casting requirements and a brief synopsis.

Contact Theatre Company

Oxford Road, Manchester M15 6JA
tel 0161 274 0600, 0161 274 0601
website www.contact-theatre.org
Artistic Director Baba Israel

Multidisciplinary arts organisation focused on working with and for young people aged 13–35.

Curve

Rutland Street, Leicester LE1 1SB
tel 0116 242 3560 0116 293 8165
email enquiries@curvetheatre.co.uk
website www.curveonline.co.uk

Regional producing theatre company.

Derby Theatre

Theatre Walk, Westfield, Derby DE1 2NF
tel (01332) 255800
email info@derbyplayhouse.co.uk
website www.derbytheatre.co.uk
Theatre Manager Gary Johnson

Regional producing and receiving theatre.

Druid Theatre Company

Druid Theatre, Flood Street, Galway, Ireland
tel +353 (0)91 568660 *fax* +353 (0)91 563109
email info@druid.ie
website www.druid.ie
Artistic Director Garry Hynes

Producing company presenting a wide range of national and international plays. Emphasis on new Irish writing.

The Dukes

Moor Lane, Lancaster LA1 1QE
tel (01524) 598505 *fax* (01524) 598519
email info@dukes-lancaster.org
website www.dukes-lancaster.org
Director Joe Sumsion

See website (www.dukes-lancaster.org) for information about the theatre's scriptreading scheme.

Dundee Repertory Theatre

Tay Square, Dundee DD1 1PB
tel (01382) 227684 *fax* (01382) 228609
website www.dundeereptheatre.co.uk
Artistic Director James Brining

Regional repertory theatre company with resident ensemble. Mix of classics, musicals and new commissions.

Everyman Theatre

7 Regent Street, Cheltenham, Glos. GL50 1HQ
tel (01242) 512515 *fax* (01242) 224305
email admin@everymantheatre.org.uk
website www.everymantheatre.org.uk
Chief Executive Geoffrey Rowe, *Creative Director* Paul Milton

Regional presenting and producing theatre promoting a wide range of plays. Small-scale experimental, youth and educational work encouraged in The Studio Theatre studio theatre. Contact the Director of ReachOut before submitting material.

Grand Theatre

Singleton Street, Swansea SA1 3QJ
tel (01792) 475715 *fax* (01792) 475379
email gerald.morris@swansea.gov.uk
website www.swanseagrand.co.uk
Assistant General Manager Gerald Morris, *Head of Marketing* Paul Hopkins

Regional receiving theatre.

Harrogate Theatre

Oxford Street, Harrogate, North Yorkshire HG1 1QF
tel (01423) 502710 *fax* (01423) 563205
email info@harrogatetheatre.co.uk
website www.harrogatetheatre.co.uk
Contact The Administrator

Regional repertory theatre and touring company producing both classic and contemporary plays. Unsolicited scripts not accepted.

Library Theatre Company

St Peter's Square, Manchester M2 5PD
tel 0161 234 1913 *fax* 0161 274 7055
email ltcadmin@manchester.gov.uk
website www.librarytheatre.com
Contact Artistic Director

Contemporary drama, modern classics and plays for children. Aims to produce drama which illuminates the contemporary world. Will consider scripts from new writers. Allow 4 months for response. Founded 1952.

Live Theatre

Broad Chare, Quayside,
Newcastle upon Tyne NE1 3DF
tel 0191 232 1232
email info@live.org.uk
website www.live.org.uk
Enquiries Wendy Barnfather, *Script Submissions* Degna Stone

New writing theatre company and venue. Stages 3–4 productions per year of new writing, comedy, musical comedy, etc.

Liverpool Everyman and Playhouse

Liverpool and Merseyside Theatres Trust Ltd, 13 Hope Street, Liverpool L1 9BH
tel 0151 706 9108 *fax* 0151 708 3701
email literary@everymanplayhouse.com
website www.everymanplayhouse.com
Executive Director Deborah Aydon, *Artistic Director* Gemma Bodinetz, *Literary Manager* Suzanne Bell

Produces and presents theatre.

The New Theatre: Dublin

The New Theatre, Temple Bar, 43 East Essex Street, Dublin 2, Republic of Ireland
tel 353 (0)1 6703361 *fax* 353 (0)1 6711943
email info@thenewtheatre.com
website www.thenewtheatre.com
Joint Artistic Directors Anthony Fox, Ronan Wilmot

Innovative theatre producing plays by classic as well as Irish writers whose work deals with issues pertaining to contemporary Irish society. Welcomes scripts from new writers. Seats 66 people. Founded 1997.

New Vic Theatre

Etruria Road, Newcastle under Lyme ST5 0JG
tel (01782) 717954 *fax* (01782) 712885
email admin@newvictheatre.org.uk
website www.newvictheatre.org.uk
Artistic Director Theresa Heskins, *Managing Director* Nick Jones

Europe's first purpose built theatre-in-the-round, presenting classics, music theatre, contemporary plays and new plays.

The New Wolsey Theatre

Civic Drive, Ipswich, Suffolk IP1 2AS
tel (01473) 295900 *fax* (01473) 295910
website www.wolseytheatre.co.uk
Chief Executive Sarah Holmes, *Artistic Director* Peter Rowe

Mix of producing and presenting in main house and studio. Hosts annual Pulse Fringe Festival. Founded 2000.

Northern Stage (Theatrical Productions) Ltd

Barras Bridge, Newcastle upon Tyne NE1 7RH
tel 0191 242 7200 *fax* 0191 242 7257
email info@northernstage.co.uk
website www.northernstage.co.uk
Chief Executive Erica Whyman

The largest producing theatre company in the north east of England. Presents local, national and international theatre across three stages and runs an extensive participation programme.

Nottingham Playhouse

Nottingham Playhouse Trust Ltd, Wellington Circus, Nottingham NG1 5AF
tel 0115 947 4361 *fax* 0115 947 5759
website www.nottinghamplayhouse.co.uk/playhouse
Chief Executive Stephanie Sirr, *Artistic Director* Giles Croft, *Director of Roundabout & Education* Andrew Breakwell

Works closely with communities of Nottingham and Nottinghamshire.

Takes six months to read unsolicited MSS.

Nuffield Theatre

University Road, Southampton SO17 1TR
tel 023-8031 5500 *fax* 023-8031 5511
email info@nuffieldtheatre.co.uk
website www.nuffieldtheatre.co.uk
Script Executive John Burgess

Repertory theatre producing straight plays and occasional musicals, and some small-scale fringe work. Interested in new plays.

Octagon Theatre

Howell Croft South, Bolton BL1 1SB
tel (01204) 529407 *fax* (01204) 556502
email info@octagonbolton.co.uk
website www.octagonbolton.co.uk
Executive Director John Blackmore, *Chief Executive* Roddy Gauld, *Artistic Director* David Thacker, *Head of Administration* Lesley Etherington, *Head of Production* Oliver Seviour, *Head of activ8* Lisa O'Neill-Rogan, *Associate Director* Elizabeth Newman

Fully flexible professional theatre. Year-round programme of own productions and visiting companies. Capacity: 320–390 depending on configuration. Also houses Bill Naughton Studio Theatre for outreach, children's theatre, new work and emerging artists. Capacity: 100.

Peacock Theatre

Abbey Theatre, 26 Lower Abbey Street, Dublin 1, Republic of Ireland
tel +353 (0)1 8787222 *fax* +353 (0)1 8729177
Director Fiach Mac Conghail

Part of the Abbey Theatre; presents new writing and contemporary classic drama.

Perth Theatre

185 High Street, Perth PH1 5UW
tel (01738) 472700 *fax* (01738) 624576
email info@horsecross.co.uk
website www.horsecross.co.uk
Creative Director (Theatre) Rachel O'Riordan

Combination of three- and four-weekly repertoire of plays and musicals, incoming tours, one-night variety events and studio productions.

Queen's Theatre, Hornchurch

(Havering Theatre Trust Ltd)
52 Billet Lane, Hornchurch, Essex RM11 1QT

tel (01708) 462362 *fax* (01708) 462363
email info@queens-theatre.co.uk
website www.queens-theatre.co.uk
Artistic Director Bob Carlton

500-seat producing theatre serving outer East London with permanent company of actors/musicians presenting eight mainhouse and 4 TIE productions each year. Treatments welcome; unsolicited scripts may be returned unread. Also offers writers' groups at various levels.

Royal Exchange Theatre Company Ltd

St Ann's Square, Manchester M2 7DH
tel 0161 833 9333 *fax* 0161 832 0881
website www.royalexchange.co.uk
Executive Director Fiona Gasper

Varied programme of major classics, new plays, musicals, contemporary British and European drama; also explores the creative work of diverse cultures. Focus on new writing, writer development, creative collaborations and community participation.

Royal Lyceum Theatre Company

Royal Lyceum Theatre, Grindlay Street, Edinburgh EH3 9AX
tel 0131 248 4800 *fax* 0131 228 3955
email info@lyceum.org.uk
website www.lyceum.org.uk
Artistic Director Mark Thomson

Edinburgh's busiest repertory company, producing a diverse year-round programme of classic, contemporary and new drama. Interested in work of Scottish writers.

Royal Shakespeare Company

The Courtyard Theatre, Southern Lane, Stratford-upon-Avon, Warks. CV37 6BB
tel (01789) 272227
email literary@rsc.org.uk
website www.rsc.org.uk
Artistic Director Michael Boyd, *Literary Manager* Pippa Hill

Based in Stratford-upon-Avon, produces a core repertoire of Shakespeare alongside modern classics and new plays as well as the work of Shakespeare's contemporaries. Works with contemporary writers, offering them open commissions for new plays. Also commissions adaptations of well-known novels and stories for Christmas shows. Works with contemporary writers, encouraging them to write epic plays. The Literary department seeks out writers it wishes to work with or commission. Does not read unsolicited work, but does monitor the work of emerging writers in production nationally and internationally. The newly revived RSC studio develops new work and invites submissions for projects. The Company has completed a rebuilding programme to transform the Theatre and the entire Waterside complex of studios, rehearsal rooms, actors' cottages and workshops in Stratford-upon-Avon.

Salisbury Playhouse

Malthouse Lane, Salisbury, Wilts. SP2 7RA
tel (01722) 320117; box office (01722) 320333
fax (01722) 421991
email info@salisburyplayhouse.com
website www.salisburyplayhouse.com
Artistic Director Phillip Wilson, *Executive Director* Michelle Carwardine-Palmer

Regional producing theatre with a broad programme of classical and contemporary plays in two auditoria. Does not accept unsolicited scripts.

Scarborough Theatre Trust Ltd

Stephen Joseph Theatre, Westborough, Scarborough, North Yorkshire YO11 1JW
tel (01723) 370540
email enquiries@sjt.uk.com
website www.sjt.uk.com
Artistic Director Chris Monks

Regional repertory theatre company which produces about six plays a year, many of which are premieres. Enclose a sae with all submissions. Send treatments rather than MSS in first instance.

Sheffield Theatres

(Crucible, Crucible Studio & Lyceum)
55 Norfolk Street, Sheffield S1 1DA
tel 0114 249 5999 *fax* 0114 249 6003
website www.sheffieldtheatres.co.uk
Chief Executive Dan Bates *Artistic Director* Daniel Evans

Large-scale producing house with distinctive thrust stage; studio; Victorian proscenium arch theatre used mainly for touring productions.

Sherman Cymru

Senghennydd Road, Cardiff CF24 4YE
tel 029-2064 6901 *fax* 029-2064 6902
email admin@shermancymru.co.uk
website www.shermancymru.co.uk
Director Chris Ricketts, *General Manager* Margaret Jones, *Literary Manager* Siân Summers, *Associate Directors* Roisin McBrill, Mared Swain

Produces new work and revivals, predominantly by Welsh or Wales-based writers, both in English and Welsh. Seeks to stage high-quality and innovative drama and dance with a local, national or international perspective. Develops writers through workshops, rehearsed readings and short courses. Participatory work with youth theatres (age 5 to 25), community engagement, and mentorship of new artists. Will accept unsolicited MSS by post, welcomed particularly from Welsh or Wales-based writers (send sae for return of script). Founded 2007.

Show of Strength Theatre Company Ltd

74 Chessel Street, Bedminster, Bristol BS3 3DN
tel 0117 902 0235

email info@showofstrength.org.uk
website www.showofstrength.org.uk
Creative Producer Sheila Hannon

Small-scale company committed to producing new and unperformed work. Founded 1986.

Theatre Royal

32 Thames Street, Windsor, Berks. SL4 1PS
tel (01753) 863444 *fax* (01753) 831673
Executive Producer Bill Kenwright, *Theatre Director* Angela Edwards

Regional producing theatre presenting a wide range of productions from classics to new plays.

Theatre Royal & Drum Theatre Plymouth

Royal Parade, Plymouth PL1 2TR
tel (01752) 668282 *fax* (01752) 230499
website www.theatreroyal.com
Artistic Director Simon Stokes

Stages small, middle and large-scale drama and music theatre. Commissions and produces new plays in the award-winning Drum Theatre. The theatre no longer accepts unsolicited playscripts but will consider plays that come through known channels – theatre practitioners, regional and national scriptwriters groups, and agents. Predominantly a receiving house, the Theatre Royal produces some shows (especially musicals) which transfer to the West End.

Theatre Royal, Bath

Sawclose, Bath BA1 1ET
tel (01225) 448815
website www.theatreroyal.org.uk

The main house presents a wide range of productions from classics to new plays. It is the base for the Peter Hall Company's middle-scale productions. The 140-seat Ustinov Theatre stages an eclectic range of drama, dance and classical music, and is the home of Britain's largest annual international festival of adult puppetry. A children's theatre, the Egg, opened in 2005.

Traverse Theatre

10 Cambridge Street, Edinburgh EH1 2ED
tel 0131 228 3223 *fax* 0131 229 8443
website www.traverse.co.uk
Literary Manager Katherine Mendelsohn

Scotland's new writing theatre with a special interest in writers based in Scotland. Will read unsolicited scripts but a sae must be included for return of script. See website for submission guidelines.

Watford Palace Theatre

20 Clarendon Road, Watford, Herts. WD17 1JZ
tel (01923) 235455 *fax* (01923) 819664
website www.watfordpalacetheatre.co.uk
Contact Artistic Director, Brigid Larmour

Regional theatre. Produces and co-produces seasonally, both classic and contemporary drama and new writing. Accepts unsolicited scripts from writers in Hertfordshire.

The West Yorkshire Playhouse

Playhouse Square, Quarry Hill, Leeds LS2 7UP
tel 0113 213 7800 *fax* 0113 213 7250
website www.wyp.org.uk
Artistic Director Ian Brown, *Associate Director (Literary)* Alex Chisholm

Twin auditoria complex; community theatre. Has a policy of encouraging new writing from Yorkshire and Humberside region. Send script with a sae for its return to the Associate Director (Literary).

York Citizens' Theatre Trust Ltd

Theatre Royal, St Leonard's Place, York YO1 7HD
tel (01904) 658162 *fax* (01904) 550164
website www.yorktheatreroyal.co.uk
Chief Executive Liz Wilson, *Artistic Director* Damian Cruden

Repertory productions, tours.

TOURING COMPANIES

Actors Touring Company

ICA, 12 Carlton Terrace, London SW1Y 5AH
tel 020-7930 6014
email atc@atctheatre.com
website www.atctheatre.com
Artistic Director Ramin Gray

Small to medium-scale company producing international new writing.

Compass Theatre Company

St Jude's Parish Hall, 175 Gibraltar Street, Sheffield S3 8UA
tel 0114 278 6931 *fax* 0114 278 6931
website www.compasstheatrecompany.com
Artistic Director Neil Sissons, *General Manager* Craig Dronfield

Touring classical theatre nationwide. Does not produce new plays.

Eastern Angles

Sir John Mills Theatre, Gatacre Road, Ipswich IP1 2LQ
tel (01473) 218202 *fax* (01473) 384999
email admin@easternangles.co.uk
website www.easternangles.co.uk
Contact Ivan Cutting

Touring company producing new work with a regional theme. Stages three–four productions per year. Welcomes scripts from new writers in the East of England region. Founded 1982.

Exeter Northcott

Stocker Road, Exeter, Devon EX4 4QB
tel (01392) 223999

email info@exeternorthcott.co.uk
website www.exeternorthcott.co.uk
Creative Director Rebecca Manson-Jones

Regional producing theatre company.

Graeae Theatre Company

Bradbury Studios,
138 Kingsland Road London E2 8DY
tel 020-7613 6900 *fax* 020-7613 6919
email info@graeae.org
website www.graeae.org
Artistic Director Jenny Sealey, *Executive Director* Judith Kilvington, *Building & Facilities Manager* Kevin Walsh, *Finance Manager* Ann Lomole, *Access Manager* Michael Achtman

Small-scale touring company. Welcomes scripts from disabled writers. Founded 1980.

Headlong Theatre

34–35 Berwick Street, London W1F 8RP
tel 020-7478 0270 *fax* 020-7434 1749
email info@headlongtheatre.co.uk
website www.headlongtheatre.co.uk
Artistic Director Rupert Goold

A mid/large-scale touring company presenting three–four productions per year: revivals and adaptations of established masterpieces, modern classics and new work.

The Hiss & Boo Company Ltd

1 Nyes Hill, Wineham Lane, Bolney,
West Sussex RH17 5SD
tel (01444) 881707 *fax* (01444) 882057
email ian@hissboo.co.uk
website www.hissboo.co.uk
Managing Director Ian Liston

Little scope for new plays, but will consider comedy thrillers/chillers and plays/musicals for children. Produces pantomimes. No unsolicited scripts – telephone first. Plays/synopses will be returned only if accompanied by a sae.

Hull Truck Theatre Co. Ltd

50 Ferensway, Hull HU2 8LB
tel (01482) 224800
email admin@hulltruck.co.uk
website www.hulltruck.co.uk

Nationally renowned new writing theatre which also tours extensively. Produces the work of living playwrights and gives regional or national premieres to new plays, including own commissions. Premieres have included works by John Godber, Alan Plater, Richard Bean, Amanda Whittington, Nick Lane and David Windass; new commissions include Tom Wells and Selma Dimitrijevic. Now operates an open submission policy for new scripts, full reader service and strong writer support programme.

The London Bubble

(Bubble Theatre Company)
5 Elephant Lane, London SE16 4JD
tel 020-7237 4434
email admin@londonbubble.org.uk
website www.londonbubble.org.uk
Creative Director Jonathan Petherbridge

M6 Theatre Company (Studio Theatre)

Hamer C.P. School, Albert Royds Street, Rochdale, Lancs. OL16 2SU
tel (01706) 355898 *fax* (01706) 712601
email info@m6theatre.co.uk
website www.m6theatre.co.uk
Contact Dorothy Wood

Theatre-in-education company providing high-quality theatre for children, young people and community audiences.

New Perspectives Theatre Company

Park Lane Business Centre, Park Lane, Basford, Nottingham NG6 0DW
tel 0115 927 2334 *fax* 0115 927 1612
email info@newperspectives.co.uk
website www.newperspectives.co.uk
Artistic Director Daniel Buckroyd

A new writing company which commissions three–four writers each year and performs small/medium-scale theatre productions to community and arts venues nationally.

NITRO

(formerly Black Theatre Co-operative Ltd)
6 Brewery Road, London N7 9NH
tel 020-7609 1331 *fax* 020-7609 1221
email info@nitro.co.uk
website www.nitro.co.uk
Artistic Director Felix Cross

Commissions and produces new and innovative musical theatre writing by black writers, that expresses the contemporary aspirations, cultures and issues that concern black people.

Northumberland Theatre Company (NTC)

The Playhouse, Bondgate Without, Alnwick, Northumberland NE66 1PQ
tel (01665) 602586 *fax* (01665) 605837
email admin@northumberlandtheatre.co.uk
website www.northumberlandtheatre.co.uk
Artistic Director Gillian Hambleton

Performs a wide cross-section of work: new plays, extant scripts, classic and modern. Particularly interested in non-naturalism, physical theatre and plays with direct relevance to rural audiences.

Out of Joint

7 Thane Works, Thane Villas, London N7 7NU
tel 020-7609 0207 *fax* 020-7609 0203
email ojo@outofjoint.co.uk
website www.outofjoint.co.uk
Contact Max Stafford-Clark

Touring company producing new plays and some revivals. Welcomes scripts from writers. Founded 1993.

Paines Plough

4th Floor, 43 Aldwych, London WC2B 4DN
tel 020-7240 4533 *fax* 020-7240 4534
email office@painesplough.com
website www.painesplough.com
Artistic Directors George Perrin, James Grieve

Commissions and produces new plays by British and Irish playwrights. Tours at least six or more plays a year nationally for small and midscale theatres. Also runs The Big Room, a concierge style development strand for professional playwrights – see website for further details. Welcomes unsolicited scripts and responds to all submissions. Seeks original plays that engage with the contemporary world and are written in a distinctive voice.

Proteus Theatre Company

Queen Mary's College, Cliddesden Road, Basingstoke, Hants RG21 3HF
tel (01256) 354541 *fax* (01256) 356186
email info@proteustheatre.com
website www.proteustheatre.com
Artistic Director Mary Swan

Small-scale touring company particularly committed to new writing and new work, education and community collaborations. Produces three touring shows per year plus several community projects. Founded 1979.

Quicksilver Theatre

The New Diorama Theatre, 15–16 Triton Street, Regents Place, London NW1 3BF
tel 020-7241 2942 *fax* 020-7254 3119
email talktous@quicksilvertheatre.org
website www.quicksilvertheatre.org
Joint Artistic Director/Ceo Guy Holland, *Joint Artistic Director* Carey English

A professional touring theatre company which brings live theatre to theatres and schools all over the country. Delivers good stories, original music, kaleidoscopic design and poignant, often humorous, new writing to entertain and make children and adults think. Two to three new plays a year for children 3–5 years, 4–7 years and age 8+ and their families. Founded 1977.

Real People Theatre Company

37 Curlew Glebe, Dunnington, York YO19 5PQ
tel/fax (01904) 488870
email sueann@curlew.totalserve.co.uk
website www.realpeopletheatre.co.uk
Contact Sue Lister, Artistic Director

Women's theatre company. Welcomes scripts from women writers. Founded 1999.

Red Ladder Theatre Company

3 St Peter's Buildings, York Street, Leeds LS9 8AJ
tel 0113 245 5311 *fax* 0113 245 5351
email rod@redladder.co.uk
website www.redladder.co.uk
Artistic Director Rod Dixon

Theatre performances with a radical and dissenting voice. National touring of theatre venues and community spaces. Commissions one or two new plays each year. Runs the Red Grit Project, a free theatre training programme for over 18s.

Red Shift Theatre Company

67 Marlborough Road, London SW19 2HF
tel/fax 020-8540 1271
email jonathan@redshifttheatreco.co.uk
website www.redshifttheatreco.co.uk
Artistic Director Jonathan Holloway

Productions include adaptations, classics, new plays.

Shared Experience Theatre

Oxford Playhouse, 11–12 Beaumont Street, Oxford OX1 2LW
tel (01865) 305305
email admin@sharedexperience.org.uk
website www.sharedexperience.org.uk
Joint Artistic Directors Nancy Meckler, Polly Teale

Middle-scale touring company presenting two productions per year: innovative adaptations or translations of classic texts, and some new writing. Tours nationally and internationally. Founded 1975.

Solent Peoples Theatre (SPT)

Bedhampton Arts Centre, Bedhampton Road, Havant, Hants PO9 3ET
tel 023-9242 3399 *fax* 023-9242 3401
website www.solentpeoplestheatre.com
Artistic Director Brendon Burns

SPT has developed its artistic programme through participatory projects, to incorporate a multimedia, cross art form approach to theatre that will offer richer opportunities and experience to both community and company. Works with diverse groups/individuals for whom an integrated approach to the creation/presentation of new work in performance makes that work more exciting, relevant and accessible.

Sphinx Theatre Company

249 Tooley Street, London SE1 2JX
email info@sphinxtheatre.co.uk
website www.sphinxtheatre.co.uk
Artistic Director Sue Parrish

Specialises in writing, directing and developing roles for women.

Talawa Theatre Company

Ground Floor, 53–55 East Road, London N1 6AH
tel 020-7251 6644 *fax* 020-7251 5969
email hq@talawa.com
website www.talawa.com
Artistic Director Patricia Cumper

Scripts from new writers considered. Particularly interested in scripts from black writers and plays portraying a black experience.

Theatre Absolute

Shop Front Theatre, 38 City Arcade,
Coventry CV1 3HW
tel (02476) 158340
email info@theatreabsolute.co.uk
website www.theatreabsolute.co.uk
Contact Julia Negus

Independent theatre producer of contemporary plays which premiere in, and then tour, the UK and Ireland. Stages one premiere and tour over two-year period. Founded 1992.

Theatre Centre

Shoreditch Town Hall, 380 Old Street,
London EC1V 9LT
tel 020-7729 3066 *fax* 020-7739 9741
email admin@theatre-centre.co.uk
website www.theatre-centre.co.uk
Artistic Director Natalie Wilson

New writing company producing and touring nationally and internationally. Professional theatre for young people – schools, arts centres, venues. Founded 1953.

Theatre Is...

The Hat Factory Arts Centre, 65-67 Bute Street,
Luton, Beds. LU1 2EY
tel (01582) 481221
email info@theatreis.org
website www.theatreis.org
Contact Michael Corley

Challenging and creating new models of live performance by, with and for young audiences across the East of England.

Theatre Workshop

34 Hamilton Place, Edinburgh EH3 5AX
tel 0131 225 7942 *fax* 0131 220 0112
email enquiries.tws@hotmail.co.uk
website www.theatre-workshop.com
Artistic Director Robert Rae

Cutting edge, professional, inclusive theatre company. Plays include new writing/community/children's/disabled. Scripts from new writers considered.

Literary agents

'I think I need an agent'

Mark Le Fanu explains when it is appropriate for an author to have an agent.

If you write fiction, having an agent is becoming almost essential. Publishers are deluged with uncommissioned proposals and rely on agents whose taste they respect to filter the best from the rest. That is why many of the major publishers tell authors they will only accept submissions from agents. But even then, there are very many more novels seeking publishers (and agents) than will ever be accepted or even looked at. This leaves many novelists – however good their work – in a depressingly difficult situation. Having a good website, self-publishing and other self-promotional activities are ways of trying to stand out from the crowd.

Further information

The Society of Authors
84 Drayton Gardens, London SW10 9SB
tel 020-7373 6642
email info@societyofauthors.org
website www.societyofauthors.org

The Society publishes a *Quick Guide to Literary Agents* (free via website), which covers the general duties of agents and the terms usually agreed between author and agent. See page 497 for further information about the Society.

For narrative non-fiction, likely to be stocked by the main booksellers, an agent may well help you to secure improved terms, but is probably not essential. A publisher can tell much about a non-fiction work from a quick glance at a proposal, which is not the case with works of fiction.

Few agents are interested in representing authors of scholarly, professional, reference or highly illustrated works, and generally they don't have the specialist knowledge to do so to great effect. Agents very rarely take on poetry, memoirs or short stories; and they are particularly hesitant about taking on authors writing in their retirement when the chances of building up a lasting full-time career are reduced.

A good agent will be likely to secure better terms (notably the advance) than you can achieve on your own and thereby more than offset their commission. Successful authors say their agent saves them an enormous amount of time looking after the business side of their work. However, an indifferent agent may be of little value; likewise one without good knowledge of rights management and contracts. Be wary of agencies seeking up-front payments, for example joining, reading or editing fees, as publishers will pay little attention to recommendations from such an agency, suspecting that its main reason for representing a work is the up-front payment rather than the quality of the material itself.

Details of approximately 150 UK agencies are listed in this *Yearbook* (see page 429). Very few literary agents take on writers other than of fiction and narrative non-fiction. Within these limitations, agencies represent a variety of authors. Some specialise in children's writers and illustrators; others in film, television and 'talent' (e.g. celebrity writers). Membership of the Association of Authors' Agents is indicative of the literary agency's expertise and professionalism; likewise membership of the Personal Managers' Association for screenwriters' and dramatists' agents. When asked how they came by their agent, many authors suggest that it was as much a matter of luck as anything else. The Society of Authors can give its members confidential advice about particular agencies and look over agency agreements they are offered.

If an agency shows interest, arrange a meeting to see if you are compatible and to discuss terms before making up your mind. If you are in the fortunate position of having more than one agent seeking to represent you, or are being courted by an agent even though you are currently happy without one, get the agent to convince you that what they can bring to the party justifies their commission. They should sell themselves to you – after all, the main skill you want from them is the ability to sell.

Most agencies give details on their websites as to how they like to be approached. The harsh reality is that many agents say they will not consider unsolicited typescripts. You will probably need to send just a synopsis and sample chapter (don't telephone) to the agency concerned with a covering letter, retaining a copy of both. Enclose stamps for return postage. Be aware that it can be a matter of weeks before you receive a response to your proposal as agents spend most of their time representing their existing clients.

It may be reassuring to know that many members of the Society of Authors do not have agents; and (whether or not you have an agent) the Society can help by scrutinising members' publishing and media contracts – without extra charge – and suggesting realistic improvements. Whatever impression publishers may like to give that their contracts, hallowed by years of experience and revered for their fairness, should simply be signed with gratitude, negotiation is invariably in order. Firm but reasonable bargaining, informed by a knowledge of what is achievable, undoubtedly pays off.

Mark Le Fanu was formerly General Secretary of the Society of Authors (see page 497).

See also...

- *How literary agencies work,* page 413
- *How to get an agent,* page 416
- *Making a successful submission to a literary agent,* page 418
- *How to attract the attention of a literary agent,* page 425
- *Literary agents UK and Ireland,* page 429

How literary agencies work

Catherine Clarke gives an insight into literary agents, both large and small.

When I joined Felicity Bryan as a literary agent in June 2001, I knew I would be making one or two adjustments to my professional mindset. But I didn't fully appreciate how different working for a small agency would be from the publishing job I had left behind – several years as a publishing director for trade books at Oxford University Press, having come up through the editorial route. OUP is a large organisation with a corporate structure and hierarchy, and several divisions which operate effectively as separate companies, not only in the UK but in offices all over the world. I was now joining an agent who had previously been a director at Curtis Brown in London, and had successfully set up her own business in 1988, and who up until this point had operated on her own, with an assistant and a bookkeeper, from a small, pretty office in north Oxford. It was with something of a sigh of relief that I left behind the regular weekly and monthly meetings with colleagues from various publishing departments, which even when they were fun and useful seemed to take up such an inordinate amount of time, and set about learning what the differences were between representing authors and publishing them.

The first eye-opening lesson was that even though the agency itself consisted of just two agents and two staff, it functioned as the hub of a vast, informal network of relationships, not only within the UK but right across the globe. On the day that I started work, an auction was in progress for a new book proposal, a memoir co-written with a ghostwriter. The authors were based in London, but the publishers bidding for it (by phone and email on this occasion) were in Germany. The bids were relayed to Felicity Bryan by our German translation sub-agent at Andrew Nurnberg Associates in London, specialists in translation rights. Felicity called the authors to keep them up to speed with what was happening, and eventually made a recommendation to them for which offer to accept. The deal, once it was done and announced in the trade press, kick-started auctions for the book in many other territories, including the UK and the USA. While all this was happening, Felicity picked up the phone and talked to a London-based agent who deals with film and television rights and agreed that, given the intense interest in the book, it would be a good time to submit it to production companies in London and Los Angeles and get the proposal on track for a film option or sale. The authors were, naturally, over the moon.

Meanwhile I, the novice agent, was learning fast from this on-the-job induction, and was also busy setting up meetings with editors and publishing directors in all the London publishing houses, particularly those who specialised in serious non-fiction – books by historians, literary biographers, and philosophers mostly, as that was my own background as a publisher, and the areas where my earliest clients would be coming from. I wanted to find out what books were selling well for each editor, and what they were looking for. In several cases they were looking for books on particular subjects, and asked if I could help find authors for them.

By the time I attended my first Frankfurt Book Fair in October 2001, I had a small list of my own clients and a few deals already done with UK publishers. In my Filofax I had a miniaturised schedule of 50 or so half-hour meetings with European and US publishers in the International Rights Centre, and several invitations to evening parties. I had already had a number of conversations about 'hot' books and who was buying what with publishers at the check-in at Heathrow airport and again waiting at the baggage claim at Frankfurt. Over the mindbogglingly expensive white wine at the Frankfurterhof bar late at night, thronging with publishers from all over the world, I handed over proposals for books that resulted in deals (which took place later, after the adrenalin rush of the Fair was over and everyone could make a sober decision on what they wanted to buy). During the evening I met the New York-based agent who was to become my first port of call for selling my clients' books on my behalf in the US market (later I added two other US agents who had different tastes and close publishing relationships so I could match each project to a really enthusiastic co-agent). I felt well and truly launched by the time I flew back home. The following spring the London Book Fair was to prove just as intense and influential, and when I went on to develop a list of children's writers, the Bologna Children's Book Fair became another annual fixture in my diary for selling rights, meeting new publishers, checking up on how existing deals were progressing, and for trailing exciting new projects that were still in the offing. Very soon I was factoring in a regular trip to New York to see publishers and co-agents, so I could get a sense of the rather different market patterns and pressures in the USA, and also talk up my clients' books.

That experience is probably not very different for any agent, whatever the size of their business, though some will have less emphasis on the international markets. It undoubtedly helps as an agent starting out to have colleagues or contacts already in the business who can effect introductions and help build the necessary networks.

So what might a prospective writer take into account when looking for an agent to represent them?

There are many literary agencies in the UK – the membership of the Association of Authors' Agents is around 90 – and they vary in size from one person working entirely on their own to very large organisations with many agents and support staff. Most agencies are somewhere in between, with several book agents specialising in fiction or non-fiction, children's and adult, or more usually a mixture, and with support staff or freelance services such as royalty management and accounts. The very large agencies, such as Curtis Brown or United Agents (set up in the wake of a mass exodus from PFD) also have agents who specialise in film and television rights, scriptwriters, directors, presenters and actors; in other words, they manage a wide range of creative talent. Jonathan Lloyd, Chairman of Curtis Brown, says, 'Compared to almost all publishers, agencies, even the bigger ones, are tiny, but an impressive client list helps us to protect our clients and the "one-stop-shop" ability allows us to exploit clients in the fullest and most effective way.'

At the other end of the spectrum, Rachel Calder at the Sayle Literary Agency, in Cambridge, feels that small is definitely beautiful: 'A small agency can afford to work in the medium- and long-term interest of their writers, not just the short term, because they are under less pressure from having to contribute to large overheads... they can be more flexible in reacting to changing industry circumstances, and still be acting in the writers' best interests.' As Sally Holloway, former publisher and now an associate agent with the Felicity Bryan Agency, says, 'Smaller agents, like smaller publishers, are much more aware of their own bottom line, and therefore will pursue that last little foreign rights deal.'

For the writer, several factors might come into the reckoning if they are thinking about who should represent them. The first is that a relationship with an agent is, ideally, for life, or at least for the longer-term career, and should not be entered into lightly on either part. Whether the agent is part of a small or larger agency is not so great a consideration as whether the writer and agent trust one another's judgement and ability to deliver: whether they can both foresee a happy and fruitful collaboration. For some writers, being part of a list of high-profile writers – or more generally of famous 'talent' – may be the highest comfort factor; they might be less concerned about having the full attention of an agent with a very big list of clients than being part of a particular 'brand' created by that list. For others, that is less of a factor than having a hands-on agent who will work hard with the writer to get a proposal or novel into the best possible shape and then doggedly pursue the best deals in all potential markets – and that would not necessarily mean the highest advances. Of course, most agents can happily combine these qualities.

Because literary agenting is a business based not only on contacts and relationships but also personal tastes, every agency will have a slightly different ethos or feel. As Rachel Calder says, 'A good agent is committed to their author's work and career, has excellent industry contacts at home and abroad, wide publishing experience, confidence about their abilities and good literary judgement... what matters is how good the deals are that the agent does for those writers.'

Catherine Clarke is Managing Director at Felicity Bryan Associates.

See also...

- *'I think I need an agent'*, page 411
- *How to get an agent*, page 416
- *Making a successful submission to a literary agent*, page 418
- *How to attract the attention of a literary agent*, page 425

How to get an agent

Philippa Milnes-Smith demystifies the role of the literary agent.

This article is for all those who are prepared to dedicate themselves to the pursuit of publication. If you are currently experiencing just a vague interest in being a writer or illustrator, stop reading now. You are unlikely to survive the rigorous commercial assessment to which your work will be subjected. If you are a children's writer or illustrator do not think that the process will be any easier. It's just as tough, if not tougher.

So, what is a literary agent and why would I want one?

Contacts for many publishers are provided in this *Yearbook*. This means that there is nothing to prevent you from pursuing publishers directly yourself. Indeed, if you can answer a confident 'yes' to all the questions below, and have the time and resources to devote to this objective, you might not need an agent:

- Do you have a thorough understanding of the publishing market and its dynamics?
- Do you know who are the best publishers for your book and why? Can you evaluate the pros and cons of each?
- Are you up to navigating the shifting world of digital publishing?
- Are you financially numerate and confident of being able to negotiate the best commercial deal available in current market conditions?
- Are you confident of being able to understand fully and negotiate a publishing or other media contract?
- Do you enjoy the process of selling yourself and your work?

An agent's job is to deal with all of the above on your behalf. A good agent will do all of these well.

So, is that all an agent does?

Agents aren't all the same. Some will provide more editorial and creative support; some will be subject specialists; some will involve themselves more in marketing and promotion; all should work in their clients' best interests.

I have decided I definitely do want an agent. Where do I begin?

Firstly, using this *Yearbook* and web research, identify the agents to whom your book will appeal. Then really think about who will buy your book and why. An agent will only take someone on if they can see how and why they are going to make money for the client and themselves. An agent also knows that if he/she does not sell a client's work, the relationship isn't going to last long.

So the agent just thinks about money?

Well, some agents may just think about money. But good agents do also care about the quality of work and the clients they represent. They are professional people who commit themselves to doing the best job they can. They also know that good personal relationships count. This means that, if and when you get as far as talking to a prospective agent, you should ask yourself the questions: 'Do I have a good rapport with this person? Do I think we will get along? Do I understand and trust what they are saying?' Follow your instinct – more often than not it will be right.

So how do I convince an agent that I'm worth taking on?

Start with the basics. Make your approach professional and only approach an appropriate agent who deals with the category of book you are writing/illustrating. Check to whom you should send your work and whether there are any specific ways your submission should be made, and only make an electronic submission if the agency in question states that it is acceptable. For hard copy submissions, only submit neat, typed work on single-sided A4 paper. Send a short covering letter with your manuscript explaining what it is, why you wrote it, what the intended audience is and providing any other *relevant* context. Always say if and why you are uniquely placed and qualified to write a particular book. Provide your professional credentials, if any. If you are writing an autobiography, justify why it is of public interest and why your experiences set you apart. Also, provide a CV (again, neat, typed, relevant) and a stamped addressed envelope for the return of your manuscript if you wish to have it returned. Think of the whole thing in the same way as you would a job application. You might only get one go at making your big sales pitch to an agent. Don't mess it up by being anything less than thorough.

And if I get to meet an agent?

Treat it like a job interview (although hopefully it will be more relaxed than this). Be prepared to talk about your work and yourself. An agent knows that a prepossessing personality in an author is a great asset for a publisher in terms of publicity and marketing – they will be looking to see how good your interpersonal and presentation skills are. Authors are sometimes required to do publicity interviews and events.

And if an agent turns my work down? Should I ask them to look again? People say you should not accept rejection.

No means no. Don't pester. It won't make an agent change his/her mind. Instead, move on to the next agency – the agent there might feel more positive. The agents who reject you may be wrong. But the loss is theirs.

Even if an agent turns my work down, isn't it worth asking for help with my creative direction?

No. Agents will often provide editorial advice for clients but will not do so for non-clients. Submissions are usually sorted into two piles of 'yes, worth seeing more' and 'rejections'. There is not another pile of 'promising writer but requires further tutoring'. Creative courses and writers' and artists' groups are better options to pursue for teaching and advice (see *Creative writing courses* on page 630). It is, however, important to practise and develop your creative skills. You wouldn't expect to be able to play football without working at your ball skills. If you want to get your work published, you will be competing with professional writers and artists – and those who have spent years working at their craft. The time you spend on your writing is still the most important you can spend.

Philippa Milnes-Smith is a past president of the Association of Authors' Agents and Managing Director of the agency LAW (Lucas Alexander Whitley). She was previously Managing Director of Penguin Children's Books.

See also...

- *How literary agencies work*, page 413
- *Making a successful submission to a literary agent*, page 418
- *Literary agents for children's books*, page 737
- *Literary agents for television, film, radio and theatre*, page 738

Making a successful submission to a literary agent

There is no magic formula to guarantee that a manuscript submitted to a literary agent will be accepted. In this article, Carole Blake suggests approaches to help authors find success with an agent.

Every client's submission letter and manuscript that I have ever taken on has been different. But there are some things a writer can do to shorten the odds of being rejected (provided your material is good of course…).

When to submit your manuscript

The most important decision to make about submitting material to an agent is 'when': far too many writers submit too early. Many manuscripts I see would definitely benefit from being put aside for a few weeks or months, then reread with a critical eye, and edited or revised again. Many contain simple mistakes – typos, bad grammar, continuity problems, plot holes – that another read-through would correct. Give your manuscript time to settle down, after you've typed 'The End': it allows reflection. I have often received a sequence of letters or emails from writers who have had second thoughts about a manuscript they've just submitted. If I'm asked to stop reading something I've started on, because a new version is coming, or – worse still – am asked to insert revised pages into a manuscript – it does make me think the writer has just been too impatient in sending it out. Impatience isn't a trait associated with professionalism.

Agents are looking for a professional approach and style. Address your letter or email personally to the agent. 'Dear agent' doesn't impress anyone.

Let there be no gimmicks, no flowers, no chocolates, no cupcakes or anything else delivered with the submission. I once received a huge package delivered by courier: it was a waste-paper bin with a submission inside. The submission letter (referring to the short journey between slush pile and rubbish bin) was witty and I put it next to my desk to read the chapters the next day. Unfortunately, our office cleaners came that night and – yes – emptied the waste-paper bin. I have never been able to respond to that submission, even though the material looked promising.

Everyone knows how difficult it is to be offered representation by an agent so don't stack the odds against yourself by showing that you haven't done your homework. I don't expect unpublished authors to know everything about the book business but I do expect them to have bothered to do at least a little research.

For instance, I don't represent science fiction, and say so quite clearly on our agency website and in my book, *From Pitch to Publication: Everything You Need to Know to Get Your Novel Published* (Pan Macmillan 1999). I don't represent it because I don't read it, and don't know enough about it to handle it well. I'm aware there are several very good agents who specialise in science fiction and who know a great deal about it, and the editors who buy it, so I leave it to them. If an author submits science fiction to me I know they haven't bothered to invest the few minutes it would take to look at our website. Which tells me they won't do even the easiest amount of research: a few minutes on their computer would have saved them an unnecessary submission.

Assuming you've done your revision and your homework, and you're certain you know which agents to submit to, you are ready to write the dreaded submission letter or email. (Agency websites will tell you if they accept submissions by email.)

By all means query multiple agents: but do be courteous and tell us you are doing so. When I have read a partial manuscript and then request more material, often at that stage I will ask for an exclusive, and in return will try to read quickly. But if you don't want to grant me an exclusive look, I will make a decision as to how far up the queue I move the reading.

A big 'don't' – don't trash other authors in your genre when submitting your material, and don't make derogatory remarks about the business, about agents, about publishers. I'm not going to look kindly on authors who complain about my clients, and showing prejudice about the business doesn't look professional. Another word of warning: if you tell me that someone I know referred you to me – please make sure that I actually know that person. Otherwise, again, it doesn't do you any favours. And please don't, ever, send us your suggested cover designs. Unfortunately nothing looks more amateur than authors who think they can design their own covers.

Successful submissions

I like submissions that show me the author is writing with such conviction that they would almost continue to write without publication. Two of my authors made that clear in their initial submissions to me – Elizabeth Chadwick and Julian Stockwin.

Elizabeth Chadwick, now the author of many award-winning and internationally published bestsellers, wrote a letter to me 23 years ago explaining that she had fallen in love with the medieval period after watching a television drama series when she was 15, and had been writing medieval novels ever since. I turned the page, started to read her chapters, and was astonished to find that after 30 minutes I had finished them and was utterly engrossed. I phoned her immediately… 20 novels and 23 years later we are still working together, and her first published novel (it was the eighth she'd completed) has now been continuously in print for 22 years. The passion for the period she was writing about just leapt off the page of that first letter to me.

Julian Stockwin's submission letter, posted on the first day of the new millennium, told me that he was writing the kind of novel he wanted to read. Having read every seafaring 'Age of Fighting Sail' action-adventure novel that he could find in print, he was now writing his own. Unlike all the others, his central character started life not as a captain or an admiral, but as an unwilling sailor – he had been press-ganged into joining the navy. Until then, I had no interest in the sea (or male action-adventure stories) but his letter expressed such a confident and calm sales pitch that I was intrigued. I remember staying in the bath to finish reading his manuscript, so engrossed that I had crinkled fingers and was sitting in cold water before I could stop. If his writing could drag me into a genre I thought I was indifferent to, then I felt he would have a wide audience. He will shortly deliver his fourteenth manuscript in the *Kydd* series.

Beryl Matthews was nearing 70 when she submitted her novel to me. I fell in love with it and thought her age an irrelevance. She has now published 13 novels.

In case you think all these successful submission stories happened years ago, the most recent client I've taken on is Liz Fenwick. I first corresponded with her via Twitter (how modern is that!) but she didn't pitch there (nor should you, ever). I then met her through the Romantic Novelists Association (RNA): she is an active and very professional member. She mentioned to me that she was about to submit her manuscript: would I like to see it? I said yes, but only on condition that she understood that I would have to respond harshly because this was my *job*: I couldn't and wouldn't be kind just because I had met her. When I started reading her manuscript I couldn't put it down, and eight weeks later had sold it to publishers in three languages. The novel was published in 2012 in English, and we are selling more languages as the months pass.

Advice from an agent

So what can be learned from these successful submissions? I would say write something you care about passionately and then get as much editorial feedback as you can, and then revise, revise, revise. Do your homework to help decide which agent to submit to and then write a short, sensible covering letter which doesn't make extravagant claims. Include anything about yourself that is relevant to your novel (and little that isn't) and have the courage to leave it at that. When it comes down to the wire, it's the writing in your manuscript that counts.

A plea to authors who have submitted material and are impatient for a response: please don't chase until at least a few weeks after sending the material. At my agency we look at every submission that comes in but we always prioritise work for our clients before we give our time to not-yet clients. Reading thousands of unsolicited submissions each year has to be fitted in around the representation of our clients. If you do decide to chase, first check the agency's website for guidelines on how long they expect to take before responding to submissions, and then please email rather than telephone: few agencies have enough staff to be able to spare people to deal with submission queries on the phone.

I like to set aside an evening, or a weekend afternoon, in the office, to go through the piles of sifted and recommended manuscripts that make their way to my office. Even though I have very little capacity to add to my client base now, I always read the submissions with a feeling of excited anticipation, remembering the wonderful authors I represent who have come to me via unsolicited submissions.

Even if you submit a good manuscript, in a professional way, there is still no guarantee of acceptance, or indeed of individual feedback if representation is not being offered. I wish it were otherwise, but my agency (in common with all the others) receives so many submissions a year (many thousands in our case), that it's just not possible to respond personally. Even though I would rather not, we have to use standard rejection letters or we would not be able to respond at all.

So what if you follow all the guidelines on agency websites but still get rejected? Don't be downhearted: it's rare to find a published author who hasn't received rejections. If you believe in your manuscript, keep sending it out. 'Faint heart never won fair lady'… or a good publishing deal. Good luck!

Carole Blake is one of the UK's foremost literary agents with a career in publishing spanning 49 years. Before starting her agency in 1977 she was marketing director for a mass-market paperback publisher. Her agency, Blake Friedmann, has been responsible for launching the international career of many bestselling authors. She is past President of the Association of Authors' Agents (AAA), past Chairman of the Society of Bookmen, and current President of the Book Trade Charity.

Letter to an unsolicited author

With the benefit of 18 years of experience as a literary agent, Simon Trewin gives valuable advice to unpublished authors on how and when to approach a literary agent with their manuscript.

Dear Author,

Being an agent is not rocket science. There is no agent training school and there is no course that I know of that exclusively trains people to do what I do. All I do, quite simply, is read work, decide if it ticks a number of boxes and then try to seek a publishing home for it. It is as clear and as simple as that – I am not a literary critic, I don't run a creative writing school and I'm not a publisher but I *am* entrepreneurial, I am clear in my mind as to my particular strengths and weaknesses and I am also a nurturer of talent. On top of all of that I continually love the fact that there are thousands and thousands of writers out there looking for book deals. So far so good.

There is an illustrated edition of *Jack and the Beanstalk* that I used to read to my son Jack when he was little and we both loved one particular page – it showed a tiny Jack knocking on the huge wooden door of the giant's castle. The door was reinforced with rivets and there was an intimidating sense of austere formality about it. Jack knocked and knocked on that door but no one came and it felt poignant and it felt uneven. I am absolutely aware that this is how unsolicited and unrepresented authors feel when they are in search of an agent – that they are knocking on a massive door which never seems to open. The reality of course is that on the other side of the publishing door there isn't an ogre or a huge author-eating giant but there are in fact hundreds of busy agents running around doing great work and all faced with a common quest – to find exciting new authors to add to their growing lists. We all want to find the Next Big Thing and any agent who says otherwise is telling porky pies. It is good to remind myself as an agent, and to remind all authors out there at the beginning of their journeys that when I started out as an agent an author called Joanne Rowling was still sitting in a café somewhere scribbling the adventures of a young wizard boy at a school called Hogwarts. She wrote to the agent Christopher Little and the rest is history. As the advert for the lottery once said, 'It could be you…'.

We are all looking for our own J.K. Rowling but, unfortunately, many writers put unnecessary barriers in between their work and the potential of an agent picking it up. There is no exact science to breaking into publishing but there are many things you should avoid like the plague.

Agents are a curious bunch (I'm not sure what the collective noun for agents should be – maybe a 'clause of agents'?) and the community I inhabit is made up of not only the mad, the bad and the dangerous to know (as in any profession) but on the whole by a huge number of truly inspiring entrepeneurial people who spend every waking hour as passionate advocates of the powers of prose. If you take a look at various agent websites (and you really should) you will see a diverse list of clients who reflect their agent's idiosyncrasies, their passion and their interests and this should be encouraging to any author in search of representation.

We agents need you – without authors we would be sitting at our desks sucking our pens and looking at empty bookshelves – but we also need you to help us make efficient use of our time and our skills. With 18 years' experience as an agent I can tell you that many prospective authors don't do themselves any favours when they approach the door.

I believe you can judge an agent's soul by their attitude to unsolicited material and, believe me, we at United Agents take it very seriously indeed. My brilliant Associate Agent colleague Ariella Feiner comes into my office every morning with the newly arrived material and we settle down and start reading. Simple as that. A wonderful hush descends over the room, the phone is set to divert, the Blackberry goes on silent mode and we read and read and read. Tea is sipped and occasionally a pencil is produced and a mark made in a margin or on a covering letter. Then we silently swap material that has grabbed our attention and get a silent second opinion. At the end of this zen-like half an hour we have a small collection of 'maybes' and a larger collection of 'no's'. The no's fall into many categories:

(a) **The Arrogant.** I once received a submission which said, and I quote, 'Dear Mr Terwin (*sic*) I am probably one of the best writers currently working in the English language and, frankly, you are lucky to be seeing this picaresque novel which my tutor at Oxford has already described as "heart-stoppingly wonderful". Personally I don't think I need an agent but someone mentioned your name as being one of the less bad ones so I am giving you an opportunity to persuade me otherwise. If you would like to visit me in Oxford next Wednesday lunchtime that would be convenient.' Sincerely, etc. Frankly I didn't bother reading any more – I knew that we weren't going to get on. I have nothing against writers being confident and passionate and displaying their work to the best of its potential but this crossed the line!

(b) **The Impersonator.** I received a mediocre thriller one day and read about 50 pages and sent it back with a note saying I didn't feel it was going to be a good fit for my list. The next morning a very indignant man called me and told me in no uncertain terms that I was mistaken. 'Oh yes,' said I, 'why is that?' He then proceeded to tell me that he had read the top ten thrillers of the previous year and had decoded each of them onto a graph. When there was a cliffhanger he coloured in the appropriate square on his chart with green crayon, when there was an explosion he whipped out the red crayon, and when there was a sex scene he used blue and so on. He then wrote his own novel based on this equation of what constituted the statistically average 'bestselling novel' and was amazed that I didn't immediately snap it up. What he had done of course was create an impersonation of a thriller rather than a thriller itself, and the book he sent me was very hollow indeed. He hadn't invested anything of himself in it and it really showed. My feeling is that you should write from the inside out and take that storytelling fire in your belly and get it down on paper. Don't analyse the market or the genre – just write.

(c) **The Misguided.** I sing in the bath. I enjoy it and I can just about carry a tune but I don't believe that I am entitled to a record deal and a seven-night residency at the O2. That doesn't bother me because, as I said, I enjoy it. Some of the manuscripts I receive are just not very good but still they come with covering letters reeking of entitlements and that say, 'My friends and family think this is better than most books being published right now'. I would be very apprehensive about suggesting to any author that they use their friends and family's reaction to their work as a selling point. Have you ever told a friend that their ugly baby was anything other than 'beautiful'? Of course not. Go figure! Don't trust anyone's judgement who you share Christmas dinner with.

(d) **The Scattergun.** I am all for authors who have a multiplicity of talents and who write prose, poetry, genre fiction, verse drama and children's books but I would advise them against sending examples of ALL OF THEM AT ONCE to an agent with a note saying, 'I love all this stuff – you decide what I should write next'. I want to hear your undivided passion for one area of your writing because if I become your agent I will need to sell you in a very focused way to a publisher. Variety may be the spice of life but I would suggest you write to an agent about one major project at a time – your publisher will want to launch you as a mini-brand and will want to package you and continue to publish you in a coherent manner that creates a sense of expectation from your growing readership.

(e) **The Misdirected.** Even though I am very open on my website as to what my likes and dislikes are, I still receive material that is in direct opposition to those stated preferences. I don't understand or represent science fiction or fantasy; I don't have an interest in sagas; I don't represent young children's books; I don't represent academic books; I don't represent illustrated books. I'm very clear about this but still, on a daily basis, letters arrive that say things like, 'Dear Simon, I know you say that you don't represent x, y or z, but I hope that once you've read my material you'll make an exception'. The short answer to that is *no* – I know it sounds harsh but it is there to save you time and to make sure that when you send your precious work out it goes to someone who is actively sitting there wanting to read it.

(f) **The Underdeveloped.** It is virtually impossible to secure a book deal for fiction in the current climate on anything less than the full manuscript, so you shouldn't approach an agent without having completed several drafts of your masterwork. Ideally you will also have put it to one side for a couple of months so you can achieve that all-important 'distance' from your work. This is crucial but it is amazing how many people approach me saying something like, 'I know the second half doesn't work at all and I will probably change the main character entirely but I would love your thoughts now'. My thoughts on this are clear – do not submit your work until you are happy to be judged by it. Again I know this sounds harsh but you wouldn't go into a job interview and say, 'I'm probably completely wrong for this job and sorry I am still wearing my pyjamas and I am half an hour late but let's have a chat ... if that's all right with you'. Take the process really seriously and present yourself in a professional way to a professional agent and you will achieve so much more.

Your one aim is to put no barriers between you, your prose and my assessment of it and it really isn't that difficult. The important thing to remember throughout this entire process is that I am sitting at my desk waiting for something wonderful to come into my life. I am looking to find storytellers – non-fiction and fiction – who can make me, for a brief moment or two, forget that I am reading a book. Authors who have a distinctive voice that carries me with it to strange lands of the imagination or simply to a place where I am viewing the mundane from an off-kilter perspective. I am looking, simply, for books that I will feel proud to share with my peers in the publishing world and who will feel the same passion for them that I do.

In 2010, Ariella texted me at home on a Sunday and told me to check my email immediately because she was sending over something amazing that I had to read *at once.* I did and she was right – it was. On the following Tuesday we met the author, Jane Casey, and we signed her up jointly. Three weeks later her chilling psychological debut *The Missing* was snapped up by Gillian Green at Ebury Press and I had that wonderful moment as an agent when you ring a client and tell them they are about to become a published author. I live for that moment and it never disappoints.

Jane's novel has now been published to huge acclaim, sold all over the world by my colleagues – the amazing Jessica Craig, Jane Willis and Zoe Ross – and the movie rights have been optioned. It all started because Jane finished the novel, did a bit of research about who best to send it to, wrote a confident letter telling me about the authors she enjoyed reading, telling me why she wanted to be a novelist and telling me about *The Missing*. She enclosed the first 10,000 words and sat back patiently while Ariella read it, enthused me and got her in for a meeting. We then suggested some changes which she carried out and then she let us get on with the business of publishing. She played to her strengths and we played to ours and it has worked out like a dream. And in 2011 she signed a new six-book (three adult and three young adult) contract. Hoorah!

If you can avoid transgressing any of the great sins of approaching an agent that I have outlined then you will raise the odds of securing an agent and publication by a factor of at least ten. And if you can avoid doing as one author did when he wrote to me and said, 'I have tried 14 publishers and nine agents and they have all said "no" so I am now approaching you', then even better!

I want to read your work and look forward to the perfect pitch from you.

Simon Trewin is head of the Books department at United Agents.

See also...

- *How to attract the attention of a literary agent*, page 425
- *How to get an agent*, page 416
- *Making a successful submission to a literary agent*, page 418
- *Literary agents UK and Ireland*, page 429
- *Dealing with rejection*, page 601

How to attract the attention of a literary agent

Having a literary agent helps you to get published. When an agent takes on a writer publishers are far more likely to take notice of that writer's work. Alison Baverstock gives advice on how to attract the attention of a literary agent.

Literary agents perform a very valuable sifting function for publishing houses. They are people with lots of publishing experience, who are offered a wide variety of work, in various stages of development. The agents bring the material they favour to the attention of the publishers they think will like them too. Of course that's not to say that all great potential writers have agents, or that all new authors taken on by publishing houses have agents, just that amongst the newly published, there will be more authors with agents than authors without. Stories of what go on to become bestselling books being spotted on a 'slush pile' (the pile of unsolicited manuscripts that all publishing houses accumulate without asking for them) do occur, but they are memorable precisely because they are rare.

The nature of literary agents

Many agents have been publishers themselves. It follows that they like to specialise (usually in the kind of titles they used to publish, or in which they have a strong personal interest) and that they have an encyclopedic view of the industry.

Agents tend to work a bit like advertising agencies, in that they tend to have just one major client in each field. So just as an advertising agency would not represent two directly competing accounts, it would be unlikely that a literary agent would take on two authors whose books were very similar. This is particularly true in the non-fiction market where having two directly competing authors would be bound to cause difficulties.

Generalising further, literary agents are gregarious, fond of being noticed (they tend to dress quite strikingly), are good talkers (they certainly seem to know everyone), dramatic travellers (fond of hopping on and off planes in a blaze of self-generated publicity), are good negotiators (their livelihood depends on it as well as that of the authors they represent) and are not immune to vanity – so mentioning that you heard them speak, or making it clear you know who they are and particularly want to be represented by *them*, tends to go down well.

What's in it for the agent?

I always think the secret of a good business proposal is to look at it from your would-be collaborator's viewpoint rather than your own. Thus when seeking sponsorship, you get a far better response if you explain what the potential sponsor will get out of a relationship with you than if you tell them how much you need the money. To paraphrase J.F. Kennedy, 'Think not what an agent can do for you, but what you can do for an agent.' Taking the same approach, agents are looking for writers (a) with talent (and can you prove it by providing quotes from satisfied readers/reviewers?); (b) who can sustain their writing beyond one book (and thus will be ongoing earners and repay the initial investment of time they make in you); (c) who are topical (all agents and publishers claim to be looking for the 'next big thing'); (d) who are different, or have a new slant to bring to an existing strand of publishing; and (e) who are *promotable* (a key publishing term meaning interesting or memorable to the media). How you come over (or are likely to come over) in the press/on the air will be a key factor in deciding whether or not to take you on.

The money side of things needs a little more consideration. Whilst most agents are book lovers, and enjoy what they do, their service is not there as a wider service to literature in general but to make a profit. As well as a talent for writing they are looking for financial remuneration. So whilst an agent may be willing to help you shape your novel, provide advice on your style, advise you on how to prepare for an interview, they will be doing these things in the hope that you will reward them with books that sell rather than out of pure altruism.

Whatever advance the author gets, their agent usually gets 15% of it, so it is in the agent's interest to sell the book for the highest amount of money, or to the publishing house that is most likely to make a long-term success of the writer's career. This may lead the cynical to conclude that agents are more likely to be interested in media-friendly (or just media-based) authors than pure literary genius, but it is through success of key names that they are able to take a punt on new writers. An agency that confined itself to literary fiction alone, and ignored the popular market completely, would probably not last long.

Top tips for securing the attention of an agent

1. Do your research. Consult *Literary agents UK and Ireland* starting on page 429 of this *Yearbook*, look at what kind of writers each agent represents and note their specialities. If they say they do not take science fiction, do not assume you are helpfully extending their range by offering it. Send an email outlining what you have in mind and ask who is the right person within their firm to send it to. Don't assume that if the agency is called 'Snodgrass and Wilkins' you must talk only to one of the two key names. The chances are their books will be full already – or they may be long deceased. A more junior member of staff may be hungrier for new authors, and don't forget that their judgement will be backed – because they are a staff member and presumably have been taken on by the partners to extend the range of those they represent. And one day they too may be on the letterhead.

2. Don't necessarily be put off by the request for no unsolicited submissions. If they say 'No unsolicited submissions' you may decide to interpret this as 'No ill-considered submissions'. All agents need some new writers; you have to make the case for their next choice being you.

3. Send in what they ask for, not more or less. Note whether they request print or email submissions and send your material in exactly the format they ask for. Three chapters and a synopsis means just that, it is not code for 'anything over three chapters' or 'as near as you can get to three chapters'. Make the three chapters sequential, not chosen at random. If the first three are not also the best, think carefully before sending anything.

4. Ensure the book has a really good title. It's tempting to think that writing the book is the really important thing and that the title can grow out of the writing later. Wrong. The title is extremely important. It should catch the agent's attention and stick in the memory. Think how the same thing works for you in bookshops. I recently bought a copy of *Fifty is Not a Four-letter Word* by Linda Kelsey simply because I liked the title. I was looking for a present for a friend and I thought her fancy would be tickled by it too.

Heather Holden-Brown of the hhb agency says: 'The title matters hugely. I want something that excites me, and that will draw a similarly instant reaction from any publisher I mention it to. So go for something that is topical, intriguing or witty and to the point.'

5. Write a synopsis. This should be an outline of what kind of book you are writing, it is not your chance to give a detailed listing of what is in each chapter. It should start by ensuring the agent can grasp in their mind very precisely what kind of writer is on offer – this is important because it may enable them to think what kind of publisher it would appeal to.

If you can, say which section of the bookshop your title would be stocked in (don't just say the table at the front!) and list writers whose books are already in this category. Booksellers are very loathed to stock titles they don't know where to put, and agents may be unwilling to back a title that has no natural home. A friend of a friend wanted to write a book on the menopause and to call it *How Long Before I Can Hang-glide?*. A bookseller friend persuaded her that whilst this would make a very good subtitle, people looking for books on the subject would be in danger of not finding it – unless they were by chance looking in the sports section.

6. Write a book blurb for your work. Think what goes on the back of most books and how important it is in attracting attention to the title inside. A book blurb should be a fair representation of the style of the book, should tempt the reader to want to know more *now*, and should not give away the ending. Writing a book blurb is harder than you think, and is an excellent way of getting yourself noticed by an agent.

7. Send an interesting CV on yourself. This is not the time to rehash your formal one; a literary agent is not interested in how you did at 'O'/GCSE or 'A' level. Rather, what they do need to know is what you have done that makes you an interesting proposition to a publishing house. Remember agents are interested in how 'promotable' any potential new author is. This could be your job, your family commitments or your past experience. Don't assume that what you consider boring or mundane will be viewed in the same light by those you are approaching. A background working in the City is not the normal path to becoming a novelist and so may be well received by an agent. Similarly your domestic arrangements may be equally ordinary to you but interesting when combined with the fact that you have written a book.

Take an imaginative approach to your past and think creatively. A friend of mine once used a revolving door in an American hotel at the same time as a well-known actor and would proudly boast that she had 'been around in New York with Cary Grant.' I have four children and have always moved house mid-pregnancy, hence the scan and the birth never took place in the same hospital. Whereas this is entirely a function of my husband's peripatetic job, my publishers got quite excited when I told them. What have you done that can be made to sound interesting?

8. Do you have anyone else who can say what you write is good? This does not have to be a celebrity (although they are always useful) but what about other readers, writers and friends with relevant job titles? It's not hard to get testimonials for your work – many people like to be asked; some will oblige out of pure friendship, others for the publicity it may bring them.

9. Can you prove that there is a market for what you write? When an agent approaches a publisher to enthuse about a new author they will have to justify the claims they make on your behalf, and the newer the feel of what you want to write, the harder they will have to work. It's not good enough to say 'everyone will want to read' this new title. So, find out the viewing figures for programmes that relate to the book you want to write, or the sales of magazines that have a strong overlap with your material. Think laterally. For example, I co-wrote a book on raising teenagers (*Whatever!*, Piatkus 2005) and there is very little published in this market. It seemed to me that my subject was really modern morality; how to provide guidance in a fast-changing world. To prove there is a market I took as examples the healthy book sales of popular philosophy titles by A.C. Grayling and the number of people who have taken an Alpha course (over 3 million in the UK and 18 million worldwide so far). The agent I approached told me this widening of the issue really made a difference to how he viewed my proposal.

If you have already self-published material say how many sales/downloads have been achieved so far. It is no longer the case that agents only consider those who have *not* self-published; today it is a good route to demonstrating demand for your writing.

10. Write a really good letter to accompany the package you send to an agent. This may take you a long time but a good letter of introduction is well worth the trouble. It should outline all of the above: what kind of book you want to publish, how far down the road you have got, what is noteworthy about you as a person, who else thinks so.

Some agents acknowledge what they receive, others do not. You could ask them to email receipt, or enclose a stamped addressed postcard with a reminder to let you know they have received it. This is a further opportunity to remind them you are a human being, so try a witty postcard or add a caption to an image to make the point that you are dying to hear from them! For inspiration, look at the card selection in a local art gallery and think which picture sums up your mood as you wait for them to respond.

Finally, do remember that agents are individuals, and perhaps more individualistic than the key protagonists in many other professions. Just as many are instantly recognisable, they also have very individual taste. It follows that what does not appeal to one may well appeal to another. So if your first choice does not immediately sign you up, there may be others who think you are the next best thing since sliced bread! But they will only find out about you if you have the gumption to keep going. In the long run, getting an agent on your side is invariably worth the effort.

Carole Blake of Blake Friedmann says: 'We receive at least 20 unsolicited manuscripts a day, our books are full and to be honest we are looking for reasons to say no – but I still get such excitement from a really new voice writing something that grabs my attention. I have known the world stand still as I ignore the rest of the post and just read on until I have finished. When that happens it's really special – and I will fight to get that author published. Sometimes it takes years, but if I believe in an author I will keep going.'

Alison Baverstock is a former publisher who has written 19 books. *Marketing Your Book: An Author's Guide* (A&C Black 2007, 2nd edn) gives writers guidance on how to present their work to agents, publishers and readers. *Is There a Book in You?* (A&C Black 2006) outlines the resources needed by writers and offers advice on how to achieve publication. Her most recent book is *The Naked Author: A Guide to Self-publishing* (A&C Black 2011). She teaches marketing – to authors, publishers and others – at Kingston University and is represented by Jenny Brown of Jenny Brown Associates. Her website is www.alisonbaverstock.com.

See also...

- *Writing a synopsis*, page 118
- *How to get an agent*, page 416
- *Making a successful submission to a literary agent*, page 418

Literary agents UK and Ireland

The *Writers' & Artists' Yearbook*, along with the Association of Authors' Agents and the Society of Authors, takes a dim view of any literary agent who asks potential clients for a fee prior to a manuscript being placed with a publisher. We advise you to treat any such request with caution and to let us know if that agent appears in the listings below. However, agents may charge additional costs later in the process but these should only arise once a book has been accepted by a publisher and the author is earning an income. We urge authors to make the distinction between upfront and additional charges.

*Full member of the Association of Authors' Agents

A & B Personal Management Ltd

PO Box 64671, London NW3 9LH
tel 020-7794 3255
email billellis@aandb.co.uk
Directors R.W. Ellis, R. Ellis

Full-length MSS, scripts for TV, theatre, cinema; also novels, fiction and non-fiction. No unsolicited material. Email or telephone before submitting anything. Founded 1982.

Sheila Ableman Literary Agency*

36 Duncan House, 7–9 Fellows Road, London NW3 3LZ
tel 020-7586 2339
email sheila@sheilaableman.co.uk
website www.sheilaableman.com
Contact Sheila Ableman

Non-fiction including history, science, biography, autobiography (home 15%, USA/translation 20%). Specialises in TV tie-ins and celebrity ghostwriting. No poetry, children's, gardening or sport. Unsolicited MSS welcome. Approach in writing with publishing history, CV, synopsis, 3 chapters and sae for return. No reading fee. Founded 1999.

The Agency (London) Ltd*

24 Pottery Lane, London W11 4LZ
tel 020-7727 1346 *fax* 020-7727 9037
email info@theagency.co.uk
website www.theagency.co.uk
Children's Book Executive Hilary Delamere

Represents authors and illustrators of children's books for all ages, preschool to teen fiction (home 15%, overseas 20%); works in conjunction with overseas subagents. Also represents screenwriters, directors, playwrights and composers (10%). Adult novels represented only for existing clients. For film/TV/theatre executives, please email. No unsolicited material. Founded 1995.

Aitken Alexander Associates Ltd*

18–21 Cavaye Place, London SW10 9PT
tel 020-7373 8672 *fax* 020-7373 6002
email reception@aitkenalexander.co.uk
website www.aitkenalexander.co.uk
Contacts Gillon Aitken, Clare Alexander, Andrew Kidd, Sally Riley, Lesley Thorne (Directors), Matthew Hamilton, Ayesha Karim, Charlotte Robertson; children's & YA fiction: Gillie Russell, Cassie Metcalf-Slovo; film/TV/stage rights: Lesley Thorne, Leah Middleton. *Associated Agents* Anthony Sheil, Mary Pachnos, Lucy Luck

Fiction and non-fiction (home 15%, USA 20%, translation 20%, film/TV 15%). No plays or scripts. Send preliminary letter with half-page synopsis and first 30pp of sample material and adequate return postage in first instance. No reading fee.

Clients include Clare Allan, Lisa Appignanesi, Pat Barker, Paul Brannigan, Jung Chang, Clare Clark, John Cornwell, John Crace, Simon Day, Sarah Dunant, Susan Elderkin, Diana Evans, Roopa Farooki, Sebastian Faulks, Helen Fielding, Germaine Greer, Mark Haddon, Mohammed Hanif, Susan Howatch, Liz Jensen, Dom Joly, Peter Kay, John Keegan, Tim Lott, Mark Lowery, Grace McCleen, Holly McQueen, Pankaj Mishra, Caroline Moorehead, Thomas Penn, Primrose Bakery, Jonathan Raban, Anna Ralph, Louise Rennison, Michèle Roberts, Jennie Rooney, Shaun Ryder, Edward St Aubyn, James Scudamore, Nicholas Shakespeare, Gillian Slovo, Rory Stewart, Nick Stone, Colin Thubron, Robert Twigger, Amanda Vickery, Penny Vincenzi, Willy Vlautin, Andrew Wilson, Robert Wilson, Moira Young. UK only – Harper Lee, J.D. Salinger.

Estates – John Betjeman, Bruce Chatwin, Paul Gallico, Ian Hamilton, Ngaio Marsh, Shiva Naipaul, Mary Norton, Slavomir Rawicz. Founded 1977.

Jacintha Alexander Associates – see LAW (Lucas Alexander Whitley Ltd)

The Ampersand Agency Ltd*

Ryman's Cottages, Little Tew, Oxon OX7 4JJ
tel (01608) 683677/683898 *fax* (01608) 683449
email info@theampersandagency.co.uk
website www.theampersandagency.co.uk
Contact Peter Buckman, Anne-Marie Doulton

Literary and commercial fiction and non-fiction (home 15%, USA 15–20%, translation 20%). No reading fee.

Clients include Helen Black, S.J. Bolton, Druin Burch, Vanessa Curtis, J.D. Davies, Will Davis, Cora Harrison, Richard Pierce, Mark Roberts, Ivo Stourton, Vikas Swarup, Henry Venmore-Rowland, Michael Walters and the estates of Georgette Heyer, Angela Thirkell, Winifred Foley and John James. Founded 2003.

Darley Anderson Literary, TV and Film Agency*

Estelle House, 11 Eustace Road, London SW6 1JB
tel 020-7386 2674
email enquiries@darleyanderson.com
website www.darleyanderson.com, www.darleyandersonchildrens.com
Contacts Darley Anderson (thrillers, women's fiction and non-fiction), Camilla Wray (crime, thrillers and mystery), Sophie Gordon (children's including young adult and crossover), Clare Wallace (general and women's fiction, Rights Manager), Vicki Le Feuvre (Editor), Mary Darby (Rights Assistant), Rosanna Bellingham (Financial Controller)

All commercial fiction and non-fiction; children's fiction (for all ages including young adult and crossover), non-fiction, picture books and illustration (home 15%, USA/translation 20%, film/TV/radio 20%). No poetry, academic books, scripts or screenplays. Send covering letter, short synopsis and first 3 chapters. Return postage/sae essential for reply. *Overseas associates* APA Talent & Literary Agency (LA/Hollywood) and leading foreign agents worldwide.

Special interests (fiction): all types of thrillers, crime and mystery. All types of American and Irish novels. All types of popular women's fiction and accessible literary/Richard and Judy Book Club-type fiction. Also comic fiction. Children's fiction for all ages (including young adult and crossover), picture books and illustration.

Special interests (non-fiction): celebrity autobiographies, biographies, sports books, 'true-life' women in jeopardy, revelatory history and science, popular psychology, self improvement, diet, beauty, health, fashion, animals, humour/cartoon, cookery, gardening, inspirational, religious.

Clients include Alex Barclay, Constance Briscoe, Chris Carter, Cathy Cassidy, Lee Child, Martina Cole, John Connolly, Jane Costello, A.J. Cross, Jason Dean, Margaret Dickinson, Clare Dowling, Tana French, Helen Grant, Michelle Harrison, Tara Hyland, Fr Ken Leech, James Leighton, Rani Manicka, Chris Mooney, Annie Murray, Lesley Pearse, Lynda Page, Adrian Plass, Carmen Reid, Rebecca Shaw, Sean Slater, Lucy Summers, Elizabeth Waite, Tim Weaver, Lee Weeks, Kimberley Willis.

Anubis Literary Agency

7 Birdhaven Close, Lighthorne, Warwick CV35 0BE
tel (01926) 642588 *fax* (01926) 642588
Contact Steve Calcutt

Genre fiction: science fiction, fantasy and horror (home 15%, USA/translation 20%). No other material considered. Send 50pp with a one-page synopsis (sae essential). No reading fee. No telephone calls. Works with The Marsh Agency Ltd on translation rights. Founded 1994.

Author Literary Agents

53 Talbot Road, London N6 4QX
tel 020-8341 0442 *mobile* 07767 022659
email agile@authors.co.uk
Contact John Havergal

Novels, thrillers, faction, non-fiction, graphic novels, children's books and graphic and illustrated media edutainment concepts (home 15%, overseas/translations 20%, advertising/sales promotion one-third). Pitches to publishers and producers. Send first chapter, scene or section, and graphics samples (if any), plus a half/one-page plot or topic outline together with sae. No reading fee. Founded 1997.

Diane Banks Associates Ltd*

email submissions@dianebanks.co.uk
website www.dianebanks.co.uk
Contact Diane Banks

Commercial fiction and non-fiction (home 15%, overseas 20%). Fiction: women's, crime, thrillers, literary fiction with a strong storyline, young adult. Non-fiction: memoir, real-life stories, celebrity, autobiography, biography, business, popular history, popular science, self-help, popular psychology, fashion, health & beauty. No poetry, children's, academic books, plays, scripts or short stories. Send brief CV, synopsis and sample chapters as Word or Open Document attachments. Aim to give initial response within 2 weeks. No reading fee.

Authors include Professor Brian Cox, Professor Jeff Forshaw, Sasha Wagstaff, Tara Moore, Polly Courtney, Adam Palmer, Alex Higgins, Andy Taylor (Duran Duran), Miss S, Shelina Janmohamed, Marisa Merico. Founded 2006.

The Bell Lomax Moreton Agency

Ground Floor, Watergate House, 13–15 York Buildings, London WC2N 6JU
tel 020-7930 4447 *fax* 020-7839 2667
email info@bell-lomax.co.uk
website www.bell-lomax.co.uk
Executives Eddie Bell, Pat Lomax, Paul Moreton, June Bell, Josephine Hayes

Quality fiction and non-fiction, biography, children's, business and sport. No unsolicited MSS without preliminary letter. No poetry, screenplays or scripts. No reading fee. Founded 2000.

Michael Berenti Literary Management

46 Warwick Way, Suite 16, London SW1 1RY
email admin@michaelberenti.com
website www.michaelberenti.com
Director Michael Berenti

Contacts Michael Berenti (thrillers, crime, suspense, current affairs, military, TV and film scripts), Natasha Hewitt (literary and commercial fiction, drama), Kate Sheldon (non-fiction, social, history, sci-fi).

Fiction: literary, general commercial, thrillers, crime, suspense, drama, fantasy, science fiction. Non-fiction: politics, social sciences, current affairs, history, military. Also film and TV scripts. Considers unpublished authors. Please check website for submission guidelines as they may change. Founded 2008.

The Blair Partnership

1st Floor, 8–14 Vine Hill, London EC1R 5DX
tel 020-7504 2534 *fax* 020-7504 2521
email info@theblairpartnership.com, submissions@theblairpartnership.com
website www.theblairpartnership.com
Agents Neil Blair, Zoe King

Considers all genres of fiction and non-fiction for adults, young readers and children. Will consider unsolicited MSS. Please email the first 10 pages of your work with a covering letter and a one-page synopsis to submissions@theblairpartnership.com. Alternatively you can submit the same via post but include sae for return of work.

Authors include Jason and Daniel Freeman, Inbali Iserles, Kieren Larwood, Pearl Lowe, Maajid Nawaz, J.K. Rowling.

Blake Friedmann Literary, TV & Film Agency Ltd*

122 Arlington Road, London NW1 7HP
tel 020-7284 0408 *fax* 020-7284 0442
email [firstname]@blakefriedmann.co.uk
website www.blakefriedmann.co.uk
Directors Carole Blake, Julian Friedmann, Isobel Dixon *Agents* Oliver Munson, Conrad Williams, Adrian Clarke

Full-length MSS. Fiction: thrillers, women's novels and literary fiction; non-fiction: investigative books, biography, travel; no poetry or plays (home 15%, overseas 20%). Specialises in film and TV rights; place journalism and short stories for existing clients only. Represented worldwide in 26 markets. Preliminary letter, synopsis and first 2 chapters preferred via email. No reading fee. See website for full submission guidelines.

Authors include Gilbert Adair, Sandy Balfour, Edward Carey, Elizabeth Chadwick, Barbara Erskine, Garen Ewing, David Gillman, Ann Granger, Ken Hom, Peter James, Deon Meyer, Lawrence Norfolk, Gregory Norminton, Joseph O'Connor, Sheila O'Flanagan, Mario Reading, Michael Ridpath, Craig Russell, Julian Stockwin. Founded 1977.

Luigi Bonomi Associates Ltd*

91 Great Russell Street, London WC1B 3PS
tel 020-7637 1234 *fax* 020-7637 2111
email info@bonomiassociates.co.uk
website www.bonomiassociates.co.uk
Directors Luigi Bonomi, Amanda Preston

Fiction and non-fiction (home 15%, overseas 20%). Fiction: commercial and literary fiction, thrillers, crime, young adult, children's, women's fiction. Non-fiction: history, science, parenting, lifestyle. No poetry. Keen to find new authors and help them develop their careers. Send preliminary letter, synopsis and first 3 chapters. No reading fee. Works with foreign agencies and has links with film and TV production companies including Endemol, HatTrick and BBC Worldwide.

Authors include Will Adams, Kirstie Allsopp, James Becker, Amanda Brooke, Fern Britton, Jo Carnegie, Sam Christer, Gennaro Contaldo, Josephine Cox, James Cracknell, Dean Crawford, A.M. Dean, Matthew Dunn, David Gibbins, Andrew Hammond, Richard Hammond, Matt Hilton, John Humphrys, Graham Joyce, Simon Kernick, Victoria Lamb, John Lucas, Colin McDowell, James May, Gavin Menzies, Mike Morley, Sue Palmer, Andrew Pepper, Melanie Phillips, Gervase Phinn, Louise Reid, Alice Roberts, Mike Rossiter, Jack Steel, Karen Swan, Prof. Bryan Sykes, Alan Titchmarsh, Phil Vickery, Sir Terry Wogan. Founded 2005.

The Book Bureau Literary Agency

7 Duncairn Avenue, Bray, Co. Wicklow, Republic of Ireland
tel/fax +353 (0)12 764996
email thebookbureau@oceanfree.net
Managing Director Geraldine Nichol

Full-length MSS (home 15%, USA/translation 20%). Fiction preferred – thrillers, crime, Irish novels, literary fiction, women's commercial novels and general fiction. No horror, science fiction, children's or poetry. Strong editorial support. No reading fee. Preliminary letter, synopsis and 3 sample chapters (single line spacing). Return postage essential, IRCs from UK and abroad. Works with agents overseas.

BookBlast Ltd

PO Box 20184, London W10 5AU
tel 020-8968 3089
email gen@bookblast.com
website www.bookblast.com
Contact Address material to the company

Full-length MSS (home 12%, overseas 20%), TV and radio (15%), film (20%). Fiction and non-fiction. Literary and general adult fiction and non-fiction (memoir, travel, popular culture, multicultural writing only). Radio, TV and film rights sold mainly in works by existing clients. No reading fee. Editorial advice given to own authors. Initiates in-house projects. Also offers translation consultancy and literary PR services. Currently not taking on new clients. Founded 1997.

Alan Brodie Representation

Paddock Suite, The Courtyard, 55 Charterhouse Street, London EC1M 6HA

tel 020-7253 6226 *fax* 020-7183 7999
email info@alanbrodie.com
website www.alanbrodie.com
Managing Director Alan Brodie, *Agents* Sarah McNair, Lisa Foster, Harriet Pennington Legh

Specialises in stage plays, radio, TV and film (home 10%, overseas 15%). No prose, fiction or general MSS. Represented in all major countries. No unsolicited scripts; recommendation from known professional required. Founded 1996.

Jenny Brown Associates*

33 Argyle Place, Edinburgh EH9 1JT
tel 0131 229 5334
email info@jennybrownassociates.com
website www.jennybrownassociates.com
Contact Jenny Brown, Mark Stanton, Lucy Juckes, Allan Guthrie, Kevin Pocklington, Bob McDevitt

Literary fiction, crime writing and writing for children; non-fiction: biography, history, sport, music, popular culture (home 12.5%, overseas/translation 20%). No poetry, science fiction, fantasy or academic. No reading fee. Check website for submission guidelines.

Clients include Lin Anderson, Robert Douglas, Jennie Erdal, Rodge Glass, Alex Gray, Doug Jackson, Sara Maitland, Tom Pow, Natasha Solomons, Paul Torday, Esther Woolfson. Founded 2002.

Felicity Bryan Associates*

2A North Parade, Banbury Road, Oxford OX2 6LX
tel (01865) 513816 *fax* (01865) 310055
email agency@felicitybryan.com
website www.felicitybryan.com

Fiction and general non-fiction with emphasis on history, biography, science and current affairs (home 15%, overseas 20%). No scripts for TV, radio or theatre, no crafts, how-to, science fiction, light romance or poetry. No email submissions.

Clients include Carlos Acosta, David Almond, Karen Armstrong, Mary Berry, Simon Blackburn, Archie Brown, Marcus Chown, Artemis Cooper, Edmund de Waal, John Dickie, Tim Harford, A.C. Grayling, Sadie Jones, Liza Klausmann, Simon Lelic, Diarmaid MacCulloch, Martin Meredith, James Naughtie, John Julius Norwich, Gemma O'Connor, Iain Pears, Rosamunde Pilcher, Matt Ridley, Eugene Rogan, Meg Rosoff, Miriam Stoppard, Roy Strong, Roma Tearne, Adrian Tinniswood, Anna Whitelock, Lucy Worsley and the estate of Humphrey Carpenter.

Juliet Burton Literary Agency*

2 Clifton Avenue, London W12 9DR
tel 020-8762 0148 *fax* 020-8743 8765
email juliet.burton@btinternet.com
Contact Juliet Burton

Handles fiction and non-fiction. Special interests include crime and women's fiction. No science fiction/fantasy, children's, short stories, plays, film scripts, articles, poetry or academic material. Commission: home 15%, US & translation 20%. Approach in writing in the first instance with synopsis and 2 sample chapters and sae. No reading fee. Founded 1999.

Campbell Thomson & McLaughlin Ltd – see The Marsh Agency Ltd

Capel & Land Ltd*

29 Wardour Street, London W1D 6PS
tel 020-7734 2414 *fax* 020-7734 8101
email rachel@capelland.co.uk
website www.capelland.com
Agents Georgina Capel (literary), Anita Land (TV)

Literary and commercial fiction, history, biography; film and TV (home/overseas 15%). No reading fee; see website for submission guidelines.

Clients include Simon Barnes, Nicky Campbell, Flora Fraser, John Gimlette, Adrian Goldsworthy, K.M. Grant, Andrew Greig, Tristram Hunt, Tobias Jones, Leanda de Lisle, Colleen McCullough, Marion McGilvary, Jonathan Meades, Adam Nicolson, Jeremy Paxman, Andrew Roberts, Ian Sansom, Simon Sebag Montefiore, Diana Souhami, Stella Rimington, Louis Theroux, Giles Tremlett, Fay Weldon. Founded 1999.

CardenWright Literary Agency

27 Khyber Road, London SW11 2PZ
mobile 07789 000608
email gen@cardenwright.com
website www.cardenwright.com
Contacts Genevieve Carden (book/theatre agent), Philippe Carden (theatre agent), Rachel Wright (TV/film consultant)

Commercial and literary fiction and non-fiction (home 15%, overseas 20%), scripts for theatre (15%), film and TV rights (10%). No reading fee. Will suggest revision. Submit by email a covering letter, one-page synopsis and CV plus the first 50pp (novel), chapter outline and sample chapter (non-fiction), or play script. No postal submissions.

Authors include Nitza Abuhatzeira Brown, Michael Butterworth, Sally Donovan, R.J. Morgan, Allen Pizzey, Daniela Norris and Shireen Anabtawi. *Playwrights* include Grant Buchanan Marshall, Miranda Walker and Nikolay Yakimchuk. Founded 2009.

Casarotto Ramsay & Associates Ltd

(formerly Margaret Ramsay Ltd and Casarotto Company Ltd)
Waverley House, 7–12 Noel Street, London W1F 8GQ
tel 020-7287 4450 *fax* 020-7287 9128
email info@casarotto.co.uk
website www.casarotto.co.uk
Directors Jenne Casarotto, Giorgio Casarotto, Tom Erhardt, Mel Kenyon, Jodi Shields, Rachel Holroyd

MSS – theatre, films, TV, sound broadcasting only (10%). Works in conjunction with agents in USA and other foreign countries. Preliminary letter essential.

Writers include Alan Ayckbourn, the estate of J.G. Ballard, Edward Bond, Howard Brenton, Caryl Churchill, the estate of Roald Dahl, Tony Grisoni, Christopher Hampton, David Hare, Nick Hornby, Amy Jenkins, Laura Jones, Neil Jordan, Frank McGuiness, Phyllis Nagy, Neal Purvis, Mark Ravenhill, Willy Russell, Martin Sherman, Shawn Slovo, Peter Straughan, Jack Thorne, Robert Wade, David Wood. For full client list see website. Founded 1989.

Celia Catchpole

56 Gilpin Avenue, London SW14 8QY
tel 020-8255 4835
email celia@celiacatchpole.co.uk, james@celiacatchpole.co.uk
website www.celiacatchpole.co.uk
Director Celia Catchpole, *Agent* James Catchpole

Agents for authors and illustrators of children's books for all ages. Commission: 10–15%. For submissions do not use the email addresses above but see website for guidelines.

Chapman & Vincent*

7 Dilke Street, London SW3 4JE
tel/fax 020-7352 5582
email chapmanvincent@hotmail.co.uk
Directors Jennifer Chapman, Gilly Vincent

Handles illustrated non-fiction work only. Not actively seeking new clients but will consider original work – not travel, domestic tragedies or academic books. Submissions require synopsis, 2 sample chapters and sae. Also considers email enquiries without attachments. Do not telephone. No reading fee. Works with The Elaine Markson Agency. Commission: home 15%; US and Europe 20%.

Clients include George Carter, Leslie Geddes-Brown, Lucinda Lambton and Eve Pollard. Founded 1992.

Mic Cheetham Associates Ltd

50 Albemarle Street, London W1S 4BD
tel 020-7495 2002 *fax* 020-7399 2801
website www.miccheetham.com
Director Mic Cheetham, *Contacts* Mic Cheetham, Simon Kavanagh

General and literary fiction, science fiction, some non-fiction (home/overseas 15–20%); film, TV and radio rights (10–20%); will suggest revision. Works with The Marsh Agency Ltd for foreign rights. No unsolicited MSS. No reading fee. Founded 1994.

Teresa Chris Literary Agency Ltd*

43 Musard Road, London W6 8NR
tel 020-7386 0633
email teresachris@litagency.co.uk
website www.teresachrisliteraryagency.co.uk
Director Teresa Chris

All fiction, especially crime, women's commercial, general and literary fiction. No science fiction, horror, fantasy, short stories, poetry, academic books (home 10%, overseas 20%). No reading fee. Send introductory letter describing work, first 3 chapters and sae. Representation in all overseas territories. Founded 1988.

Mary Clemmey Literary Agency*

6 Dunollie Road, London NW5 2XP
tel 020-7267 1290 *fax* 020-7813 9757
email mcwords@googlemail.com

High-quality fiction and non-fiction with an international market (home 15%, overseas 20%, performance rights 15%). No children's books or science fiction. TV, film, radio and theatre scripts from existing clients only. Works in conjunction with US agent. No reading fee. No unsolicited MSS and no email submissions. Approach first by letter (including sae).

US clients include Lynn C. Franklin Associates Ltd, The Miller Agency, Roslyn Targ, Weingel-Fidel Agency Inc. Founded 1992.

Jonathan Clowes Ltd*

10 Iron Bridge House, Bridge Approach, London NW1 8BD
tel 020-7722 7674 *fax* 0971-528 3647
email admin@jonathanclowes.co.uk
website www.jonathanclowes.co.uk
Directors Jonathan Clowes, Ann Evans, Nemonie Craven, Olivia Guest

Literary and commercial fiction and non-fiction, film, TV, theatre and radio (home 15%, overseas 20%). No reading fee. No unsolicited MSS. Email for general enquiries. Works in association with agents overseas. Founded 1960.

Clients include Dr David Bellamy, Sir Arthur Conan Doyle copyrights, Simon Critchley, Len Deighton, Victoria Glass, Elizabeth Jane Howard, Carla Lane, Doris Lessing, Mario Matassa, David Nobbs.

Rosica Colin Ltd

1 Clareville Grove Mews, London SW7 5AH
tel 020-7370 1080 *fax* 020-7244 6441
Directors Sylvie Marston, Joanna Marston

All full-length MSS (excluding science fiction and poetry); also theatre, film and sound broadcasting (home 10%, overseas 10–20%). No reading fee, but may take 3–4 months to consider full MSS. Send synopsis only in first instance, with letter outlining writing credits and whether MS has been previously submitted, plus return postage.

Authors include Richard Aldington, Simone de Beauvoir (in UK), Samuel Beckett (publication rights), Steven Berkoff, Alan Brownjohn, Sandy Brownjohn, Donald Campbell, Nick Dear, Neil Donnelly, J.T. Edson, Bernard Farrell, Rainer Werner

Fassbinder (in UK), Jean Genet, Franz Xaver Kroetz, Don McCamphill, Heiner Müller (in UK), Graham Reid, Alan Sillitoe, Botho Strauss (in UK), Rina Vergano, Anthony Vivis, Wim Wenders (in UK). Founded 1949.

Conville & Walsh Ltd*

2 Ganton Street, London W1F 7QL
tel 020-7287 3030 *fax* 020-7287 4545
email [firstname]@convilleandwalsh.com
website www.convilleandwalsh.com
Directors Clare Conville, Patrick Walsh, Jake Smith-Bosanquet *(Foreign Rights)*, Alan Oliver *(Finance)*

Handles all genres of fiction, non-fiction and children's worldwide (home 15%, US and translation 20%).

Fiction *clients* range from the Booker Prize winner D.B.C. Pierre to John Llewellyn Rhys Prize winner Sarah Hall, to Orwell Prize winner Delia Jarrett-Macauley and the Desmond Elliott Prize winner Ali Shaw. Other novelists include Isabel Wolff, S.J. Watson, Nick Harkaway, Stephen Kelman, John Niven, Shelley Harris, Howard Marks, Rachel Joyce, M.L. Stedman, Adam Creed, Matt Dunn and Michael Cordy.

Non-fiction *clients* include Tom Holland, Helen Castor, Simon Singh, Ben Wilson, Christian Jessen, Gavin Pretor-Pinney, Belle de Jour, Richard Wiseman, Kate Rew, Natalie Haynes, Clive Stafford-Smith, Misha Glenny, Marcus Berkmann and Jim al-Khalili. Artists represented for books include David Shrigley, Steven Appleby and the estate of Francis Bacon. Comedians and satirists represented include Vic Reeves and Charlie Brooker. Children's and young adult list includes John Burningham, Damian Dibben, Steve Voake, David Bedford, Katie Davies, Rebecca James, P.J. Lynch and the estate of Astrid Lindgren. Founded 2000.

Jane Conway-Gordon Ltd*

38 Cromwell Grove, London W6 7RG
tel 020-7371 6939
email jane@conway-gordon.co.uk

Full length MSS (home 15%, overseas 20%). No poetry, science fiction or children's. Represented in all foreign countries. No reading fee but preliminary letter and return postage essential. Founded 1982.

Coombs Moylett Literary Agency

120 New Kings Road, London SW6 4LZ
tel 020-8740 0454 *fax* 020-7736 3500
email lisa@coombsmoylett.com
website www.coombsmoylett.com
Contacts Lisa Moylett

Commercial and literary fiction (home 15%, overseas 20%, film/TV 20%). Specialises in well-written commercial fiction, particularly in the genres of historical fiction, crime/mystery/suspense and thrillers, and women's fiction across a spectrum ranging from chick-lit to sagas to contemporary and literary fiction. Does not handle non-fiction, poetry, plays or scripts for film and TV. Send synopsis, first 3 chapters and sae (essential). No disk or email submissions. No reading fee. Works with foreign agents.

Creative Authors Ltd

11A Woodlawn Street, Whitstable, Kent CT5 1HQ
email write@creativeauthors.co.uk
website www.creativeauthors.co.uk
Director Isabel Atherton

Fiction, women's fiction, literary fiction, non-fiction, humour, history, science, autobiography, biography, business, memoir, mind, body & spirit, health, cookery, arts and crafts, crime, children's fiction, picture books, young adult, graphic novels (home 15%, overseas 20%). Only accepts email submissions.

Authors include Mark Beaumont, Bompas & Parr, Clare Gee, Robert Kelsey, Fiona McDonald, Adele Nozedar, Dr Keith Souter. Founded 2008.

The Creative Rights Agency

17 Prior Street, London SE10 8SF
tel 020-8149 3955
email info@creativerightsagency.co.uk
website www.creativerightsagency.co.uk
Contact Richard Scrivener

Specialises in male interest fiction, memoirs, contemporary culture and sports. Submit via email: sample chapters, synopsis and author biog. Also handles film/tv and licensing rights. Founded 2009.

Rupert Crew Ltd*

6 Windsor Road, London N3 3SS
tel 020-8346 3000 *fax* 020-8346 3009
email info@rupertcrew.co.uk
website www.rupertcrew.co.uk
Directors Doreen Montgomery, Caroline Montgomery

International representation, handling literary and commercial fiction and non-fiction for the adult and children's markets. Home 15%; overseas, TV/film and radio 20%. No picture books, plays, screenplays, poetry, journalism, science fiction, fantasy or short stories. No reading fee. No unsolicited MSS: see website for current submission guidelines. Founded 1927 by F. Rupert Crew.

Curtis Brown Group Ltd*

Haymarket House, 28–29 Haymarket, London SW1Y 4SP
tel 020-7393 4400 *fax* 020-7393 4401
email cb@curtisbrown.co.uk
website www.curtisbrown.co.uk
Ceo Jonathan Lloyd, *Coo* Ben Hall, *Directors* Jacquie Drewe, Jonny Geller, Nick Marston, Sarah Spear
Books Jonny Geller (Managing Director), Felicity Blunt, Sheila Crowley, Anna Davis, Jonathan Lloyd,

Vivienne Schuster, Elizabeth Sheinkman, Karolina Sutton, Stephanie Thwaites (Children's & Young Adult), Gordon Wise
Film/TV/Theatre Nick Marston (Managing Director), Jessica Cooper, Amanda Davis, Tally Garner, Ben Hall, Joe Phillips, Lily Williams
Actors Sarah Spear (Head of Acting Dept), Grace Clissold, Mary FitzGerald, Maxine Hoffman, Lucy Johnson, Sarah MacCormick, Grant Parsons, Kate Staddon, Olivia Woodward
Presenters Jacquie Drewe, Richard Gibb

Founded in 1899 and today one of the UK's most dynamic agencies, Curtis Brown represents prominent writers of fiction and non-fiction, from winners of all major awards to hugely successful international bestsellers, and formats ranging from print and audio to digital and merchandise. In fiction, works across many genres, both literary and those aimed at a popular audience, and looks for strong voices and outstanding storytellers in general fiction, crime, thrillers, psychological suspense, mainstream fantasy, historical fiction, young adult and children's books. Non-fiction list includes leading commentators and thinkers, historians, biographers, scientists and writers of quality narrative non-fiction. Represents a number of well-known personalities, from world-renowned politicians to business leaders and comedians. Curtis Brown also manages the international careers of authors, with strong relationships in translation and US markets. The Book Department works closely with a team of media agents, offering full-service representation in film, TV and theatre. A creative writing school, Curtis Brown Creative, has been established with the aim of finding and fostering new talent. For more information on submissions and individual agents, please consult website.

Judy Daish Associates Ltd

2 St Charles Place, London W10 6EG
tel 020-8964 8811 *fax* 020-8964 8966
email judy@judydaish.com
website www.judydaish.com
Agents Judy Daish, Howard Gooding, Tracey Elliston

Theatre, film, TV, radio (rates by negotiation). No unsolicited MSS. No reading fee. Founded 1978.

Caroline Davidson Literary Agency*

5 Queen Anne's Gardens, London W4 1TU
tel 020-8995 5768 *fax* 020-8994 2770
email enquiries@cdla.co.uk
website www.cdla.co.uk

Handles novels and non-fiction of high quality (12.5%). Send preliminary letter with CV and detailed, well thought-out book proposal/synopsis and/or first 50pp of novel. No email submissions. Large sae with return postage essential. No reading fee. Quick response. Refer to website for further information.

Authors include Peter Barham, Andrew Dalby, Emma Donoghue, Chris Greenhalgh, Ed Husain, Tom Jaine, Helena Whitbread. Founded 1988.

Merric Davidson Literary Agency – see MBA Literary and Script Agents Ltd

Felix de Wolfe

Kingsway House, 103 Kingsway, London WC2B 6QX
tel 020-7242 5066 *fax* 020-7242 8119

Theatre, films, TV, sound broadcasting, fiction (home 10–15%, overseas 20%). No reading fee. Works in conjunction with many foreign agencies. No unsolicited submissions.

DGA Ltd

55 Monmouth Street, London WC2H 9DG
tel 020-7240 9992 *fax* 020-7395 6110
email assistant@davidgodwinassociates.co.uk
website www.davidgodwinassociates.co.uk
Directors David Godwin, Heather Godwin

Literary fiction and general non-fiction. No reading fee; send sae for return of MSS. Founded 1995.

Dorian Literary Agency (DLA)*

Upper Thornehill, 27 Church Road, St Marychurch, Torquay, Devon TQ1 4QY
tel (01803) 312095
Contact Dorothy Lumley (proprietor)

General fiction, and specialising in popular fiction (home 15%, USA 15%, translation 20%). For adults: women's fiction, romance, historicals; crime and thrillers; science fiction, fantasy, dark fantasy and horror. Reading only very selectively. No short stories, young adult or children's fiction, non-fiction, comic material, poetry or drama. No reading fee. Contact initially by post with the first 3 chapters and brief outline plus return postage/sae or email address for reply. No telephone calls, faxes or emails please.

Authors include Gillian Bradshaw, Kate Charles, Kate Hardy, Glenda Larke, Brian Lumley, Stephen Jones, Andy Remic, Rosemary Rowe, Lyndon Stacey, Julia Williams. Founded 1986.

Robert Dudley Agency

50 Rannoch Road, London W6 9SR
mobile 07879 426574
email info@robertdudleyagency.co.uk
website www.robertdudleyagency.co.uk
Proprietor Robert Dudley

Non-fiction only. Specialises in history, biography, sport, management, politics, military history, current affairs (home 15%, overseas 20%; film/TV/radio 20%). No reading fee. Will suggest revision. Email submissions preferred. All material sent at owner's risk. No MSS returned without sae.

Authors include Steve Biko, Sarah Bridge, Chris Green, David Hanrahan, Mungo Melvin, Chris Parry, Tim Phillips, Brian Holden Reid, Chris Sidwells, Martyn Whittock, Dan Wilson. Founded 2000.

Toby Eady Associates Ltd

3rd Floor, 9 Orme Court, London W2 4RL
tel 020-7792 0092 *fax* 020-7792 0879
website www.tobyeadyassociates.co.uk
Contacts Toby Eady, Jamie Coleman, Zaria Rich

Fiction and non-fiction (home 15%, overseas/ film/ TV 20%). Special interests: China, Middle East, Africa, India. No film/TV scripts or poetry. Approach by personal recommendation. *Overseas associates* La Nouvelle Agence (France), Marco Vigevani Agenzia Letteraria (Germany, Italy), Silvia Meucci (Portugal, Spain), Jan Michael (Holland), Joanne Wang (China), ICM (USA). Send submissions to submissions@tobyeadyassociates.co.uk.

Clients include Nada Awar Jarrar, Jason Burke, Mark Burnell, John Carey, Emma Chapman, Ciaron Collins, Bernard Cornwell, Shereen El Feki, Gavin Elser, Fadia Faqir, Sophie Gee, Ching-He Huang, Susan Lewis, Diane Wei Liang, Julia Lovell, Francesca Marciano, Patrick Marnham, Richard Lloyd Parry, Deborah Scroggins, Samia Serageldin, Rachel Seiffert, John Stubbs, Paul Watson, Robert Winder, Zhu Wen, Alison Wong, Fan Wu, Xinran Xue. Estates of Peter Cheyney, Ted Lewis, Margaret Powell, Mary Wesley. Founded 1968.

Eddison Pearson Ltd*

West Hill House, 6 Swains Lane, London N6 6QS
tel 020-7700 7763 *fax* 020-7700 7866
email info@eddisonpearson.com
website www.eddisonpearson.com
Contact Clare Pearson

Children's and young adult books, fiction and non-fiction, poetry (home 10%, overseas 15–20%). Small personally run agency. Enquiries and submissions by email only; email for up-to-date submission guidelines by return. No reading fee. May suggest revision where appropriate.

Authors include Valerie Bloom, Sue Heap, Caroline Lawrence, Robert Muchamore.

Edwards Fuglewicz*

49 Great Ormond Street, London WC1N 3HZ
tel 020-7405 6725 *fax* 020-7405 6726
Partners Ros Edwards, Helenka Fuglewicz

Literary and commercial fiction (but no children's fiction, science fiction or horror); non-fiction: biography, history, popular culture (home 15%, USA/translation 20%). No unsolicited MSS or email submissions. No reading fee. Founded 1996.

Faith Evans Associates*

27 Park Avenue North, London N8 7RU
tel 020-8340 9920
email faith@faith-evans.co.uk

Small agency (home 15%, overseas 20%). Co-agents in most countries. No phone calls or submissions.

Authors include Melissa Benn, Eleanor Bron, Midge Gillies, Ed Glinert, Vesna Goldsworthy, Jim Kelly, Helena Kennedy, Tom Paulin, Sheila Rowbotham, Rebecca Stott, Harriet Walter, Elizabeth Wilson, and the estates of Madeleine Bourdouxhe and Lorna Sage. Founded 1987.

Janet Fillingham Associates

52 Lowther Road, London SW13 9NU
tel 020-8748 5594 *fax* 020-8748 7374
website www.janetfillingham.com
Agents Janet Fillingham, Kate Weston

Film, TV and theatre only (home 15%, overseas 15–20%). No books. Strictly no unsolicited MSS; professional recommendation required. Founded 1992.

Film Rights Ltd

Suite 306, Belsize Business Centre, 258 Belsize Road, London NW6 4BT
tel 020-7316 1837 *fax* 020-7624 3629
email information@filmrights.ltd.uk
website www.filmrights.ltd.uk
Directors Brendan Davis, Joan Potts

Theatre, films, TV and sound broadcasting (home 10%, overseas 15%). No reading fee. Represented in USA and abroad. Founded 1932.

Laurence Fitch Ltd

(incorporating The London Play Company 1922)
Suite 306, Belsize Business Centre, 258 Belsize Road, London NW6 4BT
tel 020-7316 1837 *fax* 020-7624 3629
email information@laurencefitch.com
website www.laurencefitch.com
Directors F.H.L. Fitch, Joan Potts, Brendan Davis

Film and TV (home 10%, overseas 15%).

Authors include Carlo Ardito, John Chapman, Peter Coke, Ray Cooney OBE, Dave Freeman, John Graham, Robin Hawdon, Jeremy Lloyd (plays) Dawn Lowe-Watson, Glyn Robbins, Edward Taylor and the estate of late Dodie Smith.

JFL Agency Ltd

48 Charlotte Street, London W1T 2NS
tel 020-3137 8182
email agents@jflagency.com
website www.jflagency.com
Agents Alison Finch, Dominic Lord, Gary Wild

TV, radio, film, theatre (10%). No novels, short stories or poetry. Initial contact by preliminary letter or email; do not send scripts in the first instance. See website for further information.

Clients include Tim Brooke-Taylor, Ian Brown, Grant Cathro, Bill Dare, Phil Ford, Rob Gittins, Wayne Jackman, David Lane, Giles New and Keiron Self, Jim Pullin, Pete Sinclair, Paul Smith, Fraser Steele, Roger Williams.

Fox & Howard Literary Agency*

39 Eland Road, London SW11 5JX
tel 020-7223 9452 *fax* 020-7352 8691

email fandhagency@googlemail.com
website www.foxandhoward.co.uk
Partners Chelsey Fox, Charlotte Howard

General non-fiction: biography, history and popular culture, reference, business, mind, body & spirit, health and personal development, popular psychology (home 15%, overseas 20%). No reading fee, but preliminary letter and synopsis with sae essential for response. Founded 1992.

Fox Mason

36–38 Glasshouse Street, London W1B 5DL
tel 020-7287 0972
email info@foxmason.com, representme@foxmason.com (submissions)
website www.foxmason.com
Director Ben Mason

Literary and commercial fiction and narrative non-fiction (home 15%, overseas 20%) for worldwide exploitation. Submissions by email only. Established 2010.

Fraser Ross Associates

6 Wellington Place, Edinburgh EH6 7EQ
tel 0131 553 2759, 0131 657 4412
email lindsey.fraser@tiscali.co.uk, kjross@tiscali.co.uk
website www.fraserross.co.uk
Partners Lindsey Fraser, Kathryn Ross

Furniss & Lawton

94 Strand on the Green, London W4 3NN
tel 020-8987 6802
website furnisslawton.co.uk
Agents Eugenie Furniss, Rowan Lawton

Fiction: general commercial, thrillers, crime, suspense, women's fiction, literary, fantasy, children's and young adult from 10+. Non-fiction: biography, memoir, cookery, business, history, popular science psychology. Accept unsolicited MSS by post only. Send synopsis and 3 chapters with a sae. Home 15%, overseas 20%. Authors include Kevin Brooks, Julian Clary, Jessica Fellowes, Lindsey Kelk, Raymond Khoury, Tom Knox, Tasmina Perry, Piers Morgan, Matthew Reilly, Alex Scarrow, Alexandra Shulman.

Futerman, Rose & Associates*

91 St Leonards Road, London SW14 7BL
tel 020-8255 7755
email enquiries@futermanrose.co.uk
website www.futermanrose.co.uk
Contact Guy Rose

Fiction, biography, show business, current affairs, teen fiction and scripts for TV and film. No children's, science fiction or fantasy. No unsolicited MSS. Send brief résumé, synopsis, first 20pp and sae.

Clients include Jill Anderson, Larry Barker, Christian Piers Betley, David Bret, Tom Conti, Richard Digance, Iain Duncan Smith, Sir Martin Ewans, Susan George, Paul Hendy, Michael Kelly, Bob Langley, Keith R. Lindsay, Eric MacInnes, Paul Marx, Vartan Melkonian, Max Morgan-Witts, Judge Chris Nicholson, Mary O'Hara, Ciaran O'Keeffe, Antonia Owen, Liz Rettig, Kenneth Ross, Peter Sallis, Paul Stinchcombe, Jim Sullivan, Gordon Thomas, Bill Tidy, Toyah Willcox, Simon Woodham, Allen Zeleski. Founded 1984.

Jüri Gabriel

35 Camberwell Grove, London SE5 8JA
tel 020-7703 6186

Quality fiction and non-fiction (i.e. anything that shows wit and intelligence); radio, TV and film, but selling these rights only in existing works by existing clients. Full-length MSS (home 10%, overseas 20%); performance rights (10%). Will suggest revision where appropriate. No short stories, articles, verse or books for children. No reading fee; return postage essential. Jüri Gabriel is the chairman of Dedalus (publishers).

Authors include Tom Clempson, Clare Druce, Miriam Dunne, Matt Fox, Paul Genney, Pat Gray, Mikka Haugaard, Robert Irwin, Andrew Killeen, John Lucas, 'David Madsen', Richard Mankiewicz, David Miller, Andy Oakes, John Outram, Philip Roberts, Roger Storey, Stefan Szymanski, Jeremy Weingard, Dr Terence White.

Eric Glass Ltd

25 Ladbroke Crescent, London W11 1PS
tel 020-7229 9500 *fax* 020-7229 6220
email eglassltd@aol.com
Director Janet Glass

Full-length MSS only; also theatre, films, and TV. No unsolicited MSS. Founded 1932.

David Godwin Associates – see DGA Ltd

Graham Maw Christie

19 Thornhill Crescent, London N1 1BJ
tel 020-7609 1326
email enquiries@grahammawchristie.com
website www.grahammawchristie.com
Contacts Jane Graham Maw, Jennifer Christie

General non-fiction books, ebooks and apps: autobiography/memoir, business, web-to-book, humour and gift, food and drink, craft, health, lifestyle, parenting, self-help/how to, popular science/history/culture/reference, TV tie-in. No fiction, children's or poetry. No reading fee. Will suggest revisions. Also represents ghostwriters. See website for submission guidelines.

Authors include Jane Brocket, Simon Dawson, Cassandra Ellis, Michael Foley, Becky Jones, Cathryn Kemp, Rosie Millard, Lisa Lam, Clare Lewis, Gael Lindenfield, Alex Monroe, Nick Moran, James Ramsden, Juliet Sear, Alison Taylor, Richard Wilson. Founded 2005.

Annette Green Authors' Agency*

1 East Cliff Road, Tunbridge Wells, Kent TN4 9AD
tel (01892) 514275

website www.annettegreenagency.co.uk
Partners Annette Green, David Smith

Full-length MSS (home 15%, overseas 20%). Literary and general fiction and non-fiction, popular culture, history, science, teenage fiction. No dramatic scripts, poetry, science fiction or fantasy. No reading fee. Preliminary letter, synopsis, sample chapter and sae essential.

Authors include Andrew Baker, Charlotte Betts, Tim Bradford, Bill Broady, Meg Cabot, Victoria Connelly, Simon Conway, Terry Darlington, Elizabeth Haynes, Maria McCann, Adam MacQueen, Ian Marchant, Stephen May, Imogen Robertson, Kirsty Scott, Peter Shapiro, Bernadette Strachan, Deborah Swift. Founded 1998.

Christine Green Authors' Agent*

6 Whitehorse Mews, Westminster Bridge Road, London SE1 7QD
tel 020-7401 8844
email info@christinegreen.co.uk
website www.christinegreen.co.uk
Contacts Christine Green, Natalie Butlin

Literary and commercial fiction, narrative non-fiction (home 10%, overseas 20%). Crime and historical fiction welcome but note no science fiction, travelogues, self-help, picture books, scripts or poetry. Works in conjunction with agencies in Europe and Scandinavia. No reading fee. Preliminary queries by email welcome. Submissions should consist of synopsis and first 3 chapters. Enclose either sae or clearly indicate preference for email response. Founded 1984.

Louise Greenberg Books Ltd*

The End House, Church Crescent, London N3 1BG
tel 020-8349 1179 *fax* 020-8343 4559
email louisegreenberg@msn.com

Full-length MSS (home 15%, overseas 20–25%). Literary fiction and non-fiction. No reading fee. Return postage and sae essential. No telephone enquiries. Founded 1997.

Greene & Heaton Ltd*

37 Goldhawk Road, London W12 8QQ
tel 020-8749 0315 *fax* 020-8749 0318
email submissions@greeneheaton.co.uk
website www.greeneheaton.co.uk
Contacts Carol Heaton, Judith Murray, Antony Topping, Nicola Barr

Fiction and non-fiction (home 15%, USA/translation 20%). No poetry or original scripts for theatre, film or TV. Send a covering letter, synopsis and first 3 chapters with sae and/or return postage. Email submissions accepted but no reply guaranteed. Overseas associates worldwide.

Clients include Poppy Adams, Hugh Aldersley-Williams, Steven Amsterdam, Bill Bryson, Andy Cutbill, Jane Dalley, Suzannah Dunn, Marcus du Sautoy, Travis Elborough, Hugh Fearnley-Whittingstall, Michael Frayn, Andrea Gillies, Bill Granger, Maeve Haran, Oliver Harris, P.D. James, M.D. Lachan, Dan Lepard, William Leith, James McGee, Shona MacLean, Anna May Mangan, Thomasina Miers, C.J. Sansom, Sarah Waters, Katherine Webb, Benjamin Wood, Jackie Wullschlager. *Children's authors* include Helen Craig, Josh Lacey, Lucy Christopher. Founded 1963.

The Greenhouse Literary Agency

Stanley House, St Chad's Place, London WC1X 9HH
tel 020-7841 3959 *fax* 020-7841 3940
email submissions@greenhouseliterary.com
website www.greenhouseliterary.com
Director Sarah Davies, *Agent* Julia Churchill

Specialist children's book agency with a reputation for impressive transatlantic deals. Represents fiction from age 5 through to teen/young adult (USA/UK 15%, elsewhere 25%). Represents both US and UK authors. No picture books or non-fiction. No reading fee. Will suggest revision. Queries by email only, see website for details.

Authors include Julie Bertagna, Caroline Carlson, Sarwat Chadda, Lil Chase, Anne-Marie Conway, Donna Cooner, Elle Cosimano, Sue Cowing, S.D. Crockett, Sarah Crossan, Stephen Davies, Helen Douglas, Ashley Elston, Michael Ford, Harriet Goodwin, Jill Hathaway, Kathryn James, Sarah Lean, Lindsey Leavitt, Jon Mayhew, Megan Miranda, Leila Rasheed, Jeyn Roberts, Amy Sparkes, Tricia Springstubb, Blythe Woolston, Brenna Yovanoff. Founded 2008.

Gregory & Company Authors' Agents*

3 Barb Mews, London W6 7PA
tel 020-7610 4676 *fax* 020-7610 4686
email info@gregoryandcompany.co.uk (general enquiries), maryjones@gregoryandcompany.co.uk (submissions)
website www.gregoryandcompany.co.uk
Contacts Jane Gregory (UK, US, film rights), Claire Morris (translation rights), Stephanie Glencross and Mary Jones (editorial), Linden Sherrif (rights assistant)

Fiction (home 15%, USA/translation/radio/film/TV 20%). Special interests (fiction): literary, commercial, women's fiction, crime, suspense and thrillers. Particularly interested in books which will also sell to publishers abroad. No science fiction, fantasy, poetry, academic or children's books, original plays, film or TV scripts (only published books are sold to film and TV). No reading fee. Editorial advice given to own authors. No unsolicited MSS: send preliminary letter with CV, synopsis (3pp maximum), first 10pp of typescript and future writing plans plus return postage. Submissions can also be sent by email but due to volume we will only respond if we are interested in reading more. Represented throughout Europe, Asia and USA. Founded 1987.

David Grossman Literary Agency Ltd

118B Holland Park Avenue, London W11 4UA
tel 020-7221 2770 *fax* 020-7221 1445

Full-length MSS (home 10–15%, overseas 20% including foreign agent's commission, performance rights 15%). Works in conjunction with agents in New York, Los Angeles, Europe, Japan. No reading fee but preliminary letter required. No submissions by fax or email. Founded 1976.

Gunn Media

50 Albemarle Street, London W1S 4BD
tel 020-7529 3745
email ali@gunnmedia.co.uk
Directors Ali Gunn (managing), Doug Kean, Georgie Bean

Commercial fiction and non-fiction including literary, thrillers and celebrity autobiographies (home 15%, overseas 20%).

Authors include Jenny Colgan, Brian Freeman, Carole Malone, Mil Millington, Carol Thatcher.

Marianne Gunn O'Connor Literary Agency

Morrison Chambers, Suite 17, 32 Nassau Street, Dublin 2, Republic of Ireland
email mgoclitagency@eircom.net
Contact Marianne Gunn O' Connor

Commercial and literary fiction, non-fiction, biography, children's fiction (home 15%, overseas 20%, film/TV 20%). Email enquiry with a half-page outline. Translation rights handled by Vicki Satlow Literary Agency, Milan.

Clients include Ceclia Ahern, Chris Binchy, Claudia Carroll, Louise Douglas, Maureen Gaffney, Alan Gilsenan, Noelle Harrison, Julia Kelly, Kate Kerrigan, Style Bubble aka Suis Lau, John Lynch, Patrick McCabe, Mike McCormack, Kathleen McMahon, Paddy McMahon, David McWilliams, Sinead Moriarty, Emily Gillmor Murphy, Peter Murphy, Anita Notaro, Kevin Power.

The Hanbury Agency Ltd, Literary and Media Agents*

28 Moreton Street, London SW1V 2PE
tel 020-7630 6768
email enquiries@hanburyagency.com
website www.hanburyagency.com

Represents general fiction and non-fiction. See website for submission guidelines. Expanded in 2011 to offer media/PR service to authors.

Authors include George Alagiah, Tom Bergin, Simon Callow, Jimmy Connors, Jane Glover, Imran Khan, Roman Krznaric, Judith Lennox, Katie Price, Jerry White, Mitch Winehouse. The agency has a strong stable of ghostwriters. Founded 1983.

Antony Harwood Ltd*

103 Walton Street, Oxford OX2 6EB
tel (01865) 559615 *fax* (01865) 310660
email mail@antonyharwood.com
website www.antonyharwood.com
Contacts Antony Harwood, James Macdonald Lockhart, Jo Williamson (children's)

General and genre fiction; general non-fiction (home 15%, overseas 20%). Will suggest revision. No reading fee.

Clients include Amanda Craig, Louise Doughty, Alan Glynn, Peter F. Hamilton, Alan Hollinghurst, A.L. Kennedy, Douglas Kennedy, Dorothy Koomson, Chris Manby, George Monbiot, Garth Nix. Founded 2000.

A.M. Heath & Co. Ltd

6 Warwick Court, London WC1R 5DJ
tel 020-7242 2811 *fax* 020-7242 2711
website www.amheath.com
Contacts Bill Hamilton, Victoria Hobbs, Euan Thorneycroft, Jennifer Custer

Full-length MSS. Literary and commercial fiction and non-fiction, children's (home 15%, USA/translation 20%), film/TV (20%). No science fiction, screenplays, poetry or short stories except for established clients. No reading fee.

Clients include Prof. Christopher Andrew, Anita Brookner, Prof. David Abulafia, Stevie Davies, R.J. Ellory, Katie Fforde, Conn Iggulden, Marina Lewycka, Lucy Mangan, Hilary Mantel, Maggie O'Farrell, Barbara Trapido. Founded 1919.

Rupert Heath Literary Agency*

50 Albemarle Street, London W1S 4BD
tel 020-7060 3385
email emailagency@rupertheath.com
website www.rupertheath.com
Agents Rupert Heath, Diana Beaumont

Fiction: Thrillers, crime, historical, women's commercial fiction; non-fiction: history, biography and autobiography, lifestyle, cookery, popular science, nature, politics and current affairs, popular culture and the arts. Commission 15% UK, 20% overseas, 20% film/TV/dramatic. Visit website before submitting material. Email submissions preferred. International associates worldwide.

Authors include Michael Arnold, Ros Barber, A.K. Benedict, Mark Blake, Margot Campbell, Angela Clarke, Stephen Collishaw, Paddy Docherty, Peter Doggett, Anietie Isong, Kim Izzo, Martin Lampen, Jo Litchfield, Andrew McDonald, Reza Mahammad, Scott Mariani, Lorna Martin, Christopher Moore, James Robinson, Makiko Sana, Laura Tenison, Merryn Somerset Webb, Robyn Young. Founded 2001.

hhb agency ltd*

6 Warwick Court, London WC1R 5DJ
tel 020-7405 5525
email heather@hhbagency.com, elly@hhbagency.com, claire@hhbagency.com

website www.hhbagency.com
Contacts Heather Holden-Brown, Elly James, Claire Houghton-Price

Non-fiction: journalism, history and politics, travel and adventure, contemporary autobiography and biography, books about words, popular culture, entertainment and TV, business, family memoir, food and cookery a speciality. Fiction: commercial and literary, women's and crime. 15%. No reading fee. Founded 2005.

David Higham Associates Ltd*

(incorporating Murray Pollinger)
5–8 Lower John Street, Golden Square, London W1F 9HA
tel 020-7434 5900 *fax* 020-7437 1072
email dha@davidhigham.co.uk
website www.davidhigham.co.uk
Managing Director Anthony Goff, *Books* Veronique Baxter, Georgia Glover, Anthony Goff, Andrew Gordon, Lizzy Kremer, Caroline Walsh, *Foreign Rights* Ania Corless, Tine Nielsen, *Film/TV/Theatre* Nicky Lund, Georgina Ruffhead

Agents for the negotiation of all rights in fiction, general non-fiction, children's fiction and picture books, plays, film and TV scripts (home 15%, USA/translation 20%, scripts 10%). Represented in all foreign markets. See website for submissions policy. No reading fee. Founded 1935.

Vanessa Holt Ltd*

59 Crescent Road, Leigh-on-Sea, Essex SS9 2PF
tel (01702) 473787

General fiction and non-fiction (home 15%, overseas 20%, TV/film/radio 15%). Works in conjunction with foreign agencies in all markets. No reading fee. No unsolicited MSS and submissions preferred by arrangement. No overseas submissions. Founded 1989.

Valerie Hoskins Associates Ltd

20 Charlotte Street, London W1T 2NA
tel 020-7637 4490 *fax* 020-7637 4493
email vha@vhassociates.co.uk
website www.vhassociates.co.uk
Proprietor Valerie Hoskins, *Agent* Rebecca Watson

Film, TV and radio; specialises in animation (home 12.5%, overseas max. 20%). No unsolicited MSS; preliminary letter essential. No reading fee, but sae essential. Works in conjunction with US agents.

Tanja Howarth Literary Agency*

19 New Row, London WC2N 4LA
tel 020-7240 5553
email tanja.howarth@btinternet.com

General fiction and non-fiction, thrillers, contemporary and historical novels (home 15%, USA/translation 20%). No unsolicited MSS, and no submissions by email. No reading fee. Specialists in handling German translation rights. Represented in the USA by various agents.

Clients include Sebastian Fitzek, Markus Heitz, Erich Maria Remarque, Frank Schätzing, Patrick Süskind, Ferdinand von Schirach, and the estates of Joseph Roth and Heinrich Böll. Founded 1970.

IMG UK Ltd

McCormack House, Burlington Lane, London W4 2TH
tel 020-8233 5000 *fax* 020-8233 5268
Consultant Sarah Wooldridge

Celebrity books, sports-related books, non-fiction and how-to business books (home 15%, USA 20%, elsewhere 25%). No theatre, fiction, children's, academic or poetry. No emails. No reading fee.

Independent Talent Group Ltd

Oxford House, 76 Oxford Street, London W1D 1BS
tel 020-7636 6565 *fax* 020-7323 0101
Directors Duncan Heath, Susan Rodgers, Lyndsey Posner, Sally Long-Innes, Paul Lyon-Maris, *Literary Agents* Susan Rodgers, Jessica Sykes, Catherine King, Greg Hunt, Hugo Young, Michael McCoy, Duncan Heath, Paul Lyon-Maris, Laura Rourke, Josh Varney

Specialises in scripts for film, theatre, TV, radio (home 10%, overseas 10%).

Intercontinental Literary Agency Ltd*

Centric House, 390–391 Strand, London WC2R 0LT
tel 020-7379 6611 *fax* 020-7240 4724
email ila@ila-agency.co.uk
website www.ila-agency.co.uk
Contacts Nicki Kennedy, Sam Edenborough, Mary Esdaile, Franca Bernatavicius, Katherine West, Jenny Robson

Represents translation rights only. Founded 1965.

Janklow & Nesbit (UK) Ltd*

13A Hillgate Street, London W8 7SP
tel 020-7432 2975 *fax* 020-7376 2915
email queries@janklow.co.uk
website www.janklowandnesbit.co.uk
Agents Claire Paterson, Will Francis, Rebecca Carter, Tim Glister, *Translation rights* Rebecca Folland

Commercial and literary fiction and non-fiction. No poetry, plays, film/TV scripts. No reading fee. Send informative covering letter and return postage with full outline (non-fiction), synopsis and first 3 sample chapters (fiction). US rights handled by Janklow & Nesbit Associates in New York. Founded 2000.

Johnson & Alcock Ltd*

Clerkenwell House, 45–47 Clerkenwell Green, London EC1R 0HT
tel 020-7251 0125 *fax* 020-7251 2172
email info@johnsonandalcock.co.uk
website www.johnsonandalcock.co.uk
Contacts Michael Alcock, Andrew Hewson, Anna Power, Ed Wilson

All types of commercial and literary fiction, and general non-fiction (home 15%, USA/translation/film 20%). Young adult and children's fiction (ages 9+). No poetry, screenplays or board/picture books.

For fiction and non-fiction, send first 3 chapters, full synopsis and brief covering letter with details of writing experience. For email submission guidelines see website. No reading fee but return postage essential. Founded 1956.

Robin Jones Literary Agency

6B Marmora Road, London SE22 0RX
tel 020-8693 6062
email robijones@gmail.com
Director Robin Jones

Fiction and non-fiction: literary and commercial (home 15%, overseas 20%). No reading fee. Founded 2007.

Tibor Jones & Associates

Unit 12B, Piano House, 9 Brighton Terrace, London SW9 8DJ
tel 020-7733 0555
email enquiries@tiborjones.com
website www.tiborjones.com
Director Kevin Conroy Scott

Literary fiction and non-fiction, category fiction, music autobiographies and biographies. Send first 5pp, synopsis and covering letter via email.

Authors include V.W. Adams, Sulaiman Smy Addonia, Sophia Al-Maria, Gary Barker, Sarah Bilston, Brian Chikwava, Jason Cowley, Lewis Crofts, Peter Culshaw, Kevin Cummins, Alice de Smith, Salena Godden, Colin Grant, Matthew Green, Oscar Guardiola-Rivera, Hala Jaber, Richard T. Kelly, Rem Koolhaas, Denise Meredith, Hans Ulrich Obrist, Tali Sharot, Brian Schofield, Christopher Winn, Tod Wodicka. Founded 2007.

Jane Judd Literary Agency*

18 Belitha Villas, London N1 1PD
tel 020-7607 0273 *fax* 020-7607 0623
website www.janejudd.com

General non-fiction and fiction (home 10%, overseas 20%). Special interests: women's fiction, crime, thrillers, narrative non-fiction. No short stories, film/TV scripts, poetry or plays. No reading fee, but preliminary letter with synopsis, first chapter and sae essential. Works with agents in USA and most foreign countries. Founded 1986.

Michelle Kass Associates Ltd*

85 Charing Cross Road, London WC2H 0AA
tel 020-7439 1624 *fax* 020-7734 3394
Proprietor Michelle Kass

Full-length MSS. Literary fiction (home 10%, overseas 15–20%) and scripts for film and TV. Works with agents around the world. No reading fee. No email submissions. No unsolicited material, phone in first instance. Founded 1991.

Frances Kelly Agency*

111 Clifton Road, Kingston-upon-Thames, Surrey KT2 6PL
tel 020-8549 7830 *fax* 020-8547 0051

Full-length MSS. Non-fiction: general and academic, reference and professional books, all subjects (home 10%, overseas 20%, TV/radio 10%). No reading fee, but no unsolicited MSS; preliminary letter with synopsis, CV and return postage essential. Founded 1978.

Peter Knight Agency

20 Crescent Grove, London SW4 7AH
tel 020-7622 1467 *fax* 020-7622 1522
website www.knightfeatures.com
Director Peter Knight, *Associates* Gaby Martin, Andrew Knight, Samantha Ferris

Motor sports, cartoon books, business, history and factual and biographical material. No poetry, science fiction or cookery. No unsolicited MSS. Send letter accompanied by CV and sae with synopsis of proposed work. No email submissions. *Overseas associates* Universal Uclick (USA), Auspac Media (Australia), Puzzle Company (NZ).

Clients include David Bodycombe, Frank Dickens, John Dodd, Gray Jolliffe, Angus McGill, Barbara Minto, Lisa Wild. Founded 1985.

Knight Hall Agency Ltd

Lower Ground Floor, 7 Mallow Street, London EC1Y 8RQ
tel 020-7397 2901 *fax* 0871 918 6068
email office@knighthallagency.com
website www.knighthallagency.com
Director Charlotte Knight, Martin Knight, *Contacts* Emily Hayward, Tanya Tillett, Katie Langridge

Specialises in writers for stage, screen and radio but also deals in TV and film rights in novels and non-fiction (home 10%, overseas 15%). No reading fee.

Clients include Simon Beaufoy, Jeremy Brock, Liz Lochhead, Tim Lott, Martin McDonagh, Simon Nye, Ol Parker, Lucy Prebble, Philip Ridley, Laura Wade. Founded 1997.

LAW (Lucas Alexander Whitley Ltd)*

14 Vernon Street, London W14 0RJ
tel 020-7471 7900 *fax* 020-7471 7910
website www.lawagency.co.uk
Contacts Adult: Mark Lucas, Julian Alexander, Araminta Whitley, Alice Saunders, Peta Nightingale, Ben Clark, Guy Thompson, Sophie Hughes; Children's: Philippa Milnes-Smith, Holly Vitow

Full-length commercial and literary fiction, non-fiction and children's books (home 15%, USA/translation 20%). No fantasy (except children's), plays, poetry or textbooks. Film and TV scripts handled for established clients only. Unsolicited MSS considered; send brief covering letter, short synopsis and 2 sample chapters. Sae essential. No emailed or disk submissions. Overseas associates worldwide. Founded 1996.

LBLA (Lorella Belli Literary Agency)*

54 Hartford House, 35 Tavistock Crescent,
London W11 1AY
tel 020-7727 8547 *fax* 0870 7874194
email info@lorellabelliagency.com
website www.lorellabelliagency.com
Proprietor Lorella Belli

Fiction and general non-fiction (home 15%, overseas/dramatic 20%). Particularly interested in first-time writers, journalists, international and multicultural writing and books on Italy. No children's, science fiction, fantasy, academic, poetry, original scripts. No reading fee. May suggest revision. Send an enquiry letter or email before submitting work. Do not send attachments by email unless asked; submissions should be sent in hard copy to the office address. Do not return materials unless the correct sae postage is provided. Enclose a stamped acknowledgement card with submission if receipt acknowledgment is required. Works with dramatic and overseas associates; represents American, Canadian and Australian agencies in the UK.

Authors include Mary Bird, Susan Brackney, Zoë Brân, Gesine Bullock-Prado, Scott Carney, Sally Corner, Sandra Doran, Kristina Downing-Orr, Kasey Edwards, Marcus Ferrar, Emily Giffin, Kent Greenfield, Molly Harper, Linda Kavanagh, Ed Kritzler, Dinah Lee Kung, Diane and Bernie Lierow, William Little, Julia Macmillan, Valerie Mendes, Nisha Minhas, Alanna Mitchell, Rick Mofina, Sandro Monetti, Angela Murrills, Annalisa Coppolaro-Nowell, Judy Nunn, Jennifer Ouellette, Robert J. Ray, Anneli Rufus, Dave Singleton, Rupert Steiner, Katie Stevens, Justine Trueman, Diana Winston, Carol Wright. Founded 2002.

Susanna Lea Associates Ltd*

34 Lexington Street, London W1F 0LH
tel 020-7287 7757 *fax* 020-7287 7775
email kglencorse@susannalea.com
website www.susannalea.com
Directors Susanna Lea, Kerry Glencorse

General fiction and non-fiction with international appeal. No plays, screenplays or poetry. Send query letter, brief synopsis, the first 3 chapters and/or proposal via website. Established in Paris 2000; New York 2004; London 2008.

Barbara Levy Literary Agency*

64 Greenhill, Hampstead High Street,
London NW3 5TZ
tel 020-7435 9046 *fax* 020-7431 2063
email blevysubmissions@gmail.com
Director Barbara Levy, *Associate* John Selby (solicitor)

Full-length MSS. Fiction and general non-fiction (home 15%, overseas by arrangement). Film and TV rights for existing clients only. No reading fee, but preliminary letter with synopsis and sae essential, or by email. Translation rights handled by the Buckman Agency; works in conjunction with US agents. Founded 1986.

Limelight Celebrity Management Ltd*

10 Filmer Mews, 75 Filmer Road, London SW6 7JF
tel 020-7384 9950 *fax* 020-7384 9955
website www.limelightmanagement.com
Contacts Fiona Lindsay

Full-length and short MSS. Food, wine, health, crafts, gardening, interior design, literary fiction, biography, travel, history, women's fiction, crime, children's fiction, art, fashion, humour, business, politics (home 15%, overseas 20%), TV and radio rights (10–20%); will suggest revision where appropriate. No reading fee. Founded 1991.

Lindsay Literary Agency

East Worldham House, Alton, Hants GU34 3AT
tel (01420) 83143
email info@lindsayliteraryagency.co.uk
website www.lindsayliteraryagency.co.uk
Directors Becky Bagnell, Kate Holroyd Smith

Literary fiction, serious non-fiction, children's fiction. No reading fee. Will suggest revision.

Authors include Pamela Butchart, Gina Blaxill, Sam Gayton, Mike Lancaster, Sue Lloyd-Roberts, Rachel Valentine. Founded 2005.

Christopher Little Literary Agency LLP*

Eel Brook Studios, 125 Moore Park Road,
London SW6 4PS
tel 020-7736 4455 *fax* 020-7736 4490
email info@christopherlittle.net
website www.christopherlittle.net
Contact Christopher Little

Commercial and literary full-length fiction and non-fiction (home 15%; USA, Canada, translation, audio, motion picture 20%). No poetry, plays, science fiction, fantasy, textbooks, illustrated children's or short stories. Film scripts for established clients only. No unsolicited submissions.

Authors include Steve Barlow and Steve Skidmore, Paul Bajoria, Professor Dan Davis, Denise Deegan, Rosie Fiore, Janet Gleeson, Gorillaz, Michele Gorman, Carol Hughes, General Mike Jackson (Sir), Lise Kristensen, Alastair MacNeill, Robert Mawson, Haydn Middleton, Shiromi Pinto, Anne H. Putnam, A.J. Quinnell, Robert Radcliffe, Martina Reilly, Darren Shan, Wladyslaw Szpilman, Shane Ward, John Watson, Anne Zouroudi. Founded 1979.

London Independent Books

26 Chalcot Crescent, London NW1 8YD
tel 020-7706 0486 *fax* 020-7724 3122
Proprietor Carolyn Whitaker

Specialises in commercial, fantasy and teenage fiction, travel. Full-length MSS (home 15%, overseas 20%).

Will suggest revision of promising MSS. No reading fee.

Authors include Alex Bell, Joseph Delaney, Elizabeth Kay, Tim Mackintosh-Smith, Glenn Mitchell, Connie Monk, Richard Morgan, Steve Mosby, Dan Smith, Chris Wooding. Founded 1971.

Andrew Lownie Literary Agency*

36 Great Smith Street, London SW1P 3BU
tel 020-7222 7574 *fax* 020-7222 7576
email lownie@globalnet.co.uk
website www.andrewlownie.co.uk
Director Andrew Lownie

Full-length MSS. Biography, history, reference, current affairs, and packaging journalists and celebrities for the book market (worldwide 15%). No reading fee; will suggest revision.

Authors include Richard Aldrich, Juliet Barker, the Joyce Cary estate, Roger Crowley, Tom Devine, Duncan Falconer, Cathy Glass, Timothy Good, David Hasselhoff, John Hatcher, Kris Hollington, Robert Hutchinson, Lawrence James, Ian Knight, Christopher Lloyd, Sean Longden, the Julian Maclaren-Ross estate, Norma Major, Sean McMeekin, Tim Newark, Linda Porter, Martin Pugh, Sian Rees, David Roberts, Celia Sandys, Desmond Seward, David Stafford, Daniel Tammet, Peter Thompson, Casey Watson, Christian Wolmar; *The Oxford Classical Dictionary*, *The Cambridge Guide to Literature in English*. Founded 1988.

Lucas Alexander Whitley – see LAW (Lucas Alexander Whitley Ltd)

Lucy Luck Associates (in association with Aitken Alexander Associates Ltd)

18–21 Cavaye Place, London SW10 9PT
tel 020-7373 8672
email lucy@lucyluck.com
website www.lucyluck.com
Contact Lucy Luck

Adult quality fiction and non-fiction (home 15%, overseas 20%, films/TV 15%). No reading fee.

Authors include Kevin Barry, Greg Baxter, Ron Butlin, Jon Hotten, Catherine O'Flynn, Philip Ó Ceallaigh, Adam Thorpe, Rebbecca Ray, Jess Richards, Ray Robinson, Rupert Wright. Founded 2006.

Jennifer Luithlen Agency

88 Holmfield Road, Leicester LE2 1SB
tel 0116 273 8863, 0116 273 5697
website www.luithlenagency.com
Agents Jennifer Luithlen, Penny Luithlen

Children's fiction (home 15%, overseas 20%), performance rights (15%). See website for submission information. Founded 1986.

Lutyens & Rubinstein*

21 Kensington Park Road, London W11 2EU
tel 020-7792 4855
email submissions@lutyensrubinstein.co.uk
Directors Sarah Lutyens, Felicity Rubinstein
Submissions Susannah Godman

Fiction and non-fiction, commercial and literary (home 15%, overseas 20%). Send material by email with a covering letter and short synopsis. Submissions not accepted by hand or by post. Founded 1993.

David Luxton Associates Ltd*

23 Hillcourt Avenue, London N12 8EY
email rebecca@rebeccawinfield.com
Contact Rebecca Winfield

Duncan McAra

28 Beresford Gardens, Edinburgh EH5 3ES
tel 0131 552 1558
email duncanmcara@mac.com

Literary fiction; non-fiction: art, architecture, archaeology, biography, military, Scottish, travel (home 15%, USA/translation 20%). Preliminary letter with sae essential. No reading fee. Member of the Association of Scottish Literary Agents. Founded 1988.

The McKernan Literary Agency & Consultancy

6 Ann Street, Edinburgh EH4 1PJ
tel 0131 332 9782
email maggie@mckernanagency.co.uk
website www.mckernanagency.co.uk
Contact Maggie McKernan

Literary fiction and serious non-fiction: biography, history, current affairs, memoirs (home 15%, overseas 15%). No reading fee. Submissions only accepted if made through online form; see instructions on website. No postal submissions. No tss returned.

Authors include Michael Collins, The Rt Hon Alistair Darling, MP, Michael Fry, Jean McNeil, Michael Schmidt, Belinda Seaward. Founded 2005.

Eunice McMullen Ltd

Low Ibbotsholme Cottage, Off Bridge Lane, Troutbeck Bridge, Windermere, Cumbria LA23 1HU
tel (01539) 448551
email eunicemcmullen@totalise.co.uk
website www.eunicemcmullen.co.uk
Director Eunice McMullen

All types of children's fiction, particularly picture books and older fiction (home 10%, overseas 15%). No unsolicited scripts. Telephone or email enquiries only. Founded 1992.

Authors include Wayne Anderson, Sam Childs, Caroline Jayne Church, Jason Cockcroft, Ross Collins, Emma Dodd, Charles Fuge, Maggie Kneen, David Melling, Angela McAllister, Angie Sage, Gillian Shields. Founded 1992.

Andrew Mann Ltd*

United House, North Road, London N7 9DP
email info@andrewmann.co.uk
website www.andrewmann.co.uk
Contacts Tina Betts, Louise Burns

MSS for fiction/non-fiction. Scripts for TV, cinema and radio (home 15%, USA/Europe 20%). Email submissions only, first 3 chapters. Associated with agents worldwide. No reading fee. Founded 1968.

Sarah Manson Literary Agent

6 Totnes Walk, London N2 0AD
tel 020-8442 0396
email info@sarahmanson.com
website www.sarahmanson.com
Proprietor Sarah Manson

Specialises in fiction for children and young adults. See website for submission guidelines. Founded 2002.

Marjacq Scripts

Box 412, 19–21 Crawford Street, London W1H 1PJ
tel 020-7935 9499 *fax* 020-7935 9115
email enquiries@marjacq.com
website www.marjacq.com
Contact Philip Patterson (books), Isabella Floris (books), Luke Speed (film/TV)

All full-length MSS (home 15%, overseas 20%), including commercial and literary fiction and non-fiction, crime, thrillers, commercial, women's fiction, graphic novels, children's, science fiction, history, biography, sport, travel, health. No poetry. Send first 3 chapters with synopsis. May suggest revision. Film and TV rights, screenplays, documentaries: send full script with 1–2pp synopsis/outline. Interested in documentary concepts and will accept proposals from writer/directors: send show reel with script. Sae essential for return of submissions.

Clients include: Victoria Arch, Richard Asplin, Charles Barker, Sean Bates, Bert & Bertie, Sean Black, Catrin Collier, J.J. Connolly, John Connor, Ross Cramer, Paul Davies, Gaelle Denis, Katie Ellwood, Fern Elsdon-Baker, Helen FitzGerald, James Follett, Christopher Goffard, Stephen Graham, Ben Hatch, Rebecca Hobbs, Ros Jay, Katherine John, Jessica Kedward, Anthony Lappe, Damien Lewis, Ed Lilly, Howard Linskey, Stuart MacBride, Jane McLoughlin, Ben Marlow, Graham Oakley, Kirsty Peart, Connor Potts, Greg Read, Alex Reynolds, Stanley Reynolds, Nicholas Russell-Pavier, Jack Sheffield, Brian Sibley, Will Simpson, Michael Taylor, Toby Wagstaff, Andy Walker, Kevin Wignall, Tom Winship, Tom Wood, the estate of R.D. Wingfield and the estate of George Markstein. Founded 1974.

The Marsh Agency Ltd*

50 Albemarle Street, London W1S 4BD
tel 020-7493 4361 *fax* 020-7495 8961
website www.marsh-agency.co.uk
Contacts Camilla Ferrier (translation rights), Stephanie Ebdon and Jessica Woollard (English language), Charlotte Bruton, Sarah McFadden (finance)

Founded as international rights specialists for British, American and Canadian agencies. Expanded to act as agents to handle fiction and non-fiction, specialising in authors with international potential (home 15%, overseas/TV/film 20%). See website for agent details and submission guidelines. No reading fee. Unsolicited submissions considered. No poetry, plays, scripts, children's or picture books. Founded 1994, incorporating Paterson Marsh Ltd and Campbell, Thomson and McLaughlin Ltd as of April 2011.

Blanche Marvin, MBE

21A St John's Wood High Street, London NW8 7NG
tel 020-7722 2313 *fax* 020-7722 2313

Full-length MSS (17%), performance rights. Plays. No reading fee but return postage essential.

Authors include Christopher Bond, Mike Dorrell.

MBA Literary and Script Agents Ltd*

(incorporating Merric Davidson Literary Agency)
62 Grafton Way, London W1T 5DW
tel 020-7387 2076
email [firstname]@mbalit.co.uk
website www.mbalit.co.uk
Book agents Diana Tyler, Meg Davis, Laura Longrigg, David Riding, Susan Smith, Sophie Gorell Barnes, *Film/TV/Radio/Theatre agents* Diana Tyler, Jean Kitson

Fiction and non-fiction, children's books (commission: home 15%, overseas 20%) and TV, film, radio and theatre scripts (commission: theatre 10%, films 10–20%). See website for submission guidelines. Works in conjunction with agents in most countries. UK representative for the Donald Maass Agency and Harlequin.

Clients include Sita Brahmachari, Jeffrey Caine, Neil Forsyth, Michele Hanson, Julian Jones, Robert Jones, estate of Anne McCaffrey, Clare Morrall, Stef Penney, Cathy Woodman. Founded 1971.

Madeleine Milburn Literary, TV & Film Agency

42A Great Percy Street, London WC1X 9QR
tel/fax 020-3602 6425
email submissions@madeleinemilburn.com
website www.madeleinemilburn.com
Proprietor Madeleine Milburn

Represents leading authors from around the world. Handles all rights in the UK, US and foreign markets including film and television. Specialist areas include women's and general fiction, memoirs, crime, thrillers and mysteries, accessible literary, psychological suspense, crossover, children's and young adult books. Also considers non-fiction.

Authors include Carol Duffy, Victoria Fox, Emma Garcia, Carolyn Jess-Cooke, Martel Maxwell, Cally Taylor, J.J. Salem, Anna-Lou Weatherley.

Judith Murdoch Literary Agency*

19 Chalcot Square, London NW1 8YA
tel 020-7722 4197

Contact Judith Murdoch

Full-length fiction only, especially accessible literary, crime and commercial women's fiction (home 15%, overseas 20%). No science fiction/fantasy, poetry, short stories or children's. Approach by post, sending the first 2 chapters and synopsis. Send email address or return postage; no email submissions. Editorial advice given; no reading fee. Translation rights handled by Rebecca Winfield (email: rebecca@rebeccawinfield.com).

Clients include Trisha Ashley, Anne Bennett, Anne Berry, Frances Brody, Leah Fleming, Lola Jaye, Pamela Jooste, Jessie Keane, Catherine King, Jill McGivering, Eve Makis, Alison Mercer, Barbara Mutch, Kitty Neale, Alison Sherlock. Founded 1993.

The No.1 Manchester Literary Agency

3rd Floor, Clayton House, 59 Piccadilly, Manchester M1 2AQ
tel 0161 904 0910
website www.theno1manchesterliteraryagency.co.uk
Contacts Kathy Charvin, Karen James, Lorraine Birtwistle

Children's and adult fiction (home 15%, overseas 20%). Fiction for 5–8 and 9–12 year-olds and teenage fiction. Send covering letter, synopsis and the first 50pp (or less) with sae and return postage. No reading fee. Will suggest revision. Founded in 2009 to represent northern-based authors.

Maggie Noach Literary Agency

7 Peacock Yard, Iliffe Street, London SE17 3LH
tel 020-7708 3073
email info@mnla.co.uk
website www.mnla.co.uk
Contacts Jill Hughes, Josie Stapleton

Not currently accepting submissions. Fiction and general non-fiction for adults, plus full length fiction for older children. No illustrated books or specialist non-fiction. Home 15%, USA and translation 20%. Founded 1982.

Andrew Nurnberg Associates International Ltd*

20–23 Greville Street, London EC1N 8SS
tel 020-3327 0400
email contact@andrewnurnberg.com
website www.andrewnurnberg.com

Sells rights internationally on behalf of UK/US agencies and publishers. Agent for UK and international authors, including children's writers. See website for full information and submission guidelines.

Deborah Owen Ltd*

78 Narrow Street, Limehouse, London E14 8BP
tel 020-7987 5119/5441 *fax* 020-7538 4004
Contact Deborah Owen

Small agency specialising in only three authors: Delia Smith, Amos Oz and David Owen. No new authors. Founded 1971.

Paterson Marsh Ltd – see The Marsh Agency Ltd

John Pawsey

8 Snowshill Court, Giffard Park, Milton Keynes MK14 5QG
tel (01908) 611841
email john.pawsey@virgin.net

Specialises in general non-fiction (biography and sport). Will offer creative advice if MS sufficiently promising. Fees on application. Send brief first submission (synopsis/concept/opening chapter) by email only.

Authors include Gary Imlach, Roy Hudd OBE, William Fotheringham, Graeme McLagan, Gavin Newsham, Kathryn Spink. Founded 1981.

PBJ & JBJ Management

22 Rathbone Street, London W1T 1LA
tel 020-7287 1112 *fax* 020-7637 0899
email suzanne@pbjmgt.co.uk
website www.pbjmgt.co.uk
Chairman Peter Bennett-Jones, *Managing Director* Caroline Chignell, *Agents* Janette Linden, Suzanne Milligan, Kate Haldane

Represents writers, performers, presenters, composers, directors, producers and DJs (theatre 15%, film/TV/radio 12.5%). Specialises in comedy. No reading fee.

Founded 1987.

Maggie Pearlstine Associates*

31 Ashley Gardens, Ambrosden Avenue, London SW1P 1QE
tel 020-7828 4212 *fax* 020-7834 5546
email maggie@pearlstine.co.uk

Small agency representing a select few authors. No new authors. Translation rights handled by Aitken Alexander Associates Ltd.

Authors include Matthew Baylis, Roy Hattersley, Dr Paul Keedwell, Charles Kennedy, Quentin Letts, Mark Leonard, Gary Mulgrew, Dr Raj Persaud, Prof. Lesley Regan, Malcolm Rifkind, Winifred Robinson, Henrietta Spencer-Churchill, Prof. Kathy Sykes, Christopher Ward, Prof. Robert Winston. Founded 1989.

PFD (The Peters Fraser & Dunlop Group Ltd)*

(A literary division of The Rights House, formed through the merger of PFD (The Peters Fraser & Dunlop Group) and Michael Foster MF Management in 2010)
Drury House, 34–43 Russell Street, London WC2B 5HA
tel 020-7344 1000 *fax* 020-7836 9543
email info@pfd.co.uk
website www.pfd.co.uk
Ceo Caroline Michel, *Books* Caroline Michel, Michael

Sissons, Fiona Petheram, Annabel Merullo, Juliet Mushens, *Books & Journalism* Robert Caskie, *Foreign Rights* Rachel Mills, Alexandra Cliff *Estates* Camilla Shestopal, *TV & Film Rights* The Rights House (*Film & TV*, Michael Foster, Oriana Eli; *Head of TV & Public Speaking*, Katie Rice)

Represents authors of fiction and non-fiction, presenters and public speakers throughout the world. All children's submissions 9+, science fiction and fantasy, send to Juliet Mushens.

Covering letter, synopsis or outline and first 3 chapters as well as author biographies should be addressed to the books department or individual agents. Return postage necessary. No reading fee. Email submissions will not be answered. See website for submission guidelines. Does not represent scriptwriters.

Pollinger Limited

(formerly Laurence Pollinger Ltd, successor of Pearn, Pollinger and Higham)
9 Staple Inn, Holborn, London WC1V 7QH
tel 020-7404 0342 *fax* 020-7242 5737
email info@pollingerltd.com
website www.pollingerltd.com
Managing Director Lesley Pollinger, *Agents* Joanna Devereux, Tim Bates, Leigh Pollinger, Hayley Yeeles

All types of general trade adult and children's fiction and non-fiction books; intellectual property developments, illustrators/photographers (home 15%, translation 20%). Overseas, media and theatrical associates. For submission guidelines see website.

Clients include Kimberley Chambers, Michael Coleman, Catherine Fisher, Philip Gross, Hayley Long, Kelly McKain, Robert M. Pirsig, Jeremy Poolman, Nicholas Rhea and Robert Sellers. Also the estates of H.E. Bates, Erskine Caldwell, Rachel Carson, D.H. Lawrence, Carson McCullers, John Masters, W.H. Robinson, Eric Frank Russell, Clifford D. Simak and other notables. Founded 1935.

Shelley Power Literary Agency Ltd*

Shelley Power will be relocating in 2012 but at the time of going to press we are unable to confirm the address. Make contact by email in first instance but do not send attachments. The Agency may also be contacted at the telephone number below.
mobile 07984 202881
email sp@shelleypower.co.uk

General fiction and non-fiction. Full-length MSS (home 12.5%, USA/translation 20%). No children's books, poetry or plays. Works in conjunction with agents abroad. No reading fee, but preliminary letter with return postage as from UK or France essential. No submissions by email. Founded 1976.

PVA Media Ltd

County House, St Mary's Street,
Worcester WR1 1HB
tel (01905) 616100
email md@pva.co.uk
website www.pva.co.uk
Director Paul Vaughan

Full-length MSS. Non-fiction only (home 15%, overseas 20%, performance rights 15%). Send synopsis and sample chapters together with return postage.

Redhammer Management Ltd*

186 Bickenhall Mansions, Bickenhall Street,
London W1U 6BX
tel 020-7486 3465 *fax* 020-7000 1249
website www.redhammer.info
Vice President Peter Cox

Specialises in works with international potential (home 17.5%, overseas 20%). Unpublished authors must have major international potential, ideally book, film and/or TV. Submissions must follow the guidelines given on the website. Do not send unsolicited MSS by post. No radio or theatre scripts. No reading fee.

Clients include Richard Ashworth, Martin Bell, Mark Borkowski, Peggy Brusseau, Rebecca Hardy, Maria (M.G.) Harris, J.A. Henderson, Michelle Paver, David Yelland. Founded 1993.

The Lisa Richards Agency

108 Upper Leeson Street, Dublin 4,
Republic of Ireland
tel +353 (0)1 6375000 *fax* +353 (0)1 6671256
email faith@lisarichards.ie
website www.lisarichards.ie
Contact Faith O'Grady

Handles fiction and general non-fiction (Ireland 10%, UK 15%, USA/translation 20%, film/TV 15%). Approach with proposal and sample chapter for non-fiction and 3–4 chapters and synopsis for fiction (sae essential). No reading fee. *Overseas associate* The Marsh Agency for translation rights.

Clients include Simon Ashe-Browne, Des Bishop, Laura Jane Cassidy, Helena Close, June Considine (aka Laura Elliot), Matt Cooper, Damian Corless, Christine Dwyer Hickey, John Giles, Karen Gillece, Tara Heavey, Maeve Higgins, Paul Howard (aka Ross O'Carroll-Kelly), Amy Huberman, Arlene Hunt, Roisin Ingle, Alison Jameson, Declan Lynch, Colm O'Regan ('Irish Mammies'), Emily Mason, Roisin Meaney, Pauline McLynn, Anna McPartlin, David O'Doherty, Mary O'Donoghue, Mark O'Sullivan, Damien Owens, Nicolas Roche, Orla Tinsley, Sheena Wilkinson. Founded 1998.

Robinson Literary Agency Ltd – see Rogers, Coleridge & White Ltd

Rogers, Coleridge & White Ltd*

20 Powis Mews, London W11 1JN
tel 020-7221 3717 *fax* 020-7229 9084

email info@rcwlitagency.com
website www.rcwlitagency.com
Chairman Deborah Rogers, *Managing Director* Peter Straus, *Directors* Gill Coleridge, Georgia Garrett, David Miller, Peter Robinson, Zoe Waldie, Patricia White (children's), *Foreign Rights Directors* Stephen Edwards, Margaret Halton, Laurence Laluyaux *Agents* Sam Copeland, Jennifer Hewson (associate), Claire Wilson (children's)

Full-length book MSS, including children's books (home 15%, USA 20%, translation 20%). No unsolicited MSS, and no submissions by fax. No reading fee. Note that due to the volume of unsolicited queries, it is now policy to respond (usually within 6 weeks) only if interested in the material. Founded 1967.

Elizabeth Roy Literary Agency

White Cottage, Greatford, Nr Stamford, Lincs. PE9 4PR
tel/fax (01778) 560672
website www.elizabethroyliteraryagency.co.uk

Children's fiction and non-fiction – writers and illustrators (home 15%, overseas 20%). Send preliminary letter, synopsis and sample chapters with names of publishers and agents previously contacted. Return postage essential. No reading fee. Founded 1990.

Uli Rushby-Smith Literary Agency

72 Plimsoll Road, London N4 2EE
tel 020-7354 2718 *fax* 020-7354 2718
Director Uli Rushby-Smith

Fiction and non-fiction, literary and commercial (home 15%, USA/foreign 20%). No poetry, picture books, plays or film scripts. Send outline, sample chapters (no disks) and return postage. No reading fee. Founded 1993.

The Sayle Literary Agency*

1 Petersfield, Cambridge CB1 1BB
tel (01223) 303035 *fax* (01223) 301638
email info@sayleliteraryagency.com
website www.sayleliteraryagency.com
Proprietor & Agent Rachel Calder

Fiction: general, literary and crime. Non-fiction: current affairs, social issues, travel, biographies, history (home 15%, USA/translation 20%). No plays, poetry, textbooks, children's, technical, legal or medical books. No reading fee. See website for submission guidelines. Translation rights handled by The Marsh Agency Ltd. Film and TV rights handled by Sayle Screen Ltd. US rights handled by Dunow Carlson and Lerner. Represents UK rights for Darhansoff and Verill.

Sayle Screen Ltd

11 Jubilee Place, London SW3 3TD
tel 020-7823 3883 *fax* 020-7823 3363
email info@saylescreen.com
website www.saylescreen.com
Agents Jane Villiers, Matthew Bates, Toby Moorcroft

Specialises in scripts for film, TV, theatre and radio. No reading fee. Only accepts submissions by post; send showreel or script with CV and covering letter. Every submission carefully considered, but responds only to submissions it wishes to take further; not able to return material sent in. Represents film and TV rights in fiction and non-fiction for The Sayle Literary Agency, Greene and Heaton Ltd and Peter Robinson Ltd. Works in conjunction with agents in New York and Los Angeles.

The Science Factory Ltd

Scheideweg 34C, 20253 Hamburg, Germany
tel 020-7193 7296
email info@sciencefactory.co.uk
website www.sciencefactory.co.uk
Director Peter Tallack

Serious popular non-fiction, particularly science, history and current affairs, by academics and journalists (home 15%, overseas 20%). No fiction. In first instance send proposal with chapter summaries and sample chapter (not the first). Email submissions encouraged and given priority over hard-copy submissions (material not returned). No reading fee. Will suggest revision.

Authors include Anjana Ahuja, Anil Ananthaswamy, Jim Baggott, David Bainbridge, Vaughan Bell, Jesse Bering, Lee Billings, Piers Bizony, Daniel Bor, Dennis Bray, Dean Buonomano, Stuart Clark, Daniel Clery, Matthew Cobb, Enrico Coen, Michael Corballis, Moheb Costandi, Trevor Cox, Nicholas Dunbar, John Duncan, Richard Elwes, Georgina Ferry, Lone Frank, Christine Garwood, Simon Ings, Harris Irfan, Stephen Joseph, Jay Kennedy, Manjit Kumar, Peter Lamont, Ehsan Masood, Arthur I. Miller, Mark Miondownick, Ted Nield, Michael Nielsen, Paul Parsons, Aarathi Prasad, Angela Saini, Ian Sample, Nicholas J. Saunders, Menno Schilthuizen, P.D. Smith, Tom Stafford, Ian Stewart, Thomas Suddendorf, Frank Swain, Brian Switek, Mark Van Vugt, Geerat J. Vermeij, Adam Zeman. UK-registered limited company established 2008.

Scott Ferris Associates

22 Dunns Lane, Mumbles, Swansea SA3 4AA
tel (01792) 360453
email riversscott@btinternet.com
Partners Gloria Ferris and Rivers Scott

General fiction and non-fiction (home 15%, overseas/TV/radio 20%). No unsolicited MSS or submissions by email. Preliminary letter and postage essential. Reading fee by arrangement. Founded 1981.

Linda Seifert Management Ltd

4th Floor, 104 Great Portland Street, London W1W 6PE

tel 020-7636 9154
email contact@lindaseifert.com
website www.lindaseifert.com
Director Edward Hughes

Represents writers, directors and producers for film, TV and radio (home 10%, overseas 20%). Client list ranges from the highly established to the emerging talent of tomorrow – see website for details. Established 2002.

The Sharland Organisation Ltd

The Manor House, Manor Street, Raunds, Northants NN9 6JW
tel (01933) 626600
email tso@btconnect.com
website www.sharlandorganisation.co.uk
Directors Mike Sharland, Alice Sharland

Specialises in film, TV, stage and radio rights throughout the world (home 15%, overseas 20%). Preliminary letter and return postage is essential. No reading fee. Works in conjunction with overseas agents. Founded 1988.

Anthony Sheil in association with Aitken Alexander Associates

18–21 Cavaye Place, London SW10 9PT
tel 020-7373 8672 *fax* 020-7373 6002
website www.aitkenalexander.co.uk
Proprietor Anthony Sheil

Quality fiction and non-fiction (home 15%, overseas 20%). No plays, film/TV scripts, poetry, short stories or children's fiction. Send preliminary letter with half-page synopsis and first consecutive 30pp of sample material. Include return postage. No reading fee.

Authors include Caroline Alexander, the estate of John Fowles, John Keegan, Robert Wilson.

Sheil Land Associates Ltd*

(incorporating Richard Scott Simon Ltd 1971 and Christy & Moore Ltd 1912)
52 Doughty Street, London WC1N 2LS
tel 020-7405 9351 *fax* 020-7831 2127
email info@sheilland.co.uk
Agents UK & US Sonia Land, Vivien Green, Piers Blofeld, Ian Drury, Gaia Banks *Film/theatre/TV* Lucy Fawcett, Rachel Dench *Foreign* Gaia Banks, Virginia Ascione

Quality literary and commercial fiction and non-fiction, including: politics, history, military history, gardening, thrillers, crime, romance, drama, science fiction, fantasy, biography, travel, cookery, humour, UK and foreign estates (home 15%, USA/translation 20%). Also film, TV, radio and theatre scripts. Welcomes approaches from new clients to start or to develop their careers. Please see website for submission instructions. No reading fee. *Overseas associates* Georges Borchardt, Inc. (Richard Scott Simon). *US film and TV representation* CAA, APA and others.

Clients include Sally Abbott, Peter Ackroyd, Benedict Allen, Charles Allen, Pam Ayres, Hugh Bicheno, Melvyn Bragg, Steven Carroll, Mark Chadbourn, Lana Citron, David Cohen, Anna del Conte, Elspeth Cooper, Elizabeth Corley, Seamus Deane, Mia Dolan, Angus Donald, Alex Dryden, Joe Dunlop, Chris Ewan, Robert Fabbri, Ann Featherstone, Alan Gilbey, Jean Goodhind, Robert Green, Graham Hancock, Felicity Hayes-McCoy, Susan Hill, Richard Holmes, Brooke Kinsella, Mark Lawrence, Richard Mabey, The Brothers McLeod, Roger Pearce, Graham Rice, Leo Ruikbie, Anthony Seldon, Diane Setterfield, Tom Sharpe, Louise Soraya Black, Laura Summers, Martin Stephen, Jeffrey Tayler, Andrew Taylor, Rose Tremain, Barry Unsworth, Boris Volodarsky, Prof. Stanley Wells, Neil White, Julia Widdows, J.C. Wilsher and the estates of Catherine Cookson, Helen Forrester, Patrick O'Brian, Penelope Mortimer, Jean Rhys, F.A. Worsley and Stephen Gately. Founded 1962.

Caroline Sheldon Literary Agency Ltd*

71 Hillgate Place, London W8 7SS
tel 020-7727 9102
email carolinesheldon@carolinesheldon.co.uk, pennyholroyde@carolinesheldon.co.uk
website www.carolinesheldon.co.uk, www.carolinesheldonillustrators.co.uk
Contacts Caroline Sheldon, Penny Holroyde

Fiction and non-fiction and children's books (home 15%, USA/translation 20%, film/TV 15%). Special interests: fiction – all fiction for women, sagas, suspense, contemporary, chick lit, historical fiction, fantasy and humour; non-fiction – true life stories, animal stories, memoirs and humour; children's – fiction for all age groups, contemporary, comic, fantasy and illustration for children's books.

Send submissions by email only with Submissions/ Title of work/Name of author in subject line. Include full introductory information about yourself and your writing and the first 3 chapters only or equivalent length of work.

Does not represent TV or film scripts except for existing book writing clients. No reading fee. Gives editorial advice on work of exceptional promise. Founded 1985.

Jeffrey Simmons

15 Penn House, Mallory Street, London NW8 8SX
tel 020-7224 8917
email jasimmons@unicombox.co.uk

Specialises in fiction (no science fiction, horror or fantasy), biography, autobiography, show business, personality books, law, crime, politics, world affairs. Full-length MSS (home from 10%, overseas from 15%). Will suggest revision. No reading fee, but preliminary letter essential.

Sinclair-Stevenson

3 South Terrace, London SW7 2TB
tel 020-7581 2550 *fax* 020-7581 2550

Directors Christopher Sinclair-Stevenson, Deborah Sinclair-Stevenson

Full-length MSS (home 15%, USA/translation 20%). General – no children's books. No reading fee; will suggest revision. Founded 1995.

Robert Smith Literary Agency Ltd*

12 Bridge Wharf, 156 Caledonian Road, London N1 9UU
tel 020-7278 2444 *fax* 020-7833 5680
email robertsmith.literaryagency@virgin.net
Directors Robert Smith, Anne Smith

Non-fiction only: autobiography and biography, topical subjects, history, lifestyle, popular culture, entertainment, sport, true crime, health and nutrition, illustrated books (home 15%, overseas 20%). No unsolicited MSS. No reading fee. Will suggest revision.

Authors include Kate Adie (serialisations), Arthur Aldridge, Richard Baker, Peta Bee, Paul Begg, Ralph Bulger, Robert Clarke, Judy Cook, Rosie Dunn, Stewart Evans, Becci Fox, Neil and Christine Hamilton, Andrew Hansford, Bob Harris, Naomi Jacobs, Albert Jack, Brian and Tim Kirby, Roberta Kray, Angela Levin, Chris Lightbown, David Litchfield, Ann Ming, James Moore, Michelle Morgan, Paul Nero, Kim Noble, Theo Paphitis, Howard Raymond, Nathan Shapow, Keith Skinner, Stephen Twigg. Founded 1997.

The Standen Literary Agency

4 Winton Avenue, London N11 2AT
tel 020-8245 2606 *fax* 020-8245 2606
email submissions@standenliteraryagency.com
website www.standenliteraryagency.com
Director Yasmin Standen

Interested in discovering new writers and launching the careers of first-time writers. Literary and commercial fiction including picture books (home 15%, overseas 20%). Non-fiction: get in touch to see if genre is represented. Send submissions by email only; no submissions by post. Send first 3 chapters, a synopsis (one side of A4) and a covering letter. Submissions may be made online via the website. No reading fee. See website for further information. *Authors* include Raj & Pablo, L.H. Burswood, Zara Kane, Andrew Murray. Founded 2004.

Abner Stein*

10 Roland Gardens, London SW7 3PH
tel 020-7373 0456 *fax* 020-7370 6316
Contact Caspian Dennis, Arabella Stein, Sandy Violette

Fiction, general non-fiction and children's (home 10%, overseas 20%). Not taking on any new clients at present.

Micheline Steinberg Associates

104 Great Portland Street, London W1W 6PE
tel 020-7631 1310
email info@steinplays.com
website www.steinplays.com
Agents Micheline Steinberg, Helen MacAuley

Represents writers for theatre, TV, film, radio and animation. Film and TV rights in fiction and non-fiction on behalf of book agents (home 10%, overseas 15–20%). Works in association with agents in USA and overseas. No unsolicited submissions. Industry recommendation preferred. Founded 1987.

Rochelle Stevens & Co

2 Terretts Place, Upper Street, London N1 1QZ
tel 020-7359 3900 *fax* 020-7354 5729
email info@rochellestevens.com
website www.rochellestevens.com
Directors Rochelle Stevens, Frances Arnold

Drama scripts for film, TV, theatre and radio. Preliminary letter, CV and sae essential. Founded 1984.

Shirley Stewart Literary Agency*

3rd Floor, 4A Nelson Road, London SE10 9JB
tel 020-8293 3000
Director Shirley Stewart

Specialises in literary fiction and general non-fiction (home 10–15%, overseas 20%). No poetry, plays, film scripts, science fiction, fantasy or children's books. No reading fee. Send preliminary letter, synopsis and first 3 chapters plus return postage. Founded 1993.

Sarah Such Literary Agency

81 Arabella Drive, London SW15 5LL
tel 020-8876 4228
email info@sarahsuch.com
website twitter.com/sarahsuch
Proprietor Sarah Such

High-quality literary and commercial non-fiction and fiction for adults, young adults and children with a particular focus on debut novels, biography, memoir, history, popular culture and humour (home 15%, TV/film 20%, overseas 20%). No reading fee. Will suggest revision. Submit synopsis and a sample chapter (as a Word attachment if sending by email) plus author biography. Sae essential for postal submissions. No unsolicited MSS or telephone enquiries. TV/film scripts for established clients only. No radio or theatre scripts, poetry, fantasy, self-help or short stories. Film/TV representation: Aitken Alexander Associates Ltd.

Authors include Matthew De Abaitua, Nick Barlay, Salem Brownstone, Rob Chapman, John Harris Dunning, Rob Harris, John Hartley, Marisa Heath, Wayne Holloway-Smith, Antony Johnston, Louisa Leaman, Mathew Lyons, Sam Manning, Vesna Maric, David May, Kit McCall, Henrietta Morrison (Lily's Kitchen), Ben Osborne, Marian Pashley, Sarah Penny, Greg Rowland, John Rowley, Caroline Sanderson, Tony De Saulles, Nikhil Singh, Sara Starbuck, Emma Woolf. Founded 2006.

The Susijn Agency Ltd

3rd Floor, 64 Great Titchfield Street,
London W1W 7QH
tel 020-7580 6341 *fax* 020-7580 8626
email info@thesusijnagency.com
website www.thesusijnagency.com
Agent Laura Susijn

Specialises in world rights in English- and non-English-language literature: literary fiction and general non-fiction (home 15%, overseas 20%, theatre/film/TV/ radio 15%). Send synopsis and 2 sample chapters. No reading fee.

Authors include Peter Ackroyd, Uzma Aslam Khan, Robin Baker, Abdelkader Benali, Robert Craig, Tessa De Loo, Gwynne Dyer, Radhika Jha, Kolton Lee, Jeffrey Moore, Karl Shaw, Paul Sussman, Dubravka Ugrešić, Alex Wheatle, Adam Zameenzad. Founded 1998.

The Tennyson Agency

10 Cleveland Avenue, London SW20 9EW
tel 020-8543 5939
email submissions@tenagy.co.uk
website www.tenagy.co.uk
Theatre, Radio, Television & Film Scripts Christopher Oxford, Adam Sheldon

Scripts and related material for theatre, film and TV only (home 15%, overseas 20%). No reading fee.

Clients include Tony Bagley, Kristina Bedford, Alastair Cording, Caroline Coxon, Iain Grant, Jonathan Holloway, Philip Hurd-Wood, Steve Macgregor, Antony Mann, Elizabeth Moynihan, Ken Ross, Matthew Salkeld, Graeme Scarfe, Diane Speakman, Diana Ward and the estate of Julian Howell. Founded 2002.

JM Thurley Management

Archery House, 33 Archery Square, Walmer, Deal, Kent CT14 7JA
tel (01304) 371721
email jmthurley@aol.com
website www.thecuttingedge.biz
Contact Jon Thurley

Specialises in commercial and literary full-length fiction and commercial work for film and TV. No plays, poetry, short stories, articles or fantasy. No reading fee but preliminary letter and sae essential. Editorial/creative advice provided to clients (home 15%, overseas 20%). Links with leading US and European agents. Founded 1976.

Jane Turnbull*

Mailing address Barn Cottage, Veryan Churchtown, Truro TR2 5QA
tel (01872) 501317
email jane@janeturnbull.co.uk
London Office 58 Elgin Crescent, London W11 2JJ
tel 020-7727 9409
website www.janeturnbull.co.uk

High quality non-fiction; biography, history, natural history, lifestyle, humour; TV tie-ins, some literary fiction (home 15%, USA/translation 20%), performance rights (15%). Works in conjunction with Aitken Alexander Associates Ltd for sale of translation rights. No reading fee. Preliminary letter (NOT email) essential; no unsolicited MSS. Founded 1986.

United Agents*

12–26 Lexington Street, London W1F 0LE
tel 020-3214 0800
email info@unitedagents.co.uk
website www.unitedagents.co.uk
Agents Simon Trewin, Caroline Dawnay, Anna Webber, Sarah Ballard, Robert Kirby, Jim Gill, Rosemary Scoular, Carol McArthur, Charles Walker, Jodie Marsh *(children's and young adult)*

Fiction and non-fiction (home 15%, USA/translation 20%). No reading fee. See website for submission details. Founded 2008.

Ed Victor Ltd*

6 Bayley Street, Bedford Square, London WC1B 3HE
tel 020-7304 4100 *fax* 020-7304 4111
website www.edvictor.com
Executive Chairman Ed Victor, *Joint Managing Directors* Sophie Hicks, Margaret Phillips, *Directors* Carol Ryan, Graham C. Greene CBE, Leon Morgan, Hitesh Shah, *Editorial Director* Philippa Harrison

Fiction, non-fiction and children's books (home 15%, USA 15%, children's 15%, translation 20%). No short stories, poetry or film/TV scripts or plays. No reading fee. No unsolicited MSS. No response to submissions by email. Represented in all foreign markets.

Authors include John Banville, Herbie Brennan, Eoin Colfer, Sir Ranulph Fiennes, Frederick Forsyth, A.A. Gill, Josephine Hart, Jack Higgins, Nigella Lawson, Kathy Lette, Allan Mallinson, Andrew Marr, Frederic Raphael, Danny Scheinmann and the estates of Douglas Adams, Raymond Chandler, Dame Iris Murdoch, Sir Stephen Spender, Irving Wallace. Founded 1976.

Wade and Doherty Literary Agency Ltd

33 Cormorant Lodge, Thomas More Street, London E1W 1AU
tel 020-7488 4171 *fax* 020-7488 4172
email rw@rwla.com, bd@rwla.com
website www.rwla.com
Directors Robin Wade, Broo Doherty

General fiction and non-fiction, excluding children's books (home 10%, overseas 20%). No poetry, plays, picture books or short stories. See website for submission guidelines. Email submissions preferred. New authors welcome. No reading fee. Founded 2001.

Watson, Little Ltd*

48–56 Bayham Place, London NW1 0EU
tel 020-7388 7529 *fax* 020-7388 8501
email office@watsonlittle.com
website www.watsonlittle.com
Contact Mandy Little, James Wills, Sallyanne Sweeney

Fiction, commercial women's fiction, crime and literary fiction. Non-fiction special interests include history, science, popular psychology, self-help and general leisure books. Also children's fiction and non-fiction (home 15%, USA/translation 20%). No short stories, poetry, TV, play or film scripts. Not interested in purely academic writers. Send informative preliminary letter, synopsis and sample chapters. *Overseas associates* The Marsh Agency Ltd; *Film and TV associates* The Sharland Organisation Ltd and Ki Agency; *USA associates* Howard Morhaim Literary Agency (adult) and the Chudney Agency (children's).

Authors include Adam Hart-Davis, Christopher Fowler, Martin Edwards, James Wong, Prof. Susan Blackmore, Mark Boyle and Dr Sarah Brewer.

AP Watt Ltd*

20 John Street, London WC1N 2DR
tel 020-7405 6774
email apw@apwatt.co.uk
website www.apwatt.co.uk
Directors Caradoc King, Linda Shaughnessy, Derek Johns, Georgia Garrett, Natasha Fairweather

Full-length MSS; dramatic works for all media (home 15%, overseas 20% including commission to foreign agent). No poetry. No reading fee. Does not accept unsolicited MSS or any other material. Send a query letter and full plot synopsis in first instance.

Authors include Trezza Azzopardi, Sebastian Barry, Quentin Blake, Grace Coddington, Helen Dunmore, Nicholas Evans, Giles Foden, Janice Galloway, Martin Gilbert, Nadine Gordimer, Linda Grant, Reginald Hill, Michael Holroyd, Michael Ignatieff, Mick Jackson, Philip Kerr, Dick King-Smith, John Lanchester, Alison Lurie, Jan Morris, Andrew O'Hagan, Susie Orbach, Philip Pullman, James Robertson, Jancis Robinson, Jon Ronson, Elaine Showalter, Graham Swift and the estates of Graves and Maugham. Founded 1875.

Josef Weinberger Plays Ltd

(formerly Warner/Chappell Plays Ltd)
12–14 Mortimer Street, London W1T 3JJ
tel 020-7580 2827 *fax* 020-7436 9616

Specialises in stage plays. Works in conjunction with overseas agents. No unsolicited MSS; preliminary letter essential. Founded 1938.

Whispering Buffalo Literary Agency Ltd

97 Chesson Road, London W14 9QS
tel 020-7565 4737
email info@whisperingbuffalo.com
website www.whisperingbuffalo.com
Director Mariam Keen

Commercial/literary fiction and non-fiction, children's and young adult fiction (home 15%, overseas 20%). Special interest in book-to-screen adaptations; TV and film rights in novels and non-fiction handled in-house. No reading fee. Will suggest revision. Founded 2008.

Eve White*

54 Gloucester Street, London SW1V 4EG
tel 020-7630 1155
email eve@evewhite.co.uk
website www.evewhite.co.uk
Contact Eve White, Jack Ramm

Commercial and literary fiction and non-fiction, children's fiction (home 15%, overseas 20%). No reading fee. Will suggest revision where appropriate. See website for up-to-date submission requirements. No submissions by mail.

Authors include Saskia Sarginson, Fergus McNeill, Kate Scott, Ruth Warburton, Ellie Daines, Sarah Naughton, Michaela Morgan, Simon Nicholson, Lorrie Porter, Miriam Halahmy, Ivan Brett, Susanna Corbett, Tracey Corderoy, Jimmy Docherty, Rae Earl, Yvvette Edwards, Abie Longstaff, Jim Lusby, Kate Maryon, Rachael Mortimer, Ciaran Murtagh, Gillian Rogerson, Ruth Saberton, Alexander Stobbs, Tabitha Suzuma, Andy Stanton. Founded 2003.

Isabel White Literary Agent

14 Neville Court, Abbey Road, London NW8 9DD
tel 020-3070 1602 *fax* 020-3006 8791
email isabel@isabelwhite.co.uk (trade), query.isabelwhite@googlemail.com (submissions)
website www.isabelwhite.co.uk
Proprietor Isabel White

Fiction and non-fiction (home 15%, overseas 20%). Books only – no film, TV or stage plays, poetry, short stories or academic monographs. Email submissions only. See website for submission guidelines. No reading fee.

Authors include The Bourbon Kid, Suzi Brent, Iain Clark, Graeme Kent, Ivy Ngeow. Founded 2008.

Dinah Wiener Ltd*

12 Cornwall Grove, London W4 2LB
tel 020-8994 6011 *fax* 020-8994 6044
Director Dinah Wiener

Fiction and general non-fiction (home 15%, overseas 20%), film and TV in association (15%). No plays, scripts, poetry, short stories or children's books. No reading fee, but preliminary letter and return postage essential.

WME*

(William Morris Agency (UK) Ltd)
Centre Point, 103 New Oxford Street, London WC1A 1DD
tel 020-7534 6800 *fax* 020-7534 6900

website www.wma.com
Books Claudia Webb, Cathryn Summerhayes, *TV* Isabella Zoltowski, Coz Jackson

Literary and commercial fiction, crime, thrillers, young adult fiction, memoir, history, popular culture (film/TV 10%, UK books 15%, USA books/ translation 20%). No science fiction, fantasy, poetry, self-help or children's picture books. Accepts submissions by post only. Send a synopsis and 3 sample chapters (50pp or fewer). Worldwide talent and literary agency with offices in New York, Beverly Hills, Nashville and Miami.

The Wylie Agency (UK) Ltd

17 Bedford Square, London WC1B 3JA
tel 020-7908 5900 *fax* 020-7908 5901
email mail@wylieagency.co.uk
website www.wylieagency.co.uk
President Andrew Wylie

Literary fiction and non-fiction (home 10%, overseas 20%, USA 15%). No unsolicited MSS; send preliminary letter with 2 sample chapters and sae in first instance. Founded 1996.

Susan Yearwood Literary Agency

2 Knebworth House, Londesborough Road, London N16 8RL
tel 020-7503 0954
email susan@susanyearwood.com
website www.susanyearwood.com
Contact Susan Yearwood

Literary and commercial fiction (home 15%, overseas 20%), including crime, general and young adult. Non-fiction. Send first 30pp and a synopsis via email. No reading fee. Founded 2007.

Literary agents overseas

Before submitting material, writers are advised to send a preliminary letter with a sae/sase or to send an email to ascertain terms.

ARGENTINA

International Editors Co.

Avenida Cabildo 1156, 1426 Buenos Aires
tel +54-11-4788-2992
email costa@iecobaires.com.ar

The Nancy H. Smith Literary Agency

Margaret Murray, Ayacucho 1867, 1112 Buenos Aires
tel/fax +51-11-4084-5508
email memurray@ciudad.com.ar
Diana Stobart, 30 Acton Lane, London W4 5ED
tel 020-8995 4769 *fax* 020-8747 4012
email distobart@aol.com

No unsolicited MSS. No response to submissions by email. Founded 1938.

AUSTRALIA

Bryson Agency Australia Pty Ltd

PO Box 13327, Law Courts PO, Melbourne 8010
tel +61 (0)3 9329 2517 *fax* +61 (0)3 9600 9131
email fran@bryson.com.au
website www.bryson.com.au
Contact Fran Bryson

Represents writers operating in all media: print, film, TV, radio, the stage and electronic derivatives; specialises in representation of book writers. Query first before sending unsolicited MSS. Not accepting until further notice.

Curtis Brown (Australia) Pty Ltd

PO Box 19, Paddington, NSW 2021
tel +61 (0)2 9331 5301 *fax* +61 (0)2 9360 3935
email reception@curtisbrown.com.au
website www.curtisbrown.com.au

No reading fee.

BRAZIL

Agencia Riff

Av. Calógeras, no.6/sala 1007,
20030–070 Rio de Janeiro, RJ, Brazil
tel +55-21-2287-6299 *fax* +55-21-2287-6393
email lucia@agenciariff.com.br
website www.agenciariff.com.br
Contacts Lucia Riff, Laura Riff, João Paulo Riff

Agents for top Brazilian authors; co-agents for international publishing houses and literary agents. Home 10%, overseas 20%. No reading fee. Founded 1991.

Tassy Barham Associates

231 Westbourne Park Road, London W11 1EB
tel 020-7792 5899
email tassy@tassybarham.com
Proprietor Tassy Barham

Specialises in representing European and American authors, agents and publishers in Brazil, as well as the worldwide representation of Brazilian authors. Founded 1999.

Karin Schindler and Suely Pedro dos Santos Rights Representatives

Caixa Postal 19051, 04505–970 São Paulo, SP
tel +55-11-5041-9177 *fax* +55-11-5041-9077
email karin@agschindler.com.br, suely@agschindler.com.br

CANADA

Acacia House Publishing Services Ltd

62 Chestnut Avenue, Brantford, Ontario N3T 4C2
tel +1 519-752-0978 *fax* +1 519-752-8349
email bhanna.acacia@rogers.com
Managing Director Bill Hanna

Literary fiction/non-fiction, quality commercial fiction, most non-fiction (15% English worldwide, 25% translation, performance 20%). No horror or occult. Works with overseas agents. Query first with sample of 50pp max. Include return postage. No reading fee. Founded 1985.

Authors' Marketing Services Ltd

683 Annette Street, Toronto M6S 2C9
tel +1 416-763-8797 *fax* +1 416-763-1504
website www.hoffmanagency.ca
Directors Larry Hoffman, Antonia Hoffman, Sharon DeWynter

Adult fiction, biography and autobiography (home 15%, overseas 20%). Reading fee charged for unpublished writers; will suggest revision. Founded 1978.

The Cooke Agency

278 Bloor Street East, Suite 305, Toronto, Ontario M4W 3M4
tel +1 416-406-3390 *fax* +1 416-406-3389
email egriffin@cookeagency.ca
website www.cookeagency.ca

Agents Dean Cooke, Sally Harding, Suzanne Brandreth

Literary fiction, commercial fiction (science fiction, fantasy, mysteries and romance), non-fiction (specifically narrative-driven works in the areas of popular culture, science, history, politics and natural history), and middle-grade and young adult books. No children's picture books, poetry or screenplays. Submit query and first 4 pp by email (no attachments) to Elizabeth Griffin. Represents more than 100 writers. Co-agents: Curtis Brown Canada, Greene & Heaton, The Turnbull Agency. See website for submission guidelines. Founded 1992.

Anne McDermid & Associates Ltd

64 Bloem Avenue, Toronto, Ontario M6E 1S1
tel +1 416-324-8845 *fax* +1 416-324-8870
email info@mcdermidagency.com
website www.mcdermidagency.com
Director Anne McDermid

Literary fiction and non-fiction, and quality commercial fiction (home 15%, overseas 20%). No reading fee. Founded 1996.

Bella Pomer Agency Inc.

355 St Clair Avenue West, Suite 801, Toronto, Ontario M5P 1N5
tel +1 416-920-4949
President Bella Pomer

Not considering new clients. Founded 1978.

Carolyn Swayze Literary Agency Ltd

PO Box 39588, RPO White Rock, Surrey, BC V4A 0A9
email reception@swayzeagency.com
website www.swayzeagency.com
Proprietor Carolyn Swayze

Literary fiction, a limited list of commercial fiction and non-fiction. No romance, science fiction, poetry, screenplays or children's picture books. Eager to discover lively, thought-provoking narrative non-fiction, especially in the fields of science, history, travel, politics and memoir. No telephone calls: make contact by email or post. Send query including synopsis and short sample. Provide resume, publication credits, writing awards, education and experience relevant to the book project. If querying by post include email or sase for return of materials. No original artwork or photographs. Allow 6 weeks for a reply.

EASTERN EUROPE

Aura-Pont, Theatrical and Literary Agency Ltd

Veslařský Ostrov 62, 147 00, Prague 4, Czech Republic
tel +420 2-5155 4938 *fax* +420 2-5155 0207
email aura-pont@aura-pont.cz
website www.aura-pont.cz
Director Petra Marková

Handles authors' rights in theatre, film, TV, radio, software – both Czech and foreign (home 10%, overseas 15%). Founded 1990.

DILIA

Krátkého 1, 190 03 Prague 9, Czech Republic
tel +420 2-8389 1598 *fax* +420 2-8389 3599
email info@dilia.cz
website www.dilia.cz
Director Jiri Srstka

Theatrical and literary agency.

Andrew Nurnberg Associates Prague, s.r.o.

Jugoslávských partyzánů 17, 160 00 Prague 6, Czech Republic
tel +420 2-2278 2041
Contacts Petra Tobišková (tobiskova@nurnberg.cz), Jana Borovanova (borovanova@nurnberg.cz)

Prava I Prevodi Literary Agency Permissions & Rights Ltd

Yu-Business Centre, Blvd Mihaila Pupina 10B/I, 5th Floor, Suite 4, 11070 Belgrade, Serbia and Montenegro
tel +381 1-1311 9880 *fax* +381 1-1311 9879
email office@pravaiprevodi.org
website www.pravaiprevodi.org
Director Predraq Milenkovic, *Foreign Rights* Ana Milenkovic

Specialises in representing American and British authors in former Eastern Europe (15 languages). Founded 1983.

FRANCE

Agence Hoffman

77 Boulevard Saint-Michel, 75005 Paris
tel +33 (0)1 4326 5694 *fax* +33 (0)1 4326 3407
email info@agence-hoffman.com
Contact Georges Hoffman, Christine Scholz

Agence Michelle Lapautre

6 rue Jean Carriès, 75007 Paris
tel +33 (0)1 4734 8241 *fax* +33 (0)1 4734 0090
email agence@lapautre.com

Bureau Littéraire International

24 rue Saint Denis, F–92100 Boulogne Billancourt
tel +33 (0)1 4605 3911
Contact Geneviéve Ulmann

La Nouvelle Agence

7 rue Corneille, 75006 Paris
tel +33 (0)1 4325 8560 *fax* +33 (0)1 4325 4798

email lna@lanouvelleagence.fr
Contact Mary Kling

Susanna Lea Associates

28 rue Bonaparte, 75006 Paris
tel +33 (0)1 5310 2840 *fax* +33 (0)1 5310 2849
email fr-submission@susannalea.com
website www.susannaleaassociates.com

General fiction and non-fiction with international appeal. No plays, screenplays or poetry. Send query letter, brief synopsis, the first 3 chapters and/or proposal via the website. Established in Paris 2000, New York 2004, London 2008.

Promotion Littéraire

12 rue Pergolèse, 75116 Paris
tel +33 (0)1 4500 4210 *fax* +33 (0)1 4500 1018
email promolit@free.fr
Director Mariella Giannetti

Fiction, essays. Founded 1977.

GERMANY (SEE ALSO SWITZERLAND)

Michael Meller Literary Agency

Landwehr Strasse 17, 80336 Munich
tel +49 (0)89 366371 *fax* +49 (0)89 366372
email info@melleragency.com
website www.melleragency.com

Fiction and non-fiction (home 15%, overseas 20%). Send outline and first 50pp. No reading fee. Founded 1988.

Thomas Schlück GmbH

Literary Agency, Hinter der Worth 12, 30827 Garbsen
tel +49 (0)5131 497560 *fax* +49 (0)5131 497589
email mail@schlueckagent.com
website www.schlueckagent.com

No reading fee.

ITALY

Agenzia Letteraria Internazionale SRL

Via Valpetrosa 1, 20123 Milano
tel +39 02-865445, +39 02-861572 *fax* +39 02-876222
email barbieri@aglettinternazionale.it, info@agenzialetterariainternazionale.com
Manager Director Donatella Barbieri

Eulama SRL

Via Guido de Ruggiero 28, 00142 Rome
tel/fax +39 06-5407309
email eulama@fastwebnet.it
website www.eulama.com
President Karin von Prellwitz, *Directors* Norbert von Prellwitz, Pina Ocello von Prellwitz

International licensing agency representing publishing houses, agents and authors of adult and children's books worldwide. General and literary fiction, non-fiction, humanities. Promoting authors and publishers worldwide. Reading fee. Founded 1962.

Grandi & Associati SRL

Via Degli Olivetani 12, 20123 Milan
tel +39 02-4695541, +39 02-4818962
fax +39 02-48195108
email agenzia@grandieassociati.it
website www.grandieassociati.it
Directors Laura Grandi, Stefano Tettamanti

Provides publicity and foreign rights consultation for publishers and authors as well as sub-agent services; will suggest revision where appropriate. Reading fee. Founded 1988.

New Blitz Literary & TV Agency

Via di Panico 67, 00186 Rome
postal address CP 30047–00193, Rome 47
tel +39 06-4883268 *fax* +39 06-4883268
email blitzgacs@inwind.it
Literary Department Giovanni A.S. Congiu

No reading fee.

Piergiorgio Nicolazzini Literary Agency

Via GB Moroni 22, Milano 20146
tel/fax +39 02-48713365
email info@pnla.it
website www.pnla.it
Director Piergiorgio Nicolazzini

Literary and commerical fiction and non-fiction (home 10%, overseas 15–20%). No reading fee. Will suggest revision. Founded 1998.

JAPAN

The English Agency (Japan) Ltd

Sakuragi Building 4F, 6–7–3 Minami Aoyama, Minato-ku, Tokyo 107–0062
tel +81 (0)3-3406 5385 *fax* +81 (0)3-3406 5387
email info@eaj.co.jp
website www.eajco.jp
Managing Director Hamish Macaskill

Handles work by English-language writers living in Japan; arranges Japanese translations for internationally established publishers, agents and authors; arranges Japanese contracts for Japanese versions of all media. Standard commission: 10%. Own representatives in New York and London. No reading fee. Founded 1979.

THE NETHERLANDS

Internationaal Literatuur Bureau B.V.

Keizersgracht - 188, 1016 DW Amsterdam, The Netherlands

tel +31 20-3306658
email lkohn@planet.nl
website www.ilb.nu
Contacts Linda Kohn

NEW ZEALAND

Glenys Bean Writer's Agent

PO Box 639, Warkworth
email info@glenysbean.com
website www.glenysbean.com
Directors Fay Weldon, Glenys Bean

Adult and children's fiction, educational, non-fiction, film, TV, radio (10–20%). Send preliminary letter, synopsis and sae. No reading fee. Represented by Sanford Greenburger Associates Ltd (USA). *Translation/foreign rights* The Marsh Agency Ltd. Founded 1989.

Michael Gifkins & Associates

PO Box 6496, Wellesley Street PO, Auckland 1141
tel +64 (0)9 523 5032
email michael.gifkins@xtra.co.nz
Director Michael Gifkins

Literary and popular fiction, fine arts, substantial non-fiction (non-academic) co-publications (home 15%, overseas 20%). No reading fee. Will suggest revision. Does not accept unsolicited material. Founded 1985.

Playmarket

Level 2, 16 Cambridge Terrace, Te Aro, Wellington
PO Box 9767, Marion Square, Wellington 6141
tel +64 (0)4 382 8462
email info@playmarket.org.nz
website www.playmarket.org.nz
Director Murray Lynch

Playwrights' agent, advisor and bookshop. Representation, licensing and script development of New Zealand plays and playwrights. Currently licences over 400 productions of New Zealand plays each year, in New Zealand and around the world. Founded 1973.

Richards Literary Agency

postal address PO Box 31–240, Milford, Auckland 0620
tel/fax +64 (0)9 410 0209
email rla.richards@clear.net.nz
Staff Ray Richards, Elaine Blake, Judy Bartlam, Frances Plumpton

Full-length MSS, fiction, non-fiction, adult, juvenile, educational, academic books; films, TV, radio (home 15%, overseas 20%). Preliminary letter, synopsis with sae required. No reading fee. Co-agents in London and New York. 100 clients including Bryan Bruce, Joy Cowley, Tessa Duder, Witi Ihimaera, Brian Falkner. Founded 1977.

Total Fiction Services

PO Box 46-031, Park Avenue, Lower Hutt 5044
tel +64 (0)4 565 4429
email tfs@elseware.co.nz
website www.elseware.co.nz

General fiction, non-fiction, children's books. No poetry, or individual short stories or articles. Enquiries from New Zealand authors only. Email queries but no attachments. Hard copy preferred. No reading fee. Also offers assessment reports, mentoring and courses.

PORTUGAL

Ilidio da Fonseca Matos, Agente Literário Lda

Avenida Gomes Pereira, 105-3°–B, 1500–328 Lisbon
tel +351 21-716 2988
email ilidio.matos@oniduo.pt

No reading fee.

SCANDINAVIA, INC. FINLAND AND ICELAND

Bookman Literary Agency

Bastager 3, DK–2950 Vedbaek, Denmark
tel +45 4589 2520
email ihl@bookman.dk
website www.bookman.dk
Contact Mr Ib H. Lauritzen

Handles rights in Denmark, Sweden, Norway, Finland and Iceland for foreign authors.

Leonhardt & Høier Literary Agency A/S

Studiestraede 35, DK–1455 Copenhagen K, Denmark
tel +45 3313 2523 *fax* +45 3313 4992
email anneli@leonhardt-hoier.dk, monica@leonhardt-hoier.dk
website www.leonhardt-hoier.dk

No reading fee.

Lennart Sane Agency AB

Holländareplan 9, S–374 34 Karlshamm, Sweden
tel +46 4541 2356 *fax* +46 4541 4920
email lennart.sane@lennartsaneagency.com
website www.lennartsaneagency.com
Directors Lennart Sane, Elisabeth Sane, Philip Sane

Fiction, non-fiction, children's books. Founded 1969.

Ulf Töregård Agency AB

374 33 Karlshamn, Sweden
tel +46 4548 4340
Director Ulf Töregård

Represents authors, agents and publishers in Scandinavia and Holland for rights in fiction, non-fiction and children's books. Founded 1995.

SOUTH AFRICA

Bond Literary Agents & Specialized Services

PO Box 164, Umhlanga Rocks 4320, South Africa
tel/fax +27 (0)31 584 8888
email jeangaiser@telkomsa.net
Chief Executives Jean Davidson, Jean Gaiser, *Chief Editor* Eileen Molver, *Poetry Advisor* Irene Aarons

Full length MSS. Fiction and non-fiction; juvenile and children's literature. Consultancy service on contracts and copyright. Preliminary phone call or letter and sase required. Reading fee; terms on application. Founded 1985.

SPAIN

Carmen Balcells Agencia Literaria S.A.

Diagonal 580, 08021 Barcelona
tel +34-93-200-89-33 *fax* +34-93-200-70-41
email ag-balcells@ag-balcells.com
Contact Gloria Gutiérrez

International Editors Co., S.L.

Provenza 276, Barcelona 08008
tel +34-93-215-88-12 *fax* +34-93-487-35-83
email ieco@internationaleditors.com
Contact Isabel Monteagudo

RDC Agencia Literaria SL

C Fernando VI, No 13–15, Madrid 28004
tel +34-91-308-55-85 *fax* +34-91-308-56-00
email rdc@rdclitera.com
Director Raquel de la Concha

Representing foreign fiction, non-fiction, children's books and Spanish authors. No reading fee.

Lennart Sane Agency AB

Calle de Eraso 36, ES-28028 Madrid
tel +34-911-23-34-92
email info@lennartsaneagency.com
website www.lennartsaneagency.com
President Lennart Sane

Fiction, non-fiction, children's books, film and TV scripts. Founded 1965.

Julio F. Yañez Agencia Literaria S.L.

Via Augusta 139, 6–2A, 08021 Barcelona
tel +34-93-200-71-07 *fax* +34-93-200-76-56
email montse@yanezag.com
Director Montse F-Yañez

SWITZERLAND

Paul & Peter Fritz AG Literary Agency

Jupiterstrasse 1, CH–8032 Zürich
tel +41 44-388 4140 *fax* +41 44-388 4130
email info@fritzagency.com
website www.fritzagency.com

Represents agents and publishers in German-language areas. Representation of individual authors is restricted to German-language authors. No reading fee.

Liepman AG

Englischviertelstrasse 59, CH-8032 Zürich
tel +41 43-268 2380 *fax* +41 43-268 2381
email info@liepmanagency.com
website www.liepmanagency.com
Contacts Marc Koralnik, Ronit Zafran

Represents authors, agents and publishers from all over the world for German translation rights, and selected international authors for world rights. No reading fee.

Mohrbooks AG, Literary Agency

Klosbachstrasse 110, CH–8032 Zürich
tel +41 43-244 8626 *fax* +41 43-244 8627
email info@mohrbooks.com
website www.mohrbooks.com
Contacts Sabine Ibach, Sebastian Ritscher

No reading fee.

NPA (Neue Presse Agentur)

Haldenstrasse 5, Haus am Herterberg, 8500 Frauenfeld-Herten, Switzerland
tel +41 52-721 4374
Director René Marti

Looking for occasional contributors to write for German/Swiss papers and magazines in the German language. Founded 1950.

USA

**Member of the Association of Authors' Representatives*

The Axelrod Agency*

55 Main Street, PO Box 357, Chatham, NY 12037
tel +1 518-392-2100
email steve@axelrodagency.com
President Steven Axelrod

Full-length MSS. Fiction (home 15%, overseas 20%), film and TV rights (15%); will suggest revision where appropriate. Works with overseas agents. No reading fee. Founded 1983.

Berman, Boals & Flynn

208 West 30th Street, Room 401, New York, NY 10001
tel +1 212-500-1424 *fax* +1 212-500-1426

Dramatic writing only, and only by recommendation.

BigScore Productions Inc.

PO Box 4575, Lancaster, PA 17604
tel +1 717-293-0247 *fax* +1 717-293-1945

email bigscore@bigscoreproductions.com
Contact David A. Robie

Fiction and non-fiction (home 15%). No poetry or TV/film scripts. Contact by email only. Founded 1995.

Georges Borchardt Inc.*

136 East 57th Street, New York, NY 10022
tel +1 212-753-5785 *fax* +1 212-838-6518
Directors Georges Borchardt, Anne Borchardt, Valerie Brochardt

Full-length and short MSS (home/ British/ performance 15%, translations 20%). Agents in most foreign countries. No unsolicited MSS. No reading fee. Founded 1967.

Brandt & Hochman Literary Agents Inc.*

1501 Broadway, Suite 2310, New York, NY 10036
tel +1 212-840-5760 *fax* +1 212-840-5776
Contact Gail Hochman, *UK Representative* A.M. Heath & Co. Ltd

Full-length and short MSS (home 15%, overseas 20%), performance rights (15%). No reading fee.

The Helen Brann Agency Inc.*

94 Curtis Road, Bridgewater, CT 06752
tel +1 860-354-9580 *fax* +1 860-355-2572
email hbrann@helenbrannagency.com
President Helen Brann

Pema Browne Ltd

71 Pine Road, Woodbourne, NY 12788
email ppbltd@optonline.net
website www.pemabrowneltd.com
President Pema Browne, *Vice President* Perry J. Browne

Fiction, non-fiction and juvenile books (home/ overseas 20%). Only published children's book authors will be accepted for review. Will only review MSS if never sent out to publishers; no simultaneous submissions to other agents. Send query with sase; no phone, fax or email queries with attachments. Founded 1966.

Browne & Miller Literary Associates

(formerly Multimedia Product Development Inc.)
410 South Michigan Avenue, Suite 460, Chicago, IL 60605
tel +1 312-922-3063 *fax* +1 312-922-1905
email mail@browneandmiller.com
website www.browneandmiller.com
Contact Danielle Egan-Miller

General fiction and non-fiction (home 15%, overseas 20%). Select young adult projects. Works in conjunction with foreign agents. Will suggest revision; no reading fee. Founded 1971.

Maria Carvainis Agency Inc.*

1270 Avenue of the Americas, Suite 2320, New York, NY 10020
tel +1 212-245-6365 *fax* +1 212-245-7196
email mca@mariacarvainis.com
President & Literary Agent Maria Carvainis

Adult fiction and non-fiction (home 15%, overseas 20%). All categories of fiction (except science fiction and fantasy), especially literary and mainstream; mystery, thrillers and suspense; historical, Regency; young adult. Non-fiction: biography and memoir, health and women's issues, business, finance, psychology, popular science, popular culture. No reading fee. Query first; no unsolicited MSS. No queries by fax or email. Works in conjunction with foreign, TV and movie agents.

Frances Collin Literary Agent*

PO Box 33, Wayne, PA 19087-0033
tel +1 610-254-0555 *fax* +1 610-254-5029
email queries@francescollin.com
Owner Frances Collin, *Associate Agent* Sarah Yake

Home 15%, overseas 20%, performance rights 20%. Specialisations of interest to UK writers: literary fiction, young adult, mysteries, women's fiction, history, biography, science fiction, fantasy. No screenplays. No reading fee. No unsolicited MSS. Query via email only. Query letter in the body of the email, no attachments. Works in conjunction with agents worldwide. Founded 1948; successor to Marie Rodell-Frances Collin Literary Agency.

Don Congdon Associates Inc.*

110 William Street, Suite 2202, New York, NY 10038
tel +1 212-645-1229 *fax* +1 212-727-2688
email dca@doncongdon.com
website www.doncongdon.com
Agents Michael Congdon, Susan Ramer, Cristina Concepcion, Maura Kye-Casella, Katie Grimm, Katie Kotchman

Full-length and short MSS. General fiction and non-fiction (home 15%, overseas 19%, performance rights 15%). Works with co-agents overseas. No reading fee but no unsolicited MSS – query first with sase (no IRCs) or email for reply. Does not accept phone calls from querying authors. Founded 1983.

Richard Curtis Associates Inc.

171 East 74th Street, Floor 2, New York, NY 10021
tel +1 212-772-7363 *fax* +1 212-772-7393
website www.curtisagency.com
President Richard Curtis

All types of commercial non-fiction (home 15%, overseas 25%, film/TV 15%). Foreign rights handled by Baror International. Founded 1970.

Curtis Brown Ltd*

10 Astor Place, New York, NY 10003
tel +1 212-473-5400
Branch office 1750 Montgomery Street, San Francisco, CA 94111
tel +1-415-954 8566

Ceo Timothy Knowlton, *President* Peter Ginsberg (at CA branch office), *Contact* Query Dept (NY office), *Book* Ginger Clark, Katherine Fausset, Sarah LaPolla, Laura Blake Peterson, Maureen Walters, Mitchell Waters, *Film & TV rights* Holly Frederick, *Translation rights* Dave Barbor

Fiction and non-fiction, juvenile, film and TV rights. No unsolicited MSS; query first with sase. No reading fee; no handling fees.

DeFiore and Company*

47 East 19th Street, 3rd Floor, New York, NY 10003
email info@defioreandco.com, submissions@defioreandco.com
website www.defioreandco.com
Contact Brian DeFiore, Laurie Abkemeier, Matthew Elblonk, Kate Garrick, Meredith Kaffel, Caryn Karmatz Rudy, Adam Schear, Morris Shamah

Fiction and non-fiction (home 15%, overseas 20%). No poetry, science fiction, fantasy or romance. Query by email but if you must send by post, include SASE to ensure a response. Founded 1999.

Sandra Dijkstra Literary Agency*

PMB 515, 1155 Camino Del Mar, Del Mar, CA 92014
tel +1 858-755-3115
website www.dijkstraagency.com
President Sandra Dijkstra (adult only), *Acquiring Sub-agents* Elise Capron (adult only), Jill Marr (adult only), Thao Le (YA only), Jennifer Azantian (YA only), *Sub-rights Agent*, Andrea Cavallaro

Fiction: contemporary, women's, literary, suspense and thrillers. Non-fiction: narrative, history, business, psychology, self-help, science and memoir/biography (home 15%, overseas 20%). Works in conjunction with foreign and film agents. Email submissions only. Please see website for the most up-to-date guidelines. No reading fee. Founded 1981.

Donadio & Olson Inc.*

121 West 27th Street, Suite 704, New York, NY 10001
tel +1 212-691-8077 *fax* +1 212-633-2837
email mail@donadio.com
Associates Edward Hibbert, Neil Olson, Carrie Howland

Literary fiction and non-fiction.

Dunham Literary, Inc.*

110 William Street, Suite 2202, New York, NY 10038–3901
email dunhamlit@yahoo.com
website www.dunhamlit.com
Contact Jennie Dunham

Literary fiction and non-fiction, children's books (home 15%, overseas 20%). Send query by post or to query@dunhamlit.com. No reading fee. Founded 2000.

Dystel & Goderich Literary Management*

1 Union Square West, New York, NY 10003
tel +1 212-627-9100 *fax* +1 212-627-9313
website www.dystel.com
Contacts Jane D. Dystel, Miriam Goderich, Michael Bourret, Jim McCarthy, Lauren Abramo, Stacey Glick, Jessica Papin

General fiction and non-fiction (home 15%, overseas 19%, film/TV/radio 15%): literary and commercial fiction, narrative non-fiction, self-help, cookbooks, parenting, science fiction/fantasy, children's and young adults. Send a query letter with a synopsis and up to 50pp of sample MS. Will accept email queries. No reading fee. Will suggest revision. Founded 1994.

The Ethan Ellenberg Literary Agency*

548 Broadway, Suite 5E, New York, NY 10012
tel +1 212-431-4554
email agent@ethanellenberg.com
website www.ethanellenberg.com
President & Agent Ethan Ellenberg

Fiction and non-fiction (home 15%, overseas 20%). Commercial fiction: thrillers, mysteries, children's, romance, women's, ethnic, science fiction, fantasy and general fiction; also literary fiction with a strong narrative. Non-fiction: current affairs, health, science, psychology, new age, spirituality, pop-culture, adventure, true crime, biography and memoir. Children's fiction: interested in young adult, middle grade and younger, of all types. Will consider picture books and other illustrated works. No scholarly works, poetry, short stories or screenplays.

Will accept unsolicited MSS and seriously consider all submissions, including first-time writers. For fiction submit synopsis and first 3 chapters. For non-fiction send a proposal (outline, sample material, author CV, etc). For children's works send complete MS. Illustrators should send a representative selection of colour copies (no orginal artwork). Unable to return any material from overseas. Only an email response if interested. See website for full submission guidelines. Founded 1983.

Ann Elmo Agency Inc.*

60 East 42nd Street, New York, NY 10165
tel +1 212-661-2880 *fax* +1 212-661-2883
email elmolit@aol.com
Director Lettie Lee

Full-length fiction and non-fiction MSS (home 15%, overseas 20%), theatre (15%). Works with foreign agencies. No reading fee. Send query letter only with sase or IRC. New clients only by referral.

Diana Finch Literary Agency*

116 West 23rd Street, Suite 500, New York, NY 10011
tel +1 646-375-2081
email diana.finch@verizon.net
Owner Diana Finch

Memoirs, narrative non-fiction, literary fiction (home 15%, overseas 20%). No reading fee. Queries by email or letter only. No phone or fax. Previously agent with Ellen Levine Literary Agency since 1984. Founded 2003.

The Firm

9465 Wilshire Boulevard, Beverly Hills, CA 90212
tel +1 310-860-8000 *fax* +1 310-860-8132
Contact Alan Nevins

Full-length MSS. Fiction and non-fiction, plays, film and TV rights, performance rights. No unsolicited MSS; query first, submit outline. No reading fee.

Fletcher & Company*

78 Fifth Avenue, 3rd Floor, New York, NY 10011
email info@fletcherandco.com
website www.fletcherandco.com
Director Christy D. Fletcher

Narrative non-fiction, science, history, biography, literary and commercial fiction (home 15%, overseas 20%). Founded 2002.

The Fox Chase Agency Inc.*

701 Lee Road, Suite 102, Chesterbrook, PA 19087
tel +1 610-640-7560 *fax* +1 610-640-7562
Contact A.L. Hart

No unsolicited MSS. No reading fee. Founded 1972.

Jeanne Fredericks Literary Agency Inc.*

221 Benedict Hill Road, New Canaan, CT 06840
tel +1 203-972-3011 *fax* +1 203-972-3011
email jeanne.fredericks@gmail.com
website www.jeannefredericks.com

Quality non-fiction, especially health, science, women's issues, gardening, antiques and decorative arts, biography, cookbooks, popular reference, business, natural history (home 15%, overseas 20%). No reading fee. Query first by email or mail, enclosing sase. Member of Authors Guild and AAR. Founded 1997.

Robert A. Freedman Dramatic Agency Inc.*

(formerly Harold Freedman Brandt & Brandt Dramatic Dept Inc.)
1501 Broadway, Suite 2310, New York, NY 10036
tel +1 212-840-5760

Plays, motion picture and TV scripts. Send letter of enquiry first, with sase. No reading fee.

Samuel French Inc.*

45 West 25th Street, New York, NY 10010
tel +1 212-206-8990 *fax* +1 212-206-1429
email info@samuelfrench.com
President & Ceo Nate Collins

Play publishers; authors' representatives. No reading fee.

Sarah Jane Freymann Literary Agency

59 West 71st Street, Suite 9B, New York, NY 10023
tel +1 212-362-9277 *fax* +1 212-501-8240
email sarah@sarahjanefreymann.com
website www.sarahjanefreymann.com
President Sarah Jane Freymann

Book-length fiction and general non-fiction. Special interest in serious non-fiction, mainstream commercial fiction, contemporary women's fiction, Latino American, Asian American, African American fiction and non-fiction. Non-fiction: women's issues, biography, health/fitness, psychology, self-help, spiritual, natural science, cookbooks, pop culture. Works in conjunction with Abner Stein in London. No reading fee. Query with sase. Founded 1974.

Gelfman Schneider Literary Agents Inc.*

250 West 57th Street, Suite 2122, New York, NY 10107
tel +1 212-245-1993 *fax* +1 212-245-8678
email mail@gelfmanschneider.com
Directors Jane Gelfman, Deborah Schneider

General adult fiction and non-fiction (home 15%, overseas 20%). Will suggest revision. No reading fee. Send sase for return of material. Query by post only. Works in conjunction with Curtis Brown, London.

Frances Goldin Literary Agency*

57 East 11th Street, Suite 5B, New York, NY 10003
tel +1 212-777-0047
email agency@goldinlit.com
website www.goldinlit.com
Agents Frances Goldin, Ellen Geiger, Matt McGowan, Sam Stoloff, Sarah Bridgins, Phyllis Jenkins

Fiction (literary and high-quality commercial) and non-fiction, particularly books with a progressive political orientation. Send query with sase. No unsolicited MSS. Founded 1977.

Goodman Associates, Literary Agents*

500 West End Avenue, New York, NY 10024
tel +1 212-873-4806
Partners Arnold P. Goodman, Elise Simon Goodman

Adult book length fiction and non-fiction (home 15%, overseas 20%). No reading fee. Accept new clients by referral only. Founded 1976.

Sanford J. Greenburger Associates Inc.*

55 Fifth Avenue, New York, NY 10003
tel +1 212-206-5600 *fax* +1 212-463-8718
website www.greenburger.com
Contacts Heide Lange, Faith Hamlin, Daniel Mandel, Matt Bialer, Brenda Bowen, Lisa Gallagher, Courtney Miller-Callihan

Fiction and non-fiction, film and TV rights. No unsolicited MSS; query first. No reading fee.

The Joy Harris Literary Agency Inc.*

381 Park Avenue South, Suite 428, New York 10016
tel +1 212-924-6269 *fax* +1 212-725 5275
email joyharris@jhlitagent.com, adamreed@jhlitagent.com
website www.joyharrisliterary.com
President Joy Harris

John Hawkins & Associates Inc.*

(formerly Paul R. Reynolds Inc.)
71 West 23rd Street, Suite 1600, New York, NY 10010
tel +1 212-807-7040 *fax* +1 212-807-9555
website www.jhalit.com
President Moses Cardona, *Vice President* William Reiss, *Foreign Rights* Moses Cardona, *Other Agents* Warren Frazier, Anne Hawkins

Fiction, non-fiction, young adult. No reading fee. Founded 1893.

The Jeff Herman Agency LLC

PO Box 1522, Stockblidge, MA 01262
tel +1 413-298-0077 *fax* +1 413-298-8188
email jeff@jeffherman.com
website www.jeffherman.com

Business, reference, popular psychology, technology, health, spirituality, general non-fiction (home/overseas 15%); will suggest revision where appropriate. Works with overseas agents. No reading fee. Founded 1986.

Frederick Hill/Bonnie Nadell Inc.

8899 Beverly Bdvd, Suite 805, Los Angeles, CA 90048
tel +1 310-860-9605 *fax* +1 310-860-9672
website www.hillnadell.com

Full-length fiction and non-fiction (home 15%, overseas 20%). Send query letter initially. Works in conjunction with agents in Scandinavia, France, Germany, Holland, Japan, Spain and more. No reading fee. Founded 1979.

InkWell Management

521 Fifth Avenue, 26th Floor, New York, NY 10175
tel +1 212-922-8500 *fax* +1 212-922 0535
email info@inkwellmanagement.com
website www.inkwellmanagement.com
Contact Kimberly Witherspoon, Michael V. Carlisle, Richard Pine, Ethan Bassoff, Catherine Drayton, David Forrer, Susan Hobson, Alexis Hurley, Nathaniel Jacks, George Lucas, Elisa Petrini, Julie Schilder, Jenny Witherell, Charlie Olsen, Mairead Duffy, Rose Marie Morse

Fiction and non-fiction (home/overseas 15%). Send query with sase or by email. Obtains most clients through recommendations from others. Founded 2004.

International Creative Management Inc.*

730 Fifth Avenue, 3rd Floor, New York, NY 10019
tel +1 212-556-5600 *fax* +1 212-556-5665
London office 5th Floor, 28–29 Haymarket, London SW1Y 4SP
tel 020-7393 4400
website www.icmtalent.com

No unsolicited MSS.

Janklow & Nesbit Associates

445 Park Avenue, New York, NY 10022
tel +1 212-421-1700 *fax* +1 212-980-3671
email info@janklow.com
Partners Morton L. Janklow, Lynn Nesbit, *Agents* Anne Sibbald, Tina Bennett, Luke Janklow, Richard Morris, Cullen Stanley, Alexandra Machinist, Julie Just, P.J. Mark

Commercial and literary fiction and non-fiction. No unsolicited MSS. Works in conjunction with Janklow & Nesbit (UK) Ltd. Founded 1989.

JCA Literary Agency Inc.*

174 Sullivan Street, New York, NY 10012
tel +1 212-807-0888
email tom@jcalit.com, tony@jcalit.com
Contacts Tom Cushman, Tony Outhwait

Adult fiction, non-fiction and young adult. No unsolicited MSS; query first.

Keller Media Inc.

22631 Pacific Coast Highway, Suite 701, Malibu, CA 90265
email query@kellermedia.com
website www.kellermedia.com
Ceo/Senior Agent Wendy Keller, *Associate Agent* Megan Collins

Non-fiction for adults: business (all types); self-improvement; parenting; relationships; wellness; health and non-traditional health; science; nature; history; politics; psychology; personal finance; ecology/green movement; autobiographies (considered only by well-known people). No children's books, poetry, memoirs, screenplays or illustrated books. Founded 1989.

Virginia Kidd Agency Inc.

538 East Hartford Street, PO Box 278, Milford, PA 18337
tel +1 570-296-6205
website www.vk-agency.com
Contact Christine Cohen, Vaughne Hansen

Fiction, specialising in science fiction and fantasy (home 15%, overseas 20–25%). Send synopsis (1–3pp), cover letter and sase. Founded 1965.

Harvey Klinger Inc.*

300 West 55th Street, Suite 11V, New York, NY 10019
email queries@harveyklinger.com
website www.harveyklinger.com
Agents Harvey Klinger, David Dunton, Sara Crowe, Andrea Somberg

Commercial and literary adult and children's fiction and non-fiction – serious narrative through to self-help psychology books by authors who have already established strong credentials in their respective field. (Home 15%, overseas 25%). Send query with sase or by email. Exclusive submissions are preferred and given priority. Queries by email preferred, do not phone or fax. Founded 1977.

Barbara S. Kouts, Literary Agent*

PO Box 560, Bellport, NY 11713
tel +1 516-286-1278 *fax* +1 516-286-1538

email bkouts@aol.com
Owner Barbara S. Kouts

Fiction and non-fiction, children's (home 15%, overseas 20%). Works with overseas agents. No reading fee. No phone calls. Send query letter first. Founded 1980.

kt literary

9249 S. Broadway 200–543, Highlands Ranch, CO 80129
tel +1 720-344-4728
email contact@ktliterary.com
website www.ktliterary.com
Contact Kate Schafer Testerman

Primarily middle-grade and young adult fiction but no picture books. Seeking 'brilliant, funny, original middle-grade and young adult fiction, both literary and commercial'. Email a query letter and the first 3pp of MS in the body of the email (no attachments). No snail mail.

Clients include Maureen Johnson, Ellen Booraem, Thomas E. Sniegoski, Stephanie Perkins, Josie Bloss, Matthew Cody. Founded 2008.

Susanna Lea Associates

331 West 20th Street, New York, NY 10011
tel +1 646-638-1435 *fax* +1 646-638-1436
email us-submission@susannalea.com
website www.susannalea.com

General fiction and non-fiction with international appeal. No plays, screenplays or poetry. Send query letter, brief synopsis, the first 3 chapters and/or proposal via website. Established in Paris 2000, New York 2004, London 2008.

Lescher & Lescher Ltd*

346 East 84th Street (ground floor), New York, NY 10028
tel +1 212-396-1999 *fax* +1 212-396-1991
Director Robert Lescher

Full-length MSS (home 15%, overseas 20%). No unsolicited MSS; query first with sase. No reading fee. Founded 1966.

The Lescher Agency Inc.*

7 Peter Cooper Road, Suite 11-F, New York, NY 10010
tel +1 212-673-5748 *fax* +1 212-396-1991
Director Susan Lescher

Fiction and non-fiction (home 15%, overseas 20%). No unsolicited MSS; query first with sase, or email. No reading fee.

Donald Maass Literary Agency*

Suite 801, 121 West 27th Street, New York, NY 10001
tel +1 212-727-8383 *fax* +1 212-727-3271
email info@maassagency.com
website www.maassagency.com
Agents Donald Maass, Jennifer Jackson, Cameron McClure, Stacia Decker, Amy Boggs, Katie Shea, Jennifer Udden

Specialises in fiction, all genres (home 15%, overseas 20%). No poetry or picture books. Query with first 5pp of MS and a one-page synopsis with sase, or by email with 'query' in the subject line. Founded 1980.

Margret McBride Literary Agency*

7744 Fay Avenue, Suite 200, La Jolla, CA 92037
tel +1 858-454-1550 *fax* +1 858-454-2156
email staff@mcbridelit.com
website www.mcbrideliterary.com
President Margret McBride, *Submissions Manager* Michael Daley

Business, mainstream fiction and non-fiction (home 15%, overseas 25%). No poetry or children's books. No reading fee. Submit query letter with sase to Submissions Manager. Founded 1981.

Anita D. McClellan Associates*

464 Common Street, Suite 142, Belmont, MA 02478
website www.anitamcclellan.com
Director Anita D. McClellan

General fiction and non-fiction. Full-length MSS (USA 15%, overseas 20%). Will suggest revision for agency clients. No unsolicited MSS. Send preliminary letter and sase bearing US postage or IRC. No email submissions.

McIntosh & Otis Inc.*

353 Lexington Avenue, New York, NY 10016
tel +1 212-687-7400 *fax* +1 212-687-6894
email info@mcintoshandotis.com
website www.mcintoshandotis.com
Adult Eugene H. Winick, Elizabeth Winick Rubinstein, *Juvenile* Edward Necarsulmer IV

Adult and juvenile literary fiction and non-fiction, film and TV rights. No unsolicited MSS; query first with outline, sample chapters and sase. No reading fee. Founded 1928.

Carol Mann Agency*

55 Fifth Avenue, New York, NY 10003
tel +1 212-206-5635 *fax* +1 212-675-4809
website http://carolmannagency.com
Associates Carol Mann, Laura Yorke, Gareth Esersky, Mysini Stephanides, Joanne Wyckoff

Psychology, popular history, biography, pop culture, health, current affairs/politics, parenting, business, memoir, humour, science, general non-fiction; fiction (home 15%, overseas 20%). Works in conjunction with foreign agents. No reading fee. Founded 1977.

The Evan Marshall Agency*

1 Pacio Court, Roseland, NJ 07068
tel +1 973-882-1122 *fax* +1 973-488-7910
email evan@evanmarshallagency.com
President Evan Marshall

General fiction (home 15%, overseas 20%). Works in conjunction with overseas agents. Will suggest revision; no reading fee. Do not query. Accepting new clients by professional referral only. Founded 1987.

The Marton Agency Inc.*

1 Union Square West, Suite 815, New York, NY 10003–3303
tel +1 212-255-1908 *fax* +1 212-691-9061
email info@martonagency.com
Owner Tonda Marton

Principally foreign language licensing of US stage plays and musicals.

William Morris Agency Inc.*

(incorporating the Writers Shop, formerly Virginia Barber Literary Agency)
1325 Avenue of the Americas, New York, NY 10019
tel +1 212-903-1304 *fax* +1 212-903-1304
website www.wma.com
Senior VPs Jennifer Rudolph Walsh, Suzanne Gluck, Mel Berger, Jay Mandel, Tracy Fisher

General fiction and non-fiction (home 15%, overseas 20%, performance rights 15%). Will suggest revision. No reading fee.

Muse Literary Management

189 Waverly Place, Suite 4, New York, NY 10014–3135
tel +1 212-925-3721
email museliterarymgmt@aol.com
website www.museliterary.com
Agent Deborah Carter

Fiction and non-fiction (home 15%, overseas 20%). Special interests: literary novels and short stories with popular appeal, mysteries/thrillers, espionage fiction/non-fiction, historical fiction, literary narrative non-fiction, memoirs about extraordinary people and experiences; non-fiction: music, the arts, fashion and history; and children's fiction/non-fiction. Particularly interested in multicultural fiction for adults and children. Special call for first novels with characters in their 20s and 30s. No romance, chick lit, science fiction, fantasy, vampire stories, horror, religion, spirituality, stories of victimhood or illness. Prefers queries by email with no attachments. If no response within 2 weeks, query again.

Jean V. Naggar Literary Agency Inc.*

216 East 75th Street, Suite 1E, New York, NY 10021
tel +1 212-794-1082
email jvnla@jvnla.com
website www.jvnla.com
President Jean V. Naggar, *Vice President* Jennifer Weltz, *Agents* Alice Tasman, Jessica Regel, Elizabeth Evans

Mainstream commercial and literary fiction, non-fiction (psychology, science biography, history), young readers (picture, middle grade, young adult). Home 15%, overseas 20%. Works in conjunction with foreign agents. Submit queries via form on website. No reading fee. Founded 1978.

Harold Ober Associates Inc.*

425 Madison Avenue, New York, NY 10017
tel +1 212-759-8600 *fax* +1 212-759-9428
website www.haroldober.com
Directors Phyllis Westberg, Pamela Malpas, Jake Elwell, Craig Tenney

Full-length MSS (home 15%, UK/overseas 20%), performance rights (15%). No screenplays or playscripts. No email or fax queries; see website for submission instructions. No reading fee. Founded 1929.

Fifi Oscard Agency Inc.

110 West 40th Street, New York, NY 10018
tel +1 212-764-1100 *fax* +1 212-840-5019
email agency@fifioscard.com
website www.fifioscard.com
Agents Peter Sawyer, Carolyn French, Carmen La Via, Kevin McShane

Full-length MSS (home 15%, overseas 20%), theatrical performance rights (10%). Will suggest revision. Works in conjunction with many foreign agencies. No reading fee, but no unsolicited submissions.

James Peter Associates Inc.

PO Box 358, New Canaan, CT 06840
tel +1 203-972-1070
Contact Gene Brissie

Non-fiction, especially history, politics, popular culture, health, psychology, reference, biography (home 15%, overseas 20%). Will suggest revision. No reading fee. Foreign rights handled by JPA. Founded 1971.

The Pimlico Agency Inc.

PO Box 20490, New York, NY 10017
Contacts Christopher Shepard, *Directors* Kay McCauley, Kirby McCauley

Adult non-fiction and fiction. No unsolicited MSS.

PMA Literary and Film Management Inc.

PO Box 1817, Old Chelsea Station, New York, NY 10113
tel +1 212-929-1222 *fax* +1 212-206-0238
website www.pmalitfilm.com
President Peter Miller, *Associates* Kelly Skillen, Adrienne Rosado

Full-length MSS. Specialises in commercial fiction (especially thrillers), true crime, non-fiction (all types), and all books with global publishing and film/TV potential (home 15%, overseas 25%), films, TV (10–20%). Works in conjunction with agents worldwide. Preliminary enquiry with career goals, synopsis and résumé essential. Founded 1976.

Rees Literary Agency*

14 Beacon Street, Suite 710, Boston, MA 02108
email reesagency@reesagency.com
website www.reesagency.com
Contact Helen Rees, *Associates* Ann Collette, Lorin Rees

Business books, self-help, biography, autobiography, political, literary fiction, memoirs, history, current affairs (home 15%). No reading fee. Submit query letter with sase. Founded 1982.

The Angela Rinaldi Literary Agency*

PO Box 7877, Beverly Hills, CA 90212–7877
tel +1 310-842-7665
email amr@rinaldiliterary.com
website www.rinaldiliterary.com
President Angela Rinaldi

Mainstream and literary adult fiction; non-fiction (home 15%, overseas 25%). No reading fee. Founded 1994.

Russell & Volkening Inc.*

50 West 29th Street, Suite 7E, New York, NY 10001
tel +1 212-684-6050; +1 212-352-2055 (Lippincott, Massie, McQuilkin)
email randv@lmqlit.com
website www.randvinc.com
Contact Christina Shideler

Schiavone Literary Agency, Inc.

Corporate offices 236 Trails End, West Palm Beach, FL 33413–2135
tel/fax 516-966-9294
email profschia@aol.com
3671 Hudson Manor Terrace No 11H, Bronx, NY 10463–1139
tel/fax +1 718-548-5332
email jendu77@aol.com
400 East 11th Street, Suite 7, New York, NY 10009
email kvn.mcadams@yahoo.com
website www.publishersmarketplace.com/members/profschia
Ceo James Schiavone, *President* Jennifer DuVall, *Executive vice president* Kevin McAdams

Fiction and non-fiction, specialising in celebrity biography and memoirs (home 15%, overseas 20%). No reading fee. Accepts only one-page email queries (no attachments). No longer accepts queries by post. Founded 1996.

Susan Schulman, A Literary Agency LLC*

454 West 44th Street, New York, NY 10036
tel +1 212-713-1633 *fax* +1 212-581-8830
email schulman@aol.com

Agents for negotiation in all markets (with co-agents) of fiction, general non-fiction, children's books, academic and professional works, and associated subsidiary rights including plays and film (home 15%, UK 7.5%, overseas 20%). No reading fee. Return postage required.

Scott Meredith Literary Agency LP

200 West 57th Street, Suite 904, New York, NY 10019
tel +1 646-274-1970 *fax* +1 212-977-5997
website www.scottmeredith.com
President Arthur Klebanoff

General fiction and non-fiction. Founded 1946.

The Shukat Company Ltd

340 West 55th Street, Suite 1A, New York, NY 10019
tel +1 212-582-7614
email staff@shukat.com
President Scott Shukat, *Contacts* Maribel Rivas, Lysna Scriven-Marzani

Theatre, films, TV, radio (15%). No reading fee. No unsolicited material accepted.

The Spieler Agency

27 West 20th Street, Room 305, New York, NY 10011
tel +1 212-757-4439
Directors F. Joseph Spieler, Eric Myers

History, politics, ecology, business, consumer reference, biography, spirituality, serious non-fiction; some fiction (home 15%, overseas 20%). No reading fee. Query first with sample and sase. Founded 1982.

Philip G. Spitzer Literary Agency, Inc.*

50 Talmage Farm Lane, East Hampton, NY 11937
tel +1 631-329-3650 *fax* +1 631-329-3651
email lukas.ortiz@spitzeragency.com
website www.spitzeragency.com
Literary Manager L. Lukas Ortiz

General fiction and non-fiction; specialises in mystery/suspense, sports, politics, biography, social issues.

Rebecca Strong International Literary Agency

235 West 108th Street, Suite 35, New York, NY 10025
tel +1 212-865-1569
email info@rsila.com
website www.rsila.com
Owner/Agent Rebecca Strong

Literary and commercial fiction, narrative non-fiction, memoir and biography, self-improvement/how-to (home 15%, overseas 20%). Only accepts email submissions; see website for details. No reading fee. Founded 2003.

Trident Media Group

41 Madison Avenue, New York, NY 10010
tel +1 212-262-4810 *fax* +1 212-262-4849
website www.tridentmediagroup.com
Executive Vice President Ellen Levine

Full-length MSS: biography, contemporary affairs, women's issues, history, science, literary and commercial fiction (home 15%, overseas 20%); in conjunction with co-agents, theatre, films, TV (15%). Will suggest revision. Works direct in UK, France, Germany, Italy, Spain and Holland; co-agents in other territories. No reading fee; preliminary letter and sase and US postage essential.

Ralph M. Vicinanza Ltd*

303 West 18th Street, New York, NY 10011-4440
tel +1 212-924-7090 *fax* +1 212-691-9644
Contacts Ralph Vicinanza, Christopher Lotts, Christopher Schelling, Adam Lefton

Fiction: literary, popular (especially science fiction, fantasy, thrillers), children's. Non-fiction: history, business, science, biography, popular culture. Foreign rights specialists. New clients by professional recommendation only. No unsolicited MSS.

Austin Wahl Agency Inc.

1820 North 76th Court, Elmwood Park, IL 60707–3631
tel +1 708-456-2301
President Thomas Wahl

Full-length and short MSS (home 15%, overseas 20%), theatre, films, TV (10%). No reading fee; professional writers only. Founded 1935.

Wallace Literary Agency Inc.

301 East 79th Street, No 14–J, New York, NY 10075
tel +1 212-570-9090 *fax* +1 212-772-8979
email walliter@aol.com
Director Lois Wallace

No cookery, humour, how-to, children's or young adult; film, TV, theatre for agency clients. Will suggest revision. No unsolicited MSS; no faxed queries, no queries with attachments. Will only answer queries with return postage or email address. Founded 1988.

The Ward + Balkin Agency Inc.*

PO Box 7144, Lowell, MA 01852
tel +1 978-656-8389
email christinawardlit@mac.com
website www.wardbalkin.com
Vice President Christina Ward

Literary fiction and adult non-fiction only (home 15%, overseas 25%). Query first. No reading fee. European and British Representative: Taryn Fagerness Agency, USA.

Watkins/Loomis Agency Inc.

PO Box 20925, Park West Finance Station, New York, NY 10025
tel +1 212-532-0080 *fax* +1 212-889-0506
email assistant@watkinsloomis.com
website www.watkinsloomis.com
President Gloria Loomis

Fiction and non-fiction. No unsolicited MSS. *Representatives* Abner Stein (UK), the Marsh Agency Ltd (foreign).

Writers House LLC*

21 West 26th Street, New York, NY 10010
tel +1 212-685-2400 *fax* +1 212-685-1781
London agent: Ground Floor Flat, 24 Harvist Road, London NW6 6SH
020-8960 2966, 7534 494814
website www.writershouse.com
Chairman Albert Zuckerman, *President* Amy Berkower, *Agents* Simon Lipskar, Merrilee Heifetz, Robin Rue, Susan Ginsburg, Dan Conaway, Dan Lazar, Angharad Kowal (London)

Fiction and non-fiction, including all rights; film and TV rights. No screenplays or software. Send a one-page letter in first instance, saying what's wonderful about your book, what it is about and why you are the best person to write it. No reading fee. Founded 1974.

The Wylie Agency Inc.

250 West 57th Street, Suite 2114, New York, NY 10107
tel +1 212-246-0069 *fax* +1 212-586-8953
email mail@wylieagency.com
website www.wylieagency.com
President Andrew Wylie, *Contact* Sarah Chalfant, Scott Moyers

Literary fiction/non-fiction. No unsolicited MSS accepted. London office: the Wylie Agency UK Ltd.

Art and illustration
Freelancing for beginners

Fig Taylor describes the opportunities open to freelance illustrators and discusses types of fee and how to negotiate one to your best advantage.

Full-time posts for illustrators are extremely rare. Because commissioners' needs tend to change on a regular basis, most artists have little choice but to freelance – offering their skills to a variety of clients in order to make a living.

Illustration is highly competitive and a professional attitude towards targeting, presenting, promoting and delivering your work will be vital to your success. Likewise, a realistic understanding of how the industry works and of your place within it will be key. Without adequate research into your chosen field(s) of interest, you may find yourself approaching inappropriate clients – a frustrating and disheartening experience for both parties and a waste of your time and money.

Who commissions illustration?

Magazines and newspapers

Whatever your illustrative ambitions, you are most likely to receive your first commissions from editorial clients. The comparatively modest fees involved allow art editors the freedom to take risks, so many are keen to commission newcomers. Briefs are generally fairly loose though deadlines can be short, particularly where daily and weekly publications are concerned. However, fast turnover also ensures a swift appearance in print, thus reassuring clients in other, more lucrative, spheres of your professional status. Given then that it is possible to use magazines as a springboard, it is essential to research them thoroughly when seeking to identify your own individual market. Collectively, editorial clients accommodate an infinite variety of illustrative styles and techniques. Don't limit your horizons by approaching only the most obvious titles and/or those you would read yourself. Consider also trade and professional journals, customer magazines (such as inflight magazines and those produced for supermarkets) and those available on subscription from membership organisations or charities. You will often find obscure titles in the reference section of public or university libraries, where the periodicals they subscribe to will reflect the subjects taught. Seeking out as many potential clients as possible will benefit you in the long term. In addition to the titles listed in this *Yearbook*, the Association of Illustrators (AOI) publishes an *Editorial Directory* which gives specific client contact details, and is updated annually.

Book publishing

With the exception of children's picture books, where illustration is unlikely to fall out of fashion, many publishers are using significantly less illustration than they once did. (Hopefully this may change, as those invested in digital publishing are exploring new formats and digital platforms enabling books to be experienced in ways previously never imagined.) While publishers of traditional mass market genres, such as science fiction and fantasy, still favour strong, representational, full-colour work on their covers, photography has begun to predominate in others, such as the family saga and historical romance. However, the prevailing trend for using fashion illustration in lifestyle-related advertising has strongly influenced the packaging of contemporary women's fiction, where quirky, humorous and graphic styles are also popular. A broader range of styles can be accommodated by those smaller publishers specialising in literary, upmarket fiction, though many opt to use stock imagery in order to operate within a limited budget. Meanwhile, although specialist and technical illustrators still have a vital part to play in non-fiction publishing, there is less decorative work being commissioned for lifestyle-related subjects as photography currently predominates.

Children's publishers use a wide variety of styles, covering the gamut from baby books, activity and early learning, through to full-colour picture books, covers for young adults and black-and-white line illustrations for the 8–11-year-old age group (particularly for boys, who tend to be more reluctant readers than girls). Author/illustrators are particularly welcomed by picture book publishers – though, whatever your style, you must be able to develop believable characters and sustain them throughout a narrative. Some children's book illustrators initially find their feet in educational publishing. However, all ages are catered for within this area, including adults with learning difficulties, those learning languages for business purposes and teachers working right across the educational spectrum. Consequently, a wide variety of illustrators can be accommodated. With the exception of educational publishing, which tends to have a faster turnover, most publishing deadlines are civilised and mass market covers particularly well paid. There are numerous publishing clients listed elsewhere in this *Yearbook* and visiting individual websites is a good way to get a flavour of the kind of illustration they may favour. In addition, the AOI publishes a *Publishing Directory*, which is updated yearly and gives specific client contact details.

Greeting cards

Many illustrators are interested in providing designs for cards and giftwrap. Illustrative styles favoured include decorative, graphic, humorous, children's and cute. For specific information on the gift industry which, unlike the areas covered here, works on a speculative basis, see *Winning the greeting card game* on page 482.

Design companies

Both designers and their clients (who are largely uncreative and will, ultimately, be footing the bill) will be impressed and reassured by relevant, published work so wait until you're in print before approaching them. Although fees are significantly higher than those in newspapers, magazines and book publishing, this third-party involvement generally results in a more restrictive brief. Deadlines may vary and styles favoured range from conceptual through to realistic, decorative, humorous and technical – with those involved in multimedia and web design favouring illustrators with character development and flash animation skills.

Magazines such as *Creative Review* and the online-based *Design Week* (both published by Centaur Media Plc) will keep you abreast of developments in the design world and help you identify clients' individual areas of expertise. Meanwhile, directories such as www.chb.com, (the online version of the recently discontinued *Creative Review Handbook*), and www.creativematch.com carry many listings and weblinks. Individual contact names are also available at a price from database specialists File FX, which can provide creative suppliers with up-to-date information on commissioners in all spheres. A similar service is provided by Bikini Lists, an online subscription-based resource that specialises in providing categorised mailing lists for single or multiple usage. The AOI's annually updated *Advertising Directory* also incorporates design consultancies.

Advertising agencies

As with design, you should ideally be in print before seeking advertising commissions. Fees can be high, deadlines short and clients extremely demanding. A wide range of styles are used and commissions might be incorporated into direct mail or press advertising, featured on websites, hoardings or animated for television. Fees will vary, depending on whether a campaign is local, national or even global.

Most agencies employ an art buyer to look at portfolios. A good one will know what each creative team is currently working on and may refer you to specific art directors. These days many art buyers are open to being approached by freelance illustrators, providing the illustrator has some published work. *Creative Review* and the weekly *Campaign* (published by Haymarket Business Publications) carry agency news, while the AOI also publishes an *Advertising Directory*, updated annually.

Portfolio presentation

In general, UK commissioners prefer to see someone with a strong, consistent, recognisable style rather than an unfocused jack-of-all-trades type. Thus, when assembling your pro-

Useful addresses

Association of Illustrators (AOI)
2nd Floor, Back Building, 150 Curtain Road, London EC2A 3AR
tel 020-7613 4328 *fax* 020-7613 4417
email info@theaoi.com
website www.theaoi.com, www.aoiportfolios.com
Publishes *Images, The Illustrator's Guide to Law and Business Practice* and various client directories. See also page 505.

Bikini Lists
Unit 18, Govanhill Workspace, 69 Dixon Road, Glasgow G42 8AT
tel 0141-636 3901
email ak@bikinilists.com
website www.bikinilists.com
Contact Ann-Kirsten Neeson

Boomerang Media Ltd
Manor House, Manor Park, Church Hill, Aldershot, Hants GU12 4JU
tel (01252) 368368
email sales@boomerangmedia.co.uk
website www.boomerangmedia.co.uk

Centaur Media Plc
79 Wells Street, London W1T 3QN
tel 020-7970 4000
website www.creativereview.co.uk, www.designweek.co.uk
Publishes *Design Week* and *Creative Review.*

Contact Creative UK LLP
PO Box 397, Reigate, Surrey RH2 2ES
tel (01737) 241399
email mail@contactacreative.com
website www.contactacreative.com
Publishes *Contact Illustration.*

File FX
7 Shepperton House, 83–93 Shepperton Road, London N1 3DF
tel 020-7226 6646 *fax* 020-7288 2718
email info@filefx.co.uk
website www.filefx.co.uk
Specialises in providing creative suppliers with up-to-date information on commissioning clients in all spheres.

Haymarket Media Group
174 Hammersmith Road, London W6 7JP
tel 020-8267 5000
email campaign@haymarket.com
website www.campaignlive.com
Publishes *Campaign.*

fessional portfolio – whether print or digital – try to exclude samples which are, in your own eyes, weak, irrelevant, uncharacteristic or simply unenjoyable to do and focus on your strengths instead. Should you be one of those rare, multi-talented individuals who finds it hard to limit themselves stylistically, try splitting conflicting work into separate portfolios/sections geared towards different kinds of clients.

A lack of formal training need not be a handicap providing your portfolio accurately reflects the needs of the clients you target. Some illustrators find it useful to assemble 'mock-ups' using existing magazine layouts. By responding to the copy and replacing original images with your own illustrations, it is easier to see how your work will look in context. Eventually, as you become established you'll be able to augment these with published pieces.

If you are presenting a print portfolio, ideally it should be of the zip-up, ring-bound variety and never exceed A2 in size (A3 or A4 is industry standard these days) as clients usually have little desk space; portfolio boxes are also acceptable, though you could run the risk of samples going astray. Alternatively, you may choose to give a laptop or tablet presentation, in which case strive to keep it simple and well organised. Either bring your own device or borrow one with which you are familiar. (Also make sure it is fully charged and that you have emergency laptop back-up such as a power brick, memory sticks, DVDs, etc. If your presentation involves talking a client through your website rather than files or slideshows, check you will have wireless internet access.) Complexity of style and diversity of subject matter will dictate how many samples to include but if you are opting for a print portfolio presentation, all should be neatly mounted on lightweight paper or card and placed inside protective plastic sleeves. High-quality photographs, computer printouts and laser copies are acceptable to clients but tacky out-of-focus snapshots are not. Also avoid including multiple sketchbooks and life drawings, which are anathema to clients. It will be taken for granted that you know how to draw from observation.

Interviews and beyond

Making appointments can be hard work but clients take a dim view of spontaneous visits from passing illustrators. However, face-to-face meetings where geographically practicable can be vital to launching an illustrator's career. Having established the contact name (either from a written source or by asking the company directly), clients are still best initially approached by letter or telephone call. Emails can be overlooked, ignored or simply end up in the company spam filter. Some publishing houses are happy to see freelances, though portfolio 'drop-offs' are also quite common. Some clients will automatically take photocopies of your work for reference. However, it's advisable to have some kind of promotional material to leave behind such as a CD, postcard, broadsheet or advertising tearsheet. Always ask an enthusiastic client if they know of others who might be interested in your work. Personal recommendation almost always guarantees an interview.

Cleanliness, punctuality and enthusiasm are more important to clients than how you dress – as is a professional attitude to taking and fulfilling a brief. A thorough understanding of each commission is paramount from the outset. You will need to know your client's requirements regarding roughs; format and – if relevant – size and flexibility of artwork; preferred medium; and whether the artwork is needed in colour or black and white. You will also need to know when the deadline is. Never, under any circumstances agree to undertake a commission unless you are certain you can deliver on time and always work within your limitations. Talent is nothing without reliability.

Self-promotion

There are many ways an illustrator can ensure their work stays uppermost in the industry's consciousness, some more expensive than others. Images can be emailed in a variety of formats, put onto CD or DVD, posted in a blog, or showcased on a personal or hosting website. Advertising in prestigious hardback annuals such as Contact Creative UK's *Contact Illustration* and the AOI's *Images* – which are distributed free to commissioners – can be effective but doesn't come cheap and, in the case of *Images*, only those professionally selected are permitted to buy pages for their winning entries. However, these publications have a long shelf life and are well respected by industry professionals.

As commissioners increasingly turn to the internet for inspiration, websites are becoming an essential and affordable method of self-promotion. Make sure your website loads quickly, is simple and straightforward to negotiate and displays decent-sized images. Advertisers in *Contact Illustration* automatically qualify for a web portfolio of 20 images with links back to individual websites; these portfolios will also appear in the online version of the *US Directory of Illustration*. It is also possible for illustrators to promote their work on the *Contact* website without appearing in the annual (www.contactacreative.com). Currently, both AOI members and non-members can promote their work online at www.aoiportfolios.com, though members can do so at a reduced rate.

Free publicity can be had courtesy of Boomerang Media Ltd, which will print appropriate images to go in postcard advertising racks. Distribution includes cafés, bars, cinemas, health clubs, universities and schools.

Be organised

Once you are up and running, it is imperative to keep organised records of all your commissions. Contracts can be verbal as well as written, though details – both financial and otherwise – should always be confirmed in writing (an email fulfils this purpose) and duplicated for your files. Likewise, keep corresponding client faxes, letters, emails and order forms. The AOI publication *The Illustrator's Guide to Law and Business Practice* offers a wealth of practical, legal and ethical information. Subjects covered include contracts, fee negotiation, agents, licences, royalties and copyright issues.

Money matters

The type of client, the purpose for which you are being commissioned and the usage of your work can all affect the fee you can expect to receive, as can your own professional attitude. Given that it is *extremely* inadvisable to undertake a commission without first agreeing on a fee, you will have to learn to be upfront about funds.

Licence *v.* copyright

Put simply, according to current EU legislation, copyright is the right to reproduce a piece of work anywhere, *ad infinitum*, for any purpose, for a period ending 70 years after the death of the person who created it. This makes it an extremely valuable commodity.

By law, copyright automatically belongs to you, the creator of your artwork, unless you agree to sell it to another party. In most cases, clients have no need to purchase it, and the recommended alternative is for you to grant them a licence instead, governing the precise usage of the artwork. This is far cheaper from the client's perspective and, should they subsequently decide to use your work for some purpose other than those outlined in your initial agreement, will benefit you too as a separate fee will have to be negotiated. It's also worth noting that even if you were ill-advised enough to sell the copyright, the artwork would still belong to you unless you had also agreed to sell it.

Rejection and cancellation fees

Most commissioners will not expect you to work for nothing unless you are involved in a speculative pitch, in which case it will be up to you to weigh up the pros and cons of your possible involvement. Assuming you have given a job your best shot, i.e. carried out the client's instructions to the letter, it's customary to receive a rejection fee even if the client doesn't care for the outcome: 25% is customary at developmental/rough stage and 50% at finished artwork stage. (Clear this with the client before you start, as there are exceptions to the rule.) Cancellation fees are paid when a job is terminated through no fault of the artist or, on occasion, even the client. Customary rates in this instance are 25% before rough stage, 33% on delivery of roughs and 100% on delivery of artwork.

Fixed *v.* negotiable fees

Editorial and publishing fees are almost always fixed with little, if any, room for haggling and are generally considerably lower than advertising and design fees, which tend to be negotiable. A national full-colour 48-sheet poster advertising Marks & Spencer is likely to pay more than a local black-and-white press ad plugging a poodle parlour. If, having paid your editorial dues, you find yourself hankering after commissions from the big boys, fee negotiation – confusing and complicated as it can sometimes be – will become a fact of life. However you choose to go about the business of cutting a deal, it will help if you disabuse yourself of the notion that the client is doing you a whopping favour by considering you for the job. Believe it or not, the client *needs* your skills to bring his/her ideas to life. In short, you are worth the money and the client knows it.

Pricing a commission

Before you can quote on a job, you'll need to know exactly what it entails. For what purpose is the work to be used? Will it be used several times and/or for more than one purpose? Will its use be local or national? For how long is the client intending to use it? Who is the client and how soon do they want the work? Are you up against anyone else (who could possibly undercut you)?

Next, ask the client what the budget is. Believe it or not there's a fair chance they might tell you. Whether they are forthcoming or not, don't feel you have to pluck a figure out of thin air or agree to their offer immediately. Play for time. Tell them you need to review your current workload and that you'll get back to them within a brief, specified period of time. If nothing else, haggling over the phone is less daunting than doing it face to face. If you've had no comparable commissions to date and are an AOI member, check out the going rate by calling them for pricing advice (or check out their report on illustration fees and standards of pricing in the members-only section of the AOI website). Failing that, try speaking to a friendly client or a fellow illustrator who's worked on similar jobs.

When you begin negotiating, have in mind a bottom-line price you're prepared to do the job for and always ask for slightly more than your ideal fee as the client will invariably try to beat you down. You may find it useful to break down your asking price in order to explain exactly what it is the client is paying for. How you do this is up to you. Some people find it helpful to work out a daily rate incorporating overheads such as rent, heating, materials, travel and telephone charges, while others prefer to negotiate on a flat fee basis.

There are also illustrators who charge extra for something needed yesterday, time spent researching, model hire if applicable and so on. It pays to be flexible, so if your initial quote exceeds the client's budget and you really want the job, tell them you are open to negotiation. If, on the other hand, the job looks suspiciously thankless, stick to your guns. If the client agrees to your exorbitant demands, the job might start to look more appetising.

Getting paid

Once you've traded terms and conditions, done the job and invoiced the client, you'll then have the unenviable task of getting your hands on your fee. It is customary to send your invoice to the accounts department stating payment within 30 days. It is also customary for them to ignore this entreaty, regardless of the wolf at your door, and pay you when it suits them. Magazines pay promptly, usually within 4–6 weeks; everyone else takes 60–90 days – no matter what.

Be methodical when chasing up your invoice. Send out a statement the moment your 30 days has elapsed and call the accounts department as soon as you like. Take names, note dates and the gist of their feeble excuses, and keep on chasing. Don't worry about your incessant nagging scuppering your plans of further commissions as these decisions are solely down to the art department, and they think you're a gem. Should payment still not be forthcoming three months down the line, it might be advisable to ask your commissioner to follow things up on your behalf. Chances are they'll be horrified you haven't been paid yet and things will be speedily resolved. In the meantime, you'll have had a good deal of practice talking money, which can only make things easier next time around.

And finally...

Basic book-keeping – making a simple, legible record of all your financial transactions, both incoming and outgoing – will be crucial to your sanity once the tax inspector starts to loom. It will also make your accountant's job easier, thereby saving you money. If your annual turnover is less than £77,000, it is unnecessary to provide HM Revenue & Customs with detailed accounts of your earnings. Information regarding your turnover, allowable expenses and net profit may simply be entered on your tax return. Although an accountant is not necessary to this process, many find it advantageous to employ one. The tax system is complicated and dealing with HM Revenue & Customs can be stressful, intimidating and time consuming. Accountants offer invaluable advice on tax allowances, National Insurance and tax assessments, as well as dealing expertly with HM Revenue & Customs on your behalf – thereby enabling you to attend to the business of illustrating.

Fig Taylor initially began her career as an illustrators' agent in 1983. She has been the resident 'portfolio surgeon' at the Association of Illustrators since 1986 and also operates as a private consultant to non-AOI member artists. She lectures extensively in Professional Practice to illustration students throughout the UK and is the author of *How to Create a Portfolio and Get Hired* (Laurence King 2010).

See also...

• *Art agents and commercial studios*, page 474

Art agents and commercial art studios

Before submitting work, artists are advised to make preliminary enquiries and to ascertain terms of work. Commission varies but averages 25–30%. The Association of Illustrators (see page 505) provides a valuable service for illustrators, agents and clients.

*Member of the Society of Artists Agents
†Member of the Association of Illustrators

Advocate

56 The Street, Ashtead, Surrey KT21 1AZ
tel 020-8879 1166 *fax* (01372) 276170
email mail@advocate-art.com
website www.advocate-art.com
Director Edward Burns

Has 5 agents representing 110 artists and illustrators. Supplies work to book and magazine publishers, design and advertising agencies, greeting card and fine art publishers, and gift and ceramic manufacturers. For illustrators' submission guidelines see website. Also has an original art gallery, stock library and website in German, Spanish and French. Founded as a co-operative in 1996.

Allied Artists/Artistic License

mobile (07971) 111256
email info@alliedartists-umbrellabooks.com
website www.alliedartists-umbrellabooks.com
Contacts Gary Mills, Mary Burtenshaw

Represents over 40 artists specialising in highly finished realistic figure illustrations, stylised juvenile illustrations for children's books, and cartoons for magazines, books, plates, prints, cards and advertising. Extensive library of stock illustrations. Commission: 33%. Founded 1983.

Arena*†

Arena Illustration Ltd, 31 Eleanor Road, London E15 4AB
tel 0845 050 7600
email info@arenaillustration.com
website www.arenaillustration.com
Contact Tamlyn Francis

Represents 30 artists working mostly for book covers, children's books and design groups. Average commission 25%. Founded 1970.

The Art Agency

The Lodge, Cargate Lane, Saxlingham Thorpe, Norwich NR15 1TU
tel (01508) 471500 *fax* (01508) 470391
email artagency@me.com
website www.the-art-agency.co.uk

Represents more than 40 artists producing top-quality, highly accurate and imaginative illustrations across a wide variety of subjects and for all age groups, both digitally and traditionally. Clients are children's fiction and non-fiction publishers. Include sae with submissions. Do not email portfolios. Commission: 30%. Founded 1992.

The Art Market*†

51 Oxford Drive, London SE1 2FB
tel 020-7407 8111
email info@artmarketillustration.com
website www.artmarketillustration.com
Director Philip Reed

Represents 40 artists creating illustrations for publishing, design and advertising. Founded 1989.

Artist Partners Ltd*†

2E The Chandlery, 50 Westminster Bridge Road, London SE1 7QY
tel 020-7401 7904 *fax* 020-7401 3378
email chris@artistpartners.demon.co.uk
website www.artistpartners.com
Managing Director Christine Isteed

Represents artists, including specialists in their field, producing artwork in every genre for advertising campaigns, storyboards, children's and adult book covers, newspaper and magazine features and album covers. New artists are only considered if their work is of an exceptionally high standard, in which case submission should be by post only and include a sae. Commission: 30%. Founded 1951.

The Artworks†*

12–18 Hoxton Street, London N1 6NG
tel 020-7729 1973
email info@theartworksinc.com
website www.theartworksinc.com
Contact Lucy Scherer, Stephanie Alexander, Alex Gardner

Represents 20 artists for illustrated gift books and children's books. Commission: 25% advances, 15% royalties.

Beehive Illustration

42A Cricklade Street, Cirencester, Glos. GL7 1JH
tel (01285) 885149 *fax* (01285) 644482

email info@beehiveillustration.co.uk
website www.beehiveillustration.co.uk
Contact Paul Beebee

Represents over 100 artists specialising in education and general children's publishing illustration. Commission: 25%. Founded 1989.

Central Illustration Agency

29 Heddon Street, 1st Floor, London W1B 4BL
tel 020-7734 7187 *fax* 020-7434 0974
email info@centralillustration.com
website www.centralillustration.com
Contact Benjamin Cox

Represents 70 artists producing illustrations for design, publishing, animation and advertising. Commission: 30%. Founded 1983.

Début Art & The Coningsby Gallery†*

30 Tottenham Street, London W1T 4RJ
tel 020-7636 1064
email info@debutart.com
website www.debutart.com, www.coningsbygallery.com
Directors Andrew Coningsby, Samuel Summerskill, Jonathan Hedley

Represents 120 of the world's leading and contemporary illustrators. Commission: 20%. Worldwide commissioning clientele and artist base. Submissions from new illustrators always welcome via email. Founded 1985.

Eastwing†*

99 Chase Side, Enfield EN2 6NL
tel 020-8367 6760 *fax* 020-8367 6730
email representation@eastwing.co.uk
website www.eastwing.co.uk
Partners Andrea Plummer, Gordon Allen, *Contact* Abby Glassfield

Represents 31 artists who work across the board – advertising, design, publishing, editorial. Commission: 25–30%. Founded 1985.

Eye Candy Illustration

Pepperpot Corner, Manor Yard, Blithbury Road, Hamstall, Ridware, Staffs. WS15 3RS
tel 020-8291 0729
email info@eyecandy.co.uk
website www.eyecandy.co.uk
Managing Director Mark Wilson

Represents 40 artists producing work for advertising campaigns, packaging, publishing, editorials, greetings cards, merchandising and a huge variety of design projects. Submit printed samples with sae or email low-res jpg files via website. Founded 2002.

Ian Fleming Associates – see Phosphor Art Ltd

Folio Illustrators' & Designers' Agents

10 Gate Street, Lincoln's Inn Fields, London WC2A 3HP
tel 020-7242 9562 *fax* 020-7242 1816
email info@folioart.co.uk
website www.folioart.co.uk, www.folioboutique.com

All areas of illustration. Founded 1976.

Good Illustration Ltd

11–15 Betterton Street, London WC2H 9BP
tel 020-8123 0243, (US) +1 347-627-0243
email draw@goodillustration.com
website www.goodillustration.com
Directors Doreen Thorogood, Kate Webber, Tom Thorogood

Represents 30 artists for advertising, design, publishing and animation work. Send return postage with samples. Commission: 25% publishing, 30% advertising. Founded 1977.

Graham-Cameron Illustration

The Studio, 23 Holt Road, Sheringham, Norfolk NR26 8NB
tel (01263) 821333 *fax* (01263) 821334
email enquiry@gciforillustration.com
and Duncan Graham-Cameron, Graham-Cameron Illustration, 59 Hertford Road, Brighton BN1 7GG
tel (01273) 385890
website www.gciforillustration.com
Partners Helen Graham-Cameron, Duncan Graham-Cameron

Represents 37 artists and undertakes all forms of illustration for publishing and communications. Specialises in educational, children's and information books. Telephone before sending A4 sample illustrations with sae. Do not send MSS. Founded 1985.

The Guild of Aviation Artists

Trenchard House, 85 Farnborough Road, Farnborough, Hants GU14 6TF
tel (01252) 513123 *fax* (01252) 510505
email admin@gava.org.uk
website www.gava.org.uk
President Michael Turner FGAvA, *Secretary/ Administrator* Susan Gardner

Specialising in aviation art in all mediums and comprising 450 members, the Guild sells, commissions and exhibits members' work. Founded 1971.

Illustration Ltd*†

2 Brooks Court, Cringle Street, London SW8 5BX
tel 020-7720 5202 *fax* 020-7720 5920
email hello@illustrationweb.com
website www.illustrationweb.com
Contact Harry Lyon-Smith, Juliette Lott, Victoria Pearce, Mike Cowley, Vanessa Dell

Represents 150 artists producing illustrations and animation for international advertisers, designers, publishers and editorial clients. Artists should send submissions via the website. Founded 1929.

Image by Design Licensing

Suite 3, 107 Bancroft, Hitchin, Herts. SG5 1NB
tel (01462) 422244
email lucy@ibd-licensing.co.uk
website www.ibd-licensing.co.uk
Contact Lucy Brenham

Quality artwork, design and photography for a wide range of products including greeting cards, wall art, stationery, calendars, ceramics, table top, jigsaws, giftware and needlecraft. New artists always considered. Founded 1987.

Libba Jones Associates

Hopton Manor, Hopton, Nr Wirksworth, Derbyshire DE4 4DF
tel (01629) 540353 *fax* (01629) 540577
website www.gallery.mac.com/LJassociates
Contacts Libba Jones, Ieuan Jones

High-quality artwork and design for china, greetings cards and giftwrap, jigsaw puzzles, calendars, prints, posters, stationery, book illustration, fabric design. Submission of samples required for consideration. Founded 1983.

B.L. Kearley Ltd

16 Chiltern Street, London W1U 7PZ
tel 020-7935 9550
email christine.kearley@kearley.co.uk
website www.kearley.co.uk
Agent C.R. Kearley

We represent over 30 artists and have been supplying top quality illustrations to the publishing and advertising world for over 60 years. We mainly specialise in children's book and educational illustration for the domestic market and overseas. We are known for realistic figurative work for all countries. We also specialise in the sale of original book illustration artwork from our own artists dating back to the founding of the company. Commission 25%. Founded 1948.

Lemonade Illustration Agency

Hill House, Suite 231, 210 Upper Richmond Road, London SW15 6NP
tel (07891) 390750
email studio@lemonadeillustration.com
website www.lemonadeillustration.com
Contact Studio Manager, Justine Vincent

Represents 65 artists who create illustrations for all kinds of media from TV to children's books. Includes a specialist division, Fizzy, which represents 24 artists who provide styles suited for the children's picture book and educational market. Any submissions from illustrators by email must contain a website link (no attachments) or hard copies of samples can be sent by post with sae. There is now a New York office to help serve US clients.

David Lewis Agency

55A Crediton Hill, London NW6 1HS
tel 020-7435 7762 *mobile* (07931) 824674
email davidlewis34@hotmail.com
website www.davidlewisillustration.com
Director David Lewis, *Associate Director* Ramon Johns

Considers all types of illustration for a variety of applications but mostly suitable for book and magazine publishers, design groups, recording companies and corporate institutions. Also offers a comprehensive selection of images suitable for subsidiary rights purposes. Send return postage with samples. Commission: 30%. Founded 1974.

Frances McKay Illustration

18 Lammas Green, Sydenham Hill, London SE26 6LT
tel 020-8693 7006 *mobile* (07703) 344334
email frances@francesmckay.com
website www.francesmckay.com
Proprietor Frances McKay

Represents 20+ artists for illustration mainly for children's books, magazines and products, greetings cards and stationery. Submit colour copies of recent work or email low-res scans; sae essential for return of all unsolicited samples. Commission: 25–35%. Founded 1999.

Meiklejohn Illustration*†

5 Risborough Street, London SE1 0HF
tel 020-7593 0500 *fax* 020-7593 0501
email info@meiklejohn.co.uk
website www.meiklejohn.co.uk
Contact Claire Meiklejohn

All types of illustration.

N.E. Middleton Artists' Agency

email kathy.bishop@btinternet.com
website www.nemiddleton.co.uk

Designs for greetings cards, stationery, prints, calendars, china and jigsaws. Submissions by email only, following link from website.

The Monkey Feet Illustration Agency

Oakwood Cottage, 107 Grove Lane, Cheadle Hulme, Cheshire SK8 7NE
tel 0808 1200 996
email enquiries@monkeyfeetillustration.co.uk
website www.monkeyfeetillustration.co.uk
Director Adam Rushton

Represents 48 artists creating work for children's book publishers, design agencies, greeting card companies and toy manufacturers. Commission: 15–30%. Founded 2002.

NB Illustration

40 Bowling Green Lane, London EC1R 0NE
tel 020-7278 9131 *fax* 020-7278 9121
email info@nbillustration.co.uk
website www.nbillustration.co.uk
Directors Joe Najman, Charlotte Dowson, Paul Najman

Represents 50+ artists and will consider all material for the commercial illustration market. Sae essential. Commission: 30%. Founded 2000.

The Organisation*†

The Basement, 69 Caledonian Road, London N1 9BT
tel 0845 054 8033 *fax* 020-7833 8269
email lorraine@organisart.co.uk
website www.organisart.co.uk
Contact Lorraine Owen

Represents over 60 international illustrators. Contemporary and traditional styles for all areas of publishing. Stock illustration also available. See website for submission guidelines. Founded 1987.

Oxford Designers & Illustrators Ltd

Aristotle Lane, Oxford OX2 6TR
tel (01865) 512331 *fax* (01865) 512408
email richardcorfield@odi-illustration.co.uk
website www.o-d-i.com
Directors Peter Lawrence (managing), Richard Corfield, Andrew King

Studio of 20 staff working for educational publishers and businesses. Design for print and the web. All types of artwork including scientific, technical, medical, natural history, figures, 3D, cartoons, animation, maps and diagrams – computer generated and hand drawn. Not an agency. Founded 1968.

Phosphor Art Ltd*

41 The Pump House, Pump House Close, London SE16 7HS
tel 020-7064 4666 *fax* 020-7064 4660
email info@phosphorart.com
website www.phosphorart.com
Directors Jon Rogers, Catriona Wydmanski

Represents 46 artists and specialises in innovative graphic digital illustration with artists working in watercolour, oil and gouche methods as well as pen and ink, scraper, charcoal and engraving styles. Also animation. Incorporates Ian Fleming Associates and The Black and White Line. Commission: 33.3%.

Plum Pudding Illustration

Park House, 77-81 Bell Street, Reigate, Surrey RH2 7AN
tel (01737) 244095 *fax* 020-3004 7136
email info@plumpuddingillustration.com
website www.plumpuddingillustration.com
Contact Hannah Whitty

Represents 70+ artists, producing illustrations for children's publishing (all genres), advertising, editorial, greetings cards and packaging. See website for submission procedure. Commission: 30%. Founded 2006.

Sylvie Poggio Artists Agency

36 Haslemere Road, London N8 9RB
tel 020-8341 2722 *fax* 020-8374 1725
email sylviepoggio@blueyonder.co.uk
website www.sylviepoggio.com
Directors Slyvie Poggio, Bruno Caurat

Represents 40 artists producing illustrations for publishing and advertising. Commission: 25%. Founded 1992.

Vicki Thomas Associates

195 Tollgate Road, London E6 5JY
tel 020-7511 5767 *fax* 020-7473 5177
email vickithomasassociates@yahoo.co.uk
website www.vickithomasassociates.com
Consultant Vicki Thomas

Considers the work of illustrators and designers working in greetings and gift industries, and promotes such work to gift, toy, publishing and related industries. Written application and b&w photocopies required. Commission: 30%. Founded 1985.

How to get ahead in cartooning

Earning a living from creating cartoons is highly competitive. But if you feel that you were born to be a cartoonist, Martin Rowson offers some advice on how to get your work published.

I can't say precisely when I first realised I wanted to be a cartoonist. I personally believe that cartoonists are born and not made so perhaps I should be talking about when I realised I *was* a cartoonist. I do know that, aged ten, I nicked my sister's 1950s British history textbook, which was illustrated throughout by cartoons (from Gillray via Tenniel to Low) and somewhere inside me stirred an unquantifiable yearning to draw – to express myself in the unique style that is the equally unique talent of the 'cartoonist'. So, shortly afterwards I started copying the way Wally Fawkes (better known by his *nom de plume* 'Trog') drew the then Prime Minister Edward Heath.

I've spent most of my life drawing. I drew cartoons for school magazines, designed posters for school societies which invariably turned into political cartoons displayed, in the good old-fashioned way, on walls. I also developed a useful party trick of caricaturing teachers on blackboards. I did Art 'O' and 'A' levels (only a grade B in the latter) but that didn't have much to do with cartoons, and I certainly never contemplated for a moment going to art school. Instead I went to Pembroke College, Cambridge, to read English Literature, and as things turned out I hated it and I spent most of my time doing cartoons for two-bit student magazines, which partly explains how I ended up with a truly terrible degree. More on this later.

At the same time I was half-heartedly putting together a portfolio of work, in the hope that what I'd always done for fun (despite the fact that it was also a compulsion) might just end up being what I did for a living. I'd occasionally send off the portfolio to magazines, never to hear anything back. Then, shortly after graduating I had an idea for a series which I hoped would appeal to a particular demographic at the time (1982). It was called 'Scenes from the Lives of the Great Socialists' and consisted of a number of stylised depictions of leading socialist thinkers and politicians from history, with the added value of an appallingly bad pun thrown into the mixture. One example is 'Proudhon and Bakunin have tea in Tunbridge Wells', which showed the 19th century French and Russian anarchists sitting round a tea table, with Bakunin spitting out his cup of tea and exclaiming 'Proudhon! This tea is disgusting! This isn't proper tea at all!', to which Proudhon replied 'Ah, my dear Bakunin, but Property is Theft!'

I sent about half a dozen of these drawings to the *New Statesman* (then going through one of its periodic lefty phases) and, as usual, heard nothing for months. Then, just before Christmas 1982, in bed suffering from chickenpox, I received a phone call from the art director who said they were going to publish four of the cartoons in their Christmas issue, and would like me to do a series. (I was paid £40 a cartoon, which throughout 1983 meant I was earning £40 a month, which also meant I still had to sign on in order to stay alive.) Thus began my career as a cartoonist.

My three-year deadline

Now living in London, I found myself an agent and *She* magazine was the first offer to come in. They proposed to pay their standard fee of £6 for anything they published.

I instructed my agent to inform them that this barely covered my expenses for materials and postage and they could forget it (although I used two other words, one of them also beginning with 'f') – I don't know if he passed on the message. Then someone wanted to do a book of the *New Statesman* cartoons, with the offer of an advance of £750. This took my earned income for that year to somewhere perilously close to a thousand pounds.

At around this time I went to a College reunion and remember skulking around in my Oxfam suit listening with growing irritation to my contemporaries outlining how they'd got into computing/merchant banking/systems analysis or whatever at just the right time, and were earning 50 times more than I was. But I knew I was in for the long haul. As a slight nod to my father's ceaseless injunctions that it was time I got a proper job, I'd set myself a limit of three years, sort of promising that, if I wasn't making a fist of it by then I'd give up (although I doubt I actually meant it).

Luckily, a year into my putative career other contemporaries from university were starting out in journalism, and found they could earn important brownie points from their editors by bringing in a cartoonist to liven up the dull magazines they worked for. That's how I found myself working for *Satellite and Cable TV News* and *One Two Testing*... The fact that I neither knew nor cared about what I was illustrating and lampooning didn't matter. It was work, and also an essential lesson in how to master a brief, however obscure.

However, the true catalyst for my career came when another university acquaintance started working on *Financial Weekly* and, for the usual self-aggrandising reasons, suggested to the editor that they might use me. Again, this was something I knew and cared nothing about but it offered plenty of scope to lampoon truly awful people and of course frequently crossed over into political satire, where my real interest lay. More significantly, the editor himself was so nice, kind and amenable that he consequently drove his staff mad with frustration to the point that they would leave for better things. And when they went, they often took me with them.

Part of the *Financial Weekly* diaspora fled to Eddie Shah's infant *Today* newspaper, and so, just inside my self-imposed three-year time limit, I was producing a daily pocket cartoon for the business pages as well as drawing editorial cartoons for both *Today* and its short-lived sister paper *Sunday Today*. From there, another university friend brought me onto the books pages of the *Sunday Correspondent* and, in doing so, to broadsheet respectability. After that I never really had to solicit for work again. I'd reached cartooning critical mass; the people commissioning knew who I was and, more importantly, knew my work so the hard part was over. And, rather nicely, when I went to another College reunion, I discovered that all the smart boys in computing and banking had been sacked in the recession of the early 1990s.

How can other people get ahead in cartooning?

At one level you could say, between gritted teeth, that all that I've written above proves is that it's just about the old boy network – not what you know but who you know. To an extent that's true, but I'd like to think that none of the publications I'd worked for would have given me a second glance if I couldn't cut the mustard and deliver the goods. So, what do you need to get ahead in cartooning?

First of all, and most importantly, you need to recognise whether or not you truly are a cartoonist, and to do that you need to know what cartoons are. It won't do just to be able to draw; nor is it enough to have a sense of humour. You need to combine the two, and understand that in so doing you are creating something that can't be expressed in any other way. This requires a mindset which, I believe, is innate. Moreover, I don't believe you can teach people how to be cartoonists – they have to teach themselves, and from an early age at that. If you copy other cartoonists to find out how it's done, then slowly but surely you'll develop a style of your own which you feel comfortable with.

Once you recognise what you are, and that you're determined to embark on a career that, like poetry or acting, offers a dream of glamour out of all proportion to its guaranteed financial reward, you then need to create a frame of mind which combines, in equal measure, arrogance and sloth. In other words, you *know* that you're good, and actually better than anyone else who's ever lived, but you're also, crucially, too lazy to do anything else, like accountancy.

Then comes the hard part, which is not for the faint-hearted. You have to work very hard, to make sure what you're producing is really good, and is the best you can do (of which you will always, ultimately, be the best judge). If you're a caricaturist, practice your caricature (and by all means steal other, more established cartoonists' tricks in order to develop your own; after all, they do). If you're a gag cartoonist, hone the gag and work on the drawing so it's clear what's going on (cartooning is the last bastion of realism in the visual arts – abstract cartoons don't work). If you're a political cartoonist, immerse yourself in current affairs and, most importantly, either develop or clearly express your point of view, which can be either right or left wing (a fair, unopinionated cartoonist is as useless and boring as a newspaper columnist with no opinions and nothing to say). A good editorial cartoon is a newspaper column by other means, and is best described as visual journalism, using tricks – like irony, humour, violence and vile imagery – that the big boys in newspaper punditry are too dumb to understand. But remember – while you go through this stage you'll be papering your bedroom wall with rejection slips.

Practical advice

Always try to make your artwork look professional. This means using good paper drawn on in indelible ink, centrally placed. This might sound obvious, but I've seen many cartoons by aspiring cartoonists drawn in crayon on lined file paper going right up to the edge of the sheet. This won't even get halfway out of the envelope before any editor bins it.

Second, always remember that, although you are a genius you have to start somewhere, and some work is always better than no work. If you want to get into newspapers or magazines (which is all there really is if you want to earn some money and not just feel complacent about your beautiful website), identify parts of the press that would benefit from your input.

Journalists producing gardening or travel or, most of all, personal finance sections are crying out for something to liven their pages, something other than a photo which will mark them out as different. In other words, be arrogant enough to be sufficiently humble to illustrate copy you'd never in a million years personally read. Many famous and established cartoonists still knock out stuff for trade papers of crashing obscurity and dullness, this being as good a way as any other of paying the mortgage.

Once you've identified a potential gap in the market, *always* submit your idea or portfolio to the editor of that section, and *never* send it to the art director (despite my experience with the *New Statesman*). There are several reasons for this. First, art directors are inundated with unsolicited work, and so the odds are immediately pitched against you. Second, there's the danger that, in the endless little territorial feuds that pertain in journalism, you will become the exclusive property of the art director who, because he or she hates the gardening editor, will never pass your work on. Third, the section editor will be flattered and delighted to receive something different from the usual dross of press releases and letters of pedantic complaint. If your work tickles their fancy, then you're in, and a section editor always pulls rank over an art director, whatever anyone may imagine.

From these first steps, you will have the beginnings of a portfolio of published work which will stand you in excellent stead on your way to reaching that critical mass of recognition I mentioned earlier.

Finally, never forget that cartoons are something different from anything else. While they combine text journalism and illustration, they end up as something greater than their component parts. In a way, a cartoon is a kind of voodoo, doing harm to someone (whether a politician or a castaway on a desert island) at a distance with a sharp object, which in this case is a pen. It's hard to get established, the number of successful cartoonists earning a decent wedge is tiny and there will always be a generational logjam as the clapped-out old has-beens whose work enrages and disgusts you cling tenaciously to the precious few slots. But if you're determined and tough enough, stick with it and you, too, could become one of those clapped-out has-beens. Until then, just bear in mind that it's a small and crowded profession, and despite everything I've said, the last thing I need is anyone good coming along and muscling in on my territory. In my heart of hearts, I should really advise all aspiring young cartoonists to give up now. Such churlishness apart, however, I'll stick with wishing you good luck.

Martin Rowson is a cartoonist and writer whose work appears regularly in the *Guardian*, the *Daily Mirror*, the *Independent on Sunday* and many other publications. His awards include Political Cartoonist of the Year in 2001, 2003 and 2010, Caricaturist of the Year in 2011, and he produced the Political Cartoon of the Year in 2002 and 2007. His books include comic book versions of *The Waste Land*, *Tristram Shandy* and *Gulliver's Travels*, and *Stuff*, a memoir of clearing out his late parents' house which was longlisted for the Samuel Johnson Prize for Non-fiction. He is Chairman of the British Cartoonists' Association, a trustee of the British Humanists Association and a former vice-president of the Zoological Society of London.

See also...

- *Freelancing for beginners*, page 467
- *Design and Artists Copyright Society*, page 662
- *Marketing yourself online*, page 587
- *Managing your online reputation*, page 591

Winning the greeting card game

The UK population spends more than £1.3 billion a year on greeting cards. Jakki Brown helps to guide artists and designers to success in this fiercely competitive industry.

The UK greeting card industry leads the world on two counts – design and innovation and *per capita* send. On average people in the UK send 31 cards a year, 85% of which are bought by women.

But just how do you, as an artist or designer, go about satisfying this voracious appetite of the card-sending public? There are two main options: either to become a greeting card publisher yourself or to supply existing greeting card publishers with your artwork and be paid a fee for doing so.

The idea of setting up your own greeting card publishing company may sound exciting, but this decision should not be taken lightly. Going down this route will involve taking on all the set up and running costs of a publishing company as well as the production, selling and administrative responsibilities. This often leaves little time for you to do what you do best – creating the artwork.

Some greeting card language

Own brand/bespoke publishers. These design specific to a retailer's needs.

Spring Seasons. The industry term to describe greeting cards for Valentine's Day, Mother's Day, Easter and Father's Day. Publishers generally launch these ranges all together in June/July.

Greeting card types. Traditional; cute or whimsical; contemporary/quirky art; juvenile; handmade or hand-finished; fine art; photographic, humorous.

Finishes and treatments. Artists will not be expected to know the production techniques and finishes, but a working knowledge is often an advantage. Some of the most commonly used finishes and treatments include: embossing (raised portion of a design), die-cutting (where the card is cut into a shape or includes an aperture), foiling (metallic film) and flitter (a glitter-like substance).

There are estimated to be around 800 greeting card publishers in the UK, ranging in size from one-person operations to multinational corporations, roughly 200 of which are regarded as 'serious' publishers (see page 486).

Finding the right publishers

While some publishers concentrate on producing a certain type of greeting card (e.g. humorous, fine art or juvenile), the majority publish a variety of greeting card ranges. Unfortunately, this makes it more difficult for you as an artist to target the most appropriate potential publishers for your work. There are various ways in which you can research the market, quickly improve your publisher knowledge and, therefore, reduce the amount of wasted correspondence:

• **Go shopping.** Browse the displays in card shops and other high street shops, department stores, supermarkets, garden centres and gift shops. This will not only give you an insight into what is already available but also which publishers may be interested in your work. Most publishers include their contact details on the back of the cards.

• **Trade fairs.** There are a number of trade exhibitions held during the year at which publishers exhibit their greeting card ranges to retailers and overseas distributors. By visiting these exhibitions, you will gain a broad overview of the design trends in the industry, as well as the current ranges of individual publishers. Some publishers are willing to meet artists and look through their portfolios on the stand but others are not. Never interrupt a sale. If you believe your work could be relevant for them, when they are free, ask for a contact name and follow it up afterwards. Have a supply of business cards handy, perhaps illustrated with some of your work, to leave with publishers.

• **The Greeting Card Association website** (www.greetingcardassociation.org.uk). This resource provides advice about submitting designs and a list of publishers looking for freelance designers.

Types of publishers

There are two broad categories of publisher – wholesale and direct-to-retail – each employing a different method of distribution to reach the retailer.

Further information

The Greeting Card Association
United House, North Road, London N7 9DP
tel 020-7619 0396
email gca@max-publishing.co.uk
website www.greetingcardassociation.org.uk

The UK trade association for greeting card publishers. Its online information resource contains pages on freelance designing and writing for greeting cards complete with lists of publishers which accept freelance work. The Ladder Club is an annual one-day seminar for would-be/fledgling publishers, many of whom are artists or photographers looking to publish their own work. The seminar covers all aspects of publishing and costs approx. £40 (*tel* (01702) 480180, *email* waiteandtaitbakery@hotmail.com).

TRADE FAIRS

Spring Fair Birmingham, NEC
website www.springfair.com
Contact TPS/Emap *tel* 020-7728 5000
Takes place 3–7 Feb 2013

Progressive Greetings Live
website www.progressivegreetingslive.co.uk
Contact Max Exhibitions *tel* (01635) 297070
Takes place May 2013

Pulse, Earls Court 1
website www.pulse-london.com
Contact Clarion Events *tel* 020-7370 8207
Takes place June 2013

Home and Gift, Harrogate
website www.homeandgift.co.uk
Contact Clarion Events *tel* 020-7370 8043
Takes place mid July 2013

Autumn Fair Birmingham, NEC
website www.autumnfair.com
Contact TPS/Emap *tel* 020-7728 5000
Takes place 2–5 Sept 2012

Top Drawer Spring, Olympia
website www.topdrawer.co.uk
Contact Clarion Events *tel* 020-7370 8051
Takes place 13–15 Jan 2013

TRADE MAGAZINES

Greetings Today
Lema Publishing, Unit 1, Queen Mary's Avenue, Watford, Herts. WD18 7JR
tel (01923) 250909 *fax* (01923) 250995
Publisher-in-Chief Malcolm Naish, *Editor* Ella Hoyos
Monthly £45 p.a. (other rates on application)

Articles, features and news related to the greetings card industry. Includes Artists Directory for aspiring artists wishing to attract the eye of publishers. Runs seminars for small publishers and artists.

Progressive Greetings Worldwide
Max Publishing, United House, North Road, London N7 9DP
tel 020-7700 6740 *fax* 020-7607 6411
email jw@max-publishing.co.uk
12 p.a. (£50 p.a.)
Editor and co-owner Jakki Brown

The official magazine of the Greeting Card Association and the only monthly greeting card industry magazine in the world. Provides an insight to the industry, including news and features, an up-to-date list of publishers, a new product section and Art Source, a free showcase for artists, illustrators and verses. Special supplements include *Focus on Art Cards, Focus on Humorous Cards, Focus on Words & Sentiments* and *Focus on Kids.*

Progressive Greetings hosts The Henries, the greeting card industry awards. The September edition includes details of the finalists and the November issue features the winners.

Wholesale publishers distribute their products to the retailer via greeting card wholesalers or cash-and-carry outlets. They work on volume sales and have a rapid turnover of designs, many being used with a variety of different captions. For example, the same floral design may be used for cards for mothers, grandmothers, aunts and sisters. It is therefore usual for the artist to leave a blank space on the design to accommodate the caption. Until recently, wholesale publishers were generally only interested in traditional, cute and juvenile designs, but they now publish across the board, including contemporary and humorous ranges.

Direct-to-retail (DTR) publishers supply retailers via sales agents or reps. Most greeting cards sold through specialist card shops and gift shops are supplied by DTR publishers, which range from multinational corporations down to small, trendy niche publishing companies. These publishers market series of ranges based on distinctive design themes or characters. Categories of DTR cards include contemporary art/fun, fine art, humour, words and sentiment, children's, photographic, traditional and handmade/hand-finished and, of course, Christmas cards.

Approaching a publisher

Unfortunately, there is no standard way of approaching and submitting work to a card publisher. The first step is to establish that the publisher you wish to approach accepts work from freelance artists; then find out their requirements for submission and to whom it should be addressed.

It is always better to send several examples of your work to show the breadth of your artistic skills. Some publishers prefer to see finished designs while others are happy with well-presented sketches. Never send originals: instead supply your images on disk, or as photocopies, laser copies or photographs, and include at least one design in colour. You can initially send your designs to as many publishers as you like, but never be tempted to sell similar designs to two publishers – a bad reputation will follow you around.

Some publishers will be looking to purchase individual designs for specific sending occasions (e.g. new baby, new home, sympathy) while others will be more intent on looking for designs which could be developed to make up a range. Bear in mind that publishers work a long way in advance, for example Christmas ranges are launched to the retailers the previous January. Development of a range may take up to six months prior to launching.

Also remember that cards in retail outlets are rarely displayed in their entirety with many of the racking display systems obscuring part of the design. Therefore, when designing a card make sure that some of the 'action' appears in the top half.

When interest is shown

Some publishers respond to submissions from artists immediately while others prefer to deal with them on a monthly basis. A publisher's response may be in the form of a request for more submissions of a specific design style or of a specific character. This speculative development work is usually carried out free of charge. Always meet your deadline (news travels fast in the industry).

A publisher interested in buying your artwork will probably then issue you with a contract. This may cover aspects such as the terms of payment; rights of usage of the design (e.g. is it just for greeting cards or will it include giftwrap and/or stationery?);

territory of usage (most publishers want worldwide rights); and ownership of copyright or license period.

There is no set industry standard rate of pay for greeting card artists. Publishers pay artists either on a per design or per range basis in one of the following ways:

• **Flat fee.** A one-off payment is made to the artist for ownership of a design for an unlimited period. The industry standard is around £200–£250 for a single design, and payment on a sliding scale for more than one design.

• **Licensing fee.** The publisher is granted the right to use a piece of artwork for a specified number of years, after which the full rights revert to the artist. Payment to the artist is approximately £150 upwards per design.

• **Licensing fee plus royalty.** As above plus a royalty payment on each card sold. Artists would generally receive a minimum of £100 for the licensing fee plus 3%–7% of the trade price of each card sold.

• **Advance royalty deal.** A goodwill advance on royalties is paid to the artist. In the case of a range, the artist would receive a goodwill advance of say £500–£1,000 plus 5%–8% additional royalty payment once the threshold is reached.

• **Royalty only.** The artist receives regular royalty payments, generally paid quarterly, based on the number of cards sold. Artists should expect to receive a 5%–8% royalty, sales reports and royalty statements.

The fees stated above should only be regarded as a rough guideline. Fees and advances are generally paid on completion of artwork. Publishers which have worldwide rights pay royalties for sales overseas to artists, although these will be on a pro rata basis to the export trade price.

Jakki Brown is editor of *Progressive Greetings Worldwide* and general secretary of the Greeting Card Association.

See also...

- *Freelancing for beginners*, page 467
- *Art agents and commercial studios*, page 474
- *Card and stationery publishers that accept illustrations and verses*, page 486
- *Design and Artists Copyright Society, page 662*

Card and stationery publishers that accept illustrations and photographs

Before submitting work, artists and photographers are advised to ascertain requirements of the company they are approaching, including terms and conditions. Only top quality material should be submitted; inferior work is never accepted.

*Member of the Greeting Card Association

Card Connection Ltd*

Park House, South Street, Farnham, Surrey GU9 7QQ
tel (01252) 892300 *fax* (01252) 892363
email ho@card-connection.co.uk
website www.card-connection.co.uk
Managing Director Michael Johnson

Everyday and seasonal designs. Styles include cute, fun, traditional, contemporary, humour and photographic. Humorous copy and jokes plus sentimental verse. Founded 1992.

Carlton Cards Ltd

Mill Street East, Dewsbury, West Yorkshire WF12 9AW
tel (01924) 465200 *fax* (01924) 453908
website www.carltoncards.co.uk
Group Marketing Director Keith Auty, *Product Development Director* Josephine Loughran

All types of artwork, any size; submit as colour roughs, colour copies or transparencies. Especially interested in humorous artwork and ideas.

Caspari Ltd*

Linden House, John Dane Player Court, East Street, Saffron Walden, Essex CB10 1LR
tel (01799) 513010 *fax* (01799) 513101
email info@caspari.co.uk
website www.casparionline.com
Director of Sales Lynn Briody

Traditional fine art/classic images; 5 x 4in transparencies. No verses. Founded 1990.

Colneis Marketing Ltd*

York House, 2–4 York Road, Felixstowe IP11 7QQ
tel (01394) 271668 *fax* (01394) 275114
email colneiscards@btconnect.com
website www.colneisgreetingcards.com
Proprietor John Botting

Photographs (preferably medium format) and colour artwork of nature and cute images. Founded 1994.

Colour House Graphics Ltd*

York House, 2–4 York Road, Felixstowe IP11 7QQ
tel (01394) 271668 *fax* (01394) 275114
email colourhousegraphics@hotmail.com
website www.colourhousegraphics.co.uk
Contact John Batting

Contemporary styles of painting of subjects relating to people's everyday lives. Particularly interested in sophisticated, loose, graphic styles. No verses. Founded 1990.

Simon Elvin Ltd*

Wooburn Industrial Park, Wooburn Green, Bucks. HP10 0PE
tel (01628) 526711 *fax* (01628) 531483
email studioadmin@simonelvin.com
website www.simonelvin.com
Art Director Fiona Buszard, *Studio Manager* Rachel Green

Female/male traditional and contemporary designs, female/male cute, wedding/anniversary, birth congratulations, fine art, photographic animals, flowers and male imagery, traditional sympathy, juvenile ages, special occasions and giftwrap.

Looking for submissions that show flair, imagination and an understanding of greeting card design. Artists should familiarise themselves with the ranges, style and content. Submit a small collection of either colour copies or prints (no original artwork) and include a sae for return of work. Alternatively email jpg files.

4C For CardsWorld Ltd

114 High Street, Stevenage, Herts. SG1 3DW
tel 0845 230 0046 *fax* 0845 230 0048
email 4c@charitycards.org
website www.charitycards.org

Traditional and contemporary Christmas cards for the corporate and charity market. Submit artwork by email. No verses. Works for 70+ charities. Founded 1966.

Gallery Five Ltd*

The Old Bakery, 1 Bellingham Road, London SE6 2PN
tel 020-8697 1629 *fax* 020-8461 5015
website www.galleryfive.co.uk

Send samples of work FAO 'Gallery Five Art Studio'. Colour photocopies, Mac-formatted zip/CD acceptable, plus sae. No verses.

Gemma International Ltd*

Linmar House, 6 East Portway, Andover, Hants SP10 3LU
tel (01264) 388400 *fax* (01264) 366243
email esales@gemma-international.co.uk
website www.gemma-international.co.uk
Directors William Harris, A. Parkin, T. Rudd-Clarke, David Wesson

Cute, contemporary, leading-edge designs for children, teens and young adults. Founded 1984.

Graphic Humour Ltd

PO Box 717, North Shields, Tyne & Wear NE30 4WR
tel 0191-215 5006 *fax* (01207) 566842
email enquiries@graphichumour.com
website www.graphichumour.com

Risqué and everyday artwork ideas for greetings cards; short, humorous copy. Founded 1984.

The Great British Card Company

Waterwells Drive, Gloucester, Glos. GL2 2PH
tel (01452) 888999 *fax* (01452) 888912
email art@paperhouse.co.uk
website www.greatbritishcards.co.uk

Products include greetings cards; gift wrap and social stationery; birthday and blank cards; Christmas cards; Spring Seasons cards; occasions cards; family relations cards; and calendars. Brands include Paper House; Medici Cards; Elgin Court; Royle Publications; National Geographic; Royal Horticultural Society (RHS); English Heritage; Peter Cross; Madeleine Floyd; Eric The Penguin; Stripy Horse; The Humour Factory; Young at Heart; I Can't Believe I'm Not Human; Everybody Smile; Word for Word; Blue Label Art; Medici Cards Wildlife; Darkroom.

Green Pebble Publications

Roos Hall Studio, Bungay Road, Beccles, Suffolk NR34 7JE
tel (01502) 710427
email ruby@greenpebble.co.uk
website www.greenpebble.co.uk
Director Michael Charles

Publisher of fine art and photography cards by artists. Humorous, friendship, reflective, and contemporary still lifes with a twist. Send a minimum of 6 design thumbnails via post (with sae) or email. Founded 2010.

Hallmark Cards Plc*

Hallmark House, Bingley Road, Heaton, Bradford BD9 6SD
tel (01274) 252523
email creativesubmissions@hallmark-uk.com
website www.hallmark.co.uk

See website for freelance opportunities and submission details.

Hanson White – UK Greetings

2nd Floor, AMP House, Dingwall Road, Croydon CR0 2LX
tel 020-8260 1200 *fax* 020-8260 1213
email hannah.turpin@ukgreetings.co.uk, sally.england@ukgreetings.co.uk
Submissions Editors Hannah Turpin, Sally England

Humorous artwork and cartoons/photographs for greeting cards, including Christmas, Valentine's Day, Mother's Day, Father's Day, general birthday and everyday occasions. Humorous copy lines and punchline jokes, funny poems and rhymes – guidelines available on request. Founded 1958.

Hotchpotch Publishing Ltd

PO Box 264, Hampton, Middlesex TW12 2ZT
tel 020-8941 0126
email art@hotchpotchpublishing.com
website www.thegreetingsfactory.com
Design Manager Kathryn Clague

Colour artwork for greetings cards, giftwrap and social stationery. Considers verses. Founded 1997.

Jodds*

PO Box 353, Bicester, Oxon OX27 0GS
tel (01869) 278550 *fax* (01869) 278551
email joddscard@hotmail.co.uk
website www.joddscards.com
Partners M. Payne and J.S. Payne

Children's and contemporary art style greetings cards. Prefers low resolution jpg files by email. Will reply if interested. The company appreciates the time taken to submit. Established 1988.

Leeds Postcards

4 Granby Road, Leeds LS6 3AS
email xtine@leedspostcards.com
website www.leedspostcards.co.uk
Contact Christine Hankinson

Publisher and distributor of satirical radical postcards for the wall and post. Archives and more information on www.leedspostcards.com. Suitable and relevant postcard ideas send jpg files to email above. Please check catalogue to make sure work is appropriate. Paid by advance royalty on print run.

Lima Design*

1 Lordship Lane, London SE22 8EW
tel 020-8693 4257 *fax* 020-8693 8723
email info@limadesign.co.uk
website www.limadesign.co.uk
Proprietor Lisa Breakwell

Produces contemporary, design-conscious cards which are all hand applied using resisters and capacitors, ribbon, indoor sparklers, animal-shaped rubber bands, metallic thread and beads. Founded 2002.

Ling Design Ltd*

Westmoreland House, Westmoreland Street, Bath BA2 3HE

tel (01225) 489760 *fax* (01225) 448190
email info@lingdesign.co.uk
website www.lingdesign.co.uk
Creative Director Isabel Scott Evans

Artwork for greetings cards, stationery and giftwrap.

Medici Cards Limited

Waterwells Drive, Gloucester, Glos. GL2 2PH
tel (01452) 888999 *fax* (01452) 888912
email art@medicicards.co.uk
website www.medicicards.co.uk

Specialises in market leading art and photographic cards. Brands include National Geographic, English Heritage, RHS, C'est La Vie, Medici Cards Wildlife and Medici Cards Blue Label.

Paper House

Waterwells Drive, Gloucester, Glos. GL2 2PH
tel (01452) 888999 *fax* (01452) 888912
email art@paperhouse.co.uk
website www.paperhouse.co.uk

Producers of everyday greetings cards; brands include Viva, Humour Factory, Two Fat Gherkins, Birdwit, Floreo, Animal Magic, Love the Moment, Eric, Look at it This Way, Up the Garden Path, Fred & Ginger, Life As We Know It, Darkroom, Elgin Court, Thoughts of You, Cherry Boom Boom, Pearls.

Paperlink Ltd*

356 Kennington Road, London SE11 4LD
tel 020-7582 8244 *fax* 020-7587 5212
email info@paperlink.co.uk
website www.paperlink.co.uk
Directors Louise Tighe, Tim Porte, Tim Purcell

Publishers of ranges of humorous and contemporary art greetings cards. Produce products under licence for charities. Founded 1986.

Pineapple Park*

Unit 9, Henlow Trading Estate, Henlow Camp, Beds. SG16 6DS
tel (01462) 814817 *fax* (01462) 819443
email info@pineapplepark.co.uk
website www.pineapplepark.co.uk
Directors Peter M. Cockerline, Sarah M. Parker

Illustrations and photographs for publication as greetings cards. Contemporary, cute, humour: submit artwork or laser copies with sae. Photographic florals always needed. Humour copy/jokes accepted without artwork. Also concepts for ranges. Founded 1993.

Powell Publishing*

Millyard House, Millyard Way, Eythorne, Dover, Kent CT17 4NL
tel (01304) 833550 *fax* (01304) 833555
email richard@powellpublishing.co.uk
website www.powellpublishing.co.uk
Directors D.J. Powell, T.J. Paulett, *Art & Design Manager* Richard Oram

Greetings card publishers. Interested in Christmas designs for the charity card market. Division of Powell Print Ltd.

The Publishing House

PO Box 81, Banbury, Oxon OX16 3YL
tel (01295) 271144 *fax* (01295) 277403
email naval@thepublishinghouse.co.uk
Contact Naval Phandey

General and multicultural cards across all faiths. No verses.

Nigel Quiney Publications Ltd*

Cloudesley House, Shire Hill, Saffron Walden, Essex CB11 3FB
tel (01799) 520200 *fax* (01799) 520100
email alison.butterworth@nigelquiney.com
website www.nigelquiney.com
Contact Alison Butterworth, Creative Director

Everyday and seasonal greetings cards including fine art, photographic, humour, contemporary and cute. Submit by email or colour copies, photographs, transparencies or disk by post: no original artwork.

Really Good*

The Old Mast House, The Square, Abingdon, Oxon OX14 5AR
tel (01235) 537888 *fax* (01235) 537779
email ello@reallygood.uk.com
website www.reallygood.uk.com
Director David Hicks

Always looking for fun, funny and quirky artwork to publish on cards, stationery or gifts. Check the website first, and if there is a fit email website/blog link or small jpg or pdf files to view. Please do not post submissions. Really Good is the sister company of Soul. Founded 1987.

Felix Rosenstiel's Widow & Son Ltd

Fine Art Publishers, 33–35 Markham Street, London SW3 3NR
tel 020-7352 3551 *fax* 020-7351 5300
email artists@felixr.com
website www.felixr.com

Invites offers of artwork of a professional standard for reproduction as picture prints for the picture framing trade. Any type of subject considered. See our website for submission details.

Royle Publications Ltd – see Medici Cards Limited

J. Salmon Ltd

100 London Road, Sevenoaks, Kent TN13 1BB
tel (01732) 452381 *fax* (01732) 450951
email enquiries@jsalmon.co.uk
website www.jsalmon.co.uk

Picture postcards, calendars, greeting cards and local view booklets.

Santoro London

Rotunda Point, 11 Hartfield Crescent,
London SW19 3RL
tel 020-8781 1100 *fax* 020-8781 1101
email submissions@santorographics.com
website www.santoro-london.com
Directors Jason Freeman

Publishers of innovative and award-winning designs for greeting cards, giftwrap and gift stationery. Bold, contemporary images with an international appeal. Subjects covered: contemporary, pop-up, cute, quirky, fashion, retro. Submit samples as colour copies or digital files (jpg or pdf files). Founded 1985.

Second Nature Ltd*

10 Malton Road, London W10 5UP
tel 020-8960 0212 *fax* 020-8960 8700
email rods@secondnature.co.uk
website www.secondnature.co.uk
Publishing Director Rod Schragger

Contemporary artwork for greetings cards and handmade cards; jokes for humorous range; short modern sentiment; verses. Founded 1981.

Solomon & Whitehead Ltd

Lynn Lane, Shenstone, Staffs. WS14 0DX
tel (01543) 483000 *fax* (01543) 481619

Fine art prints, limited editions and originals, framed and unframed.

Soul*

Old Mast House, The Square, Abingdon,
Oxon OX14 5AR
tel (01235) 537816 *fax* (01235) 537817
email smile@souluk.com
website www.souluk.com
Director David Hicks

Publishers of contemporary art cards with modern sentiment. Also wrapping paper and notebooks. Please look at the website, and if there is a fit please email website/blog link, or small jpg or pdf files to view. Please do not post artwork. Soul is the sister company of Really Good.

Noel Tatt Group/Impress Publishing*

Appledown House, Barton Business Park,
Appledown Way, New Dover Road, Canterbury,
Kent CT1 3TE
tel (01227) 811600 *fax* (01227) 811601
email mail@noeltatt.co.uk
website www.noeltatt.co.uk
Directors Jarle Tatt, Diane Tatt, Richard Parsons, Ian Hylands

General everyday cards – broad mix; Christmas. Will consider verses. Founded 1964.

The Webb Group

Queen Street, Burton-on-Trent, Staffs. DE14 3LP
tel 0845 218 4530 *fax* (01283) 506306
website www.thewebbgroup.co.uk

High-quality Christmas cards and paper products.

Wishing Well Studios (cbg)*

The Granary, Wallgate, Wigan WN1 1BA
tel (01243) 792642
email nicky.harrison@cbg.co.uk
website www.wishingwell.co.uk
Contact Nicky Harrison

Part of Carte Blanche Group. Rhyming and prose verse 4–24 lines long; also jokes. All artwork styles considered but do not send originals (enclose a sae for return of work). Email attachements no larger than 3mb.

Woodmansterne Publications Ltd*

1 The Boulevard, Blackmoor Lane, Watford,
Herts. WD18 8UW
tel (01923) 200600 *fax* (01923) 200601
website www.woodmansterne.co.uk

Publisher of greeting cards and social stationery featuring fine and contemporary art and photography (colour and b&w). Submit colour copies, photographs or jpg files by email.

The freelance photographer

Becoming a successful freelance photographer is as much about marketing as photographic talent. Professional photographer Ian Thraves highlights possibilities for the freelance.

Having an outstanding portfolio is one thing, but to receive regular commissions takes a good business head and sound market knowledge. Although working as a professional photographer can be tough, it is undoubtedly one of the most interesting and rewarding ways of earning a living.

Entering professional photography

A good starting point is to embark on one of the many college courses available, which range from GCSE to degree level, and higher. These form a good foundation, though most teach only the technical and artistic aspects of photography and very few cover the basics of running a business. But a good college course will provide students with the opportunity to become familiar with photographic equipment and develop skills without the restrictions and pressures found in the workplace.

In certain fields, such as commercial photography, it is possible to learn the trade as an assistant to an established photographer. A photographer's assistant will undertake many varied tasks, including preparing camera equipment and lighting, building sets, obtaining props and organising locations, as well as general mundane chores. It usually takes only a year or two for an assistant to become a fully competent photographer, having during that time learnt many technical aspects of a particular field of photography and the fundamentals of running a successful business. There is, however, the danger of a long-standing assistant becoming a clone of the photographer worked for, and it is for this reason that some assistants prefer to gain experience with various photographers rather than working for just one for a long period of time. The Association of Photographers (AOP) can help place an assistant.

However, in other fields of photography, such as photojournalism or wildlife photography, an assistant is not generally required, and photographers in these fields are usually self-taught.

Identifying your market

From the outset, identify which markets are most suitable for the kind of subjects you photograph. Study each market carefully and only offer images which suit the client's requirements.

Usually photographers who specialise in a particular field do better than those who generalise. By concentrating on one or two subject areas they become expert at what they do. Those who make a name for themselves are invariably specialists, and it is far easier for the images of, for example, an exceptional fashion photographer or an award-winning wildlife photographer to be remembered than the work of someone who covers a broad range of subjects.

In addition, photographers who produce work with individual style (e.g. by experimenting with camera angles or manipulating images to create unusual and distinctive effects) are far more likely to make an impact. Alternative images which attract attention and can help sell a product or service are always sought after. This is especially true of advertising photography, but applies also to other markets such as book and magazine publishers, who are continually seeking eye-catching images, especially for front cover use.

Promoting yourself

Effective self-promotion tells the market who you are and what service you offer. A first step should be to create an outstanding portfolio of images, tailored to appeal to the targeted market. Photographers targeting a few different markets should create an individual portfolio for each rather than presenting a single general one, including only a few relevant images. A portfolio should only contain a photographer's most outstanding work. Including substandard images will show inconsistent quality, leaving a potential client in doubt about the photographer's ability.

Images should be presented in a format that the client is used to handling. Usually, a high-quality printed portfolio, backed up by a well-designed website is adequate. Many photographers also produce an additional portfolio in the form of a DVD slideshow or movie. These can be very cheap to create and duplicate and can be handed or posted out to potential and existing clients. Any published material (often referred to as 'tearsheets') should also be added to a portfolio. Tearsheets are often presented mounted and laminated in plastic.

Business cards and letterheads should be designed to reflect style and professionalism. Consider using a good graphic designer to create a logo for use on cards, letterheads and any other promotional literature. Many photographers produce postcard-size business cards and include an image as well as their name and logo.

Other than word of mouth, advertising is probably the best way of making your services known to potential clients. Whether targeting local or global markets, web-based advertising has become the photographer's preferred method of gaining business. Compared to print advertising media, web-based marketing is generally much cheaper and more acces-

Professional organisations

The Association of Photographers (AOP)
Co-Secretary Gwen Thomas, 81 Leonard Street, London EC2A 4QS
tel 020-7739 6669 *fax* 020-7739 8707
email general@aophoto.co.uk
website www.the-aop.org
See page 505.

British Institute of Professional Photography (BIPP)
The Coach House, The Firs, High Street, Whitchurch, Aylesbury, Bucks. HP22 4SJ
tel (01296) 642020
email info@bipp.com
website www.bipp.com
See page 510.

Master Photographers Association
Jubilee House, 1 Chancery Lane, Darlington, Co. Durham DL1 5QP
tel (01325) 356555 *fax* (01325) 357813
email info@mpauk.com
website www.thempa.com
See page 525.

The Royal Photographic Society
Fenton House, 122 Wells Road, Bath BA2 3AH
tel (01225) 325733 *fax* (01225) 325733
email rps@rps.org
website www.rps.org
See page 532.

BAPLA (British Association of Picture Libraries and Agencies)
See page 506.

sible to potential markets, plus it allows the photographer more opportunity to showcase a greater number of portfolio images, supported by an unlimited amount of text/copy. However, for more specific commercial markets (such as advertising and design), high-quality printed directories are still popular. These include titles like *The Creative Handbook* and *Contact Photography* (see page 493), which both still take pride-of-place on the bookshelves of many who work in the creative marketplace.

Cold calling by telephone is probably the most cost-effective and productive way of making contacts, and these should be followed up by an appointment to meet potential clients in person, if possible.

Photographers should regard the internet as a primary promotion medium. A cleverly designed website is essential and is a stylish and cost-effective way to expose a photographer's portfolio to a global market, as well as being a convenient way for a potential client to view a photographer's work. Your website address should be included in all business stationery and other forms of advertising.

Creating a website can be much cheaper than advertising using conventional published print media. However, its design should be carefully composed and is probably best left to a professional website designer. Although many images and details about your business can be placed on a website, one limiting factor is the time it can take to navigate an over-complicated site. Unless this is a relatively quick process the viewer may lose patience.

In addition to a traditional website, many photographers have taken to 'blogging' as another form of web-based marketing. The beauty of a blog is the ease at which the owner can update the content. Updatable items may include your latest images, news articles and equipment reviews, plus any other interesting posts that relate to the industry. Blogs and other types of social media, such as Twitter, Facebook and LinkedIn, can all work hand-in-hand to increase a photographer's 'fan-base' or 'following', all serving to strengthen a photographer's market presence on a global basis.

A well-organised exhibition of images is a very effective way of bringing a body of work to the attention of current and potential new clients. Some photographers promote themselves by throwing a preview party with refreshments for friends, colleagues and specially invited guests from the industry. A show that is well reviewed by respected newspaper and magazine journalists can generate additional interest.

As a photographer's career develops, the budget for self-promotion should increase. Many established photographers will go as far as producing full-colour mailers, posters, and even calendars, which all contain examples of their work.

Digital photography

Most photographers now use digital cameras, and image-enhancement and manipulation using computer technology are widely used in the photographic industry. There are various levels of quality produced by digital cameras and photographers should consider the requirements of their market prior to investing in expensive hardware which is prone to rapid change and improvement. At the cheaper level, digital SLR cameras (DSLRs) manufactured by companies such as Nikon and Canon can produce outstanding quality images suitable for many end uses. Cameras like these are used predominantly for press, PR and general commercial work.

At a higher level, many commercial studio photographers have invested in a medium or large format 'digital capture back', which is a high-quality chip that can be adapted to fit many of the conventional studio cameras. This system is far more expensive, but is capable of producing file sizes which closely compare in quality to a high-resolution scan from large format film. Thus the images are suitable for any end use, such as top-quality advertisements. Photographers thinking of supplying stock libraries with digital images should consider the quality of the camera they use. Stock libraries often supply a diverse range of clients, including advertising, and will therefore only accept the highest standard in order to meet the demands of the market.

Image-enhancement and manipulation using a computer program such as Adobe Photoshop provides photographers with an onscreen darkroom where the possibilities for creating imaginative images are endless. As well as being useful for retouching purposes and creating photo compositions, it provides the photographer with an opportunity to create images that are more distinctive.

Using a stock library

As well as undertaking commissions, photographers have the option of selling their images through a photographic stock library or agency. There are many stock libraries in the UK, some specialising in specific subject areas, such as wildlife photography, and others covering general subjects (see *Picture agencies and libraries* listed on this *Yearbook's* website, www.writersandartists.co.uk).

Stock libraries are fiercely competitive, all fighting for a share of the market, and it is therefore best to aim to place images with an established name, although competition amongst photographers will be strong. Each stock library has different specific requirements and established markets, so contact them first before making a submission. Some agencies will ask to see a large number of images from a photographer in order to judge for consistency of quality and saleability, while others will consider an initial submission of just a few images.

Images placed with a library usually remain the property of the photographer and libraries do not normally sell images outright to clients, but lease them for a specific use for a fee, from which commission is deducted. This means that a single image can accumulate many sales over a period of time. The commission rate can be up to 50% of every sale generated by the library. This may sound high, but it should be borne in mind that the library takes on all overheads, marketing costs and other responsibilities involved in

Useful information

Bureau of Freelance Photographers
Focus House, 497 Green Lanes, London N13 4BP
tel 020-8882 3315
email info@thebfp.com
website www.thebfp.com
Chief Executive John Tracy
Membership £54 p.a.
Helps the freelance photographer by providing information on markets and a free advisory service. Publishes *Market Newsletter* (monthly).

Directories

Centaur Communications
50 Poland Street, London W1F 7AX
tel 020-7970 4000
website www.creativereview.co.uk
Publishes *The Creative Handbook.*

Contact Creative UK LLP
PO Box 397, Reigate, Surrey RH2 2ES
tel (01737) 241399
email mail@contactacreative.com
website www.contactacreative.com
Publishes *Contact Photography.*

the smooth running of a business, allowing the photographer the freedom to spend more time taking pictures.

Photographers should realise, however, that stock photography is a long-term investment and it can take some time for sales to build up to a significant income. Clearly, photographers who supply the right images for the market, and are prolific, are those who do well, and there are a good number of photographers who make their entire living as full-time stock photographers, never having to undertake commissioned work.

Royalty-free CD companies

Many stock photography agencies now market royalty-free images on CD or as 'virtual CD' downloads. This method of purchasing images as sets is popular with graphic designers since it is possible to create their own in-house image library of popular subjects. Once the CD has been purchased, the images can be used commercially as often as required without paying any further fees. Images are usually purchased as themes, such as health and beauty, sports and fitness, business and industry, etc. Typically, a stock agency will obtain images from photographers by either purchasing them outright, or by paying royalties based on CD sales.

Although photographers may be tempted to sell images to these companies in order to gain an instant fee, they should be aware that placing images with a traditional stock library can be far more fruitful financially in the long term, since a good image can accumulate very high fees over a period of time and go on selling for many years to come. Furthermore, the photographer always retains the rights to his or her own images.

Running your own library

Photographers choosing to market their own images or start up their own library have the advantage of retaining a full fee for every picture sale they make. But it is unlikely that an individual photographer could ever match the rates of an established library, or make the same volume of sales per image. However, the internet has opened a new marketing avenue for photographers, who now have the opportunity to sell their images worldwide. Previously, only an established stock library would have been able to do this. Before embarking on establishing a 'home' library, photographers should be aware that the business of marketing images is essentially a desk job which involves a considerable amount of paperwork and time, which could be spent taking pictures.

When setting up a picture library, your first consideration should be whether to build up a library of your own images, or to take on other contributing photographers. Many photographers running their own libraries submit additional images to bigger libraries to increase the odds of making a good income. Often, a photographer's personal library is made up of work rejected by the larger libraries, which are usually only interested in images that will regularly sell and generate a high turnover. However, occasional sales can generate a significant amount of income for the individual. Furthermore, a photographer with a library of specialised subjects stands a good chance of gaining recognition with niche markets, which can be very lucrative if the competition for those particular subjects is low.

If you take on contributing photographers, the responsibility for another's work becomes yours, so it is important to draw up a contract with terms of business for both your contributing photographers and your clients. Since images are now predominantly distributed in digital formats, via CD/DVD or broadband, there is no real problem with loss or damage, which used to be a big problem in the days of film-based originals. However, another issue has emerged since the advent of digital technology in the form of copyright abuse, which is now rife in the industry. Therefore, if representing another's work, it will be the library or agent's responsibility to protect image copyright on behalf of the photographer and also take any necessary legal steps in cases where copyright has been abused.

Reproduction fees should also be established on a strict basis, bearing in mind that you owe it to your contributing photographers to command fees which are as high as possible when selling the rights to their images. It is also essential that you control how pictures will be used and the amount of exposure they will receive. The fees should be established according to the type of client using the image and how the image itself will be reproduced. Important factors to consider are where the image will appear, to what size it will be reproduced, the size of the print run, and the territorial rights required by the client. However, many online agencies have now simplified their pricing structure and base fees on the specific image file size that's required by the client. A smaller file size (or lower resolution) limits the extent to which an image can be reproduced and therefore dictates final reproduction quality.

Working in any field of professional photography is fiercely competitive and successful businesses commonly spend a great deal of time researching their client's needs and marketing accordingly – the ultimate goal to ensure their name is always ahead of the ever-increasing competition.

Ian Thraves is a self-employed photographer and former picture editor at Bruce Coleman The Natural World Photo Agency (www.thravesphoto.co.uk).

See also...

- *Freelancing for beginners,* page 467
- *Marketing yourself online,*page 587
- *Managing your online reputation,* page 591
- *Design and Artists Copyright Society,* page 662

Societies, prizes and festivals

The Society of Authors

The Society of Authors is an independent trade union, representing writers' interests in all aspects of the writing profession, particularly publishing, but also broadcasting, television and film, theatre and translation.

Founded over 100 years ago, the Society now has more than 9,000 members. It has a professional staff, responsible to a Management Committee of 12 authors, and a Council (an advisory body meeting twice a year) consisting of 60 eminent writers. Specialist groups within the Society serve particular needs: the Broadcasting Group, the Children's Writers and Illustrators Group, the Educational Writers Group and the Translators Association (see page 538). There are also groups representing Scotland and the North of England.

Membership

The Society of Authors
84 Drayton Gardens, London SW10 9SB
tel 020-7373 6642
email info@societyofauthors.org
website www.societyofauthors.org
General Secretary Nicola Solomon

Membership is open to authors who have had a full-length work published, broadcast or performed commercially in the UK and to those who have had a full-length work accepted for publication, but not yet published; and those who have had a significant number of items broadcast or performed, or translations, articles, illustrations or short stories published. The owner or administrator of a deceased author's copyright can become a member on behalf of the author's estate. Writers who have been offered a contract may apply for associate membership and have the contract vetted.

The annual subscription (tax deductible) is £95 (£90 by direct debit after the first year). Authors under 35 and not yet earning a significant income from writing may pay a lower subscription of £68. Authors over 65 may pay at the reduced rate after their first year of membership.

The Society and members

Through its permanent staff (including a solicitor), the Society is able to give its members a comprehensive personal and professional service covering the business aspects of authorship, including:

- advising on negotiations, including the individual vetting of contracts, clause by clause, and assessing their terms both financial and otherwise;
- helping with members' queries, major or minor, over any aspect of the business of writing;
- taking up complaints on behalf of members on any issue concerned with the business of authorship;
- pursuing legal actions for breach of contract, copyright infringement, and the non-payment of royalties and fees, when the risk and cost preclude individual action by a member and issues of general concern to the profession are at stake;
- holding conferences, seminars, meetings and social occasions;
- producing a comprehensive range of publications, free of charge to members, including the Society's quarterly journal, the *Author*. The *Quick Guides* series covers many aspects of the profession such as: copyright, publishing contracts, libel, income tax, VAT, authors'

agents, permissions, indexing and self-publishing. The Society also publishes occasional papers on subjects such as film agreements and packaged books.

The Society frequently secures improved conditions and better returns for members. It is common for members to report that, through the help and facilities offered, they have saved more, and sometimes substantially more, than their annual subscription.

Further membership benefits include special offers and discounts on books, places to stay, insurance and other products and services, and free membership of the Authors' Licensing and Collecting Society (ALCS; see page 660).

The Society and authors

The Society lobbies Members of Parliament, ministers and government departments on all issues of concern to writers, litigates in matters of importance to authors and campaigns for better terms for writers. It is recognised by theBBC for the purpose of negotiating rates for writers' contributions to radio drama, as well as for the broadcasting of published material. It was instrumental in setting up the ALCS, which collects and distributes fees from reprography and other methods whereby copyright material is exploited without direct payment to the originators.

> 'It does no harm to repeat, as often as you can, "Without me the literary industry would not exist: the publishers, the agents, the sub-agents, the accountants, the libel lawyers, the departments of literature, the professors, the theses, the books of criticism, the reviewers, the book pages – all this vast and proliferating edifice is because of this small, patronised, put-down and underpaid person."' – *Doris Lessing*

The Society keeps in close touch with the Association of Authors' Agents, the Booksellers Association and Publishers Association, the British Council, the Department for Culture, Media and Sport, the National Union of Journalists and the Writers' Guild of Great Britain. It is a member of the European Writers Council and the British Copyright Council.

Awards

The following awards are administered:

• the Authors' Foundation and Kathleen Blundell Trust, which give grants to assist authors working on their next book;

• the Francis Head Bequest and the Authors' Contingency Fund, which assist authors who, through physical mishap, are temporarily unable to maintain themselves or their families;

• Travelling Scholarships, which give honorary awards;

• two prizes for first novels: the Betty Trask Awards and the McKitterick Prize;

• the Somerset Maugham Awards for a full-length published work;

• two poetry awards: the Eric Gregory Awards and the Cholmondeley Awards;

• the Tom-Gallon Award for short story writers;

• two radio drama prizes: the Imison Award for a writer new to radio drama and the Tinniswood Award;

• awards for translations from Arabic, Dutch/Flemish, French, German, Greek, Italian, Portuguese, Spanish and Swedish into English;

• educational book awards.

The Writers' Guild of Great Britain

The Writers' Guild of Great Britain is the TUC-affiliated trade union for writers.

The Writers' Guild of Great Britain is a trade union, affiliated to the TUC, and represents writers' interests in film, television, radio, theatre, books and video games. Formed in 1959 as the Screenwriters' Guild, the union gradually extended into all areas of freelance writing activity and copyright protection. In 1974, when book authors and stage dramatists became eligible for membership, substantial numbers joined. In June 1997 the Theatre Writers' Union membership unified with that of the Writers' Guild to create a larger, more powerful writers' union.

Apart from necessary dealings with Government and policies on legislative matters affecting writers, the Guild is, by constitution, non-political, has no involvement with any political party, and members pay no political levy.

The Guild employs a permanent general secretary and other permanent staff and is administered by an Executive Council of 20 members. The Guild comprises professional writers in all media, united in common concern for one another and regulating the conditions under which they work.

Membership

The Writers' Guild of Great Britain
40 Rosebery Avenue, London EC1R 4RX
tel 020-7833 0777
email admin@writersguild.org.uk
website www.writersguild.org.uk
General Secretary Bernie Corbett
Full Membership: 1.2% of earnings from professional writing (min. £180, max. £1,800 p.a.)
Candidate Membership: £100 p.a. (restricted to writers who have not had work published or produced at Guild-approved rates)
Student Membership: £20 p.a. (open to anyone on an accredited writing course or on attachment with a theatre)
Affiliate Membership: £275 p.a. (for people who work professionally with writers, e.g. agents, technical advisers)

Members receive the Guild's quarterly *UK Writer* magazine, which carries articles, letters and reports written by members, plus a weekly email newsletter every Friday afternoon. Other benefits include: legal advice and contract vetting; free entry to the British Library reading rooms.

The Writers' Guild and agreements

The Guild's basic function is to negotiate minimum terms in those areas in which its members work. Those agreements form the basis of the individual contracts signed by members. Further details are given below. The Guild also gives individual advice to its members on contracts and other matters which the writer encounters in his or her professional life. It also organises informative and social events for members, and maintains a benevolent fund to help writers in financial trouble.

Television

The Guild negotiates minimum terms agreements with the BBC, ITV, Pact (Producers' Alliance for Cinema and Television) and has also talked to Channel 4 and Five about various new internet services.

The Guild also has a minimum terms agreement in place with TAC (representing Welsh-language television producers), which has been reviewed because of the early analogue/digital switchover in Wales.

These agreements regulate minimum fees, residuals and royalties, copyright, credits, and general conditions for television plays, series and serials, dramatisations and adaptations, soaps and sitcoms. One of the Guild's most important achievements has been the establishment of pension rights for members. The BBC, ITV and independent producers pay a pension contribution on top of the standard writer's fee on the understanding that the Guild member also pays a contribution.

The advent of digital and cable television channels, video-on-demand and download-to-own services, mobile phone technology and the expansion of the BBC's commercial arm have seen the Guild in constant negotiation over the past decade. The Guild now has agreements for all of the BBC's digital channels and for its joint venture channels.

Film

In 1985 an important agreement was signed with the two producer organisations: the British Film and Television Producers' Association and the Independent Programme Producers' Association (now known as Pact). Since then there has been an industrial agreement covering UK film productions. Pension fund contributions have been negotiated for Guild members in the same way as for the BBC and ITV. The Agreement was renegotiated in February 1992 and consultations on an updated arrangement, led by the Guild's Film Committee, are in progress. The Guild now has a presence at the Cannes Film Festival each year. The Guild has recently published updated guidelines for film writers.

Radio

The Guild has a standard agreement for Radio Drama with the BBC, establishing a fee structure that is reviewed annually. This agreement was comprehensively renegotiated in 2005, with input from the Guild's Radio Committee, resulting in an agreement covering various new developments such as digital radio. In 1985 the BBC agreed to extend the pension scheme already established for television writers to include radio writers. The Guild has special agreements for Radio 4's the *Archers* and for the online streaming of BBC Radio services (iPlayer). A separate agreement covers the reuse of old comedy and drama material on digital BBC Radio 4 Extra. The Guild has opened discussions with the Radio Independents Group to establish a minimum terms agreement covering its members' ouptut.

Books

The Guild fought long, hard and successfully for the loans-based Public Lending Right (see page 324) to reimburse authors for books lent in libraries. This is now law and the Guild is frequently in touch with the Registrar of the scheme.

The Guild has an active Books Committee, which works on behalf of book writers and poets. Recently, the committee has been discussing and advising members about new trends in self-publishing, print-on-demand services and ebooks. It has also announced a new co-operative self-publishing venture: www.writersguildbookscoop.co.uk.

Theatre

In 1979 the Guild, together with the Theatre Writers' Union, negotiated the first industrial agreement for theatre writers. The Theatres National Committee Agreement (TNC) covers the Royal Shakespeare Company, the Royal National Theatre Company and the English Stage Company at the Royal Court. When their agreement was renegotiated in 2007 the Guild achieved a long-standing ambition of a minimum fee of £10,000 for a new play.

In June 1986, a new agreement was signed with the Theatrical Management Association (TMA), which covers 95 provincial theatres. In 1993, this agreement was comprehensively revised and included a provision for a year-on-year increase in fees in line with the Retail Price Index. The TMA agreement is now being renegotiated.

After many years of negotiation, an agreement was concluded in 1991 between the Guild and the Independent Theatre Council (ITC), which represents 200 of the smaller and fringe theatres as well as educational and touring companies. This agreement was revised in 2002 and the minimum fees are reviewed annually. The Guild is currently talking to the ITC about updating the agreement again and making it more user-friendly.

The Guild's Theatre Committee holds an annual forum for Literary Managers, runs a Theatre Encouragement Award scheme and has regular meetings with Arts Council England to inform its theatre policy.

Other activities

The Guild is in touch with Government and national institutions wherever and whenever the interests of writers are in question or are being discussed. It holds cross-party Parliamentary lobbies with Equity and the Musicians' Union to ensure that the various artforms they represent are properly cared for.

Working with the Federation of Entertainment Unions, the Guild makes its views known to Government bodies on a broader basis. It keeps in touch with Arts Council England, the BBC Trust, Ofcom and other national bodies.

The Guild is an active affiliate of the British Copyright Council, Creators' Rights Alliance, Save Kids' TV, Voice of the Listener and Viewer, and other organisations whose activities are relevant to professional writers. It has an Anti-Censorship Committee, which has intervened strongly to protect freedom of speech.

Internationally, the Guild plays a leading role in the International Affiliation of Writers Guilds, which includes the American Guilds East and West, the Canadian Guilds (French and English), and the Irish, Mexican, Australian and New Zealand Guilds. When it is possible to make common cause, the Guilds act accordingly. The Guild takes a leading role in the European Writers' Council and the Fédération des Scénaristes d'Europe. The Guild is becoming more involved with matters at the European level where the harmonisation of copyright law and the regulation of a converged audiovisual/telecommunications industry are of immediate interest.

On a day-to-day basis, the Guild helps with problems on behalf of individual members, gives advice on contracts, and takes up issues that affect the lives of its members as professional writers. Members have access to free legal advice and professional contract vetting. Regular committee meetings are held by the Guild's various specialist Craft Committees. The writer is an isolated individual in a world in which individual voices are not always heard. The Guild brings together those writers to make common cause on many vitally important matters, making full use of its collective strength.

Societies, associations and clubs

The societies, associations and clubs listed here will be of interest to both writers and artists. They include appreciation societies devoted to specific authors, professional bodies and national institutions. Some also offer prizes and awards (see page 543).

Academi – see Literature Wales

Academic Writers Group – see The Society of Authors

All Party Parliamentary Writers Group

tel 020-7264 5709 *fax* 020-7264 5755
email barbara.hayes@alcs.co.uk
website www.allpartywritersgroup.co.uk
Chair John Whittingdale MP, *Administrator* Barbara Hayes

The Group has some 60 Members from both Houses and seeks to represent the interests of all writers; to safeguard their intellectual property rights and ensure they receive a fair level of recognition and reward for their contribution to the economy and society as a whole. Founded 2007.

Alliance of Literary Societies

Chair Linda J. Curry, 59 Bryony Road, Birmingham B29 4BY
tel 0121 475 1805
email l.j.curry@bham.ac.uk
website www.allianceofliterarysocieties.org.uk
Membership Charge depends on size of society

Membership comprises 100+ affiliated literary societies. Aims to act as a valuable liaison body between member societies as a means of sharing knowledge, skills and expertise, and may also act as a pressure group when necessary. The Alliance can assist in the preservation of buildings, places and objects which have literary associations. Produces 2 newsletters a year, plus a literary magazine.

American Literary Translators Association (ALTA)

c/o University of Texas at Dallas, 800 W. Campbell Road, J051 Richardson, TX 75080–3021, USA
tel +1 972-883-2092 *fax* +1 972-883-6303
email maria.suarez@utdallas.edu
website www.literarytranslators.org

A broad-based organisation dedicated to the promotion of literary translation through services to literary translators, forums on the theory and practice of translation, collaboration with the international literary community, and advocacy on behalf of the library translator. Founded 1978.

American Society for Indexing (ASI)

(formerly American Society of Indexers)
10200 West 44th Avenue, Suite 304, Wheat Ridge, CO 80033, USA
tel +1 303-463-2887 *fax* +1 303-422-8894
email info@asindexing.org
website www.asindexing.org
Executive Director Annette Rogers

Aims to increase awareness of the value of high-quality indexes and indexing; offer members access to educational resources that enable them to strengthen their indexing performance; keep members up to date on indexing technology; defend and safeguard the professional interests of indexers.

American Society of Composers, Authors and Publishers

One Lincoln Plaza, New York, NY 10023, USA
tel +1 212-621-6000 *fax* +1 212-621-8453
London contact: 8 Cork Street, London W1S 3LT
website www.ascap.com
President & Chairman Paul Williams

Arts Club

40 Dover Street, London W1S 4NP
tel 020-7499 8581 *fax* 020-7409 0913
email bc@theartsclub.co.uk
website www.theartsclub.co.uk
Club Secretary Brian Clivaz

For all those connected with or interested in the arts, literature and science.

Arts Council England

14 Great Peter Street, London SW1P 3NQ
tel 0845 300 6200 *fax* 0161 934 4426
email enquiries@artscouncil.org.uk
website www.artscouncil.org.uk
Chief Executive Alan Davey

The national development agency for the arts in England, distributing public money from Government and the National Lottery. Arts Council England's main funding programme is Grants for the Arts, which is open to individuals, arts organisations, national touring companies and other people who use the arts in their work.

Arts Council England has one national and 9 regional offices. It has a single contact telephone and email address for general enquiries (see above). Founded 1946.

East

Eastbrook, Shaftesbury Road, Cambridge CB2 8BF
tel 0845 300 6200 *textphone* (01223) 306893
fax 0870 242 1271

East Midlands

St Nicholas Court, 25–27 Castle Gate, Nottingham NG1 7AR
tel 0845 300 6200 *fax* 0115 950 2467

London
14 Great Peter Street, London SW1P 3NQ
tel 0845 300 6200 *textphone* 020-7973 6564
fax 020-7608 4100

North East
Central Square, Forth Street, Newcastle upon Tyne NE1 3PJ
tel 0845 300 6200 *textphone* 0191 255 8585
fax 0191 230 1020

North West
The Hive, 49 Lever Street, Manchester M1 1FN
tel 0845 300 6200 *textphone* 020-7973 6564
fax 0161 934 4426

South East
Sovereign House, Church Street, Brighton BN1 1RA
tel 0845 300 6200 *textphone* (01273) 710659
fax 0870 242 1257

South West
Senate Court, Southernhay Gardens, Exeter EX1 1UG
tel 0845 300 6200 *textphone* (01392) 433503
fax (01392) 98546

West Midlands
82 Granville Street, Birmingham B1 2LH
tel 0845 300 6200 *textphone* 0121 643 2815
fax 0121 643 7239

Yorkshire
21 Bond Street, Dewsbury, West Yorkshire WF13 1AX
tel 0845 300 6200 *textphone* (01924) 438585
fax (01924) 38585

Arts Council/An Chomhairle Ealaíon

70 Merrion Square, Dublin 2, Republic of Ireland
tel +353 (0)1 6180200 *fax* +353 (0)1 6761302
email stephanie.ocallaghan@artscouncil.ie
website www.artscouncil.ie
Arts Programme Director John O'Kane

The national development agency for the arts in Ireland. Founded 1951.

Arts Council of Northern Ireland

77 Malone Road, Belfast BT9 6AQ
tel 028-9038 5200 *fax* 028-9066 1715
email info@artscouncil-ni.org
website www.artscouncil-ni.org
Chief Executive Roisín McDonough, *Literature Officer* Damian Smyth, *Visual Arts Officer* Suzanne Lyle

Promotes and encourages the arts throughout Northern Ireland. Artists in drama, dance, music and jazz, literature, the visual arts, traditional arts and community arts can apply for support for specific schemes and projects. The value of the grant will be set according to the aims of the application. Applicants must have contributed regularly to the artistic activities of the community, and been resident for at least one year in Northern Ireland.

Arts Council of Wales

Bute Place, Cardiff CF10 5AL
tel 0845 873 4900 *fax* 029-2044 1400
email info@artswales.org.uk
website www.artswales.org.uk
Chairman Prof. Dai Smith, *Arts Director* David Alston, *Head of Communications* Betsan Moses, *Head of Wales Arts International* Eluned Haf

National organisation with specific responsibility for the funding and development of the arts in Wales. Arts Council of Wales receives funding from the Welsh Government and also distributes National Lottery funds for the arts in Wales. From these resources, Arts Council of Wales makes grants to support arts activities and facilities. Some of the funds are allocated in the form of annual revenue grants to full-time arts organisations such as Literature Wales. It also operates schemes which provide financial and other forms of support for individual artists or projects. Arts Council of Wales undertakes this work in both the English and Welsh languages. Wales Arts International is the unique partnership between the Arts Council of Wales and British Council Wales, which works to promote knowledge about contemporary arts and culture from Wales and encourages international exchange and collaboration.

North Wales Regional Office
36 Princes Drive, Colwyn Bay LL29 8LA
tel (01492) 533440 *minicom* (01492) 532288
fax (01492) 533677

Mid and West Wales Regional Office
6 Gardd Llydaw, Jackson Lane, Carmarthen SA31 1QD
tel (01267) 234248 *minicom* (01267) 223496
fax (01267) 233084

South Wales Office
Bute Place, Cardiff CF10 5AL
tel 0845 873 4900 *fax* 029-2044 1400

Aslib (The Association for Information Management)

Howard House, Wagon Lane, Bingley BD16 1WA
tel (01274) 777700 *fax* (01274) 785201
website www.aslib.co.uk
Director Rebecca Marsh, *Editor-in-Chief* Graham Coult

Actively promotes best practice in the management of information resources. It represents its members and lobbies on all aspects of the management of and legislation concerning information at local, national and international levels. Aslib provides consultancy and information services, professional development training, conferences, specialist recruitment, internet products, and publishes primary and secondary journals, conference proceedings, directories and monographs. Founded 1924.

Association for Scottish Literary Studies (ASLS)

c/o Dept of Scottish Literature, 7 University Gardens, University of Glasgow G12 8QH
tel 0141 330 5309
email office@asls.org.uk
website www.asls.org.uk
President Ian Brown, *Secretary* Lorna Borrowman Smith, *Director* Duncan Jones
Membership £45 p.a. individuals, £10 UK students, £75 corporate

Promotes the study, teaching and writing of Scottish literature and furthers the study of the languages of Scotland. Publishes annually *New Writing Scotland*, an anthology of new Scottish writing; an edited text of Scottish literature; a series of academic journals; and a newsletter (2 p.a.) Also publishes *Scotnotes* (comprehensive study guides to major Scottish writers), literary texts and commentary CDs designed to assist the classroom teacher, and a series of occasional papers. Organises 3 conferences a year. Founded 1970.

Association of American Correspondents in London (AACL)

AACL, PO Box 645, Pinner HA5 9JJ
email secretary@theaacl.co.uk
website www.theaacl.co.uk
Contact Monique Jessen

Association of American Publishers Inc.

71 Fifth Avenue, New York, NY 10003-3004, USA
tel +1 212-255-0200 *fax* +1 212-255-7007
email info@publishers.org
website www.publishers.org
President & Ceo Tom Allen

Founded 1970.

Association of Art Historians (AAH)

70 Cowcross Street, London EC1M 6EJ
tel 020-7490 3211 *fax* 020-7490 3277
email admin@aah.org.uk
website www.aah.org.uk
Administrator Claire Davies (Senior Programme Coordinator), Matt Lodder (Senior Administrator)
Membership Various options for personal membership; institutional membership available

Formed to promote the study of art history and ensure wider public recognition of the field. Publishes *Art History* journal, *The Art Book* magazine, *Bulletin* newsletter. Manages the Artists' Papers Register (APR). Annual conference and book fair in March/April. Founded 1974.

Association of Assistant Librarians – see Careers Development Group

The Association of Authors' Agents

10 Iron Bridge House, Bridge Approach, London NW1 8BD
tel 020-7722 7674
website www.agentsassoc.co.uk
President Peter Straus, *Secretary* Olivia Guest

Maintains a code of professional practice to which all members commit themselves; holds regular meetings to discuss matters of common professional interest; provides a vehicle for representing the view of authors' agents in discussion of matters of common interest with other professional bodies. Founded 1974.

Association of Authors' Representatives Inc.

676A, Suite 312 9th Avenue, New York, NY 10036, USA
tel +1 212-840-5770
email administrator@aaronline.org
website www.aaronline.org

Founded 1991.

Association of British Science Writers (ABSW)

The Dana Centre, 165 Queen's Gate, London SW7 5HD
tel 0870 770 3361 *fax* 0870 770 7102
email absw@absw.org.uk
website www.absw.org.uk
Chair Dr Natasha Loder

Association of science writers, editors, and radio, film and TV producers concerned with the presentation and communication of science, technology and medicine. Aims to improve the standard of science writing and to assist its members in their work.

Association of Canadian Publishers

174 Spadina Avenue, Suite 306, Toronto, Ontario M5T 2C2, Canada
tel +1 416-487-6116 *fax* +1 416-487-8815
email admin@canbook.org
website www.publishers.ca
Executive Director Carolyn Wood

Founded 1976; formerly Independent Publishers Association, 1971.

Association of Christian Writers

Administrator Ms Jennifer Allong-Bratt, 5 Cranston Close, Hounslow, Middlesex TW3 3DQ
tel 07542 918929
email admin@christianwriters.org.uk
website www.christianwriters.org.uk
Membership £28 p.a. (£25 DD), £33 (overseas)

Resigtered charity that aims to see the quality of writing in every area of the media, either overtly Christian or shaped by a Christian perspective, reaching the widest range of people across the UK and beyond. To inspire and equip people to use their talents and skills with integrity to devise, write and market excellent material which comes from a Christian world view. Founded 1971.

Association of Freelance Editors, Proofreaders and Indexers

Contact 1 Brenda O'Hanlon, 11 Clonard Road, Sandyford, Dublin 16, Republic of Ireland
tel +353 (0)1 2952194
email brenda@ohanlonmedia.com
Contact 2 Tess Tattersall, Howth, Co. Dublin, Republic of Ireland
tel +353 (0)1 8395345
email tesstattersall@gmail.com
website www.afepi.ie

Provides information to publishers on freelances through a list of members and their qualifications. Also protects the interests of freelances, and provides social contact for isolated workers.

The Association of Illustrators

2nd Floor, Back Building, 150 Curtain Road, London EC2A 3AT
tel 020-7613 4328 *fax* 020-7613 4417
email info@theaoi.com
website www.theaoi.com
Contact Membership Coordinator

Exists to support illustrators, promote illustration and encourage professional standards in the industry. Publishes *Varoom* magazine (3 p.a.); presents an annual programme of events; annual competition, exhibition and tour of Images – the Best of British Contemporary Illustration (call for entries: July/August). Founded 1973.

The Association of Learned and Professional Society Publishers

Acting Chief Executive Audrey McCulloch, 1–3 Ship Street, Shoreham-by-Sea, West Sussex BN43 5DH
tel (01442) 828928 *fax* (01442) 311328
email audrey.mcculloch@alpsp.org
website www.alpsp.org
Membership Open to not-for-profit publishers and allied organisations

The International trade association for non-profit publishers. Founded 1972.

The Association of Photographers (AOP)

Co-Secretary Gwen Thomas, 81 Leonard Street, London EC2A 4QS
tel 020-7739 6669 *fax* 020-7739 8707
email general@aophoto.co.uk
website www.the-aop.org
Membership £280 p.a.

Managing Director Kingsley Marten

Exists to protect and promote the interests of fashion advertising and editorial photographers. Founded 1968.

The Jane Austen Society

Secretary Maureen Stiller, 20 Parsonage Road, Henfield, West Sussex BN5 9JG
email hq@jasoc.co.uk
website www.janeaustensoci.freeuk.com
Membership £20 p.a., student for 3 years £10, UK, on production of tutor reference or ID; £30 overseas; £25 joint membership for 2 people living at same address.

Aims to promote interest in, and enjoyment of, the life and works of Jane Austen (1775–1817). Regular publications, meetings and conferences. Eleven branches in UK. Founded 1940.

Australia Council

PO Box 788, Strawberry Hills, NSW 2012, Australia
located at 372 Elizabeth Street, Surry Hills, NSW 2010, Australia
tel +61 (0)2 9215 9000 *fax* +61 (0)2 9215 9111
email mail@australiacouncil.gov.au
website www.australiacouncil.gov.au
Ceo Kathy Keele

Provides a broad range of support for the arts in Australia, embracing music, theatre, literature, visual arts, crafts, Aboriginal arts, community and new media arts. It has 7 Boards: Literature, Visual Arts, Music, Theatre, Dance, Major Performing Arts, as well as the Aboriginal and Torres Strait Islander Arts Board.

The Literature Board's chief objective is to support the writing of all forms of creative literature – novels, short stories, poetry, plays and literary non-fiction. It also assists with the publication of literary magazines, has a book publishing subsidies programme, and initiates and supports projects of many kinds designed to promote Australian literature both within Australia and abroad.

Australian Copyright Council

PO Box 1986, Strawberry Hills, NSW 2012, Australia
tel +61 (0)2 8815 9777 *fax* +61 (0)2 8815 9799
email info@copyright.org.au
website www.copyright.org.au

An independent non-profit organisation which aims to assist creators and other copyright owners to exercise their rights effectively; raise awareness in the community generally about the importance of copyright; research and identify areas of copyright law which are inadequate or unfair; seek changes to law and practice to enhance the effectiveness and fairness of copyright; foster cooperation amongst bodies representing creators and owners of copyright.

The Council comprises 23 organisations or associations of owners and creators of copyright material, including the Australian Society of Authors, the Australian Writers' Guild and the Australian Publishers Association. Founded 1968.

Australian Publishers Association (APA)

60–89 Jones Street, Ultimo, NSW 2007, Australia
tel +61 (0)2 9281 9788 *fax* +61 (0)2 9281 1073

email apa@publishers.asn.au
website www.publishers.asn.au
Ceo Maree McCaskill

The Australian Society of Authors

Suite C1.06, 22–36 Mountain Street, Ultimo, NSW 2007, Australia
tel +61 (0)2 9211 1004 *fax* +61 (0)2 9211 0125
email asa@asauthors.org
website www.asauthors.org
Executive Director Angelo Loukakis

Australian Writers' Guild (AWG)

5 Blackfriars Street, Chippendale, NSW 2008
tel +61 (0)2 9319 0339 *fax* +61 (0)2 9319 0141
email admin@awg.com.au
website www.awg.com.au
Executive Director Jacqueline Woodman

The professional association for all performance writers, i.e. writers for film, TV, radio, theatre, video and new media. The AWG is recognised throughout the industry in Australia as being the voice of performance writers. Founded 1962.

Authors' Club

Blacks, 67 Dean Street, London W1D 4QH
website www.authorsclub.co.uk
Chairman Chris Schuler *President* John Walsh
Membership Apply to Chairman

Founded by Sir Walter Besant, the Authors' Club welcomes as members writers, publishers, critics, journalists, academics and anyone involved with literature. Administers the Authors' Club Best First Novel Award, the Sir Banister Fletcher Award and the Dolman Best Travel Book Award. Founded 1891.

Authors' Licensing and Collecting Society Ltd – see page 660

Axisweb – contemporary art radar

Studio 17/18, 46 The Calls, Leeds LS2 7EY
tel 0113 242 9830 *fax* 0113 217 9665
email info@axisweb.org
website www.axisweb.org
Membership Artist/art professional/organisational membership from £15 p.a.

Axisweb.org is the leading online directory of contemporary artists and art professionals, profiling the contemporary arts scene in the UK. On Axisweb you can promote your practice, find work opportunities, take a look at commissioned writing showcasing the artists to watch, interviews, videos, art world news and debates.

Signing up to e-bulletins and contacting the artists and art professionals is free; or apply as an artist, art professional or organisation to have your own profile. Axisweb was established as a charity in 1991 and is funded by Arts Council England.

BAFTA (The British Academy of Film and Television Arts)

195 Piccadilly, London W1J 9LN
tel 020-7734 0022 *fax* 020-7734 1792
email info@bafta.org
website www.bafta.org
Chief Executive Amanda Berry

The UK's pre-eminent, independent charity supporting, developing and promoting the art forms of the moving image (film, TV and video games) by identifying and rewarding excellence, inspiring practitioners and benefiting the public. In addition to its Awards ceremonies, BAFTA's year-round Learning & Events programme offers unique access to some of the world's most inspiring talent through workshops, masterclasses, lectures and mentoring schemes, connecting with audiences of all ages and backgrounds across the UK, Los Angeles and New York. Founded 1947.

BANA (Bath Area Network for Artists)

The Old Malthouse, Comfortable Place, Upper Bristol Road, Bath BA1 3AJ
tel (07526) 428280
email enquiries@banaarts.co.uk
website www.banaarts.co.uk
Membership From £20 p.a.

An artist-led network that is committed to developing members' professional practice through connecting their creativity. BANA aims to raise the profile of arts activity in and around the Bath area, to establish and strengthen links between artists, artists' groups and art promoters, and advocate for increased investment in local arts activities. Founded 1998 and a company limited by guarantee since 2003.

BAPLA (British Association of Picture Libraries and Agencies)

59 Tranquil Vale, Blackheath, London SE3 0BS
tel 020-8297 1198 *fax* 020-8852 7211
email enquiries@bapla.org.uk
website www.bapla.org.uk
Membership & Communications Manager Susanne Kittlinger

The British Association of Picture Libraries and Agencies (BALPA) is the trade association for picture libraries in the UK, and has been a trade body since 1975. Members include the major news, stock and production agencies as well as sole traders and cultural heritage institutions.

The Beckford Society

The Timber Cottage, Crockerton, Warminster BA12 8AX
tel (01985) 213195
email sidney.blackmore@btinternet.com
website http//beckford.c18.net/wbsocietyintro.html
Membership £20 p.a. minimum

Aims to promote an interest in the life and works of William Beckford of Fonthill (1760–1844) and his circle. Encourages Beckford studies and scholarship through exhibitions, lectures and publications, including *The Beckford Journal* (annual) and occasional newsletters. Founded 1995.

The Arnold Bennett Society

Secretary Carol Gorton, 4 Field End Close, Trentham, Stoke-on-Trent ST4 8DA
email arnoldbennettscty@btinternet.com
website www.arnoldbennettsociety.org.uk
Membership £12 p.a. individuals, £14 p.a. family plus £2 if living outside Europe

Aims to promote the study and appreciation of the life, works and times not only of Arnold Bennett (1867–1931) himself, but also of other provincial writers with particular relationship to North Staffordshire. Registered charity 1140053.

The E.F. Benson Society

The Old Coach House, High Street, Rye, East Sussex TN31 7JF
tel (01797) 223114
website www.efbensonsociety.org
Secretary Allan Downend
Membership £12 p.a. single, £15 p.a. for 2 people at same address, £20 overseas

Aims to promote interest in the author E.F. Benson (1867–1940) and the Benson family. Arranges annual literary evening, annual outing to Rye (July) and other places of Benson interest, talks on the Bensons and exhibitions. Archive includes the Austin Seckersen Collection, transcriptions of the Benson diaries and letters. Publishes postcards, anthologies of Benson's works, a Benson biography, books on Benson and an annual journal, *The Dodo*. Also sells out-of-print Bensons to members. Founded 1984.

Bibliographical Society

c/o Institute of English Studies, University of London, Senate House, Malet Street, London WC1E 7HU
tel 020-7782 3279
email admin@bibsoc.org.uk
website www.bibsoc.org.uk
President David Pearson, *Secretary* Meg Ford

Acquisition and dissemination of information on subjects connected with historical bibliography. Publishes the journal *The Library*. Founded 1892.

The Blackpool Art Society

The Studio, Wilkinson Avenue, Off Woodland Grove, Blackpool FY3 9HB
tel (01253) 768297
email sec@blackpoolartsociety.co.uk
website www.blackpoolartsociety.co.uk
Hon. Secretary E. Potter

Autumn exhibition (members' work only). Studio meetings, practicals, lectures, etc, out-of-door sketching, workshops. Founded 1884.

Book Aid International

39–41 Coldharbour Lane, London SE5 9NR
tel 020-7733 3577 *fax* 020-7978 8006
email info@bookaid.org
website www.bookaid.org
Director Clive Nettleton

Works in 12 countries in sub-Saharan Africa and Palestine, providing half a million new books each year to libraries in hospitals, refugee camps and schools. Also supports training of librarians and development of community libraries.

The Booksellers Association of the United Kingdom & Ireland Ltd

6 Bell Yard, London WC2A 2JR
tel 020-7421 4640 *fax* 020-7421 4641
email mail@booksellers.org.uk
website www.booksellers.org.uk
Chief Executive T.E. Godfray

Founded 1895.

Booktrust

(formerly the National Book League, founded 1925)
Book House, 45 East Hill, London SW18 2QZ
tel 020-8516 2977
email query@booktrust.org.uk
website www.booktrust.org.uk
Director Viv Bird, *Chairman* Sue Horner

An independent charity dedicated to encouraging people of all ages and cultures to engage with books. It is responsible for a number of successful national reading promotions, sponsored book prizes and creative reading projects aimed at encouraging readers to discover and enjoy books. These include the Orange Prize for Fiction, the Children's Laureate, the Roald Dahl Funny Prize and Bookstart, the national programme that works through locally based organisations to give a free pack of books to young children, with guidance materials for parents and carers. Booktrust has developed 2 further free book programmes in the UK: Booktime, run in association with Pearson, gives a free book to every Year 1 pupil, and Booked Up, which gives a free book, from a selection, to every Year 7 pupil.

The George Borrow Society

Membership Secretary Michael Skillman, 60 Upper Marsh Road, Warminster, Wilts. BA12 9PN
email mkskillman@onetel.com
website http://georgeborrow.org
Membership £17 p.a., £25.50 joint members at same address, £10 students, £170 life membership

Promotes knowledge of the life and works of George Borrow (1803–81), traveller and author. Publishes *Bulletin* (bi-annual). Founded 1991.

British Academy

10 Carlton House Terrace, London SW1Y 5AH
tel 020-7969 5200 *fax* 020-7969 5300
email pubs@britac.ac.uk
website www.britac.ac.uk
President Sir Adam Roberts, *Publications Secretary* Prof. Christopher Wickham, *Chief Executive & Secretary* Dr Robin Jackson

The national Academy for the humanities and social sciences: an independent and self-governing fellowship of scholars, elected for distinction and achievement in one or more branches of the academic disciplines that make up the humanities and social sciences. Its primary purpose is to promote research and scholarship in those areas: through research grants and other awards, the sponsorship of a number of research projects and of research institutes overseas; the award of prizes and medals (including the Crawshay prizes for critical literary studies by a female scholar); and the publication both of sponsored lectures and seminar papers and of fundamental texts and research aids prepared under the direction of Academy committees. It also acts as a forum for the discussion of issues of interest and concern to scholars in the humanities and the social sciences, and it provides advice to the Government and other public bodies. Founded 1901.

British Academy of Songwriters, Composers and Authors

British Music House, 26 Berners Street,
London W1T 3LR
tel 020-7636 2929 *fax* 020-7636 2212
email info@basca.org.uk
website www.basca.org.uk
Contact Graham Jackson, Head of Membership

The Academy represents the interests of composers and songwriters across all genres, providing advice on professional and artistic matters. It administers a number of major events, including the annual Ivor Novello Awards and British Composer Awards.

British Association of Journalists

General Secretary Denise Richardson, 89 Fleet Street,
London EC4Y 1DH
tel 020-7353 3003 *fax* 020-7353 2310
email office@bajunion.org.uk
website www.bajunion.org.uk
Membership £18.25 per month national newspaper staff, national broadcasting staff and national news agency staff; £10.50 p.m. other seniors including magazine journalists, PRs, freelances; £7.50 p.m. under age 24

Aims to protect and promote the industrial and professional interests of journalists. Founded 1992.

British Association of Picture Libraries and Agencies – see BAPLA (British Association of Picture Libraries and Agencies)

British Centre for Literary Translation (BCLT)

University of East Anglia, Norwich NR4 7TJ
tel (01603) 592785 *fax* (01603) 592737
email bclt@uea.ac.uk
website www.bclt.org.uk

Jointly funded by Arts Council England and the University of East Anglia, BCLT raises the profile of literary translation in the UK through events, publications, activities and research aimed at professional translators, the publishing industry, students and the general reader. Activities include the annual Sebald Lecture in London, Summer School, a mentorship programme and public talks and events. It is joint sponsor of the John Dryden Translation Prize and publishes the journals *In Other Words* and *New Books in German*. Member of the international RECIT literary translation network. Founded 1989 by the author and UEA Professor W.G. Sebald.

British Copyright Council

Copyright House, 29–33 Berners Street,
London W1T 3AB
tel (01986) 788122
email info@britishcopyright.org
website www.britishcopyright.org
Vice-Presidents Prof. Adrian Sterling, Geoffrey Adams, *President of Honour* Maureen Duffy, *Chairman* Paul Mitchell, *Directors* Bernie Corbett, John Smith, Andrew Yeates, Derek Brazell, Peter Leatham, Richard Combes, Frances Lowe, *Ceo* Janet Ibbotson, *Treasurer* Hugh Jones

Aims to defend and foster the true principles of copyright and its acceptance throughout the world, to bring together bodies representing all who are interested in the protection of such copyright, and to keep watch on any legal or other changes which may require an amendment of the law.

The British Council

London office 10 Spring Gardens, London SW1A 2BN
tel 020-389 4385 *fax* 020-7839 6347
email general.enquiries@britishcouncil.org
Headquarters Bridgewater House, 58 Whitworth Street, Manchester M1 6BB
tel 0161 957 7000
website www.britishcouncil.org, www.britishcouncil.org/arts, www.contemporarywriters.com, www.encompassculture.com
Chair The Rt Hon. Lord Kinnock, *Chief Executive* Martin Davidson, *Director of Arts* Graham Sheffield

The British Council connects people worldwide with learning opportunities and creative ideas from the UK, and builds lasting relationships between the UK and other countries. It has 6,000 staff in offices, teaching centres, libraries, and information and resource centres in the UK and 110 countries and territories worldwide.

Working in close collaboration with book trade associations, British Council offices participate in major international book fairs.

The British Council is an authority on teaching English as a second or foreign language. It also gives advice and information on curriculum, methodology, materials and testing.

The British Council promotes British literature overseas through writers' tours, academic visits, workshops, conferences, seminars and exhibitions. It publishes *New Writing*, an annual anthology of unpublished short stories, poems and extracts from works in progress and essays; and a series of literary bibliographies, including *Tbooks: UK Teenage Literature*, *Crime Literature* and *Reading in the City*. Through its Literature Department, the British Council provides an overview of UK literature and a range of online resources (see above). This includes a literary portal, information about UK and Commonwealth authors, translation workshops and a worldwide online book club and reading group for adults, teenagers and children with over 10,000 books plus reading group advice.

The Visual Arts Department, part of the British Council's Arts Group, develops and enlarges overseas knowledge and appreciation of British achievement in the fields of painting, sculpture, printmaking, design, photography, the crafts and architecture, working closely with the British Council's overseas offices and with professional colleagues in the UK and abroad.

Further information about the work of the British Council is available from Arts Press at the above address, or from British Council offices overseas by emailing arts@britishcouncil.org.

The British Fantasy Society

email secretary@britishfantasysociety.org
website www.britishfantasysociety.org
Membership £35 p.a. single; £40 joint; £45 Europe; £60 rest of world

For devotees of fantasy, horror and related fields, in literature, art and the cinema. Publications include *Prism* (quarterly) featuring news and reviews, and *Dark Horizons* or a new third magazine which alternate every quarter. There is a small-press library and an annual convention, FantasyCon, and fantasy awards sponsored by the Society. Founded 1971.

BFI (British Film Institute)

21 Stephen Street, London W1T 1LN
tel 020-7255 1444 *fax* 020-7436 0439
website www.bfi.org.uk
Chair Greg Dyke *Chief Executive* Amanda Nevill

In its mission to achieve a creative and prosperous film culture and industry base, the BFI drives creative, economic and cultural success through a linked portfolio of activities. Its diverse public programme presents over 1,000 films a year across BFI Southbank, BFI IMAX and the BFI London film festivals. As the biggest distributor of cultural cinema in the UK, it supplies film to over 600 venues across the UK and over 2,000 hours of material are available free online. The BFI cares for the world's most significant film and television collections in the BFI National Archive, its vibrant DVD label releases around 50 titles a year and its publications include *Sight & Sound* magazine. The BFI works through key partnerships. As the Lottery distributor for film, the BFI provides funding for film development and training; and in education through Skillset and First Light. It also has strategic partnerships for film across the devolved nations and funding in the English regions; responsibility for UK certification, which is the gateway to the UK film tax credit; and MEDIA Desk UK. In supporting Film London and the British Film Commission, the BFI also takes on promoting British film and talent internationally. Founded 1933.

British Guild of Agricultural Journalists

General Secretary Clemmie Gleeson, 1 Rose Villa, Anchor Road, Spa Common, North Walsham, Norfolk NR28 9AJ
tel (01692) 402313
email gajsec@gmail.com
website www.gaj.org.uk
President Lord Cameron of Dillington, *Chairman* Adrian Bell

Established in 1944, the Guild promotes high standards among journalists, photographers and communicators who specialise in agriculture, horticulture food production and other rural affairs, and contributes towards a better understanding of agriculture.

British Guild of Beer Writers

Secretary Adrian Tierney-Jones, Woodcote, 2 Jury Road, Dulverton, Somerset TA22 9DU
tel (01398) 324314
email tierneyjones@btinternet.com
website www.beerwriters.co.uk
Membership £40 p.a

Aims to improve standards in beer writing and at the same time extend public knowledge of beers and brewing. Awards are given annually to writers and broadcasters judged to have made the most valuable contribution to this end. Publishes a directory of members with details of their publications and their particular areas of interest, which is circulated to the media. Founded 1988.

The British Guild of Travel Writers

335 Lordship Road, London N16 5HG
tel 020-8144 8713
email secretariat@bgtw.org
website www.bgtw.org

Arranges meetings, discussions and visits for its 220 members (who are all professional travel journalists) to promote and encourage the public's interest in travel. Publishes a monthly newsletter (for members only), website and annual *Yearbook*, which contain details of members and lists travel industry PRs and contacts. Annual awards for journalism (members only) and the travel trade.

The British Haiku Society

Longholm, East Bank, Sutton Bridge, Spalding, Lincs PE12 9YS

website www.britishhaikusociety.org
General Secretary Janet Blundell

Promotes appreciation and writing of haiku and related forms. Provides tutorials, workshops, readings, critical comment and information. Specialist advisors are available. Runs a library and administers a contest. The Journal, *Blithe Spirit*, is produced quarterly. The Society has active local groups and issues a regular newsletter. Welcomes overseas members. Current membership details can be found on the website. For notes on the development of Haiku in the West, see www.anotherkindofpoetry.org.uk/anotherkind/slideshow. Founded 1990.

British Institute of Professional Photography

The Coachhouse, The Firs, High Street, Whitchurch, Aylesbury, Bucks. HP22 4SJ
tel (01296) 642020 *fax* (01296) 641553
email info@bipp.com
website www.bipp.com

Represents all who practise photography as a profession in any field; to improve the quality of photography; establish recognised qualifications and a high standard of conduct; to safeguard the interests of the public and the profession. Admission can be obtained by submission of work and other information to the appropriate examining board. Fellows, Associates and Licentiates are entitled to the designation FBIPP, ABIPP or LBIPP in accordance with the qualification awarded. Organises numerous meetings and conferences in various parts of the country throughout the year; publishes *The Photographer* magazine (bi-monthly), plus various pamphlets and leaflets on professional photography. Founded 1901; incorporated 1921.

British Interactive Media Association (BIMA)

The Lightwell, 12–16 Laystall Street, London EC1R 4PF
tel 020-7843 6797
email info@bima.co.uk
website www.bima.co.uk
Membership Open to any organisation or individual with an interest in multimedia

Established to promote a wider understanding of the benefits of interactive multimedia to industry, government and education and to provide a regular forum for the exchange of views amongst members. Founded 1984.

The British Science Fiction Association Ltd

email sf@pwilkinson.cix.co.uk
website www.bsfa.co.uk
Chair Ian Whates, *Membership Secretary*, Peter Wilkinson

For authors, publishers, booksellers and readers of science fiction, fantasy and allied genres. Publishes *Matrix*, an informal magazine of news and information; *Focus*, an amateur writers' magazine; *Vector*, a critical magazine and the Orbiter Service, a network of postal writers workshops. Trophies are awarded annually to the winner in each category of the BSFA Awards: best UK-published novel, best short story, best artwork. Founded 1958.

British Society of Comedy Writers

President Kenneth Rock, 61 Parry Road, Ashmore Park, Wolverhampton, West Midlands WV11 2PS
tel (01902) 722729 *fax* (01902) 722729
email info@bscw.co.uk
website www.bscw.co.uk
Membership £75 p.a. full, £40 p.a. subscriber

Aims to bring together writers and industry representatives in order to develop new projects and ideas. Holds an annual international comedy conference, networking days and workshops to train new writers to professional standards. Founded 1999.

British Society of Magazine Editors

137 Hale Lane, Edgware, Middlesex HA8 9QP
tel 020-8906 4664
email admin@bsme.com
website www.bsme.com

British Society of Miniaturists

13 Manor Orchards, Knaresborough, North Yorkshire HG5 0BW
tel (01423) 540603
email info@britpaint.co.uk
website www.britpaint.co.uk
Membership By selection

The world's oldest miniature society. Holds 2 open exhibitions a year. Founded 1895.

British Society of Painters

13 Manor Orchards, Knaresborough, North Yorkshire HG5 0BW
tel (01423) 540603
email info@britpaint.co.uk
website www.britpaint.co.uk
Director Leslie Simpson
Membership By selection

Promotes interest and encourages high quality in the work of painters in these media. Holds 2 open exhibitions a year. Founded 1988.

British Watercolour Society

13 Manor Orchards, Knaresborough, North Yorkshire HG5 0BW
tel (01423) 540603
email info@britpaint.co.uk
website www.britpaint.co.uk

Promotes the best in traditional watercolour painting. Holds 2 open exhibitions a year. Founded 1830.

Broadcasting Entertainment Cinematograph and Theatre Union (BECTU)

373–377 Clapham Road, London SW9 9BT
tel 020-7346 0900 *fax* 020-7346 0901
email info@bectu.org.uk
website www.bectu.org.uk
General Secretary G. Morrissey

Aims to defend the interests of writers in film, TV and radio. By virtue of its industrial strength, the Union is able to help its writer members to secure favourable terms and conditions. In cases of disputes with employers, the Union can intervene in order to ensure an equitable settlement. Its production agreement with PACT lays down minimum terms for writers working in the documentary area. Founded 1991.

Broadcasting Group – see The Society of Authors, page 497

The Brontë Society

Society Administrator The Brontë Parsonage Museum, Haworth, Keighley, West Yorkshire BD22 8DR
tel (01535) 642323 *fax* (01535) 647131
email bronte@bronte.org.uk
website www.bronte.info

Acquisition, preservation, promotion of the memoirs and literary remains of the Brontë family; exhibitions of MSS and other subjects. Publishes *Brontë Studies* (3 p.a.) and *The Brontë Gazette* (tri-annual). Its Museum is open throughout the year, except for the month of January.

The Browning Society

Acting Hon. Secretary, Dr Simon Avery, Department of English, Linguistics and Cultural Studies, University of Westminster, 32-38 Wells Street, London W1T 3UW
email s.avery@westminster.ac.uk
website www.browningsociety.org
Contact Dr Simon Avery, Acting Hon. Secretary
Membership £15 p.a.

Aims to widen the appreciation and understanding of the lives and poetry of Robert Browning (1812–89) and Elizabeth Barrett Browning (1806–61), as well as other Victorian writers and poets. Founded 1881; refounded 1969.

The John Buchan Society

Membership Secretary Dr Dee Dunne-Thomas, 31 Walmley Ash Road, Walmley, Sutton Coldfield B76 1JA
tel 0121 351 3121
email thomasmdrb@btinternet.com
website www.johnbuchansociety.co.uk
Membership £15 p.a. – full; overseas and other rates on application

Promotes a wider understanding of the life and works of John Buchan (1875–1940). Encourages publication of Buchan's works, and supports the John Buchan Heritage Museum in the Scottish Borders. Holds regular meetings and social gatherings; produces a Newsletter and a Journal. Founded 1979.

Bureau of Freelance Photographers

Focus House, 497 Green Lanes, London N13 4BP
tel 020-8882 3315
email mail@thebfp.com
website www.thebfp.com
Chief Executive John Tracy
Membership £54 p.a. UK; £70 p.a. overseas

Exists to help the freelance photographer by providing information on markets, and free advisory service. Publishes *Market Newsletter* (monthly). Founded 1965.

Byron Society (International)

Acushla, Halam Road, Southwell, Notts. NG25 0AD
website www.internationalbyronsociety.org
Chairman P.K. Purslow
Membership £30 p.a.

Aims to promote research into the life and works of Lord Byron (1788–1824) by seminars, discussions, lectures and readings. Publishes *The Byron Journal* (annual, £6.50 plus postage). Founded 1971.

Randolph Caldecott Society

Secretary Kenn Oultram, Blue Grass Cottage, Clatterwick Lane, Little Leigh, Northwich, Cheshire CW8 4RJ
tel (01606) 891303 (office), 781731 (evening)
website www.randolphcaldecott.org.uk
Membership £12.50 p.a. individual, £17.50 p.a. families/corporate

Aims to encourage an interest in the life and works of Randolph Caldecott (1846–86), the Victorian artist, illustrator and sculptor. Meetings held in Chester. Liaises with the American Caldecott Society. Founded 1983.

Cambridge Bibliographical Society

University Library, West Road, Cambridge CB3 9DR
tel (01223) 333123 *fax* (01223) 333160
email cbs@lib.cam.ac.uk
website www.lib.cam.ac.uk/cambibsoc

To encourage the study of bibliography, including book and MS production, book collecting and the history of libraries. It publishes *Transactions* (annual) and a series of monographs, and arranges a programme of lectures and visits. Founded 1949.

Campaign for Freedom of Information

Suite 102, 16 Baldwins Gardens, London EC1N 7RJ
tel 020-7831 7477 *fax* 020-7831 7461
email admin@cfoi.demon.co.uk
website www.cfoi.org.uk

A non-profit organisation working to improve public access to official information and to ensure that the Freedom of Information Act is implemented effectively.

Campaign for Press and Broadcasting Freedom

2nd Floor, Vi & Garner Smith House, 23 Orford Road, London E17 9NL
tel 07729 846146
email freepress@cpbf.org.uk
website www.cpbf.org.uk

Canadian Authors Association

PO Box 851, Stn Main Orillia, Ontario L3V 6KS, Canada
tel +1 705-653-0323, +1 866-216-6222 (toll free)
email admin@canauthors.org
website www.canauthors.org
President Matthew Bin, *Executive Director* Anita Purcell

Canadian Publishers' Council

250 Merton Street, Suite 203, Toronto, Ontario M4S 1B1, Canada
tel +1 416-322-7011 *fax* +1 416-322-6999
website www.pubcouncil.ca
Executive Director Jacqueline Hushion

CANSCAIP (Canadian Society of Children's Authors, Illustrators & Performers)

40 Orchard View Boulevard, Suite 104, Toronto, Ontario M4R 1B9, Canada
tel +1 416-515-1559
email office@canscaip.org
website www.canscaip.org
Administrative Director Jennifer Gordon
Membership $85 p.a. Full member (published authors and illustrators), $45 Friend

A non-profit support network for children's artists. Promotes children's literature and performances through Canada and internationally. Founded 1977.

Careers Development Group

Carlton Plaza, 111 Upper Richmond Road, London SW15 2TJ
tel 0300 247 2000
email info@cdguk.org
website www.cdguk.org
Ceo Roy O'Shaughnessy

Represents the development needs of new and existing library and information workers. Founded 1895.

Careers Writers' Association

Membership Secretary Ann Goodman, 16 Caewal Road, Llandaff, Cardiff CF5 2BT
tel 029-2056 3444 *fax* 029-2065 8190
email gm.sharp@virgin.net
website www.careerswriting.co.uk
Membership £40 p.a.

Society for established writers on the interrelated topics of education, training and careers. Holds occasional meetings on subjects of interest to members, and circulates details of members to information providers. Founded 1979.

The Lewis Carroll Society

Secretary Bob Cole, 50 Lauderdale Mansions, Lauderdale Road, London W9 1NE
email markrichards@aznet.co.uk
website www.lewiscarrollsociety.org.uk
Membership £20 p.a. UK, £23 Europe, £26 elsewhere; special rates for institutions

Aims to promote interest in the life and works of Lewis Carroll (Revd Charles Lutwidge Dodgson) (1832–98) and to encourage research. Activities include regular meetings, exhibitions, and a publishing programme that includes the first annotated, unexpurgated edition of his diaries in 9 volumes, the Society's journal *The Carrollian* (2 p.a.), a newsletter, *Bandersnatch* (quarterly) and the *Lewis Carroll Review* (occasional). Founded 1969.

Lewis Carroll Society (Daresbury)

Secretary Kenn Oultram, Blue Grass Cottage, Clatterwick Lane, Little Leigh, Northwich, Cheshire CW8 4RJ
tel (01606) 891303 (office), (01606) 781731 (evening)
Membership £7 p.a., £10 families/corporate

Aims to encourage an interest in the life and works of Lewis Carroll (1832–98), author of *Alice's Adventures*. Meetings take place at Carroll's birth village (Daresbury, Cheshire). Founded 1970.

Cartoonists Club of Great Britain

17 Eliot Road, Worcester WR3 8DP
email secretary@thecartoonistsclub.com
website www.ccgb.org.uk
Membership £44 p.a.

Aims to encourage social contact between members and endeavours to promote the professional standing and prestige of cartoonists.

The Chartered Institute of Journalists

General Secretary Dominic Cooper, 2 Dock Offices, Surrey Quays Road, London SE16 2XU
tel 020-7252 1187 *fax* 020-7232 2302
email memberservices@cioj.co.uk
website www.cioj.co.uk
Membership £195 p.a. maximum, £97.50 trainees, £133 affiliate

The senior organisation of the profession, the Chartered Institute has accumulated funds for the assistance of members. A Freelance Division links editors and publishers with freelances and a Directory is published of freelance writers, with their specialisations. There are special sections for broadcasters, motoring correspondents, public relations practitioners and overseas members. Occasional contributors to the media may qualify for election as Affiliates. Founded in 1884; incorporated by Royal Charter in 1890.

Chartered Institute of Linguists (IoL)

Saxon House, 48 Southwark Street, London SE1 1UN
tel 020-7940 3100 *fax* 020-7940 3101
email info@iol.org.uk
website www.iol.org.uk

An international professional membership organisation. It promotes proficiency in modern languages worldwide amongst professional linguists, including translators, interpreters and educationalists, as well as those in the public and private sectors for whom languages are an important skill. Through its wholly owned subsidiary IoL Language Services Ltd (LSL) it offers translation, production and recruitment services, validation of language qualifications and assessments as well as training courses. The IoL Educational Trust, an associated charity, is an accredited awarding body offering high level exams. The Institute helps to ensure equal access for all to the public services (law, health, local government) by providing interpreting qualifications in most of the languages spoken in the UK and running the National Register of Public Service Interpreters (NRPSI Ltd).

The Chartered Society of Designers

1 Cedar Court, Royal Oak Yard, Bermondsey Street, London SE1 3GA
tel 020-7357 8088 *fax* 020-7407 9878
email info@csd.org.uk
website www.csd.org.uk
President Christopher Ramsden

Works to promote and regulate standards of competence, professional conduct and integrity, including representation on government and official bodies, design education and awards. The services to members include general information, publications, guidance on copyright and other professional issues, access to professional indemnity insurance, as well as the membership magazine *The Designer*. Activities in the regions are included in an extensive annual programme of events and training courses.

The Chesterton Society

6 Sunningwell Road, Oxford OX1 4SX
email contactus@gkchesterton.org.uk
Membership £12 p.a.

Aims to promote interest in the life and work of G.K. Chesterton (1874–1936) and those associated with him or influenced by his writings. Two lectures a year. Publishes the *Chesterton Quarterly Review* (4 p.a.). Founded 1974.

The Children's Book Circle

67A Holly Street, Hackney, London E8 3HS
website www.childrensbookcircle.org.uk
Membership £20 p.a. if working inside M25; £15 outside

Provides a discussion forum for anybody involved with children's books. Meetings are addressed by a panel of invited speakers and topics focus on current and controversial issues. Holds the annual Patrick Hardy lecture and administers the Eleanor Farjeon Award. Founded 1962.

Children's Books Ireland

17 North Great Georges Street, Dublin 1, Republic of Ireland
tel +353 (0)1 8727475 *fax* +353 (0)1 8727476
email info@childrensbooksireland.com
website www.childrensbooksireland.ie
Director Mags Walsh, *Publications and Communications* Jenny Murray, *Programme Officer* Aoife Murray
Membership €30/£20 p.a. individual, €60/£55 p.a. insitutions (Ireland & UK), €70/£70/$105 (Europe and R.O.W)

CBI is the national children's books organisation of Ireland. Through many activities and events CBI aims to engage young people with books, foster a greater understanding of the importance of books for young people and act as a core resource for those with an interest in books for children in Ireland. CBI is dedicated to ensuring that books are at the centre of young people's lives, through advocacy, resource and innovative programming and outreach. Founded 1996.

Children's Writers and Illustrators Group – see The Society of Authors, page 497

CILIP (Chartered Institute of Library and Information Professionals)

7 Ridgmount Street, London WC1E 7AE
tel 020-7255 0500 *fax* 020-7255 0501
email info@cilip.org.uk
website www.cilip.org.uk
Chief Executive Annie Mauger
Membership Varies according to income

The leading professional body for librarians, information specialists and knowledge managers. CILIP's vision is a fair and economically prosperous society underpinned by literacy, access to information and the transfer of knowledge. CILIP is a registered charity, no. 313014.

Circle of Wine Writers

Administrator Andrea Warren, Scots Firs, 70 Joiners Lane, Chalfont St Peter, Bucks. SL9 0AU
tel/fax (01753) 882320
email administrator@winewriters.org
website www.winewriters.org
Membership By election, £50 p.a.

An association for those engaged in communicating about wines and spirits. Produces *Circle Update* newsletter (5 p.a.), organises tasting sessions as well as a programme of meetings and talks. Founded 1960.

The John Clare Society

Hon. Secretary 9 The Chase, Ely, Cambs. CB6 3DR
tel (01353) 668438
email l.j.curry@bham.ac.uk, sueholgate@hotmail.co.uk
website http://johnclaresociety.blogspot.com/
Membership £15 p.a. UK individual; other rates on application

Promotes a wider appreciation of the life and works of the poet John Clare (1793–1864). Founded 1981.

Classical Association

Senate House, Malet Street, London WC1E 7HU
tel 020-7862 8706 *fax* 020-7862 8729
email office@classicalassociation.org
website www.classicalassociation.org
Joint Hon. Secretaries, Dr E.J.Stafford, Mrs B. Finney

Exists to promote and sustain interest in classical studies, to maintain their rightful position in universities and schools, and to give scholars and teachers opportunities for meeting and discussing their problems.

The William Cobbett Society

1 Meadow View Cottages, Spring Grove, Burlesdon SO31 8BB
email information@williamcobbett.org.uk
website www.williamcobbett.org.uk

Aims to make the life and work of William Cobbett (1763–1835) better known. Founded 1976.

The Wilkie Collins Society

Membership Secretary Paul Lewis, 4 Ernest Gardens, London W4 3QU
email paul@paullewis.co.uk
website www.wilkiecollins.org
Membership £12 p.a. EU, £18 international

Aims to promote interest in the life and works of Wilkie Collins (1824–89). Publishes a newsletter, an annual scholarly journal and reprints of Collins's lesser known works. Founded 1981.

Comhairle nan Leabhraichean/The Gaelic Books Council

32 Mansfield Street, Glasgow G11 5QP
tel 0141 337 6211
email brath@gaelicbooks.net
website www.gaelicbooks.org
Chair Donald-Iain Brown

Stimulates Scottish Gaelic publishing by awarding publication grants for new books, commissions new works from established and emerging authors and provides editorial advice and guidance to Gaelic writers and publishers. Has its own bookshop of all Gaelic and Gaelic-related books in print. All the stock is listed on the website and a paper catalogue is also available. Founded 1968.

The Joseph Conrad Society (UK)

The Honorary Secretary c/o The Polish Social and Cultural Association, 238–246 King Street, London W6 0RF
email theconradian@aol.com
website www.josephconradsociety.org
Chairman Keith Carabine, *Honorary Secretary* Hugh Epstein, *Editor* Allan Simmons

Activities include an annual international conference; publication of *The Conradian* and a series of pamphlets; and maintenance of a substantial reference library as part of the Polish Library at the Polish Social and Cultural Association, 238–246 King Street, London W6 0RF. Administers the Juliet McLauchlan Prize, £200 annual award for the winner of an essay competition, and travel grants for scholars wishing to attend Conrad conferences. Founded 1973.

Copyright Clearance Center Inc.

222 Rosewood Drive, Danvers, MA 01923, USA
tel +1 978-750-8400 *fax* +1 978-646-8600
email info@copyright.com
website www.copyright.com

Copyright Council of New Zealand Inc.

PO Box 331488, Takapuna 0740, North Shore City, New Zealand
tel +64 (0)9 486 6250 *fax* +64 (0)9 486 6260
email info@copyright.org.nz
website www.copyright.org.nz

The Copyright Licensing Agency Ltd – see page 658

Creative Scotland

Waverley Gate, 2-4 Waterloo Place, Edinburgh EH1 3EG
tel 0330 333 2000
email enquiries@creativescotland.com
website www.creativescotland.com

The lead body for Scotland's arts, screen and creative industries. Helps Scotland's creativity shine at home and abroad. Creative Scotland, established on 1 July 2010, took over the functions and resources of Scottish Screen and the Scottish Arts Council but also has a wider set of responsibilities for developing the sector.

Crime Writers' Association

email info@thecwa.co.uk
website www.thecwa.co.uk
Membership Associate membership open to publishers, journalists, booksellers specialising in crime literature and literary agents

Full membership open to professional writers of crime novels, short stories, plays for stage, TV and radio, or of other serious works on crime. Publishes *Red Herrings* (monthly), available to members only. Founded 1953.

The Critics' Circle

Contact William Russell, c/o 50 Finland Road, Brockley, London SE4 2JH

tel 020-7732 9636
email williamfinland@gmail.com
website www.criticscircle.org.uk
President Tom Sutcliffe, *Hon. General Secretary* William Russell
Membership By invitation of the Council

Aims to promote the art of criticism, to uphold its integrity in practice, to foster and safeguard the professional interests of its members, to provide opportunities for social intercourse among them, and to support the advancement of the arts. Such invitations are issued only to persons engaged professionally, regularly and substantially in the writing or broadcasting of criticism of drama, music, films, dance and the visual arts. Founded 1913.

Cwlwm Cyhoeddwyr Cymru

Bethan Mair, Gellimanwydd, 54 Stryd Fawr, Rhydarnan SA18 2NB
tel 07779 102224
website www.cwlwmcyhoeddwyr.com (Welsh language only)

Represents and promotes Welsh-language publishers. Founded 2002.

Cyngor Llyfrau Cymru – see Welsh Books Council/Cyngor Llyfrau Cymru

Data Publishers Association (DPA)

Queen's House, 28 Kingsway, London WC2B 6JR
tel 020-7405 0836 *fax* 020-7404 4167
email info@dpa.org.uk
website www.dpa.org.uk
Membership £490–£2,570 p.a.

Maintains a code of professional practice; aims to raise the standard and professional status of UK directory and data publishing and to protect (and promote) the legal, statutory and common interests of directory and data publishers. Annual Conference and Awards. Founded 1970.

Walter de la Mare Society

PO Box 25351, London NW5 1ZT
tel 020-8886 1771
Membership £15 p.a.

To promote the study and deepen the appreciation of the works of Walter de la Mare (1873–1956) through a magazine, talks, discussions and other activities. Founded 1997.

Design and Artists Copyright Society – see page 662

Dickens Fellowship

The Charles Dickens Museum, 48 Doughty Street, London WC1N 2LX
tel 020-7405 2127 *fax* 020-7831 5175
website www.dickensfellowship.org
Joint Hon. Secretaries Mrs Lee Ault, Mrs Joan Dicks
Membership On application

Based in house occupied by Charles Dickens (1812–75) during the period 1837–9. Publishes *The Dickensian* (3 p.a.). Founded 1902.

Directory of Writers' Circles, Courses and Workshops

39 Lincoln Way, Harlington, Beds. LU5 6NG
tel (01525) 873197
website www.writers-circles.com
Editor Diana Hayden

Directory of writers' groups published annually.

Diversity in Publishing Network (DIPNET)

Booktrust, Book House, 45 East Hill, London SW18 2QZ
tel 020-8875 4824
website www.booktrust.org.uk, www.dipnet.org.uk
Contact Sue Evans

DIPNET was established to promote the status and contribution of groups traditionally underrepresented within all areas of publishing, as well as to support those seeking to enter the industry. It aims to redress the balance of equality in the UK publishing sector. DIPNET is an initiative funded by Arts Council England and managed at Booktrust. Membership is free and members are able to access a network of informal publishing contacts, gain inside information for job seekers, and read case studies of people in publishing jobs and tips about getting published. Founded 2004.

The Arthur Conan Doyle Society

PO Box 1360, Ashcroft, BC V0K 1A0, Canada
tel +1 250-453-2045 *fax* +1 250-453-2075
email sirhenry@telus.net
website www.ash-tree.bc.ca/acdsocy.html

Promotes the study of the life and works of Sir Arthur Conan Doyle (1859–1930). Publishes *ACD* journal (bi-annual) and occasional reprints of Conan Doyle material. Occasional conventions. Founded 1989.

Early English Text Society

Lady Margaret Hall, Oxford OX2 6QA
website www.eets.org.uk
Hon. Director Prof. Anne Hudson *Executive Secretary* Prof. V. Gillespie
Membership £20 p.a.

Aims to bring unprinted early English literature within the reach of students in sound texts. Founded 1864.

Edinburgh Bibliographical Society

Rare Book Collections, National Library of Scotland, George IV Bridge, Edinburgh EH1 1EW
email h.vincent@nls.uk
website http://mcs.qmuc.ac.uk/ebs/

Secretary H. Vincent, *Treasurer* D. Finkelstein
Membership £15 p.a., £20 corporate; £10 full-time students

Encourages bibliographical activity through organising talks for members, particularly on bibliographical topics relating to Scotland, and visits to libraries. See website for submission guidelines and prizes. Publishes *Journal* (annual, free to members) and other occasional publications. Founded 1890.

Educational Writers Group – see The Society of Authors, page 497

The George Eliot Fellowship

Chairman John Burton, 39 Lower Road, Barnacle, Coventry CV7 9LD
tel 024-7661 9126
email jkburton@tiscali.co.uk
website www.georgeeliot.org
President Jonathan G. Ouvry
Membership £15 p.a. (£12 concessions) individuals; £20 p.a. (£15 concessions) for couples

Promotes an interest in the life and work of George Eliot (1819–80) and helps to extend her influence; arranges meetings, study days and conferences; produces an annual journal (*The George Eliot Review*), newsletters and other publications. Works closely with educational establishments in Nuneaton area. Awards the annual George Eliot Fellowship Prize (£500) for an essay on Eliot's life or work, which must be previously unpublished and not exceed 4,000 words. Founded 1930.

English Association

University of Leicester, University Road, Leicester LE1 7RH
tel 0116 229 7622 *fax* 0116 229 7623
email engassoc@leicester.ac.uk
website www.le.ac.uk/engassoc
Chair Adrian Barlow, *Chief Executive* Helen Lucas

Aims to further knowledge, understanding and enjoyment of English literature and the English language, by working towards a fuller recognition of English as an essential element in education and in the community at large; by encouraging the study of English literature and language by means of conferences, lectures and publications; and by fostering the discussion of methods of teaching English of all kinds.

English Speaking Board (International) Ltd

9 Hattersley Court, Burscough Road, Ormskirk L39 2AY
tel (01695) 573439 *fax* (01695) 228003
email admin@esbuk.org
website www.esbuk.org
Ceo Lesley Cook
Membership £39.50 p.a. individuals, £75 p.a. corporate, £20 for new individual members

Aims to foster all activities concerned with oral communication. Offers assessment qualifications in practical speaking and listening skills for candidates at all levels in schools, vocational and business contexts; also for those with learning difficulties and those for whom English is an acquired language. Also provides training courses in teaching and delivery of oral communication. Offers membership to all those concerned with the development and expression of the English language. Members receive *Speaking English* (2 p.a.); articles are invited on any special aspect of spoken English.

The English-Speaking Union

Dartmouth House, 37 Charles Street, London W1J 5ED
tel 020-7529 1550
email esu@esu.org
website www.esu.org
Membership Various categories

Aims to promote international understanding and human achievement through the widening use of the English language throughout the world. The ESU is an educational charity which sponsors scholarships and exchanges, educational programmes promoting the effective use of English, and a wide range of international and cultural events. Members contribute to its work across the world. Administers several awards, including the Marsh Biography Award, the Marsh Award for Children's Literature in Translation (see page 559) and various English language book awards. Founded 1918.

European Broadcasting Union

General Headquarters, Ancienne Route 17A, CH–1218 Grand Saconnex (Geneva), Switzerland
tel +41 22-717 2111 *fax* +41 22-747 4000
email ebu@ebu.ch
website www.ebu.ch
Director General Ingrid Deltenre

The EBU serves 85 national media organisations in 56 countries in and around Europe. It represents its members and promotes the values and distinctiveness of public service media in Europe and around the world. The Eurovision and Euroradio networks deliver news, sports, events and music to EBU members and other media organisations. Services to members range from legal advice, technical standardisation and development to co-productions and exchange of quality European content.

Fabian Society

11 Dartmouth Street, London SW1H 9BN
tel 020-7227 4900 *fax* 020-7976 7153
email info@fabians.org.uk
website www.fabians.org.uk
General Secretary Andrew Harrop

Current affairs, political thought, economics, education, environment, foreign affairs, social policy.

Also controls NCLC Publishing Society Ltd. Founded 1884.

Federation Against Copyright Theft Ltd (FACT)

Europa House, Church Street, Old Isleworth, Middlesex TW7 6DA
tel 020-8568 6646 *fax* 020-8560 6364
email contact@fact-uk.org.uk
website www.fact-uk.org.uk
Contact Kieron Sharp, Director General

Aims to protect the interests of its members and others against infringement in the UK of copyright in cinematograph films, TV programmes and all forms of audiovisual recording. Founded 1982.

Federation of British Artists

17 Carlton House Terrace, London SW1Y 5BD
tel 020-7930 6844 *fax* 020-7839 7830
email info@mallgalleries.com
website www.mallgalleries.org.uk

Administers 9 major National Art Societies, as well as BITE: Artists Making Prints, and the Threadneedle Prize at the Mall Galleries, The Mall, London SW1.

Federation of European Publishers

Rue Montoyer 31 Bte 8, B–1000 Brussels, Belgium
tel +32 2-7701110 *fax* +32 2-7712071
email info@fep-fee.eu
website www.fep-fee.be
President Fergal Tobin, *Director* Anne Bergman-Tahon

Represents the interests of European publishers on EU affairs; informs members on the development of EU policies which could affect the publishing industry. Founded 1967.

The Federation of Indian Publishers

18/1c, Institutional Area,
Aruna Asaf Ali Marg (Near JNU),
New Delhi 110067, India
tel +91 11-26852263, +91 11-26964847
fax +91 11-26864054
email fip1@sify.com
website www.fipindia.org
President Shri Sudhir Malhotra

Federation of Spanish Publishers' Association

(Federación de Gremios de Editores de España)
Cea Bermúdez, 44–2 Dcha. 28003 Madrid, Spain
tel +34 915 345 195 *fax* +34 915 352 625
email fgee@fge.es
website www.federacioneditores.org
President Sr D. Antoni Comas

The Federation of Worker Writers and Community Publishers

email membership@fedonline.org.uk
website www.fedonline.org.uk
Chair, Roger Druy
Membership £25 p.a. funded groups; £15 unfunded

A network of writers groups and community publishers which promotes working-class writing and publishing. Founded 1976.

The Fine Art Trade Guild

16–18 Empress Place, London SW6 1TT
tel 020-7381 6616 *fax* 020-7381 2596
email info@fineart.co.uk
website www.fineart.co.uk
Ceo Louise Hay

Promotes the sale of fine art prints and picture framing in the UK and overseas markets; establishes and raises standards amongst members and communicates these to the buying public. The Guild publishes *Art Business Today*, the trade's longest established magazine, and various specialist books. Founded 1910.

FOCAL International Ltd (Federation of Commercial AudioVisual Libraries International Ltd)

79 College Road, Harrow, Middlesex HA1 1BD
tel 020-3178 3535
email info@focalint.org
website www.focalint.org
Commerical Manager Anne Johnson, *General Manager* Julie Lewis

Founded 1985.

The Folklore Society

c/o The Warburg Institute, Woburn Square, London WC1H 0AB
tel 020-7862 8564
email enquiries@folklore-society.com
website www.folklore-society.com
Hon. Secretary Prof James H. Grayson
Membership £45 p.a.

Collection, recording and study of folklore. Founded 1878.

Foreign Press Association in London

Registered Office 25 Northumberland Avenue, London WC2N 5AP
tel 020-7930 0445
email briefings@foreign-press.org.uk
website www.foreign-press.org.uk
Director Christopher Wyld
Membership Full membership open to those working for news media organisations with headquarters overseas. Associate membership also available.

Aims to promote access for journalists from overseas. Founded 1888.

Free Painters & Sculptors

Registered office 14 John Street, London WC1N 2EB
email info@freepaintersandsculptors.co.uk
website www.freepaintersandsculptors.co.uk

Promotes group shows 2 times a year in prestigious galleries in London. Sponsors all that is exciting in contemporary art.

Free Word

Free Word Centre, 60 Farringdon Road,
London EC1R 3GA
tel 020-7324 2570 *fax* 020-7490 0566
email info@freewordonline.com
website www.freewordonline.com
Fees for associates Individuals from UK, Western Europe, USA and Australia: £150 p.a., Rest of the World: £80 p.a.; organisations: £300 p.a. (2–4 employees), £500 p.a. (4–8 employees), £700 p.a. (more than 8 employees)

Free Word is a charity that works to promote, protect and democratise the power of the written and spoken word, nationally and internationally. People who are involved in literature, literacy and free expression are brought together with unique programmes and events and invited to work collaboratively.

Free Word is a venue, a meeting place, an office space, a thinking space, a place of debate and risk taking, a window to the world, a robust voice for the word. Together with Free Word, there are 9 resident organisations: Apples & Snakes, Article 19, Booktrust, English PEN, Index on Censorship, Arvon, The Literary Consultancy, The Reading Agency and Dalkey Archive.

The Centre's facilities include a lecture theatre, meeting rooms, atrium and a café, which are also open to associates, including UK and international literary, literacy and free expression organisations and individuals, as well as writers and journalists. Associates are granted full access to the Free Word website to seek collaborations, network, stay in touch, and profile themselves and their work. They may also use the Free Word base as a 'members club'; other benefits include smart card access and café discounts.

French Publishers' Association

(Syndicat National de l'Edition)
115 Blvd St Germain, 75006 Paris, France
tel +33 (0)1 4441 4050 *fax* +33 (0)1 4441 4077
website www.sne.fr

The Gaelic Books Council – see Comhairle nan Leabhraichean/The Gaelic Books Council

The Garden Media Guild

(Formerly the Garden Writers' Guild)
Katepwa House, Ashfield Park Avenue,
Ross-on-Wye, Herefordshire HR9 5AX
tel (01989) 567393 *fax* (01989) 567676
email admin@gardenmediaguild.co.uk
website www.gardenmediaguild.co.uk
Membership £62 p.a.

Aims are to raise the quality of garden writing, photography and broadcasting, to help members operate efficiently and profitably, to improve communication between members and to promote liaison between members and the broader horticultural industry. The Guild administers annual awards to encourage excellence in garden writing, photography, trade and consumer press journalism, TV and radio broadcasting. Founded 1991.

The Gaskell Society

37 Buckingham Drive, Knutsford,
Cheshire WA16 8IH
tel (01565) 651761
email pam.griffiths@talktalk.net
website www.gaskellsociety.co.uk
Secretary Mrs Pam Griffiths
Membership £20 p.a., £25 corporate/overseas

Promotes and encourages the study and appreciation of the work and life of Elizabeth Cleghorn Gaskell (1810–65). Holds regular meetings in Knutsford, London, Manchester and Bath, visits and residential conferences; produces an annual journal and bi-annual newsletters. Founded 1985.

Gay Authors Workshop

Kathryn Byrd, BM Box 5700, London WC1N 3XX
email eandk2@btinternet.com
Membership £8 p.a., £4 unwaged

Exists to encourage writers who are lesbian, gay or bisexual. Quarterly newsletter, bi-annual magazine and monthly meetings. Founded 1978.

German Publishers' and Booksellers' Association

(Börsenverein des Deutschen Buchhandels e.V.)
Postfach 100442, 60004 Frankfurt am Main, Germany
tel +49 (0)69 13060 *fax* +49 (0)69 1306201
email info@boev.de
website www.boersenverein.de
General Manager Alexander Skipis, *President* Gottfried Honnefelder

The Ghost Story Society

PO Box 1360, Ashcroft, British Columbia V0K 1A0, Canada
tel +1 250-453-2045 *fax* +1 250-453-2075
email nebuly@telus.net
website www.ash-tree.bc.ca/GSS.html
Secretary Barbara Roden
Membership £25/US$45/Can.$45 p.a.

Provides enthusiasts of the classic ghost story with a forum to discuss and appreciate the genre. Publishes *All Hallows* (3 p.a.) journal which contains news, articles, reviews and approx. 100pp of new fiction. Founded 1989.

Graham Greene Birthplace Trust

Yan Christensen, 9 Briar Way, Berkhamsted HP4 2JJ
tel (01442) 873604
email secretary@grahamgreenebt.org
website www.grahamgreenebt.org
Membership £11 p.a., £27 for 3 years

Exists to study the works of Graham Greene (1904–91). The Trust promotes the Annual Graham Greene Festival and Graham Greene trails. It publishes a quarterly newsletter, occasional papers, videos and CDs, and maintains a small library. It administers the Graham Greene Memorial Awards. Founded 1997.

The Greeting Card Association

United House, North Road, London N7 9DP
tel 020-7619 0396
website www.greetingcardassociation.org.uk
Chief Executive Sharon Little

The trade association for greeting card publishers. See website for information on freelance designing and writing for greeting cards. Official magazine: *Progressive Greetings Worldwide* (see page 483).

Guernsey Arts Commission

North Esplanade, St Peter Port Guernsey GY1 2LQ
tel (01481) 709747
email info@arts.gg

The Guild of Aviation Artists

(incorporating the Society of Aviation Artists)
Trenchard House, 85 Farnborough Road, Farnborough, Hants GU14 6TF
tel (01252) 513123 *fax* (01252) 510505
email admin@gava.org.uk
website www.gava.org.uk
President Michael Turner FGAvA, *Secretary/Administrator* Susan Gardner
Membership £65 p.a. Full (by invitation), £50 Associates (by selection), £30 Friends

Formed to promote aviation art through the organisation of exhibitions and meetings. Holds annual open exhibition in July in London; £1,000 prize for 'Aviation Painting of the Year'. Quarterly members' newsletter. Founded 1971.

Guild of Food Writers

Administrator Jonathan Woods,
255 Kent House Road, Beckenham, Kent BR3 1JQ
tel 020-8659 0422
email guild@gfw.co.uk
website www.gfw.co.uk
Membership £85 p.a.

Aims to bring together professional food writers including journalists, broadcasters and authors, to print and issue an annual list of members, to extend the range of members' knowledge and experience by arranging discussions, tastings and visits, and to encourage the development of new writers by every means, including competitions and awards. There are 12 awards and entry is not restricted to members of the Guild. Founded 1984.

Guild of Health Writers

Administrator Jatinder Dua, Dale Lodge,
88 Wensleydale Road, Hampton,
Middlesex TW12 2LX
tel 020-8941 2977
email admin@healthwriters.com
website www.healthwriters.com
Membership £50 p.a., Student £12 p.a.

The Guild of Health Writers is a national, independent membership organisation representing Britain's leading health journalists and writers. It was founded to encourage the provision of readable and accurate health information to the public. Members write on every aspect of health and wellbeing, from innovative medical science to complementary therapies and lifestyle issues. They value the training and networking opportunities that the Guild provides. Founded 1994.

The Guild of International Songwriters & Composers

Sovereign House, 12 Trewartha Road, Praa Sands, Penzance, Cornwall TR20 9ST
tel (01736) 762826 *fax* (01736) 763328
email songmag@aol.com
website www.songwriters-guild.co.uk
Secretary Carole Ann Jones
Membership £55

Gives advice to members on contractual and copyright matters; assists with protection of members rights; assists with analysis of members' works; international collaboration register free to members; outlines requirements to record companies, publishers, artists. Publishes *Songwriting & Composing* (quarterly).

The Guild of Motoring Writers

Contact The Guild of Motoring Writers' Secretariat, 40 Baring Road, Bournemouth BH6 4DT
tel (01202) 422424
email generalsec@gomw.co.uk
website www.guildofmotoringwriters.co.uk

A representative body with more than 500 members including journalists, authors, broadcasters, photographers and web editors reporting on the automotive industry, both in the UK and overseas. Aims to raise the standard of motoring journalism, to encourage motoring, motorsport and road safety, to provide a link between fellow members around the world and to safeguard the interests of members in relation to the aims of the Guild.

Guild of Railway Artists

Chief Executive Officer F.P. Hodges, Hon. GRA,
45 Dickins Road, Warwick CV34 5NS
tel (01926) 499246
email frank.hodges@virgin.net
website www.railart.co.uk

Aims to forge a link between artists depicting railway subjects and to give members a corporate identity; also stages railway art exhibitions and members' meetings and produces books of members' works. Founded 1979.

Hakluyt Society

c/o The Map Library, The British Library, 96 Euston Road, London NW1 2DB
tel (01428) 641850 *fax* (01428) 641933
email office@hakluyt.com
website www.hakluyt.com
President Michael Barritt

Publication of original narratives of voyages, travels, naval expeditions, and other geographical records. Founded 1846.

Hampshire Writers' Society

c/o Research and Knowledge Exchange, University of Winchester, Winchester, Hants SO22 4NR
email barbara.large@winchester.ac.uk
website www.writersconference.co.uk/hws
Contact Barbara Large, MBE

Welcomes all aspiring and published writers to enjoy a broad range of talks, readings, discussions, panels and performances by well-known novelists, authors, poets, playwrights, children's authors, scriptwriters, literary agents, commissioning editors and industry specialists. Meetings are held on the second Tuesday of each month in The Stripe Building, University of Winchester, at 7.30 p.m. Monthly competitions. Annual membership £25, half-yearly membership £15, students £5/£3.

The Thomas Hardy Society

c/o Dorset County Museum, High West Street, Dorchester, Dorset DT1 1XA
tel (01305) 251501 *fax* (01305) 251501
email info@hardysociety.org
website www.hardysociety.org
Membership £24 p.a., £35 overseas

Aims to promote and celebrate the work of Thomas Hardy (1840–1928). Publishes *The Thomas Hardy Journal* (annual) and *The Hardy Society Journal* (2 p.a.). Biennial conference held in Dorchester. Founded 1967.

Harleian Society

College of Arms, Queen Victoria Street, London EC4V 4BT
tel 020-7236 7728 *fax* 020-7248 6448
email chester@college-of-arms.gov.uk
website http://harleian.org.uk
Chairman T. Woodcock LVO, DL, FSA, Garter King of Arms, *Hon. Secretary* T.H.S. Duke, Chester Herald of Arms

Instituted for transcribing, printing and publishing the heraldic visitations of Counties, Parish Registers and any manuscripts relating to genealogy, family history and heraldry. Founded 1869.

Hesketh Hubbard Art Society

17 Carlton House Terrace, London SW1Y 5BD
tel 020-7930 6844 *fax* 020-7839 7830
email info@mallgalleries.com
website www.mallgalleries.org.uk
President Simon Whittle

Weekly life drawing classes.

The Hilliard Society of Miniaturists

The Executive Officer Priory Lodge, 7 Priory Road, Wells, Somerset BA5 1SR
tel (01749) 674472
website www.hilliardsociety.org
President Paddy Davison
Membership From £40 p.a.

Aims to increase knowledge and promote the art of miniature painting. Annual exhibition held in June at Wells; produces a newsletter. Member of the World Federation of Miniaturists. Founded 1982.

The James Hilton Society

Hon. Secretary Dr J.R. Hammond, 49 Beckingthorpe Drive, Bottesford, Nottingham NG13 0DN
website www.jameshiltonsociety.co.uk
Membership £13 p.a. (£10 concessions)

Aims to promote interest in the life and work of novelist and scriptwriter James Hilton (1900–54). Publishes quarterly newsletter and an annual scholarly journal, and organises conferences. Founded 2000.

Historical Novel Society

Contact Richard Lee, Marine Cottage, The Strand, Starcross, Devon EX6 8NY
tel (01626) 891962
email richard@historicalnovelsociety.org
website www.historicalnovelsociety.org
Membership £30 p.a.

Promotes the enjoyment of historical fiction. Based in the US and UK but welcomes members (who can be readers or writers) from all over the world. Publishes print magazines, organises conferences and has an active website. Founded 1997.

The Sherlock Holmes Society of London

General enquiries Roger Johnson, Press & Publicity Officer shj@waitrose.com
Membership Secretary David Jones, audav@hotmail.co.uk
email www.sherlock-holmes.org.uk
President Guy Marriott, guym144@googlemail.com

The Society is open to anyone with an interest in Sherlock Holmes, Dr John H. Watson and their world. A literary and social society, publishing a bi-annual scholarly journal and occasional papers, and holding meetings, dinners and excursions. Founded 1951.

Horror Writers Association (HWA)

244 5th Avenue, Suite 2767, New York, NY 10001
email hwa@horror.org
UK Jo Fletcher, *Italy* Alessandro Manzetti

email jo.fletcher@fletcherbooks.co.uk, a.manzetti@hotmail.it
website www.horror.org
Membership $65 p.a. (individual), $45 (supporting), $110 (corporate), $85 (family)

A worldwide organisation of writers and publishing professionals dedicated to promoting the interests of writers of horror and dark fantasy. There are 5 levels of membership: for new writers, established writers, professionals, academics and non-writing horror professionals. Founded 1987.

Housman Society

80 New Road, Bromsgrove, Worcs. B60 2LA
tel (01527) 874136
email info@housman-society.co.uk
website www.housman-society.co.uk
Chairman Jim Page
Membership £10 p.a.

Aims to foster interest in and promote knowledge of A.E. Housman (1859–1936) and his family. Sponsors a lecture at the Guardian Hay Festival. Publishes an annual journal and bi-annual newsletter. Founded 1973.

Incorporated Society of Musicians

10 Stratford Place, London W1C 1AA
tel 020-7629 4413 *fax* 020-7408 1538
email membership@ism.org
website www.ism.org
President Paul Max Edlin, *Chief Executive* Deborah Annetts
Membership £150 p.a., £12 students

Professional body for musicians. Aims to promote the art of music; protect the interests and raise the standards of the musical profession; provide services, support and advice for its members. Publishes *Music Journal* (6 p.a.) and a yearbook annually.

Independent Publishers Guild

PO Box 12, Llain, Login SA34 0WU
tel (01437) 563335 *fax* (01437) 562071
email info@ipguk.com
website www.ipg.uk.com
Executive Director, Bridget Shine
Membership Open to new and established publishers and book packagers

Provides an information and contact network for independent publishers. Also voices concerns of member companies within the book trade. Founded 1962.

Independent Theatre Council (ITC)

The Albany, Douglas Way, London SE8 4AG
tel 020-7089 6821
email admin@itc-arts.org
website www.itc-arts.org
Chief Executive Charlotte Jones
Membership Varies

Represents a wide range of performing arts organisations, venues and individuals in the fields of drama, dance, opera, music theatre, puppetry, mixed media, mime, physical theatre and circus. These organisations predominantly work on the middle and small scale around the UK. It has around 700 members across the performing arts who are united by their commitment to producing innovative, contemporary work (24% of the membership work specifically in the educational field reaching over 2 million children and young people). Founded 1974.

Institute of Designers in Ireland

The Digital Hub, Roe Lane, Thomas Street, Dublin 8, Republic of Ireland
tel +353 (0)1 4893650 *fax* +353 (0)1 4885801
email info@idi-design.ie
website www.idi-design.ie
Membership €225 p.a. full, €85 associate

Irish design profession's representative body, covering every field of design. Founded 1972.

Institute of Internal Communication

Oak House, Woodlands Business Park, Breckland, Milton Keynes MK14 6EY
tel (01908) 313755 *fax* (01908) 313661
email enquiries@ioic.org.uk
website www.ioic.org.uk

The market leader in internal communications for those involved in corporate media management and practice by providing professional, authoritative, dynamic, supportive and innovative services. Founded 1949.

The Institute of Translation & Interpreting (ITI)

Contact The Chief Executive, Suite 165, Milton Keynes Business Centre, Linford Wood, Milton Keynes MK14 6DG
tel (01908) 325250 *fax* (01908) 325259
email info@iti.org.uk
website www.iti.org.uk

A professional association of translators and interpreters which aims to promote the highest standards in translating and interpreting. It has a strong corporate membership and runs professional development courses and conferences, sometimes in conjunction with its language, regional and subject networks. Membership is open to those with a genuine and proven involvement in translation and interpreting of all kinds. As a full and active member of the International Federation of Translators, it maintains good contacts with translators and interpreters worldwide. ITI's directory of members (online) and its bi-monthly bulletin are available from the Secretariat.

International Amateur Theatre Association (IATA)

c/o Norsk teaterrad, Postbox 1129 Sentrum, 0104 Oslo, Norway

tel +47 24 14 1100
email secretariat@aitaiata.org
website www.aitaiata.org
English Speaking Secretary Anne Gilmour

Aims to encourage, foster and promote exchanges of community and non-professional theatre; student, educational, adult, theatre activities at international level. To organise international seminars, workshops, courses and conferences, and to collect and collate information of all types for national and international dissemination. UK centre of IATA.

International Association of Conscious & Creative Writers (IACCW)

PO Box 3703, Trowbridge BA14 6ZW
tel (01380) 871331
email info@iaccw.com
website www.iaccw.com
Founder/Creative Director Julia McCutchen
Membership £97 p.a.

Membership-based organisation for writers offering monthly teleseminar training and interviews with best-selling authors and experts from around the world. Topics include all aspects of creativity, writing and contemporary publishing options, plus marketing and building an author platform. The range of member benefits includes a complimentary audio CD set presenting the current year's best interviews collection, a welcome pack and opportunities to share information and resources. Highlights the importance of discovering an authentic voice both on the page and in the world. Established 2010.

International Publishers Association

3 avenue de Miremont, CH–1206 Geneva, Switzerland
tel +41 22-704 1820 *fax* +41 22-704 1821
email secretariat@internationalpublishers.org
website www.internationalpublishers.org
President Youngsuk (Y.S.) Chi, *Secretary-General* Mr Jens Bammel

Founded 1896.

International Society of Typographic Designers

ISTD Ltd, PO Box 7002, London W1A 2TY
email mail@istd.org.uk
Co-chairs David Coates, Becky Chilcott, *Past President* Freda Sack

Working closely with graphic design educationalists and the professional community, the International Society of Typographic Designers establishes, maintains and promotes typographic standards through the forum of debate and design practice. Membership is awarded to practising designers, educators and students who demonstrate, through the quality of their work, their commitment to achieving the highest possible quality of visual communication. It publishes a journal, *Typographic*. Students of typography and graphic design are encouraged to gain membership of the Society by entering the annual student assessment scheme. Founded 1928.

International Visual Communication Association (IVCA)

1st Floor, 23 Golden Square, London W1F 9JP
tel 020-7512 0571 *fax* 020-7512 0591
email info@ivca.org
website www.ivca.org
Chief Executive Officer Marco Forgione
Membership membership@ivca.org

For those who work in business communication. Aims to promote the industry and provide a collective voice; provides a range of services, publications and events to help existing and potential users to make the most of what video, film, multimedia and live events can offer their business. Founded 1987.

The Irish Book Publishers' Association – see Publishing Ireland – Foilsiú Éireann

The Irish Copyright Licensing Agency

25 Denzille Lane, Dublin 2, Republic of Ireland
tel +353 (0)1 6624211 *fax* +353 (0)1 6624213
email info@icla.ie
website www.icla.ie
Executive Director Samantha Holman

Licences schools and other users of copyright material to photocopy extracts of such material, and distributes the monies collected to the authors and publishers whose works have been copied. Founded 1992.

Irish Playwrights and Screenwriters Guild

(formerly the Society of Irish Playwrights)
Art House, Curved Street, Temple Bar, Dublin 2, Republic of Ireland
tel +353 (0)1 6709970
email info@script.ie
website www.script.ie
Chairperson Joe O'Byrne

Represents writers' interests in theatre, radio and screen. Founded 1969.

Irish Translators' and Interpreters' Association

Irish Writers' Centre, 19 Parnell Square, Dublin 1, Republic of Ireland
tel +353 (0)87 673 8386
website www.translatorsassociation.ie
Hon. Secretary Mary Phelan

Membership p.a. €100 professional, €50 ordinary, €25 student, €250 corporate

Promotes translation in Ireland, the translation of Irish authors abroad and the practical training of translators, and promotes the interests of translators and interpreters. Maintains a detailed register of translators and interpreters. Founded 1986.

Irish Writers' Centre

19 Parnell Square, Dublin 1, Republic of Ireland
tel +353 (0)1 872 1302 *fax* +353 (0)1 872 6282
email info@writerscentre.ie
website www.writerscentre.ie
Chairperson Jack Harte

National organisation for the promotion of writers, writing and literature in Ireland. Provides a wide range of services and facilities to individual writers. Runs an extensive programme of events at its headquarters, including readings and book launches, seminars and discussions. Offers an education programme of workshops and masterclasses in writing and provides a venue for visiting international writers. Founded 1987.

Irish Writers' Union/Comhar na Scríbhneoirí

Irish Writers' Centre, 19 Parnell Square, Dublin 1, Republic of Ireland
tel +353 (0)86 233 0084 *fax* +353 (0)1 872 6282
email iwu@ireland-writers.com
website www.ireland-writers.com
Chairperson Liz Clarty, *Secretary* Kate Walsh

The Union aims to advance the cause of writing as a profession, to achieve better remuneration and more favourable conditions for writers and to provide a means for the expression of the collective opinion of writers on matters affecting their profession. Founded 1986.

The Johnson Society

Johnson Birthplace Museum, Breadmarket Street, Lichfield, Staffs. WS13 6LG
tel (01543) 264972
email info@thejohnsonsociety.org.uk
website www.thejohnsonsociety.org.uk
Hon. General Secretary Barbara Hattersley

Aims to encourage the study of the life and works of Dr Samuel Johnson (1709–84); to preserve the memorials, associations, books, manuscripts and letters of Dr Johnson and his contemporaries; and to work with the local council in the preservation of his birthplace.

Johnson Society of London

Secretary Mrs Zandra O'Donnell MA, 255 Baring Road, London SE12 0BQ
email alanzandy@btinternet.com
website www.johnstonsocietyoflondon.org
President Lord Harmsworth

Aims to study the life and works of Dr Johnson (1709–84), and to perpetuate his memory in the city of his adoption. Founded 1928.

Journalists' Charity

Dickens House, 35 Wathen Road, Dorking, Surrey RH4 1JY
tel (01306) 887511 *fax* (01306) 888212
email enquiries@journalistscharity.org.uk
website www.journalistscharity.org.uk
Director David Ilott

For the relief of hardship amongst journalists, their widows and dependants. Financial assistance and retirement housing are provided.

The Sheila Kaye-Smith Society

Secretary Christine Hayward, 22 The Cloisters, St John's Road, St Leonards-on-Sea, East Sussex TN37 6JT
tel (01424) 422139
Membership £8 p.a. single, £12 joint

Aims to stimulate and widen interest in the work of the Sussex writer and novelist, Sheila Kaye-Smith (1887–1956). Produces a Newsletter (3 p.a.) now incorporating *The Gleam* and occasional papers; also organises talks and an annual walk. Founded 1987.

Keats-Shelley Memorial Association

Bedford House, 76A Bedford Street, Leamington Spa CV32 5DT
tel (01926) 427400 *fax* (01926) 335133
Chairman Hon. Mrs H. Cullen, *Hon. Secretary* David Leigh-Hunt
Membership £15 p.a. minimum

Owns and supports house in Rome where John Keats died, as a museum open to the public; celebrates the poets Keats (1795–1821), Shelley (1792–1822) and Leigh Hunt (1784–1859). Regular meetings; poetry competitions; annual *Review;* 2 literary awards; and progress reports. Founded 1903.

Kent and Sussex Poetry Society

Contact John Arnold, 39 Rockington Way, Crowborough, East Sussex TN6 2NJ
tel (01892) 662781
email info@kentandsussexpoetrysociety.org
website www.kentandsussexpoetrysociety.org
Secretary Jo Hemmant
President Laurence Lerner, *Chairman* Sarah Salway
Membership £15 p.a. full, £10 country members/concessions

Based in Tunbridge Wells, the Society was formed to create a greater interest in poetry. Well-known poets address the Society, a Folio of members' work is produced and a full programme of recitals, discussions, competitions (see page 556) and readings is provided. Founded 1946.

The Kipling Society

Hon. Secretary Jane Keskar, 6 Clifton Road, London W9 1SS

email jmkeskar@btinternet.com
website www.kipling.org.uk
Membership £24 p.a., £12 under age 23

Aims to honour and extend the influence of Rudyard Kipling (1865–1936), to assist in the study of his writings, to hold discussion meetings, to publish a quarterly journal, and to maintain a Kipling Library in London and a Kipling Room in The Grange, Rottingdean, near Brighton.

The Charles Lamb Society

BM Elia, London WC1N 3XX
Chairman Nicholas Powell, *Membership Secretary* Cecilia Powell
Membership Personal: £18/$35 p.a. (single), £24 (double); Corporate: £24/$48 p.a.

Publishes the academic journal *The Charles Lamb Bulletin* (twice a year). The Society's extensive library of books and MSS by and about Charles Lamb (1775–1834) is housed at the Guildhall Library, Aldermanbury, London EC2P 2EJ. Founded 1935.

The Lancashire Authors' Association

General Secretary Michael Finney, 53 Loch Street, Orrell, Wigan, Lancs. WN5 0AN
tel (01942) 216748
Membership £15 p.a. single, £19.50 p.a. joint

For writers and lovers of Lancashire literature and history. Publishes *The Record* (quarterly). Founded 1909.

The D.H. Lawrence Society

Secretary Brenda Sumner, 1 Church Street, Swepstone, Leics. LE67 2SA
tel (01530) 207367
Membership £18 p.a. UK, £20 rest of world, £16 UK retired persons and students

Aims to bring together people interested in D.H. Lawrence (1885–1930), to encourage study of his work, and to provide information and guides for people visiting Eastwood. Founded 1974.

The T.E. Lawrence Society

PO Box 728, Oxford OX2 9ZJ
email memsec@telsociety.org.uk
website www.telsociety.org.uk
Membership £18 p.a., £23 overseas

Promotes the memory of T.E. Lawrence (1888–1935) and furthers knowledge by research into his life; publishes *Journal* (bi-annual) and *Newsletter* (quarterly). Founded 1985.

League of Canadian Poets

312–192 Spadina Avenue, Toronto, Ontario M5T 2C2, Canada
tel +1 416-504-1657 *fax* +1 416-504 0096
email joanna@poets.ca
website www.poets.ca
Executive Director Joanna Poblocka
Membership $185 p.a.

Aims to promote the interests of poets and to advance Canadian poetry in Canada and abroad. Administers 3 annual awards; runs National Poetry Month; publishes a newsletter and *Poetry Markets for Canadians, Who's Who in The League of Canadian Poets*, and *Poets in the Classroom* (teaching guide). Founded 1966.

Literature Wales

(formerly Academi)
Main Office 3rd Floor, Mount Stuart House, Mount Stuart Square, Cardiff CF10 5FQ
tel 029-2047 2266 *fax* 029-2049 2930
email post@literaturewales.org
Glyn Jones Centre, Wales Millennium Centre, Cardiff Bay, Cardiff CF10 5AL
tel 029-2047 2266 *fax* 029-2047 0691
email post@literaturewales.org
North West Wales Office Tŷ Newydd, Llanystumdwy, Cricieth, Gwynedd LL52 0LW
tel (01766) 522817 *fax* (01766) 523095
email tynewydd@literaturewales.org
website www.literaturewales.org
Chief Executive Lleucu Siencyn

The national organisation responsible for developing and promoting literature. It is made up of Yr Academi Gymreig (Welsh Academy), the Society for Writers of Wales, and Tŷ Newydd Writers' Centre. Its activities include Wales Book of the Year, the National Poet of Wales, Writers on Tour funding scheme, writing courses at Tŷ Newydd, Translators' House Wales, funding and advice for writers, the BayLit and Tŷ Newydd festivals, Young People's Writing Squads and fieldworkers in the south Wales valleys and north Wales.

Literature Wales represents the interests of Welsh writers in all genres and languages, both inside Wales and internationally. It offers advice, support, bursaries, mentoring and opportunities to meet other writers. It works with the support of the Arts Council of Wales and the Welsh Assembly Government. It is one of the resident organisations of the Wales Millennium Centre, where it runs the Glyn Jones Centre.

Little Theatre Guild of Great Britain

Guild Secretary Caroline Chapman, Satley House, Satley, near Bishop Auckland, Co. Durham DL13 4HU
tel (01388) 730042
website www.littletheatreguild.org

Aims to promote closer cooperation amongst the little theatres constituting its membership; to act as coordinating and representative body on behalf of the little theatres; to maintain and advance the highest standards in the art of theatre; and to assist in encouraging the establishment of other little theatres.

Magazines Canada (Canadian Magazine Publishers Association)

425 Adelaide Street West, Suite 700, Toronto, Ontario M5V 3C1, Canada

tel +1 416-504-0274 *fax* +1 416-504-0437
email friends@magazinescanada.ca
website www.magazinescanada.ca
Chief Executive Mark Jamison

The Marlowe Society

Honorary Chairman Valerie Colin-Russ, 27 Melbourne Court, Little Venice, London W9 1BJ
tel 020-7289 2535
email valerie.colin-russ@marlowesociety.org
Newsletter Editor Roger Hards, Parkhyde, 70 Park Road, Congresbury, North Somerset BS49 5HH
tel (01934) 834780
email roger.hards@marlowesociety.org
website www.marlowe-society.org
Membership £18 p.a., £15 concessions, £30 joint (couple), £300 life.

Registered charity that aims to extend appreciation and widen recognition of Christopher Marlowe (1564–93) as the foremost poet and dramatist preceding Shakespeare, whose development he influenced. Holds meetings and cultural visits, and issues a bi-annual magazine and an occasional research journal. Founded 1955.

The John Masefield Society

Chairman Peter J.R. Carter, The Frith, Ledbury, Herefordshire HR8 1LW
tel (01531) 633800
email carter-p@btconnect.com
website www.ies.sas.ac.uk/cmps/projects/masefield/society/jmsws.htm
Membership £5 p.a., £10 overseas, £8 family/institution

Aims to stimulate interest in, and public awareness and enjoyment of, the life and works of the poet John Masefield (1878–1967). Holds an annual lecture and other, less formal, readings and gatherings; publishes an annual journal and frequent newsletters. Founded 1992.

Master Photographers Association

Jubilee House, 1 Chancery Lane, Darlington, Co. Durham DL1 5QP
tel (01325) 356555 *fax* (01325) 357813
email general@mpauk.com
website www.thempa.com
Membership £165 p.a.

Exists to promote and protect professional photographers. Members qualify for awards of Licentiate, Associate and Fellowship.

The Media Society

website www.themediasociety.com
President Geraldine Sharpe-Newton
Membership £35 p.a.

Exists to promote and encourage collective and independent research into the standards, performance, organisation and economics of the media and hold regular discussions, debates, etc on subjects of topical or special interest and concern to print and broadcast journalists and others working in or with the media. Founded 1973.

Mediawatch-UK

(formerly National Viewers' and Listeners' Association)
Director Vivienne Pattison, 3 Willow House, Kennington Road, Ashford, Kent TN24 0NR
tel (01233) 633936 *fax* (01233) 633836
email info@mediawatchuk.org
website www.mediawatchuk.org
Membership £15 p.a.

Aims to encourage viewers and listeners to react effectively to programme content; to initiate and stimulate public discussion and parliamentary debate concerning the effects of broadcasting, and other mass media, on the individual, the family and society; to secure effective legislation to control obscenity and pornography in the media. Founded 1965.

Medical Writers Group – see The Society of Authors, page 497

The Memoir Writing Club

tel +353 (0)86 2523428
email office@thememoirwritingclub.com
website www.thememoirwritingclub.com
Founder & Director Irene Graham

Created from Irene Graham's long established writing workshops using right-brain/left-brain learning techniques, the Memoir Writing Club is an online membership writing community providing a memoir writing course, memoir workbook, audio tutorials, online publishing, writing rooms, book club, writers' network, memoir critique, story consultancy, memoir archive and alumni benefits. Founded 2008.

William Morris Society

Kelmscott House, 26 Upper Mall, London W6 9TA
tel 020-8741 3735 *fax* 020-8748 5207
email uk@morrissociety.org
website www.williammorrissociety.org
Secretary Phillippa Bennett

Aims to spread knowledge of the life, work and ideas of William Morris (1834–96); publishes *Newsletter* (quarterly) and *Journal* (2 p.a.). Library and collections open to the public Thurs and Sat, 2–5pm. Founded 1955.

Music Publishers Association Ltd

6th Floor, British Music House, 26 Berners Street, London W1T 3LR
tel 020-7580 0126 *fax* 020-7637 3929
email info@mpaonline.org.uk
website www.mpaonline.org.uk
Chief Executive Stephen Navin
Membership Details on request

Trade organisation representing over 200 UK music publisher members: promotes and safeguards its members' interests in copyright, trade and related matters. Sub-committees and groups deal with particular interests. Founded 1881.

National Acrylic Painters' Association (NAPA)

49 Cortsway, Greasby, Wirral, Merseyside CH49 2NA
tel 0151 678 4034
email hillhouse_david@hotmail.com
website www.napauk.org, www.isap-usa.com
President Alwyn Crawshaw, *Director/Treasurer/ Exhibitions* David Hillhouse, *Founder* Kenneth J. Hodgson

Promotes interest in, and encourages excellence and innovation in, the work of painters in acrylic. Holds an annual exhibition and regional shows: awards are made. Worldwide membership. Publishes a newsletter known as the *International NAPA Newspages*. Founded 1985; American Division established 1995, now known as International Society of Acrylic Painters (ISAP).

National Association of Press Agencies (NAPA)

Suite 302, 3rd Floor, Queens Dock Business Centre, 67–83 Norfolk Street, Liverpool L1 0BG
tel 0870 240 0311 *fax* 0151 708 8079
email enquiries@napa.org.uk
website www.napa.org.uk
Directors Denis Cassidy, Chris Johnson, Matt Bell, Mark Solomons
Membership £250 p.a.

A network of independent, established and experienced press agencies serving newspapers, magazines, TV and radio networks. Founded 1983.

National Association of Writers' Groups

Secretary Chris Huck, PO Box 9891, Market Harborough LE16 0FU
tel (01484) 844056
email secretary@nawg.co.uk
website www.nawg.co.uk
Membership £40 p.a. per group; £20 Associates (individuals)

Aims 'to advance the education of the general public throughout the UK, including the Channel Islands, by promoting the study and art of writing in all its aspects'. Publishes *LNK*, a bi-monthly magazine. Festival of Writing held annually in September. New members always welcome. Founded 1995.

National Campaign for the Arts (NCA)

1 Kingly Street, London W1B 5PA
tel 020-7287 3777 *fax* 020-7287 4777
email nca@artscampaign.org.uk
website www.artscampaign.org.uk
Acting Director Selina Mehra

The UK's only independent lobbying organisation representing all the arts. It provides a voice for the arts world in all its diversity and seeks to safeguard, promote and develop the arts and win public and political recognition for their importance as a key element in our national culture. The NCA is a membership organisation.

National Council for the Training of Journalists (NCTJ)

The New Granary, Station Road, Newport, Essex CB11 3PL
tel (01799) 544014 *fax* (01799) 544015
email info@nctj.com
website www.nctj.com

A registered charity which aims to advance the education and training of trainee journalists, including press photographers. Full-time courses run at 40 colleges/universities in the UK. Distance learning courses also available in newspaper and magazine journalism and sub-editing. A variety of short courses are also available. Founded 1951.

National Literacy Trust

68 South Lambeth Road, London SW8 1RL
tel 020-7587 1842
email contact@literacytrust.org.uk
website www.literacytrust.org.uk

An independent charity that aims to help change lives through literacy. It campaigns to improve public understanding of the importance of literacy, as well as delivering projects and working in partnership to reach those most in need of support.

National Society for Education in Art and Design

3 Mason's Wharf, Potley Lane, Corsham, Wilts. SN13 9FY
tel (01225) 810134 *fax* (01225) 812730
website www.nsead.org
General Secretary Lesley Butterworth MA, BA (HONS),

The leading national authority concerned with art, craft and design across all phases of education in the UK. Offers the benefits of membership of a professional association, a learned society and a trade union. Has representatives on National and Regional Committees concerned with Art and Design Education. Publishes *International Journal of Art and Design Education* (3 p.a.; Wiley Blackwell) and *AD* magazine for schools. Founded 1888.

National Society of Painters, Sculptors and Printmakers

Hon. Secretary Gwen Spencer, 122 Copse Hill, London SW20 0NL
tel 020-8946 7878
website www.nationalsociety.org

An annual exhibition at the Menier Gallery, Southwark Street, London SE1. An open exhibition and artists are welcome to apply for membership. Newsletter (2 p.a.) for members. Founded 1930.

National Union of Journalists

Head Office Headland House,
308–312 Gray's Inn Road, London WC1X 8DP
tel 020-7843 3700 *fax* 020-7837 8143
email info@nuj.org.uk
website www.nuj.org.uk

Trade union for journalists and photographers, including freelances, with 38,000 members and 136 branches in the UK, Republic of Ireland, Paris, Brussels and the Netherlands. It covers the newspaper press, news agencies, magazines, broadcasting, periodical and book publishing, public relations departments and consultancies, information services and new media. The NUJ mediates disputes, provides training and general and legal advice. Official publications: *The Journalist* (bi-monthly), the online *Freelance Directory* and *Freelance Fees Guide*, *The NUJ Code of Conduct* and policy pamphlets.

National Viewers' and Listeners' Association – see Mediawatch-UK

NCTJ – see National Council for the Training of Journalists (NCTJ)

The Edith Nesbit Society

21 Churchfields, West Malling, Kent ME19 6RJ
email edithnesbit@googlemail.com
website www.edithnesbit.co.uk
Membership £7 p.a., £14 organisations/overseas

Aims to promote an interest in the life and works of Edith Nesbit (1858–1924) by means of talks, a regular newsletter and and other publications, and visits to relevant places. Founded 1996.

New English Art Club

17 Carlton House Terrace, London SW1Y 5BD
tel 020-7930 6844 *fax* 020-7839 7830
email alexfowler@newenglishartclub.co.uk
website www.newenglishartclub.co.uk
President Jason Bowyer

For all those interested in the art of painting, and the promotion of fine arts. Open Annual Exhibition at the Mall Galleries, The Mall, London SW1, open to all working in painting, drawing, pastels and prints.

New Writers UK

PO Box 9310, Nottingham NG5 0DZ
tel 07969 516158
email john@newwritersuk.co.uk, julie@newwritersuk.co.uk
website www.newwritersuk.co.uk
Chairman John Baird, *Founder & President* Julie Malone
Membership £30 p.a.

Created to support and advise independently published authors and those who have been published by small mainstream publishers who do not have financial backing or marketing to promote their books. This is an organisation of authors working on a voluntary basis to assist other authors and encourage imaginative literacy in young people and adults. NWUK holds a number of events throughout the year and produces a quarterly newsletter distributed nationally. Established 2006.

New Writing North

PO Box 1277, Newcastle upon Tyne NE99 5BP
tel 0191 233 3850 *fax* 0191 447 7686
email office@newwritingnorth.com
website www.newwritingnorth.com
Director Claire Malcolm

The literature development agency for the North East. Offers advice and support to writers of poetry, prose and plays. See website for details. Founded 1996.

New Writing South

9 Jew Street, Brighton, East Sussex BN1 1UT
tel (01273) 735353
email admin@newwritingsouth.com
website www.newwritingsouth.com
Director Chris Taylor
Membership £45/£26 concs. p.a./£20 under 25s/ students p.a.

Supports and encourages writers at all stages of their careers and new writing in all its forms. Activities include a script-reading service, workshops, mentoring, fortnightly *E News*, masterclasses and events. New Writing South is open to all creative writers in south east England.

New Zealand Writers Guild

PO Box 47 886, Ponsonby, Auckland 1144, New Zealand
tel +64 (0)9 360 1408 *fax* +64 (0)9 360 1409
email info@nzwg.org.nz
website www.nzwritersguild.org.nz
Membership $175–$400 p.a. full, $125 associate

Aims to represent the interests of New Zealand writers (TV, film, radio and theatre); to establish and improve minimum conditions of work and rates of compensation for writers; to provide professional services for members. Founded 1975.

The Newspaper Publishers Association Ltd

8th Floor, St Andrew's House,
18–20 St Andrew Street, London EC4A 3AY
tel 020-7632 7430 *fax* 020-7632 7431
website www.n-p-a.org.uk

Newspaper Society

8th Floor, St Andrew's House,
18–20 St Andrew Street, London EC4A 3AY
tel 020-7632 7400 *fax* 020-7632 7401

email ns@newspapersoc.org.uk
website www.newspapersoc.org.uk
Director David Newell

Outdoor Writers and Photographers Guild

83 Glenshiels Avenue, Hoddlesden, Darwen, Lancs. BB3 3LS
tel (01254) 773097
email secretary@owpg.org.uk
website www.owpg.org.uk
Membership £80 p.a.

Association of the leading practitioners in outdoor media; represents members' interests to representative bodies in the outdoor industry; circulates members with news of media opportunities; provides a forum for members to meet colleagues and others in the outdoor industry. Presents annual literary and photographic awards. Members include writers, journalists, broadcasters, illustrators, photographers, editors and publishers. Founded 1980.

Wilfred Owen Association

29 Arthur Road, London SW19 7DN
website www.wilfredowen.org.uk
Membership £10 p.a. individual, £15 p.a. couple, £8 concessions, £13 couple concession, £15 overseas, £20 overseas couple; special rates for joint membership of The Wilfred Owen Association and the Siegfried Sassoon Fellowship

Aims to commemorate the life and work of Wilfred Owen (1893–1918), and to encourage and enhance appreciation of his work through visits, public events and a bi-annual journal. Founded 1989.

Oxford Bibliographical Society

Bodleian Library, Broad Street, Oxford OX1 3BG
email membership@oxbibsoc.org.uk
Honorary Secretary Dr Christina Neagu, Christ Church, Oxford
website www.oxbibsoc.org.uk
Membership £20 p.a.

Exists to encourage bibliographical research. Founded 1922.

Pact (Producers' Alliance for Cinema and Television)

3rd Floor, Fitzrovia House,
153–157 Cleveland Street, London W1T 6QW
tel 020-7380 8230
email info@pact.co.uk
website www.pact.co.uk

The UK trade association that represents and promotes the commercial interests of independent feature film, television, animation and interactive media companies. Headquartered in London, it has regional representation throughout the UK, in order to support its members. An effective lobbying organisation, it has regular and constructive dialogues with government, regulators, public agencies and opinion formers on all issues affecting its members and contributes to key public policy debates on the media industry, both in the UK and in Europe. It negotiates terms of trade with all public service broadcasters in the UK and supports members in their business dealings with cable and satellite channels. It also lobbies for a properly structured and funded UK film industry and maintains close contact with the UK Film Council and other relevant film organisations and government departments.

The Pastel Society

17 Carlton House Terrace, London SW1Y 5BD
tel 020-7930 6844 *fax* 020-7839 7830
email info@mallgalleries.com
website www.thepastelsociety.org.uk
President John Ivor Stewart

Pastel and drawings in pencil or chalk. Annual Exhibition open to all artists working in dry media held at the Mall Galleries, The Mall, London SW1. Members elected from approved candidates' list. Founded 1899.

PEN International

Brownlow House, 50–51 High Holborn, London WC1V 6ER
tel 020-7405 0338 *fax* 020-7405 0339
email info@internationalpen.org.uk
website www.internationalpen.org.uk
International President John Ralston Saul, *International Secretary*, Hori Takeaki
Membership Apply to Centres

A world association of writers. PEN was founded by C.A. Dawson Scott under the presidency of John Galsworthy, to promote friendship and understanding between writers and to defend freedom of expression within and between all nations. The initials PEN stand for Poets, Playwrights, Editors, Essayists, Novelists – but membership is open to all writers of standing (including translators), whether men or women, without distinction of creed or race, who subscribe to these fundamental principles. PEN takes no part in state or party politics.

Membership of any one Centre implies membership of all Centres; at present 145 autonomous Centres exist throughout the world. Associate membership is available for writers not yet eligible for full membership and for persons connected with literature. Founded 1921.

English PEN Centre

email enquiries@englishpen.org
website www.englishpen.org

Scottish PEN Centre

email info@scottishpen.org
website www.scottishpen.org

Irish PEN Centre
email info@irishpen.com.com
website www.irishpen.com

The Personal Managers' Association Ltd

27 College Gardens, Brighton, BN2 1HP
tel 0845 602 7191
email info@thepma.com
website www.thepma.com

Membership organisation for agents representing talent in film, television and theatre.

The Picture Research Association

email chair@picture-research.org.uk
website www.picture-research.org.uk

Professional organisation of picture researchers and picture editors. Its aims are:

- to promote the recognition of picture research, management, editing, picture buying and supplying as a profession requiring particular skills and knowledge;
- to bring together all those involved in the picture profession and provide a forum for information exchange and interaction;
- to encourage publishers, TV and video production organisations, internet companies, and any other users of images to use the PRA freelance register and engage a member of PRA to obtain them, thus ensuring that professional standards are maintained;
- to advise those specifically wishing to embark on a profession in the research and supply of pictures for all types of visual media information, providing guidelines and standards in so doing.

Player–Playwrights

Secretary Peter Thompson, 9 Hillfield Park, Muswell Hill, London N10 3QT
email publicity@playerplaywrights.co.uk
website www.playerplaywrights.co.uk
Membership £12 in first year and £8 thereafter (plus £2 per attendance)

Meets on Monday evenings downstairs in the Phoenix Artists Club, 1 Phoenix Street, Charing Cross Road, London WC2H 0DT. The society reads, performs and discusses plays and scripts submitted by members, with a view to assisting the writers in improving and marketing their work. Newcomers and new acting members are always welcome. Founded 1948.

The Poetry Book Society – see page 346

The Poetry Society – see page 347

The Beatrix Potter Society

c/o The Lodge, Salisbury Avenue, Harpenden, Herts. AL5 2PS
tel (01582) 769755
email beatrixpottersociety@tiscali.co.uk
website www.beatrixpottersociety.org.uk
Membership £25 p.a. UK (£31 overseas), £30/£36 commercial/institutional

Promotes the study and appreciation of the life and works of Beatrix Potter (1866–1943) as author, artist, diarist, farmer and conservationist. Regular lecture meetings, conferences and events in the UK and USA. Quarterly newsletter. Small publishing programme. Founded 1980.

The Powys Society

Hon. Secretary Chris Thomas, Flat D, 87 Ledbury Road, London W11 2AG
tel 020-7243 0168
email chris.d.thomas@hotmail.co.uk
website www.powys-society.org
Membership (from 2013) £22 p.a. UK (£26 overseas)

Aims to promote the greater public recognition and enjoyment of the writings, thought and contribution to the arts of the Powys family, particularly John Cowper (1872–1963), Theodore (1875–1953) and Llewelyn (1884–1939) Powys, and the many other family members and their close friends. Publishes an annual scholarly journal (*The Powys Journal*) and 3 newsletters per year as well as books by and about the Powys family, and holds an annual weekend conference in August, as well as organising other activities throughout the year. Founded 1967.

The Press Complaints Commission

Halton House, 20–23 Holborn, London EC1N 2JD
tel 020-7831 0022, 0845 600 2757 (helpline)
fax 020-7831 0025
email complaints@pcc.org.uk
website www.pcc.org.uk

The PCC is an independent body which administers the system of self-regulation for the press. It does so primarily by dealing with complaints, framed within the terms of the Editors' Code of Practice, about the editorial content of newspapers and magazines (and their websites, including editorial audio-visual material) and the conduct of journalists. It can also assist individuals by representing their interests to editors in advance of an article about them being published. Founded 1991.

The J.B. Priestley Society

Secretary Rod Slater, 24 St Lawrence Quay, Salford Quays, Manchester M50 3XT
tel 0161 872 0332
email rodslater@btinternet.com
Membership £12 p.a. single, £18 family, £7 concessions

Aims to widen the knowledge, understanding and appreciation of the published works of J.B. Priestley (1894–1984) and to promote the study of his life and career. Holds lectures and discussions and shows films. Publishes a newsletter and journal. Organises walks to areas with Priestley connections, Annual Priestley Night and other social events. Founded 1997.

Printmakers Council

Ground Floor Unit, 23 Blue Anchor Lane, London SE16 3UL
tel/fax 020-7237 6789
email printpmc@googlemail.com
website www.printmakerscouncil.com
Acting Chair Steve Mumberson
Membership £65 p.a., £30 students

Artist-led group which aims to promote the use of both traditional and innovative printmaking techniques by:

- holding exhibitions of prints;
- providing information on prints and printmaking to both its membership and the public;
- encouraging cooperation and exchanges between members, other associations and interested individuals. Founded 1965.

Private Libraries Association

Leader House, Carfraemill, nr Oxton, Lauderdale TD2 6RA
website www.plabooks.org
President Keith Fletcher, *Hon. Journal Editors* David Chambers, David Butcher
Membership £30 p.a.

International society of book collectors and private libraries. Publications include *The Private Library* (quarterly), annual *Private Press Books*, and other books on book collecting. Founded 1956.

Professional Cartoonists' Organisation

65 Victoria Road, Cambridge CB4 3BW
tel (01223) 517737 *fax* 020-7900 1677
email info@procartoonists.org
website www.procartoonists.org, www.thebloghorn.org
Secretary Clive Goddard, 25 Paget Road, Oxford OX4 2TB
Membership £80 p.a.

An organisation dedicated to the promotion of UK cartoon art in new media and old. Cartoons provide much-needed humour and satire to society and are a universally appreciated, effective method of communication for business. The organisation showcases UK cartoonists via its magazine, *Foghorn*, cartoon news blog (*Bloghorn*), and public events such as the annual Big Draw and cartoon festivals. Established 2006.

Professional Publishers Association

Queens House, 28 Kingsway, Holborn, London WC2B 6JR
tel 020-7404 4166
email info1@ppa.co.uk
website www.ppa.co.uk
Chief Executive Barry McIlheney

PRS for Music

Copyright House, 29–33 Berners Street, London W1T 3AB
tel 020-7580 5544 *fax* 020-7306 4455
website www.prsformusic.co.uk

The Publishers Association

29B Montague Street, London WC1B 5BW
tel 020-7691 9191 *fax* 020-7691 9199
email mail@publishers.org.uk
website www.publishers.org.uk
Ceo Richard Mollet, *President* Rod Bristow, *Director of International & Trade Services* Emma House, *Director of Educational, Academic & Professional Publishing* Graham Taylor, *Operations Director* Mark Wharton

Founded 1896.

Publishers Association of New Zealand (PANZ)

4 Whetu Place, Mairangi Bay, Auckland 0632, New Zealand
tel +64 (0)9 477 5589 *fax* +64 (0)9 477 5570
email anne@publishers.org.nz
website www.publishers.org.nz
Association Director Anne de Lautour

Publishers' Association of South Africa (PASA)

PO Box 18223, Wynberg, 7824, South Africa
tel +27 (0)21 762 9083 *fax* +27 (0)21 762 2763
email pasa@publishsa.co.za
website www.publishsa.co.za

Publishers Licensing Society Ltd (PLS)

37–41 Gower Street, London WC1E 6HH
tel 020-7299 7730 *fax* 020-7299 7780
email pls@pls.org.uk
website www.pls.org.uk
Chairman Mark Millar, *Chief Executive* Sarah Faulder

PLS serves the UK publishing industry by working to protect publishers' rights, and leads on industry-wide initiatives involving rights management and collective licensing. It is a not-for-profit organisation and has mandates from over 2,700 publishers. PLS is dedicated to protecting and strengthening the copyright framework by motivating good practice in rights management. One of the most important ways it does this is by facilitating licence solutions that protect rights and provide revenue for publishers through collective licensing. PLS strives to ensure a high level of service that works on behalf of publishers and readers to uphold copyright legislation. Founded 1981.

Publishers Publicity Circle

Secretary/Treasurer 65 Airedale Avenue, London W4 2NN
tel 020-8994 1881
email ppcemail@virgimedia.com
website www.publisherspublicitycircle.co.uk

Enables all book publicists to meet and share information regularly. Monthly meetings provide a forum for press journalists, TV and radio researchers and producers to meet publicists collectively. Awards are presented for the best PR campaigns. Monthly newsletter includes recruitment advertising. Founded 1955.

Publishing Ireland – Foilsiú Éireann

25 Denzille Lane Dublin 2, Republic of Ireland
tel +353 (0)1 6394868
email info@publishingireland.com
website www.publishingireland.com
Executive Director Jean Harrington

Publishing Scotland

(formerly Scottish Publishers Association)
Scottish Book Centre, 137 Dundee Street, Edinburgh EH11 1BG
tel 0131 228 6866 *fax* 0131 228 3220
email enquiries@publishingscotland.org
website www.publishingscotland.org
Chair Caroline Gorham, *Chief Executive* Marion Sinclair

Founded 1973.

ReadWell

26 Nailsworth Mills, Avening Road, Nailsworth, Glos. GL6 0BS
tel 0845 606 1151
website www.readwell.org.uk

Books and stories are important for the well-being of all children and are especially important for children in hospital. As well as helping to prevent children falling behind in their school work while they are in hospital, books act as a diversion, they entertain, reduce stress, reassure and comfort. ReadWell is a new initiative from Read for Good which provides books and stories to children in hospital. Currently in 3 hospitals in the UK, with hopes to expand, ReadWell provides a mobile book unit for hospitals and fills it with new books every month. In addition, a storyteller visits hospitals each month and travels around wards entertaining and comforting young patients.

Regional Arts Offices – see Arts Council England

Ridley Art Society

50 Crowborough Road, London SW17 9QQ
tel 020-8682 1212
President Ken Howard RA

Represents a wide variety of attitudes towards the making of art. In recent years has sought to encourage younger artists. At least one Central London Members' exhibition a year. Founded 1889.

The Romantic Novelists' Association

Chairman Anne Ashurst
Hon. Secretary Jay Dixon
email rnahonsec@romanticnovelistsassociation.org
website www.romanticnovelistsassociation.org

Aims to promote romantic fiction and encourage good writing within the genre. Represents more than 700 writers, agents, editors and other publishing professionals. See also page 563.

Royal Academy of Arts

Burlington House, Piccadilly, London W1J 0BD
tel 020-7300 8000
website www.royalacademy.org.uk
President Christopher Le Brun, *Keeper* Eileen Cooper

Royal Academicians are elected from the most distinguished artists in the UK. Holds major loan exhibitions throughout the year including the Annual Summer Exhibition (June–Aug). Also runs Royal Academy Schools for 60 postgraduate students in painting and sculpture.

Royal Birmingham Society of Artists

RBSA Gallery, 4 Brook Street, St Paul's, Birmingham B3 1SA
tel 0121 236 4353
email rbsagallery@rbsa.org.uk
website www.rbsa.org.uk
Membership Friends £33 p.a.

The Royal Birmingham Society of Artists (RBSA) is an artist-led charity, which supports artists and promotes engagement with the visual arts through a range of exclusive activities: exhibitions, workshops, demonstrations and other events. The RBSA Gallery is owned by the Society, making it one of the rare few galleries to be owned by artists and run for artists. It has a changing programme of exhibitions on 2 floors and on the ground floor cafe and craft wall spaces. The ground floor also houses the RBSA Craft Gallery, which has established a reputation as the place to find unique handmade jewellery. Entrance is free. See the website for further details.

Royal Institute of Oil Painters

17 Carlton House Terrace, London SW1Y 5BD
tel 020-7930 6844 *fax* 020-7839 7830
email enquiries@theroi.org.uk
website www.theroi.org.uk
President Peter Wileman

Promotes and encourages the art of painting in oils. Open Annual Exhibition at the Mall Galleries, The Mall, London SW1.

Royal Institute of Painters in Water Colours

17 Carlton House Terrace, London SW1Y 5BD
tel 020-7930 6844 *fax* 020-7839 7830
website www.royalinstituteofpaintersinwatercolours.org
President Ronald Maddox Hon. RWS
Membership Elected from approved candidates' list

Promotes the appreciation of watercolour painting in its traditional and contemporary forms, primarily by means of an annual exhibition at the Mall Galleries,

The Mall, London SW1 of members' and non-members' work and also by members' exhibitions at selected venues in Britain and abroad. Founded 1831.

The Royal Literary Fund

3 Johnson's Court, off Fleet Street, London EC4A 3EA
tel 020-7353 7159 *fax* 020-7353 1350
email rlitfund@btconnect.com
website www.rlf.org.uk
President Ronald Harwood CBE, *General Secretary* Eileen Gunn

Founded in 1790, the Fund is the oldest charity serving literature, set up to help writers and their families who face hardship. It does not offer grants to writers who can earn their living in other ways, nor does it provide financial support for writing projects. But it sustains authors who have for one reason or another fallen on hard times – illness, family misfortune, or sheer loss of writing form. Applicants must have published work of approved literary merit. The literary claim of every new applicant must be accepted by the General Committee before the question of need can be considered.

The Royal Musical Association

Executive Officer Dr Jeffrey Dean, 4 Chandos Road, Chorlton-cum-Hardy, Manchester M21 0ST
tel 0161 861 7542 *fax* 0161 861 7543
email jeffrey.dean@stingrayoffice.com
website www.rma.ac.uk

The Royal Photographic Society

Fenton House, 122 Wells Road, Bath BA2 3AH
tel (01225) 325733
email reception@rps.org
website www.rps.org

Membership organisation open to everyone which promotes the art and science of photography and digital imaging. It acts as an advocate for photographers and photography. Publishes *The RPS Journal* (10 p.a.) and *Imaging Science Journal* (quarterly). Founded 1853.

The Royal Scottish Academy of Art and Architecture

The Mound, Edinburgh EH2 2EL
tel 0131 225 6671
email info@royalscottishacademy.org
website www.royalscottishacademy.org
Director, Colin R. Greenslade

Led by eminent artists and architects, the Royal Scottish Academy (RSA) is an independent voice for cultural advocacy and one of the largest supporters of artists in Scotland. The Academy administers a number of scholarships, awards and residencies and has an historic collection of Scottish artworks and an archive, recognised by the Scottish Government as being of national significance. The Academy cherishes its independence from local or national government funding, relying instead on bequests, legacies, sponsorship and earned income. This allows the RSA the autonomy to develop and present a wide range of initiatives without restriction. For information on open submission exhibitions, artist scholarships and residencies, or to discuss making a bequest to the Academy, contact the RSA office or visit the website. Founded 1826.

The Royal Society

6–9 Carlton House Terrace, London SW1Y 5AG
tel 020-7451 2500 *fax* 020-7930 2170
email library@royalsociety.org
website royalsociety.org
President Sir Paul Nurse Kt, PRS, *Treasurer* Sir Peter Williams CBE, FRS, *Biological Secretary* Dame Jean Thomas DBE FRS, *Physical Secretary* Prof. John Pethica FRS, *Foreign Secretary* Prof. Martyn Poliakoff FRS, *Executive Director* Dr Julie Maxton

The Royal Society for Asian Affairs

2 Belgrave Square, London SW1X 8PJ
tel 020-7235 5122 *fax* 020-7259 6771
email info@rsaa.org.uk
website www.rsaa.org.uk
President The Lord Denman CBE, MC TD, *Chairman of Council* Sir David John KCMG, *Secretary* Colonel Neil Porter
Membership £70 p.a. London, £60 if more than 60 miles from London and overseas, £10 up to age 25

For the study of all Asia present and recent past; fortnightly lectures, etc; library. Publishes *Asian Affairs* (3 p.a.), free to members. Founded 1901.

Royal Society for the Encouragement of Arts, Manufactures and Commerce (RSA)

8 John Adam Street, London WC2N 6EZ
tel 020-7930 5115
email general@rsa.org.uk
website www.thersa.org

Works to remove the barriers to social progress, driving ideas, innovation and social change through an ambitious programme of projects, events and lectures. Supported by over 27,000 Fellows, an international network of influencers and innovators from every field and background across the UK and overseas. Welcomes women and men of any nationality and background who will support the organisation's aims. Its activities are detailed in the *RSA Journal*. Founded 1754.

Royal Society of British Artists

17 Carlton House Terrace, London SW1Y 5BD
tel 020-7930 6844 *fax* 020-7839 7830
email info@mallgalleries.com
website www.royalsocietyofbritishartists.org.uk
President James Horton

Incorporated by Royal Charter for the purpose of encouraging the study and practice of the arts of painting, sculpture and architectural designs. Annual Open Exhibition at the Mall Galleries, The Mall, London SW1, open to artists working in any 2- or 3-dimensional medium.

Royal Society of Literature

Somerset House, Strand, London WC2R 1LA
tel 020-7845 4676 *fax* 020-7845 4679
email info@rslit.org
website www.rslit.org
Membership Secretary Hazel Tsoi-Wiles
Membership £50 p.a.

For the promotion of literature and encouragement of writers by way of lectures, discussions, readings, and by publications. Administers the VS Pritchett Memorial Prize, the Royal Society of Literature Ondaatje Prize, and the Royal Society of Literature/ Jerwood Awards. Founded 1820.

Royal Society of Marine Artists

17 Carlton House Terrace, London SW1Y 5BD
tel 020-7930 6844 *fax* 020-7839 7830
email info@rsma-web.co.uk
website www.rsma-web.co.uk
President David Howell

Aims to promote and encourage marine painting. Open Annual Exhibition at the Mall Galleries, The Mall, London SW1 for any artists whose main interest is the sea, or tidal waters, or some object essentially connected therewith.

The Royal Society of Miniature Painters, Sculptors and Gravers

email info@royal-miniature-society.org.uk
website www.royal-miniature-society.org.uk
President Elisabeth R. Meek, PRMS, PPSWA, HS, FRSA,
Executive Secretary Patricial Houchell
Membership By selection and standard of work over a period of years (ARMS associate, RMS full member)

Annual Open Exhibition in October at the Mall Galleries, The Mall, London SW1. Hand in August; schedules available in July (send sae). Applications and enquiries to the Executive Secretary. Founded 1895.

Royal Society of Painter-Printmakers

Bankside Gallery, 48 Hopton Street, London SE1 9JH
tel 020-7928 7521
email info@banksidegallery.com
website www.banksidegallery.com
President Bren Unwin PRE
Membership Open to British and overseas artists. An election of Associates is held annually; for particulars apply to the Secretary. Friends membership is open to all those interested in artists' original printmaking

Organises workshops and lectures on original printmaking. Holds two members' exhibitions per year. Founded 1880.

Royal Society of Portrait Painters

17 Carlton House Terrace, London SW1Y 5BD
tel 020-7930 6844 *fax* 020-7839 7830
email enquiries@therp.co.uk
website www.therp.co.uk
President Alastair Adams

Annual Exhibition at the Mall Galleries, The Mall, London SW1, of members' work and that of selected non-members. Four high-profile artists' awards are made: the Ondaatje Prize for Portraiture (£10,000), the De Laszlo Prize (£3,000), the Prince of Wales's Award for Portrait Drawing (£2,000), the Changing Faces Prize (£2,000). Also commissions consultancy service. Founded 1891.

Royal Television Society

7th Floor, Kildare House, 3 Dorset Rise, London EC4Y 8EN
tel 020-7822-2810
email info@rts.org.uk
website www.rts.org.uk

The leading forum for discussion and debate on all aspects of the TV community. In a fast changing sector, it reflects the full range of perspectives and views. Holds awards, conferences, seminars, lectures and workshops. Founded 1927.

Royal Watercolour Society

Bankside Gallery, 48 Hopton Street, London SE1 9JH
tel 020-7928 7521
email info@banksidegallery.com
website www.banksidegallery.com
President Thomas Plunkett, PRWS, Hon RE
Membership Open to British and overseas artists; election of Associates held annually. Friends membership is open to all those interested in watercolour painting

Arranges lectures and courses on watercolour paintings; holds an annual open exhibition in February. Exhibitions in the spring and autumn. Founded 1804.

Royal West of England Academy

Queens Road, Clifton, Bristol BS8 1PX
tel 0117 973 5129 *fax* 0117 923 7874
email info@rwa.org.uk
website www.rwa.org.uk
President Derek Balmer

An art academy/gallery/museum whose objectives are to advance the education of the public in the fine arts and in particular to promote the appreciation and practice of the fine arts and to encourage and develop talent in the fine arts. Founded 1844.

The Ruskin Society

Membership Secretary and Treasurer The Hon. Mrs Catherine Edwards, The Old Brewhouse, 20 Cole Green. Nr Hertford SG14 2NL
email secretary@theruskinsociety.com
website www.theruskinsociety.com
Membership £10 p.a.

Aims to encourage a wider understanding of John Ruskin (1819–1900) and his contemporaries. Organises lectures and events which seek to explain to the public the nature of Ruskin's theories and to place these in a modern context. Affiliated to the Ruskin Foundation. Founded 1997.

SAA (Society for All Artists)

PO Box 50, Newark, Notts. NG23 5GY
tel 0845 877 0775 *fax* 0845 300 7753
email info@saa.co.uk
website www.saa.co.uk
Membership from £27.50 p.a.

Aims to encourage and inspire all artists. Members range from complete beginners to professionals. SAA is the largest art society with over 47,000 members, and welcomes new members. Membership includes paintings insurance for exhibitions and third party public liability, discounted art materials from the society's *Home Shop* catalogue and the *Paint* newsletter (bi-monthly). Founded 1992.

The Malcolm Saville Society

35 Chapel Road, Penketh, Warrington WA5 2NG
email mystery@witchend.com
website www.witchend.com
Membership £10 p.a. (£12.50 Europe, £16 elsewhere)

Aims to remember and promote interest in the work of Malcolm Saville (1901–82), children's author. Regular social activities, library, contact directory and magazine (4 p.a.). Founded 1994.

The Dorothy L. Sayers Society

Gimsons, Kings Chase, Witham, Essex CM8 1AX
tel (01376) 515626
email info@sayers.org.uk
website www.sayers.org.uk
Acting Chair Seona Ford, *Secretaries* Lenelle Davis, Jasmine Simeone
Membership £18 p.a. UK, £21 Europe, $44 USA, £24 rest of world; under 25 rates available

Aims to promote and encourage the study of the works of Dorothy L. Sayers (1893–1957); to collect archive materials and reminiscences about her and make them available to students and biographers; to hold an annual conference and other meetings; to publish *Proceedings*, pamphlets and a bi-monthly Bulletin; to make grants and awards. Founded 1976.

Scattered Authors Society

Secretary Elen Caldecott
email membership@scatteredauthors.org
website www.scatteredauthors.org

Aims to provide a forum for informal discussion, contact and support for professional writers in children's fiction. Founded 1998.

Scottish Arts Club

24 Rutland Square, Edinburgh EH1 2BW
tel 0131 229 8157
email scottishartsclub@btconnect.com
website www.scottishartsclub.co.uk
Hon. Secretary tel 0131 229 8157

Art, literature, music.

Scottish Arts Council – see Creative Scotland

Scottish Book Trust (SBT)

Sandeman House, 55 High Street, Edinburgh EH1 1SR
tel 0131 524 0160 *fax* 0131 524 0161
email info@scottishbooktrust.com
website www.scottishbooktrust.com

With a responsibility towards Scottish writing, SBT exists to inspire readers and writers, and through the promotion of reading, to reach and create a wider reading public. Programmes include: management of Live Literature funding, a national initiative enabling Scottish citizens to engage with authors, playwrights, poets, storytellers and illustrators; Writer Development, offering mentoring and professional development for emerging and established writers; an ambitious children's programme including national tours, a children's festival and the Scottish Children's Book Awards; and readership development programmes. An information service for readers, writers and occasional exhibitions and publications all contribute to SBT's mission to bring readers and writers together.

Scottish Fellowship of Christian Writers

c/o Diana Lynch, 56 Oak Drive, Kirkintilloch G66 4BU
email info@sfcw.info
website www.sfcw.info
Membership Secretary Diana Lynch
£10 p.a.

To encourage Christians living in Scotland to make use of their creative writing talents. Over 130 members. Founded 1980.

Scottish Newspaper Publishers Association

108 Holyrood Road, Edinburgh EH8 8AS
tel 0131 220 4353 *fax* 0131 220 4344
email info@snpa.org.uk
website www.snpa.org.uk
President Michael Johnston

Scottish Newspaper Society

email info@scotns.org.uk

Seven Stories – the Centre for Children's Books

30 Lime Street, Ouseburn Valley, Newcastle upon Tyne NE1 2PQ

tel 0845 271 0777
email info@sevenstories.org.uk
website www.sevenstories.org.uk

Seven Stories champions the art of children's books to ensure its place as an integral part of childhood and national cultural life. The world of children's books is celebrated through exhibitions, events and an archive. Seven Stories is the only gallery dedicated to children's literature in the UK and one of just a few in the world. It is housed in a specially converted warehouse. Arts Council England and Newcastle City Council regularly fund Seven Stories' work, giving children's literature status and establishing new ways of engaging young audiences.

The Shaw Society

1 Buckland Court, 37 Belsize Park, London NW3 4EB
tel 020-435 6497
email contact@shawsociety.org.uk
website www.shawsociety.org.uk
Chairman Alan Knight
Membership £15/$30 p.a.

Works towards the improvement and diffusion of knowledge of the life and works of Bernard Shaw (1856–1950) and his circle. Publishes *The Shavian.*

Society for Editors and Proofreaders (SfEP)

Apsley House, 176 Upper Richmond Road, London SW15 2SH
tel 020-8785 6155
email administrator@sfep.org.uk
website www.sfep.org.uk

Works to promote high editorial standards and achieve recognition of its members' professional status, through local and national meetings, an annual conference, email discussion groups, a regular magazine and a programme of reasonably priced workshops/training sessions. These sessions help newcomers to acquire basic skills, enable experienced editors to update their skills or broaden their competence, and also cover aspects of professional practice or business for the self-employed. An online directory of editorial services is available. The Society supports moves towards recognised standards of training and accreditation for editors and proofreaders and has developed its own Accreditation in Proofreading qualification. It has close links with the Publishing Training Centre and the Society of Indexers, is represented on the BSI Technical Committee dealing with copy preparation and proof correction (BS 5261), and works to foster good relations with all relevant bodies and organisations in the UK and worldwide. Founded 1988.

The Society for Theatre Research

c/o The National Theatre Archive, 83–191 The Cut, London SE1 8LL
email contact@str.org.uk
website www.str.org.uk
Hon. Secretaries Eileen Cottis, Valerie Lucas

Publishes journal *Theatre Notebook* (3 p.a.) and at least one major book per annum, holds lectures and makes annual research grants (current annual total sum approx. £5,000). Also awards an annual prize of up to £500 for best book published in English on the historical or current practice of the British Theatre.

Society of Artists Agents

website www.saahub.com

Formed to promote professionalism in the illustration industry and to forge closer links between clients and artists through an agreed set of guidelines. The Society believes in an ethical approach through proper terms and conditions, thereby protecting the interests of the artists and clients. Founded 1992.

The Society of Authors – see page 497

The Society of Botanical Artists

Executive Secretary Mrs Pam Henderson, 1 Knapp Cottages, Wyke, Gillingham, Dorset SP8 4NQ
tel (01747) 825718
email pam@soc-botanical-artists.org
website www.soc-botanical-artists.org
President Vickie Marsh
Membership Through selection. £140 p.a.; £20 friend members

Aims to encourage the art of botanical painting. Annual Open Exhibition held in April at Westminster Central Hall, London SW1. Submit work in February. Entry schedules available from the Executive Secretary from January on receipt of sae. Founded 1985.

Society of Children's Book Writers and Illustrators (SCBWI)

36 Mackenzie Road, Beckenham, Kent BR3 4RU
email ra@britishscbwi.org
website www.britishscbwi.org
Regional Adviser, SCBWI–British Isles Natascha Biebow
Membership £50 p.a.

An international network for the exchange of knowledge between professional writers, illustrators, editors, publishers, agents, librarians, educators, booksellers and others involved with literature for young people. Sponsors conferences on writing and illustrating children's books and multimedia – in New York (February, annual), Los Angeles (August, annual) and Bologna (spring, bi-annual) – as well as dozens of regional conferences and events throughout the world. Publishes a bi-monthly newsletter, *The Bulletin*, and information publications. Awards grants for works in progress and for marketing your book. The SCBWI also presents the annual Golden Kite and Crystal Awards for the best fiction and non-fiction books.

The SCBWI British Isles region meets regularly for speaker, networking or professional development events, including the professional series and masterclasses for writers and illustrators. Also sponsors local critique groups and publishes *Words and Pictures* newsletter blog, which includes up-to-date events and marketing information, interviews and articles on the craft of children's writing and illustrating. The yearly 2-day Writers' and Illustrators' Conference includes workshops, one-to-one manuscript and portfolio reviews, a mass book launch and the opportunity to meet publishing professionals. Founded 1971.

The Society of Civil and Public Service Writers

Secretary Mrs J.M. Lewis, 17 The Green, Corby Glen, Grantham, Lincs. NG33 4NP
email joan@lewis5634.fsnet.co.uk
website www.scpsw.co.uk
Membership £15 p.a.; Poetry Workshop add £5

Welcomes serving and retired members of the Civil Service, Armed Forces, Post Office and BT, the nursing profession, and other public servants. Members can be aspiring or published writers. Holds annual competitions for short stories, articles and poetry, plus occasional for longer works. Offers postal folios for short stories and articles; holds an AGM and occasional meetings; publishes *The Civil Service Author* (quarterly) magazine. Poetry Workshop offers magazine, postal folio, anthology and weekend. Send sae for details. Founded 1935.

Society of Editors

Director Bob Satchwell, University Centre, Granta Place, Mill Lane, Cambridge CB2 1RU
tel (01223) 304080 *fax* (01223) 304090
email info@societyofeditors.org
website www.societyofeditors.org
Membership £230 p.a.

Formed from the merger of the Guild of Editors and the Association of British Editors, the Society has more than 400 members in national, regional and local newspapers, magazines, broadcasting, new media, journalism education and media law, campaigning for media freedom. Founded 1999.

Society of Graphic Fine Art

c/o The Skylight Studio, 55 Wray Park Road, Reigate RH2 0EQ
email enquiries@sgfa.org.uk
website www.sgfa.org.uk
President Jo Hall PSGFA, *Hon. Secretary* Christine Hopkins, SGFA
Membership by election twice yearly

The Society of Graphic Fine Art (The Drawing Society) exists to promote and exhibit works of high quality in colour or black and white, with the emphasis on good drawing and draughtsmanship, in pencil, pen, brush, charcoal or any of the forms of original printmaking. The Society holds an annual Open Exhibition with prizes and awards in many categories. Founded 1919.

Society of Heraldic Arts

10–12 Ridgeway, Ottery St Mary, Devon EX11 1DT
email sha.hon-sec@tiscali.co.uk
website www.heraldic-arts.com
Secretary Kevin Arkinstall HSDAD SHA, *Membership Secretary* David Hopkinson SHA (*email* chris-david.hopkinson3@ntlworld.com)
Membership Craft £25 p.a., Associate £17

Aims to serve the interests of heraldic artists, craftsmen, designers and writers, to provide a 'shop window' for their work, to obtain commissions on their behalf and to act as a forum for the exchange of information and ideas. Also offers an information service to the public. Candidates for admission as craft members should be artists or craftsmen whose work comprises a substantial element of heraldry and is of a sufficiently high standard to satisfy the requirements of the Society's advisory council. Founded 1987.

Society of Indexers – see page 619

The Society of Limners

Contact Richard East, 16 Tudor Close, Hove, East Sussex BN3 7NR
tel (01273) 770628
email rgeast.limners@ntlworld.com
website www.societyoflimners.co.uk
Membership £35 p.a., £15 Friends (open to non-exhibitors); £40/£20 overseas

The Society's aims are to promote an interest in miniature painting (in any medium), calligraphy and heraldry and encourage their development to a high standard. New members are elected after the submission of 4 works of acceptable standard and guidelines are provided for new artists. Members receive up to 3 newsletters a year and an annual exhibition is arranged. Seminars and painting weekends are held at least every two years. Founded 1986.

The Society of Medical Writers

Dr R. Cutler, 30 Dollis Hill Lane, London NW2 6JE
website www.somw.org.uk

Aims to recruit members from all branches of the medical profession, together with all professions allied to medicine, to foster interest in literature and in writing – not solely about medicine but also about art, history, music, theatre, etc. Members are encouraged to write fiction, poetry, plays, book reviews, non-fiction articles. Poetry, short story and biography (Roger Bacon Award) prizes, for best non-fiction and best written clinical paper. Publishes *The Writer* (2 p.a.) and a register of members and their writing interests. Holds a bi-annual conference in which various aspects of literature and writing are explored in a relaxed and informal atmosphere. Founded 2001.

Society of Scribes and Illuminators (SSI)

Hon. Secretary 6 Queen Square, London WC1N 3AT
email honsec@calligraphyonline.org
website www.calligraphyonline.org
Membership £40 Fellows; £32 Lay members; £26 Friends

Aims to advance the crafts of writing and illumination. Holds regular exhibitions, provides opportunities for discussion, demonstration and sharing of research. Founded 1921.

The Society of Sussex Authors

Secretary David Arscott, Dolphin House, 51 St Nicholas Lane, Lewes, East Sussex BN7 2JZ
tel (01273) 470100 *fax* (01273) 470100
email sussexbooks@aol.com
Membership £10 p.a.

Aims to encourage social contact between members, and to promote interest in literature and authors. Membership is open to writers living in Sussex who have had at least one book commercially published or who have worked extensively in journalism, radio, TV or the theatre. Founded 1969.

Society of Wildlife Artists

17 Carlton House Terrace, London SW1Y 5BD
tel 020-7930 6844 *fax* 020-7839 7830
website www.swla.co.uk
President Harriet Mead

Aims to promote and encourage the art of wildlife painting and sculpture. Open Annual Exhibition at the Mall Galleries, The Mall, London SW1, for any artist whose work depicts wildlife subjects (botanical and domestic animals are not admissable).

The Society of Women Artists

Executive Secretary 1 Knapp Cottages, Wyke, Gillingham, Dorset SP8 4NQ
tel (01747) 825718
email pamhenderson@dsl.pipex.com
website www.society-women-artists.org.uk
President Sue Jelley SPF
Membership Election by invitation, based on work submitted to the exhibition

Founded in 1855 when women were not considered as serious contributors to art and could not compete for professional honours, the Society continues to promote art by women. Receiving day in April for annual open exhibition held in June/July at Mall Galleries, The Mall, London SW1.

Society of Women Writers & Journalists (SWWJ)

email membership@swwj.co.uk
website www.swwj.co.uk
Membership Secretary W.L. Hughes
Membership £45 p.a. Full, £35 Associate, £30 overseas, £20 joining fee

For women writers: the SWWJ upholds professional standards and literary achievements through regular workshops for all genre of writing where work-in-progress can be evaluated. Regional group meetings; residential weekends; postal critique service; competitions and outings. For Full members, membership card doubles as a press card. Publishes *The Woman Writer* (5 p.a.). Men writers are accepted as Associate members. Founded 1894.

Society of Young Publishers

Contact The Secretary, c/o The Publishers Association, 29B Montague Street, London WC1B 5BW
email sypchair@thesyp.org.uk
website www.thesyp.org.uk
Membership Open to anyone employed in publishing or hoping to be soon; £30 p.a. standard, £24 student/unwaged

Organises monthly events which offer the chance to network and hear senior figures talk on topics of key importance to the publishing industry. Runs a job database advertising the latest vacancies and internships as well as a blog, InDigital, and a print magazine, *InPrint*. Also has branches in Oxford, Scotland and the North. Founded 1949.

South African Writers' Circle

Suite 522, Private Bag X4, Kloof 3640, South Africa
fax +27 (0)31 564 2059
website www.sawriters.org.za
Membership R160 p.a. local, R210 p.a. overseas

Aims to help and encourage all writers, new and experienced, in the art of writing. Publishes a monthly *Newsletter*, and runs competitions with prizes for the winners. Founded 1960.

Southwest Scriptwriters

email info@southwest-scriptwriters.co.uk
website www.southwest-scriptwriters.co.uk
Artistic Director Tim Massey
Membership £6 p.a.

Workshops members' drama scripts for stage, screen, radio and TV with the aim of improving their chances of professional production, meeting at Watershed in Bristol. Also hosts talks by professional dramatists. Projects to present members' work to a wider audience have included theatre and short film productions, as well as public rehearsed readings. Bi-monthly e-newsletter. Founded 1994.

Sports Journalists' Association of Great Britain (SJA)

c/o Start2Finish Event Management, Unit 92, Capital Business Centre, 22 Carlton Road, Surrey CR2 0BS

tel 020-8916 2234 *fax* 020-8916 2235
website www.sportsjournalists.co.uk
President Michael Parkinson CBE
Membership £30 p.a., £20 regional

Represents sports journalists across the country and is Britain's voice in international sporting affairs. Offers advice to members covering major events, acts as a consultant to organisers of major sporting events on media requirements. Member of the BOA Press Advisory Committee. Founded 1948.

Spread the Word

The Albany, Douglas Way, London SE8 4AG
tel 020-8692 0231 extension 248/249
email info@spreadtheword.org.uk
website www.spreadtheword.org.uk

The Robert Louis Stevenson Club

Secretary John W.S. Macfie, 17 Heriot Row, Edinburgh EH3 6HP
tel/fax 0131 556 1896
email mail@stevenson-house.co.uk
Membership £20 p.a., £150 for 10 years

Aims to foster interest in Robert Louis Stevenson's life (1850–94) and works through various events and its newsletter. Founded 1920.

Sussex Playwrights' Club

Hon. Secretary, 24 Highcroft Villas, Brighton BN1 5PS
email mail@sussexplaywrights.com
website www.sussexplaywrights.com

Founded 1935.

Swedish Publishers' Association

(Svenska Förläggareföreningen)
Drottninggaten 97, 113 60 Stockholm, Sweden
tel +468-7 361940 *fax* +468-7 361944
email info@forlaggare.se
website www.forlaggare.se
Director Kristina Ahlinder

Founded 1843.

The Tennyson Society

Central Library, Free School lane, Lincoln LN2 1EZ
tel (01522) 687837
email kathleen.jefferson@lincolnshire.gov.uk
website www.tennysonsociety.org.uk
Membership £14 p.a., £16 family, £25 institutions

Promotes the study and understanding of the life and work of the poet Alfred, Lord Tennyson (1809–92) and supports the Tennyson Research Centre in Lincoln. Holds lectures, visits and seminars; publishes the *Tennyson Research Bulletin* (annual), Monographs and Occasional Papers; tapes/recordings available. Founded 1960.

Theatre Writers' Union – see page 499

Angela Thirkell Society

Chairman Mrs P. Aldred, 54 Belmont Park, London SE13 5BN
tel 020-8244 9339
Membership enquiries Dr Sarah Preston, 59 Kings Hedges Road, Cambridge CB4 2QD
tel (01223) 426438
email smrpreston@gmail.com
website www.angelathirkellsociety.com
Membership £10 p.a.

Aims 'to honour the memory of Angela Thirkell (1890–1960) as a writer, and to make her works available to new generations'. Publishes an *Annual Journal*, and encourages Thirkell studies. Founded 1980.

The Edward Thomas Fellowship

1 Carfax, Undercliff Drive, St Lawrence, Isle of Wight PO38 1XG
tel (01983) 853366
email colingthornton@btopenworld.com
website www.edward-thomas-fellowship.org.uk
Hon. Secretary Colin G. Thornton
Membership single £10 p.a., joint £15 p.a.

Aims to perpetuate the memory of Edward Thomas (1878–1917), poet and writer, foster an interest in his life and work, to assist in the preservation of places associated with him and to arrange events which extend fellowship amongst his admirers. Founded 1980.

Dylan Thomas Society of Great Britain

4 Bishops Grove, Sketty, Swansea SA2 8BE
website thedylanthomassocietyofgb.co.uk
Chair Mr John Rhys Thomas
Membership £10 p.a. single, £15 p.a. double, Patrons £25

Aims to promote an interest in the works of Dylan Thomas (1914–53) and other writers. Founded 1977.

The Tolkien Society

Membership Secretary Marion Kershaw, 655 Rochdale Road, Walsden, Todmorden, Lancs. OL14 6SX
email membership@tolkiensociety.org
website www.tolkiensociety.org
Membership £25 p.a. (Full), £12.50 p.a. (Associate), £2 p.a. (Entings)

The Translators Association

84 Drayton Gardens, London SW10 9SB
tel 020-7373 6642
email info@societyofauthors.org
website www.societyofauthors.org/translators-association

Specialist unit within the membership of the Society of Authors (see page 497), exclusively concerned with the interests and special problems of translators into English whose work is published or performed commercially in Great Britain. Members are entitled to general and legal advice on all questions connected with their work, including remuneration and contractual arrangements with publishers, editors, broadcasting organisations. Founded 1958.

The Trollope Society

PO Box 505, Tunbridge Wells, TN2 9RW
tel (01747) 8397998
email info@trollopesociety.org
website www.trollopesociety.org
Chairman Michael Williamson JP DL
Membership £26 p.a.

Has produced the first ever complete edition of the novels of Anthony Trollope (1815–82). Founded 1987.

The Turner Society

BCM Box Turner, London WC1N 3XX
website www.turnersociety.org.uk
Chairman Andrew Wilton
Membership £25 p.a. individuals, £25 p.a. overseas surface mail, £37.50 p.a. overseas airmail, Life Member £500

Aims to foster a wider appreciation of all facets of the work of J.M.W. Turner RA (1775–1851); to encourage exhibitions of his paintings, drawings and engravings. Publishes *Turner Society News* (2 p.a.). Founded 1975.

Ver Poets

Secretary Daphne Schiller
email daphneschiller8@gmail.com
website www.verpoets.org.uk
Contact Daphne Schiller (tel: 01727-864898)
Membership £18 p.a. UK, £24 overseas, £12 students

Encourages the writing and study of poetry. Holds evening meetings and daytime workshops in the St Albans area. Holds members' competitions and the annual Open Competition. Founded 1966.

Visiting Arts

c/o ICA, The Mall, London SW1Y 5AH
tel 020-3463 4560
email information@visitingarts.org.uk
website www.visitingarts.org.uk
Director Yvette Vaughan Jones

Aims to strengthen intercultural understanding through the arts. It provides information and intelligence in order to strengthen intercultural dialogue, and creates opportunities to experience intercultural exploration. This is done through mediated performances, exhibitions, and by initiating and promoting collaborations. Visiting Arts seeks to expand the skills and knowledge of existing cultural players and develop new talent to ensure a wide, diverse and sustainable group of players.

Visiting Arts creates, produces and distributes authoritative directories and help-sheets, targeted briefings and the latest advice through print, web and word of mouth. It organises seminars, conferences and networking events to deepen intercultural understanding; establishes and fosters opportunities for ground-breaking artist exchanges; promotes cutting edge exhibitions; and contributes to some of the world's biggest and most innovative festivals. It works with the most exciting next generation of artists and cultural players, inviting them to the UK, expanding knowledge and horizons and championing intercultural working.

Visiting Arts is an independent registered charity. It is funded by the British Council, Arts Council England, Creative Scotland, the Arts Council of Wales, the Arts Council of Northern Ireland and the Department of Culture, Media and Sport. Founded 1977.

Voice of the Listener & Viewer Ltd (VLV)

PO Box 401, Gravesend, Kent DA12 9FY
tel (01474) 338711/338716 *fax* (01474) 325440
email info@vlv.org.uk
website www.vlv.org.uk
Administrative Secretary Sue Washbrook

Represents the citizen and consumer interests in broadcasting: it is an independent, non-profit-making society working to ensure independence, quality and diversity in broadcasting. VLV is funded by its members and is free from sectarian, commercial and political affiliations. It holds public lectures, seminars and conferences, and has frequent contact with MPs and other relevant parties. It provides an independent forum where all with an interest in broadcasting can speak on equal terms. It produces a quarterly news bulletin and holds its own archive and those of the former Broadcasting Research Unit (1980–90) and BACTV (British Action for Children's Television). It maintains a panel of speakers, the VLV Forum for Children's Broadcasting, the VLV Forum for Educational Broadcasting, and acts as a secretariat for the European Alliance of Listeners' and Viewers' Associations (EURALVA). VLV does not handle complaints. Founded 1984.

The Walmsley Society

Secretary Fred Lane, April Cottage, 1 Brand Road, Hampden Park, Eastbourne, East Sussex BN22 9PX
website www.walmsleysoc.org
Membership Secretary Mrs Elizabeth Buckley, 21 The Crescent, Hipperholm, Halifax, West Yorkshire HX3 8NQ

Aims to promote and encourage an appreciation of the literary and artistic heritage left to us by Leo Walmsley (1892–1966) and J. Ulric Walmsley (1860–1954). Founded 1985.

Mary Webb Society

Secretary Sue Higginbotham, Old Barn Cottage, 10 Barrow Hall Farm, Village Road, Great Barrow, Chester, Cheshire CH3 7JH

tel (01829) 740592
email suehigginbotham@yahoo.co.uk
website www.marywebbsociety.co.uk

For devotees of the literature and works of Mary Webb (1881–1927) and of the beautiful Shropshire countryside of her novels. Publishes a bi-annual Journal, organises summer schools and other events in various locations related to Webb's life and works. Archives, lectures; tours arranged for individuals and groups. Founded 1972.

The H.G. Wells Society

Eric Fitch, 20 Upper Field Close, Hereford HR2 7SW
email hgwellssociety@gmail.com
website www.hgwellsusa.50megs.com
Membership £18 p.a. UK/Eu, £21 p.a. rest of world

Promotes an active interest in and an appreciation of the life, work and thought of H.G. Wells (1866–1946). Publishes *The Wellsian* (annual) and *The Newsletter* (bi-annual). Founded 1960.

Welsh Academy – see Literature Wales

Welsh Books Council/Cyngor Llyfrau Cymru

Castell Brychan, Aberystwyth, Ceredigion SY23 2JB
tel (01970) 624151 *fax* (01970) 625385
email castellbrychan@cllc.org.uk
website www.cllc.org.uk, www.gwales.com
Ceo Elwyn Jones

A national body funded directly by the Welsh Government which provides a focus for the publishing industry in Wales. Awards grants for publishing in Welsh and English. Provides services to the trade in the fields of editing, design, marketing and distribution. The Council is a key enabling institution in the world of books and provides services and information in this field to all who are associated with it. Founded 1961.

The West Country Writers' Association

Fiona McAughey, Trevean, Yeolmbridge, Launceston PL15 8NJ
tel (01566) 773615
website www.westcountrywriters.com
President Lady Rachel Billington, *Chair* Lyn Carnaby
Membership Open to published authors, joining fee plus first year membership £20 – thereafter £25 p.a.

Aims to foster love of literature in the West Country and to give authors an opportunity of meeting to exchange news and views. Holds Annual Weekend Congress and Regional Meetings. Plus newsletters.

The Oscar Wilde Society

Kambah, Harcourt Hill, Oxford OX2 9AS
email cressida.battersby@virgin.net
website www.oscarwildesociety.co.uk
Membership Secretary Cressida Battersby, *Hon. Secretary* Michael Seeney

Aims to promote knowledge, appreciation and study of the life, personality and works of the writer and wit Oscar Wilde (1854–1900). Activities include meetings, lectures, readings and exhibitions, and visits to associated locations. Members receive a journal, *The Wildean* (2 p.a.), and a newsletter, *Intentions* (5 p.a.). Founded 1990.

Charles Williams Society

Secretary Richard Sturch, 35 Broomfield, Stacey Bushes, Milton Keynes MK12 6HA
email charles_wms_soc@yahoo.co.uk
website www.charleswilliamssociety.org.uk

Aims to promote interest in the life and work of Charles Walter Stansby Williams (1886–1945) and to make his writings more easily available. Founded 1975.

The Henry Williamson Society

General Secretary Sue Cumming, 7 Monmouth Road, Dorchester, Dorset DT1 2DE
tel (01305) 264092
email zseagull@aol.com
Membership Secretary Margaret Murphy, 16 Doran Drive, Redhill, Surrey RH1 6AX
tel (01737) 763228
email mm@misterman.freeserve.co.uk
website www.henrywilliamson.co.uk
Chairman Tony Boakes
Membership £15 p.a.

Aims to encourage a wider readership and greater understanding of the literary heritage left by Henry Williamson (1895–1977). Two meetings annually; also weekend activities. Publishes an annual journal. Founded 1980.

The P.G. Wodehouse Society (UK)

Details Tony Ring, 34 Longfield, Great Missenden, Bucks. HP16 0EG
tel (01494) 864848
website www.pgwodehousesociety.org.uk
Membership £20 p.a.

Aims to promote enjoyment of P.G. Wodehouse (1881–1975). Publishes *Wooster Sauce* (quarterly) and *By The Way* papers (4 p.a.) which cover diverse subjects of Wodehousean interest. Holds events, entertainments and meetings throughout Britain. Founded 1997.

Women in Publishing (WiP)

c/o Kathryn King, Multilingual Matters/Channel View Publications, Frankfurt Lodge, Clevedon Hall, Victoria Road, Clevedon BS21 7HH
email info@wipub.org.uk
website www.wipub.org.uk
Membership £27.50 p.a.

Promotes the status of women within publishing; encourages networking and mutual support among women; provides a forum for the discussion of ideas, trends and subjects to women in the trade; offers advice on publishing careers; supports and publicises women's achievements and successes. Each year WiP presents 2 awards: the Pandora Award is given in recognition of significant personal contributions to women in publishing, and the New Venture Award is presented to a recent venture which reflects the interests and concerns of women or minority groups in the 21st century. Founded 1979.

Virginia Woolf Society of Great Britain

Stuart N. Clarke, Membership Secretary, Fairhaven, Charnleys Lane, Banks, Southport PR9 8HJ
tel (01704) 225232
email stuart.n.clarke@btinternet.com
website www.virginiawoolfsociety.co.uk
Membership £17 p.a., £22 Europe, £23 outside Europe

Acts as a forum for British admirers of Virginia Woolf (1882–1941) to meet, correspond and share their enjoyment of her work. Publishes the *Virginia Woolf Bulletin*. Founded 1998.

The Wordsworth Trust

Dove Cottage, Grasmere, Cumbria LA22 9SH
tel (01539) 435544 *fax* (01539) 435748
email enquiries@wordsworth.org.uk
website www.wordsworth.org.uk
Membership Officer Sally Robinson
Membership £25 p.a. (individual)

To preserve and enhance Dove Cottage, the Collection and the historic environment of Town End for future generations; to give people of all ages the chance to fulfil their creative potential; to develop the education and lifelong learning programmes for the benefit of the widest possible audience. Founded 1891.

Worshipful Company of Stationers and Newspaper Makers

Stationers' Hall, London EC4M 7DD
tel 020-7246 0999 *fax* 020-7489 1975
email info@stationers.org
Master Kevin Dewey, *Clerk* William Alden MBE DL

One of the Livery Companies of the City of London. Connected with the printing, publishing, bookselling, newspaper and allied trades. Founded 1403.

Writers Advice Centre for Children's Books

16 Smith's Yard, London SW18 4HR
tel 07979 905353
email info@writersadvice.co.uk
website www.writersadvice.co.uk
Managing Editor Louise Jordan

Dedicated to helping new and published children's writers by offering both editorial advice and tips on how to get published. The Centre also runs an online children's writing correspondence course plus a mentoring scheme for both ideas and manuscripts. Founded 1994.

Writers Guild of America, East Inc. (WGAE)

250 Hudson Street, 7th Floor, New York, NY 10013, USA
tel +1 212-767-7800
website www.wgaeast.org
President Michael Winship
Membership 1.5% of covered earnings

Represents writers in screen, TV and new media for collective bargaining. It provides member services including pension and health, as well as educational and professional activities. Founded 1954.

Writers Guild of America, West Inc. (WGA)

7000 West 3rd Street, Los Angeles, CA 90048, USA
tel +1 323-951-4000 *fax* +1 323-782-4800
website www.wga.org
Membership $2,500 initiation, $25 quarterly, 1.5% of income annually

Union representing and servicing 9,000 writers in film, broadcast, cable and multimedia industries for purposes of collective bargaining, contract administration and other services, and functions to protect and advance the economic, professional and creative interests of writers. Monthly publication, *Written By*, available by subscription. Founded 1933.

Writers Guild of Canada

366 Adelaide Street West, Suite 401, Toronto, Ontario M5V 1R9, Canada
tel +1 416-979-7907; toll free +1-800-567-9974
fax +1 416-979-9273
email info@wgc.ca
website www.wgc.ca
Executive Director Maureen Parker

Represents over 2,000 professional writers of film, TV, animation, radio, documentary and digital media. Negotiates and administers collective agreements with independent producers and broadcasters. The Guild also publishes *Canadian Screenwriter* magazine.

The Writers' Guild of Great Britain – see page 499

Writers in Oxford

email wio_membership@yahoo.co.uk
website www.writersinoxford.org
Chair Denise Cullington
Membership £25 p.a.

Promotes social mixing, networking and professional discussion among published writers in and around Oxfordshire. Activities include: suppers, literary talks, parties and outings. Publishes a regular newsletter, *The Oxford Writer*. Founded 1992.

The Writers' Union of Canada

90 Richmond Street East, Suite 200, Toronto, Ontario M5C 1P1
tel +1 416-703-8982 *fax* +1 416-504-9090
email info@writersunion.ca
website www.writersunion.ca

Yachting Journalists' Association

Chris English, Secretary, 16 Wanderdown Way, Ovingdean, Brighton BN2 7BX
tel (07711) 717470
email secretary@yja.co.uk
website www.yja.co.uk
Membership £40 p.a.

Aims to further the interests of yachting, sail and power, and yachting journalism. Members vote annually for the Yachtsman of the Year and the Young Sailor of the Year Award. Founded 1969.

The Yorkshire Dialect Society

Publicity & Information Officer 19 Prospect Close, Swinefleet, East Yorkshire DN14 8FB
enquiries@yorkshireidialectsociety.org.uk
website www.yorkshiredialectsociety.org.uk
Membership £10 p.a.

Aims to encourage interest in: dialect speech, the writing of dialect verse, prose and drama; the publication and circulation of dialect literature; the study of the origins and the history of dialect and kindred subjects. Organises meetings; publishes *Transactions* (annual) and *The Summer Bulletin* free to members; list of other publications on request. Founded 1897.

Francis Brett Young Society

Secretary Mrs J. Hadley, 92 Gower Road, Halesowen, West Midlands B62 9BT
tel 0121 422 8969
email michael.hall10@gmail.com
website www.fbysociety.co.uk
Chairman Dr Michael Hall
Membership £7 p.a., £70 p.a. life

Aims to provide opportunities for members to meet, correspond, and to share the enjoyment of the works of Francis Brett Young (1884–1954). Publishes a journal (2 p.a.). Founded 1979.

Prizes and awards

This list provides details of many British prizes, competitions and awards for writers and artists, including grants, bursaries and fellowships, as well as details of major international prizes. See page 741 for a quick reference to its contents.

Academi Cardiff International Poetry Competition – see Literature Wales Cardiff International Poetry Competition

J.R. Ackerley Prize for Autobiography

English PEN, 60 Farringdon Road, London EC1R 3GA
tel 020-7324 2535
email enquiries@englishpen.org
website www.englishpen.org

An annual prize of £2,000 is given for an outstanding work of literary autobiography written in English and published during the previous year by an author of British nationality. No submissions: books are nominated by the judges only. Founded 1982.

The Aeon Award

8 Bachelor's Walk, Dublin 1, Republic of Ireland
email fraslaw@yahoo.co.uk
website www.albedo1.com

An annual contest for short fiction (up to 10,000 words) in genres of fantasy, science fiction, horror or anything in between. A grand prize of €1,000 will be awarded to the winner (2nd prize €200, 3rd €100) plus publication in Albedo One. The contest runs for 4 rounds throughout the year; deadlines are 31 March (1st round), 30 June (2nd round), 30 September (3rd round) and 30 November (final round). At the end of each round the best story submissions will be shortlisted for the award. Online and postal submissions accepted. Entry fee: €7.50.

The Hans Christian Andersen Awards

International Board on Books for Young People, Nonnenweg 12, Postfach, CH–4003 Basel, Switzerland
tel +41 61-272 2917 *fax* +41 61-272 2757
email ibby@ibby.org, liz.page@ibby.org
website www.ibby.org

The Medals are awarded every 2 years to a living author and an illustrator who by the outstanding value of their work are judged to have made a lasting contribution to literature for children and young people.

Arts Council England

The Literature Dept, Arts Council England, 14 Great Peter Street, London SW1P 3NQ
tel 0845 300 6200 *textphone* 020-7973 6564
fax 0161 934 4426
email enquiries@artscouncil.org.uk
website www.artscouncil.org.uk

Arts Council England presents national prizes rewarding creative talent in literature. These are awarded through the Council's flexible funds and are not necessarily open to application: the David Cohen Prize for Literature, and the Independent Foreign Fiction Prize.

Arts Council England, London

Literature Administrator, Arts Council England, 14 Great Peter Street, London SW1P 3NQ
tel 0845 300 6200 *fax* 020-7973 6590
website www.artscouncil.org.uk/regions/london/
Contact Gemma Seltzer

Arts Council England, London is the regional office for the Capital, covering 33 boroughs and the City of London. Grants are available through the 'Grants for the Arts' scheme throughout the year to support a variety of literature projects, concentrating particularly on:

- original works of poetry and literary fiction and professional development for individual writers, including writers of children's books;
- touring and live literature;
- small independent literary publishers; and
- literary translation into English.

Contact the Literature Unit for more information, or see website for an application form.

The Arts Council/An Chomhairle Ealaíon

70 Merrion Square, Dublin 2, Republic of Ireland
tel +353 (0)1 6180200 *fax* +353 (0)1 6761302
email info@artscouncil.ie
website www.artscouncil.ie

Outlines all of its funding opportunities for individuals, groups and organisations on website. Also publishes an email newsletter that provides monthly updates on grants and awards, news and events, and arts policy. Register to receive the newsletter by visiting http://www.artscouncil.ie/en/newsletter.aspx.

Arts Council site YouWriteOn.com Book Awards

tel (07948) 392634
email edward@youwriteon.com
website www.youwriteon.com

Arts Council funded site publishing awards for new fiction writers. Random House and Orion, the publishers of authors such as Dan Brown and Terry Pratchett, provide free professional critiques for the highest rated new writers' opening chapters and short stories on YouWriteOn.com each month. The highest rated writers of the year are then published, 3 in each of the adult and children's categories, through YouWriteOn's free paperback publishing service for writers. The novel publishing awards total £1,000. Writers can enter at any time throughout the year: closing date is 31 December each year. Join YouWriteOn.com to participate. Previous YouWriteOn.com winners have been published by mainstream publishers such as Random House, Orion, Penguin and Hodder including Channel 4 TV Book Club winner and bestseller *The Legacy* by Katherine Webb. Founded 2005.

The Asham Award

Details The Administrator,
Asham Literary Endowment Trust, c/o Town Hall, High Street, Lewes, East Sussex BN7 2QS
email carole.buchan@btinternet.com
website www.ashamaward.com

A biennial national short story competition for women writers over the age of 18 and currently resident in the UK, who have not previously had a novel or anthology of their work published. Twelve winning writers will receive cash prizes (sponsored by Much Ado Books of Alfriston, East Sussex) and their stories will be published in an anthology alongside specially commissioned established writers. The next Award is scheduled to be launched in early summer 2012. The shortlist will be announced in February 2013 and the results will be announced in August 2013 to coincide with publication by Virago of the anthology of winning and commissioned stories. See website or send sae for details. Founded 1996.

The Australian/Vogel's Literary Award

email vogel@allenandunwin.com
website www.allenandunwin.com

An annual award of $20,000 for a chosen unpublished work of fiction, Australian history or biography. Entrants must be under 35 years of age on the closing date and must normally be residents of Australia. The MS must be between 30,000 and 100,000 words and must be an original work entirely by the entrant written in English. It cannot be under consideration to any publisher or award. See website for details. Closing date: 31 May. Founded 1980.

Authors' Club Awards

Blacks, 67 Dean Street, London W1D 4QH
website www.theartsclub.co.uk

Best First Novel Award

An award of £1,000 is presented at a dinner held in the Club, to the author of the most promising first novel published in the UK during each year. Entries are accepted during August and must be full-length novels – short stories are not eligible. Instituted by Lawrence Meynell in 1954.

Sir Banister Fletcher Award for Authors' Club

The late Sir Banister Fletcher, a former President of both the Authors' Club and the Royal Institute of British Architects instituted an annual prize 'for the book on architecture or the arts most deserving'. Books eligible are those written by British authors or those resident in the UK and published under a British imprint and should be submitted by the end of May of the year after publication. The prize of £1,000 is awarded by the Authors' Club during October. First awarded in 1954.

Dolman Best Travel Book Award

An award of £2,500 is presented annually for the best literary travel book (no guidebooks accepted). Instituted by William Dolman in 2005.

The Authors' Contingency Fund

Sarah Baxter, The Society of Authors,
84 Drayton Gardens, London SW10 9SB
tel 020-7373 6642 *fax* 020-7373 5768
email info@societyofauthors.org
website www.societyofauthors.org

This fund makes modest grants to established, published authors who find themselves in sudden financial difficulty. Apply for guidelines and application form.

The Authors' Foundation

The Society of Authors, 84 Drayton Gardens, London SW10 9SB
tel 020-7373 6642
email info@societyofauthors.org
website www.societyofauthors.org

Grants are available to novelists, poets and writers of non-fiction who are published authors working on their next book. The aim is to provide funding (in addition to a proper advance) for research, travel or other necessary expenditure. Closing dates: 30 April and 30 September. Download or send sae for an information sheet. Founded in 1984 to mark the centenary of the Society of Authors.

BAFTA (British Academy of Film and Television Arts)

195 Piccadilly, London W1J 9LN
tel 020-7734 0022 *fax* 020-7292 5868
email info@bafta.org
website www.bafta.org
Chief Executive, Amanda Berry

The UK's pre-eminent independent charity supporting, developing and promoting the art forms of the moving image (film, TV and video games) by identifying and rewarding excellence, inspiring practitioners and benefiting the public. BAFTA Awards are awarded annually by members to their peers in recognition of their skills and expertise. In addition, BAFTA's year-round Learning & Events programme offers unique access to some of the world's most inspiring talent through workshops, masterclasses, lectures and mentoring schemes, connecting with audiences of all ages and backgrounds across the UK, Los Angeles and New York. Founded 1947.

Bardd Plant Cymru (Welsh-Language Children's Poet Laureate)

Welsh Books Council, Castell Brychan, Aberystwyth, Ceredigion SY23 2JB
tel (01970) 624151 *fax* (01970) 625385
email castellbrychan@wbc.org.uk
website www.cllc.org.uk

The main aim is to raise the profile of poetry amongst children and to encourage them to compose and enjoy poetry. During his/her term of office the bard will visit schools as well as helping children to create poetry through electronic workshops.

The scheme's partner organisations are: S4C, the Welsh Books Council, Urdd Gobaith Cymru, Literature Wales and the Welsh Language Board.

Verity Bargate Award

Writers' Centre Assistant, Soho Theatre, 21 Dean Street, London W1D 3NE
email writers@sohotheatre.com
website www.sohotheatre.com

This biennial award is made to the writer of a new and previously unperformed full-length play. It is the only award in the UK designed specifically for emerging writers and is only eligible to playwrights with less than 3 professional credits. The winner receives: a prize of £5,000, a residency at the Soho Theatre, and the prize-winning play may be professionally produced by the Soho Theatre Company. Next award: 2013. Closing date for submissions: March. See website for information on workshops and events associated with the award. Established 1982.

BBC FOUR Samuel Johnson Prize for Non-Fiction

Four Colman Getty, The Communications Building, 48 Leicester Square, London WC2H 7FG
tel 020-3032 9900
email lisa.perkins@fourcolmangetty.co.uk
website www.thesamueljohnsonprize.co.uk
Contact Lisa Perkins

This annual prize is the biggest non-fiction prize in the UK and is worth £20,000. Closing date: mid-January. Founded 1999.

BBC National Short Story Award

Booktrust, Book House, 45 East Hill, London SW18 2QZ
tel 020-8516 2972
email prizes@booktrust.org.uk
website www.theshortstory.org.uk
Contact Claire Shanahan

Part of the Booktrust campaign to celebrate short stories, a prize of £15,000 is awarded for the winning story, plus £3,000 for the runner-up and £500 for the 3 other shortlisted writers. One of the most prestigious prizes for a single short story, the BBC NSSA is run in partnership with Booktrust. Closing date: May. Winner announced: September. Founded 2005.

The David Berry Prize

Administrative Secretary of the Royal Historical Society, University College London, Gower Street, London WC1E 6BT
tel 020-7387 7532
email royalhistsoc@ucl.ac.uk
website www.royalhistoricalsociety.org/prizes.php

Candidates may select any subject dealing with Scottish history. Value of prize: £250. Closing date: 31 December each year.

Besterman/McColvin Medals – see The ISG Reference Awards

The Biographers' Club Tony Lothian Prize

Prize Administrator, 119A Fordwych Road, London NW2 3NJ
tel 020-8452 4993
email anna@annaswan.co.uk
website www.biographersclub.co.uk
Contact Anna Swan

The £2,000 Tony Lothian Prize (sponsored by her daughter, Elizabeth, Duchess of Buccleuch) supports uncommissioned first-time writers working on a biography. Applicants should submit a proposal of no more than 20 pages including a synopsis and 10-page sample chapter (double-spaced, numbered pages), CV and a note on the market for the book and competing literature, to the prize administrator. Entry fee: £10. For further details and mandatory entry form, see website.

The Bisto Book of the Year Awards – see The CBI Book of the Year Awards

The K. Blundell Trust

K. Blundell Trust, The Society of Authors, 84 Drayton Gardens, London SW10 9SB
tel 020-7373 6642
email info@societyofauthors.org
website www.societyofauthors.org

Awards are given to published writers under the age of 40 to assist them with their next book. The author's work must 'contribute to the greater understanding of existing social and economic organisation', but fiction is not excluded. Closing dates: 30 April and 30 September. Download from the website or send sae for an information sheet.

The Boardman Tasker Prize

Steve Dean, 8 Bank View Road, Darley Abbey, Derby DE22 1EJ
email steve@people-matter.co.uk
website www.boardmantasker.co.uk

This annual prize of £3,000 is given for a work of fiction, non-fiction or poetry, the central theme of which is concerned with the mountain environment. Authors of any nationality are eligible but the work must be published or distributed in the UK. Entries from publishers only. Founded 1983.

The Bollinger Everyman Wodehouse Prize for Comic Fiction

Lucy Hinton, Four Colman Getty, The Communications Building, 48 Leicester Square, London WC2H 7FG
tel 020-3023 9900
email lucy.hinton@fourcolmangetty.co.uk

UK's only prize for comic fiction. Awarded to the most original comic novel of the previous 12 months. The winner receives a case of Bollinger Special Cuvée, a jeroboam of Bollinger, a complete set of the Everyman Wodehouse collection and a rare breed pig named after the winning novel. Eligible novels are published in the UK between 1 May and 30 April. The winner is announced at the Daily Telegraph Hay Festival in late May/early June. Closing date: late February; shortlist announced in mid-April. Launched in 2000 on the 25th anniversary of the death of P.G. Wodehouse.

The Book to Talk About

email worldbookday@blueyonder.co.uk
website www.worldbookday.com, www.spread-the-word.org.uk

Online voting determines the winning title, which is announced on World Book Day. The winning author will receive a £5,000 prize. See World Book Day (page 580).

The *Bookseller* Industry Awards

The Bookseller, Ground Floor, 56–68 Southwark Street, London SE1 1UN
tel 020-3358 0387
website www.thebookseller.com/awards
Contact Ashley Baugh, Events & Marketing Executive

Awards to celebrate the best in bookselling, publishing, and other aspects of the UK book industry. Closing date: end February/March.

Booktrust Early Years Awards

(formerly the Sainsbury's Baby Book Award)
Booktrust, Book House, 45 East Hill, London SW18 2QZ
tel 020-8516 2972
email prizes@booktrust.org.uk
website www.booktrust.org.uk
Contact Claire Shanahan

The winners of each of 3 categories, The Best Book for Babies under one year old, The Best Picture Book for children up to 5 years old, and Best Emerging Illustrator, each receive a cheque for £2,000 and a crystal award. The winner of the Best Emerging Illustrator also receives a specially commissioned piece of artwork from a well-known children's illustrator.

The Booktrust Teenage Prize

Booktrust, Book House, 45 East Hill, London SW18 2QZ
tel 020-8516 2972
email prizes@booktrust.org.uk
website www.booktrust.org.uk
Contact Claire Shanahan

The first annual national book prize to recognise and celebrate the best in young adult fiction. The author of the best book for teenagers receives £2,500 and is chosen from a shortlist of 6–8. The prize is open to works of fiction and non-fiction (including short story collections, graphic novels, poetry and reference books), aimed at teenagers aged 13–16 and written in English by a citizen of the UK, or an author resident in the UK. The work must be published between 1 July and the following 30 June by a UK publisher.

Harry Bowling Prize for New Writing

MBA Literary and Script Agents, 62 Grafton Way, London W1T 5DW
tel 020-7387 2076
website www.harrybowlingprize.co.uk

Established in honour of Harry Bowling, 'the King of Cockney Sagas' who died in 1999, this biannual award offers a winning prize of £1,000 and a £100 runner-up prize. Sponsored by Headline Book Publishing and in partnership with the Romantic Novelists' Association. Administered by MBA Literary and Script Agents. Open to anyone who has not published fiction previously. Judges are looking for great storytelling in an urban setting, with a romantic theme. For details of entry fees, entry forms and submission guidelines, see website. The winner of the 2012 award: Natalie Lloyd-Evans for *A Dark Flowering*.

Alfred Bradley Bursary Award

website www.bbc.co.uk/writersroom

This biennial development opportunity is awarded to a writer or writers resident now or in the past in the North of England. The scheme also allows for a group of finalists to receive small bursaries and develop ideas for radio drama commissions. Founded 1992.

The Branford Boase Award

8 Bolderwood Close, Bishopstoke, Eastleigh, Hants SO50 8PG

Societies, prizes and festivals

tel 023-8060 0439
email anne.marley@tiscali.co.uk
website www.branfordboaseaward.org.uk

An annual award of £1,000 is made to a first-time writer of a full-length children's novel (age 7+) published in the preceding year; the editor is also recognised. Its aim is to encourage new writers for children and to recognise the role of perceptive editors in developing new talent. The Award was set up in memory of the outstanding children's writer Henrietta Branford and the gifted editor and publisher Wendy Boase who both died in 1999. Closing date for nominations: end of December. Founded 2000.

The Bridport Prize

The Bridport Prize, PO Box 6910, Dorset DT6 9BQ
tel (01308) 428333
email frances@bridportprize.org.uk
website www.bridportprize.org.uk

Annual prizes are awarded for poetry and short stories (1st £5,000, 2nd £1,000, 3rd £500) in both categories, and £1,000 for short short stories (under 250 words). Entries should be in English, original work, typed or clearly written, and never published, read on radio/TV/stage. Winning stories are read by a leading London literary agent, without obligation, and an anthology of winning entries is published each autumn. Top 4 poems are submitted to the Forward Poetry Prizes and top 13 eligible stories are submitted to the National Short Story Award and *The Sunday Times* Short Story Prize. Send sae for entry form or enter online. Closing date: 31 May each year.

Bristol Festival of Ideas Book Prize

Bristol Festival of Ideas,
Bristol Cultural Development Partnership,
Leigh Court, Abbots Leigh, Bristol BS8 3RA
email ideas@gwebusinesswest.co.uk
website www.ideasfestival.co.uk

A prize of £10,000 is awarded to the book which is judged to present new, important and challenging ideas, which is rigorously argued, and which is engaging and accessible. A book of ideas may be a work of fiction or non-fiction, poetry or prose. Submission deadline: October. Awarded in association with Arts & Business and Blackwell bookshops. Founded 2008.

British Academy Medals and Prizes

The British Academy, 10 Carlton House Terrace, London SW1Y 5AH
tel 020-7969 5200 *fax* 020-7969 5300
email secretary@britac.ac.uk
website www.britac.ac.uk

A number of medals and prizes are awarded for outstanding work in various fields of the humanities on the recommendation of specialist committees: Burkitt Medal for Biblical Studies; Derek Allen Prize (made annually in turn for musicology, numismatics and Celtic studies); Sir Israel Gollancz Prize (for English studies); Grahame Clark Medal for Prehistoric Archaeology; Kenyon Medal for Classical Studies; Rose Mary Crawshay Prize (for English literature); Serena Medal for Italian Studies; Leverhulme Medal and Prize; The John Coles Medal for Landscape Archaeology, The Wiley Prize in Psychology.

British Book Awards – see Galaxy National Book Awards

British Czech & Slovak Association Writing Competition

24 Ferndale, Tunbridge Wells, Kent TN2 3NS
tel (01892) 543206
email prize@bcsa.co.uk
website www.bcsa.co.uk
Contact BCSA Prize Administrator

Annual competition (1st prize: £300; 2nd prize: £100) for fiction or non-fiction on the theme of the links between Britain and the Czech and Slovak Republics, at any time in their history, or society in transition in those republics since the Velvet Revolution in 1989. Winning entries published in *British Czech & Slovak Review*. Length: 2,000 words max. Closing date: 30 June each year. Established 2002.

British Press Awards

Press Gazette, Brunel House,
55–57 North Wharf Road, London W2 1AL
tel 020-7936 6433
email pged@pressgazette.co.uk
website www.britishpressawards.com, www.pressgazette.co.uk

Annual awards for British journalism judged by more than 80 respected, influential judges as well as representatives from all the national newspaper groups. Closing date: mid-January.

British Sports Book Awards

c/o Agile Marketing, Magnolia House,
172 Winsley Road, Bradford-on-Avon,
Wiltshire BA15 1NY
tel (01580) 212041
email merric@agile-ideas.com
website www.britishsportsbookawards.co.uk
Contact Merric Davidson

Sports books published in the UK in hardback or paperback in the calendar year are eligible. Categories include biography, cricket, football, golf, horse racing, motorsports and rugby. Nominations are called in December/January over a 4-week period. Winners are announced at an annual awards ceremony in May. See website for full details.

The Caine Prize for African Writing

Lizzy Attree, Administrator, The Menier Gallery,
Menier Chocolate Factory, 51 Southwark Street,
London SE5 1RU

tel 020-7378 6234
email info@caineprize.com
website www.caineprize.com

An annual award of £10,000 for a short story published in English (may be a translation into English) by an African writer in the 5 years before the closing date, and not previously submitted. Indicative length 3,000–10,000 words. Submissions only by publishers. Closing date: 31 January each year. Founded 1999.

Carnegie Medal – see The CILIP Carnegie and Kate Greenaway Awards

The CBI Book of the Year Awards

Children's Books Ireland,
CBI Book of the Year Awards,
17 North Great Georges Street, Dublin 1,
Republic of Ireland
tel +353 (0)1 8727475 *fax* +353 (0)1 8727476
email info@childrensbooksireland.ie
website www.childrensbooksireland.ie

These awards are made annually to authors and illustrators born or resident in Ireland and are open to books written in Irish or English. Closing date: December for work published between 1 January and 31 December of an awards year. Winners announced in May. Founded 1990.

The CBI Book of the Year Award

The award is presented to the overall winner (text and/or illustration).

The CBI Honour Awards

Three separate awards: one given for excellence in fiction, one for illustration and an overall special judges award.

The CBI Eilís Dillon Award

An award presented to an author for a first children's book.

Cheltenham Illustration Awards

The CIA, Francis Close Hall Campus,
University of Gloucestershire, Swindon Road,
Cheltenham, Glos. GL50 4AZ
email cheltillustrationawards@glos.ac.uk
website www.cheltenham-illustration-awards.com

Now in their sixth year, the Awards are for students and new illustrators. The winning entries, together with a selection of runners up, will have their work exhibited and also published as a full-colour annual. The Emerging Talent first prize is £1,000 and the runner up will receive £500; the Student prize will be an Apple Mac computer and both will have their work showcased. Artwork must be supplied digitally; up to 5 entries per person. Entry fee: £12.50 per entry. See website for details.

The Children's Laureate

Booktrust, Book House, 45 East Hill,
London SW18 2QZ
tel 020-8516 2977
email childrenslaureate@booktrust.org.uk
website www.childrenslaureate.org.uk

The role of Children's Laureate, which has a bursary of £15,000, is awarded once every 2 years to honour a writer or illustrator of children's books to celebrate outstanding achievement. It highlights the importance of exceptional children's book creators in developing the readers of tomorrow. Children's Laureates: Julia Donaldson (2011–13), Anthony Browne (2009–11), Michael Rosen (2007–9), Jacqueline Wilson (2005–7), Michael Morpurgo (2003–5), Anne Fine (2001–3), Quentin Blake (1999–2001). Founded 1998.

Cholmondeley Awards

Paula Johnson, Awards Secretary,
The Society of Authors, 84 Drayton Gardens,
London SW10 9SB
tel 020-7373 6642
email info@societyofauthors.org
website www.societyofauthors.org

These honorary awards are to recognise the achievement and distinction of individual poets. Submissions are not accepted. Total value of awards about £8,000. Established by the then Dowager Marchioness of Cholmondeley in 1965.

The CILIP Carnegie and Kate Greenaway Awards

CILIP, 7 Ridgmount Street, London WC1E 7AE
tel 020-7255 0650 *fax* 020-7255 0651
email ckg@cilip.org.uk
website www.carnegiegreenaway.org.uk

Recommendations for the following 2 awards are invited from members of CILIP (the Chartered Institute of Library and Information Professionals), who are asked to submit a preliminary list of not more than 2 titles for each award, accompanied by a 50-word appraisal justifying the recommendation of each book. The awards are selected by the Youth Libraries Group of CILIP.

Carnegie Medal

Awarded annually for an outstanding book for children (fiction or non-fiction) written in English and first published in the UK during the preceding year or co-published elsewhere within a 3-month time lapse.

Kate Greenaway Medal

Awarded annually for an outstanding illustrated book for children first published in the UK during the preceding year or co-published elsewhere within a 3-month time lapse. Books intended for older as well as younger children are included, and reproduction will be taken into account. The Colin Mears Award (£5,000) is awarded annually to the winner of the Kate Greenaway Medal.

Arthur C. Clarke Award

website www.clarkeaward.com

An annual award of £2,011 plus engraved bookend is given for the best science fiction novel with first UK publication during the previous calendar year. Titles are submitted by publishers. Founded 1985.

The David Cohen Prize for Literature

Booktrust, Book House, 45 East Hill, London SW18 2QZ
tel 020-8516 2972
email prizes@booktrust.org.uk
Contact Claire Shanahan

Awarded biennially, this £40,000 prize recognises a lifetime's achievement in literature, honouring a writer in the English language who is a citizen of the UK or the Republic of Ireland. The winner of the prize is nominated and selected by a panel of judges comprising authors, literary critics and academics; no shortlist is announced. The John S. Cohen Foundation finances the prize and Arts Council England provides a further £12,500 for the Clarissa Luard Award, which the winner of the David Cohen Prize awards to a literature organisation that supports young writers or an individual writer under the age of 35. 2011 winner: Julian Barnes. Founded 1991.

Commonwealth Writers

Commonwealth Foundation, Marlborough House, Pall Mall, London SW1Y 5HY
email writers@commonwealth.int
website www.commonwealthwriters.org

Commonwealth Writers – A World of New Fiction is an ongoing cultural programme within the Commonwealth Foundation which develops, connects and inspires writers. By awarding prizes and running activities it works in partnership with international literary organisations, the wider cultural industries and civil society to help writers develop their craft in the 54 countries of the Commonwealth. The website provides a forum where members from anywhere in the world can exchange ideas and contribute to debates. There are 2 prizes awarded by Commonwealth Writers. The Commonwealth Book Prize is open to writers who have had their first novel (full-length work of fiction) published between 1 January and 31 December 2012. The overall winner receives £10,000. Regional winners will receive £2,500. The Commonwealth Short Story Prize is awarded for the best piece of unpublished short fiction (2,000-5,000 words). The overall winner receives £5,000. Regional winners will receive £1,000.

The Duff Cooper Prize

Artemis Cooper, 54 St Maur Road, London SW6 4DP
tel 020-7736 3729
website www.theduffcooperprize.org

An annual prize for a literary work in the field of biography, history, politics or poetry published in English or French and submitted by a recognised publisher during the previous 12 months. The prize of £5,000 comes from a Trust Fund established by the friends and admirers of Duff Cooper, 1st Viscount Norwich (1890–1954) after his death.

Cordon d'Or – Gold Ribbon Culinary Academy Awards

PO Box 40868, St Petersburg, FL 33743–0868, USA
email cordondor@aol.com
website www.goldribboncookery.com
Contact Noreen Kinney, President

Awards for authors, writers, journalists, photographers, newsletters, websites, cookbooks and culinary literature. Overall winner receives $1,000. See website for details. Founded 2003.

Costa Book Awards

(formerly the Whitbread Book Awards)
The Booksellers Association, 6 Bell Yard, London WC2A 2JR
tel 020-74214640
email info@costabookawards.com
website www.costabookawards.com
Contact Naomi Gane

The awards celebrate and promote the most enjoyable contemporary British writing. Judged in 2 stages and offering a total of £55,000 prize money, there are 5 categories: Novel, First Novel, Biography, Poetry and Children's. They are judged by a panel of 3 judges and the winner in each category receives £5,000. Nine final judges then choose the Costa Book of the Year from the 5 category winners. The overall winner receives £30,000. Authors of submitted books must have been resident in the UK or Ireland for over 6 months of each of the previous 3 years (although UK or Irish nationality is not essential). Books must have been first published in the UK or Ireland between 1 November of the previous year and 31 October of the current year. Books previously published elsewhere are not eligible. Submissions must be received from publishers. Closing date: end of June.

The Rose Mary Crawshay Prizes

The British Academy, 10 Carlton House Terrace, London SW1Y 5AH
tel 020-7969 5200 *fax* 020-7969 5300
email secretary@britac.ac.uk
website www.britac.ac.uk

One or more prizes are awarded each year to women of any nationality who, in the judgement of the Council of the British Academy, have written or published within the 3 calendar years immediately preceding the date of the award an historical or critical work of sufficient value on any subject connected with English literature, preference being given to a work regarding Byron, Shelley or Keats. Founded 1888.

Creative Scotland

tel 0330 333 2000
email enquiries@creativescotland.com
website www.creativescotland.com

A limited number of writers' bursaries of up to £15,000 each are offered to enable professional writers based in Scotland, including writers for children, to devote more time to writing. Priority is given to writers of fiction and verse and playwrights, but writers of literary non-fiction are also considered. Applications may be discussed with Gavin Wallace. See also Scottish Children's Book Awards (page 565).

Scottish Mortgage Investment Trust Book Awards

email aly.barr@scottisharts.org.uk
Contact Aly Barr, Literature Officer

Scotland's largest literary prize, which recognises and rewards literary excellence and merit. There are 4 awards, each worth £5,000, selected by a distinguished panel of judges at the end of February. They are: Fiction, First Book, Non-fiction, and Poetry. The 4 category winning titles will be considered for the Book of the Year award and the winning title will secure an overall prize of £30,000.

Eligible books are those published for the first time between January and December and should be submitted by 31 December each year. While preference is given to literary fiction and poetry, many other types of books are eligible, in particular literary non-fiction such as biography, history, essays, etc. Reprints, technical or scientific books, and books that are highly specialised will not be considered. Authors of submitted books should be Scottish or resident in Scotland but books of particular Scottish interest by other authors are eligible for consideration. Posthumous awards cannot be made. Publishers are invited to enter suitable books on behalf of their authors by submitting 6 copies of each title, together with biographical information on the author. Publishers of books selected for the shortlist will be requested to submit additional copies. Writers may not submit entries.

The John D. Criticos Prize

The London Hellenic Society, The Hellenic Centre, 16–18 Paddington Street, London W1U 5AS
email msmoschos@yahoo.com, jason.leech@criticosprize.org
website www.criticosprize.org
Prize Coordinator, Michael Moschos, *Assistant*, Jason Leech

Established in 1996 and funded by the Criticos-Fotinelli Foundation, the Prize, worth £10,000, will be awarded to the author of an original work in English printed in 2012 and inspired by Greek or Hellenic culture: ancient, Hellenistic, Byzantine or modern. Areas of interest are not restricted but, because the work must be accessible to a broad readership, shortlists revolve around archaeology, art, history and literature (fiction, poetry, travel). Individual applicants or their publishers may submit any number of titles (2 copies of each). Closing date 31 January 2013. The winner will be announced in June.

CWA Awards

email secretary@thecwa.co.uk
website www.thecwa.co.uk

Awards for crime writing: the Cartier Diamond Dagger; the New Blood Dagger; the CWA International Dagger; the CWA Gold Dagger for Fiction; the Gold Dagger for Non-Fiction; the CWA Ellis Peters Historical Award; the CWA Short Story Award; the Debut Dagger; the Ian Fleming Steel Dagger, the Dagger in the Library. See website for details.

The Rhys Davies Trust

Details Prof Meic Stephens, The Secretary, The Rhys Davies Trust, 10 Heol Don, Whitchurch, Cardiff CF14 2AU
tel 029-2062 3359

The Trust aims to foster Welsh writing in English and offers financial assistance to English-language literary projects in Wales, directly or in association with other bodies.

Deutsche Börse Photography Prize

The Photographers' Gallery, 16–18 Ramillies Street, London W1F 7LW
tel 020-7087 9310
email info@photonet.org.uk
website www.thephotographersgallery.org.uk

Aims to reward a living photographer, of any nationality, who has made the most significant contribution to the medium of photography during the past year (1st prize £30,000; 3 runners up will each receive £3,000). Photographers will be nominated for a significant exhibition that took place or publication that was published in Europe during that time, and 4 shortlisted photographers will be selected and invited to present their work in an exhibition at the Gallery. Founded in 1996 by the Photographers' Gallery.

The Dundee International Book Prize

email book.prize@dundeecity.gov.uk
website www.dundeebookprize.com

A prize (£10,000 and the chance of publication by Polygon) awarded for an unpublished novel. Founded 1996.

Edge Hill Short Story Prize

Edge Hill University, St Helens Road, Ormskirk, Lancs. L39 4QP
tel (01695) 584121
email ailsa.cox@edgehill.ac.uk
website www.edgehill.ac.uk/shortstory
Contact Ailsa Cox

This prize is awarded annually by Edge Hill University for excellence in a published single author short story collection. The winner will receive £5,000 and a Readers' Choice prize of £1,000 is awarded to a writer from the shortlist. Publishers are entitled to submit collections published during the preceding year. Authors must be born or normally resident in the British Isles (including Ireland). Deadline: 1 March.

The T.S. Eliot Prize

Poetry Book Society, 4th Floor, 2 Tavistock Place, London WC1H 9RA
tel 020-7833 9247
email info@poetrybooks.co.uk
website www.poetrybooks.co.uk, www.poetrybookshoponline.com

An annual prize of £15,000, with £1,000 for each of the ten shortlisted poets, is awarded by the Poetry Book Society to the best collection of new poetry published in the UK or the Republic of Ireland during the year. Submissions are invited from publishers in the summer. The prize money is provided by Valerie Eliot. The prize is accompanied by a Shadowing Scheme for schools, which enables students to read the best new poetry and shadow the judges. Founded 1993.

The Desmond Elliott Prize

Emma Manderson, Administrator, The Desmond Elliott Charitable Trust, 84 Godolphin Road, London W12 8JW
tel 020-8222 6580
email ema.manderson@googlemail.com
website www.desmondelliottprize.org

An annual prize for a first novel written in English by an author resident in the UK or Ireland and published in the UK. Worth £10,000 to the winner, the prize is named after the literary agent and publisher, Desmond Elliott, who died in 2003. Qualities the judges will be looking for are: a debut novel of depth and breadth with a compelling narrative, original and arresting characters, vividly written and confidently realised. Founded 2007.

Encore Award

email encoreprize@hotmail.co.uk

The prize of £10,000 is awarded annually to a UK or Commonwealth writer whose second novel is first published in the UK between 1 January and 31 December. All books must be submitted via the publisher; direct submissions from authors cannot be accepted. Self-published books or those published by vanity publishers cannot be accepted. The closing date for submissions is 1 November. Submission suggestions should be sent by email.

The European Publishers Award

Dewi Lewis Publishing, 8 Broomfield Road, Heaton Moor, Stockport SK4 4ND
tel 0161 442 9450 *fax* 0161 442 9450
email mail@dewilewispublishing.com
website www.dewilewispublishing.com

Annual competition for the best set of photographs suitable for publication as a book. All photographic material must be completed and unpublished in book form and be original. Projects conceived as anthologies are not acceptable. Copyright must belong to the photographer. See website for details. Founded 1994.

The Geoffrey Faber Memorial Prize

An annual prize of £1,000 is awarded in alternate years for a volume of verse and for a volume of prose fiction, first published originally in the UK during the 2 years preceding the year in which the award is given which is, in the opinion of the judges, of the greatest literary merit. Eligible writers must be not more than 40 years old at the date of publication of the book and a citizen of the UK and Colonies, of any other Commonwealth state or of the Republic of Ireland. The 3 judges are reviewers of poetry or fiction who are nominated each year by the literary editors of newspapers and magazines which regularly publish such reviews. Faber and Faber invite nominations from reviewers and literary editors. No submissions for the prize are to be made. Established in 1963 by Faber and Faber Ltd, as a memorial to the founder and first Chairman of the firm.

The Alfred Fagon Award

c/o Talawa Theatre Company, 53–55 East Road, London N1 6AH
email info@alfredfagonaward.co.uk
website www.alfredfagonaward.co.uk

An annual award of £5,000 for the best new play (which need not have been produced) for the theatre in English. TV and radio plays and film scripts will not be considered. Only writers from the Caribbean or with Caribbean antecedence and who are resident in the UK are eligible. Applicants should submit 2 copies of their play plus sae for return of their script and a CV which includes details of the writer's Caribbean connection. Closing date: end August. Founded 1997.

The Eleanor Farjeon Award

website www.childrensbookcircle.org.uk

An annual award may be given to an individual or an organisation. Librarians, authors, publishers, teachers, reviewers and others who have given exceptional service to the children's book industry are eligible for nomination. It was instituted in 1965 by the Children's Book Circle (page 513) for distinguished services to children's books and named after the much-loved children's writer Eleanor Farjeon.

Financial Times and Goldman Sachs Business Book of the Year Award

email bookaward@ft.com
website www.ft.com/indepth/business-book-award-2012

To identify the book that provides the most compelling and enjoyable insight into modern business issues, including management, finance and economics. Submissions should come via the publisher. The winner will receive £30,000 and each runner up will receive £10,000. Closing date: end of June.

Fish Short Story Prize, Short Memoir Prize, Flash Fiction Prize, and Poetry Prize

Contact Clem Cairns, Fish Publishing, Durrus, Bantry, Co. Cork, Republic of Ireland
email info@fishpublishing.com
website www.fishpublishing.com

International writing prizes set up to publish and encourage new writers. The best 10 or more from each competition are published in the annual Fish Anthology in July.

• Fish Short Story Prize: €3,000 first, second €300 and a week at Anam Cara Writers and Artists' Retreat in West Cork. Entry €20 for 5,000 words or less. Closing date: 30 November. Results: mid-March. *Hon. Patrons* Roddy Doyle, Colum McCann, Dermot Healy. Established 1994.
• Fish Short Memoir Prize: €2,000. Closing date: 30 January. Results: March. €15 entry for entries of 4,000 words or less.
• Fish Flash Fiction Prize: €1,000. Closing date: mid-March. Results: end April. €14 entry for stories up to 300 words.
• Fish Poetry Prize: €1,000. Closing date: end March. Results: end April. €14 entry for poems up to 200 words.
• The Fish Critique service is available all year for help with short fiction and poetry, and the Editorial Consultancy is for writers of longer works or screenplays. See website for details.
• Online writing courses is Flash Fiction and Memoir (Life Writing). Three month courses to do in your own time with one-to-one tuition.

Established 1994.

The Paul Foot Award

tel 020-7590 8909
email tracey.jennings@midaspr.co.uk
website www.private-eye.co.uk
Contact Margot Weale

An award to honour campaigning journalism in the UK, in memory of revered investigative journalist Paul Foot. Submissions will be accepted for material that has been published in a newspaper, magazine or online between 1 September and 31 August each year. No broadcast material is eligible. Individual journalists, teams of journalists or entire publications may enter and entries will be considered for anything from single pieces to entire campaigns. The overall winner will be awarded £5,000, with the 5 runners up each receiving £1,000. See website for downloadable application form. Closing date: September. Sponsored by *Private Eye* and the *Guardian*.

E.M. Forster Award

American Academy of Arts and Letters, 633 West 155th Street, New York, NY 10032, USA
tel +1 212-368-5900
website www.artsandletters.org

The distinguished English author, E.M. Forster, bequeathed the American publication rights and royalties of his posthumous novel *Maurice* to Christopher Isherwood, who transferred them to the American Academy of Arts and Letters, for the establishment of an E.M. Forster Award, currently $20,000, to be given annually to a British or Irish writer for a stay in the USA. Applications for this award are not accepted.

Forward Prizes for Poetry

Forward Poetry Prize Administrator, Four Colman Getty, The Communications Building, 48 Leicester Square, London WC2H 7FG
tel 020-3032 9900
email info@fourcolmangetty.com
website www.fourcolmangetty.com

3 prizes are awarded annually:

• The Forward Prize for best collection published between 1 October and 30 September (£10,000);
• The Felix Dennis Prize for best first collection published between 1 October and 30 September (£5,000); and
• The Forward Prize for best single poem in memory of Michael Donaghy, published but not as part of a collection between 1 May and 30 April (£1,000).

All poems entered are also considered for inclusion in the *Forward Book of Poetry*, an annual anthology. Entries must be submitted by book publishers and editors of newspapers, periodicals and magazines in the UK and Eire. Entries from individual poets of their unpublished or self-published work will not be accepted. Established 1992.

Miles Franklin Literary Award

The Trust Company, GPO Box 4270, Sydney, NSW 2001, Australia
tel +61 (0)2 8295 8100
email trustawards@thetrustcompany.com.au
website www.milesfranklin.com.au

This annual award of $50,000 is for a novel or play first published in the preceding year, which presents Australian life in any of its phases. More than one entry may be submitted by each author. Biographies, collections of short stories or children's books are not eligible. Closing date: December, check website for date. Founded 1954.

Galaxy National Book Awards

Merric Davidson, PO Box 60, Cranbrook, Kent TN17 2ZR

tel (01580) 212041
email merric@agile-ideas.com
website www.galaxynationalbookawards.com

Award categories include: Popular Fiction, Non-fiction, Food and Drink, New Writer, Children's Book, Biography, Author, International Author plus Outstanding Achievement. Sponsored by Galaxy. Founded 1989.

The Lionel Gelber Prize

Prize Manager, The Lionel Gelber Prize, c/o Munk Centre for International Studies, University of Toronto, 1 Devonshire Place, Toronto, Ontario M5S 3K7, Canada
tel +1 416-946 8901 *fax* +1 416-946 8915
email gelberprize.munk@utoronto.ca
website www.utoronto.ca/mcis/gelber

This international prize is awarded annually in Canada to the author of the year's most outstanding work of non-fiction in the field of international relations. Submissions must be published in English or in English translation. Books must be submitted by the publisher. Full eligibility details are on website. Established 1989.

Gladstone History Book Prize

Administrative Secretary, Royal Historical Society, University College London, Gower Street, London WC1E 6BT
tel 020-7387 7532
email royalhistsoc@ucl.ac.uk
website www.royalhistsoc.org/prizes.php

An annual award (value £1,000) for a history book. The book must:

• be on any historical subject which is not primarily related to British history;
• be its author's first solely written history book;
• have been published in English during the calendar year of 2012 by a scholar normally resident in the UK;
• be an original and scholarly work of historical research.

One non-returnable copy of an eligible book should be submitted by the publisher before 31 December. Should the book be shortlisted, 2 further copies will be required.

Kate Greenaway Medal – see The CILIP Carnegie and Kate Greenaway Awards

The Eric Gregory Trust Fund

Paula Johnson, Awards Secretary, The Society of Authors, 84 Drayton Gardens, London SW10 9SB
tel 020-7373 6642
email info@societyofauthors.org
website www.societyofauthors.org

A number of substantial awards are made annually for the encouragement of young poets who can show that they are likely to benefit from an opportunity to give more time to writing. An eligible candidate must:

• be a British subject by birth, but not a national of Eire or any of the British dominions or colonies, and be ordinarily resident in the UK or Northern Ireland;
• be under the age of 30 on 31 March in the year of the Award (i.e. the year following submission).
Download or send sae for entry form. Closing date, 31 October.

Griffin Poetry Prize

The Griffin Trust for Excellence in Poetry, 363 Parkridge Crescent, Oakville, Ontario L6M 1A8
tel +1 905-618 0420
email info@griffinpoetryprize.com
website www.griffinpoetryprize.com

Two annual prizes of Can$65,000 will be awarded for collections of poetry published in English during the preceding year. One prize will go to a living Canadian poet, the other to a living poet from any country. Collections of poetry translated into English from other languages are also eligible and will be assessed for their literary quality in English. Submissions only from publishers. Closing date: 31 December. Founded 2000.

The Guardian Children's Fiction Prize

email childrensprize@guardian.co.uk

The *Guardian's* annual prize of £1,500 is for a work of fiction for children over 8 (no picture books) published by a British or Commonwealth writer. The winning book is chosen by the Children's Book Editor together with a team of 3–4 authors of children's books.

The Guardian First Book Award

email firstbook@guardian.co.uk

Open to first-time authors published in English in the UK across all genres of writing, the award will recognise and reward new writing by honouring an author's first book. The winner will receive £10,000 plus an advertising package within the *Guardian* and the *Observer*. Publishers may submit up to 3 titles per imprint with publication dates between January and December each year.

The Guardian Research Fellowship

Academic Administrator, The Guardian Research Fellowship, Nuffield College, Oxford OX1 1NF
tel (01865) 278542

A biennial Fellowship to be held for one year at Nuffield College, Oxford, to research or study any project related to the experience of working in the media. It is hoped that the Fellow will produce a book or substantial piece of written work. The Fellow will be asked to give the *Guardian* lecture following the end of their Fellowship. The Fellowship is open to people working in newspapers, TV, the internet or other media. Founded 1987.

Hawthornden Fellowships

The Director, International Retreat for Writers, Hawthornden Castle, Lasswade, Midlothian EH18 1EG
tel 0131 440 2180 *fax* 0131 440 1989

Applications are invited from novelists, poets, dramatists and other creative writers whose work has already been published by reputable or recognised presses. Four-week fellowships are offered to those working on a current project. Translators may also apply. Application forms are available from January for Fellowships awarded in the following year. Deadline for applications 30 June.

The Hawthornden Prize

The Director, International Retreat for Writers, Hawthornden Castle, Lasswade, Midlothian, Scotland EH18 1EG

This prize of £10,000 is awarded annually to the author of what, in the opinion of the Committee, is the best work of imaginative literature published during the preceding calendar year by a British author. Books do not have to be specially submitted.

Francis Head Bequest

Sarah Baxter, The Society of Authors, 84 Drayton Gardens, London SW10 9SB
tel 020-7373 6642 *fax* 020-7373 5768
email info@societyofauthors.org
website www.societyofauthors.org

This fund provides grants to published British authors over the age of 35 who need financial help during a period of illness, disablement or temporary financial crisis. Apply for guidelines and application form.

The Felicia Hemans Prize for Lyrical Poetry

Dr Judi Turner-Gill, School Manager, The Felicia Hemans Prize for Lyrical Poetry, School of Arts, The University of Liverpool, 19 Abercromby Square, Liverpool L69 7ZG
tel 0151 795 0563
email judi.turner-gill@liverpool.ac.uk

This annual prize of books or money, open to past and present members and students of the University of Liverpool only, is awarded for a lyrical poem, the subject of which may be chosen by the competitor. Only one poem, either published or unpublished, may be submitted. The prize shall not be awarded more than once to the same competitor. Poems, endorsed Hemans Prize', must be submitted by 1 May.

Hessell-Tiltman Prize

English PEN, 60 Farringdon Road, London EC1R 3GA
tel 020-7324 2535
email enquiries@englishpen.org
website www.englishpen.org

An annual prize made possible by a bequest to the PEN Literary Foundation of £100,000 from PEN member Marjorie Hessell-Tiltman. Each year the prize is awarded to a non-fiction work of high literary merit covering any historical period until the end of the Second World War. Submissions are not accepted. Founded 2002.

William Hill Sports Book of the Year Award

Graham Sharpe, William Hill Organisation, Greenside House, 50 Station Road, London N22 4TP
tel 020-8918 3731
website www.williamhillmedia.com

This award is given annually in November for a book with a sporting theme (record books and listings excluded). The title must be in the English language, and published for the first time in the UK during the relevant calendar year. Total value of prize is £25,000, including £23,000 in cash. An award for the best cover design has total value of £1,000. Founded 1989.

The Calvin and Rose G. Hoffman Memorial Prize for Distinguished Publication on Christopher Marlowe

Applications The Hoffman Administrator, The King's School, Canterbury, Kent CT1 2ES
tel (01227) 595544 *fax* (01227) 595589
email bursar@kings-bursary.co.uk

This annual prize of around £9,000 is awarded to the best unpublished work that examines the life and works of Christopher Marlowe and the relationship between the works of Marlowe and Shakespeare. Closing date: 1 September.

L. Ron Hubbard's Writers and Illustrators of the Future Contests

Administrator Andrea Grant-Webb, PO Box 218, East Grinstead, West Sussex RH19 4GH
website www.writersofthefuture.com

Aims to encourage new and aspiring writers and illustrators of science fiction and fantasy. In addition to the quarterly prizes there is an annual prize of £2,500 for each contest. All 24 winners are invited to the annual L. Ron Hubbard Achievement Awards, which include a series of writers' and illustrators' workshops, and their work is published in an anthology. Write for an entry form.

Writers of the Future Contest

Entrants should submit a short story of up to 10,000 words or a novelette of less than 17,000 words. Prizes of £600 (1st), £450 (2nd) and £300 (3rd) are awarded each quarter. Founded 1984.

Illustrators of the Future Contest

Entrants should submit 3 b&w illustrations on different themes. Three prizes of £300 are awarded each quarter. Founded 1988.

The Ted Hughes Award for New Work in Poetry

Competition Organiser, The Poetry Society, 22 Betterton Street, London WC2H 9BX
tel 020-7420 9880 *fax* 020-7240 4818
email info@poetrysociety.org.uk
website www.poetrysociety.org.uk

An annual award of £5,000 for a living UK poet, working in any form, who has made the most exciting contribution to poetry over the year. Organised by the Poetry Society and funded by Carol Ann Duffy with the honorarium which the Poet Laureate traditionally receives from H.M. the Queen.

Images – The Best of British Contemporary Illustration

Association of Illustrators, 2nd Floor, Back Building, 150 Curtain Road, London EC2A 3AT
tel 020-7613 4328 *fax* 020-7613 4417
email info@theaoi.com
website www.theaoi.com, www.aoiimages.com
Contact Images Programme Manager

Illustrators are invited to submit work for possible inclusion in the *Images* annual, a jury-selected showcase of the best of contemporary British illustration, which is distributed to 4,000 commissioners. Selected work forms the Images exhibition, which tours the UK. UK illustrators or illustrators working for UK clients are all eligible. See website for entry details. Founded 1975.

The Imison Award

The Secretary, The Broadcasting Committee, The Society of Authors, 84 Drayton Gardens, London SW10 9SB
tel 020-7373 6642 *fax* 020-7373 5768
email info@societyofauthors.org
website www.societyofauthors.org

This annual prize of £1,500 is awarded to any new writer of radio drama first transmitted within the UK during the previous 18 months by a writer new to radio. Founded 1995.

The Impress Prize for New Writers

Innovation Centre, Rennes Drive, University of Exeter, Devon EX4 4RN
tel (01392) 262301 *fax* (01392) 262303
email enquiries@impress-books.co.uk
website www.impress-books.co.uk
Contact Richard Willis, Colin Morgan

This prize aims to find exciting new, unpublished writing talent. The winner will receive a publishing contract from Impress Books and will be chosen from a shortlist by a panel of judges working in the book industry. Entry fee: £10. Established 2006.

Independent Foreign Fiction Prize

Booktrust, Book House, 45 East Hill, London SW18 2QZ
tel 020-8516 2972
email prizes@booktrust.org.uk
website www.translatedfiction.org.uk
Contact Claire Shanahan

This prize honours the best work of fiction by a living author which has been translated into English and published in the UK during the prize year. Uniquely, this prize gives the winning author and translator equal status: they each receive £5,000. The prize ran until 1995 and was then revived in 2000 with the support of Arts Council England, which continues to fund the award in association with Champagne Tattinger and the *Independent*. This prize also forms part of the Booktrust campaign to celebrate translated fiction. Closing date: late September. 2010 winner: Phillippe Claudel (author) and John Cullen (translator) for *Brodeck's Report* (Quercus). Established 1990.

Insight Guides Travel Photography Prize

APA Publications (UK) Ltd, 58 Borough High Street, London SE1 1XF
tel 020-7403 0284 *fax* 020-7403 0290
website www.insightguides.com

An annual competition open to amateur and professional photographers resident in the UK. First prize is a commission to photograph for an *Insight Guide* worth £3,000. Closing date: September. Founded 2000.

International IMPAC Dublin Literary Award

Ms Cathy McKenna, The International IMPAC Dublin Literary Award, Dublin City Library & Archive, 138–144 Pearse Street, Dublin 2, Republic of Ireland
tel +353 (0)16 744802 *fax* +353 (0)16 744879
email literaryaward@dublincity.ie
website www.impacdublinaward.i'

This award is the largest and most international prize of its kind. Administered by Dublin City Public Libraries, nominations are made by libraries in capital and major cities throughout the world. Novels are nominated solely on the basis of 'high literary merit' and books may be written in any language.

The prize is €100,000 which is awarded to the author if the book is written in English. If the winning book is in English translation, the author receives €75,000 and the translator €25,000. The Award, an initiative of Dublin City Council, is a partnership between Dublin City Council, the Municipal Government of Dublin City, and IMPAC. Established 1996.

International Playwriting Festival

Festival Administrator, Warehouse Theatre, Dingwall Road, Croydon CR0 2NF
tel 020-8681 1257 *fax* 020-8688 6699

email info@warehousetheatre.co.uk
website www.warehousetheatre.co.uk

An annual competition for full-length unperformed plays. Selected plays are showcased during the festival weekend in November. Plays are also presented in Italy at the leading Italian playwriting festival Premio Candoni Arta Terme. Entries are welcome from all parts of the world. Send sae for further details or visit the website. Deadline for entries: 30 June. See also page 575. Founded 1985.

The ISG Reference Awards

CILIP, 7 Ridgemount Street, London WC1E 7AE
tel 020-7255 0500 *fax* 020-7255 0501
email isgrefawards@cilip.org.uk/isg
website www.cilip.org.uk/isg

The Besterman/McColvin Medals

Awarded annually for outstanding works of reference that have become available and relevant to the library and information sector in the UK within the preceding year. There are 2 categories, one for electronic formats and one for printed works. Recommendations are invited from Members of CILIP (the Chartered Institute of Library and Information Professionals), publishers and others, who are asked to submit a preliminary list of not more than 3 titles via email. Winners receive a certificate.

The Walford Award

Awarded annually to an individual for outstanding contribution to the world of reference and information services. Recommendations may be made for the work of a living person or persons, or for an organisation. The winner receives a certificate and a cheque for £100.

Jewish Quarterly – Wingate Literary Prizes

Jewish Quarterly, ORT House, 126 Albert Street, London NW3 2EP
tel 020-7267 9442
email editorial@jewishquarterly.org
website www.jewishquarterly.org

Annual prize of £4,000 awarded for a work of fiction or non-fiction which best stimulate an interest in and awareness of themes of Jewish concern among a wider reading public. Founded 1977.

Samuel Johnson Prize for Non-Fiction – see BBC FOUR Samuel Johnson Prize for Non-Fiction

Kent and Sussex Poetry Society Open Poetry Competition

The Competition Organiser, 26 Courtlands, Teston, Maidstone, Kent ME18 5AS

This competition is open to all unpublished poems, no longer than 40 lines in length. Prizes: 1st £800, 2nd £300, 3rd £150, 4th 4 at £75. Closing date: 31 January. Entries should include an entry fee of £5 per poem, the author's name and address and a list of poems submitted. Founded 1985.

Kerry Group Irish Novel of the Year Award

Writers' Week, 24 The Square, Listowel, Co. Kerry, Republic of Ireland
tel +353 (0)68 21074
email info@writersweek.ie
website www.writersweek.ie

An annual award of €15,000 for a published novel by an Irish author; must be published between 1 March 2012 and 1 March 2013. No entry fee. Submit 8 copies. Closing date: 28th February 2013.

Kraszna-Krausz Awards

email info@kraszna-krausz.org.uk
website www.kraszna-krausz.org.uk

Awards totalling over £10,000 are made each year for the best photography book and best moving image book published in English. Entries to be submitted by publishers only. The Foundation also presents the Outstanding Contribution to Publishing Award and supports the National Media Museum First Book Award. Instituted in 1985.

Leverhulme Research Fellowships

The Leverhulme Trust, 1 Pemberton Row, London EC4A 3BG
tel 020-7042 9861
email agrundy@leverhulme.ac.uk
website www.leverhulme.ac.uk

The Leverhulme Trust Board offer annually approximately 90 fellowships to experienced researchers in aid of original research. These awards are not available as replacement for past support from other sources. Applications in all subject areas are considered. Applications must be completed online by mid November 2012 for 2013 awards. Refer to the website for further details. Founded 1933.

Literary Review Grand Poetry Prize

44 Lexington Street, London W1F 0LW
tel 020-7437 9392
email editorial@literaryreview.co.uk
website www.literaryreview.co.uk

Runs a competition each month for poems on a given subject which rhyme, scan and are no more than 24 lines. Monthly prizes of £300 and £150 are awarded. The Grand Prize of £5,000 is awarded to the best of these each year. Closing date: September. Founded 1990.

Literature Wales Cardiff International Poetry Competition

(formerly Academi Cardiff International Poetry Competition)

Literature Wales, Mount Stuart House,
Mount Stuart Square, Cardiff, Wales CF10 5FQ
tel 029-2047 2266
email post@literaturewales.org
website www.literaturewales.org
Chief Executive Peter Finch

Eight prizes awarded annually for unpublished poetry written in English and not a translation of another author's work (1st £5,000; 2nd £500; 3rd £250; plus 5 prizes of £50). For submission details, see website or send sae. Closing date: March.

John Llewellyn Rhys Prize

Booktrust, Book House, 45 East Hill,
London SW18 2QZ
tel 020-8516 2972
email prizes@booktrust.org.uk
website www.booktrust.org.uk
Contact Claire Shanahan

This annual prize of £5,000 (plus £500 to each shortlisted author) is made to an author aged 35 or under for a work of literature (fiction, poetry, drama, non-fiction, etc) which has been published in the UK during the calendar year of the prize. The author must be a UK or Commonwealth national. The prize was inaugurated in memory of the writer John Llewellyn Rhys who died in World War II, by his widow Jane Oliver. Established 1942.

London Press Club Awards

London Press Club, St Bride Institute, 14 Bride Lane,
Fleet Street, London EC4Y 8EQ
tel 020-7353 7086 *fax* 020-7353 7087
email info@londonpressclub.co.uk
website www.londonpressclub.co.uk

Business Journalist of the Year, Consumer Affairs Journalist of the Year, Daily Newspaper of the Year, Sunday Newspaper of the Year and Broadcasting Journalist of the Year.

Scoop of the Year Award

Chosen by a panel of senior editors, this annual award of a bronze statuette is given for the reporting scoop of the year, appearing in a newspaper. Founded 1990.

Edgar Wallace Award

Chosen by a panel of senior editors, this annual award of a silver inkstand is given for outstanding writing or reporting by a journalist. Founded 1990.

The Elizabeth Longford Grants

Paula Johnson, Awards Secretary,
The Society of Authors, 84 Drayton Gardens,
London SW10 9SB
tel 020-7373 6642 *fax* 020-7373 5768
email info@societyofauthors.org
website www.societyofauthors.org

Grants of £2,500 are made payable to 2 historical biographers each year whose publisher's advance is insufficient to cover the costs of research involved. Send sae for information. Sponsored by Flora Fraser and Peter Soros. Entry dates: 30 April and 30 September.

The Elizabeth Longford Prize for Historical Biography

Paula Johnson, Awards Secretary,
The Society of Authors, 84 Drayton Gardens,
London SW10 9SB
tel 020-7373 6642 *fax* 020-7373 5768
email info@societyofauthors.org
website www.societyofauthors.org

A prize of £5,000 is awarded annually for a historical biography published in the year preceding the prize. No unsolicited submissions. Established in 2003 in affectionate memory of Elizabeth Longford, the acclaimed biographer, and sponsored by Flora Fraser and Peter Soros.

The Sir William Lyons Award

The Guild of Motoring Writers' Secretariat,
40 Baring Road, Bournemouth BH6 4DT
tel (01202) 422424
email generalsec@gomw.co.uk
website www.guildofmotoringwriters.co.uk

Sponsored by Jaguar Cars in memory of Sir William Lyons, founder and president of Jaguar Cars, this annual award – trophy, £2,000 and two years' probationary membership of The Guild of Motoring Writers – was set up to encourage young people to foster interest in motoring and the motor industry through automotive journalism. Open to any person of British nationality resident in the UK aged 17–23 years at the closing date of 1 October. The entry consists of writing two essays and a shortlist interview with the Award Committee.

The McKitterick Prize

Paula Johnson, Awards Secretary,
The Society of Authors, 84 Drayton Gardens,
London SW10 9SB
tel 020-7373 6642
email info@societyofauthors.org
website www.societyofauthors.org

This annual award of £4,000 is open to first published novels (excluding works for children) and unpublished typescripts by authors over the age of 40. Closing date: 31 October. Endowed by the late Tom McKitterick. Download or send sae for entry form.

The Franco-British Society's Enid McLeod Literary Prize

Executive Secretary, Franco–British Society,
3 Dovedale Studios, 465 Battersea Park Road,
London SW11 4LR
tel 020-7924 3511
email francobritish@googlemail.com
website www.francobritishsociety.org.uk

This annual prize of £500 is given for a full-length work of literature which contributes most to Franco–British understanding. It must be first published in the UK between 1 January and 31 December, and written in English by a citizen of the UK, British Commonwealth or the Republic of Ireland. Closing date: 31 December.

Bryan MacMahon Short Story Award

Writers' Week, 24 The Square, Listowel, Co. Kerry, Republic of Ireland
tel +353 (0)68 21074
email info@writersweek.ie
website www.writersweek.ie

An annual award for the best short story (up to 3,000 words) on any subject. Prize: €2,000. Entry fee: €10. No entry form required. Closing date: 28 February 2013. Founded 1971.

The Macmillan Prize for Children's Picture Book Illustration

Macmillan Children's Books, 20 New Wharf Road, London N1 9RR
email macmillanprize@macmillan.co.uk

Five prizes are awarded annually for unpublished children's book illustrations by art students in higher education establishments in the UK. Prizes: £1,000 (1st), £500 (2nd) and £250 (3rd) , the Lara Jones award for the entry that shows most promise as an illustrator of books for preschool (£500) and the new digital prize (£1,000). 2011 winner: Gemma Merino for *The Crocodile Who Didn't Like Water*.

Man Asian Literary Prize

email info@manasianliteraryprize.org
website www.manasianliteraryprize.org
Contact Prize Manager, Marina Ma

An annual award (US$10,000) for an unpublished Asian novel in English. Submissions accepted online between December and March. See website for details. Supported financially by the Man Group plc. Founded 2007.

The Man Booker International Prize

Four Colman Getty, The Communications Building, 48 Leicester Square, London WC2H 7FG
tel 020-3032 9900
email info@fourcolmangetty.co.uk
website www.themanbookerprize.com

A prize of £60,000 to complement the annual Man Booker Prize by recognising one writer's achievement in continued creativity, development and overall contribution to world fiction. The prize does not invite submissions; a list is drawn up by the judges. It is awarded once every 2 years to a living author who has published fiction either originally in English, or generally available in translation in the English language.

The Man Booker International Prize will echo and reinforce the annual Man Booker Prize for Fiction in that literary excellence will be its sole focus. The winner will be announced in May. Sponsored by Man Group plc.

The Man Booker Prize

Four Colman Getty, The Communications Building, 48 Leicester Square, London WC2H 7FG
tel 020-3032 9900
website www.themanbookerprize.com

This annual prize for fiction of £50,000, including £2,500 to each of 6 shortlisted authors, is awarded to the best novel published each year. It is open to novels written in English by citizens of the British Commonwealth and Republic of Ireland and published for the first time in the UK by a British publisher, although previous publication of a book outside the UK does not disqualify it. Entries only from UK publishers who may each submit not more than 2 novels with scheduled publication dates between 1 October of the previous year and 30 September of the current year, but the judges may also ask for other eligible novels to be submitted to them. In addition, publishers may submit eligible titles by authors who have either won or been shortlisted in the past. Sponsored by Man Group plc.

The Manchester Fiction Prize

Contact James Draper,
Manager: The Manchester Writing School at MMU, Dept of English,
Manchester Metropolitan University,
Rosamund Street West, Off Oxford Road,
Manchester M15 6LL
tel 0161 247 1787
email j.draper@mmu.ac.uk
website www.manchesterwritingcompetition.co.uk

The Manchester Writing School, home of creative writing within the Department of English at Manchester Metropolitan University (MMU), hosts this competition which is designed to attract and celebrate the best new writing from around the world. An award of £10,000 will be made to the overall winner, or winners of the 2013 prize. The competition alternates annually between poetry and fiction (short stories). See website for further information and to enter online.

The Manchester Poetry Prize

Contact James Draper, Manager,
The Manchester Writing School at MMU,
Dept of English,
Manchester Metropolitan University,
Rosamond Street West, Off Oxford Road,
Manchester M15 6LL
tel 0161 247 1787
email j.draper@mmu.ac.uk
website www.manchesterwritingcompetition.co.uk

The Manchester Writing School, the home of creative writing within the Department of English at

Manchester Metropolitan University (MMU), hosts this competition which is designed to attract and celebrate the best new writing from around the world. An award of £10,000 will be made to the overall winner, or winners. The competition will alternate between poetry and fiction on an annual basis. The deadline for entries for the 2012 competition is mid-August and the award ceremony will be held in October 2012. The next competition will take place in 2014. See website for further information.

The Michael Marks Awards for Poetry Pamphlets

Wordsworth Trust, Dove Cottage, Grasmere, Cumbria LA22 9SH
tel (01539) 435544 *fax* (01539) 463538
website www.wordsworth.org.uk

Inaugurated by the British Library in 2009 to raise the profile of poetry pamphlets and also recognise and reward the enormous contribution that poets and their pamphlet publishers make to the poetry world in the UK. There are 2 awards worth £5,000 each:

• The Michael Marks Poetry Award to recognise a single outstanding work of poetry published in pamphlet form in the UK during the eligible period. This award is open to self-published work.
• The Michael Marks Publishers' Award to recognise an outstanding UK publisher of poetry in pamphlet form, based on their publishing programme during the eligible period.

See website for full details and submission guidelines. Supported by the Michael Marks Charitable Trust. Deadline: March.

Marsh Award for Children's Literature in Translation

Administered by The English-Speaking Union, Dartmouth House, 37 Charles Street, London W1J 5ED
tel 020-7529 1550
email education@esu.org
website www.esu.org

This biennial award of £2,000 is given to the translator of a book for children (aged 4–16) from a foreign language into English and published in the UK by a British publisher. Electronic books, and encyclopedias and other reference books, are not eligible. Next award: January 2013 (entries from mid-2012).

Marsh Biography Award

Administered by The English-Speaking Union, Dartmouth House, 37 Charles Street, London W1J 5ED
tel 020-7529 1550 *fax* 020-7495 6108
email education@esu.org

This major national biography prize of £5,000 plus a trophy is presented every 2 years. Entries must be serious biographies written by British authors and published in the UK. Next award: October 2013. Founded 1985–6.

The John Masefield Memorial Trust

Sarah Baxter, The Society of Authors, 84 Drayton Gardens, London SW10 9SB
tel 020-7373 6642 *fax* 020-7373 5768
email info@societyofauthors.org
website www.societyofauthors.org

This trust makes occasional grants to professional poets who find themselves with sudden financial problems. Apply for guidelines and application form.

The Somerset Maugham Awards

Paula Johnson, Awards Secretary, The Society of Authors, 84 Drayton Gardens, London SW10 9SB
tel 020-7373 6642
email info@societyofauthors.org
website www.societyofauthors.org

These annual awards, totalling about £10,000, are for writers under the age of 35. Candidates must be British subjects by birth, and ordinarily resident in the UK or Northern Ireland. Poetry, fiction, non-fiction, belles-lettres or philosophy, but not dramatic works, are eligible. Entries should be submitted by the publisher. Closing date: 30 November.

Kathleen Mitchell Award

Christina Piazza, Level 15, 20 Bond Street, Sydney, NSW 2000, Australia
tel +61 (0)2 8295 8118
email trustawards@thetrustcompany.com.au
website www.thetrustcompany.com.au

A biennial literary award ($7,500) for authors 30 years of age, or under, for the advancement and improvement of Australian literature. Eligible authors must be born in Australia or the UK and must have been resident in Australia for the 12 months preceeding close of entries, or be a naturalised Australian. Founded 1996.

Sheridan Morley Prize for the Best Theatre Biography

Administered by Oberon Books Ltd, 521 Caledonian Road, London N7 9RH
tel 020-7607 3637 *fax* 020-7607 3629
email info@oberonbooks.com
Contact The Administrator

In memory of the late critic and biographer Sheridan Morley, a cash prize of £2,000 will be awarded to the winner chosen by the panel of judges chaired by critic, broadcaster and biographer Ruth Leon. Awarded in the spring of each year for biographies published in English in the preceding calendar year. Launched 2008.

The Melissa Nathan Award for Comedy Romance

website www.melissanathan.com

Set up in memory of Melissa Nathan, who died in 2006, this award of £5,000 honours the criteria that

Melissa drew up herself: she wanted to encourage and reward writers who can combine in a novel the magical, life-enhancing elements of humour and love. Books published between January and December each year are eligible.

National Poetry Competition

Competition Organiser, The Poetry Society, 22 Betterton Street, London WC2H 9BX
tel 020-7420 9880 *fax* 020-7240 4818
email info@poetrysociety.org.uk
website www.poetrysociety.org.uk

One of the UK's major annual open poetry competitions. Accepts poems up to 40 lines long on any theme (previously unpublished and written in English). Prizes: 1st £5,000, 2nd £2,000, 3rd £1,000, plus 7 commendations of £100. Judged by a panel of 3 leading poets. For rules and an entry form send a sae or visit the website. Closing date: 31 October each year. Founded 1978.

The New Writer Prose and Poetry Prizes

PO Box 60, Cranbrook, Kent TN17 2ZR
tel (01580) 212626
email admin@thenewwriter.com
website www.thenewwriter.com

Annual international competition. Categories include: short stories of 500–5,000 words, micro fiction up to 500 words, essays and articles; single poems plus collection of 6–10 previously unpublished poems. Total prize money £2,000 as well as publication for the prize-winners in *The New Writer* magazine. Entry fees: various. Send for an entry form or visit the website for information about all categories. Closing date: 30 November each year. Founded 1997.

New Zealand Post Book Awards

c/o Booksellers New Zealand, PO Box 25033, Panama Street, Wellington 6146, New Zealand
tel +64 (0)4 472 1908 *fax* +64 (0)4 472 1912
email info@booksellers.co.nz
website www.booksellers.co.nz/awards

Annual awards to celebrate excellence in, and provide recognition for, the best books written and illustrated by New Zealanders each year. Awards are presented in 8 categories. The winner of each category wins $5,000. Category winners are considered for the Montana Medal for Non-Fiction or the Montana Medal for Fiction or Poetry. Medal winners each receive an additional $10,000. Eligible authors' and illustrators' books must have been published in New Zealand in the calendar year preceding the awards year. Closing date: December. Founded 1996.

New Zealand Post Book Awards for Children and Young Adults

c/o Booksellers New Zealand, PO Box 25033, Panama Street, Wellington 6146, New Zealand
tel +64 (0)4 472 1908 *fax* +64 (0)4 472 1912
email info@booksellers.co.nz
website www.bookseller.co.uk/awards

Annual awards to celebrate excellence in, and provide recognition for, the best books for children and young adults published annually in New Zealand. Awards are presented in 4 categories: non-fiction, picture book, junior fiction and young adult fiction. The winner of each category wins $7,500. One category winner is chosen as the *New Zealand Post* Book of the Year and receives an additional $7,500. Eligible authors' and illustrators' books must have been published in New Zealand in the calendar year preceding the awards year. Closing date: December. Founded 1990.

Nielsen Gold and Platinum Book Awards

tel (01483) 712200 *fax* (01483) 712201
email marketing.book@nielsen.com

The awards are a recognition of sales purchases of a book by the general public. Eligible books are those that reach 500,000 unit sales (Gold) or 1,000,000 unit sales (Platinum) as measured by Nielsen BookScan within a 5-year period. All qualifying titles may receive an award funded for the author by their publisher. Founded 2000.

The Nobel Prize in Literature

Awarding authority Swedish Academy, Box 2118, S–10313 Stockholm, Sweden
tel +46 8-55512554 *fax* +46 8-55512549
email sekretariat@svenskaakademien.se
website www.svenskaakademien.se

This is one of the awards stipulated in the will of the late Alfred Nobel, the Swedish scientist who invented dynamite. No direct application for a prize will be taken into consideration. For authors writing in English it was bestowed upon Rudyard Kipling in 1907, W.B. Yeats in 1923, George Bernard Shaw in 1925, Sinclair Lewis in 1930, John Galsworthy in 1932, Eugene O'Neill in 1936, Pearl Buck in 1938, T.S. Eliot in 1948, William Faulkner in 1949, Bertrand Russell in 1950, Sir Winston Churchill in 1953, Ernest Hemingway in 1954, John Steinbeck in 1962, Samuel Beckett in 1969, Patrick White in 1973, Saul Bellow in 1976, William Golding in 1983, Wole Soyinka in 1986, Nadine Gordimer in 1991, Derek Walcott in 1992, Toni Morrison in 1993, Seamus Heaney in 1995, V.S. Naipaul in 2001, Harold Pinter in 2005 and Doris Lessing in 2007.

Northern Writers' Awards

Administered by New Writing North, PO Box 1277, Newcastle upon Tyne NE99 5BP
tel 0191 233 3850
email office@newwritingnorth.com
website www.newwritingnorth.com
Contact Olivia Mantle

Awards (£1,000–£5,000) are aimed at developing writers at different stages in their careers. A panel of professional writers shortlists and makes awards once a year. Applicants must be resident in the Arts Council England North East region (Northumberland, Tyne & Wear, Durham, Tees Valley). See website for details. Deadline for applications: end January.

The Observer/Jonathan Cape/Comica Graphic Short Story Prize

website www.comicafestival.com

An annual graphic short story competition offering a £1,000 cash prize and the chance to see your story printed in the Observer. Founded 2007.

Frank O'Connor International Story Award

Frank O' Connor House, 84 Douglas Street, Cork, Ireland
tel +353 (0)21 431 2955
email munsterlit@eircom.net
website www.munsterlit.ie, www.frankoconnor-shortstory-award.net

This prestigious international short story award in the memory of Frank O'Connor is the single biggest prize in the world for a collection of short stories. The Frank O'Connor International Short Story prize is worth €25,000 to the winning author of a collection of short stories published for the first time, in English, anywhere in the world between 1 July and 30 June. Deadline for entries: March. See website for submission guidelines.

Orange Award for New Writers

Booktrust, Book House, 45 East Hill, London SW18 2QZ
tel 020-8516 2973
email claire.shanahan@booktrust.org.uk
website www.orangeprize.co.uk
Contact Claire Shanahan

This award of £10,000 is awarded annually to recognise emerging female fiction-writing talent published in the UK. The prize will be awarded to a woman for her first work of fiction – a novel, novella or collection of short stories. Women of any age or nationality may be entered providing their first work of fiction is published in the UK between 1 April and the following 31 March. The emphasis of the award is on emerging talent and the evidence of future potential. Founded 2005.

Orange Prize for Fiction

Booktrust, Book House, 45 East Hill, London SW18 2QZ
tel 020-8516 2973
email claire.shanahan@booktrust.org.uk
website www.orangeprize.co.uk
Contact Claire Shanahan

This award of £30,000 and a bronze statuette known as 'The Bessie' is for a full-length novel written in English by a woman of any nationality and first published in the UK between 1 April and 31 March the following year. Any woman writing in English – whatever her nationality, country of residence, age or subject matter – is eligible. Sponsored by Everything Everywhere. 2011 winner: Tea Obreht for *The Tiger's Wife* (Weidenfeld & Nicolson). Founded 1996.

The Orwell Prize

5/7 Vernon Yard, Portobello Road, London W11 2DX
tel 020-7229 5722
website www.theorwellprize.co.uk

The Orwell Prize consists of 3 prizes; a book prize, a journalism prize and a blog prize. The work in each category that comes closest to George Orwell's ambition 'to make political writing into art' is awarded £3,000 in May. All work with a British or Irish connection first published in the calendar year before the date of the prize is eligible. Founded 1994.

The Jeremy Paul Award for Theatre Writing

email rosie@creativethoughtsproductions.co.uk
website www.creativethoughtsproductions.co.uk
Contact Rosie Jones

An annual award in honour of Jeremy Paul, actor, director and playwright (and patron and judge of the Prequel to Cannes film script competition) who died in 2011. Organised by Creative Thoughts Productions, organisers/founders of the Prequel and Sequel to Cannes script competitions, the Award is open to plays written in English of no longer than 60 pages and which must be a resolved story within 3 acts. The winner will receive a rehearsed reading of their play at Lighthouse, Poole Centre for the Arts, in 2013, with a cast of professional actors from Dramatic Productions. Entry fee: £50 (£40 for early entries). Closing date for entries: 5 November. For full guidelines, entry information and details of prizes, see website.

Penguin Prize for African Writing

website www.penguinbooks.co.za/african-winners/index.php

A new literary award for writers from the African continent with 2 categories: one each for a previously unpublished full-length work of adult fiction and non-fiction. The prize in each category will be R50,000 and a publishing contract with Penguin Books South Africa, with worldwide distribution via Penguin Group companies. Submissions deadline: end January. See website for further details. Founded 2009.

The Samuel Pepys Award

Paul Gray, Haremoor House, Faringdon, Oxon SN7 8PN

website www.pepys-club.org.uk

A biennial prize is given to a book published in English making the greatest contribution to the understanding of Samuel Pepys, his times, or his contemporaries. The winner receives £2,000 and the Robert Latham Medal. Founded by the Samuel Pepys Award Trust in 2003 on the tercentenary of the death of Pepys. Closing date: June.

Charles Pick Fellowship

School of Literature, Drama and Creative Writing, University of East Anglia, Norwich NR4 7TJ
tel (01603) 592286 *fax* (01603) 504154
email charlespickfellowship@uea.ac.uk
website www.uea.ac.uk/lit/fellowships/charles-pick-fellowship

An annual fellowship to assist and support the work of a new and unpublished writer of fiction or non-fiction, dedicated to the memory of the distinguished publisher and literary agent, Charles Pick. Writers of any age or nationality are eligible to apply. The award is £10,000 plus free accommodation on UEA campus. Residential: 1 Oct–31 March. Closing date for applications: 31 January each year. Founded 2002.

The Plough Prize

The Plough Arts Centre, 9–11 Fore Street, Great Torrington, Devon EX38 8HQ
tel (01805) 624624
website www.theploughprize.co.uk

Entries are invited in 2 categories: Open Poem (up to 40 lines) and Short Poem (up to 10 lines). Both postal and online entry are eligible. See website for rules. Entry fee: £4, 4 poems £14, £3.50 thereafter. Closing date: 30 November; free tick-box critiques will be available to entries that arrive before 30 October.

The Poetry Business Book & Pamphlet Competition

Competition Administrator The Poetry Business, Bank Street Arts, 32–40 Bank Street, Sheffield S1 2DS
tel 0114 346 3037
email office@poetrybusiness.co.uk
website www.poetrybusiness.co.uk
Directors Peter Sansom, Ann Sansom

An annual award is made for a poetry collection. The judges select up to 5 short collections for publication as pamphlets; on further submission of more poems, one of these will be selected for a full-length collection. To be published under the Poetry Business's Smith/Doorstop imprint. All winners share a cash prize of £1,000. Poets over the age of 18 writing in English from anywhere in the world are eligible. Entry fee £20/£25. Founded 1986.

The Corneliu M. Popescu Prize for Poetry in Translation

Competition Organiser, The Poetry Society, 22 Betterton Street, London WC2H 9BX
tel 020-7420 9880 *fax* 020-7240 4818
email info@poetrysociety.org.uk
website www.poetrysociety.org.uk

Awarded biennially by the Poetry Society and the Ratiu Family Charitable Foundation, this award of £1,500 rewards a published collection of poetry translated from a European language into English. Founded 2003.

The Portico Prize

Miss Emma Marigliano, Librarian, Portico Library, 57 Mosley Street, Manchester M2 3HY
tel 0161 236 6785 *fax* 0161 236 6803
email librarian@theportico.org.uk
website www.theportico.org.uk

This biennial prize is awarded for a published work of fiction or non-fiction, of general interest and literary merit set wholly or mainly in the North of England with prizes for fiction and non-fiction totaling £8,000. Next award: 2014. Founded 1985.

Prequel and Sequel to Cannes Feature Film Script Competition

Creative Thoughts Productions Ltd
tel (01202) 691994
email rosie@prequel.biz, info@creativethoughtsproductions.co.uk
website www.prequeltocannes.biz, www.creativethoughtsproductions.co.uk
Contact Rosie Jones

This prize gives writers the opportunity to receive industry feedback on their script. All entries which meet the terms and conditions of entry will have the chance to win one of the 2 cash prizes (1st £200, 2nd £50); have their script (max. 90pp) read by a film production company; receive a 3pp feedback document on the merits and opportunities of their script from a professional film industry script reader. Submissions accepted from 1 March 2013. Entry £45. Previous winners include Dom Carver, 'Faith' and Lisa Barass, 'Since you've been gone'. See website for details. Closing date: 5 November 2013.

Prequel to Cannes Short Film Script Competition

Creative Thoughts Productions Ltd
tel (01202) 691994
email rosie@prequel.biz, info@creativethoughtsproductions.co.uk
website www.prequeltocannes.biz, www.creativethoughtsproductions.co.uk
Contact Rosie Jones

Competition for film scripts. Prizes of £100, £75 and £50 will be awarded to writers of the top 3 scripts by a prestigious film industry judging panel. Scripts will be read by a professional script reader and selected production companies and a one-page script summary on the strengths and opportunities of the script will be supplied. See website for details. Entry fee: £25. Submissions accepted from 1 March 2013. Deadline: 5 November 2013. Founded 2009.

The V.S. Pritchett Memorial Prize

The Royal Society of Literature, Somerset House, Strand, London WC2R 1LA
tel 020-7845 4676 *fax* 020-7845 4679
email info@rslit.org
website www.rslit.org

An annual prize of £1,000 is awarded for a previously unpublished short story of up to 5,000 words. Entry fee: £5 per story. For entry forms contact the Secretary from mid-November. The writer must be a citizen of the UK or Ireland. Founded 1999.

The Peggy Ramsay Foundation

G. Laurence Harbottle, Hanover House, 14 Hanover Square, London W1S 1HP
tel 020-7667 5000 *fax* 020-7667 5100
email laurence.harbottle@harbottle.com
website www.peggyramsayfoundation.org

Grants are made to established writers of stage plays and to theatrical organisations to facilitate new writing for the stage. Awards are made at intervals during each year. A total of approx. £200,000 is expended annually. Founded 1992.

The Red House Children's Book Award

Karen Hellewell, Hampton Farm, Bowerhill, Melksham, Wilts. SN12 6QZ
tel (01225) 353710
email info@fcbg.org.uk
website www.redhousechildrensbookaward.co.uk

This award is given annually to authors of fiction for children published in the UK. Children participate in the judging of the award. 'Pick of the Year' book list is published in conjunction with the award. Founded in 1980 by the Federation of Children's Book Groups.

Trevor Reese Memorial Prize

Institute of Commonwealth Studies, School of Advanced Study, University of London, Senate House, Malet Street, London WC1E 7HU
tel 020-7862 8844 *fax* 020-7862 8813
email ics@sas.ac.uk
website www.commonwealth.sas.ac.uk/reese.htm

The Trevor Reese Memorial Prize was established by the Institute of Commonwealth Studies in 1979. It is in the name of Dr Trevor Reese, a distinguished scholar of Australian and Commonwealth history, who was Reader in Imperial Studies at the Institute until his death in 1976. He was the author of several leading works in his field, and was both founder and first editor of the *Journal of Imperial and Commonwealth History*. The prize was established with the proceeds of contributions to a memorial fund by friends and colleagues of Trevor Reese throughout the Commonwealth and United States. The prize of £1,000 is awarded every 3 years to the author of a work which has made a wide-ranging, innovative and scholarly contribution in the broadly-defined field of Imperial and Commonwealth History. The next award of the prize will be in 2013, for books in the relevant field published in 2010, 2011 or 2012. A public call for nominations will be made in September 2012. Queries regarding this prize should be sent by email.

The RoNAs and the Romantic Novel of the Year Awards

For the name of the current organiser, check the Romantic Novelists' Association (RNA) website at www.romanticnovelistsassociation.org/index.php/contact
email rnaawardorganiser@hotmail.com
website www.romanticnovelistsassociation.org

The Romantic Novelists' Association recognises and gives annual awards for the very best romantic fiction. These awards, presented in early March, have recently been restructured to consist of six catagories of Romantic Novel Awards (RoNAs): Contemporary, Epic, Historical, Romantic Comedy and Young Adult romantic novels, and the RoNA Rose (formerly called Love Story of the Year) for shorter/category novels. The winners of the first five RoNAs go forward to a panel of judges that selects an overall winner for the Romantic Novel of the Year Award, presented later in the year. The awards are open to both members and non-members of the RNA. For further information go to the RNA website. Novels must be first published in the UK between 1 January and 31 December of the year of entry and in the case of the first five categories, be published in paperback. Four copies of each novel are required and there is a small entry fee. The entry form can be found on the website or obtained from the organiser.

Joan Hessayon Award

For the name of the current organiser visit www.romanticnovelistsassociation.org/index.php/contact
This award is only open to members of the Romantic Novelists' Association's New Writers' Scheme who submit a MS from January until the end of August. All will receive a critique. Any MSS subsequently accepted for publication become eligible for the Award.

The RoNA Rose Award

See website for details.

The Royal Society of Literature Jerwood Awards

Paula Johnson, The Royal Society of Literature, Somerset House, Strand, London WC2R 1LA
tel 020-7845 4676 *fax* 020-7845 4679
email paulaj@rslit.org
website www.rslit.org

Awards offering financial assistance to authors engaged in writing their first major commissioned works of non-fiction. Three awards – one of £10,000 and 2 of £5,000 – will be offered annually to writers working on substantial non-fiction projects. The awards are open to UK and Irish writers and writers who have been resident in the UK for at least 3 years. See website for further details.

The Royal Society of Literature Ondaatje Prize

Paula Johnson, The Royal Society of Literature, Somerset House, Strand, London WC2R 1LA
tel 020-7845 4676 *fax* 020-7845 4679
email paulaj@rsl.org
website www.rslit.org

This annual £10,000 award, administered by the Royal Society of Literature and endowed by Sir Christopher Ondaatje, is awarded to a book of literary merit, fiction, poetry or non-fiction, best evoking the spirit of a place. All entries must be published within the calendar year and should be submitted between 1 September and 10 December. The writer must be a citizen of the UK, Commonwealth or Ireland. See website for further details.

The Royal Society Winton Prize

The Royal Society, 6–9 Carlton House Terrace, London SW1Y 5AG
tel 020-7451 2500 *fax* 020-7930 2170
email sciencebooks@royalsociety.org
website www.royalsociety.org/awards/science-books/

This prize rewards books that make science more accessible to readers of all ages and backgrounds. The winner will receive £10,000 and each shortlisted author will receive £1,000.

Eligible books should be written in English and their first publication in the UK must have been between 1 January and 31 December each year. Publishers may submit any number of books for each prize. Entries may cover any aspect of science and technology but educational textbooks published for professional or specialist audiences are not eligible. Founded 1988.

RSPCA Young Photographer Awards (YPA)

Publications Department, RSPCA, Wilberforce Way, Southwater, Horsham, West Sussex RH13 9RS
tel 0300 123 0455 *fax* 0303 123 0455
email publications@rspca.org.uk
website www.rspca.org.uk/ypa

Annual awards are made for animal photographs taken by young people in categories: under 12; 12–18 year-olds; Portfolio (5 pictures); Pets Personalities. Prizes: overall winner (photography break, £1,000-worth of Olympus vouchers), age group winners (cameras, photoshoots). Four runners-up in each age group receive a camera. Closing date for entries: September. Founded 1990.

RTÉ P.J. O'Connor Radio Drama Awards

RTÉ Radio Drama, Dublin 4, Republic of Ireland
tel +353 (0)1 2083111 *fax* +353 (0)1 2083304
email radiodrama@rte.ie
website www.rte.ie/radio1/drama
Contact Fionnuala Hayes

An annual competition for a 55-minute play open to writers with a maximum of one hour of professionally produced radio drama who are born or living in Ireland. See website for details.

RTÉ Radio 1 Francis MacManus Awards

RTÉ Radio 1 Short Story Competition, RTÉ Radio Centre, Features & Drama Dept, Dublin 4, Republic of Ireland
tel +353 (0)1 2083111
website www.rte.ie/radio1/francismacmanus/
Producer Seamus Hosey

An annual competition for short stories of 1,800–2,000 words, open to writers born or living in Ireland. First prize €3,000. Entries, in Irish or English, should not have been previously published or broadcast. See website for details. Winning entries are broadcast on RTÉ Radio 1.

Rubery Book Award

PO Box 15821, Birmingham, B31 9EA
email submissions@ruberybookaward.com
website www.ruberybookaward.com

An annual award for published books on any subject, with prizes totalling £1,000. Books published by independent presses and self-published books are eligible. Short story competition for unpublished short stories on any subject; the best stories will be published in an anthology. See website for entry fees and submission guidelines. Deadline (book award) end March; (short story competition) end September.

Runciman Award

The Administrator, The Anglo-Hellenic League, 16–18 Paddington Street, London W1U 5AS
tel 020-7486 9410
fax 020-7486 4254 (mark FAO The Anglo-Hellenic League)
email info@anglohellenicleague.org
website www.anglohellenicleague.org

An annual award of £9,000 to promote Anglo–Greek understanding and friendship. Works must be wholly or mainly about some aspect of Greece or the world of Hellenism, which has been published in English in any country in its first edition during the previous year. Shortlisted books must be available for purchase to readers in the UK at the time of the award ceremony. No category of writing will be excluded from consideration, e.g. history, literary studies, biography, travel and topography, the arts, architecture, archaeology, the environment, social and political sciences or current affairs; fiction, poetry or drama. Works in translation, with the exception of translations from Greek literature, will not be considered. Final entries: late January; award presented in May/June. Sponsored by the National Bank of Greece and named after Sir Steven Runciman, former Chairman of the Anglo-Hellenic League. Established 1985.

Sainsbury's Baby Book Award – see Booktrust Early Years Awards

The David St John Thomas Charitable Trust Competitions & Awards

The David St John Thomas Charitable Trust,
PO Box 6055, Nairn IV12 4YB
tel (01667) 453351 *fax* (01667) 452365
website www.dstjthomascharitabletrust.co.uk
Contact Anne Hill

Two annual competitions – The Self-Publishing Awards are open to anyone who has self-published a book during the preceding 18 months with a total award of £2,250 and the Anthology Trophy, an annual award to writers' groups for anthologies published in the last 18 months. For details of either send a large sae or see the website for details.

The Saltire Society Awards

The Saltire Society, 9 Fountain Close, 22 High Street, Edinburgh EH1 1TF
tel 0131 556 1836
email saltire@saltiresociety.org.uk
website www.saltiresociety.org.uk
Contacts Jim Tough, Executive Director; Sarah Mason, Office Manager

Books published between 1 September and 31 August are eligible for the following awards:

Scottish Book of the Year

An annual award of £5,000 open to authors of Scottish descent or living in Scotland, or for a book by anyone which deals with a Scottish topic. Established 1982.

Scottish First Book of the Year

An annual award of £1,500 open to any author who has not previously published a book. Authors of Scottish descent or living in Scotland, or for any book which deals with the work or life of a Scot or with a Scottish problem, event or situation are eligible. Established 1988.

Scottish Research Book Award

An annual award of £1,500 is open to the authors of books which represent a significant body of research; offer new insight or dimension to the subject; and add knowledge and understanding of Scotland and the Scots. Established 1998.

Scottish History Book of the Year

An annual award of £1,500 for a work of Scottish historical research. Editions of texts are not eligible. Nominations are invited from professors of Scottish History and editors of historical reviews.

The Kim Scott Walwyn Prize

Booktrust, Book House, 45 East Hill,
London SW18 2QZ
tel 020-8516 2972
email prizes@booktrust.org.uk
website www.booktrust.org.uk, www.thesyp.org.uk, www.train4publishing.co.uk
Contact Claire Shanahan

Relaunched in 2011 as part of a new partnership between the Kim Scott Walwyn committee, the Society of Young Publishers (SYP) and the Publishing Training Centre (PTC), this prize celebrates emerging talent and achievement amongst women working in any area of UK publishing. Open to women who have worked in publishing for seven years or less, it commemorates the life and career of Kim Scott Walwyn, Publishing Director at Oxford University Press until her death in 2002. The winner is awarded a cheque for £1,000 sponsored by the SYP and a one-day training course of their choice, courtesy of the PTC. Applicants nominate themselves and their application must be supported by 2 referee statements. Closing date: March. Founded 2004.

Scottish Book of the Year – see The Saltire Society Awards

Scottish Children's Book Awards

Scottish Book Trust, Sandeman House,
Trunk's Close, 55 High Street, Edinburgh EH1 1SR
tel 0131 524 0160 *fax* 0131 524 0161
email chris.newton@scottishbooktrust.com/scottishchildrensbookawards
website www.scottishbooktrust.com
Contact Chris Newton, ActingChildren's Programme Manager

Awards totalling £12,000 are given to new and established authors of published books in recognition of high standards of writing for children in 3 age group categories: Bookbug Readers (0–7 years), Younger Readers (8–11 years) and Older Readers (12–16 years). A shortlist is drawn up by a panel of children's book experts and then a winner in each category is decided by children and young people by voting for their favourites in book groups in schools and libraries across Scotland. An award of £3,000 is made for the winner in each category and £500 for runners-up. Books published in the preceding calendar year are eligible. Authors should be resident in Scotland. Guidelines available on request. Closing date: 31 March. Award presented: February. Administered by Scottish Book Trust, in partnership with Creative Scotland.

Scottish First Book of the Year – see The Saltire Society Awards

Scottish Research Book Award – see The Saltire Society Awards

Short Sentence

Short Sentence, Bloomsbury Publishing plc,
50 Bedford Square, London WC1B 3DP

tel 020-7631 5727
email shortsentence@bloomsbury.com
website www.shortsentence.co.uk
Contact Jude Drake

Short Sentence is a crime story competition open to authors of crime stories of 1,000 words or less. See website for full submission guidelines. The winner will be announced during National Short Story Week in November.

The André Simon Memorial Fund Book Awards

Katie Lander, 1 Westbourne Gardens, Glasgow G12 9XE
tel 07801 310973
email katie@andresimon.co.uk

Celebrating excellent new writing in the fields of food and drink. Two awards of £2,000 are given annually, one each for the best new books on food and on drink. There is also a Special Commendation of £1,000 in either category. All works first published in the calendar year of the award are eligible (publisher entry only). Closing date: November each year. Awards are given in the spring of the following year. Founded 1978.

The Jill Smythies Award

The Linnean Society of London, Burlington House, Piccadilly, London W1J 0BF
tel 020-7434 4479 *fax* 020-7287 9364
email info@linnean.org
website www.linnean.org

Established in honour of Jill Smythies whose career as a botanical artist was cut short by an accident to her right hand. The rubric states that 'the Award, to be made by Council usually annually consisting of a silver medal and a purse ... is for published illustrations, such as drawings and paintings, in aid of plant identification, with the emphasis on botanical accuracy and the accurate portrayal of diagnostic characteristics. Illustrations of cultivars of garden origin are not eligible.' Closing date for nominations: 31 December. Founded 1988.

The Society of Authors Medical Book Awards

The Secretary, Medical Book Awards, The Society of Authors, 84 Drayton Gardens, London SW10 9SB
tel 020-7373 6642
email info@societyofauthors.org
website www.societyofauthors.org

Please contact The Society of Authors and see the website for up-to-date information.

Sony Radio Academy Awards

Sony Radio Academy Awards Secretariat, Zafer Associates, 47–48 Chagford Street, London NW1 6EB
tel 020-7723 0106 *fax* 020-7724 6163
website www.radioawards.org

The Sony Radio Academy Awards celebrate excellence in UK radio broadcasting. The Awards offer an opportunity to enter work in a range of categories which reflect today's local, regional and national radio. The Awards are for everyone regardless of resources – for stations big and small, for a team or for one person with a microphone. See website for further information. Founded 1982.

Spear's Book Awards

John Carpenter House, John Carpenter Street, London EC4Y 0AN
tel 020-7936 6445
email emily.rookwood@spearswms.com
website www.spearswms.com

These annual awards celebrate the best writing talent and British books of the year – from finance to fiction. The awards – Outstandingly Produced Book, Best First Book and Lifetime Achievement – are presented at a glamorous sit-down lunch for 100 guests. All books must have been first published or made available in English (electronic versions excluded) between 1 May and 30 April of the following year. Closing date: May. Established 2009.

The Sunday Times EFG Private Bank Short Story Award

Booktrust, Book House, 45 East Hill, London SW18 2QZ
tel 020-8516 2972
email claire.shanahan@booktrust.org.uk
website www.theshortstory.org.uk
Contact Claire Shanahan

This annual literary prize has built on the success of the weekly short story slot in the *Sunday Times Magazine*. Judges shortlist 6 authors from a longlist of 20 and the winner is announced in April at the Sunday Times Oxford Literary Festival. Authors compete for a prize of £30,000, the largest short story prize in the UK and Ireland, and shortlisted authors will receive £500 each. Closing date: October. Founded 2010.

The James Tait Black Memorial Prizes

Department of English Literature, David Hume Tower, George Square, Edinburgh EH8 9JX
tel 0131 650 3619 *fax* 0131 650 6898
website www.ed.ac.uk/about/people/tait-black

Two prizes of £10,000 are awarded annually: one for the best biography or work of that nature, the other for the best work of fiction, published during the calendar year 1 January to 31 December. The adjudicators are Professors of English Literature at the University of Edinburgh, with the assistance of teams of postgraduate readers. Eligible novels and biographies are those written in English and first published or co-published in Britain in the year of the award. Both prizes may go to the same author, but neither to the same author a second time.

Publishers should submit a copy of any appropriate biography, or work of fiction, as early as possible with a note of the date of publication, marked 'James Tait Black Prize'. Closing date for submissions: 1 December. Founded in memory of a partner in the publishing house of A&C Black, these prizes were instituted in 1918.

TAPS Cymru (Training and Performance Showcase Cymru)

West Farm, Southern Down, Vale of Glamorgan, Wales CF32 0PY
tel (01932) 592151 *fax* (01932) 592233
email admin@tapsnet.org
website www.tapsnet.org

A national scheme to train and promote new writers for film and TV. TAPS workshop training courses are open to all British scriptwriters. Full-length drama (min. 60 mins), comedy (30 mins) or shorts (10 mins) will be accepted as qualifying script submissions for the appropriate courses. Scripts selected from each course are showcased by professional actors, taped and screened to industry executives.

Reginald Taylor and Lord Fletcher Essay Competition

John McNeill, Hon. Secretary,
British Archaeological Association, 18 Stanley Road, Oxford OX4 1QZ
email jsmcneill@btinternet.com

A prize of a medal and £500 is awarded biennially for the best unpublished essay of high scholarly standard, which shows original research on a subject of archaeological, art-historical or antiquarian interest within the period from the Roman era to AD1830. The successful competitor will be invited to read the essay before the Association and the essay may be published in the Association's *Journal*. Competitors should notify the Hon. Editor in advance of the intended subject of their work. Next award: Spring 2014. The essay should be submitted not later than 1 November 2013 to the Honorary Editor, Dr Julian Luxford, School of Art History, St Andrews University, 79 North Street, St Andrews, Fife KY16 9AL. Founded in memory of E. Reginald Taylor FSA and Lord Fletcher FSA.

Dylan Thomas Literary Prize

The Dylan Thomas Centre, Ty Llen, Somerset Place, Swansea SA1 1RR
tel (01792) 474051
email sian@dylanthomasprize.com
website www.dylanthomasprize.com

An award of £60,000 is given to the winner of this prize, which was established to encourage, promote and reward exciting new writing in the English-speaking world and to celebrate the poetry and prose of Dylan Thomas. Entrants should be the author of a published book (in English), under the age of 30, writing within one of the following categories: poetry, novel, collection of short stories by one author, play that has been professionally performed, a broadcast radio play, a professionally produced screenplay that has resulted in a feature-length film. Authors need to be nominated by their publishers, or producers in the case of performance art. Closing date: May. Founded 2005.

The Times/Chicken House Children's Fiction Competition

Chicken House, 2 Palmer Street, Frome, Somerset BA11 IDS
tel (01373) 454488
email tina@doublecluck.com
website www.doublecluck.com
Contact Tina Waller

This annual competition is open to unpublished writers of a full-length children's novel (age 7–18). Entrants must be over 18 and novels must not exceed 80,000 words in length. The winner will be announced in *The Times* and will receive a worldwide publishing contract with Chicken House with a royalty advance of £10,000. The winner is selected by a panel of judges which includes children's authors, journalists, publishers, librarians and other key figures from the world of children's literature. Submissions are invited between April and October, with a shortlist announced the following February and the winner chosen at Easter. See website for further details.

Tir na n-Og Awards

Welsh Books Council, Castell Brychan, Aberystwyth, Ceredigion SY23 2JB
tel (01970) 624151 *fax* (01970) 625385
email wbc.children@wbc.org.uk
website www.wbc.org.uk

The Tir na n-Og Awards were established with the intention of raising the standard of children's and young people's books in Wales. Three awards are presented annually by the Welsh Books Council and are sponsored by the Chartered Institute of Library and Information Professionals Cymru/Wales and Cymdeithas Lyfrau Ceredigion:

- The best English-language book of the year with an authentic Welsh background. Fiction and factual books originally in English are eligible; translations from Welsh or any other language are not eligible. Prize: £1,000.
- The best original Welsh-language book aimed at the primary school sector. Prize: £1,000.
- The best original Welsh-language book aimed at the secondary school sector. Prize: £1,000.

Founded 1976.

The Tom-Gallon Trust Award

Awards Secretary, The Society of Authors, 84 Drayton Gardens, London SW10 9SB
tel 020-7373 6642
email info@societyofauthors.org
website www.societyofauthors.org

A biennial award of £1,000 is made on the basis of a submitted short story to fiction writers of limited means who have had at least one short story accepted for publication. Send a sae or download entry forms. Closing date: 31 October each year.

The Translation Prizes

The Awards Secretary, The Society of Authors, 84 Drayton Gardens, London SW10 9SB
tel 020-7373 6642
email info@societyofauthors.org
website www.societyofauthors.org

The Society of Authors administers a number of prizes for published translations into English. There are prizes for translations of Arabic, Dutch, French, German, Greek, Italian, Portuguese, Spanish and Swedish works. Closing date 31 January. Entries should be submitted by the publisher.

The Betty Trask Awards

Paula Johnson, Awards Secretary, The Society of Authors, 84 Drayton Gardens, London SW10 9SB
tel 020-7373 6642
email info@societyofauthors.org
website www.societyofauthors.org

These awards are for the benefit of young authors under the age of 35 and are given on the strength of a first novel (published or unpublished) of a traditional or romantic nature. It is expected that prizes totalling approximately £20,000 will be presented each year. The winners are required to use the money for a period or periods of foreign travel. Send a sae or download from the website for entry form. Closing date: 30 November. Made possible through a generous bequest from the novelist Betty Trask.

The Travelling Scholarships

Administered by The Society of Authors, 84 Drayton Gardens, London SW10 9SB
tel 020-7373 6642
email info@societyofauthors.org
website www.societyofauthors.org

These are honorary awards established in 1944 by an anonymous benefactor. Submissions are not accepted.

John Tripp Award for Spoken Poetry

Literature Wales, Mount Stuart House, Mount Stuart Square, Cardiff CF10 5FQ
tel 029-2047 2266 *fax* 029-2049 2930
email post@literaturewales.org
website www.literaturewales.org
Contact Peter Finch, Chief Executive

A competition for any form of spoken poetry in the English language. There are regional heats around Wales, with the winners from each heat going forward to a Grand Final. Performers have 5 minutes to read their work at each stage of the competition and are judged on the content of their poetry and their performance skills. Anyone either born or currently living in Wales is eligible to enter, and all works must be unpublished. Founded 1990.

The V&A Illustration Awards

Enquiries The Word & Image Dept, Victoria & Albert Museum, London SW7 2RL
tel/fax 020-7942 2385
email villa@vam.ac.uk
website www.vam.ac.uk/illustrationawards
Contact Martin Flynn

These annual awards are given to practising book and magazine illustrators living or publishing in the UK for work first published during the 12 months preceding the closing date of the awards. Cash prizes will be awarded for best book cover, illustrated book and newspaper, magazine and comic illustration. Also student illustrator of the year category. Closing date: December.

Venture Award

website www.flippedeye.net/venture
Contact Ian Somers, Publicist

Annual poetry pamphlet award worth £1,750 named after Wilfred Albert Venture. Open to anyone over the age of 16. Enter up to 15 A4 pages of poetry of any length. Entries by email only to venture@flippedeye.net. Email enquiries to ian.somers@apron-pr.com. Fee: £20 per entry. Closing date: end of September. Winners announced mid-April.

Ver Poets Open Competition

Competition Secretary Gill Knibbs, 181 Sandridge Road, St Albans, Herts. AL1 4AH
tel (01727) 762601
email gillknibbs@yahoo.co.uk
website www.verpoets.org.uk

A competition open to all for poems of up to 30 lines of any genre or subject matter, which must be unpublished work in English. Prizes: £600 (1st), £300 (2nd), £100 (3rd). Send 2 copies of each poem with no name or address; either put address on separate sheet or send sae or email for entry form. Closing date: 30 April. Anthology of winning and selected poems with Adjudicator's Report usually available from mid-June, free to those included. See website for details.

The Walford Award – see The ISG Reference Awards

Warwick Prize for Writing

Contact Helen May, Warwick Prize for Writing, Communications Office, University House, University of Warwick CV4 8UW

tel (0247) 615 0708
email prizeforwriting@warwick.ac.uk
website www.warwick.ac.uk/go/prizeforwriting/

An international cross-disciplinary biennial prize awarded for an excellent and substantial piece of writing in the English language, in any genre or form. Nominations are invited from University of Warwick and Monash University staff, students, honorary and emeritus professors, and honorary graduates. See website for full details.

The Wellcome Trust Book Prize

tel 020-7611 8540
email bookprize@wellcome.ac.uk, k.nevin-ridley@wellcome.ac.uk
website www.wellcomebookprize.org
Contact Katrina Nevin-Ridley

Celebrates the best of medicine in literature by awarding £25,000 each year for the finest fiction or non-fiction book centred around medicine. With this prize, the Wellcome Trust aims to stimulate interest, excitement and debate about medicine and literature, reaching audiences not normally engaged with medical science. Closing date for submission forms: 31 March. See website for further details. Founded 2009.

Whitbread Book Awards – see Costa Book Awards

The Whitfield Prize

Administrative Secretary, Royal Historical Society, University College London, Gower Street, London WC1E 6BT
tel 020-7387 7532 *fax*
email royalhistsoc@ucl.ac.uk
website www.royalhistoricalsociety.org/prizes.php

The Prize (value £1,000) is announced in July each year for the best work on a subject within a field of British or Irish history. It must be its author's first solely written history book, an original and scholarly work of historical research and have been published in the UK or Republic of Ireland in the preceding calendar year. One non-returnable copy of an eligible book should be submitted by the publisher before 31 December to the Administrative Secretary. Should the book be shortlisted, 2 further copies will be required.

Wildlife Photographer of the Year

The Natural History Museum, Cromwell Road, London SW7 5BD
tel 020-7942 5015
website www.nhm.ac.uk/wildphoto

An annual award given to the photographer whose individual image or portfolio is judged to be the most striking and memorable. The overall adult winner receives £10,000. The Young Wildlife Photographer of the Year receives £500, plus a day out with a photographer. Open to all ages. Closing date: March.

Winchester Writers' Conference Competitions

Contact Barbara Large, Centre for Research and Knowledge Exchange, University of Winchester, Winchester, Hants SO22 4NR
tel (01962) 827238
email barbara.large@winchester.ac.uk
website www.writersconference.co.uk
Honorary Patrons Jacqueline Wilson OBE, Maureen Lipman, Baroness James OBE, Colin Dexter OBE

Eighteen writing competitions are attached to this major international Festival of Writing, which takes place at the end of June/early July (see page 633). Each entry is adjudicated and 70 sponsored prizes are presented at the Writers' Awards Dinner. Categories are the First Three Pages of the Novel, Short Stories, Shorter Short Stories, Writing for Children, A Page of Prose, Lifewriting, Slim Volume, Small Edition, Poetry, Retirement, Writing Can be Murder, Local History, Young Writers' Poetry Competition, Sustainability of our Climate and the Enrico Charles Literary Award for non-fiction describing physical disability. Deadline for entries: 1 June. Fee, £7 if attending the conference; otherwise £9. Each entrant will receive an adjudication of their work.

The Wolfson Foundation

The Prize Administrator, The Wolfson Foundation, 8 Queen Anne Street, London W1G 9LD
tel 020-7323 5730 ext. 202 *fax* 020-7323 3241
website www.wolfson.org.uk

Annual awards are made to encourage and recognise books by British historians that can be enjoyed by a general readership and will stimulate public interest in history. The awards total up to £40,000. Authors must be British citizens and normally resident in the UK. The book must be published in the calendar year of the prize. Closing date: January following the prize year. Founded 1972.

David T.K. Wong Fellowship

School of Literature, Drama and Creative Writing, University of East Anglia, Norwich NR4 7TJ
tel (01603) 592286 *fax* (01603) 507728
email davidtkwongfellowship@uea.ac.uk
website www.uea.ac.uk/lit/fellowships/david-wong-fellowship

This annual fellowship (award £26,000) at the University of East Anglia will give a writer of exceptional talent the chance to produce a work of fiction in English which deals seriously with some aspect of life in the Far East. Applications will be considered from established published as well as unpublished writers of any age and any nationality. Residential: 1 Oct–30 June. Closing date for applications: 17 January. Founded in 1997 by David T.K. Wong, retired senior civil servant, journalist and businessman.

Write A Story for Children Competition

The Academy of Children's Writers, PO Box 95, Huntingdon, Cambs. PE28 5RL
tel (01487) 832752
website www.childrens-writers.co.uk

Three prizes (1st £2,000, 2nd £300, 3rd £200) are awarded annually for a short story for children, maximum 1,500 words, by an unpublished writer of children's fiction. Send a sae for details or see website. Founded 1984.

Writers' & Artists' Yearbook 2013 Short Story Competition

website www.writersandartists.co.uk

See information panel opposite About the Yearbook in this edition or visit our website for details.

Writers' Week Poetry Competitions

Writers' Week, 24 The Square, Listowel, Co. Kerry, Republic of Ireland
tel +353 (0)68 21074
email info@writersweek.ie
website www.writersweek.ie

Holds 3 poetry competitions, with various prizes. Contact as above for full details, and submission guidelines. No entry form required. Closing date: 28 February.

Young Writers Programme

Young Writers Programme,
Royal Court Young Writers Programme,
Sloane Square, London SW1W 8AS
tel 020-7565 5050 *fax* 020-7565 5001
email studio@royalcourttheatre.com
website www.royalcourttheatre.com

Playwright development programme for 18–25 year olds. See website for further information on how to submit plays and programme dates.

YouWriteOn.com – see Arts Council site YouWriteOn.com Book Awards

Literature festivals

There are hundreds of arts festivals held in the UK each year – too many to mention in this *Yearbook* and many of which are not applicable specifically to writers. We give here a selection of literature festivals and general arts festivals which include literature events. Space constraints and the nature of an annual publication together determine that only brief details are given; contact festival organisers for a full programme of events. The British Council will supply a list of forthcoming literature festivals on receipt of a large sae.

Ageas Salisbury International Arts Festival

87 Crane Street, Salisbury, Wilts. SP1 2PU
tel (01722) 332977
email info@salisburyfestival.co.uk
website www.salisburyfestival.co.uk
Takes place May–June

An annual multi-arts festival that includes a thriving literature programme. Programme published in March.

Aldeburgh Poetry Festival

The Poetry Trust, 9 New Cut, Halesworth, Suffolk IP19 8BY
tel (01986) 835950
email info@thepoetrytrust.org
website www.thepoetrytrust.org
Director Naomi Jaffa
Takes place annually on the first weekend in November

Annual festival of contemporary poetry with readings, workshops, talks, discussions, public masterclass, children's event. Features leading international and national poets, including the winner of the Aldeburgh First Collection Prize.

Appledore Book Festival

Brenda Daly, ABF Festival Office,
Docton Court Gallery, 2 Myrtle Street, Appledore, Bideford, Devon EX39 1PH
website www. appledorebookfestival.co.uk
Takes place 29 September–7 October 2012

Founded by children's author Nick Arnold this 9-day annual festival includes a schools programme covering north Devon and public events for all ages; also book fairs and a bookshop. Programme published in July. Founded 2007.

Asia House Festival of Asian Literature

Asia House, 63 New Cavendish Street, London W1G 7LP
tel 020-7307 5454 *fax* 020-7307 5459
email enquiries@asiahouse.co.uk
website www.asiahouse.co.uk, www.festivalofasianliterature.com
Takes place May

The only festival in the UK dedicated to writing about Asia and Asians. It covers Asia in the broadest context, from the Persian Gulf in the West to Indonesia in the East. Tickets go on sale in March.

Contact Adrienne Loftus Parkins (Festival Director) at adrienne.parkins@asiahouse.co.uk

Aspects Irish Literature Festival

Town Hall, The Castle, Bangor, Co. Down BT20 4BT
tel +353 (0)28-9127 8032, +353 (0)28-9127 1200 (box office) *fax* +353 (0)28-9127 1370
website www.northdown.gov.uk
Contact Gail Prentice, Arts Officer/Festival Director
Takes place 26–30 September 2012

An annual celebration of contemporary Irish writing with novelists, poets and playwrights. Includes readings, discussions, workshops and an Aspects showcase day for young writers.

Autumn International Literary Festival

University of East Anglia, Norwich NR4 7TJ
tel (01603) 592286 *fax* (01603) 504154
email literaryevents@uea.ac.uk
website www.uea.ac.uk/litfest
Contact Festival Administrator
Takes place Late September–early December

An annual festival of events bringing established writers of fiction, biography and poetry to a public audience in the Eastern region.

Ballymena Arts Festival

The Braid Ballymena Town Hall,
Museums & Arts Centre, 1–29 Bridge Street, Ballymena, Co. Antrim BT43 5EJ
tel 028-2565 7161, 028-2563 5988
email rosalind.lowry@ballymena.gov.uk
website www.ballymena.gov.uk
Festival Director Rosalind Lowry
Takes place March–April

Bath Literature Festival

Bath Festivals, Abbey Chambers, Kingston Buildings, Bath BA1 1NT
tel (01225) 462231 *fax* (01225) 445551
Box Office *tel* (01225) 463362
email info@bathfestivals.org.uk
website www.bathlitfest.org.uk
Artistic Director James Runcie
Takes place 1–10 March 2013

An annual 9-day festival with leading guest writers. Includes readings, debates, discussions and workshops, and events for children and young people. Programme available in December.

Bay Lit

Literature Wales, Mount Stuart House, Mount Stuart Square, Cardiff CF10 5FQ
tel 029-2047 2266 *fax* 029-2049 2930
email post@literaturewales.org
website www.literaturewales.org
Contact Peter Finch, Chief Executive
Takes place varies

A bilingual (Welsh and English) literature festival, held in Cardiff Bay. It is organised by Literature Wales (formerly Academi), the Welsh National Literature Promotion Agency and Society for Authors, and features an array of writers from Wales and beyond.

Ulster Bank Belfast Festival at Queen's

Culture & Arts Unit, Queen's University, 8 Fitzwilliam Street, Belfast BT9 6AW
tel 028-9097 1034
email festival.operations@qub.ac.uk
website www.belfastfestival.com
Director Graeme Farrow
Takes place 19 October–3 November 2012

The largest annual arts event in Ireland. Includes literature events. Programme available end August.

Beverley Literature Festival

Wordquake, Council Offices, Skirlaugh, East Riding of Yorkshire HU11 5HN
tel (01482) 392745
email john.clarke@eastriding.gov.uk
website www.beverley-literature-festival.org
Festival Director John Clarke
Takes place October

This festival offers author readings, readers' group sessions, writers' workshops and masterclasses. It involves all kinds of good writing but a special emphasis is placed on poetry.

Birmingham Book Festival

Unit 204, The Custard Factory, Gibb Street, Birmingham B9 4AA
tel 0121 246 2770 *fax* 0121 246 2771
email sara@birminghambookfestival.org
website www.birminghambookfestival.org
Director Sara Beadle
Takes place October

Annual festival which presents a range of events, workshops and seminars focused on reading, writing and ideas. A project of Writing West Midlands.

Brighton Festival

29 New Road, Brighton BN1 1NG
tel (01273) 700747 *fax* (01273) 707505
email info@brightonfestival.org
website www.brightonfestival.org.uk
Takes place May

An annual arts festival with an extensive national and international programme featuring theatre, dance, music, opera, literature, outdoor and family events. Programme published end of February.

Bristol Poetry Festival

Poetry Can, 12 Great George Street, Bristol BS1 5RH
tel 0117 933 0900
email admin@poetrycan.co.uk
website www.poetrycan.co.uk
Festival Director Colin Brown
Takes place April–May and September

An annual celebration of language. Features award-winning poets and performers from all over the UK and abroad. Venues include Bristol Old Vic, Arnolfini and elsewhere.

Buxton Festival

3 The Square, Buxton, Derbyshire SK17 6AZ
tel (01298) 70395
email info@buxtonfestival.co.uk
website www.buxtonfestival.co.uk
Artistic Director Stephen Barlow, *Chief Executive* Randall Shannon
Takes place July (provisional dates for 2013 are 5–23 July)

The incredible opera and music programme is complemented by a much envied Literary Series, featuring distinguished authors, which takes place every morning and afternoon.

Canterbury Festival

8 Orange Street, Canterbury, Kent CT1 2JA
tel (01227) 452853 *fax* (01227) 379164
email info@canterburyfestival.co.uk
website www.canterburyfestival.co.uk
Takes place 13–27 October 2012

An annual international arts festival with 200 events in 2 weeks. Programme published in July.

Charleston Festival

The Charleston Trust, Charleston, Firle, Lewes, East Sussex BN8 6LL
tel/fax (01323) 811626
email info@charleston.org.uk
website www.charleston.org.uk
Artistic Director Diana Reich, *Festival Manager* Niamh Pearce
Takes place 10 days at end of May

Charleston, country home of Bloomsbury artists Duncan Grant and Vanessa Bell hosts an annual literary festival involving writers, performers, politicians and thinkers – both high profile and up and coming, national and international.

The Times Cheltenham Literature Festival

109–111 Bath Road, Cheltenham, Glos. GL53 7LS
tel (01242) 774400

website www.cheltenhamfestivals.com
Artistic Director Sarah Smyth
Takes place 5–14 October 2012

This annual festival is the largest of its kind in Europe. Events include talks and lectures, poetry readings, novelists in conversation, exhibitions, discussions, workshops and a large bookshop. *Book It!* is a festival for children within the main festival with an extensive programme of events. Brochures are available in August.

Chester Literature Festival

Chester Festivals, 1st Floor, West Wing Offices, Chester Railway Station, Chester CH1 3NT
tel (01244) 405605
email p.lavin@chesterfestivals.co.uk
website www.chesterfestivals.co.uk
Festival Manager Paul Lavin
Takes place Every October

A leading literature festival, grown in stature and scale in recent years, with scores of events spread over a fortnight featuring writers from the internationally acclaimed to emerging local talent. The festival incorporates GobbleDeeBook, an annual week-long children's literature festival with workshops, plays and parties as well as events featuring dozens of children's authors.

Chichester Festivities

Canon Gate House, South Street, Chichester, West Sussex PO19 1PU
tel (01243) 785718 *fax* (01243) 528356
email info@chifest.org.uk
website www.chifest.org.uk
Takes place June/July

City of London Festival

Fitz Eylwin House, 25 Holborn Viaduct, London EC1A 2BP
tel 020-7583 3585 *fax* 020-7353 0455
email admin@colf.org
website www.colf.org
Director Ian Ritchie
Takes place Last week of June and first 2 weeks of July

An annual multi-arts festival with a programme predominantly of music. Programme published in April.

The Cúirt International Festival of Literature

Galway Arts Centre, 47 Dominick Street, Galway, Republic of Ireland
tel +353 (0)91 565886 *fax* +353 (0)91 568642
email info@galwayartscentre.ie
website www.galwayartscentre.cuirt
Progamme Director Dani Gill
Takes place 23–28 April 2013

An annual week-long festival to celebrate writing, bringing together national and international writers to promote literary discussion. Events include readings, performances, workshops, seminars, lectures, poetry slams and talks. The festival is renowned for its convivial atmosphere ('cúirt' means a 'bardic court or gathering').

Dublin Book Festival

Publishing Ireland, 25 Denzille Lane, Dublin 2, Republic of Ireland
tel +353 (0)1 6394868
email info@dublinbookfestival.com
website www.dublinbookfestival.com
Takes place 16–18 November 2012

Dublin Book Festival brings together the best of Irish publishing, offering a chance for the voices of both established and up and coming authors to be heard. Held in Dublin's City Hall, the festival's events include an *In conversation with...* series.

Dublin Writers Festival

c/o Dublin City Council, Arts Office, The Lab, Foley Street, Dublin 1, Republic of Ireland
tel +353 (0)1 2225455
email info@dublinwritersfestival.com
website www.dublinwritersfestival.com
Takes place June

The Dublin Writers Festival is one of Ireland's most important literary events celebrating the best of Irish and international writers.

Durham Book Festival

c/o New Writing North, Holy Jesus Hospital, City Road, Newcastle NE1 2AS
tel 0191 233 3850
email office@newwritingnorth.com
website www.durhambookfestival.com
Takes place October

A book festival for new and established writers, taking place in the historic city of Durham.

Edinburgh International Book Festival

5A Charlotte Square, Edinburgh EH2 4DR
tel 0131 718 5666 *fax* 0131 226 5335
email admin@edbookfest.co.uk
website www.edbookfest.co.uk
Director Nick Barley
Takes place August

Now established as Europe's largest book event for the public. In addition to a unique independent bookselling operation, more than 800 writers contribute to the programme of events. Programme details available in June.

Ennis Book Club Festival

c/o Clare Library HQ, Mill Road, Ennis, Co. Clare, Republic of Ireland
tel +353 (0)87 2262259
email info@ennisbookclubfestival.com
website www.ennisbookclubfestival.com

Chairperson Frances O'Gorman
Takes place First weekend in March

An annual literary weekend which brings together book club members, book lovers and writers. Includes lectures, readings, discussions, workshops and exhibitions.

Essex Poetry Festival

2 The Drive, Hullbridge, Essex SS5 6LN
tel (01702) 230596
email derek@essex-poetry-festival.co.uk
website www.essex-poetry-festival.co.uk
Contact Derek Adams
Takes place October

A poetry festival across Essex. Also includes the Young Essex Poet of the Year Competition.

Exeter Arts and Events

Civic Centre, Exeter EX1 1JJ
tel (01392) 265200 *fax* (01392) 265265
website www.exeter.gov.uk
Arts & Events Manager Val Wilson

Supports a programme of arts and events throughout the year.

Festival at the Edge

The Morgan Library, Aston Street, Wem, Shrops. SY4 5AU
tel (01939) 236626
email info@festivalattheedge.org
website www.festivalattheedge.org
Contact Sue Chand
Takes place July

A storytelling festival with a mix of stories, music and performance, held in Much Wenlock, Shropshire.

The Festival of Writing

The Writers' Workshop, 7 Market Street, Charlbury, Oxon OX7 3PH
tel 0845 459 9560
email info@writersworkshop.co.uk
website www.festivalofwriting.com
Director Harry Bingham
Takes place in York in September

A festival for new writers providing the opportunity to meet literary agents, publishers, professional authors and book doctors. Keynote speakers from across the industry. Also workshops, competitions, networking events, Q&A panels and the chance to pitch work directly to literary agents.

Folkestone Book Festival

Creative Foundation Offices, The Block, 65–69 Tontine Street, Folkestone, Kent CT20 1JR
tel (01303) 245799
email info@creativefoundation.org.uk (FAO Folkestone Book Festival)
website www.folkestonebookfest.com
Takes place November

An annual festival with over 40 events, including a Children's Day.

Free the Word!

PEN International, Brownlow House, 50–51 High Holborn, London WC1V 6ER
tel 020-7405 0338 *fax* 020-7405 0339
email info@internationalpen.org.uk
website www.internationalpen.org.uk/go/literary-events/free-the-word-
Takes place April

'Free the Word! is International PEN in spirit and action – a festival for authors and readers to make sparks across the divide between national literatures' – Sir Tom Stoppard. Presents writers from countries worldwide at events in London.

Guildford Book Festival

c/o Tourist Information Office, 155 High Street, Guildford GU1 3AJ
tel (01483) 444334
email assistant@guildfordbookfestival.co.uk
website www.guildfordbookfestival.co.uk
Festival Director Glenis Pycraft
Takes place Last 2 weeks in October

An annual festival. Diverse, provocative and entertaining, held throughout the historic town and drawing audiences from throughout London and the south-east. Author events, workshops and schools programme. Its aim is to further an interest and love of literature by involvement and entertainment. Founded 1989.

Hay Festival – see The Telegraph Hay Festival

Huddersfield Literature Festival

School of Humanities, Music and Media, University of Huddersfield HD1 3DH
tel (01484) 430528
email litfest@hud.ac.uk
website www.litfest.org.uk
Festival Director Michael Stewart

The festival programmes events to support and showcase new, emerging and established writers/artists, offering a platform to promote new work as well as the opportunity to attend intensive writing workshops and masterclasses. Founded 2006.

Ilkley Literature Festival

The Manor House, 2 Castle Hill, Ilkley LS29 9DT
tel (01943) 601210 *fax* (01943) 817079
email admin@ilkleyliteraturefestival.org.uk
website www.ilkleyliteraturefestival.org.uk
Festival Director Rachel Feldberg
Takes place First 2 weeks in October

The north of England's most prestigious literature festival with over 200 events, from author's discussions to workshops, readings, literary walks, children's events and a festival fringe.

International Playwriting Festival

Warehouse Theatre, Dingwall Road,
Croydon CR0 2NF
tel 020-8681 1257
email info@warehousetheatre.co.uk
website www.warehousetheatre.co.uk
Contact Rose Marie Vernon
Takes place March

It starts with the competition, which has entries accepted from all over the world and is judged by a panel of distinguished theatre practitioners. Closing date for entries is the end of June each year. The festival itself forms second part, which features a showcase of the best work from the IPF competition, and selected plays from the festival's international partners – the leading Italian playwriting festival, Extra Candoni, and Theatro Ena, Cyprus.

Jewish Book Week

Jewish Book Council, ORT House, 126 Albert Street, London NW1 7NE
tel 020-7446 8771
email info@jewishbookweek.com
website www.jewishbookweek.com
Administrator Pam Lewis
Takes place Feb/March

A festival of Jewish writing, with contributors from around the world and sessions in London and nationwide. Includes events for children and teenagers.

King's Lynn Festival

5 Thoresby College, Queen Street, King's Lynn, Norfolk PE30 1HX
tel (01553) 767557
website www.kingslynnfestival.org.uk
Administrator Joanne Mawson
Takes place 14–27 July 2013 (tbc)

An annual general arts festival with literature events featuring leading guest writers. Founded 1951.

King's Lynn Literature Festivals

19 Tuesday Market Place, King's Lynn,
Norfolk PE30 1JW
tel (01553) 691661 *fax* (01553) 691779
website www.lynnlitfests.com
Chairman Tony Ellis
Takes place Sept/March

28th Poetry Festival (21–23 Sept 2012): An annual festival which brings 12 published poets to King's Lynn for the weekend for readings and discussions.

24th Fiction Festival (March 2013): An annual festival which brings 10 published novelists to King's Lynn for the weekend for readings and discussions.

Kingston Readers' Festival

Kingston University, River House,
53–57 High Street, Kingston upon Thames KT1 1LQ
tel 020-8417 9000
email events@kingston.ac.uk
website www.kingston.ac.uk/krf
Festival Director Sandy Williams
Takes place April/May

A small non-profit-making limited company with charitable and educational aims to:

• Foster and celebrate a love of reading
• Promote a broad range of events for all ages, including short story, poetry and writing for performance competitions
• Develop an outreach programme comprising workshops and authors' talks
• Promote the work of Kingston University and the Rose Theatre, Kingston
• Raise money for local good causes and other reading-related charities. Established 2002.

Knutsford Literature Festival

1 Green Lane Close, Winwick, Warrington,
Cheshire WA2 8RG
tel (01925) 575556
email christinebhatt@gmail.com
website www.knutsfordlitfest.org
Contact Christine Bhatt
Takes place First 3 weeks of October

An annual festival to celebrate writing and performance, with distinguished national, international and local authors. Events include readings and discussions, a literary lunch and theatrical performances.

Laureate na nÓg

Children's Books Ireland,
17 North Great Georges Street, Dublin 1, Ireland
tel +353 (0)18 727475 *fax* +353 (0)18 727476
email info@childrenslaureate.ie
info@childrensbooksireland.ie
website www.childrenslaureate.ie

This is a project recognising the role and importance of literature for children in Ireland. This unique honour was awarded for the first time in 2010 to author Siobhan Parkinson. The position is held for a period of two years. The laureate participates in selected events and activities around Ireland and internationally during their term. The laureate is chosen as a result of their widely recognised high-quality children's writing or illustration and the considerably positive impact they have had on readers as well as other writers and illustrators.

Ledbury Poetry Festival

Town Council Offices, Church Street,
Ledbury HR8 1DH
tel 0845 458 1743
email admin@poetry-festival.com
website www.poetry-festival.com
Festival Director Chloe Garner
Takes place June/July

An annual festival featuring top poets from around the world, together with a poet-in-residence programme, competitions (see rules and download form from website), workshops and exhibitions. Full programme available in May.

Lewes Live Literature (LLL Productions)

PO Box 2766, Lewes, East Sussex BN7 2WF
tel (07972) 037612
email info@leweslivelit.co.uk
website www.leweslivelit.co.uk
Artistic Director Mark Hewitt
Takes place See website for dates

A live literature production company developing performances and projects with writers for presentation as part of a season or festival of new work. LLL is not able to respond to unsolicited enquiries about performance opportunities.

Lincoln Book Festival

Freeschool Lane, Lincoln, Lincs. LN2 1EY
tel (01522) 545458 *fax* (01522) 842718
email sara.bullimore@lincoln.gov.uk, info@lincolnbookfestival.co.uk
website www.lincolnbookfestival.co.uk
Contact Sara Bullimore (Arts & Cultural Sector Officer)
Takes place May

A festival that celebrates books but also includes other art forms that books initiate and inspire – comedy, film, performance, conversation. It aims to celebrate local, national and international writers and artists, historical and contemporary works of art as well as offering the public a chance to see both emerging and well-known writers and artists. Includes a programme of children's events.

Lit.com

Arts Development, Origin One, One Origin Way, Europarc, Grimsby DN37 9TZ
tel (01472) 323382
email charlotte.bowen@nelincs.gov.uk
website www.nelincs.gov.uk/leisure/arts
Contact Arts Development Unit
Takes place October

Reflecting the heritage and culture of the area, this combined literature and comedy festival aims to be accessible to all ages and abilities through a varied and unusual programme.

Litfest

The Storey Creative Industries Centre, Meeting House Lane, Lancaster LA1 1TH
tel (01524) 62166
email all@litfest.org
website www.litfest.org
Artistic Director Andrew Darby
Takes place October

Annual literature festival featuring prose and poetry from local, national and international writers. Litfest is the literature development agency for the Northwest. Year round programme of seasonal readings and workshops. Publisher of new writing from Lancashire and Cumbria via Flax imprint.

London Literature Festival

Southbank Centre, Belvedere Road, London SE1 8XX
tel 020-7960 4200
email customer@southbankcentre.co.uk
website www.southbankcentre.co.uk, www.londonlitfest.com
Takes place July

A 2-week festival featuring international and prize-winning authors, historians, poets, performers and artists, children's events, specially commissioned work, debate and discussion, interactive and improvised writing and performance. Founded 2007.

Lowdham Book Festival

c/o The Bookcase, 50 Main Street, Lowdham NG14 7BE
tel 0115-966 4143
email info@fiveleaves.co.uk
website www.lowdhambookfestival.co.uk
Contact Jane Streeter, Ross Bradshaw
Takes place June

An annual 10-day festival of literature events for adults and children, with a daily programme of high-profile national and local writers. The last day always features dozens of free events and a large book fair.

Manchester Children's Book Festival

The Manchester Writing School at MMU, Dept of English, Manchester Metropolitan University, Rosamond Street West, Off Oxford Road, Manchester M15 6LL
tel 0161 247 1787/1966
email mcbf@mmu.ac.uk
website www.manchesterchildrensbookfestival.co.uk
Festival Directors Carol Ann Duffy (Creative Director), James Draper (Public Events), Kaye Tew (Education)
Takes place June/July

A biennial festival celebrating the very best writing for children, inspiring young people to engagee with literature and creative projects across the curriculum, and offering training for teachers, writers, librarians and arts practitioners.

Manchester Literature Festival

Beehive Mill, Jersey Street, Manchester M4 6JG
tel 0161 236 5555
email admin@manchesterliteraturefestival.co.uk
website www.manchesterliteraturefestival.co.uk
Director Cathy Bolton
Takes place 8–21 October 2012

An annual festival celebrating new literature, new

technology and the original modern city of Manchester.

National Eisteddfod of Wales

40 Parc Ty Glas, Llanisien, Cardiff CF14 5DU
tel 029-2076 3777 *fax* 029-2076 3737
email gwyb@eisteddfod.org.uk
website www.eisteddfod.org.uk
Chief Executive Elfed Roberts
Takes place August

Wales's largest cultural festival, based on 800 years of tradition. Activities include competitions in all aspects of the arts, fringe performances and majestic ceremonies. In addition to activities held in the main pavilion, it houses over 300 trade stands along with a literary pavilion, a music studio, a movement and dance theatre, outdoor performance stages and a purpose-built theatre. The event is set in a different location each year, and will take place in the Vale of Glamorgan in 2012 and in Denbighshire in 2013.

National Short Story Week

PO Box 1302, Berkhamsted, Herts. HP4 9AE
tel (01442) 862628
email admin@shortstoryweek.org.uk
website www.nationalshortstoryweek.org.uk
Director Ian Skillicorn
Takes place 12–18 November 2012

An annual awareness week aimed at encouraging more people to write, read and listen to short stories. Events held around the UK with involvement from publishers, writers, libraries, universities, writing organisations and readers. Founded 2010.

Norfolk & Norwich Festival

Augustine Steward House, 14 Tombland, Norwich NR3 1HF
tel (01603) 877750 *fax* (01603) 877766
email info@nnfestival.org.uk
website www.nnfestival.org.uk
Artistic Director William Galinsky
Takes place annually in May

Northern Children's Book Festival

Newcastle City Library, Charles Avison Building, 33 Newbridge Street, Newcastle upon Tyne NE1 8AX
website www.ncbf.org.uk
Chairperson Janice Hall
Takes place November

An annual festival to bring authors, illustrators, poets and performers to children in schools, libraries and community centres across the North East of England. About 36 authors visit the North East over the 2-week period for 2–8 days, organised by the 12 local authorities. The climax of the festival is a huge public event in a different part of the North East each year when over 4,000 children and their families visit to take part in author seminars, drama workshops, and to enjoy a variety of book-related activities.

Off the Shelf Literature Festival

Central Library, Surrey Street, Sheffield S1 1XZ
tel 0114 273 4716
email offtheshelf@sheffield.gov.uk
website www.offtheshelf.org.uk
Contact Maria de Souza, Su Walker, Lesley Webster
Takes place October

The festival comprises a wide range of events for adults and children, including author visits, writing workshops, storytelling, competitions and exhibitions. Programme available in September.

Oundle Festival of Literature

email enquiries@oundlelitfest.org.uk
website www.oundlelitfest.org.uk
Takes place March (festival fortnight) plus all-year-round programme

Featuring a full programme of author events, poetry, philosophy, politics, storytelling, biography, illustrators and novelists for young and old. Includes events for children.

The Sunday Times Oxford Literary Festival

Christ Church, Oxford OX1 1DP
tel (01865) 276152
website www.oxfordliteraryfestival.com
Festival Chief Executive Sally Dunsmore
Takes place March/April

An annual 6-day festival for both adults and children. Presents topical debates, fiction and non-fiction discussion panels, and adult and children's authors who have recently published books. Topics range from contemporary fiction to discussions on politics, history, science, gardening, food, poetry, philosophy, art and crime fiction. An additional 2 days of events for schools.

Oxford Literary Festival – see The Sunday Times Oxford Literary Festival

Poetry International

Literature Department, Southbank Centre, Belvedere Road, London SE1 8XX
tel 020-7921 0904
website www.southbankcentre.co.uk
Contact Martin Colthorpe
Takes place October 2012 (biennial)

The biggest poetry festival in the British Isles, bringing together a wide range of poets from around the world. Includes readings, workshops and discussions. The Literature + Spoken Word department also runs a year-round programme of readings, talks and debates.

Port Eliot Festival

Port Eliot Estate, St Germans, Saltash, Cornwall PL12 5ND

tel (01503) 232783
email info@porteliotfestival.com
website www.portelitfestival.com
Contact M. Clayton

The idyllic Port Eliot estate in Cornwall plays host to the UK's most imaginative arts festival; over 100 performances on 10 different stages, presenting a wealth of creative talent from the worlds of books, music, fashion, food and film. Port Eliot aims to raise the spirits of and inspire its audience, and the festival prides itself on offering something a little bit different. In 2011, Kate Winslet gave an impromptu reading, Martin Scorcese curated the outdoor cinema and world-renowned milliner Stephen Jones demonstrated the best way to make and eat a hat. Each year the festival is developed in order to broaden its appeal to younger audiences and others who might never before have considered attending a literary festival.

Quite Literary

The Plough Arts Centre, 9–11 Fore Street, Torrington, Devon EX38 8HQ
tel (01805) 622552
email richard@theploughartscentre.org.uk
website www.theploughartscentre.co.uk
Contact Richard Wolfenden-Brown
Takes place Throughout the year

An occasional literature programme including workshops, readings, performances and exhibitions, as part of a larger programme of arts work, including community and educational workshops, projects, residencies and performances. For info on The Plough Prize international poetry competition, visit www.theploughprize.co.uk.

Redbridge Book and Media Festival

London Borough of Redbridge, Arts & Events Team, 3rd Floor, Central Library, Clements Road, Ilford IG1 1EA
tel 020-8708 2855
website www.redbridge.gov.uk
Contact Arts & Events Team
Takes place April and May

Features author talks, performances, panel debates, Urdu poetry events, an exhibition, workshops, children's activities and events, and a schools outreach programme.

Richmond upon Thames Literature Festival, Arts Service

Orleans House Gallery, Riverside, Twickenham TW1 3DJ
tel 020-8831 6000 *fax* 020-8744 0501
email artsinfo@richmond.gov.uk
website www.richmondliterature.com
Takes place November

An annual literature festival covering a broad range of subjects. Leading contemporary authors hold discussions, talks, debates and readings. There are also exhibitions and storytelling sessions for children and adults.

Royal Court Young Writers Festival

The Royal Court Theatre, Sloane Square, London SW1W 8AS
tel 020-7565 5050
email studio@royalcourttheatre.com
website www.royalcourttheatre.com
Contact Tom Lyons, Studio
Takes place See website for dates

Debut plays from young British playwrights with original and diverse stories to tell. Anyone aged 18–25 can submit a script for the Festival. Selected plays are presented at the Royal Court Theatre as full productions and staged readings (see page 400).

Rye Festival

Literary Events Director, Court Lodge Oast, Udimore, Rye, East Sussex TN31 7YB
tel (01797) 224442
website www.ryefestival.co.uk
Chairman and Literary Events Director Catherine Bingham
Takes place Last 2 weeks of September (15 days)

Annual festival of literary events featuring biographers, novelists, political and environmental writers with book signings and discussions. Runs concurrently with festival of music and visual arts.

Small Wonder: The Short Story Festival

The Charleston Trust, Charleston, Firle, Lewes, East Sussex BN8 6LL
tel/fax (01323) 811626
email info@charleston.org.uk
website www.charleston.org.uk
Artistic Director Diana Reich, *Festival Manager* Niamh Pearce
Takes place 4 days at end of September

Charleston, country home of Bloomsbury artists Duncan Grant and Vanessa Bell, hosts the only festival in the UK dedicated to the short story. Provides the opportunity to sample the best and the most innovative short fiction in a variety of forms from recognised top practitioners of the art. It is interactive and experimental, as well as traditional.

Spring International Literary Festival

University of East Anglia, Norwich NR4 7TJ
tel (01603) 592286 *fax* (01603) 504154
email literaryevents@uea.ac.uk
website www.uea.ac.uk/litfest
Contact Festival Administrator
Takes place Late January–May

An annual festival of events to bring well-established international writers of fiction, biography, poetry, etc to a public audience in the Eastern region.

Spring Literary Festival

University of East Anglia, Norwich NR4 7TJ
tel (01603) 592286 *fax* (01603) 504154

email literaryevents@uea.ac.uk
website www.uea.ac.uk/litfest
Contact Festival Administrator
Takes place February–May

An annual festival of events bringing established writers of fiction, biography and poetry to a public audience in the Eastern region.

St Ives Literature Festival

St Ives Arts Club, The Warren, St Ives, Cornwall TR26 2DY
email info@stiveslitfest.co.uk
website www.stiveslitfest.co.uk
Contact Bob Devereux
Takes place First week in May

Organised in association with a number of Cornwall and West Country publishers, the festival consists of readings, talks, workshops and performance events.

StAnza: Scotland's International Poetry Festival

tel (01334) 475000 (box office), (01334) 474610 (programmes)
email info@stanzapoetry.org
website www.stanzapoetry.org
Festival Director Eleanor Livingstone
Takes place March

The festival engages with all forms of poetry: read and spoken verse, poetry in exhibition, performance poetry, cross-media collaboration, schools work, book launches and poetry workshops, with numerous UK and international guests and weekend children's events.

States of Independence

c/o Five Leaves Publications, PO Box 8786, Nottingham NG1 9AW
email info@fiveleaves.co.uk
website www.statesofindependence.co.uk
Contact Ross Bradshaw

Takes place March

An annual one-day festival celebrating independent publishing. Held in mid-March at De Montfort University in Leicester. Involves independent publishers from the region and elsewhere in the country. A free event with 30 sessions and a book fair.

Stratford-upon-Avon Poetry Festival

Shakespeare Centre, Henley Street, Stratford-upon-Avon CV37 6QW
tel (01789) 204016 *fax* (01789) 296083
email info@shakespeare.org.uk
website www.shakespeare.org.uk
Takes place June/July

An annual festival to celebrate poetry past and present with special reference to the works of Shakespeare. Events include: evenings of children's verse, a Poetry Mass and a local poets' evening. Full details available on the website from March. Sponsored by The Shakespeare Birthplace Trust.

Swindon Festival of Literature

Lower Shaw Farm, Shaw, Swindon, Wilts. SN5 5PJ
tel (01793) 771080
email swindonlitfest@lowershawfarm.co.uk
website www.swindonfestivalofliterature.co.uk
Festival Director Matt Holland
Takes place May

An annual celebration of live literature through prose, poetry, drama and storytelling, with readings, discussions, performances and talks in theatres, arts centres, parks and pubs. A festival of ideas with leading authors, speakers and performers.

The Telegraph Hay Festival

Festival Office, The Drill Hall, 25 Lion Street, Hay-on-Wye HR3 5AD
tel (01497) 822620 (admin)
email admin@hayfestival.org
website www.hayfestival.org
Takes place May/June

This annual festival of literature and the arts in Hay-on-Wye, Wales, brings together writers, musicians, film-makers, historians, politicians, environmentalists and scientists from around the world to communicate challenging ideas. More than 700 events over 10 days. Within the annual festival is a festival for families and children, Hay Fever, which introduces children, from toddlers to teenagers, to their favourite authors and holds workshops to entertain and educate. Programme published April.

Theakstons Old Peculier Crime Writing Festival

Raglan House, Raglan Street, Harrogate, North Yorkshire HG1 1LE
tel (01423) 562303 *fax* (01423) 521264
email crime@harrogate-festival.org.uk
website www.harrogate-festival.org.uk/crime
Takes place July

Four days of events featuring the best of UK and international crime writers.

The Dylan Thomas Festival

The Dylan Thomas Centre, Somerset Place, Swansea SA1 1RR
tel (01792) 463980 *fax* (01792) 463993
email dylanthomas.lit@swansea.gov.uk
website www.dylanthomas.com
Events Manager Jo Furber
Takes place 27 October–9 November 2012

An annual festival celebrating the life and work of Swansea's most famous son: performances, lectures, debates, poetry, music and film. Also, regular events throughout the year and talks and tours by arrangement.

Warwick Words – Festival of Literature and Spoken Word

The Court House, Jury Street, Warwick CV34 4EW
tel (07944) 768607
email info@warwickwords.co.uk
website www.warwickwords.co.uk
Takes place beginning of October

Founded 1999.

Ways With Words Festivals of Words and Ideas

Droridge Farm, Dartington, Totnes, Devon TQ9 6JG
tel (01803) 867373 *fax* (01803) 863688
email admin@wayswithwords.co.uk
website www.wayswithwords.co.uk
Contact Kay Dunbar

Leading writers give talks, interviews and discussions. Events: Words by the Water Festival of Words and Ideas (Cumbria, March), Words in the Park (London, May) The Telegraph Ways With Words Festival of Words and Ideas (Devon, July), the Southwold Literature Festival (Suffolk, November) and writing and art holidays in Italy and Devon. .

Wells Festival of Literature

60 St Thomas Street, Wells BA5 2UZ
tel (01749) 671658
website www.wellslitfest.org.uk
Takes place mid-October

A week-long festival featuring leading writers and poets. As well as talks on literature, science and current affairs, also includes crime novel, short story and poetry competitions, cinema, book groups and events for primary and secondary schools. Most events take place in the historic Bishop's Palace. Founded 1992.

Wigtown Book Festival

Wigtown Festival Company, County Buildings, Wigtown, Dumfries & Galloway DG8 9JH
tel (01988) 402036
email mail@wigtownbookfestival.com
website www.wigtownbookfestival.com
Festival Director Anne Barclay
Takes place 28 September–7 October 2012

An annual celebration of literature and the arts in Scotland's National Book Town. Over 180 events including author events, theatre, music, film and a full children's programme.

Word – University of Aberdeen Writers Festival

University of Aberdeen, Office of External Affairs, University of Aberdeen, King's College, Aberdeen AB24 3FX
tel (01224) 273874 *fax* (01224) 272086
email word@abdn.ac.uk
website www.abdn.ac.uk/word
Artistic Director Alan Spence
Takes place May

Over 70 of the world's finest writers and artists take part in a packed weekend of readings, music, art exhibitions and film screenings. The festival hosts some of the UK's best-loved children's writers and some of the richest talents in Gaelic literature.

World Book Day

c/o The Booksellers Association, 6 Bell Yard, London WC2A 2JR
020-7421 4640
email wbd@education.co.uk
website www.worldbookday.com
Takes place March

An annual celebration of books and reading aimed at promoting their value and creating the readers of the future. Every schoolchild in full-time education receives a £1 book token. Events take place all over the UK in schools, bookshops, libraries and arts centres. World Book Day was designated by UNESCO as a worldwide celebration of books and reading, and is marked in over 30 countries. It is a partnership of publishers, booksellers and interested parties who work together to promote books and reading for the personal enrichment and enjoyment of all.

See also the Book to Talk About (page 546).

Writers' Week

24 The Square, Listowel, Co. Kerry, Republic of Ireland
tel +353 (0)68 21074
email info@writersweek.ie
website www.writersweek.ie
Administrators Eilish Wren, Máire Logue
Takes place 29 May–2 June 2013

Aims to promote the work of Irish writers in both the English and Irish language, and to provide a platform for new and established writers to discuss their works. Events include readings, seminars, lectures, book launches, workshops and art exhibitions.

Young Readers Birmingham

Children's Office, Central Library, Chamberlain Square, Birmingham B3 3HQ
tel 0121 303 3368 *fax* 0121 464 1004
website www.youngreadersbirmingham.org
Contact Debbie Mynott
Takes place June and throughout the year

An annual festival targeted at children, young people and families. It aims to promote the enjoyment of reading, to provide imaginative access to books, writers, performers and storytellers and to encourage families to use libraries and to share reading for pleasure.

Writers and artists online

Electronic publishing

Ebooks continue to change the face of the publishing industry and possibilities for e-publishing are rapidly developing all the time. With new author-to-reader routes opening up, Philip Jones sets the scene and explains the implications for authors.

If 2011 was the year the ebook arrived, and 2012 the year when the ebook became big business, then 2013 could be the year when ebooks begin to overtake print. This trajectory has been far steeper than anyone predicted: and has raised fundamental questions over what we understand as the trade publishing business, and indeed what we think of as a book.

In 2011, ebook sales went from being perhaps 3% of a typical publisher's sales to 10% and beyond. Ebook sales in 2012 began the year at about 20%, following the usual Christmas jump in device sales, and it is predicted they could end the year as high as 40%. For example, the general trade publisher Hachette reported in April 2012 that its ebook sales were running at over 20%, and for fiction were already over 30%.

In terms of the market size, that is growth from £15 million to £150 million to £500 million in two 12-month periods. In the USA, an equivalent market to the UK in lots of ways, publishers experienced three years of treble-digit ebook growth before the rate of ascent began to plateau. In the UK, 2013 will be that third year.

Since Nielsen BookScan, which tracks sales of physical books on the high street and online, does not yet track ebook sales, we know very little about the make-up of this new market. Of course, Amazon dominates, with Barnes & Noble, Apple and Kobo being the next biggest players. Genres such as romance, crime/thrillers, science fiction and fantasy do very well, while non-fiction titles are, in the main, doing less well, along with literary fiction. As many have remarked: throw-away books do well digitally, books for keeps do less well.

With regard to the overall book market, we do know that the number of print books sold has fallen consistently since its high point in 2008, thanks first to the recession, then a minor collapse in celebrity titles, and now the transfer to digital reading. This downturn has been in the range of 3%–5% annually, but since the beginning of 2012 the rate of decline has accelerated with paperback fiction sales down as much as 30%. Digital is not just taking away, however, it is adding sales – just not at a value high enough to grow the wider market. According to data published in 2012 by research company Book Marketing Ltd, British consumers bought 344 million [individual] books in 2011, a slight rise, but the money they spent on those titles collectively (£2.1 billion) still dropped. Statistics put out by the UK Publishers Association further emphasised this point: in 2011 the value of print fiction sales fell by £57 million, the value of ebook fiction rose to £50 million. There is transference taking place, but it is not necessarily a direct replacement.

The conclusion is that, in the early years at least, the rise of digital reading has impacted high street booksellers, killing off those fragile companies that owned them and could not withstand any downturn in sales. But so far publishers have been unharmed, partly because though overall sales may be stagnant, digital sales are a higher margin business for most publishers. Many fear, however, that this state of affairs may be subject to change as the digital market develops, as the range of digital formats grows along with the costs of supplying to them, as Amazon's publishing business begins to fight for talent, and as more authors choose to publish direct.

What's in it for writers?

How does this changing market affect writers? Publishers may look like swans gliding across the publishing waters, but the reality is that these bookish cygnini are working furiously to keep themselves afloat as the waters around them swirl malevolently and predators await signs of fatigue.

What this means is that the people authors do business with are likely to become extremely busy as befits an industry straddling two different marketplaces: some may have new job titles, or they make work for new imprints; some may not work on books at all anymore; some contacts may disappear entirely as publishing begins its cultural shift to the networked world. As Anthony Forbes Watson, Managing Director of Pan Macmillan, told the *Bookseller* at the beginning of 2012: publishing needs to migrate 'from being an industry for arts graduates who can count, into an industry for science graduates who can write a paragraph'.

The better news for authors is that the routes to readers will get easier to see as the barriers to the consumer break down. However, they will also become more complex to navigate as different pathways grow. As you write your book, or begin to think about sending it out for submission, there are new questions to ask yourself. Do you wait for a publisher to discover you? Or do you publish direct to a retailer's website? Do you use a third-party aggregator? Or pay for professional help?

All that glisters

Should you choose to self-publish, then Amazon's Kindle Desktop Publishing platform promises to provide a map to a veritable City of Gold, with direct access to millions of ebook-hungry customers. In the examples of Amanda Hocking, Joe Konrath, Mark Williams and Louise Voss, and Kerry Wilkinson, this path has led either to strong sales or a traditional publishing deal – and sometimes both. It is also deceptively simple: you can publish within hours (no more waiting months for a rejection slip), as was evidenced following the death of Whitney Houston when within hours a dozen self-published 'tributes' appeared online. In fact the most difficult decision to make on the Amazon platform is whether to price your book above £1.49 and thereby qualify for the 70% royalty, or between 70p and £1.49 and opt for a rate of 35%.

At the moment, this market – like many in this new world – is dominated by Amazon. In fact, when most 'indie' authors talk about self-publishing they are in fact talking about Kindle self-publishing. However, with the launch of Apple's iBook Author app in early 2012, Kobo developing its self-publishing portal and Barnes & Noble's Pubit platform likely to be replicated in the UK, the marketplace where creative writing can be sold, without the need for a traditional intermediary, is only going in one direction: forwards.

But – and this is important – as an author you will at some point need to engage an expert. This *Yearbook* will help, of course. But you may not be looking for the kind of help traditionally sought before. An agent will be your first call, of course, but don't expect the agent of the future to be the only, or even the best, conduit to a publisher. Some agents may actually be just too busy publishing themselves (or at least trying it out), some may be concentrating on fewer and bigger brands, while others may be looking at how the books fare on the digital slush pile before making a commitment.

New wine

Even if you do find an agent, and they in turn find a publisher, don't expect an advance – at least not a big one. However, you should expect (and push for) a bigger digital royalty (you may not think that spending 90% of your negotiating time on 20% of the market is a wise idea, but watch that market grow and think again). Publishers *are* making more money from digital, so should you. Ask for a strategic plan for both print and digital (and occasionally app) versions of your writing. Interrogate them about the marketing plan: publishers may want to offer less up-front, but they need to deliver more on publication than ever before, if they are going to remain competitive.

Sadly, none of this is going to make it easier to make that first deal.

However, look at new publishers, or old publishers publishing in new bottles: the rise of digital-only lists will be a growing phenomenon, with the Macmillan New Writing imprint likely to make a comeback in ebook format. Publishers will begin looking for new talent more aggressively, and they'll be jumping earlier to get at that talent, and, in the case of HarperCollins' Authonomy platform or Penguin's Bookcountry they will be looking to incubate that talent in their own walled gardens.

Even if you eschew the traditional experts, such as agents or publishers, you will still need an editor, a cover designer, and perhaps even a 'social media guru'. But as ever, be careful what you pay for up-front, and make sure you understand what you are getting in return for your money. The rebranding of the self-published into 'indie' writers has not meant an end to the traditional vanity operations: many have simply transformed into online author platforms offering to publish a book and make it available worldwide for a fee. Just as there is much more to publishing than simply printing a book, there is also much more to digital publishing that merely acquiring an ISBN. Consult the giant ebook aggregators, such as Ingram (www.ingrambook.com), Lulu (www.lulu.com) and Smashwords (www.smashwords.com): these companies will ensure the ebook basics are covered and that the ebooks are featured on third-party websites at a fraction of the cost of a typical vanity publisher.

And if you get this far, it's only just beginning – the digital route to consumers is proving to be no less complicated than the print circuit, as both ebooksellers and e-reading devices proliferate.

Major players

In the UK (as in the USA) Amazon dominates digital sales, with a market share of perhaps 70%–80% of consumer ebook sales. It also dominates device sales. The Kindle is by far the most popular device for pure digital reading, with Sony something of a legacy player these days (try and buy the new Sony device in the high street), and Kobo coming up falteringly from the rear. By the time this edition of the *Yearbook* is published there may be more (perhaps many more). Waterstones is working on creating a device, which is expected to be unveiled by Summer 2012, and Barnes & Noble's Nook will make its way across the Atlantic, either via Waterstones or on the Windows platform, after Microsoft took a stake in that business. Google is also thought to be working on an e-reader.

And then there are the tablets. These devices are for interacting with multimedia content, including enhanced ebooks and book apps. Here Apple does have a play, with its iPad, and iPhone devices, the runaway leaders. Kobo (KoboVox), Amazon (Kindle Fire), Nook (NookTablet) and Sony (Sony Tablet S) are also all pushing into this developing space. We do not yet know how much e-reading goes on using tablets, or whether heavily illustrated books (such as children's picture books) will migrate, but we do know that Apple has yet to pull off this trick, and that is worrying.

Apple's share of the ebooks market via the iBookstore has disappointed (its market share in the USA is about 20% and decreasing, and in the UK perhaps half that). This is not due to the lack of devices in people's hands (hundreds of millions, in fact) or because those users are not engaging with book content on them (people read ebooks via their Kindle apps, and download separate books apps). The reason is simply that Apple has not yet come up with a compelling retail platform to sell enhanced digital content on.

Three things may quickly change this view of tablets and open them up as a vehicle for published content. First, the launch of Apple's iBooks Author app promises to do for tablets what the Amazon Kindle Desktop Publishing initiative has done for e-readers: get authors on the inside creating their own content. Though initially aimed at those wanting to build textbooks, the tool actually allows anyone to publish an enhanced ebook. We may see creative authors or publishers build a new kind of story-book or non-fiction title – one with music, images, animation and voice-over – that engages the reader and sells at a reasonable price.

Second, the launch of Amazon Kindle Fire tablet worldwide will see the giant bookseller ratchet up its output of content specifically created for a multimedia device. Shortly before the Kindle Fire launched in the USA, for example, Amazon bought the entire children's list of the US publishing house Marshall Cavendish, promising to digitise those texts. It did this to establish a market, as it has done with e-reading.

Third, we are now beginning to witness a second wave of book apps, that are seeing publishers not just regurgitate new content in app format, but look at apps as standalone products using both backlist and frontlist content in a way that befits the medium. For example, in early 2012 Collins published Brian Cox's *Wonders of the Universe* app, based on Cox's two BBC series, *Wonders of the Solar System* and *Wonders of the Universe*, both of which Collins had published in print. Profile also released an app version of the feature film *Frankenstein Reborn* that allows the reader to engage with the story and dictate how it evolves: a truly interactive use of an interactive medium. In their own ways, both show how publishers are now engaging with the technology, rather than simply expecting texts to seamlessly transfer across and find a receptive audience, already distracted by music, films and apps.

Reading rules

Up to now, ebooksellers without devices have failed to gain a foothold in the growing digital market, with Waterstones' diminishing ebook market share showing what happens when the bookseller does not also own the device. But with new ebook players emerging, such as Bilbary and Anobii, the promise to sell so-called 'universal' ebooks that can be read on any device, as well as social media websites dedicated to the 'discoverability' of ebooks, Amazon's price-led stranglehold over the UK ebook market may finally be coming to an end.

If this does happen, then 27 March 2012 should be taken as the day when it all changed. This was when for the first time legal ebook editions of the Harry Potter books went on sale, with the vendor not Amazon, or Barnes & Noble, or even Google, but Pottermore, a company created by the author J.K. Rowling to run that digital business. The trick Pottermore pulled off was to convince Amazon (and others) to list the ebooks on its website, but then push the customer to Pottermore to make the payment, before allowing the file to be delivered to the device of the customer's choice. It was a truly exceptional shift in author power, one that had many publishers agog. Pottermore had in fact created the world's first 'universal' ebook, and did it by facing down Amazon.

Could other content owners/creators follow suit? Difficult yes, but no longer impossible. If a universal ebook does emerge, or if Amazon's hold over the Kindle weakens, then the whole shape of the ebook world could shift as readers start to look beyond one retailer, and away from the bestseller lists and the cheap ebooks that have come to dominate. In short, the ebook reading market will begin to professionalise, and perhaps more closely resemble the print market, with both publishers and booksellers better at understanding what digital readers want and a truly diverse marketplace able to serve their needs.

But print will survive.

Keeping in mind that all predictions about the ebook market have so far been wrong, most people now predict that the ebook market will plateau at around 40% –50% of overall sales – as most heavy book readers will have migrated and resistance among those who wish to resist grows (and publishers actively begin to publish to readers who 'love' print, better print books).

By the end of 2013 we could then see the beginnings of an uneasy truce between the ebook forces and the print troops, as both markets settle into their trenches. Certainly, no-one is yet imagining a world without bookshops, but with commercial fiction likely to have by then moved predominantly into digital format – we will all, publishers, booksellers, authors and readers be looking at a world remarkably different from the one we currently inhabit: but one still with the author at its heart.

Philip Jones is deputy editor of the *Bookseller*, and co-founder of the digital blog FutureBook.net. He also hosts a fortnightly radio show devoted to discussing how digital is changing book publishing, *The Naked Book*.

E-PUBLISHING RESOURCES

This is a fast-moving area: sites and businesses appear and others cease year by year. Writers are reminded to check carefully what each service offers and to check all details of any contractual arrangements before entering into these. This *Yearbook* cannot be held responsible for any content on any of these sites.

Axis

website www.axisweb.org

Opportunities site for practising artists. Free to register – quality control in operation. Artists can advertise work on a web page starting at £15 p.a. (included in paid-for membership).

Book Submit

website www.book-submit.com

An automated book submission system that sends book information to literary agents.

eBooks.com

website www.ebooks.com

Internet Digital Bookstore. Invites authors to let their publisher or agent know about new work; authors should check rights deals with their publisher.

eBook Versions

website www.ebookversions.com

Specialists in conversions to Kindle, ePub, and PDF formats. Conversion packages start at £95.

fotoLIBRA

website www.fotolibra.com

Picture library. Photographers can upload and sell pictures for a monthly subscription. Terms: 50%.

KDP Select

website https://kdp.amazon.com/self-publishing/

A quick and easy way to self-publish ebooks into the Amazon Kindle bookstore.

Nielsen's BookData Services

website www.nielsenbookdata.co.uk

ISBN, SAN and DOI agents. Bibliographic records of books in print.

International Digital Publishing Forum

website www.idpf.org

Format specifications, sponsored by the National Institute of Standards and Technology (formerly the Open Book Forum).

E-READING DEVICES

Apple iPad

website www.apple.com/uk/ipad

A 'must have' piece of kit for internet surfers. It is also very effective as a reading device. Apple iPads start at £399.

Android

This tablet comes in 2 sizes, starting at £149 and theoretically vying as a PC version of the iPad.

Kindle

website www.amazon.co.uk/kindle

UK-compatible Kindle Wireless Reading Device. Affordable at £89.

Microsoft Reader

website www.microsoft.com/reader

Free downloadable software for reading ebooks on Windows-based platforms.

Nook

website www.barnesandnoble.com/nook

Contender to the Kindle; not yet UK-compatible.

Sony Reader

website www.sony.co.uk/reader

Large and pocket formats and starting at £149.

See also...

- *Self-publishing in ebook*, page 294
- *A year in view of the publishing industry*, page 313

Marketing yourself online

Simon Appleby and Mathew F. Riley outline how writers can use the internet to get noticed.

Make some noise!

Some basic things have not changed since the 2012 edition of this *Yearbook* was published. Writers are writing. Readers are reading, whether it's a physical book or an ebook. This is good, but whether you're a published writer with an ongoing deal, or an aspiring writer with a whole load of ideas, and even a finished manuscript, the challenge will always be the same: how do you get your name known, your words read, your manuscripts taken on, your book bought, and then sell *more* books to justify a second book?

Important aspects of the literary environment are unquestionably changing: more people are reading and writing *online*. This trend will continue. Another change: readers have *become* writers. The ceaseless development of the internet enables anyone to say anything at anytime to anyone who's reading. Whether fiction, news, opinion or reviews, everybody's having their say, shouting the loudest to lure readers to their writing; readers and critics wanting to attract writers and publishers to their reviews. One more change: risk-averse publishers (and agents) look to the internet for inspiration (see *Books published from blogs* on page 269), and will do so increasingly to gauge marketability, because books as hold-in-the-hand, textured entertainment will *always* be published. Much of your activity should be geared towards demonstrating to a publisher that people like your work and would pay to read more of it. Hence an author (budding or otherwise) who is entrepreneurial, has developed a loyal fan-base, and a positive vibe about their work, has a chance of standing out from the crowd, with more to put on their CV (and in their covering letter to a publisher) and evidence that they really have put in the effort to try to achieve publication.

The technologies, platforms and communities involved are constantly evolving, but the concepts behind developing a manageable approach to promoting you and your writing on the internet, *to get you closer to your readers and them closer to you*, will absolutely hold true. This article won't give you detailed DIY instructions, but it will hopefully provide you with a focus from which to develop your presence on the internet in a structured and achievable fashion.

There's a lot of noise out there, and to be heard you will have to make some of your own. So, how do you do it?

The technical side of things is not rocket science – the numerous (and free) solutions available out there do most of it for you, but it does take persistence and require an idea of where you want to be, and who you want to talk to. At the risk of teaching an old dog new tricks this means setting aside an amount of time to plan your approach. Just like writing. Once you've put the building blocks in place, it *is* writing. And (you already know this) when you start writing, you won't be able to stop!

Set up your own blog

Chances are you're already doing this: check out the authors who are selling themselves well (and badly). Look at professional authors with well-designed websites, as well as lesser-known authors who are simply utilising the blogging platforms available to all of us. Note what blogging platform these authors are using. You don't need to have an all-singing, all-dancing, beautifully designed website and blog from day one.

A blog is *your* website. It can be whatever you want it to be. Publish your work to find out what people think about it, discuss other authors' work, the writing market, and the places on the internet where they hang out. Give readers extra content they cannot get anywhere else. Study the statistics (try to avoid becoming addicted!) that your blog automatically provides and follow the links. Make yourself accessible. When someone sends you a message or leaves you a comment it's an opportunity to enter into a discussion about your writing. Get back to them while they're still interested. Make your blog the centre of your online universe, and explore the threads that will grow from this centre. To aid this you must exploit and be a willing participant of the social internet.

> *At my publisher's behest, and very reluctantly, I began my online marketing with a MySpace profile. Facebook and Twitter swiftly followed. More recently, with fellow Bloody Books author Bill Hussey, we set up www.horrorreanimated.com. The blog promotes the resurgence in horror, our publisher and our books. Awareness and sales of my novels have spread globally and it has cost me almost nothing.* – Joseph D'Lacey

Social networking and communities

There are innumerable communities on the internet – each one an island floating on an ocean of 'noise'. Navigating your way to these oases of context is vital and you'll find them just as you find a good book – by searching according to your tastes, and listening to the recommendations of your friends. With Bookgeeks (www.bookgeeks.co.uk) we have been doing all that follows for three years, and slowly but surely it works: your friends and visitors increase, your words are read and your name and reputation spreads. Here are the main categories to think about:

- **Writing communities** – where you can get your work evaluated and rate the work of others. These are both a source of useful feedback and encouragement, and a place to get noticed by publishers (even leading to book deals for the best).
- **General book communities** – where book owners, librarians, collectors and authors come together, an instant source of like-minded people.
- **Forums** – these can be wide ranging or frighteningly focused on one subject, but if you find one you like, hang around and join in. You should not expect to drop in, plug your work and have other users be grateful for your contribution if you don't stick around.
- **Social networking** – this is the broadest category, encompassing thousands of sites large and small. Find the one that's right for you.

'Friends'

Set up a Facebook page and a Twitter profile. Thousands of writers have already done so, and they're talking to each other and their fans right now. Facebook and Twitter are *all* about talking. Use these platforms to promote your work – friendships may even develop too. It's an excuse to talk to complete strangers and you'll soon find things in common. Search for the topics that interest you, the areas you write about and the markets you work in. It's no exaggeration to say that you'll be sure to find people and groups who like what you do. As well as your profile you can set up pages for your books and invite people to be fans. You can import the content from your blog and send people updates as your content changes. All this can be done automatically. Ten minutes a day is all you'll need after the initial set-up.

A tool for every job

As in life, so online, there is a tool for every possible situation. We can't tell you everything a good toolkit should contain, but we can suggest some general principles and a few key tools, all of which are free and easy to use.

• **Stay on 'brand'** – keep handy a standard biography and a decent photo of yourself when setting up user profiles. It helps to represent yourself consistently wherever people encounter you. Try to always use the same username as well.

• **Social conversation** – use social networking sites, micro-blogging services (like Twitter) and your own site to get engaged with your current and potential readers and your fellow authors.

• **Share and enjoy** – for any type of content you create, there's a platform to share it on, whether it's video (YouTube), photos (Flickr or Photobucket), audio/podcasts and, of course, writing of all kinds. When you share content, consider whether it needs to be under copyright or whether Creative Commons licensing might help it be more widely seen.

• **Listening tools** – when people are talking about you and your work, or linking to your website, you can drop in and make a contribution, or link to the content in question. For this, Google Alerts is your friend. More broadly, use Really Simple Syndication (RSS) to follow the blogs that interest you and keep track of new writers, industry trends and more – we suggest Google Reader, but there are numerous feed readers available.

• **Keep current** – wherever there is information about you, make sure it's current and as detailed as possible. Keep your Wikipedia entry up to date (taking care to stay factual); update information about yourself on sites like LibraryThing (www.librarything.com); and make sure your publisher knows about your online activities so they can link to them.

Engagement

As a writer spending time online, you are inevitably going to come in contact with criticism of your work at some point, perhaps even abuse. Keep your cool and when deciding how to react to something, one of these four responses will usually be appropriate:

• **Endorse** – if something's really positive (a good review, or creativity inspired by your work) link to it, shout about it, tell your publisher, encourage the creator.

• **Engage** – enter in to discussion with fans and critics alike on their forum of choice; respond to constructive criticism professionally and never take it personally.

• **Ignore** – if you can't say anything nice....

• **Enforce** – if anyone is getting abusive, infringing your rights or going too far, take measured steps to do something about it (like contacting their forum moderator or ISP), but never descend to their level.

One other thing – *never* pretend to be someone you're not, anywhere, for any reason. Always represent yourself honestly as 'the author in question'.

Online PR

This is a glorified way of saying 'Talk to people about your work in order to get them to write about it'. If you are willing to put in the time to contact bloggers and offer review copies, interviews, competition prizes or other content they can use, some of them are likely to respond positively. Understand their pressures – they want to find things to write about, and that's where you come in.

Use some of the same organisational skills that you use researching and talking to agents and publishers – much as you do when you look through the *Writers' & Artists' Yearbook* for suitable publishers and agents, do your homework on blogs too. Read a blog thoroughly before you approach the blogger to make sure your work is right for that blog, and read any submission guidelines the site may have. Keep a record of who you contact and when, to make sure you don't repeat yourself. Follow up after a suitable time any sites that offer to look at your work. Present yourself professionally: it's all good common sense, but in our experience that doesn't mean everyone does it right.

> *I went down the independent publishing route and got my book out in the USA and UK with BookSurge, a branch of Amazon. The pivotal moment for me was reading an article in the* Guardian, *'Is it curtains for critics?', describing the eclipse of professional critics by bloggers, and mentioning an influential book blogger, dovegreyreader. I emailed her and most of the other bloggers listed on her page, asking if they would review an independently published book. Most said they would, and most of those read and reviewed my book. This led to enquiries by publishers. The result: 'War on the Margins: A Novel' was released by Duckworth Publishers in the UK in July 2009.* – Libby Cone

Getting creative on a budget

You can get creative and get noticed even if you have little or no money to spend: write a blog or an article 'in character'. Set up a Twitter feed in your character's name, or write micro-fiction. Enlist the services of friends and family, and their cameras, video cameras, computers and, most importantly, skills to create images or videos that you can promote yourself with. We know you're creative, or you wouldn't be reading this, so we bet you can think of something imaginative (and don't get hung up on being wholly original, or you might never get started).

What does the future look like?

You don't need us to tell you this is a hard question to answer – especially for anything relating to the online world. What we do know is that the internet is rapidly eroding the barriers between writers, readers and publishers, posing new challenges for all three groups, and that's without mentioning the changes being wrought by the growth of the ebook market. This is an opportunity for you as a writer: it's a chance to get feedback earlier, from more people than ever before; a chance to hone your own marketing and presentational skills not just to literary agents, but to a much broader base of enthusiastic bloggers and fans; and most importantly, a chance to take your destiny into your own hands in a way that writers would not have imagined possible only a few years ago.

So let us hear you make some noise!

Simon Appleby and **Mathew F. Riley** have a combined total of 28 years' experience working with digital media, including setting up many publisher and author websites. They jointly own Bookswarm (www.bookswarm.co.uk), a company dedicated to providing digital marketing services to publishers and authors.

See also...

- *Managing your online reputation*, page 591
- *Writing a blog*, page 594

Managing your online reputation

These days, most people who want to find out about someone they haven't met instinctively reach for their phone, laptop or computer and key the name into Google. Antony Mayfield offers guidelines to help determine what is found as a result.

Managing your reputation has become part of every professional's career these days, and for aspiring and published authors alike it is especially important to understand what the web says about you and why that matters. Rather than think of this as another onerous responsibility in the ever-expanding job description of the professional writer, however, it may be better to view managing what the web says about you as both an opportunity and part of a powerful new way of working.

As the saying goes, reputation is what you do plus what others say about you. Translated for the web age, that means when someone puts your name into a search engine or social networking website, your reputation is what they find about you and your work.

Most importantly, for writers looking to get published, an established online reputation being part of a strong network or community of peers and fans adds to the chances that a book will be a success. This is not just about direct sales: an online community that values a writer's work will be likely to help spread the word, write reviews and generally support that writer's efforts.

In the best tradition of *Writers' & Artists' Yearbook*, the advice in this article comes from a personal perspective, and should be taken and made your own. One of the most important things to understand about the web is that it is a machine, a tool, and you should feel like it works for you rather than the other way around.

Understanding your online world

Just as being a good writer means being a good reader, it helps to get to know your online world and pay attention to what is going on there. Who are the people who are talking about subjects you are interested in and write about, or if you have a public profile already, where are they talking about your work?

It can even be helpful to sketch a map of what your online world looks like: over here are the people blogging about your subject matter, over there the specialist community site dedicated to it, over there the Twitter conversations.

Being found for yourself

The next job is to look at what people find when they look for you online. What happens when you key your name into Google, Facebook, or other websites? If you have a common name, what keywords would a stranger (a publisher or journalist wanting to know more about you, for instance) use to narrow their search? Would they add the name of your school or university, the town where you live, your employer or profession for instance?

One fairly useful measure of success for your efforts in managing your reputation is how much easier you can make it for others to find you online and how much useful stuff they find (on your sites and others). Ideally, you want the first page on Google – or any other search engine – that appears for your name to be yours. Not least, this means that whatever the rest of the world says about you, you get your say first.

A page you can call home

Developing your online presence these days can mean having profiles on several websites (for most authors at least a personal website or blog, Twitter and Facebook). Ensure that one is your hub, where you organise your online presence and connect to others.

Some people find that a Facebook page (a fan page, not a personal profile) can serve this purpose. Bear in mind, though that not everyone has a Facebook account and a few even object to it – so making this your central online presence can have drawbacks.

For me, the most versatile and future-proof approach is to have a personal blog or website and to link writing and other content you put there to other sites and social networks.

Ideally, a hosted Wordpress (www.wordpress.com) blog at a personal web address is the way to go (a little help from a moderately tech-savvy friend can get you up and running). Alternatives like SquareSpace (www.squarespace.com) charge a reasonable monthly fee and make it relatively simple to run a professional-looking blog or personal web page.

Another option is to use a personal homepage service like Flavors.me or About.me. These are attractive, simple web pages which are easy to set up, free or low-cost and can sit on your personal web address. Your homepage will link to and even show excerpts from your Twitter, Facebook and other social websites. This is a low maintenance approach, but will still stand a good chance of appearing high in the search engine listings for your name.

Public and private lives online

Early on in managing your online reputation, there is an important personal policy you need to draw up. How much of your life are you going to live in public? To put it another way, where are you going to draw the line between your personal life and your work as a writer?

For some people, living publicly is something they are very happy to do. For others, they want a complete division between their professional persona and their private self. Most people draw their personal division somewhere in between.

It is not just a case of protecting your personal privacy. The word 'over-share' crept into the dictionaries a couple of years back, largely to describe people sharing too many personal details online. It is not just a privacy issue as you may annoy readers of your blog or Twitter by posting a stream of personal trivia.

Once you are clear on your approach to public and private, pay careful attention to what you are posting and where. If you use services like Facebook for personal and family communication, take some time to understand the privacy settings and how you can use them to make sure that you are, for instance, not sharing 200 photos of a birthday party with your professional Facebook page instead of just your family and friends.

Make it a way of working

You already have a job that takes up most of your time: writing. The danger of online reputation management is that it can either be too daunting a job to take on at all, or become an addictive distraction (I'll just check my Twitter feed, just look at the visitor statistics on my blog, etc).

The best way of adding to your online presence and growing your reputation is to be useful to the communities around you, your networks of contacts, connections and readers. As a writer this can be done by complementing your working routine (research, reading, thinking) with social media tools.

Thinking of your blog as a public notebook can be a liberating and useful experience. At a conference on storytelling, science fiction writer and blogger Cory Doctorow shared his approach to blogging as a way of collecting ideas and research. I noted his method (on my own blog) like this:

• Blog about why something is interesting in five sentences.
• By doing that you are creating a searchable database.
• If it is interesting, people will annotate it with comments.
• After a while, there are enough posts and emerging themes that the case for a long-form piece of writing becomes clear.

Dealing with the dark side of online reputation

Many people feel trepidation about writing on the web because of a fear of being attacked by unkind commentators and critics. This shouldn't be an issue for authors though, right? If it is, then consider the web an excellent opportunity to develop a thicker skin when it comes to criticism.

There is a useful maxim among community managers and web editors that is worth sharing: 'don't feed the trolls'. Trolls are people who – usually anonymously – like to bait others with deliberately provocative comments online. The simple advice therefore, is to ignore them and refuse to be drawn into arguments you are unlikely ever to win.

Lastly, remember that when it comes to any online space, even a seemingly intimate or private one, you are on the record when you post anything on the web, and a permanent record at that. Effectively, all electronic communication – emails, texts and instant messages included – should be thought of as semi-public.

Useful resources and links

Managing your online reputation then, is an art that authors should learn. It should not interfere with the day job much though; think of it as a way of making the most of what you already have in terms of thoughts, ideas, reputation and writing. If you want to find out more, see my blog (www.antonymayfield.com/writers) for a list of resources and links to the websites and services mentioned in this article, along with some others that would be useful for any author looking to manage their online reputation.

Antony Mayfield is a founding partner of Brilliant Noise, a digital strategy consultancy working with major brands, media and marketing agencies. He founded the content and social media teams at iCrossing, which became the largest independent digital marketing firm in the world, before being sold to Hearst Media in 2010. His book, *Me and My Web Shadow* (Bloomsbury 2010), is about how to manage your personal reputation online.

See also...

• *Marketing yourself online*, page 587
• *Writing a blog*, page 594

Writing a blog

A blog is a way to publish your ideas instantaneously for an online audience. It allows readers to comment swiftly on what you have to say. Isabella Pereira introduces the world of blogging and describes how to set up a blog of your own.

Whether you're finishing a feature or crafting a novel, writing can be a lonely life. And while some might argue that seclusion is the only way to produce half decent work, unless you're an Emily Dickinson type, staring at a blank screen waiting for the 'flow' is probably going to send you potty. So, should the four walls of your 'room of one's own' be closing in, writing a blog could be the perfect tonic: both a steam vent for your inspirations and a gateway to the real world and real readers. All you'll need are a little time, energy and – if you're lucky enough to attract lots of readers – a thick skin.

What is a blog?

A blog (short for 'weblog') is a personal website to which you can make regular updates ('posts') – an online platform for your thoughts, laced with links to other websites, pictures and even sound or video clips. The latest material appears at the top, where readers can comment on it, link to it, or (worst of all) ignore it. Your posts are tagged by date and category, and stored chronologically in an archive which you can access through links on your site. You can use a blog to publish journalism, opinion, creative writing or technical expertise. It's completely free because the 'hosting' of your site (in other words, your webspace) is paid for by advertising revenue generated by the website you use to create the blog. And, in the finest spirit of the web, it's a living thing, part of a global community of the sophisticated, the sympathetic, the opinionated and the downright rude.

The glory of blogging lies not just in its immediacy but in its lack of rules, its openness and in the sheer diversity of the 'blogosphere'. The best bloggers can open a window into private worlds and passions, or provide a blast of fresh air in an era when corporate giants control most of our media. From new mums to teachers to Whitehall wonks, bloggers will tell you the unadulterated truth, often artfully veiled in the anonymity of cyberspace. Indeed anonymity has been the key to the success of many blogs, liberating the voices of writers who have taken politics and journalism by the scruff of the neck, demystified the web and quite simply made people laugh and look at the world differently.

What are writers blogging about?

Bloggers are a far from homogenous bunch and, unlike the competitive, sometimes forbidding, world of getting between hard covers, there is absolutely nothing to stop you joining them. Unsurprisingly, more than a handful of established writers are among their number.

Some have put blogging firmly at the centre of their universe, happily dedicating the weekly stints it takes to make a site take off. Adult and children's writer Neil Gaiman's site is one of the best. A blogger since 2001, Gaiman continues to make the most of blogging's potential with a rich, regularly updated and very personal site which has his thousands of fans addicted. His daily posts tell fans about new enthusiasms: music, books, tour news and work-in-progress. Poet George Szirtes's blog is home to elegant daily disquisitions on politics, art and, sometimes, domesticity – an example of how wonderful writing can make the most mundane of life's occurrences. And short story writer, novelist and poet Sarah Salway uses her blog for 'regular writing prompts and inspiration, but mostly random notes of things that take my fancy' – reassuring reading for her fellow writers.

And what about the others?

You don't have to be an established wordsmith to write a cracking blog. Some of the best online opinions about books, publishing and writing can be found on the blogs of 'amateur' writers, whose work is often anything but. See box for a list of some of today's best book bloggers who comment on 'bookworld' debate, opinion and news. And publishers haven't wanted to miss the boat: on the Penguin blog you'll find details of the travails of writing a blurb, creating a jacket and the pleasures and pains of being a commissioning editor.

Recommended book blogs

Cornflower Books
website www.cornflowerbooks.co.uk
Reviews a wide range of books and has a monthly online book club, debates cover designs and includes a 'writing and publishing' section.

Ready Steady Book
website www.readysteadybook.com/Blog.aspx
Very professional site, with book reviews and links for purchase. Highlights up-coming book events and has an extensive list of interviews with authors.

The Write Practice
website http://thewritepractice.com
Focuses on how to get published; includes posts on different stages of the writing process (e.g. '8 Tips for Naming Characters' and 'Your Dream vs. Rejection').

Dear Author
website www.dearauthor.com
Focuses on romanctic novels. All reviews are written in the form of a letter to the author.

Jane Friedman
website http://janefriedman.com
Tips for writers on how to beat writers' block, DIY ebook publishing and marketing your writing.

The Creative Penn
website www.thecreativepenn.com
Focuses on how to write, market and sell your book.

The Book Shelf Muse
website http://thebookshelfmuse.blogspot.co.uk
Writing tools for authors, including multiple thesauruses such as the 'Character Trait Thesaurus', 'Emotion Thesaurus' and 'Setting Thesaurus'.

Romance University
website http://romanceuniversity.org
An online 'university' for all who are hoping to learn the craft of writing romance. Three new lectures are added weekly.

Courage 2 Create
website http://ollinmorales.wordpress.com
Ollin Morales shares the experience of writing his first novel: pitfalls to avoid, dealing stress and inspirational quotes.

Terrible Minds
website http://terribleminds.com/ramble/blog
Comical, easy-to-read blog about author Chuck Wendig's trials and tribulations whilst writing.

The Artist's Road
website http://artistsroad.wordpress.com
Dedicated to the cross-USA road trip that the author took in the summer of 2010 whilst interviewing over 40 artists.

Wordplay
website http://wordplay-kmweiland.blogspot.co.uk
Tips on story structure, character and plot development; extensive list of books for aspiring authors.

Writer Unboxed
website http://writerunboxed.com
Comical tips on writing fiction, including interviews from established authors also offering advice.

A Newbie's Guide to Publishing
website http://jakonrath.blogspot.co.uk/
Looks at the publishing industry as a whole, with a slant towards the author's perspective.

Why should I write a blog?

Blogs are a great place to test out new material, get some feedback from the like-minded and enjoy the gratifying experience of actually seeing yourself in print. If you've already got a website, you should take heed of how blogs are used by writers to keep fans coming back, with juicy new material that is updated regularly. This is as true for writers with a profile as for those without. A blog is also a fine way to control your public image. Many writers use their sites as their 'official mouthpiece' to dispel rumours and give their opinion from the horse's mouth. A blog can help you construct and manage what you present to the public. Whether you prefer a greater openness or less speculation, blogging means that you can have the final word rather than leaving it to the press.

But what if no one's heard of me?

That's the point! With or without the public profile, a blog can be the perfect place to cut your teeth or test new material – with the additional kick of seeing yourself published straight away. If you're having trouble motivating yourself to write 2,000 words a day, the regular deadline of a blog update can be an excellent way of accumulating material. Blogs can be fertile ground for fiction: Dean Esmay and John Eddy, authors of the recent blog-turned-novel *Methuselah's Daughter*, wrote such a heartrending story of immortal life that it was a Blooker Prize finalist in 2007 and turned into a novel in 2011. (The Blooker Prize – formerly the Lulu Blooker Prize – is the world's first literary prize for 'blooks' – or books based on blogs, websites or other online content.) Bestselling author of *Labyrinth*, Kate Mosse, generated her novel through a blog, sharing characters, scenarios and her motivation for writing the book with her audience and drawing directly on their responses. Some of book industry's most successful recent finds have been blogs first of all, notably those of self-professed London call girl Belle de Jour and Salam Pax, the famous 'Baghdad Blogger'. For these writers, the success of their blogs brought their writing to the attention of agents and publishers – in the same way that what Helen Fielding's long-running column in the Independent*Independent* did for *Bridget Jones' Diary*. The only difference these days is that you don't have to be an established writer to try it. Which takes us to the next pressing question about blogs.

How do I get started?

A blogging 'portal' (a website for creating and hosting blogs) will lead you through all the steps to setting up a personal blog. Some of the best-known are: www.blogger.com, www.posterous.com, www.typepad.com and www.wordpress.org. You simply register on the site, choose a name under which to write, select a layout for the page from the templates on offer and you're practically ready to go. All you need now is something to say.

What should I write?

The best blogs have a distinctive voice – they're warm, witty, acerbic, opinionated, emotional or all of the above. Most of all, they're honest. Blogs work best when they have an unusual viewpoint. They aren't usually high art – they're timely and bitesized. To capture the notoriously short attention span of the internet audience you'll need to be short, sharp and, ideally, have an unusual angle for your blog. You don't have to be trapped in a war zone (though it definitely helps). If you're short of ideas, think about an aspect of your life that you could write about in a distinctive way: your job, your family, an organisation you're involved with. You can keep an account of an event you're taking part in, a hobby or art form you're passionate about and, of course, if you're writing fiction you could try your characters for size.

Guidelines

Strictly speaking, there are no rules in cyberspace. But if you want your blog to have regular readers, and even better, to have people linking to you, it may help if you:

- keep your posts short – the average internet reader doesn't dawdle;
- write in the first person and use declarative sentences;
- keep your writing uncomplicated and avoid jargon at all costs;
- use short paragraphs – web readers need white space, because it is difficult to read a solid block of text on a computer screen;
- use subheadings, and bold and italicised text liberally;
- if you can't be brief, be very, very interesting and make sure you entertain your readers. This goes for all kinds of writing but never more so than when trying to fix the attention of ruthlessly surf-happy web-readers;
- be conversational, funny and opinionated — the internet is not a formal place and a sense of humour is essential, not just in your content but in readiness for animated feedback on your work;
- use your headlines and tell as much of the story as possible in them – the headline should not only hook the reader but express the content explicitly. Many people use 'news feeders' which scan headlines for keywords, so keep this in mind when writing if you're looking to get picked up in searches;
- use lots of links – links uniquely enrich writing for the web and readers expect them. Make sure you link to all the blogs, articles, biographies and sites you mention and use links wherever they can help clarify or add depth to your post. It pays to be as original with links as your writing – seek out some of the more offbeat material on the web, and offer a full opinion on sites you link to;
- express yourself – blogging is an opportunity to be published with complete artistic freedom, so make sure you make the most of it;
- be thick-skinned – opinions online are untrammelled, so be ready for unwelcome 'flamings' from fellow bloggers who might not like your style. What's more, irony is rife and taking yourself too seriously can be asking for trouble.

How often should I write?

Blogs die if they're not updated but blogger burnout is an equally likely cause of death. If you try to update every day but don't have the time or the energy, your site will be the next burnout casualty, so it's important to decide upon a realistic schedule for posting. Updating daily makes perfect sense if you're doing something newsworthy each day but if not, save your thoughts for the next post. It's fine not to post for a few days or even weeks but don't go completely silent. A blog is a living thing and it needs feeding.

What about pictures?

You can get away without them but it would be a shame not to use photos to make the most of the web's all-singing, all-dancing capacities. Good writing is vital but visual layout is also important on the web. Pictures break up blocks of text and can bring your blog to life. All custom blogging websites allow you to add simple pictures and, for a larger catalogue of images, you can link to a photo-sharing site (see box for some links). Use some judgement in which pictures you post up, though – even your die-hard fans won't want to plough through every holiday snap. On the web this makes for very tedious 'scrolling through' time.

How will people find me?

Keywords in the headlines of your blog posts will ensure that you're picked up by searches made through blogging portals and search engines. Be aware people can sign up for email updates from blog aggregators and through RSS feeds (RSS stands for 'Rich Site Summary' and is a digested version of the new content on a website) to keep them updated with new posts they are interested in. Your blogging portal will give you the option to add RSS feeds to your own site. Finally, start exploring your community: make friends with other like-minded bloggers and swap links on your sites.

Vlog and Twitter

When you've got the pictures licked, you might want to graduate to adding 'podcasts' (regular digital audio clips) or a 'vlog' (a 'video log', i.e. regularly updated digital video clips) to your site. As digital video is becoming increasingly simple to use, vlogs are becoming more common on sites. If you can beg or borrow a digital video camera, it's worth considering adding this extra dimension.

Brevity being the soul of the blog, if you haven't the energy to write an entire post you can of course now tweet instead. Twitter is blogging-lite – you simply update your site with what you're doing right at that moment and all those signed up in your online social circle are instantly updated on your activities.

A final word

Writing a blog means you can see yourself published in minutes, test out material and ensure you're writing regularly. Yet without the time-honoured authority of the printed page behind you, you're vulnerable to the many sharpened wits of cyberspace – or even their indifference. As much of a marketplace as any bookshop but many millions of times bigger, browsers on the web are disinclined to linger. But good writing and engaging with the blogging community can compel readers to come back and ensure your blog develops a life of its own. Most of all, blogging is simple, free and has huge creative potential – don't be afraid to try it.

Isabella Pereira is an editor and intermittent blogger who has worked in book publishing. The *Writers' & Artists'* website (www.writersandartists.co.uk) has a host of regular and guest bloggers: authors, editors and other publishing professionals.

BLOGGING SITES

This is a fast-moving area: sites and businesses appear and others cease year by year. Writers are reminded to check carefully what each service offers and to check all details of any contractual arrangements before entering into these. This *Yearbook* cannot be held responsible for any content on any of these sites.

Bebo

website www.bebo.com

The name means 'Blog early, blog often' and is an online social media network.

Blogger

website http://blogger.com

One of the first, and easiest to use, sites for starting a blog. All blogs are hosted on Google's servers.

Facebook

website www.facebook.com

Social networking site with profile pages and password access.

LinkedIn

website www.linkedin.com

Business networking site, mainly used for professional networking.

LiveJournal

website www.livejournal.com

A virtual community where Internet users can keep a blog, journal or diary.

MySpace

website www.myspace.com

Cult social networking site that offers email, a forum, communities, videos and blog space.

TravelPod

website www.travelpod.com

A blogging site specifically targeted at travellers.

See also...

- *Books published from blogs*, page 269
- *Self-publishing in ebook*, page 294
- *Marketing yourself online*, page 587
- *Managing your online reputation*, page 591

Tumblr

website www.tumblr.com

An image-focused blogging platform. Users tend to post mostly about fashion, design, art, architecture.

Twitter

website http://twitter.com

Users share their daily activities for anyone to follow. Well-known writers use it.

TypePad

website www.typepad.com

A blogging site where users can upload video and music. Offers a service that fights against spam.

Wordpress

website http://wordpress.org

A 'personal publishing platform': in other words a free home for blogs.

YouTube

website www.youtube.com

A video sharing website where users can upload, view and share video clips.

Resources for writers

Dealing with rejection

Alison Straw discusses how to deal with rejection by building resilience.

When you look back over the careers of the most successful writers and artists you will see that they've managed to navigate their way through rejection and failure. William Golding's *Lord of the Flies* was rejected by 20 publishers, one of which denounced the future classic as 'An absurd and uninteresting fantasy which was rubbish and dull'. One publisher rejected George Orwell's *Animal Farm* with the comment, 'It is impossible to sell animal stories in the USA'. Perhaps one of the most quoted examples is that of the first *Harry Potter* book, which is reported to have been rejected by 14 publishers.

It's almost inevitable that at some point in your literary career your work will be rejected too. So how you manage rejection and build resilience is essential to your success. In fact the only way to avoid your work being rejected is to keep it to yourself.

It's not about you

What sets resilient people apart from others is that they don't take rejection personally. Rejection hurts. It can be like a body blow but it's not about you or your value as a person. It's about your work and in the world of publishing rejection comes with the territory. In building your resilience, you need to make sure that this hurt doesn't translate into a loss of faith in yourself or in your work.

Ray Bradbury said that the secret of being a good writer was knowing when to reject success and when to accept rejection. Others interpret a 'no thank you' not as a rejection but rather an acknowledgement that you are trying: you are getting your work out there; you are a real writer and you believe in your work. You merely need to find the right person who shares your belief; and the publisher, agent or editor who has decided not to take your work is simply not that person.

There are many reasons for your work being rejected – it could be that it's just not good enough yet, that the typescript is too long, too short, too good, too similar to a story recently published, or it is simply not right for the reader at that moment in time.

Remind yourself that when you experience a setback it is temporary. So avoid blowing it out of proportion, otherwise you may predict the future negatively without considering other, more positive outcomes. Setbacks are difficult, but they are experiences which give you the opportunity to create a different and more positive future.

Pause

Even though you know that the bad news of rejection is not a reflection of you personally, it is important to take time out and recognise its impact. There is some truth to the old adage of dusting yourself off, but first let the dust settle. Everyone reacts differently, so create a natural pause by doing something that you find recuperative, such as going for a walk in nature, having a nice meal, or talking it through with friends. Do whatever helps to lift your spirits and get a balanced perspective on the situation.

Reflect

One of the best ways to deal with rejection is to reflect. We make sense of things retrospectively, gathering valuable wisdom from reflecting on our experiences. People who don't do this miss the opportunity of learning from their rejection experience and can become stuck. For some people this can lead to feeling helpless, becoming bitter, being frozen in negative thinking or blaming others for not recognising the quality or importance of the work. In contrast, the traits of resilience, creativity, growth and optimism all demand that you look forward.

Once you have recovered from your initial reaction to a rejection, take the time and effort to work things out. Often the quality of feedback you receive doesn't provide the information you need so you may need to make the connections yourself. Keep writing as most people write better if they practise. One of the best methods of reflecting on your work is to think of it in the context of others. So read widely and this may help you adapt and alter your thinking, or simply inspire you.

Creating a book is a difficult and exacting process. If you look back, you may feel that some of the work you've submitted to a publisher or literary agent is the best you can do. But other work, even though you thought it was good at the time you wrote it, may make you cringe when you reread it now. Reflect and hone your work, making sure that you present your best work in most appropriate way.

Move on

Resilience is the result of managing strong feelings, emotions and impulses, and channelling these emotions into positive activity. People who are not resilient stay in a place where their thoughts feed their insecurities and lack of belief. If you believe that your work has simply not reached the right person at the right time, then moving on is critical to your success.

So plan your action. You may need to ask yourself questions about what change is necessary to achieve success. Have I contacted the right individuals? Have I approached them in the appropriate way? Who has found success and what are they doing that I could learn from? Used well, this *Yearbook* can give you many ideas. Or maybe it's time to do something completely different, and new technology offers new and creative ways of both publishing and promoting your work which are not too costly.

Ask for advice

When you receive a rejection for your work, you may get a standard response like 'we can see no market for that' or 'this doesn't fit with our current list', both of which don't give you much to work on. Ask for advice from people whose opinion you respect. It's always refreshing to experience how genuinely helpful people can be if approached in the right way. A starting point could be questions such as: Who else should I be talking to? What could I do differently? Where can I see examples of a successful proposal? If you feel awkward about this approach, perhaps you should seek out someone who can give professional editorial advice, appraisal and mentoring (see www.writersandartists.co.uk for listings of such services). Whilst this kind of feedback may come at a cost, it should result in receiving valuable advice or making the right contact which could generate the desired result. Alternatively, join a writing group, either in person or on the internet. Just being in contact with like-minded people immediately removes the sense of isolation that writers sometimes experience and can also short-cut your learning by understanding what others have done, what has been successful and why.

Also, get out and meet people in the publishing world. Go to writing group meetings; attend events at one of the many literary festivals (see *Literature festivals* on page 571); go to book launches and author talks – go anywhere you think is relevant. In time you may meet someone who provides another contact or whose experience makes you think again about your approach. Again, simple questions work best, such as: What advice would you give to a new author? If you were starting again what would you do differently? What's the best advice you've been given? Also explore opportunities on the internet, including www.writersandartists.co.uk.

Focus on success

It's important to understand what success looks and feels like and to make it part of your daily life. Think about the times you have felt successful. What leads to a sense of achievement? A solid and firm foundation builds resilience and will counterbalance the affect of receiving a rejection. All effective techniques for developing skills at feeling good will help you to understand about achievement.

Set realistic goals

Focusing on success means keeping the end goal in mind. By keeping your focus and expressing it repeatedly, whatever you are aiming for will become real. The goals of resilient people remain constant; however, their journey may take a variety of twists and turns.

Develop some realistic goals for yourself and do something regularly which moves you towards them, even if it seems like a small accomplishment at the time. Instead of focusing on tasks that seem unachievable, ask yourself, 'What's the one thing I know I can accomplish today or this week that helps me move in the direction I want to go?'

Become a problem solver

It's likely that in working towards a goal you will experience an impasse, but don't let this knock you. Think laterally and apply all your problem-solving skills to the situation. Reflect on an experience when you faced a similar challenge and how you managed the problem or navigated the obstacle. Alternatively, think about the approaches you've used to problem solve in the past and consider the options. These may be to walk away from the situation, share your thoughts on it, or view the problem from another angle. Hopefully a creative solution will develop.

Try again

The more risks you take, the more successes you are likely to celebrate. Don't give up; bounce back, persevere, try something new – as a successful golfer once said, 'the more I practise the luckier I get'.

Sir Winston Churchill said: 'Success is the ability to go from one failure to another with no loss of enthusiasm.' I may replace the word 'failure' with 'rejection' or 'setback', but the sentiment remains the same. So keep trying, keep talking to others about your work and your aspirations, and success will follow.

Alison Straw is a coach and trainer. She works with individuals and organisations on developing their capability to deal with challenges and change.

The writer's ultimate workspace

Arranging for a space to write in a domestic environment can be a mammoth challenge for some people. Rib Davis gives the benefit of his experience of writing from home.

This is a work of fiction. It is based on fact – as much of the best fiction is – but there is certainly more of the wish than the accomplishment in what follows. I have been asked to write an article giving advice to the prospective writer about some of the day-to-day material conditions and habits of mind that one should attempt to establish in order to be able to work happily and efficiently. I assume that I was chosen on the basis that I have, over 30 years, failed to do these so spectacularly that I am now considered an expert in the field. I may not have learned much from my mistakes but at least I can list some of them, and let the reader do the learning.

Finding the ideal workspace

Where should the workspace be located? When we have to, we can write anywhere. At my most desperate I have written parts of scripts on trains, in crowded offices, in pubs and even leaning on a car steering wheel while waiting for the AA to rescue me. Such is the power of the deadline. Sometimes, strangely, I have produced some rather good work while battling with the distractions and other limitations of the immediate environment; I would hesitate, however, to recommend the practice too highly.

So what would be the ideal workspace location? It seems to be generally agreed that a writer (or writers, if you are working collaboratively) should work in a place where distractions are minimal. Some highly successful writers have taken this to the extreme of working in a shed or a caravan at the bottom of the garden, with only elves for company. I have never owned a caravan, and unless I learn to write seated on a bicycle I will always have trouble squashing into our slowly rotting shed, so that has never been an option. But where possible a degree of isolation – and particularly isolation from family activities and domestic duties – does seem desirable. Sustained concentration is extremely important for any sort of creative work, and such a location helps to facilitate it. In my own case, when I am actually scripting (as opposed to researching or planning) I usually find that I have to read my notes and then the latest part of the script for about an hour before I can even begin to put new words onto the page, so anything that breaks the concentration is unwelcome.

At the same time, though, we are only as strong as our will-power. Many of us could stick ourselves in an arctic igloo to write and yet still manage to find distractions (examining snowflakes can be so fascinating). For about a year I did my writing in a room at the back of a bookshop in Milton Keynes, well away from my home. It seemed to offer the ideal combination of relative isolation along with a congenial, supportive and vaguely arty environment. But the lure of the books and the customers ultimately proved too much; I soon found myself helping out at the till rather than tapping away at my *magnum opus*.

Perhaps my need to write was not sufficiently urgent. Certainly it is true that in those days I was driven by blind hope rather than deadlines, but I don't think that was the problem. The problem was (and is) fear: fear of writing badly, of not living up to one's own – and others' – expectations. For me, at least, it is this fear above all that gets in the way of creativity. First I fear the blank page (of course), then the writing, and then the finishing. This is why those awful distractions can seem, in fact, very welcome indeed. And it is part of the reason why we should try to avoid them as far as possible.

For a few years, remarkably, I did work in a suitable location. Quite simply, this was a room in the house that I was able to turn into my study. It was not totally cut off from the rest of Life, but it was sufficiently separate to allow generally uninterrupted concentration. My small son had difficulty understanding why, if I was behind the door, I refused to open it, but apart from that it worked well. For most of my working life, though, I have done my writing on the living room table. My laptop and notes have been moved away at meal times; people have traipsed through the living room to get to the kitchen (why didn't we think of this when we bought the house?); the television has been in the same room. In short, my workplace has been set in the teeming hub of the house. Big mistake.

Cordial domestic relations

A word on educating one's family. A writer's partner and/or children will generally recognise and respect the writer's need to focus on the work in hand, but there is at least one point which needs clarifying. When I write, I take breaks. These breaks can occur for a variety of reasons. Perhaps I have reached an interim target, or I have become stuck, or I am thirsty, or just tired. So I might stop and play the piano, or make a cup of coffee, or – exceptionally – even do some washing up, and then return to the writing with a clearer head. No problem, except that this might be observed, and the observing partner/child may think, 'Ah, so he doesn't mind his concentration being broken after all'. This can be a problem. You have to be selfish. You have to make clear that you can break your own concentration as and when you feel the need – you can wrong-note your way through a whole Beethoven sonata if you feel like it – but that does not give others the green light to break your concentration as and when they feel the need. Be unreasonable.

So much for location. Now, what should the workspace look like? My answer would simply be: pleasant. It should be a welcoming place, where you will feel comfortable and not oppressed. For me, this means well decorated in soft colours, with the desk facing out to a window, preferably with a view, and a temperature that's warm but not sleep-inducing. For others, windows may present yet another distraction, colours should be severe, the radiator should be off and the whole place should be tatty. The point is that you should feel comfortable in it – it should feel like *your* space.

Where I have been able to, I have turned my space into an almost self-sufficient world. This requires at the very least coffee (stimulation), Scotch (counter the extreme effects of coffee) and a variety of non-laxative snacks (counter the other effects of coffee). Ideally I suppose an en suite bathroom would be a good idea, but we should keep to the feasible. When I am really rich and famous I will also have an extra piano in my study, but for now I make do with a stereo. I find music (at least, some music) can create a less intense atmosphere when I am researching or planning, but when I am actually scripting I tend to turn it off, as otherwise I find the writing being influenced moment-to-moment by every passing mood of the music, which does not tend to improve the quality of my literary product at all.

Working efficiently

Writing is of course more than simply tapping words onto a page. It is also thinking, researching, planning and finally doing all the administrative work connected to the sale and then either publication or production of the work, whether through an agent or otherwise. So your workspace must be able to accommodate all this too. Give yourself as much work surface as possible, so that you can refer to as many materials as you need simultaneously, and you can even have materials left out for more than one project at a time. And set up an efficient filing system from the start. Or if, as in my case, this is certainly not the start, do it now anyway. Do not simply put every new publisher's letter, piece of research and pizza takeaway leaflet together in an in-tray. The in-tray eventually overflows; you get a second one; that overflows too. You will eventually be surrounded by in-trays. File everything as it comes along, and don't hesitate to open a new file for even the germ of a new project.

This filing particularly applies to emails. One can make the mistake of thinking that because something is there on the computer it has been filed. It hasn't. Electronic documents – and emails most of all – can be just as much of a mess as a physical desktop. When you receive an email, save it in the relevant project file elsewhere in the computer. If you are feeling super-efficient, you could also print it off and keep it in that same project's hard-copy file.

Mention of emails leads me on to phones. Both can take over your whole existence if you allow them to; they will certainly try. Deal with emails when you are at your least productive as a writer. If you think of yourself as a 'morning person' then that is when you should be writing; do the emails in the evening. Or if mornings tend to be barren periods of grogginess and haze, those are the times for doing emails. And try to deal with all the day's emails in one sitting; certainly don't let them interrupt you whenever they feel like it. Set up your computer in such a way that it does not let you know when emails have arrived; instead, just check them once or twice per day.

Similarly, don't simply answer the phone whenever it rings. The phone can of course be very useful for your writing, particularly for research, but in general – switch it to silent. If the caller doesn't leave a message, it can't be very important.

A great deal of research is now done on the web, but I still like having books around. In particular, despite the existence of online dictionaries I still believe a writer should have a really good book dictionary (some of the larger ones give a date for each word usage, which is particularly helpful for period writing), and I also find a large thesaurus very useful (the original format, not the alphabetical kind; the latter is simpler to use but as it is necessarily so repetitive it contains far fewer options). Then, of course, there are always the books needed for the particular project in hand.

Most writers actually fit their research and other writing activities in with other work, whether writing-related or not. This means that time becomes a very precious commodity. I have always worked best when I have been able to arrange my writing time in large chunks, preferably whole days. An hour here or there really is hardly any use. And whenever possible I have tried to establish routines. The truth is that I have been particularly bad at this, perhaps because I have often had too many projects at different stages simultaneously, but I would still recommend adopting a daily routine as far as possible. It means there is just one less decision to have to make: your writing times have been decided and that's it.

Writer's block

So now you are all set. You have bought yourself Final Draft software (or something similar) and you have the workspace, the materials, the books, the filing – the lot. You write and write. You pin the best rejection slips onto the wall (we've all had them). You write and write. And then you don't. You get writer's block. I have had this. It is a particularly nasty affliction as in almost everyone else's eyes 'writer's block' translates as 'laziness'. This is not the place for a full discussion, but I can pass on a couple of pieces of advice I received, which worked for me. Firstly, don't always try to see the whole piece of work, as that may be overwhelming to you. Instead, try to focus on a particular section of it and nothing more. Secondly, when you have writer's block a whole day of writing ahead of you looks interminable. So don't do it. Strictly limit yourself to writing for two hours and no more. You may well find yourself writing with real urgency, trying to cram all that you can into those two allotted hours. Only much later can you gradually increase the limit back to a normal day.

Well, it worked for me. But then there are all sorts of writers. My old friend Jack Trevor Story had a writer's solution for insomnia: he wrote right through the night. Every night. It worked for him.

Now, as usual, I am going to try to learn from what I've written.

Rib Davis has been writing professionally for 30 years. He has over 60 credits, including scripts for radio, television and stage, as well as two books on the art of writing scripts. He is close to sorting out his domestic writing arrangements. Having finally sorted out his domestic arrangements he has now moved house, so is starting all over again.

Writers' retreats

Some writers find that spending time at a writers' retreat proves bountiful. One author who has benefited from this experience is Maggie Gee.

Writers' retreats are not for everyone. They aren't, for example, for the poet who once said to me, *a propos* of Hawthornden Castle International Writers' Retreat, 'But it's so quiet. And Edinburgh is *half an hour away* by bus.' For him, to be half an hour from the metropolis was a penance.

Before going into the desert, think long and hard. Are you quarrelsome, or over-sensitive, or both? The other writers will, for the most part, be busy and quiet, but mealtimes are generally communal. People are more vulnerable when they are off their own territory and away from loved ones. Do not always eat the last piece of cake (food gains an emotional significance when other props are missing) or be competitive about how much you have written, or how much you get paid. Actual numbers of words and pounds should never be quoted. Do not give a reading from your new work unless asked.

Ask yourself hard questions before you go. Do you mind very much being away from your loved ones, your cat, your garden? Will you be wracked by guilt? Are you addicted to television? Do you feel anxious if you can't pick up emails or vary the monotony of your work with half-hourly binges on Google, Facebook or Twitter? Most retreats have no televisions and some still have no internet connection.

But if you are a writer who can never get enough time uninterrupted by phone calls, plumbers, pets, children and the washing-machine, writers' retreats are absolute heaven. For me personally, three widely spaced four-week stays at Hawthornden Castle produced the first drafts of two novels, *Where are the Snows* (1991) and *The Flood* (2004), and the second half of my memoir, *My Animal Life* (2011). When I am away from all the things I ought to do at home, 200–300 words a day swells into 2,000–3,000.

Prose writers have to come to terms with the leaden truth that you cannot write a book without hours of immobility. I personally prefer concentrating those hours into a smaller number of weeks and months. I speak as one whose eighth novel (*The White Family*), took seven years to write and rewrite (no retreats), whereas *The Flood*, after 18 months of mulling over, took just a month to dream up and write at a retreat, and six months to rewrite at home. Poets enjoy retreats too: the second time I was at Hawthornden I was with Jean Sprackland, and the collection she wrote, *Hard Water*, was later shortlisted for the T.S. Eliot Prize and the Whitbread Award for Poetry.

In the USA there is a wide choice of retreats. Google will present you with a bewildering variety of retreats there, many of them luxurious, long established and highly competitive. Most of them are free, but you have to find the air fare. In the UK there are fewer choices and just one retreat is free, Hawthornden Castle in Scotland. Writers can only go there once every five years. You must make a formal application and if you are accepted you can

Retreats overseas

Chateau de Lavigny
website www.chateaudelavigny.ch

Creative Cauldron
website www.creativecauldron.com/retreats
A useful list of retreats in the USA.

El Gouna
website www.elgouna.com/writers-residency/how-to-apply.html

look forward to a stay in a beautiful castle in dramatic wooded grounds. The rooms are small but attractive, the food is good and the five or six writers who are in residence at any one time pay only for their pre-prandial sherry. The Arvon Foundation, famous for tutored retreats, also offers one week for untutored retreats to Arvon Friends at its four beautiful, remote centres. Ireland has scenic Anam Cara, on the coast of Western Cork.

It is common for American writers to spend much of their life going from retreat to retreat, but British writers are less well served. I can recommend only three retreats from personal experience: Hawthornden, as above; the Chateau de Lavigny, a very beautiful and special European mansion on the hilly slopes of Lac Leman above Lausanne; and El Gouna, an amazing free retreat in a hotel in an 'eco-village' in Egypt, not far from Hurghada.

Lavigny – ah, Lavigny. This free retreat was founded by Jane Rowohlt in memory of her husband, famous German publisher Heinrich Mari Ledig-Rowohlt, who lived there and sometimes entertained the writers he published, among them his friend Vladimir Nabokov – my room was only a wall away from the narrow bed where my Russian hero slept. I was there in summer, watched the cornfields below turn golden for the harvest, and took long walks through rows of vines, coming back to write the end of my novel about Uganda as I looked towards the white tip of Mont Blanc. Lavigny is luxurious, relaxed, and truly international – I was there with an Egyptian, a Pole, an American, a Frenchwoman and a Scotsman.

El Gouna, Egypt, was totally different, a modern four-star hotel set beside dry, sparkling vistas over blue canals to the sea. I was there in May 2011, not long after the Revolution, and I managed to write half my new novel in my cool room, printing it off and correcting it in the open air in the hot square which was hazy with aromatic smoke from the hubble-bubble pipes. Unforgettable, but entry to El Gouna has been suspended for now.

Do not despair. There are always bargain deals at out-of-season seaside hotels, or if you once went to a college or university, you could find out if they let *alumni* stay there cheaply in empty rooms. Many do, and they should have decent desks and chairs. As a last resort, send yourself on 'day retreats' to the local library or park, and don't go home until the pages are done. I like to flee to the British Library. Once the washing-machine, the telephone and the pets have fallen silent, the dream of the book will begin.

Maggie Gee OBE has written a memoir, *My Animal Life*, a collection of short stories, *The Blue*, and 11 acclaimed novels, including *The White Family*, shortlisted for the Orange Prize. Her most recent novels are two comedies about the UK and Uganda, *My Cleaner* and *My Driver* (Telegram 2009). She was the first female Chair of the Royal Society of Literature (2004–8) and is currently one of its vice-presidents. Her forthcoming novel brings Virginia Woolf back to life in the 21st century in New York and Istanbul. The first international conference about her work will be held at St Andrew's University, Scotland, in August 2012.

Anam Cara

website www.anamcararetreat.com

Arvon

Free Word, 60 Farringdon Road, London EC1R 3GA
tel 020-7324 2554
website www.arvonfoundation.org
Chief Executive Ruth Borthwick

See individual entries for Arvon's 4 centres: The Hurst – The John Osborne Arvon Centre, Lumb Bank – The Ted Hughes Arvon Centre, Moniack Mhor and Totleigh Barton. Arvon hosts week-long residential creative writing courses in 4 beautiful writing houses. Grants available.

The Creative Writer's Workshop

Kinvara, Co. Galway, Republic of Ireland
tel +353 (0)86 2523428
email info@thecreativewritersworkshop.com
website www.thecreativewritersworkshop.com
Contact Irene Graham

Residential writing retreats in fiction, memoir and work-in-progress using right-brain/left-brain learning techniques. Founded 1991.

Resources for writers

Hawthornden Castle

International Retreat for Writers, Lasswade, Midlothian EH18 1EG
tel 0131 440 2180 *fax* 0131 440 1989
Contact The Director

Exists to provide a peaceful setting where published writers can work without disturbance. The Retreat houses up to 6 writers at a time, who are known as Hawthornden Fellows. Writers from any part of the world may apply for the fellowships. No monetary assistance is given, nor any contribution to travelling expenses, but fellows board as guests of the Retreat. Application forms are available from January for the following calendar year. Deadline for applications 30 June.

The Hurst – The John Osborne Arvon Centre

Arvon, The Hurst, Clunton, Craven Arms, Shropshire SY7 0JA
tel (01588) 640658
email thehurst@arvonfoundation.org
website www.arvonfoundation.org
Centre Directors Kerry Watson, Ilona Leighton-Goodall, *Administrator* Dan Pavitt

Offers residential writing courses April to December. Grants available. The Hurst is situated in the beautiful Clun Valley in South Shropshire, 12 miles from Ludlow, and is set in 30 acres of woodland, with gardens and a lake.

Irish Writers' Centre

19 Parnell Square, Dublin 1, Republic of Ireland
tel +353 (0)1 8721302 *fax* +353 (0)1 8726282
email info@writerscentre.ie
website www.writerscentre.ie
Contact Chairperson, Jack Harte

Residencies at the Irish Writers' Centre awarded on an occasional basis to enable writers to work on specific projects, for a period up to 3 months. Most recent Writer-in-Residence was Catherine Morris, who completed her biography of the poet Alice Milligan at the Irish Writers' Centre, in collaboration with University College Dublin and the National Library of Ireland. See website for further details.

Lumb Bank – The Ted Hughes Arvon Centre

Arvon, Lumb Bank, Heptonstall, Hebden Bridge, West Yorkshire HX7 6DF
tel (01422) 843714 *fax* (01422) 843714
email lumbbank@arvonfoundation.org
website www.arvonfoundation.org
Centre Directors Liz Flanagan, Rebecca Evans, *Administrator* Ilona Jones

Offers residential writing courses April to December. Grants available. Lumb Bank is an 18th-century former mill-owner's house set in 20 acres of steep pasture land.

Moniack Mhor

Arvon, Moniack Mhor, Teavarran, Kiltarlity, Beauly, Inverness-shire IV4 7HT
tel (01463) 741675
email moniackmhor@arvonfoundation.org
website www.arvonfoundation.org, www.moniackmhor.org.uk
Centre Directors Cynthia Rogerson, Rachel Humphries

Moniack Mhor is a traditional croft house commanding panoramic views over Highland landscapes with forest walks nearby. Courses run from April to November and are mainly tutored. Grants available. Centre available at other times for schools, writing groups, etc.

Totleigh Barton

Arvon, Totleigh Barton, Sheepwash, Beaworthy, Devon EX21 5NS
tel (01409) 231338 *fax* (01409) 231144
email totleighbarton@arvonfoundation.org
website www.arvonfoundation.org
Centre Directors Claire Berliner, Oliver Meek, *Administrator* Stephanie Wardle

Offers residential writing courses April to December. Grants available. Totleigh Barton is a thatched, pre-Domesday manor house, surrounded by farmland in Devon, 2 miles from the village of Sheepwash.

Tŷ Newydd

Tŷ Newydd Writers' Centre, Llanystumdwy, Cricieth, Gwynedd LL52 0LW
tel (01766) 522811 *fax* (01766) 523095
email post@tynewydd.org
website www.tynewydd.org

Writers' retreats are organised at different times during the year to give writers the opportunity to find a week's peace and quiet in a stimulating environment. Everyone has a single room and stays on a self-catering basis with a shared meal in the evening.

Upton Cressett Foundation

Upton Cressett Hall, Upton Cressett, Nr Bridgnorth, Shrops. WV16 6UH
tel (01746) 714616
email foundation@uptoncressett.co.uk
website www.uptoncressett.co.uk

Guest fellows (approximately 6 per year) are invited to stay in the Foundation's historic Elizabethan gatehouse for between 2 and 6 weeks to make progress with a literary or academic project. The idea is to give established UK and international writers an opportunity to make accelerated headway with a work-in-progress in a remote and beautiful creative environment away from domestic or second career distractions. This could be 100 pages of a new novel, a major rewrite after an editor's marks, a play/screenplay or a policy think-tank monograph.

Perfect proofs

Even the most trivial of errors on a printed page can result in embarrassment, delay or unexpected costs. In this article, Lauren Simpson identifies the skills, knowledge and processes required to produce a perfect publication.

Writing is only one part of the journey to producing publishable material. In addition to transforming thoughts into elegant or cogent words and phrases, there are a number of other processes involved – chiefly, copy-editing and proofreading, in addition to typesetting and printing.

What happens when?

While processes differ from publisher to publisher, the chain of events from draft copy to printed copy can be *broadly* summarised as follows:

• Author delivers completed manuscript to publisher. It is important that the author supplies the manuscript in accordance with the publisher's editorial style guide and format requirements, to avoid the time and expense of revising material later down the line.

• Publisher arranges for the manuscript to be copy-edited and any queries arising from this process (including any necessary rewriting or cutting overmatter) are passed to the author to be resolved in advance of typesetting. Some books, including directories and reference books, have no 'author' as such; instead, content is supplied, updated or edited by many contributors, often via remote access to a secure database.

• Copy-edited material is typeset or put through an electronic 'page layout' process.

• Typeset page proofs are produced and (1) first page proofs are proofread and corrections marked up; (2) corrections are incorporated and revised page proofs are produced; (3) revised page proofs are corrected and signed off.

• Printing takes place.

Copy-editing and proofreading

Copy-editing and proofreading are crucial stages of the publishing process and, while the two can often be confused, there are important differences. The copy-editing function normally takes place when the writing of an article, document, book, etc is completed, and involves checking that the content is accurate, clearly and logically expressed, conveys the appropriate message or tone, and comes together to form a coherent and cohesive whole. Copy-editors must be analytical in their approach and able to weed out factual errors, as well as annotate diagrams, cross-check references and impose a publisher's house style on a text. They may also be required to have general or specialist knowledge of the written subject matter, particularly in the case of science and maths.

Traditionally, manuscripts have been copy-edited on paper; increasingly, publishers prefer copy-editing to be carried out electronically, usually using Word. The 'track changes' function allows the copy-editor to make alterations to the manuscript in 'real time': deletions/additions can be highlighted so that the copy-editor's work can be easily monitored; comments and queries for the author or publisher can be inserted into the margins of the document; and the 'find and replace' function enables inaccuracies and inconsistencies to be corrected globally. Furthermore, tracking changes electronically allows changes to the

Marks/symbols for general instructions

INSTRUCTIONS	MARGIN	TEXT
Leave the text in its original state and ignore any marks that have been made, commonly referred to as 'stet'	(✓)	---- under the characters to be left as they were
Query for the author/typesetter/printer/publisher.	(?)	A circle should be placed around text to be queried
Remove non-textual marks	×	A circle should be placed around marks to be removed
End of change	/	None

Marks/symbols for inserting, deleting and changing text

INSTRUCTIONS	MARGIN	TEXT
Text to be inserted	New text, followed by ⋏	⋏
Additional text supplied separately	⋏ followed by a letter in a diamond which identifies additional text ◇A	⋏
Delete a character	⁊	/ through the character
Delete text	⁊	⊢⊣ through text
Delete character and close space	⁊	through the character
Delete text and close space	⁊	through text
Character to replace marked character	New character, followed by /	/ through the character
Text to replace marked text	New text, followed by /	⊢⊣ through text

Marks/symbols for grammar and punctuation

INSTRUCTIONS	MARGIN	TEXT
Full stop	⊙	⋏ at insertion point or / through character
Comma	,	As above
Semi-colon	;	As above
Colon	(:)	As above
Hyphen	⊢–⊣	As above
Single quote marks	‘ or ’	As above
Double quote marks	“ or ”	As above
Apostrophe	’	As above
Ellipses or leader dots	(...)	As above
Insert/replace dash	1en Size of dash to be stated between uprights	As above

Marks/symbols for altering the look/style/layout of text

INSTRUCTIONS	MARGIN	TEXT
Put text in italics	⌊⌊⌋	—— under text to be changed
Remove italics, replace with roman text	⌊+⌋	Circle text to be changed
Put text in bold	~~~	~~~ under text to be changed
Remove bold	~/~	Circle text to be changed
Put text in capitals	≡	≡ under text to be changed
Put text in small capitals	=	= under text to be changed
Put text in lower case	≢ or ≠	Circle text to be changed
Change character to superscript	Y under character	/ through character to be changed
Insert a superscript character	Y under character	⅄ at point of insertion
Change character to subscript	⅄ above character	/ through character to be changed
Insert a subscript character	⅄ above character	⅄ at point of insertion
Remove bold and italics	~⊥~	Circle text to be changed
Paragraph break	_⌐	_⌐
Remove paragraph break, run on text	⌒	⌒
Indent text	⊏	⊏
Remove indent	⊐	⊐
Insert or replace space between characters or words	Y	⅄ at relevant point of insertion or / through character
Reduce space between characters or words	T	|
Insert space between lines or paragraphs	Mark extends into margin	—(or)—
Reduce space between lines or paragraphs	Mark extends into margin	—) or (—
Transpose lines	⊑	⊑
Transpose characters or words	⌊⌉	⌊⌉
Close space between characters	⊂⊃	character ⊂⊃ character
Underline words	(underline)	◯ circle words
Take over character(s) or word(s) to next line/column/page	Mark extends into margin	⊏
Take back character(s) or word(s) to previous line/column/page	Mark extends into margin	⊐

Marked proof of text

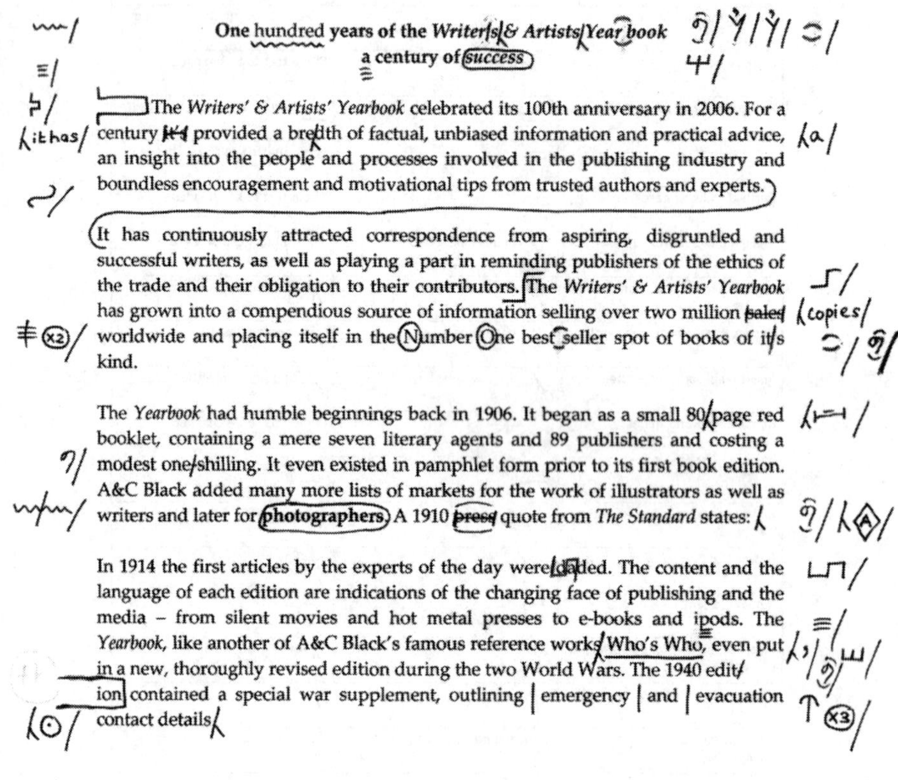

One hundred years of the *Writers & Artists Year book*
a century of *success*

The *Writers' & Artists' Yearbook* celebrated its 100th anniversary in 2006. For a century it's provided a bredth of factual, unbiased information and practical advice, an insight into the people and processes involved in the publishing industry and boundless encouragement and motivational tips from trusted authors and experts.

It has continuously attracted correspondence from aspiring, disgruntled and successful writers, as well as playing a part in reminding publishers of the ethics of the trade and their obligation to their contributors. The *Writers' & Artists' Yearbook* has grown into a compendious source of information selling over two million sales worldwide and placing itself in the Number One best seller spot of books of it's kind.

The *Yearbook* had humble beginnings back in 1906. It began as a small 80 page red booklet, containing a mere seven literary agents and 89 publishers and costing a modest one-shilling. It even existed in pamphlet form prior to its first book edition. A&C Black added many more lists of markets for the work of illustrators as well as writers and later for **photographers**. A 1910 press quote from *The Standard* states:

In 1914 the first articles by the experts of the day were daded. The content and the language of each edition are indications of the changing face of publishing and the media – from silent movies and hot metal presses to e-books and ipods. The *Yearbook*, like another of A&C Black's famous reference works Who's Who, even put in a new, thoroughly revised edition during the two World Wars. The 1940 edit-ion contained a special war supplement, outlining emergency and evacuation contact details

A 'Professional and amateur dabblers in ink no longer have any excuse for sending the offspring of their brains on the wrong road to public admiration and emolument'.

Revised proof of text incorporating corrections

One hundred years of the *Writers' & Artists' Yearbook*
A century of success

The *Writers' & Artists' Yearbook* celebrated its 100th anniversary in 2006. For a century it has provided a breadth of factual, unbiased information and practical advice, an insight into the people and processes involved in the publishing industry and boundless encouragement and motivational tips from trusted authors and experts. It has continuously attracted correspondence from aspiring, disgruntled and successful writers, as well as playing a part in reminding publishers of the ethics of the trade and their obligation to their contributors.

The *Writers' & Artists' Yearbook* has grown into a compendious source of information selling over two million copies worldwide and placing itself in the number one bestseller spot of books of its kind.

The *Yearbook* had humble beginnings back in 1906. It began as a small 80-page red booklet, containing a mere seven literary agents and 89 publishers and costing a modest one shilling. It even existed in pamphlet form prior to its first book edition. A&C Black added many more lists of markets for the work of illustrators as well as writers and later for photographers. A 1910 quote from *The Standard* states: 'Professional and amateur dabblers in ink no longer have any excuse for sending the offspring of their brains on the wrong road to public admiration and emolument'.

In 1914 the first articles by the experts of the day were added. The content and the language of each edition are indications of the changing face of publishing and the media – from silent movies and hot metal presses to e-books and iPods. The *Yearbook,* like another of A&C Black's famous reference works, *Who's Who,* even put in a new, thoroughly revised edition during the two World Wars. The 1940 edition contained a special war supplement, outlining emergency and evacuation contact details.

manuscript to be accepted or rejected by the publisher on an individual basis, giving them more control over the final version. Another advantage of copy-editing electronically is that an edited manuscript can be emailed – saving time and money.

Proofreading, on the other hand, involves scrutinising the content in very fine detail after copy-editing (and, usually, typesetting) has taken place, to ensure that errors relating to syntax, grammar, punctuation, design and format are eliminated. Proofreaders, therefore, must have good technical language skills and an excellent eye for detail. Attention to detail is especially important in order to effectively deal with errors in technical or complex text, or when applying a style guide.

The importance of exemplary proofreading is highlighted by the fact that in addition to publishers, typesetters and reproduction teams often employ people whose job it is to ensure that the finished article is as finely polished and technically accurate as possible.

Authors will usually be expected to proofread just the first page proofs of their work. It is important for authors to keep changes to a minimum as corrections to page proofs are costly, time-consuming and can have a negative impact on aspects such as the index or cross-referencing. It is far better practice to amend a manuscript *before* pages have been typeset and corrections on page proofs should be limited to typos, amending inaccurate or out-of-date material, and resolving problems relating to page layout, design, etc.

A word about typesetting and printing

Page layout has traditionally been undertaken by a typesetter. However, nowadays it is often carried out by the publisher using either bespoke or off-the-peg page production software, especially if a book has an uncomplicated layout or structure. This gives the publisher greater control over production processes and schedules and helps to reduce costs. In addition to laying out pages in-house, many publishers make use of print on demand (POD) which allows books to be produced as and when they are required. This is beneficial for two main reasons: firstly, there is greater flexibility for factual errors or time-sensitive material to be updated on an ongoing basis and, secondly, the expense of printing and warehousing books in bulk is eliminated.

Proofreading symbols

Despite occupying very distinct roles, both copy-editors (to a lesser extent due to onscreen editing) and proofreaders require knowledge of the 'shorthand' for correcting written material. Typesetters, designers and printers also require this knowledge as part of correcting page layout, style and format.

Correcting proofs or 'marking up' copy effectively relies on the use of proofreading symbols (or 'marks') which instruct the typesetter, printer, or whoever, what changes need to be made, in a uniform and concise way. The full set of proofreading marks is defined by the British Standards Institute (BS 5261). However, most proofreading can be carried out using only the most common proofreading symbols.

Proofreading marks fall into separate categories:

- Marks/symbols for general instructions
- Marks/symbols for inserting, deleting and changing text
- Marks/symbols for grammar and punctuation
- Marks/symbols for altering the look/style/layout of text.

Depending on the nature of the changes needed, proofreading marks are typically positioned in the margin of the document undergoing correction, with some changes requiring a mark within the text or some additional instruction.

Marked proofs

Anyone who has ever seen a marked-up proof will probably acknowledge the fact that proof corrections are not always executed perfectly. Pressured schedules, last-minute changes and familiarity between colleagues often result in shortcuts to the way corrections are applied. That said, proof corrections should, in accordance with BS 5261, be made in the following way:

• Alterations and instructions made by the publisher and/or his agents should be marked up using dark blue or black ink.
• Errors made by the typesetter/printer should be marked up by the publisher and/or his agents using red ink.
• Errors made by the typesetter/printer should be marked up by the typesetter/printer using green ink.

A page covered in proofreading marks can look rather daunting to the untrained eye but with experience, the application and deciphering of proof corrections becomes second nature.

Mistakes to look out for

Clearly, no two manuscripts will have exactly the same problems. However, there are a number of mistakes that commonly crop up for which authors and proofreaders need to be on the constant look out.

• Similar words used incorrectly, e.g. effect/affect.
• Phrases used inappropriately, e.g. 'should of' instead of 'should have'.
• Apostrophe misuse, especially in respect of its/it's.
• Words with similar spelling or pronunciation but different meanings used incorrectly, e.g. their/they're/there.
• References in text that do not correspond to footnotes.
• Inaccurate or inadequate cross-referencing.
• Index listings which cannot be found on the page given in the index.
• Text inadvertently reordered or cut during the typesetting process.
• Headings formatted as ordinary text.
• Running heads that do not always correspond to chapter headings.
• Fonts and font sizes used incorrectly.
• Inconsistent use of abbreviations and acronyms.
• Format inconsistencies such as poorly aligned margins or uneven columns.
• Captions/headings omitted from illustrations, photographs or diagrams.
• Illustrations/photographs/diagrams without appropriate copyright references.
• Missing bullet points or numbers in a sequenced list.
• Word processing errors, e.g. '3' instead of '£'.
• Incorrect layout of names, addresses, telephone numbers and email/web addresses.
• Incorrect use of trademarks, e.g. blackberry instead of BlackBerry™.
• Abbreviations that have not been defined in full.
• Widows and orphans, e.g. text which runs over page breaks and leaves a word or line stranded.
• Past and present tenses mixed within a piece of text.
• Use of plural verb conjugations with single subjects, e.g. 'one in five children are…' instead of 'one in five children is…'.

Tips for perfect page proofs

Effective and accurate proofreading takes time and practice. These tips will help ensure a top-notch finished product, every time.

• Set aside adequate time for proofreading. It is a job that requires concentration and should not be rushed.

• Before starting on a proofreading task, make sure you have easy access to a dictionary and thesaurus, and ensure that you have appropriate style guides for language style and format/design.

• If possible, proofread a document several times and concentrate on different aspects each time, e.g. sense/tone, format, grammar/punctuation/use of language.

• Try not to proofread copy that you wrote yourself to avoid repeating mistakes. When proofreading scientific or mathematical material, ensure you are confident with the subject matter. If not, seek an expert opinion.

• Spot typos by reading the text backwards – that way you will not be distracted by the meaning of the text.

• Always double check scientific, mathematical or medical symbols as they can often be corrupted during the typesetting process.

• If possible, have a version of the marked-up copy-edited text alongside you while you proofread – it might help solve minor inaccuracies or inconsistencies, or at least help you flag up whether text needs to be referred back to the author for clarification.

Lauren Simpson is a freelance editor and publisher who has worked in reference publishing for nearly 20 years. She has contributed to and developed a wide range of print and electronic publications covering subjects as diverse as agriculture, local government, banking, marketing, business, English language teaching, boating, social work and counselling & psychotherapy. In addition, she has been editor of a number of prestigious reference works including *The Municipal Year Book* and *Whitaker's Almanack*.

See also...

- *Understanding the publishing process*, page 215
- *Who will edit your book?*, page 299
- *Print on demand*, page 317

Indexing

A good index is a joy to the user of a non-fiction book; a bad index will downgrade an otherwise good book. The function of indexes, and the skills needed to compile them, are examined here.

An index is a detailed key to the contents of a document, in contrast to a contents list, which gives only the titles of the parts into which the document is divided (e.g. chapters). Precisely, an index is 'A systematic arrangement of entries designed to enable users to locate information in a document'. The document may be a book, a series of books, an issue of a periodical, a run of several volumes of a periodical, an audiotape, a map, a film, a picture, a CD-Rom, a website, a database, an object, or any other information source in print or non-print form.

The objective of an index is to guide enquirers to information on given subjects in a document by providing the terms of their choice (single words, phrases, abbreviations, acronyms, dates, names, and so on) in an appropriately organised list which refers them to specific locations using page, column, section, frame, figure, table, paragraph, line or other appropriate numbers or hyperlinks.

An index differs from a catalogue, which is a record of the documents held in a particular collection, such as a library; though a catalogue may require an index, for example to guide searchers from subject words to class numbers.

A document may have separate indexes for different classes of heading, so that personal names are distinguished from subjects, for example, or a single index in which all classes of heading are interfiled.

The Society of Indexers

The Society of Indexers was founded in 1957 and is the only autonomous professional body for indexers in the UK. It is affiliated with the American Society for Indexing, the Australian and New Zealand Society of Indexers, the China Society of Indexers, the Indexing Society of Canada, and the Association of Southern African Indexers and Bibliographers, and has close ties with the Chartered Institute of Library and Information Professionals (CILIP) and the Society for Editors and Proofreaders (SfEP).

Further information

Society of Indexers
Woodbourn Business Centre, 10 Jessell Street, Sheffield S9 3HY
tel 0114-244 9561
email admin@indexers.org.uk
website www.indexers.org.uk
Office Manager Paul Machen
Membership (2012) £110 p.a. UK/Europe, £138 overseas; £220 corporate

Publishers and authors seeking to commission an indexer should consult *Indexers Available* on the website.

The main objectives of the Society are to promote high standards in all types of indexing and highlight the role of indexers in the organisation of knowledge; to provide, promote and recognise facilities for both the initial and the further training of indexers; to establish criteria for assessing conformity to indexing standards; and to conduct research and publish guidance, ideas and information about indexing. It seeks to establish good relationships between indexers, librarians, publishers and authors, both to advance good indexing and to ensure that the contribution of indexers to the organisation and retrieval of knowledge is properly recognised.

Services to indexers

The Society publishes a learned journal *The Indexer* (quarterly), a newsletter and *Occasional Papers on Indexing*. Additional resources for members are published in electronic form on the Society's website (www.indexers.org.uk). Local and special interest groups provide the chance for members to meet to discuss common interests, while email discussion lists have encouraged the development of a virtual community of indexers. A two-day conference is held every year. All levels of training are supported by regular workshops held at various venues throughout the country, plus online tutorials.

Professional competence is recognised in three stages by the Society. Professional Members (MSocInd) have successfully completed initial training (usually the Society's open-learning course – see below) or have many years' continuous experience. Advanced Professional Members (MSocInd(Adv)) have demonstrated skills and experience gained since their initial training, while Fellows of the Society of Indexers (FSI) have been through a rigorous assessment procedure to demonstrate the quality of their work. All trained and experienced members have the opportunity to take an annual entry in *Indexers Available*, a directory available on the Society's website to help publishers find an indexer.

The Society recommends minimum rates for indexing (£21.95 per hour; approx. £2.45 per page; £6.64 per 1,000 words in 2012) and provides advice on the business side of indexing to its members.

Services to publishers and authors

Anyone who commissions indexes needs to be certain of engaging a professional indexer working to the highest standards and able to meet deadlines. *Indexers Available* lists qualified and experienced members of the Society and gives basic contact details, subject specialisms and professional grade. The website also includes much useful advice on commissioning indexes, including a sample contract.

The Society awards the Wheatley Medal for an outstanding index.

Training in indexing

The Society's training course has received the CILIP Seal of Recognition and is based on the principle of open learning, so that individuals can learn in their own way and at their own pace. A web-based platform offers seamless access to study materials, practice exercises and quizzes, and links to a wide range of useful resources. Online tutorials are undertaken at various stages during the course. After completing the four assessed modules, which cover the core indexing skills, trainees undertake a practical indexing assignment to prepare them for work in the commercial world. The course is open to members of the Society and to members of the affiliated societies in Australia/New Zealand, Canada and Southern Africa. Successful completion of the course leads to Accreditation, designation as a Professional Indexer (MSocInd), and entry in the Society's online directory, *Indexers Available* (members of other indexing societies receive a certificate).

Further reading

Booth, P.F., *Indexing: the manual of good practice*, K.G. Saur, 2001

British Standards Institution, *British Standard recommendations for examining documents, determining their subjects and selecting indexing terms*, (BS6529:1984)

International Standards Organisation, *Information and documentation – guidelines for the content, organization and presentation of indexes* (ISO 999:1996)

Why libraries matter

Maggie Gee shares her love of libraries and presents the case for supporting the fight to keep them open and accessible to all.

I must be less than five years old. I look down at my feet as they climb the six high steps leading up from the rainy street, see I am wearing gaiters over my brown Start-rite shoes, and think: 'I have got gaiters, I am nearly grown up, and I am going to the library'. And I am happy. So happy. Because of gaiters, because my mother is holding my hand, but mostly because soon we will be out of the rain and into the library, and I will be dragging her to the display stand where the astonishing coloured covers of new library books can be inspected, pictures of another world far away from the wet, sepia postwar Midlands.

Then the best bit of all: I will be able to choose six new books, six (one for nearly every day of the week until I come back again), and take them home to my bedroom, where I will read and read and read until I am eight or nine and my father will come in on the way to bed and say, 'If you don't stop reading like this, you'll have to wear glasses, Margaret.' But I will go on reading and, though it will make me myopic, it will also make me a writer.

I have lived the life I have because, as a skinny white-haired child, I made regular weekly visits to the Bromsgrove Public Library. This story is from the past, but it is still being retold in different forms in public libraries all over the country at teatime as parents or child-minders push buggies flanked by toddlers up other steps, as teenagers slope in after school, tilted to the left by heavy schoolbags, joining pensioners and students and the unemployed in the safe, warm, free places where anyone can learn to read, to dream, to use English, sometimes, or a computer – or, perhaps, to be a writer.

As an adult, libraries are still home to me. Before I had a study of my own, I wrote two entire novels, *Light Years* and *Grace*, in the British Library. I've borrowed books from public libraries wherever I've lived, and taught writing in libraries as far apart as Salford and Southampton. *The White Family*, perhaps my best-known book, had a librarian, Thomas, as its narrator-hero.

It's not surprising, then, that for the past two years I have been part of the campaign for my local library, Kensal Rise in Brent, London. Libraries should be hives of quietly buzzing calm, but recently they have featured in the press only in a context of crisis. According to a March 2012 statement by CILIP, the Chartered Institute of Library and Information Professionals, we are 'in the eye of the storm': 'more than 100 libraries across the country have either closed, are now run by volunteers, or have been turned into social enterprises since April 2011', and 20% of staff will have been lost by April 2013. Public Libraries News (www.publiclibrariesnews.com/p/cuts-and-closures-by-local-authority.html) claims that up to 600 libraries are now threatened – something unimaginable even five years ago.

What seems to be happening is that two waves from different angles are hitting the shore at the same time: one technological, the assault of the virtual on the real, the second financial, the global economic downturn.

It's undeniable that more people are reading electronically now. Some ask, do we therefore still need stores for physical books? Books will be virtual and float in a cloud, the argument goes; clouds are cheap, space on earth expensive....

But let's not rush. According to an August 2011 RNIB survey, three-quarters of UK library authorities still do not even offer ebooks. And outside the library system, e-readers are still, for the most part, luxury goods: as long as the hardware costs around £100, the bulk of the UK's population will not be giving up on print just yet.

No one can deny, on the other hand, that money is tight. Tim Coates, the most persistent gadfly on behalf of libraries, recently explained in the Huffington Post how central government and local councils played the pass-the-blame-game with each other over the cuts. This was 'fine and fun if you are a highly paid official of the state' – but not 'if you are a single parent who wants to help your child to love and enjoy books.'

There it is in a nutshell. The public want free libraries: the politicians, local and national, don't want to pay for them. But councils across the country have been shocked to find that cutting branch libraries is not a soft option. Local people did not see their library, however neglected and underfunded, only as a store for physical books, and did not consider a 'cloud' a good substitute. They knew the library building as a safe shared place, somewhere that was theirs, somewhere that mattered. For the 30% of UK households that don't own a computer, it is also the best way of getting online: a 2012 Society of Chief Librarians' press release said, 'Public library staff and volunteers… have helped more than 2.5 million people to go online in the past 18 months. Most… were completely new internet users'.

Protest nation-wide has been strong. Oxfordshire campaigners fighting to save 20 out of 43 libraries from threatened closure were led to victory by Philip Pullman, and in November 2011 Gloucestershire and Somerset protesters won a court ruling that library closures were 'unlawful' because councils had not properly considered equalities law, i.e. how closures might affect the most vulnerable citizens.

But other battles have been lost. On the Isle of Wight, five of 11 libraries are now closed. Despite a very high-profile campaign in Brent and a high court appeal that was also argued on 'equalities' grounds, six of Brent's 12 libraries, including Kensal Rise, have shut their doors. Many writers have helped the Save Kensal Rise Library campaign, but most of the time it's an uphill struggle and I often wonder if it's worth the trouble. Aren't I supposed to be writing the books that go on the shelves, I think, rather than attending another sodding meeting about libraries?

Then I go back to basics.

A place for wandering, wondering strangers

What is a book, whether print or digital? Before books, what was a scroll, a papyrus, or a stone tablet?

They are all, at bottom, devices for recording and storing knowledge, ideas and stories. A way of taking the contents of one head and heart and putting them out in the world so other human minds can take them in. Books carry ideas to the other side of the planet, and see that stories aren't lost when the individual gets old or dies or forgets. They help human beings escape the limits of our narrow lifespan.

Libraries take this idea further. If a book is a collection of ideas, a great library is a collection of collections, an unknown city of thought where all of us who visit become wandering, wondering strangers. There were libraries of a sort 5,000 years ago – one collection of 30,000 clay tablets was found in ancient Mesopotamia. The most famous public library of them all, the library of Alexandria, opened to readers in about 300 BCE. Pharaoh Ptolemy I wanted to establish a universal library by the purchase, confiscation and copying of texts throughout the known world; at its height, it held around 600,000 scrolls. When Julius Caesar occupied Alexandria in 48 BCE, however, fire destroyed some of the great library, and the replacement of papyrus by the book-like 'codex' may help explain its eventual end. Power passed to Rome: by 4 CE there were 28 public libraries there, often sited by public baths and open to the masses, including slaves. But in 378 CE, the historian Ammianus Marcellinus commented, 'The libraries are closing forever, like so many tombs'. As libraries fell into disuse, the Roman Empire, too, was crumbling.

Maybe the closure of libraries tells us that something is wrong with a society. I think the British public library is a sign of civic decency, whispering (as the pages turn on communal tables, gazed at by readers from every country and culture in the world) that we are ready to share what we have, the words, the knowledge and the hopefulness. These things have value, but it is not monetary.

Philip Pullman linked the threatened closures of libraries in 2011 to the ruthless money-grubbing of globalised publishing. 'I think… old Karl Marx had his finger on the heart of the matter when he pointed out that the market in the end will destroy everything we know, everything we thought was safe and solid. It is the most powerful solvent known to history. "Everything solid melts into air," he said. "All that is holy is profaned."'

Secular temples

And yet, and yet. In 2012 many excellent public libraries continue to survive, some of them no longer staffed by professional librarians but still looked after by dedicated people who treat their readers with courtesy and kindness. Good libraries embody a belief in shared talent and shared happiness. Don't forget that usage figures are closely monitored by cash-strapped local authorities: even if you have books at home, it is important to have a library card and use your local library so it will continue to flourish.

I do see free public libraries as secular temples. Like free art galleries, they preserve the best and most beautiful human artefacts and make them available to everyone, not just the rich and the lucky. When I sat writing *Grace* under the blue dome of the British Library, then housed in the great central cupola of the British Museum, I could be, somehow, more than myself, small and stupefied with sleepiness, a young woman in her first pregnancy. I could draw on the work and the words of all the great minds who left their writings in the library, as well as those who actually wrote there, ghosts around my desk – Virginia Woolf, Charles Dickens, and Karl Marx himself. Woolf wrote, in *Jacob's Room*, about liking the 'dusty bookish atmosphere', and though 'dusty' is the last adjective that would appeal to a modern library professional, it catches something of the old Reading Room's quietness, the dust-motes dancing in thin golden light from the dome's windows high above my bowed head.

Now the British Library is rehoused in a bold, sturdy, late 20th century building between Euston and King's Cross. Though I now have my own study, I still go in, when I can escape, to write my new novel, my twelfth, *Virginia Woolf in Manhattan*, because without email and domestic duties I can squeeze three days' worth of quiet work into one. There are always other writers there: at random, A.N. Wilson, Kwame Dawes, and most recently Jacqueline Rose. Today's BL is an open, dramatic space that is always full and shows how a great library can stay alive and flourish.

My local public library, by contrast, launched with brio by moustachio-ed Mark Twain in 1900 – the only library that the great man of American letters, himself self-educated in public libraries, personally opened – is now rehoused in a glorified plastic tent on the pavement outside it, renamed the 'Kensal Rise Popup Library'. In it our local group struggles in wind and rain to keep free books available to everybody. We have a tent, a ginger cat, and hope. The cat warms the lap of the 'librarian' on duty, but it is not ideal, and we still hope to negotiate our way back in past the padlocked doors.

Every generation makes and remakes its own shared sacred spaces. It's good to take stock of what we have, and what it means to a literate, civilised society. It's up to us to see that our stories, in whatever form, are still there for our readers; available to anyone who wants them, keeping open house for the future, a place for the next generation of writers to grow.

Maggie Gee OBE has written a memoir, *My Animal Life*, a collection of short stories, *The Blue*, and 11 acclaimed novels, including *The White Family*, shortlisted for the Orange Prize. Her most recent novels are two comedies about the UK and Uganda, *My Cleaner* and *My Driver* (Telegram 2009). She was the first female Chair of the Royal Society of Literature (2004–8) and is currently one of its vice-presidents. Her forthcoming novel brings Virginia Woolf back to life in the 21st century in New York and Istanbul. The first international conference about her work will be held at St Andrew's University, Scotland, in August 2012.

Libraries

LIBRARIES OF LEGAL DEPOSIT IN THE UK AND IRELAND

A library of legal deposit is a library that has the power to request (at no charge) a copy of anything published in the UK. There are 6 legal deposit libraries in the UK and Ireland. To obtain a copy of a book, 5 out of the 6 legal deposit libraries must make a request in writing to a publisher within one year of publication of a book, newspaper or journal. Different rules apply to the British Library in that all UK libraries and Republic of Ireland publishers have a legal responsibility to send a copy of each of their publications to the library, without a written request being made. The British Library is the only legal deposit library with its own Legal Deposit Office.

Agency for the Legal Deposit Libraries

161 Causewayside, Edinburgh, EH9 1PH
tel 0131 623 4680 *fax* 0131 623 4681
email publisher.enquiries@legaldeposit.org.uk
website www.legaldeposit.org.uk

The legal deposit libraries belong to the Agency for the Legal Deposit Libraries, which sends out written requests on behalf of member libraries and acts as a depot for books received.

Bodleian Libraries of the University of Oxford

Broad Street, Oxford OX1 3BG
tel (01865) 277162 *fax* (01865) 277182
email reader.services@bodleian.ox.ac.uk
website www.bodley.ox.ac.uk

With 11 million volumes, the Bodleian Libraries form the second-largest library in the UK after the British Library, and are the main reference library of Oxford University.

The British Library

St Pancras Building, 96 Euston Road,
London NW1 2DB
tel 0843-208 1144 (Switchboard), 020-7412 7676 (Advance Reservations, St Pancras Reading Rooms and Humanities enquiries), 020-7412 7702 (Maps), 020-7412 7513 (Manuscripts), 020-7412 7772 (Music), 020-7412 7873 (Asia, Pacific & Africa Collections)
Legal Deposit Office: The British Library, Boston Spa, Wetherby, West Yorkshire LS23 7BY
tel (01937) 546268 (books), (01937) 546267 (serials)
email legal-deposit-books@bl.uk, legal-deposit-serials@bl.uk
website www.bl.uk

The British Library holds books, journals, newspapers, sound recordings, patents, original MSS, maps, online images and texts, plays, digital books, and poet and author recordings. With a holding of 14 million UK books, 150 million published items from around the globe, almost a million journals and newspapers, and 3 million sound recordings, it is the largest library in the world in terms of number of items held.

Cambridge University Library

West Road, Cambridge CB3 9DR
tel (01223) 333000 *fax* (01223) 333160
email library@lib.cam.ac.uk
website www.lib.cam.ac.uk

Cambridge University Library houses its own collection and also comprises 4 other libraries within the university. The library dates back to the 15th century and now has a collection of 8 million books. It is the only legal deposit library that keeps a large percentage of its books on open access.

National Library of Scotland

George IV Bridge, Edinburgh, EH1 1EW
tel 0131 623 3700 *fax* 0131 623 3701
email enquiries@nls.uk
website www.nls.uk

The National Library of Scotland holds 7 million books, 14 million printed items and more than 2 million maps. It is the world's central source for research relating to Scotland and the Scots. The library also holds a copy of the Gutenberg Bible, a First Folio of Shakespeare, and the last letter written by Mary Queen of Scots. In 2005 the library bought the John Murray Archive for £31 million and it contains important items relating to Jane Austen, Lord Byron and Sir Arthur Conan Doyle.

The National Library of Wales

Aberystwyth, Ceredigion SY23 3BU
tel (01970) 632800 *fax* (01970) 615709
email holi@llgc.org.uk
website www.llgc.org.uk

The National Library of Wales was established in 1907 and holds over 5 million books, including many important works such as the first book printed in Welsh and the first Welsh translation of the Bible.

Trinity College Library Dublin

College Street, Dublin 2, Republic of Ireland
tel +353 (0)1 896 1661 *fax* +353 (0)1 896 3774
website www.tcd.ie/library

Trinity College Library is the largest library in Ireland and is home to the *Book of Kells* – 2 of the 4 volumes are on permanent public display. The library houses sound recordings, maps, databases, and a digital collection.

YOUR LOCAL LIBRARY

Libraries have always been essential to writers, for both the resources they offer and their atmosphere. Local libraries are the best places to find information about the surrounding area. Aside from lending books, local libraries now offer a whole range of services, from specialist activities that aim to engage children in the reading process, to access for everyone to audiobooks, the internet and local newspaper archives. Contact your local council for a list of libraries in your area.

TEN OF THE BEST

In addition to small local libraries, most cities in the UK have large central public lending libraries, many of which have undergone major refurbishments in recent years in order to adjust to their changing role. Britain has such a wealth of these comprehensive and historic libraries that a full list of them is not possible in this publication. Here are just 10 of the best.

Barbican Library

Barbican Centre, London EC2Y 8DS
tel 020-7638 0569 (general enquiries) 020-7628 9447 (Children's Library), 020-7638 0672 (Music Library)
email barbicanlib@cityoflondon.gov.uk
website www.cityoflondon.gov.uk/barbicanlibrary

The largest of the City of London's lending libraries with a strong arts and music section, a London collection, literature events programme, and reading groups.

Belfast Central Library

Royal Avenue, Belfast BT1 1EA
tel 028-9050 9150 *fax* 028-9033 2819
email info.belb@librariesni.org.uk
website www.ni-libraries.net

The library's reference library is the largest in stock terms in Northern Ireland. The library houses a number of special collections including a digital film archive and the Northern Ireland Music Archive.

Birmingham Central Library

Chamberlain Square, Birmingham B3 3HQ
tel 0121 303 4511 *textphone* 0121 303 4547
fax 0121 233 4458
email central.library@birmingham.gov.uk
website www.birmingham.gov.uk/centrallibrary

A new Central Library is currently under construction and is due to open in September 2013. The library will change its name to the Library of Birmingham. The new site has been dubbed a 'super-library' and will house 1.5 million books, 6,000 archive collections, and 25 km of shelving. The library will include extensive internet facilities and gallery space.

Cardiff Central Library

The Hayes, Cardiff CF10 1FL
tel 029-2038 2116
email centrallibrary@cardiff.gov.uk
website www.cardiff.gov.uk/centrallibrary

The largest public library in Wales, opened in 2009, houses 90,000 books, 10,000 of which are in Welsh.

Liverpool Central Library

William Brown Street, Liverpool L3 8EW
tel 0151 233 5829
email refbt.central.library@liverpool.gov.uk
website www.liverpool.gov.uk

This library is undergoing a major refurbishment and will re-open in Spring 2013. A temporary service is available until then at Horseshoe Gallery, World Museum, William Brown Street, L3 8EN.

The London Library

14 St James's Square, London SW1Y 4LG
tel 020-7930 7705 *fax* 020-7766 4766
email reception@londonlibrary.co.uk
website www.londonlibrary.co.uk

Subscription lending library holding approximately one million books in all European languages and a subject range across the humanities, with particular emphasis on literature, history and related subjects. Membership is open to all.

Manchester Central Library

St Peter's Square, Manchester M2 5PD
tel 0161 234 1900 *fax* 0161 274 7053
email libraries@manchester.gov.uk
website www.manchester.gov.uk/libraries/central

Manchester's main library is undergoing returbishment and will re-open in 2013.

The Mitchell Library

North Street, Glasgow G3 7DN
tel 0141 287 2999 *fax* 0141 287 2815
email archives@glasgowlife.org.uk
website www.mitchelllibrary.org

The largest public reference library in Europe housing almost 2 million volumes. Holds an unrivalled collection of material relating to the City of Glasgow.

Newcastle City Library

City Library, Charles Avison Building,
33 Newbridge Street West,
Newcastle upon Tyne NE1 8AX
tel 0191 277 4100
email information@newcastle.gov.uk
website www.newcastle.gov.uk/libraries

The city's main public library re-opened in a new building in 2009 and includes a café, exhibition spaces, a rare books and watercolours collection, a viewing deck, and six floors of books.

Westminster Reference Library

35 St Martin's Street, London WC2H 7HP
tel 020-7641 1300 (Contact Centre: ask for Westminster Reference Library) *fax* 020-7641 5232
email referencelibrarywc2@westminster.gov.uk
website www.westminster.gov.uk/libraries/findalibrary/westref.cfm

General reference library with special collections in Performing Arts and Art & Design. Also has a range of business resources including market research, company and legal databases.

DESIGNATED OUTSTANDING COLLECTIONS

The Designated Outstanding Collections scheme was established in 1997 by the Museums and Galleries Commission to identify collections of national and international importance in non-national museums and galleries. In 2005 the scheme was extended to include libraries and archives. The scheme is now administered by Arts Council England and there are 140 Designated Outstanding Collections in England. To find out if there is a Designated Outstanding Collection library near you, visit the Designation section of the Arts Council website (www.artscouncil.org.uk).

SPECIALIST LIBRARIES IN THE UK

Writers often need access to specialised information sources in order to research their work. The following listing provides a sample of the kind of specialist libraries the UK has to offer.

BBC Written Archives Centre

Peppard Road, Caversham Park, Reading RG4 8TZ
tel 0118-948 6281 *fax* 0118-946 1145
email heritage@bbc.co.uk
website www.bbc.co.uk/historyofthebbc/contacts/wac.shtml

Home of the BBC's written records. Holds thousands of files, scripts and working papers from the BBC's formation in 1922 to c. 2000 together with information about past programmes and the history of broadcasting. Does not have recordings or information about current programmes.

BFI National Library

21 Stephen Street, London W1T 1LN
tel 020-7255 1444 *fax* 020-7436 0165
email library@bfi.org.uk
website www.bfi.org.uk/nationallibrary

A major national research collection. Provides coverage of British film and television primarily but is also international in scope. Includes over 60,000 books, 5,000 periodical titles and over 25,000 scripts.

British Library for Development Studies (BLDS)

Institute of Development Studies at the University of Sussex, Brighton BN1 9RE
tel (01273) 915659 *fax* (01273) 621202
email blds@ids.ac.uk
website www.blds.ids.ac.uk

Europe's largest research collection on economic and social change in developing countries.

Catholic National Library

St Michael's Abbey, Farnborough Road, Farnborough, Hants GU14 7NQ
tel (01252) 543818
email library@catholic-library.org.uk
website www.catholic-library.org.uk

Holds 65,000 books and periodicals on theology, spirituality and related subjects, biography and history.

Chawton House Library

Chawton, Alton, Hants GU34 1SJ
tel (01420) 541010 *fax* (01420) 595900
email info@chawton.net
website www.chawtonhouse.org

A collection of over 8,000 volumes focusing on women's writing in English from 1600 to 1830 including some manuscripts. The library also houses the Knight Collection.

City Business Library

Aldermanbury, London EC2V 7HH
tel 020-7332 1812
email cbl@cityoflondon.gov.uk
website www.cityoflondon.gov.uk/citybusinesslibrary

One of the leading business information sources in the UK.

City of London Libraries – see City Business Library, Guildhall Library and Barbican Library

Civil Aviation Authority Library and Information Centre (CAA)

Aviation House, Gatwick Airport South, West Sussex RH6 0YR
tel (01293) 567781
email infoservices@caa.co.uk
website www.caa.co.uk/library/default.asp

Holds books, reports, directories, statistics, videos and periodicals on most aspects of civil aviation and related subjects.

The Library of the Commonwealth Secretariat

Commonwealth Secretariat, Marlborough House, Pall Mall, London SW1Y 5HX

tel 020-7747 6164 (librarian), 020-7747 6167 (archivist)
fax 020-7747 6168 (librarian) 020-7747 6168 (archivist)
email library@commonwealth.int
website www.thecommonwealth.org/subhomepage/191529/library_and_archives

Collection covers politics and international relations, economics, education, health, gender, environment and management. Holds a comprehensive collection of Commonwealth Secretariat publications and its archives.

Crafts Council Research Library

Crafts Council, 44A Pentonville Road, London N1 9BY
tel 020-7806 2501
email reference@craftscouncil.org.uk
website www.craftscouncil.org.uk

A unique collection of materials mapping the development of contemporary craft since the mid-20th century. Holdings include over 7,000 books and catalogues, and 100 journals and magazines. Online access to Photostore, the national register of makers, and funding resources also provided. Open every Weds and Thurs 10a.m.–5p.m. (excluding 1p.m.–2p.m.) by appointment.

Goethe-Institut London Library

50 Princes Gate, Exhibition Road, London SW7 2PH
tel 020-7596 4040 *fax* 020-7594 0230
email library@london.goethe.org
website www.goethe.de/london

Specialises in German literature, especially contemporary fiction and drama, film DVDs, and books/audiovisual material on German culture and recent history. New e-library gives access to Goethe Institut libraries in the UK, Ireland and the Netherlands and allows electronic downloading of ebooks, e-audiobooks and electronic newspapers for a predetermined period of time.

Guildhall Library

Aldermanbury, London EC2V 7HH
tel 020-7332 1868/1870 *textphone* 020-7332 3803
email guildhall.library@cityoflondon.gov.uk
website www.cityoflondon.gov.uk/guildhalllibrary

Specialises in the history of London, especially the City, as well as holding other significant collections including business history, maritime history, clock and watchmaking, food and wine.

Lambeth Palace Library

15 Galleywall Road, London SE1 7JU
tel 020-7898 1400
email archives@churchofengland.org
website www.lambethpalacelibrary.org

The historic library of the archbishops of Canterbury and the principal library and record office for the Church of England.

The Linen Hall Library

17 Donegall Square North, Belfast BT1 5GB
tel 028-9032 1707 *fax* 028-9043 8586
email info@linenhall.com
website www.linenhall.com

Renowned for its Irish and Local Studies Collection ranging from early Belfast and Ulster printed books to the 300,000 items in the internationally acclaimed Northern Ireland Political Collection (NIPC). Also expansive General Lending Collection. Open free to the public.

National Art Library

Victoria & Albert Museum, South Kensington, London SW7 2RL
tel 020-7942 2400
email vanda@vam.ac.uk
website www.vam.ac.uk/nal

A major reference library and the Victoria & Albert Museum's curatorial department for the art, craft and design of the book.

National Maritime Museum

Greenwich, London SE10 9NF
tel 020-8858 4422 *fax* 020-8312 6632
email library@rmg.co.uk
website www.rmg.co.uk/national-maritime-museum (astronomy information)

Specialist maritime research library.

Natural History Museum Library and Information Services

Cromwell Road, London SW7 5BD
tel 020-7942 5011 (main information desk), 020-7942 5507/5873 (archives), 020-7942 5460 (general library), 020-7942 6156 (Ornithology Library, Tring)
website www.nhm.ac.uk

Online catalogue contains all library material acquired since 1989 and about 80% of earlier items. The collections are of international importance with extensive holdings of early works, periodicals and current literature, including over 800,000 books, 20,000 periodical titles (about half of them current) and original watercolour drawings, as well as maps, manuscripts and archives of the Museum.

Open Library

Open University, Walton Hall, Milton Keynes, MK7 6AA
tel (01908) 659001
email lib-help@open.ac.uk
website http://library.open.ac.uk

The Open University's electronic library service.

Press Association News Library

Central Park, New Lane, Leeds LS11 5DZ
tel 0870 830 6824
email palibrary@pressassociation.co.uk
website www.pressassociation.co.uk

Holds electronically over 10 years of Press Association articles.

RNIB National Library Service

Far Cromwell Road, Bredbury, Stockport SK6 2SG
tel 0303 123 9999
email library@rnib.org.uk
website www.rnib.org.uk/library

The largest specialist library for readers with sight loss in the UK. Offers a comprehensive range of books and accessible information for children and adults in a range of formats including braille, large print and unabridged audio. Also provides free access to online reference material, braille sheet music, themed book lists and a quarterly reader magazine.

Science Museum Library

Imperial College Road, London SW7 5NH
tel 020-7942 4242 *fax* 020-7942 4243
email SMLinfo@sciencemuseum.org.uk
website www.sciencemuseum.org.uk/about_us/about_the_museum/science_library.aspx

In recent years the Library has specialised in the history of science and technology as its key role as part of the National Museum of Science & Industry.

Tate Library & Archive

Hyman Kreitman Reading Rooms, Tate Britain, Millbank, London SW1P 4RG
tel 020-7887 8838
email visiting.britain@tate.org.uk
website www.tate.org.uk/research/library

Broadly covers those areas in which the Tate collects. Library collects British art from the Renaissance to the present day and international modern art from 1900. Archive covers British art from 1900 and contains a wealth of unpublished material on artists, art world figures and organisations.

Wellcome Library

183 Euston Road, London NW1 2BE
tel 020-7611 8722 *fax* 020-7611 8369
email library@wellcome.ac.uk
website http://library.wellcome.ac.uk

Wellcome Images

tel 020-7611 8348 *fax* 020-7611 8577
email images@wellcome.ac.uk
website http://images.wellcome.ac.uk

Moving Image and Sound Collections

tel 020-7611 8766 *fax* 020-7611 8765
email misc@wellcome.ac.uk
website http://library.wellcome.ac.uk/misc.html

Westminster Music Library

Victoria Library, 160 Buckingham Palace Road, London SW1W 9UD
tel 020-7641 1300
email musiclibrary@westminster.gov.uk
website www.westminster.gov.uk/musiclibrary

Housed in Victoria Library, the Westminster Music Library holds a wide range of scores, orchestral sets, books on music, music journals and a collection of Mozart sound recordings, formerly the GLASS collection.

Working Class Movement Library

51 The Crescent, Salford M5 4WX
tel 0161 736 3601
email enquiries@wcml.org.uk
website www.wcml.org.uk

Records over 200 years of organising and campaigning by ordinary men and women. The collection provides an insight into working people's daily lives. Collection contains: books, pamphlets, archives, photographs, plays, poetry, songs, banners, posters, badges, cartoons, journals, biographies, reports.

The Zoological Society of London Library

Outer Circle, Regent's Park, London NW1 4RY
tel 020-7449 6293
email library@zsl.org
website www.zsl.org

Creative writing courses

Anyone wishing to participate in a writing course should first satisfy themselves as to its content and quality. For day and evening courses consult your local Adult Education Centre. Details of postgraduate writing courses follow on page 634.

Alston Hall College

Alston Lane, Longridge, Preston PR3 3BP
tel (01772) 784661 *fax* (01772) 785835
email alstonhall.general2@lancashire.gov.uk
website www.alstonhall.com

Arvon

Lumb Bank – The Ted Hughes Arvon Centre, Heptonstall, Hebden Bridge, West Yorkshire HX7 6DF
tel (01422) 843714 *fax* (01422) 843714
email lumbbank@arvonfoundation.org
website www.arvonfoundation.org
Contact Ilona Jones
Moniack Mhor, Teavarran, Kiltarlity, Beauly, Inverness-shire IV4 7HT
tel (01463) 741675 *fax* (01463) 741733
email moniackmhor@arvonfoundation.org
Contact Lyndy Batty
The Arvon Foundation, Totleigh Barton, Sheepwash, Beaworthy, Devon EX21 5NS
tel (01409) 231338 *fax* (01409) 231144
email totleighbarton@arvonfoundation.org
Contact Stephanie Wardle
The Hurst – The John Osborne Arvon Centre Clunton, Craven Arms, Shrops. SY7 0JA
tel (01588) 640658 *fax* (01588) 640509
email thehurst@arvonfoundation.org
Contact Dan Pavitt

The Book Doctor Academy

Canalot Studios, Kensal Road, London W10 5BN
tel 020-8964 1444
email philippa.pride@btinternet.com
website www.thebookdoctor.co.uk
Contact Philippa Pride

How to Free Your Creativity, Write a Book and Get it Published writing course held in glorious locations in the UK and abroad.

University of Cambridge

Institute of Continuing Education, Madingley Hall, Madingley, Cambridge CB23 8AQ
tel (01223) 746262 *fax* (01223) 746200
email registration@ice.cam.ac.uk
website www.ice.cam.ac.uk
Contact The Registration Team

A wide range of part-time courses at introductory and advanced levels on literature, creative writing, art and art history. See website for details.

Centerprise Trust

136 Kingsland High Street, London E8 2NS
tel 020-7254 9632
website www.centerprisetrust.org.uk

Central St Martins College of Arts & Design, Short Course Office

Granary Square, 1 Granary Building, King's Cross, London N1 4AA
tel 020-7514 7015 *fax* 020-7514 7016
email shortcourse@csm.arts.ac.uk
website http://courses.csm.arts.ac.uk
Contact The Short Course Office

Evening and day-time courses for beginners and intermediate levels.

Community Creative Writing and Publishing

Sea Winds, 2 St Helens Terrace, Spittal, Berwick-upon-Tweed, Northumberland TD15 1RJ
tel/fax (01289) 305213
email mavismaureen@btinternet.com
Author/Tutor Moderator Maureen Raper MBE, (member of Society of Authors)

Classes for beginners and intermediates in Writing Crime and Mystery, Writing for Radio and Television, Romantic Fiction, Writing for Children, Writing Comedy. Writing groups fortnightly; reading groups monthly at Berwick Library. Distance learning available.

Cove Park

Peaton Hill, Cove, Dunbartonshire, Scotland G84 0PE
tel (01436) 850123 *fax* (01436) 850445
email information@covepark.org
website www.covepark.org, www.fieldingprogramme.com
Director Julian Forrester, *Founders & Trustees* Peter Jacobs, Eileen Jacobs

The Fielding Programme is a series of retreats for artists of all types and mentored residencies for writers with a project in hand, offered by Cove Park. Artists may stay for one week or more any time between September and April. Residents stay in the Cove Park's spectacular self-catering accommodation overlooking Loch Long. Retreats are £310 for 7 nights; a mentored week for writers is £450. A studio can be hired for £20 per day. For more information and bookings visit the website. Established 2000.

Dingle Writing Courses

Ballintlea, Ventry, Co Kerry, Republic of Ireland
tel +353 (0)66 9159815
email info@dinglewritingcourses.ie
website www.dinglewritingcourses.ie
Directors Abigail Joffe, Nicholas McLachlan

Emerson College

Emerson College, Forest Row, East Sussex RH18 5JX
tel (01342) 822238 *fax* (01342) 826055
email info@emerson.org.uk
website www.emerson.org.uk

The Faber Academy

Faber and Faber Ltd, Bloomsbury House,
74–77 Great Russell Street, London WC1B 3DA
tel 020-7927 3827 *fax* 020-7927 3801
email iane@faber.co.uk
website www.faberacademy.co.uk
Contact Ian Ellard

Committed to innovation, with both an international and UK focus, the Faber Academy delivers high-quality events, from one-day workshops to 6-month mentoring schemes, devised by the foremost practitioners in their fields. As part of Faber and Faber, Faber Academy offers tuition from hand-picked authors, editors and agents, on focused, practical writing courses. Launched October 2008.

Fire in the Head

tel (01548) 821004
email roselle.angwin@internet-today.co.uk
website www.fire-in-the-head.co.uk
Contact Roselle Angwin

Poetry, novel, life writing, therapeutic writing, journaling and personal development; retreats, eco-retreats and short courses; correspondence courses, mentoring.

The French House Party

The Jaylands, Abberley, Worcs. WR6 6BN
mobile 07900 322791
email enquiries@frenchhouseparty.co.uk
website www.frenchhouseparty.eu
Director Moira Martingale

Learning retreat in South of France which includes creative writing and songwriting courses.

Indian King Arts

Garmoe Cottage, 2 Trefrew Road, Camelford, Cornwall PL32 9TP
tel (01840) 212161
email indianking@btconnect.com

Weekly poetry morning group, occasional all day poetry workshop, and bi-monthly novel workshop led by Karen Hayes. Also the home of the Poetry Society's Camelford Stanza.

The Inkwell Group

The Old Post Office, Kilmacanogue, Co. Wicklow, Republic of Ireland
tel +353 (0)1 2765921, +353 087 2835382
website www.inkwellwriters.ie
Contact Vanessa O'Loughlin

One-day intensive fiction-writing workshops facilitated by bestselling authors. Full manuscript critiquing service and publishing consultancy. Online workshops. Inkwell 4 Kids Summer Camps. Inkwell are scouts for leading Irish and UK agents and publishers. Founded 2006.

Irish Writers' Centre

19 Parnell Square, Dublin 1, Republic of Ireland
tel +353 (0)1 8721302 *fax* +353 (0)1 8726282
email courses@writerscentre.ie
website www.writerscentre.ie
Contact Chairperson, Jack Harte

National organisation for the promotion of writers, writing and literature in Ireland. Runs an extensive education programme offering courses, workshops, masterclasses and seminars, calibrated to assist new and emerging writers at every stage in their development. All courses are facilitated by published authors and poets. See website for further details.

Kilkenny Campus NUI Maynooth

College Road, Kilkenny, Republic of Ireland
tel +353 (0)56 7775910 *fax* +353 (0)56 7761369
email kilkenny.campus@nuim.ie
website http://kilkenny.nuim.ie

NUI Certificate in Creative Writing for Publication held over 10 weekends.

Knuston Hall

Irchester, Wellingborough, Northants NN29 7EU
tel (01933) 312104 *fax* (01933) 357596
email enquiries@knustonhall.org.uk
website www.knustonhall.org.uk

Liberato

16 Middle King, Braintree, Essex CM7 3XY
tel (01376) 551379 *mobile* (07718) 339636
email liberato@talktalk.net
website www.liberato.co.uk
Contact Maureen Blundell, Tutor and novelist

Weekend fiction courses and MS critiques. Editing of fiction MS via post or email. Mentoring offered for dedicated novelists.

London Writers' Workshop

5a Arundel Square, London N7 8AT
tel 020-7609 1839
email londonwritersworkshop@hotmail.co.uk
website www.londonwritersworkshop.co.uk
Contact Susan Oudot

Offers a range of one-day workshops and courses led by acclaimed novelist and scriptwriter Susan Oudot and best-selling author David Wingrove. Workshops range from Basics in Creative Writing through to Developing Your Skills, with specialist classes on How to Write and Pitch TV Drama and Writing Science Fiction. The tutors are able to draw on their wide-ranging experience to answer students' questions about the book and broadcasting industries.

Marlborough College Summer School

Marlborough, Wilts. SN8 1PA
tel (01672) 892388 *fax* (01672) 892476

email admin@mcsummerschool.org.uk
website www.mcsummerschool.org.uk
Contact Jon Copp

A 3-week summer school where students can attend for 1, 2 or 3 weeks. There are a large variety of courses, including 7 creative writing courses, with each course being 5 half days Monday-Friday. Accommodation available.

Middlesex University Summer School

Summer School Office, Middlesex University, Trent Park, Bramley Road, London N14 4YZ
tel 020-8411 5782 *fax* 020-8411 2297
email sschool@mdx.ac.uk
website www.mdx.ac.uk/study/summer

Offers a number of creative writing courses.

Missenden Abbey

Great Missenden, Bucks. HP16 0BD
tel (01296) 383582 *fax* (01753) 783756
email dcevreham@buckscc.gov.uk
website www.missendenabbey-al.co.uk/arca

Weekend and summer-school writing courses.

Morley College

61 Westminster Bridge, London SE1 7HT
tel 020-7450 1889 *fax* 020-7928 4074
email enquiries@morleycollege.ac.uk
website www.morleycollege.ac.uk

Offers a number of creative writing courses – one day, one week and part-time day and evening throughout the year.

The National Academy of Writing

email rena@thenationalacademyofwriting.org.uk
website www.thenationalacademyofwriting.org.uk
Director Richard Beard, *Course Coordinator* Rena Brannan

The National Academy of Writing (NAW) runs a course designed to prepare full-length works of prose fiction and non-fiction for publication. Twelve writers are selected each year as members of the Academy. They will receive close attention to their work with a mixture of tuition, editorial feedback, one-to-one mentoring and workshops. This advanced, intensive course takes place in London over an 8-month period between April and November, and is delivered by the Academy's Director and NAW patrons. Established 2000.

Newcastle University

School of English, Percy Building, Newcastle upon Tyne NE1 7RU
tel 0191 222 7619 *fax* 0191 222 8708
email melanie.birch@ncl.ac.uk
website www.ncl.ac.uk/elll/creative
Contact Melanie Birch

Short courses, spring and summer schools, a postgraduate certificate (available via distance learning) and degrees at MA and PhD level.

North West Kent College

Oakfield Lane, Dartford DA1 2JT
tel (0800) 0741447 *fax* (01322) 629468
email enquiries@nwkcollege.ac.uk
website www.nwkmedia.com
Contact Neil Nixon, Pathway Leader, Professional Writing

Offers full-time, part-time and one-off courses in professional writing.

Open College of the Arts

The Michael Young Arts Centre, Redbrook Business Park, Wilthorpe Road, Barnsley S75 1JN
tel (0800) 731 2116
email enquiries@oca-uk.com
website www.oca-uk.com

Distance learning writing courses to develop skills or gain credits towards a degree.

Open Studies – Part-time Courses for Adults: Office of Lifelong Learning

Office of Lifelong Learning, University of Edinburgh, Paterson's Land, Holyrood Road, Edinburgh EH8 8AQ
tel 0131 650 4400 *fax* 0131 667 6097
email oll@ed.ac.uk
website www.lifelong.ed.ac.uk

Offers a large number of creative writing courses.

Oxford University Summer School for Adults

Dept for Continuing Education, Rewley House, 1 Wellington Square, Oxford OX1 2JA
tel (01865) 270396 *fax* (01865) 270429
email oussa@conted.ox.ac.uk
website www.conted.ox.ac.uk/oussa
Contact Programme Administrator

A 4-week programme consisting of over 40 week-long courses, including creative writing and specialist literature courses.

Scottish Universities', International Summer School

21 Buccleuch Place, Edinburgh EH8 9LN
tel 0131 650 4369 *fax* 0131 662 0275
email suiss@ed.ac.uk
website www.summer-school.hss.ed.ac.uk/suiss
Directors Dr Konstantina Georganta, Julia Boll

A 3-week creative writing course for undergraduates, postgraduates and teachers, as well as published writers keen to widen their skills.

Swanwick, The Writers' Summer School

Hayes Conference Centre, Swanwick, Derbyshire DE55 1AU

tel (01572) 720674
email secretary@swanwickwritersschool.co.uk
website www.swanwickwritersschool.co.uk
Takes place 11–17 August 2012 / 10–16 August 2013

A week-long programme for writers of all ages, abilities and genres featuring courses, talks, workshops, panels and one-to-one sessions, all run by expert tutors. Attracts top speakers such as Iain Banks, Kate Mosse, Simon Brett, Katie Fforde and other best-selling authors, playwrights, journalists and comedy writers plus the literary agents and publishers who represent them. Full-board accommodation available onsite; day tickets also available. Founded 1949.

Travellers' Tales

92 Hillfield Road, London NW6 1QA
email info@travellerstales.org
website www.travellerstales.org
Director Jonathan Lorie, Contributing Editor of *Traveller* magazine

UK's leading training agency for travel writers and photographers. Offers vocational courses with the UK's top travel photographers and writers in London, Marrakech, Istanbul and Andalucia including beginners' weekends, masterclasses and creative retreats. Hosts the annual Travellers' Tales Festival of the world's leading travel writers and photographers. Online tuition also available.

Tŷ Newydd

Tŷ Newydd, National Writers' Centre for Wales, Llanystumdwy, Cricieth, Gwynedd LL52 0LW
tel (01766) 522811 *fax* (01766) 523095
email post@tynewydd.org
website www.tynewydd.org

Week and weekend courses on all aspects of creative writing. Full programme available.

Urchfont Manor College

Urchfont, Devizes, Wilts. SN10 4RG
tel (01380) 840495 *fax* (01380) 840005
email urchfontmanor@wiltshire.gov.uk
website www.urchfontmanor.co.uk

Wedgwood Memorial College

Station Road, Barlaston, Stoke-on-Trent ST12 9DG
tel (01782) 372105
email wedgewood.memorial@stoke.gov.uk
website www.stoke.gov.uk

The Winchester Writers' Conference Festival and Bookfair, Centre for Research and Knowledge Exchange

University of Winchester, Winchester, Hants SO22 4NR
tel (01962) 827238
email barbara.large@winchester.ac.uk
website www.writersconference.co.uk
Conference Director Barbara Large MBE, FRSA, HFUW, *Honorary Patrons* Jacqueline Wilson OBE, Maureen Lipman, Colin Dexter OBE, Baroness James OBE
Takes place University of Winchester, last week in June

This Festival of Writing, celebrating its 32nd year in 2012, attracts 65 internationally renowned authors, poets, playwrights, agents and commissioning editors who give 12 mini-courses, 22 workshops, 60 talks, seminars and 500 one-to-one appointments to help writers harness their creativity and develop their writing, editing and marketing skills. Eighteen writing competitions, including Writing for Children, Haiku, Writing Can Be Murder, Short Story, Shorter Short Story, First Three Pages of the Novel and Sustainability are adjudicated and 70 prizes are awarded at the Writers' Awards Reception. All first place winners are published annually in *The Best of* series.

The Bookfair offers delegates a wide choice of exhibits including authors' and internet services, publishers, booksellers, printers and trade associations.

For details of Pitstop Refuelling Writers' Weekend Workshops visit the website. How to Self-Publish Your Book workshops will take place on 6 July and 12 October 2012 at a major book production company, CPI Antony Rowe, Chippenham or Croydon.

A retreat in Mallorca, the Great Fiction Workshop, is planned for 10–15 October 2012 (www.centromallorca.com) to cover creating, writing, editing and marketing fiction.

The Write Retreat

Contact Katherine Bolton-Parris,
The Write Retreat Ltd, Kerivoa, 22390, Bourbriac, Cotes d'Armor, Brittany, France
tel +33 (0)2 9643 6361 *mobile* +33 (0)6 3594 5754
email info@thewriteretreat.com
website www.thewriteretreat.com

Set in historic Kerivoa in Brittany, The Write Retreat Ltd offers residential creative writing holidays and writing retreats throughout the year. Accommodation is in a renovated farmhouse within in a secluded spot offering tranquility and peacefulness. Inspiring accompanied walks from the farmhouse include a Dolmen, Menhir, ancient woodlands and local villages. Free wi-fi. The food is mostly home grown, reared or baked and special diets can be catered for. Non-writing partners are welcome and there is one dedicated pet-friendly room.

Courses are bespoke and run by experienced creative writing tutor Katherine Bolton-Parris (member of SWWJ, NAWG, IBBY).

Writers' Holiday at Caerleon

School Bungalow, Church Road, Pontnewydd, Cwmbran, South Wales NP44 1AT
tel (01633) 489438

email gerry@writersholiday.net
website www.writersholiday.net
Contact Gerry Hobbs

A 6-day annual conference for writers of all standards from absolute beginner to bestselling author. The event includes 14 courses. Also weekend workshops.

The Writers' Workshop

7 Market Street, Charlbury, Oxon OX7 3PH
tel 0845 459 9560
email info@writersworkshop.co.uk
website www.writersworkshop.co.uk
Contacts Harry Bingham, Laura Wilkins, Nikki Holt

The range of online courses tutored by professional authors includes: How to Write a Novel, Screenwriting, Writing for Children, Writing from Life, Self-editing your Novel and the Complete Novel Writing Course. Plus events, editorial critiques, mentoring and the Festival of Writing. See website for full details.

The Writing College

The Glebe House, Whitestone, Exeter EX4 2LF
tel (01392) 811642
email enquiries@writingcollege.com
website www.writingcollege.com
Director Richard Littler

'The Complete Writer' correspondence course: 28 modules divided into the practice and art of writing, writing genres and the business of writing. An MS appraisal service is also available. Founded 2000.

Written Words

5 Queen Elizabeth Close, London N16 0HL
tel 020-8809 4725
email henrietta@writtenwords.net
website www.writtenwords.net
Contact Henrietta Soames

Workshops, tutorials and mentoring offered to all writers by experienced author, lively discussion and clear constructive feedback.

www.writing.ie

The Old Post Office, Kilmacanogue, Co. Wicklow, Republic of Ireland
tel +353 (0)1 2765921, +353 (0)87 2835382
email info@writing.ie
Contact Vanessa O'Loughlin

Arts Council-backed online magazine and writing resources website. Features author interviews and tips plus information on festivals, events, book launches and readers' days as well as writing courses and workshops across Ireland. Agent and publisher listings, guest blogs, plus services for writers listings, this site is packed full of information for new and established writers. Book reviews, book club information, a complete library listing, competitions and giveaways.

POSTGRADUATE COURSES

Aberystwyth University

Department of English and Creative Writing, Hugh Owen Building, Aberystwyth University, Penglais Campus, Aberystwyth, Ceredigion SY23 3DY
tel (01970) 621946
website www.aber.ac.uk/english
Contact The Administrator

MA in Creative Writing. PhD in Creative Writing.

Bath Spa University

School of Humanities and Cultural Industries, Bath Spa University, Newton Park, Newton St Loe, Bath BA2 9BN
tel (01225) 875875 *fax* (01225) 875503
email s.may@bathspa.ac.uk
website www.bathspa.ac.uk

MA in Creative Writing. MA in Writing for Young People. MA in Scriptwriting. MA in Travel and Nature Writing. PhD in Creative Writing.

Birkbeck College, University of London

Malet Street, London WC1E 7HX
tel 020-7631 6000
email a.taylor@english.bbk.ac.uk
website www.bbk.ac.uk
Contact Anne-Marie Taylor

MA in Creative Writing: full- and part-time evening teaching. Applications from students writing fiction for young adults welcome. Tutors include: Julia Bell, Toby Litt and Russell Celyn Jones. PhD students also welcome but prospective students should consult with individual tutors before making an application. BA Creative Writing: four-years part-time, evening study. Course covers all genres from fiction to playwriting to poetry and practical courses on publishing and journalism. Certificate in Creative Writing: short courses in creative writing covering fiction, poetry and life writing.

University of Bolton

School of Arts, Media and Education, University of Bolton, Dean Campus, Bolton BL3 5AB
tel (01204) 900600 *fax* (01204) 903232
email j.glover@bolton.ac.uk
website www.bolton.ac.uk
Contact John Glover, Programme Leader, Creative Writing

MA in Creative Writing.

Brunel University

School of Arts, Brunel University, Uxbridge, Middlesex UB8 3PH
tel (01895) 267214 *fax* (01895) 2697686
email pg-arts-admissions@brunel.ac.uk
website www.brunel.ac.uk/arts

MA Creative Writing: The Novel with Celia Brayfield and Fay Weldon (Visiting Professor).

Cardiff University

Cardiff School of English and Philosophy, Humanities Building, Colum Drive, Cardiff CF10 3EU
tel 029-2087 4722 *fax* 029-2087 4502

email encap-pg@cardiff.ac.uk
website www.cf.ac.uk/encap
Contact Rachel Thomas

MA in Creative Writing.

The Central School of Speech and Drama

Embassy Theatre, Eton Avenue, London NW3 3HY
tel 020-7722 8183
website www.cssd.ac.uk

MA in Advanced Theatre Practice: Playwriting. MA in Writing for Stage and Broadcast Media.

University of Chichester

Bishop Otter Campus, College Lane, Chichester, West Sussex PO19 6PE
tel (01243) 816000
email s.norgate@chi.ac.uk
website www.chi.ac.uk
Contact Stephanie Norgate, MA in Creative Writing Programme Coordinator

MA in Creative Writing.

City University

Dept of Creative Practice and Enterprise,
School of Arts, City University,
Northampton Square, London EC1V 0HB
tel 020-7040 5060 *fax* 020-7040 8887
email journalism@city.ac.uk
website www.city.ac.uk
Contact The Course Officer

MA Creative Writing (Plays and Screenplays), MA Creative Writing (The Novel), MA Creative Writing (Creative Non-Fiction); these are all two-year part-time courses.

University of Cumbria

Bowerham Road, Lancaster LA1 3JD
tel (01524) 384328
website www.cumbria.ac.uk

MA in Scriptwriting.

De Montfort University

Faculty of Arts,
Design and Humanities Admission Team,
De Montfort University, The Gateway,
Leicester LE1 9BH
tel 0116 257 7555
email adh@dmu.ac.uk
website www.dmu.ac.uk/tvscriptwriting
Contact Promotion and Recruitment Centre

MA in TV Scriptwriting.

University of East Anglia

Admissions Office, School of Literature,
Drama and Creative Writing,
Faculty of Arts and Humanities,
University of East Anglia, Norwich Research Park,
Norwich NR4 7TJ
tel (01603) 592154
email ldc.pgt.admiss@uea.ac.uk
website www.uea.ac.uk/ldc
Contact Admissions Office

MA in Creative Writing: Prose Fiction. MA in Creative Writing: Poetry. MA in Creative Writing: Scriptwriting. MA in Biography and Creative Non-fiction. MA in Writing the Modern World.

Edge Hill University

Department of English and History, St Helens Road, Ormskirk L39 4QP
tel (01695) 584274 *fax* (01695) 579997
email shepparr@edgehill.ac.uk
website www.edgehill.ac.uk
Contact Prof Robert Sheppard

MA in Creative Writing (full time and part time). PhD programmes in creative writing. BA in Creative Writing (single honours included): contact Daniele Pantano (pantanod@edgehill.ac.uk)

University of Edinburgh

Graduate School of Literatures,
Languages & Cultures, Room 12.15,
David Hume Tower, Edinburgh EH8 9JX
tel 0131 650 4114
website www.ed.ac.uk/englit/
Contact The Graduate Secretary

MSc in Creative Writing.

University of Essex

Wivenhoe Park, Colchester CO4 3SQ
tel (01206) 873333
email thorj@essex.ac.uk
website www.essex.ac.uk
Contact Dept of Literature, Film & Theatre Studies

MA in Literature with option to specialise in creative writing.

University of Exeter

College of Humanities, Department of Drama,
Thornlea, New North Road, Exeter EX4 4LA
tel (01392) 724580 *fax* (01392) 724594
email drama@ex.ac.uk
website www.exeter.ac.uk/drama

MA in Theatre Practice: Playwriting and Dramaturgy.

University College Falmouth

Falmouth, Cornwall TR11 4RH
tel (01326) 213730
email admissions@falmouth.ac.uk
website www.falmouth.ac.uk
Contact Admissions Office

MA Professional Writing, MA Professional Writing (Distance Learning), BA (Hons) English with Creative Writing, BA (Hons) Creative Writing.

University of Glamorgan

Faculty of Business and Society,
University of Glamorgan, Treforest,
Pontypridd CF37 1DL

tel (01443) 654195
email pgross@glam.ac.uk
website www.glam.ac.uk
Contact Prof. P. Gross, Director of Studies

Master's in Writing programme.

University of Glasgow

English Literature, University of Glasgow,
6 University Gardens, Glasgow G12 8QQ
tel 0141 330 7493
email michael.schmidt@glasgow.ac.uk
website www.glasgow.ac.uk/creativewriting
Head of Creative Writing Programmes Prof. Michael Schmidt

MLitt, MFA and PhD in Creative Writing.

University of Greenwich

School of Humanities and Social Sciences,
University of Greenwich, Old Royal Naval College,
30 Park Row, Greenwich, London SE10 9LS
tel/fax 020-8331 8800
website www.greenwich.ac.uk
Contact Prof. Susan Rowland

MA by Research (Creative Writing).

University of Hull

Dept of English, University of Hull,
Cottingham Road, Hull HU6 7RX
tel (01482) 465623
email m.j.goodman@hull.ac.uk
website www.hull.ac.uk
Contact Prof. Martin Goodman

MA/PhD in Creative Writing.

Kingston University

River House, 53–57 High Street,
Kingston upon Thames, Surrey KT1 1LQ
tel 020-8417 9000
website www.kingston.ac.uk
Contact Postgraduate Admissions Administrator

MAs in Creative Writing, Travel Writing, Writing Fiction and Writing Children's Literature.

Lancaster University

Dept of English & Creative Writing, County College,
Lancaster University, Lancaster LA1 4YD
tel (01524) 594169
email l.kellett@lancaster.ac.uk
website www.lancs.ac.uk/fass/english
Contact The Secretary

MA in Creative Writing. MA in Creative Writing by Distance Learning.

University of Leeds

School of Performance and Cultural Industries,
Leeds LS2 9JT
tel 0113 343 8710 *fax* 0113 343 8711
email enquiries-pci@leeds.ac.uk
website www.leeds.ac.uk
Contact Postgraduate Secretary

MA in Writing for Performance and Publication.

Leeds Metropolitan University

School of Film, Television and Performing Arts,
Electric Press Building, 1 Millennium Square,
Leeds LS2 3AD
tel 0113 812 3860
email filmenquiries@leedsmet.ac.uk
website www.leedsmet.ac.uk
Contact Chris Pugh, Course Administrator

MA in Film-making.

Liverpool John Moores University

School of Media, Critical and Creative Arts,
Liverpool John Moores University,
Dean Walters Building, Upper Duke Street,
Liverpool L1 7BT
tel 0151 231 5196 *fax* 0151 231 5049
website www.ljmu.ac.uk
Contact Programme Administrator

MA in Screenwriting and MA in Writing.

University of London, Goldsmiths

Dept of English and Comparative Literature,
Goldsmiths, University of London,
London SE14 6NW
tel 020-7919 7752 *fax* 020-7919 7453
email r.bolley@gold.ac.uk
website www.goldsmiths.ac.uk
Contact Richard Bolley, Departmental Administrator

MPhil/PhD in Creative Writing, MA in Creative and Life Writing, BA in English with Creative Writing.

University of London, Goldsmiths College

Dept of Theatre and Performance,
Goldsmiths College, University of London,
London SE14 6NW
tel 020-7919 7171 *fax* 020-7919 7413
website www.gold.ac.uk
Contact Drama Secretary

MA in Writing for Performance.

University of London, King's College

School of Humanities, University of London,
King's College, Strand, London WC2R 2LS
tel 020-7836 5454 *fax* 020-7848 2257
email englishdept@kcl.ac.uk
website www.kcl.ac.uk
Contact Helene Hokland (course administrator)

MA in Text and Performance Studies; scriptwriting option supervised at RADA.

University of London, Royal Holloway

Dept of English, Royal Holloway,
University of London, Egham, Surrey TW20 0EX
tel (01784) 434455/437520
website www.rhul.ac.uk/English

Contacts Prof. Andrew Motion (Creative Writing), Dr Redell Olsen (Poetic Practice)

MA in Creative Writing. MA in Poetic Practice, taught in central London.

University of London, Royal Holloway

Dept of Media Arts, Royal Holloway,
University of London, Egham, Surrey TW20 0EX
tel (01784) 443214
email mediaarts@rhul.ac.uk
website www.rhul.ac.uk/media-arts
Contact Sue Clayton (Retreat Programme)

MA in Screenwriting for Film and TV (Retreat Programme).

London College of Communication

LCC School of Media, Elephant & Castle,
London SE1 6SB
tel 020-7514 6569
email info@lcc.arts.ac.uk
website www.lcc.arts.ac.uk
Contact S. Paskell, Postgraduate Administrator

MA in Screenwriting (2-year part-time degree).

The London Film School

London Film School, 24 Shelton Street,
London WC2H 9UB
tel 020-7836 9642 *fax* 020-7497 3718
email screenwriting@lfs.org.uk
website www.lfs.org.uk
Contact Brian Dunnigan

MA in Screenwriting.

University of Manchester

Centre for New Writing, Mansfield Cooper Building,
University of Manchester, Oxford Road,
Manchester M13 9PL
tel 0161 306 1240 *fax* 0161 306 1241
email info-cnw@manchester.ac.uk
website www.manchester.ac.uk/arts/newwriting

MA and PhD in Creative Writing. MA and PhD in Contemporary Literature.

The Manchester Writing School at Manchester Metropolitan University

Dept of English, Rosamond Street West,
Off Oxford Road, Manchester M15 6LL
tel 0161 247 1787 *fax* 0161 247 6345
email j.draper@mmu.ac.uk
website www.mmu.ac.uk/english/writingschool
Contact James Draper, Manager: The Manchester Writing School at MMU

MA in Creative Writing: Novel, Poetry and Writing for Children (campus-based and international online distance learning); short courses in Teaching Creative Writing, Literary Translation, Crime Fiction and Scriptwriting Practice.

Middlesex University

Oakleigh Road South, London N11 1QS
tel 020-8411 5555
email admissions@mdx.ac.uk
website www.mdx.ac.uk
Contact Admissions Office

MA/Postgraduate Diploma/Postgraduate Certificate in Writing (Prose Fiction) and MPhil/PhD in Creative Writing.

National Film and Television School

National Film and Television School,
Beaconsfield Studios, Station Road, Beaconsfield,
Bucks. HP9 1LG
tel (01494) 671234 *fax* (01494) 674042
email info@nfts.co.uk
website www.nfts.co.uk

MA in Screenwriting and Diploma in Script Development. See website for application information.

Newcastle University

School of English Literature,
Language and Linguistics, Newcastle University,
Newcastle upon Tyne NE1 7RU
tel 0191 222 7625 *fax* 0191 222 8708
website www.ncl.ac.uk/elll
Contact Postgraduate Admission Secretary

MA in Creative Writing. Postgraduate Certificate in Creative Writing. PhD in Creative Writing.

Northumbria University

School of Arts and Social Sciences,
University of Northumbria at Newcastle, Room 126,
Lipman Building, Sandyford Road,
Newcastle upon Tyne NE1 8ST
tel 0191 227 4473
website www.northumbria.ac.uk
Contact The Admissions Tutor

MA in Creative Writing, combining prose and script.

Nottingham Trent University

School of Arts and Humanities,
Nottingham Trent University, Clifton Lane,
Nottingham NG11 8NS
tel 0115 848 4200
email hum.enquiries@ntu.ac.uk
website www.ntu.ac.uk/creativewriting
Contact Sarah Jackson

MA in Creative Writing.

Oxford University

Dept for Continuing Education,
1 Wellington Square, Oxford OX1 2JA
tel (01865) 270369 *fax* (01865) 270309
email ppaward@conted.ox.ac.uk
website www.conted.ox.ac.uk/mstcw
Contact MSt Administrator

Master of Studies (MSt) in Creative Writing from Oxford University: a 2-year part-time course covering prose fiction, radio and TV drama, poetry, stage drama and screenwriting. A 2-year part-time Diploma and Summer Schools in creative writing are also offered.

Plymouth University

Faculty of Arts, University of Plymouth,
Drake Circus, Plymouth PL4 8AA
tel (01752) 585100
email anthony.caleshu@plymouth.ac.uk,
artspostgrad@plymouth.ac.uk
website www.plymouth.ac.uk
Contact Dr Anthony Caleshu, Senior Lecturer in English and Creative Writing

MA/Postgraduate Diploma in Creative Writing. PhD in Creative Writing.

Queen's University, Belfast

School of English, Queen's University, Belfast,
Belfast BT7 1NN
tel 028-9024 5133 ext. 5103 *fax* 028-9031 4615
website www.qub.ac.uk
Contact Linda Drain (Postgraduate Secretary)

MA/Postgraduate Diploma in Creative Writing. PhD in Creative Writing.

University of St Andrews

School of English, University of St Andrews,
St Andrews, Fife KY16 9AJ
tel (01334) 462666 *fax* (01334) 462655
email english@st-andrews.ac.uk
website www.st-andrews.ac.uk
Contact Postgraduate Director

MLitt/Graduate Diploma in Creative Writing.

University of Salford

University of Salford, Adelphi Building, Peru Street,
Salford, Greater Manchester M3 6EQ
tel 0161 295 6026 *fax* 0161 295 6027
email course-enquiries@salford.ac.uk
website www.salford.ac.uk
Contact Admission Tutor

MA/Postgraduate Diploma in Television and Radio Scriptwriting.

Sheffield Hallam University

Admissions Office,
Faculty of Development and Society,
Sheffield Hallam University, Sheffield S1 1WB
tel 0114 225 3636 *fax* 0114 225 5880
email fdsenquiries@shu.ac.uk
website www.shu.ac.uk/english

MA/Postgraduate Diploma/Postgraduate Certificate in Creative Writing. Recognised by Don Paterson (winner of the Whitbread Poetry Prize and two-time winner of the TS Eliot Prize) as one of the leading postgraduate courses in England. There are 2 intakes per year and applications should be received by the end of October for the January intake and by the end of March for the September intake.

Trinity College, Carmarthen

School of Creative Arts & Humanities,
Trinity College, Carmarthen, Dyfed SA31 3EP
tel (01267) 676767 *fax* (01267) 676766
email p.wright@trinity-cm.ac.uk
website www.trinity-cm.ac.uk
Contact Dr Paul Wright

MA in Creative Writing.

University of Warwick

Dept of English and Comparative Literary Studies,
Humanities Building, University of Warwick,
Coventry CV4 7AL
tel 024-7652 3665
email cheryl.cave@warwick.ac.uk
website www.warwick.ac.uk
Contact Cheryl Cave, Programme Secretary

MA in Writing.

University of Winchester

Winchester SO22 4NR
tel (01962) 841515
email course.enquiries@winchester.ac.uk
website www.winchester.ac.uk
Contact Course Enquiries & Admissions

MA Writing for Children and MA Creative and Critical Writing.

Copyright and libel

Copyright questions

Gillian Davies answers questions to draw out some of the legal issues and explain the basics of how copyright works, or should work, for the benefit of the writer.

What is copyright?

Copyright is a negative right in the sense that it is not a right of possession but is a right of exclusion. However, if you know your rights it can be a strong legal tool because copyright law affords remedies in both the civil and criminal courts. Material will automatically be protected by copyright without registration if it is original, i.e. not copied. The onus is on you, the writer, and your publisher to do the work of protecting, policing and enforcing your valuable intellectual property. Unfortunately, generally speaking people do not respect copyright and there are ongoing issues to do with copyright, especially online.

I am leaving my unpublished manuscript to my daughter when I die, but I haven't written a will yet. What are the implications?

Charles Dickens was involved in just this scenario. What happens to the physical lump of paper might be different from what happens to the intellectual property (copyright) in your work. In your will you could bequeath the physical manuscript to your daughter; but you could leave the copyright in the text to someone else (or split it up into different rights to different people); and the copyright in the pictures to someone else. Specifying this in a will gives you control. If you have no will, the property in the manuscript will be dealt with in one way and the intellectual property in the text/pictures another way when being handled by the personal representative.

I am a freelance writer and submitted an article to a magazine editor and heard nothing back. Six months later I read a feature in a Sunday newspaper which looks very similar. Can I sue someone?

Pitching ideas can be fraught with difficulty. In legal terms you do not have any protection under copyright law for 'ideas', but only for 'the expression of those ideas' – for the way in which the ideas have been 'clothed in words' to paraphrase a Learned Judge. It could be argued that in many ways this distinction between ideas and their expression does not work for writing and 'literary works'. But that won't help you in court or get you legal recompense if you are ripped off.

In the situation described, you would need to prove that your work came first in time; that your work was seen by the second writer or publisher; and that the second person copied unlawfully a 'substantial part' of your work, which these days involves a very woolly and subjective judicial comparison of one work weighed against the other. You would also need to be able to counter any claims that the subject matter is not capable of being monopolised by you and that there is actual language copying. Avoid this happening in the first place by taking practical steps: mark your speculative pieces 'in confidence' and add '© Your Name 201X'. Using the © puts people on notice that you are aware of your rights. It would also have an effect later on if it came to litigation evidentially, i.e. if a person sees the copyright sign but nevertheless goes ahead and uses work without permission, the defence of 'innocent dissemination' cannot be relied upon. But all that is evidential.

A couple of caveats: if the subject matter is 'out there', i.e. common knowledge, copyright law may not protect the first work. The law is very contradictory in this area, as can be seen in these three cases which went to court: the persistent lifting of facts from another newspaper, even with rewriting, was deemed a copyright infringement; copyright protected a detailed sequence of ideas where precise wording was not copied; the fact that an author went to primary sources did not necessarily ensure that he was not copyright infringing. However, copyright law does weigh heavily in favour of protecting the originator.

If a newspaper pays for an article and I then want to sell the story to a magazine, am I free under the copyright law to do so?

Yes, provided that you have not assigned copyright or licensed exclusive use to the newspaper. When selling your work to newspapers or magazines make it clear, in writing, that you are selling only First or Second Serial Rights, not your copyright.

Does being paid a kill fee affect my copyright in a given piece?

No, provided that you have not sold the magazine or newspaper your copyright.

Am I legally required to inform an interviewee that our conversation is being recorded?

The interviewee owns the copyright of any words that he or she speaks as soon as they are recorded on your voice recorder. Unless you have received permission to use those words in direct quotation, you could be liable to an action for infringement of copyright. You should therefore certainly inform the interviewee that the conversation is being recorded and seek permission to quote what is said directly. However, if you record someone talking and use their words for reporting on current events, then you will be able to use the recorded words if they are relevant to what you are reporting on.

I want to use a quote from another book but can't remember the original source. Can I just put it in quotes and use it?

Using extracts and quotes is a very difficult area and there is no easy answer to this. If the author has definitely been deceased for 70 years or more, you may be fine; the work may have passed into the 'public domain'. However, unpublished works require caution. In general, unpublished works are protected by copyright as soon as they are 'expressed' and copyright belongs to the author until/unless published and rights are transferred to a publisher. Protection for unpublished works lasts for 50 years (usually); Crown copyright lasts for 125 years for unpublished works – it's a legal minefield!

Generally, copyright law demands that you ask permission and (usually) pay a fee for reuse. There is no exact recipe for the amount of money payable or the number of words you can 'take' before you need to pay. The original author or publisher may let you use it for free, usually with an appropriate acknowledgement, or a sum of money may be requested.

If you cannot identify the source of the quote, we enter the tricky arena of 'orphan works'. There are plans for an agency (called the 'Digital Copyright Exchange' at the time of writing) to be set up to help people trace copyright owners. In the meantime, all you can do is make serious and diligent efforts to trace the copyright owner. You can contact publishers, search the WATCH (Writers Artists and their Copyright Holders) database (www.watch-file.com, http://norman.hrc.utexas.edu/watch), place an advertisement in the *TLS*, the *Bookseller*, etc) and use a legal disclaimer. Keep a record of all your efforts in case the copyright question comes back to bite you later.

In an ideal world, all content would be tagged with details of what is permissible and how to contact the owner. A new Copyright Licensing Agency scheme (http://WhatCanIDoWithThisContent.com) attempts just that by letting any online content provider add an icon which has an embedded code into the website's CMS (Content Management System).

My publisher has forgotten to assert my copyright on the imprint page. What does that mean for me?

Technically, what is usually asserted on the imprint page is the moral right to be identified as author of the work. This 'paternity right' is lost if it is not 'asserted', so if it is not on the imprint page or anywhere else (say, the contract) you lose the right. Moral rights are copyrights, separate to and additional to what we normally refer to as 'copyright': they protect the personal side of creation, in that they are about the integrity of the work and the person/reputation of the creator. Whereas the 'main'/economic copyright protection is there to ensure you get revenues from your work, for example licence fees and royalties. Both economic copyrights and moral rights were conferred by the 1988 UK statute and derive from the Berne Convention. They exist separately, so you can keep moral rights and 'licence away' copyright (economic copyrights). And so in reverse, even if your moral right to be identified as author is lost, your other rights – economic copyright and the moral right to not have your work subjected to 'derogatory treatment' – remain with you. Moral rights cannot be licensed or assigned because they are personal to the author, but they can be 'waived', for example a ghostwriter may well waive the right to be identified as author. Moral rights are very flexible and useful, but are not widely used.

I've found an illustration I want to use for the cover of a book that I'm self-publishing. I chose the picture (dated 1928) on purpose because the artist is out of copyright and the picture is in the 'public domain'. Why is the picture library, who holds the image, charging a reproduction fee?

You have to pay a reproduction fee under copyright law because of the separate copyright issue for photography. Because the original artwork was photographed, copyright vests separately in the photograph (of the artwork) as opposed to the artwork itself. It is a controversial area and one where the UK/US legal systems are split.

I included someone's work on my blog, but as I blog for free and it's not a money-making exercise, can I be sued for copyright infringement?

Yes you can. If the person alleging copyright infringement can show she has copyright in the work, that you had access to her work, can show you copied the whole of that work or a 'substantial part' of it, and that you did not have permission, you could well be infringing criminal and civil copyright laws. The point of copyright law – the economic as opposed to the moral rights aspect – is to protect the economic interests of the original copyright owner. If she can show that her position has been undermined by your blog in terms of her market share having diminished and/or that sales have been adversely affected, etc or if she can show that you have not paid her any reuse fee or asked permission or acknowledged her authorship, you are on very thin ice.

My book has been made available by a free book download site but I never agreed to this. What can I do?

Contact your publisher or ask the site direct (if it's a self-published work) to remove it from their website. If they do not act or do not respond get legal advice: a lawyer will be able to issue a warning followed by a 'take down notice', followed if necessary by a court injunction. However, this is very difficult for cases worth under £25,000. Take practical steps to protect copyright in your own works yourself by setting up a Google Alert for every title you own.

First steps legal advice may be available from the Society of Authors, the Writers' Guild, the National Union of Journalists (NUJ), the Society for Editors and Proofreaders (SfEP) or your local BusinessLink or an intellectual property specialist adviser like Own-It.

DISCLAIMER

I am an editor and writer not a lawyer and am not providing legal advice. My work brings to bear my practical experience of the issues to unfold legal issues and to try to explain the issues in plain English. I use the names Gillian Davies and Gillian Haggart. I am not the Gillian Davies, barrister who currently co-edits the leading copyright text for lawyers, Copinger & Skone James on Copyright, and has recently co-authored Moral Rights with Kevin Garnett QC (Sweet & Maxwell 2011).

Gillian Davies MA (Hons), LLB is the author of *Copyright Law for Artists, Designers and Photographers* (A&C Black 2010) and *Copyright Law for Writers, Editors and Publishers* (A&C Black 2011).

See also...

- *UK copyright law*, page 643
- *The laws of Privacy and Confidentiality*, page 664
- *Defamation*, page 668

UK copyright law

Amanda Michaels (with updates by Jonathan Moss) describes the main types of work which may qualify for copyright protection, or related protection as a design, together with some of the problems which may be faced by readers of this *Yearbook* in terms of protecting their own works or avoiding infringement of existing works in the UK. This is a technical area of the law, and one which is constantly developing; in an article of this length, it is not possible to deal fully with all the complexities of the law. It must also be emphasised that copyright is national in scope, so whilst works of UK authors will be protected in many other countries of the world, and works of foreign authors will generally be protected in the UK, foreign laws may deal differently with questions of subsistence, ownership and infringement.

Copyright law creates and protects a property right in a number of different kinds of works. UK copyright arises immediately upon creation of a relevant work, and provides its owner with the right to take action to prevent others from doing a number of 'restricted acts' without the owner's consent.

Copyright law in the UK has developed over many years; since the first Copyright Act (the Statute of Anne) in 1709, a series of statutes has extended copyright protection to a widening range of copyright works, often reflecting changes in technology, but also reflecting the requirements of a number of international conventions on the protection of copyright and related works, such as in particular the Berne and Universal Copyright Conventions. In addition, UK copyright law has been significantly shaped and affected by a series of EU harmonisation Directives, and the Act must be interpreted in accordance with them; they must be applied in a uniform manner across the EU. The impact of those Directives can perhaps best be described as 'a work in progress', in particular because the Court of Justice of the EU (CJEU) has been asked to provide guidance on numerous questions referred to it by national courts; some such questions are pending and the implications of some of the Court's answers have yet to be resolved.

Useful websites

www.ipo.gov.uk

Useful information, guidance notes and legislation are available on the website of the UK Intellectual Property Office (previously the Patent Office).

www.wipo.int

Website of the World Intellectual Property Organisation.

www.bailii.org

Provides free and broadly comprehensive access to UK case-law and legislation, with links to equivalent foreign websites. Legislation on the site may be in an unamended form.

The major UK statute is the Copyright, Designs & Patents Act 1988 ('the Act') which came into force on 1 August 1989. It replaced the Copyright Act 1956, which had replaced the first modern Act, the Copyright Act 1911. All three Acts remain relevant because a property right which may last for many years (see below) and questions of the subsistence, ownership and protection of works may be tested according to the law in force at the time a work was made or first published.

Since the 1988 Act came into force it has been amended pretty much continuously, mainly in the light of various EU Directives. An important change occurred on 1 January 1996, when the duration of copyright protection in respect of most works (see below) was extended from 'life of the author' plus 50 years to life plus 70 years. New rights have been created, such as the database right which came into existence on 1 January 1998, and the important Community registered and unregistered design rights which came into effect in 2003. Numerous other changes have been made, some of the most significant arose out of the Information Society Directive (2001/29), implemented by the Copyright and Related Rights Regulations 2003, which sought in particular to meet the challenges posed by the Internet and electronic rights management, and changes to remedies required by the Enforcement Directive, 2004/48, and by the Digital Economy Act 2010. Further important changes were made by the Broadcasting Acts of 1990 and 1996.

These continuing changes do mean that it is important to check that you are using the current version of the Act. The website of the UK Intellectual Property Office (see box) is a useful resource.

Continuing relevance of old law

In this article, I discuss the law as it currently stands, but where a work was made before 1 August 1989 one needs to consider the law in force at the time of creation (or, possibly, first publication) in order to assess the existence or scope of any rights. Particular difficulties arise with foreign works, which may qualify for protection in the UK as a matter of international obligation. Each Act has contained transitional provisions and these, as well as the substantive provisions of any relevant earlier Act, need to be considered where, for instance, you wish to use an earlier work and need to decide whether permission is needed and, if so, who may grant it. In addition, publishing or licence agreements designed for use under older Acts and prior to the development of modern technologies may be unsuitable for current use.

Copyright protection of works

According to the CJEU in Case C-5/08, *Infopaq International A/S* v. *Danske Dagblades Forening*, 16 July 2009 [2010] FSR 20: 'copyright within the meaning of [the Information Society] Directive 2001/29 is liable to apply only in relation to a subject matter which is original in the sense that it is its author's own intellectual creation'. This reflects, but may not be identical to, the UK concept of the policy justifying copyright protection, i.e. 'to prevent the unauthorised copying of material forms of expression (literary, dramatic, artistic and musical, for example) resulting from intellectual exertions of the human mind.... The important point is that copyright can be used to prevent copying of a substantial part of the relevant form of expression, but it does not prevent use of the information, thoughts or emotions expressed in the copyright work. It does not prevent another person from coincidentally creating a similar work by his own independent efforts' (see Mummery LJ in *Sawkins* v. *Hyperion Records* [2005] 1 WLR 3281).

Copyright does not subsist in ideas – that is the province of patents and the law of confidence. Copyright protects the expression of ideas, the particular form of the subject matter in which the author's idea has been expressed, not the idea itself. This distinction was examined in *Baigent & Leigh* v. *The Random House Group* [2007] FSR 24: Dan Brown was alleged to have copied the 'Central Theme', consisting of a series of historical facts, conjectures or theories, from the Claimants' book, *The Holy Blood and the Holy Grail*, in writing his bestselling novel *The Da Vinci Code*. Whilst the judge found evidence of copying, the Court of Appeal held that what Dan Brown took from HBHG 'amounted to generalised propositions, at too high a level of abstraction to qualify for copyright protection, because it was not the product of the application of skill and labour by the authors of HBHG in the creation of their literary work. It lay on the wrong side of the line between ideas and their expression.' (Lloyd LJ at para. 99). Copyright does not 'extend to clothing information, facts, ideas, theories and themes with exclusive property rights, so as to enable the Claimants to monopolise historical research or knowledge and prevent the legitimate use of historical and biographical material, theories... arguments... general hypotheses... or general themes' (Mummery LJ at para. 156).

The difficulty in seeking to apply this guidance to other cases is that the Court of Appeal emphasised that case-law cannot lay down any clear principle from which one may tell whether what is sought to be protected in any particular case is on the 'ideas' side of the dividing line, or on the 'expression' side. What can be said is that in cases of artistic copyright at least, '...the more abstract and simple the copied idea, the less likely it is to constitute a substantial part. Originality, in the sense of the contribution of the author's skill and labour, tends to lie in the detail with which the basic idea is presented.' (Lord Hoffman in *Designers Guild* v. *Russell Williams (Textiles) Ltd* [2000] 1 WLR 2416). What is more, these pre-2009 UK decisions may need to be re-evaluated in the light of the breadth of the CJEU's decision in *Infopaq* (see below).

One area of particular difficulty for establishing a dividing line between ideas and expression is photography. This problem was as issue in the case of *Temple Island Collections* v. *New English Teas* [2012] FSR 9 where a photographer had taken a picture of a red London bus going over Westminster Bridge with the houses of Parliament in the background. The picture had then been manipulated to remove all colour except for that of the red London bus. A similar, but not identical photo was then created by the defendant. The judge held that the later photograph was an infringing copy. Whether this case of similar works infringing will be applied outside of manipulated photographs remains to be seen. The case is currently subject to an appeal.

Of course, if someone has written an outline, script or screenplay for a television show, film, etc and that idea is confidential, then dual protection may arise in the confidential idea embodied in the documents and in the literary (and sometimes artistic) works in which the idea is recorded. If the idea is used, but not the form, this might give rise to an action for breach of confidence, but not for infringement of copyright. Copyright prevents the copying of the *material form* in which the idea has been presented, or of a substantial part of it, measured in terms of quality, not quantity (see further below). One result is that so-called 'format right' cases rarely succeed.

Section 1 of the Act sets out a number of different categories of works which can be the subject of copyright protection. These are:

- original literary, dramatic, musical or artistic works,
- sound recordings, films or broadcasts, and
- typographical arrangements of published editions.

These works are further defined in ss.3–8 (see box for examples).

However, no work of any description enjoys copyright protection until it has been recorded in a tangible form, as s.3(2) provides that no copyright shall subsist in a literary, musical or artistic work until it has been recorded in writing or otherwise.

On the other hand, all that is required to achieve copyright protection is to record the original work in an appropriate medium. Once that has been done, copyright will subsist in the work in the UK (assuming that the qualifying features set out below are present) without any formality of registration or otherwise. There is, for instance, no need to publish a work to protect it. However, where a work is unpublished, it will be more difficult for a party to prove that another party copied that work.

Nonetheless, you can derive practical benefits from keeping a proper record of the development, design and creation of a work. Drafts or preliminary sketches should be kept and dated, as should source or research material, so as to be able to show the development of your work. It is also a wise precaution (especially where works are to be submitted to potential publishers or purchasers) to take a complete copy of the documents and send them to yourself or lodge them with a responsible third party, sealed and dated, so as to be able to provide cogent evidence of the form or content of the work at that date. Such evidence may help the author, whether as claimant or defendant, to prove the independence of the creation of his work and its originality in a copyright infringement or breach of confidence action. If, as is often the case, a work is being prepared on a computer, it is advisable to keep separate electronic copies for each stage at which the work is potentially revealed to third parties.

Originality

Under the 1988 Act, literary, dramatic, artistic and musical works must be 'original' to qualify for copyright protection. According to the CJEU in *Infopaq* (above), originality means that a work must be 'its author's own intellectual creation'. Subject to that point, UK law does not impose any concept of objective originality. Originality relates to the 'expression of the thought', rather than to the thought itself. The policy of copyright protection and its limited scope (set out above) explain why the threshold requirement of originality does not impose 'any objective standard of novelty, usefulness, inventiveness, aesthetic merit, quality or value'; so, a work may be 'complete rubbish', yet have copyright protection (see again Mummery LJ in *Sawkins*). A work need only be original in the sense of being the product of skill and labour on the part of the author.

There may be considerable difficulty, at times, in deciding whether a work is of sufficient originality, or has sufficient original features to attract copyright, particularly if there have been a series of similar designs, see e.g. *L.A. Gear Inc.* [1993] FSR 121, *Biotrading* [1998] FSR 109. There are similar difficulties where there has been amendment of an existing work. In *Sawkins* (above), the question was whether or not the editorial work done by Dr Sawkins on works by the baroque composer, Lalande, had created new musical works. The result turned partly on the definition of 'music', but the nature of Dr Sawkins' input was such that he was found to have created an original musical work with its own copyright. So an adaptation of an existing work may have its own copyright protection (see *Cala Homes* [1995] FSR 818) but making a '*slavish* copy' of a work will not create an original work: (*Interlego AG* [1989] AC 217). This is a matter of degree – some copying may take skill (Jacob LJ in *Sawkins*). If the work gives particular expression to a commonplace idea or an old tale, copyright may subsist in it, for example in *Christoffer* v. *Poseidon Film Distributors Limited* (6/10/99) a script for an animated film of a story from Homer's *Odyssey* was found to be an original literary work. But, as the *Da Vinci* case showed, whilst copyright may subsist in the work, the unlicensed use only of facts or ideas contained in it may not infringe that copyright. Copyright protection will be limited to the original features of the work, or those features created or chosen by the author's input of skill and labour.

Historically, the titles of books and periodicals, headlines, or phrases like advertising slogans, were not generally given copyright protection, however much original thought was involved in their creation, because they were too short to be deemed literary works. Following *Infopaq*, that may no longer be the case, because the CJEU said that even a short part of a longer work may be entitled to copyright protection if that part also amounts to its author's 'own intellectual creation'. In *Newspaper Licensing Agency Ltd* v. *Meltwater Holding BV* [2011] RPC 7, it was therefore held that headlines were capable of being literary works, whether independently or as part of the articles to which they related, depending upon the process of creation and the identification of the skill and labour that had gone into it.

The CJEU has also held, in relation to portrait photographs, that the level of creativity required for a work to be original is minimal (*Painer* [2012] ECDR 6). Thus for photographs the angle, composition and special techniques used may be enough to give even the most basic photograph copyright protection. Therefore, even very short excerpts of text, from a headline or from a book, or very simple photographs, could theoretically infringe another person's copyright. However, it is very hard to determine where exactly this line will get drawn.

Sound recordings or films which are copies of pre-existing sound recordings or films, and broadcasts which infringe rights in another broadcast are not protected by copyright.

Computer 'languages', and the ideas or logic underlying them, are not protected as copyright works; such protection extends only to the computer programs: see *Navitaire* v. *Easyjet* [2004] EWHC 1725. So it is legitimate to emulate a program for a computer game and produce a game with similar characteristics, as long as the program code and the graphics are not copied (*Nova Productions Limited* v. *Mazooma Games Limited* [2007] RPC 25).

Qualification

The Act is limited in its effects to the UK (and for example to colonies to which it may be extended by Order). It is aimed primarily at protecting the works of British citizens, or works first published in the UK. However, in line with various international conventions,

Definitions under the Act

Literary work is defined as: 'any work, other than a dramatic or musical work, which is written, spoken or sung, and accordingly includes: (a) a table or compilation other than a database, (b) a computer program, (c) preparatory design material for a computer program and (d) a database.'

A musical work means: 'a work consisting of music, exclusive of any words or action intended to be sung, spoken or performed with the music.'

An artistic work means: '(a) a graphic work, photograph, sculpture or collage, irrespective of artistic quality, (b) a work of architecture being a building or model for a building, or (c) a work of artistic craftsmanship.' What constitutes a sculpture or work of artistic craftsmanship was discussed in relation to *Star Wars* stormtrooper helmets in *Lucasfilm* v. *Ainsworth*. The Supreme Court held that the stormtrooper helmet (and the rest of the armour) was a work of neither sculpture nor artistic craftsmanship, instead it was properly protected by design law.

These categories of work are not mutually exclusive, e.g. a film may be protected both as a film and as a dramatic work. See *Norowzian* v. *Arks* [2000] FSR 363. However, the position as to databases is particularly complicated: rights may arise under the Act or under the Database Directive 96/9, the question of how this works has been referred to the CJEU: see *Football Dataco Ltd* v. *Yahoo! UK Ltd* [2010] EWCA Civ 1380, 9 Dec 2010.

copyright protection in the UK is also accorded to the works of nationals of many foreign states, as well as to works first published in those states, on a reciprocal basis.

There is a principle of equal treatment for works of nationals of other member states of the European Union, so that protection must be offered to such works here: see *Phil Collins* [1993] 3 CMLR 773.

The importance of these rules mainly arises when one is trying to find out whether a foreign work is protected by copyright here, for instance, to make a film based upon a foreign novel.

Traditionally, if a work was not protected in the UK then it could be copied in the UK, even if it was in copyright elsewhere, i.e. copyright was a territorial right limited in its scope. This is still the case, but a corollary of this was that a defendant could only be sued in the country where the infringement occurred. However, the recent decision of the Supreme Court in *Lucasfilm* v. *Ainsworth* [2012] 1 AC 208 means that an action can now be brought in England for the infringement of US copyright in the USA (e.g. if a party sells into the USA through the internet). This still requires an infringement to occur *in the USA* but this is relatively easy due to the presence of the internet.

Ownership

The general rule is that the copyright in a work will first be owned by its author, the creator of the work. The definition of 'author' in relation to films and sound recordings has changed over the years; currently, the author of a sound recording is its producer, and the authors of a film are the producer and principal director.

One important exception to the general rule is that the copyright in a work made by an employee in the course of his or her employment will belong to their employer, subject to any agreement to the contrary. However, this rule does not apply to freelance designers, journalists, etc and not even to self-employed company directors. This obviously may lead to problems if the question of copyright ownership is not dealt with when an agreement is made to create, purchase or use a work. In the absence of an appropriate agreement, the legal title may simply not be owned by the apparent owner, who will generally need it if he wishes to sue for infringement, and it is often difficult to formalise the position long after creation of the work. More importantly, perhaps, there have been numerous cases in which the extent of the rights obtained in a 'commissioned' work has been disputed, simply because of the lack of any clear agreement at the outset between the author and the 'commissioner'. See for example *Griggs* v. *Evans* (below). It is very important for writers and artists of all kinds to agree about ownership/terms of use at the outset and record them in writing, particularly where you are being paid to create a work – any such arrangement may be a 'commission'. It is equally important to understand the difference between an assignment and a licence (again, see below).

Where a work is produced by several people who collaborate so that each one's contribution is not distinct from that of the other(s), then they will be joint authors of the work, for example where two people write a play, each rewriting what the other produces, there will be a joint work. But where two people collaborate to write a song, one producing the lyrics and the other the music, there will be two separate copyright works, the copyright of which will be owned by each of the authors separately. The importance of knowing whether the copyright is joint or not arises:

- in working out the duration of the copyright, and

• from the fact that joint works can only be exploited with the agreement of all the joint authors, so that all of them have to join in any licence, although each of them can sue for infringement without joining the other(s) as a claimant in the proceedings. In 2005 Matthew Fisher claimed that he had been a joint author of the music of Procol Harum's hit record *Whiter Shade of Pale*. The song had been written in 1967. He was found to be a joint author, having added the distinctive organ solo to the song, and the House of Lords held that even his 40-year delay in making his claim did not bar it: *Fisher* v. *Brooker* [2009] UKHL 41.

For example, in a recent decision in the Patents County Court, it was held that copyright in a film of a skydive was owned both by the person who took the film and the person who commissioned it (*Slater* v. *Wimmer* [2012] EWPCC 7). The upshot of this being that neither party could use it, as both were owners who could stop the other using it without their permission.

Duration of copyright

With effect from 1 January 1996, copyright in literary, dramatic, musical or artistic works expires at the end of the period of 70 years from the end of the calendar year in which the author dies (s.12(1)). Where there are joint authors, then the 70 years runs from the death of the last of them to die. If the author is unknown, there will be 70 years protection from the date the work was made or (where applicable) first made available to the public. Previously, the protection was for 'life plus 50'. (NB See 'Infringement' below for important limits on the copyright protection of artistic works.)

The extended 70-year term also applies to films, and runs from the end of the calendar year in which the death occurs of the last to die of the principal director, the author of the screenplay or the dialogue, or the composer of any music created for the film (s.13B). This obviously may be a nightmare to establish, and there are certain presumptions in s.66A which may help someone wishing to use material from an old film.

However, sound recordings are still protected by copyright only for 50 years from the year of making or release (s.13A). This affects many 'classic' recordings of pop music, and (after much international negotiation) it is possible, though not certain, that the term may be extended to 70 or even 95 years. Broadcasts and computer-generated works get only 50 years protection.

The new longer term applies without difficulty to works created after 1 January 1996 and to works in copyright on 31 December 1995. The owner of the extended copyright will be the person who owned it on 31 December 1995, unless he had only a limited term of ownership, in which case the extra 20 years will be added on to the reversionary term.

Where copyright had expired here, but the author died between 50 and 70 years ago, the position is more complicated. EC Directive 93/98 provided that if a work was protected by copyright anywhere in the EU on 1 July 1995, copyright would revive for it in the other EU states until the end of the same 70-year period. This may make it necessary to look at the position in the states offering a longer term of protection, namely Germany, France and Spain.

Ownership of the *revived* term of copyright will belong to the person who was the owner of the copyright when the initial term expired, though if that person died (or a company, etc ceased to exist) before 1 January 1996, then the revived term will vest in his personal representatives.

Any licence affecting a copyright work which was in force on 31 December 1995 and was for the full term of the copyright continues to have effect during any extended term of copyright, subject to any agreement to the contrary.

The increased term offered to works of other EU nationals as a result of the Term Directive is not offered automatically to the nationals of other states, but will only apply where an equally long term is offered in their state of origin.

Where acts are carried out in relation to such revived copyright works as a result of things done whilst they were in the public domain, protection from infringement is available. A licence as of right may also be available, on giving notice to the copyright owner and paying a royalty.

Dealing with copyright works

Ownership of the copyright in a work gives the exclusive right to deal with the work in a number of ways, and essentially stops all unauthorised exploitation of the work. Ownership of the copyright is capable of being separated from ownership of the material form in which the work is embodied, depending upon the terms of any agreement or the circumstances. So, buying an original piece of artwork will not in general carry with it the legal title to the copyright, as an effective assignment must be in writing signed by the assignor (although beneficial ownership might pass: see below).

Copyright works can be exploited by their owners in two ways:

• **Assignment**. In an assignment, rights in the work are sold, with the owner retaining no interest in it (except, possibly, for a claim to royalties). An assignment must be in writing, signed by or on behalf of the assignor, but no other formality is required. One can make an assignment of future copyright under s.91: Where the author of a work not yet made agrees in writing that he will assign the rights in the future work to another, copyright vests in the assignee immediately upon the creation of the work, without further formalities.

These rules do not affect the common law as to beneficial interests in copyright. A Court may, in the right circumstances, find or infer an agreement to assign the copyright in a work. For example where a sole trader who had title to the copyright used in his business later incorporated the business and allowed the company to exploit the software as if it were its own, an agreement to assign was inferred (see *Lakeview Computers plc* 26/11/99). Alternatively, if the court finds that a work was commissioned to be made, and that there was a common intention that the purchaser should own the copyright, the Court may order the author to assign the copyright to him. 'Commission' in this context means only to order a particular piece of work to be done: see *Apple Corps Ltd* v. *Cooper* [1993] FSR 286 (a 1956 Act case). Where a freelance designer produced a logo for an advertising agency, a term was implied in the contract that the client (Doc Martens) for which the logo was designed was to be the owner of the worldwide copyrights in the logo: see *R. Griggs Group* v. *Ross Evans* [2005] FSR 31.

• **Licensing**. A licence arises where permission is granted to another to exploit the right whilst the licensor retains overall ownership. Licences do not need to take any particular form, and may be granted orally. However, an exclusive licence (i.e. one which excludes even the copyright owner himself from exploiting the work) must be in writing if the licensee is to enjoy rights in respect of infringements concurrent with those of the copyright owner. Non-exclusive licensees get more limited rights. See ss.101 and 101A of the Act.

Agreements dealing with copyright should make it clear whether an assignment or a licence is being granted. There may be significant advantages for an author in granting only a licence, for a third party who acquires the assignee's rights will not necessarily be subject to the assignee's obligations, for example to pay royalties (see *Barker* v. *Stickney* [1919] 1 KB 121). However, an assignment may expressly provide for the rights to revert to the author if the assignee breaches the agreement (see *Crosstown Music* v. *Rive Droite Music* [2011] FSR 5). If it is unclear whether a licence or an assignment was intended or agreed, the Court is likely to find that the grantee took the minimum rights necessary for his intended use of the work, quite probably an exclusive licence rather than an assignment (*Ray* v. *Classic FM plc* [1998] FSR 622), unless the work was 'commissioned' from the author. This case, *Griggs* (see above), and many other similar disputes, show how very important it is, if you make an agreement to create a work for someone else, or ask someone to make a work for you or your business, to discuss who is to own the copyright, or what is to be the extent of any licence, and to record the agreed position in writing. The question of moral rights (see below) should also be considered by the parties.

Assignments and licences often split up the various rights contained within the copyright. So, for instance, a licence might be granted to one person to publish a novel in book form, another person might be granted the film, television and video rights, and yet another the right to translate the novel into other languages. Obviously, the author should seek to grant the narrowest possible rights on each occasion and retain other rights for future exploitation. All such agreements must be drafted carefully; the author must negotiate as best he can. Failure to make clear what is covered by a licence can lead to problems. It is particularly important to make clear what forms of exploitation are licensed, and whether the licence will extend to new technologies. See for example *MGN Ltd* v. *Grisbrook* [2011] ECDR 4: photos held in a picture library were not licensed for use on a website.

Assignments and licences may also confer rights according to territory, dividing the USA from the EU or different EU countries one from the other. Any such agreement should take into account divergences between different national copyright laws. Furthermore, when seeking to divide rights between different territories of the EU there is a danger of infringing the competition rules of the EU. Professional advice should be taken, as breach of these rules may attract a fine and can render the agreement void in whole or in part.

Licences can, of course, be of varying lengths. There is no need for a licence to be granted for the whole term of copyright. Well-drafted licences will provide for termination on breach, including the failure of the licensee to exploit the work, and on the insolvency of the licensee and will specify whether the rights may be assigned or sub-licensed.

Copyright may be assigned by will. A bequest of an original document, etc embodying an unpublished copyright work will carry the copyright.

Infringement

The main type of infringement is what is commonly thought of as plagiarism, that is, copying the work. In fact, copyright confers on the owner the exclusive right to do a number of specified acts, so that anyone doing those acts without his permission will normally infringe. It is not necessary to copy a work exactly or use all of it; it is sufficient if a substantial part is used. That question is to be judged on a qualitative not a quantitative basis, bearing in mind that it is the skill and labour of the author which is to be protected (see *Ravenscroft* v. *Herbert* [1980] RPC 193 and *Designers Guild*). The ECJ has recently held that an extract just 11 words long might be protected, if it reproduced 'the expression of the intellectual creation of their author' – see *Infopaq* (above), as might a newspaper headline: see *Meltwater* (above). Primary infringement, such as copying, can be committed innocently of any intention to infringe.

The form of infringement common to all forms of copyright works is that of copying. This means reproducing the work in any material form. Infringement may occur from direct copying or where an existing work provides the inspiration for a later one, for example by including edited extracts from a history book in a novel (*Ravenscroft*), using a photograph as the inspiration for a painting (*Baumann* v. *Fussell* [1978] RPC 485), or words from a verse of one song in another (*Ludlow Music* v. *Williams* [2001] FSR 271). Infringement will not necessarily be prevented merely by the application of significant new skill and labour by the infringer, nor by a change of medium.

In the case of a two-dimensional artistic work, reproduction can mean making a copy in three dimensions, and vice versa. However, s.51 of the Act provides that in the case of a 'design document or model' (for definition, see 'Design right' below) for something which is not *itself* an artistic work, it is no infringement to make an article to that design. This means that whilst it would be an infringement of copyright to make an article from a design drawing for, say, a sculpture, it will not be an infringement of copyright to make a handbag from a copy of the design drawing for it, or from a handbag which one has purchased. In *Lucasfilm* (above) a Star Wars helmet was found not to be protected as a 'sculpture'. The defendant (who had made the original model and was selling replicas) had a defence under s.51. Instead, such designs are generally protected by design right or as registered designs (for both see below). Some cases fall into a gap between the two rights. UK design right does not protect 'surface decoration', but nor (because of s.51) does copyright protect elements of surface decoration if they are dictated by the shape of the article on which the decoration appears. The decision in *Lucasfilm* was recently affirmed by the Supreme Court. Hence, the design of stripes on a T-shirt was not protected either by copyright or by UK design right. However, such designs may well now be protected as Community designs. See *Lambretta* v. *Teddy Smith* [2005] RPC 6. Contrast *Flashing Badge* v. *Groves* [2007] FSR 36 which found no s.51 defence to infringement of the artistic works designed to decorate badges, where the artistic works could have been used in other ways.

Copying a film, broadcast or cable programme can include making a copy of the whole or a substantial part of any image from it (see s.17(4)). This means that copying one frame of the film will be an infringement. It is not an infringement of copyright in a film to reshoot the film (*Norowzian*) (though there would doubtless be an infringement of the copyright in underlying works such as the literary copyright in the screenplay).

Copying is generally proved by showing substantial similarities between the original and the alleged copy, plus an opportunity to copy. Surprisingly often, minor errors in the original are reproduced by an infringer.

Copying need not be direct, so that, for instance, where the copyright is in a fabric design, copying the material without ever having seen the original drawing will still be an infringement, as will 'reverse engineering' of industrial designs, for example to make unlicensed spare parts (*British Leyland* [1986] AC 577; *Mars* v. *Teknowledge* [2000] FSR 138).

Issuing copies of a work to the public (e.g. by putting them on sale) when they have not previously been put into circulation in the UK is also a primary infringement of all types of work.

Other acts which may amount to an infringement depend upon the nature of the work. It will be an infringement of the copyright in a literary, dramatic or musical work to perform it in public, whether by live performance or by playing recordings. Similarly, it is an infringement of the copyright in a sound recording, film, broadcast or cable programme to play or show it in public. Many copyright works will also be infringed by the rental or lending of copies of the work.

It is also an infringement to 'communicate' a work to the public, especially by making it available electronically, such as on the internet (s.20). See, for example, *Twentieth Century Fox* v. *Newzbin* [2010] EWHC 608 (infringement by facilitating illegal downloading). The Digital Economy Act 2010 is designed to control online infringement of copyright (especially in music, films and games) by imposing duties on ISPs, with an industry code to be approved or made by Ofcom.

It is also possible to infringe by making an adaptation of a literary, dramatic or musical work. An adaptation includes, in the case of a literary work, a translation, in the case of a non-dramatic work, making a dramatic work of it, and vice versa. A transcription or arrangement of a musical work is an adaptation of it.

There are also a number of 'secondary' (but nonetheless very common and commercially important) infringements – see box.

It is also an infringement to authorise another person to commit any act of primary infringement.

As copyright law is territorial, it is only an infringement of UK copyright to carry out the prescribed acts in the UK, save that it is possible to infringe by authorising an infringement in the UK even where the act of authorisation takes place abroad. This is a tricky issue in terms of where there is communication to the public (i.e. electronically) from an off-shore server: see *Football Dataco Ltd* v. *Sportradar GmbH* [2011] EWCA 330, 29 March 2011 in which the Court of Appeal referred this question to the CJEU.

Exceptions to infringement

The Act provides a large number of exceptions to the rules on infringement. They are far too numerous to be dealt with here in full, but they include:

- fair dealing with literary, dramatic, musical or artistic works for the purpose of non-commercial research or private study (s.29). See e.g. *HMSO* v. *Green Amps Limited* [2007] EWHC 2755;
- fair dealing for the purpose of criticism or review or reporting current events, as to which see e.g. *Pro Sieben Media* [1999] FSR 610; *Hyde Park* v. *Yelland* [2001] Ch. 143; *NLA* v. *Marks & Spencer Plc* [2002] RPC 4 (s.30);

'Secondary' infringements

Secondary infringements consist not of making infringing copies, but of dealing with existing infringing copies in some way. It is an infringement to import an infringing copy into the UK, and to possess in the course of business, or to sell, hire, offer for sale or hire, or distribute in the course of trade an infringing copy. However, none of these acts will be an infringement unless the alleged infringer knew or had reason to believe that the articles were infringing copies. What is sufficient knowledge will depend upon the facts of each case (see *LA Gear Inc.* [1992] FSR 121, *ZYX Records* v. *King* [1997] 2 All ER 132 and *Pensher Security* [2000] RPC 249). Merely putting someone on notice of a dispute as to ownership of copyright may not suffice to give him or her reason to believe in infringement for this purpose. But someone who is informed that he is infringing 'yet carries out no sensible enquiries, and does nothing in the face of continued assertions of the copyright' may become someone with 'reason to believe' the claim: *Nouveau Fabrics* v. *Voyage Decoration* [2004] EWHC 895; *Hutchison* [1995] FSR 365.

Other secondary infringements consist of permitting a place to be used for a public performance in which copyright is infringed and supplying apparatus to be used for infringing public performance, again, in each case, with safeguards for innocent acts.

• incidental inclusion of a work in an artistic work, sound recording, film, broadcast or cable programme (s.31);
• educational exceptions (ss.32–36A);
• exceptions for libraries (ss.37–44A) and public administration (ss.45–50);
• making transient copies as part of a technological process (s.28A) and backing-up, or converting a computer program or accessing a licensed database (s.50A–D);
• dealing with a work where the author cannot be identified and the work seems likely to be out of copyright (s.57).

The effect of the Human Rights Act on copyright in relation to the right to free speech seems likely to be limited, as sufficient protection is to be found in the fair dealing provisions: *Ashdown* v. *Telegraph Group Limited* [2002] Ch. 149.

There is no defence of parody, though the recent Hargreaves Review has called for a review of the defences to copyright and suggested that a parody defence be included.

Remedies for infringements

The copyright owner will usually want to prevent the repetition or continuation of the infringement and will want compensation.

In almost all cases an injunction will be sought to stop the infringement. The Courts have useful powers to grant an injunction at an early stage, even before any infringement takes place, if a real threat of damage can be shown. Such an interim injunction can be applied for on three days' notice (or without notice in appropriate cases), but will not be granted unless the claimant has a reasonably good case and can show that he would suffer 'unquantifiable' damage if the defendant's activities continued pending trial. Delay in bringing an interim application may be fatal to its success. An injunction may not be granted where the claimant clearly only wants financial compensation (*Ludlow Music*).

Financial compensation may be sought in one of two forms. First, damages. These will usually be calculated upon evidence of the loss caused to the claimant, sometimes based upon loss of business, or upon the basis of what would have been a proper licence fee for the defendant's acts. Additional damages may be awarded in rare cases for flagrant infringements, and can be substantial. See for example *Notts. Healthcare* v. *News Group Newspapers* [2002] RPC 49.

Damages will not be awarded for infringement where the infringer did not know, and had no reason to believe, that copyright subsisted in the work. This exception is of limited use to a defendant, though, in the usual situation where the work was of such a nature that he should have known that copyright would subsist in it.

The alternative to damages is an account of profits, that is, the net profits made by the infringer by virtue of his illicit exploitation of the copyright. Where an account of profits is sought, no award of flagrant damages can be made; see *Redrow Homes Limited* [1999] 1 AC 197. But there may now be an overlap between damages and profits, by reason of Article 13 of the Enforcement Directive, 2004/48.

A copyright owner may also apply for delivery up of infringing copies.

Finally, there are various criminal offences relating to the making, importation, possession, sale, hire, distribution, etc of infringing copies. The criminal sanctions are most commonly sought in piracy and counterfeiting cases, though technically they could be used in more standard actions.

UK design right

Many designs are excluded from copyright protection by s.51 (see above). Section 52 of the Act may also limit the term of copyright protection given to certain types of artistic works, if they are applied industrially, to 25 years from first industrial application. Such artistic works may instead be protected by the UK unregistered 'design right' created by ss.213–64 of the Act or by Community design right. Like copyright, design right depends upon the creation of a suitable design by a 'qualifying person'.

UK unregistered design right is granted to original designs consisting of the shape or configuration (internal or external) of the whole or part of an article, not being merely 'surface decoration'. Even very simple designs may be protected. However, a design is not original if it was commonplace in the design field in question at the time of its creation, meaning a design of a type which would excite no 'peculiar attention' amongst those in the trade, or one which amounts to a run-of-the-mill combination of well-known features (*Farmers Build* [1999] RPC 461). Designs are not protected if they consist of a method or principle of construction, or are dictated by the shape, etc of an article to which the new article is to be connected or of which it is to form part, the so-called 'must-fit' and 'must-match' exclusions. In *Ocular Sciences* [1997] RPC 289, these exclusions had a devastating effect upon design rights claimed for contact lens designs. See also *Dyson* v. *Qualtex* [2006] RPC 31 in which these exclusions were applied to spare parts for Dyson vacuum cleaners.

UK design right subsists in designs made by or for qualifying persons (see, broadly, 'Qualification', above) or first marketed in the UK or EU or any other country to which the provision may be extended by Order.

UK design right lasts only 15 years from the end of the year in which it was first recorded or an article made to the design, or (if shorter) ten years from the end of the year in which articles made according to the design were first sold or hired out. During the last five years of the term of protection, a licence to use the design can be obtained 'as of right' on payment of a proper licence fee. Hence, design right may give only five years 'absolute' protection, as opposed to the 'life plus 70' of copyright.

The designer will be the owner of the right, unless it was commissioned, in which case the commissioner will be the first owner. An employee's designs made in the course of employment will belong to the employer. The right given to the owner of a design right is the exclusive right to reproduce the design for commercial purposes. The rules as to assignments, licensing and infringement, both primary and secondary, are substantially similar to those described above in relation to copyright, as are the remedies available.

The law on UK registered designs coexists with the right given by the unregistered UK design right discussed above. The Registered Design Act 1949 has been amended (and expanded) in line with EU legislation, and permits the registration of designs consisting of the appearance of the whole or any part of a product resulting from features of the product itself, such as shape, materials, etc or from the ornamentation of the product. It covers industrial or handicraft items, their packaging or get-up, etc. Designs must be novel and not solely dictated by function. The range of designs which may be registered is wider than under the old law, and designs need not necessarily have 'eye appeal'. Such designs provide a monopoly right renewable for up to 25 years. For further explanation see the guidance on the Patent Office website.

Community designs

In addition to UK design right and registered designs, EU Regulation 6/2002 created two Community design regimes, one for registered and one for unregistered designs. It is increasingly common for designers to rely on Community design right, especially where there are problems in relying on UK design right, for example where a surface decoration, pattern or colouring is central to the design. Artists and industrial designers may wish to consider registering their designs, whilst infringements should now generally be considered under both the UK and Community design right regimes.

It is not possible in the space available here to describe these new regimes in detail but the Regulation is available online (www.europa.ue.int/eur-lex). In brief, Community designs are *very* broadly defined in Article 3 and can include the outward appearance of a product or part of it, shape, texture, materials and/or its ornamentation. 'Products' include any industrial or handicraft item, packaging, graphic symbols and typographic typefaces but not computer programs. Huge numbers of designs have been registered, especially for furniture and for packaging; see *Procter & Gamble* v. *Reckitt Benckiser* [2008] FSR 8 about the design of an air-freshener spray can. However, the designs must be 'new' and have 'individual character'. This means that the 'overall impression' the design has on an 'informed user' (someone who is familiar with the existing designs in the field) is different from that of prior designs. The registered right lasts up to 25 years in five-year tranches, but an unregistered Community design right lasts only three years. The unregistered right protects the design from copying, but the registered right gives 'absolute' exclusivity, in that it may be infringed without copying. This benefit, when the registration process is relatively cheap and quick, doubtless explains why some quarter of a million Community designs have already been registered.

The breadth of protection for unregistered designs has also been of huge benefit; numerous UK infringement actions have been based on unregistered Community design right.

Moral rights

The Act also provides for the protection of certain 'moral rights'.

The right of 'paternity' is for the author of a copyright literary, dramatic, musical or artistic work, or the director of a copyright film, to be identified as the author/director, largely whenever the work is commercially exploited (s.77). See *Sawkins.*

However, the right does not arise unless it has been 'asserted' by appropriate words in writing (see end), or in the case of an artistic work by ensuring that the artist's name appears on the frame, etc. There are exceptions to the right, in particular where first ownership of the copyright vested in the author's or director's employer.

The right of 'integrity' protects work from 'derogatory treatment', meaning an addition to, deletion from, alteration or adaptation of a work which amounts to distortion or mutilation of the work or is otherwise prejudicial to the honour or reputation of the author/director. Again, infringement of the right takes place when the maltreated work is published commercially or performed or exhibited in public. There are various exceptions set out in s.81 of the Act, in particular where the publication is in a newspaper, etc and the work was made for inclusion in it or made available with the author's consent.

Where the copyright in the work vested first in the author's or director's employer, he or she has no right to 'integrity' unless identified at the time of the relevant act or on published copies of the work.

These rights subsist for as long as the copyright in the work subsists.

A third moral right conferred by the Act is not to have a literary, dramatic, musical or artistic work falsely attributed to one as author, or to have a film falsely attributed to one as director, again where the work in question is published, etc. This right subsists until 20 years after a person's death.

None of these rights can be assigned during the person's lifetime, but all of them either pass on the person's death as directed by his or her will or fall into his residuary estate.

A fourth but rather different moral right is conferred by s.85. It gives a person who has commissioned the taking of photographs for private purposes a right to prevent copies of the work being issued to the public, etc.

The remedies for breach of these moral rights again include damages and an injunction, although s.103(2) specifically foresees the granting of an injunction qualified by a right to the defendant to do the acts complained of, if subject to a suitable disclaimer.

Moral rights are exercisable in relation to works in which the copyright has revived subject to any waiver or assertion of the right made before 1 January 1996 (see details as to who may exercise rights in paragraph 22 of the Regulations).

NOTICE
AMANDA LOUISE MICHAELS hereby asserts and gives notice of her right under s.77 of the Copyright, Designs & Patents Act 1988 to be identified as the author of the foregoing article.
AMANDA MICHAELS

Amanda L. Michaels is a barrister in private practice in London, and specialises in copyright, designs, trade marks, and similar intellectual property and 'media' work. She is author of *A Practical Approach to Trade Mark Law* (OUP, 4th edn, 2010) and is a Civil Recorder and an Appointed Person under the Trade Marks Act 1994, hearing appeals from decisions of the UK Registrar of Trade Marks. **Jonathan Moss** is a barrister in private practice in London, and specialises in patents, copyright, designs, trade marks, and similar intellectual property and 'media' work. He is also a qualified US lawyer, being a member of the New York State Bar.

Further reading

Cornish, William, *Intellectual Property: Patents, Copyrights, Trademarks & Allied Rights* (Sweet & Maxwell, 2010)

Bently, Lionel and Sherman, Brad, *Intellectual Property Law*, OUP, 2008

Garnett, Rayner James and Davies, *Copinger and Skone James on Copyright*, Sweet & Maxwell, 16th edn, 2010

Copyright Acts

Copyright, Designs and Patents Act 1998 (but it is vital to use an up-to-date amended version). See www.ipo.gov.uk

The Duration of Copyright and Rights in Performances Regulations 1995 (SI 1995 No 3297)

The Copyright and Rights in Databases Regulations 1997 (SI 1997/3032) amended by the Copyright and Rights in Databases (Amendment) Regulations 2003 (SI 2003/2501)

The Copyright and Related Rights Regulations 2003 (SI 2003 No 2498)

The Intellectual Property (Enforcement, etc) Regulations 2006 (SI 2006 No 1028)

The Performances (Moral Rights, etc) Regulations 2006 (SI 2006 No 18)

see also Numerous Orders in Council

Council Regulation 6/2002

Directive 2006/116/EC (codifying provisions)

See also...

- *Copyright questions*, page 639

The Copyright Licensing Agency Ltd

The Copyright Licensing Agency (CLA) licenses organisations to copy extracts from copyright publications on behalf of the authors, publishers and visual creators it represents.

CLA's licences permit limited copying from print and digital publications. This copying includes photocopying, scanning and emailing of articles and extracts from books, journals and magazines, as well as digital copying from electronic publications, online titles and websites. CLA issues its licences to schools, further and higher education, businesses and government bodies. The money collected is distributed to the copyright owners to ensure that they are fairly rewarded for the use of their intellectual property.

Why was CLA established?

CLA was set up by its owners, the Authors' Licensing and Collecting Society (ALCS) and the Publishers Licensing Society (PLS) and has an agency agreement with the Design and Artists Copyright Society (DACS), which represents visual artists, such as photographers, illustrators and painters.

Further information

The Copyright Licensing Agency Ltd
Saffron House, 6–10 Kirby Street,
London EC1N 8TS
tel 020-7400 3100 *fax* 020-7400 3101
email cla@cla.co.uk
website www.cla.co.uk

CLA represents creators and publishers by licensing the copying of their work and promoting the role and value of copyright generally. By championing copyright it is helping to sustain creativity and maintain the incentive to produce new work.

How CLA helps creators and users of copyright work

CLA allows licensed users access to millions of titles worldwide. In return, CLA ensures that creators, artists, photographers and writers, along with publishers, are fairly recompensed by the payment of royalties derived from the licence fees which CLA collects and distributes.

Through this collective licensing system CLA is able to provide users with the simplest and most cost-effective means of obtaining authorisation for photocopying and scanning of published works, albeit under strict copy limits.

CLA has licences which enable digitisation of existing print material, enabling users to scan and electronically send extracts from print copyright works.

CLA has more recently launched a series of new licences for business and government which allow users to reuse and copy from digital electronic and online publications, including websites. Writers and publishers can benefit further from the increased income generated from these enhanced licences which operate under the same copy limits as the established photocopying licences.

Who is licensed?

CLA's licences are available to three principal sectors:

- education (schools, further and higher education);
- government (central departments, local authorities, public bodies); and
- business (businesses, industry and the professions).

CLA offers licences to meet the specific needs of each sector and user groups within each sector. Depending on the requirement, there are both blanket and transactional licences available. Every licence allows copying from most books, journals, magazines and periodicals published in the UK. Most licences include digital copying permissions granted by copyright owners on an opt-in basis.

International dimension

Many countries have established equivalents to CLA and the number of such agencies is set to grow. Nearly all these agencies, including CLA, are members of the International Federation of Reproduction Rights Organisations (IFRRO).

Through reciprocal arrangements covering more than 30 overseas territories including the USA, Canada and most EU countries, CLA's licences allow copying from an expanding list of international publications. CLA receives monies from these territories for the copying of UK material abroad, passing it on to UK rightsholders.

Distribution of licence fees

The fees collected from licensees are forwarded to PLS, ALCS and DACS for distribution to publishers, writers and visual artists respectively. The allocation of fees is based on subscriptions, library holdings and detailed surveys of copying activity. CLA has collected and distributed to rightsholders over £700 million since 1983. For the year 2010/11, £66 million was paid to creators and publishers in the UK and abroad.

Enabling access, protecting creativity

CLA believes it is important to raise awareness of copyright and the need to protect the creativity of artists, authors and publishers. To this end, it organises a range of activities such as copyright workshops in schools, seminars for businesses and institutions and an extensive programme of exhibitions and other events.

CLA believes in working positively together with representative bodies in each sector, meaning legal action is rare. However, organisations – especially in the business sector – are made aware that copyright is a legally enforceable right and not a voluntary option. CLA's compliance arm, Copywatch (www.copywatch.org), is active in these sectors to educate users and seek out illegal copying.

By supporting rightsholders in this way, CLA plays an important role in maintaining the value of their work, thereby sustaining creativity and its benefit to all. Through protection of this sort the creative industries in the UK have been able to grow to support millions of jobs and contribute 6.4% of GVA to the economy.

See also...

- *Authors' Licensing and Collecting Society*, page 660
- *Design and Artists Copyright Society*, page 662

Authors' Licensing and Collecting Society

The Authors' Licensing and Collecting Society is the rights management society for UK writers.

The Authors' Licensing and Collecting Society (ALCS) is the UK collective rights management society for writers. Established in 1977, it represents the interests of all UK writers and aims to ensure that they are fairly compensated for any works that are copied, broadcast or recorded.

A non-profit company, ALCS was set up in the wake of the campaign to establish a Public Lending Right to help writers protect and exploit their collective rights. Today, it is the largest writers' organisation in the UK with a membership of approximately 85,000. In the financial year of 2011/12, £28.1 million (gross) in royalties were paid out to writers.

ALCS is committed to ensuring that the rights of writers, both intellectual property and moral, are fully respected and fairly rewarded. It represents all types of writers and includes educational, research and academic authors drawn from the professions: scriptwriters, adaptors, playwrights, poets, editors and freelance journalists, across the print and broadcast media.

Internationally recognised as a leading authority on copyright matters and authors' interests, ALCS is committed to fostering an awareness of intellectual property issues among the writing community. It maintains a close watching brief on all matters affecting copyright both in the UK and internationally and makes regular representations to the UK government and the European Union.

ALCS collects fees that are difficult, time-consuming or legally impossible for writers and their representatives to claim on an individual basis, money that is nonetheless due to them. To date, it has distributed over £280 million in secondary royalties to writers. Over the years, ALCS has developed highly specialised knowledge and sophisticated systems that can track writers and their works against any secondary use for which they are due payment. A network of international contacts and reciprocal agreements with foreign collecting societies also ensures that British writers are compensated for any similar use overseas.

The primary sources of fees due to writers are secondary royalties from the following.

Membership

Authors' Licensing and Collecting Society Ltd
The Writers' House, 13 Haydon Street,
London EC3N 1DB
tel 020-7264 5700 *fax* 020-7264 5755
email alcs@alcs.co.uk
website www.alcs.co.uk
Chief Executive Owen Atkinson

Membership is open to all writers and successors to their estates at a one-off fee of £25 for Ordinary membership. Members of the Society of Authors and the Writers' Guild of Great Britain have free Ordinary membership of ALCS. Operations are primarily funded through a commission levied on distributions and membership fees. The commission on funds generated for Ordinary members is currently 9.75%. Most writers will find that this, together with a number of other membership benefits, provides good value.

Photocopying

The single largest source of income, this is administered by the Copyright Licensing Agency (CLA, see page 658). Created in 1982 by ALCS and the Publishers Licensing Society (PLS),

CLA grants licences to users for copying books and serials. This includes schools, colleges, universities, central and local government departments as well as the British Library, businesses and other institutions. Licence fees are based on the number of people who benefit and the number of copies made. The revenue from this is then split between the rightsholders: authors, publishers and artists. Money due to authors is transferred to ALCS for distribution. ALCS also receives photocopying payments from foreign sources.

Digitisation

In 1999, CLA launched its licensing scheme for the digitisation of printed texts. It offers licences to organisations for storing and using digital versions of authors' printed works that have been scanned into a computer. Again, the fees are split between authors and publishers.

Foreign Public Lending Right

The Public Lending Right (PLR) system pays authors whose books are borrowed from public libraries. Through reciprocal agreements ALCS members receive payment whenever their books are borrowed from German, Belgian, Dutch, French, Austrian, Spanish and Irish libraries. Please note that ALCS does not administer the UK Public Lending Right, this is managed directly by the UK PLR Office; see page 324.

ALCS also receives other payments from Germany. These cover the loan of academic, scientific and technical titles from academic libraries; extracts of authors' works in textbooks and the press, together with other one-off fees.

Simultaneous cable retransmission

This involves the simultaneous showing of one country's television signals in another country, via a cable network. Cable companies pay a central collecting organisation a percentage of their subscription fees, which must be collectively administered. This sum is then divided by the rightsholders. ALCS receives the writers' share for British programmes containing literary and dramatic material and distributes it to them.

Educational recording

ALCS, together with the main broadcasters and rightsholders, set up theEducational Recording Agency (ERA) in 1989 to offer licences to educational establishments. ERA collects fees from the licensees and pays ALCS the amount due to writers for their literary works.

Other sources of income include a blank tape levy and small, miscellaneous literary rights.

Tracing authors

ALCS is dedicated to protecting and promoting authors' rights and enabling writers to maximise their income. It is committed to ensuring that royalties due to writers are efficiently collected and speedily distributed to them. One of its greatest challenges is finding some of the writers for whom it holds funds and ensuring that they claim their money.

Any published author or broadcast writer could have some funds held by ALCS for them. It may be a nominal sum or it could run into several thousand pounds. Either call or visit the ALCS website – see box for contact details.

Design and Artists Copyright Society

Established by artists for artists, the Design and Artists Copyright Society (DACS) is the UK's leading visual arts rights management organisation.

As a not-for-profit organisation, DACS translates rights into revenues and recognition for a wide spectrum of visual artists. It offers three rights management services – Payback, Artist's Resale Right and Copyright Licensing – in addition to lobbying, advocacy and legal advice for visual artists.

Contact details

Design and Artists Copyright Society (DACS)
33 Great Sutton Street, London EC1V 0DX
tel 020-7336 8811 *fax* 020-7336 8822
email info@dacs.org.uk
website www.dacs.org.uk

DACS is part of an international network of rights management organisations. Today DACS represents nearly 70,000 artists and in 2011 it distributed over £8 million to artists and their beneficiaries. See website for more information about DACS and its services.

Payback

Each year DACS pays a share of royalties to visual artists whose work has been reproduced in UK magazines and books or broadcast on UK television channels. DACS operates this service for situations where it would be impractical or near impossible for rights to be licensed on an individual basis, for example when a university wants to photocopy pages from a book that features your work. Every kind of visual artist can claim Payback.

Artist's Resale Right

The Artist's Resale Right entitles artists to a royalty each time their work is resold by an auction house, gallery or dealer subject to certain conditions. Visual artists who benefit from this service include fine artists, bookbinders, photographers, sculptors, furniture designers and ceramicists to name but a few. See website for details of eligibility criteria. DACS ensures artists receive their royalties from qualifying sales not just in the UK but also internationally through our network of rights management organisations. The Right is capped at €12,500 to protect the art market. Since 1 January 2012 in the UK, artists' heirs and beneficiaries can now benefit from these royalties.

Copyright Licensing service

For artists to manage their copyright it can be a complex and time-consuming process. However, DACS' Copyright Licensing service provides an effective way for artists to manage the licensing of their rights, by ensuring terms, fees and contractual arrangements are all in order and in their best interests. Copyright licensing benefits artists and their estates when their work is reproduced for commercial purposes, for example on t-shirts or greetings cards, in a book or on a website. DACS provides advice and support if an artist's work is used without their permission. Artists who use this service are also represented globally through our international network of rights management organisations.

Copyright facts

- Copyright is a right granted to visual artists under law.
- Copyright in all artistic works is established from the moment of creation – the only qualification is that the work must be original.

• There is no registration system in the UK; copyright comes into operation automatically and lasts the lifetime of the visual artist plus a period of 70 years after their death.
• After death, copyright is usually transferred to the visual artist's heirs or beneficiaries. When the 70-year period has expired, the work then enters the public domain and no longer benefits from copyright protection.
• The copyright owner has the exclusive right to authorise the reproduction (or copy) of a work in any medium by any other party.
• Any reproduction can only take place with the copyright owner's consent.
• Permission is usually granted in return for a fee, which enables the visual artist to derive some income from other people using his or her work.
• If a visual artist is commissioned to produce a work, he or she will usually retain the copyright unless an agreement is signed which specifically assigns the copyright. When visual creators are employees and create work during the course of their employment, the employer retains the copyright in those works.

See also...

• *Freelancing for beginners*, page 467
• *The Copyright Licensing Agency Ltd*, page 658

The laws of Privacy and Confidentiality

Privacy is a developing area of law and in a short article it is not possible to do justice to its many complexities or to identify all the instances where it may apply. In this article Keith Schilling guides writers and artists through the main principles of English law to assist him or her in gauging when specialist legal advice may be required.

Privacy and confidentiality issues may affect writers and artists (hereinafter 'the Writer') in a number of different ways, namely:

• **The Writer as a publisher.** In law a writer is also regarded as a publisher because he causes his work to be published. When writing/publishing an article, a press release, a work of non-fiction (and even a work of fiction), or a blog, the Writer needs to take care to ensure that the privacy rights of others are not infringed. Generally, the privacy rights of others are *engaged* when they have *a reasonable expectation of privacy in respect of the information in question*. This could include information disclosed orally or overheard, or contained in correspondence, journals, telephone calls or emails, or posted on social networking sites, if it concerns medical and family details, financial issues, sexual preferences or orientation or other information of a private nature. This potential liability is of particular importance in the field of book publishing (and the making of television programmes and films) since the Writer will generally give a warranty to the book publisher (or producer of the television programme or film) that nothing contained in the work will infringe the privacy or confidentiality rights of any third person and, if it does, the Writer agrees to fully indemnify the publisher. Often a book publisher will take out insurance and may carry out pre-publication checks but the insurance will not usually benefit the Writer and, if the pre-publication checks are inadequate or fail to identify a particular risk, it may be the Writer who has to make full restitution for all claims. The extent of his liability may go far beyond any financial benefit he is due to receive from the publication of his work. Due to Privacy law being a relatively recent development in English law, its importance is not always appreciated, particularly in the pre-publication process.

• **The Writer as public figure or celebrity.** The private life of a successful Writer may be of great interest to the public. This may result in the unwanted publication of details of the Writer's private life, as well as of the private life of members of his or her family. This can occur when, for example, the Writer is photographed surreptitiously whilst engaged in private activities such as sunbathing on holiday, or when on a family outing. Phone messages can be illicitly intercepted (as occurred on an industrial scale by the now defunct *News of the World)*, or their computers, social networking sites or email accounts can be accessed. The Writer may therefore wish to take steps to prevent the publication of private information about himself or his family. This could include managing his or her digital (online) reputation by removing, where appropriate and practicable, private information available on the internet, checking the privacy settings of social networking sites used by her and her family or, in a more extreme case, by taking legal action to have private information taken down from the internet, before it is widely published.

• **The Writer as the originator of confidential ideas (or, conversely the Writer as the recipient of such ideas from another writer).** The law of confidentiality may be invoked by the Writer where he or she submits an original idea, in confidence, for the consideration of a third party (perhaps a potential partner or television production company) and that other person decides to use those ideas without the consent of the Writer. This is a form of plagiarism but it is not a copyright infringement since it is said 'there is no copyright in ideas'. However, there may be confidentiality in ideas provided that certain conditions are met. Where a protectable idea has been stolen, the Writer may have been deprived not only of the fee that he or she might have received for their work but any repeat fees, any buy-out fees and, importantly, the loss of opportunity to enhance their reputation through the commercial exploitation of their idea.

In each of the above three instances there is a tension, or conflict, between freedom of speech and rights of privacy or confidentiality. This article therefore outlines some of the principles which are applied to resolving those conflicts.

The law of Privacy

Article 8 of the European Convention on Human Rights was incorporated into English law by the Human Rights Act 1998 and states: 'Everyone has the right to respect for his private and family life, his home, and his correspondence'.

The case of *Naomi Campbell* v. *The Mirror* in 2004 established our modern law of privacy. The *Mirror* had published a series of photographs and an accompanying article which revealed that Campbell was attending a drug addiction support group, a fact which she had publicly denied.

The newspaper unsuccessfully argued that (1) the publication was in the public interest to expose her (false) denials of drug use, and (2) the photographs had been taken on a public street and, therefore, were not private.

Campbell accepted that the newspaper was entitled to publish the fact that she was receiving treatment for her addiction. She argued that publishing *details* of the treatment she was receiving, including how often she attended meetings of the group, was unnecessary and went too far. Publication of photographs of her leaving the treatment centre were objectionable as they might inhibit her future attendance, and others as well, and it was in the public interest that people should be able to attend unhindered.

The Court held that on these facts the publication by the *Mirror* had been in breach of Naomi Campbell's rights of privacy and she was awarded damages and an injunction.

Photographs

As the *Campbell* case shows, the courts regard photographs, and long lens photography, as particularly intrusive. A picture 'tells a thousand words' and can provide a degree of intrusive detail which a mere description cannot.

As such, where photographs are concerned, the courts are generally willing to afford claimants a higher degree of protection in the information depicted. However, photographs can be a very powerful medium to impart information and present a story. Whilst photographs published pursuant to a genuine 'public interest' (which does not mean 'what is of interest to the public') will undoubtedly be hard to challenge, photographs depicting, say, sexual relationships or activity intended to titillate, or private family activities, will be harder to justify.

Children and privacy

Children have a right to privacy which is distinct from that of their parents, even where a parent is a world-famous celebrity (and writer). In 2008, Harry Potter author J.K. Rowling and her husband brought proceedings on behalf of their 19-month-old son against a paparazzi agency which was responsible for the publication of a picture of their son in his pram which was taken as she was walking to a café near her home. The photographs had been taken by a long lens camera and were published in a national newspaper. The court held that the child had a reasonable expectation of privacy and the law should protect children from unwarranted and unjustifiable media intrusion.

Free speech

Where there is a strong public interest in publication, then the publisher's right to freedom of expression (protected by Article 10 of the European Convention on Human Rights) *may* outweigh rights to privacy. In such cases, where privacy and freedom of expression rights are in conflict, the court must carry out a careful balancing act to decide which right should prevail, on those particular facts. There is no exhaustive list of what is or is not 'in the public interest'. It is possible to conclude, however, that some things possess a higher level of public interest than others, for example the reporting of a crime, political conduct and integrity, matters of national health and security, and matters of general public concern. Those who feel that there is a public interest in knowing about medical procedures undergone by an actress or intimate details of the sex lives of celebrities may have an uphill task in persuading a court that publication of this information is in the public interest.

Damages and injunctions

If a claim in privacy is made out at trial a claimant may be entitled to damages and legal costs. In 2008, Max Mosley was awarded £60,000 damages for invasion of his privacy – the highest award made to date – against the *News of the World* for publishing details of his sexual preferences (including a video on their website which was accessed over one million times).

However, most claimants will want to prevent the publication of the information in the first place, rather than recover damages after the event, and may therefore apply for an interlocutory (i.e. interim) injunction restraining publication. Such an injunction may prevent an article being published or could prevent a book, television programme or film being published and distributed in that form.

Key points

The relevant questions to ask in such cases are usually the following (bearing in mind that in the event of a dispute it will be for the court to answer them definitively):

- Is there a reasonable expectation of privacy in the relevant information?
- Does the privacy right outweigh other countervailing rights – in particular the right of free speech?

Before publication the Writer may wish to ask himself the following questions:

- Has the information in question already been published and, if so, to what extent? If it has been widely published it may no longer be entitled to protection.
- Has the person spoken openly about the particular information or otherwise consented to its publication?
- Are sensitive photographs involved and/or were they taken in inappropriate circumstances?
- Are the privacy rights of children or other private family members engaged?
- Is there an overwhelming public interest in the publication of this particular material?

The law of Confidentiality

Whilst the law of Privacy is apposite to protect private information, the law of Confidentiality may protect confidential ideas. In (Donald) *Fraser and Others* v. *Thames Television* in 1983, the claimants devised an idea for a television series and conveyed this idea orally to producers at Thames. Thames subsequently broadcast an award-winning series, called *Rock Follies*, based upon that idea. The court found that to be protectable such an idea must be:

• *Clearly identifiable*, in other words not too vague
• *Original*, i.e. not in the public domain
• *Of potential commercial attractiveness*
• *Capable of being realised in actuality* (These last two conditions were established by Thames broadcasting a series based upon the idea.)
• *Communicated in confidence* to the defendant.

This law may also protect, in appropriate circumstances, unpublished television formats which are often not protectable in copyright.

Key points

If you are submitting an idea for a novel, a television programme or format or a film, or a business idea, it is recommended that you:

• Reduce it into writing, and keep a copy in a safe place and/or with a trusted third party to establish the date by which it was created
• Do not overexpose the idea by sending it out too widely as it could then be said it is no longer confidential
• Prominently mark the document and any covering letter with the word 'Confidential'.

If you have *received* an idea which may be confidential, consider carefully whether you are entitled to use it.

Keith Schilling is Senior Partner of Schillings, a business specialising in the protection of privacy and reputations (www.schillings.co.uk). He successfully represented Naomi Campbell, J.K. Rowling and Donald Fraser in the cases cited in the text.

See also...

• *Copyright questions*, page 639
• *UK copyright law*, page 643
• *Defamation*, page 668

Defamation

The law of defamation affects writers in particular, but also artists and others involved in the creative industries. In this article, Alex de Jongh summarises its main principles. However, specific legal advice should be taken when practical problems arise – or better still, prior to publication, if problems are anticipated. The law discussed is that of England and Wales. Scottish law is similar, but there are a number of differences between the two systems and these are briefly described.

1. Introduction

Defamation is a tort (a civil wrong). Its purpose is to vindicate an injured party's reputation. Where the claimant is an individual, his or her reputation may be part of their right (under Article 8 of the European Convention on Human Rights, ECHR) to respect for their private and family life. The law seeks to balance that right against the competing right to freedom of expression under Article 10 of the ECHR.

Publication of a defamatory allegation can result in a civil claim for damages and/or an injunction to prevent repetition. Libel is no longer actionable under the criminal law.

There are two categories of defamation: libel and slander. A defamatory statement in permanent form is *libel*; where the form is transient, it is *slander*. 'Permanent form' includes writing, printing, drawings and photographs, radio and television broadcasts, film and tape recordings, and theatrical performances. Publications on the internet or in other electronic form will generally fall into the category of libel. Slander tends to be spoken, and claims are comparatively rare. Thus libel is more likely than slander to concern writers and artists professionally, and the slightly differing rules applicable to slander are not covered here.

Claims for libel almost invariably relate to the published word, but can be brought in respect of any other matter which conveys meaning, such as paintings or photographs. A colourful and often cited example is an 1894 claim against Madame Tussaud's, arising out of the positioning of a waxwork of the claimant adjacent to the entrance of the Chamber of Horrors (the claimant successfully argued that this amounted, by innuendo, to an allegation that he was guilty of murder, but recovered damages of only one farthing).

Libel claims can be tried by a judge or jury, but there has been a recent trend in favour of trial by judge alone and new draft legislation (see below) would, if enacted, remove the presumption that trial will be by jury.

Law reform?

Defamation law and procedure in England and Wales has long been criticised as being open to abuse by powerful interests, which many view as creating a 'chilling effect' on freedom of speech. Particular concern has arisen in relation to coverage of scientific and academic debate. At the 2010 general election all three main parties pledged to reform the libel laws in the new Parliament, and in 2011 the coalition government published a new draft Defamation Bill. A joint parliamentary committee reported on the Bill in October 2011 and the government published its reply in February 2012, but it remains unclear whether, and if so when and what form, legislation will be enacted. Some of the main proposals in the Bill are discussed below.

2. The ingredients of a claim: what does the Claimant need to prove?

The claimant must prove that the statement about which s/he complains:

- is defamatory;

- refers to him or her (or is capable of being understood as referring to him or her); and
- has been published by the defendant to a third party.

Each of these requirements is discussed in greater detail below. If the claimant can establish all three elements, s/he has a *prima facie* case, and the burden shifts to the defendant. The defendant will escape liability if s/he can show that s/he has a good defence.

2.1. What is defamatory?

Before it is possible to decide whether a statement is defamatory, it is necessary to determine what it means. The meaning decided by a court will not necessarily be the same as the meaning intended by the publisher: intention is irrelevant.

The law will treat a given statement as having only one 'natural and ordinary' meaning, i.e. the meaning that an ordinary reasonable person would understand from it. This 'single meaning rule' is not, of course, reflective of the reality that a statement may be open to more than one equally valid interpretation. The natural and ordinary meaning will not necessarily be the literal meaning: the law recognises that the ordinary reader is not naive and will be able to detect (for example) a degree of sarcasm, irony or insinuation.

A statement may also have an 'innuendo meaning' (which can coexist with the natural and ordinary meaning). In the legal sense, this is not a simple insinuation which could be understood by anyone reading between the lines based on matters of general knowledge, but a meaning which will only be apparent to individuals with particular knowledge. The words may appear quite innocent but acquire a defamatory meaning when read by a person in possession of this special knowledge. For example, to state that a person has been seen entering a particular house would be an innocuous statement to some readers, but not to those who knew the address to be a brothel or a crack house.

Meaning is derived from a reading of the publication as a whole, so if a damaging allegation is made in one part but corrected with sufficient prominence in another (so called 'bane and antidote') the overall meaning will not be defamatory.

Having established their meaning, the claimant must show that the words complained of are defamatory. There is no single definition of 'defamatory', but various tests have been established and it is sufficient that any one of these is satisfied. A statement is defamatory if it would tend to:

- lower the subject in the estimation of reasonable or right-thinking members of society;
- bring the subject into ridicule, hatred or contempt with society;
- make the subject shunned, avoided or cut off from society.

The first of these definitions is most commonly encountered in practice, but the others cannot be ignored. For example, it may seem surprising that a statement that an individual was 'hideous-looking' could be held to be defamatory, but that was the outcome of a 1997 case, on the grounds that the statement exposed the claimant to ridicule (however, mere 'vulgar abuse' will not be regarded as defamatory; it is a fine dividing line). Similarly, an allegation that an individual is seriously ill or mentally unstable may imply no fault on the part of the claimant, but would be likely to cause them to be shunned or avoided.

A statement may be inaccurate (and damaging) but if it does not impact adversely on the claimant's reputation, it is not defamatory. Such a statement may still give rise to regulatory sanction (e.g. if it breaches the Ofcom or PCC codes of conduct) or to a claim for malicious falsehood (see below). For example, merely to overstate a person's income is not defamatory; but it will be if the context implies s/he has not fully declared it to the tax authorities.

'Society' means right-thinking members of society generally. It is by reference to such people that the above tests must be applied. A libel claim will fail if the statement would bring the claimant into disrepute with a section of society, but not 'right-thinking' society as a whole. So, an allegation that an individual was a police informer may have brought the claimant into grave disrepute with the underworld, but would not be defamatory.

Proposed reform: The 2011 draft Bill proposed a statutory hurdle for claimants – a test of 'substantial harm'. This merely restates the common law, which already recognises that trivial allegations may not be actionable because they do not meet a 'threshold of seriousness'. The government now proposes to 'raise the bar' with a test of 'serious harm'. If this is enacted, a statement will not be defamatory unless it causes, or is likely to cause, serious harm. This is intended to deter frivolous threats and claims.

2.2. Identification – and who can sue

A claimant will usually be named, but an unnamed claimant may still be able to bring a claim: s/he may be identifiable to readers from other published information or pointers, which may range from an address or job description to references to physical characteristics. The intention of the publisher is irrelevant, so a statement intended to refer to one person may give rise to a claim by another person of the same name, if the statement could be understood to refer to him (even if this is based on knowledge derived from other sources rather than the publication itself). For example, in a 1996 case a newspaper article accused an author of plagiarism. It was illustrated with a photograph of an artist of the same name. The artist claimed, successfully, that some readers would understand that he, not the author, was the plagiarist in question.

Generalised references to classes of individuals are, broadly speaking, not successfully actionable, because it is not possible to establish that any individual has been identified. To say that 'all lawyers are corrupt' does not give any single lawyer a cause of action, because the statement does not point a finger at any individual. The smaller the class, however, the more likely it becomes that an individual within it will be able to show that they are identified by the libel.

As well as individuals, a company (in its trading reputation), officials of unincorporated association or trustees of a charity can all be defamed, and bring libel claims seeking vindication.

Defamation claims cannot be brought by political parties or departments of central or local government (although individuals within them may be able to sue in respect of similar allegations).

Civil claims for defamation cannot be brought on behalf of the dead. Any claim will be extinguished if the claimant dies before the judge or jury deliver their verdict. In those circumstances, the claim 'abates', and cannot be carried on by the deceased's estate.

Proposed reform: corporate reputations. It has been suggested that corporate claimants should be restricted in their ability to sue for defamation, due to widespread concern that companies may be able to stifle criticism by virtue of financial clout alone. Such a provision already exists in Australia. But the government now appears to have ruled out any similar statutory provision for England and Wales. It has, however, stated that 'in order to satisfy the serious harm test in Clause 1 a corporation would in practice be likely to have to demonstrate actual or likely financial loss'.

2.3. Publication – and who can be sued

There will be no civil claim for defamation if the statement has been made to the claimant alone. In order for a cause of action to arise, it must be communicated to a third party.

'Publication' in the legal sense is therefore much wider than (but includes) the lay usage applied to books and newspapers: any communications to a person other than the claimant is sufficient. It follows that the content of a book is published in the legal sense when the manuscript is first submitted to the publishing firm just as it is when the book is later placed on sale to the public. The first publication, however, is obviously much narrower in scope, and the extent of the publication will affect the measure of any damages awarded.

All those responsible for a given publication, including the author (or artist or photographer), the editor and the publisher, can be sued. Where publication takes place online, website publishers and internet hosts and service providers will similarly be treated as publishers. However, those whose involvement in the publication is limited may have a defence of innocent dissemination (see below). Libel claims will not qualify for legal aid, unless the Legal Services Commission considers a case incapable of being fairly tried without it. Such cases will be extremely rare.

3. Defences

If the claimant can show that s/he has a *prima facie* cause of action, the defendant must establish a defence. There are several, although by far the most common are justification, honest comment and privilege.

3.1. Justification

The defendant will have a complete defence to a libel claim if s/he can show that the statement is a true or substantially true statement of fact. S/he must show this on the balance of probability, i.e. that there is a greater than 50% likelihood that the statement is substantially true. In other words, the law presumes that a defamatory statement is false, and the burden is on the defendant to show otherwise. The defendant does not have to show that the statement is entirely accurate. Minor errors will be disregarded, but s/he must show that the statement is sufficiently true so as to substantiate the 'sting' of the libel. Similarly, where a number of distinct charges are made against a claimant, some of which turn out to be inaccurate, the publisher will be safe if the claimant's reputation is made no worse, in the light of what is shown to be true, by the unprovable defamatory allegations. For example, an allegation that a man is a burglar, and arsonist and a shoplifter could be justified on the basis of evidence proving the first two charges, even if the defendant has no evidence to prove the third. However, this would not help the defendant if the claimant sued only in respect of the allegation of shoplifting. One point requires special mention. It is insufficient for the defendant to prove that s/he has accurately repeated what a third person has written or said or that such statements have gone uncontradicted when made on occasions in the past. If X writes 'Y told me that Z is a liar', it is no defence to an action against X merely to prove that Y did indeed say that. X has given currency to a defamatory statement concerning Z and has so made it his own. His only defence is to prove that Z is a liar by establishing a number of instances of Z's untruthfulness. Nor does it help a defence of justification to prove that the defendant genuinely believed what s/he published to be true. This may, however, form part of a qualified privilege defence (see below). *Bona fide* belief may also be relevant to the assessment of damages. Special care should be taken in relation to references to a person's convictions, however accurately described. Under the Rehabilitation of Offenders Act 1974, a person's less serious convictions may become 'spent' and reference to them may then incur liability. Reference to the 1974 Act and its subordinate legislation must be made in order to determine the position in any particular case.

3.2. Honest comment

This defence protects the expression of the writer's genuinely held opinion. It applies to statements of comment, opinion or value judgement, as opposed to statements of fact (the distinction between comment and fact is not always easy to draw in practice). It was known, until recently, as 'fair comment' – a misleading name, because there was no requirement for the comment to be objectively fair. It may be exaggerated or prejudiced: the requirement is only that it be honestly held in good faith and without malice.

In order to benefit from the defence, the statement must relate to a matter of public interest, be based on facts which are true, sufficiently true or privileged, and be honestly held.

The facts on which the comment is based must be drawn to the reader's attention, at least indirectly. The purpose of this is to enable the reader to exercise his or her own judgement and to agree or disagree with the comment. It is not necessary to state every single detail of the facts but, in general, the fuller the facts set out or referred to with the comment, the better. The new draft Bill would significantly relax this requirement, bringing welcome clarity to a difficult area (see below).

The defence will remain available if, for example, only three out of five factual claims can be proved true (or privileged) provided that these three are by themselves sufficient to sustain, and are proportionate to, the fairness of the comment.

The flipside to the requirement that the opinion be honestly held is that a defence of honest comment will fail if the claimant can prove malice. In the legal sense, 'malice' means any dishonest or improper motive but, in contrast to its application in the context of qualified privilege (see below), it does not include actuation by spite or animosity, even if this is the dominant or sole motive. However, evidence of such motivation could also be seen as a lack of genuine belief in the view expressed.

The defence only applies where the matters commented on are of public interest, i.e. of legitimate concern to the public or a substantial section of it. Thus the conduct of national and local government, international affairs, the administration of justice, etc are all matters of public interest, whereas other people's private affairs may very well not be, although they undoubtedly interest the public, or provoke curiosity.

Matters of which criticism has been expressly or impliedly invited, such as publicly performed plays and published books, are a legitimate subject of comment. Criticism need not be confined merely to their artistic merit but equally may deal with the attitudes and opinions they expressed.

Proposed reform: The 2011 draft Bill will, if enacted, abolish the common law defence described above. It would be replaced with a new statutory defence of 'honest opinion'. This would be available for statements of opinion which are honestly held on the basis of a pre-existing fact or privileged statement. It would be defeated by evidence that the defendant did not in fact hold the opinion. The requirement that the statement be made on a matter of public interest is likely to be dropped.

3.3. Privilege

The law recognises situations in which it is in the public interest that freedom of expression should trump a claimant's right to protect their reputation. Statements made on such occasions will be privileged (i.e. the publisher will have a defence) regardless of the truth or accuracy of the statement, and the harm it may do to the claimant's reputation. There are two broad categories of privilege: *absolute privilege*, where there will be a complete defence regardless of the truth of the statement and the motivation of the publisher; and *qualified privilege*, where the publisher's motives may prevent the defence from succeeding. The 2011 draft Defamation Bill provides for some widening of the circumstances in which absolute and qualified privilege may arise.

3.3.1. Absolute privilege

A person defamed by a statement made on an occasion of absolute privilege has no remedy whatsoever, even if the statement is demonstrably false or the maker of the statement has an improper motive (malice) for making it.

Absolute privilege applies to statements in parliamentary proceedings and papers, statements made in the course of proceedings in the courts and certain tribunals, and reports published by certain quasi-judicial bodies.

It also applies to fair, accurate and contemporaneous reports of public judicial proceedings in the UK, the European Courts of Justice and Human Rights, and any international criminal tribunal established by the Security Council.

3.3.2. Qualified privilege

Qualified privilege differs from absolute privilege in that the defence will fail if the claimant can prove malice (i.e. an improper motive or carelessness or recklessness as to the truth of the publication). There are two subcategories of qualified privilege.

First, there are various examples of *statutory qualified privilege*, established under section 15 of the Defamation Act 1996. These are set out in Schedule 1 to the 1996 Act, and include fair and accurate reports of public proceedings before a legislature, a court, a government inquiry and an international organisation or conference anywhere in the world, and of certain documents, or extracts from such documents, issued by those bodies. There is no requirement to correct or publish explanations concerning these reports. Such an obligation does arise in respect of a separate category of potentially privileged reports. These include fair and accurate reports of notices issued by various bodies within the European Community and of proceedings of certain organisations within the UK.

Second, there are instances of *qualified privilege at common law*. Here, the law recognises that a statement made by a person with a legal, social or moral duty to make it, to someone with legal, social or moral duty or interest in receiving it. Examples include employment references, credit references and statements made to the police in response to enquiries or in relation to a crime. Normally the scope of publication must be no wider than necessary: if the material is published to those with no interest in receiving it, the defence of qualified privilege will be lost.

However, the protection of qualified privilege has been extended to publications by the media to the public at large since the 1999 case of *Reynolds* v. *Times Newspapers*. In order to benefit from the defence, the reporting must be responsible, and relate to a matter of significant public interest. Relevant factors may include the seriousness of allegation, the nature of its source, the steps taken to verify it, the urgency of the publication, whether the claimant's side of the story has been obtained and reported, and the tone of the publication.

Proposed reform: The 2011 draft Bill would create a new statutory defence of responsible publication. This appears similar to, but is arguably intended to widen, the common law defence of *Reynolds* qualified privilege. This will protect a publisher who cannot show that what it published was true (or honest comment) but can show that it acted responsibly in publishing material on a matter of public interest. 'Neutral reportage' – even-handed coverage of both sides of a controversy, which does not adopt either side's position – will also gain statutory protection.

3.4. Secondary responsibility

This defence may be available where the publisher publishes a defamatory statement inadvertently. 'Innocent disseminators', such as printers, distributors, broadcasters, internet service providers (ISPs) and retailers, who can show they took reasonable care and had no reason to believe what they were handling contained a libel, will have a defence under section 1 of the Defamation Act 1996 or Electronic Commerce Regulations 2002.

The defence will only be available if the broadcaster, ISP or other publisher is not the 'author, editor or publisher' of the offending words. Typically, this might occur where the offending statement is made by an interviewee in a live broadcast, or a website or ISP publishes a defamatory user-generated comment, for example on a message board, without vetting it first (where any pre-publication moderation is carried out, this element of editorial control will mean that the defence is unlikely to be available). There is some recent case law which suggests that ISPs such as Google may not be regarded as publishers at all in certain cases, in respect of material they carry online.

3.5. Offer of amends

Section 2 of the Defamation Act 1996 creates a procedure which aims to nip in the bud disputes in which the claimant has been defamed unintentionally. Under this procedure, the defendant must offer to publish a suitable correction and sufficient apology, and pay damages (if any) and the claimant's costs, to be assessed by a judge if not agreed. If an offer of amends is not accepted by the claimant, the defendant can rely on it as a defence, unless the claimant can prove malice. While reliance on an offer of amends prevents the defendant from relying on any other defences, it offers a considerable incentive to settle complaints and will save substantially on costs.

3.6. Other defences and restrictions

Limitation. A claim for libel can be defeated on the grounds that it has been issued too late: section 4 of the Limitation Act 1990 provides that any claim for libel must be issued within one year from date of publication. Currently, each new publication (e.g. every hit on a website) is regarded as a separate tort, giving rise to a fresh one-year limitation period. This puts online publishers at a disadvantage, but the position will change if the 2011 draft Bill comes into force. The Bill introduces a 'single publication' rule, preventing claimants from suing more than a year after the date of the original publication, even if the material remains online. This will not protect republication in a materially different manner, or by other publishers.

A claim may be *struck out* on the grounds that it is an abuse of the process of the courts. For example, if the scope of the publication is so small as to be insignificant, the court may prevent the claim from continuing. The Court of Appeal did so in a case involving the *Wall Street Journal* in 2005, where there was evidence that the article in question had been viewed only five times in this jurisdiction, and that three of those viewings were by individuals closely connected to the claimants or their lawyers.

There are a number of other, rarely used, defences:

- *Consent:* there will be a defence where the claimant has given their consent to the publication in question. Consent may be express or implied.
- *Release* (aka accord and satisfaction): where the claimant has agreed that he will not sue (or continue to sue) the defendant in respect of a given publication, the terms of settlement have contractual force and may be relied on as a defence.
- *Apology under 1843 and 1845 Acts:* this defence only applies to actions in respect of libels in newspapers and periodicals and is used so rarely that it is only mentioned here for the sake of completeness.

4. Remedies

A successful claimant will be compensated for the damage done to his or her reputation by an award of damages. He will usually also be awarded an injunction to prevent further publication of the offending words. The losing party will usually be ordered to pay the winner's costs. However, the costs claimed by the winning party will be assessed by the court, and it is unusual for the winner to recover 100% of his costs.

4.1. Damages

At present, where libel cases are heard by a judge and jury, the jury decides the amount of any award, which is tax-free. Awards will be made by the judge when, as seems likely, the presumption of trial by jury is abolished. It is not necessary for the claimant to prove that s/he has actually suffered any loss: some damage is presumed. It is generally very difficult to forecast the amounts juries are likely to award; the Court of Appeal has power to reduce excessive awards of damages.

There are four categories of damages:

- *'Ordinary' or 'general' damages:* the law presumes that a successful claimant will suffer some damage to their reputation. This is compensated by an award of general damages. At the top end, these may be in the region of £250,000 for the most serious libels. At the bottom end, the court may award nominal damages of as little as £1 where the libel is trivial (and in such cases the claimant would be unlikely to recover his costs). Awards of general damages are considerably lower now than they have been in the past, notably in the 1980s when a number of seven-figure awards were made. The courts may take into account the damages which would be recoverable in personal injury claims when deciding what is an appropriate figure to compensate a claimant.
- *'Special' damages:* where the claimant can prove that the publication of the libel has caused him to suffer some specified loss, for example the loss of a sponsorship contract.
- *'Aggravated' damages:* where the defendant's conduct after publication has been malevolent or spiteful, and as such has 'rubbed salt in the wound', for example by repeating the libel or attacking the claimant in some other way.
- *'Exemplary' or 'punitive' damages:* where there is evidence that the defendant has calculated that any libel damages awarded against it will be outweighed by the boost that the publication will give to its sales revenues.

4.2. Injunctions

A claimant who wins at trial will normally be entitled to an injunction restraining repetition of the libel. A claimant may also seek an injunction before trial, most commonly to prevent the threatened publication of defamatory material. Such interim injunctions are rare. Section 12 of the Human Rights Act 1998 requires the courts to balance the competing rights to private life and freedom of expression under ECHR Article 10 and ECHR Article 8. There is a long-standing common law rule against 'prior restraint' and discretion will be exercised in favour of freedom of expression if the publisher (intended defendant) indicates that s/he will defend any claim on the grounds of justification (truth).

5. Settlement and summary disposal

Most claims settle before trial. Matters likely to be dealt with in any settlement agreement include the terms of any apology to be published by the defendant, undertakings by the defendant not to repeat the libel, the making of a statement in open court (in which the defendant formally retracts the allegation), whether any damages are to be paid, and who is to bear the legal costs on each side. The Defamation Act 1996 introduced a 'fast-track' or 'summary disposal' procedure, providing a simplified mechanism for dealing with less serious complaints. This recognised the costly and time-consuming nature of libel litigation. Sections 8, 9 and 10 of the 1996 Act enable a judge alone to dismiss unrealistic claims at the outset; and s/he will also be able to dispose 'summarily' of relatively minor, but well-founded, claims, on the basis of an award of up to £10,000, a declaration that the publication was libelous, an order for the publication of an apology and an order forbidding repetition.

6. Malicious falsehood

Where a false statement is published which is not defamatory, a claimant may still be able to bring a claim under the separate (but related) tort of malicious falsehood. Claims for defamation and malicious falsehood are not mutually exclusive and may be brought together in respect of the same statement. In a claim for malicious falsehood, the claimant needs to prove that the statement:

- has been published to a third party;
- is false;
- was published maliciously (i.e. knowing it to be untrue or careless as to whether it is true); and
- is likely to cause (or has caused) the claimant to suffer financial loss (however, there are exceptions so this final requirement will not always be present).

An example is a false statement by the proprietor of a business to a member of the public that a rival proprietor has closed his business, thereby deliberately diverting the person away from his rival. The statement is not defamatory, but it is false and is calculated to cause the rival loss.

7. Scotland

The Scottish law of defamation is very similar to English law. The principal differences are as follows. There is no distinction between libel and slander. There is no requirement that the publication be made to a third party. There is no summary disposal procedure (otherwise, the 1996 Defamation Act applies). The limitation period is three years, not one. So a claimant who is too late to bring a claim in England and Wales may still be able to do so in Scotland.

8. Insurance

For an author, the importance of at least an awareness of this branch of law lies first, in the fact that most book contracts contain a clause enabling the publisher to look to him should any libel claims result; and second, in the unpredictable awards of damages. It is therefore advisable to check what libel insurance a publisher carries, and whether it also covers the author who, if s/he is to have the benefit of it, should always alert the publisher to any potential risk. Insurance for authors can only be obtained through an insurance broker or company registered with the Financial Services Authority. Insurers may require authors to obtain (at their own expense) a legal opinion before they will provide cover.

9. The privacy dimension

A developing law of privacy has emerged over the past decade, and this poses an additional risk for writers. Whilst pre-publication injunctions in respect of libelous material are very hard to obtain, injunctions to restrain publication of information which is said to be private have been dispensed much more readily by the courts. Post-publication, damages have been awarded for publication of material the truth of which is not challenged, but the publication of which may be to an individual's discredit and regarded by them as private.

The most prominent examples are the decisions that the model Naomi Campbell was entitled to damages for the revelation of her attendance at a drug addiction clinic, and more recently (July 2008) that Max Mosley was entitled to damages of £60,000 against the *News of the World*, confirming Mosley's right to privacy for a sex party.

Many claimants in voicemail interception claims against News International have settled out of court for six-figure sums, but Mosley may remain the benchmark in non-phone hacking cases for the foreseeable future.

Historically, there was no clearly defined right to privacy under English law. Claims tended to be brought on the basis of a breach of confidence: that confidential information has been imparted to the defendant in circumstances giving rise to an obligation of confidence, and that unauthorised use of that information has been (or would be) detrimental to the claimant. An action for breach of confidence may be defended on the grounds that publication is a matter of legitimate public interest.

The Human Rights Act 1998 incorporated the European Convention on Human Rights (ECHR) into English law. Claims for privacy are now viewed through the prism of Articles 8 and 10 of the ECHR. Article 8 protects an individual's right to respect for his or her private and family life, home and correspondence, and Article 10 protects freedom of expression. These two Articles are inherently likely to conflict, and often do, as recent case law has shown. Since *Campbell*, the courts have recognised a claim for 'misuse of private information' based on Article 8, so the criteria for a claim for breach of confidence, which are not always apposite, no longer needs to be satisfied.

In order to succeed in a claim based on interference with his (and it is usually a he) or her Article 8 rights, a claimant will need to show the court that the information is such that there would be a reasonable expectation of privacy. If so, the court will have to consider whether that right is outweighed by the publisher's Article 10 right and the public interest in the information.

There was a great deal of press coverage in 2011 of so-called 'super-injunctions'. These are injunctions granted in circumstances the courts consider to be so secret that the very existence of the injunction cannot be reported. Such injunctions may be necessary in commercial disputes where any 'tipping-off' might defeat the injunction's purpose. It is harder to see how they can be justified in privacy cases, and the courts have latterly backed away from awarding them. Instead, privacy injunctions now tend to be anonymised, but their existence can be reported and the basis on which they have been awarded will be set out in a written judgement.

The law in this area is likely to develop on a case-by-case basis. There is concern in many quarters as to the apparent ease with which celebrities have been able to restrain publication of information relating to marital infidelity and other indiscretions, but each case will turn on its own facts. For example, a super-injunction obtained by the footballer John Terry was discharged when the judge took the view that Terry was more concerned with preventing damage to his commercial interests than protecting his privacy. Politicians criticise the *ad hoc*, judge-made development of privacy law but Parliament has so far shown no imminent intention of legislating on the subject.

Alex de Jongh is a commercial litigation solicitor at Bates Wells and Braithwaite (www.bwbllp.com). He frequently advises claimants and defendants in defamation and other media-related disputes.

See also...

- *Copyright questions*, page 639
- *UK copyright law*, page 643
- *The laws of Privacy and Confidentiality*, page 664

Finance for writers and artists

FAQs for writers

Peter Vaines, a chartered accountant and barrister, addresses some frequently asked questions.

What can a working writer claim against tax?

A working writer is carrying on a business and can therefore claim all the expenses which are incurred wholly and exclusively for the purposes of that business. A list showing most of the usual expenses can be found in the article on *Income tax* (see page 681) but there will be other expenses that can be allowed in special circumstances.

Strictly, only expenses which are incurred for the sole purpose of the business can be claimed; there must be no 'duality of purpose' so an item of expenditure cannot be divided into private and business parts. However, HM Revenue & Customs are now able to allow all reasonable expenses (including apportioned sums) where the amounts can be commercially justified.

Allowances can also be claimed for the cost of business assets such as a car, personal computers, fax, copying machines and all other equipment (including books) which may be used by the writer. An allowance of 100% of the cost can now be claimed for most assets except cars, for which a lower allowance can be claimed. See the article on *Income tax* for further details of the deductions available in respect of capital expenditure.

Can I request interest on fees owed to me beyond 30 days of my invoice?

Yes. A writer is like any other person carrying on a business and is entitled to charge interest at a rate of 8% over bank base rate on any debt outstanding for more than 30 days – although the period of credit can be varied by agreement between the parties. It is not compulsory to claim the interest; but it is your decision whether to enforce the right.

What can I do about bad debts?

A writer is in exactly the same position as anybody else carrying on a business over the payment of his or her invoices. It is generally not commercially sensible to insist on payment in advance but where the work involved is substantial (e.g. a book), it is usual to receive one third of the fee on signature, one third on delivery of the manuscript and the remaining one third on publication. On other assignments, perhaps not as substantial as a book, it could be worthwhile seeking 50% of the fee on signature and the other 50% on delivery. This would provide a degree of protection in case of cancellation of the assignment because of changes of policy or personnel at the publisher.

What financial disputes can I take to the Small Claims Court?

If somebody owes you money you can take them to the Small Claims section of your local County Court, which deals with financial disputes up to £5,000. The procedure is much less formal than normal court proceedings and involves little expense. It is not necessary to have a solicitor. You fill in a number of forms, turn up on the day and explain the background to why you are owed the money (see www.courtservice.gov.uk).

If I receive an advance, can I divide it between two tax years?

Yes. There is a system known as 'averaging'. This enables writers (and others engaged in the creation of literary, dramatic works or designs) to average the profits of two or more consecutive years if the profits for one year are less than 75% of the profits for the highest year. This relief can apply even if the work takes less than 12 months to create and it allows the writer to avoid the higher rates of tax which might arise if the income in respect of a number of years' work were all to be concentrated in a single year.

How do I make sure I am taxed as a self-employed person so that tax and National Insurance contributions are not deducted at source?

To be taxed as a self-employed person you have to make sure that the contract for the writing cannot be regarded as a contract of employment. This is unlikely to be the case with a professional author. The subject is highly complex but one of the most important features is that the publisher must not be in a position to direct or control the author's work. Where any doubt exists, the author might find the publisher deducting tax and National Insurance contributions as a precaution and that would clearly be highly disadvantageous. The author would be well advised to discuss the position with the publisher before the contract is signed to agree that he or she should be treated as self-employed and that no tax or National Insurance contributions will be deducted from any payments. If such agreement cannot be reached, professional advice should immediately be sought so that the detailed technical position can be explained to the publisher.

Is it a good idea to operate through a limited company?

It can be a good idea for a self-employed writer to operate through a company but generally only where the income is quite large. The costs of operating a company can outweigh any benefit if the writer is paying tax only at the basic rate. Where the writer is paying tax at the higher rate of 40% (or 50%), being able to retain some of the income in a company at a tax rate of only 20% is obviously attractive. However, this will be entirely ineffective if the writer's contract with the publisher would otherwise be an employment. The whole subject of operating through a company is complex and professional advice is essential.

When does it become necessary to register for VAT?

Where the writer's self-employed income (from all sources, not only writing) exceeds £77,000 in the previous 12 months or is expected to do so in the next 30 days, he or she must register for VAT and add VAT to all his/her fees. The publisher will pay the VAT to the writer, who must pay the VAT over to the Customs and Excise each quarter. Any VAT the writer has paid on business expenses and on the purchase of business assets can be deducted. It is possible for some authors to take advantage of the simplified system for VAT payments which applies to small businesses. This involves a flat rate payment of VAT without any need to keep records of VAT on expenses.

If I make a loss from my writing can I get any tax back?

Where a writer makes a loss, HM Revenue & Customs may suggest that the writing is only a hobby and not a professional activity thereby denying any relief or tax deduction for the loss. However, providing the writing is carried out on a sensible commercial basis with an expectation of profits, any resulting loss can be offset against any other income the writer may have for the same or the previous year.

Income tax

Despite attempts by successive governments to simplify our taxation system, the subject has become increasingly complicated. Peter Vaines, a chartered accountant and barrister, gives a broad outline of taxation from the point of view of writers and other creative professionals. The proposals in the March 2012 Budget are broadly reflected in this article.

How income is taxed

Generally

Authors are usually treated for tax purposes as carrying on a profession and are taxed in a similar fashion to other self-employed professionals. This article is directed to self-employed persons only, because if a writer is employed he or she will be subject to the much less advantageous rules which apply to employment income.

Employed persons may try to shake off the status of 'employee' to attain 'freelance' status so as to qualify for the tax advantages, but such attempts meet with varying degrees of success. The problems involved in making this transition are considerable and space does not permit a detailed explanation to be made here – individual advice is necessary if difficulties are to be avoided.

Particular attention has been paid by HM Revenue & Customs (HMRC) to journalists and to those engaged in the entertainment industry with a view to reclassifying them as employees so that PAYE is deducted from their earnings. This blanket treatment has been extended to other areas and, although it is obviously open to challenge by individual taxpayers, it is always difficult to persuade HMRC to change its views.

There is no reason why employed people cannot carry on a freelance business in their spare time. Indeed, aspiring authors, artists, musicians, etc often derive so little income from their craft that the financial security of an employment, perhaps in a different sphere of activity, is necessary. The existence of the employment is irrelevant to the taxation of the freelance earnings, although it is most important not to confuse the income or expenditure of the employment with that of the self-employed activity. HMRC is aware of the advantages which can be derived by an individual having 'freelance' income from an organisation of which he or she is also an employee, and where such circumstances are contrived, it can be extremely difficult to convince an Inspector of Taxes that a genuine freelance activity is being carried on. Where the individual operates through a company or partnership providing services personally to a particular client, and would be regarded as an employee if the services were supplied directly by the individual, additional problems arise from the notorious IR35 legislation and professional advice is essential.

For those starting in business or commencing work on a freelance basis HMRC produces a very useful booklet, *Thinking of Working for Yourself?* (SE1), which is available from any tax office.

Income

For income to be taxable it need not be substantial, nor even the author's only source of income; earnings from casual writing are also taxable but this can be an advantage because occasional writers do not often make a profit from their writing. The expenses incurred in connection with writing may well exceed any income receivable and the resultant loss may then be used to reclaim tax paid on other income. Certain allowable expenses and capital allowances may be deducted from the income, and these are set out in more detail below. The possibility of a loss being used as a basis for a tax repayment is fully appreciated by HMRC, which sometimes attempts to treat casual writing as a hobby so that any losses incurred cannot be used to reclaim tax; of course by the same token any income receivable would not be chargeable to tax. This treatment may sound attractive but it should be resisted vigorously because HMRC does not hesitate to change its mind when profits begin to arise. In the case of exceptional or non-recurring writing, such as the autobiography of a sports personality or the memoirs of a politician, it could be better to be treated as pursuing a hobby and not as a professional author. Sales of copyright cannot be charged to income tax unless the recipient is a professional author. However, the proceeds of sale of copyright may be charged to capital gains tax, even by an individual who is not a professional author.

Royalties

Where the recipient is a professional author, a series of cases has laid down a clear principle that sales of copyright are taxable as income and not as capital receipts. Similarly, lump sums on account of, or in advance of royalties are also taxable as income in the year of receipt, subject to a claim for averaging relief (see below).

Copyright royalties are generally paid without deduction of income tax. However, if royalties are paid to a person who normally lives abroad, tax must be deducted by the

Arts Council awards

Arts Council category A awards

- Direct or indirect musical, design or choreographic commissions and direct or indirect commission of sculpture and paintings for public sites.
- The Royalty Supplement Guarantee Scheme.
- The Contract Writers' Scheme.
- Jazz bursaries.
- Translators' grants.
- Photographic awards and bursaries.
- Film and video awards and bursaries.
- Performance Art Awards.
- Art Publishing Grants.
- Grants to assist with a specific project or projects (such as the writing of a book) or to meet specific professional expenses such as a contribution towards copying expenses made to a composer or to an artist's studio expenses.

Arts Council category B awards

- Bursaries to trainee directors.
- Bursaries for associate directors.
- Bursaries to people attending full-time courses in arts administration (the practical training course).
- In-service bursaries to theatre designers and bursaries to trainees on the theatre designers' scheme.
- In-service bursaries for administrators.
- Bursaries for actors and actresses.
- Bursaries for technicians and stage managers.
- Bursaries made to students attending the City University Arts Administration courses.
- Awards, known as the Buying Time Awards, made not to assist with a specific project or professional expenses but to maintain the recipient to enable him or her to take time off to develop his personal talents. These include the awards and bursaries known as the Theatre Writing Bursaries, awards and bursaries to composers, awards and bursaries to painters, sculptures and print makers, literature awards and bursaries.

payer or his agent at the time the payment is made unless arrangements are made with HMRC for payments to be made gross under the terms of a Double Taxation Agreement with the other country.

Grants, prizes and awards

Persons in receipt of grants from the Arts Council or similar bodies will be concerned whether or not such grants are liable to income tax. HMRC issued a Statement of Practice after detailed discussions with the Arts Council regarding the tax treatment of the awards. Grants and other receipts of a similar nature have now been divided into two categories (see box) – those which are to be treated by HMRC as chargeable to tax and those which are not. Category A awards are considered to be taxable; awards made under category B are not chargeable to tax.

This Statement of Practice has no legal force and is used merely to ease the administration of the tax system. It is open to anyone in receipt of a grant or award to disregard the agreed statement and challenge HMRC view on the merits of their particular case. However, it must be recognised that HMRC does not issue such statements lightly and any challenge to their view would almost certainly involve a lengthy and expensive action through the Courts.

The tax position of persons in receipt of literary prizes will generally follow a decision by the Special Commissioners in connection with the Whitbread Book Awards (now called the Costa Book Awards). In that case it was decided that the prize was not part of the author's professional income and accordingly not chargeable to tax. The precise details are not available because decisions of the Special Commissioners were not, at that time, reported unless an appeal was made to the High Court; HMRC chose not to appeal against this decision. Details of the many literary awards that are given each year start on page 543, and this decision is of considerable significance to the winners of these prizes. It would be unwise to assume that all such awards will be free of tax as the precise facts which were present in the case of the Whitbread awards may not be repeated in another case; however, it is clear that an author winning a prize has some very powerful arguments in his or her favour, should HMRC seek to charge tax on the award.

Allowable expenses

To qualify as an allowable business expense, expenditure has to be laid out wholly and exclusively for business purposes. Strictly there must be no 'duality of purpose', which means that expenditure cannot be apportioned to reflect the private and business usage, for example food, clothing, telephone, travelling expenses, etc. However, HMRC will usually allow all reasonable expenses (including apportioned sums) where the amounts can be commercially justified.

It should be noted carefully that the expenditure does not have to be 'necessary', it merely has to be incurred 'wholly and exclusively' for business purposes. Naturally, however, expenditure of an outrageous and wholly unnecessary character might well give rise to a presumption that it was not really for business purposes. As with all things, some expenses are unquestionably allowable and some expenses are equally unquestionably not allowable – it is the grey area in between which gives rise to all the difficulties and the outcome invariably depends on negotiation with HMRC.

Great care should be taken when claiming a deduction for items where there may be a duality of purpose and negotiations should be conducted with more than usual care and courtesy – if provoked the Inspector of Taxes may well choose to allow nothing. An appeal is always possible although unlikely to succeed as a string of cases in the Courts has clearly demonstrated. An example is the case of *Caillebotte* v. *Quinn* where the taxpayer (who normally had lunch at home) sought to claim the excess cost of meals incurred because he was working a long way from his home. The taxpayer's arguments failed because he did not eat only in order to work, one of the reasons for his eating was in order to sustain his life; a duality of purpose therefore existed and no tax relief was due.

Other cases have shown that expenditure on clothing can also be disallowed if it is the kind of clothing which is in everyday use, because clothing is worn not only to assist the pursuit of one's profession but also to accord with public decency. This duality of purpose may be sufficient to deny relief – even where the particular type of clothing is of a kind not otherwise worn by the taxpayer. In the case of *Mallalieu* v. *Drummond* a barrister failed to obtain a tax deduction for items of sombre clothing that she purchased specifically for wearing in Court. The House of Lords decided that a duality of purpose existed because clothing represented part of her needs as a human being.

Allowances

Despite the above, Inspectors of Taxes are not usually inflexible and the following list of expenses are among those generally allowed.

(a) Cost of all materials used up in the course of the work's preparation.

(b) Cost of typewriting and secretarial assistance, etc; if this or other help is obtained from one's spouse then it is entirely proper for a deduction to be claimed for the amounts paid for the work. The amounts claimed must actually be paid to the spouse and should be at the market rate, although some uplift can be made for unsocial hours, etc. Payments to a spouse are of course taxable in their hands and should therefore be most carefully considered. The spouse's earnings may also be liable for National Insurance contributions and it is important to take care because otherwise you may find that these contributions outweigh the tax savings. The impact of the National Minimum Wage should also be considered.

(c) All expenditure on normal business items such as postage, stationery, telephone, email, fax and answering machines, agent's fees, accountancy charges, photography, subscriptions, periodicals, magazines, etc may be claimed. The cost of daily papers should not be overlooked if these form part of research material. Visits to theatres, cinemas, etc for research purposes may also be permissible (but not the cost relating to guests). Unfortunately, expenditure on all types of business entertaining is specifically denied tax relief.

(d) If work is conducted at home, a deduction for 'use of home' is usually allowed providing the amount claimed is reasonable. If the claim is based on an appropriate proportion of the total costs of rent, light and heat, cleaning and maintenance, insurance, etc (but not the Council Tax), care should be taken to ensure that no single room is used 'exclusively' for business purposes, because this may result in the Capital Gains Tax exemption on the house as the only or main residence being partially forfeited. However, it would be a strange household where one room was in fact used exclusively for business purposes and for no other purpose whatsoever (e.g. storing personal bank statements and other private papers); the usual formula is to claim a deduction on the basis that most or all of the rooms in the house are used at one time or another for business purposes, thereby avoiding any suggestion that any part was used exclusively for business purposes.

(e) The appropriate business proportion of motor running expenses may also be claimed although what is the appropriate proportion will naturally depend on the particular circumstances of each case. It should be appreciated that the well-known scale of benefits, whereby employees are taxed according to the size of the car's CO_2 emissions, do not apply to self-employed persons.
(f) It has been long established that the cost of travelling from home to work (whether employed or self-employed) is not an allowable expense. However, if home is one's place of work then no expenditure under this heading is likely to be incurred and difficulties are unlikely to arise.
(g) Travelling and hotel expenses incurred for business purposes will normally be allowed but if any part could be construed as disguised holiday or pleasure expenditure, considerable thought would need to be given to the commercial reasons for the journey in order to justify the claim. The principle of 'duality of purpose' will always be a difficult hurdle in this connection – although not insurmountable.
(h) If a separate business bank account is maintained, any overdraft interest thereon will be an allowable expense. This is the only circumstance in which overdraft interest is allowed for tax purposes.
(i) Where capital allowances (see below) are claimed for a personal computer, laptop, iPad, fax machine, mobile phone, television, CD or DVD player, etc used for business purposes the costs of maintenance and repair of the equipment may also be claimed.

Clearly many other allowable items may be claimed in addition to those listed. Wherever there is any reasonable business motive for some expenditure it should be claimed as a deduction although it is necessary to preserve all records relating to the expense. It is sensible to avoid an excess of imagination as this would naturally cause the Inspector of Taxes to doubt the genuineness of other expenses claimed.

The question is often raised whether the whole amount of an expense may be deducted or whether the VAT content must be excluded. Where VAT is reclaimed from HMRC by someone who is registered for VAT, the VAT element of the expense cannot be treated as an allowable deduction. Where the VAT is not reclaimed, the whole expense (inclusive of VAT) is allowable for income tax purposes.

Capital allowances

Where expenditure of a capital nature is incurred, it cannot be deducted from income as an expense – a separate and sometimes more valuable capital allowance being available instead. Capital allowances are given for many different types of expenditure, but authors and similar professional people are likely to claim only for 'plant and machinery'; this is a very wide expression which may include cars, personal computers, laptops, iPads, fax machines, televisions, CD and DVD players used for business purposes. Plant and machinery generally qualifies for an allowance of 100% (reduced to 20% for expenditure over £25,000). Where the useful life of an asset is expected to be short, it is possible to claim special treatment as a 'short life asset' enabling the allowances to be accelerated.

The reason capital allowances can be more valuable than allowable expenses is that they may be wholly or partly disclaimed in any year that full benefit cannot be obtained – ordinary business expenses cannot be similarly disclaimed. Where, for example, the income of an author is not large enough to bring him above the tax threshold, he would not be liable to tax and a claim for capital allowances would be wasted. If the capital allowances were to be disclaimed their benefit would be carried forward for use in subsequent years. This would also be advantageous where the income is likely to be taxable at the higher rate of 40% (or even the 50% rate) in a subsequent year. Careful planning with claims for capital allowances is therefore essential if maximum benefit is to be obtained.

As an alternative to capital allowances, claims can be made on the 'renewals' basis whereby all renewals are treated as allowable deductions in the year; no allowance is obtained for the initial purchase, but the cost of replacement (excluding any improvement element) is allowed in full. This basis is no longer widely used, as it is considerably less advantageous than claiming capital allowances as described above.

Leasing is a popular method of acquiring fixed assets, and where cash is not available to enable an outright purchase to be made, assets may be leased over a period of time. Whilst leasing may have financial benefits in certain circumstances, in normal cases there is likely to be no tax advantage in leasing an asset where the alternative of outright purchase is available.

Books

The question of whether the cost of books is eligible for tax relief has long been a source of difficulty. The annual cost of replacing books used for the purposes of one's professional activities (e.g. the cost of a new *Writers' & Artists' Yearbook* each year) has always been an allowable expense; the difficulty arose because the initial cost of reference books, etc (e.g. when commencing one's profession) was treated as capital expenditure but no allowances were due as the books were not considered to be 'plant'. However, the matter was clarified by the case of *Munby* v. *Furlong* in which the Court of Appeal decided that the initial cost of law books purchased by a barrister was expenditure on 'plant' and eligible for capital allowances. This is clearly a most important decision, particularly relevant to any person who uses expensive books in the course of exercising his or her profession.

Pension contributions

Where a self-employed person makes contributions to a pension scheme, those contributions are usually deductible.

These arrangements are generally advantageous in providing for a pension as contributions are usually paid when the income is high (and the tax relief is also high) and the pension (taxed as earned income when received) usually arises when the income is low and little tax is payable. There is also the opportunity to take part of the pension entitlement as a tax-free lump sum. It is necessary to take into account the possibility that the tax advantages could go into reverse. When the pension is paid it could, if rates rise again, be taxed at a higher rate than the rate of tax relief at the moment. From 6 April 2006 a whole new regime for pensions was introduced to create a much simpler system. Each individual has a lifetime allowance of £1.8 million and when benefits crystallise, which will generally be when a pension begins to be paid, this is measured against the individual's lifetime allowance; any excess will be taxed at 25%, or at 55% if the excess is taken as a lump sum.

Each individual also has an annual allowance for contributions to the pension fund which is set at £50,000 for 2011/12 but may change in later years. If the annual increase in an individual's rights under all registered schemes of which he is a member exceeds the annual allowance, the excess is chargeable to tax.

For many writers and artists this means that they can contribute a large part of their earnings to a pension scheme (if they can afford to do so) without any of the previous complications. It is still necessary to be careful where there is other income giving rise to a pension because the whole of the pension entitlement has to be taken into account.

Flexible retirement is possible allowing members of occupational pension schemes to continue working while also drawing retirement benefits. As part of this reform, however, the normal minimum pension age was raised from 50 to 55 on 6 April 2010.

Class 4 National Insurance contributions

Allied to pensions is the payment of Class 4 National Insurance contributions, although no pension or other benefit is obtained by the contributions; the Class 4 contributions are designed solely to extract additional amounts from self-employed persons and are payable in addition to the normal Class 2 (self-employed) contributions. The rates are changed each year and for 2012/13 self-employed persons will be obliged to contribute 9% of their profits between the range £7,605–£42,475 per annum plus 2% on earnings above £42,475. This amount is collected in conjunction with the annual income tax liability.

Averaging relief

Relief for copyright payments

Professional authors and artists engaged in the creation of literary or dramatic works or designs may claim to average the profits of two or more consecutive years if the profits for one year are less than 75% of the profits for the highest year. This relief can apply even if the work took less than 12 months to create and is available to people who create works in partnership with others. It enables the creative artist to utilise their allowances fully and to avoid the higher rates of tax which might apply if all the income were to arise in a single year.

Collection of tax: self-assessment

Under 'self-assessment' you submit your tax return and work out your tax liability for yourself. If you get it wrong, or if you are late with your tax return or the payment of tax, interest and penalties will be charged. Completing a tax return is a daunting task but the term 'self-assessment' is not intended to imply that individuals have to do it themselves; they can (and often will) engage professional help. The term is only intended to convey that it is the taxpayer, and not HMRC, who is responsible for getting the tax liability right and for it to be paid on time.

The deadline for filing your tax return is 31 January following the end of the tax year. You must now file online; there is no longer any opportunity to file a paper tax return.

Income tax on self-employed earnings remains payable in two instalments on 31 January and 31 July each year. Because the accurate figures may not necessarily be known, these payments in January and July will therefore be only payments on account based on the previous year's liability. The final balancing figure will be paid the following 31 January together with the first instalment of the liability for the following year.

When HMRC receives the self-assessment tax return, it is checked to see if there is anything obviously wrong; if there is, a letter will be sent to you immediately. Otherwise, HMRC has 12 months from the filing date in which to make further enquiries; if it doesn't, it will have no further opportunity to do so and your tax liabilities are final – unless it contains a careless error. In that event, HMRC can raise an assessment later to collect any extra tax together with appropriate penalties. It is essential that all records relevant to your tax return are retained for at least 12 months after the filing date in case they are needed by HMRC. For the self-employed, the record-keeping requirement is much more onerous because the records need to be kept for nearly six years. If you claim a tax deduction for an expense, it will be necessary to have a receipt or other document proving that the expenditure has been made. Because the existence of the underlying records is so important to the operation of self-assessment, HMRC will treat them very seriously and there is a penalty of £3,000 for any failure to keep adequate records.

Interest

Interest is chargeable on overdue tax at a variable rate, which is 3% per annum. It does not rank for any tax relief, which can make HMRC an expensive source of credit.

However, HMRC can also be obliged to pay interest (known as repayment supplement) tax-free where repayments are delayed. The rules relating to repayment supplement are less beneficial and even more complicated than the rules for interest payable but they do exist and can be very welcome if a large repayment has been delayed for a long time. Unfortunately, the rate of repayment supplement is only 0.5% and is always less than the rate charged by HMRC on overdue tax.

Value added tax

The activities of writers, painters, composers, etc are all 'taxable supplies' within the scope of VAT and chargeable at the standard rate. (Zero rating which applies to publishers, booksellers, etc on the supply of books does not extend to the work performed by writers.) Accordingly, authors are obliged to register for VAT if their income for the past 12 months exceeds £77,000 or if their income for the coming month will exceed that figure.

Delay in registering can be a most serious matter because if registration is not effected at the proper time, HMRC can (and invariably do) claim VAT from all the income received since the date on which registration should have been made. As no VAT would have been included in the amounts received during this period the amount claimed by HMRC must inevitably come straight from the pocket of the author.

The author may be entitled to seek reimbursement of the VAT from those whom he or she ought to have charged VAT but this is obviously a matter of some difficulty and may indeed damage his commercial relationships. Apart from these disadvantages there is also a penalty for late registration. The rules are extremely harsh and are imposed automatically even in cases of innocent error. It is therefore extremely important to monitor the income very carefully because if in any period of 12 months the income exceeds the £77,000 limit, the Customs and Excise must be notified within 30 days of the end of the period. Failure to do so will give rise to an automatic penalty. It should be emphasised that this is a penalty for failing to submit a form and has nothing to do with any real or potential loss of tax. Furthermore, whether the failure was innocent or deliberate will not matter. Only the existence of a 'reasonable excuse' will be a defence to the penalty. However, a reasonable excuse does not include ignorance, error, a lack of funds or reliance on any third party.

However, it is possible to regard VAT registration as a privilege and not a penalty, because only VAT registered persons can reclaim VAT paid on their expenses such as stationery, telephone, professional fees, etc and even computers and other plant and machinery (excluding cars). However, many find that the administrative inconvenience – the cost of maintaining the necessary records and completing the necessary forms – more than outweighs the benefits to be gained from registration and prefer to stay outside the scope of VAT for as long as possible.

Overseas matters

The general observation may be made that self-employed persons resident and domiciled in the UK are not well treated with regard to their overseas work, being taxable on their worldwide income. It is important to emphasise that if fees are earned abroad, no tax saving can be achieved merely by keeping the money outside the country. Although exchange control regulations no longer exist to require repatriation of foreign earnings, such income remains taxable in the UK and must be disclosed to HMRC; the same applies to interest or other income arising on any investment of these earnings overseas. Accordingly, whenever foreign earnings are likely to become substantial, prompt and effective action is required to limit the impact of UK and foreign taxation. In the case of non-resident authors it is important that arrangements concerning writing for publication in the UK, for example in newspapers, are undertaken with great care. A case concerning the wife of one of the great train robbers who provided detailed information for a series of articles published in a Sunday newspaper is most instructive. Although she was acknowledged to be resident in Canada for all the relevant years, the income from the articles was treated as arising in this country and fully chargeable to UK tax.

The UK has double taxation agreements with many other countries and these agreements are designed to ensure that income arising in a foreign country is taxed either in that country or in the UK. Where a withholding tax is deducted from payments received from another country (or where tax is paid in full in the absence of a double taxation agreement), the amount of foreign tax paid can usually be set off against the related UK tax liability.

Many successful authors can be found living in Eire because of the complete exemption from tax which attaches to works of cultural or artistic merit by persons who are resident there. However, such a step should only be contemplated having careful regard to all the other domestic and commercial considerations and specialist advice is essential if the exemption is to be obtained and kept; a careless breach of the conditions could cause the exemption to be withdrawn with catastrophic consequences. Consult the Revenue Commissioners in Dublin (www.revenue.ie) for further information concerning the precise conditions to be satisfied for exemption from tax in Eire.

Companies

When an author becomes successful the prospect of paying tax at the higher rate may drive them to take hasty action such as the formation of a company, etc which may not always be to their advantage. Indeed some authors seeing the exodus into tax exile of their more successful colleagues even form companies in low tax areas in the naive expectation of saving large amounts of tax. HMRC is fully aware of these possibilities and have extensive powers to charge tax and combat avoidance. Accordingly, such action is just as likely to increase tax liabilities and generate other costs and should never be contemplated without expert advice; some very expensive mistakes are often made in this area which are not always able to be remedied.

To conduct one's business through the medium of a company can be a very effective method of mitigating tax liabilities, and providing it is done at the right time and under the right circumstances very substantial advantages can be derived. However, if done without due care and attention the intended advantages will simply evaporate. At the very least it is essential to ensure that the company's business is genuine and conducted properly with regard to the realities of the situation. If the author continues his or her activities unchanged, simply paying all the receipts from his work into a company's bank account, he cannot expect to persuade HMRC that it is the company and not himself who is entitled to, and should be assessed to tax on, that income.

It must be strongly emphasised that many pitfalls exist which can easily eliminate all the tax benefits expected to arise by the formation of the company. For example, company directors are employees of the company and will be liable to pay much higher National Insurance contributions; the company must also pay the employer's proportion of the contribution and a total liability of nearly 26% of gross salary may arise. This compares most unfavourably with the position of a self-employed person. Moreover, on the commencement of the company's business the individual's profession will cease and the possibility of revisions being made by HMRC to earlier tax liabilities means that the timing of a change has to be considered very carefully.

The Tax Return

No mention has been made above of personal reliefs and allowances; this is because these allowances and the rates of tax are subject to constant change and are always set out in detail in the explanatory notes which accompany the Tax Return. The annual Tax Return is an important document and should be completed promptly with extreme care. If filling in the Tax Return is a source of difficulty or anxiety, *Money Which? – Tax Saving Guide* (Consumer Association, annual, March) is very helpful.

Peter Vaines FCA, CTA, barrister, is a partner in the international law firm of Squire Sanders (UK) LLP and writes and speaks widely on tax matters. He is on the Editorial Board of *Personal Tax Planning Review*, tax columnist of the *New Law Journal* and author of a number of books on taxation..

See also...

- *FAQs for writers*, page 679
- *Social security contributions and benefits*, page 691

Social security contributions and benefits

In general, everyone who works in Great Britain either as an employee or as a self-employed person is liable to pay social security contributions. The law governing this subject is complex and Peter Arrowsmith FCA summarises it here for the benefit of writers and artists. This article, which also contains an outline of the benefits system, should be regarded as a general guide only.

All contributions are payable in respect of years ending on 5 April. See box (below) for the classes of contributions.

Classes of contributions

Class 1 Payable by employees (primary contributions) and their employers (secondary contributions), based on earnings

Class 1A Payable only by employers in respect of all taxable benefits in kind

Class 1B Payable only by employers in respect of PAYE Settlement Agreements entered into by them

Class 2 Weekly flat rate contributions payable by the self-employed

Class 3 Weekly flat rate contributions, payable on a voluntary basis in order to provide, or make up entitlement to, certain social security benefits

Class 4 Payable by the self-employed in respect of their trading or professional income, based on earnings.

Employed or self-employed?

The question as to whether a person is employed under a contract *of* service and is thereby an employee liable to Class 1 contributions, or performs services (either solely or in partnership) under a contract for service and is thereby self-employed liable to Class 2 and Class 4 contributions, often has to be decided in practice. One of the best guides can be found in the case of *Market Investigations Ltd* v. *Minister of Social Security* (1969 2 WLR 1) when Cooke J. remarked:

'...the fundamental test to be applied is this: "Is the person who has engaged himself to perform these services performing them as a person in business on his own account?" If the answer to that question is "yes", then the contract is a contract for services. If the answer is "no", then the contract is a contract of service. No exhaustive list has been compiled and perhaps no exhaustive list can be compiled of the considerations which are relevant in determining that question, nor can strict rules be laid down as to the relative weight which the various considerations should carry in particular cases. The most that can be said is that control will no doubt always have to be considered, although it can no longer be regarded as the sole determining factor; and that factors which may be of importance are such matters as:

- whether the man performing the services provides his own equipment,
- whether he hires his own helpers,
- what degree of financial risk he takes,
- what degree of responsibility for investment and management he has, and
- whether and how far he has an opportunity of profiting from sound management in the performance of his task.'

The above case has often been considered subsequently in Tribunal cases, but there are many factors to take into account. An indication of employment status can be obtained using a tool on the HM Revenue & Customs (HMRC) website (www.hmrc.gov.uk/calcs/esi.htm). Please note, however, that this tool sometimes gives dubious results and in some cases will not give a conclusive answer at all.

Exceptions

There are exceptions to the above rules, those most relevant to artists and writers being:

• The employment of a wife by her husband, or vice versa, is disregarded for social security purposes unless it is for the purposes of a trade or profession (e.g. the employment of his wife by an author would not be disregarded and would result in a liability for contributions if her salary reached the minimum levels). The same provisions also apply to civil partners from 5 December 2005.

• The employment of certain relatives in a private dwelling house in which both employee and employer reside is disregarded for social security purposes provided the employment is not for the purposes of a trade or business carried on at those premises by the employer. This would cover the employment of a relative (as defined) as a housekeeper in a private residence.

Personal service companies

From 6 April 2000, those who have control of their own 'one-man service companies' are subject to special rules. If the work carried out by the owner of the company for the company's customers would be – but for the one-man company – considered as an employment of that individual (i.e. rather than self-employment), a deemed salary may arise. If it does, then some or all of the company's income will be treated as salary liable to PAYE and National Insurance contributions (NICs). This will be the case whether or not such salary is actually paid by the company. The same situation may arise where the worker owns as little as 5% of a company's share capital.

The calculations required by HMRC are complicated and have to be done very quickly at the end of each tax year (even if the company's year-end does not coincide). It is essential that affected businesses seek detailed professional advice about these rules which may also, in certain circumstances, apply to partnerships.

In order to escape the application of these rules, a number of workers have arranged their engagements through 'managed service companies', etc where the promoter is heavily involved in all the company management to the exclusion of the workers themselves. Such companies are now subjected to similar, but different, rules from 6 April 2007 for tax and 6 August 2007 for NICs.

For further information see the HMRC website at www.hmrc.gov.uk/ir35 and www.hmrc.gov.uk/employment-status/msc.htm.

State pension age

The current state pension age for men is 65. In the case of women the previous age of 60 no longer applies as from 6 April 2010 to 5 April 2020 the female pensionable age is now rising to 66 (and that for men will rise from the current 65 to 66 over the period from November 2018 to April 2020). NICs are payable up to the extended pension age. In 2013 women will reach state pension age on the following dates dependent on date of birth:

Date of birth	Pension age
6 August 1951 to 5 September 1951	6 January 2013
6 September 1951 to 5 October 1951	6 March 2013
6 October 1951 to 5 November 1951	6 May 2013
6 November 1951 to 5 December 1951	6 July 2013
6 December 1951 to 5 January 1952	6 September 2013
6 January 1952 to 5 February 1952	6 November 2013

From late 2018 the pensionable age for both men and women will rise to 66 (by March 2020), and will rise further to 67 over the two-year period from 2034–6 and then similarly to 68 from 2044–6. The increases to 67 and 68 are under review by the coalition government and may yet be accelerated.

Class 1 contributions

As mentioned above, these are related to earnings, the amount payable depending upon whether the employer has applied for his employees to be 'contracted-out' of the State earnings-related pension scheme; such application can be made where the employer's own pension scheme provides a requisite level of benefits for his or her employees and their dependants (salary related, COSR). From 6 April 2012, contracting out is no longer possible in the case of a money purchase scheme (COMPS).

Contributions are payable by employees and employers on earnings that exceed the earnings threshold. Contributions are normally collected via the PAYE tax deduction machinery, and there are penalties for late submission of returns and for errors therein. Interest is charged automatically on PAYE and social security contributions paid late.

Employees' liability to pay

Contributions are payable by any employee who is aged 16 years and over (even though they may still be at school) and who is paid an amount equal to, or exceeding, the earnings threshold. Nationality is irrelevant for contribution purposes and, subject to special rules covering employees not normally resident in Great Britain, Northern Ireland or the Isle of Man, or resident in EEA countries or those with which there are reciprocal agreements, contributions must be paid whether the employee concerned is a British subject or not provided he is gainfully employed in Great Britain.

Persons over state pension age are exempt from liability to pay primary contributions, even if they have not retired. However, the fact that an employee may be exempt from liability does not relieve an employer from liability to pay secondary contributions in respect of that employee.

Employees' (primary) contributions

From 6 April 2012, the rate of employees' contributions on earnings from the employee earnings threshold to the upper earnings limit is 12% (for contracted-out employment 10.6% up to the upper accrual point, then 12% to the upper earnings limit). Certain married women who made appropriate elections before 12 May 1977 may be entitled to pay a reduced rate of 5.85%. However, they will have no entitlement to benefits in respect of these contributions. It should be noted that from 6 April 2011 the employee and employer earnings thresholds are no longer the same.

From April 2003, earnings above the upper earnings limit attract an employee contribution liability at the additional rate. Previously, this was 1% but from 6 April 2011 is 2%.

Employers' (secondary) contributions

All employers are liable to pay contributions on the gross earnings of employees. As mentioned above, an employer's liability is not reduced as a result of employees being exempted from contributions, or being liable to pay only the reduced rate (5.85%) of contributions.

For earnings paid on or after 6 April 2012 employers are liable at a rate of 13.8% on earnings paid above the employer earnings threshold (without any upper earnings limit),

10.4% where the employment is contracted out (salary related). In addition, special rebates apply in respect of earnings falling between the lower earnings limit and the earnings threshold. This provides, effectively, a negative rate of contribution in that small band of earnings. It should be noted that the contracted-out rate of 10.4% now applies only up to the upper accrual point. Thereafter, the not contracted-out rate of 13.8% is applicable. Prior to 6 April 2009 the contracted-out rate applied up to the upper earnings limit.

The employer is responsible for the payment of both employees' and employer's contributions, but is entitled to deduct the employees' contributions from the earnings on which they are calculated. Effectively, therefore, the employee suffers a deduction in respect of his or her social security contributions in arriving at his weekly or monthly wage or salary. Special rules apply to company directors and persons employed through agencies.

Items included in, or excluded from, earnings

Contributions are calculated on the basis of a person's gross earnings from their employment. This will normally be the figure shown on the deduction working sheet or computer equivalent record, except where the employee pays superannuation contributions and, from 6 April 1987, charitable gifts under payroll giving – these must be added back for the purposes of calculating Class 1 liability.

Earnings include salary, wages, overtime pay, commissions, bonuses, holiday pay, payments made while the employee is sick or absent from work, payments to cover travel between home and office, and payments under the statutory sick pay, statutory maternity pay, statutory paternity pay and statutory adoption pay schemes.

However, certain payments, some of which may be regarded as taxable income for income tax purposes, are ignored for Class 1 purposes. These include:

- certain gratuities paid other than by the employer;
- redundancy payments and some payments in lieu of notice;
- certain payments in kind;
- reimbursement of specific expenses incurred in the carrying out of the employment;
- benefits given on an individual basis for personal reasons (e.g. birthday presents);
- compensation for loss of office.

Booklet CWG 2 (2012 edition) gives a list of items to include in or exclude from earnings for Class 1 contribution purposes. Some such items may, however, be liable to Class 1A (employer only) contributions.

Rates of Class 1 contributions and earnings limits from 6 April 2012

Earnings per week	*Rates payable on earnings in each band*			
	Not contracted out		*Contracted out*	
	Employee	*Employer*	*Employee*	*Employer*
£	%	%	%	%
Below 107.00	–	–	–	–
107.00–143.99	–	–	– (*)	– (*)
144.00–145.99	–	13.8	– (*)	10.4
146.00–769.99	12	13.8	10.6	10.4
770.00–817.00	12	13.8	12	13.8
Over 817.00	2	13.8	2	13.8

* Special rebates deductible in respect of this band of earnings.

Miscellaneous rules

There are detailed rules covering a person with two or more employments; where a person receives a bonus or commission in addition to a regular wage or salary; and where a person is in receipt of holiday pay. From 6 April 1991 employers' social security contributions arise under Class 1A in respect of the private use of a company car, and of fuel provided for private use therein. From 6 April 2000, this charge was extended to cover most taxable benefits in kind. The rate is now 13.8%. From 6 April 1999, Class 1B contributions are payable by employers using PAYE Settlement Agreements in respect of small and/or irregular expense payments and benefits, etc. This rate is also currently 13.8%.

Upper accrual point

From 6 April 2009 there was introduced a new upper accrual point (UAP) from which entitlement to benefit (principally earnings-related state pension) ceases, even though main rate Class 1 contributions continue to be due. This impacts on contracted-out employees in particular. The UAP is fixed at a constant cash amount of £770 per week and would eliminate any earnings-related element of the state pension by around 2031, although the government is planning to accelerate this change to the latter half of the current decade.

Class 2 contributions

Class 2 contributions are payable at the weekly rate of £2.65 as from 6 April 2012. Exemptions from Class 2 liability are:

- A person over state pension age.
- A person who has not attained the age of 16.
- A married woman or, in certain cases, a widow either of whom elected prior to 12 May 1977 not to pay Class 2 contributions.
- Persons with small earnings (see below).
- Persons not ordinarily self-employed (see below).

Small earnings

Application for a certificate of exception from Class 2 contributions may be made by any person who can show that his or her net self-employed earnings per his profit and loss account (as opposed to taxable profits):

- for the year of application are expected to be less than a specified limit (£5,595 in the 2012/13 tax year); or
- for the year preceding the application were less than the limit specified for that year (£5,315 for 2011/12) and there has been no material change of circumstances.

Certificates of exception must be renewed in accordance with the instructions stated thereon. At the discretion of HMRC the certificate may commence up to 13 weeks before the date on which the application is made. Despite a certificate of exception being in force, a person who is self-employed is still entitled to pay Class 2 contributions if they wish, in order to maintain entitlement to social security benefits.

Persons not ordinarily self-employed

Part-time self-employed activities (including as a writer or artist) are disregarded for contribution purposes if the person concerned is not ordinarily employed in such activities and has a full-time job as an employee. There is no definition of 'ordinarily employed' for this purpose. Persons qualifying for this relief do not require certificates of exception but are well advised to apply for one nonetheless.

Payment of contributions

Class 2 contributions may be paid by monthly or six-monthly direct debit in arrears or, alternatively, by cheque, bank giro, etc following receipt of a six-monthly (in arrears) bill.

If, following the payment of Class 2 contributions, it is found that the earnings are below the exception limit (e.g. the relevant accounts are prepared late), the Class 2 contributions that have been overpaid can be reclaimed, provided a claim is made between 6 April and 31 January immediately following the end of the tax year. Such a refund may, however, prejudice entitlement to contributory benefits.

Class 3 contributions

Class 3 contributions are payable voluntarily, at the weekly rate of £13.25 per week from 6 April 2012, by persons aged 16 or over with a view to enabling them to qualify for a limited range of benefits if their contribution record is not otherwise sufficient. In general, Class 3 contributions can be paid by employees, the self-employed and the non employed.

Broadly speaking, no more than 52 Class 3 contributions are payable for any one tax year, and contributions cannot be paid in respect of tax years after the one in which the individual concerned reaches state pension age. Class 3 contributions may be paid by monthly direct debit, quarterly bill or by annual cheque in arrears.

Class 4 contributions

In addition to Class 2 contributions, self-employed persons are liable to pay Class 4 contributions. These are calculated at the rate of 9% on the amount of profits or gains chargeable to income tax which exceed £7,605 per annum but which do not exceed £42,475 per annum for 2012/13. Profits above the upper limit of £42,475 attract a Class 4 charge at the rate of 2%. The income tax profit on which Class 4 contributions are calculated is after deducting capital allowances and losses, but before deducting personal tax allowances or retirement annuity or personal pension or stakeholder pension plan premiums.

Class 4 contributions produce no additional benefits, but were introduced to ensure that self-employed persons as a whole pay a fair share of the cost of pensions and other social security benefits, yet without those who make only small profits having to pay excessively high flat rate contributions.

Payment of contributions

In general, Class 4 contributions are self-assessed and paid to HMRC together with the income tax as a result of the self-assessment income tax return, and accordingly the contributions are due and payable at the same time as the income tax liability on the relevant profits. Under self-assessment, interim payments of Class 4 contributions are payable at the same time as interim payments of tax.

Class 4 exemptions

The following persons are exempt from Class 4 contributions:

- Persons over state pension age at the commencement of the year of assessment (i.e. on 6 April).
- An individual not resident in the UK for income tax purposes in the year of assessment.
- Persons whose earnings are not 'immediately derived' from carrying on a trade, profession or vocation (e.g. sleeping partners).
- A person under 16 on 6 April of the year of assessment.
- Persons not ordinarily self-employed.

Married persons and partnerships

Under independent taxation of husband and wife from 1990/91 onwards, each spouse is responsible for his or her own Class 4 liability.

In partnerships, each partner's liability is calculated separately. If a partner also carries on another trade or profession, the profits of all such businesses are aggregated for the purposes of calculating their Class 4 liability.

When an assessment has become final and conclusive for the purposes of income tax, it is also final and conclusive for the purposes of calculating Class 4 liability.

Maximum contributions

There is a form of limit to the total liability for social security contributions payable by a person who is employed in more than one employment, or is also self-employed or a partner.

Where only not contracted-out Class 1 contributions, or not contracted-out Class 1 and Class 2 contributions, are payable, the maximum contribution payable at the main rates (12%, 10.6% or 5.85% as the case may be) is limited to 53 primary Class 1 contributions at the maximum weekly not contracted-out standard rate. For 2012/13 this 'maximum' will thus be £4,238.63 (amounts paid at only 2% are to be excluded in making this comparison).

However, where contracted-out Class 1 contributions are payable, the maximum primary Class 1 contributions payable for 2012/13 where all employments are contracted out are £3,804.55 (again excluding amounts paid at only 2%).

Where Class 4 contributions are payable in addition to Class 1 and/or Class 2 contributions, the Class 4 contributions payable at the full 9% rate are restricted for 2012/13 so that they shall not exceed the excess of £3,278.75 (i.e. 53 Class 2 contributions plus maximum Class 4 contributions) over the aggregate of the Class 1 and Class 2 contributions paid at the full (i.e. other than 2%) rates.

Merger with income tax

It was announced in the 2011 Budget that consultation will take place on a possible merger of the operation of income tax and social security contributions. After some initial working groups set up by HM Treasury at the end of 2011, a consultation document was due to be issued in Spring 2012. Even if this ambition proceeds, it will take many years to come to fruition.

Social security benefits

Certain benefits which were formerly available to men from the age of 60 are, from 6 April 2010, only available – to either sex – from the now rising female state pension age (see 'State pension age' above).

Benefits may be contributory (i.e. dependent upon set levels of social security contributions and/or NIC-able earnings arising in all or part of one or more tax years) or means-tested (i.e. subject to a full assessment of the income and capital of the claimant and their partner). Child benefit is one of a handful falling outside either category being neither contributory nor means tested, though there is an income tax clawback from January 2013 where anyone in the household has taxable income over £50,000 per annum.

Most benefits are administered by the Department for Work and Pensions and its agencies (such as Jobcentre Plus and The Pension Service). Some are administered wholly or partly by HMRC and the latter are marked with an asterisk in the following lists.

Universal benefits

- Child Benefit*
- Carer's Allowance (for those looking after a severely disabled person)
- Disability Living Allowance (DLA)

Contributory benefits

- State Pension – basic and earnings related
- Bereavement benefits
- Contribution-based Jobseeker's Allowance (JSA) (time limited, i.e. unemployment)
- Contribution-based Employment and Support Allowance (ESA) (time limited for some, i.e. sickness and incapacity)
- Statutory Sick Pay* (SSP) (for employees only, paid by the employer)
- Statutory Maternity Pay* (SMP) (for employees only, paid by the employer)
- Maternity Allowance (for self-employed and others meeting the conditions)
- Statutory Paternity Pay* (SPP) (for employees only, paid by the employer)
- Statutory Adoption Pay* (SAP) (for employees only, paid by the employer)
- Guardian's Allowance*

Further information

website www.hmrc.gov.uk/leaflets/index.htm
www.hmrc.gov.uk/ni/index.htm

Booklets published by HMRC are available from local Enquiry Centres and on their website.

DWP benefits

website www.dwp.gov.uk/publications/catalogue-of-information/a-to-z-of-all-dwp-information
www.direct.gov.uk/en/MoneyTaxAndBenefits/index.htm
www.direct.gov.uk/en/Pensionsandretirementplanning/index.htm

HMRC benefits

website www.hmrc.gov.uk/taxcredits/index.htm
www.hmrc.gov.uk/childbenefit/index.htm

For SSP, SMP, SPP and SAP contact your employer in the first instance.

National Insurance Contributions & Employer Office, International Caseworker

Newcastle upon Tyne NE98 1ZZ
tel (08459) 154811 (local call rates apply)

For enquiries for individuals resident abroad.

Means-tested benefits

- Jobseeker's Allowance (JSA) (i.e. unemployment)
- Employment and Support Allowance (ESA) (i.e. sickness and incapacity)
- Income Support (low-income top up for those of working age, not working but neither unemployed nor sick/incapacitated)
- Working Tax Credits* (WTC) (low-income top up for those of working age)
- Child Tax Credit* (low-income top up for those of working age with children, in addition to Working Tax Credit if applicable)
- Disabled Person's Tax Credits* (DPTC) (low-income top up for disabled people)
- Pension Credit (low-income top up for those of pension age)
- Social Fund grants (one-off assistance for low-income household with unexpected, emergency expenditure)

In addition, help with rent and rates is available on a means-tested basis from local authorities.

Many of the working age benefits are to be replaced with 'Universal Credit' on a phased basis from October 2013.

Peter Arrowsmith FCA is a sole practitioner specialising in National Insurance matters. He is a member and former chairman of the Employment Taxes and National Insurance Committee of the Institute of Chartered Accountants in England and Wales.

Magazines by subject area

These lists provide a broad classification and pointer to possible markets. Listings for magazines start on page 28.

Fiction

Puzzles and quizzes

The following take puzzles and/or quizzes on an occasional or, in some cases, regular basis. Ideas must be tailored to suit each publication: approach in writing in the first instance.

Magazines aimed at women

Magazines aimed at men

Children's and young adult magazines

Subject articles

Advertising, design, printing and publishing

Agriculture, farming and horticulture

Architecture and building

Art and collecting

Aviation

Business, industry and management

Cinema and films

Computers

Economics, accountancy and finance

Education

Engineering and mechanics

Gardening

Health and home

History and archaeology

Hotel, catering and leisure

Humour and satire

Legal and police

Leisure interests, pets

Literary (see also Poetry)

Local government and civil service

Marketing and retailing

Medicine and nursing

Military

Motor transport and cycling

Music and recording

Natural history

Nautical and marine

Photography

Poetry

Some magazines only take the occasional poem. Check with the Editor before submitting.

Politics

Radio, TV and DVD

Religion, philosophy and New Age

Rural life and country

Sciences

Sports and games

TGO (The Great Outdoors) Magazine 87
Today's Golfer 88
Total Off-Road 88
Trail 89
Trout and Salmon 89
World Fishing Magazine 94
World Soccer 94

Theatre, drama and dancing (see also Cinema and films, Music and recording)

AS Magazine 31
Canadian Screenwriter 102
Dance Australia 99
Dance Today 45
Dancing Times 45
New Theatre Quarterly 70
Radio Times 78
The Stage 84
Tribune 89
TVTimes Magazine 89

Travel and geography

Australian Geographic 97
Caravan Magazine 38
Condé Nast Traveller 42
France 53
Geographical 54
Geographical Journal 54
Living France Magazine 64
Traveller 89
Traveltalk 101
Wanderlust 91
Wild 101
The Witness 109

Publishers of fiction

Addresses for *Book publishers UK and Ireland* start on page 123.

Adventure/thrillers

Crime/mystery/suspense

Erotic

Ethnic

Gay/lesbian

General

Graphic

Historical

Horror

Humour

Literary

New/experimental

Romantic

Science fiction

Short stories

Teenage/young adult

Translations

War

Westerns

Publishers of non-fiction

Addresses for *Book publishers UK and Ireland* start on page 123.

Academic and professional

Agriculture, farming and horticulture

Animals and birds

Archaeology

Architecture and building

Art and craft

Astronomy

Aviation

Bibliography

Biography, autobiography and memoir

Business, industry and management

Cartography/maps

Computers and computing

Cookery, food and drink

Crime

Cultural studies

Current affairs

Design

Economics, accountancy and finance

Education

Engineering and mechanics

Environment and development

Fashion

Film and cinema

Fine art and antiques

Gardening

Gender studies and gay and lesbian

General non-fiction

Gift books

Health

Heritage

History

Hotel, catering and leisure

Humour

Illustrated books

International issues

Irish interest

Subject indexes

Languages and ELT

Law

Leisure interests and hobbies

Lifestyle, home and DIY

Literary criticism and essays

Local government and civil service

Local interest

The media

Medicine and nursing

Military

Mind, Body & Spirit

Music

Natural history

Nautical and marine

Parenting, relationships and self-help

Performing arts

Photography

Politics

Popular culture

Popular reference

Puzzles and crosswords

Reference

Subject indexes

Religion, philosophy and New Age

Rural life and country

Sciences

Scottish interest

Social sciences

Sports and games

Transport, including cycling

Travel and geography

TV, TV tie-ins and radio

Welsh interest

Writers' guides

Children's book publishers and packagers

Listings for *Book publishers UK and Ireland* start on page 123 and listings for *Book packagers* start on page 210.

Children's fiction

Book publishers

Book packagers

Children's non-fiction

Book publishers

Book packagers

Picture books

Book publishers

Book packagers

Other

Activity and novelty

Book publishers

Book packagers

Audiobooks

Book publishers

Multimedia

Book publishers

Book packagers

Poetry

Book publishers

Book packagers

Religion

Book publishers

Book packagers

Publishers of plays

Playwrights are reminded that it is unusual for a publisher of trade editions of plays to publish plays which have not had at least reasonably successful, usually professional, productions on stage first. See listings beginning on page 123 for addresses.

Publishers of poetry

Addresses for *Book publishers UK and Ireland* start on page 123.

Literary agents for children's books

The following literary agents will consider work suitable for children's books, from both authors and illustrators. Listings start on page 429. See also *Art agents and commercial art studios* on page 474.

Literary agents for television, film, radio and theatre

Listings for these and other literary agents start on page 429.

Newspapers and magazines that accept cartoons

Listed below are newspapers and magazines which take cartoons – either occasionally, or on a regular basis. Approach in writing in the first instance (for addresses see listings starting on page 11 for newspapers and page 28 for magazines) to ascertain the Editor's requirements.

Newspapers and colour supplements

Consumer and special interest magazines

Business and professional magazines

Prizes and awards by subject area

This index gives the major subject area(s) only of each entry in the main listing which begins on page 543, and should be used with discrimination.

Biography

Children

Drama – theatre, TV and radio

Essays

Fiction

Grants, bursaries and fellowships

Illustration

Journalism

Non-fiction

Photography

Poetry

Short stories

Translation

Specialist

General index

Key topics and terms that appear in the articles within this *Yearbook* are listed here.

Listings index

All companies, public and commercial organisations, societies, festivals and prize-giving bodies, that have a listing in the *Yearbook* are included in this index.

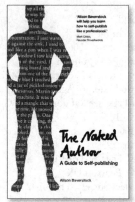